25 Largest Non-Financial Transnational Corporations from Developed Economies by Assets

(millions of dollars and number of employees)

Rank	Corporation	Home Economy	Industry	Assets		Sales		Employment	
				Foreign	Total	Foreign	Total	Foreign	Total
1	General Electric	United States	Electrical and electronic equipment	401,290	797,769	97,214	182,515	171,000	323,000
2	Deutsche Post	Germany	Transport and storage	30,765	365,990	55,170	79,699	283,699	451,515
3	Toyota	Japan	Motor vehicles	169,569	296,249	129,724	203,955	121,755	320,808
4	Royal Dutch/ Shell	United Kingdom	Petroleum expl./ref./distr.	222,324	282,401	261,393	458,361	85,000	102,000
5	Eléctricité de France	France	Utilities (electricity, gas, and water)	133,698	278,759	43,914	94,044	51,385	160,913
6	CITIC	China	Diversified	43,750	238,725	5,427	22,230	18,305	90,650
7	Volkswagen	Germany	Motor vehicles	123,677	233,708	126,007	166,508	195,586	369,928
8	GDF Suez	France	Utilities (electricity, gas, and water)	119,374	232,718	68,992	99,377	95,018	196,592
9	BP	United Kingdom	Petroleum expl./ref./distr.	188,969	228,238	283,876	365,700	76,100	92,000
10	ExxonMobil	United States	Petroleum expl./ref./distr.	161,245	228,052	321,964	459,579	50,337	79,900
11	Ford	United States	Motor vehicles	102,588	222,977	85,901	146,277	124,000	213,000
12	Vodafone	United Kingdom	Telecommunications	201,570	218,955	60,197	69,250	68,747	79,097
13	E.On	Germany	Utilities (electricity, gas, and water)	141,168	218,573	53,020	126,925	57,134	93,538
14	Daimler	Germany	Motor vehicles	87,927	184,021	108,348	140,268	105,463	273,216
15	Deutsche Telekom	Germany	Telecommunications	95,019	171,385	47,960	90,221	96,034	227,747
16	Total	France	Petroleum expl./ref./distr.	141,442	164,662	177,726	234,574	59,858	96,959
17	Walmart	United States	Retail & trade	62,514	163,429	98,645	401,244	648,905	2,100,000
18	Eni	Italy	Petroleum expl./ref./distr.	95,818	162,269	95,448	158,227	39,400	78,880
19	Chevron	United States	Petroleum expl./ref./distr.	106,129	161,165	153,854	273,005	35,000	67,000
20	Conocophillips	United States	Petroleum expl./ref./distr.	77,864	142,865	74,346	240,842	15,128	33,800
21	BMW	Germany	Motor vehicles	63,201	140,690	62,119	77,830	26,125	100,041
22	Telefonica	Spain	Telecommunications	95,446	139,034	54,124	84,778	197,096	251,775
23	Siemens	Germany	Electrical and electronic equipment	104,488	135,102	84,322	116,089	295,000	427,000
24	Procter & Gamble	United States	Diversified	62,942	134,833	47,949	79,029	99,019	135,000
25	ArcelorMittal	Luxembourg	Metal and metal products	127,127	133,088	112,689	124,936	239,455	315,867

Source: UNCTAD World Investment Report 2010, Annex Table 26. World's Top 100 Non-Financial TNCs Ranked by Foreign Assets.

Largest Transnational Corporations from Each Emerging Market, Ranked by Foreign Assets, 2008

(millions of dollars and number of employees)

Corporation	Home Economy	Industry	Assets		Sales		Employment	
			Foreign	Total	Foreign	Total	Foreign	Total
Hutchison Whampoa	Hong Kong, China	Diversified	70,762	87,745	25,006	30,236	182,148	220,000
CITIC	China	Diversified	43,750	238,725	5,427	22,230	18,305	90,650
Cemex	Mexico	Non-metalic mineral products	40,258	45,084	17,982	21,830	41,586	56,791
Samsung Electronics	Korea, Republic of	Electrical and electronic equipment	28,765	83,738	88,892	110,321	77,236	161,700
Petronas	Malaysia	Petroleum expl./ref./distr.	28,447	106,416	32,477	77,094	7,847	39,236
Lukoil	Russian Federation	Petroleum and natural gas	21,515	71,461	87,637	107,680	23,000	152,500
Vale	Brazil	Mining & quarrying	19,635	79,931	30,939	37,426	4,725	62,490
Petróleos De Venezuela	Venezuela, Bolivarian Republic of	Petroleum expl./ref./distr.	19,244	131,832	52,494	126,364	5,140	61,909
Zain	Kuwait	Telecommunications	18,746	19,761	6,034	7,452	1,151	15,000
Singtel	Singapore	Telecommunications	17,326	21,887	6,745	10,374	9,058	20,000
Formosa Plastics	Taiwan Province of China	Chemicals	16,937	76,587	17,078	66,259	70,519	94,268
Tata Steel	India	Metal and metal products	16,826	23,868	26,426	32,168	45,864	80,782
Abu Dhabi National Energy Company	United Arab Emirates	Utilities (electricity, gas, and water)	13,519	23,523	3,376	4,576	1,839	2,383
MTN Group	South Africa	Telecommunications	13,266	18,281	7,868	12,403	10,870	16,452
Evraz	Russian Federation	Metal and metal products	11,196	19,448	12,805	20,380	29,480	134,000
Qatar Telecom	Qatar	Telecommunications	10,598	20,412	4,077	5,582	1,539	1,832
Ternium	Argentina	Metal and metal products	7,063	10,671	5,357	8,465	10,042	15,651
Orascom Telecom	Egypt	Telecommunications	6,718	9,757	2,947	5,305	11,376	16,522
Enka Insaat ve Sanayi	Turkey	Construction and real estate	3,540	7,767	3,256	6,956	19,286	40,886
San Miguel	Philippines	Food, beverages and tobacco	2,655	7,117	458	3,774	2,383	15,344
PTT	Thailand	Petroleum expl./ref./distr.	2,525	25,252	5,993	59,931	798	7,989

Source: UNCTAD/Erasmus University database.

International Financial Management

The Prentice Hall Series in Finance

 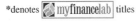

International Financial Management

Geert Bekaert

Columbia University and the National Bureau of Economic Research

Robert Hodrick

Columbia University and the National Bureau of Economic Research

PEARSON

Boston   Columbus   Indianapolis   New York   San Francisco   Upper Saddle River
Amsterdam   CapeTown   Dubai   London   Madrid   Milan   Munich   Paris   Montréal   Toronto
Delhi   Mexico City   São Paulo   Sydney   Hong Kong   Seoul   Singapore   Taipei   Tokyo

Editorial Director: Sally Yagan
Editor-in-Chief: Donna Battista
Acquisitions Editor: Tessa O'Brien
Editorial Project Manager: Amy Foley
Editorial Assistant: Elissa Senra-Sargent
Director of Marketing: Patrice Jones
Marketing Assistant: Ian Gold
Senior Managing Editor: Nancy H. Fenton
Senior Production Project Manager: Meredith Gertz
Permissions Project Supervisor: Michael Joyce
Permissions Editor: Maria Leon Maimone
Art Director: Jayne Conte
Cover Designer: Suzanne Behnke
Cover Photo: Kentoh/Shutterstock
Senior Manufacturing Buyer: Carol Melville
Media Producer: Nicole Sackin
Production Coordination, Composition, and Art Creation: PreMediaGlobal

Credits and acknowledgments borrowed from other sources and reproduced, with permission, in this textbook appear on appropriate page within the text.

Many of the designations by manufacturers and seller to distinguish their products are claimed as trademarks. Where those designations appear in this book, and the publisher was aware of a trademark claim, the designations have been printed in initial caps or all caps.

Library of Congress Cataloging-in-Publication Data

Bekaert, Geert.
  International financial management / Geert Bekaert, Robert J. Hodrick.—2nd ed.
    p. cm.
  ISBN-13: 978-0-13-216276-0
  ISBN-10: 0-13-216276-8
  1. International finance.   2. International business enterprises—Finance.   3. Foreign exchange.   I. Hodrick, Robert J.   II. Title.
  HG3881.B436 2012
  658.15'99—dc23

                                                                 2011023449

10 9 8 7 6 5 4 3 2 1
ISBN-13: 978-0-13-216276-0
ISBN-10: 0-13-216276-8

To my world of women, Emma, Britt, Laura and Ann
— Geert

To my wife, Laurie, and my children, Reid and Courtney,
with love — Bob

BRIEF CONTENTS

CONTENTS

When we were graduate students, we chose to study international finance because we wanted to understand issues such as how exchange rates are determined and how people manage the risks that fluctuations in exchange rates create. We also recognized that the economic forces that people now call *globalization* were trends that would only increase in importance over time. We like to think that we made a good call on our careers because, without a doubt, globalization of business is now a fact. Our goal with this book is to equip future global business leaders with the tools they need to understand the issues, to make sound international financial decisions, and to manage the myriad risks that their businesses face in a competitive global environment.

Over the years, the markets for goods and services as well as capital and labor have become increasingly open to the forces of international competition. All business schools have consequently "internationalized" their curriculums. Nevertheless, our combined 54 years of teaching experience indicates that most students will not be ready for the real world, with its global complications, unless they know the material in this book. They will not really understand how fluctuations in exchange rates create risks and rewards for multinational corporations and investment banks, and they will not understand how those risks can be managed. They will not really understand how to determine the value of an overseas project or the nature of country risk. The purpose of this book is to prepare students to deal with these and other real-world issues.

THIS BOOK'S APPROACH: MAKING BETTER DECISIONS BY BLENDING THEORY AND PRACTICE WITH REAL-WORLD DATA ANALYSIS

International Financial Management, 2nd Edition, continues to blend theory, the analysis of data, examples, and practical case situations to allow students to truly understand not only what to do when confronted with an international financial decision but why that decision is the correct one. When we explore international financial markets, we do so with an eye on risk management. We thereby incorporate practical considerations into what other textbooks take as background theory or institutional detail.

Multinational companies face a daunting array of risks, but they also have a wide variety of financial instruments available to manage them. In this book, we detail the sources of risks that arise in international financial markets and how these risks can be managed. For example, a basic risk of international trade involves the fact that goods are being shipped out of the country. How does an exporter make sure that he is paid? We do not stop at identifying the risks and showing how to manage them; we also reflect on why a firm should manage them and how that management affects the firm's value. We do this by developing the valuation methodologies needed to determine the value of any foreign project—from the establishment of a foreign subsidiary to the takeover of a foreign company. Because we have a well-defined valuation methodology, we present international financial management using a modern, theoretically correct approach, building on the newest insights from international corporate finance. How international risk management affects the value of a firm falls out naturally from our framework. We also provide considerable detail about the institutional aspects of international financial markets for debt and equity. For example, we show how firms can obtain international equity financing, but we also discuss theories and empirical work on the costs and benefits of these decisions.

WHAT'S NEW IN THE SECOND EDITION

In the new edition, all data have been updated to reflect the most recent information. The newest research ideas in international finance are reflected in the text. Some examples include an in-depth discussion of novel research on why the carry trade makes money and the risks involved in Chapter 7; a discussion of new research on exchange rate determination that explains why exchange rates are so hard to predict in Chapter 10; and new terminal value calculations in Chapter 16.

Between the writing of the first edition and this one, a global financial crisis has roiled markets and economies, and its ramifications are explored in many different chapters. Chapter 1 contains a general discussion of the crisis, and Chapter 2 explores the effects of the crisis on transactions costs in the foreign exchange market. Chapter 6 covers the breakdown of covered interest rate parity during the crisis, and Chapter 18 examines its effects on trade finance. Chapter 20 reflects on how emerging-market companies dabbling in exotic options got burned when the dollar became a safe haven during the crisis. Lessons from the crisis are drawn throughout the book. Chapter 20 now also includes an appendix that discusses the valuation of foreign currency options, and a spreadsheet is available to do the calculations.

While the first edition explored the developments leading up to monetary union in Europe, we now put this material to good use to more fully understand the recent European sovereign debt crisis in Chapter 5. Our swaps chapter (Chapter 21) now also includes a section on credit default swaps, which are important in understanding global sovereign debt markets and also played a role in the 2007 to 2010 global financial crisis.

This new edition also more prominently recognizes the increased importance of emerging markets. The so-called BRICs (Brazil, Russia, India, and China) account for an increasingly larger portion of the global economy, global trade, and global financial markets, with China dominating many debates about international business. Several of our new illustration boxes and examples provide insights about the Chinese economy and its place in global business. Chapter 1 discusses the attempted takeover of a U.S. oil company by a Chinese company; the *Point–Counterpoint* in Chapter 4 discusses the balance of payments imbalances between the United States and China and their consequences; Chapter 5 discusses China's capital controls; Chapter 12 its equity markets; and so on. We also analyze how Brazil's capital controls affect covered interest rate parity in Chapter 6.

PEDAGOGY FOR STUDENTS

This book necessarily combines theory and business practice. We provide plenty of real-world examples and case studies, and at the same time, we stress fundamental concepts, principles, and analytical theories that are bound to be more resilient to the constantly changing challenges of operating in a competitive global marketplace.

To help students develop an in-depth and enduring knowledge of international financial management, *International Financial Management,* 2nd Edition, incorporates the following features:

- **Real data analysis:** We incorporate the analysis of data in each relevant chapter to allow students to learn how well or poorly the current theories are supported by the data. All Exhibits in the 2nd Edition use the most recent data possible.
- **Extended cases:** Where relevant, we introduce and solve intricate cases that illustrate the application of theory. These case solutions can serve as templates for future analyses.
- *Point–Counterpoint* **features:** We reinforce the subtleties of many international financial management issues by presenting a *Point–Counterpoint* feature for each chapter. Many textbooks provide short, easy answers to difficult questions. That approach is fine when there is general agreement about an issue, but many situations are more subtle and intricate than standard books may lead the reader to believe. The *Point–Counterpoint* features are designed to raise issues that are contentious and that are often not fully resolved or well understood by the academic and practitioner communities. Each *Point–Counterpoint* feature ends by summarizing the state-of-the-art thinking on the issue.
- **Boxes:** We provide boxes to serve two purposes. First, they may contain concrete historical or current illustrations of important concepts introduced during the chapter. Second, they explore and illustrate basic finance concepts that are used in the chapter.
- **Appendixes:** We have included some mathematical and statistical material in appendixes to various chapters in an effort to make the book self-contained. We intend the book to be accessible to students with limited financial backgrounds.
- **End-of-chapter questions and problems:** At the end of each chapter, we have provided a set of interesting questions and problems that are designed to help students ensure that they have mastered the chapter material.
- **Bibliographies:** Each chapter contains a bibliography of further reading that contains not only citations to the books and articles mentioned in the text but also some additional readings that interested students can explore.

MATERIALS FOR INSTRUCTORS

At the Instructor Resource Center, located at www.pearsonhighered.com/irc, instructors can download a variety of print, digital, and presentation resources available for this textbook, including the following:

Solutions Manual
Test Item File
TestGen EQ
PowerPoint slides

Solutions Manual—Prepared by the authors, Geert Bekaert and Robert Hodrick. The Solutions Manual contains fully worked out solutions for all the end-of-chapter questions and problems.

Test Item File—Prepared by Dr. April Knill. The Test Item File for each chapter will contain approximately 25 multiple choice questions with fully worked out solutions, 5 short answer questions with answers, and 2 essays with answers. The question difficulty levels of each chapter will be approximately 60% easy, 30% moderate, and 10% difficult.

TestGen—The computerized TestGen package allows instructors to customize, save, and generate classroom tests. The test program permits instructors to edit, add, or delete

Chapter 1

Globalization and the Multinational Corporation

1.1 INTRODUCTION

The world economy is becoming increasingly globalized. Campuses have students from many different countries. The chips in your laptop computer may have come from Korea, and its software could have been developed by Indian engineers. We hope that during your study break, you savor some Italian espresso, although the "Italian" coffee beans that were roasted in Italy were likely grown in Indonesia or Brazil. The concept of **globalization** refers to the increasing connectivity and integration of countries and corporations and the people within them in terms of their economic, political, and social activities.

Because of globalization, multinational corporations dominate the corporate landscape. A **multinational corporation (MNC)** produces and sells goods or services in more than one nation. A prototypical example is the Coca-Cola Company, which operates in more than 200 countries. An MNC probably produces your favorite brew. For example, Anheuser-Busch In-Bev is a publicly traded company headquartered in Belgium with origins dating back to 1366. Over time, the local Belgian firm grew into an MNC called Interbrew, with famous brands such as Stella Artois and Leffe. In 2004, Interbrew and Companhia de Bebidas das Américas (AmBev), from Brazil, merged to create InBev; and in 2008, InBev acquired Anheuser-Busch, the brewer of Budweiser beer, to become Anheuser-Busch InBev. The company is now the largest brewer in the world by volume, producing 91 million hectoliters (hl) of beer in the first quarter of 2010.

The link between a large European company and a large company from an emerging economy is no coincidence. Recent years have seen strong growth in Brazil, Russia, India, and China (sometimes called the BRICs). Today, the BRICs account for 15% of the world's **gross domestic product (GDP)** and more than 50% of the GDP of all emerging countries. The integration of these emerging economies into the global economy was forcefully illustrated in 2006, with the creation of the world's largest steel company, ArcelorMittal. Mittal Steel, an Indian company, took over Arcelor, a European steel producer, which was created by an earlier merger of steel companies in France, Belgium, Luxembourg, and Spain. The fact that Arcelor's management at first opposed the takeover shows that globalization does not necessarily proceed smoothly.

The international scope of business creates new opportunities for firms, but it also poses many challenges as became abundantly clear in 2008 when a housing and mortgage crisis in the United States morphed into a global financial crisis. This book provides a guide to financial management in an increasingly globalized world and, in particular, to the financial management problems that multinational firms face. In this introductory chapter, we first reflect generally on the globalization phenomenon. We then discuss multinational firms in more detail, including their effects on the economy and society at large. We also survey the different important players in this globalizing world, ranging from international banks to international institutions and institutional investors. We end with a quick preview of the book.

1.2 GLOBALIZATION AND THE GROWTH OF INTERNATIONAL TRADE AND CAPITAL FLOWS

Globalization affects all aspects of society, but economically, two main trends define it. First, countries continue to expand their trade in goods and services. Second, countries continue to reduce their barriers to capital flows. We discuss each in turn.

The Growth of International Trade

Trade Liberalization

Beginning with the writings of David Ricardo in the 19th century, economists have known that countries gain from trade if each nation specializes in the production of those goods in which it has a **comparative advantage**. Even if one country is more productive at producing a given item than other countries, it should still focus its production on those goods in which it is relatively most efficient, and doing so will make all trading partners better off.[1] There also appears to be a link in the data between trade and growth: More open countries tend to grow faster.[2]

Unfortunately, protectionist tendencies have long kept the world relatively closed, with many countries restricting international trade through tariffs on imports, non-tariff barriers such as subsidies to local producers, quotas on imported products, onerous regulations applying to imported products, and so forth. Wacziarg and Welch (2008) pinpointed when various countries liberalized their trade regimes—in other words, when the countries became open to trade. They looked at a variety of criteria, including the extent of the countries' tariffs and non-tariff barriers, and state control on major export sectors. In 1960, only about 20% of countries were open to trade. These countries included the United Kingdom and the United States, who had a long tradition of openness to international trade, and many European countries that liberalized in 1959 or 1960, after the creation of the **European Economic Community (EEC)**. The EEC set out to establish free trade among a number of European countries, later turning into the European Union, which we describe further in Section 1.4.

The idea that economies should be open to trade got a further boost in the early 1980s, when Western governments started to deregulate their economies and privatize government firms. The fall of the Iron Curtain in 1990 and subsequent trade liberalizations occurring in many developing countries increased trade openness dramatically, with more than 70% of countries open to trade by 2000.

International Efforts to Promote Free Trade

The **General Agreement on Tariffs and Trade (GATT)**, signed in 1947, was designed to encourage free trade between member states by regulating and reducing tariffs on traded

---

[1]This law of comparative advantage will show up again when we discuss the foreign currency swap market in Chapter 21.
[2]Articles confirming such a link include Frankel and Romer (1999), Sachs and Warner (1995), Alcalá and Ciccone (2004), and Wacziarg and Welch (2008).

goods and by providing a common mechanism for resolving trade disputes. GATT signatories occasionally negotiated new trade agreements to reduce tariffs, called "Rounds," to which countries would agree.

The Tokyo Round in 1979 also reduced non-tariff barriers to trade, and the Uruguay Round, begun in 1986, established the **World Trade Organization (WTO)** in 1995 to replace the GATT Treaty. GATT succeeded in lowering trade barriers in a multilateral, worldwide way, but a number of important regional trade agreements have slashed trade barriers even more in particular regions. The best known of these regional agreements are the **European Union (EU)**, the **North America Free Trade Agreement (NAFTA)**, **Mercosur** in South America, and the **Association of Southeast Asian Nations (ASEAN)**.

In the meantime, advances in information technology increased the share of services and made the world seem smaller, allowing outsourcing to become an important phenomenon. **Outsourcing** is the shifting of non-strategic functions—such as payroll, information technology (IT), maintenance, facilities management, and logistics—to specialist firms to reduce costs. Today, outsourcing IT work to low-cost countries, such as India, has become commonplace. These developments led to a new focus for trade policy: increasing the international tradability of services. During the Doha Round, which began in 2001, trade in services was put on the agenda. In addition, the Doha Round focused on agriculture, industrial goods, and updated custom codes. Unfortunately, the trade talks have been going far from smoothly, and, at the time of writing, WTO officials hoped to conclude the round by the end of 2011.

The Growth in Trade

The evolution of trade openness dramatically increased trade flows between countries. One measure of trade openness is the sum of exports and imports in a given year divided by a measure of output, such as GDP. Exhibit 1.1 presents some data on this relative size of the trade sector.

In Panel A, the data for large, developed countries reveal a significant increase in trade-to-GDP ratios between 1970 and 1985. Between 1985 and 2000, the trade sectors mostly grew, especially in France, Germany, and Australia, but over the past decade, only Germany has witnessed a substantial increase in its trade sector. Of the countries shown, Germany is the most open, with its trade sector comprising 75% of GDP in 2009, while Japan is the least open, with trade comprising just 27% of its GDP.

In Panel B, large, developing countries such as Brazil, India, and China witnessed increases in the relative size of their trade sectors. India's trade sector evolved from less than 10% of GDP in 1970 to over 45% in 2009. China's trade sector nearly doubled between 1985 and 2000 and was over 50% of GDP in 2009. This increase reflects the major trade reforms China undertook during the 1980s and 1990s, including China's accession to the WTO in 2001. The accession, in turn, led to a steady decrease in tariffs on imports. Because of its large size and increased openness, China has become a major player in the world economy.

As Exhibit 1.1 demonstrates, although the global trend is toward freer trade, some countries are clearly more open than others. Many factors affect why, how much, and with whom countries trade. For example, countries that border oceans tend to trade more than inland countries. Large countries tend to trade relatively less than smaller countries as evidenced by the U.S. numbers relative to most other countries; and, indeed, China is a relative outlier. Small open countries such as Belgium and Singapore (see Panel C of Exhibit 1.1) have trade-to-GDP ratios well over 150% and 350%, respectively.

How Multinational Corporations Are Affecting Trade

The phenomenal growth of MNCs after World War II also boosted international trade. According to the **United Nations Conference on Trade and Development (UNCTAD)**, there are now 82,053 international companies with about 810,000 subsidiaries, whereas in the

Exhibit 1.1 International Trade as a Percentage of GDP

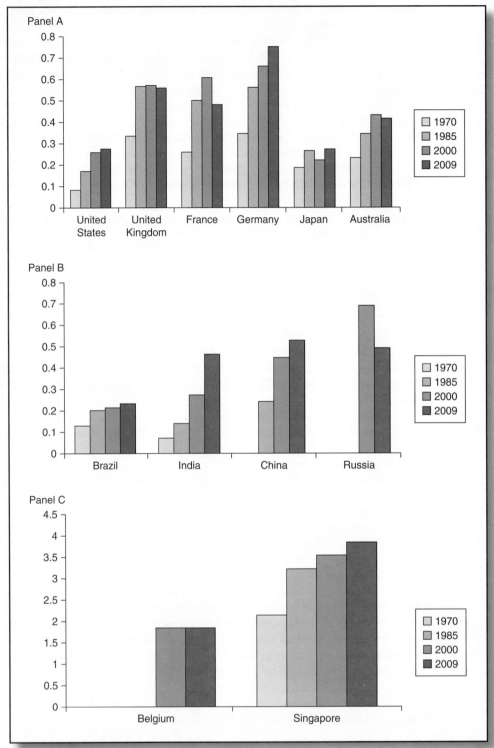

Note: The data are from UNCTAD and are the sum of exports and imports divided by gross domestic product (GDP), a measure of total output.

early 1990s, there were only 37,000 companies with 175,000 subsidiaries. More than 50% of international trade actually occurs within MNCs (that is, firms trading with themselves). By 2008, more than 25% of MNCs were headquartered in emerging markets.

In MNCs, capital, labor, management skills, and technology are all transferred to other countries to produce abroad rather than export from a domestic factory. Sometimes, the components of different goods are produced in different countries, depending on their relative advantages in terms of costs and technological ability. A classic example is the Barbie doll. The raw materials for dolls come from Taiwan and Japan; their assembly takes place in the Philippines, Indonesia, and China (due to the low labor costs); and the design and the final coat of paint come from the United States, which still has an edge in design and marketing.

The Globalization of Financial Markets

The globalization of financial markets and the profound changes they have undergone since 1980 have also dramatically changed how MNCs manage their business risks, improved their access to foreign capital, and enhanced their ability to reduce financing costs. We provide a short overview of the major developments.

Trends in Financial Openness

A country is financially open if it allows foreigners to invest in its capital markets and allows its citizens to invest abroad. After World War II, most countries had controls or restrictions in place that prevented the free flow of capital across borders. However, in the 1980s, many developed countries began liberalizing their capital markets. For example, Japan started to liberalize in 1984; in Europe, the movement toward the Single Market forced many countries to abolish their capital controls, with France abolishing capital controls in 1986, Italy in 1988, and Belgium in 1990.

In the late 1980s and during the 1990s, many developing countries began a financial liberalization process, relaxing restrictions on foreign ownership of their assets and taking other measures to develop their capital markets, often in tandem with macroeconomic and trade reforms. These developments created a new asset class in which to invest: emerging markets, which we discuss in more detail in Chapter 12.

AMB: Betting on Global Trade

AMB, which owns and develops industrial real estate, is a **real estate investment trust (REIT)** that trades on the New York Stock Exchange. You might think that real estate is not an easily exchangeable asset and consequently that AMB has little to do with international business. But in fact, the fortunes of AMB totally depend on globalization.

You see, AMB develops, acquires, and operates distribution facilities in locations tied to global trade, such as international airports, seaports, and major highway systems. AMB has investments in 11 countries, ranging from Spain to Brazil to China. With increased international trade and the need to minimize inventories, companies have realized that distribution efficiency is a key to their success. Therefore, AMB targets properties that are built for the efficient movement of goods and are strategically located in the world's global distribution markets. Although the value of the property depends to a certain degree on local factors, as is the case for any piece of real estate, AMB's business is primarily a bet on globalization. Investors in AMB are betting on continued growth of international trade and the increasing demand for such strategically located distribution facilities.

The 2007 to 2010 global crisis was particularly dire for AMB. Not only did the crisis cause a worldwide recession that reduced trade flows, but it also prompted protectionist pressures in many countries, undermining the core of AMB's growth strategy. AMB's stock price dropped from about $60 before the crisis to less than $10 in March 2009, a drop of more than 80%! It has since partially recovered.

Deregulation of foreign investment considerably increased the degree of financial openness in the world between 1980 and now. While measuring financial openness is difficult, most relevant studies agree that financial openness has not yet evolved as far as trade openness.[3]

One way to assess how open countries are to capital flows is to examine their foreign assets and liabilities.[4] The ratio of foreign assets plus foreign liabilities to GDP has grown rapidly for industrial countries. In 1970, this financial ratio for industrial countries as a group was slightly less than 50%. By 1985, the ratio was 100%, whereas in 2008, the ratio was over 400%. Financial openness in emerging markets progressed more gradually, with the ratio of foreign assets and liabilities over GDP increasing from 60% to about 150% in 2008.[5]

The New Financial Landscape

The deregulatory zeal of governments worldwide happened against the background of and perhaps as a reaction to a vastly different financial landscape that emerged in the 1980s. Most importantly, the markets for financial derivatives exploded, backed by advances in financial economics and computer technology. A **derivative security** is an investment whose payoff over time is *derived* from the performance of underlying assets (such as commodities, equities, or bonds), interest rates, exchange rates, or indices (such as a stock market index, a consumer price index, or an index of weather conditions). The main types of derivatives are futures, forwards, options, and swaps. These derivatives are traded over the counter (that is, on a bilateral basis among financial institutions or between financial institutions and their clients) and on organized exchanges. Chapters 20 and 21 discuss some of these derivative contracts in more detail.

Another important development was the increased use of **securitization**—the repackaging of "pools" of loans or other receivables to create a new financial instrument that can be sold to investors. For example, financial institutions package mortgages or car loans into complex securities that are sold to investors, thereby spreading the risks involved. Moreover, banks earn fees on these securities and need not hold a capital buffer on their balance sheets to protect against possible losses as required for a regular loan. As Acharya et al. (2010) report, securitized assets worldwide increased from $767 billion at the end of 2001 to $2.7 trillion in December 2006.

The spectacular growth in derivatives and securitization considerably increased the complexity in the financial intermediation business. These developments dramatically improved the ability of banks and corporations to manage risk. For example, corporations with earnings denominated in foreign currencies could now easily hedge their risks using derivatives contracts. Similarly, companies could now easily tap foreign investors for capital with bond issues denominated in different currencies, while using the derivative markets to convert the loans back to their domestic currency if they desired to do so.

The new financial landscape also made it increasingly difficult for governments to regulate their domestic capital markets without smart financiers finding loopholes around the rules. For example, a major impetus to the growth of the swap market was regulatory arbitrage, where financial institutions exploited country-specific regulations or taxes to lower the cost of funding for multinational companies. In Chapter 11, we give some concrete examples of such regulatory arbitrage.

With derivative contracts and securitization techniques becoming ever more sophisticated, a degree of complexity and opaqueness crept into the financial system that put stress on the risk management systems of banks and companies. For instance, mortgage loans were

---

[3]See Quinn and Toyoda (2008) and Chinn and Ito (2008) for indices of financial openness.
[4]See Chapter 4 for a discussion of the relationship between flows of capital that are recorded in a country's balance of payments and the balance sheet position of the country's foreign assets and liabilities.
[5]These numbers are reported and discussed in Lane and Milesi-Ferretti (2007) and Milesi-Ferretti et al. (2010).

offers support at various levels, and may even initially invest in the franchise in exchange for periodic fees. McDonald's is the best-known franchising firm. Another way to penetrate foreign markets is through a **joint venture**, a company that is jointly owned and operated by two or more firms. For example, Walmart, the gigantic U.S. retailer, set up a joint venture with India's Bharti Enterprises in 2007 to start a chain of wholesale cash-and-carry stores in India.

MNCs also enter foreign markets by setting up production and distribution facilities abroad either by acquiring or merging with foreign companies or by simply establishing new operations in the countries (in what are called *greenfield investments*). These latter categories constitute the bulk of **foreign direct investment (FDI)**, which we discuss in more detail later in this chapter.

Today, there is much talk about the globally integrated corporation. As IBM chief executive officer (CEO) Samuel Palmisano put it in a 2006 speech, such a firm shapes its strategy, management, and operations as a single global entity. True to form, Mr. Palmisano's speech took place not at its corporate headquarters in Armonk, New York, but in Bangalore, India, where IBM now has more than 50,000 employees.

The Goals of an MNC

The premise of this book is that the appropriate goal of the management of any corporation, including a multinational corporation, is to maximize shareholder wealth. This is the tradition in what are called the "Anglo-American" countries, including Australia, Canada, the United Kingdom, and especially the United States. The management of a corporation maximizes shareholder wealth by making investments in projects whose returns are sufficiently large to compensate its shareholders, through dividends and capital gains, for the risk involved in the projects.

The Investment Time Horizon
The appropriate time horizon for management to consider is the long term. When deciding if an investment today maximizes shareholder value, the current value of all its future benefits must be compared to the cost of the investment. It is sometimes argued that shareholder maximization leads management to be too short-term focused on meeting the quarterly expectations of stock analysts, and it is certainly possible for management to mislead the markets in the short run, as the U.S. accounting scandals discussed shortly aptly demonstrate. Yet, we believe that markets are pretty efficient at finding and aggregating information. Thus, good management should not be willing to trade off an increase in the stock price today for a major fall in the stock price shortly thereafter. Rather, it is the job of management to inform the markets about the costs and future profitability of the firm's investments.

The Stakeholder Alternative
Shareholder wealth maximization is not traditionally practiced by large European or Asian firms who tend to lump shareholder interests together with those of other "stakeholders," including management, labor, governments (both local and national), banks and other creditors, and suppliers. Because management must juggle these various interests, its objectives are less clear in the stakeholder model than in the shareholder model.

Agency Theory and Corporate Governance
In a modern corporation, stockholders hire managers who make decisions about production and marketing. How can the ultimate owners of the assets motivate the managers to act in the owners' interest? The economic field of **agency theory** (see, for instance, Jensen and Meckling, 1976) explores the problems that arise from the separation of ownership and control and devises ways to resolve them. A manager of a firm, in particular the CEO, is viewed as an agent who contracts with various principals—most importantly the firm's shareholders,

but also the firm's creditors, suppliers, clients, and employees. The principals must design contracts that motivate the agent to perform actions and make decisions that are in the best interests of the principals.

Unfortunately, the world is too complicated for investors to write a contract that specifies all the actions that managers will take in the future. Yet, the managers will surely acquire important information that the shareholders do not have and thus retain a great deal of discretion about which actions to take in response to such "private" information.

The legal and financial structure that controls the relationship between a company's shareholders and its management is called **corporate governance**. Its role is to establish the framework within which the managers operate and to mitigate the principal–agent problem. The importance of poor corporate governance was forcefully illustrated in a series of recent corporate scandals.

Corporate Scandals

One of the most spectacular cases of corporate fraud involved the Enron Corporation of Houston, Texas. By late 2001, the company, which was founded in 1985, had transformed itself from a regional gas pipeline operator into the largest buyer and seller of natural gas and electricity in the United States, as well as a major trader in numerous other commodities. A criminal investigation begun in 2001 revealed that Enron's meteoric rise in value was fed mostly by institutionalized, systematic, creative accounting fraud, which landed its top executives in jail. The Enron bankruptcy was a disaster for many of the company's 21,000 employees who lost their jobs and any retirement savings in Enron stock. The market price of an Enron share fell from a high of $90 in August 2000 to zero in 2006, as creditors eventually liquidated the company. The CEOs of Worldcom, a telecommunications firm, and Tyco, a sprawling conglomerate, also received prison sentences around the same time for corporate misdeeds.

Lest you think that only managers of large U.S. companies are capable of fraud, consider the case of Parmalat, an Italian dairy and food-processing company founded in 1961 by Calisto Tanzi. Parmalat is the global leader in the production of ultra high temperature (UHT) milk, which sterilizes food in 1 to 2 seconds by exposing it to temperatures exceeding 135°C. Such milk can be kept on the shelf, unrefrigerated, for between 6 and 9 months. In 2003, accounting irregularities were uncovered in Parmalat's books implying that €3.95 billion of assets were missing from the accounts of Bonlat, a Parmalat subsidiary in the Cayman Islands. Parmalat declared bankruptcy, and Tanzi was arrested. He eventually admitted to illegally diverting funds from Parmalat into other ventures he controlled and was sentenced to prison.

More recently, asset management scandals dominated the press. The investment firms of Bernard Madoff (in 2008) and of Allen Stanford (in 2009) were shown to have run massive Ponzi schemes for years. A Ponzi scheme is an investment fraud that dupes investors into believing they are earning fabulous returns from good investments, whereas actual payouts use funds contributed by new investors. As long as assets under management grow, the scheme can continue indefinitely. Both cases, and especially the Madoff case, with total losses reportedly amounting to $21 billion, raise serious issues about the regulatory oversight of the investment industry.

Corporate Governance Around the World

It is clear from these corporate scandals that management does not always act in the interest of shareholders. Yet, most corporations function without fraud and corruption. This section examines how shareholders deal with management not only to try to prevent outright illegal activities but to align the interests of management with those of shareholders.

Multinationals must worry about more than "in-house" corporate governance. Whether they acquire an existing foreign firm, set up a joint venture, or simply adopt a licensing agreement may depend on the corporate governance practices in that country. Corporate

Exhibit 1.4 Methods of Overcoming Agency Problems Due to the Separation of Ownership and Control

Method	Pros	Cons
1. Independent board of directors	Protection of minority shareholders' interests. Increased risk sharing.	Often not sufficiently independent of management and therefore ineffective.
2. Partial concentration of ownership and control in the hands of a large shareholder	A large shareholder has the self-interest to monitor management's activities to prevent abuses.	Possible collusion between management and large shareholder against smaller shareholders. Reduced liquidity in the stock.
3. Executive compensation with options or bonuses related to performance.	Provides a direct incentive to maximize stock price.	Rewards management for good luck. Subject to monipulation and possible short-term focus to allow management to get rich.
4. Clearly defined fiduciary duties for CEOs with class-action law suits.	Provides a complementary disciplining device.	Increases legal costs and enriches lawyers at the expense of stockholders.
5. Hostile takeovers and proxy contests.	Directly disciplines bad management.	Provides an incentive for raiders to expropriate wealth from creditors and employees.

governance differences across countries and firms affect a firm's valuation and may lead firms to cross-list shares in stock markets with a legal environment that fosters good corporate governance, or MNCs may improve their own corporate governance standards to attract international investors.

In their review of corporate governance and control, Becht et al. (2007) examine five ways of overcoming agency problems. The pros and cons of the different approaches are discussed in the following sections and are summarized in Exhibit 1.4.

An Independent Board of Directors

In the Anglo-American model, the board of directors has the most important role in corporate governance. It is the board's responsibility to help management develop a strategy and to approve its major investments. The board controls management's activities by appointing and compensating the management with the goal of making the organization accountable to its owners and the authorities.

How well the board of directors functions depends on whether the directors are independent of the management. If the board is dominated by the CEO's friends, the board may not be able to represent the interests of shareholders. If the board is not independent, international expansion of the activities of the firm could be a manifestation of empire building; why else would you need a corporate jet?

While the Anglo-American model of corporate governance embraces the independent board of directors, things are different in Europe. In Germany, for example, the *Aufsichtsrat*, or supervisory board, of a large corporation has 20 members. Shareholders elect 10 members, and the other 10 members are employee representatives. The supervisory board oversees and appoints the members of the *Vorstand*, or management board, which must approve major business decisions.

Concentrated Ownership

The most common method of overcoming agency problems in developed countries outside of the United Kingdom and the United States is through concentrated ownership. A block of stock is held by either a wealthy investor or a financial intermediary, which might be a bank, a holding company, a hedge fund, or a pension fund. A large shareholder clearly has a vested interest in monitoring management and has the power to implement changes in management. Negative aspects of this approach include possible collusion between the large shareholder and the management to expropriate wealth from the smaller shareholders and the fact that the stock may be more difficult to trade on the stock market if a substantial block of shares is withdrawn from the market but still available to be sold should the large shareholder want to sell.

Executive Compensation

An important aspect in aligning the interests of an agent and a principal is how the agent is compensated. The compensation committee of the board of directors has the responsibility to design appropriate executive compensation that overcomes shareholder/management conflicts. Here, ownership of stock by the management and grants of stock options should encourage the management to think like the shareholders.

Positive aspects of this method include the fact that people respond to incentives, and the economics of the problem indicate the need to pay for performance. Unfortunately, it is often difficult to ascertain why stock prices increase. Was it management's actions or simply luck? An increase in the price of oil raises the value of the large firms that extract oil and sit on large reserves, and consequently, oil price increases can lead to big paydays for managers whose decisions had nothing to do with the increase in the oil price.

The recent global crisis certainly raised a variety of knotty corporate governance issues. Within banks, the compensation of traders and executives was based too much on short-term gains and failed to account for the riskiness of their actions, whereas risk managers were insufficiently compensated for halting excessive risk taking. Rating agencies failed to correctly assess the risks of the complex securities issued by the banks. In the wake of the global financial crisis, the large compensation packages offered to executives and successful employees by several financial institutions, especially those that received taxpayers' money during the crisis, were heavily criticized.

Shareholder Activism and Litigation

Poor corporate performance eventually leads to unhappy shareholders. If the performance isn't too bad, the shareholders may just bide their time and allow management to improve performance. Alternatively, the unhappy shareholders may sell their shares to someone who is more optimistic about the firm's prospects. Disgruntled shareholders also may try to use the legal system to sue the board of directors for failure to perform their fiduciary duty. Clearly defining the fiduciary responsibilities of the CEO raises the threat of litigation and keeps managers from expropriating shareholder value, thus providing a complementary method of aligning management's actions with shareholders' interests.

If shareholders disagree with the management's strategy or its implementation, they may actively try to change the management or vote for different directors. For example, in November 2010, Carl Icahn, a billionaire investor, and Seneca Capital, a hedge fund, blocked the takeover of Dynegy, an energy company, by The Blackstone Group, a private equity group. They also sought to replace several board members who were deemed not to be acting in the interest of the firm. The saga continues at the time of writing as Seneca Capital now tries to halt a counter-bid by Icahn to take over Dynegy.

Hostile Takeovers

Ultimately, management is disciplined by the market for hostile takeovers. In a hostile takeover, the candidate acquiring company, the "raider," bids for a majority of the voting rights of the "target" company and, if successful, uses the acquired voting power to replace the CEO and redirect the strategy of the target.

Such takeovers are common in the United States, the United Kingdom, and France, but they are rare in Germany. Nevertheless, in 2000, Vodafone of the United Kingdom completed a $199 billion cross-border hostile takeover of the German company Mannesmann, in the largest-ever European takeover. Hostile takeovers are also rare in Japan because of the presence of keiretsu, an arrangement in which a group of firms is linked, usually with a prominent bank, through cross-shareholding agreements.

The Sarbanes-Oxley Act

In response to the corporate scandals, the U.S. Congress passed legislation to attempt to improve corporate governance. The Sarbanes-Oxley Act of 2002 covers issues such as auditor independence, corporate governance, and enhanced financial disclosure. It established the Public Company Accounting Oversight Board, charged with overseeing, regulating, inspecting, and disciplining accounting firms in their roles as auditors of public companies. It requires that public companies and their internal auditors evaluate and disclose the effectiveness of their internal controls as they relate to financial reporting, because CEOs and chief financial officers (CFOs) of publicly traded companies must certify their financial reports. Companies can no longer make loans to corporate directors. Finally, the audit committee of the board of directors, which oversees the relationship between the corporation and its auditor, must be composed of independent directors.

Note that the Sarbanes-Oxley Act's insistence that only independent directors serve on the audit committee conflicts with European and Asian traditions. For example, the German supervisory board has employee representatives, who are clearly not independent.

The issue is really one of getting the right form for corporate governance. While the Sarbanes-Oxley Act may further improve corporate governance in the United States, the United States was already considered the country with the best corporate governance. Moreover, implementing the new requirements is expensive, and it is likely one of the factors behind the decision of many international companies not to list their stock on the U.S. stock market but in European countries with less onerous regulations.

What the Data Show

Differences across countries in corporate governance are examined in a series of influential and controversial articles by La Porta et al. (1997, 1998, 2000a, 2000b), known as LLSV. The LLSV articles show that measures of investor protection across countries correlate strongly with a classification of legal systems based on the idea of "legal origin"—the primary distinction being between English common law countries, such as Canada, the United Kingdom, and the United States; French civil law countries, such as Belgium, France, and Italy; German civil law countries, such as Austria, Germany, and Switzerland; and Scandinavian civil law countries, such as Denmark, Finland, and Sweden. The English common law countries provide more investor protections than the civil law countries.

LLSV show that legal origin correlates well with concentration of ownership, the size of the stock market, and the level of dividend payments. For example, in civil law countries with low ownership protection, corporate ownership is much more concentrated than in the English common law countries. LLSV also show that countries with greater legal protection of investor rights have more firms listed on public stock markets, larger corporate valuations, and greater economic growth.

China provides an important counterexample to the findings on the importance of legal systems in promoting the growth of financial systems and the overall economy. Allen et al. (2005) note that neither China's legal system nor its financial system is particularly well developed, yet China has experienced extraordinary real growth. While China retains a large state-controlled sector, it is the private sector that has been the engine of growth. This suggests that alternative financing channels and corporate governance mechanisms, possibly based on reputation considerations, promote the growth of the private sector.

Multinational Corporations and Foreign Direct Investment

Foreign direct investment (FDI) occurs when a company from one country makes a significant investment that leads to at least a 10% ownership interest in a firm in another country. The outstanding stock of FDI was estimated to be worth around $18 trillion in 2009 and has grown 30-fold between 1980 and 2009.

Exhibit 1.5 shows the sum of FDI inflows and outflows relative to GDP between 1980 and 2009 for developed countries, for developing countries, and for two countries in Asia (Japan and China). Between 1980 and 2000, the FDI/GDP ratio essentially grew by a factor of 10 in both developed countries (from 1% to 9%) and in developing countries (from 0.4% to 4.3%). Over the last decade, FDI flows stalled, and they decreased during the global crisis. Although much was made of Japan's international investments in the 1980s, it now has a lower FDI/GDP ratio than China, whose FDI flows have grown quickly. There is another notable difference between the two countries. Japan's FDI outflows are about six times as large as FDI inflows to Japan. In contrast, China's inflows in 2009 were twice as large as its outflows. Overall, the United States remains the country with the largest dollar amount of FDI inflows and outflows.

International Mergers and Acquisitions

An important part of FDI involves international mergers and acquisitions (M&A), in which a corporation in one country merges with or acquires a corporation in another country. Exhibit 1.6 presents UNCTAD data on cross-border mergers and acquisitions broken down by country of purchaser on the left side and by country of seller on the right side. We only report countries with a minimum amount of deals.

Exhibit 1.6 shows that $250 billion of cross-border M&A occurred in 2009. This was substantially above the roughly $100 billion in 1990 but substantially below the $900 billion of 2000. Exhibit 1.6 clearly indicates that most M&A activity remains primarily a developed country phenomenon. Of the $250 billion of M&A activity in 2009, purchasers in developed

Exhibit 1.5   Foreign Direct Investment as a Percentage of GDP

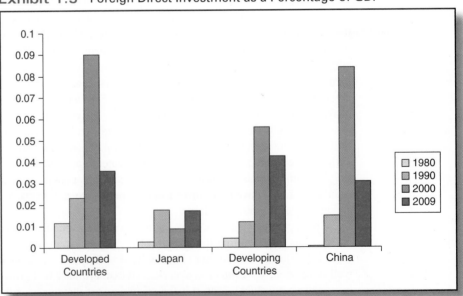

Notes: The data are compiled from UNCTADstat (http://unctadstat.unctad.org). Foreign inflows, foreign outflows, and GDP are reported in nominal U.S. dollars.

Exhibit 1.6 Cross-Border Mergers and Acquisitions, 1990–2009 (in millions of dollars)

Region/Economy	By Purchaser			By Seller		
	1990	2000	2009	1990	2000	2009
World	98,903	905,214	249,732	98,903	905,214	249,732
Developed Economies	87,188	828,662	160,785	89,310	852,265	203,530
Europe	60,676	671,695	102,709	42,945	515,547	133,871
Belgium	660	18,856	(9,638)	2,770	1,991	12,089
France	18,704	114,581	41,565	7,036	33,544	724
Germany	3,898	9,996	24,313	4,391	232,554	12,790
Italy	1,678	18,722	17,505	1,067	11,151	1,109
Netherlands	3,127	42,816	(3,273)	1,321	27,004	17,988
Spain	4,312	31,984	(1,278)	2,198	19,823	32,173
Switzerland	3,502	59,164	7,385	3,349	6,046	15,275'
United Kingdom	5,593	321,784	(3,546)	17,958	112,630	25,164
North America	13,158	127,223	40,477	40,651	303,142	51,475
Canada	1,966	33,119	16,718	4,175	31,421	11,389
United States	11,192	94,105	23,760	36,475	271,721	40,085
Other Developed Countries	13,354	29,744	17,598	5,714	33,576	18,185
Japan	13,532	13,901	17,440	1,223	12,695	22,206
Australia	(75)	3,423	(2,981)	1,223	12,695	22,206
Developing Economies	7,551	57,599	73,975	9,593	52,320	39,077
Africa	499	3,069	2,702	411	2,355	5,140
South Africa	290	2,852	1,491	(15)	308	4,215
Latin America and the Caribbean	1,159	3,584	3,740	8,748	35,798	(4,358)
Brazil	—	189	2,501	(32)	17,274	(1,369)
Mexico	302	4,082	3,247	2,005	4,477	104
Asia and Oceania	5,893	50,946	67,534	434	14,167	38,295
Qatar	—	2	10,266	—	—	298
United Arab Emirates	48	3	14,831	—	(10)	300
China	1,340	(307)	21,490	—	37,316	10,898
Hong Kong, China	501	37,704	7,461	286	(35,699)	3,028
Korea, Republic of	46	1,286	6,951	—	6,345	1,956
Malaysia	58	236	3,277	(186)	976	354
Singapore	88	8,013	2,762	461	1,309	9,693
Turkey	13	49	—	113	112	2,849
Russian Federation	—	157	7,599	—	421	5,079

Notes: Compiled from UNCTAD's cross-border M&A database (www.unctad.org/fdistatistics). The data cover deals involving the acquisition of an equity stake of more than 10 percent. The data are "net"; that is, purchases by home-based MNCs minus the sales of foreign affiliates of home-based MNCs, or sales in the host economy to foreign MNCs minus sales of foreign affiliates in the host economy. For the developed countries, we select countries that either purchased or sold more than $10 billion worth of companies internationally in 2009; for emerging markets, the cutoff is $2 billion. Negative numbers are indicated with parentheses.

countries accounted for $160 billion, while sellers in developed countries accounted for more than $200 billion. France, Germany, and the United States were among the largest acquirers, whereas Spain, the United Kingdom, and the United States were the largest sellers.

Valuing a cross-border acquisition is clearly an important financial skill, and Chapter 15 explains how this can be done. Financial mergers are increasingly coming from emerging markets, as the trend of emerging market companies competing for targets in the West continues. Not all mega deals are value enhancing. Karnani (2010) argues that many of the high-profile deals where Indian MNCs bought well-known Western companies failed to increase shareholder value, and the desire for empire building and nationalistic pride often played a role. One example he analyzes is Tata Motor's 2008 acquisition of Jaguar and Land Rover, two classic British car brands, from the Ford Motor Company.

In a study of over 6,000 acquisitions covering data from 61 countries from 1990 to 2007, Ellis et al. (2011) assess the effect of measures of corporate governance on the benefits of an international acquisition for the acquiring shareholders. They find that acquirers from countries with better governance show the highest stock price reaction to such acquisitions and that the stock price reaction is largest when targets are from countries with worse governance.

1.4 OTHER IMPORTANT INTERNATIONAL PLAYERS

In the course of its international business activities, an MNC may need financing from an internationally active bank, use economic information provided by an international organization, operate within a regulatory framework set by local governments or international institutions, and deal with investor relations in several countries. We briefly survey these other important players in international finance.

International Banks

Major banks operate internationally to service their MNC clients. The globalization of business is well expressed in the banking sector. For example, Citibank, part of the Citigroup financial services company, operates in virtually every country in the world, and it has a long tradition of foreign activity, having established offices in Europe and Asia in 1902.

Cross-border mergers have also created a few top global asset management firms. In 2009, U.S.-based Blackrock became the world's largest asset manager with over $3 trillion under management by buying Barclays Global Investors (BGI) from Barclays, a major British bank. BGI was created in 1995 when Barclays bought Wells Fargo Nikko Advisors, which combined the asset management activities of Wells Fargo, a California bank, and Nikko Securities, a leading Japanese broker.

The emergence of more consolidated financial institutions at the global level is a recent phenomenon. One reason is that banks were often protected from foreign takeovers, either through explicit regulation or through political maneuvering, because they are considered to be important and strategic components of the economy. It was the Uruguay Round that paved the way for the deregulation of the financial services sector. Chapter 11 presents a fuller discussion of these issues.

International Institutions

The International Monetary Fund (IMF)

The IMF is an international organization of 187 member countries, based in Washington, DC, which was conceived at a United Nations conference convened in Bretton Woods, New Hampshire, in 1944. The 45 governments represented at that conference sought to build a framework for economic cooperation that would avoid a repetition of the disastrous economic policies that had contributed to the Great Depression of the 1930s.

The main goals of the IMF are to ensure the stability of the international monetary and financial system (the system of international payments and exchange rates among national currencies that enables trade to take place between countries), to help resolve crises when they occur, and to promote growth and alleviate poverty. To meet these objectives, the IMF offers *surveillance* and *technical assistance*. Surveillance is the regular dialogue about a country's economic condition and policy advice that the IMF offers to each of its members.

Technical assistance and training are offered to help member countries strengthen their capacity to design and implement effective policies, including fiscal policy, monetary and exchange rate policies, banking and financial system supervision and regulation, and statistics.

Economic crises often occur when countries borrow excessively from foreign lenders and subsequently experience difficulties financing their balance of payments. We discuss the balance of payments in detail in Chapter 4. The IMF is set up to offer temporary financial assistance to give member countries the breathing room they need to correct balance-of-payment problems. A policy program supported by IMF financing is designed by the national authorities in close cooperation with the IMF, and continued financial support is conditional on effective implementation of this program. This is known as IMF conditionality. The IMF charges market interest rates for these loans. In addition, the IMF also actively works to reduce poverty in countries around the globe, independently and in collaboration with the World Bank and other organizations. Here, loans are provided at below-market rates. The IMF's main resources are provided by its member countries, primarily through the payment of quotas, which broadly reflect each country's economic size.

The World Bank

This institution was also created in 1944, as the **International Bank for Reconstruction and Development (IBRD)**, to facilitate postwar reconstruction and development. Over time, the IBRD's focus shifted toward poverty reduction, and in 1960, the **International Development Association (IDA)** was established as an integral part of the World Bank. Whereas the IBRD focuses on middle-income countries, the IDA focuses on the poorest countries in the world. Together they provide low-interest loans, interest-free credits, and grants to developing countries for investments in education, health, infrastructure, communications, and other activities.

The World Bank also provides advisory services to developing countries and is actively involved with efforts to reduce and cancel the international debt of the poorest countries. Rogoff (2004) describes the World Bank as a complex hybrid of a long-term development bank, an aid agency, and a technical assistance outsourcing center.

Because the contributions from its 187 member countries are relatively modest, the World Bank is an important borrower in international capital markets. It then lends these funds to developing countries at a small markup.

A number of other closely associated development organizations are part of the World Bank Group. The best known is the **International Finance Corporation (IFC)**. The IFC is a global investor and advisor committed to promoting private-sector development in developing countries. One priority is the development of domestic financial markets through institution building and the use of innovative financial products.

Multilateral Development Banks (MDBs)

These institutions provide financial support and professional advice for economic and social development activities in developing countries. The term typically refers to the World Bank Group and four regional development banks: the African Development Bank, the Asian Development Bank, the European Bank for Reconstruction and Development, and the Inter-American Development Bank. These banks have a broad membership that includes both developing countries (borrowers) and developed countries (donors), and their membership is not limited to countries from the region of the regional development bank. While each bank has its own independent legal and operational status, their similar mandates and a considerable number of joint owners lead to a high level of cooperation among MDBs.

The MDBs provide financing for development in three ways. First, they provide long-term loans at market interest rates. To fund these loans, the MDBs borrow on the international capital markets and re-lend to borrowing governments in developing countries. Second, the MDBs offer long-term loans (often termed *credits*) with interest rates set well below market rates. These credits are funded through direct contributions of governments in donor countries. Finally, grants are sometimes offered mostly for technical assistance, advisory services, or project preparation.

The World Trade Organization (WTO)

In 1995, the GATT members created the WTO, headquartered in Geneva, Switzerland, which had 153 member countries in 2010. Whereas GATT was a set of rules, the WTO is an institutional body. The WTO expanded its scope from traded goods to trade within the service sector and intellectual property rights. Various WTO agreements set the legal ground rules for international commerce to hopefully ensure that the multilateral trading system operates smoothly. The agreements are negotiated and signed by a large majority of the world's trading nations and are ratified in the parliaments of the member countries.

If there is a trade dispute between countries, the WTO's dispute settlement process helps interpret the agreements and commitments, and it ensures that countries' trade policies conform to them. In the past decade, for example, Europe and the United States have bickered over international trade rules regarding steel and bananas and have needed WTO rulings to end the conflicts.

The Organization for Economic Cooperation and Development (OECD)

The OECD operates from Paris, France, and is a group of 34 relatively rich member countries. It provides a setting to examine, devise, and coordinate policies that foster sustainable economic growth and employment, rising standards of living, and financial stability in member countries and beyond. Analysis by the OECD staff and representatives of the member countries in specialized committees may culminate in formal agreements or treaties between member countries. Negotiations at the OECD on taxation and transfer pricing, for example, have paved the way for bilateral tax treaties around the world.

The OECD is renowned for its high-quality economic and social databases. Its country reviews and surveys are a must-read for policymakers and provide useful information for businesses. The OECD is funded by national contributions from its members.

The Bank for International Settlements (BIS)

The BIS, established in 1930, is headquartered in Basel, Switzerland. It fosters international monetary and financial cooperation to promote stability and serves as a bank for central banks. Bimonthly meetings of the governors and other senior officials of the BIS member central banks to discuss monetary and financial matters are instrumental in pursuing this goal. BIS standing committees support central banks and authorities in charge of financial stability more generally, by providing background analysis and policy recommendations. The best known is the Basel Committee on Banking Supervision, which developed into a standard-setting body on all aspects of banking supervision, including the framework that regulates the amount of capital international banks must hold. We discuss this in detail in Chapter 11.

The European Union (EU)

The member states of the EU seek to create a common market in which goods, services, people, and capital can move around freely and to achieve economic and political

International Organizations and the 2007 to 2010 Global Crisis

Whereas the OECD is busy writing policy briefs on the corporate governance lessons of the crisis and the BIS knows that the Basel III standards will be scrutinized more than ever, the crisis means a reversal of fortunes of sorts for the IMF. First, it reacted quickly to mitigate the effects of the crisis on low-income countries by increasing lending and making the conditions attached less onerous. Second, although many developing countries had became reluctant to tap IMF support after financial crises in the 1990s, the IMF was called in several times during the 2007 to 2010 crisis to provide emergency support to both developing (Colombia, El Salvador, Jamaica, Mexico, Poland, and Ukraine) and developed countries (Greece and Ireland). Third, a 2009 summit of the G20, the largest developed and developing economies, increased the IMF's capital by $500 billion and put the organization at the center of the fight against future financial crises by asking it to develop new early warning systems. Finally, in early 2011, the IMF announced that it would also start surveillance of capital flows and capital controls, rather than being restricted to overseeing current account imbalances. It also announced, in another reversal of previous policy, that it may support some forms of capital controls. The IMF has claimed a central role in the new post-crisis international financial architecture.

integration. The EU grew out of the post–World War II desire to prevent such wars from ever happening again. In the early years, the cooperation was between six countries (Belgium, West Germany, Luxembourg, France, Italy, and the Netherlands) and was mainly about trade and the economy, but the EU has grown to 27 members with successive waves of country accessions. The most recent additions were Bulgaria and Romania in 2007. The EU developed common policies in a wide range of fields—agriculture, culture, consumer affairs, competition, the environment, energy, transport, and trade. The 1992 Treaty of Maastricht introduced new forms of cooperation between the member state governments—for example, on defense and in the area of justice and home affairs—and created the EU.

While all original goals of the EU have not yet been completed, its importance for everyday life in Europe is undeniable. Although the Single Market was formally completed at the end of 1992, work must still be done in some areas (for example, creating a genuinely single market in financial services). During the 1990s, it became increasingly easy for people to move around Europe, as passport and customs checks were abolished at most of the EU's internal borders.

In 1992, the EU decided to go for **economic and monetary union (EMU)**, involving the introduction of a single European currency managed by a European central bank. The single currency, the euro, became a reality on January 1, 1999. While the euro was initially a success, the global financial crisis laid bare deep economic problems in Greece, Ireland, Italy, Portugal, and Spain that could no longer be resolved by independent monetary policies. In 2010, the situation deteriorated into a sovereign debt crisis, initially focused on Greece and Ireland, and some have come to doubt the survival of the EMU. We discuss exchange rate policies in the EU and the current crisis in more detail in Chapter 5. The EU also negotiates major trade and aid agreements with other countries and is developing a common foreign and security policy. Decision power within the EU rests with the European Commission, a collection of bureaucrats, the Council of Ministers (for example, ministers of finance of the member states who get together regarding financial decisions), and the European Parliament (which is chosen through direct elections).

Governments

Governments are important players in international financial management because they set the regulatory environment in which multinationals operate. Chapter 14 describes how corporations ought to assess political risk—the risk that government decisions may adversely affect the MNC's cash flows. Governments (central banks in particular) also affect important asset prices, such as interest rates, which constitute the main component of a firm's cost of debt. Chapter 5 examines how central banks influence the value of exchange rates, another critical asset price.

Individual and Institutional Investors

Individual Investors

You may wonder what role individual investors play in a book about international financial management. First, they are the company's shareholders, the ultimate owners of the company, and we argued earlier that the management should act in the interest of shareholders. More importantly, though, individual and institutional investors determine bond and stock prices.

Institutional Investors

These organizations invest pools of money on behalf of individual investors or other organizations. Examples include banks, insurance companies, pension funds, mutual funds, and university endowments. The 1980s and 1990s displayed a slow trend of institutionalization, with more savings channeled through institutional investors, which were more sophisticated and more interested in the international diversification of their portfolios.

Institutional investors, together with individual investors, determine the prices of bonds and stocks, implicitly determining the expected rates of return on these assets and thereby setting the MNC's cost of capital (see Chapter 13). The cost of capital, in turn, affects project valuations, which determines a company's investments (see Chapters 15 and 16).

Institutional investors often own relatively large portions of the shares of particular companies and are consequently well positioned to try to exert control on management. The California Public Employees' Retirement System (CalPERS) has become the poster child for shareholder activism. In 2010, CalPERS urged changes in the board of BP, the oil company, following the disastrous oil spill in the Gulf of Mexico.

Sovereign Wealth Funds

Over the past decade, a new set of institutional investors has received much attention. **Sovereign wealth funds** are state-owned investment funds, managing a global portfolio much like a pension fund would do. Many of these funds are located in countries with substantial oil revenues, such as Norway's oil fund or the Kuwait Investment Authority, which dates back to the 1950s. Sovereign wealth funds became particularly prominent during the 2007 to 2010 crisis when several funds took large stakes in struggling U.S. banks, such as the Abu Dhabi Investment Authority acquiring a $7.5 billion stake in Citigroup.

It is not always oil that provides the base revenue stream of sovereign wealth funds. One of the first funds, created in 1956, is the Revenue Equalization Reserve Fund of Kiribati, a tiny island in the Pacific Ocean. Kiribati's luck was that migrating birds produce tons of guano on its soil, which proved to be a much sought after fertilizer!

Hedge Funds and Private Equity Firms

In recent years, much of investors' money has flowed to **hedge funds**. Like mutual funds, hedge funds pool investors' money and invest in financial instruments to make a positive return. Many hedge funds seek to profit in all kinds of markets by pursuing speculative investment practices that may increase the risk of loss. The number of such funds has grown exponentially, particularly in the United States and Europe. Whereas mutual funds are strictly regulated—in the United States, they fall under the Investment Company Act of 1940—hedge funds operate under exemptions to the law. Theoretically, this limits their investors to people who are sophisticated and affluent. For example, hedge fund investors must have a minimum marketable wealth to qualify. Because of their light regulation, hedge funds can invest in just about anything and may make extensive use of derivatives. They also charge fees as a function of performance, whereas mutual funds charge fees as a percentage of assets under management. As the hedge fund industry continues to grow, hedge funds may become more and more important in determining asset prices.

Operating under a structure similar to that of hedge funds are private equity firms, which raise money from rich individual investors and institutions and invest in a number of individual companies. These companies can be private (that is, not traded on a stock market), but larger private equity firms, such as Kohlberg Kravis Roberts & Co. and The Blackstone Group, also invest in companies listed on public exchanges and take them private (that is, de-list from the exchange). Private equity firms typically control the management of their companies, often bringing in new teams that focus on making the overall company more valuable. Private equity firms are increasingly involved in international acquisitions and may own genuine MNCs. Hedge funds and private equity firms are often actively looking for firms with poor corporate governance as potential targets for their value-enhancing activities.

1.5 GLOBALIZATION AND THE MULTINATIONAL FIRM: BENEFACTOR OR MENACE?

The past few decades witnessed enormous momentum toward trade and capital liberalization, deregulation, and the privatization of state-owned companies. The multinationalization of business is proceeding at a rapid pace. Yet, in the late 1990s and the beginning of the current century, several events and developments threatened the trend toward increasing globalization. These events include the recent problems experienced by multilateral trade liberalization, the currency and banking crises many countries experienced at the end of the 1990s, derivatives and corporate scandals that put capitalism more generally in a negative light, and the rise of the so-called anti-globalist movement. The watershed event may be the 2007 to 2010 global crisis.

In this section, we reflect on the possibility that these events may lead to a slowing or halting of the globalization process. This is a critical question that every international financial manager should ponder regularly. Managing financial risks in an integrated world economy is very different from managing risk in a world where governments fully assert their sovereignty, hamper international trade, and limit international capital flows. While nobody can foresee the future, it is our opinion that if societal trends are generally welfare enhancing, they will likely continue. Much ink has flowed on this topic, and the effects of trade liberalization (economic integration) and capital market liberalization (financial integration) on economic welfare are controversial. We turn to the rapidly growing academic literature on the real effects of globalization and foreign direct investment to find some objective clues as to whether recent events really have the potential to undermine globalization.

A Rocky Road to Free Trade

Several recent developments have slowed the trend toward more trade openness. First, unilateral trade liberalization in the developing world has slowed down considerably. There seems to be more emphasis on preferential trade agreements in particular regions, but these may challenge the viability of multilateral trade rules. Second, recent efforts to open the European services markets to increased competition in the context of the European Union fell short of initial ambitions. Third, multinational trade talks in the Doha Round, after 10 years, have yet to yield concrete results. Moreover, violent demonstrations by opponents of free trade interrupted several meetings. Finally, the global crisis led to what Baldwin and Everett (2009) call "murky" protectionism. This includes measures that are allowed under WTO obligations but still discriminate against foreign companies, goods, workers, and investors.

Many developing countries raised tariffs while adhering to the ceilings imposed by the WTO (such as Russia on used cars), or they used trade litigation or technical barriers to shield domestic industries from foreign competition. Legislatures imposed rules in bailout packages following the crisis implicitly favoring domestic companies or labor, such as UK banks being encouraged to lend to the home market or the U.S. requirement that banks receiving bailout money replace laid-off workers with American workers. The United States did not set a good example for free trade: The U.S. government bailout of the car company GM is a blatant example of protectionism, and its September 2009 decision to slap a 35% tariff on imported Chinese tires threatened to ignite a trade war.

The sudden increase in economic protectionism is dangerous, as trade openness seems to unambiguously create economic growth. Increased protectionism likely only worsened the recessionary impact of the financial crisis. Here, we review two critiques of the trade liberalization process that have some merit. They do not call for less trade openness but for a different emphasis and process toward trade openness.

Trade Openness and Economic Risk

Countries should care not only about their long-term rate of economic growth but also about its variability. If a global economy exposes countries to additional risks and causes deeper recessions than a closed economy would face, many policymakers and their citizens may prefer the calmer waters of slower, steady growth in a relatively closed economy. Rodrik (1998) argued that trade openness increases external risk because open economies are more buffeted by international shocks (changes in commodity prices, exchange rates, foreign business cycles, and so forth). These shocks may create volatile swings in the fortunes of internationally oriented businesses, with adverse implications for the job security of the people employed in these companies.

Such increases in real variability call for government transfers to mitigate external risk: social security, unemployment benefits, job training, and so on. Indeed, small European countries, such as those in Scandinavia, have simultaneously opened their economies and developed extensive welfare states to protect their citizens against the economic insecurities generated by globalization. However, the social safety nets in most developing countries are anemic, which suggests that unbridled trade openness without the existence of government welfare programs may be ill advised.

Fairer Trade Openness?

Within the EU, the Common Agricultural Policy protects farmers through subsidies and other measures. In the 1980s, enormous dairy subsidies led to such overproduction of butter and milk that increasingly drastic measures had to be taken to get rid of the "butter mountain" and "milk lake." This unfortunately also included disposing of vast quantities of butter on the world market at low prices. While the introduction of production quotas has reduced this problem, it has not gone away completely. In the United States, growers of corn, wheat, cotton, soybeans, and rice receive more than 90% of all farm subsidies; Japan is notorious for the protection of its rice farmers.

Clearly, developed countries have maintained protectionist measures and subsidies in the agricultural sector. Yet, it is in that sector that the comparative advantage of developing countries is likely largest. Nobel Laureate Joseph Stiglitz, in his 2002 book *Globalization and Its Discontents*, has railed against such inequalities. Other examples include the Uruguay Round opening up markets for financial services (benefiting developed countries with large international banks) but not for maritime and construction services (benefiting developing countries). As often happens, what is desirable at an economic level is not always achievable politically. For example, while the agricultural sector has shrunk considerably in most developed countries, its political power remains disproportionately large.

Do International Capital Flows Cause Havoc?

In the 1990s, a number of emerging markets that had previously opened up their capital markets to foreign investment experienced significant currency and banking crises. First, Mexico was hit in 1994, then Southeast Asia in 1997, and Russia in 1998. These crises caused real economic pain as output fell and unemployment rose dramatically. The crises also resulted in a reversal of capital flows, and many developing countries are now exporting capital to rather than importing capital from developed countries. We discuss these issues further in Chapter 4. Many blamed the crises on foreigners—either foreign investors or international organizations such as the IMF. The crises also intensified the political and economic debate about the benefits and costs of financial globalization. Are these criticisms well-founded? Let's examine the theoretical benefits and costs of financial globalization and what the record shows.

Benefits of Financial Openness

Economic theory suggests undeniable benefits of financial globalization. A free international capital market can channel savings to its most productive uses, wherever they may be. Residents of different countries can pool risks internationally, achieving more effective insurance than purely domestic arrangements allow. A country suffering a temporary recession, a natural disaster, or simply a lack of capital can borrow abroad. Because risks are shared, the cost of capital decreases, leading firms to invest more, which increases growth.

Costs of Financial Globalization

Of course, foreign capital need not be efficiently invested. One view of the global financial crisis sees foreign capital as a problem. Low interest rates led to a consumption binge and unrealistically high asset prices with worldwide booms in construction and real estate. These phenomena were greatly helped by weak banking sectors in the capital-receiving countries that failed to stop excessive borrowing using inflated assets as collateral. A boom–bust cycle resulted. Fickle foreign capital can leave at the first hint of trouble, and financial volatility easily turns into real volatility when businesses go broke and banks collapse. This view suggests that liberalization dramatically increased financial-sector vulnerability in many countries and increased real volatility.

Financial globalization may also mean a loss of fiscal autonomy as it is difficult to tax internationally footloose capital relative to less mobile factors of production, notably labor. MNCs can also shift "profits" across countries, reducing tax revenue in high-tax countries.

Nevertheless, in a globalizing world where multinational corporations account for much economic activity, the effectiveness of capital controls likely decreases. Desai et al. (2009) show that multinational corporations employ "internal capital markets" (between the affiliates of the MNC) to circumvent capital controls. They also demonstrate that MNCs in countries with capital controls shift profits to other countries and invest less than in other, similar countries. Consequently, imposing capital controls can have potentially severe economic costs and lead to reduced tax revenues.

What the Data Show

Because a large number of emerging economies have liberalized at different times, the data allow us to see what has happened in countries that liberalized relative to countries that did not. While such exercises are never definitive, they give us a better overall picture of the evidence than some well-chosen case studies. Recent work by Bekaert et al. (2005) demonstrates that countries with open equity markets grow 1% faster per year than countries with closed markets and that countries with open capital accounts also grow faster than countries with severe capital controls. Although not everyone agrees with these findings, they appear to be robust. It is generally accepted that countries with better financial development (a stronger banking sector, for instance) and better institutions (higher-quality governments) are more likely to experience growth benefits after opening up their capital markets than countries with weak development and poor institutions.

The evidence on real volatility is more mixed (see Bekaert et al., 2006; and Kose et al., 2009). Liberalizing countries, on average, appear to experience a small decrease in real volatility, but the institutional background of the countries is important. Countries with highly (less) developed banking sectors or high- (low-) quality government institutions experience decreases (increases) in real volatility. The assertion that globalization has gone too far for emerging economies is consequentially not supported by empirical analysis. Nevertheless, the recent crises suggest that financial integration is best accompanied with vigorous reforms of the domestic financial sector and local institutions.

Interestingly, MNCs can provide a buffer during an economic crisis. When emerging markets suffer a currency crisis, severe economic recessions usually follow. While the currency depreciation should improve the international competitiveness of local firms, imperfect capital markets often make it difficult for local companies to avail themselves of these opportunities. Desai et al. (2008) show that multinational affiliates are both better able to capitalize on these competitiveness effects and better able to circumvent the financing difficulties that local firms face. In doing so, multinational affiliates expand activity precisely when local firms are handicapped. They can do so because they can sell products within the multinational network and obtain intra-firm borrowing and equity infusions. In short, an MNC's enhanced access to global product and capital markets allows them to buffer crisis economies from the severity of economic shocks.

The Anti-Globalist Movement and MNCs

Recent trade rounds have not only had to cope with political squabbling between countries but also with a powerful anti-globalist movement that has organized often violent demonstrations around trade talk centers. The anti-globalist movement is particularly important because it has identified multinational corporations as one of the main "villains" of globalization.

What Are Anti-Globalists?

Anti-globalization is an umbrella term encompassing separate social movements, united in their opposition to the globalization of corporate economic activity and the free trade with developing nations that results from such activity. Anti-globalists generally believe that global laissez-faire capitalism is detrimental to poor countries and to disadvantaged people in rich countries.[6]

Anti-globalists also criticize global financial institutions such as the World Bank, the IMF, and the WTO. Especially under attack is the so-called Washington consensus model of development, which, as promoted by international financial institutions (especially the IMF), is interpreted as requiring macroeconomic austerity, privatization, and a relatively laissez-faire approach to economic management. It is believed that these policies exacerbate unemployment and poverty. While there are serious criticisms of IMF-supported policies, the point should be made that seeing a doctor near a patient does not mean the doctor made the patient sick. Too often, unsustainable policies in the developing countries are the root of the problem, and the IMF arrives later.

Many anti-globalists are part of nongovernmental organizations (NGOs), which advocate global human rights, protection of the environment, poverty alleviation, fair trade, and so on. The movement's largest and most visible mode of organizing remains mass demonstrations against international meetings, which unfortunately often turn violent. At the Rostock, Germany, Group of Eight (G8) Summit in 2007, hundreds of people were injured.

---

[6]*No Logo*, the book by the Canadian journalist Naomi Klein (2000), which criticized the production practices of multinational corporations and the omnipresence of brand-driven marketing in popular culture, has become a manifesto of the movement.

Why Do Anti-Globalists Dislike Multinationals So Much?

One worry is that multinational activities harm the environment because governments keen on FDI degrade environmental standards (the race-to-the-bottom effect) or because heavily polluting industries relocate to countries with lower standards, in particular to developing countries (the pollution-haven effect). The evidence to date is inconclusive. A second critique is the "sweatshop" argument: People in developing nations slave away for MNCs at low wages and for excruciating long hours under horrific conditions.

Finally, globalization is seen as a threat to employment in home countries. The internationalization of the labor market is arguably the most contentious issue in the societal debate about the effects of globalization. Originally, worries focused on international trade sucking blue-collar manufacturing jobs to lower-cost countries, but more recently, the outsourcing phenomenon is seen as also threatening white-collar jobs. Because telecom charges have tumbled worldwide, workers in far-flung locations are easily and inexpensively connected to customers in the developed world. Moreover, not only are basic data processing and call centers being outsourced to lower-wage countries but also software programming, medical diagnostics, engineering design, law, accounting, finance, and even business consulting. These services can now be delivered electronically from anywhere in the world, exposing skilled white-collar workers to increased competition.

The Economic Effects of FDI and Multinational Activity

Setting aside nationalistic pride and anti-globalist slogans, scholars have studied the economic effects of FDI quite thoroughly, and some firm conclusions can be drawn.[7] The bleak view that FDI simply leads to unemployment in the company's home country and depressed wages and exploited workers in the host country does not hold up to close scrutiny.

In the home country, there is no denying that job losses occur when production facilities are shifted abroad or certain tasks are outsourced. However, FDI is a two-way street. Foreign companies investing in the home country create jobs. For example, studies indicate that over the past 30 years, the jobs and output created by foreign-owned affiliates offset the losses suffered by the U.S. manufacturing sector. Moreover, Desai et al. (2006) show that U.S. firms investing abroad also increase their U.S. investment and employment. Hence, a company's investment abroad could end up protecting jobs at home by strengthening the parent company, for example, by shielding it from the damaging effects of currency fluctuations and trade-inhibiting tax policies in the home country. Analysis by Amiti and Wei (2005) also suggests that outsourcing so far has not led to net job losses because globalizing firms also create jobs as they become more profitable.

Let's turn to the effects of FDI on host countries. While some working conditions may be less than ideal (definitely compared to what workers are used to in developed countries), the preponderance of the evidence suggests that MNCs pay higher wages than local firms. Unfortunately, there is only sparse evidence of those higher wages having a "spillover" effect on the wages local companies pay.

Proponents of FDI argue that its main advantages are an improvement in allocative efficiency (employing capital where it is most productive) and technology transfer and productivity spillovers. Foreign direct investors presumably have access to productive knowledge that is otherwise not available to producers in the host country: technological know-how, marketing and managing skills, export contacts, coordinated relationships with suppliers and customers, and reputation. FDI

---

[7]Most of what is written here builds on the review article by Lipsey (2004). Other articles include one by Goldberg (2007), which focuses on the financial services sector, and an article by Aitken and Harrison (1999), which is a nice example of a careful empirical study with detailed data for one country (Venezuela).

may consequently help close the "idea gap" between developing and developed countries. Yet the empirical evidence on FDI-induced improvements in productivity is somewhat inconclusive to date.[8] Nevertheless, there is general agreement that FDI boosts economic growth in host countries, with one authoritative study suggesting that the growth effects are only significant when the host countries boast a sufficiently educated population (see Borensztein et al., 1998).

Pondering the economic effects of FDI for host countries is important because many countries offer incentives (outright subsidies or reduced taxes) to attract FDI, and host countries must make sure the benefits from FDI justify the costs.

Some Final Thoughts on Globalization

Can globalization withstand all the challenges already discussed? The 2007 to 2010 crisis gave additional ammunition to anti-globalization voices. On the surface, it looked as if greedy American bankers enriched themselves by dumping worthless assets on the rest of the world, causing a worldwide recession. The chance that the globalization process may be halted is now real.

We believe globalization is desirable, yet the arguments of the critics should not be ignored. There does seem to be some evidence that, on average, workers in developed countries have not benefited from globalization and that the benefits of globalization in developing countries have not, as of yet, brought widespread welfare enhancements. It is possible that this is because of the incompleteness of the process; it is equally possible that governments must intervene to help better spread the newly created wealth. For example, whereas it was generally believed that the IT revolution increased the relative value of skilled workers relative to nonskilled ones, it is now becoming clear that globalization also contributes to this trend. With the vast labor forces of India and China gradually becoming integrated into the world's labor force, this massive increase in labor relative to capital is likely to have affected their relative returns. High returns to capital typically mean that the rich get richer. At the same time, the skill level in emerging markets is rising so that even some skilled labor in the Western world will feel the brunt. Because globalization destroys some jobs and creates others, it is natural that it creates uncertainty and that trade-displaced workers feel left behind by the benefits. This should put pressure on governments to help as much as possible those displaced by globalization, for example, by effective retraining and employment policies. If the average worker does not feel better off due to the globalization process, resentment will rise.

Similarly, developing countries must ensure that the benefits of openness are shared widely. The dialogue between developing countries and developed countries should change. A fair globalization involves developed countries opening their markets more to products in which developing countries can be highly competitive (such as agricultural products). 1987 Nobel Peace Prize Laureate and former president of Costa Rica, Oskar Arias Sánchez, said it best: "We [the developing countries] don't want your [the developed countries'] handouts; we want the right to sell our products in the world markets."

1.6 OVERVIEW OF THE BOOK

The field of international financial management addresses decisions facing corporate managers regarding trade and investment across national borders. While practical examples and case studies are useful study guides, we stress fundamental concepts, principles, and analytical

---

[8]Branstetter (2006) uses citations of patents to demonstrate that Japanese FDI in the United States increases the flow of knowledge spillovers both from the Japanese investing firms to American companies and vice versa. However, Aitken and Harrison (1999) find that the net gains from foreign investment are small as FDI improves the productivity of the foreign-owned plant but negatively affects the productivity of domestically owned plants.

theories that are bound to be more resilient to the constantly changing challenges of operating in a competitive global marketplace.

The fundamental idea of this book is to present international financial management in a modern, theoretically correct approach that incorporates analysis of data and thus allows the student to learn how well or poorly the current theories are supported by the data. Throughout the book, we emphasize the sources of risks that arise in international financial markets and how these risks can be managed.

This book is divided into five parts: I: Introduction to Foreign Exchange Markets and Risks; II: International Parity Conditions and Exchange Rate Determination; III: International Capital Markets; IV: International Corporate Finance; and V: Foreign Currency Derivatives.

Part I: Introduction to Foreign Exchange Markets and Risks

Part I examines the spot foreign exchange market in Chapter 2, the forward foreign exchange market in Chapter 3, the balance of payments in Chapter 4, and alternative exchange rate systems in Chapter 5. These chapters allow you to understand the nature of transactions foreign exchange risk and how it can be managed and to understand the links between the balance of payments and the demands and supplies of currencies that flow through the foreign exchange market. The fact that different countries choose different exchange rate systems implies that risks of loss due to fluctuations in exchange rates and the ability to manage these risks differ across countries.

Part II: International Parity Conditions and Exchange Rate Determination

Part II examines the relationships between interest rates and exchange rates and between prices and exchange rates. Chapter 6 explains the foremost building block of international finance: the theory of interest rate parity. This crucial concept explains why differences in interest rates across countries are neither a profit opportunity for investors nor an opportunity for corporations to lower their borrowing costs. Chapter 7 discusses speculation and risk in the foreign exchange market. We examine the issue of whether the uncertainty of future exchange rates affects the expected profitability from investing abroad. Chapter 8 examines the concept of purchasing power parity, which describes the relationship between the prices of goods in different countries and the exchange rate. It also discusses the links between inflation rates and rates of change of exchange rates. We will show that purchasing power parity works quite poorly in contrast to interest rate parity. Chapter 9 discusses management issues that arise in such an environment. The competitive pricing of products in different countries and the evaluation of foreign subsidiaries are examined. With all the building blocks out of the way, Chapter 10 explains how economists think about exchange rate determination and explores alternative methods that are used to forecast future exchange rates.

Part III: International Capital Markets

Part III surveys the international capital markets. The international bond market is examined in Chapter 11. When an MNC issues debt, it must consider the currency of the debt, the maturity of the debt, the type of interest rate payments that are promised and when the principal will be repaid, and who to use as a marketing agent for the debt. The international equity markets are explored in Chapter 12. As discussed earlier, a key consideration for firms is the cost of capital. Chapter 13 explains how international investors determine the expected return on equity and thus set the costs of capital for corporations. Chapter 14 explores the ideas of political risk and country risk. The history of direct foreign investment by multinational corporations is replete with instances in which MNCs have lost either part or all of the value of an investment because of a political decision in the host country.

Part IV: International Corporate Finance

Part IV contains a blueprint for valuing international projects. Chapter 15 lays the foundations of international capital budgeting using the adjusted net present value (ANPV) framework. Chapter 16 continues with some more advanced issues in international capital budgeting. Foreign projects can be valued, as in Chapter 15, by discounting expected foreign currency cash flows. They can also be valued by discounting expected domestic currency cash flows. Chapter 16 explains how these two approaches are related. Although risk management issues arise throughout the book, Chapter 17 uses the ANPV framework to show how risk management can add value to a multinational corporation.

Part IV also considers two basic topics that are part of the tool kit of any international financial manager. Chapter 18 examines how firms finance international trade. Managing working capital is the topic of Chapter 19, including allocating assets and liabilities efficiently and transfer pricing.

Part V: Foreign Currency Derivatives

Part V introduces foreign currency options in Chapter 20 and interest rate and foreign currency swaps in Chapter 21. These derivative instruments are incredibly useful in managing foreign exchange risks. Option strategies can be described as purchasing insurance in the sense that you pay up front to protect yourself against bad events, but you participate in the profitability if the bad event doesn't occur. Interest rate swaps allow a financial manager to change a firm's debt from fixed interest rate payments to floating interest rate payments, while currency swaps allow the financial manager to change the currency of denomination of the debt.

A Final Introduction

We still have one introduction to make. Throughout the book, two brothers, Ante and Freedy Handel, discuss various international financial management problems and controversial issues in international finance in *Point–Counterpoint* features. These brothers, who are enrolled in an international finance class, don't share a common viewpoint. Ante typically rails against free trade and free markets as he believes financial markets are inefficient and that prices do not necessarily correctly reflect information about a firm's prospects. Freedy believes more in the power of the capitalist system to allocate resources efficiently, and he consequently believes that financial markets by and large get things right.[9]

The *Point–Counterpoint* feature is designed to explore areas of controversy and is consistent with the philosophy of this book. Many textbooks often provide short, easy answers to difficult questions. That approach is fine when there is general agreement about an issue, but often the situation is more subtle and intricate than standard books may make you believe. The *Point–Counterpoint* feature is designed to raise issues that are contentious and that are often not fully resolved or well understood by the academic and practitioner communities. Luckily, the two brothers have a sober thinking cousin, Suttle Trooth, who moderates their discussions and reflects state-of-the-art thinking on the issues. Here, we start the brothers off discussing a takeover attempt of a U.S. oil company by a Chinese company.

---

[9]For the language buffs, *handel* is Dutch for "trade" or "commerce." In German, it means "trade" or "transaction," but *händel suchen* also means "making trouble" or "quarreling," and the brothers do a lot of that.

POINT–COUNTERPOINT

China Goes Global and Gets Rebuffed

It's August, and Ante and Freedy Handel enjoy their vacation, relaxing at home. Ante, comfortably lounging in a splendid sofa designed and produced in Milan, Italy, looks up from his newspaper and barks to Freedy: "Hey, that Chinese company withdrew its bid on Unocal. Our Congressional Representatives finally got something right because we don't want the Chinese government owning our strategic assets." Freedy, savoring a refreshing Leffe, sounds baffled. "I have not heard of this case; can I see the paper? I thought FDI is good for the world economy as it places the control of assets into the hands of the people that value them the most."

Ante gives the article to Freedy, who grows increasingly agitated as he reads. Here are the facts. On April 4, 2005, directors of Unocal, the 12th-largest U.S. oil company, accepted a $16.5 billion offer to be bought by Chevron, the second-largest U.S. oil company. However, on June 22, 2005, the Chinese National Offshore Oil Corporation (CNOOC), the third-largest Chinese oil company and a company smaller than Unocal, made an $18.5 billion counteroffer to purchase Unocal. In mid-July 2005, Chevron increased its bid to $17.3 billion, still below CNOOC's bid. However, CNOOC's offer was facing unprecedented political opposition in Washington. For example, in a letter to the Treasury Department, 41 politicians, both Republicans and Democrats, raised concerns that a Chinese takeover of Unocal could compromise national security. Many other high-ranking U.S. government officials also expressed doubts about the desirability of CNOOC's purchase of Unocal. The situation was resolved August 2, 2005, when CNOOC withdrew its bid, thus allowing Chevron to complete the takeover.

"See!" blurts Ante. "Clearly, the Chinese want to grab strategic U.S. oil assets, and that simply is a threat to U.S. national security." Freedy gasps, "Mercantilism is dead, Ante. You have got to be joking. Unocal is a small player. It only produces 0.8% of total U.S. crude oil production. Most of what you buy is international anyway. Where do you think your sofa is from?"

"Wait a minute, wise guy," Ante retorts. "Read the article! Unocal is a significant provider of natural gas to Southeast Asia (the Philippines, Bangladesh, and Thailand), where 70% of its oil and gas reserves are located. It is also a primary investor in the Baku-Tbilisi-Ceyhan (BTC) Pipeline, which carries oil from the Caspian to the Mediterranean. If China acquired a share through CNOOC, it would gain a foothold in a region of utmost strategic importance to the United States."

At that point, Suttle Trooth strolls in, sporting a cool red iPod Nano. "Hey guys, have you heard that new killer CD by Radiohead?" Noting Ante and Freedy's agitated faces, he quickly gets the picture. "Boy, you really are quarreling again."

Ante and Freedy show the article to Suttle, both smirking confidently and thinking that Suttle will prove them right. "Aha." Suttle sighs, "What else is new? The American public and its politicians were up in arms in the 1970s when the Saudis recycled their petrodollars buying into U.S. industries, and again in the 1980s when Japan embarked on a buying spree of American assets including a real estate icon like Rockefeller Center in New York. Americans just do not like foreigners getting their hands on important, 'symbolic,' American assets. Nevertheless, it remains bad economics. The results on the economic effects of FDI for host countries are rather unanimously positive. Freedy is hence correct that much of the economic protectionism that goes on is simply bad politics catering to some latent xenophobic feelings that exist everywhere. I also do not believe the strategic value of Unocal is large or that a Chinese takeover of a relatively small American oil and gas firm is a risk to U.S. national security. However, there is one thing about the takeover that is a bit unfair. Look at what the article says about the financing of the deal."

Suttle continues, "CNOOC planned to pay for Unocal by using substantial loans ($7 billion) from its parent company (also called CNOOC), $6 billion from a major Chinese government-owned bank (Industrial and Commercial Bank of China), and only $3 billion from its financial advisers (JPMorgan and Goldman Sachs). The problem is that the $7 billion loan from the government-owned parent company would require interest payments at 3.6% (lower than the U.S. government Treasury bonds yield), and the loan from the government-owned bank was interest free. While these rates are certainly 'off-market,' the fact of the matter is that governments routinely subsidize firms all around the world, and such subsidies are quite valuable to those who can obtain them. Overall, though, I think this situation was much ado about nothing. China's tremendous economic growth requires tons of energy, and the country simply must be assertive in securing oil and gas supplies from the Middle East, Central Asia, South America, and Africa, regions that provide the United States with a large share of its own imported oil, as well. Oil and natural gas are commodities that are traded on world markets. I just hope China doesn't find a way to retaliate against the United States after being rebuffed this blatantly. After all, CNOOC's bid should have won." Freedy smiles while Ante sinks a bit deeper in the Italian sofa.

1.7 SUMMARY

This chapter introduces the globalization phenomenon and the resulting dominance of the corporate landscape by multinational corporations. The main points and concepts of the chapter are as follows:

1. Globalization refers to the increasing connectivity and integration of countries and corporations and the people within them in terms of their economic, political, and social activities. A multinational corporation produces and sells goods or services in more than one country.

2. Globalization proceeded through a process of trade and financial liberalization. Trade liberalizations happened through countries reducing trade barriers unilaterally, within regional arrangements such as the European Union, and through multilateral action within the context of GATT. The abolition of capital controls, occurring first in many developed countries in the 1980s and then in many emerging markets in the 1990s, led to increasingly globalized financial markets.

3. Financial markets also became more sophisticated, especially because of a derivatives revolution. A derivative security is an investment from which the payoff is derived from the performance of underlying assets or asset prices, such as exchange rates. Derivatives make it easy to hedge various business risks, including the risks of changes in the value of the exchange rate.

4. In 2007, a global financial crisis erupted, leading to bank failures and a deep recession worldwide.

5. Multinationals enter foreign markets through exports and imports, licensing arrangements, franchising, joint ventures, or simply local production and distribution facilities. Globally integrated firms with strategy, management, and operations all streamlined in one global entity are also appearing.

6. In the Anglo-American countries, the goal of an MNC is to maximize shareholder wealth, whereas in many other countries, the interests of other stakeholders (such as labor, governments, creditors, and suppliers) are also taken into account. Modern corporate finance holds that shareholder wealth maximization should be the goal of each corporation.

7. Agency theory explores the problems that arise because the owners of the firm do not typically manage the firm, and it devises ways to resolve these problems.

8. Corporate governance is the legal and financial structure that controls the relationship between the company's owners and its management. Corporate scandals demonstrate that corporate governance can be rather poor, even in developed countries.

9. Corporate governance can be enhanced at the firm level by an independent board of directors, concentrated share ownership, executive compensation that motivates management to act in the interest of

the shareholders, shareholder activism and litigation, and ultimately hostile takeovers.

10. The Sarbanes-Oxley Act of 2002 attempts to improve corporate governance in the United States, but many domestic and international companies view it as costly to implement.

11. Foreign direct investment (FDI) occurs when a company from one country invests at least 10% in a firm in another country. FDI flows across countries have increased manifold over the past decades.

12. Important international organizations that provide financing to countries include the IMF, the World Bank, and various multilateral development banks.

13. The WTO sets the legal ground rules for international trade, whereas the BIS is the central bank for the central banks and promotes monetary and financial stability.

14. The EU unites 27 European countries in a common market with common policies for a wide range of fields—essentially free mobility of capital and people, and, for a subset of countries, a common currency and monetary policy.

15. Both trade liberalization and financial globalization have beneficial economic effects, yet the process toward globalization is less than smooth and has many critics. One criticism is that globalization increases "real risk"—that is, it increases the chance that economies will suffer recessions and temporary slumps in employment.

16. The anti-globalist movement encompasses a number of social movements that are opposed to globalization because it is supposedly detrimental to poor countries and disadvantaged people in rich countries. However, the academic evidence strongly suggests that FDI typically has genuinely positive effects, both in target and in host countries. However, globalization may destroy jobs and leave some people worse off; it is not clear yet how its macroeconomic benefits have been distributed throughout society at large.

17. The field of international financial management addresses financial decisions facing corporate managers regarding trade and investment across national borders.

QUESTIONS

1. Define globalization. How has it proceeded in trade in goods and services versus capital markets?
2. Describe fours ways that a company can supply its products to a foreign country. How do they differ?
3. What is a *greenfield investment*?
4. What percentage ownership typically defines FDI?
5. What is agency theory? How does corporate governance address the issues raised by agency theory?
6. Why is ownership more concentrated in developing countries than in developed countries?
7. What is the IMF? What is its role in the world economy?
8. What is the World Bank? What is its role in the world economy?
9. What are the major multilateral development banks?
10. What is the WTO? What is its role in the world economy?
11. What is an institutional investor? Along with individual investors, what do they determine?
12. What are anti-globalists?
13. Who are Ante and Freedy Handel? How do their views on the world economy differ?

PROBLEMS

1. Go to the Web site of your favorite multinational firm and determine where it operates throughout the world. How many employees does it have worldwide? Has it done any interesting cross-border mergers and acquisitions during the past year?
2. Go to UNCTADstat at http://unctadstat.unctad.org. Update the data in Exhibit 1.6 on cross-border mergers and acquisitions for the most recent years.
3. Go to the IMF's Web site at www.imf.org and download the 2011 *World Economic Outlook*. Pick your favorite country and determine if this is a good time to invest in it or not.
4. Go to the WTO's Web site at www.wto.org and determine which goods or services are the sources of trade disputes between countries this year.

BIBLIOGRAPHY

Acharya, Viral V., Thomas Cooley, Matt Richardson, and Ingo Walter, eds., 2010, *Regulating Wall Street: The Dodd-Frank Act and the New Architecture of Global Finance*, New York: NYU Stern School of Business, Wiley.

Aitken, Brian J., and Ann E. Harrison, 1999, "Do Domestic Firms Benefit from Direct Foreign Investment? Evidence from Venezuela," *American Economic Review* 89, pp. 605–618.

Alcalá, Francisco, and Antonio Ciccone, May 2004, "Trade and Productivity," *Quarterly Journal of Economics* 119, pp. 613–646.

Allen, Franklin, Jun Qian, and Meijun Qian, 2005, "Law, Finance, and Economic Growth in China," *Journal of Financial Economics* 77, pp. 57–116.

Amiti, Mary, and Shang-Jin Wei, 2005, "Fear of Service Outsourcing: Is It Justified?" *Economic Policy* 42, p. 307.

Baldwin, Richard, and Simon J. Everett, eds., 2009, *The Collapse of Global Trade, Murky Protectionism, and the Crisis: Recommendations for the G20*, Geneva: VOX.

Becht, Marco, Patrick Bolton, and Ailsa Röell, 2007, "Corporate Law and Governance and Control," Chapter 12 in A. Polinsky and S. Shavell, eds., *Handbook of Law and Economics Volume 2*, Amsterdam: North-Holland Elsevier.

Bekaert, Geert, Campbell R. Harvey, and Christian Lundblad, 2005, "Does Financial Liberalization Spur Growth?" *Journal of Financial Economics* 77, pp. 3–55.

_____, 2006, "Growth, Volatility and Financial Liberalization," *Journal of International Money and Finance* 25, pp. 370–403.

Bloom, Nicholas, 2009, "The Impact of Uncertainty Shocks," *Econometrica* 77, pp. 623–685.

Borensztein, Eduardo, José De Gregorio, and Jong-Wha Lee, 1998, "How Does Foreign Direct Investment Affect Economic Growth?" *Journal of International Economics* 45, pp. 115–135.

Branstetter, Lee, 2006, "Is Foreign Direct Investment a Channel of Knowledge Spillovers? Evidence from Japan's FDI in the United States," *Journal of International Economics* 53, pp. 325–344.

Chinn, Menzie D., and Hiro Ito, 2008, "A New Measure of Financial Openness," *Journal of Comparative Policy Analysis* 10, pp. 309–322.

Desai, Mihir, C. Fritz Foley, and Kristin Forbes, 2008, "Financial Constraints and Growth: Multinational and Local Firm Responses to Currency Crises," *Review of Financial Studies* 21, pp. 2857–2888.

Desai, Mihir, C. Fritz Foley, and James R. Hines, Jr., 2006, "Capital Controls, Liberalizations and Foreign Direct Investment," *Review of Financial Studies* 19, pp. 1399–1431.

_____, 2009, "Domestic Effects of the Foreign Activities of Multinationals," *American Economic Journal: Economic Policy* 1, pp. 181–203.

Ellis, Jesse, Sara B. Moeller, Frederik P. Schlingemann, and René M. Stulz, 2011, "Globalizaton, Governance, and the Returns to Cross-border Acquisitions," Dice Center Working Paper.

Frankel, Jeffrey A., and David Romer, 1999, "Does Trade Cause Growth?" *American Economic Review* 89, pp. 379–399.

Goldberg, Linda, 2007, "Financial-Sector Foreign Direct Investment and Host Countries: New and Old Lessons," *Federal Reserve Bank of New York Economic Policy Review* 13, pp. 1–17.

Gorton, Gary B., 2010, "Questions and Answers About the Financial Crisis," NBER Working Paper 15787.

Jensen, Michael, and William Meckling, 1976, "The Theory of Firm-Managerial Behavior, Agency Costs and Ownership Structure," *Journal of Financial Economics* 3, pp. 305–360.

Karnani, Aneel, 2010, "Dubious Value of International Acquisitions by Emerging Economy Firms: The Case of Indian Firms," Ross School of Business Working Paper No. 1140.

Klein, Naomi, 2000, *No Logo: Taking Aim at the Brand Bullies*, Canada: Knopf.

Kose, M. Ayhan, Eswar S. Prasad, and Marco E. Terrones, 2009, "Does Financial Globalization Promote International Risk Sharing?" *Journal of Development Economics* 89, pp. 258–270.

La Porta, Rafael, Florencio Lopez-de-Silanes, Andrei Shleifer, and Robert W. Vishny, 1997, "Legal Determinants of External Finance," *Journal of Finance* 52, pp. 1131–1150.

_____, 1998, "Law and Finance," *Journal of Political Economy* 106, pp. 1113–1155.

_____, 2000a, "Agency Problems and Dividend Problems Around the World," *Journal of Finance* 55, pp. 1–33.

_____, 2000b, "Investor Protection and Corporate Governance," *Journal of Financial Economics* 53, pp. 3–27.

Lane, Philip R., and Gian Maria Milesi-Ferretti, 2007, "The External Wealth of Nations Mark II: Revised and Extended Estimates of Foreign Assets and Liabilities, 1970–2004," *Journal of International Economics* 73, pp. 223–250.

Leeson, Nicholas, with Edward Whitley, 1996, *Rogue Trader: How I Brought Down Barings Bank and Shook the Financial World*, London: Little, Brown & Co.

Lipsey, Robert E., 2004, "Home and Host Country Effects of FDI," in R. E. Baldwin and L. A. Winters, eds., *Challenges to Globalization*, Chicago: University of Chicago Press, pp. 333–379.

Mankiw, N. Gregory, and Laurence Ball, 2011, *Macroeconomics and the Financial System*, New York: Worth Publishers.

Milesi-Ferretti, Gian Maria, Francesco Strobbe, and Natalia Tamirisa, 2010, "Bilateral Financial Linkages and Global Imbalances: A View on the Eve of the Financial Crisis," International Monetary Fund Working Paper 10/257.

Quinn, Dennis, and Maria Toyoda, 2008, "Does Capital Account Liberalization Lead to Growth?" *Review of Financial Studies* 21, pp. 1403–1449.

Rodrik, Dani, 1998, "Why Do More Open Economies Have Bigger Governments?" *Journal of Political Economy* 106, pp. 997–1032.

Rogoff, Kenneth, July 24, 2004, "The Sisters at 60," *The Economist*, pp. 63–65.

Sachs, Jeffrey D., and Andrew M. Warner, 1995, "Economic Convergence and Economic Policies," National Bureau of Economic Research Working Paper W5039.

Stiglitz, Joseph E., 2002, *Globalization and Its Discontents*, New York: W.W. Norton and Company.

United Nations Conference on Trade and Development, "World Investment Report," 2010.

Wacziarg, Romain, and Karen Horn Welch, 2008, "Trade Liberalization and Growth: New Evidence," *World Bank Economic Review* 22, pp. 187–231.

Chapter 2

The Foreign Exchange Market

Whether you are a Dutch exporter selling Gouda cheese to a U.S. supermarket for dollars or a U.S. mutual fund investing in Mexican stocks, you will need to find a way to exchange foreign currency into your own currency and vice versa. These exchanges of monies occur in the **foreign exchange market**. Because different countries use different kinds of money, the globalization process of the past 30 years, described in Chapter 1, has led to spectacular growth in the volumes traded on this market.

This chapter introduces the institutional structure that allows corporations, banks, international investors, and tourists to convert one money into another money. We discuss the size of the foreign exchange market, where it is located, and who the important market participants are. We then examine in detail how prices are quoted in the foreign exchange market, and in doing so, we encounter the important concept of **arbitrage**. Arbitrage profits are earned when someone buys something at a low price and sells it for a higher price without bearing any risk.

At the core of the foreign exchange market are traders at large financial institutions. We study how these people trade with one another, and we consider the clearing mechanisms by which funds are transferred across countries and the risks these fund transfers entail. We also examine how foreign exchange traders try to profit by buying foreign money at a low price and selling it at a high price.

Finally, the chapter introduces the terms used to discuss movements in exchange rates. Developing the ability to use these terms correctly makes it easier to discuss the risks involved in doing business in an increasingly global marketplace.

2.1 THE ORGANIZATION OF THE FOREIGN EXCHANGE MARKET

The foreign exchange (sometimes abbreviated "forex") market typically conjures up images of a hectic trading room, full of computers and information networks, with traders talking excitedly on telephones. This image is a reality on the trading floors of the world's major banks and other financial institutions that make up the **interbank market**. It may help to think of the interbank market as the wholesale part of the forex market where banks manage inventories of currencies. There is also a less hectic retail side of the forex market, where the customers of the foreign exchange dealers buy and sell foreign currencies. These customers are the multinational corporations that market goods and services throughout the world and the institutional investors and money managers that invest capital or speculate throughout the world.

Exhibit 2.1   The Structure of the Foreign Exchange Market

Note: Our own design, inspired by Figure 1 in Gallaugher and Melville (2004).

Exhibit 2.1 displays the various components of the foreign exchange market. In the middle of the diagram sits the interbank market, which is a very large, diverse, over-the-counter market, not a physical trading place where buyers and sellers gather to agree on a price to exchange currencies. Traders, who are employees of financial institutions in the major financial cities around the world, deal with each other via computer or over the phone, with back-office confirmations of transactions occurring only later.

The foreign exchange market operates 24 hours per day because the major financial centers where currencies are traded are geographically spread out. When it is midnight in London, England, it is morning in the Pacific and Asian markets. The first market activity is in Sydney (Australia) and Wellington (New Zealand), and it is quickly followed by trading in Tokyo and Osaka (Japan), Hong Kong, and Singapore. An abrupt decline in trading then occurs at hour 4, which is lunchtime in those markets. Market intensity picks up again in the afternoon of the Eastern Asian trading session, and it continues as Hong Kong and Singapore close and Frankfurt and London open. Other centers in Europe include Zurich, Switzerland; Copenhagen, Denmark; and Paris, France. Trading intensity increases when New York opens and overlaps with European activity, and trading declines after New York closes until the Eastern Asian markets open again. Other trading centers in the United States include Chicago and Los Angeles.

Because most transactions in the interbank market are large trades with values of $1 million or more, most retail investors and small businesses cannot access the foreign exchange market directly. As a result, many in need of foreign exchange deal with small regional banks or branches of money center banks that quote less advantageous rates than would be prevalent in the interbank market. Retail investors also participate in the foreign exchange markets through their stockbrokers, who can place orders in derivative markets on futures and options exchanges. As Exhibit 2.1 shows, large multinational corporations, such as IBM, and very large money-management firms, such as the mutual fund company Fidelity, can directly access the foreign exchange interbank market. Some multinational companies even have their own foreign exchange trading desks. An important recent trend is the rapid growth in electronic trading both in the interbank market (through electronic brokering) and on the retail side of the market. We provide further details below.

Size of the Market

The foreign exchange market is the largest market in the world, measured by dollar volume of trade. This volume has increased rapidly since the 1970s. In 1973, the estimated daily volume of currency trading was roughly $10 to $20 billion. By the late 1980s, daily volume had grown to around $500 billion. By September 1993, the estimated daily volume in all currencies had grown to over $1 trillion, and by 2004, it had grown to almost $2 trillion. The Bank for International Settlements (BIS) (2010) estimated that daily trading volume in April 2010 was $3.9 trillion. This dollar volume of trade dwarfs the corresponding dollar volume of transactions on stock markets such as the New York Stock Exchange (NYSE), where average daily dollar volume was roughly $50 billion in 2010. Of course, the $3.9 trillion includes all markets and all currencies around the world, not just trade conducted in New York.

The main factor behind the large increase in volumes is undoubtedly the globalization process, which led to increased cross-border trades in goods, services, and securities, all requiring transactions in the forex market. More recently, the speculative activities and high-volume, high-frequency trading by hedge funds have also played an increasingly important role.

Exhibit 2.2 gives an idea of the relative trading activity in the major financial centers around the world and how it grew between 1995 and 2010. The United Kingdom, with London as the major financial center, is the dominant market, accounting for 37% of all trading in 2010, followed by the United States, with the bulk of the trades occurring in New York. London's dominance has increased since 1995.

Exhibit 2.2   Foreign Exchange Trading Activity Across the World

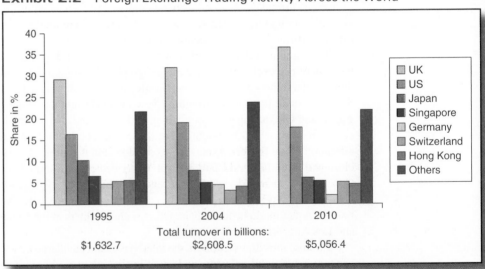

Notes: Amounts are average daily turnover in billions of U.S. dollars. The numbers are not adjusted for interdealer double-counting, which explains why the total turnover in 2010 is about $1 trillion higher than $3.9 trillion.

Source: From the Central Bank Survey of Foreign Exchange and Derivatives Marketing Activity 2010; BIS, September 2010; Table 5, MED Publications for the Bank for International Settlements.

Types of Contracts Traded

Many different types of trades can be conducted in the foreign exchange market. In this chapter, we examine the **spot market**, where "spot" implies the market for immediate exchanges of monies. Another part of the interbank foreign exchange market involves trade in swaps and forward contracts, transactions that involve exchanges of currencies in the future. We discuss these types of trades in Chapter 3. A third part of the market involves derivative securities such as foreign currency futures and options. These contracts are discussed in Chapter 20.

When currencies in the interbank spot market are traded, certain business conventions are followed. For example, when the trade involves the U.S. dollar, business convention dictates that spot contracts are settled in 2 business days—that is, the payment of one currency and receipt of the other currency occurs in 2 business days. One business day is necessary because of the back-office paperwork involved in any financial transaction. The second day is needed because of the time zone differences around the world.

Several exceptions to the 2-business-day rule are noteworthy. First, for exchanges between the U.S. dollar and the Canadian dollar or the Mexican peso, the rule is 1 business day. Second, if the transaction involves the dollar and the first of the 2 days is a holiday in the United States but not in the other settlement center, the first day is counted as a business day for settlement purposes. Third, Fridays are not part of the business week in most Middle Eastern countries, although Saturdays and Sundays are. Hence, Middle Eastern currencies transacted on Wednesday settle on Saturday, not on Friday.

Foreign Exchange Dealers

The main participants in the foreign exchange market are the commercial banks, investment banks, and brokerage firms in the major financial cities around the world. Traders at these banks and firms function as **foreign exchange dealers**, simultaneously "making a market" in several currencies. These **market makers** stand ready to buy and sell the currencies in which they specialize. By standing ready to transact with retail customers or other dealers, they provide **liquidity** to the market—that is, they make it easier and less costly to match buyers and sellers. When there are large numbers of buyers and sellers, markets are very liquid, and transaction costs are low. The foreign exchange markets for the major currencies of the world, such as the markets for the U.S. dollar, the euro, the Japanese yen, and the British pound, are among the most liquid markets in the world.

Forex dealers try to buy a foreign currency at a low rate and sell the foreign currency at a higher rate, thus making a profit. Hence, their provision of liquidity does not go unrewarded. We examine the size of these profits in Section 2.3.

Foreign Exchange Brokers

Foreign exchange brokers do not attempt to buy low and sell high. Instead, brokers fulfill the role of a financial intermediary. They match buyers and sellers but do not put their own money at risk. They then receive a brokerage fee on their transactions.

Forex brokers typically have many lines of communication open to various foreign exchange dealers, and they provide information to dealers on the best available prices. Foreign exchange dealers often use these brokers to unwind very large positions in a particular currency in order to preserve their anonymity. For example, suppose that Citibank finds itself stuck with a very large amount of Australian dollars toward the end of the day. Citibank would like to sell Australian dollars for U.S. dollars before the end of the trading day. Without anonymity in trading, competing dealers would try to profit from the knowledge that Citibank has a short-term excess supply of Australian dollars. If Citibank were to call JPMorgan Chase, for example, the prices quoted to Citibank would likely be unfavorable. By contrast, a broker may be able to negotiate trades with several foreign exchange dealers, thereby "unwinding" the large position in Australian dollars in small portions, while preserving Citibank's anonymity.

While these "voice brokers" continue to play an important role in foreign exchange trading, a large part of the brokering business now happens through computerized trading systems. In the early 1990s, Reuters (now Thomson Reuters), a large financial information provider, and Electronic Brokering Service (EBS), started by a consortium of 12 banks but now part of the interdealer broker ICAP, launched the first anonymous electronic brokering systems for trading spot foreign exchange. Trading is carried out through a network of linked computer terminals among the participating forex dealers. Currency prices are displayed on computer screens, and deals are completed by keystroke or by automatic deal matching within the system. Before a trade gets executed, either the systems check for mutual credit availability between the initiator of the deal and the counterparty of the deal or each counterparty must have its creditworthiness prescreened.

Trading in each major currency pair has over time become very highly concentrated on only one of the two systems. The top two traded currency pairs, euro–dollar and dollar–yen, trade primarily on EBS, whereas the third, pound–dollar, trades primarily on Reuters. As a result, the exchange rates on EBS and Reuters for these particular currency pairs have become the reference rates for dealers across the world. When EBS allowed institutional investors and hedge funds on its platform in 2005, it confirmed a trend towards the blurring of the distinction between the interbank and retail side of the foreign exchange market, ushered in by the emergence of electronic trading.

Other Participants in the Forex Market

The central banks of different governments around the world periodically participate in the foreign exchange market as they try to influence the foreign exchange value of their currencies. (We discuss how this works in Chapter 5.) Other participants include multinational corporations, which need to exchange currencies to conduct their international trade; institutional investors buying and selling foreign securities; hedge funds speculating on currency movements; and smaller domestic banks that service firms or individuals wanting to exchange currencies. If the trades are large enough, the highly liquid interbank market can be tapped. The more removed from the interbank market participants are (see Exhibit 2.1), the higher the transaction costs likely are.

The interbank market used to dominate the foreign exchange market, accounting for over 80% of trading volume, but this has recently drastically changed. The 2010 BIS survey on foreign exchange activity reports that turnover accounted for by trading between foreign exchange dealers fell below 50% of the total trading volume for the first time ever. Corporations accounted for 13.4% of transactions, a proportion that has not changed much over time. However, almost 48% of total volume is now accounted for by what the BIS survey calls "other financial institutions," which include smaller banks, mutual funds, pension funds, hedge funds, central banks, and so on. This change reflects a change in the dominant clientele of foreign exchange dealers. Before the 1980s, international trade was the main source of non-bank demand and supply. Since then, the explosion in international capital flows and the growth of the hedge fund industry have made professional money managers increasingly important participants in the forex market. The emergence of electronic trading has also contributed to this trend.

Electronic Foreign Exchange Trading (eFX)

The Internet revolution has not bypassed the foreign exchange market. The fastest growing segment of the foreign exchange market, already representing more than 30% of all trading volume (and more than 50% in spot markets), is electronic "online" trading. It is possible that the old telephone-based system will eventually be supplanted by pure electronic trading.

Electronic trading platforms may offer multiple quotes from a number of foreign exchange dealers and/or can house an electronic communication network (ECN). An ECN electronically collects and matches buy and sell orders, and it displays the best available prices.

In such a system, it is possible that a pension fund trades with a hedge fund, so that banks lose their traditional role of market makers. Trades are often totally anonymous. Because the market price for a particular currency is visible for all participants on the platform, electronic trading ensures price transparency. Another advantage of electronic trading is the possibility of straight-through processing (STP): A foreign exchange trade takes place from placement of the order to settlement and even entry in accounting systems in an automated fashion without errors induced by faulty paperwork. Electronic trading has greatly enhanced the liquidity of the foreign exchange market and reduced trading costs.

There are three different categories of "eFX," as electronic trading has come to be known: single bank–sponsored platforms (or "portals"), multi-bank portals, and independent companies offering electronic trading. To offer better services to their clients, many banks developed electronic trading platforms. For example, Deutsche Bank's platform is imaginatively called the "Autobahn," perhaps to make potential clients associate its speed of execution with the German highway, which has no speed limits. By far, the best known and most active platform is FXConnect from State Street. This platform was launched in 1996, originally to serve the foreign exchange trading needs of State Street's client base, consisting mostly of institutional investors making use of State Street's custody services. It has since been expanded to include quotes from a large number of other foreign exchange dealers; that is, it evolved into a multi-bank portal. Another market leader is the portal FXall, offered by a consortium of banks. FXall started operations in May 2001 and focuses primarily on corporate clients. Finally, there are a number of independent companies trying to muscle their way into online foreign exchange trading, such as HotSpot and Currenex. The Currenex box discusses the success story of Currenex, a Silicon Valley technology firm that created a successful forex electronic trading platform.

Electronic platforms were originally focused on attracting either corporate clients or institutional investors, but they got a great boost by the rapid development of hedge funds trading currencies and the emergence of "retail aggregators." Currency speculation happens in three different types of hedge funds. First, there are funds, such as FX Concepts, dedicated solely to currency trading. Second, the so-called "global macro" funds trade a wide variety of international securities, including currencies. Finally, algorithmic trading firms connect their computers directly to the ECN to trade currencies, typically at a very high frequency. Such funds use computer algorithms to attempt to profit from incremental price movements by conducting frequent small trades, executed in milliseconds. These systems make up an increasingly larger portion of trading (some estimates suggest 25% of spot trading!) and can be viewed as liquidity providers to the market, further undermining the traditional market-making role of the money center banks (see Chaboud et al., 2009). The advent of such systems accounts for why foreign exchange turnover has grown much faster than underlying economic activity as measured by gross domestic product (GDP), equity turnover, or gross trade flows (see King and Rime, 2010).

The growing importance of hedge funds in foreign exchange trading went hand-in-hand with the increased prevalence and availability of prime brokerage. The prime broker, typically a large security firm such as Morgan Stanley, offers the hedge fund a bundle of services, including securities lending, cash management, and access to various markets. Importantly, the prime broker's customers trade in the prime broker's name using its existing credit lines with the foreign exchange dealers, so that a hedge fund does not need to establish credit relationships with numerous banks.

A retail aggregator is a financial firm that acts as an intermediary, aggregating bid-offer quotes from the top foreign-dealing banks and electronic platforms, which are then streamed live to customers via the aggregator's online platform at very competitive spreads. Retail aggregators cater to the smallest accounts, including households, as well as small corporations, asset managers, trading firms, and institutional investors. A well-known example is

Currenex

At the end of the 1990s, the foreign exchange market was an over-the-counter dealer market dominated by major banks such as Citibank and Deutsche Bank. It seems almost foolhardy to think that a small technology firm with a handful of people could compete with these giants. Yet, this is what Currenex, founded in 1999, attempted. The key to Currenex's success was its anticipation of the usefulness of increased automation in foreign exchange trading and the fact that it managed to stay at the technological frontier of trading systems. Its initial strategy was to attract multi-national companies to its trading platform, and the oil company, Shell, was an early financial backer of the company. Currenex's corporate clients not only had to be convinced to use Currenex's services, but they also had to convince their foreign exchange dealers to quote prices on Currenex's platform. Currenex's focus on technology eventually paid off. Over time, the company offered an increasingly larger variety of trading possibilities to its clients. Clients could request a particular quote from the participating dealers (with whom they had a credit relationship). The platform also offered transactable quotes, leading to automated trade execution ("executable streaming prices"), and in 2004, Currenex started an ECN, called FXTrades, attracting liquidity from as many sources as it possibly could. The ECN allowed anonymous trading and worked essentially like an organized exchange with a clearinghouse and central counterparty (see Chapter 20).

Currenex foresaw more quickly than other market participants the need for speedy execution required by hedge funds and algorithmic traders. It also successfully leveraged the business of order flow aggregators. These wholesale or retail aggregators are financial institutions (e.g., Man Financial) that provide eFX trading platforms to their clients. These clients include small institutions, mutual funds, pension funds, and retail investors (such as foreign exchange day traders) that do not have sufficient resources or credit characteristics to access market makers directly. The aggregator firms incur the credit risk of these end-users by operating like a futures exchange with margins (see Chapter 20). All major prime brokers also participated on Currenex. Its platform could also be used and branded by a broker, aggregator, prime broker, or bank to deploy to their customers.

Having successfully taken advantage of the new technological trends, Currenex became an important player in foreign exchange markets. It now offers both spot and forward trading in a very large number of currency pairs. However, its independence would not last. State Street realized that Currenex's technological edge and client base provide good synergies with its own currency offerings, such as FXConnect, and bought the firm in 2007.

Oanda, whose Web site has become a retail benchmark for currency quotes. Retail aggregators now account for over 10% of foreign exchange trading volume, with this percentage being by far the highest in Japan. The stories about Japanese housewives (the proverbial Mrs. Watanabes) speculating in the currency markets from their kitchens are real!

The Competitive Marketplace

Retail customers of banks should pay only slightly more than participants in the interbank market if the foreign exchange market is competitive. In what economists refer to as a *perfectly competitive market*, many firms compete with one another, and the cost of entering the market is low. Competition is most intense when the product being sold is the same across the firms. We already know that the foreign exchange market satisfies this latter condition: A dollar is a dollar and a euro is a euro wherever and by whomever they are bought or sold. In such markets, firms are unable to earn abnormally high profits. On the other hand, when the number of firms in a market is small and entering the market is costly, firms may possess market power, which leads to less competitive pricing.

Exhibit 2.3 lists the major foreign exchange dealers and their market shares and shows that there has been tremendous consolidation in foreign exchange trading. The top four dealers now account for over 45% of trading volume and the top 20 for over 90%. In the past, the top four dealers accounted for less than 30% of the trading, the top 20 for less than 75%, and Citibank, helped by its global presence, was consistently the top foreign exchange

Exhibit 2.3 Top 20 Dealers in the Foreign Exchange Market

Rank 2010	Company	Market Share	Rank 2009	Market Share 2000[1]
1	Deutsche Bank	18.06%	1	12.53%
2	UBS[2]	11.30%	2	5.02%
3	Barclays	11.08%	3	2.07%
4	Citigroup	7.69%	5	8.07%
5	Royal Bank of Scotland[3]	6.50%	4	2.71%
6	JPMorgan Chase[4]	6.35%	6	12.10%
7	HSBC	4.55%	7	4.55%
8	Credit Suisse	4.44%	9	2.89%
9	Goldman Sachs	4.28%	8	4.38%
10	Morgan Stanley	2.91%	11	2.87%
11	BNP Paribas	2.89%	10	—
12	Bank of America	2.27%	12	1.86%
13	Société Générale	2.06%	13	0.60%
14	Commerzbank	1.46%	—	—
15	Standard Chartered	1.25%	16	0.62%
16	State Street	1.11%	15	1.95%
17	Calyon	0.81%	18	—
18	Nomura	0.80%	—	—
19	SE Banken	0.74%	—	—
20	Royal Bank of Canada	0.71%	17	1.96%
	Total	91.26%		

Note: Based on the Foreign Exchange Polls by *Euromoney* in 2010 and 2001.

[1]If the bank was not in the top 25 in 2000, we do not have market share information. The market share missed would then in any case be less than 0.60%.

[2]Market share for 2000 is for Warburg Dillon Read, then the investment banking division of UBS.

[3]Market share for 2000 is for NatWest, which was later acquired by the Royal Bank of Scotland.

[4]Market share for 2000 also includes the share of Chase Manhattan, which was later acquired by JPMorgan.

dealer. Now, the three European banks, Deutsche Bank, UBS, and Barclays, have overtaken Citibank as the major foreign exchange dealers after making significant investments in foreign exchange trading. These three banks account for 40% of the trading volume.

Competitive pressures and the growing importance of online trading have made foreign exchange trading a high volume–low margin business, which requires tremendous investments in technology. Smaller banks can no longer afford to make markets in the major currencies, but they now tend to specialize in regional currencies.

Despite the somewhat increased market shares of the major traders, no single dealer dominates the market, and the foreign exchange market remains very competitive. We examine how this competition affects pricing later in this chapter, when we discuss bid–ask spreads. According to guidelines by the U.S. Department of Justice regarding industry concentration, the foreign exchange market would not even be considered "moderately concentrated" (see Cetorelli et al., 2007).

2.2 CURRENCY QUOTES AND PRICES

You now know about the participants in the forex market and its organization but have yet to learn about the currencies that are traded and how their prices are quoted. Because more than 150 countries in the world have their own currencies, it makes sense that currency trading is governed by an intricate set of conventions and practices.

Exchange Rates

An **exchange rate** is the relative price of two monies, such as the Japanese yen price of the U.S. dollar, the British pound price of the euro, or the Brazilian real price of the Mexican peso. Rather than write out the full name of these currencies, contractual parties use abbreviations. In banking and commercial transactions, it is important that all parties understand which currencies are being used. Hence, there is a need for standardization of the abbreviations. The International Organization for Standardization (called ISO from the Greek word for equal) sets these standards. Exhibit 2.4 provides a list of some of the ISO currency abbreviations used to represent the different currencies. In most cases, the abbreviation is the ISO two-digit country code plus a letter from the name of the currency.

For example, the notation for the U.S. dollar is USD, the British pound is GBP, the Japanese yen is JPY, and the euro is EUR. In examples throughout the book, we use these codes to illustrate the units involved in different transactions. At other times, though, common symbols for the major currencies are used, such as $ for the U.S. dollar, £ for the pound, € for the euro, and ¥ for the yen.

If it takes 100 yen to purchase 1 dollar, we can write

$$JPY100 = USD1$$

The exchange rate can be written as JPY100/USD, or ¥100/$, where the 1 dollar in the denominator is implicit. Similarly, if it takes 1.75 U.S. dollars to purchase 1 British pound, then

$$USD1.75 = GBP1$$

and the exchange rate can be written as USD1.75/GBP or simply $1.75/£.

Notice that we treat the slash symbol (/) as a divisor in a ratio to indicate the amount of the first currency that is necessary to purchase one unit of the second currency. While we continue to use this logical notation throughout the book, you will encounter foreign exchange quotations, such as EUR/USD or EURUSD, in which the first currency in the quote is the base currency and the second currency is the numerator currency or "quote currency." In other words, if you type EUR/USD into Google, it will return the price of the euro in terms of dollars, or how many dollars you can buy with 1 euro. Presentations that use this convention typically contain lists of numbers without letters or symbols. We retain our ratio presentation with either letters or symbols throughout the book to make it easy for the reader to understand the relative price aspect of exchange rates.

Exchange Rate Quotes

Because exchange rates are relative prices, they can be expressed in two ways. Exchange rates can be quoted in direct terms as the domestic currency price of the foreign currency or in indirect terms as the foreign currency price of the domestic currency.

Because direct prices are, perhaps, the most natural way to discuss exchange rates, let's consider **direct quotes** first. For example, in the United Kingdom, people discuss the pound prices of various goods and assets. If you were in the United Kingdom, you might inquire, "How many pounds does it take to purchase that car?" or "What does that car cost?" In each case, you want to know the number of pounds that must be given up to purchase a specific car. An economist would say the answer to these questions is the value of the car in terms of the pound.

Now, suppose you were in the United Kingdom, and you wanted to travel to Germany. If you thought you might need 1,000 euros on your trip, it would also be natural for you to inquire, "How many pounds does it take to purchase 1,000 euros?" or "What do 1,000

Exhibit 2.4 Currencies and Currency Symbols

Country	Currency	ISO Currency Code
Argentina	Peso	ARS
Australia	Dollar	AUD
Bahrain	Dinar	BHD
Brazil	Real	BRL
Canada	Dollar	CAD
Chile	Peso	CLP
China	Yuan	CNY
Colombia	Peso	COP
Czech Republic	Koruna	CZK
Denmark	Krone	DKK
Ecuador	US dollar	USD
Egypt	Pound	EGP
European Union	Euro (€)	EUR
Hong Kong	Dollar	HKD
Hungary	Forint	HUF
India	Rupee	INR
Indonesia	Rupiah	IDR
Israel	Shekel	ILS
Japan	Yen (¥)	JPY
Jordan	Dinar	JOD
Kuwait	Dinar	KWD
Lebanon	Pound	LBP
Malaysia	Ringgit	MYR
Mexico	Neuvo Peso	MXN
New Zealand	Dollar	NZD
Norway	Krone	NOK
Pakistan	Rupee	PKR
Peru	New Sol	PEN
Philippines	Peso	PHP
Poland	Zloty	PLZ
Russia	Ruble	RUR
Saudi Arabia	Riyal	SAR
Singapore	Dollar	SGD
South Korea	Won	KRW
South Africa	Rand	ZAR
Sweden	Krona	SEK
Switzerland	Franc	CHF
Taiwan	Dollar	TWD
Thailand	Baht	THB
Turkey	Lira	TRL
United Arab Emirates	Dirham	AED
United Kingdom	Pound (£)	GBP
United States	Dollar ($)	USD
Uruguay	Peso	UYU
Venezuela	Bolivar	VEB
Vietnam	Dong	VND

Note: For a more complete list of ISO Currency Codes, see www.iso.org.

euros cost?" In each case, you want to know the number of pounds that must be given up to purchase this specific number of euros. Once again, economists would say that the answer is the value of 1,000 euros in terms of the pound.

If the pound price of the euro is £0.90/€, the pound cost of 1,000 euros is

$$€1,000 \times (£0.90/€) = £900$$

Notice that with direct exchange rates, converting from a foreign currency amount (in this case, the euro) into a domestic currency value (in this case, the pound) simply involves multiplying the amount of foreign currency by the exchange rate expressed in units of domestic currency per foreign currency.

For the U.S. dollar, it is common for many exchange rates to be quoted in **indirect quotes**, such as ¥100/$ for the Japanese yen or CHF1.8/$ for the Swiss franc. These exchange rates represent the amount of foreign currency that is equivalent to 1 dollar, which is also the amount of foreign currency required to purchase 1 dollar.

Conventions in the foreign exchange market have converged on an order for how exchange rates are usually quoted. This clearly facilitates communication between traders across the world. For major currencies, the base currency or denominator of the exchange rate in a quote follows this order: euro, British pound, Australian dollar, New Zealand dollar, U.S. dollar, Canadian dollar, Swiss franc, and Japanese yen. Thus, people quote the pound price of the euro, as in our earlier example, but they quote the U.S. dollar price of the pound. Similarly, traders quote the Australian dollar price of the British pound but quote the New Zealand dollar (or "kiwi," as it is often referred to) price of the Australian dollar. Exchange rates between Asian and Latin American currencies and the U.S. dollar are also quoted in indirect terms from the U.S. perspective.

Because exchange rates are the relative prices of monies, an exchange rate expressed in direct terms is the reciprocal (inverse) of the exchange rate expressed in indirect terms. For example, suppose it takes 100 yen to purchase 1 dollar—that is, the exchange rate in indirect terms from the U.S. perspective is ¥100/$. Then, the exchange rate in direct terms from the U.S. perspective, which is the dollar price of the Japanese yen, is the reciprocal of the exchange rate quoted in indirect terms:

$$1/(¥100/\$) = \$1/¥100 = \$0.01/¥$$

The reciprocal nature of direct and indirect terms often confuses students. Earlier in the chapter, we converted money between pounds and euros when traveling between the United Kingdom and Germany. Now, suppose you are in the United States, and you want to travel to Japan. If you were advised that you needed 500,000 yen for your trip, it would be natural for you to inquire, "How many dollars does it take to purchase 500,000 yen?" Now, though, because the exchange rate is typically quoted as ¥100/$, the dollar cost of the ¥500,000 is

$$¥500,000/(¥100/\$) = \$5,000$$

Notice that with the exchange rate quoted as an indirect price, converting from a foreign currency amount (the yen, in this case) into a domestic currency value (the dollar, in this case) involves dividing the amount of foreign currency (the yen) by the exchange rate expressed in units of foreign currency per domestic currency (¥ per $). Because such currency conversions lie at the heart of all international financial transactions, it clearly pays to be careful to remember how the exchange rate is being quoted before converting from one currency into another.

The indirect method of quoting exchange rates is also commonly referred to as a **European quote** (the amount of foreign currency needed to buy dollars) because most former European currencies, such as the Deutsche mark and the French franc, were quoted this way relative to the dollar. The phrase **American quote** refers to the dollar price of a foreign currency—that is, the number of dollars it takes to purchase one unit of the foreign currency. Exchange rates of the British pound versus the dollar and the euro versus the dollar are commonly expressed directly in dollars per pound (for example, as $1.65/£) and in dollars per euro (for example, $1.15/€).

The following table summarizes the different ways of quoting exchange rates:

DIRECT AND INDIRECT, EUROPEAN AND AMERICAN QUOTES		
	In the United States	**In Britain**
$ per £	Direct	Indirect
$ per £	American	American
£ per $	Indirect	Direct
£ per $	European	European
	In Thailand	**In the European Union**
Thai baht per €	Direct	Indirect

When you are in the United States, quoting the pound exchange rate as $ per £ means you are using domestic currency per foreign currency; it is a direct quote. Similarly, when you are in Thailand, quoting the euro exchange rate as Thai baht per € is an example of a direct quote. When you are in Europe, quoting the Thai baht as Thai baht per € is an example of an indirect quote because you use foreign currency per domestic currency. The terminology *American* and *European* only refers to exchange rates relative to the dollar.

Major financial newspapers such as the *Wall Street Journal* and the *Financial Times* provide daily lists of foreign exchange rates, and many Web sites such as www.oanda.com provide currency converters. Exhibit 2.5 presents a typical listing from the *Wall Street Journal*. These exchange rates are supplied to the *Wall Street Journal* from the interbank market by Reuters. The exchange rate information pertains to Tuesday, December 21, 2010.

One set of quotes is in direct terms from the U.S. perspective (American quotes) and is reported "in US$." These columns indicate the number of U.S. dollars equivalent to one unit of the other currency, which is also the U.S. dollar price of one unit of the other currency. The second set of quotes is in indirect terms from the U.S. perspective (European quotes). These columns are labeled "per US$," which is the foreign currency price of 1 U.S. dollar.

Notice that many of the exchange rates listed under the columns titled "per US$" are greater than one in value (although there are a number of exceptions, including the euro, the British pound, the Swiss franc, and the SDR[1]). Most people find this way of discussing exchange rates superior to discussing small fractions. It is much easier to state the yen rate as "83.74 yen per dollar" (¥83.74/$) than it is to state its reciprocal, which is "Eleven thousand, nine hundred, and forty-two millionths of a dollar per yen" ($0.011942/¥). No doubt this is why indirect terms have become the common way of discussing many dollar exchange rates.

Most of the quotations in Exhibit 2.5 represent spot exchange rates, but the currencies of Britain, Canada, Japan, and Switzerland have quotes for 1-month, 3-month, and 6-month forward contracts. These financial instruments are discussed in Chapter 3.

Vehicle Currencies and Currency Cross-Rates

Our focus on the U.S. dollar exchange rates versus other currencies of the world is warranted because the U.S. dollar is a **vehicle currency**, meaning it is actively used in many international financial transactions around the world. The transaction costs of making markets in many currencies lead the market to use only a few currencies as the major vehicles for international transactions.

[1] SDR stands for *Special Drawing Right*, a unit of account created by the International Monetary Fund (IMF). The IMF and the SDR are discussed in Chapter 5.

Exhibit 2.5 U.S. Dollar Currency Quotes from Tuesday, December 21, 2010

G-10 Currencies	Code	Per USD	In USD	Emerging Markets	Code	Per USD	In USD
Australian dollar	AUD	1.0138	0.9864	Brazilian real	BRL	1.7118	0.5842
Canadian dollar	CAD	1.0207	0.9797	Brunei dollar	BWP	1.2202	0.8195
Swiss franc	CHF	0.9719	1.0289	Bulgarian lev	BGN	1.3716	0.7291
Euro	EUR	0.7636	1.3096	Cambodian riel	KHR	4080	0.0002451
UK pound	GBP	0.6461	1.5477	Chinese yuan	CNY	6.6681	0.1500
Japanese yen	JPY	84.12	0.011888	Columbian peso	COP	1929.51	0.0005183
Norwegian krone	NOK	6.0052	0.1665	Egyptian pound	EGP	5.7841	0.1729
New Zealand dollar	NZD	1.3606	0.7350	Hong Kong dollar	HKD	7.7794	0.1285
Swedish krona	SEK	6.8661	0.1456	Indian rupee	INR	46.292	0.02160
				Indonesian rupiah	IDR	8952	0.0001117
Other OECD	**Code**	**Per USD**	**In USD**	Iranian rial	IRR	10,555	0.0000947
Chilean peso	CLP	470.21	0.002127	Jamaican do Mar	JMD	84.052	0.0119
Czech koruna	CZK	17.259	0.0579	Jordanian dinar	JOD	0.7035	1.4215
Estonian kroon	EEK	11.713	0.0854	Kazakhstan tenge	KZT	143.55	0.006966
Hungarian forint	HUF	188.37	0.005309	Kuwaiti dinar	KWD	0.2826	3.5386
Icelandic krona	ISK	115.42	0.008664	Lebanese pound	LBP	1499.41	0.0006669
Israeli shekel	ILS	3.6154	0.2766	Malaysian ringgit	MYR	3.1467	0.3178
South Korean won	KRW	1155.67	0.0008653	Nigerian naira	NGN	156.75	0.006380
Mexican peso	MXN	12.4278	0.0805	Pakistani rupee	PKR	85.751	0.01166
Polish zloty	PLN	2.7875	0.3587	Peruvian new sol	PEN	2.877	0.3476
Slovak koruna	SKK	0.7014	1.4257	Philippines peso	PHP	44.473	0.0225
Turkish lira	TRL	1.5622	0.6401	Russian ruble	RUB	28.195	0.0355
				Saudi Arabian riyal	SAR	3.7499	0.2667
Emerging Markets	**Code**	**Per USD**	**In USD**	Singapore dollar	SGD	1.3225	0.7561
Argentine peso	ARS	3.9874	0.2508	South African rand	ZAR	6.8872	0.1452
Azerbijan manat	AZN	0.7983	1.2527	Taiwan dollar	TWD	29.925	0.03342
Bahraini dinar	BHD	0.3773	2.6504	Tajikistani somoni	TJS	4.5926	0.2177
Bangladeshi taka	BDT	69.286	0.01443	Thai baht	THB	30.168	0.03315
Belarusian ruble	BYR	4947.8	0.0002021	UAE dirham	AED	3.6735	0.2722
Belize dollar	BZD	1.9536	0.5119	Uruguayan peso	UYU	19.39	0.05157
Bhutan ngultrum	BTN	45.173	0.02214	Venezuelan bolivar	VEB	4.2705	0.2342
Botswana pula	BWP	6.5081	0.1537	Vietnamese dong	VND	19500	0.00005128

Note: Original data in foreign currency per dollar are from www.oanda.com and are the highest bid prices of the day.

For example, if there are N different currencies issued by various countries throughout the world, there are $N(N-1)/2$ possible exchange rates. With more than 150 different currencies, there are more than 11,175 possible exchange rates. Because the demands to trade between many of these different currency pairs are often low or nonexistent, there is no direct market made. Rather, traders make a direct market in one or two important currencies, referred to as *vehicle currencies*. In the 19th century, the world's primary vehicle currency was the British pound; now, it is the U.S. dollar.

Exchange rates between two currencies that do not involve the dollar are often called **cross-rates**. Exhibit 2.6 provides examples of cross-rates taken from the *Wall Street Journal* for December 21, 2010.

The rows represent "direct quotes" from the perspective of the country whose currency begins the row. For example, 83.47 is the Japanese yen price of 1 dollar. The columns thus represent the indirect quotes from the perspective of the country whose currency is at the top

Exhibit 2.6 Representative Cross-Rate Quotes from December 21, 2010

	USD	EUR	GBP	CHF	MXN	JPY	CAD
Canada CAD	1.0207	1.3367	1.5798	1.0502	0.08217	0.01213	....
Japan JPY	84.118	110.16	130.19	86.5495	6.7715	....	82.411
Mexico MXN	12.422	16.268	19.226	12.781	....	0.14768	12.170
Switzerland CHF	0.97191	1.2728	1.5042	....	0.07824	0.01155	0.95218
United Kingdom GBP	0.64612	0.84616	....	0.66479	0.05201	0.00768	0.63300
Euro	0.76359	....	1.1818	0.78566	0.06147	0.00908	0.74809
United States USD	....	1.3096	1.5477	1.0289	0.08050	0.01189	0.97970

Source: www.oanda.com and authors' calculations.

of the column. For example, the Swiss franc column tells you how many foreign currency units it takes to buy 1 Swiss franc.

Although there appears to be a trend toward more cross-rate transactions, an estimated 85% of all transactions have the dollar as one side. Some analysts think the euro, which replaced 11 different currencies in Europe in 1999, may someday replace the dollar as a vehicle currency. In fact, a BIS (2010) survey of foreign exchange activity reveals that about 40% of all trades during 2010 involved the euro.

Triangular Arbitrage

Triangular arbitrage is a process that keeps cross-rates (such as euros per British pound) in line with exchange rates quoted relative to the U.S. dollar. A trader can conduct a triangular arbitrage in many ways. For example, a trader might start with euros, buy pounds with the euros, then simultaneously sell those pounds for dollars and sell those dollars for euros. In other words, instead of exchanging just two currencies, the trader exchanges three (hence the term "triangular" arbitrage). If the number of euros the trader has at the end of these three transactions is greater than the number of euros at the beginning, there is a profit.

If such transactions can be done profitably, the trader can generate pure arbitrage profits—that is, earn risk-free profits. Obviously, in perfectly competitive financial markets, it is impossible to earn arbitrage profits for very long. If the euro price of the pound were not equal to the euro price of the U.S. dollar multiplied by the U.S. dollar price of the pound, arbitrage activity would immediately restore equality between the quoted cross-rate and the cross-rate implied by two dollar quotes:

$$(\text{Euros}/\text{Pound}) = (\text{Euros}/\text{Dollar}) \times (\text{Dollars}/\text{Pound})$$

In other words, the direct quote for the cross-rate should equal the implied cross-rate, using the dollar as an intermediary currency.

To see how a triangular arbitrage works, suppose that the euro price of the pound quoted in the market is €1.1555/£. Also, suppose that this quoted cross-rate is lower than the indirect rate, using the dollar as the intermediary currency. That is,

$$(\text{Euros}/\text{Pound}) < (\text{Euros}/\text{Dollar}) \times (\text{Dollars}/\text{Pound})$$

This means there is some room to make a profit. In this situation, buying the pound first with euros (or selling euros for pounds), and then selling those pounds for dollars, and finally selling that number of dollars for euros would make a profit because we would be buying the pound at a low euro price and selling the pound at a high euro price.

To check this logic, let's go through the steps in a triangular arbitrage.

Example 2.1 A Triangular Arbitrage

Suppose David Sylvian, a trader at the foreign exchange desk of Goldman Sachs in London, observes the following exchange rates of the euro relative to the pound and the dollar and the dollar relative to the pound:

EUR1.1555/GBP or GBP0.86543/EUR

EUR0.76388/USD or USD1.3091/EUR

USD1.5386/GBP or GBP0.64994/USD

Determine the arbitrage profits when David starts with EUR10,000,000 and buys GBP. Exhibit 2.7 presents the situation in a triangle diagram.

Exhibit 2.7 Triangular Arbitrage Diagram

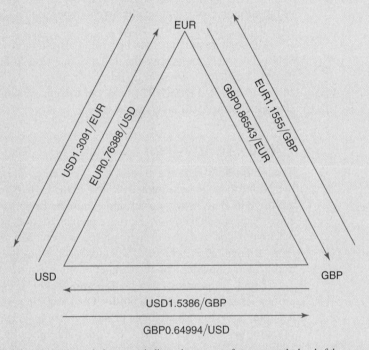

Notes: The exchange rates beneath the arrows indicate the amount of currency at the head of the arrow obtained by selling one unit of the currency at the tail of the arrow. For example, at the EUR node, selling 1 euro yields 0.86543 GBP going in the clockwise direction, and it yields 1.3091 USD going in the counterclockwise direction.

The exchange rates beneath the arrows in Exhibit 2.7 indicate the relevant prices, denominated in the currency at the next node (the buyer's node), of selling one unit of the currency at the starting node (the seller's node). You can use these prices to follow along on the transactions, recognizing that in some cases, we want to buy a currency, and in others, we want to sell.

Step 1. The revenue in pounds of selling EUR10,000,000 at the direct cross-rate would be

$$EUR10,000,000 \times (GBP0.86543/EUR) = GBP8,654,300$$

Step 2. Because the exchange rate of dollars per pound is (USD1.5386/GBP), David would be able to sell GBP8,654,300 for dollars to get

$$GBP8,654,300 \times (USD1.5386/GBP) = USD13,315,506$$

Step 3. Then, because the exchange rate of euros per dollar is EUR0.76388/USD, he would sell the USD13,315,506 for euros to get

$$USD13,315,506 \times (EUR0.76388/USD) = EUR10,171,449$$

If David had truly been able to make these transactions simultaneously, he would have made

$$EUR10,171,449 - EUR10,000,000 = EUR171,449$$

for an instantaneous rate of return of

$$1.71\% = (EUR171,449/EUR10,000,000)$$

Example 2.1 demonstrates how triangular arbitrage provides an instantaneous opportunity for profit *if* these were the actual market quotes. The data for the dollar exchange rates are, in fact, from Exhibit 2.6—quotes from the *Wall Street Journal* on December 21, 2010. We can use them to calculate the true cross-rate of EUR/GBP using the dollar as an intermediary currency:

$$(EUR0.76388/USD) \times (USD1.5386/GBP) = EUR1.1753/GBP$$

as in Exhibit 2.7. This is 1.71% larger than the rate quoted in Example 2.1 of EUR1.1555/GBP. Traders in the foreign exchange market will quickly capitalize on such a situation, figuring out which direction to move around the triangle in order to make a profit. David Sylvian made money by going in the clockwise direction; he first sold euros for pounds, then obtained dollars with the pounds, and finally euros with dollars. He knew this was the way to go because he compared the direct revenue in pounds (GBP0.86543/EUR) with the implied one we computed using the dollar:

$$1/[EUR1.1753/GBP] = GBP0.85085/EUR$$

You should convince yourself that going in the counterclockwise direction loses money. Three things are important to note about triangular arbitrage. First, to be an effective arbitrage, the transactions must all be conducted simultaneously. Because it is not physically possible to do all three transactions simultaneously, there is some risk involved in any attempted triangular arbitrage because prices might change between transactions. Second, as traders place orders to conduct the arbitrage in Exhibit 2.7, market forces are created that bring the quoted direct cross-rate back into alignment with the indirect cross-rate—the rate we calculated. In our example, we have

$$GBP0.86543/EUR > GBP0.64994/USD \times USD1.3091/EUR$$

As traders sell euros for pounds to conduct the arbitrage, the supply of euros (that is, the demand for pounds) increases in this market, which tends to drive down the GBP/EUR rate. Selling pounds for dollars tends to drive up the GBP/USD rate because it increases the supply of pounds (demand for dollars) in this market, and selling dollars for euros tends to drive up the USD/EUR rate because it increases the supply of dollars (that is, the demand for euros) in this market. Eventually, the two sides of the equation will once again equal one another. At that point, arbitrage profits will no longer be possible.

The third point is that the arbitrage need not start by using the euro to purchase pounds. The triangular arbitrage would be profitable starting from any of the currencies, as long as we trade in the same direction and go completely around the triangle.

Example 2.2 Ringgits and Bahts

Suppose you would like to know the Thai baht (THB) price of the Malaysian ringgit (MYR). For these emerging market currencies, it is unlikely that cross-rate quotes will be available except possibly at Thai or Malaysian banks. However, quotes relative to the dollar are easy to find. For example, the December 21, 2010, Reuters quotes were as follows:

$$MYR3.1348/\$$$

$$THB30.157/\$$$

By using triangular arbitrage, we would expect the THB/MYR exchange rate to be

$$(THB30.157/\$)/(MYR3.1348/\$) = THB9.6201/MYR$$

Of course, in our examples, we ignored bid–ask spreads, the main source of transaction costs in the forex market. From our discussion in the next section, you will see that the bid–ask spreads in the spot foreign exchange market are quite small and are often ignored in this book. We also assume that triangular arbitrage works perfectly from now on.

2.3 INSIDE THE INTERBANK MARKET I: BID–ASK SPREADS AND BANK PROFITS

A foreign exchange trader is typically responsible for buying and selling a particular currency or a small group of currencies and holds an inventory or portfolio of positions in those currencies. One reason for the activity in the interbank market is that forex traders at one bank use forex traders at other banks to adjust their portfolios in response to transactions that arise from their customers in the corporate market. They also trade with other banks to try to make a profit, and their desired positions in various currencies change in response to the news events of the day.

For example, suppose corporate customers buy yen from a trader at Deutsche Bank. The trader's inventory is now imbalanced, and the trader is likely to use the interbank market to buy yen, thereby "passing along" the original corporate order. For example, after completing the corporate trade, the Deutsche Bank trader may enter the interbank market to buy yen from Nomura to replenish his inventory of yen. The repeated passing of inventory imbalances among dealers has been dubbed "hot potato trading" and may be one reason for the large volumes we see in the interbank market (see Lyons, 2001).

Bid–Ask Spreads

Ultimately, traders in the interbank market try to buy and sell various foreign currencies with the goal of generating profits. To do so, they quote two-way prices. The **bid rate** is the rate at which they want to buy a base currency (to remember this, think *b* for buy), and the **ask rate** is the rate at which they sell base currency (think *s* for sell). The difference between these two rates is known as the **bid–ask spread**. The bid price is always less than the ask price because the trader bids for the base currency when they buy it and asks a price for the base currency when they sell it. Let's illustrate the concept of bid–ask spreads with an example.

Example 2.3 Yen–Dollar and Dollar–Yen Bid and Ask Rates

A yen–dollar bank trader would quote a bid price of yen per dollar at which she is willing to buy dollars in exchange for yen of, say, ¥110.25/$. The trader would then quote a higher ask price of yen per dollar (also called the **offer price**) at which she is willing to sell dollars for yen, say, at an exchange rate of ¥110.30/$. In this latter transaction, the trader can be said to be offering dollars, the base currency in the denominator, to the market, and she is willing to accept yen in return.

What are the dollar per yen bid and ask rates? The bid rate is the dollar price of yen at which the bank trader is willing to buy yen with dollars from the market, and the ask rate is the dollar price at which the bank trader is willing to sell yen for dollars to the market. Since buying yen from the market is equivalent to selling dollars to the market, the dollar per yen bid rate must be the reciprocal of the yen per dollar ask rate, $[1/¥110.30/\$]^{ask} = (\$0.009066/¥)^{bid}$. Similarly, selling yen to the market is the equivalent of buying dollars from the market, thus $[1/(¥110.25/\$)^{bid}] = (\$0.009070/¥)^{ask}$

We can summarize the reciprocal nature of bid–ask spreads with a line diagram, as represented in Exhibit 2.8. Each node in the diagram represents a currency at a point in time. In Exhibit 2.8, we have only the dollar and the yen at the current time period.

The arrows indicate the direction of sale. The exchange rates under the arrows are direct revenues to the seller (in terms of the currency at the next node) from selling one unit of the currency at the starting node. We take the perspective of the seller being a corporation or a client (with foreign currency) and the buyer being a bank trader. In selling yen for dollars, the seller will receive the bid price of $(\$ \text{ per } ¥)^{bid}$, which is the reciprocal of the bank's ask yen price per dollar. That is

$$(\$ \text{ per } ¥)^{bid} = 1/(¥ \text{ per } \$)^{ask}$$

The person selling yen to the bank for dollars gets the lower dollar bid price because the bank trader buying yen with dollars wants to make a profit when reselling the yen she obtains. Similarly, in going from dollars to yen, the seller of dollars to the bank receives the bank's bid price of $(¥ \text{ per } \$)^{bid}$, which Exhibit 2.8 demonstrates is the reciprocal of the bank's ask price of dollars for yen. That is,

$$(¥ \text{ per } \$)^{bid} = 1/(\$ \text{ per } ¥)^{ask}$$

If you are confused about whether to use the bid or ask exchange rate in a particular transaction, just remember that you will *always* transact with the bank to your disadvantage. If you are purchasing dollars with yen, you will have to pay the high price of ¥ per $, which is the bank's ask price for dollars. Similarly, if you are selling dollars to the bank to obtain yen, you will get the low price of ¥ per $, which is the bank's bid price for dollars.

The Magnitude of Bid–Ask Spreads

The competitive nature of the foreign exchange market and the growth of electronic trading have greatly compressed bid–ask spreads over the last decade. In the interbank market, spreads for major currencies have become negligible.

Even in the customer market, bid–ask spreads are now also within 5 "pips" for the major currencies and large transaction sizes. **Pip** is trader jargon for the fourth decimal point in a currency

Exhibit 2.8 The Reciprocal Nature of Bid and Ask Exchange Rates

Notes: The exchange rates beneath the arrows indicate the amount of currency at the head of the arrow obtained by selling one unit of the currency at the tail of the arrow to the bank. We take the perspective of a corporation or individual at the starting node and a bank trader at the ending node.

quote.[2] For example, Exhibit 2.5 shows that the USD/EUR quote on December 21, 2010, is \$1.3096/€. Assuming a spread of 2 pips and taking the \$1.3096/€ rate as the midpoint, the ask rate is \$1.3097/€ and the bid rate is \$1.3095/€. Therefore, 1 pip reflects 1/100 of a U.S. cent in this case. However, to get an idea of transaction costs involved in trading currencies, it's better to express the bid–ask spread in percentage points. The percentage bid–ask spread is computed as:

$$\text{Percentage spread} = \frac{(\text{ask} - \text{bid})}{\text{midpoint}}$$

Hence, for the example, we obtain

$$\frac{1.3097 - 1.3095}{1.3096} = 0.00015$$

That is, the bid–ask spread represents 0.015% or 1.5 basis points. The difference between the ask price and the bid price actually represents two transaction costs. In the first transaction, you buy from a bank at its ask price; then you turn around and sell to another bank at its bid price. To understand how small these transaction costs are, consider the following example.

Example 2.4 Paying the Bid–Ask Spread

Suppose the treasurer of a U.S. company purchases pounds with dollars in anticipation that the manufacturing manager will want to purchase some British goods, but the treasurer is told immediately after the purchase of the pounds that the deal for the goods is off. The treasurer then sells the pounds back to the bank for dollars. Because the treasurer bought pounds at the bank's ask price of \$/£ and immediately sold the pounds

---

[2]For the currencies not trading around a value of 1, the convention is different. For example, for a quote of ¥110.25/\$, a pip represents 0.01.

back to the bank at the bank's bid price of $/£, the treasurer has made two transactions and has lost the bid–ask spread on every pound bought and sold. (Of course, this presupposes that the quoted exchange rates did not change.)

Assume that the percentage bid–ask spread the treasurer faced for the pound–dollar exchange rate is 4 pips. If the ask rate is $1.50/£, then the bid rate is $1.4996/£, and the percentage spread is:

$$[(\$1.50/£) - (\$1.4996/£)]/(\$1.4998/£) = 0.03\%$$

Thus, if the treasurer bought, say, £1,000,000 at $1.5000/£, the cost would have been

$$£1,000,000 \times (\$1.5000/£) = \$1,500,000$$

Selling £1,000,000 back to the bank at the bank's bid price for pounds of $1.4996/£ would provide

$$£1,000,000 \times (\$1.4996/£) = \$1,499,600$$

Hence, the treasurer would lose $400 on the two transactions, which is 0.03% of $1.5 million.

The cheapest currencies to trade are the major ones like the EUR versus USD (with spreads sometimes as low as 1 pip), the GBP versus USD, and the USD versus JPY. The most liquid currencies, typically trading at less than 10 pips, are called the "G10" currencies and also include the AUD, CHF, CAD, NZD, SEK, and NOK (see Exhibit 2.4 for the meaning of these acronyms). Emerging market currencies trade at higher spreads.

Bid–ask spreads are not constant over time and even vary through the day. Traders seek to profit from their currency positions on a daily basis and do not want to be stuck with large open positions at the end of the day. Varying the magnitude of the bid–ask spread as a function of market conditions helps traders manage their inventory risk. For example, when markets are more volatile (that is, exchange rate values are undergoing relatively large changes), bid–ask spreads tend to increase. The effect of volatility is even apparent within each trading day, with spreads being wider at the open or close of particular markets (because there is more uncertainty then) or around the time important economic statistics are released.

The volatility in currency markets varies considerably through time, as was abundantly clear during the 2008 global financial crisis. After Lehman Brothers failed, volatility in the foreign exchange market rose to unprecedented heights, increasing bid–ask spreads on the major currencies by a factor of 4 to 5 times (see Melvin and Taylor, 2009).

Bid–ask spreads also vary with the nature of the particular customer order. For example, bid–ask spreads tend be lower for larger orders. While processing costs could explain this size pattern, recent research suggests that dealers tend to pay for informative order flow in the form of lower spreads (see, for example, Mende et al., 2007; Osler, 2009; and Ding, 2009). Foreign exchange dealers use information in order flow to speculate on foreign exchange movements and manage the risk of their trading books. Recent research also finds that financial customers obtain better spreads than corporate customers and that better performing money managers obtain better spreads than poorly performing ones (see Ramadorai, 2008; and Bjonnes and Rime, 2005).

While retail customers can now also obtain competitive spreads on certain online trading Web sites, spreads for exchanging physical currencies in the tourist market continue to be quite large at 5% or more. Banks and currency exchanges quote larger bid–ask spreads in this market because they must hold physical inventories of different monies, and these inventories are not interest bearing. They must also transact with brokers who move physical amounts of currencies between different countries in response to excess supplies and demands. It is interesting to note that using credit cards when traveling as a tourist actually saves on transaction costs because the credit card companies give their customers an exchange rate that is quite close to the interbank rate on the day of the transaction. However, be careful because some card companies also charge steep fees for international transactions.

POINT–COUNTERPOINT

Are Speculative Trading Profits in the Foreign Exchange Market Excessive?

The top foreign exchange banks, such as Deutsche Bank, UBS, Barclays, and Citibank, earn billions of dollars per year from foreign exchange trading. Our two sidekick brothers engage in a heated discussion of this fact. Ante Handel views these profits as a typical example of speculative excess. "Compare the dollar volume of interbank foreign exchange trading to the dollar volume of international trade flows," he fumes. "The difference is enormous. All that trading only makes the banks rich, and it causes exchange rates to be more volatile than they should be, which hurts our exporters. The government ought to tax speculative trading and make sure our banks simply support our exporters, who need these foreign currencies," he concludes.

Freedy Handel, on the other hand, claims that foreign exchange dealers are primarily market makers who trade with one another to adjust their portfolios in response to fundamental buy and sell transactions from the corporate world. "These banks' profits are simply the normal reward for providing liquidity in a market, and liquidity is of vital importance to the well-being of our economy," he politely argues.

As often happens, their cousin, Suttle Trooth, comes in and reconciles their differences by analyzing the available facts. "First," Suttle says, "Freedy, you are wrong in presuming that banks do not speculate. There is plenty of evidence that they do." (In this book, we will encounter several examples of speculative trading strategies that major banks follow in order to profit from exchange rate movements. As we mentioned in this section, large banks may attempt to exploit information from their order flow to predict exchange rate movements and develop a position before their competitors do. Many banks apparently attempt to profit from short-term, within-the-day, trading strategies.)

"Second," Suttle continues, "Ante, you are wrong to conclude that the profits are necessarily due to speculative excess. If most of the enormous trading volume in the foreign exchange market is trading between banks, you should realize that as a whole, the interbank market cannot profit from interbank trades. Interbank trading is a 'zero sum' game: Some other bank must lose every dollar one bank gains."

"Third," Suttle goes on, "Freedy might be right to think that market making alone may indeed lead to substantial profits for foreign exchange dealers because of the huge trading volumes. Let's make a quick back-of-the-envelope computation." Suttle produces the following numbers. Suppose that 50% of all trading is between banks and their customers. In 2010, Citibank's share of the total market is 7.69%. Hence, if total volume in the foreign exchange market is $3.9 trillion, the volume of transactions per day handled by Citibank is

$$0.0769 \times \$3.9 \text{ trillion} = \$299.9 \text{ billion}$$

However, 50% of these transactions involve other foreign exchange dealers, and we assume that overall, Citibank does not earn money on these deals. However, it does earn the bid–ask spread from dealing with corporate and other customers, which represents 50% of their market or $0.50 \times \$299.9$ billion $= \$149.96$ billion.

If a typical bid–ask spread is 0.015%, the annual revenue from pure market making is

$$\$149.96 \text{ billion/day} \times \frac{1}{2} \times (0.015/100) \times 250 \text{ trading days/year} = \$2.812 \text{ billion/year}$$

The $\frac{1}{2}$ arises because the volume applies to both sell and buy transactions, and Citibank needs a round-trip transaction to earn the full spread. Of course, these numbers represent revenues, not profits. Moreover, it is also possible that part of the customer flow is no longer intermediated by forex dealers, given the rapid growth in "eFX."

Yet, for a number of reasons, this estimate still probably understates Citibank's earnings from providing liquidity services in the foreign exchange market. First, we used indicative spreads for large transaction sizes for major currency pairs. Smaller orders and transactions involving other currency pairs carry higher spreads. Second, spreads are much higher for less liquid emerging currencies, in which Citibank tends to have a larger market share. Finally, spreads are larger on the part of the foreign exchange trading volume that involves forward contracts and other derivative contracts. Given our computations, it seems very likely that the bulk of Citibank's profits arise from its market-making function and not from its taking of speculative positions.

Several academic studies have examined whether speculative position taking was a major source of earnings from foreign exchange trading for a number of banks.[3] While there are some caveats to these studies, they all confirm that most profits come from conventional market-making activities rather than from speculation.

While Suttle's arguments have reconciled our two brothers on their main points of disagreement, Suttle has to concede that he is not sure whether the taking of speculative positions by banks could drive up exchange rate volatility, as Ante claimed. He promises to revisit this issue in later chapters.

2.4 INSIDE THE INTERBANK MARKET II: COMMUNICATIONS AND FUND TRANSFERS

The enormous volume of trade in the foreign exchange market requires an extensive communication network between traders and a sophisticated settlement system to transfer payments in different currencies between the buyers and sellers in different countries.

Communication Systems

Until the introduction of computers in the 1970s, the participants in the foreign exchange market communicated with their clients and each other on the telephone and via telex. Today, traders watch information displayed on computer screens, provided by major commercial information distributors such as Reuters and Bloomberg. The firms distributing financial information have long provided information about market prices of different currencies that is *not* contractually binding. Traders then contact each other to obtain actual prices and negotiate deals. For example, suppose Citibank wants to obtain a large number of euros. Citibank has three avenues to conduct a trade. First, it may contact traders at other major banks, such as BNP Paribas. Second, it may contact a foreign exchange broker to obtain quotes and broker a deal. Third, Citibank can trade on an electronic brokerage system, where quotes on a screen are transactable.

When a trade is agreed upon, banks communicate and transfer funds electronically through computer networks. The most important interbank communications network is the **Society of Worldwide Interbank Financial Telecommunications (SWIFT)**, which began operations in Europe in 1973 and is jointly owned by more than 2,000 member banks. The SWIFT network links more than 9,000 financial institutions in more than 200 countries. Banks use SWIFT to send and receive messages pertaining to foreign exchange transactions, payment confirmations, documentation of international trade, transactions in securities, and other financial matters. In particular, SWIFT is used to confirm foreign exchange deals agreed upon on the phone. In 2010, SWIFT's global network processed close to 4 trillion messages.

---

[3]See, for example, Ammer and Brunner (1997), Lyons (1998), and Mende and Menkhoff (2006).

After the verbal deal is electronically confirmed over SWIFT, the deal also has to be settled. Citibank will transfer dollars to BNP Paribas in the United States, and Citibank will receive euros from BNP Paribas in Europe. The transfer of dollars will be done through the **Clearing House Interbank Payments System (CHIPS)**, and the transfer of euros will be done through the **Trans-European Automated Real-time Gross Settlement Express Transfer (TARGET)**.

CHIPS is a private-sector system, owned and operated by The Clearing House Interbank Payments Company L.L.C. (CHIPCo), whose membership consists of many of the world's largest commercial banks. CHIPS is an electronic payment system that transfers funds and settles transactions in U.S. dollars. It is the central clearing system in the United States for international transactions, handling the bulk of all dollar payments moving between countries around the world. On a typical day in New York, about $1.5 trillion in business payments pass through CHIPS computers. This amount corresponds to more than 350,000 international transactions, such as foreign trade payments, foreign exchange transfers, securities settlements, and money market transactions, as well as a growing number of domestic payments. CHIPS participants receive same-day settlement of funds through a special Fedwire account at the Federal Reserve Bank of New York.

Fedwire is a real-time gross settlement (RTGS) system operated by the Federal Reserve System of the United States. Fedwire links the computers of more than 7,000 U.S. financial institutions that have deposits with the Federal Reserve System. Transactions on Fedwire instantly move dollar balances between financial institutions. A transfer occurs when the originating office transmits a message to a Federal Reserve Bank, indicating who the paying and receiving banks are. The Federal Reserve Bank then debits the account of the paying bank and credits the account of the receiving bank. "Real time" means that the transactions are settled as soon as they are processed, and "gross settlement" means that the transactions are settled on a one-to-one basis without bunching or netting with other transactions.

Transactions on CHIPS are facilitated with a universal identifier (UID), a unique identification number for a bank or a corporation that tells the CHIPS system what private account and bank information to use for sending or receiving payments. Because Citibank owes dollars to BNP Paribas, it uses BNP Paribas's UID to ensure that it is paying to the right account.

Cross-border transactions in euros are facilitated through the Trans-European Automated Real-time Gross settlement Express Transfer (TARGET2) system, which is the euro counterpart of Fedwire. For each of the European countries using the euro, the national RTGS systems were superseded by an international RTGS system (TARGET2) run through the European Central Bank. Hence, BNP Paribas would indicate to TARGET2 that it was paying euros to a particular European Citibank office, and TARGET2 would debit BNP Paribas's account and credit that of Citibank. The system also allows clearing of foreign exchange transactions between the members of the European Union that do not use the euro and those that do, although Sweden and the United Kingdom do not participate in TARGET2. Switzerland links to the euro through the Swiss Interbank Clearing (SIC) system. Exhibit 2.9 summarizes the communication systems used in the foreign exchange market, using two banks, Citibank and BNP Paribas, as an example.

Cross-Currency Settlement (or Herstatt) Risk

Of course, the settlement of a foreign exchange trade requires the payment of one currency and the receipt of another. However, the settlement procedures described previously do not guarantee that the final transfer of one currency occurs if and only if the final transfer of the other currency occurs as well. Because foreign currency transactions often involve the payment systems of two countries in different time zones, simultaneous exchange of currencies

Exhibit 2.9 Communication Systems in the Forex Market

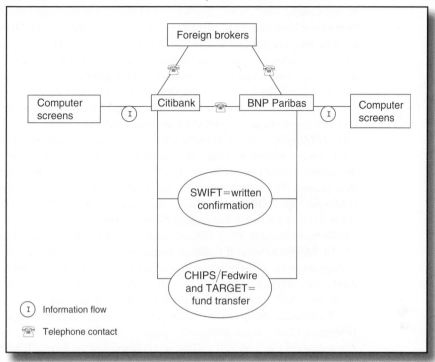

is difficult. The risk that only one leg of the transaction may occur is very real. It is known as **cross-currency settlement risk**, or **Herstatt risk**.

The term *Herstatt risk* derives from the first modern occurrence of settlement risk. On June 26, 1974, Bankhaus Herstatt, a small bank in Cologne, Germany, went bankrupt at a very inopportune time for some of its foreign exchange trading partners. Herstatt had purchased Deutsche marks with dollars, and it was expected to wire dollars to various trading partners in the United States that day in return for the Deutsche marks. But that same day, the German regulatory authorities withdrew Herstatt's banking license and ordered it into liquidation after several of its U.S. counterparties in the foreign exchange market had irrevocably paid Deutsche marks to Herstatt. However, Herstatt had not yet delivered the U.S. dollars it owed its trading partners because the U.S. trading day had only just begun. After Herstatt's closure, its New York correspondent bank suspended outgoing U.S. dollar payments from Herstatt's account.

Herstatt risk is thus the risk that a bank will fail to deliver on one side of a foreign exchange deal even though the counterparty to the trade has delivered its promised payment. With the growing volumes of foreign exchange trading, the major central banks have understandably been worried about the ramifications of another Herstatt crisis. In particular, there is fear among government authorities that a large settlement failure could create an international liquidity crisis and jeopardize the health of the worldwide financial system.

Indeed, after the 1974 Herstatt event, several U.S. banks suddenly faced a short-term liquidity crisis because the millions of dollars they expected to receive failed to materialize. Daily gross funds transfers in the United States fell by half. Fortunately, the crisis was short-lived. The banks gradually regained confidence in each other, and normal operations soon resumed, indicating that the banks were basically solvent despite their losses from Herstatt's failure to deliver.

With the explosion in trading volume that is occurring today, systemic risk is much larger. Central banks worry that foreign exchange trading is so large that even highly capitalized major banks could be wiped out by a Herstatt-style event. Recently, foreign exchange dealers, encouraged by the BIS, have developed a number of practices to limit settlement risk. First, banks now have strict limits on the amount of transactions they are willing to settle with a single counterparty on a given day. This generally helps curtail Herstatt risk.

Second, banks have started to engage in a variety of netting arrangements, in which they agree to wire the net traded amounts only at the end of a trading day. That is, a series of gross currency payments going both ways are converted into a single netted payment. When Citibank owes JPMorgan Chase $50 million from one foreign exchange transaction, and JPMorgan Chase owes Citibank $30 million from another transaction, it sounds reasonable to have only one wiring of funds from Citibank to JPMorgan Chase for the net amount of $20 million rather than to have JPMorgan Chase wire $30 million to Citibank and Citibank wire $50 million to JPMorgan Chase. **Bilateral netting** reduces the amount of settlement risk by lowering the number and size of payments that would otherwise be needed to settle the underlying transactions on a trade-by-trade basis. SWIFT has recently started to offer netting services for its users.

In the 1990s, several financial institutions set up organizations that offered multilateral netting services. The multilateral systems take all of a given bank's foreign exchange payments with other members of the system and then net them down to a single payment. This results in a further reduction in the number of payments actually required at the end of the day.

To illustrate these various netting arrangements, suppose that, in addition to Citibank and JPMorgan Chase, Bank of America participates in a multinetting system. Suppose Bank of America owes Citibank $30 million and is owed $20 million by JPMorgan Chase. Exhibit 2.10 illustrates this numeric example to demonstrate how gross flows, in which every payment is made, differ from the payments made under both bilateral and multilateral netting.

When there is no netting at all, the gross flows equal the sum of all transactions $(30 + 20 + 50 + 30 = 130)$. Under bilateral netting, Citibank and JPMorgan Chase recognize that one payment between them ($20 million from Citibank to JPMorgan Chase) settles their net position, reducing the gross flows to $70 million. With all three banks in the netting organization, JPMorgan Chase does not have to pay anything because it owes Bank of America 20, but it is owed 20 by Citibank. The netting organization simply settles the overall net debt and credit positions, significantly reducing the amount of payment flows between banks.

Third, settlement risk is eliminated if the exchange of the two monies happens simultaneously in a process known as payment versus payment (PvP). The dream of a global clearing bank that would ensure the simultaneous settlement of all currency transactions between members of its system became a reality with the establishment of CLS Bank in 2002. CLS Bank (where CLS stands for *Continuous Linked Settlement*) is owned by the world's largest financial groups. CLS Bank collects details of all the currency trades between its member banks, uses multilateral netting to figure net payments for each bank, and finalizes pay-ins and pay-outs to the system over a 5-hour window. This window represents the overlapping hours of the participating settlements systems. Because of its multilateral netting feature, CLS estimates that for each $1 trillion of value settled, only $50 billion has to be transferred between counterparties.

While CLS Bank is a private institution, its creation and operation require unprecedented cooperation between central banks, as the accounts that the financial institutions hold at central banks are used for all the transactions. The Federal Reserve organizes and administers the CLS Oversight Committee on behalf of the other participating central banks, and CLS bank now covers 17 currencies, including the G10 currencies and the currencies of Denmark, Hong Kong, Israel, Mexico, Singapore, South Korea, and South Africa. CLS Bank handles over 1.5 million transactions per day. Recent data suggest that well over 50% of foreign exchange trades are now settled through CLS bank, but over 30% of transactions still use the classic correspondent banking model. The CLS bank continued to operate seamlessly throughout the 2007 to 2010 global crisis, facing in fact record levels of transactions.

Exhibit 2.10 Netting Arrangements

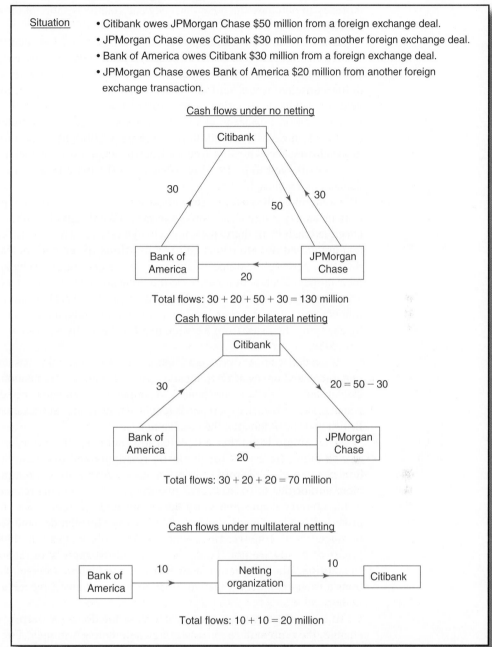

Situation
- Citibank owes JPMorgan Chase $50 million from a foreign exchange deal.
- JPMorgan Chase owes Citibank $30 million from another foreign exchange deal.
- Bank of America owes Citibank $30 million from a foreign exchange deal.
- JPMorgan Chase owes Bank of America $20 million from another foreign exchange transaction.

Cash flows under no netting

Citibank

30   50   30

Bank of
America   20   JPMorgan
Chase

Total flows: 30 + 20 + 50 + 30 = 130 million

Cash flows under bilateral netting

Citibank

30   20 = 50 − 30

Bank of
America   20   JPMorgan
Chase

Total flows: 30 + 20 + 20 = 70 million

Cash flows under multilateral netting

Bank of
America   10   Netting
organization   10   Citibank

Total flows: 10 + 10 = 20 million

2.5 DESCRIBING CHANGES IN EXCHANGE RATES

Section 2.3 explains how exchange rates are quoted at one point in time. Now, we turn to the topic of how to describe changes in exchange rates that occur over time. The first thing to remember about describing changes in exchange rates is that they are relative prices. Consequently, there are always two ways to describe the same situation. After the change in the exchange rate, it will always be true that it takes relatively less of one currency to purchase the other currency and relatively more of the latter currency to purchase the former.

Consider an example. Suppose the exchange rate between the dollar and the yen changes from ¥120/$ to ¥100/$. Because it now takes fewer yen to purchase the dollar, the yen is said to have *strengthened*, or appreciated, in value relative to the dollar. The dollar consequently is said to have *weakened*, or depreciated, in value relative to the yen. After this depreciation of the dollar, it will take more dollars to purchase a given number of yen. Formerly, at ¥120/$, it took $8,333.33 to purchase ¥1,000,000. Now, at ¥100/$, it takes $10,000.00 to purchase ¥1,000,000. The terms **appreciation** and **depreciation** are typically used to describe changes in exchange rates when exchange rates are allowed to be flexible—that is, to fluctuate freely in response to changes in demand and supply.

Sometimes, the government authorities of a country "fix," or "peg," the exchange rate of their money relative to a foreign money. (We discuss how they do this in Chapter 5.) Discrete changes in the values of exchange rates under such a fixed exchange rate system are called **devaluations** and **revaluations** of the currencies. If the monetary authorities increase the domestic currency price of foreign exchange, they are *devaluing* their money. Such actions increase the domestic currency prices of foreign monies and are often the result of a failure in government policy. One famous historical devaluation occurred in November 1967, when Britain devalued the pound relative to the dollar by changing the price from $2.80/£ to $2.40/£, or by over 14% $[(2.40 - 2.80)/2.80 = -14.29\%]$.

If the dollar prices of foreign imports into Britain remain constant after such a devaluation, the pound prices of foreign goods will rise with the devaluation. This is because, after the devaluation, it takes more pounds to purchase a given number of dollars. Similarly, if the pound prices of British export goods remain constant after the devaluation, the dollar price of British goods will fall after the devaluation.

The simple logic that a devaluation increases the prices of foreign goods relative to domestic goods for domestic residents and decreases the relative prices of domestic goods to foreign buyers makes devaluations a tempting way for government authorities to try to "cure" unemployment problems in a country at the expense of the country's consumers. By devaluing their currency, which changes the relative prices of goods, the government induces more foreign demand for the domestic goods produced in its country. Unfortunately, the policy does not always work because the prices of goods are not fixed. They can adjust rapidly in response to devaluations. In addition, if a devaluation does work, it can lead to a cycle of competitive devaluations as countries across the world try to gain a competitive advantage in international trade.

If the authorities of a country decrease the domestic currency price of foreign exchange, they are said to be *revaluing* the country's money. For example, in October 1969, Germany lowered the DEM price of the dollar from DEM4/$ to DEM3.66/$, a change of $8.5\% = (4 - 3.66)/4.0$. This action decreased the DEM cost of imports to Germany and increased the dollar cost of goods exported from Germany. If a revaluation changes the relative prices across countries, it benefits domestic consumers but hurts domestic workers and producers. This is because the goods and services produced in the country have to compete with imports that have become cheaper after the revaluation. In recent years, the U.S. government has exerted much political pressure on the Chinese government to revalue its currency relative to the dollar and other Western currencies, claiming that its weak currency gives Chinese companies an unfair trade advantage.

Example 2.5 Baseball Caps in Turkey

Suppose a Turkish importer buys American baseball caps for $10 per cap. The exchange rate is 685,000 Turkish lira (TRL) per dollar, and the baseball caps are put up for sale in Ankara, with a 50% markup over the export price. Hence, the price of the baseball caps for Turkish consumers is

$$\$10 \times TRL685,000/\$ \times 1.50 = TRL10,275,000$$

The Turkish lira was pegged to a "basket" (combination) of the dollar and the euro until February 23, 2001. A political crisis earlier that week led to a financial crisis: Interest rates soared, and the Turkish stock market plummeted. On February 23, the Turkish government let the lira "float," or fluctuate, rather than keep it pegged to the dollar–euro basket. In just 1 day, the value of the dollar increased to TRL962,499/$, which represents a 40.51% increase in the value of the dollar relative to the lira. If the baseball cap export price and the markup remain unchanged, the Turkish lira price becomes

$$\$10 \times TRL962,499/\$ \times 1.50 = TRL14,437,402$$

This increase in price should certainly decrease the demand for baseball caps in Turkey. In 2005, the Turkish government dropped 6 zeroes from the lira, and the Turkish lira traded at a rate of TRL1.5591/$ on December 21, 2010.

Rates of Appreciation and Depreciation

Now that you know how to describe the movements in exchange rates, you can quantify those changes. The rate of appreciation or depreciation of one currency relative to another can be calculated as the percentage rate of change of the exchange rate:

$$\frac{(\text{New exchange rate} - \text{Old exchange rate})}{\text{Old exchange rate}}$$

It is important to note that technically, the description of an appreciation or a depreciation refers to the currency that is in the denominator of the exchange rate. For example, for dollar–pound exchange rates, the percentage change in the exchange rate describes an appreciation or a depreciation of the pound:

$$\text{Percentage appreciation or depreciation of the pound} = \frac{(\text{new \$ per £}) - (\text{old \$ per £})}{(\text{old \$ per £})}$$

For example, if the exchange rate changes from $2.00/£ to $2.50/£, the pound is said to have appreciated relative to the dollar by 25%:

$$25\% = \frac{(\$2.50/£) - (\$2.00/£)}{(\$2.00/£)}$$

Now, let's examine the rate of depreciation of the dollar relative to the pound in the same situation. Unfortunately, it will turn out to be a slightly different percentage change. Because the old exchange rate of pounds per dollar is £1/$2.00 = £0.50/$, and the new exchange rate is £1/$2.50 = £0.40/$, the dollar is said to have depreciated relative to the pound by 20%, because

$$\frac{(£0.40/\$) - (£0.50/\$)}{(£0.50/\$)} = -20\%$$

The fact that these rates of appreciation and depreciation are not the same causes some confusion. The explanation for the difference begins with the observation that the exchange rate quoted in direct terms from the U.S. perspective is the reciprocal (inverse) of the exchange rate quoted in indirect terms. Let $S(t, \$/£)$ be the dollar–pound exchange rate at time t. Then, the rate of appreciation of the pound relative to the dollar is $\dfrac{S(t+1, \$/£) - S(t, \$/£)}{S(t, \$/£)}$. If we want to find the rate of appreciation of the dollar relative to the pound, we must consider the indirect quotes. Let us denote these exchange rates with a different symbol, $E(t, £/\$)$. Then, the rate of appreciation of the dollar relative to the pound is $\dfrac{E(t+1, £/\$) - E(t, £/\$)}{E(t, £/\$)}$.

But, by definition, the indirect and direct quotes are each other's reciprocal, $S(t, \$/£) = 1/[E(t, £/\$)]$. Hence, the rate of appreciation of the dollar relative to the pound can be rewritten as $\dfrac{[1/S(t+1, \$/£)] - [1/S(t, \$/£)]}{[1/S(t, \$/£)]}$. If we multiply the numerator and the denominator of the rate of appreciation of the dollar by $S(t, \$/£)$, we find

$$\frac{S(t, \$/£)}{S(t+1, \$/£)} - 1 = \frac{S(t, \$/£) - S(t+1, \$/£)}{S(t+1, \$/£)}$$

Hence, the numerator in the rate of appreciation of the dollar is the negative of the numerator in the rate of appreciation of the pound, but the denominators are different. One uses the exchange rate at time t, and the other uses the exchange rate at time $t+1$.

While the distinction in terminology (that appreciation or depreciation refers to the currency in the denominator of the exchange rate) may seem like little more than an annoying and potentially confusing curiosity, the different descriptions are sometimes used for political purposes, which makes the distinction important to understand.[4] In Greece, before the advent of the euro, for example, different newspapers tended to describe the change in the exchange rate in the way that was most favorable to the political party that the newspaper supported. For example, suppose the Greek drachma value of the dollar rose from GRD200/\$ to GRD220/\$. Newspapers that wanted to heighten concern about the event would report "Dollar Strengthens Relative to Drachma by 10%," while newspapers that wanted to reduce concern would announce "Drachma Weakens Relative to Dollar by 9%." You should be able to explain why these statements actually describe the same event.

Continuously Compounded Rates of Appreciation (Advanced)

It turns out that using continuously compounded rates of change reconciles the two descriptions of the same event and makes them equal but opposite in sign. Let's look at what happens to the description as we change the time interval over which the event happened. For example, if the appreciation of the pound, from \$2.00/£ to \$2.50/£, took place over the course of a year, we would say that the annual rate of appreciation of the pound was 25%. That is, to go from the old rate at the end of a year to the new rate at the end of the current year requires multiplication by 1.25:

$$(\$2.00/£) \times (1.25) = (\$2.50/£)$$

If portfolio decisions are made monthly, we might also be interested in describing the rate of appreciation on a compound monthly basis while still expressing the percentage change at an annual rate. In this case, we ask what value of a in $[1 + (a/12)]$ when raised to the 12th power satisfies the following equation:

$$(\$2.00/£)[1 + (a/12)]^{12} = (\$2.50/£)$$

---

[4]Thanks to Ekaterini Kryiazidou for this example.

To solve for a, we first divide both sides by $2.00/£$ and then take the $(1/12)$ power on each side:

$$[1 + (a/12)] = [(\$2.50/£)/(\$2.00/£)]^{1/12}$$

Try this with your calculator. Then, subtract 1 and multiply by 12. The answer is $a = 0.2256$, or an annualized compound monthly rate of appreciation of the pound of 22.56%. The annualized compound monthly rate of depreciation of the dollar, d, can analogously be calculated as

$$(£0.50/\$)[1 - (d/12)]^{12} = (£0.40/\$)$$

and we find through similar steps that $d = 0.2208$, or 22.08%. Notice that the difference in the two descriptions of the same event is now smaller.

If we drive the compounding interval smaller and smaller, we will eventually ask what continuous rate of appreciation of the pound relative to the dollar over the course of a year caused the pound to strengthen from $2.00/£ to $2.50/£. Continuous compounding uses the symbol e, which represents the base of natural logarithms, and the value of e rounded to five decimal places is 2.71828.[5]

Now, the annualized continuously compounded rate of appreciation of the pound is the value of a that satisfies

$$(\$2.00/£)e^a = \$2.50/£$$

To solve for the value of a, we take the natural logarithm of both sides of the equation and find

$$a = \ln(\$2.50/£) - \ln(\$2.00/£) = 0.2231$$

or 22.31%. Similarly, the annualized continuously compounded rate of depreciation of the dollar is the value of d that satisfies

$$(£0.50/\$)e^{-d} = £0.40/\$$$

To solve for the value of d, we take the natural logarithm of both sides of the equation and find

$$d = -[\ln(£0.40/\$) - \ln(£0.50/\$)] = 0.2231$$

or 22.31%. With continuous compounding, the rates of appreciation of the pound and depreciation of the dollar are the same.

2.6 SUMMARY

This chapter discusses the foreign exchange market. The main points in the chapter are as follows:

1. The foreign exchange market is a large, over-the-counter market composed of banks and brokerage firms and their customers in the financial centers of countries around the world. Volume of trade in the market is estimated to be almost $4 trillion on active days.

2. The traditional phone-based system, where trades are agreed upon over the phone and confirmed later, is increasingly being supplanted by electronic trading.

3. The foreign exchange market is very competitive, with no single bank dominating the worldwide trading of currencies, but the top three banks nonetheless capture more than 40% of the trading volume.

---

[5]The appendix to this chapter discusses logarithms and continuous compounding.

4. Exchange rates—that is, the prices of currencies—are relative prices. They can be quoted in direct terms as the domestic currency price of the foreign currency (sometimes called *American terms* in the United States) or in indirect terms as the foreign currency price of the domestic currency (sometimes called *European terms* in the United States).
5. Exchange rates between two currencies that do not involve the dollar are called *cross-rates*. Triangular arbitrage keeps cross-rates in line with exchange rates quoted relative to the U.S. dollar.
6. Traders quote two-way prices in a bid–ask spread. They attempt to buy one currency at their low bid price and to sell that currency at their higher ask, or offer, price. Competition keeps bid–ask spreads in the market quite small.
7. In the interbank market, traders agree on currency transactions by phone or through electronic trading systems. Confirmation and settlement of a trade occurs later through SWIFT and CHIPS.
8. Settlement risk, the risk that one leg of the currency transaction may not occur, is also called Herstatt risk. In recent years, more and more foreign exchange transactions are settled through the CLS bank, which drastically mitigates settlement risk using a centralized, simultaneous settlement system.
9. Changes in flexible exchange rates are described as currency appreciations and depreciations. When it takes fewer yen to purchase the dollar, the yen is said to have *strengthened*, or *appreciated*, in value relative to the dollar. The dollar consequently has *weakened*, or *depreciated*, in value relative to the yen. It will take more dollars to purchase a given number of yen.

QUESTIONS

1. What is an exchange rate?
2. What is the structure of the foreign exchange market? Is it like the New York Stock Exchange?
3. What is a spot exchange rate contract? When does delivery occur on a spot contract?
4. What was the Japanese yen spot price of the U.S. dollar on December 21, 2010?
5. What was the U.S. dollar spot price of the Swiss franc on December 21, 2010?
6. How large are the bid–ask spreads in the spot market? What is their purpose?
7. What was the euro price of the British pound on December 21, 2010? Why?
8. If the direct euro price of the British pound is higher than the indirect euro price of the British pound using the dollar as a vehicle currency, how could you make a profit by trading these currencies?
9. What is an appreciation of the dollar relative to the pound? What happens to the dollar price of the pound in this situation?
10. What is a depreciation of the Thai baht relative to the Malaysian ringgit? What happens to the baht price of the ringgit in this situation?

PROBLEMS

1. Mississippi Mud Pies, Inc., needs to buy 1,000,000 Swiss francs (CHF) to pay its Swiss chocolate supplier. Its banker quotes bid–ask rates of CHF1.3990–1.4000/USD. What will be the dollar cost of the CHF1,000,000?
2. If the Japanese yen–U.S. dollar exchange rate is ¥104.30/$, and it takes 25.15 Thai bahts to purchase 1 dollar, what is the yen price of the baht?
3. As a foreign exchange trader, you see the following quotes for Canadian dollars (CAD), U.S. dollars (USD), and Mexican pesos (MXN): USD0.7047/CAD, MXN6.4390/CAD, and MXN8.7535/USD. Is there an arbitrage opportunity, and if so, how would you exploit it?
4. The Mexican peso has weakened considerably relative to the dollar, and you are trying to decide whether this is a good time to invest in Mexico. Suppose the current exchange rate of the Mexican peso relative to the U.S. dollar is MXN9.5/USD. Your investment advisor at Goldman Sachs argues that the peso will lose 15% of its value relative to the dollar over the next year. What is

Goldman Sachs's forecast of the exchange rate in 1 year?

5. Deutsche Bank quotes bid–ask rates of $1.3005/€ –$1.3007/€ and ¥104.30–104.40/$. What would be Deutsche Bank's direct asking price of yen per euro?

6. Alumina Limited of Australia has called Mitsubishi UFJ Financial Group to get its opinion about the Japanese yen–Australian dollar exchange rate. The current rate is ¥67.72/A$, and Mitsubishi UFJ thinks the Australian dollar will weaken by 5% over the next year. What is Mitsubishi UFJ's forecast of the future exchange rate?

7. Go to www.fxstreet.com, find the "Live Charts Window," and plot the exchange rate of the dollar versus the euro with a "candle stick" high–low chart at 5-minute intervals for 1 day, daily intervals for 1 month, and weekly intervals for 1 year. Now, cover the units and ask a classmate to identify the different graphs. Are you surprised?

8. Pick three currencies, and go to www.oanda.com to get their current bilateral exchange rates. Is there an arbitrage opportunity?

9. Go to the CLS Bank Web site, www.cls-group.com, and read about In/Out Swaps. How do they help participants manage their risks?

BIBLIOGRAPHY

Bank for International Settlements, 2010, "Central Bank Survey of Foreign Exchange and Derivatives Market Activity, 2010," Bank for International Settlements.

Bjonnes, Geir H., and Dagfinn Rime, 2005, "Dealer Behavior and Trading Systems in Foreign Exchange Markets," *Journal of Financial Economics* 75, pp. 571–605.

Cetorelli, Nicola, Beverly Hirtle, Donald P. Morgan, Stavros Peristiani, and Joao A.C. Santos, 2007, "Trends in Financial Market Concentration and their Implications for Market Stability," *Federal Reserve Bank of New York Economic Policy Review* 13, pp. 33–51.

Chaboud, Alain, Benjamin Chiquoine, Erik Hjalmarsson, and Clara Vega, 2009, "Rise of the Machines: Algorithmic Trading in the Foreign Exchange Market," Board of Governors of the Federal Reserve System, International Finance Discussion Paper 980.

Ding, Liang, 2009, "Bid-Ask Spread and Order Size in the Foreign Exchange Market: An Empirical Investigation," *International Journal of Finance and Economics* 14, pp. 98–105.

Gallaugher, John, and Nigel Melville, 2004, "Electronic Frontiers in Foreign Exchange Trading," *Communications of the ACM* 47, pp. 81–87.

King, Michael R., and Dagfinn Rime, 2010, "The $4 Trillion Question: What Explains FX Growth Since the 2000 Survey?" *BIS Quarterly Review*, December, pp. 27–42.

Lyons, Richard K., 1998, "Profits and Position Control: A Week of FX Dealing," *Journal of International Money and Finance* 17, pp. 97–115.

_____, 2001, *The Microstrucutre Approach to Exchange Rates*, Cambridge, MA: MIT Press.

Melvin, Michael, and Mark P. Taylor, 2009, "The Crisis in the Foreign Exchange Market," *Journal of International Money and Finance* 28, pp. 1317–1330.

Mende, Alexander, and Lukas Menkhoff, 2006, "Profits and Speculation in Intra-Day Foreign Exchange Trading," *Journal of Financial Markets* 9, pp. 223–245.

Mende, Alexander, Lukas Menkhoff, and Carol Osler, 2007, "Price Discovery in Currency Markets," working paper.

Osler, Carol, 2009, "Foreign Exchange Microstructure: A Survey of the Empirical Literature," in Robert B. Meyers, ed., *Springer Encyclopedia of Complexity and System Science*, pp. 5404–5438.

Ramadorai, Tarun, 2008, "What Determines Transaction Cost in Foreign Exchange Markets," *International Journal of Finance and Economics* 13, pp. 14–25.

Appendix

Logarithms

Logarithms are useful because they simplify growth calculations. The logarithm of a number is taken with respect to a particular base number, such as base 10 or base 2. The logarithm of a number X under base B is the number Y to which the base number B must be raised to make it equal to X. That is, because

$$B^Y = X$$

Base B logarithm of X is Y.

For example, if the base number is 10, and $X = 1{,}000$, then $Y = 3$, because $10^3 = 1{,}000$. Thus, in base 10, we say the logarithm of 1,000 is 3, and we can write $\log 10(1{,}000) = 3$.

In finance, we often encounter the *natural logarithm*. Natural logarithms arise because of continuous compounding and discussions of growth at continuous rates.

Banks usually quote interest rates at annual rates such as 10%, and they specify a compounding period, which might be annual, semiannual, monthly, daily, or even continuously. We know that the more often the bank credits interest to our account, the more money we will have at the end of a year because we will earn interest on previously credited interest. For example, if the quoted interest rate is 10%, at the end of 1 year, we will have the following amounts, depending on the compounding interval:

Compounding Interval	Amount in 1 Year
Annual	$(1 + 0.1) = 1.1$
Semiannual	$(1 + (0.1/2))^2 = 1.1025$
Quarterly	$(1 + (0.1/4))^4 = 1.1038$
Monthly	$(1 + (0.1/12))^{12} = 1.1047$
Daily	$(1 + (0.1/365))^{365} = 1.10516$

The return from continuously compounding at an interest rate, i, is obtained by taking the limit as the number of compounding intervals goes to infinity:

$$\lim_{n \to \infty} (1 + (i/n))^n = e^i$$

where e turns out to be the number that is the base for natural logarithms, which is approximately equal to 2.71828. In our example with a 10% annual interest rate, the amount of money in 1 year if interest is continuously compounded is $e^{0.1} = 1.10517$.

The natural logarithm of 1.10517 is 0.1 because raising 2.71828 to the 0.1 power is 1.10517. Sometimes, people write $\exp(i)$ rather than e^i to mean evaluate the exponential function, $\exp(i)$, at the value of i, which means simply to raise the number e to the i-th power.

Because raising the number e to a power tells you how much your principal grows when it is compounded continuously at a certain interest rate, the exponential function can be used to describe other growth rates, such as rates of appreciation or depreciation of currencies and rates of inflation. For example, if the dollar price of the pound were to grow at a continuous rate of 5% during 2012, then the exchange rate at the end of the year would be

$$S(\$/£, 2012) = S(\$/£, 2011)e^{0.05}$$

There are several useful properties of natural logarithms, which are represented by ln and their base number, e, that we will exploit:

1. $\ln(\exp(A)) = A$
2. $\exp(\ln(A)) = A$
3. If $A = BC$, then $\ln(A) = \ln(B) + \ln(C)$
4. If $A = B/C$, then $\ln(A) = \ln(B) - \ln(C)$
5. If $A = B^C$, then $\ln(A) = C \ln(B)$

We can combine these properties to establish that differences in natural logarithms are growth rates or percentage differences at continuous rates.

For instance, you can use the rules to demonstrate that

$$\ln[S(\$/£, 2012)] - \ln[S(\$/£, 2011) = 0.05]$$

Chapter 3

Forward Markets and Transaction Exchange Risk

Comercial Mexicana, Mexico's third largest retailer and a competitor of Walmart, sells many goods imported from the United States. Because Comercial's revenues are in Mexican pesos, a strengthening of the dollar relative to the Mexican peso increases Comercial's costs and lowers its earnings. In general, when the delivery of and payment for goods takes some time, future fluctuations in exchange rates give rise to potential losses, and possible gains, for the parties involved. The possibility of taking a loss in such a transaction is called **transaction exchange risk**.

In Chapter 2, we examined the organization of the spot foreign exchange market, in which the exchange of currencies typically happens in 2 business days. This chapter examines the **forward foreign exchange market** (or the *forward market*, for short). It is the market for exchanges of currencies in the future.[1] One of the major reasons for the existence of forward markets is to manage foreign exchange risk in general and transaction exchange risk in particular.

The forward markets for foreign exchange allow corporations, such as Comercial Mexicana, to protect themselves against transaction exchange risks by **hedging**.[2] To hedge against such risks, the corporation enters into an additional contract that provides profits when the underlying transaction produces losses. To evaluate the costs and benefits of hedging for a future transaction involving foreign currencies, the hedging party must have some way to quantify the degree of uncertainty it faces about future spot exchange rates. It accomplishes this by figuring out the likelihood of observing various ranges for future exchange rates.

Unfortunately, prior to the global financial crisis, Comercial Mexicana neither assessed nor hedged its transaction exchange risk properly. Instead, it dabbled excessively in complex foreign exchange derivatives contracts. As the dollar strengthened in the fall of 2008, Comercial lost $1.4 billion and was forced into bankruptcy. Numerous other companies throughout the developing world took enormous losses on foreign exchange contracts, including CITIC Pacific of Hong Kong, an infrastructure firm, which lost $1.89 billion, and Aracruz Celulose SA of Brazil, the world's biggest eucalyptus pulp maker, which lost $0.92 billion.[3]

---

[1] This chapter studies the over-the-counter forward markets. The other type of market for the exchange of currencies in the future is the organized futures foreign exchange market, which is discussed in Chapter 20.

[2] In Chapter 17, we explore more generally why firms might want to hedge currency risk.

[3] See *Euromoney* (2008); many of these losses were related to option-like derivatives, which are also discussed in Chapter 20.

We begin the chapter by defining *transaction exchange risk* and continue by formalizing how to think about the uncertain future exchange rate movements that cause it. Next, we introduce forward contracts and discuss how transaction exchange risk can be hedged using these contracts. We then provide more details about the conventions and trading practices of the forward exchange market. Finally, we introduce the concept of a forward premium, which describes how forward rates are related to spot rates, a relationship that we will come back to many times throughout the book.

3.1 TRANSACTION EXCHANGE RISK

Corporations, institutional investors, and individuals incur transaction exchange risk if they enter into a transaction in which they are required to pay or to receive a specific amount of foreign currency at a particular date in the future. Because the future spot exchange rate cannot be known with certainty, and the exchange rate can move in an unfavorable direction, such a transaction could lead to a loss. Our next task is to determine the precise nature of the risks associated with these transactions.

Suppose Motorola, a U.S. firm, is importing some electronic equipment from Hitachi, a Japanese company. Motorola orders the equipment and promises to pay a certain amount of yen in, say, 90 days. Suppose that Motorola does nothing between the time that it enters into the transaction and the time that the payment of yen is scheduled to occur. Motorola consequently will be required to purchase the amount of yen that it owes Hitachi with dollars in the future spot market. If the dollar weakens unexpectedly relative to the yen, Motorola will end up paying more dollars than it expected to pay.

Analogously, suppose Oracle, a U.S. firm, exports some Sun SPARC Enterprise Servers to Europe and agrees to receive euro payments in the future, when it delivers the servers. If Oracle does nothing between the time that it enters into the contracts and the date of delivery and payment, Oracle will convert the euros into dollars in the future spot market. If the euro depreciates unexpectedly, Oracle will receive fewer dollars for the transaction than it had anticipated receiving.

Whenever you engage in an international financial transaction that involves an exchange of currencies in the future, you will almost always be unsure about what the spot exchange rate will be in the future when you conduct this transaction. This is true even under regimes of fixed exchange rates because political and economic events can always trigger devaluation or revaluation of the domestic currency relative to foreign currencies. Under the flexible exchange rate system that has characterized the foreign exchange markets for the major currencies for nearly 40 years, exchange rates fluctuate a good deal from day to day. As a financial manager, you must be able to gauge where the exchange rate might head and how likely such fluctuations may be. This range of possible future values for the exchange rate and the likelihood of their occurring will give you an idea of the foreign exchange risk your firm faces and whether it's a good idea to hedge.

Often, people in corporations discuss the possibility or magnitude of a potential foreign exchange loss by valuing the foreign currency that is scheduled to be paid or received in the future at today's spot exchange rate. However, this is not the proper way to think about transaction exchange risk *unless there is no expected change to the exchange rate*. The potential loss or the possible gain from uncertain future exchange rates is appropriately measured relative to the expected future spot rate.

To see why, let's look at an example regarding transaction exchange rate risk at a fictitious company, Fancy Foods. We return to this example in the next section, after we have discussed how to formally describe uncertainty in future spot rates.

Example 3.1   Transaction Exchange Risk at Fancy Foods

Suppose Fancy Foods, a U.S. firm, is importing meat pies from the British firm Porky Pies. Assume that Fancy Foods is obligated to pay £1,000,000 in 90 days, in return for meat pies that will be delivered at that time by Porky Pies. Suppose that Fancy Foods owns no pounds currently and is going to wait until 90 days in the future to purchase pounds. How many dollars does Fancy Foods expect to have to pay? If Fancy Foods waits until 90 days from now to transact, it will have to purchase the £1,000,000 at whatever the spot exchange rate is at that time. Its dollar cost will consequently be

$$\text{Realized dollar cost in 90 days} = S(t{+}90, \$/£) \times (£1{,}00{,}000)$$

Suppose the current exchange rate is $1.50/£ and that Fancy Foods expects the pound to appreciate relative to the dollar by 2% over the next 90 days. Then the expected value of the future spot rate in 90 days is $1.53/£ = ($1.50/£) × (1 + 0.02). Hence, Fancy Foods expects to pay

$$(\$1.53/£) \times (£1{,}000{,}000) = \$1{,}530{,}000$$

This is the amount that will be paid *if* Fancy Foods's expectations are realized and the pound actually appreciates by 2%. But in currency markets, as in most other financial markets, what is expected usually does not happen. If the pound appreciates relative to the dollar by more than 2%, the future exchange rate will be higher than $1.53/£, and Fancy Foods will have to pay more dollars to offset its pound liability. On the other hand, if the dollar strengthens relative to the pound or does not weaken from the current spot rate of $1.50/£ to the expected spot of $1.53/£, Fancy Foods will experience a gain because the number of dollars required to eliminate the pound obligation will be reduced relative to what it expected.

If, instead, another U.S. company, Nancy Foods, agrees to receive some number of British pounds 90 days in the future in return for delivering frozen quiches to the British firm Quirky Pies, our calculations of gains and losses will be exactly the opposite: A depreciation of the pound relative to the dollar will cause Nancy Foods to receive fewer dollars than it expected to receive. Conversely, if the pound appreciates (that is, if the dollar weakens) by more than is expected, Nancy Foods will experience a gain because it has a pound asset.

3.2 DESCRIBING UNCERTAIN FUTURE EXCHANGE RATES

To quantify the potential losses or gains due to a transaction exchange risk, we must think more about describing the uncertainty surrounding *future* spot exchange rates. Although we do not know exactly what value exchange rates will have in the future, we can quantify the possible changes that may occur and thus quantify how much risk we are bearing in international financial transactions. In doing so, we use some statistical concepts that you probably know, but if not, the appendix "A Statistics Refresher," at the end of this chapter, should bring you up to speed.

Assessing Exchange Rate Uncertainty Using Historical Data

Historical data provide insight not only to what has happened in the past but what might happen in the future. Exhibit 3.1 presents a histogram of monthly percentage changes in the exchange rate of the U.S. dollar per British pound ($/£). The exhibit also superimposes on the graph a normal distribution curve, with the same **mean** and **standard deviation** as the data. We will explore this in more detail shortly.

Exhibit 3.1 Dollar/Pound Monthly Exchange Rate: 1975–2010

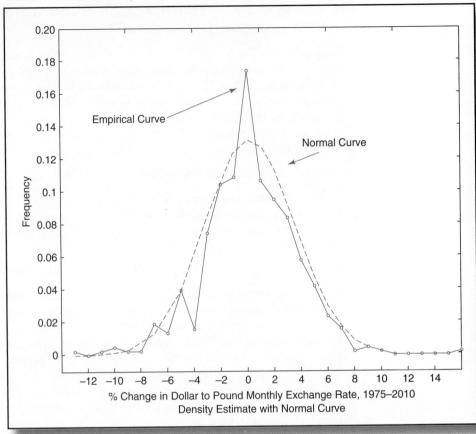

Notes: We compute monthly percentage changes in the dollar–pound exchange rate as $s(t) = \dfrac{S(t) - S(t-1)}{S(t-1)}$,

where $S(t)$ represents the exchange rate at time t (the end of a particular month). If $s(t)$ is a negative (positive) number, the pound depreciated (appreciated) that month. The graph creates a histogram of the $s(t)$ data. We consider small ranges (bins) of possible percentage changes (for example, between -0.167% and 0.167%) and compute the number of observations within the bin. The dots on the graph represent the midpoint of the bin and its frequency (the number of observations divided by the total number of observations). The curve connecting them is the histogram. The smooth curve is the density corresponding to a normal distribution.

The data in Exhibit 3.1 cover January 1975 to November 2010, or 431 observations. With the spot exchange rate at time t denoted $S(t)$, the percentage change in the exchange rate between time t–1 and time t is

$$s(t) = \lceil S(t) - S(t{-}1) \rceil / S(t{-}1) \tag{3.1}$$

Chapter 2 notes that these percentage rates of change are *appreciations* of the pound (if positive) and *depreciations* of the pound (if negative).

The horizontal axis in Exhibit 3.1 describes the percentage changes historically observed for the $/£ rate, which range from about -12% to $+14.5\%$. To create the histogram, we create ranges (bins) of equal width. The dots on the curve are the midpoints of the bins. The vertical axis represents the percentage frequency of occurrence of the rates of exchange rate change for each bin. The average (mean) monthly percentage change was -0.05% for the dollar–pound. Because the mean "centers" the distribution, and because the distribution is bell shaped, observations near the mean are likely to occur. The standard deviation is a measure of the dispersion of possibilities *around* the mean. For the monthly percentage changes in the exchange rates, the standard deviation was 3.03%. Exchange rate changes within 1 standard deviation of the mean (between $-0.05\% - 3.03\% = -3.08\%$ and $-0.05\% + 3.03\% = 2.98\%$) occur more frequently than changes further away from the mean. For the curve in Exhibit 3.1, exchange rate changes 2 standard deviations away from the mean (either smaller than $-0.05\% - (2 \times 3.03\%) = -6.12\%$ or larger than 6.01%) occurred very infrequently as the vertical distances become very small. For example, our detailed data reveal that exchange rate changes higher than 7.42% have occurred less than 1% of the time.

If we think that the histogram is a useful guide for the future, we can translate it into a probability distribution of future exchange rate changes. You have no doubt encountered probability distributions in other financial applications, such as describing the uncertainty regarding returns on investments in equity. Here, we use a probability distribution to summarize our ignorance about what will happen to future exchange rate changes.

The second curve in Exhibit 3.1 represents a normal probability distribution with the same mean and standard deviation as the historical data. Exhibit 3.1 reveals that the assumption of a normal distribution, characterized by its classic bell-shaped curve, is very reasonable for the dollar–pound rate, as it is for exchange rate changes between all major currencies for monthly rates of change. However, many emerging market currencies exhibit probability distributions that are distinctively non-normal. An example is Exhibit 3.2, which shows the distribution for monthly percentage changes of the Mexican peso relative to the U.S. dollar (MXN/USD) and the normal distribution with the same mean and standard deviation.

The historical distribution in Exhibit 3.2 is obviously not symmetric. Using historical data, we calculate a mean of 0.79% and a standard deviation of 4.76%. But, the most prominent feature of the historical distribution is the long right-hand tail. Statisticians say the distribution is skewed to the right. This indicates that large depreciations or devaluations of the peso relative to the dollar have occurred, and the absence of a large left-hand tail indicates

Exhibit 3.2 Peso/Dollar Monthly Exchange Rate: 1994–2010

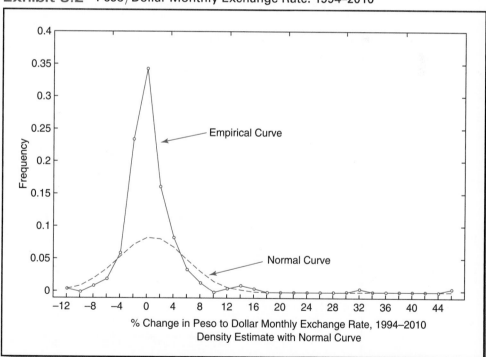

Notes: We perform the same exercise as in Exhibit 3.1, but using peso per dollar exchange rates.

that there have been no analogously large appreciations or revaluations of the peso. Also, many more of the observations are centered around the mean (relative to the normal distribution), which was also true for the pound in Exhibit 3.1. This is always true when distributions have more observations in the tails (both left and right) than the normal, as the area underneath the distribution must add up to 1. This phenomenon is called "**fat tails**" or **leptokurtosis**. For now, you should remember that a normal probability distribution is a reasonable description of monthly percentage changes for the major floating currencies, but it is not a good description of emerging market currencies.

The Probability Distribution of Future Exchange Rates

Financial managers are also interested in the probability distribution of future spot exchange rates. Given that we observe an exchange rate of $S(t)$ today, we can find the probability distribution of future exchange rates in, say, 90 days from the probability distribution of the percentage change in the exchange rate. From Equation (3.1), we see that the possible future spot exchange rates are

$$S(t+90) = S(t) \times [1 + s(t+90)] \qquad (3.2)$$

where $s(t+90)$ denotes the percentage change in the exchange rate over the next 90 days, $s(t+90) = [S(t+90) - S(t)]/S(t)$.

Exhibit 3.3 provides an example of a normal probability distribution for the dollar–pound spot exchange rate at time $t + 90$, which is 90 days in the future relative to today.

Conditional Means and Volatilities

Because the probability distribution of the future exchange rate depends on all the information available at time t, we say that it is a **conditional probability distribution** (see the appendix to this chapter). Consequently, the mean, which is the expected value of this distribution, is also referred to as the **conditional mean**, or the **conditional expectation**, of the

Exhibit 3.3 Probability Distribution of $S(t+90)$

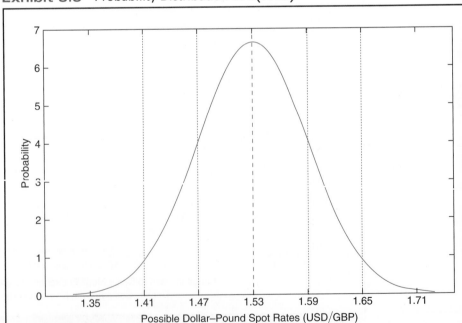

future exchange rate. Because the conditional expectation of the future exchange rate plays an important role in what is to follow, we use the following symbolic notation to represent it:

Conditional expectation at time t of the future spot exchange
rate at time $t+90 = E_t\left[S(t+90)\right]$

One nice feature of the normal distribution is that the probability of any range of possible future exchange rates is completely summarized by its mean and the standard deviation, which is also often referred to as **volatility**. The conditional mean ties down the location of the probability distribution; the conditional standard deviation describes how spread out the distribution is. Notice that if the mean and the standard deviation of $s(t+90)$ are denoted μ and σ, then from Equation (3.2), we see that the conditional mean and conditional standard deviation of $S(t+90)$ are $\left[S(t)(1 + \mu)\right]$ and $\left[S(t)\sigma\right]$, respectively.

Let's look at how Exhibit 3.3 is constructed. Suppose, as in Example 3.1, that the current exchange rate is \$1.50/£, and that people expect the pound to appreciate relative to the dollar by 2% over the next 90 days. The conditional expectation of the future spot rate in 90 days is then \$1.53/£ = (\$1.50/£) × (1 + 0.02). Suppose that the standard deviation of the rate of appreciation over the next 90 days is 4%. Because 4% of \$1.50/£ is \$0.06/£, the standard deviation of the conditional distribution of the expected future spot exchange rate is \$0.06/£. To summarize,

	Formula	Example
Conditional expectation of the future exchange rate (mean)	$S(t) \times (1 + \mu)$	\$1.50/£ × (1 + 0.02) = \$1.53/£
Conditional volatility of the future expected exchange rate (standard deviation)	$S(t) \times \sigma$	\$1.50/£ × 0.04 = \$0.06/£

Armed with the conditional mean and conditional standard deviation of the future exchange rate, we can determine the probability that the future exchange rate will fall within any given range of exchange rates. For example, for the normal distribution, slightly more than two-thirds, or 68.27%, of the probability distribution is within plus or minus 1 standard deviation of the mean. In our example, this range is from

$$\$1.47/£ = \$1.53/£ - \$0.06/£$$

to

$$\$1.59/£ = \$1.53/£ + \$0.06/£$$

Consequently, the area under the curve between the two vertical lines emanating from \$1.47/£ and \$1.59/£ represents 68.27% of the total area. Also, for the normal distribution, 95.45% of the probability distribution is within plus or minus 2 standard deviations of the mean. Thus, the range of future exchange rates that encompasses all but 4.55% of the future possible values of dollar–pound exchange rates is \$1.41/£ to \$1.65/£.

Assessing the Likelihood of Particular Future Exchange Rate Ranges

Given a probability distribution of future exchange rates, we can also determine the probability that the exchange rate in the future will be greater or less than a particular future spot rate. For example, suppose we want to know how likely it is that the pound will strengthen over the next 90 days to at least an exchange rate of \$1.60/£. Because \$1.60/£ is \$0.07/£ greater than the conditional mean of \$1.53/£ and the standard deviation is \$0.06/£, we want to know how likely it is that we will be 0.07/0.06 = 1.167 standard deviations above the mean. For the normal distribution, this probability is 12.16%—that is, the probability of the exchange rate rising to $1.60/£ or higher from $1.50/£ is 12.16%.

Now that you can describe the possible changes in exchange rates that you may experience, you are in a better position to define and understand the concept of transaction exchange risk, so let's revisit the Fancy Foods example.

Example 3.2   Transaction Exchange Risk at Fancy Foods Revisited

Fancy Foods must pay Porky Pies £1,000,000 in 90 days, and the current exchange rate is $1.50/£. The conditional distribution of future $/£ rates is based on the information that the firm has when it is making its decision. Let's assume that the firm bases its decision on the probability distribution in Exhibit 3.3. Our calculations of the range of possible future exchange rates calculated earlier tell us that with 95.45% probability, the exchange rate will fall between $1.41/£ and $1.65/£. Hence, there is a 95.45% chance that Fancy Foods will pay between $1,410,000 = $1.41/£ × £1,000,000 and $1,650,000 = $1.65/£ × £1,000,000 to offset its pound liability. Remember that Fancy Foods expects to pay $1,530,000. If the dollar weakens to $1.65/£, we can think of Fancy Foods as losing

$$\$1,650,000 - \$1,530,000 = \$120,000,$$

compared to what it expected to pay. In contrast, if the dollar strengthens to $1.41/£, we can think of Fancy Foods as gaining

$$\$1,530,000 - \$1,410,000 = \$120,000,$$

compared to what it expected to pay. Of course, Fancy Foods is exposed to potentially larger losses and possibly bigger gains because something more extreme than this range of exchange rates could happen, but the probability of such extreme events is less than 4.55% if our probability distribution accurately reflects rational beliefs about the future.

3.3 HEDGING TRANSACTION EXCHANGE RISK

Fancy Foods can totally eliminate the risk of loss due to a change in the exchange rate if it uses a **forward contract**. Let's see why.

Forward Contracts and Hedging

A forward contract between a bank and a customer calls for delivery, at a fixed future date, of a specified amount of one currency against payment in another currency. The exchange rate specified in the contract, called the **forward rate**, is fixed at the time the parties enter into the contract. If you owe someone foreign currency at some date in the future, you can "buy the foreign currency forward" by contracting to have a bank deliver a specific amount of foreign currency to you on the date that you need it. At that time, you must pay the bank an amount of domestic currency equal to the forward rate (domestic currency per foreign currency) multiplied by the amount of foreign currency. Because the total amount you would owe the bank is determined today, it does not depend in any way on the actual value of the future exchange rate. Thus, using a forward contract eliminates transaction exchange risk.

Similarly, if you are scheduled to receive some foreign currency on a specific date in the future, you can "sell it forward" and entirely eliminate the foreign exchange risk. You contract to have the bank buy from you the amount of foreign currency you will receive in the future on that date in the future. Your forward contract establishes today the amount of domestic currency that you will receive in the future, which is equal to the forward exchange rate (domestic currency per foreign currency) multiplied by the amount of foreign currency you will be selling. The amount of domestic currency that you receive in the future consequently does not depend in any way on the future spot exchange rate.

Notice that in both cases, you have completely hedged your transaction exchange risk. Basically, you eliminate your risk by acquiring a foreign currency asset or liability that exactly offsets the foreign currency liability or asset that is given to you by your business.

Hedging Currency Risk of Fancy Foods

Consider again Example 3.1, in which Fancy Foods owes Porky Pies £1,000,000 in 90 days. Let the forward rate at which Fancy Foods can contract to buy and sell pounds be $1.53/£. Fancy Foods can wait to transact in 90 days, but it risks losing money if the pound strengthens against the dollar. Contracting with a bank in the forward market to buy £1,000,000 at $1.53/£ gives Fancy Foods a foreign currency asset that is equivalent to its foreign currency liability. Fancy Foods's £1,000,000 liability from its business transaction is offset by a £1,000,000 asset, which is the bank's promise to pay Fancy Foods on the forward contract. Fancy Foods is left with an offsetting dollar liability of $1,530,000 = ($1.53/£) × (£1,000,000). We can summarize this position using the asset and liability accounts on Fancy Foods's balance sheet:

FANCY FOODS PARTIAL BALANCE SHEET	
Assets	**Liabilities**
£1,000,000 due from the bank in 90 days	£1,000,000 payable to Porky Pies in 90 days
	$1,530,000 payable to the bank in 90 days

Hedging at Nancy Foods

Now let's consider Nancy Foods, which is scheduled to receive £1,000,000 from Quirky Pies in 90 days. The sale of the quiches gives Nancy Foods a foreign currency asset. Entering into a forward contract to sell £1,000,000 to the bank provides Nancy Foods with an equivalent foreign currency liability and a domestic currency asset. This hedges its foreign exchange risk. In this example, Nancy Foods's asset and liability positions would look like this:

NANCY FOODS PARTIAL BALANCE SHEET	
Assets	**Liabilities**
£1,000,000 receivable from Quirky Pies in 90 days	£1,000,000 payable to the bank in 90 days
$1,530,000 receivable from the bank in 90 days	

These asset and liability accounts demonstrate that using forward contracts can turn the underlying British pound asset or liability that arises in the course of a U.S. firm's normal business transactions into a dollar asset or liability that has no foreign exchange risk associated with it.

Exposure of Hedged Versus Unhedged Strategies

Exhibit 3.4 summarizes the exposures to transaction exchange risk of various strategies for buying or selling foreign currency. On the horizontal axis of Exhibit 3.4 (Panel A) are the future spot rates that can be realized in terms of the domestic currency (for example, dollars) per unit of foreign currency (for example, pounds). As you move to the right, the price of the foreign currency (pounds) in terms of the domestic currency (dollars) rises. In other words, the foreign currency is appreciating in value. On the vertical axis are the domestic currency costs per unit of foreign currency (if you must buy the foreign currency in the future) or the domestic currency revenue per unit of foreign currency (if you must sell the foreign currency in the future). Hence, we can represent the domestic currency revenue or cost of hedging or not hedging as a function of the actual value of the future spot exchange rate using simple lines.

Exhibit 3.4 Gains and Losses Associated with Hedged Versus Unhedged Strategies

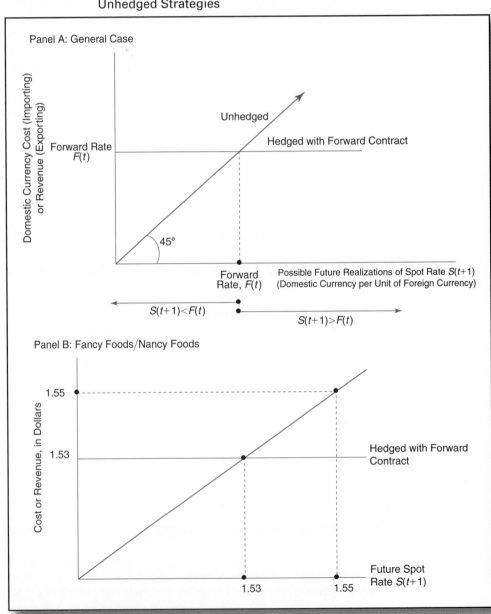

The 45-degree line represents the unhedged strategy. If you must buy foreign currency in the future and you are unhedged, your cost will fluctuate one-for-one with the domestic currency price of foreign currency that is realized in the future. As the domestic currency weakens, your cost rises, and as the domestic currency strengthens, your cost declines. Your risk is unlimited in the sense that your cost keeps rising one-for-one with the future exchange rate. Conversely, your costs decline directly with any strengthening of the domestic currency relative to the foreign currency. Theoretically, your costs could fall to zero, although it's highly unlikely that the domestic currency would strengthen to that extent.

The horizontal line in Exhibit 3.4 represents the strategy of hedging with a forward contract. If an international transaction requires you to buy foreign currency in the future, and you completely hedge by buying a forward contract today, your cost will be the same (equal to the forward rate) no matter what spot exchange rate is realized in the future. You bear no risk because the price you will pay is fixed, even if the domestic currency weakens relative to the foreign currency. But the price you pay also cannot decline if the domestic currency strengthens relative to the foreign currency.

In Panel B, we consider the cases of Fancy Foods and Nancy Foods. Suppose that after 90 days, when the contracts must be settled, the spot rate is $1.55/£. If the companies entered a forward contract at $1.53/£, this is entirely immaterial. Fancy Foods will avoid paying $1.55/£ as it has locked in $1.53/£, and Nancy Foods will receive only $1.53/£, even though it could have done better in the spot market by selling its pounds at $1.55/£.

The Costs and Benefits of a Forward Hedge

In light of the discussion of hedging transaction exchange risk, what is the appropriate way to think about the cost of a forward hedge? First, it is important to ascertain when the cost is computed. Are we looking *ex post* (after the fact) and examining whether we paid more or less with our forward contract than we would have paid had we waited to transact at the realized future spot rate? Or are we thinking of cost in an *ex ante* (before the fact) sense, in which case we have to examine the expected cost? In the latter case, you should remember that if you do not hedge, you will bear the foreign exchange risk, and the actual exchange rate at which you will transact in the future is very likely not going to be the expected future spot rate.

If you are buying foreign currency with domestic currency because your underlying transaction gives you a foreign currency liability, you will be glad to have hedged *ex post* if the future spot rate (domestic currency per foreign currency) is above the forward rate. You will have regrets *ex post* if the future spot rate is below the forward rate. These costs and benefits are summarized in Exhibit 3.5.

When you are trying to determine whether to hedge, how the forward rate relates to the expected future spot exchange rate dictates whether there is an expected cost or an expected benefit to hedging. If you are buying foreign currency because your underlying transaction gives you a foreign currency liability, you will think that there is an expected cost to hedging if the expected future spot rate of domestic currency per unit of foreign currency is below the forward rate (domestic currency per foreign currency). Hedging would require you to

Exhibit 3.5 Costs and Benefits of Hedging

	$F(t, k) < S(t+k)$	$F(t, k) < S(t+k)$
Foreign currency assest	Cost of hedging	Benefit of hedging
Foreign currency liability	Benefit of hedging	Cost of hedging

Notes: The spot rate and the forward rate are in domestic currency per unit of foreign currency. $F(t, k)$ is the forward rate at time t for delivery at time $t+k$. The costs/benefits are calculated *ex post*, after the realization of $S(t+k)$. If we replace $S(t+k)$ by $E_t[S(t+k)]$, they become expected costs/benefits.

transact at a domestic currency price higher than you expect to have to pay if you do not hedge. Conversely, you will think there is an expected benefit to hedging if the expected future spot rate (domestic currency per foreign currency) is above the forward rate. In this case, hedging allows you to purchase foreign currency with domestic currency more cheaply than you would have expected to have to pay. Of course, complete hedging removes all potential benefits as well as all possible losses.

Examples of Using Forward Contracts to Hedge Transaction Risk

Let's look at some examples to see the nature of different exposures, the extent of the possible losses, and how the exposures might be fully hedged with forward contracts.

Example 3.3 Hedging Import Payments

Assume that you are the financial manager of Zachy's, a wine store in Scarsdale, New York, that imports wine from France. You have just contracted to import some Chateau Margaux wine, and your invoice is for €4 million. You have agreed to pay this number of euros when you have received the wine and determined that it is in good condition. Payment of the euros and delivery of the wine are scheduled for 90 days in the future. The following data are available:

$$\text{Today's sport rate} = \$1.10/\text{€}$$

$$\text{Today's 90-day forward rate} = \$1.08/\text{€}$$

What is the source of your transaction exchange risk, and how much could you lose? First, as the U.S. importer, you have a euro-denominated liability because you have agreed to pay euros in the future. You are exposed to losses if the euro strengthens relative to the dollar unexpectedly to, say, $1.12/€. In this case, the dollar cost of the euros would be higher. If you do nothing to hedge your risk, your loss is theoretically unlimited in the sense that the dollar cost of the euros could go to infinity because the dollar amount that you will pay is $S(t+90, \$/\text{€}) \times \text{€}4$ million. Although this extreme loss is very unlikely, there is always some downside risk due to possible weakening, or depreciation, of the dollar relative to the euro.

You can eliminate the transaction exchange risk completely by buying €4 million in the forward market. The dollars that will be paid in 90 days are

$$(\text{€}4,000,000) \times (\$1.08/\text{€}) = \$4,320,000$$

Notice that the cash inflow of euros that you generate from the forward contract (€4,000,000) exactly matches the cash outflow of euros that you have from your underlying transaction. In other words, you have neutralized the euro liability that arises from your business by acquiring an equivalent euro asset, which is the promise by the bank to deliver euros to you. Hence, as long as you trust the bank that is your counterparty, you are not exposed to the risk of loss from fluctuations in exchange rates.

Of course, if you buy euros forward and the dollar strengthens substantially over the next 90 days (for example, to $1.05/€), you will still have to buy your euros from the bank at the forward price of $1.08/€ because that is the price you agreed to in the contract with the bank. In this sense, the forward contract eliminates your risk of loss, but it does so by keeping you from participating in possible gains in the future.

Example 3.4 Hedging Export Receipts

Now, place yourself in the position of Shetland Sweaters, a British manufacturer. Consider your transaction exchange risk if you agree to ship sweaters to Japan and are willing to accept ¥500,000,000 in payment from the Japanese sweater importer Nobu Inc. Delivery of the goods and receipt of the yen are scheduled for 30 days from now, and the following data are available:

$$\text{Today's spot rate} = \text{¥}176/\text{£}$$

$$\text{Today's 30-day forward rate} = \text{¥}180/\text{£}$$

What are the nature and extent of your transaction exchange risk? Because you have agreed to accept yen in payment for your sweaters, you have a yen-denominated asset. You are exposed to losses if you wait to sell the yen in the future spot market and the yen depreciates, or weakens, unexpectedly relative to the pound. In this case, the yen you receive in payment for your sweaters will purchase fewer pounds than you expect. If you do nothing between the time you enter into the contract and the time you receive your yen, you risk everything in the sense that, theoretically, the pound value of your yen receivable could go to zero. Although that is very unlikely, there certainly is a downside risk due to a possible weakening of the yen relative to the pound. Of course, there is also a possible gain if the yen strengthens relative to the pound.

How can you fully hedge, or eliminate, this transaction risk from your business? You can eliminate the risk of loss by selling ¥500,000,000 in the forward market for pounds. The pounds that will be received in 30 days are

$$\text{¥}500,000,000/(\text{¥}180/\text{£}) = \text{£}2,777,778$$

Notice again that your contractual yen cash outflow (¥500,000,000) to pay the bank for the forward purchase of pounds in 30 days exactly matches the cash inflow of yen that you will have from your underlying transaction. You have neutralized the foreign exchange exposure of your business by acquiring a foreign currency liability that is exactly equivalent to your foreign currency asset. Your promise to deliver yen to the bank is your yen liability. Hence, as long as you are willing to trust that the bank will be able to deliver pounds to you in the future and that Nobu Inc. will pay yen for the goods, you are not exposed to risk of loss due to an unanticipated change in the exchange rate.

Of course, if the yen strengthens relative to the pound over the next 30 days, you will still have to sell your yen at the forward price specified by your agreement with the bank because the forward contract is not contingent on the future exchange rate. The rate is carved in stone, so to speak, by your contract with the bank. In this sense, the forward contract eliminates your risk of loss, but it does so by not allowing you to participate in possible gains in the future.

POINT–COUNTERPOINT
"Refining" a Hedging Strategy

With the *Financial Times* in hand, Ante Handel bursts into his brother's room, shouting, "I told you non-financial companies should stay out of the forex markets! Another Japanese company has been pounded in the forward market. Kashima Oil has just announced a loss of ¥61.9 billion. At least it is only half the loss that other Japanese oil refinery, Showa Shell, had to swallow last year. I wonder what the stock market will think of this baby. Showa's equity value dropped in half when the news of their foreign exchange loss broke!"

Ante's brother, Freedy, responded surprisingly fast. "Come off it. Kashima is an oil refinery. They were just trying to hedge their currency risk. Oil is priced in dollars, and they were buying dollars in the forward market, and the exchange rate moved against them. It's just bad luck. It could have gone the other way."

Fortunately, their cousin, Suttle Trooth, had overheard everything through the thin walls of their dorm rooms, and he was intrigued. "This is not so simple," he thought. "Should an oil company be hedging in the foreign exchange market? What really happened? Did they simply get a bad shock?" Rather than disturb the raucous discourse of the two brothers, Suttle put on his headphones, cranked up his iPod, and started searching the Internet. The facts soon became clear.

Suttle quickly learned that the Japanese oil refineries, Showa Shell and Kashima, are exposed to foreign exchange risk. All contracts in the oil business are settled in dollars, implying that these companies have dollar costs because they import crude oil, and they have yen revenues because they sell their refined oil in Japan. Showa Shell and Kashima face the risk that their yen costs will escalate if the dollar appreciates unexpectedly. To hedge that risk, both companies routinely buy dollars in the forward market for several months and sometimes years ahead. It happened to be the case that the forward yen price of the dollar was usually lower than the prevailing spot rate when most of these contracts were struck. So the forward contracts reduced the cost of the dollars relative to the prevailing spot rate and protected the companies against the risk of a dollar appreciation. However, the relevant comparison rate to judge the *ex post* benefit of the hedge is the future exchange rate at which crude oil would have been bought had the oil refineries not hedged. There were quite a few instances where the dollar did not appreciate relative to the yen; and, in fact, the actual yen price of the dollar in the future turned out to be lower than the forward rate the companies had agreed to. In such cases, the companies would have been better off, *ex post*, not to hedge. They would have had lower yen costs by buying the dollars they needed in the spot market with the stronger yen.

Unfortunately, as Suttle read on, he learned that these companies did not just hedge. People in the companies' finance departments who were authorized to make forward contracts expected the dollar to appreciate. They thought they could profit from this outlook, and they agreed to forward contracts for much more than the actual currency exposure the companies had from their underlying oil businesses. In other words, people at both companies were **speculating** in an effort to make a profit! When the yen continued to appreciate and the speculators' losses mounted, they did not disclose these losses to their superiors. They instead hid the losses from the companies' accounting statements and simply entered into additional forward contracts with their banks, hoping that the yen would eventually fall in value. Showa's total losses finally amounted to ¥125 billion and Kashima's to ¥152.5 billion.

Hedging Versus Speculating. Suttle Trooth decided to analyze this case step by step. The first thing to do is to separate the hedging part from the speculation part. Pure speculation in the currency markets does not seem to be a great idea for any corporate finance department. In addition, not disclosing mounting losses to your shareholders is illegal in most countries. So on that part, Ante is right, Suttle mused. Kashima should not have dabbled in foreign exchange markets the way it did. Not surprisingly, Japan's regulatory authorities cracked down on the practice of non-disclosure, and new disclosure rules regarding unrealized losses or profits from forward contracts in the foreign exchange markets were instituted in the wake of the oil companies' debacles.

To Hedge or Not to Hedge? Now, Suttle wondered whether hedging made sense in this case. Why was Freedy so convinced this was absolutely a normal thing to do? Certainly, if Kashima has a number of contracts to buy oil in the future with dollars, and we view this as a source of transaction exposure, it makes sense to hedge, right? After all, Kashima has a dollar liability, and by buying dollars forward, it obtains a dollar asset in exchange for a yen liability. This allows it to lock in the future transaction price in yen, getting rid of the effect of uncertain future exchange rates. Of course, *ex post* there may be a cost to hedging because the yen may keep appreciating, but at least they do not lose sleep over exchange rate movements, and they can better budget future operations.

But Suttle Trooth had a nagging feeling this might not be the full story. You see, Kashima's and Showa Shell's whole businesses are structured around buying oil with dollars, refining the oil, and selling it for yen in the local Japanese market. Not only do they do this now, but they plan to be doing the same thing for the conceivable future. In other words, their exchange rate exposures do not just arise from a single transaction. Exchange rate movements can really affect the bottom line of the companies. Consequently, if they hedge, they should at least have a long-term hedging plan in place. Also, it may be that forward contracts are not the right hedging vehicles. Suttle had heard that these contracts are only liquid when the maturity is shorter than 1 year and that the transaction costs for longer-term contracts are higher. In lieu of forward contracts, are there other contracts out there for longer-term hedging?

If the companies think long term, don't they also need to worry about inflation and oil price movements? Maybe an increase in the oil price or an increase in the yen–dollar rate is not so bad for the oil refining companies if the general price level in Japan goes up, too, and they can pass the increase in their costs through to their customers in the form of higher yen prices for the refined oil they sell.

Suttle Trooth started to have some doubts about the benefits of hedging, even for firms such as Kashima and Showa Shell. He concluded that he better keep reading the international financial management text he had just picked up from his bookshelf.

We will discuss the fundamental issue of why a firm should or should not hedge in Chapter 17. By that time, we will have developed all the tools necessary to answer all of Suttle's questions.

3.4 THE FORWARD FOREIGN EXCHANGE MARKET

Now that you understand how forward contracts can be used to manage foreign exchange risk, let's examine the organization of the forward market in more detail.

Market Organization

The organization of trading for future purchase or delivery of foreign currency in the forward foreign exchange market is similar to the spot market discussed in Chapter 2. Whereas some traders focus on spot contracts, other traders focus on forward contracts. As mentioned previously, forward contracts greatly facilitate corporate risk management, and bank traders happily quote forward exchange rates for their corporate and institutional customers. However, such simple forward contracts, called **outright forward contracts**, are a relatively unimportant component of the foreign exchange market. In fact, a Bank for International Settlements (2010) survey found that only 12% of all transactions in the foreign exchange market are outright forward contracts. The survey also found that forward contracts are much more often part of a package deal, called a **swap**. In fact, about 44% of forex market transactions are swaps. A swap transaction involves the simultaneous purchase and sale of a certain amount of foreign currency for two different dates in the future. Given the importance of swaps, we discuss the swap market after we describe some of the details regarding the trading of forward contracts.

Forward Contract Maturities and Value Dates

Forward exchange rates are contractual prices, quoted today, at which trade will be conducted in the future. The parties agree to the price today, but no monies change hands until the maturity of the contract, which is called the **forward value date**, or **forward settlement date**.

The most active maturities in the forward market tend to be the even maturities of 30, 60, 90, and 180 days. Because the forward market is an over-the-counter market, however, it is possible for the corporate and institutional customers of banks and traders at other banks to arrange odd-date forward contracts with maturities of, say, 46 or 67 days.

The exchange of currencies in a forward contract takes place on the forward value date. Determination of the value date for a forward contract begins by finding today's spot value date. As we saw in Chapter 2, this is 2 business days in the future for trades between U.S. dollars and European currencies or the Japanese yen. Exchange of monies in a 30-day forward contract occurs on the calendar day in the next month that corresponds to today's spot value date, assuming that it is a legitimate business day. So, if today is July 28 and the spot value date is July 30, the forward value date for a 30-day contract is August 30. If the forward value date is a weekend or a bank holiday in either country, settlement of the forward contract occurs on the next business day. If the next business day moves the settlement of the forward contract into a new month, the forward value day becomes the *previous* business day. For example, in our previous example, it is possible that August 30 and 31 are weekend days. In that case, the value date would be August 29. This rule is followed except when the spot value day is the last business day of the current month, in which case the forward value day is the last business day of the next month (this is referred to as the *end–end rule*).

Let's consider an example.

Example 3.5 Finding the Forward Value Date

Suppose we purchase euros with dollars in the spot market on Friday, November 11, 2011. The dollars will come from our Citibank account in New York, and the euros will be paid into our Deutsche Bank account in Germany. The spot value day for such a trade is Tuesday, November 15, 2011, a legitimate business day in both countries. If we also initiated a 30-day forward contract to buy euros with dollars on Friday, November 11, 2011, when would the exchange of currencies take place? We can find the forward value date by following the logic just described. Because the spot value date is November 15, 2011, the forward value date is Thursday, December 15, 2011, a legitimate business day in both countries. Notice that the exchange of currencies on the 30-day forward contract is actually 34 days in the future in this example.

Of course, you don't have to actually own the currency that you contract to deliver when entering into a forward contract. It may be that you expect to receive the currency in the future in the normal course of your business, or you may plan to acquire the currency in the spot market sometime between when the forward contract is made and when the exchange of monies takes place on the forward value date. Suppose you have contracted to deliver euros as part of a forward contract (as in the previous example), but you do not own any euros. When is the last day that you could purchase euros in the spot market? We know that you must have euros on Thursday, December 15, 2011. Thus, you could buy the euros in the spot market 2 business days before this day, or on Tuesday, December 13, 2011, which is 32 days in the future relative to the date the forward contract was initiated.

Forward Market Bid–Ask Spreads

We noted in Chapter 2 that bid–ask spreads are quite narrow in the spot market. In the forward market, however, they tend to widen as the maturity of the forward contract increases. Yet forward bid–ask spreads for active maturities remain small and are typically less than 0.05% for the major currencies. In particular, for 90-day forward contracts, spreads are mostly less than a pip wider than the spot spread. For very long-dated contracts, especially extending beyond 1 year, bid–ask spreads are wider.[4]

Liquidity in the Forward Market

The bid–ask spreads are larger in the forward market than in the spot market because the forward market is less liquid than the spot market. Liquid markets allow traders to buy and sell something without incurring large transaction costs and without significantly influencing the market price. The liquidity of the market depends on the number of people who are actively trading in the market and on the sizes of the positions they are willing to take. In very liquid markets, it is easy to find a buyer if you want to be a seller and vice versa. It is also easy to conduct large transactions without having to provide concessions to the party taking the opposite side of the transaction. Illiquid markets are sometimes referred to as *thin* markets.

The reasons forward markets are less liquid than spot markets are subtle and are best explained in the context of an example.

Example 3.6 The Source of Low Liquidity in the Forward Market

Suppose Canada Beer, a Canadian company, exports beer to the United States and receives regular payments in U.S. dollars. Suppose Canada Beer enters into a 30-day forward contract with Bank of America to sell USD1,000,000 in exchange for Canadian dollars. That is, Canada Beer is selling its dollar revenues forward for Canadian dollars. Assume that the forward rate is $0.90/CAD. We are interested in seeing what risk this transaction creates for Bank of America. Consider Panel A in Exhibit 3.6.

The forward contract implies that Bank of America is now short Canadian dollars in the forward market—that is, it owes Canadian dollars for future delivery. Conversely, in the forward contract, Canada Beer is long Canadian dollars and short U.S. dollars, but Canada Beer expects to receive U.S. dollar revenues from its beer sales, which hedges this position.

What are the risks involved for Bank of America? The most obvious risk is currency risk. In 30 days, Bank of America must deliver CAD1,111,111 = $1,000,000/($0.90/CAD) to Canada Beer in exchange for $1,000,000. In the meantime, the Canadian dollar may increase in value relative to the U.S. dollar, yet Bank of America will receive only the $1,000,000 specified in the forward contract. For example, suppose the spot exchange rate in 30 days moves up to $1.00/CAD. Then the cost of CAD1,111,111 would be $1,111,111, not the $1,000,000 Bank of America is receiving!

It is tempting to think that this position carries more transactions exchange risk than a spot position with delivery 2 days from now because adverse exchange rate movements are more likely over the longer time span. Although it is true that the size of possible adverse exchange rate movements increases over the longer time span,

---

[4]The relatively high transaction costs in the long-term forward market contributed to the development of an entirely new market, the long-term currency swap market, which is discussed in Chapter 21.

Exhibit 3.6 Risks in Forward Contracts

Panel A: Original Positions

BANK OF AMERICA

Assets	Liabilities
$1,000,000 due from Canada Beer in 30 days	CAD1,111,111 payable to Canada Beer in 30 days

CANADA BEER

Assets	Liabilities
$1,000,000 Export revenues in 30 days	$1,000,000 payable to Bank of America
CAD1,111,111 due from Bank of America in 30 days	

Panel B: Bank of America Risk Management—Case 1

BANK OF AMERICA

Assets	Liabilities
$1,000,000 due from Canada Beer in 29 days	CAD1,111,111 payable to Canada Beer in 29 days
CAD1,111,111 due from interbank counterparty in 29 days	$1,022,222 payable to interbank counterparty in 29 days

Panel C: Bank of America Risk Management—Case 2

BANK OF AMERICA

Assets	Liabilities
$1,000,000 due from Canada Beer in 30 days	CAD1,111,111 payable to Canada Beer in 30 days
CAD1,111,111 payable to interbank counterparty in 30 days	$1,000,000 payable to interbank counterparty in 30 days

---

Notes: Since the forward rate is $0.90/CAD, the amount of Canadian dollars involved in the forward contract is $\frac{\$1,000,000}{\$0.90/CAD} = CAD1,111,111$. We assume the next day's forward rate for a 29-day contract is $0.92/CAD.

the forward position does not pose a larger currency risk than the spot position as long as the forward market is liquid enough to allow a fast reversal of the forward position. That is, if Bank of America thinks that it may take a loss on the forward contract because of an adverse movement in the Canadian dollar exchange rate, the bank will want to close its position by buying Canadian dollars forward for the remaining life of the contract. Let's reconsider Exhibit 3.6. In Case 1 (Panel B), Bank of America waits 1 day and sees the spot rate increase. It suddenly feels that the risk of a short position in Canadian dollars is not worth taking and goes long Canadian dollars in the interbank market with a 29-day contract. We assume that the forward rate for this contract is $0.92/CAD, making the dollar equivalent of CAD1,111,111 equal to

CAD1,111,111 × $0.92/CAD = $1,022,222. In 29 days, Bank of America's counterparty bank will deliver the CAD1,111,111 to Bank of America, and Bank of America in turn will deliver them to Canada Beer. The forward price with the bank's counterparty is set only 1 day after the Canada Beer contract was signed. So the adverse currency movement pertains only to 1 day. Nevertheless, because the Canadian dollar strengthened in that 1 day, Bank of America has already lost $1,022,222 − $1,000,000 = $22,222 on the deal. In fact, more often than not, banks immediately hedge their positions with corporate customers, as illustrated in Panel C of Exhibit 3.6. As soon as the trader records the trade with Canada Beer, he may start looking for a counterparty in the interbank market to conclude a 30-day forward contract to buy Canadian dollars.

As long as forward contracts are traded actively enough for this transaction to occur at fair prices, the bank does not have to worry much about the currency risk in the forward contract. But there is another risk that Bank of America faces: Bank of America expects that Canada Beer will deliver U.S. dollars to it in exchange for Canadian dollars. But Canada Beer may not honor the forward contract if it goes bankrupt between now and 30 days from now. This is an example of default risk. Recall from Chapter 2 that counterparty default occurs when the party on the other side of a contract fails to deliver what it promised. If Canada Beer does not deliver the U.S. dollars, Bank of America does not need to deliver the Canadian dollars to Canada Beer, but Bank of America was counting on having U.S. dollars in its portfolio, not additional Canadian dollars. In fact, if it indeed hedged the original transaction as in Exhibit 3.6, it will receive Canadian dollars from its bank counterparty and must wire U.S. dollars to that bank. Hence, if Bank of America does not want to build up an inventory of Canadian dollars, it will have to sell Canadian dollars for U.S. dollars in the spot market if Canada Beer defaults. This spot transaction will occur about 28 days from now, so that it settles 2 business days later, at the same date the forward contract with the bank counterparty does. In other words, currency risk reappears because the future Canadian versus U.S. dollar exchange rate may be disadvantageous for Bank of America.

There are two main reasons why forward markets are less liquid than spot markets. First, banks are exposed to counterparty default risk for a much longer time interval in a forward contract than in a spot contract. In fact, banks are so worried about counterparty default risk in forward contracts that they impose limits on the total magnitude of the contracts (the "positions") traders can enter into with their counterparty banks in the interbank market. The limits vary with the creditworthiness and reputation of the other trading bank. In retail transactions, the dealer bank also often requires the non-bank counterparty either to maintain a minimum deposit balance with the dealer bank, to accept a reduction in its normal credit line, or to provide some other form of collateral. Second, because increased counterparty default risk reduces the number of forward transactions banks are willing to do, banks find it more difficult to manage open positions in forward contracts. Because it may take longer to find a counterparty with whom to trade at reasonable prices, forward contracts are more susceptible to foreign exchange risk. The increased inventory risk reduces liquidity even more.

Given these concerns, the lack of liquidity in the interbank forward market and the resulting increase in bid–ask spreads are not so surprising. In addition, some contracts are less heavily traded than others and are therefore less liquid. As a result, the bid–ask spread for these contracts is greater. Odd-maturity forward contracts—that is, contracts that do not have standard value dates 30, 60, or 90 days in the future—are an example.

The 2008 Global Financial Crisis and Forward Market Bid–Ask Spreads[5]

The role of counterparty risk and inventory risk in driving the bid–ask spreads of forward contracts became painfully obvious during the 2008 global financial crisis. When Lehman Brothers declared bankruptcy in September of 2008, there was no longer any doubt that there was substantial credit risk attached to dealing even with major financial institutions. Not only did the volatility of exchange rate changes increase substantially, but so did bid–ask spreads. Bid–ask spreads on spot contracts for the major currencies increased by about 400%. However, the spreads on forward contracts widened much more than the spreads on spot contracts. Three-month forward contract spreads were double those of spot contracts, instead of being just fractionally higher. Foreign exchange dealers did not want to be exposed to counterparties with questionable credit risk for a full 3 months.

Net Settlement

Most outright forward contracts are settled by payment and delivery of the amounts in the contract. It is possible, however, to settle a contract by paying or receiving a net settlement amount that depends on the value of the contract. For example, suppose you think you will owe a Mexican company MXN20,000,000 in 30 days, and you would like to pay with dollars. You could enter into a forward contract to purchase MXN20,000,000 with dollars at a forward rate of, say, MXN10/USD. On the settlement day of the forward contract, you could expect to receive MXN20,000,000 from the bank and expect to pay $2 million for it:

$$MXN20,000,000/(MXN10/USD) = USD2,000,000$$

Suppose that 1 business day before the forward value date, the spot exchange rate is MXN 12/USD, and you learn that you no longer need to purchase MXN20,000,000 because the underlying transaction has been cancelled. Must you still follow through with the forward contract, paying the USD2 million and receiving the MXN20,000,000 that you will now have to sell for dollars? It turns out that the bank will let you make a net payment. Notice that the MXN20,000,000 is now worth only

$$\frac{MXN20,000,000}{MXN12/USD} = USD1,666,667$$

Hence, if you pay the bank

$$USD2,000,000 - USD1,666,667 = USD333,333$$

this is equivalent to carrying out the original transaction and then entering into a new spot transaction in which you immediately sell the MXN20,000,000 back to the original seller of pesos at the current spot rate.

Net settlement is often used in the forex futures market, which we discuss in Chapter 20, and for emerging market currencies. In many emerging markets, there are capital controls in place, making it more difficult to trade foreign exchange for non-residents. Foreign exchange dealers have responded by developing offshore markets in forward contracts that do not require physical delivery of currency but are cash settled, mostly in U.S. dollars. These non-deliverable forward contracts (NDFs) have become an important market segment for currencies such as the Korean won, the Chinese yuan, the Indian rupee, the Brazilian real, and the Russia ruble. EBS now even offers electronically traded NDFs in over 10 currencies.

---

[5]See Melvin and Taylor (2009) for further details on this topic.

The Foreign Exchange Swap Market

Most of the trading of forward contracts happens in the swap market. We now discuss in more detail what swap contracts are, how swap rates are quoted, and why swaps are so popular.

A swap simultaneously combines two foreign exchange transactions with different value dates but in opposite directions. The most common example of a swap is the combination of a spot and a forward contract, for example, buying the foreign currency spot against purchasing the foreign currency forward. Other swaps involve the purchase (sale) of foreign currency short-term forward against the sale (purchase) of foreign currency long-term forward. The main reason swaps are so popular is that simultaneous spot and forward transactions in opposite directions occur quite naturally. In Chapter 6, we discuss interest rate arbitrage, and we show that arbitrage transactions in the money markets across two countries involve spot and forward transactions in opposite directions. Similarly, in Part IV, we discuss investments in international bond and equity markets. Many portfolio managers want to invest in the bond and equity markets of foreign countries without being exposed to changes in the values of those countries' currencies. To buy a foreign equity, these people must first buy the foreign currency in the spot market. To hedge the currency risk, they sell that currency forward. Hence, it is again natural to combine the spot and forward transaction in one trade.

Banks also actively use swaps to manage the maturity structure of their currency exposure. If they think they have too much exposure at one particular maturity, they can conveniently switch their position to another maturity, using a single swap transaction without changing their overall exposure to that currency. For example, when a bank has a short Swiss franc position of CHF1,000,000 (that is, when it sold CHF1,000,000 forward for dollars) with a maturity of 180 days and would like to shorten the maturity of these contracts to 90 days, it can simply enter into a swap to buy CHF1,000,000 at a 180-day value date and sell CHF1,000,000 at a 90-day value date. Because of the existence of the swap market, these transactions can be carried out with one phone call to a swap trader.

How Swap Prices Are Quoted

Before we examine the details of the cash flows associated with a swap, let's look at how prices are quoted. We focus on swaps involving a spot transaction and a forward transaction. The following is an example of a swap quote:

Spot	30-day
¥/$ 104.30–35	15/20

A quote mentions the spot rates (first column) and the swap points (second column). The spot rates quoted by a bank in this example are ¥104.30/$ bid and ¥104.35/$ ask. Remember that the bank's bid price is the rate at which the bank buys dollars from someone in exchange for yen. In contrast, the bank's ask or offer price is the rate at which the bank sells dollars to someone and receives yen from them. The **swap points** are a set of pips that must be either added to or subtracted from the current spot bid and ask prices to yield the actual 30-day bid and ask forward prices.

A Rule for Using Swap Points

A confusing aspect of moving from swap quotes to outright forward quotes is knowing whether to add the swap points to or to subtract the points from the bid and ask prices. Here's the rule: If the first number in the swap quote is smaller than the second, you add the points to the spot bid and ask prices to get the outright forward quotes; if the first number in the swap points is larger than the second, you subtract the points.

Let's examine the logic behind this rule, using the sample prices. With the swap points quoted as 15/20, the points should be added, so the outright forward quotes for 30 days would be

$$¥104.30/\$ \text{ spot bid} + ¥0.15/\$ = ¥104.45/\$ \text{ forward bid for dollars}$$

and

$$¥104.35/\$ \text{ spot ask} + ¥0.20/\$ = ¥104.55/\$ \text{ forward ask for dollars}$$

Notice that adding the swap points in this case makes the bid–ask spread in the forward market larger than the bid–ask spread in the spot market, which it should be.

When the first swap point quote is larger than the second, the points must be subtracted. Traders could quote negative numbers to indicate subtraction, but they follow a different convention. Rather than quote negative numbers when they want to indicate that the forward exchange rates are less than the spot prices, traders are assumed to understand that a swap quote of, say, 20/15 indicates that the swap points must be subtracted from the spot bid and ask rates. In this second example, the outright forward quotes for 30 days would be

$$¥104.30/\$ \text{ spot bid} - ¥0.20/\$ = ¥104.10/\$ \text{ forward bid for dollars}$$

and

$$¥104.35/\$ \text{ spot ask} - ¥0.15/\$ = ¥104.20/\$ \text{ forward ask for dollars}$$

Notice that in both of these examples, the bid–ask spread in the forward market is 10 points (or pips), which is larger than the 5-point spread in the spot market. If we had, in error, added the points in the second example, the forward market bid–ask spread would have fallen to 0 points, which is less than the 5-point spot bid–ask spread. This would tell us that we made an error because we know that the forward market is less liquid than the spot market. Hence, if you are having trouble remembering the rule and are trying to determine whether to add the swap points or to subtract them, you can always check to make sure that the forward bid–ask spread is larger than the spot bid–ask spread.

Cash Flows in a Swap

Let's consider an example of a swap to see what the cash flows look like.

Example 3.7 Swapping Out of Dollars and into Yen

Nomura, a Japanese investment bank, quotes the spot rates ¥104.30/\$ bid and ¥104.35/\$ ask and swap points of 20/15. Suppose that IBM wants to swap out of \$10,000,000 and into yen for 30 days. To do so, IBM sells dollars in the spot market in exchange for yen, but also wants to buy dollars for yen 30 days from now using a forward transaction. Both transactions can be combined in a swap. IBM swaps out of \$10,000,000 and into an equivalent amount of yen for 30 days. The swap diagram in Exhibit 3.7 summarizes the cash flows for both IBM and Nomura.

IBM is selling \$10,000,000 to Nomura in the spot market. Consequently, the amount of yen IBM receives is determined by Nomura's spot bid rate of ¥104.30/\$. In the first leg of the swap, IBM would receive

$$\$10,000,000 \times (¥104.30/\$) = ¥1,043,000,000$$

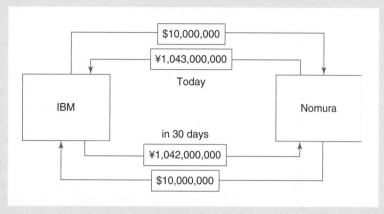

Exhibit 3.7 Cash Flows in a Spot–Forward Swap

When IBM gets its $10,000,000 back in 30 days, how many yen will it have to pay the bank? Because in the future Nomura is selling dollars to IBM for yen, Nomura will charge its forward ask price of ¥104.20/$ (¥104.35/$ − ¥0.15/$). Hence, IBM will pay Nomura

$$\$10,000,000 \times (¥104.20/\$) = ¥1,042,000,000$$

Hence, IBM gives up $10,000,000 for 30 days, and it receives ¥1,043,000,000 for 30 days. Nomura receives $10,000,000 for 30 days and in exchange gives up the use of ¥1,043,000,000. At the swap contract's maturity, IBM has to give Nomura only ¥1,042,000,000 rather than the original ¥1,043,000,000, which means that IBM gets to keep

$$¥1,043,000,000 - ¥1,042,000,000 = ¥1,000,000$$

Why is Nomura willing to accept ¥1,000,000 less in return when it buys $10,000,000 from IBM for 30 days? The answer is related to the interest rates on the two currencies.

Fundamentally, in a swap, each party is giving up the use of one currency and gaining the use of a different currency for the period of time of the swap. The two parties could charge each other the going market rates of interest on the respective currencies for this privilege. Instead of doing this, however, swaps are priced so that the party that is borrowing the high-interest-rate currency pays the party that is borrowing the low-interest-rate currency the difference in basis points. We will see in Chapter 6 precisely how the swap rates are related to the interest differential between the two currencies. Here we merely note that the yen must be the low-interest-rate currency relative to the dollar in this example because IBM had the use of yen while Nomura had the use of dollars, and IBM paid Nomura less yen in the future than the amount of yen Nomura paid IBM for its use of the dollars.

3.5 FORWARD PREMIUMS AND DISCOUNTS

Now that you understand how forward contracts are traded, it is time to introduce some important terminology regarding the relationship between forward and spot exchange rates.

If the forward price of the euro in terms of dollars (that is, USD/EUR) is higher than the spot price of USD/EUR, the euro is said to be at a **forward premium** in terms of the dollar. Conversely, if the forward price of the euro in terms of dollars (USD/EUR) is less than the spot price of USD/EUR, the euro is said to be at a **forward discount** in terms of the dollar. Remember, as with the terms *appreciation* and *depreciation*, the terms *forward premium* and *forward discount* refer to the currency that is in the denominator of the exchange rate.

Because the forward premium and forward discount are related to the interest rates on the two currencies, these premiums and discounts are often expressed as annualized *percentages*. That is, the difference between the forward rate and the spot rate is divided by the spot rate and then multiplied by the reciprocal of the fraction of the year over which the forward contract is made. The result is then multiplied by 100 to convert it to a percentage:

% per annum forward premium or discount of an *N* day forward rate

$$= \left(\frac{\text{forward} - \text{spot}}{\text{spot}} \right) \times \left(\frac{360}{N \, \text{days}} \right) \times 100 \qquad (3.3)$$

Here, N is the number of days in the forward contract. A 360-day year is used for most currencies, corresponding to the conventions for quoting interest rates. Exceptions to this convention include the British pound and the Kuwaiti dinar, which are quoted on a 365-day year.

We explore the formal linkage between the forward premium or discount and the interest differential between the two currencies in Chapter 6. Intuitively, however, you should realize that there must be a strong link among the spot rate (the relative price of two monies for immediate trade), the forward rate (the relative price of two monies for trade at a future date), and the two interest rates, which are the time values of the two monies between today and the future date.

Sizes of Forward Premiums or Discounts

Exhibit 3.8 presents some information on historical forward premiums and discounts for several of the major currencies versus the dollar. We use the Deutsche mark to fill in data for the euro prior to 1999.

Both for 30-day and 90-day yen–dollar contracts, the average forward premium is negative. In other words, on average, the dollar traded at a discount in the forward market versus the yen. The yen-denominated forward prices of the dollar were about 2.8% lower than the spot prices. For the euro and the pound, the exchange rates are expressed in $ per € and $ per £. For the dollar–euro rates, the 30-day forward premium of 1.046% indicates that the euro was at a premium versus the dollar, and the negative values for the dollar–pound rates indicate that the pound traded at a forward discount relative to the dollar. The discount was 1.649% for 30-day forward contracts and 1.541% for 90-day contracts. These numbers only represent averages (the means) because the forward discount changes over time. For example, Exhibit 3.8 shows that in 2010, the pound and the euro traded at small discounts relative to the dollar, whereas the dollar traded at a historically low discount of 0.399% relative to the yen.

Forward Premiums and Swap Points

Because forward contracts are typically traded as part of a swap, the swap points tell us whether the denominator currency is at a premium or a discount. Consider the example given using the JPY/USD exchange rate. If the dollar is at a forward premium, it is more expensive to purchase dollars in the future, so the forward rate should be larger than the spot rate. This happens if the swap points are added to the spot rates to yield larger forward rates. Hence,

Exhibit 3.8 Historical Means of Forward Premiums or Discounts

	$/£	$/€	¥/$
30-day forward (full sample)	−1.649%	1.046%	−2.822%
30-day forward (2010 only)	−0.182%	−0.040%	−0.378%
90-day forward (full sample)	−1.541%	0.754%	−2.848%
90-day forward (2010 only)	−0.183%	−0.013%	−0.399%

Notes: We report the mean of the time series on forward premiums for three currencies versus the dollar. Thirty-day premiums are reported for the sample period 1976 to 2010, whereas 90-day premiums are reported for the period 1991 to 2010. We use monthly data for 1976 to 1990 and daily data for 1991 to 2010. A negative sign indicates that the currency in the denominator is at a discount. The forward premiums and discounts are annualized. We also report the averages for the first 11 months of 2010.

when the first number in the swap points is less than the second number, as in our earlier example of 15/20, the swap points should be added, and the currency in the denominator is at a premium. If there is a discount on the dollar, the first number in the swap price will be greater than the second number, as in the second example of 20/15, and the swap points should be subtracted.

In the swap in Example 3.7, the dollar is at a discount relative to the yen because the forward rate of yen per dollar is smaller than the spot rate (the swap points were subtracted from the spot rate). In this example, IBM sold USD10,000,000 at the spot bid and bought them at the forward ask. Because of the forward discount on the dollar, the example involves an additional negative yen cash flow at maturity for Nomura because the bank bought dollars in the spot market, and the dollar is the high-interest-rate currency. That is, Nomura gets less yen back than it paid to IBM to begin with. Thus, Nomura is said to be "paying the points," or "dealing against oneself." Conversely, because IBM gave up the use of the high-interest currency (dollars) for the use of the low-interest currency (the yen), it is said to be "earning the points," or "dealing in its favor." Consequently, if the dollar is at a discount, swapping out of dollars today and into yen generates a positive yen cash flow. A good rule to remember is that swapping into the currency that is at a premium generates a positive cash flow.

3.6 CHANGES IN EXCHANGE RATE VOLATILITY (ADVANCED)

To judge the extent of transaction exchange risk, understanding volatility is critical. The wider the conditional distribution of future exchange rates, the higher is your risk; and the width of the distribution in turn depends on the volatility or standard deviation of changes in exchange rates. Exhibit 3.1 uses information from several different decades to graph the probability distribution of monthly changes in the $/£ rate. But what if volatility has increased (decreased) over time? In this case, using a probability distribution based on a historical standard deviation underestimates (overestimates) the true uncertainty about future exchange rates.

Volatility Clustering

Many financial researchers have spent considerable computer time examining exchange rate data, and they have come to the conclusion that exchange rate volatility is not constant over time. In fact, as is true for the returns on many assets, percentage changes in exchange rates

Exhibit 3.9 Monthly Standard Deviations of Daily Rates of Appreciation

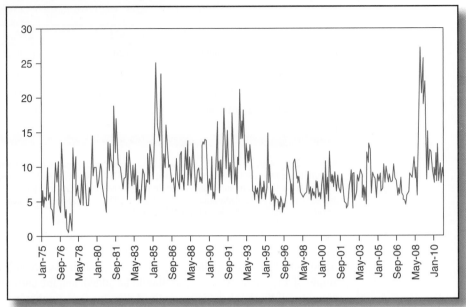

Notes: We obtained daily changes in the $/£ exchange rate from Datastream and computed the sample volatility for each month using these daily percentage changes. The graph plots these volatilities, annualized to be comparable to the way volatilities are plotted in financial markets. The data span January 1, 1975, through November 30, 2010.

show a pattern known as **volatility clustering**. When volatility is high, it tends to remain high for a while; periods of low volatility are likewise persistent. Asset markets in general, and the foreign exchange market in particular, appear to go through periods of tranquility and periods of turbulence. To illustrate this pattern, we use daily data on the dollar/pound exchange rate to compute monthly standard deviations. That is, for each month in our sample, we use the available daily observations to compute the sample standard deviation for each month. Exhibit 3.9 plots these monthly standard deviations.

The graph clearly reveals quiet periods (for example, 1977 to 1979 or 1999) and turbulent periods (for example, 1985 and 1991 to 1993) during which volatility exceeded 20% at times. The most volatile period of all is the autumn of 2008, in particular, October 2008, when volatility in both equity and foreign exchange markets reached unprecedented heights during the crisis.

A number of models have been developed to fit the observed pattern of volatility clustering in these data. The most popular model to date is the GARCH model developed by Bollerslev (1986).[6] Remember that the squared value of the volatility is the variance. Let v denote the variance. The relevant variance for assessing our uncertainty about future exchange rate changes is the conditional variance, $v(t) = var_t[s(t+1)]$ (see the appendix to this chapter). Let us denote the deviation of the actual percentage change in the exchange rate from its conditional expectation by $e(t) = s(t) - E_{t-1}[s(t)]$. We can interpret $e(t)$ as an economic shock that represents "news" because that part of the exchange rate change was not expected to occur. For example, suppose you expected the exchange rate change

---

[6]GARCH is an acronym that stands for Generalized Auto-Regressive Conditional Heteroskedasticity. A conditionally heteroskedastic time series does not have a constant variance. The future of an auto-regressive process depends on its own past. You will be happy to know that other models of conditional heteroskedasticity, such as SPARCH, QGARCH, and FIGARCH models, are gaining in popularity, but we will not discuss them here. A precursor to the GARCH model was Robert Engle's ARCH model, for which Engle won the Nobel Prize in Economics in 2003.

over the past month to be 5%, but it was actually 7%. The additional 2% change is "news" to you; it is an unexpected change in the exchange rate. The GARCH model for the conditional variance is

$$v(t) = a + bv(t-1) + ce(t)^2$$

The constants a, b, and c are parameters that can be estimated from the data; b reflects the sensitivity of the current conditional variance to the past conditional variance; c reflects its sensitivity to current news; and a is the minimum variance we would predict even if the past volatility and news terms are zero. Depending on the frequency of the data, b is between 0.85 and 0.95, and c is much lower (for example, between 0.05 and 0.15) (see Baillie and Bollerslev, 1989).

This model accommodates persistence in volatility. If the conditional variance is high today, it is likely to be high tomorrow. This persistence in $v(t)$ can generate the patterns of volatility clustering we see in the data. If we are in a quiet period today, but the exchange rate suddenly and unexpectedly moves in either direction, volatility immediately shifts to a higher level for a while through the e^2 term. This shift will tend to persist because of the feedback the model allows through the $bv(t-1)$ term. That is, because $v(t)$ is now higher, $v(t+1)$ will be higher as well because b is positive. Let's illustrate this positive feedback effect with an example.

Example 3.8 Positive Feedback in Volatility

Suppose last month's dollar–euro exchange rate stood at $1.20/€, and the market expected no change for the next month. However, after a number of opaque statements by the policy makers in Europe, the euro has weakened to $1.08/€. Note that this depreciation of the euro, $\left(s(t) = \dfrac{1.08 - 1.20}{1.20} = -0.10 \right)$, is unexpected, and hence it constitutes news [an $e(t)$-shock]. What does the GARCH model predict next month's currency volatility to be, assuming that $a = 0.00072$, $b = 0.90$, and $c = 0.05$ and the previous market volatility of the $/€ rate of depreciation was 8.0%? The GARCH model predicts $v(t)$, according to

$$v(t) = a + bv(t-1) + ce(t)^2$$
$$= 0.00072 + 0.90(0.08)^2 + 0.05(-0.10)^2 = 0.00698$$

Hence, volatility today, which is the square root of v_t, is 8.35% $\left(\sqrt{0.00698} \right)$. The large unexpected depreciation drives up volatility by 0.35%. Whatever the "shock" next month, today's volatility increase will tend to persist. If the GARCH model is correct, next month's volatility will be $v(t+1) = 0.00072 + 0.90(0.0835)^2 + 0.05(e(t+1))^2$. Today, we do not know what next month's shock will be, but we assign a high weight $(b = 0.90)$ to this period's higher volatility in computing next period's volatility. This is why we say the coefficient b implies positive feedback, or persistence, for the volatility process. Not everyone is convinced that GARCH is the right volatility model, but alternative models are beyond the scope of this book. Although some of these statistical models capture the volatility patterns well, they do not tell us why volatility moves the way it does. Possibilities include the clustering of macroeconomic news events (see Andersen and Bollerslev, 1998), the reaction of risk-averse agents to small changes in uncertainty regarding macroeconomic fundamentals (see Bekaert, 1996; and Hodrick, 1989), and the trading process itself (see Laux and Ng, 1993).

3.7 Summary

The purpose of this chapter is to introduce forward foreign exchange markets and to examine their use in hedging transaction exchange risk. The following are the main points in the chapter:

1. A transaction exchange risk arises when an individual or a firm enters into a transaction in which it is required to receive or pay a specific amount of foreign currency at some date in the future. If the firm does nothing to hedge the risk, there is a possibility that the firm will incur a loss if the exchange rate moves in an unfavorable direction.

2. One can fully hedge a transaction exchange risk by either buying or selling foreign currency in the forward foreign exchange market. If you are importing (exporting) goods and will contractually owe (receive) foreign currency, you have a foreign currency–denominated liability (asset) and must acquire an equivalent foreign currency–denominated asset (liability) to be hedged. Buying (selling) foreign currency from (to) the bank in the forward market provides the hedge.

3. Outright forward exchange rates are contractual prices at which trade will be conducted in the future. The parties agree to the price today, but no currencies change hands until the maturity, or value, date in the future.

4. Bid–ask spreads in the forward market are larger than in the spot market because the forward market is less liquid.

5. Forward contracts are sometimes cash settled, especially for emerging markets with foreign exchange trading restrictions ("non-deliverable forwards").

6. A swap involves the simultaneous purchase and sale of a certain amount of foreign currency for two different value dates. Traders quote swap rates as the number of pips that must be either added to the spot bid and ask rates or subtracted from the spot rates. When the points must be added, they are quoted with the smaller number first, and when they must be subtracted, they are quoted with the smaller number second. This ensures that the bid–ask spread in the forward market is always larger than the spread in the spot market.

7. If the forward price of a currency is higher than the spot price, that currency is said to be trading at a forward premium. If the forward price of a currency is lower than the spot price, that currency is said to be trading at a forward discount.

8. The extent of transaction exchange risk is proportional to the (conditional) volatility of exchange rate changes. This volatility changes over time.

Questions

1. What is a forward exchange rate? When does delivery occur on a 90-day forward contract?
2. If the yen is selling at a premium relative to the euro in the forward market, is the forward price of EUR per JPY larger or smaller than the spot price of EUR per JPY?
3. What do we mean by the expected future spot rate?
4. How much of the probability distribution of future spot rates is between plus or minus 2 standard deviations?
5. If you are a U.S. firm and owe someone ¥10,000,000 in 180 days, what is your transaction exchange risk?
6. What is a spot–forward swap?
7. What is a forward–forward swap?

Problems

1. If the spot exchange rate of the yen relative to the dollar is ¥105.75/$, and the 90-day forward rate is ¥103.25/$, is the dollar at a forward premium or discount? Express the premium or discount as a percentage per annum for a 360-day year.
2. Suppose today is Tuesday, January 18, 2011. If you enter into a 30-day forward contract to purchase euros, when will you pay your dollars and receive your euros? (Hints: February 18, 2011, is a Friday, and the following Monday is a holiday.)
3. As a foreign exchange trader for JPMorgan Chase, you have just called a trader at UBS to get quotes for the British pound for the spot, 30-day, 60-day, and 90-day forward rates. Your UBS counterpart stated, "We trade sterling at $1.7745-50, 47/44, 88/81, 125/115." What cash flows would you pay and

receive if you do a forward foreign exchange swap in which you swap into £5,000,000 at the 30-day rate and out of £5,000,000 at the 90-day rate? What must be the relationship between dollar interest rates and pound sterling interest rates?

4. Consider the following spot and forward rates for the yen per euro exchange rates:

Spot	30 Days	60 Days	90 Days	180 Days	360 Days
146.30	145.75	145.15	144.75	143.37	137.85

Is the euro at a forward premium or discount? What are the magnitudes of the forward premiums or discounts when quoted in percentage per annum for a 360-day year?

5. As a currency trader, you see the following quotes on your computer screen:

Exch. Rate	Spot	1-Month	2-Month	3-Month	6-Month
USD/EUR	1.0435/45	20/25	52/62	75/90	97/115
JPY/USD	98.75/85	12/10	20/16	25/19	45/35
USD/GBP	1.6623/33	30/35	62/75	95/110	120/130

a. What are the outright forward bid and ask quotes for the USD/EUR at the 3-month maturity?

b. Suppose you want to swap out of $10,000,000 and into yen for 2 months. What are the cash flows associated with the swap?

c. If one of your corporate customers calls you and wants to buy pounds with dollars in 6 months, what price would you quote?

6. Intel is scheduled to receive a payment of ¥100,000,000 in 90 days from Sony in connection with a shipment of computer chips that Sony is purchasing from Intel. Suppose that the current exchange rate is ¥103/$, that analysts are forecasting that the dollar will weaken by 1% over the next 90 days, and that the standard deviation of 90-day forecasts of the percentage rate of depreciation of the dollar relative to the yen is 4%.

a. Provide a qualitative description of Intel's transaction exchange risk.

b. If Intel chooses not to hedge its transaction exchange risk, what is Intel's expected dollar revenue?

c. If Intel does not hedge, what is the range of possible dollar revenues that incorporates 95.45% of the possibilities?

7. Go to the *Wall Street Journal*'s Market Data Center (http://online.wsj.com/mdc/public/page/market data.html) and find New York closing prices for currencies. Calculate the 180-day forward premium or discount on the dollar in terms of the yen.

8. Go to the St. Louis Federal Reserve Bank's database, FRED, at http://research.stlouisfed.org/fred2/ and download data for the exchange rate of the Brazilian real versus the U.S. dollar. Calculate the percentage changes over a 1-month interval. What loss would you take if you owed BRL 1 million in 1 month and the dollar depreciated by 2 standard deviations?

BIBLIOGRAPHY

Andersen, Torben G., and Tim Bollerslev, 1998, "Deutsche Mark–Dollar Volatility: Intraday Activity Patterns, Macroeconomic Announcements, and Longer Run Dependencies," *Journal of Finance* 53, pp. 219–265.

Baillie, Richard, and Tim Bollerslev, 1989, "The Message in Daily Exchange Rates: A Conditional Variance Tale," *Journal of Business and Economic Statistics* 7, pp. 297–305.

Bank for International Settlements, September 2010, "Central Bank Survey of Foreign Exchange and Derivatives Market Activity, 2010," Basel, Switzerland: Bank for International Settlements.

Bekaert, Geert, 1996, "The Time-Variation of Risk and Return in Foreign Exchange Markets: A General Equilibrium Perspective," *Review of Financial Studies* 9, pp. 427–470.

Bollerslev, Tim, 1986, "Generalized Autoregressive Conditional Heteroskedasticity," *Journal of Econometrics* 31, pp. 307–327.

Euromoney, November 2008, "Is Foreign Exchange the New Sub-Prime?" www.euromoney.com/Article/2038259/Is-foreign-exchange-the-new-sub-prime.html.

Hodrick, Robert J., 1989, "Risk, Uncertainty, and Exchange Rates," *Journal of Monetary Economics* 23, pp. 433–459.

Laux, Paul A., and Lilian K. Ng, 1993, "The Sources of GARCH: Empirical Evidence from an Intraday Returns Model Incorporating Systematic and Unique Risks," *Journal of International Money and Finance* 12, pp. 543–560.

Melvin, Michael, and Mark P. Taylor, 2009, "The Crisis in the Foreign Exchange Market," *Journal of International Money and Finance* 28, pp. 1317–1330.

Appendix

A Statistics Refresher

Statistics is a very valuable tool in business, and you will encounter the concepts discussed here on many occasions throughout the book. In Exhibit 3.1, we used historical data on end-of-month dollar per pound exchange rates between December 1974 and November 2010, yielding 431 observations on the percentage change from one month to the next. We denote the exchange rate itself by $S(t)$, where t indicates the date, and we denote the percentage rate of change of the exchange rate, by

$$s(t) = [S(t) - S(t-1)]/S(t-1)$$

One goal of statistics is to use past data to describe what the future will be like. Eventually, we would like to attach "likelihoods of occurrence" to different possible realizations of the future exchange rate. We start by looking at simple properties of the past data. In statistics, we would say we have T (in this case, 431) observations on a time series $\{s(t), t = 1, \dots, T\}$ or $\{S(t), t = 1, \dots, T\}$. The average, or **sample mean**, of a time series is the sum of all these observations divided by T. Focusing on $s(t)$, we denote this sample mean by $\hat{\mu}$, and in symbols, it is given by $\hat{\mu} = (1/T) \sum_{t=1}^{T} s(t)$. The sample mean for our example is -0.05%. To the extent that the future is like the past, the sample mean may tell us something about the central tendency of future rates of depreciation. But we know it will not tell us enough as there are months in which the dollar appreciated by 4.5% and months in which the dollar depreciated by more than 4%, and these observations are quite different from the mean of –0.05%. One way to summarize how spread out our past observations were and how spread out they may be in the future is to compute the standard deviation of our $s(t)$ time series. The standard deviation is a measure of the dispersion of possibilities around the sample mean. The sample standard deviation is the square root of the **sample variance**. In symbols, the sample variance is computed as

$$\hat{\sigma}^2 = \frac{1}{T-1} \sum_{t=1}^{T} [s(t) - \hat{\mu}]^2.$$

An extreme observation relative to the sample mean in either direction (such as 4.5% in this example) makes the sample variance bigger. The sample variance squares the deviations from the mean so that an extreme positive observation, such as 4.5%, does not get partially cancelled out by an extreme negative observation, such as -5%.

Common sense suggests that such extreme observations are less likely to occur than observations near the mean, and statistical analysis bears this out. To find out how much less likely these observations might be, we can construct a **histogram** of the data. A histogram groups our observations into intervals of equal magnitude and records the number of observations in each interval. That is exactly what we did in Exhibit 3.1.

The intervals are represented on the horizontal axis, and the percent of the total of observations in each interval on the vertical axis. Because we have so many observations, we used quite a few intervals, too many for all their midpoints to be denoted on the horizontal axis. The width of an interval is 0.8959%. Often, we denote the number of observations as a fraction of the total, and it is then called the *frequency of occurrence*. For example, in Exhibit 3.1, there is a 17.4% frequency that dollar–pound changes are in the middle bin, which is between -0.6466% and $+0.2492\%$ (that is, 75 observations out of 431). There is also only one observation above 14%, so that the frequency for the highest bin is 1/431 = 0.23%. A histogram expressed in frequencies is also called a **frequency distribution**.

It turns out that many natural and economic data show frequency distributions that can be approximated by smooth curves and simple mathematical expressions. Such a smooth curve is called a **probability distribution**, and the mathematical formula that describes it is called a **density function**. Probability distributions summarize information about the likelihood of different events (for example, future exchange rates) occurring. It is easiest to think about probability distributions when there are a finite, distinct number of possible events. In this case, the probability distribution describes the events and their associated probabilities, and the distribution is said to be *discrete*.

There are several important things to remember about probabilities. First, if there is more than one thing that can happen in the future, the probability of each future event must be a fraction between 0 and 1. Second, if we know all the possible future events, the sum of the probabilities of all the events must be 1 because one of the events will actually happen.

Now that you understand the concept of a probability distribution, we can also more formally define the mean, or **expected value**, and the **variance**, associated with a distribution. The expected value is easily defined in the case of discrete probability distributions. The expected value of the future events is the sum of the values in each state of the world, say x_k in state k, multiplied, or "weighted," by the probability of that particular state, say p_k. That is, the expected value of event x is

$$E(x) = (p_1 x_1 + p_2 x_2 + \ldots + p_N x_N)$$

Notice that if there are N possible events that are equally likely, the probability of any one event is $(1/N)$. In this case, the expected value is the average of the possible outcomes. The sample mean implicitly assigns an equal weight to each observation. When the probabilities of the events differ, the expected value is the *probability-weighted average* of the possible events.

The variance, $V(x)$, is the expected value of the squared deviations from the means:

$$V(x) = E[(x - E[x])^2]$$
$$= p_1(x_1 - E[x])^2 + p_2(x_2 - E[x])^2$$
$$+ \ldots + p_N(x_N - E[x])^2$$

The sample variance we defined is an estimate of this variance, treating each observed exchange rate change as having equal probability of occurrence. The square root of the variance is called the *standard deviation*, or *volatility*, when it concerns financial data.

In Exhibit 3.1, for example, we also draw a smooth bell-shaped curve that approximates the histogram. In fact, the approximation would become more accurate if we had many more data points on exchange rate changes and let the intervals in which we measure the frequencies become smaller and smaller. The probability distribution described by the curve in Exhibit 3.1 is called the **normal distribution**, and it describes many phenomena well. (For example, the heights of people in the general population are normally distributed.)

The normal distribution has a number of important characteristics. First, it is symmetric around its mean—that is, the same amount of the probability distribution of possibilities is below as above the mean. If the mean is -0.05%, statisticians would say that the probability of observing $s(t)$ larger than -0.05% is 50%. Because the normal distribution is symmetric, the mean and median of the distribution of the future exchange rate coincide. The **median** is the exchange rate that has 50% of the possible exchange rates above it and 50% of the possible exchange rates below it. Not all distributions are symmetrical. For example, suppose that, as in Example 3A.1, there are only three possible exchange rate changes (-5.00%, 0%, and 8.00%), which are equally likely to occur. The mean exchange rate change is 1%, but the median exchange rate change is 0%, which is lower than the mean. The distribution is said to be *positively skewed* in this case.[7]

Example 3A.1 Calculating with a Discrete Distribution

Suppose there are only three possible exchange rate changes, which are equally likely to occur: -5, 0, and 8 (in percentages). The probability distribution refers to the events $[-5, 0, 8]$ and the associated probabilities $[1/3, 1/3, 1/3]$.

The mean is $(1/3)(-5) + (1/3)(0) + (1/3)(8) = 1$.

The variance is $(1/3)(-5 - 1)^2 + (1/3)(-1)^2 + (1/3)(8 - 1)^2 = 86/3$.

The standard deviation therefore equals $\sqrt{86/3} = 5.35\%$.

If the possible exchange rate percentage changes were $[-3, 0, 3]$ instead, you should demonstrate to yourself that the mean would be 0, and the standard deviation would be smaller (2.45%).

Although discrete distributions are useful in many circumstances, describing uncertainty of future rates of depreciation for flexible exchange rates should allow for all possible values over a very wide range. This is best done using a continuous probability distribution and a density function that expresses probabilities of occurrence for any range of depreciation between $-\infty$ and $+\infty$.

---

[7]The mean is the first moment or the center of the distribution, and the variance is the second moment around the mean, and it measures the dispersion of the distribution. Skewness is the third moment around the mean, and it measures asymmetry. For the normal distribution, skewness is 0. Another moment of interest in financial data is the fourth moment around the mean, called kurtosis. Kurtosis measures how "fat" the tails of the distribution are; that is, it measures the likelihood of extreme outcomes.

Second, the normal probability distribution is completely summarized by its mean and its standard deviation. When a statistician is given the mean and standard deviation of the normal distribution, she has all the information necessary to assess the probability of any range of possible exchange rate changes. These probabilities can be assessed using computers or tables that are reported in any statistics textbook. For example, suppose the possible dollar–pound exchange rate changes are well described by a normal distribution with a mean of -0.05% and a standard deviation of 3.03%. How likely is it that we will observe an exchange rate change larger than 8% or an exchange rate change smaller than -5%? We can look up the answer in any statistics book. Most books describe the probabilities for standard normal distributions—this is, normal distributions with a mean of 0 and a standard deviation of 1. To use the tables in statistics books, we must "standardize" our numbers by figuring out how many standard deviations from the mean the number we are interested in is. For example, an exchange rate change of 8% is $\dfrac{8\% - (-0.05\%)}{3.03\%} = 2.66$ standard deviations from the mean. According to the normal distribution table, there is only a 0.39% chance that an exchange rate change will occur that is larger than that. Likewise, an exchange rate change smaller than -5%, which is 1.63 standard deviations away from the mean, has a 5.16% probability of occurrence.

Throughout this book, we are interested in describing our uncertainty about future exchange rates. To do so, we look at the distribution of exchange rate changes, conditional on the information we have today (which includes the current exchange rate). Because the probability distribution of the future exchange rate depends on all the information available at time t, we say that it is a *conditional probability distribution*. Consequently, the expected value of this distribution is also referred to as the *conditional expectation* of the future exchange rate (conditional mean). Likewise, we can define a **conditional standard deviation**, or **conditional volatility**, as the square root of the conditional variance. With $E_t[s(t+1)]$, the conditional mean of exchange rate changes, the conditional variance $v(t)$ is

$$v(t) = E_t\{s(t+1) - E_t[s(t+1)]\}^2$$

The conditional means and volatilities of future exchange rate changes and their distribution allow us to make inferences about future exchange rates. Because $s(t+1) = [S(t+1) - S(t)]/S(t)$, we can solve for the future exchange rate as a function of future exchange rate changes and the current exchange rate (which is part of our information set). That is,

$$S(t+1) = S(t)[1 + s(t+1)]$$

Hence, the conditional mean of the future exchange rate will simply be

$$E_t[S(t+1)] = S(t)[1 + E_t[s(t+1)]]$$

Note that we do not take an expectation of the current exchange rate because it is a part of our information set today.

Likewise, the conditional volatility of the future exchange rate will be $S(t)\sqrt{v(t)}$.[8]

If the distribution of exchange rate changes never varied over time, there would be no need to distinguish between the conditional and the unconditional distributions we talked about earlier. However, throughout this book, you will see how both the mean and volatility can, and do, vary through time. Section 3.6 summarizes recent research on how the volatility of exchange rate changes seems to move through quiet and turbulent periods.

You may wonder why we did not look at the distribution of actual exchange rates instead of percentage changes in exchange rates. This is because it is more reasonable to assume that percentage changes in exchange rates are drawn from some well-defined probability distribution, such as the normal distribution, than to assume that the levels of exchange rates are from a common distribution. The logic that leads us to use percentage changes in exchange rates in describing future distributions of exchange rates is the same as the logic that dictates using rates of return on stocks rather than the levels of stock prices to describe future distributions of stock prices. Both the stock price and the exchange rate are asset prices, and the percentage changes in asset prices provide part of the rate of return to holding the asset. For most of our applications, we are interested in how much the exchange rate is likely to change from today's level.

---

[8]If we take a random variable, say x, with a certain distribution and multiply it by a constant, say b, the variance of bx is $V(bx) = b^2 V(x)$. From the perspective of today's information set, $S(t)$ is a constant because it is known, and the conditional variance is $S(t)^2 v(t)$.

Chapter 4

The Balance of Payments

*T*he first three chapters of this book provide insights into the nature of foreign exchange markets and foreign exchange risks. To understand these concepts more deeply, you need to understand the economic forces that cause exchange rates to fluctuate. Exchange rates respond to demand and supply to trade currencies. These demands and supplies arise from international trade flows and international capital flows.

Plenty of useful information about these international flows is provided by the balance of payments, which records the payments between residents of one country and the rest of the world over a given time period. As such, it helps shed a great deal of light on the supply and demand for various currencies, the possible evolution of their exchange rates, and the global financial marketplace in general.

Balance of payments statistics are discussed daily by politicians, the news media, and currency analysts at corporations, commercial banks, investment banks, and mutual funds. Currency traders eagerly await the release of new balance of payments statistics because they know exchange rates will move with the new information. We will see how the balances on various subaccounts are linked to domestic and international saving and investment decisions and ultimately how they may determine a country's financial and economic health. For example, multinational firms should recognize that persistent current account deficits in developing countries can signal that currency devaluations are likely to occur there, with potentially dire economic ramifications. In developed countries, persistent current account deficits can lead legislators to unleash protectionist policies, such as tariffs and embargoes on imported goods and services. Every company in the world doing business with China keenly follows the effect that the U.S. trade deficit with China is having on the two countries' trade policies.

4.1 THE BALANCE OF PAYMENTS: CONCEPTS AND TERMINOLOGY

A country's **balance of payments (BOP)** records the value of the transactions between its residents, businesses, and government with the rest of the world for a specific period of time, such as a month, a quarter, or a year. Hence, the balance of payments summarizes the international flows of goods and services and changes in the ownership of assets across countries.

Major Accounts of the Balance of Payments

There are two major BOP accounts: the current account and the capital account. In recent years, most countries have renamed the capital account as the "financial account" in order to comply with the recommendations of the International Monetary Fund (IMF). Because the terminology *capital account* has a long tradition and continues to be used in the financial press, we continue to use it here.

The **current account** records the following:

Goods and services transactions (**imports**, which are purchases of goods and services from foreign residents; and **exports**, which are sales of goods and services to foreign residents).

Transactions associated with the income flows from the ownership of foreign assets (dividends and interest paid to domestic residents who own foreign assets as well as dividends and interest paid to foreign residents who own domestic assets).

Unilateral **transfers** of money between countries (foreign aid, gifts, and grants given by the residents or governments of one country to those of another).

The **capital account** records the purchases and sales of foreign assets by domestic residents as well as the purchases and sales of domestic assets by foreign residents. The definition of an asset is all inclusive: It encompasses both financial assets (bank deposits and loans, corporate and government bonds, and equities) and real assets (factories, real estate, antiques, and so forth).

One type of capital account transaction merits special attention: transactions involving the purchase or sale of official international reserve assets by a nation's central bank. International reserves are the assets of the central bank that are not denominated in the domestic currency. Gold and assets denominated in foreign currency are the typical international reserves. Exhibit 4.1 surveys the various types of transactions and accounts of the BOP and splits the capital account into two parts: a regular capital account and an **official settlements account**, or **official reserves account**. The regular capital account records all transactions other than

Exhibit 4.1 Summary of the Accounts of the Balance of Payments

Debits (recorded with a −)	Credits (recorded with a +)
I. CURRENT ACCOUNT	
(A) TRADE BALANCE (Transactions in goods, services, and transfers)	
Imports to the United States	Exports from the United States
(B) INVESTMENT INCOME ACCOUNT	
Payment by the United States of dividends and interest to foreigners	Receipt by the United States of dividends and interest from foreigners
II. CAPITAL ACCOUNT	
Capital Outflows	Capital Inflows
Increase in U.S. ownership of foreign assets	Increase in foreign ownership of U.S. assets
Decrease of foreign ownership of U.S. assets	Decrease in U.S. ownership of foreign assets
III. OFFICIAL RESERVES ACCOUNT	
Increase in official reserves of the U.S. central bank	Decrease of official reserves of the U.S. central bank
Decrease in dollar reserves of foreign central banks	Increase in dollar reserves of foreign central banks

Notes: This exhibit summarizes the various accounts of the balance of payments and indicates the types of transactions that are booked there. We use the U.S. perspective, but the structure applies to any country.

those involving international reserves. We discuss the official settlements account in detail in Section 4.2. Throughout this chapter, Exhibit 4.1 provides a useful guide.

A Double-Entry Accounting System

The balance of payments uses a double-entry system. Each transaction gives rise to two entries: One entry is a credit, and the other entry is a debit of equal value. The rules for determining credits and debits on the balance of payments are analogous to those in financial accounting. Any transaction resulting in a payment to foreigners is entered in the BOP accounts as a debit. Any transaction resulting in a receipt of funds from foreigners is entered as a credit. In presentations of the balance of payments that merely list the values of the items, it is traditional that credit items are listed with a positive sign $(+)$ and debit items are listed with a negative sign $(-)$.

An Intuitive Rule for Determining Credits and Debits

Determining which items are credits or debits can be easily done if you suppose that all transactions between the residents of a country and the rest of the world must be conducted with foreign money, which flows through the foreign exchange market. Thus, a credit transaction on a country's balance of payments corresponds to an inflow, or source, of foreign currency, whereas a debit transaction constitutes an outflow, or use, of foreign currency.

In summary:

Credit transactions give rise to *conceptual inflows or sources of foreign exchange*. The purchases of goods and assets by foreign residents from domestic residents are credits because they are a source of foreign exchange. That is, they increase the supply of foreign money in the foreign exchange market.

Debit transactions give rise to *conceptual outflows or uses of foreign exchange*. The purchases of goods and assets by domestic residents from foreign residents are debits because they cause an outflow of foreign exchange. Debit transactions increase the demand for the foreign money in the foreign exchange market.

Let's apply these rules in some example situations to make sure that you understand them and the double-entry system.

Current Account Transactions

Every current account transaction can be considered to have a corresponding flow of foreign money associated with it, and this flow of foreign money is recorded as a capital account transaction. To illustrate the double-entry system, let's begin with two simple examples that illustrate the recording on the BOP of export and import transactions.

Example 4.1 Commercial Exports of Goods

Suppose the U.S. computer maker Dell sells $20 million of computers to Komatsu, a Japanese manufacturer of construction and mining equipment. Komatsu pays Dell by transferring dollars from its dollar-denominated bank account at Citibank in New York to Dell's bank account. What are the credit and debit items on the U.S. balance of payments?

First, a U.S. firm is selling goods to a foreign firm. This transaction is an export of goods from the United States and is a credit on the U.S. balance of payments because it gives rise to a conceptual inflow of foreign money—in this case, yen—to the United

States. Second, in this example, Komatsu already owned dollars and thus did not need to enter the foreign exchange market, but the payment of dollars by Komatsu does reduce the foreign ownership of U.S. assets. This action is a debit transaction because if it were done as a separate transaction, Komatsu would have taken the dollars it owned and converted them back into yen, which would have increased the demand for yen in the foreign exchange market. In summary, we record the following transactions on the U.S. BOP:

U.S. BOP	Credit	Debit
Computer purchase by Komatsu from Dell (Current account; U.S. goods export)	$20 million	
Citibank foreign deposit decrease (Capital account; capital outflow from the United States)		$20 million

If these transactions were listed without the credit and debit titles, the export of goods would receive a $(+)$, and the capital outflow item would receive a $(-)$.

Example 4.2 examines how French imports of foreign services affect the French balance of payments.

Example 4.2 Commercial Imports of Services

Suppose LVMH, a French luxury goods company, buys €1.5 million of consulting services from the British subsidiary of the Boston Consulting Group (BCG). LVMH pays by writing a check on its euro-denominated bank account at its Paris bank, Société Générale, and BCG deposits the check in its euro-denominated bank account at a different Paris bank, BNP Paribas. What are the credit and debit items on the French balance of payments?

First, a French firm, LVMH, is buying services from a foreign firm, BCG. This is a French import of services. This gives rise to an outflow of funds from France, so it is a debit on the French current account. BCG could have demanded British pounds, which would have forced LVMH to enter the foreign exchange market to purchase pounds, thus increasing the demand for pounds. Second, the receipt of the euro funds by the British firm increases foreign (British) ownership of French assets. This is a credit transaction on the French capital account because if it were done as a separate transaction, BCG would have had to buy euros directly with pounds, which would have supplied foreign currency to the French foreign exchange market. Hence, the underlying transaction by BCG of depositing the euro-denominated check in a Paris bank is one that conceptually supplies foreign money to France and is thus a credit on the French balance of payments.

In summary, the transactions on the French BOP are as follows:

French BOP	Credit	Debit
LVMH purchase of consulting services from BCG (Current account; French import of services)		€1.5 million
BNP Paribas foreign deposit increase (Capital account; capital inflow to France)	€1.5 million	

If these transactions were listed without the credit and debit titles, the import of services would receive a $(-)$, and the capital inflow would receive a $(+)$.

Interest and Dividend Receipts and Payments

The current account also records receipts and payments of dividend and interest income across countries. Dividends from foreign stocks and interest income on foreign bonds give rise to inflows of foreign money and are, therefore, credit items on the balance of payments. These investment income flows are also recorded on the current account of the balance of payments because they are considered returns to the owners of capital for the services of productive capital. The service flows from capital assets are comparable to the service flows from labor, such as the consulting services LVMH purchased from BCG in Example 4.2.

It is important to distinguish between these income flows that are returns to previously made investments and the values of the outstanding assets. The outstanding asset or stock position is analogous to an item on the balance sheet of a firm. Changes in the ownership of assets are booked on the capital account.

Example 4.3 is a concrete example of how investment income is recorded on the Indonesian balance of payments.

Example 4.3   The Receipt of Income from Foreign Assets

Consider an Indonesian resident who in previous years invested in Japanese government bonds. Each year, the Indonesian receives ¥500,000 of coupon payments from her Japanese bonds. Suppose that these payments are paid to her Tokyo bank, where she keeps a yen-denominated bank account. What are the credit and debit items on the Indonesian balance of payments?

When the Indonesian resident receives coupon payments from the Japanese government, these receipts are credits to Indonesia's investment income part of the current account (see Exhibit 4.1). They provide an inflow of foreign currency to Indonesia. The fact that the Indonesian resident receives the yen and deposits them at a Tokyo bank implies that there is an increase in Indonesian ownership of foreign assets. This is a debit on the Indonesian capital account because if the Indonesian resident had set out to increase the value of her yen bank account in Tokyo directly, she would have had to use rupiah to purchase yen in the foreign exchange market. Hence, the increase in Indonesian ownership of foreign assets would have increased the demand for foreign exchange, and it is consequently a debit item on the Indonesian balance of payments. In summary, if the rupiah–yen exchange rate is IDR89/JPY, so that ¥500,000 represents IDR44,500,000, the transactions on the Indonesian BOP would be as follows:

Indonesian BOP	Credit	Debit
Coupon receipts from Japanese Treasury (Current account; interest income)	IDR44.5M	
Tokyo bank, foreign deposit increase (Capital account; capital outflow from Indonesia)		IDR44.5M

Transfer Payments Between Countries

The last items recorded on the current account of the balance of payments are transfers between countries. Transfers are indicated as unilateral transfers in the U.S. BOP and unrequited transfers in the IMF's *Balance of Payments Manual*. Both terms indicate that the items are given by the individual, without an explicit receipt of an item of equivalent value in return. Typical examples are a U.S. resident sending a gift to her relatives in the "old country" or foreign aid from one country to another. Clearly, gifts to foreign countries or to a family abroad lead to an increase in the demand for foreign exchange and, by our rule, must be debit items on the U.S. BOP.

You may be thinking that because the gift is a debit, there must be a way of describing this transaction that makes it seem more like imports of goods or services to United States, which are also debit items on the U.S. BOP. There is a way—you just need to understand the motivation behind the transaction. Presumably, the U.S. resident hoped that the gift would improve relations with her foreign relatives. That is, she sought to import goodwill to the United States. Hence, the gift is an import of goodwill and is therefore a debit (on the current account).

To clarify how transfers are recorded on the BOP, let's look at an example that considers the Japanese balance of payments.

Example 4.4 Gifts to Foreign Residents

Consider the effect on the Japanese BOP of a gift of $2 million by a Japanese firm to a U.S. university to create an endowed chair. Suppose, also, that the Japanese firm finances the gift by selling U.S. Treasury bonds in which it had previously invested. What should we record as credit and debit items on Japan's balance of payments?

The action by the Japanese firm clearly uses $2 million of foreign exchange from Japan's perspective. Hence, by our rule, the gift must be a debit item on the Japanese balance of payments because it leads to an outflow of foreign exchange. Notice that the gift by the Japanese firm improves relations with the U.S. university and is a Japanese import of goodwill from the United States.

Now, consider the offsetting credit transaction on the Japanese balance of payments. The Japanese firm sold U.S. Treasury bonds, which reduces the Japanese ownership of foreign assets. This transaction is a credit on the capital account of the Japanese balance of payments because it supplies dollars to the Japanese foreign exchange market.

In summary, if the yen–dollar exchange rate is ¥100/$, in which case the $2 million equals ¥200 million, the transactions would be as follows:

Japanese BOP	Credit	Debit
Gift by Japanese firm to U.S. university (Current account; Japanese import of goodwill)		¥200 million
Sale of U.S. Treasury bonds (Capital account; capital inflow to Japan)	¥200 million	

We turn now to transactions in assets that are recorded on the capital account.

Capital Account Transactions

Some capital account transactions arise naturally, as demonstrated in the case of payment flows associated with current account transactions. However, some transactions involve situations in which both entries are recorded exclusively on the capital account. For example, suppose a Mexican resident buys a U.S. Treasury bond. You can think of this as Mexico "importing" a foreign asset (a bond). Thus, the transaction should have the same sign as an import of a regular good. This transaction is therefore a debit on the Mexican capital account because it represents an outflow, or use, of foreign exchange. In other words, this transaction gives rise to an increase in the demand for foreign currency—dollars in this case— because the Mexican resident needs dollars to purchase the U.S. Treasury bond. Notice that in presentations of the balance of payments in which credits are given a $(+)$ and debits are given a $(-)$, the acquisition of foreign assets by a Mexican resident would be a debit and would receive a $(-)$, even though Mexican ownership of foreign assets is increasing!

Capital Outflows

There is an alternative way of describing the acquisition of foreign assets. When the residents of Mexico purchase foreign assets rather than investing in domestic assets, there is said to be a **capital outflow** from Mexico. In this case, the "capital" refers to the money that could have financed an investment in Mexico. Because this money is no longer available to finance local investment projects, local governments often try to discourage this outflow of capital, which is often called **capital flight** when it occurs rapidly in response to a deteriorating investment climate in the home country.

Capital Inflows

If a U.S. resident purchases Mexican Cetes (Treasury bills), Mexico is said to have a **capital inflow**. This transaction is recorded as a credit on the Mexican balance of payments because it supplies foreign money to Mexico's foreign exchange market. Generally, capital inflows to Mexico occur when foreigners buy Mexican assets or when Mexicans reduce the amount of wealth they hold abroad (for example, a Mexican sells U.S. stocks).

Summarizing Capital Account Transactions

All the transactions discussed so far are easily matched with the capital account categories mentioned in Exhibit 4.1, when viewed from the Mexican perspective. The U.S. purchase of Cetes corresponds to an "increase in foreign ownership of assets in Mexico," and the Mexican selling of U.S. stocks corresponds to a "decrease in Mexican ownership of foreign assets." Both are capital inflows to Mexico. Similarly, capital outflows from Mexico (debits on the Mexican BOP) happen when Mexicans increase their assets abroad, as they do when buying U.S. Treasury bonds, or when foreigners decrease their ownership of assets in Mexico.

We have now discussed how the buying and selling of assets is recorded on the Mexican BOP, but what about the payment flows associated with these transactions? When a Mexican resident buys a U.S. Treasury bond, he must pay in dollars. This reduction of his dollar holdings is a Mexican capital inflow ("decrease in Mexican ownership of foreign assets") and provides the credit transaction that balances the debit transaction of the original foreign bond purchase. Similarly, when a U.S. investor buys Cetes (a capital inflow into Mexico), he must pay in Mexican pesos. If we conceptually assume that he had a peso-denominated account with a Mexican bank, the reduction in his peso bank account is a capital outflow, which is the debit on the Mexican BOP that balances the credit generated when the American purchases Cetes.

Official Reserves Account Transactions

Changes in the **official international reserves** of a country's central bank are also recorded on the country's balance of payments—in this case, in the country's official reserves account. The rules for determining credits and debits are identical to the rules that govern the private sector's capital account. If the central bank acquires international reserves, a debit is entered on the official settlements account, just as it is recorded on the private capital account if private residents acquire foreign assets. Once again, this debit receives a $(-)$ in a presentation of the BOP that just lists items even though the reserves of the central bank are increasing. If, on the other hand, the central bank draws down its international reserves, there is a credit on the official settlements account, just as there is on the private capital account if private residents sell their foreign assets. In this case, the transaction would be recorded with a $(+)$ even though the central bank's reserves are declining.

Implications for Fixed Exchange Rates

In some developing countries, the central bank fixes the exchange rate at a particular value relative to the dollar, for example, and the country's residents are required to deal directly with the central bank to conduct international transactions. If a resident of the country wants to purchase U.S. equities, the person must first purchase dollars from the central bank with local currency at the fixed exchange rate determined by the central bank. The official settlements account records a credit that offsets the debit associated with the use of the dollars (the increase in foreign assets represented by the equity purchase). Conversely, when residents of this country acquire dollars in international transactions, they must also sell the dollars to the central bank for local currency at the fixed exchange rate. In this way, the central bank's stock of dollars increases, and the transaction is recorded as a debit on the official settlements account, offsetting the private sector's credit transaction that originally gave rise to the dollars.

4.2 SURPLUSES AND DEFICITS IN THE BALANCE OF PAYMENTS ACCOUNTS

Because the balance of payments system uses a double-entry accounting system, the value of credits on a country's balance of payments must equal the value of its debits. The overall balance of payments therefore must always sum to zero. Nevertheless, the total value of credits generated by a particular set of economic transactions, such as the sales of goods and services *to* foreigners (exports), need not be equal to the value of debits generated by the purchase of goods and services *from* foreigners (imports). If credit transactions on a particular account are greater than debit transactions on that account, the account is said to be in **surplus**. If debit transactions on a particular account are greater than credit transactions on that account, the account is said to be in **deficit**.

An Important Balance of Payments Identity

Because the two major accounts of the balance of payments are the current account and the capital account, we see immediately that a current account deficit must have a capital account surplus as its counterpart. In other words, if we list credit items with a $(+)$ and debit items with a $(-)$, we can add the accounts, and they must sum to zero:

$$\text{Current account} + \text{Capital account} = 0$$

If we highlight the transactions that change a country's stock of international reserves at its central bank as a separate part of the balance of payments, as in Exhibit 4.1, we have

$$\text{Current account} + \text{Regular capital account} + \text{Official settlements account} = 0 \quad \text{(4.1)}$$

To better understand the economic meaning of the various surpluses and deficits, we next study the U.S. BOP statistics in more detail. We then look at the special role of the official settlements account. Finally, we investigate recent BOP statistics around the world. Detailed statistics of the U.S. BOP are provided in Exhibits 4.2 and 4.3. Exhibit 4.4 presents the data from these exhibits for 2009 in the format of Exhibit 4.1. We now discuss the various subaccounts, one by one.

The U.S. Current Account

Let's look at the current account of the United States and its various subcategories, which are shown in Exhibit 4.2.

Goods

The first category in Exhibit 4.2 is "exports and imports of goods." This account covers trade in commodities such as oil or wheat and in physical goods such as cars, airplanes, DVD players, and computers. The goods can be raw materials, semi-finished goods, or finished goods. In 2009, the U.S. exported $1,068 billion of goods and imported $1,575 billion of goods. Because debits (imports) exceeded credits (exports) by $507 billion, we say the United States had a $507 billion **merchandise trade balance** deficit in 2009.

Services

We only show the net amount, or balance, on the services account, which was a $132 billion surplus in 2009. Typically, economists classify services as economic transactions that must be produced and utilized at the same time. Services thus include the export and import of education, financial services, insurance, consulting, telecommunications, medical services, royalties on films, and the fees and royalties repatriated to U.S. corporations. Fees and royalties repatriated to U.S. corporations are earned when the corporations license technology to their foreign subsidiaries or to other foreign companies.

In the U.S. current account, services also include military transactions even when they involve purchases of goods. Because personnel at U.S. military bases in foreign countries are considered to be U.S. residents, their purchases of local goods and services, including supplies for the bases themselves, are imported goods. The primary U.S. military exports are sales of aircraft.

Another important subcategory of services is travel and transportation. When foreigners spend more while traveling in the United States for food, lodging, recreational activities, and gifts than U.S. residents spend while traveling in foreign countries, this account is in surplus. Because it is impossible to know how much each foreign tourist spends, the U.S. Department of Commerce estimates expenditures on this account by multiplying an average expenditure obtained from surveys by the known number of travelers (obtained from immigration and naturalization statistics).

Exhibit 4.2 The U.S. Current Account, 1970–2009 (billions of dollars; credits, +; debits, −)

Year	Goods Exports	Goods Imports	Goods Balance on Goods	Services Balance on Services	Balance on Goods and Services	Income Receipts and Payments Receipts	Income Receipts and Payments Payments	Balance on Income	Unilateral Current Transfers, Net	Balance on Current Account
1970	42	−40	2	0	2	12	−6	6	−6	2
1980	224	−250	−26	6	−20	73	−43	30	−8	2
1990	389	−498	−109	30	−79	172	−143	29	−27	−77
2000	772	−1,224	−452	74	−378	353	−331	22	−54	−410
2005	895	−1,677	−782	66	−716	475	−463	12	−86	−790
2009	1,068	−1,575	−507	132	−375	588	−467	121	−125	−379

Note: Data are from the U.S. Department of Commerce, Bureau of Economic Analysis, Survey of Current Business, April 2010, and are rounded to the nearest billion.

Balance on Goods and Services

The sum of the net positions on the goods account and the services account gives the balance on the goods and services account, which was −$375 billion in 2009. Notice that the absolute value of this account is substantially smaller than in 2005. Much of this change can be attributed to the global recession, which was more severe in the United States than its trading partners, because between 2008 and 2009, U.S. imports of goods and services declined by $770 billion, but U.S. exports of goods and services only declined by $477 billion.

Investment Income

The next columns in Exhibit 4.2 report income receipts and payments, which are the dividend and interest income received by U.S. residents (credits) because of their ownership of assets in foreign countries as well as the dividend and interest income paid to foreigners (debits) who own U.S. assets. In 2009, the United States received $588 billion of investment income from foreigners and made $467 billion of payments to foreigners, for a net figure of $121 billion. Because credits on this account outweigh debits, we say that there is a surplus on this account.

Unilateral Current Transfers, Net

The second-to-last column in Exhibit 4.2 is "Unilateral Current Transfers, Net." The figure for 2009 is −$125 billion. This indicates that the U.S. government and other U.S. residents gave more money to foreign countries and residents as gifts and grants than the United States received from abroad. The deficit on this account represents a net import of goodwill into the United States.

Balance on Current Account

When the investment income account and the unilateral transfers account are added to the balance on goods and services, the result is the *current account surplus or deficit*, which is recorded in Exhibit 4.2 as the balance on the current account. Exhibit 4.2 indicates that the 2009 U.S. current account balance was −$379 billion, which is a current account deficit.

The U.S. Capital and Financial Accounts

Exhibit 4.3 presents the details of the U.S. capital and financial accounts. As noted earlier, the current account and the capital account must sum to zero. Hence, if there is a current account deficit, it must be financed by a capital account surplus.

Exhibit 4.3 The U.S. Capital and Financial Accounts, 1970–2009 (billions of dollars; credits, + ; debits, −)

	U.S.–Owned Assets Abroad, Net, [increase/financial outflow (−)]			Foreign-Owned Assets in the U.S., Net, [increase/financial inflow (+)]						
Year	Total	U.S. Official Reserve Assets	Other U.S. Government Assets	U.S. Private Assets	Total	Foreign Official Assets	Other Foreign Assets	Financial Derivatives, Net	Capital Account Transfers	Balance on Capital Account	Statistical Discrepancy
1970	−9	3	−2	−10	6	7	−1	—	—	−3	1
1980	−86	−7	−5	−74	63	16	47	—	—	−23	21
1990	−81	−2	2	−81	142	34	108	—	−7	54	23
2000	−606	−0.3	−0.3	−605	1,016	38	978	—	1	411	−1
2005	−427	14	5	−446	1,212	199	1,013	—	−4	781	9
2009	−141	−52	541	−630	306	450	−144	51	0	216	163

Notes: Data are from the Department of Commerce, Bureau of Economic Analysis, Survey of Current Business, April 2010, and are rounded to the nearest billion. Financial Derivatives are excluded from U.S.–Owned Assets Abroad and Foreign-Owned Assets in the U.S. The statistical discrepancy is the sum of the current account and the capital account with the sign reversed.

A surplus in the capital account can occur in several ways. First, there could be a decrease in U.S. private and official assets abroad. A country can sell its foreign assets to finance a current account deficit, just as an individual can consume more than his current income by selling his assets. Such sales of foreign assets are credits on the capital account.

A second way that a current account deficit can be financed is through a net increase in foreign private and official assets in the United States. Just as an individual might consume more than her income by taking out a loan or selling someone her assets, a country might borrow from abroad or sell assets to foreigners. For the United States, these activities correspond to an increase in foreign claims on the United States. Any combination of these capital account transactions that results in a capital account surplus of the appropriate magnitude will also finance the current account deficit. From Exhibit 4.3, we see that the particular combination of capital account transactions that financed the current account deficit in 2009 was an increase in foreign ownership of U.S. assets that was much larger than the increase in U.S. ownership of foreign assets.

U.S.–Owned Assets Abroad, Net

The total of credits and debits recorded for changes in the category "U.S.–Owned Assets Abroad, Net" was −$141 billion for 2009. This indicates that during 2009, on net, U.S. residents increased their outstanding stock of claims on foreigners by $141 billion. This represents a capital outflow from the United States.

Foreign-Owned Assets in the United States, Net

The category "Foreign-Owned Assets in the U.S., Net" shows that foreign residents increased their claims on the United States by $306 billion in 2009, which constitutes a capital inflow to the United States. Notice how the composition of foreign capital flows to the U.S. changed from 2005 to 2009. In 2005, the foreign private sector acquired $1,013 billion of U.S. assets, whereas in 2009, the foreign private sector actually sold $144 billion of U.S. assets. During the same time, foreign officials increased their purchases of U.S. assets from $199 billion to $450 billion.

Financial Derivatives, Net

Beginning in 2006, the U.S. Department of Commerce began reporting the net value of transactions in financial derivatives as a separate item in the capital account. In 2009, the value of this account was $51 billion, indicating that foreigners purchased derivatives from U.S. residents worth $51 billion more than the value of derivatives that U.S. residents purchased from foreigners.

Capital Account Transfers

In 1997, the U.S. Department of Commerce began separating capital transfers—primarily transactions involving the forgiveness of debt and the value of goods and assets accompanying migrants as they cross borders—from other unilateral transfers involving current income. The latter transactions continue to be recorded on the current account. The transactions involving debt forgiveness and the value of assets accompanying migrants are now recorded on the capital account. In 2009, that amount was −$0.10 billion, which is rounded to zero in Exhibit 4.3. The terminology can get a bit confusing here. The U.S. balance of payment statistics uses the word *capital account* very narrowly to indicate the category "capital account transfers," whereas the financial account records all transactions that belong in what we called the "capital account." Therefore, we will refer to the transactions booked under the "capital account" in the United States as "capital account transfers."

Balance on the Capital Account

By adding together the debits that result from the increase in U.S.–owned foreign assets (−$141 billion), the credits from the increase in foreign ownership of U.S. assets ($306 billion), the credits in the net derivatives account ($51 billion), and the debits from the capital account transfers (0), the balance on the capital account in 2009 was a surplus of $216 billion.

The Statistical Discrepancy

Exhibits 4.2 and 4.3 show that in 2009, the value of the U.S. current account was −$379 billion, and the value of the U.S. capital account was $216 billion. Hence, the sum of the two accounts is −$163 billion. However, we explained that because of the double-entry system, the sum of the current account and the capital account should be zero because capital must flow into a country if it has a current account deficit. Why then was the sum −$163 billion in 2009? The fact is that the government misses some transactions, and it estimates other transactions.

To make the balance of payments add to zero, government statisticians must add a balancing item (or fudge factor) equal to the sum of all the measured items with the sign reversed. The technical term for the balancing item in the U.S. accounts is the **statistical discrepancy**. Formerly, this balancing account was called "errors and omissions," and such a term is often encountered in other presentations of the balance of payments. The statistical discrepancy is reported in column 12 of Exhibit 4.3 as $163 billion.

Because the statistical discrepancy is the sum of all the measured items with the sign reversed, the United States was missing over $163 billion of credits in 2009. These credits are probably capital account transactions such as unmeasured U.S. sales of foreign assets and unmeasured purchases of U.S. assets by foreign residents, although freer trade and the emergence of the Internet have increased the difficulty that governments face in accurately measuring international trade.

Because one country's borrowing is another country's lending, theoretically, the sum of all the individual current account balances of countries across the world should also sum to zero. Unfortunately, this is not the case because of the statistical discrepancies around the world.

The Official Settlements, or Reserves, Account

In our discussion of the U.S. capital account so far, we have not made any distinction between the transactions of private individuals and those of the government. The U.S. Department of Commerce breaks the total net change in U.S. assets abroad into three categories of transactions: transactions in "U.S. Official Reserve Assets" (column 3 of Exhibit 4.3), transactions in "Other U.S. Government Assets" (column 4 of Exhibit 4.3), and transactions in "U.S. Private Assets" (column 5 of Exhibit 4.3).

The U.S. official reserves account measures changes in the official stock of international reserve assets, consisting of gold, foreign currencies, special drawing rights, and the U.S. reserve position with the IMF. In 2009, there was a deficit on this account of $52 billion. The deficit indicates that official reserves increased by that amount. Transactions in other U.S. government assets are primarily the changes in the outstanding quantities of official loans to foreigners and of capital subscriptions to international financial institutions. In 2009, there was a surplus on this account of $541 billion. Here, the surplus indicates that U.S. official loans to foreigners were reduced by this amount, which amounts to a capital inflow. Column 5 of Exhibit 4.3 indicates a deficit of $630 billion in transactions in U.S. private assets. The deficit in this account indicates the net amount by which private U.S. residents increased their ownership of foreign assets, which amounts to a capital outflow.

Similarly, the U.S. Department of Commerce decomposes the total net change in foreign-owned U.S. assets into transactions in "foreign official assets" and "other foreign

Exhibit 4.4 U.S. Balance of Payment for 2009 (billions of dollars; credits, +; debits, −)

Current Account	
Trade Account	
Exports of Goods	1,068
Imports of Goods	−1,575
Exports of Services	502
Imports of Services	−370
Net Unilateral Transfers	−125
(A) Trade Balance	**−500**
Investment Income Account	
Receipts on U.S. Assets Abroad	588
Payments on Foreign Assets in the U.S.	−467
(B) Investment Account Balance	**121**
Current Account Balance (A) + (B)	**−379**
Regular Capital Account	
U.S. Assets Abroad (net) of which:	−89
Other U.S. Government Assets	541
U.S. Private Assets	−630
Foreign Private Assets in the U.S.	−144
Financial Derivatives, Net	51
Capital Account Transfers, Net	0
Balance on Regular Capital Account	**−182**
Official Settlements Account	
U.S. Official Reserve Assets	−52
Foreign Official Assets	450
Balance on Official Settlements Account	**398**
Balance on Capital Account	**216**
Statistical Discrepancy	**163**
(Sum of all the items with the sign reversed)	

assets." In 2009, foreign official assets in the United States increased by $450 billion, whereas foreign private individuals decreased their ownership of U.S. assets by $144 billion. The former category is important for the United States because other countries use dollar-denominated assets as international reserves. Hence, the increase in foreign official assets indicates that the dollar reserves of foreign central banks increased substantially.

Although the Department of Commerce separately records transactions in U.S. international reserves and foreign official assets within the capital account, it does not separate this account into an official settlements account as we did in Exhibit 4.1. So, we do it ourselves in Exhibit 4.4. Exhibit 4.4 shows that in 2009, the balance on the official settlements account was a $398 billion surplus: Although the U.S. central bank increased its official reserves by $52 billion (a debit), central banks across the world increased their dollar assets by $450 billion (a credit). This buildup in dollar reserves has been going on for a while and is primarily concentrated in Southeast Asia, particularly China.

Balance of Payment Deficits and Surpluses and the Official Settlements Account

One often hears that the central bank gained international reserves because the balance of payments was in "surplus." This statement refers to the fact that if the sum of the private and government transactions on the current account and the regular capital account is positive, the central bank must have increased its holdings of foreign money. Hence, there is a deficit on the official settlements account when the other accounts are in surplus.

Conversely, if private residents and government agencies other than the central bank have more debits than credits in their accounts, the central bank must be in surplus. It will be supplying foreign assets out of its stock of international reserves. Because the central bank is losing international reserves (that is, it is reducing its ownership of foreign assets), the official settlements account is credited, but there is said to be a deficit on the balance of payments. This indicates that private residents and other government agencies of the country are purchasing more goods, services, and assets from abroad than foreigners are purchasing domestic goods, services, and assets.

The official settlements account plays a critical role if a central bank wants to maintain a "fixed" exchange rate, a situation we discuss in detail in Chapter 5. To fix the exchange rate, the central bank must be prepared to buy and sell its domestic currency with its stock of international reserves. However, if the central bank depletes its stock of international reserves, the central bank will not be able to maintain the fixed exchange rate, and the country will be forced to devalue its currency. Hence, looking closely at a country's balance of payments and the variation over time in the country's stock of international reserves can help exporters, importers, and investors get an idea about how probable a devaluation of the currency will be in the future. We explore these issues in more detail in Chapter 5.

Balance of Payment Statistics Around the World

Although we have focused the discussion so far in this chapter on the United States, the principles are applicable to the balance of payments statistics of all countries. Exhibit 4.5 presents data for the current account balances of the G7 countries, which are the United States, the United Kingdom, Germany, Japan, Italy, France, and Canada.[1]

Each of these balances is expressed as a percentage of the country's **gross domestic product (GDP)**, the value of all final goods and services produced within a country. (See the appendix to this chapter for a review of GDP and a country's national income and product accounts.) Notice that in any given year, some of the G7 countries have a current account deficit, whereas other countries have a current account surplus. This situation is to be expected because a country with a current account deficit must borrow from or sell assets to another country to finance the deficit.

Several features of these data are noteworthy. Notice that during the six annual snapshots over 50 years in Exhibit 4.5, the largest current account deficit as a percentage of GDP is

Exhibit 4.5 Current Account Balances for the G7 Countries as a Percentage of GDP

Year	United States	United Kingdom	Japan	Italy	Germany	France	Canada
1960	0.6	−1.0	0.5	0.6	1.6	2.2	−3.2
1970	0.4	1.3	1.0	0.8	0.6	0.8	0.9
1980	0.4	1.5	−1.0	−2.4	−1.7	−0.6	−0.9
1990	−1.3	−3.4	1.5	−1.5	3.5	−0.8	−3.5
2000	−4.3	−2.6	2.5	−0.5	−1.6	1.4	2.8
2009	−2.6	−1.2	3.4	−4.6	7.4	−3.0	−3.7

Note: Data are from the Organization for Economic Cooperation and Development, 2010.

---

[1] The data are from the Organization for Economic Cooperation and Development (OECD). Go to www.oecd.org to find data on your favorite country.

Exhibit 4.6 Current Account Balances as a Percentage of GDP for Some Emerging Market Countries

	Brazil	China	India	Indonesia	Korea	Malaysia	Philippines	Singapore	Russia	Thailand
1990	−0.7	3.1	−2.4	−2.5	−0.7	−2.1	−6.1	8.0	N/A	−8.3
1996	−2.8	0.8	−1.6	−2.9	−4.0	−4.4	−4.6	14.7	2.8	−7.9
2000	−3.8	1.7	−1.0	4.8	2.3	9.0	−2.9	10.8	18.0	7.6
2004	1.8	3.6	0.1	0.6	3.9	12.1	1.9	17.1	10.1	1.7
2008	−1.7	9.6	−2.0	0.0	−0.6	17.5	2.2	18.5	6.2	0.6
2010	−2.6	4.7	−3.1	0.9	2.6	14.7	4.1	20.5	4.7	3.6

Notes: Data are from the IMF's *World Economic Outlook*, October 2010. Data for 2010 are IMF estimates. N/A, not available.

Italy's 4.6% in 2009. The largest surplus is Germany's 7.4%, also in 2009. During the post–World War II era, developed countries have rarely run current account deficits or surpluses in excess of 6% of GDP. Germany's large surplus and Italy's large deficit reflect the tensions within the European Union that have arisen as some countries have rebounded nicely from the global financial crisis, while others have become mired in slow growth and high unemployment. Although we have left out the intervening years, we note that current account deficits and surpluses are quite persistent. The United States has run a deficit every year since 1981, and Japan has run a surplus every year since 1980.

The balance of payments is also a critical set of statistics for developing countries. In Exhibit 4.6, we show current account balances between 1990 and 2010 for some emerging markets. In 1997, several of these countries faced severe currency and banking crises. You might wonder whether large current account deficits in these countries helped trigger the crises. Indeed, Thailand's current account deficit in 1996 was 7.9% of GDP, whereas South Korea's was 4.0%. Note that Singapore and China had surpluses prior to the crises and that these countries did not experience large depreciations of their currencies. After the crises, the crisis countries experienced large current account reversals, moving from large deficits to large surpluses. The surpluses in emerging Asia, Japan, and the oil-producing countries (benefiting from increases in oil prices) therefore form the counterpart to the sizable U.S. current account deficit. The fact that these surpluses and the deficit in the United States are so large has led economists and reporters alike to refer to them as "global imbalances." To evaluate whether this moniker is accurate, you must understand how current accounts and the balance of payments evolve over time.

4.3 THE DYNAMICS OF THE BOP

Now that you understand the meaning of the surpluses and deficits on various subaccounts of a country's BOP, it is time to reflect on the economic importance of these surpluses and deficits. For example, the experience of Southeast Asia in the late 1990s shows how large current account deficits led to an accumulation of foreign debt that eventually became unsustainable and led to currency crises in Thailand, Malaysia, Indonesia, and South Korea. We leave the discussion of these currency crises to Chapter 10; here, we discuss how current account deficits today affect the balance of payments in the future and ultimately the country's debt position relative to the rest of the world.

The Trade Account and the Investment Income Account

In Exhibits 4.1 and 4.4, we intentionally lumped in the current account all the items other than those associated with flows of investment income into what can be called the **trade account** of the balance of payments. The flows of payments that service assets and liabilities were put into the **international investment income account**. The current account is the sum of the trade account and the investment income account:

$$\text{Current account} = \text{Trade account} + \text{International investment income account} \quad \textbf{(4.2)}$$

Note that the "trade account" in this case is not the same thing as the goods or merchandise trade balance, which the Department of Commerce calculates. The trade account includes transactions in the economic services, such as education, banking, tourism, shipping, insurance, and transfers, that the merchandise trade balance does not. This breakdown of the balance of payments is desirable because it will help us discuss the dynamics of the balance of payments and the accumulation of international assets or debt.

Investment income flows come from previously made foreign direct investments and previously made portfolio investments. Recall from Chapter 1 that a *foreign direct investment (FDI)* implies that an investor has a long-term interest in a business enterprise in a foreign country and some ability to affect how the company is managed, whereas a *portfolio investment* is typically thought to be more short term in nature and does not involve control over a foreign company. Income from previous FDI is the return a parent firm earns on its foreign affiliates, including the dividends repatriated from those affiliates plus the interest paid by affiliates to the parents on loans made by the parents. Dividends and interest earned on equity and debt securities are examples of portfolio investment income.

There is considerable estimation involved in determining the flows of income related to portfolio investments. In the United States, the Department of Commerce uses information from the monthly and quarterly Treasury International Capital reporting system to estimate the outstanding stocks of various asset classes. It then uses market interest rates and bond yields to estimate the income flows to these asset classes.

Countries as Net Creditors or Net Debtors

A country's balance of payments records the flows of goods and assets over a period of time, just like the income statement of a firm. A country's **net international investment position**, or **net foreign assets**, with the rest of the world is similar to a firm's balance sheet. It is the difference between the value of a country's ownership of foreign assets and the value of the foreign ownership of the country's assets at a given point in time. If the net international investment position is positive, the country is often referred to as a *net creditor*, and if the net international investment position is negative, the country is often called a *net debtor*, even though the investments in question are not restricted to debt securities.

The statement that a country such as Brazil is a net debtor means that ownership of foreign assets by Brazilian residents is less than foreign ownership of Brazilian assets. This typically implies that the country has a deficit on its investment income account, which in this case may also be called its debt service account.

Suppose that a country is a net debtor and that it cannot take on additional foreign debt because foreign lenders do not want to increase their claims on the country. As a consequence, the country's capital account cannot be positive. From Equation (4.1), we see that the country's current account cannot be negative because it must be equal and opposite in sign to the capital account. From Equation (4.2), we see that the country's trade account must be in surplus if there is a deficit on the investment income account. Because the country must pay more interest and dividends to foreigners than it receives from them in asset income, the country must sell more goods and services abroad than it buys from abroad. We will see shortly that this means the country must consume less than its income.

Now, consider a country such as Japan that is a net creditor to the rest of the world. It has a positive international investment income account. From Equation (4.2), we see that Japan could have a trade balance deficit while still having a balanced current account. This means that Japan could import more goods and services from abroad than it exports out of the country without incurring foreign debt or selling assets to foreigners because it has a surplus on its investment income account.

The U.S. Net International Investment Position

Exhibit 4.7 shows the net international investment position of the United States, which is U.S. assets owned abroad minus foreign assets owned in the United States. At the end of 2009, the U.S. Department of Commerce estimates that the net international investment position of the United States was −$2,737 billion. This figure is negative because foreign-owned assets in the United States ($21,167 billion) were substantially larger than U.S.–owned assets abroad ($18,379 billion). In fact, as Exhibit 4.7 shows, the estimated U.S. net international investment position turned negative in 1986.

Of course, because current account deficits must be balanced by capital account surpluses, the deterioration in the U.S. international investment position parallels the deterioration of its current account that we discussed earlier. Yet, a change in the international investment position is not only due to international transactions involving the selling and buying of assets across borders, but it also reflects valuation adjustments attributable to changes in the market prices of assets and in exchange rates. For example, even though the United States ran a current account deficit of $379 billion in 2009, the U.S. Department of Commerce reports that its investment position actually improved from −$3,494 billion in 2008 to −$2,737 in 2009. The general weakening of the dollar during 2009 increased the value of U.S.–owned assets abroad, improving the U.S. net international investment position,

Exhibit 4.7 International Investment Positions

Notes: The chart plots the value of U.S. assets owned abroad, the value of foreign-owned assets in the United States, and their difference, which is the U.S. net international investment position. All values are trillions of U.S. dollars. Data are from the U.S. Department of Commerce, Bureau of Economic Analysis.

and the local currency capital gains that the United States earned on its investments in foreign bonds and equities substantially exceeded the capital gains that foreigners had on their U.S. assets. These capital gains offset the deterioration in the net international investment position that would have been caused by the current account deficit. The continuing globalization of the world economy has made the outstanding stocks of foreign assets and liabilities much larger than they used to be, causing such valuation effects to be relatively more important than they once were. Gourinchas and Rey (2007) and Lane and Milesi-Ferretti (2007) provide economic analyses stressing the importance of these valuation effects.

Many economists worry about the large negative international investment position of the United States because they worry about its implications for the U.S. current account. In theory, the magnitude of a country's net international investment position should determine the balance on its investment income account. For example, suppose that interest on all assets is 5%. Then, a −$2,737 billion net international investment position implies a deficit on the investment income account of 0.05 × $2,737 billion = $137 billion.

From Exhibit 4.4, though, we see that the United States had a surplus of $121 billion on its investment income account in 2009. In fact, since 1986, the United States has managed to combine a negative net international investment position with a surplus on its investment income account. Some economists called this the best deal in international finance: Americans borrowed trillions of dollars from abroad to buy big SUVs and build fancy homes, sold low-yielding assets to foreigners, and always managed to earn more from their foreign assets than they had to pay to foreigners.

The U.S. net income balance has in fact remained positive because of a composition effect and a return effect. The composition effect arises because the U.S. portfolio of assets abroad contains a relatively large share of higher-risk, higher-yielding FDI, whereas a relatively large share of foreign liabilities is made up of lower-risk, lower-yielding portfolio debt. In 2009, the market value of U.S. foreign direct investment was $4.3 trillion, whereas the market value of foreign direct investment in the United States was $3.1 trillion. The return effect arises because there has been a large and persistent yield differential between U.S. direct investment abroad and FDI in the United States. One recurring explanation for why the return on U.S. FDI would be relatively high is that FDI in the United States is relatively young compared with U.S. direct investment abroad, and it appears that the income generated by new investments increases over time. A study by the Bank for International Settlements (2010) also suggests that foreign MNCs have tax incentives to minimize income reported in the United States, lowering the measured yield on their investments.

It is rather obvious that if the U.S. net international investment position continues to deteriorate, the net income balance cannot remain in surplus. This has fueled intense debate over the sustainability of the situation.

First, although the net international investment position has grown considerably, when viewed as a percentage of the total wealth of the country, it remains relatively small. The Federal Reserve's Flow of Funds Accounts estimate total U.S. net wealth at the end of 2009 to be $53,791 billion. Hence, the ratio of the outstanding net international investment position of $2,737 billion to the wealth of the United States is 5.1%. In 1998, this figure was 5.9%. Thus, although the net international investment position has deteriorated substantially, wealth in the United States has also grown.

Second, the current account deficit viewed as a percentage of GDP is not particularly alarming. The current account deficit as a percentage of GDP was less than 3% in 1998; it was 6.1% in 2006; and it fell to 2.65% in 2009. We showed earlier that current account deficits of 3% of GDP are relatively common for developed countries.

A third observation, though, involves the changing composition of foreigners' claims on the United States. Since 2000, foreigners have primarily bought U.S. bonds, especially Treasury bonds, with central banks in Asia particularly keen on building up official reserves denominated in dollars. So the United States borrows money relatively cheaply and then invests in risky assets. What might happen if foreign central banks suddenly diversify out of U.S. bonds? To better understand the macroeconomic background to these figures, it is necessary to understand the relationship between income, saving, and investment, to which we now turn.

4.4 SAVINGS, INVESTMENT, INCOME, AND THE BOP

In this section, we explore how current account surpluses and deficits are linked to the saving and spending patterns of a country, including its government. Understanding these links allows us to see how the policies of different governments around the world affect the international economic environment and the determination of exchange rates, a topic we take up in Chapter 10. The discussion that follows uses the information in a country's **national income and product accounts (NIPA)**. The appendix to this chapter reviews the most important concepts.

Linking the Current Account to National Income

From NIPA, we know that gross national income (GNI) equals gross domestic product (GDP) plus net foreign income (NFI):

$$\text{Gross national income} = \text{Gross domestic product} + \text{Net foreign income}$$
$$\text{GNI} = \text{GDP} + \text{NFI} \tag{4.3}$$

If we subtract the country's total expenditures—that is, its consumption purchases (C), investment purchases (I), and government purchases (G)—from both sides of Equation (4.3), and we use the definition of GDP as the sum of C, I, G, and NX (net exports), we obtain:

$$\text{Gross national income} - \text{National expenditures} = \text{Net exports} + \text{Net foreign income}$$
$$\text{GNI} - (\text{C} + \text{I} + \text{G}) = \text{GDP} + \text{NFI} - (\text{C} + \text{I} + \text{G}) = \text{NX} + \text{NFI} \tag{4.4}$$

The right-hand side of Equation (4.4) is of course the current account of the balance of payments (CA) because net exports correspond to the overall trade balance, and net foreign income represents the investment account.[2]

Thus, we now have an important national income accounting identity:

$$\text{Gross national income} - \text{National expenditures} = \text{Current account}$$
$$\text{GNI} - (\text{C} + \text{I} + \text{G}) = \text{CA} \tag{4.5}$$

From Equation (4.5), we see that if a country has a current account surplus, it must have national income that exceeds national expenditures. If a country has a current account deficit with the rest of the world, the country's expenditures exceed its income.

Because the overall balance of payments must always balance, if a country has a current account surplus, it must have a capital account deficit. Remember that the capital account records transactions that generate changes in ownership of net foreign assets. Let's denote the stock of net foreign assets by NFA and changes in NFA by ΔNFA. The symbol Δ indicates the change in a stock variable from the end of the previous period to the end of the current period. A capital account deficit means that the debit items on the capital account must outweigh credit items on the capital account. Hence, a current account surplus is associated with an increase in net foreign assets. Therefore, we can write

$$\text{Current account} = \text{Change in net foreign assets}$$
$$\text{CA} = \Delta\text{NFA} \tag{4.6}$$

---

[2] In fact, this is true only if we ignore transfers. In our definition of the trade balance, we have included transfers that are not part of net exports but of net foreign income.

If there is a current account surplus, the economy is adding net foreign assets. Substituting from Equation (4.5) into Equation (4.6),

$$\text{National income } - \text{ National expenditure } = \text{ Change in net foreign assets}$$
$$\text{GNI} - (\text{C} + \text{I} + \text{G}) = \Delta\text{NFA} \tag{4.7}$$

This identity makes perfectly good intuitive sense. Just as an individual whose income is greater than her expenditures must be acquiring assets, similarly, if a country has total income that is greater than the country's total expenditures, the country must be acquiring assets. Of course, the only assets that the country can acquire are those of foreign countries. Hence, the country's net foreign assets must increase when its expenditures are less than its income. Viewed this way, the concept of net foreign assets is simply the net debtor or net creditor position of the country.

National Savings, Investment, and the Current Account

Another way to understand the current account is to see that it is the difference between national savings and national investment. If an individual consumes more (less) than her income, her savings are negative (positive). In the case of a country, both the private (C) and public (G) sectors consume. So, by definition, national savings are equal to national income minus the consumption of the private and public sectors:

National savings = Gross national income − Consumption of the private and public sectors

In symbols, this becomes:

$$\text{S} = \text{GNI} - \text{C} - \text{G} \tag{4.8}$$

After substituting the definition of GNI from Equation (4.3), we find

$$\text{S} = \text{GDP} + \text{NFI} - \text{C} - \text{G}$$

Substituting the components of GDP gives

$$\text{S} = \text{C} + \text{I} + \text{G} + \text{NX} + \text{NFI} - \text{C} - \text{G}$$

Upon canceling out the consumption of the private and public sectors and rearranging terms, we find

$$\text{S} - \text{I} = \text{NX} + \text{NFI} = \text{CA} \tag{4.9}$$
$$\text{National saving } - \text{ National investment } = \text{ Current account}$$

If a country's purchases of investment goods are more than its savings, the country must run a current account deficit; that is, the country's investment spending must be financed from abroad with a capital account surplus.

Current Accounts and Government Deficits

It is often argued that current account deficits are caused by government budget deficits. We now show that there is indeed an identity that links current accounts and government budget deficits, although the identity does not at all suggest causality from government budget deficits to current account deficits.

Consider total national savings; it consists of private savings and government savings. Private savings are what is left over after households spend out of their disposable income. Total disposal income for the residents of the country is gross national income, plus the transfer payments received from the various levels of government (TR), plus interest on government debt (iD), but minus taxes (T) paid to the government. Hence, we have

$$\text{National income} + \text{Transfers} + \text{Interest on government debt} - \text{Taxes}$$
$$= \text{Consumption} + \text{Private saving}$$

Using symbols, we have

$$GNI + TR + iD - T = C + S^P \tag{4.10}$$

where S^P is private savings. But we know that GNI is linked to the current account:

$$GNI = C + I + G + NX + NFI = C + I + G + CA \tag{4.11}$$

By rearranging terms and canceling the two consumption terms, we find

$$(\text{Private saving} - \text{Investment}) + (\text{Taxes} - \text{Transfers} - \text{Interest on government debt}$$
$$- \text{Government purchases}) = \text{Current account}$$

or

$$(S^P - I) + (T - TR - iD - G) = CA \tag{4.12}$$

The first term in parentheses on the left-hand side of Equation (4.12) is **net private saving**, which is the difference between **private saving** and the private sector's expenditures on investment goods. The second term is **national government saving**, which is the **surplus on the government budget**. If there is a deficit on the government budget because total government expenditures (including spending on goods and services, transfer payments, and interest on government debt) exceed taxes, government saving is negative. There are a number of ways to interpret Equation (4.12).

If the current account is negative, private savings are inadequate to finance both private investment purchases and the government budget deficit. Therefore, foreign funds (borrowing from the rest of the world in the form of an accumulation of foreign debt) are required. Equation (4.12) also indicates that the government and private industry are competitors in capital markets for the pool of private savings: If the government borrows more of that capital, there is less capital available for private investment.

Because Equation (4.12) is an identity, a government budget deficit must be matched by some combination of higher private saving, lower investment, or a current account deficit. So it is quite conceivable that a large government deficit will be associated with a large current account deficit. This was the case in the United States, for example, during the 1980 to 1985 period, when the federal budget deficit coincided with a large current account deficit. But must it be the case?

What Causes Current Account Deficits and Surpluses?

Why did France run a current account deficit during most of the 1980s but a current account surplus in the 1990s, whereas the opposite happened in Germany (refer to Exhibit 4.5)? The discussion in this section reveals that it must be related to savings and investment decisions by the citizens and governments of these countries.

Let's start with governments. If a government chooses not to finance its current purchases of goods and services, its transfer payments, and the interest payments on outstanding government debt from its current tax receipts, the government must either issue more government debt to be held by the public or print money. On the other hand, if current tax receipts exceed current government outlays, government debt can be retired or money can be removed from the economy.

To induce investors to hold its debt, a government must pay a competitive interest rate on its outstanding stock of government bonds. In the future, though, these interest payments must be financed through some form of taxation, including possibly money creation. For every dollar of taxes not raised this period, the government must raise 1 dollar plus interest in the future. This long-run budget constraint is called an **intertemporal budget constraint**.

Hence, we are left with a puzzle. Why does a country's government not balance its current total expenditures with its current tax receipts? The answer is that the economic costs of distortions due to taxes are minimized if the government sets permanent tax rates that balance the government budget only over the long run and not every period. Roughly, this appears to be what governments try to do.

Suppose, for example, there were a recession. During a recession, people's incomes fall, so the government's tax revenues fall as well. Hence, if the government were to attempt to balance the budget during the recession, it would have to cut spending and increase tax rates. However, governments are reluctant to cut spending because spending stimulates the economy. Raising taxes during a recession puts a serious damper on the economy and would be politically unpalatable. Therefore, instead of adjusting their spending and tax rates, governments tend to run deficits during recessions and surpluses during economic booms.

Ricardian Equivalence

Another serious problem in understanding how government budget deficits affect the economic behavior of the overall economy is the important idea of **Ricardian equivalence** between government debt and taxes.[3] The issue is the extent to which taxpayers look into the future and see their future tax liabilities increasing when the government runs a deficit (that is, the government dissaves). If private saving increases one for one with any government budget deficit, budget deficits have no real effect. In particular, from Equation (4.12), we see that the current account of the balance of payments would not be affected by government saving and dissaving if taxpayers are Ricardian. Alternatively, it may be that current taxpayers feel wealthier when governments run budget deficits because some future generation is going to have to pay the increased taxes. In this case, government budget deficits reduce national savings and cause current account deficits.

Individuals' Intertemporal Budget Constraints

Individuals are also subject to intertemporal budget constraints when it comes to their consumption and savings decisions. The decisions of how much to work, how much to consume, and how to invest any accumulated wealth are heavily influenced by the prices and opportunities that individuals have in current markets and by their expectations of what those prices and opportunities are likely to be in the future. For example, high interest rates might induce people to save more rather than to consume. And good investment opportunities in other countries might lead to a capital outflow.

Investment Spending

The last of the components that determine the current account is private investment in businesses and residential housing. Businesses continually evaluate investment projects. They contemplate adding new product lines and changing their scales of operation to generate additional future income. When firms consider investment projects, they are subject to an intertemporal budget constraint as well. An investment project is worth doing only if it is a

---

[3]The effect is named after the economist David Ricardo (1772–1823), who first analyzed arguments for the equivalence of government debt and taxes in his *Principles of Political Economy and Taxation* (1817). Although the effect bears his name, Ricardo did not believe that the result would hold in actual economies. In particular, he argued that high public debt could create an incentive for both labor and capital to migrate abroad to avoid future taxes necessary to service the public debt (see Ricardo, 1951, pp. 247–249).

positive net present value project. We will explain this concept in more detail in Chapter 15; for now, assume that it means that the project's expected return in future periods must provide adequate compensation to those who have supplied the capital to the firm. Put differently, businesses invest in new projects by purchasing new plants and equipment when managers believe the returns on projects will be high relative to the cost of capital required to launch them. Analogously, new residential housing is constructed only when expected rents in the future provide the developer with an expected return that exceeds the cost of the project. The cost of funding a project rises with higher interest rates so that higher interest rates typically decrease investments.

Investment expenditures are also highly pro-cyclical because during expansions in the business cycle, businesses perceive that future demand for their products will be high and they invest to meet that future demand. If a country's growth prospects slow down or if there is fear of possible tax increases on the income earned from capital, investment declines. When the desired investments of a country's businesses exceed the desired savings of its citizens and government, the country must borrow from abroad and run a current account deficit.

As you can see, it is very difficult to disentangle the exact determinants of the current account because it depends on so many individual decisions. Taxes, interest rates, the cost of capital, the relative expected investment returns in different countries, and business cycles all play a role.

POINT–COUNTERPOINT

U.S.–China Current Account Imbalances and Their Consequences

It is a sunny Sunday afternoon in New York, and Ante and Freedy Handel are enjoying some Central Park greenery at the Boathouse Café while digesting a refreshing beer. Ante is perusing some statistics on bilateral U.S.–China current account deficits for his international finance class, when he suddenly blurts out, "This is a crazy, untenable situation. If we do not do something about this U.S. current account deficit, the dollar will tank. Did you know that these large cumulative deficits have made the United States a huge debtor relative to the rest of the world?"

Because Freedy was enjoying the sunshine too much to put up a fight, Ante was able to continue: "The Chinese simply exploit their workers, making them work long hours for next to nothing, then they dump their products here at cheap prices to keep their workers employed. That is the main cause of it all: unfair competition. I tell you what we should do. We should slap tariffs on these Chinese products. We must force them to make their markets more open to American products and enact decent social laws for their workers or pay the price."

Now, Freedy had finally had too much. He countered, "Ante, you can't be serious. Free trade has been the cornerstone of world economic growth for the past few decades, and you propose to turn back the clock? The U.S. current account deficit does not matter at all. Remember, it is just national savings minus national investment. Americans do not save very much, and they love to consume foreign goods and gadgets. They are enjoying the current account deficit enormously. Look at the Corona you are drinking: a smooth and rich taste from Mexico, brother! Besides, the flip side of the current account deficit is the capital account surplus; that just means that foreigners are buying U.S. stocks and bonds more than Americans are investing overseas. Do you know why? Foreigners buy U.S. assets because they are considered to be very attractive investments with high expected returns."

"Wow, I never heard you spout so much," blurted Ante. "It must be that foreign beer! I cling to my story. Besides, do you know what the Chinese are buying here? Treasury bonds!!! Heaps of them. I can't believe the Chinese don't realize what a bad investment our bonds are.

The U.S. budget deficit was over $1 trillion last year, and the Federal Reserve runs this complex policy of quantitative easing, which looks like dropping money on people. I think it is a recipe for future inflation, lower bond prices, and an incredibly weak dollar. The Chinese will rue the day they invested here."

Freedy responds, "Do you really think the Chinese are that stupid? They are investing in America because they believe in our way of life. They are signaling to their population that it is okay to be capitalist. Besides, they peg the yuan to the dollar, so if the dollar weakens, the yuan weakens. They don't take any currency risk versus the dollar. Their biggest risk is Senator Chuck Schumer, who keeps threatening China with tariffs if they don't appreciate the yuan. Schumer just doesn't get it that the Chinese want to be capitalists, just like us."

Ante is about to answer, when a familiar voice shouts, "Hey, guys, what are you up to?" As Suttle Trooth walks up to their table, Freedy says, "Hey, look Ante, he's drinking foreign beer, too, although it's only a Heineken. I see that deficit going up even more!"

After hearing the topic of discussion, Suttle frowns and says, "I think some of your arguments make good sense, but as usual, the issues are more complex than they seem. Ante, you cite the lack of openness of foreign markets as a cause of the large U.S. trade balance deficit. Such an argument misses the point that the Chinese savings rate is much larger than the U.S. savings rate; Freedy is definitely right that current account deficits reflect an imbalance between savings and investment. But Ante has a point that Chinese government policies may play a role; for example, a better social safety net would reduce the need to save so much for a rainy day. That being said, I recently read an article suggesting that the Chinese savings rate became so high because there are too many men in China relative to women. The uneven sex ratio makes families with men save an enormous amount of money to improve their prospects in the marriage market" (see Wei and Zhang, 2009).

"The bottom line is that if we are to understand the current account, we must understand the determinants of private saving, private investment, and government budget surpluses and deficits. It is conceivable that the U.S. current account reflects a large pool of profitable investment opportunities that cannot be financed by domestic savings alone, given the consumption preferences of U.S. citizens. The fact that the United States now runs large government deficits cannot exactly help close the U.S. current account deficit. However, the current account deficit has recently been going down, while the government deficit has been ballooning.

"However, as Ante correctly points out, one reason for concern is that a good portion of the recent deficits has been financed by the Chinese central bank buying Treasury bonds. In fact, the Chinese are holding a lot of dollar assets. In October 2010, China had $2.648 trillion of international reserves, most of which are in dollars. They also are accumulating international reserves at a rate of $23 billion per month. The United State does not need to worry about paying off foreign debt in a different currency, but what if the Chinese are no longer willing to hold such large positions in U.S. bonds? If that happens, Ante is probably right that the dollar would depreciate to induce higher expected returns on U.S. assets and to make U.S. goods more attractive to foreigners so that the current account deficit can be reversed."

Suttle continues, "Let's consider the exchange rate situation a bit. The Chinese control the yuan's currency value relative to the dollar (see Chapter 5), and the yuan appreciated steadily from 2005 until the financial crisis hit in the summer of 2008. I think the yuan is probably weaker than it would be if the Chinese didn't intervene in the foreign exchange market, and that undervaluation gives Chinese producers a competitive advantage in international markets. The Chinese know this, and they know that they'll have to accumulate dollars as international reserves to continue their policy."

Ante interjects, "See, I told you that the Chinese are going to take a massive loss. They lose over $265 billion for every 10% that the dollar weakens versus the yuan. When the big depreciation comes, they'll be sorry."

Suttle nods and says, "You're right there, but you may be wrong about the future. The dollar in fact appears to do well when the world's economic situation is bad. The major alternative, the euro, has problems of its own. The situation in Europe is a mess with the bailouts of Greece and Ireland. Some people even think the European Monetary Union may break up if the Germans get fed up with supporting the peripheral countries. It isn't clear that investing in euro assets is a good idea. The real question is, why are the Chinese willing to undervalue their currency and acquire massive quantities of international reserves? I think the answer is that the Chinese authorities want the country to grow as quickly as possible so that they can get their massive population of underemployed rural peasants into jobs. But, they don't want just any jobs. They want world-class manufacturing jobs. Right now, they do not have well-developed local capital markets to allocate capital efficiently. One solution of course is to have foreigners allocate capital in the form of foreign direct investment. Now, how do you get multinational firms to invest in China if they are afraid of being expropriated by the communists? The answer is that the Chinese acquire massive international reserves that are the debt of the U.S. government. If the Chinese are ever tempted to expropriate multinational corporations, they know that the United States could expropriate them back by reneging on the debt. The system is quite stable and symbiotic. China grows, the U.S. consumes, and both countries are safer in the long run. China also develops some leverage over future U.S. policy because it could dump U.S. bonds, which would send dollar interest rates skyrocketing and cause economic chaos. Of course, China would lose a lot of wealth in the process, so I don't think that will happen."[4]

"Thanks, Suttle," said Ante. "Now, I feel much more comfortable drinking foreign beer. Let's have another one." Freedy nods approvingly.

Assessing the Openness of International Capital Markets

In a closed economy, national saving and national investment are forced to move together. When two variables move perfectly together, statisticians say their correlation is one. However, access to international capital markets allows the correlation between national savings and national investment to be less than one. An increase in savings can finance a foreign project rather than a domestic one, and domestic investment can be conducted by raising funds from the savings of other countries rather than from domestic savings.

In an important, but controversial, article in 1980, Feldstein and Horioka demonstrated that there was a very strong correlation between the average national savings rate and the average national investment rate in 16 countries. This suggests that countries with relatively high average savings rates also have relatively high investment rates. Feldstein and Horioka concluded that international capital markets were not very open and international capital mobility was quite low during their sample period. More recent studies, such as that by Bai and Zhang (2010), largely confirm the significant positive correlation between the national savings rates and national investment rates of developed countries but note that the positive correlation appears to be declining over time.

Are the Feldstein and Horioka findings that international capital markets are not very open accurate? Or can the data be interpreted another way? There are several important caveats to the Feldstein and Horioka interpretation that have been noted in the literature. One line of argument asserts that the high correlation between savings and investment could be produced by common forces that move both variables even though the international capital market is open and competitive.

---

[4] Formal arguments regarding the insurance function of the Chinese bond holdings can be found in Dooley et al. (2008); whereas the idea that the Chinese send capital out of the country and efficiently recycle it into the country through foreign direct investment can be found in Ju and Wei (2010).

Authors such as Baxter and Crucini (1993) and Mendoza (1991) argue that economic shocks affecting productivity can increase both saving and investment over the business cycle. The argument goes like this: An increase in productivity causes output and income to increase. Some of the increase in income is consumed, but some of it is saved because the shock is not expected to be permanent. But because productivity is temporarily high and is expected to be high for awhile, it is also a good time to invest. Hence, investment and saving both increase. Bai and Zhang (2010) argue that financial frictions, such as default risk, prevent people in different countries from sharing risk adequately, leading to the positive correlation between savings and investment.

Finally, Frankel (1991) has argued that high correlations between national investment rates and national saving rates should not really be surprising because the world economy during the 1960s, 1970s, and even much of the 1980s and 1990s was not characterized by perfect capital mobility. That is, capital markets were not completely open around the world. For example, there were significant barriers to international investment in many European countries and Japan that persisted well into the 1980s. (See also Chapter 1.) Hence, it would stand to reason that in countries in which the saving rates are high, investment rates would be high as well because there is nowhere else for the capital to go. We noted earlier that the savings–investment correlation appears to be falling. This is consistent with Exhibit 4.5, which suggests that current account imbalances have substantially increased in magnitude over the last decade. Frankel argues that to assess how integrated the world's capital markets are, we must look at the various rates of return offered around the world and not merely at the flows of saving and investment stressed by Feldstein and Horioka. We do so in Chapter 13.

4.5 SUMMARY

This chapter introduced the concepts associated with a country's balance of payments and its net international investment position and examined how these concepts are related to national income and product accounts. Knowledge of this information is useful in discussions of the determination of exchange rates. The main points in the chapter are the following:

1. A country's balance of payments records the economic transactions between its residents and government and those of the rest of the world.

2. There are two major accounts on the balance of payments: the current account and the capital account.

3. The current account records transactions in goods and services, transactions that are associated with the income flows from asset stocks, and unilateral transfers.

4. The capital account, which is also called the financial account in some presentations of the BOP, records the purchases and sales of assets—that is, changes in the domestic ownership of the assets of other nations and in the foreign ownership of assets of the domestic country.

5. The balance of payments uses a double-entry accounting system. Each transaction gives rise to two entries—a credit and a debit of equal value.

6. The purchases of goods and assets by foreign residents from domestic residents are recorded as credits. Credit transactions result in an inflow, or source, of foreign currency.

7. The purchases of goods and assets by domestic residents from foreign residents are debits. Debit transactions result in an outflow, or use, of foreign currency.

8. Sales of domestic goods and services to foreign residents are domestic exports. Sales of domestic assets to foreigners are capital inflows to the home country. Both types of transaction are credits on the domestic balance of payments.

9. Purchases of foreign goods and services by domestic residents are domestic imports. Purchases of foreign assets by domestic residents are capital outflows from the home country. Both types of transaction are debits on the domestic balance of payments.

10. If the sum of the credits on a particular account is greater than the sum of the debits on that account,

the account is said to be in surplus. If the sum of the debits on a particular account is greater than credits on that account, the account is said to be in deficit.

11. The current account is sometimes decomposed into the sum of the trade account and the international investment income account. The trade account is a broader concept than the merchandise trade balance because the former includes trade in economic services such as education, banking, tourism, shipping, insurance, and transfers, whereas the latter does not.

12. International reserves are the assets of a country's central bank that are not denominated in the domestic currency. Gold and assets denominated in foreign currency are the typical international reserves.

13. The official settlements account of the capital account measures changes in the international reserves that a country's central bank holds. If a central bank wants to maintain a fixed exchange rate, it must use its international reserves to fix the price of the domestic currency in terms of a foreign currency. International reserves will rise and fall with the surpluses and deficits on the current account and the private capital account.

14. Because many balance of payments entries are estimated, the sum of the current account and the capital account does not always equal zero as it should in a double-entry system. If the sum of the current and capital accounts is not zero, statisticians add a balancing item equal to the sum of all the measured items with the sign reversed. This term is called the statistical discrepancy or errors and omissions.

15. The balance of payments records flows of goods and assets over a period of time, just like the income statement of a firm. By analogy, just as a firm has a balance sheet, at a point in time, a country owns a certain stock of foreign assets, and foreigners own a certain stock of domestic assets. The difference between the values of these two stocks is called net foreign assets. Consequently, at any given point in time, a country has a net international investment position; it is either a net creditor or a net debtor with the rest of the world.

16. The value of all the final goods and services produced within a country is called the country's gross domestic product (GDP).

17. The value of what is produced in a country must be purchased either by domestic residents or foreign residents. Hence, the country's total consumption purchases, C, plus its total government purchases, G, plus its total investment purchases, I, plus the value of its net exports, NX, must equal its GDP: $GDP = C + I + G + NX$.

18. The value of all the final goods and services must be paid to factors of production. In an open economy, net factor income from abroad (NFI) from either labor that works in foreign countries or capital that is invested in foreign countries provides a flow of resources that separates gross national income (GNI) from GDP ($GNI = GDP + NFI$).

19. By subtracting a country's total expenditures on consumption, investment, and government purchases from its gross national income, we are left with net exports plus net factor income from abroad, which is equal to the current account (CA) of the balance of payments.

20. If a country has a current account surplus, it must have national income that exceeds national expenditures. If a country has a current account deficit, the country's expenditures exceed its income.

21. The owners of a country's factors of production receive its national income plus transfer payments from the government and interest on government debt, but they must pay taxes to the government. After-tax disposable income must be either spent on consumption or saved in some form of asset.

22. Net private saving, which is private saving in excess of expenditures on investment goods, plus national government saving, which is taxes minus total government spending or the surplus on the government budget, equals the current account of the balance of payments.

23. Because national savings and national investment decisions affect a country's current account, interest rates and other rates of return around the world influence, and in turn are influenced by, the current account.

24. Feldstein and Horioka demonstrated that there is a very strong cross-sectional correlation between the national savings rate and the national investment rate of countries. They argued that this is evidence of strong international capital market imperfections, but there is a large debate regarding this interpretation.

QUESTIONS

1. What are the major accounts of the balance of payments, and what transactions are recorded on each account?
2. Why is it important for an international manager to understand the balance of payments?
3. What are the rules that determine the residency requirements on the balance of payments?
4. Which items on the balance of payments are recorded as credits, and which items are recorded as debits? Why?
5. How are gifts and grants handled in the balance of payments?
6. What does it mean for a country to experience a capital inflow? Is this associated with a surplus or a deficit on the country's capital account?
7. If you add up all the current accounts of all countries in the world, the sum should be zero. Yet this is not so. Why?
8. What is the investment income account of the balance of payments?
9. What is the official settlements account of the balance of payments? How are official settlements deficits and surpluses associated with movements in the international reserves of the balance of payments?
10. What is the meaning of an account labeled "statistical discrepancy" or "errors and omissions"? If this account is a credit, what does that imply about the measurement of other items in the balance of payments?
11. Why must the national income of a closed economy equal the national expenditures of that economy? What separates the two concepts in an open economy?
12. Explain why private national saving plus government saving equals the current account of the balance of payments.
13. It has been argued that the high correlation between national saving and national investment that Feldstein and Horioka first measured in 1980 is not evidence of imperfect capital mobility. What arguments can you offer for why they might have misinterpreted the data, and what do recent investigations of this issue imply about the degree of capital mobility throughout the world?

PROBLEMS

1. Suppose that the following transactions take place on the U.S. balance of payments during a given year. Analyze the effects on the merchandise trade balance, the international investment income account, the current account, the capital account, and the official settlements account.
    a. Boeing, a U.S. aerospace company, sells $3 billion of its 747 airplanes to the People's Republic of China, which pays with proceeds from a loan from a consortium of international banks.
    b. Mitsubishi UFJ Financial Group purchases $70 million of 30-year U.S. Treasury bonds for one of its Japanese clients. Mitsubishi draws down its dollar account with Bank of America to pay for the bonds.
    c. Eli Lilly, a U.S. pharmaceutical company, sends a dividend check for $25,255 to a Canadian investor in Toronto. The Canadian investor deposits the check in a U.S. dollar-denominated bank account at the Bank of Montreal.
    d. The U.S. Treasury authorizes the New York Federal Reserve Bank to intervene in the foreign exchange market. The New York Fed purchases $5 billion with Japanese yen and euros that it holds as international reserves.
    e. The president of the United States sends troops into a Latin American country to establish a democratic government. The total operation costs U.S. taxpayers $8.5 billion. To show their support for the operation, the governments of Mexico and Brazil each donate $1 billion to the United States, which they raise by selling U.S. Treasury bonds that they were holding as international reserves.
    f. Honda of America, the U.S. subsidiary of the Japanese automobile manufacturer, obtains $275 million from its parent company in Japan in the form of a loan to enable it to construct a new state-of-the-art manufacturing facility in Ohio.

2. Consider the situation of La Nación, a hypothetical Latin American country. In 2010, La Nación was a net debtor to the rest of the world. Assume that all of La Nación's foreign debt was dollar

denominated, and at the end of 2010, its net private foreign debt was $75 billion and the official foreign debt of La Nación's treasury was $55 billion. Suppose that the interest rate on these debts was 2.5% per annum (p.a.) over the London Interbank Offering Rate (LIBOR), and no principal payments were due in 2011. International reserves of the Banco de Nación, La Nación's central bank, were equal to $18 billion at the end of 2010 and earn interest at LIBOR. There were no other net foreign assets in the country. Because La Nación is growing very rapidly, there is great demand for investment goods in La Nación. Suppose that residents of La Nación would like to import $37 billion of goods during 2011. Economists indicate that the value of La Nación's exports is forecast to be $29 billion of goods during 2011. Suppose that the Banco de Nación is prepared to see its international reserves fall to $5 billion during 2011. The LIBOR rate for 2011 is 4% p.a.

a. What is the minimum net capital inflow during 2011 that La Nación must have if it wants to see the desired imports and exports occur and wants to avoid having its international reserves fall below the desired level?

b. If this capital inflow occurs, what will La Nación's total net foreign debt be at the end of 2011?

3. True or false: If a country is a net debtor to the rest of the world, its international investment service account is in deficit. Explain your answer.

4. Choose a country and analyze its balance of payments for the past 10 years. Good sources of data include official bulletins of the statistical authority of a country or its central banks; *International Financial Statistics*, which is a publication of the IMF (www.imf.org); and *Main Economic Indicators*, which is a publication of the Organization for Economic Cooperation and Development (www. oecd.org).

a. Examine how trade in goods and services has evolved over time. Is the country becoming more or less competitive in world markets?

b. Consider the relationship between the country's net foreign asset position and its international investment income account.

c. If the country has run a current account deficit, what capital inflows have financed the deficit? If the country has run a current account surplus, how have the capital outflows been invested?

5. Pick a country and search the Internet for newspaper or magazine articles that contain information related to the balance of payments of the country and corresponding movements in the foreign exchange value of the country's currency. Does an unexpectedly large current account deficit cause the country's currency to strengthen or weaken on the foreign exchange market?

6. What are the effects on the British balance of payments of the following set of transactions? U.K. Videos imports £24 million of movies from the U.S. firm Twenty-First Century Wolf (TFCW). The payment is denominated in pounds, is drawn on a British bank, and is deposited in the London branch of a U.S. bank by TFCW because TFCW anticipates purchasing a film studio in the United Kingdom in the near future.

7. What are the effects on the French balance of payments of the following set of transactions? Les Fleurs de France, the French subsidiary of a British company, The Flowers of Britain, has just received €4.4 million of additional investment from its British parent. Part of the investment is a €0.9 million computer system that was shipped from Britain directly. The €3.5 million remainder was financed by the parent by issuing euro-denominated Eurobonds to investors outside of France. Les Fleurs de France is holding these euros in its Paris bank account.

8. In December 1994, a major earthquake rocked Kobe, Japan, destroying the housing stock of more than 300,000 people and ruining bridges, highways, and railroad tracks. What impact, if any, do you think this event had on the Japanese current account deficit? Why?

9. After running high current account surpluses in the second half of the 1980s, Germany ran sizable deficits in the early 1990s. The most important reason for the current account deficit was the surge in demand from eastern Germany after reunification, causing imports to rise sharply. At the same time, Germany went from being a net creditor country to being a net debtor. Explain why this is a logical implication of the current account deficits. Interest rates in Germany were historically high during this period. Why might that have been the case? Could East Germany have been developed without running a current account deficit? How?

Bai, Yan, and Jing Zhang, 2010, "Solving the Feldstein-Horioka Puzzle with Financial Frictions," *Econometrica* 78, pp. 603–632.

Bank for International Settlements (BIS), 2010, *80th Annual Report*, Basel, Switzerland: BIS.

Baxter, Marianne, and Mario J. Crucini, 1993, "Explaining Saving–Investment Correlations," *American Economic Review* 83, pp. 416–436.

Dooley, Michael P., David Folkerts-Landau, and Peter M. Garber, 2008, *Asia, Interest Rates, and the Dollar*, Frankfurt, Germany: Deutsche Bank, March.

Feldstein, Martin, and Charles Horioka, 1980, "Domestic Savings and International Capital Flows," *Economic Journal* 90, pp. 314–329.

Frankel, Jeffrey A., 1991, "Quantifying International Capital Mobility in the 1980's," in B. Douglas Bernheim and John B. Shoven, eds., *National Saving and Economic Performance*, Chicago: University of Chicago Press, pp. 227–260.

Gourinchas, Pierre-Olivier, and Hélène Rey, 2007, "International Financial Adjustment," *Journal of Political Economy* 115, pp. 665–703.

International Monetary Fund (IMF), 1993, *Balance of Payments Manual*, Washington, DC: IMF.

International Monetary Fund (IMF), 2010, *World Economic Outlook*, Washington, DC: IMF.

Ju, Jiandong, and Shang-Jin Wei, 2010, "Domestic Institutions and the Bypass Effect of Financial Globalization," *American Economic Journal: Economic Policy* 2, pp. 173–204.

Lane, Philip R., and Gian Maria Milesi-Ferretti, 2007, "A Global Perspective on External Positions," in Richard Clarida, ed., *G7 Current Account Imbalances: Sustainability and Adjustment*, Chicago: University of Chicago Press.

Mendoza, Enrique G., 1991, "Real Business Cycles in a Small Open Economy," *American Economic Review* 81, pp. 797–818.

Organization for Economic Cooperation and Development (OECD), "National Accounts," Brussels, Belgium: OECD.

Ricardo, David, 1951, *On the Principles of Political Economy and Taxation*, Piero Sraffa, ed., Cambridge, UK: Cambridge University Press.

United Nations (UN), *National Accounts Statistics*, New York: UN.

U.S. Department of Commerce, *Survey of Current Business*, www.bea.gov/scb/.

Wei, Shang-Jin, and Xiaobo Zhang, 2009, "The Competitive Saving Motive: Evidence from Rising Sex Ratios and Savings Rates in China," NBER Working Paper No. 15093.

Appendix

A Primer on National Income and Product Accounts

The **gross national income (GNI)** of a country is the flow of resources over a period of time that allows residents of the country to consume during that period and to provide for their future consumption through saving and the accumulation of wealth. All countries attempt to measure their national income and production. In the United States, national income is recorded in the **national income and product accounts (NIPA)**, which are reported by the Department of Commerce. The national income accounts of other countries are available from the *National Accounts* of the Organization for Economic Cooperation and Development (OECD) and from the *National Accounts Statistics* of the United Nations.

There are three ways to record national income and production during a given time interval, such as a year or a quarter of a year. The first records the incomes that accrue to the country's factors of production—its labor and capital. The second records the expenditures by residents of the country on different classes of goods and services. The third records the value of new production of final goods and services within the country. The value of all the final goods and services produced by a country within a certain time period is called the country's gross domestic product (GDP). Because a percentage of the capital goods (assets) used in the production process depreciate or wear out while being used, some of what a country produces will be used to replace the equipment and structures that have worn out during a given period. Subtracting a measure of this depreciation from a country's GDP gives us a country's net domestic product. In what follows, however, we will ignore depreciation and focus on GDP.

Gross Domestic Production and Expenditures

Purchases of goods and services fall under four general categories of expenditures: personal consumption expenditures, gross private domestic investment, government purchases, and net exports of goods and services.

Consumption Expenditures (C)

The personal consumption expenditures of domestic residents are the purchases of final goods (such as cars and clothing) and services (such as education or the imputed rental value of owner-occupied housing). In most developed countries, roughly two-thirds of GDP is purchased by domestic consumers.

Gross Private Domestic Investment (I)

Gross private domestic investment includes investment by corporations (that is, purchases of new machines and buildings), residential investment (including the construction of both single-family homes and multifamily buildings such as apartments), and the change in business inventories. Business inventories are stocks of finished goods, goods in process, and raw materials for the production process. The change in business inventories measures the investment firms have made in the current period to improve the firms' profitability in future periods. For example, if firms add finished goods to their stocks of inventories, this is positive investment, and if firms draw down their stocks of finished goods, this is negative investment. In developed countries, gross private domestic investment (I) ranges between 15% and 30% of GDP.

Government Purchases (G)

The different levels of government of a country—federal, state or provincial, and local—purchase a substantial amount of the final goods and services that are produced in a country. In the United States, government purchases of goods and services equal approximately 20% of GDP, but in a small European country, such as Sweden, they equal approximately 25%.

Overall outlays of the federal government, which are the total expenditures in the government budget, are much larger than a government's purchases of goods and services. This is because federal government outlays include transfer payments and interest on the federal debt. Examples of transfer payments in the United States include Social Security, Medicare benefits, and welfare. Although these programs provide income to the recipients of the transfers, the programs do not provide additional income to the economy. The government merely taxes some individuals in the economy and transfers the money to other individuals in the economy.

Net Exports (NX)

If the economy were completely closed to international trade, the value of what is produced as final goods and services would equal the value of the purchases of goods and services for consumption, investment, and government. What is produced as a final good would either be sold to someone in the economy or placed into business inventories. But in an open economy, the foreign sector can buy some of an economy's final goods and services. In the United States, the fraction of exports to GDP sold to foreigners is lower than in many other major countries, but it has been growing rapidly and now exceeds 10% of GDP. In a smaller, more open economy, such as that of Sweden, the fraction of exports to GDP is almost 40%.

Because the consumers, businesses, and various governmental organizations of a country need not limit their expenditures to goods and services that are produced in that country, part of a country's total purchases of goods and services for consumption, investment, and government will be imports of foreign goods and services. Net exports are exports minus imports, and they roughly correspond to the trade balance concept introduced in Section 4.1.

Gross Domestic Product and Expenditures

Our discussion of the relationship between the value of what is produced in a country and the purchases of various goods and services by individuals in the country can be summarized in our first fundamental national income identity:

$$\text{Gross domestic product} = \text{Consumption} + \text{Investment} + \text{Government} + \text{Net exports}$$

or, using symbols:

$$\text{GDP} = C + I + G + NX \qquad \textbf{(4A.1)}$$

Basically, this equation states that the value of what is produced in a country, GDP, equals the total purchases of final goods and services of individuals, firms, and the government of the country plus the purchases by foreigners of domestic exports, but minus the value of what is imported into the country because these are goods and services that are not produced in the country. There are, of course, serious measurement issues in quantifying GDP.

In 2006, the Greek statistical office reminded us of this fact by suddenly declaring GDP to be 25% higher. The change was designed to better capture a fast-growing service sector, including parts of the illegal economy, such as prostitution and money laundering. Although this led the *Financial Times* to write "Oldest profession helps boost Greek national output by 25%," the potential consequences were quite important: The higher GDP meant that the ratio of Greece's budget deficit to its GDP would also be lower. Thus, Greece would not be subject to certain European Union (EU) limits on the size of this ratio. However, the higher Greek GDP also meant that Greece would lose some financial aid from the EU.

From Gross Domestic Product to Gross National Income

In a closed economy, the value of GDP must equal the income of the factors of production in the economy. Thus, the value of what is produced domestically (GDP) would equal the gross national income (GNI) of the country. In an open economy that trades and invests with other countries in the world, GNI need not equal GDP.

There are three reasons why GNI does not equal GDP in an open economy. First, the capital and labor used to produce the goods in the domestic country need not be owned by domestic residents. Hence, the income that accrues to the factors of production used in producing goods in the country would go to foreign residents and not domestic residents.

For example, Germany has historically imported many temporary workers from eastern Europe. These foreign workers take substantial amounts of their wage income back to their home countries. Similarly, in most countries, some fraction of the capital stock that is used to produce output in the country is owned by foreign residents. In the United States, Japanese car manufacturers have made substantial investments in production facilities. As a result, many of the Toyotas and Hondas sold in the United States are actually "made in America" with American labor, but the income attributable to the capital stock goes to the owners of the equity of these firms, who are primarily Japanese.

The second related reason why GDP does not equal GNI in an open economy is that capital and labor owned by the country can be located and used to produce goods in different countries. Hence, the income of the residents of the country is augmented relative to the value of the goods produced in the country by the income from these factors of production located abroad. For example, Japan has a large capital investment in foreign countries that adds to its income. Pakistan also generates important income from workers who supply labor in other countries. In recent years, Ireland's GDP has been much higher than its GNI because the country has attracted a great deal of foreign investment, drawn to Ireland by its low corporate tax rates. Consequently, much of Ireland's GDP is accounted for by non-Irish factors of production.

The third reason why GNI does not equal GDP is that the country may receive unilateral transfers (gifts and grants) from abroad or may give unilateral transfers to other countries. Gifts from abroad increase a country's income.

In summary, in an open economy, net factor income from abroad plus net unilateral transfers from abroad, which we combine and define as **net foreign income (NFI)**, provide a flow of resources that separates the income of the country from the value of final goods and services produced in a country. Thus, we have our second open-economy national income accounting identity:

$$\text{GNI} = \text{GDP} + \text{NFI} \qquad \text{(4A.2)}$$

Notice that both net factor income and net unilateral transfers from abroad can be either positive or negative. Hence, net foreign income can be either positive or negative.

For many countries, such as the United States and Japan, the primary source of net factor income from abroad is the asset income generated by the country's net international investment position.

Chapter 5

Exchange Rate Systems

Currencies such as the euro, the yen, and the dollar trade freely in the world's forex markets, and their values fluctuate from minute to minute. The Hong Kong Monetary Authority, on the other hand, has kept the Hong Kong dollar between HKD7.75 = USD1 and HKD7.85 = USD1 since 1983. Between these extremes of freely floating exchange rates and fully fixed exchange rates is a wide variety of exchange rate systems. Understanding how these systems differ is critically important because the differences affect the currency risks international businesses face.

This chapter examines the many different currency arrangements around the world. An important part of this discussion involves understanding the key role central banks and their international reserves play in the exchange rate systems.

This chapter also describes how European countries created the European Monetary Union and came to adopt the euro as a common currency. This discussion is topical for three reasons. First, countries continue to adopt the euro as their currency; second, other groups of countries around the world may someday follow a similar scheme; and third, stresses within the euro zone have caused some European politicians to advocate abandonment of the euro and return to domestic currencies. Understanding the constraints that adopting the euro has placed on different countries clarifies the desirability of such a system.

5.1 ALTERNATIVE EXCHANGE RATE ARRANGEMENTS AND CURRENCY RISK

This section first surveys the spectrum of existing exchange rate arrangements. Then we summarize how different systems impose different currency risks on international businesses. Finally, we reflect on past and future trends in exchange rate arrangements.

Exchange Rate Systems Around the World

Exhibit 5.1 surveys the current arrangements in place across the world, using information from the International Monetary Fund (IMF). Although the IMF distinguishes more categories, the exchange rate systems can be split up into roughly three broad categories: currencies with floating exchange rates, currencies that have fixed or pegged exchange rates, and currencies in which the exchange rate is kept in a target zone or allowed to follow a crawling peg.

Exhibit 5.1 Exchange Rate Systems Around the World

No Separate Legal Tender	
Uses the U.S. Dollar	Ecuador, El Salvador, Marshall Islands, Micronesia, Palau, Panama, Timor-Leste, Zimbabwe
Uses the Euro	Kosovo, Montenegro, San Marino; **European Monetary Union** – Austria, Belgium, Cyprus, Estonia, Finland, France, Germany, Greece, Ireland, Italy, Luxembourg, Malta, Netherlands, Portugal, Slovak Republic, Slovenia, Spain
Uses the Australian Dollar	Kiribati

Currency Board	
Fixed to the U.S. Dollar	**ECCU** – Antigua and Barbuda, Dominica, Grenada, St. Kitts and Nevis, St. Lucia, St. Vincent and the Grenadines
	Djibouti, Hong Kong
Fixed to the Euro	Bosnia and Herzegovina, Bulgaria, Lithuania
	CFA Franc Zone: WAEMU – Benin, Burkina Faso, Côte d'Ivoire, Guinea-Bissau, Mali, Niger, Senegal, Togo; **CEMAC** – Cameroon, Central African Republic, Chad, Republic of Congo, Equatorial Guinea, Gabon
Fixed to the Singapore Dollar	Brunei Darussalam

Conventional Fixed Rate	
Fixed to the U.S. Dollar	Aruba, Bahamas, Bahrain, Barbados, Belize, Eritrea, Jordan, Maldives, Netherlands Antilles, Oman, Qatar, Saudi Arabia, Turkmenistan, United Arab Emirates, Venezuela
Fixed to the Euro	Cape Verde, Comoros, Denmark, Latvia, São Tomé and Principe
Fixed to a Composite Currency	Fiji, Kuwait, Libya, Morocco, Samoa
Fixed in Other Way	Bhutan, Lesotho, Namibia, Nepal, Swaziland

Crawling Pegs and Other Stabilization Arrangements Involving Active Intervention	
Versus the Dollar	Angola, Algeria, Azerbaijan, Bangladesh, Bolivia, Cambodia, Costa Rica, China, Ethiopia, Guyana, Honduras, Iraq, Kazakhstan, Lebanon, Liberia, Nicaragua, Suriname, Trinidad and Tobago, Uzbekistan, Vietnam
Versus the Euro	Croatia, Macedonia
Versus Composite	Algeria, Belarus, Botswana, Iran, Russia, Singapore, Solomon Islands, Syria, Tonga, Vanuatu
Other	Burundi, Dominican Republic, Egypt, Georgia, Guinea, Haiti, Kyrgyz Republic, Jamaica, Lao P.D.R., Malawi, Malaysia, Mauritania, Myanmar, Nigeria, Paraguay, Rwanda, Sri Lanka, Tajikistan, Ukraine, Tunisia, Yemen

Floating Rates	
Managed Floating	Afghanistan, Albania, Argentina, Armenia, Brazil, Colombia, Democratic Republic of Congo, Gambia, Ghana, Guatemala, Hungary, Iceland, India, Indonesia, Israel, Kenya, Republic of Korea, Madagascar, Mexico, Moldova, Mongolia, Mozambique, Pakistan, Papua New Guinea, Peru, Philippines, Romania, Serbia, Seychelles, Sierra Leone, South Africa, Switzerland, Sudan, Tanzania, Thailand, Uganda, Uruguay, Zambia
Free Floating	Australia, Canada, Chile, Czech Republic, Japan, Mauritius, New Zealand, Norway, Somalia, Sweden, Turkey, United Kingdom, United States

Note: The information is based on the International Monetary Fund's 2010 Annual Report (Appendix Table II-9).

Floating Currencies

At one extreme, some countries allow the value of their currency to be determined freely in the foreign exchange markets without any government restrictions or interventions in the foreign exchange market. These currencies are said to be **floating currencies**, and major currencies such as the dollar, yen, euro, and pound fall into this category, as do the currencies of other developed countries, such as the Australian dollar and the Swedish krona, and emerging market currencies, such as the Czech koruna and the Turkish lira.

Managed Floating

Although a number of countries can be classified as have floating exchange rates, the monetary authorities in the managed floating countries intervene in the foreign exchange market sufficiently often that IMF does not classify them as freely floating. A number of the prominent emerging market countries, such as Argentina, Brazil, Colombia, Indonesia, Israel, Mexico, and South Africa, fall into this category.

Fixed, or Pegged, Currencies

In exchange rate systems with **fixed rates**, or **pegged currencies**, governments attempt to keep the values of their currencies at particular pegged values in the foreign exchange market, relative to another currency or a basket of currencies. A **basket of currencies** is a composite currency consisting of various units of other currencies. The two most well-known examples of currency baskets are the **special drawing right (SDR)**, which is a unit of account created by the IMF (see Section 5.5), and the historical **European currency unit (ECU)**, which was formerly a unit of account in the European Monetary System (see Section 5.6). The SDR is sometimes used to denominate contracts, as Example 5.1 demonstrates.

Example 5.1 The Thai Baht Value of the SDR

As an exporter of rice from Thailand, ThaiRice contracted to receive the Thai baht (THB) value of SDR 1 million on December 24, 2010, for its rice exports. How many baht did it receive?

The Thai baht value of the SDR is found by multiplying the exchange rates of the baht versus the individual currencies by the given amounts of each currency in the basket. In December 2010, the SDR consisted of the following amounts of four major currencies: €0.41, ¥18.4, £0.0903, and $0.632. The exchange rates for these currencies on December 24, 2010, were THB40.2821/EUR, THB0.3704/JPY, THB47.3875/GBP, and THB30.6860/USD.

Thus, on December 24, 2010, the Thai baht value of the SDR was

$$\frac{THB40.2821}{EUR} \times €0.41 + \frac{THB0.3704}{JPY} \times ¥18.4 + \frac{THB47.3875}{GBP} \times £0.0903$$

$$+ \frac{THB30.6860}{USD} \times \$0.632 = \frac{THB47.0037}{SDR}$$

Because ThaiRice received the Thai baht value of SDR 1 million, ThaiRice received

$$\frac{THB47.0037}{SDR} \times SDR \ 1 \ million = THB47,003,700$$

Between July 2005 and July 2008, China pegged the value of the yuan relative to a basket of currencies including the major ones (dollar, euro, and yen) and a number of Asian currencies. Following Singapore's example, China did not disclose the amounts of the currencies in the basket. Other examples of pegged currencies include the Namibian dollar, which is pegged to the South African rand, and the Latvian lat, which is pegged to the euro.

No Separate Legal Tender

Some countries have actually adopted the currency of another country, thereby importing both that country's money and its monetary policy. Ecuador, El Salvador, and Panama have all adopted the U.S. dollar, whereas Kiribati uses the Australian dollar. Kosovo, Montenegro, and San Marino use the euro, as do the 17 euro-zone countries.

The category also includes arrangements such as the CFA franc zone, where a regional central bank controls the exchange rate system for several countries. The CFA franc zone is a group of 14 African countries with two currencies, the West African CFA franc (with currency symbol XOF), which is used in eight countries in the West African Economic and Monetary Union, and the Central African CFA franc (with currency symbol XAF), which is used in six countries in the Economic and Monetary Community of Central Africa.[1] The values of the two CFA francs are pegged at CFA francs $655.957 =$ EUR 1. The area is called the *franc zone* because the countries formerly pegged their currencies to the French franc. CFA is an acronym that originally stood for *Colonies Françaises d'Afrique* ("French Colonies of Africa") and now stands either for *Coopération Financière en Afrique Centrale* ("Financial Cooperation in Central Africa") in the Central African countries and *Communauté Financière d'Afrique* ("Financial Community of Africa") in the West African countries.

Currency Boards

A fixed, or pegged, exchange rate fully hinges on the commitment of a country's central bank to defend the currency's value. Some countries have created **currency boards** to accomplish this. A currency board limits the ability of the central bank to create money (see Section 5.4). The most well-known currency board is run by Hong Kong. The countries in the Eastern Caribbean Currency Union (ECCU) also have a currency board.

Target Zones and Crawling Pegs

The IMF also distinguishes some other categories including *target zone systems* and *crawling peg systems*. In such systems, the exchange rate is either kept within a fixed band (the target zone), or exchange rate changes are kept lower than preset limits that are adjusted regularly, typically with inflation (crawling pegs). For example, in 2007, the currency of Cyprus, the Cypriot pound, moved in a 15% band around the value of the euro. The ability of Cyprus to remain in this band was a condition for joining the EMU, and the euro replaced the Cypriot pound in January 2008.

Currency Risks in Alternative Exchange Rate Systems

It may seem that exporters or importers face more uncertainty conducting business in a country with a flexible exchange rate than in a country with a target zone, or even better, a pegged exchange rate system. Unfortunately, things are not that simple.

Quantifying Currency Risks

We know that the transaction exchange risk faced by an importer or exporter depends on the conditional distribution of the future exchange rate. It is easier to assess the conditional distribution of future exchange rates in some regimes than in others.

A critical characteristic of the conditional distribution is its dispersion, typically measured by the standard deviation (also called volatility). Exporters and importers can use this volatility to help quantify a possible range of future exchange rates, and hence quantify their currency risks. Exhibit 5.2 provides a general guide to the currency risks related to various exchange rate regimes.

A second important characteristic of the conditional distribution of future exchange rate changes is its skewness, which tells us whether large exchange rate changes in a particular direction are more likely than in the other direction.

---

[1]The West African countries are Benin, Burkina Faso, Côte d'Ivoire, Guinea-Bissau, Mali, Niger, Sénégal, and Togo. The Central African countries are Cameroon, Central Africa Republic, Chad, Republic of the Congo, Equatorial Guinea, and Gabon.

Exhibit 5.2   Currency Risk in Alternative Exchange Rate Systems

	Central Bank Objective	Exchange-Rate Volatility		Inflation Variability	Countries Adhering to System
		Historical	Latent		
Pure Floating	Domestic	—	—	—	0
Dirty Float	Domestic and Exchange Rate	Large	None	Large	51
Target Zone or Crawling Bands/Pegs	Domestic and Exchange Rate	Small	Large	Small	53
Pegged Exchange Rates	Exchange Rate	None	Large	Small	30
Currency Board	Exchange Rate	None	Small	Small	6
Dollarized	Domestic	None	Small	Small	12
Monetary Union	Domestic	None	Very Small	Small	17

Notes: The first column indicates whether the central bank focuses its policy on exchange rates or domestic objectives, such as inflation targeting. We classified "managed floating systems" under dirty float, but some of these currencies may more appropriately fit into the pegged or target zone categories. We did not classify the currencies in the ECCU and the CFA zones. The two exchange rate volatility columns classify the various currency systems according to the expected magnitude of volatility. The next column does the same with respect to inflation variability. The last column records the number of countries in each currency system, using the information provided in Exhibit 5.1.

Currency Risks in Floating Exchange Rate Systems

A completely pure floating rate system does not really exist. In reality, central banks *intervene* episodically in the foreign exchange market. That is, they buy and sell their own currencies to attempt to affect their values. Whether such a **dirty float currency system** is more or less volatile than a true floating system depends on whether you believe central bank intervention increases or decreases exchange rate volatility. In any case, one advantage of the floating exchange rate system is that history provides data that indicate past currency volatility. Although this volatility varies through time, because most major currencies have been freely floating since 1973, the historical data are useful in pinning down a realistic volatility number for the future. However, if you randomly pick two countries in the world that have substantial trade with one another, chances are their currencies are not floating relative to one another.

The risks of a large movement of the exchange rate in one direction or another in a floating exchange rate system are reasonably symmetric unless a currency has strengthened or weakened systematically for several years, as the dollar did in the early 1980s. Then, the risk of a large reversal in direction typically begins to manifest itself—often while the currency continues to defy this prediction.

Currency Risk in Target Zones

Target zones try to limit exchange rate variability and achieve inflation convergence within the participating countries. As long as the exchange rate remains within the preset band, day-to-day currency fluctuations are bound to be smaller than what is observed for floating currencies. However, when the monetary authorities devalue or revalue a currency (by resetting the bands), the discrete changes in rates are often large. The effect of this behavior for currency risk is well illustrated with an historical example.

The annualized historical volatility of the rate of change of the French franc–Deutsche mark (FRF/DEM) exchange rate between 1979 and 1999 was 3.01%. This is much lower than the typical volatilities observed for the major floating currencies, such as the $/£ and ¥/$, which tend to be around 11% (see Chapter 13). This suggests that the European Monetary System—the target zone system under which the franc and the mark traded at the time—successfully reduced the volatility of the exchange rate between the two currencies to below what it would have been in a floating currency system. However, the comparison is somewhat strained.

The United States, United Kingdom, and Japan do not have similarly close geographical proximity and trading relationships as do France and Germany. A more comparable country duo, which has not established a formal currency system between them, is Canada and the United States. The volatility of changes in the CAD/USD exchange rate was only 4.53% over the same time period, which is closer to the volatility of the FRF/DEM series than to the volatility of the major currencies.

When we graph the CAD/USD and the FRF/DEM exchange rate changes (see Exhibit 5.3), we see that the volatility of the FRF/DEM exchange rate came in bursts.

Exhibit 5.3 Contrasting the FRF/DEM and CAD/USD Exchange Rates

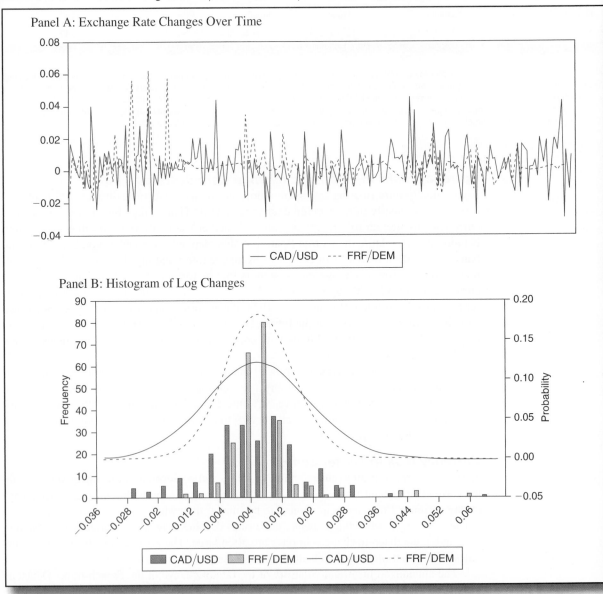

Notes: In Panel A, we graph monthly exchange rate changes over time (using data from April 1979 to December 1998), whereas in Panel B, we show histograms for logarithmic differences. These logarithmic differences are relatively close to the simple percentage differences computed as $[S(t+1)/S(t)]-1$, with $S(t)$ being the spot rate. For each histogram, we also graph the normal distribution with the same mean and standard deviation as the data.

When there was a speculative crisis and the weak currency was eventually devalued, volatility suddenly and sharply increased.[2] For example, the exchange rate would abruptly move to the edge of the band. Indeed, the FRF witnessed devaluations of as much as 5.75%. Such large, 1-day movements do not tend to occur with floating exchange rates, where a weak currency may lose ground more gradually. As a result, more extreme observations occurred for changes in the FRF/DEM than for changes in the CAD/USD. If more extreme observations are observed than what we would see in a normal distribution, the distribution is said to exhibit "fat tails," or leptokurtosis (see Chapter 3). We can see this leptokurtic behavior clearly in the histograms in Panel B of Exhibit 5.3. From the perspective of a multinational business, dealing with such exchange rate behavior is much more difficult than dealing with the smoother changes over time characterizing flexible exchange rate changes. If the possibilities of devaluations or revaluations are not symmetrical, the conditional distribution will also be skewed. This risk also arises in pegged exchange rate systems, as you will see.

Currency Risk in Pegged Exchange Rate Systems

The difficulties in assessing currency risk are amplified in pegged exchange rate systems. If the peg holds for a long time, historical volatility appears to be zero, but this may not accurately reflect underlying tensions that may ultimately result in a devaluation of the currency. Hence, the true currency risk does not show up in day-to-day fluctuations of the exchange rate. Therefore, we say this situation exhibits "latent volatility."

The key reason we discovered that the behavior of the FRF/DEM exchange rate was not all that different from the behavior of the CAD/USD exchange rate is that we used a long enough historical period, so that a number of devaluations of the FRF were part of the sample. In pegged exchange rate systems, such history is sometimes completely lacking. For example, before the Thai baht succumbed to speculative pressure in the crisis of 1997, it had only been devalued twice in the previous 30 years and not at all in the prior 10 years. From these few observations, it was impossible to determine the true latent volatility of the baht in 1997. What can be done is to look at other countries with similar systems and policies. Economists have built sophisticated models to forecast devaluations and quantify currency risk, which we will discuss in Chapter 10. The great challenge of these models often is to be forward looking without the benefit of a long span of historical data.

Fortunately, it is usually clear in a pegged exchange rate system whether the pegged currency will be devalued or revalued. This one-sided view helps importers and exporters to assess who faces the greater risk. Nevertheless, it is still difficult to know the probabilities associated with devaluations or revaluations and the potential magnitudes of these changes.

Currency Risk in Currency Boards and Monetary Unions

Currency boards attempt to further limit the risk of devaluation by severely reducing the scope of a country's monetary policy in exchange rate matters. The problem is that currency boards frequently collapse. For example, the currency boards of all the former British colonies ceased to exist after the colonies became independent, although their demise was not always accompanied by a currency crisis. The Argentine currency board that began in 1991 collapsed in 2002 when the county faced a banking crisis, which plunged the country into a deep recession and a currency crisis.

The only truly credible fixed exchange rate regime may well be a common currency in a monetary union, such as the euro. (We study the European experience with currency arrangements in the final section of this chapter and offer a brief introduction to monetary unions there.) Nevertheless, even a monetary union can be broken apart, so while the probability of devaluation under such a system is quite low, it is not zero.

---

[2]See Bekaert and Gray (1998) for a detailed study of the currency volatility around speculative crises in the FRF/DEM market.

Exhibit 5.4 Exchange Rate Arrangements

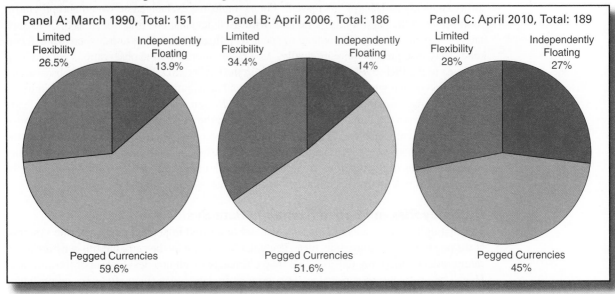

Panel A: March 1990, Total: 151
Limited Flexibility 26.5%
Independently Floating 13.9%
Pegged Currencies 59.6%

Panel B: April 2006, Total: 186
Limited Flexibility 34.4%
Independently Floating 14%
Pegged Currencies 51.6%

Panel C: April 2010, Total: 189
Limited Flexibility 28%
Independently Floating 27%
Pegged Currencies 45%

Note: Data are from various International Monetary Fund Annual Reports.

The lessons from this analysis are clear: For currencies that are not freely floating, the historical volatility of their exchange rates may not be an accurate measure of currency risk. Even though such exchange rate systems might provide short-term exchange rate stability, they do not guarantee the absence of currency risk. Currencies in pegged exchange rate systems can still be devalued, and even currency boards can be, and have been, abandoned.

Trends in Currency Systems

Exhibit 5.4 puts the currencies into the three categories mentioned earlier, comparing the current situation (Panel C) with the situations in 1990 (Panel A) and 2006 (Panel B). Needless to say, there have been many changes in recent years.

First of all, there are now more currencies than there used to be. One main reason is the splitting of the Soviet Union into separate states, each with its own currency. Second, there was an increase in systems with limited flexibility between 1990 and 2006 that has reversed itself. Third, pegged currency systems still dominate, but they are less dominant than they used to be. Fourth, the world has seen a modest increase in floating exchange rate systems.

Exchange rate systems are in constant flux, and international businesses must be watchful for potential dramatic events. One prediction that we venture to make from studying the history of currency systems is that there is now a trend toward the extremes. Countries opt either for a very credible fixed exchange rate system, such as a currency board or monetary union, or a free-float system. The popularity of pegged and target zone systems is declining. When doing business with countries operating such systems, the potential for regime shifts is large.

5.2 CENTRAL BANKS

To understand how the exchange rate systems operate, you must first understand the functioning of central banks.

Exhibit 5.5 Central Bank Balance Sheet

Assets	Liabilites
Official international reserves	Deposits of private financial institutions (Bank reserves)
Domestic credit	Currency in circulation
• Government bonds	Other
• Loans to domestic financial institutions	
Other	

The Central Bank's Balance Sheet

Exhibit 5.5 shows a simplified central bank balance sheet.[3]

Bank Reserves and Currency in Circulation

The first item on the liabilities side of the balance sheet consists of the reserves that financial institutions have on deposit at the central bank. Countries require their commercial banks to hold a certain percentage of the deposits the banks accept from the public as reserves at the central bank. These reserves are called **required reserves**, and they are often non-interest bearing. Even if the central bank did not force banks to hold reserves, banks would still hold some reserves to facilitate transfers across banks and because they always face withdrawals, many of which have to be met immediately. Currency physically held in banks, called *vault cash*, is also part of reserves.

The other liability of the central bank is currency in circulation, which includes the coins and bills used by the public. Because the central bank operates the only authorized printing press in the country, it can actually print money to pay its bills or to acquire assets.

The sum of the two central bank liabilities is called the **monetary base** of the country, or simply *base money*. If the central bank buys an asset (for example, a government bond) from a financial institution, it credits the financial institution's reserve account at the central bank for the purchase price of the bond. Because this financial institution can now use these funds to lend money to individuals and businesses, the central bank has, essentially, created money. During the financial crisis that began in 2007, many central banks engaged in a policy known as "quantitative easing," which essentially amounts to the purchase of additional assets from commercial banks that expanded the banks' reserves. Although definitions of *money* in a modern economy vary, we define it here as the sum of bills in circulation and demand deposits at commercial banks (a measure called M1).

One dollar of additional base money eventually leads to much more than 1 dollar of actual money. Further money creation happens as financial institutions lend out part of the additional reserve dollar. This money is spent and, in turn, is deposited at some other financial institution, swelling that bank's deposits and its reserves. This bank will not leave that money idle but will lend it out and keep only a fraction as reserves. Consequently, the process of money creation continues in what monetary economists call the money multiplier effect: 1 dollar of additional base money leads to multiple dollars of new money. The money multiplier effect is smaller when financial institutions fail to lend out new deposits or when people hold cash rather than depositing money in the banking system.

Domestic Credit

The asset side of the central bank's balance sheet in Exhibit 5.5 records its investment portfolio. One important category here is domestic government bonds. In the United States and many other countries, these assets are used to influence the money supply through **open market operations**, which are the purchases or sales of government bonds by the central

---

[3]See Mishkin (2010) for more details about central banks and monetary policy.

bank. In the United States, the Federal Reserve (the Fed) is the central bank, and if the Fed buys a U.S. Treasury bond, it pays by crediting the account of the bank selling the bond. By doing so, the Fed injects dollars into the financial system. The converse is also true; the Fed can reduce the money supply by selling government bonds to the public. Open market operations are the main channel through which the Fed affects the money supply.

The interest rate at which the Fed's supply of reserves matches the financial institutions' demand for reserves is called the federal funds rate. It is also the rate at which banks lend reserves to each other overnight. Using open market operations, the Fed controls the federal funds rate, which in turn affects the interest rates at which banks lend to households and firms.

Another category of assets on a central bank's balance sheet that is often extremely important for developing countries is "credit to the domestic financial sector," which corresponds to "loans to domestic financial institutions" in Exhibit 5.5. The central bank in most countries is also a lender of last resort—that is, it can and should extend credit to the banking sector to prevent bank runs in times of panic and financial crisis. Inflationary problems often arise, though, when financial institutions become dependent on the central bank for funds.

Official Reserves

The item "official international reserves" on the balance sheet in Exhibit 5.5 is at the core of the role central banks play in the foreign exchange market. **Official reserves** consist of three major components: foreign exchange reserves, gold reserves, and IMF-related reserve assets. (We discuss the last two items in Section 5.4.) Around the world, **foreign exchange reserves** constitute the largest component of official international reserves, accounting for 86% of total reserves at the end of 2009. Gold accounted for 10% and IMF-related reserve assets accounted for 4% of total reserves.

Chapter 4 noted that international reserves are the central bank's foreign currency–denominated assets (bonds, deposits, and credit lines). In terms of currency denomination, the dollar is the dominant foreign reserve asset held by most central banks around the world. Exhibit 5.6, constructed from IMF Annual Reports, indicates that the dollar's dominance has waned in recent times, falling from close to 80% in 1975 to about 61% today.

Exhibit 5.6 Foreign Exchange Reserves

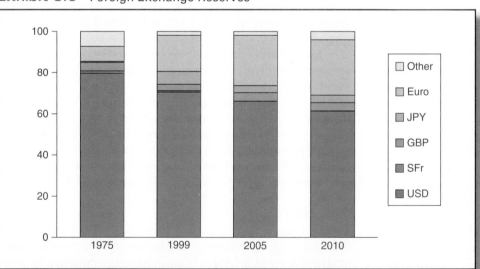

Notes: The data are from Table I-2 in the International Monetary Fund Annual Reports, various issues. For 1975, the numbers for the euro reflect the sum of reserve positions in the Deutsche mark and the French franc.

Other important reserve assets are the euro, the pound sterling, and the yen. A much-discussed issue is whether the arrival of the euro will cause the relative importance of the dollar to decrease (see Galati and Wooldridge, 2009; and Papaioannou et al., 2006). Comparing the 1999 and 2010 numbers, it does appear to be the case that the share of the euro has increased relative to that of the dollar, but at times during the 1980s and 1990s, the total share of international reserves of the currencies replaced by the euro (the Deutsche mark, French franc, and ECU) was higher than that of the euro today.

International reserves are depleted or increased when a central bank intervenes in the foreign exchange market. If the central bank buys its currency in the foreign exchange market, it must sell foreign currency assets and its international reserves are depleted. If the central bank sells its currency in the foreign exchange market, it buys foreign currency assets and its international reserves are increased.

Central banks usually limit the risk of their portfolios by not investing in equities. Most official reserves are held as foreign Treasury bills and bonds.

Whereas 10 years ago, the largest stock of official reserves was found in developed countries, at the end of 2009, developing countries held more than 65% of the global stock of reserve assets. After currency crises in Mexico in 1994, Southeast Asia in 1997, and Russia in 1998, many developing countries built up substantial reserves, partially as insurance against future crises. Traditionally, the level of reserves is compared to the amount of imports a country must fund. However, in an increasingly financially globalized world, reserves can also protect against sudden stops in capital flows from abroad (see Jeanne and Ranciere, 2009). China, in particular, has built up substantial reserves, which at the end of September 2010 stood at $2,987 billion, of which $2,648 billion was foreign exchange and $339 billion was gold.

Money Creation and Inflation

The central bank's right to create money is a valuable tool. Central banks finance their physical operations and pay their staff from the interest income on their assets, which are obtained by creating base money. Any residual income is given to the country's treasury. The value of the real resources that the central bank obtains through the creation of base money is called **seigniorage**. By setting the amount of nominal money circulating in the economy at each point in time, the bank establishes the growth rate of the nation's money supply over time. Monetary authorities hope to use their policies to achieve low inflation while promoting growth and lowering unemployment. This is a difficult task because the demand for money ultimately depends on the amount of real transactions in the economy and how much money is needed to facilitate these transactions.

For example, if the authorities double the money supply in the hope of stimulating the economy, they will probably only succeed in doubling the overall level of prices in the economy. The increase in the money supply is unlikely to make people consume more or work harder. But with more money supporting the same number of real transactions, prices will inevitably rise. Whereas economists have formulated theories in which changes in the supply of money do have real effects on the economy in the short run, it is generally believed that the long-run impact of additional money growth on real activity is negligible. This long-run property of the growth in the money supply is called *money neutrality*.

Sometimes, central banks forget that creating money cannot solve real problems. For example, governments may use open market operations to monetize fiscal deficits to help finance a large budget deficit. The deficit arises because government expenditures exceed tax revenues, and the deficit must be financed by the sale of government bonds to the public. If the bonds are bought by the central bank, the central bank's holdings of government bonds increase, and the money supply expands. The deficit is monetized. A government that "runs the printing presses" to finance its deficits undermines its central bank's ability to control the money supply and eventually creates inflation.

Central banks fall into this trap because the open market purchase of bonds does not immediately increase the price level. Prices only rise over time as the banking system's increased reserves finance additional lending to the public, which increases aggregate demand. In 2010, the Fed's policy of quantitative easing essentially monetized a large part of the U.S. budget deficit, but inflation remained low. When questioned by Congress if this policy would eventually create inflation, Chairman Bernanke responded that the Fed had the tools to reverse the policy in the future should inflationary pressures appear.

Deficit finance was an acute problem in many Latin American economies in the 1970s and 1980s. Argentina and Bolivia eventually faced hyperinflation (triple-digit annual inflation or worse) because they created too much money. Similarly, if central banks frivolously extend credit to the banking sector, the money supply will likely expand beyond the amount that individuals and firms need to conduct transactions, and inflation inevitably results.

The Impossible Trinity or Trilemma

Standard open-economy macroeconomic theory holds that there is an intrinsic incompatibility between perfect capital mobility (that is, no capital controls on international financial transactions), a fixed exchange rate, and domestic monetary autonomy (that is, using monetary policy to achieve domestic policy goals). The fact that only two of these three policies are possible is called the **impossible trinity** or **trilemma**.[4] If a country wants to fix its exchange rate and has perfect capital mobility, capital flows will determine the country's money supply, making it impossible to run an independent monetary policy.

Some economists argue that combining an independent monetary policy and control of the exchange rate with capital controls is the best way to deal with the impossible trinity, but in practice, such policies do not always work. Even when a currency is flexible, problems can arise. For example, in December 2006, Thailand imposed capital controls on foreign capital inflows (essentially slapping a tax on foreign portfolio investment into Thailand) after facing a strong appreciation of the Thai baht that hurt Thai exporters. The Thai authorities did not want to lower local interest rates to lessen the attractiveness of foreign investment in Thailand. Why? Because that would boost local demand and further overheat the economy. As you will see in the next section, any effort by the central bank to intervene to lower the value of the baht would have a similar effect. After the equity market declined by 15% in 1 day in response to the imposition of capital controls, the controls were hastily removed from equity investments and relaxed for debt investments. Yet, in the wake of the 2007 to 2010 global crisis, a number of emerging economies, including Brazil and South Korea, imposed capital controls on short-term or "hot" capital inflows, and capital controls are an integral ingredient of China's monetary policy (see the box titled *The Trilemma in China* later in this chapter).

Foreign Exchange Interventions

Central banks sometimes intervene in foreign exchange markets to affect exchange rates directly. By supplying more of their currency, they weaken it; and by demanding their currency, they strengthen it. Exhibit 5.7 shows the effects of two different types of interventions on a central bank balance sheet.

With either intervention, the central bank ends up buying foreign currency. (In practice, central banks do not just buy foreign currency; they eventually buy foreign currency assets that earn interest, such as foreign bonds.) There are two types of interventions, depending on whether the interventions are "sterilized." We discuss the non-sterilized intervention first and then explain sterilization.

---

[4]**Capital controls** are the set of regulations and taxes pertaining to flows of capital into and out of the country. See Obstfeld and Shambaugh (2005) for some historical perspectives on the trilemma and Aizenman et al. (2010) for an analysis of the current situation.

Exhibit 5.7   Sterilized and Non-Sterilized Foreign Exchange Intervention

Panel A: A Non-Sterilized Intervention

Central Bank Balance Sheet			
Assets		**Liabilities**	
International reserves	+50	Deposits of financial institutions	+50
Domestic credit	0		

Financial Intermediary Balance Sheet		
Assets		**Liabilities**
Reserves at Federal Reserve	+50	
Foreign currency interbank deposits	−50	
Government bonds	0	

Panel B: A Sterilized Intervention

Central Bank Balance Sheet			
Assets		**Liabilities**	
International reserves	+50	Deposits of financial institutions	+50
Domestic credit	**−50**		**−50**
	0		0

Financial Intermediary Balance Sheet		
Assets		**Liabilities**
Reserves at Federal Reserve	+50	
	−50	
Foreign currency interbank deposits	−50	
Government bonds	**+50**	
	0	

Notes: The Fed buys USD 50 million worth of yen on the foreign exchange market in Panel A. In Panel B, the bold transaction shows how the Fed sterilizes the original transaction by selling government bonds to financial intermediaries.

Non-Sterilized Interventions

Consider the situation in Exhibit 5.7. Imagine that the Fed wants to depreciate the dollar relative to the yen, to make U.S. products more attractive to potential Japanese buyers. Suppose the exchange rate is ¥100/$, and the Fed buys ¥5,000 million in the foreign exchange market from a major U.S. commercial bank. How does the Fed pay for the yen? It simply credits the account of the commercial bank at the Fed by $50 million = (¥5,000 million)/ (¥100/$). The commercial bank in turn wires ¥5,000 million to the Fed. This transaction decreases the assets of the commercial bank by ¥5,000 million, but it increases the assets of the commercial bank by $50 million. At the central bank, this **non-sterilized intervention** increases foreign assets and increases the U.S. money supply. Essentially, the Fed pays the bank by creating $50 million of base money. By increasing the demand for yen and increasing the supply of dollars to the foreign exchange market, the Fed hopes to lower the yen price of the dollar.

Sterilized Interventions

An unwelcome side effect of a non-sterilized foreign exchange intervention is its effect on the money supply. A higher money supply eventually leads to higher inflation, and the foreign exchange objective of the central bank's policy may conflict with its domestic goal of price stability. A potential solution is to "sterilize" the foreign exchange intervention— that is, to remove the new money from circulation to remove the inflation threat. **Sterilized interventions** involve conducting an offsetting open market transaction to restore the monetary base to its original size.

Panel B of Exhibit 5.7 presents a sterilized intervention. Here, the Fed uses an open market transaction to offset the effect of the foreign exchange intervention on the domestic money supply. That is, at the same time as the Fed buys ¥5,000 million for $50 million, it sells $50 million worth of domestic government bonds in the bond market. Because a financial institution pays for these bonds using its reserve account at the Fed, money is taken out of circulation at the same time that money is injected into circulation through the foreign exchange intervention. These two transactions cancel each other out, as Exhibit 5.7 shows. The net effect is that the Fed has replaced domestic bonds with foreign assets, but there is no effect on the money supply. The private sector now holds more domestic bonds and fewer foreign currency bonds.

How Do Central Banks Peg a Currency?

Although most central banks—even those with free-floating currencies—intervene in the foreign exchange market, some central banks go further and attempt to fix the value of their currencies relative to a benchmark currency. How does a central bank peg a currency? To establish and maintain a fixed value when a currency is freely traded, the central bank has to be willing to "make a market" in its currency. The central bank has to be willing and able to supply its currency when there is excess private demand for it (buying the foreign currency), and if there is excess private supply of the domestic currency, the central bank must demand any excess supply that arises (selling its foreign currency reserves). As the central bank buys or sells the foreign currency, its international reserves increase or decrease.

Pegging the Exchange Rate

Suppose that the Bank of England, the U.K. central bank, wants to peg the value of the pound relative to the dollar at $\bar{S} = \$1.25/\pounds$. Exhibit 5.8 presents the aggregate demand and supply for the pound. The horizontal axis represents quantities of pounds demanded or supplied in the foreign exchange market over some time interval, such as a quarter or a year. The vertical axis represents the price of the pound in terms of the dollar—in other words, the dollar/pound exchange rate, S.

Why is the demand (supply) schedule downward (upward) sloping? Let us assume that the United Kingdom and the United States are the only countries in the world and

Exhibit 5.8 Fixing the $/£ Exchange Rate

assume for simplicity that the demands to trade currencies arise only from importers and exporters. The quantity of pounds demanded by U.S. importers will go down as the dollar price of the pound increases. If the U.K. product prices remain fixed, a higher dollar/pound exchange rate raises the dollar prices of U.K. goods to U.S. importers. Consequently, the demand schedule for pounds, Demand$_£$, is downward sloping. Similarly, the supply of pounds to the foreign exchange market—for example, by U.K. importers needing dollars to import goods or services from the United States—will tend to increase the higher the exchange rate (the more dollars a pound buys) because the price of U.S. goods is going down from the U.K. perspective. The supply schedule, Supply$_£$, is therefore upward sloping. The equilibrium exchange rate that equates the private sector's demand and supply schedules is denoted by S and equals $1.50/£. If the exchange rate were freely floating without government intervention, this would be the market exchange rate.

The level at which the government wants to fix the value of the pound, $\overline{S}$, is represented by a horizontal line. In this case, the value is below the equilibrium exchange rate. At $\overline{S}$, there is an excess private demand for pounds, and the pound is undervalued relative to its equilibrium value. Hence, if the Bank of England wants to keep the exchange rate at that level, it will have to supply these excess pounds (represented by $Q_D - Q_S$) to the foreign exchange market and obtain foreign currency (dollars) in return. In other words, this situation causes the Bank of England to increase its foreign reserves.

Exhibit 5.8 also summarizes the essence of the economic content of the balance of payments (BOP) statistics we discussed in Chapter 4. The demand for pounds over a certain time interval is every item that gives rise to a credit on the BOP, a source of foreign currency. The supply of pounds over that same time interval is every item that gives rise to a debit item, a use of foreign currency. In a purely floating exchange rate system, the exchange rate is always at its equilibrium value, S; the private sector's balance of payments is always balanced; and there is no need for central bank intervention. However, if the Bank of England wants to peg the currency at $\overline{S}$, its foreign exchange reserves will increase when there is excess private-sector demand for pounds, and there will be an official settlements deficit because the Bank of England is building up foreign assets.

The Trilemma in China

Because China pegs the value of the yuan to the dollar, the impossible trinity or trilemma implies that China can only run an independent monetary policy by imposing capital controls. Indeed, China incurs huge costs to control capital flows. The controls are asymmetric: Certain types of inflows are allowed (especially foreign direct investment [FDI] and limited equity flows), but outflows are prohibited. However, with growing international trade, China's current account transactions are now relatively unrestricted, making it more difficult to contain capital flows masked as current account transactions. The fixed exchange rate coupled with large trade surpluses and substantial FDI inflows necessarily imply that China has been building up massive international reserves. To prevent this from affecting the local money supply, China must sterilize the foreign reserve buildup. Because China does not have well-developed financial and Treasury bond markets, the People's Bank of China, its central bank, has resorted to issuing central bank bills and raising reserve requirements to reduce the money multiplier. As Wang (2010) reports, between July 2006 and September 2008, reserve requirements for the commercial banks were raised 19 times, from 8.0% to 17.5%. Wang also demonstrates that China's ability to fully sterilize the foreign exchange buildup has diminished over time, as has the effectiveness of its capital controls. As China slowly continues on a path toward more financial openness, it may have to give up the exchange rate peg or risk losing monetary independence.

Although the central banks of the major developed countries mostly let competitive market forces determine the values of their exchange rates, they nonetheless have a variety of tools at their disposal to influence the path of exchange rates. For example, they can use domestic monetary policy (by varying the money supply or interest rates under their control); they can attempt to restrict capital movements; or they can tax or subsidize international trade to influence the demand for foreign currency. We will come back to these alternative tools later on in this chapter. Here we focus on direct foreign exchange intervention—that is, the sale or purchase of foreign assets against domestic assets by the central bank.

The Effects of Central Bank Interventions

Despite their prevalence, foreign exchange interventions are a controversial policy option for central banks. In one view, intervention policy is not only ineffective in influencing the level of the exchange rate, but it is viewed as dangerous because it can increase foreign exchange volatility. Others argue that intervention operations can influence the level of the exchange rate and can "calm disorderly markets," thereby decreasing volatility. Yet others, including Nobel Laureate Milton Friedman (1953), argue that interventions are ineffective and a waste of taxpayers' money.

To better understand this debate, let's consider how interventions can affect exchange rates. We distinguish two main channels: direct and indirect. The direct channel stresses the importance of the volume and the intensity of the intervention operations themselves, whereas the indirect channel stresses the importance of the market response to the intervention and how expectations of private investors and their investment portfolios may be altered as a result. We summarize these channels in Exhibit 5.9, which takes us through the potential effects of the Fed buying euros. In the discussion here, we move from left to right in the diagram.

Direct Effects of Interventions

The direct channel is easiest to understand. The central bank's action directly affects the supply and demand of foreign currency. In Exhibit 5.9, the supply of dollars to the foreign exchange market increases, and the demand for euros increases. Most economists believe that the direct effects of interventions must be negligible because the magnitude of interventions is typically like a drop in the ocean of overall foreign exchange trading. The daily trading volume in the foreign exchange markets across all currencies is around $4 trillion per day, whereas interventions rarely exceed $20 billion at a time. Of course, when the intervention is not sterilized, buying euros has the same effect as an expansion of the U.S. money supply. However, the U.S. money supply also dwarfs the size of a typical intervention so that this money supply effect is likely to be small as well. Moreover, both the Fed and the European Central Bank routinely *sterilize* their interventions, implying that the money supply is typically not affected by direct interventions.

Although sterilized interventions have no effect on the domestic money supply, they do change the composition of the assets held by private investors. For example, a Fed purchase of euros with dollars would increase the U.S. money supply and must be offset with a sale of government bonds, which reduces the U.S. money supply, if the intervention is sterilized. The net effect in private-sector portfolios in Exhibit 5.9 is that dollar bonds replace euro bonds, which we term the *bond portfolio effect*. The central bank forces this change in portfolio composition upon private investors, who may require changes in the prices and expected returns on the bonds before they are willing to buy them. Whether these changes in portfolio composition generate any direct effect on the exchange rate is questionable, given the size of

Exhibit 5.9 The Effects of Foreign Exchange Interventions

Notes: The Federal Reserve buys euros to attempt to reduce the value of the dollar relative to the euro. Because it wants to hold interest-bearing instruments, it uses the euro to buy a 5-year Bund, a German government bond with a maturity of 5 years.

worldwide bond portfolios relative to the typical size of an intervention. The U.S. government bond market alone, for example, has a market capitalization over to $9 trillion.

Interventions may still be effective in generating short-term effects on the exchange rate through creating inventory imbalances for foreign exchange dealers or by creating order flow that dealers try to exploit (see Pasquariello, 2010). For example, if the Fed intervenes to reduce the value of the dollar by buying euros with dollars from several dealers, the efforts of these dealers to either reduce their inventory imbalances (by re-buying the euros) or to exploit the order flow may well decrease the value of the dollar. In this sense, "smallish" interventions may still have an exchange rate effect by squeezing foreign exchange inventories at dealer banks.

Indirect Effects of Interventions

Even though an intervention may fail to move the exchange rate directly, it can still alter people's expectations and affect their investments, thus helping to push the exchange rate in the direction the central bank desires. For example, the intervention may be a signal to the public of the central bank's monetary policy intentions, or it may signal the central bank's inside information about future market fundamentals, such as future GDP growth.

Alternatively, the central bank may signal to investors that the exchange rate is deviating too far from its long-run equilibrium value. However, the market might not take a mere announcement of a policy change seriously because "talk is cheap," as the saying goes. By contrast, an actual intervention makes the signal more credible because the central bank is putting its own resources on the line when it intervenes. When a central bank incorrectly assesses the equilibrium value of the exchange rate, the intervention will result in a loss. For example, if the central bank buys foreign currency when it feels the foreign currency is undervalued and bound to appreciate, but subsequently the foreign currency depreciates, the bank suffers a loss. The marketplace, recognizing these costs, is likely to take the central bank's policy statement more seriously if it is backed up by intervention. This reasoning, though, makes standard secretive interventions of central banks quite mysterious.

Empirical Evidence on the Effectiveness of Interventions

After the advent of floating exchange rates in 1973, policymakers gradually discovered that exchange rates were much more variable than they had envisioned. Several years of undisciplined and uncoordinated national monetary and fiscal policies created huge current account imbalances and a sizable misalignment of the dollar, which had appreciated strongly since the end of 1979. The Plaza Accord of September 1985 ushered in a period of quasi-regular interventions by the major central banks. With the Plaza Accord, the central banks of Germany, Japan, and the United States conducted a coordinated intervention to lower the value of the dollar after its sustained rise during the first half of the 1980s. Since then, there have been other coordinated interventions (for example, the Louvre Accord in 1987) and many unilateral interventions by a single central bank, which provide useful data to examine whether interventions are effective. Surveys of the literature by Neely (2008) and Menkhoff (2010) suggest that interventions are more successful when coordinated among central banks and when they are consistent with market fundamentals.

Dominguez and Frankel (1993) draw an engaging analogy between the foreign exchange market and a cattle drive. In the analogy, the market is the herd of steers, and the central banks are the herd dogs. In any cattle drive, the steers clearly outnumber the herd dogs in both size and number, yet the dogs can still influence the steers' path by barking and nipping at their heels. The steers at the edge of the pack influence the rest of the herd to stay on the right path. In much the same way, central banks, while clearly outnumbered in terms of market participants and the sheer volume of market trading activity, may be able to exert greater influence on exchange rates than their size and number would suggest because they can affect market expectations. But the herd dogs likely have less chance of success when the cattle are going full speed toward a ravine and must be turned around 180 degrees. Interventions that fly in the face of powerful economic fundamentals are unlikely to work. Although the Plaza Accord was deemed successful because the dollar did indeed decline in its wake, the decline in the value of the dollar had already started, and the Plaza Accord may have just endorsed a market movement already under way.

Many studies have tested whether central bank intervention has served to stabilize exchange rates. While the results differ across countries, the empirical evidence so far suggests that central bank interventions have increased or not changed volatility rather than decreased it (see Beine et al., 2007; and Dominguez, 2006).[5] One problem with assessing the efficacy of interventions to reduce volatility is the possibility that central banks intervene during periods that are relatively more volatile.

A final perspective is to try to assess directly whether central bank interventions indeed waste taxpayers' money by examining the profitability of interventions. One example of a loss was the Swiss National Bank's (SNB) loss on euro intervention in 2010. The Swiss franc is often viewed as a safe haven currency and tends to attract many investors in crisis times. In March 2009, the SNB thought that Swiss franc appreciation had gone too far and intervened

---

[5]This is true despite central bankers themselves believing that their interventions do not increase volatility. See the survey in Neely (2008).

against the euro to prevent the Swiss franc from appreciating below CHF1.50/EUR. The SNB was successful throughout 2009, but during the first half of 2010, they acquired CHF132 billion of international reserves, mostly euro denominated. This intervention was unsuccessful in preventing appreciation of the Swiss franc as the exchange rate reached CHF1.25/EUR by July 2010, at which time the SNB announced that it had lost CHF14 billion on its intervention. In contrast, Neely (2008) notes that several studies show central bank interventions to be profitable, both in the United States and Australia. Given the inconclusiveness of much of the research in this area, the debate on the usefulness of interventions in otherwise freely floating currencies will probably continue for a long time to come.

5.4 FIXED EXCHANGE RATE SYSTEMS

Until 1971, an essentially fixed exchange rate system based on gold dominated the international monetary system. From then onward, fixed exchange rate systems have been primarily prevalent in developing countries.

The International Monetary System Before 1971: A Brief History

The Gold Standard

At the start of the 18th century, Great Britain made its paper currency notes exchangeable for gold, thereby establishing the first official **gold standard**. By the end of the 19th century, all major industrial countries had adopted the gold standard. Because coins and bills could be converted into gold at fixed rates at central banks, the gold standard essentially resulted in a system of fixed exchange rates among the major countries. Central banks also used gold to pay for balance of payments deficits. That is, gold was sent from the deficit country (which faced an excess demand for the foreign currency) to the surplus country. This transfer helped restore equilibrium on the balance of payments because the loss of international reserves by deficit countries also meant that their money supply decreased, putting downward pressure on prices. Lower prices increased demand for the country's products from foreign residents, which automatically improved the BOP.

Hyperinflation and the Interwar Period

During World War I, the gold standard was suspended as governments printed massive amounts of paper money to finance their war efforts. The result was substantial inflation, with Germany as the most dramatic example. Germany faced hyperinflation between 1919 and 1923, with prices rising by a factor of 481.5 billion in those 4 years alone! People literally had to use wheelbarrows full of money to make their purchases.

The interwar period was an era of international economic disintegration punctuated by the Great Depression starting in 1929.[6] Some countries allowed their currencies to float in the foreign exchange markets. Others maintained some form of gold standard; for example, the United States and Great Britain restored gold convertibility at prewar parities after the war. That is, the number of dollars or pounds needed to obtain an ounce of gold was kept at the same value as before the war. However, gold standard countries regularly devalued their currencies relative to gold and hence relative to other currencies. These devaluations were intentionally aimed at making locally produced goods more competitive—that is, cheaper for foreign buyers. At the same time, protectionist measures were taken, aimed at keeping out foreign products. International cooperation and coordination of economic policies declined precipitously, and international tensions grew.

---

[6]Eichengreen (1992) provides an excellent economic history of the interwar period.

The Bretton Woods System

In 1944, the International Monetary Fund (IMF) was created by an international agreement called the **Bretton Woods Agreement** because it was signed at Bretton Woods, New Hampshire. The participating countries agreed to an exchange rate regime that linked their exchange rates to the dollar. The dollar itself had a fixed gold parity ($35 per ounce).

The Bretton Woods Agreement grew out of a desire to avoid the monetary chaos of the interwar period. Fixed exchange rates were meant to provide stability and discipline, but the Great Depression had convinced the IMF's architects that fixed exchange rates should not come at the price of long-term domestic unemployment. Therefore, the IMF agreement incorporated some flexibility into the application of the fixed exchange rate system. Countries were allowed to devalue their currencies if they experienced "fundamental disequilibrium," a term that was never formally defined. Policymakers in different countries debated who should do the adjustments and who was at fault for protracted balance of payments deficits. In contrast, if a country encountered a temporary balance of payments problem (a current account deficit) that threatened its currency peg, it could draw on the lending facilities of the IMF to help it defend the currency.

Each IMF member contributed both gold and its own national currency to the fund. A member was entitled to use its own currency to temporarily purchase gold or foreign currencies from the fund equal in value to its gold contribution. Further gold or foreign currencies (up to a limit) could be borrowed from the fund, but only under increasingly stringent IMF supervision of the borrower's macroeconomic policies. This *IMF conditionality* (see also Chapter 1) is still applied to countries when they borrow from the IMF. The Bretton Woods Agreement allowed exchange rates to fluctuate in a 1% band around the chosen parity value.

Individual Incentives Versus Aggregate Incentives

Because the United States was required to trade gold for dollars with foreign central banks, it maintained large gold reserves. During the 1950s, the world demand for international reserves grew more rapidly than world gold supplies, and foreign countries happily accumulated interest-earning dollar international reserves without converting them into gold at the Federal Reserve. As these dollar claims became larger and larger relative to the size of the U.S. gold reserves, though, foreign confidence in the dollar–gold parity understandably fell. The market began to predict a devaluation of the dollar in terms of gold, which increased the incentive of individuals and central banks to hold gold, not dollars.

If individual foreign countries exercised their right to convert their dollar claims into gold, the United States would eventually not be able to honor all these requests and would be forced to abolish convertibility at $35 an ounce. Yet, if the aggregate of all countries did not ask to convert their dollar assets into gold, the system could continue indefinitely, with dollar assets forming the foundation of international reserves. Some countries, such as France, found this politically unacceptable.

Special Drawing Rights

In 1968, the IMF created special drawing rights (SDRs) as an alternative reserve asset with the same gold value as the dollar, in an attempt to provide an internationally acceptable asset other than the dollar. However, the United States kept running BOP deficits, and the pressure on the U.S. gold reserves continued to mount, prompting President Nixon to abolish the convertibility of the dollar into gold in August 1971.

An international agreement reached in December 1971 at the Smithsonian Institution in Washington, DC, devalued the dollar by about 8% relative to most other currencies, but speculation against the dollar continued. By March 19, 1973, the Bretton Woods system collapsed, and the currencies of Japan and most European countries began to float freely relative to the dollar.

The value of the SDR remained expressed in gold until 1976, after which it became a basket currency. Since then, gold has lost its official role in the international monetary system, although most central banks continue to keep part of their official reserves in the form of gold. The price of gold has fluctuated considerably over the years and exceeded $1,400 per ounce at the end of 2010.

Pegged Exchange Rate Systems in Developing Countries

As we saw in Exhibit 5.1, many developing countries have pegged exchange rate systems. It is often the case that the authorities in these countries set the exchange rate at a level that overvalues the local currency. This situation is opposite that in Exhibit 5.8, in which the equilibrium exchange rate is below the pegged value. Exhibit 5.10 repeats Exhibit 5.8 for the Malaysian ringgit, with S being 0.10 dollars per ringgit (10 ringgits to the dollar) and $\overline{S}$ being equal to 0.20 dollars per ringgit (5 ringgits to the dollar).

At 0.20 dollars per ringgit, there is an excess supply of Malaysian ringgits ($Q_S - Q_D$): Everybody wants to turn in ringgits to the central bank, receive dollars, and buy goods abroad or invest abroad. The fixed exchange rate overvalues the domestic currency (the ringgit) and undervalues the foreign currency (the dollar), thereby subsidizing buyers of foreign currency (such as importers and those investing abroad) and taxing sellers of foreign exchange (such as exporters and foreign buyers of domestic assets). (The *Point–Counterpoint* feature in this chapter further analyzes the ramifications of such an overvalued exchange rate.)

Needless to say, this situation is not tenable indefinitely. Because of the implicit tax on sellers of foreign exchange, exporters would fail to repatriate their foreign currency earnings, and because of the subsidies to buyers of foreign exchange, domestic residents would invest in foreign assets (a phenomenon known as capital flight; see Chapter 4). At the exchange rate the central bank wants to maintain (0.2 dollars per ringgit), the supply of ringgits to the central bank is larger than the demand for ringgits; or, equivalently, the demand for foreign currency from the central bank is larger than the supply of foreign currency to the central bank. The country runs a BOP deficit, and the central bank must artificially restore equilibrium by

Exhibit 5.10 Pegging an Exchange Rate in a Developing Country

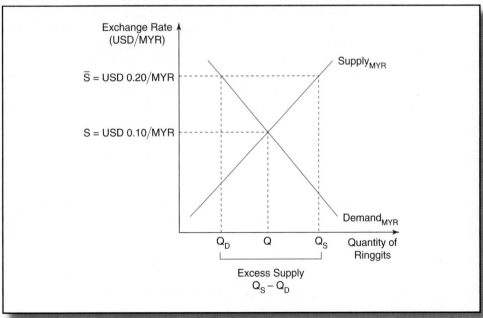

using its international reserves to satisfy the excess demand. If this situation persists, the central bank's foreign reserves will dwindle fast.

The only way to sustain such a system indefinitely is to impose exchange controls. The central bank of the developing country must ration the use of foreign exchange, manage who gets access to it, and restrict capital flows; in short, it must strictly control financial transactions involving foreign currencies. More often than not, most frontier and some emerging market country currencies are inconvertible, which makes the use of exchange controls easier.[7] Inconvertible currencies are primarily traded by the central bank of the country or by financial institutions with strict controls on their use of foreign currency.

Illegal Currency Markets

The private market response to the incorrectly valued exchange rate is often the development of an illegal or parallel currency market where foreign currencies command a higher domestic-currency price than the one offered by the central bank. The differences between official and illegal market rates can often be very large. For example, the Venezuelan government devalued the Bolivar Fuerte to VEF4.3/USD in January 2011, but in the parallel market, U.S. dollars sold for VEF9.25, more than double the official rate. Tourists sometimes take advantage of illegal market rates simply by selling dollars to informal dealers stationed in front of their hotel, but such activity can result in severe penalties.

Although maintaining capital controls may be feasible for inconvertible currencies, it is much harder for countries with freely traded currencies because the government can exert less direct control over the use of its currency. Nevertheless, capital controls were the norm in many European countries during the 1970s and 1980s (see Section 5.6).

POINT–COUNTERPOINT

The Burden of the Baguette

Freedy, Ante, and Suttle are in Paris, where they are visiting their cousin, Jean Patie, who grew up in France, received his MBA at Columbia Business School in May 1993, and then decided to go back to France. Jean suggested that they meet at Chez Jerry, a cozy bar on the Place du Tertre, and over a delightful glass of Sancerre, Ante asks Jean what life was like when Jean took his first job.

"Well," Jean begins, "I spent half of my time in Africa, as I was working for Painargent, a French company that exported sourdough baguettes to Africa. Their main markets were the 14 French-speaking countries in the Communauté Financière d'Afrique." "Hey," Freedy interjects, "we just learned about those countries in the international finance class that Ante and I are taking. Those countries all peg the CFA franc to the euro, right?" Jean responds, "Very good, Freedy. So, if you guys are such international finance hot shots, are you up for a little quiz?" Ante and Freedy respond enthusiastically, with shouts of "Bring it on," as Suttle just smiles.

Jean begins, "Well, when I left school, the CFA countries had been pegging their exchange rate versus the French franc, without devaluation, for an impressive 45 years. My bosses spoke volumes about how wonderful the stability of the fixed exchange rate was for business. Painargent even accepted CFA francs from the African importers because they were fully convertible into French francs at the fixed exchange rate. Because of the stability of the CFA franc's value, exchange rate issues really had not played any part in Painargent's business."

---

[7]A convertible currency is one that may be freely used in international transactions by citizens of any country. After World War II, Europe only restored currency convertibility (and then mostly only for current account transactions) in 1958.

Jean continued, "When I was hired, economic growth in the CFA region had recently lagged behind economic growth in other countries. Many in the region blamed an overvalued CFA franc, and some politicians were calling for a devaluation of the CFA franc relative to the French franc. These politicians noted that non-CFA neighbors Nigeria and Ghana had recently devalued their own currencies, which seemed to improve the competitiveness of their exports and provided additional jobs in their export industries. Nevertheless, some of my bosses expressed anger at those CFA *canailles* and said that devaluation would crush Painargent's profit margin." Ante and Freedy, remembering their international finance class, nod approvingly. Jean asks Ante, "What would devaluation mean for Painargent?"

Ante quickly responds, "A CFA devaluation would mean that every CFA franc Painargent earns would turn into fewer French francs, resulting in lower French franc revenues." Freedy, quick to show that he had been paying attention in class, adds, "A CFA devaluation would definitely have cut into Painargent's profits because its primary cost would be wages paid to French bakers, which would not be affected by the devaluation. Thus, profits would fall."

Jean then asks, "So, did the CFA countries devalue or not?" Ante agitatedly exhorts, "Surely they did not devalue! The system worked well for over 45 years, it brought stability to the region, and besides, devaluation would have been a disaster for too many people. Think of all the French companies, like Painargent, with assets, real and financial, in the CFA countries. It would have been devastating for them to have to endure devaluation!" Freedy is less sure. "If their currency was really overvalued, this would have put pressure on their foreign reserves because foreign goods would have appeared cheaper than domestic goods. People in the CFA countries would also have sold the overvalued currency and bought foreign exchange if they thought devaluation might occur. The central bank would have to supply that foreign exchange to keep the exchange rate fixed, but their reserves would have been limited. Devaluation was probably inevitable," he concludes.

While Ante and Freedy continue their heated discussion about the likelihood of devaluation, Jean notices that his other cousin, Suttle, has decided to join in. Suttle interjects, "Let's list who gains and who loses by the devaluation. Once we figure this out, it should be easy to infer what was likely to happen." Ante gushes, "Good idea! Here is why they would never devalue: French businesses such as Painargent would never tolerate the loss of stability and monetary discipline that the fixed CFA franc brought. Moreover, these firms would be willing to use a lot of political capital to prevent devaluation because such an event would mean an instant loss of wealth for these companies." Suttle nods. "You're right, but I think the decision to devalue was not entirely up to the French businesses. I think it is also important to think about the rich Africans, including the ones wielding political power and the civil servants. Devaluation would reduce their purchasing power abroad as the CFA franc would buy fewer French francs, and hence, fewer bottles of Moët & Chandon and fewer vacations in Saint-Tropez. It would also make French schools more expensive for their kids." Ante, now ecstatic, shouts, "And import prices would rise, which fuels inflation. It would also be harder for the CFA governments and firms to repay any debt denominated in foreign currency because it would cost more in local currency."

"Hold it," cries a surprisingly agitated Freedy. "A government simply cannot keep the exchange rate at what is clearly not its equilibrium value without severe exchange controls that would eventually cripple the country. If the CFA countries had lost their competitiveness relative to the countries with which they trade, a devaluation would make imports more expensive, but exports to the rest of the world would be cheaper, leading to a competitive edge for local businesses." Suttle notes, "Yes, that is true, too." Jean adds, "At the time, there were also lots of rumors of rich Africans spotted arriving in Marseilles with suitcases stuffed full of CFA francs that they immediately converted to French francs while the rate was good."

Freedy interjects, "Right, we learned that such capital flight removes critical capital, which could be used to finance development. Moreover, it is likely that the IMF and the World Bank probably were insisting on devaluation before they would lend more money to those countries."

"Hmmm, this is a hard one," Suttle admits. "I am not convinced that devaluation helps in the long run. After all, import prices will likely rise, and that in turn may put upward pressure on other prices and wages. If that is true, the competitive advantage for local firms gets squandered pretty quickly. In the short run, however, appropriate government policies can make sure the higher import prices do not filter through immediately into higher wage demands. I'm not sure I know how this one turned out," he muses.

Finally, Jean decides it is time to explain what happened. "Well, the devaluation happened shortly after I started working. In January 1994, the exchange rate was changed from 50 CFA francs per French franc to 100 CFA francs per French franc, a 100% increase in the value of the French franc relative to the CFA franc. The results of the devaluation were decidedly mixed. After years of dismal growth, the Ivory Coast, for example, started growing again, but in Cameroon, problems persisted, and inflation was rife.[8] The profitability of Painargent was definitely affected for a few years, but we persisted as best we could. We raised our baguette prices as much as we could, and we had to fire some of our bakers. We also started selling more in Nigeria."

Why Not Simply Float?

Why do countries go through the trouble of trying to keep the exchange rate fixed at a particular value instead of letting market forces determine the equilibrium value of their currency? As in the *Point–Counterpoint* feature, the political elite may prefer a strong exchange rate for their own private benefit, potentially to the detriment of the country's citizens. However, the economics profession has most definitely not reached a consensus about the choice of the exchange rate regime. The most-often-quoted advantages ascribed to fixed exchange rates can be summarized with two words: discipline and stability.

Discipline refers to the "straitjacket" that a fixed-rate regime imposes on fiscal and monetary policies. If a country with a fixed exchange rate runs higher inflation than its trading partners, it loses competitiveness (see Chapters 8 and 9). The fear of this occurring should discourage over-expansionary fiscal or monetary policies, which in turn, should keep inflation down. According to fixed-rate proponents, the currency volatility that characterizes floating exchange rates can hardly be beneficial for international trade. Fluctuating currencies make importers more uncertain about the prices they will have to pay for goods in the future and exporters more uncertain about the prices they will receive. Of course, this argument can be easily countered by noting that this risk can be rather cheaply hedged (for example, using forward contracts) and by noting that the stability offered by pegged exchange rate systems appears more illusory than real. In fact, the 1990s witnessed a number of important currency crises where speculators successfully attacked pegged currencies.

These currency crises are not isolated phenomena. Klein and Shambaugh (2008) examine the dynamics of exchange rate regimes in 125 countries over a 35-year period. The average duration of a fixed-rate regime is 4.67 years, and the median is only 2 years. Most fixed-rate periods end with a devaluation of the currency and a continuation of the pegged system, but often a new exchange rate regime is adopted. The risk that the currency will devalue plagues any system in which exchange rates are not allowed to trade at market values.

---

[8]See "After a Devaluation, Two African Countries Fare Very Differently," 1995; and Amegbeto and Winter-Nelson, 1998.

If pegged systems have such short durations and devaluations occur frequently, can they really be expected to yield the benefits of inflation credibility and exchange rate stability the authorities expect? Although Klein and Shambaugh argue that fixed-rate regimes effectively lower exchange rate volatility, many believe that such systems are doomed to fail. In recent times, a number of governments have resorted to an alternative monetary system, the currency board, which enhances the credibility of the peg. In their quest for exchange rate stability, the European Union (EU) countries went one step further and established a monetary union, where one central bank issues one currency for all the participating countries. Other countries have adopted the currency of a larger country, a phenomenon known as *dollarization*. We discuss currency boards and dollarization next but defer the discussion of monetary unions to Section 5.6, where we survey Europe's experimentation with different currency arrangements.

Currency Boards

A currency board is a type of fixed exchange rate system, a monetary institution that issues base money (notes and coins and required reserves of financial institutions) that is fully backed by a foreign reserve currency and fully convertible into the reserve currency at a fixed rate and on demand. Hence, the domestic currency monetary base is 100% backed by assets payable in the reserve currency. In practical terms, this requirement bars the currency board from extending credit to either the government or the banking sector. Exhibit 5.11 shows the balance sheet of a currency board.

In the past, currency boards have existed in more than 70 countries. The first currency board was established in the British Indian Ocean colony of Mauritius in 1848, and currency boards were subsequently adopted in many British colonies and a few other countries. However, when those countries became independent after World War II, most of them decided to replace their currency boards with central banks. More recently, currency boards have been adopted by Hong Kong (since 1983), Argentina (1991 to 2001), and Estonia (1992 to 2010).

In recent policy debates, currency boards are often mentioned as a miracle cure for cutting inflation without high costs to the economy. The main success story is Hong Kong (see Kwan and Liu, 2005). The Hong Kong Monetary Authority has kept the Hong Kong dollar at HKD7.8/USD since 1983, and it successfully weathered the Southeast Asian currency crisis of 1997. Argentina's experience offers a cautionary tale. Argentina's Convertibility Law of April 1991 instituted a currency board. In the 1980s, inflation in Argentina averaged 750.4% per year; in the 1990s, inflation averaged 2.4% per year. The reason some believe a currency board imparts more monetary credibility than a conventional exchange rate peg is that a currency board has no discretionary powers. Its operations are completely passive and automatic. It cannot lend to the government and hence cannot monetize fiscal deficits. This also means that a currency board cannot rescue banks when they get into trouble. In other words, a currency board cannot function as a lender of last resort.

It has to be said that the practical implementations of currency boards are not always this strict. For example, the reserve requirements for Argentine banks were quite high; hence, the central bank could inject liquidity into the banking system by lowering reserve requirements, and it did so following the Mexican crisis in 1994.

Exhibit 5.11 The Balance Sheet of a Currency Board

Assets	Liabilities
International reserves	Currency in circulation
	Required reserves of financial institutions

Whether a currency board is more credible than a standard pegged exchange rate system is hard to determine from the limited historical experiences we have. Speculators attacked the Argentine peso in the wake of the Mexican currency crisis, and they attacked the Hong Kong dollar in the wake of the Southeast Asian currency crisis, but the currency boards survived. As always in speculative crises, interest rates did increase, and the economies suffered. Whether other systems would have generated smaller economic costs is difficult to guess.

Argentina's good luck did not last. While Argentina enjoyed the success of a seemingly well-functioning currency board, its government was able to borrow at competitive rates, and the country's public debt grew substantially. In addition, a crisis in Brazil in 1999 led to a large devaluation of the Brazilian real, making Argentine exports less competitive. Also, the dollar was strong relative to the euro, which undermined the competitiveness of Argentine exports to Europe. The Argentine economy began to sputter, with economic growth becoming negative, making the public debt burden suddenly seem much less sustainable. In mid-2001, the government started to tinker with the currency board (introducing a special exchange rate for international trade transactions, for example) in the hope of improving Argentina's international competitiveness. But the policy changes only managed to further undermine the confidence of investors in the sustainability of the currency board.

Argentina had trouble meeting interest payments on its international bonds, and in November 2001, the country effectively defaulted on its international debt. This led to a bank run by Argentine citizens, who dumped their pesos in favor of dollars. The government responded by restricting bank deposit withdrawals. Soon the country was engulfed in a deep economic crisis, with looting and rioting accompanying close to 20% unemployment rates.

In January 2002, the new interim president of Argentina, Eduardo Duhalde, abandoned the currency board and devalued the peso to 1.4 pesos per dollar for most transactions, while allowing all other transactions to be made at market rates. Other ill-devised temporary measures to deal with the crisis (converting debts denominated in dollars to debts denominated into pesos, for example) only further deepened the economic crisis. The year 2002 was disastrous for Argentina: Output collapsed, and inflation increased to double-digit levels. The idea that a currency board entailed no currency risk was buried with it. The peso was eventually allowed to float, and it depreciated to over 3.5 pesos per dollar.[9]

Dollarization

Interestingly, Argentina's Minister of Finance, Domingo Cavallo, who was the architect of the Convertibility Plan, ascribed Argentina's initial success in controlling inflation and maintaining the exchange rate peg not as much to the currency board as to the dual-currency feature of the system. During the hyperinflation of the 1970s, Argentina's money was superseded by the U.S. dollar. The phenomenon of foreign currencies (often the dollar) driving out local currencies as a means of payment (at least for big transactions) and a savings vehicle is known as **dollarization**.[10]

"Unofficial" dollarization occurs when residents of a country extensively use foreign currency alongside or instead of the domestic currency. The foreign currency often is the U.S. dollar, as is the case in much of Latin America, but it can also be another currency, such as the euro, as is often true in southeastern Europe. Researchers at the Federal Reserve gauge the extent of unofficial dollarization by estimating the use of dollars by nonresidents. They estimate that foreigners hold 55% to 70% of U.S. dollar notes.

"Official" dollarization occurs when foreign currency has exclusive or predominant status as full legal tender. In Andorra, a small country in the Pyrenees, the euro is legal tender.

---

[9]See Dornbusch (2001) for more detail about the pros and cons of currency boards.

[10]Kurt Schuler maintains a Web site with information on dollarization and currency boards (http://users.erols.com/kurrency). Edwards and Magendzo (2003) provide a rather skeptical view of the economic benefits of dollarization.

Unofficial Dollarization Turns Official: The Disappearance of the Zimbabwe Dollar

Before January 2009, the Zimbabwe dollar was nominally pegged relative to the U.S. dollar, but it was devalued regularly. Mugabe's regime not only mismanaged the economy, causing a decline in GDP per capita of over 75% in the course of a decade, but it also made ample use of the printing press, generating inflation. At the end of 2001, inflation in Zimbabwe reached over 100% per month; by the end of 2008, it reached astronomical levels, over 450 billion percent per month! The hyperinflation not only sent the exchange rate of Zimbabwe dollars per dollar to astronomical levels in the parallel market, but people also simply stopped using the worthless Zimbabwe dollar bills, resorting to several international currencies instead. In January 2009, the Zimbabwe government made dollarization official by abolishing the Zimbabwe dollar and rendering the U.S. dollar, the British pound, the euro, the South African rand, and the Botswanan pula legal tender. What made the introduction of the multicurrency system inevitable was that the payment systems of the banking sector and the central bank could no longer cope with the increased volumes and multiple digits in the transaction values that had to be handled.

Similarly, the 1991 Convertibility Law in Argentina officially condoned the use of the dollar, allowing Argentines to open checking and savings accounts and to conduct most transactions in the currency of their choice.

Most officially dollarized countries, however, are tiny, using the currency of the "mother" country from colonial times or from a large neighboring country. Kiribati, a Polynesian island, for example, uses the Australian dollar, but it issues its own coins. The largest and most well-known dollarized country is Panama, where dollarization has existed since 1904. Ecuador (in 2000) and El Salvador (in 2001) have also officially adopted the U.S. dollar as their currency. In contrast to a currency board, a dollarized system can no longer collect seigniorage. This may discourage larger countries such as Mexico and Argentina from adopting such a system.

5.5 LIMITED-FLEXIBILITY SYSTEMS: TARGET ZONES AND CRAWLING PEGS

In between fixed and floating exchange rate systems are systems where exchange rate fluctuations are kept within a certain range.

Target Zones

The Bretton Woods system in effect between 1944 and 1971 is an example of a **target zone system**. Whereas the dollar was fixed relative to gold (at $35 per ounce), all other currencies had particular dollar par values (a specified exchange rate versus the dollar), but the actual exchange rates were allowed to move within a range of 1% on either side of these par values. The most famous target zone system in recent times is the European Monetary System (EMS), and, given its historical importance, we discuss it in greater detail later.

To see how a target zone operates, consider Exhibit 5.12, which once again looks at the French franc–Deutsche mark (FRF/DEM) exchange rate between early 1987 and August 1993. Although the exchange rate shows substantial variability, it fluctuates within a band until the very end of that period. The EMS specified a central parity of FRF3.3539/DEM, but the exchange rate was allowed to fluctuate in a 2.25% band around this value.

Exhibit 5.12 An Example of a Target Zone

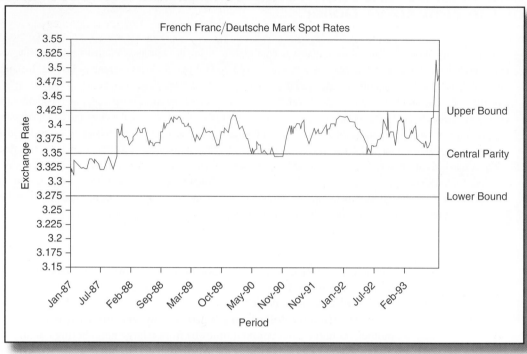

French Franc/Deutsche Mark Spot Rates

Example 5.2 Determining the Intervention Exchange Rates

Let's use the FRF/DEM information to determine the intervention exchange rates. With a central parity of FRF3.3539/DEM, the monetary authorities need to determine the exchange rates for the upper and lower intervention limits such that the band is a 2.25% band around the central parity. The computation also must guarantee that the width of the band is the same, no matter how the exchange rates were expressed (in FRF/DEM or DEM/FRF).

Let S be the central parity in FRF/DEM, let the upper intervention limit be $(1 + y)S$, and let the lower intervention limit be $S/(1 + y)$. Clearly, expressing exchange rates in DEM/FRF by taking reciprocals results in the same intervention points. Then, because the width of the band is 4.5% of the central parity, we can solve the following equation for y:

$$(1 + y)S - S/(1 + y) = 0.045S$$

The solution is $y = 0.022753$. Thus, the upper value of the band is $1.022753 \times$ (FRF3.3539/DEM) = FRF3.4302/DEM, and the lower value of the band is (FRF 3.3539/DEM)/1.022753 = FRF 3.2793/DEM.

During this period, francs and marks were freely traded in the forex market. What keeps the actual exchange rate in the prespecified band? As long as private market participants deem the central rate reasonable and recognize a credible commitment by the monetary authorities to defend the rate, market participants will not expect the currency value to go outside the bands, and no currency crisis will occur. A previously announced strategy of monetary policy is *credible* if it remains an optimal strategy for the central bank over time. A strategy will continue to be optimal if it is more costly for policymakers to abandon their commitment to the strategy rather than to honor it. Unless a strategy is credible, the private sector's expectations and consequent behavior will not support the strategy's goal, and it will not be achieved.

Hence, a crucial element for the stability of a target zone system is the perception on the part of investors and speculators that the authorities are committed to defend their exchange rate. This holds all the more for a pegged exchange rate system, which can be thought of as a target zone with a very thin band. From our description of how a central bank functions, we know that such an exchange rate target necessarily means that the authorities will not be able to use monetary policy to reach other goals, such as pushing the economy toward full employment. When the commitment of the authorities becomes less certain—for example, because of unfavorable domestic economic conditions—a currency can come under pressure and move toward the edge of the band. In Exhibit 5.12, the franc is the weak currency when the exchange rate approaches the higher edge of the band.

Although Denmark is a member of the EU, the Danes did not vote to adopt the euro. Policymakers have chosen, though, to remain in the Exchange Rate Mechanism II that requires specification of a central parity and allows for deviations of ±2.25%. Exhibit 5.13 shows that in recent years the Danish National Bank has actually kept the spot rate very close to the central parity of DKK7.46038/EUR. The maximum deviation is only 0.30%, which has prompted the IMF to classify the Danish krone as a pegged currency.

Speculative Attacks

Policymakers invariably blame downward pressure on the foreign exchange value of their currency on nasty speculators. We will discuss speculation explicitly in Chapter 7, so here we just give a verbal description. During a speculative attack, speculators hope to profit from a devaluation of the currency or a resetting of the bands of a target zone by massively borrowing the weak currency and investing the proceeds in assets (typically short-term money market instruments) denominated in the strong currency. If the amount of the devaluation exceeds any differential between the interest they pay and the interest they receive, speculators win.

Exhibit 5.13 A Tight Target Zone

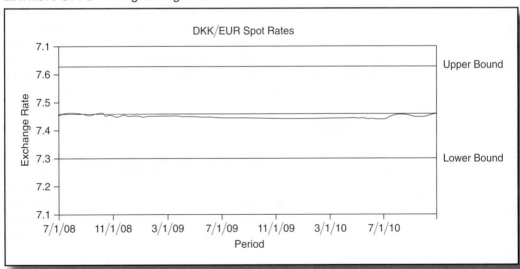

Defending the Target Zone

To defend their currency, the monetary authorities in the countries with weaker currencies have three basic mechanisms available. First, they can simply intervene in the currency markets. When a central bank intervenes to support its currency, it buys its own currency with official reserves. An intervention by the central bank of the weak currency country, if not sterilized, reduces the money supply. The reduced liquidity in the money market tends to put upward pressure on interest rates. This raises the costs of speculators (which include financial institutions), who try to borrow the money to invest abroad.

The second defense mechanism of the central bank is to raise the interest rates they control (typically, the rate at which banks can borrow at the central bank), both to make currency speculations more costly and to signal commitment to the central rate.[11] The behavior of central banks and private market participants results in higher short-term interest rates, which drive up the cost of speculation. The magnitude of the interest rate hike needed to stave off a speculative attack depends on the probability that the currency will devalue and hence on the credibility of the authorities.

Although a policy of high interest rates discourages speculation, it also increases the short-term funding costs for businesses borrowing money, which is a drag on the economy. Not surprisingly, many countries resort to a third line of defense: limiting foreign exchange transactions through capital controls. At the simplest level, the authorities may tax or simply prohibit the purchase of most foreign securities by the country's residents. At one time, Italy and Spain, countries that had participated in the EMS, forced purchasers of foreign currency or foreign assets to make a non-interest-bearing deposit at their central banks equal to 50% of the value of the foreign investment. Such rules considerably increase the cost of speculation but at a loss of freedom for the citizens of the country.

Lead–Lag Operations

Most countries with capital controls also impose restrictions on trade financing. Whereas currency speculation may conjure up images of wicked financiers plotting the fall of a currency behind a computer screen, often a more serious problem arises from the financing practices of exporters and importers. In international business, it is customary for exporters to allow their customers to pay some time after the goods have been shipped or even after they have arrived. When devaluation is expected, exporters from the country tend to extend the maturity of these "trade credits" (because they hope to exchange currency they receive for a greater amount of local currency than they could have before the devaluation). This is called a **lag operation** because it postpones the inflow of foreign currency. Conversely, domestic importers prepay for goods that they plan to purchase from abroad in order to beat the increase in costs the devaluation will impose on them. This effectively grants a credit to foreign exporters and is therefore called a **lead operation**. Lead and lag operations often put pressure on the foreign reserves of the central bank because the volume of foreign trade is large relative to the reserves of the central bank for small open economies.

Crawling Pegs

In many developing countries, where inflation is especially a problem, the bands have been allowed to move ("crawl") over time. Such mini-devaluations or resets of the bands take place quite frequently, sometimes even daily, and are mostly preannounced.

To understand the logic behind this system, you must understand the effects of inflation on a quasi-fixed exchange rate system. (These issues are addressed in more detail in Chapters 8 and 9.) Consider the example of Mexico and the United States. Suppose the Mexican

---

[11]Earlier, we argued that monetary authorities can set the rate of money growth, unless they focus on another policy goal, in which case money growth becomes endogenous (see Section 5.2).

central bank wants to fix the Mexican peso's value relative to the dollar, as it has tried to do many times in the past. If the exchange rate remains fixed, and Mexico experiences higher inflation than the United States, it loses competitiveness because the prices of Mexican goods increase relative to the prices of U.S. goods. The resulting reduction in Mexican exports to the United States is likely to hurt Mexico's economy severely because the United States is its largest trading partner.

Knowing the perverse effects of the loss of competitiveness that high inflation entails, governments should be motivated to follow non-inflationary policies. Hence, the fixed exchange rate can potentially buy inflation credibility, and Mexico can "import" low inflation from the United States by pegging its currency to the U.S. dollar. Again, credibility is important, and in developing countries, maintaining the same level of inflation as in developed countries is a tall order. Also, the consequences of the loss of competitiveness are particularly dire. Anticipating a gradual loss of competitiveness, a **crawling peg** system adjusts the fixed rate or band over time, where the adjustment is often a function of the inflation differential between the developing country and the country to which its currency is pegged.

Exhibit 5.14 illustrates such a policy. From November 1, 1991, to December 21, 1994, the Mexican peso traded within a formal intervention band set by the Bank of Mexico relative to the dollar. The floor of the band remained fixed at MXP3.052/USD, while the upper band rose (allowing for peso depreciation) at a predetermined rate: increasing at MXP0.0002/USD per day from November 11, 1991, to October 20, 1992, and MXP0.0004/USD per day from October 21, 1992, to December 21, 1994. The history of the crawling peg in Mexico ended with the famous currency crisis in December 1994 and early 1995.

Exhibit 5.14 An Example of a Crawling Peg

It turns out that the changes in the band did not fully correct for the inflation difference between the United States and Mexico, and Mexican firms gradually lost competitiveness. With a large current account deficit and insufficient capital inflows, Bank of Mexico intervention in the foreign exchange market was necessary. By December 1994, international reserves had dwindled until they were almost depleted. An attempt to devalue the peso by 15% in December only caused a run on the currency, and Mexico was forced to float the peso. Currently, the Mexican peso floats freely. Costa Rica has successfully run a crawling band system (relative to the USD) since 2006, but the currency did come under pressure in 2010, causing the central bank to intervene. The problem was not that the colón was too weak but too strong, as the dollar depreciated substantially against many emerging currencies during 2010.

5.6 How to See an Emu Fly: The Road to Monetary Integration in Europe

One of the most important financial developments in recent years is the emergence of the economic and monetary union (EMU), with the euro as a common currency, first for 11 countries and now for 17 countries. All 27 countries in the EU are eligible to join the monetary union if they comply with certain monetary requirements. Although the United Kingdom and Denmark participated in the Maastricht Treaty (discussed later) and the European Monetary System (EMS), they negotiated exemptions from the requirement that they adopt the euro as their currency. Any country joining the EU since the 1993 implementation of the Maastricht Treaty has had to pledge to adopt the euro in due course.

Because the euro did not arrive overnight, this section chronicles the history of currency systems in Europe, starting with the EMS and leading to the introduction of the euro. We also discuss the economic issues related to whether countries should use a common currency—what economists term the "optimum currency area" issue. When the euro was initially proposed, some economists voiced concern that Europe was not an optimal currency area. The problems that were predicted took 10 years to manifest themselves, but the sovereign debt crisis of 2010 has led some economists to predict the eventual dismantling of the euro. The history of the euro may hold important lessons for other regions of the world that may set up similar currency systems. In particular, regional associations of countries promoting free trade and other forms of economic and political cooperation in Latin America (Mercosur), Asia (the ASEAN countries), and Africa (the East African Community [EAC] countries) are prime candidates for a similar currency arrangement sometime in the foreseeable future.[12]

The European Monetary System (EMS)

The desire for currency stability in Europe dates back many decades. It was actively pursued in the context of the European Community (EC). One reason these countries desired monetary stability is that most western European countries are not only quite open to foreign trade but their main trading partners are also their neighboring countries, making costs of exchange rate variability particularly acute within Europe. Another reason the EC countries wanted to limit exchange rate fluctuations was to facilitate the operation of a common market for agricultural products. Finally, the desire for stable exchange rates in Europe should also be

---

[12]The Mercosur countries are Argentina, Brazil, Paraguay, and Uruguay, whereas Bolivia, Chile, Colombia, Ecuador, and Peru have associate member status. The ASEAN countries are Brunei Darussalam, Cambodia, Indonesia, Laos, Malaysia, Myanmar, the Philippines, Singapore, Thailand, and Vietnam. The EAC countries are Burundi, Kenya, Rwanda, Tanzania, and Uganda.

viewed as an integral part of the wider drive toward economic, monetary, and political union between European countries in the EC.

From 1944 to 1973, stability was supplied by the Bretton Woods system of fixed exchange rates. Although old plans to establish a monetary union got bogged down during the breakup of the Bretton Woods system, the EC countries kept their currencies in a target zone system and eventually established the **European Monetary System (EMS)** in 1979. All EC countries joined, although Britain, characteristically, did not fully participate until 1990. The EMS had three components: the Exchange Rate Mechanism (ERM), a set of intervention rules and intervention financing mechanisms, and a set of rules for realignments. We discuss each in turn.

The ERM

The ERM was a grid of bilateral fixed central parities, from which exchange rates could deviate by 2.25% on each side, with the exception of the Italian lira, which was allowed a margin of 6%.

Intervention Rules

Interventions by both central banks were compulsory whenever either bilateral margin was reached. The central bank of the strong currency was required to grant the central bank of the weak currency an unlimited credit line to assist in the defense of its currency. Of course, a central bank could intervene to support its currency before the outer limits were reached, which happened quite frequently.

Realignment Rules

When the bilateral central parity could not be sustained at reasonable cost, the finance ministers of the EMS countries gathered secretively to establish new central parities, devaluing the weaker currencies and revaluing the stronger currencies.

ECUs, Euros, and Franken

The central parities were expressed in terms of the **European Currency Unit (ECU)**, which was a currency basket, consisting of specified amounts of each member currency. Exhibit 5.15 presents the last composition of the ECU basket, which was fixed in 1989, after which the Maastricht Treaty prevented any changes. Consequently, the currencies of countries joining the EC later were never part of the ECU basket. The amounts of the different currencies were revised every 5 years to reflect the economic importance of each country.

Exhibit 5.15 also reports the central parities expressed in terms of the ECU. Using the ECU as the numeraire obviates the need for a complex bilateral grid of central rates. For example, knowing the exchange rates of FRF/ECU and DEM/ECU provides the FRF/DEM central parity:

$$(FRF6.63186/ECU)/(DEM1.97738/ECU) = FRF3.35386/DEM$$

However, the actual exchange rates differed from the central parities because exchange rates only needed to stay within a 2.25% band around the central rates. This also meant that the market weights in the ECU basket could differ from the official weights. In fact, with the basket amounts fixed, stronger currencies slowly gained weight in the basket.

Apart from its role as a numeraire, the ECU was the unit of account for all interventions and thus came to serve as a reserve asset for transactions among the EC's central banks. In addition, some companies used the ECU for invoicing and in their financial statements, and contracts denominated in ECUs became important in financial markets. Banks offered ECU-denominated deposits and loans, bonds were issued in ECU, and derivative contracts traded on exchanges allowed traders to bet on the direction of ECU interest rates. As a consequence,

Exhibit 5.15 Composition of the ECU Basket

Currency	Amounts of Currencies Included in the ECU Basket[a]	ECU Central Rates[b]	Relative Weight of Each Currency in the ECU Basket (in %)	
			9-21-89	10-22-98
Deutsche mark	0.6242	1.97738	30.09	31.57
French franc	1.332	6.63186	19.00	20.08
British pound	0.08784	0.653644	13.00	13.44
Italian lira	151.8	1957.61	10.16	7.75
Dutch guilder	0.2198	2.22799	9.40	9.87
Belgian and Luxembourg franc	3.431	40.7844	7.89	8.41
Spanish peseta	6.885	168.22	5.31	4.09
Danish krone	0.1976	7.54257	2.45	2.62
Irish punt	0.008552	0.796244	1.10	1.07
Portuguese escudo	1.393	202.692	0.80	0.69
Greek drachma	1.44	357	0.80	0.41

[a]As of September 21, 1989.
[b]As of October 23, 1998.
Note: Data are from the Bank for International Settlements.

banks started to quote ECU-denominated exchange rates without strict reference to its synthetic value—that is, the value of the ECU in terms of the market value of the constituent currencies. Soon, this "private" ECU no longer necessarily had a 1 to 1 value with the market-determined value of the basket of currencies.

The Treaty of Maastricht in 1991, which mapped out the road to monetary integration, named the ECU as the single European currency, and when the single currency came into existence, on January 1, 1999, its external value was set equal to the theoretical value of one ECU. However, the new currency was not called the ECU, but the euro. This is somewhat surprising because the name "euro" confusingly added to a list of existing but quite different "Euro-financial assets" such as Eurobonds and Eurocurrencies (see Chapter 11).

The Politics of Naming the Euro

The seemingly insignificant issue of the single currency's name is a nice illustration of the amazing development in Europe that brings together very different cultures in one monetary arrangement. Despite the familiarity of Europeans with the ECU and its use in scores of financial contracts, the Germans, who were very attached to their beloved Deutsche mark, felt that the name "ECU" sounded too French. The name of an old French coin also was the écu. Rumor has it that to ensure that the name "euro" would replace the name "ECU," the Germans pushed for an alternative name, the "Franken." Appalled, the French agreed to a compromise.

Was the EMS Successful?

The main goal of the EMS was to reduce exchange rate volatility and consequently to narrow inflation and interest differentials between countries. Was it successful?

Day-to-Day Variability Was Down

Overall, the EMS record was mixed. First, although the day-to-day variability of European exchange rates decreased beginning in 1979, large currency movements still occurred because of realignments and the currency crises of 1992 to 1993. The realignments were frequent at first, but they became less frequent over the years. Interestingly, the Deutsche mark never devalued during the history of the EMS. With the exception of the Dutch guilder, the currencies of other countries in the EMS fell by more than 20% relative to the Deutsche mark through seven realignments in the early 1980s.

Inflation and Interest Differentials Narrowed

Although inflation and interest rate differentials narrowed during the EMS period, the EMS might not have been the main cause of the narrowing. For instance, inflation cooled down in most countries around the world during the 1980s. After the currency realignments mentioned earlier, two traditionally weak currencies, the Belgian franc and the Danish krone, actually became "hard" currencies.

A country's monetary and fiscal authorities practice a hard currency policy when they try to prevent their currency from depreciating by maintaining staunch anti-inflationary monetary and fiscal policies. The benefit of such a policy in the context of the EMS was lower interest rates, which meant important interest rate savings for a high public debt country such as Belgium. Unfortunately, the Maastricht Treaty started a period of currency turmoil that peaked in September 1992, when the pound and the lira were forced to leave the system. This currency turmoil led to a widening of the bands to 15% on each side of the central parities in August 1993.

Asymmetric Adjustments

The original plans for the EMS envisioned a symmetric system with the ECU as the center of the EMS and the adjustment burden in times of crises shared across countries. An anatomy of the realignment episodes and the turbulent events in the 1990s strongly indicates an asymmetric system with an anchor role for the Deutsche mark. That is, the Bundesbank, the German central bank, maintained the purchasing power of the Deutsche mark, and the other countries adopted monetary and financial market policies that were consistent with maintaining a stable exchange rate vis-à-vis the Deutsche mark. In tense and speculative times, countries with weak currencies intervened in the currency markets and increased their interest rates.

Some claim the system proved beneficial to inflation-prone countries, such as Italy and France, by improving the credibility of authorities in pursuing non-inflationary policies. The EMS made it costly for an economy to experience inflation because it led to an erosion of the competitiveness of the country's currency between realignments. It could also lead to a permanent erosion of competitiveness if the realignment didn't compensate fully for the inflation that had occurred, which was often the case. Others admit that the Bundesbank played a central and at times disciplinary role in the EMS, but they believe that in times of crises, the Bundesbank stubbornly stuck to its policies, even if that put the entire adjustment burden on the other countries. For example, the Bundesbank only intervened when it was required to do so according to the EMS rules.

The Maastricht Treaty and the Euro

In 1991, the European heads of state met in Maastricht in the Netherlands to map out the road to economic and monetary union, including a single EC currency, to be reached by 1999. When a number of countries establish a **monetary union**, they fix their exchange rates relative to one another, possibly by introducing a single currency, and they establish a single central bank to conduct a single monetary and exchange rate policy across the region. The Maastricht Treaty specified a number of criteria that member countries had to satisfy in order to be able to join the monetary union. These "convergence criteria" were to be measured 1 year before the start of the EMU and were as follows:

1. Inflation within 1.5% of that of the three best-performing states.
2. Interest rate on long-term government bonds within 2% of the long-term interest rates of the three best-performing countries in terms of inflation.
3. A budget deficit of less than 3% of gross domestic product.
4. Government debt less than 60% of gross domestic product.
5. No devaluation within the exchange rate mechanism within the past 2 years.

The convergence criteria garnered a lot of controversy, and the fiscal criteria almost became a stumbling block for the EMU. At one point, only one country readily qualified for EMU entry—tiny Luxembourg—and even Germany barely made it.

The road to EMU was completed in three stages. In Phase I, all remaining restrictions on the movement of capital and payments between member states and between member states and third countries were removed. This phase was completed by January 1, 1994.

In Phase II, a new European Monetary Institute (EMI) was created, with headquarters in Frankfurt, Germany, to administer the EMS and prepare the ground for the European Central Bank to be established in Phase III by strengthening the coordination of monetary policies of the member states. Phase II also introduced EC supervision of fiscal policy of the member states and forbade monetary financing of budget deficits. Central banks of the member countries were also made politically independent.

In Phase III, the European Central Bank (ECB) replaced the EMI. The European System of Central Banks (ESCB), composed of the ECB and the national central banks, conducts monetary and exchange rate policy for the whole of the single-currency area. Its primary objective, as specified in the Maastricht Treaty, is to maintain price stability. This phase started on January 1, 1999, at which time the conversion rates into the euro were fixed. The first 11 countries were Austria, Belgium, Finland, France, Germany, Ireland, Italy, Luxembourg, Netherlands, Portugal, and Spain. The United Kingdom and Denmark opted out. To join, a country must satisfy the convergence criteria, and the following countries have joined: Greece (2001), Slovenia (2007), Cyprus and Malta (2008), Slovakia (2009), and Estonia (2011).

ERM II

When a country joins the EU, it negotiates a time at which it joins the ERM II, which requires that the country establish a central parity for its currency versus the euro and pledge to remain within a ±15% band. In practice, countries keep their currencies in a much tighter band, as Exhibit 15.13 demonstrates.

If a country successfully keeps its currency within the ERM II band for 2 years and satisfies the other Maastricht criteria, it is eligible to adopt the euro as its currency and become a member of the **eurozone**. The EMU may eventually include most countries in Europe and may inspire other regions to form monetary unions, but are they really a good idea?

Pros and Cons of a Monetary Union

Since the signing of the Maastricht Treaty, economists have heatedly debated whether monetary union in Europe makes economic sense. The debate typically centers on the question of whether Europe is, or is not, an optimum currency area.

Optimum Currency Areas

In 1961, Robert Mundell, a Nobel Laureate, published a theory of **optimum currency areas**. Mundell defines an optimum currency area as one that balances the microeconomic benefits of perfect exchange rate certainty against the costs of macroeconomic adjustment problems.

Sharing a currency across a border enhances price transparency (prices are easier to understand and compare across countries), lowers transactions costs, removes exchange rate uncertainty for investors and firms, and enhances competition. A currency union may therefore promote trade and economic growth.

The potential cost of a single currency is the loss of independent monetary policies for the participating countries. Losing this monetary independence is especially grave if a region is likely to suffer from *asymmetric economic shocks*. Asymmetric shocks can include a sudden fall in demand for a country's main export product or sudden increases in the prices of the main inputs for a country's manufacturing sector, where the shocks affect that country differently from the other countries in the single-currency area. In a monetary union, the affected country no longer has the ability to respond to economic shocks by relaxing its monetary policy.

The country also cannot devalue its currency. The inability to react with monetary policy is thought to deepen recessions and exacerbate unemployment. Rockoff (2003) notes that such problems plagued different regions of the United States especially in the 19th century.

These problems became apparent in 2010 when the financial markets realized that Greece, Ireland, Portugal, and Spain were experiencing much deeper recessions than Germany. The Organization for Economic Cooperation and Development (OECD) reports that unemployment in Germany in 2010 was 6.9%, compared to Portugal's 10.7%, Greece's 12.2%, Ireland's 13.6%, and Spain's 19.8%. The fall in income during a recession also manifests itself in government budget deficits. In 2010, Germany's budget deficit as a percentage of GDP was 4%, compared to Portugal's 7.3%, Greece's 8.3%, Spain's 9.2%, and Ireland's 32.3%. The optimum currency area theory concludes that for a currency area to have the best chance of success, asymmetric shocks should be rare. This is likely to be the case when the economies involved face similar business cycles and have similar industrial structures. Failing that, other mechanisms must absorb the shocks. This requires mobility of labor and capital or a central fiscal authority that has the power to make transfers across regions.

An analogy to the United States is useful. For example, if California experiences lower demand from Asia, which increases unemployment in California, while Texas booms due to high oil prices, workers moving from California to Texas can restore unemployment rates back to normal. Labor mobility is enhanced if wages are flexible because wages would be increasing in Texas and decreasing in California. Moreover, federal fiscal transfers to California may help it get out of the economic doldrums.

Is Europe an Optimum Currency Area?

Many prominent U.S. economists conclude that Europe is not particularly well suited to be a monetary union: The shocks hitting European countries are quite asymmetric; labor mobility is very limited due to cultural, linguistic, and legal barriers between countries; and the EC budget is too small to transfer huge resources into recessionary areas. An adjustment to a bad shock requires a relative price change, which could be more quickly accomplished, if countries had separate currencies, by an exchange rate change.

Nevertheless, substantial academic research documents sizable economic benefits following the introduction of the euro in terms of price convergence, lower costs of capital, and increased trade.[13] None of the articles have incorporated the very recent data though. The severity of the recessions following the 2007 to 2010 global financial crisis and the lack of an overall European fiscal authority led to the sovereign debt crisis of 2010. Greece was the first to encounter problems funding its budget deficit when the new government announced in late 2009 that the previous government had understated the magnitude of the deficit by 50%. Confronted with a possible Greek default, European finance ministers and the IMF cobbled together a €110 billion package of loans for Greece on May 2, 2010, forcing Greece to announce cutbacks in government services and increases in taxes. On May 4, riots erupted throughout Athens. Problems came to a head later in 2010 for Ireland as the ramifications of Ireland's bailout of its banking system during the financial crisis led to its massive budget deficit and the prospect of an Irish default. While Irish politicians initially fought a bailout from the EU, they eventually agreed on November 28 to a €67.5 billion rescue deal.

Proponents of the EMU argue that the skeptics have too much confidence in the real effects of monetary or exchange rate policy. They argue that devaluing a currency may only cause local inflation, and the competitive advantage gained may be very temporary. Furthermore, the proponents question the effectiveness of labor mobility as a shock absorber, even in the United States. The theory talks about temporary business cycle shocks that would require

---

[13]The literature is reviewed in Baldwin (2006) and Bekaert et al. (2010). One concern with much of the literature is that the benefits ascribed to the single currency may simply reflect the benefits of economic (not monetary) integration. See Silva and Tenreyro (2010) for a skeptical view on the economic benefits of the euro.

a temporary movement into regions where work is abundant and productivity high, and vice versa. But even in the United States, such a temporary migration of workers across states is unlikely to occur on a large scale because moving is so costly.

The ability of a central fiscal authority to make transfers across regions in the United States has also come into question. By the end of 2010, many U.S. states including California, Illinois, New Jersey, and New York faced large fiscal deficits that were leading some economists to forecast that there would be defaults on state and municipal debt. The presence of a federal fiscal authority with its 2009 stimulus package had allowed these states to put off the hard issues of how they were going to balance their budgets, but in 2011, it seemed unlikely that Congress would agree on further bailouts.

On the other hand, the leaders of the EU realized that a sovereign default would possibly wreak havoc in European government debt markets and engulf the region in an even worse recession. To avoid this fate, the 27 members of the EU agreed to the creation of the European Financial Stability Facility, which has the ability to borrow up to €440 billion with the backing of all EU governments in order to lend to a country in financial difficulty. These funds can be combined with €60 billion of funds from the EU budget and €250 billion from the IMF for a total of €750 billion.

The backing of these loans is proportional to the capital contributed by each country to the ECB. Thus, Germany's share is 27.13%. Should some of these loans end up in default, German tax payers would be shouldering a burden that they might not enjoy. Of course, the German banking system also holds substantial amounts of the debts of the troubled countries, so the German tax payers may be forced to do a bank bailout if they abandon the euro. It is this tension that has economists discussing situations in which the euro unravels. Others argue that Europe's troubles will only force the countries into greater cooperation and integration.

5.7 SUMMARY

This chapter has analyzed the large variety of currency arrangements around the world. The main points in the chapter are the following:

1. There are three main exchange rate systems: floating exchange rates, target zones, and pegged or fixed exchange rate systems. Different systems entail different currency risks.
2. Currency risk can be summarized by a forward-looking conditional distribution of exchange rate changes and the distribution's volatility (dispersion) and skewness. This distribution depends on the exchange rate system and is more difficult to estimate when currencies are not freely floating.
3. The government, through its central bank, controls the money supply. When too much money is issued relative to the demand for money, inflation results.
4. The central bank's balance sheet contains currency in circulation and reserves held by financial institutions as its main liabilities. Together, these are called base money. The assets of the central banks are foreign currency–dominated securities (official international reserves), domestic government bonds, and loans to the domestic financial sector.
5. When a currency is freely floating, no official reserves are needed, but in reality, pure freely floating exchange

rate systems do not exist. Instead, governments either intervene to influence a currency's value (dirty float) or formally try to peg the exchange rate (fixed exchange rate system) or limit its variability within certain bands around a central value (target zone or crawling peg when the bands are automatically reset over time).
6. In dirty float systems, forex interventions are often sterilized; that is, the central bank performs an open market operation that counteracts the effect of the original intervention on the money supply. There is no consensus on whether central banks can really affect the level and volatility of exchange rates through their interventions.
7. To peg a currency, the government must make a market in foreign currencies buying any private excess supply of foreign currency and delivering additional foreign currency if there is excess private demand for it.
8. The impossible trinity or trilemma holds that there is an intrinsic incompatibility between perfect capital mobility, fixed exchange rates, and domestic monetary autonomy.
9. After World War II, countries adopted the Bretton Woods system of fixed exchange rates, based on gold and the dollar. This system lasted until 1971.

10. Currently, many developing countries peg their exchange rates, often at unrealistically high values. Devaluations and currency crises resulting in changes in the exchange rate regime occur regularly. To increase credibility, a number of governments have introduced currency boards, where base money is backed 100% by foreign currency–denominated assets.

11. The most important historical example of a target zone is the European Monetary System, which operated between 1979 and 1999. Exchange rates were maintained between bands of 2.25% around central parities.

12. The EU experimented with various exchange rate systems in an attempt to limit exchange rate variability. Since 1999, 17 countries in Europe are now joined in a monetary union with a single currency, the euro, and a single monetary policy.

QUESTIONS

1. How can you quantify currency risk in a floating exchange rate system?
2. Why might it be hard to quantify currency risk in a target zone system or a pegged exchange rate system?
3. What is likely to be the most credible exchange rate system?
4. How can a central bank create money?
5. What are official international reserves of the central bank?
6. What is likely to happen if a central bank suddenly prints a large amount of new money?
7. What is the effect of a foreign exchange intervention on the money supply? How can a central bank offset this effect and still hope to influence the exchange rate?
8. How can a central bank peg the value of its currency relative to another currency?
9. Describe two channels through which foreign exchange interventions may affect the value of the exchange rate.
10. What was the Bretton Woods currency system?
11. How do developing countries typically manage to keep currencies pegged at values that are too high? Who benefits from such an overvalued currency? Who is hurt by an overvalued currency?
12. What are the potential benefits of a pegged currency system?
13. Describe two different currency systems that have been introduced in countries such as Hong Kong and Ecuador to improve the credibility of pegged exchange rate systems.
14. What is the difference between a target zone and a crawling peg?
15. How can central banks defend their currency—for example, if the currency is within a target zone or pegged at a particular value?
16. What was the EMS?
17. What is a basket currency?
18. What did the Maastricht Treaty try to accomplish?
19. What is an optimum currency area?
20. Do you believe its monetary union will be beneficial for Europe?
21. Do you think the euro will survive?

PROBLEMS

1. Toward the end of 1999, the central bank (Reserve Bank) in Zimbabwe stabilized the Zimbabwe dollar, the Zim for short, at Z$38/USD and privately instructed the banks to maintain that rate. In response, at the end of 1999, an illegal market developed wherein the Zim traded at Z$44/USD. Are you surprised at rumors that claim corporations in Zimbabwe were "hoarding" USD200 million? Explain.

2. In Chapter 3, we described how exchange rate risk could be hedged using forward contracts. In pegged or limited-flexibility exchange rate systems, countries imposing capital controls sometimes force their importers and exporters to hedge. First, assuming that forward contracts are to be used, and an exporter has future foreign currency receivables, what will the government force him to do? Second, how does this help the government in defending their exchange rate peg?

3. In years past, Belgium and South Africa operated a two-tier, or dual, exchange rate market. The two-tier market was abolished in March 1990 in Belgium and in March 1995 in South Africa. Import and export transactions were handled on the official market, and capital transactions were handled on the financial market, where the "financial" exchange rate was freely floating. Discuss why such a system may prevent speculators from profiting when betting on a devaluation.

4. The kuna is the currency of Croatia. Find the Web site of Croatia's central bank and determine the exchange

rate system Croatia runs. Suppose the kuna weakens substantially relative to the euro. Which action can the central bank take to keep its currency system functioning properly?

5. Type "People's Bank of China" into your favorite search engine and go to the English versions of the Web site. Under "Statistics," find the Balance Sheet of the Monetary Authority. Calculate the growth rate of base money and the growth rate of international assets for the past few years. How much foreign exchange intervention is China doing? Are they sterilizing it?

BIBLIOGRAPHY

"After a Devaluation, Two African Countries Fare Very Differently," May 10, 1995, *Wall Street Journal.*

Aizenman, Joshua, Menzie D. Chinn, and Hiro Ito, 2010, "The Emerging Financial Architecture: Tracing and Evaluating the New Patterns of the Trilemma's Configurations," *Journal of International Money and Finance* 29, pp. 614–641.

Amegbeto, Koffi, and Alex Winter-Nelson, 1998, "Currency Devaluation and Resource Mobilization. A Computable General Equilibrium Analysis of Adjustment in Cameroon," *Review of Development Economics* 2, pp. 94–105.

Baldwin, Richard E., 2006, "The Euro's Trade Effects," ECB Working Paper.

Beine, Michel, Jerome Lahaye, Sebastien Laurent, Christopher J. Neely, and Franz C. Palm, 2007, "Central Bank Intervention and Exchange Rate Volatility, Its Continuous and Jump Components," *International Journal of Finance and Economics* 12, pp. 201–224.

Bekaert, Geert, and Stephen Gray, 1998, "Target Zones and Exchange Rates: An Empirical Investigation," *Journal of International Economics* 45, pp. 1–45.

Bekaert, Geert, Campbell Harvey, Christian Lundblad, and Stephan Siegel, 2010, "The European Union, the Euro and Equity Market Integration," working paper.

Dominguez, Kathryn M. E., 2006, "Why Do Central Bank Interventions Influence Intra-Daily and Longer-Term Exchange Rate Movements," *Journal of International Money and Finance* 25, pp. 1051–1071.

Dominguez, Kathryn, and Jeffrey Frankel, 1993, "Does Foreign Exchange Intervention Matter? The Portfolio Effect," *American Economic Review* 83, pp. 1356–1369.

Dornbusch, Rudiger, 2001, "Fewer Monies, Better Monies," *American Economic Review* 91, pp. 238–242.

Edwards, Sebastian, and I. Igal Magendzo, 2003, "Dollarization and Economic Performance: What Do We Really Know?" *International Journal of Finance and Economics* 8, pp. 351–363.

Eichengreen, Barry, 1992, *Golden Fetters: The Gold Standard and the Great Depression, 1919-1939*, Oxford, U.K.: Oxford University Press.

Friedman, Milton, 1953, "The Case for Flexible Exchange Rates," *Essays in Positive Economics*, Chicago: University of Chicago Press, pp. 157–203.

Galati, Gabriele, and Philip Wooldridge, 2009, "The Euro as a Reserve Currency: A Challenge to the Pre-Eminence of the Dollar," *International Journal of Finance & Economics* 14, pp. 1–23.

Jeanne, Olivier, and Romain Ranciere, 2009, "The Optimal Level of International Reserves for Emerging Market Countries: A New Formula and Some Applications," Johns Hopkins Working Paper.

Klein, Michael W., and Jay C. Shambaugh, 2008, "The Dynamics of Exchange Rate Regimes: Fixes, Floats and Flips," *Journal of International Economics* 92, pp. 70–92.

Kwan, Yum K., and Francis T. Liu, 2005, "How Well Has the Currency Board Performed? Evidence from Hong Kong," Chapter 10, in Y. K. Kwan and Eden S. M. Yu, eds., *Critical Issues in China's Growth and Development*, Aldershot, U.K.: Ashgate Press.

Menkhoff, Lukas, 2010, "High Frequency Analysis of Foreign Exchange Interventions: What Do We Learn?" *Journal of Economic Surveys* 24, pp. 85–112.

Mishkin, Frederic S., 2010, *The Economics of Money, Banking, and Financial Markets*, 9th ed., Boston: Addison-Wesley.

Mundell, Robert, 1961, "A Theory of Optimum Currency Areas," *The American Economic Review*, LI, No. 4, pp. 509–517.

Neely, Christopher J., 2008, "Central Bank Authorities' Beliefs About Foreign Exchange Intervention," *Journal of International Money and Finance* 27, pp. 1–25.

Obstfeld, Maurice, and Jay C. Shambaugh, 2005, "The Trilemma in History: Tradeoffs Among Exchange Rates, Monetary Policies, and Capital Mobility," *Review of Economics and Statistics* 87, pp. 423–438.

Papaioannou, Elias, Richard Portes, and Gregorios Siourounis, 2006, "Optimal Currency Shares in International Reserves: The Impact of the Euro and the Prospects for the Dollar," *Journal of the Japanese and International Economies* 20, pp. 508–547.

Pasquariello, Paolo, 2010, "Central Bank Intervention and the Intraday Process of Price Information in the Currency Markets," *Journal of International Money and Finance* 29, pp. 1045–1061.

Rockoff, Hugh, 2003, "How Long Did It Take the United States to Become an Optimal Currency Area," in Forrest H. Capie and Geoffrey E. Wood, eds., *Monetary Unions: Theory, History, Public Choice*, London: Routledge.

Silva, João, M.C. Santos, and Silvana Tenreyro, 2010, "Currency Unions in Prospect and Retrospect," *Annual Review of Economics* 2, pp. 51–74.

Wang, Yongzhong, 2010, "Effectiveness of Capital Controls and Sterilizations in China," *China and the World Economy* 18, pp. 106–124.

Chapter 6

Interest Rate Parity

In January 2011, Brazilian real-denominated Treasury bill rates exceeded 11%, whereas U.S. Treasury bill rates were less than 20 basis points. Why would U.S. investors accept such low returns when they could invest in Brazil? First and foremost, U.S. investors face transaction foreign exchange risk when investing in a Brazilian security. The Brazilian real might weaken, wiping out the interest gain. If investors hedge this risk, the relative return on Brazilian Treasury bills versus U.S. Treasury bills is driven by four variables: the Brazilian interest rate, the spot and forward exchange rates, and the U.S. interest rate. After hedging, perhaps the dollar return on the Brazilian Teasury bill looks much lower.

Interest rate parity describes a no-arbitrage relationship between spot and forward exchange rates and the two nominal interest rates associated with these currencies. The relationship is called **covered interest rate parity**. This chapter shows that interest rate parity implies that forward premiums and discounts in the foreign exchange market offset interest differentials to eliminate possible arbitrage that would arise from borrowing the low-interest-rate currency, lending the high-interest-rate currency, and covering the foreign exchange risk. Interest rate parity is a critical equilibrium relationship in international finance. However, it does not always hold perfectly, and we discuss why, which will bring us back to the Brazilian example above.

The availability of borrowing and lending opportunities in different currencies allows firms to hedge transaction foreign exchange risk with money market hedges. We demonstrate that when interest rate parity is satisfied, money market hedges are equivalent to the forward market hedges of transaction exchange risk that were presented in Chapter 3. Moreover, we can use interest rate parity to derive long-term forward exchange rates. Knowledge of long-term forward rates is useful in developing multiyear forecasts of future exchange rates, which are an important tool in the valuation of foreign projects.

6.1 THE THEORY OF COVERED INTEREST RATE PARITY

In international money markets, the interest rate differential between two currencies approximately equals the percentage spread between the currencies' forward and spot rates. If this is not the case, traders have an opportunity to earn arbitrage profits. In this section, we first derive intuition for this interest rate parity relationship using a number of examples, and then we derive it formally. We end the section by illustrating how an arbitrage would result when the parity relationship is violated. For students rusty on concepts related to interest rates, the box titled *The Time Value of Money* in this chapter provides a brief review.

Example 6.1 Kim Deal's Investment Opportunities

Let's consider the situation of Kim Deal, a portfolio manager at BNP Paribas, a French bank. Kim is trying to decide how to invest €10 million, and she must choose between 1-year euro deposits and 1-year yen investments. In the latter case, she knows she must worry about transaction foreign exchange risk, but she also understands that she can use the appropriate forward contract to eliminate it.

Suppose Kim has the following data:

EUR interest rate:	3.5200% per annum (p.a.)
JPY interest rate:	0.5938% p.a.
Spot exchange rate:	¥146.0300/€
1-year forward exchange rate:	¥141.9021/€

Which of these investments should Kim choose to get the highest euro return?

To do the analysis, let's first calculate the euro return from investing in the euro-denominated asset. If Kim invests €10,000,000 at 3.52%, after 1 year, she will have

$$€10,000,000 \times 1.0352 = €10,352,000$$

Next, let's calculate the euro return if Kim invests her €10,000,000 in the yen-denominated asset. This analysis requires three steps:

Step 1. Convert the euro principal into yen principal in the spot foreign exchange market. The €10,000,000 buys

$$€10,000,000 \times (¥146.03/€) = ¥1,460,300,000$$

at the current spot exchange rate.

Step 2. Calculate yen-denominated interest plus principal. Kim can invest her yen principal at 0.5938% for 1 year. Hence, Kim knows that in 1 year, she will have a return of yen principal plus interest equal to

$$¥1,460,300,000 \times 1.005938 = ¥1,468,971,261$$

Step 3. Hedge the transaction exchange risk with a 1-year forward contract.

Kim knows that if she does nothing today to eliminate the transaction foreign exchange risk, she will sell the ¥1,468,971,261 at the future spot rate in 1 year to get back to euros, and she will bear the foreign exchange risk that the yen weakens relative to the euro. Kim also realizes that this unhedged investment does not have the same risk characteristics as the euro-denominated bank investment. The unhedged investment is subject to foreign exchange risk; the euro investment returns a sure amount of euros. As we saw in Chapter 3, the transaction foreign exchange risk can be eliminated by selling yen forward for euros. In this case, Kim would contract to sell ¥1,468,971,261 for euros at the 1-year forward rate of ¥141.9021/€. In 1 year, she would receive

$$¥1,468,971,261/(¥141.9021/€) = €10,352,005$$

So, even though she has the opportunity to invest euros at 3.52% versus investing yen at 0.5938%, Kim is slightly better off making the yen-denominated investment and covering the foreign exchange risk. But the difference between the two euro returns is an additional €5 of interest on €10,000,000 after 1 year for the yen investment, and this is 5 thousandths of a basis point. We conclude that the two returns are essentially the same.

The Intuition Behind Interest Rate Parity

Forward exchange rates allow investors to contract to buy and sell currencies in the future. Because the future value of one unit of currency depends on the interest rate for that currency, the forward exchange rate must be linked to the current spot exchange rate and to the nominal interest rates in the two currencies. Interest rate parity relates the spot and forward exchange rates and the nominal interest rates denominated in the two currencies. Instead of memorizing a formula that requires you to remember which way spot and forward rates are quoted, think of interest rate parity as the equality of the returns on comparable money market assets when the forward foreign exchange market is used to eliminate foreign exchange risk. With interest rate parity satisfied in Example 6.1, the two euro-denominated returns were equal.

Interest rate parity holds if markets are efficient and there are no government controls to prevent arbitrage. In the absence of these conditions, traders could make an extraordinary profit via **covered interest rate arbitrage**. Once again, the term *covered* means the investment is not exposed to transaction foreign exchange risk. The return Kim Deal obtained by investing in yen, for example, and "covering" the yen exchange rate risk is sometimes called the *covered yield*. The next example demonstrates how to exploit the covered yield if interest rate parity is not satisfied.

Example 6.2 Kevin Anthony's Arbitrage Opportunity

Suppose Kevin Anthony has $10,000,000 to invest, and he faces the following data: USD interest rate, 8.0% p.a.; GBP interest rate, 12.0% p.a.; spot exchange rate, $1.60/£; and 1-year forward exchange rate, $1.53/£. Doing the calculations analogous to Example 6.1 indicates that if Kevin invests $10,000,000 in the dollar asset at 8%, he will have

$$\$10,000,000 \times 1.08 = \$10,800,000$$

If Kevin converts his $10,000,000 into pounds at the current spot exchange rate, he'll get

$$\$10,000,000/(\$1.60/£) = £6,250,000$$

which he can invest at 12% to get

$$£6,250,000 \times 1.12 = £7,000,000$$

of pound principal plus interest. Selling this amount forward gives a dollar return of

$$£7,000,000 \times (\$1.53£) = \$10,710,000$$

So, even though Kevin has the opportunity to invest in pounds at 12% versus investing dollars at 8%, he is better off making the dollar-denominated investment. But would Kevin stop there?

Let's allow Kevin to borrow or lend at the dollar interest rate of 8% and the pound interest rate of 12%. Now, instead of simply choosing to invest in dollars instead of pounds, Kevin can borrow pounds and invest in dollars. Does it make sense for him to do this?

For each £1,000,000 that Kevin borrows, in 1 year he will owe

$$£1,000,000 \times 1.12 = £1,120,000$$

Let's see how many pounds he will have after 1 year if he converts the pound principal to dollars in the spot market, invests the dollars at 8%, and covers the foreign exchange risk by selling the dollar interest plus principal in the forward market. Once again, this takes three steps:

Step 1. Convert from pounds to dollars at the spot rate of $1.60/£:

$$£1,000,000 \times (\$1.60/£) = \$1,600,000$$

Step 2. Calculate dollar interest plus principal at 8%:

$$\$1,600,000 \times 1.08 = \$1,728,000$$

Step 3. Cover the foreign exchange risk by engaging in a forward contract to sell the dollar interest plus principal at $1.53/£:

$$\$1,728,000/(1.53/£) = £1,129,411.76$$

The covered interest arbitrage produces a riskless profit of

$$£1,129,411.76 - £1,120,000.00 = £9,411.76$$

for every £1,000,000 that is borrowed.

If interest rates and spot and forward exchange rates were actually as they are in Example 6.2, many banks and investors would borrow pounds, convert to dollars, invest the dollars, and sell the dollar interest plus principal in the forward market for pounds. This arbitrage activity would quickly eliminate the profit opportunity. The additional demand to borrow pounds would drive up the pound interest rate. The sale of pounds for dollars would lower the dollar–pound spot exchange rate. The lending of dollars would lower the dollar interest rate, and the forward purchase of pounds with dollars would raise the dollar–pound forward exchange rate. Each of these movements would reduce the arbitrage profits that are present at the current prices.

The Time Value of Money

Interest rates provide market prices for buying and selling a given currency between different points in time. If you sell someone a dollar for 1 year (that is, you lend them $1), they must pay you $1 plus the 1-year dollar interest rate after 1 year. Similarly, if you buy pounds from someone today, promising payment in pounds in 1 year (that is, you borrow pounds), the price paid in 1 year for £1 today is £1 plus the 1-year pound interest rate. Thus, interest rates provide prices for moving currencies between different time periods. Interest rates are therefore said to be the *time values* of monies.

The two fundamental concepts associated with the time value of money are **present value** and **future value**. The following are examples of each.

Example 6.3 Lisa Dowling's Lottery Choices

Suppose Lisa Dowling has just won the London daily lottery and has been offered a choice of prizes. The lottery is willing to pay her either £100,000 today or £110,000 in 1 year. Suppose that London banks are paying 11% interest on deposits for the next year. Which offer should she accept and why?

First, we know that if Lisa deposits £100,000 in the bank today, she will receive an amount of pounds in 1 year, denoted FV (for future value), equal to

$$FV = £100,000 + 0.11 \times £100,000 = £100,000 \times 1.11 = £111,000$$

$$FV = \text{Return of Principal} + \text{Interest on Principal}$$

We say that £111,000 is the future value in 1 year of £100,000 today when the interest rate is 11% p.a. Because this is more than the lottery has promised her in 1 year, she should take the money today.

An alternative way to analyze Lisa's choice is to ask how much money she must set aside today if she wants to have £110,000 in 1 year. This approach calculates the present value (PV) of the future cash flow promised by the lottery. We want to know the amount of pounds, denoted PV, that is equal to £110,000 in 1 year after Lisa earns interest on the PV pounds at 11% p.a. Algebraically, we have

$$PV \times 1.11 = £110,000$$

Solving for PV gives the present value of the future pounds:

$$PV = £110,000/1.11 = £99,099.10$$

$$PV = \frac{\text{Future Value}}{1 + \text{Interest Rate}}$$

Lisa's decision is still the same. She should take the £100,000 today. If she wants to have £110,000 in 1 year, she can deposit £99,099.10 in the bank, and she can spend the residual £900.90 today. When interest rates appear in the denominator of a present value relation, as in the formula here, they are called **discount rates**. Both present value analysis and future value analysis lead Lisa to the same solution. This is true in all problems involving the time value of cash flows, whether they are denominated in pounds, dollars, or yen. Because the interest rates denominated in different currencies are not the same, we must use an interest rate quoted on a particular currency to understand the time value of that currency.

Deriving Interest Rate Parity

A General Expression for Interest Rate Parity

Now let's consider the derivation of interest rate parity in algebraic terms. Our goal is to derive an expression that summarizes the relationship between the interest rates denominated in two different currencies and the spot and forward exchange rates between those currencies when there are no arbitrage opportunities in the money markets. The notation is as follows:

i = the domestic currency interest rate appropriate for one period
i^* = the foreign currency interest rate appropriate for one period
S = the spot exchange rate (domestic currency per foreign currency)
F = the one-period forward exchange rate (domestic currency per foreign currency)

Consider an investor who has one unit of domestic currency and two alternative investments at time t.

Alternative 1: Invest one unit of domestic currency. Get $\left[1 + i\right]$ units of domestic currency (the return of the principal plus interest) after the investment period.

where the dollar interest rate is $i(\$)$, the pound interest rate is $i(£)$, and the units of the exchange rates are dollars per pound. In numbers, we had

$$1 + 0.08 > \frac{1}{\$1.60/£} \times (1 + 0.12) \times (\$1.53/£) = 1.071$$

Example 6.2 drew out the implication of Equation (6.6). Investors facing these interest rates and exchange rates would be able to profit by borrowing pounds, converting the pounds into dollars in the spot market, investing the dollars, and contracting in the forward market to cover the foreign exchange risk by selling the dollar amount of principal plus interest. To see this, multiply both sides of the inequality in Equation (6.6) by S and by $[1/F]$ to get

$$S \times [1 + i(\$)] \times [1/F] > [1 + i(£)]. \qquad (6.7)$$

The right-hand side of the inequality in Equation (6.7) is the cost per pound to an investor who borrows pounds. For Kevin Anthony, this was £1.12. The left-hand side is the pound return per pound invested from converting the borrowed pound into dollars, investing the dollars, and contracting to sell dollar interest plus principal forward for pounds. For Kevin, the transaction would yield £1.1294. The inequality indicates that there is an arbitrage possibility at these interest rates and exchange rates, amounting to 0.94 pounds per £100 borrowed in Kevin's case.

Because the lending return is greater than the borrowing cost, a covered interest arbitrage opportunity would be available. Everyone would want to borrow an infinite amount of pounds, convert those pounds to dollars, invest the dollars, and sell the dollars forward for pounds. Clearly, such interest rates and exchange rates would not be in equilibrium.

A Box Diagram

The idea of covered interest arbitrage can be represented in a box diagram that is similar to the diagrammatic representation of triangular arbitrage in Exhibit 2.7. Exhibit 6.1 presents a box diagram that represents covered interest arbitrage.

In Exhibit 6.1, each node represents either dollars or pounds today or dollars or pounds in 1 year. As in Exhibit 2.7, the arrows indicate the direction of movement from one node to another, and they are labeled with the associated revenue or price in terms of the currency at the final node as a result of delivering one unit of currency at the initial node. The interest rates provide the prices for moving monies between today and the future. The exchange rates provide the prices for moving from one currency to another currency either today for the spot rate or in the future period for the forward rate.

For example, if you are at the node representing pounds today and you move 1 pound to the future, the future pound revenue is $[1 + i(£)]$. You invested 1 pound and earned interest. Similarly, if you place yourself at the dollar node in the future, and you move 1 dollar to the present, you receive $\frac{1}{1 + i(\$)}$ dollars in the current period. Obtaining dollars today with payment of dollars in the future is equivalent to borrowing dollars today. You will owe interest plus principal on your loan. In order for the repayment to be $1, you borrow only $\frac{1}{1 + i(\$)}$ today. If you are at the node representing dollars today and move to pounds today, you receive $\frac{1}{S(\$/£)}$ pounds for 1 dollar, and if you are at the future pound node and move to the future dollar node, you get $F(\$/£)$ dollars for your 1 pound.

In the covered interest arbitrage of Example 6.2, we moved clockwise around the box, starting from the future pound node. We first bought current pounds (that is, we borrowed a fraction of a pound by promising to repay 1 pound in the future) and used the borrowed pounds to buy dollars today, yielding the dollar principal of $\frac{S(\$/£)}{1 + i(£)}$. We then sold our

Exhibit 6.1 Diagram of Covered Interest Arbitrage

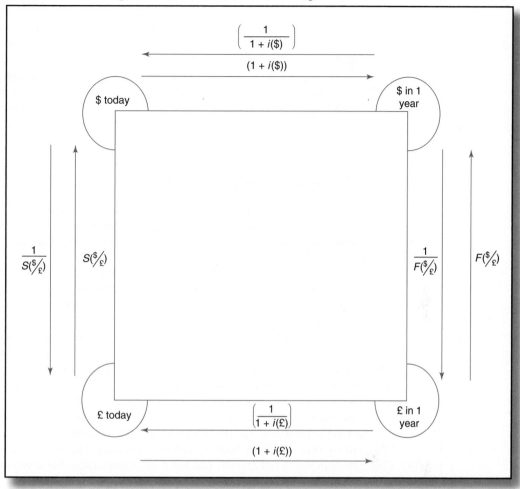

Note: The exchange rates and interest rates associated with each arrow indicate the funds obtained in the currency at the arrow's point from selling one unit of the currency at the arrow's tail. For example, at the $ today node, selling 1 dollar for $ in 1 year gives $(1 + i(\$))$ dollars in 1 year.

current dollars for dollars in the future (by investing the dollars today), and we sold future dollars for future pounds by using a forward contract. This set of transactions made a profit.

If we start at the future pound node by selling 1 pound and move completely around the box in a clockwise direction, selling the amount of currency that we have at each node, our total revenue is found by multiplying the four prices of selling one unit together:

$$(\text{Current } \pounds/\text{Future } \pounds) \times (\text{Current } \$/\text{Current } \pounds) \times (\text{Future } \$/\text{Current } \$)$$

$$\times (\text{Future } \pounds/\text{Future } \$) = \left[\frac{1}{1 + i(\pounds)}\right] \times [S(\$/\pounds)] \times [1 + i(\$)] \times \left[\frac{1}{F(\$/\pounds)}\right] \quad \text{(6.8)}$$

If interest rate parity is not satisfied, the right-hand side of Equation (6.8) gives us more than 1. (To see this, divide both sides of the inequality in Equation (6.7) by the value on its right-hand side.) We made a profit when we did the arbitrage because we were able to sell 1 pound in the future for more than 1 pound in the future. You should convince yourself that, with these prices, you could start at any node and move around the box in the clockwise direction to make a profit because the price of one unit starting at any node is always more than 1 with this particular violation of interest rate parity.

Covered interest arbitrage not only requires transacting in the foreign exchange market, but also borrowing and lending. This is typically done in the *external currency market*, the interbank market most closely related to the foreign exchange market. To evaluate the possibility of arbitrage opportunities, we must take transaction costs into account. In addition to the bid–ask spreads in the foreign exchange markets, arbitrageurs also face transaction costs in the external currency market. The lending rate that banks charge their customers is above the rate that the banks are willing to pay on deposits. We now discuss how transaction costs affect covered interest rate parity.

The External Currency Market

The **external currency market** is a bank market for deposits and loans that are denominated in currencies that are not the currency of the country in which the bank is operating. Its settlement procedures are identical to those of the foreign exchange market, and its interest rates flicker on the same computer screens.

The first of these deposits and loans were called eurodollars because they were dollar-denominated deposits at European banks. Although the external currency market was once limited to eurodollars, the idea quickly spread. Now, there are external currency markets for many currencies in financial centers around the world. A few of the examples include pound-denominated deposits and loans made by banks in Frankfurt, euro deposits and loans made by banks in Hong Kong or Tokyo, and yen deposits and loans made by banks in Paris or New York. Many market participants still use the terminology *euro-currency* for this market, but given its international nature and especially the emergence of the euro as a currency, *external currency market* now seems more appropriate.

One reason that the external currency market continues to grow is that the banks accepting the deposits and making the loans are subject to the regulations of the government of the country in which the bank is operating, not the government of the country that issues the money in which the deposits and loans are denominated. These regulations include how much banks must keep on reserve with their nation's central bank (see Chapter 5). Because reserve requirements are often lower for foreign currency deposits than for domestic currency deposits, banks can lend out a larger part of these deposits. Thus, the foreign currency deposits are potentially more profitable.

The demand by domestic banks to meet the foreign competition from the external currency market has also resulted in some government authorities allowing external currency deposits that are internal to the country issuing the currency. In short, the domestic bank gets to act like a foreign bank in the domestic country. For example, U.S. financial regulations allow U.S.–chartered depository institutions to establish international banking facilities (IBFs) that accept dollar deposits from and make dollar loans to noncitizens of the United States. The IBF is not a separate physical or legal entity, but its asset and liability accounts are segregated from the rest of the bank's. The IBF's accounts are subject to different regulations and reserve requirements.

Transaction Costs in the External Currency Market

In practice, the reduced regulatory burden and the strong competition in the external currency market have resulted in very small spreads between the interest rates at which banks are willing to pay for deposits and the interest rates that banks charge for loans. This has lowered transaction costs. Exhibit 6.2 provides borrowing and lending rates from the *Financial*

Exhibit 6.2   Interest Rates in the External Currency Market

			Currency					
			USD	EUR	GBP	JPY	CAD	CHF
Maturity	1 Month	Bid	0.27	0.73	0.56	0.05	0.95	0.01
		Ask	0.57	0.88	0.76	0.30	1.05	0.30
	3 Month	Bid	0.33	0.96	0.73	0.30	1.05	0.29
		Ask	0.58	1.06	0.93	0.40	1.15	0.39
	6 Month	Bid	0.53	1.19	1.04	0.25	1.56	0.43
		Ask	0.83	1.31	1.24	0.46	1.88	0.55
	1 Year	Bid	0.91	1.35	1.46	0.46	1.80	0.56
		Ask	1.11	1.65	1.76	0.58	1.90	0.68

Note: Data are from the *Financial Times,* January 19, 2011.

Times for January 18, 2011. For example, at the 3-month maturity, banks are willing to make Canadian dollar (CAD) loans at 1.15% (ask rate) and accept CAD deposits at 1.05% (bid rate). These interest rates are quoted in percentage points per annum. The spread is therefore 10 basis points. To determine the appropriate interest rate for a 3-month basis, we must "de-annualize" the quoted interest rates by dividing by 100 (to convert from a percentage quotation to a decimal value) and then multiply by the fraction of a year over which the investment is made.

Most annualized external currency interest rates are based on a 360-day year, except for the pound sterling, which is quoted on a 365-day year. The interest received is the annualized interest rate multiplied by the ratio of actual days of deposit to the postulated number of days in a year. Thus, if the 3-month CAD deposit actually corresponds to 90 days, the de-annualized deposit interest rate is

$$1.05 \times (1/100) \times (90/360) = 0.002625$$

For the 3-month CAD borrowing rate, the de-annualized interest rate is

$$1.15 \times (1/100) \times (90/360) = 0.002875$$

Hence, for each CAD1,000,000 that you deposit, you would receive

$$CAD1,000,000 \times 1.002625 = CAD1,002,625$$

in principal and interest after 90 days, and for each CAD1,000,000 you borrow, you would owe

$$CAD1,000,000 \times 1.002875 = CAD1,002,875$$

in 90 days. If you borrowed first and then deposited, you would lose CAD250, or 0.0250%, of your principal in the two transactions, which is a bid–ask spread comparable to the ones in the foreign exchange market. Notice that this bid–ask spread is simply one-fourth of the quoted annualized spread of 0.10%.

These deposit and lending quotations are available in the interbank market on the same telecommunications networks as the spot and forward quotations discussed in Chapters 2 and 3. The minimum amount traded in the external currency markets is typically $1 million. The maximum amount varies because lending banks limit the amount they lend to borrowing banks, depending on their default risk.

How the External Currency Market Affects Other Capital Markets

External currency quotations in the interbank market form the basis for the interest rates at which investors and corporations can borrow and lend. An investor or a corporation that wants to participate in this market depositing funds typically earns less than the interbank rate. For example, in Exhibit 6.2, banks accept 3-month CAD deposits at 1.05% in the interbank market, but the deposit interest rate available to a corporate customer may be 10 basis points less, or 0.95%.

The lending rate that banks and other financial intermediaries charge investors and corporations is typically quoted as a fixed spread or margin over the external currency market interbank lending rate. The spreads depend on the borrower's creditworthiness. For example, in Exhibit 6.2, the 3-month CAD interbank lending rate is 1.15%. If a corporation's spread over the interbank rate is 0.50%, the corporation would borrow at 1.65% = 1.15% + 0.50%.

The most important interbank reference rates are calculated daily in London by the British Bankers' Association (BBA) for 10 currencies and 15 maturities ranging from overnight to 1 year. Each currency's interest rate is known as the **London Interbank Offer Rate (LIBOR)** for that currency. The BBA officially defines USD LIBOR as the "trimmed" arithmetic mean of 16 multinational banks' interbank offered rates; that is, only the eight middle rates are used in calculating the mean. These rates are sampled at approximately 11:00 A.M. London time.[1] Other currency LIBORs are calculated using the middle half of the rates quoted from eight, 12, or 16 banks. Borrowing agreements involving corporations and sovereign nations often specify that the interest rate on a loan is a fixed spread over LIBOR. The determination of the spread depends on the possibility that the borrower will default on the loan. We examine these issues in detail in Chapter 14. LIBOR also plays a large role in the swap market, which we discuss in Chapter 21.

Covered Interest Arbitrage with Transaction Costs (Advanced)

In the presence of transaction costs in the foreign exchange and external currency markets, the absence of profitable covered interest arbitrage opportunities can be characterized by two inequalities. Arbitrage must be impossible either by borrowing the domestic currency and lending the foreign currency or by borrowing the foreign currency and lending the domestic currency. In each case, the transaction foreign exchange risk must be eliminated with the appropriate forward market transaction.

We can express these two inequalities symbolically by defining the dollar bid and ask interest rates, $i(\$)^{\text{bid}}$ and $i(\$)^{\text{ask}}$; the foreign currency bid and ask interest rates, $i(\text{FC})^{\text{bid}}$ and $i(\text{FC})^{\text{ask}}$; and the bid and ask spot and forward exchange rates of dollars per foreign currency, S^{bid}, S^{ask}, F^{bid}, and F^{ask}. The appropriate modifications to the box diagram in Exhibit 6.1, which used the pound as an example, are made in Exhibit 6.3.

Thus, if we go clockwise around the box in Exhibit 6.3, starting at £ in 1 year, we borrow pounds at $i(\pounds)^{\text{ask}}$; we convert from pounds to dollars in the spot market at S^{bid}; we lend the dollars at $i(\$)^{\text{bid}}$; and we sell the dollars forward for pounds at F^{ask}. The failure of this attempt to do covered interest arbitrage out of pounds into dollars can be summarized by the fact that the revenue of selling 1 pound in the future is less than 1:

$$\frac{1}{[1 + i(\pounds)^{\text{ask}}]} \times [S^{\text{bid}}] \times [1 + i(\$)^{\text{bid}}] \times \frac{1}{F^{\text{ask}}} < 1 \qquad \textbf{(6.9)}$$

---

[1] For more information on LIBOR, see the BBA Web site at www.bbalibor.com. Other reference interest rates include EURIBOR (Euro Interbank Offered Rate), CIBOR (Copenhagen), MIBOR (Moscow), and SIBOR (Singapore).

Exhibit 6.3 Covered Interest Rate Parity with Bid–Ask Rates

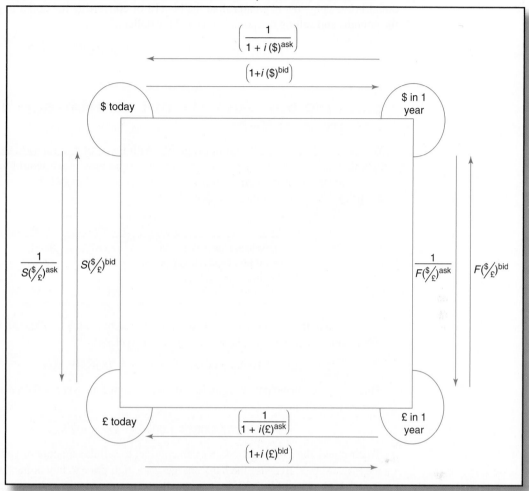

Note: The exchange rates and interest rates associated with each arrow indicate the funds obtained in the currency at the arrow's point from selling one unit of the currency at the arrow's tail. For example, at the $ today node, selling 1 dollar for $ in 1 year gives $(1 + i(\$)^{\text{bid}})$ dollars in 1 year.

Alternatively, rearranging the terms in the inequality in Equation (6.9), we see that the pound borrowing cost is greater than the benefit of converting the pounds to dollars, lending the dollars, and selling the dollars forward for pounds:

$$[1 + i(\pounds)^{\text{ask}}] > S^{\text{bid}} \times [1 + i(\$)^{\text{bid}}] \times \frac{1}{F^{\text{ask}}} \qquad (6.10)$$

The failure of an attempt to do covered interest arbitrage out of the dollar into the pound is summarized by going counterclockwise around the box in Exhibit 6.3. We start at the future dollar node and find out that the future revenue of selling 1 future dollar is less than 1:

$$\frac{1}{[1 + i(\$)^{\text{ask}}]} \times \frac{1}{S^{\text{ask}}} \times [1 + i(\pounds)^{\text{bid}}] \times F^{\text{bid}} < 1 \qquad (6.11)$$

Alternatively, rearranging the terms in the inequality in Equation (6.11), we see that the dollar borrowing cost is greater than the benefit of converting the dollar to pounds, lending the pounds, and selling the pounds forward for dollars:

$$[1 + i(\$)^{\text{ask}}] > [1/S^{\text{ask}}] \times [1 + i(\pounds)^{\text{bid}}] \times F^{\text{bid}} \qquad \textbf{(6.12)}$$

Example 6.4 An Attempt at Arbitrage Using Dollars and Yen

We use the data from Exhibit 6.2 together with the spot and forward exchange rates that also appear in the *Financial Times* to examine how much would have been lost in attempting to arbitrage between, say, the U.S. dollar and the yen at the 1-year maturity. The relevant data are as follows:

	Bid	Ask
Spot exchange rates (¥ per $):	82.67	82.71
Forward exchange rates (¥ per $):	82.32	82.37
Dollar interest rates:	0.91	1.11
Yen interest rates:	0.46	0.58

To make the magnitudes interesting, let's first borrow $10,000,000. If we convert this to yen, we do so at the bank's bid price for dollars:

$$\$10,000,000 \times ¥82.67/\$ = ¥826,700,000$$

This is our yen principal. We can invest this amount for 1 year at 0.46% p.a. Hence, in 1 year, we will have

$$¥826,700,000 \times 1.0046 = ¥830,502,820$$

To eliminate the exchange risk, we can contract to sell this amount of yen for dollars at the forward rate. Because the bank charges us a high price to buy dollars, we transact at forward ask price of ¥82.37/$. Hence, selling our yen principal plus interest for dollars yields

$$(¥830,502,820)/(¥82.37/\$) = \$10,082,589$$

Thus, if we borrow $10,000,000 for 1 year at 1.11%, we would owe

$$\$10,000,000 \times 1.0111 = \$10,111,000$$

Notice that if we were to do these transactions, we would lose

$$\$10,111,000 - \$10,082,589 = \$28,411$$

Notice also that the loss is $0.284\% = 28,411/10,000,000$ of the principal that we borrow.

Given that we lose money by attempting arbitrage by borrowing dollars, you should try to make money by doing a covered interest arbitrage that begins by borrowing yen. You will find that you would also lose money doing that. Hence, no profitable arbitrage exists in these data.

Does Covered Interest Parity Hold?

Because the settlement procedures in the external currency markets are identical to the settlement procedures in the forward markets, and because transaction costs are small, banks operating in this market should arbitrage away all deviations from covered interest rate parity. In fact, it is often the case that banks use interest rate parity to quote forward rates in outright forward transactions.

Prior to the financial crisis that began in 2007, documented violations of interest rate parity were exceedingly rare. Because prices move quickly within the day, careful analysis of the issue requires time-stamped data. Akram et al. (2008) assembled such data from Reuters for the pound, euro, and yen, all versus the dollar, for a short period from February 13 to September 30 of 2004. They detected multiple short-lived deviations from covered interest rate parity that provided possible arbitrage profits. Nevertheless, the deviations tended to persist only for a few minutes and represented a tiny fraction of all possible transactions. Hence, unless you are a trader in a bank, it is safe to assume that covered interest rate parity holds, at least in normal times.

The frequency, size, and duration of apparent arbitrage opportunities do increase with market volatility. This became very apparent during the 2007 to 2010 financial crisis, which we discuss in the box titled *Deviations from Interest Rate Parity During the Financial Crisis*.

6.3 WHY DEVIATIONS FROM INTEREST RATE PARITY MAY SEEM TO EXIST

If you observe foreign exchange prices and interest rates that appear to provide an arbitrage opportunity, you must make sure the arbitrage opportunity is real before plunging headlong into arbitrage trading. We now examine three reasons apparent arbitrage opportunities might not result in riskless profitable trades: default risk, exchange controls, and political risk.

Default Risks

In all our derivations so far, we have ignored the possibility that one of the counterparties may fail to honor its contract. When this possibility is reflected in interest rates, we may find an apparent deviation from interest rate parity that does not represent a riskless arbitrage opportunity. Default risk or credit risk is the possibility that a borrower will not repay the lender the entire amount promised in a loan contract. Let's explore the implications of default risk in more detail.

Because there is always some risk that a bank will fail, depositors (lenders) must assess the possibility that they will not be repaid. To make a rational investment, the depositors must determine what possible events in the future could trigger a default, and they must ascertain what probabilities are associated with these events. For example, let p denote the probability that the borrowing bank will default, so $(1 - p)$ is the probability that the borrowing bank will not default. Suppose that if the borrowing bank defaults, the depositing bank receives nothing. When the borrowing bank does not default, the depositing bank will receive $(1 + i)$, where i is the promised interest rate on the deposit of one unit of currency. Then the expected return to the depositing bank is

$$\left[(1 - p) \times (1 + i) \right] + (p \times 0) = (1 - p) \times (1 + i)$$

If depositors require a particular expected return in order to make a deposit, riskier banks (ones with larger values for p) must offer higher deposit rates to increase the expected return on their deposits in order to compete effectively for funds. Therefore, observing different interest rates on bank deposits denominated in the same currency in the interbank market need not be evidence of market inefficiency. If we see a deviation from interest rate parity, we cannot be certain that we are observing a true profit opportunity without knowing more about the particular banks making the quotations.

There may also be some risk of default on the forward contracts (again, because some banks are risky), and this could also lead to deviations from interest rate parity that do not represent arbitrage opportunities. Banks must continually assess the risk of their counterparties, and a bank's risk managers put limits on the amount of trading that can be done with any particular counterparty.[2] Assessing credit risk became of paramount importance during the 2007 to 2010 crisis, as the box discusses in detail.

Deviations from Interest Rate Parity During the Financial Crisis[3]

Exhibit 6.4, adapted from an article by Baba and Packer (2009b), shows deviations from covered interest parity between January 2007 and January 2009. Let's call them DEV; DEV is computed as

$$\text{DEV} = [1 + i(\text{FC})]\frac{F}{S} - [1 + i(\$)].$$

The three currencies considered are the euro, the pound, and the Swiss franc (quotes are in dollars per foreign currency), and the interest rates are 3-month euro-currency rates. Two important dates are indicated, the summer of 2007 when the first signs of trouble appeared (on August 9, 2007, BNP Paribas froze the assets of three of its investment funds, as

Exhibit 6.4 Covered Interest Parity Deviations During the Financial Crisis

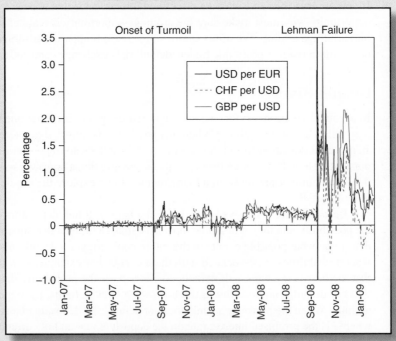

Notes: Reprinted from *Journal of Banking and Finance* 33, Naohiko Baba and Frank Packer, "Interpreting Deviations from Covered Interest Parity during the Financial Market Turmoil of 2007–2008," p. 195 (2009b), Copyright 2009 with permission from Elsevier. The covered interest rate parity deviations are defined in the text.

---

[2]Banks rely on information from firms that rate the creditworthiness of financial institutions and corporations; see Chapter 11 for additional discussion of these issues.
[3]Much has been written about this fascinating episode. We primarily relied on information in Baba and Packer (2009a, 2009b), Griffoli and Ranaldo (2010), and Coffey et al. (2009).

it failed to value the subprime mortgage–backed assets they were holding) and the failure of Lehman Brothers in September 2008. The graph clearly shows that the problems at several financial institutions in the United States, Europe, and elsewhere created apparent arbitrage opportunities in the foreign exchange market, which widened considerably after the Lehman failure. Apparently, borrowing dollars, converting them into any of the three currencies at the spot rate, investing them in those external currency markets, and then selling the known proceeds forward for dollars should have yielded juicy profits during this tumultuous period.

But were there truly arbitrage opportunities here? A first point is that the graph was created using only LIBORs and averages of bid and ask forward and spot rates. However, an arbitrageur would borrow dollars at the ask rate (correctly represented by LIBOR) but would lend at bid rates for the different currencies, not the LIBORs used in the calculations. The exchange rate quotes should also reflect transaction costs. As noted in Chapter 3, the crisis caused forex volatility to increase, which caused an increase in the transaction costs in the spot and especially the forward markets. The spreads between deposit and lending rates likewise increased substantially during the crisis. However, Griffoli and Ranaldo (2010) show that adjusting properly for transaction costs does not make the profit opportunities disappear.

Second, the creditworthiness of many financial institutions worsened as the crisis unfolded and deteriorated dramatically following the Lehman bankruptcy. Because different banks had very different exposures to "toxic" assets, LIBOR showed a lot of dispersion across banks, and many financial institutions had trouble obtaining funds in the money markets. However, the graph uses LIBOR for both the foreign currencies and the dollar. Because the different currency LIBOR bank panels use the same banks (for example, 14 of the 16 LIBOR panel banks in the dollar and euro panels are the same), the banks' default risks should affect both the euro and the dollar interest rates. Hence, default risk is unlikely to explain the large differences we observe in the graph.

So, what caused the large deviations? The studies reveal that the mispricing came mostly from the forward rate; the forward dollar price of the euro was too high, making F in the computation of DEV too high. Although there is still debate about the exact reasons, the most plausible mechanism seems to be a combination of credit risk and the desire for dollar liquidity.

Most financial institutions have long-term assets funded by short-term liabilities, which they roll over in typically well-functioning money markets. When the ramifications of the subprime crisis started to manifest themselves, many financial institutions, initially primarily in Europe, were stuck with long-term assets (mostly linked to American mortgages), which were hard to value and hard to sell. To pay off dollar loans that funded these dollar-denominated assets, the financial institutions needed either to borrow short-term dollars or engage in fire sales of the assets themselves. Because there was much uncertainty about the banks' credit risk, the money markets started to freeze up, and several banks found it increasingly difficult to obtain dollar funding via the usual channels.

The foreign exchange market provides a potential solution: The bank borrows in another currency, say the euro, but uses the foreign exchange markets to transform the euro proceeds of the loan into the dollars it needs. Of course, it must pay off the euro loan, but it can do so by buying the euros forward with dollars. The cost of the operation is exactly $\left[1 + i(\text{\euro})\right]\dfrac{F}{S}$, the left term in DEV. Now, if everyone is trying to use the forward markets to do this, there may be upward pressure on the forward rate.

This is exactly what happened in the crisis. Many financial institutions were scrambling to find dollar funding. As a safe haven currency, the dollar was appreciating in the spot markets (S decreased), but the actions of many banks prevented the dollar from appreciating proportionally in the forward market (F did not decrease as much as it should have). The situation got much worse after Lehman failed. With many more financial institutions in trouble and money market funds that invested in commercial paper issued by Lehman Brothers losing money, the liquidity in the money markets almost completely dried up. A global dollar shortage followed, leading to the substantial interest rate parity deviations shown in Exhibit 6.4 after the Lehman bankruptcy.

What gives much credence to this interpretation of events is how central banks around the world managed to mitigate the crisis. As we discussed in Chapter 5, a central bank should be able to help banks in a liquidity crisis by acting as a lender of last resort. It can do so by lending to its banks, essentially creating money. But in this particular crisis, banks around the world needed dollars, not euros or pounds. This was recognized by the central bankers, and the Federal Reserve essentially provided global dollar liquidity by lending dollars to central banks in Europe, Latin America, and Asia. The study by Baba and Packer (2009b) shows that the Fed's actions really helped reduce the deviations from covered interest rate parity, at least after the Lehman crisis.

Let's look at Exhibit 6.4 again from the perspective of an arbitrageur. The arbitrage profits from borrowing dollars and investing in these currencies while covering the currency risk would have been between 30 basis points and over 2% at the height of the crisis. Some canny investors may have taken advantage of this, but the fact that the deviations were so persistent shows that arbitrage activity must have been fairly limited. When there is a global dollar shortage, who can borrow dollars? Moreover, the crisis went hand in hand with a massive flight to safety, with most investors buying safe Treasury bills and bonds. As a result, many investment funds faced redemptions from risk-averse investors and had little speculative capital to deploy. This confirms an important idea in finance: As Shleifer and Vishny (1997) stress, arbitrage has its limits; it requires capital and is often risky.

Exchange Controls

Another problem with assessing the validity of interest rate parity is caused by **exchange controls**. Governments of countries periodically interfere with the buying and selling of foreign exchange. They may tax, limit, or prohibit the buying of foreign currency by their residents. They may also tax, limit, or prohibit the inflow of foreign investment into their country. Such exchange controls were common in several developed countries (including the United Kingdom, Switzerland, France, and Italy) until the mid-1980s, after which they were gradually abandoned. In more recent times, exchange controls are found in many developing countries. In 2010, a number of emerging economies (including Brazil and Thailand) reimposed controls or made existing controls more severe to stem the inflow of what authorities perceived as hot speculative capital attracted by high interest rates. Whenever you examine historical data on interest rates and exchange rates, you should be aware that not taking into account exchange controls or differential taxes can cause the appearance of a covered interest arbitrage opportunity that really doesn't exist, as the controls prevent an effective arbitrage.

One way to understand the effects of exchange controls and differential taxes on foreign versus domestic investors is to examine internal interest rates within a country versus external interest rates outside of the country. A large differential may not indicate an arbitrage opportunity but binding exchange controls. Suppose the onshore interest rate is higher than its offshore counterpart. This has often been the case for the Chinese renminbi in recent years.[4] An arbitrageur would like to borrow at low offshore renminbi rates and invest at higher onshore renminbi rates, but investment controls prevent such transactions. The onshore–offshore renminbi yield gap averaged more than 250 basis points during 2004 to 2006, but it has since narrowed considerably. It is possible that the narrowing partially reflects exchange controls becoming less effective at preventing capital inflows into China.

Analogously, when the onshore interest rate is lower than the offshore rate, domestic residents have an incentive to invest abroad, but capital controls prevent them from doing so. Of course, the differences between onshore and offshore interest rates may reflect other factors as well. For example, the instruments used to borrow and lend may have differential liquidity, which could lead to differences in interest rates. We already mentioned the possibility of default risk. Offshore interest rates reflect the credit risk of major financial institutions. In the United States, the difference between 3-month LIBOR and the 3-month Treasury bill rate is known as the TED spread. The TED spread is typically positive because it reflects the credit risk of the major banks in the LIBOR panel. It became particularly large in 2007 to 2010, during the subprime mortgage crisis.

---

[4]See the articles by Cheung and Qian (2010) and Ma and McCauley (2008). Because offshore borrowing and lending in Chinese renminbi is not yet possible, the offshore rate is computed using the offshore non-deliverable (NDF) forward rate, the spot exchange rate (which is controlled by the Chinese government), and dollar LIBOR. We show how to do this in Section 6.4.

When onshore interest rates reflect the default risk of the local government, it is called political risk, to which we turn next. But first, let's reexamine those very high Brazilian interest rates mentioned in the introduction.

Example 6.5 Investing in Brazil

Consider the following data from January 25, 2011.

> USD 3-month LIBOR: 0.37% p.a.
>
> Brazilian 3-month Treasury bill rate: 11.92% p.a.
>
> Spot exchange rate: BRL1.67/USD
>
> 3-month forward rate: BRL1.7042/USD

If covered interest rate parity holds, the 11.92% BRL rate should turn into a measly 0.37% USD return after covering the currency risk of investing in the Brazilian real. To find this "covered yield," we convert dollars into reais at the spot rate of BRL1.67/USD, invest in the Brazilian Treasury bill, and sell the reais at the forward rate (BRL1.7042/USD). Doing so, gives

$$\text{BRL1.67} \, (1 + 0.1190/4) \, (1/\text{BRL1.7042/USD}) - 1 = 0.91\%$$

In annualized terms, this yields 3.65%, much higher than the USD LIBOR. Clearly, covered interest rate parity does not hold.

Nevertheless, the high Brazilian Treasury bill rates will not attract many foreign investors because the Brazilian government taxes fixed-income investors. It initialized a flat tax on foreigners investing in the Brazilian fixed-income market at the end of 2008, and it has raised the tax rate in several installments to 6%! A foreign investor must give up 6 cents of every investment dollar to the Brazilian government. Obviously, the 0.91% return earned over 3 months does not overcome such a steep tax. The longer the investor's horizon, the less impact the tax has on returns. Therefore, the tax mostly affects short-term fixed-income flows, which is exactly the government's intent. During 2009 and 2010, the Brazilian real appreciated by more than 30%, hurting Brazilian exporters. The government felt that this appreciation was primarily driven by speculative capital flows, attracted by the high Brazilian interest rates.

In fact, covered interest rate parity is alive and well for the Brazilian real. International banks do borrow and lend in reais. It turns out that the offshore BRL LIBOR is 8.62%. You should verify that, at this rate, the annualized covered yield on a 3-month Brazilian investment is reduced to 52 basis points, very close to the USD interest rate.

Political Risk

Even if no exchange controls are currently present, foreign investors may rationally believe that a government will impose some form of exchange controls or taxes on foreign investments in the future. Or, perhaps the government will declare a "bank holiday," closing the nation's banks for a period of time.[5] All such events would affect an investor's return. The possibility of any of these events occurring is called **political risk**. Recent history is riddled with examples of political risk causing onshore interest rates to be larger than offshore interest rates. Chapter 14 examines political risk in detail. Next, Ante and Freedy discuss a famous historical case involving investing in Mexico.

---

[5]*Bank holidays* are situations in which governments close banks for periods of time to allow information to be obtained about the solvency of various banks—that is, whether the value of their assets exceeds the value of their liabilities.

Mexican Cetes or U.S. Treasury Bills?

Ante and Freedy are working on a case for their international finance class. Their professor has asked them to examine some data from June 20, 1995, to look for arbitrage opportunities between Mexico and the United States. Ante storms into Freedy's room with *Wall Street Journal* quotes in his hand and shouts, "Here is the definite proof. Markets are totally inefficient. Look at these prices. People must have made a killing investing in Cetes. These Mexican treasury bills were offering 44.85% p.a. on a 3-month deposit. And look, the Mexican peso–U.S. dollar forward rate was really attractive, so they could have covered the currency risk cheaply and locked in immediate profits of 1.19% per dollar invested." Freedy peruses the data and urges Ante to stay calm so he can explain why this apparent arbitrage opportunity was illusory.

Ante says, "Look, the USD Treasury bill rate was 5.60% p.a., so you could borrow a dollar at 1.40% for 3 months. Because the spot rate was MXN6.25/USD, each dollar borrowed yielded 6.25 pesos. By investing these pesos at the Cetes rate of 44.85%, they would have grown to

$$\text{MXN6.25} \times (1 + 44.85/400) = \text{MXN6.95078}$$

With the forward at a rate of MXN6.775/USD, one could sell them for dollars to lock in the profit.[6] In other words, for each dollar that someone borrowed, they got

$$\text{MXN6.95078}/(\text{MXN6.775/USD}) = \text{USD1.0259}$$

back, and they only need \$1.014 to pay back the 1-dollar loan. So their profit was a whopping \$1.0259 − \$1.0140 = \$0.0119 per dollar invested. Now that was a money machine, buddy!"

Freedy is totally puzzled. "But that is impossible. Financial markets would not tolerate a money machine. Traders would quickly take advantage of the situation and, via arbitrage, eliminate any opportunity for profit. Maybe these Mexican peso investments were much less liquid than other contracts, or maybe these are just typos in the newspaper. I bet you this opportunity was gone the next day."

At this point, Suttle leisurely walks in, sighing, "Are you guys at it again? What are you fighting about now?" After hearing both Ante's and Freedy's accounts of the great Mexican investment opportunity, Suttle smiles and says there is nothing mysterious about those rates. "It was not a money machine, and it wasn't explained by transaction costs. The higher Cetes rates simply reflected country risk or default risk on the part of the Mexican government. The U.S. government may be expected to always repay its dollar debts, but this is not necessarily true for the governments of developing countries," he says. "As you may remember, Mexico had come close to totally running out of official international reserves at the end of 1994, and it was building up its international reserves during 1995, after having been bailed out by an international aid package early in 1995. In this context, the interest rate differential can be split up into two parts. One part is the Mexican interest rate that would result if the Mexican government had the same credit risk as the U.S. government. This rate can be inferred from spot and forward exchange rates (if conducted with creditworthy counterparties) and the U.S. Treasury bill rate. The remainder is an additional return offered by the Mexican government to compensate for the political risk that investors perceive to be present," he continues.

---

[6]The forward exchange rate used here is actually calculated from the price of the peso futures contract trading on the Chicago Mercantile Exchange. (See Chapter 20 for a full account of futures contracts and exchanges.) For our purposes, it is important to realize that the forward rate and the futures rate are virtually identical for identical maturities and that the counterparty in the futures contract (the Chicago Mercantile Exchange) is very likely to honor its contract with you.

Seeing Ante's and Freedy's puzzled faces, Suttle decides to use the actual numbers. "So, if we look at the numbers, the Cetes investment, hedged for foreign currency risk, represents a 10.37% annualized return (2.5945% times 4), which is 4.77% higher than the U.S. Treasury bill rate of return. Because the investment is totally hedged against foreign currency risk, this extra reward must be due to default risk, and it is typically called the **country risk premium**. I remember that for 1993 and 1994, country risk premiums on 3-month Mexican Cetes averaged 2.25%," he finally offers (see Domowitz et al., 1998). Ante and Freedy know that Suttle has taught them a very valuable lesson!

Epilogue

The Mexican government did not default on the Cetes investments discussed here. Consequently, Ante was right, *ex post*, that investors would have found them to be a good investment relative to USD Treasury bills. Nevertheless, government defaults do happen. For example, both Russia and Ecuador defaulted in the late 1990s on obligations to foreign investors that had similar risk characteristics to Mexican Cetes investments in 1995, Argentina also defaulted on its international debt in 2002, and Ecuador defaulted again in 2008. Therefore, it is difficult to know exactly whether Ante or Freedy is right in an *ex ante* sense.

6.4 HEDGING TRANSACTION RISK IN THE MONEY MARKET

If you have an open position (either an account receivable or an account payable) denominated in foreign currency, you are exposed to transaction foreign exchange risk. When interest rate parity holds, there are two equivalent ways to hedge your transaction exchange risk:

1. Having an appropriate forward contract to buy or sell the foreign currency
2. Borrowing or lending the foreign currency coupled with making a transaction in the spot market

We examined the first technique in Chapter 3. Now let's look at the second, which is also known as a **synthetic forward**. There are several reasons for using such hedges. First, in some currency markets (for instance, those in certain developing countries), forward contracts may not be available. Nevertheless, a forward contract can be manufactured using a **money market hedge**. Second, individual companies are not able to borrow and lend at the interest rates available in the interbank market, which means the two strategies may not be equivalent, depending on the forward quote that the company receives. Third, when time horizons are long, forward contracts can be expensive as the bid–ask spread widens substantially. Therefore, it may be advantageous to consider borrowing and lending to hedge one's currency risk. We discuss this long-term issue explicitly in Section 6.5. For now, we focus on short-term money market hedges to get the logic correct.

The general principal is that if the underlying transaction gives you a liability (an account payable) denominated in foreign currency, you need an equivalent asset in the money market to provide a hedge. If, on the other hand, the underlying transaction gives you an asset (an account receivable) denominated in foreign currency, you need an equivalent liability in the money market to provide a hedge.

Hedging a Foreign Currency Liability

Example 6.6 Zachy's Money Market Hedge

Assume, as in Chapter 3, that you are managing Zachy's Wine and Spirits, and you have just contracted to import some Chateau Margaux wine from France. As before, the wine is valued at €4 million, and you have agreed to pay this amount when you have received the wine and determined that it is in good condition. Payment of the money and delivery of the wine are scheduled for 90 days in the future. The spot exchange rate is \$1.10/€; the 90-day forward exchange rate is \$1.08/€; the 90-day dollar interest rate is 6.00% p.a.; and the 90-day euro interest rate is 13.519% p.a.

Remember that because the underlying transaction gives you a euro-denominated account payable, you are exposed to losses if you do not hedge and the euro appreciates relative to the dollar. In this case, the dollar cost of the euros would be higher in the future, which would increase the cost of your wine. In Chapter 3, we eliminated this risk by buying euros forward. Numerically, the dollar cost, which is paid in 90 days, is €4,000,000 × (\$1.08/€) = \$4,320,000.

Let's look at the alternative money market hedging strategy. Because you have a euro liability, you must acquire an equivalent euro asset. You can do this by buying the present value of your euro liability at the spot exchange rate and investing these euros in a money market asset. You then use the principal plus interest on this euro asset to offset your underlying euro liability at maturity. The present value of €4,000,000 at 13.519% p.a. is

$$€4,000,000/[1 + (13.519/100)(90/360)] = €3,869,229.71$$

This amount of euros must be purchased in the spot foreign exchange market:

$$€3,869,229.71 × (\$1.10/€) = \$4,256,152.68$$

Notice that with the money market hedge, the payment is made today unless you borrow dollars. To compare the money market hedge to the forward market hedge, we must take the present value of the \$4,320,000 at 6% p.a.:

$$\$4,320,000/[1 + (6/100)(90/360)] = \$4,256,157.64$$

At these interest rates and exchange rates, the two strategies are basically equivalent. The dollar present value of the forward contract is only \$4.96 more expensive.

Hedging a Foreign Currency Receivable

Example 6.7 A Shetland Sweater Exporter's Money Market Hedge

Now, consider the example in Chapter 3 of the British manufacturer Shetland Sweaters. As in that example, you have agreed to ship sweaters to Japan, and you will receive ¥500,000,000 in payment. Shipment of the goods and receipt of the yen are scheduled for 30 days from now, and the following data are available:

Spot exchange rate:	¥179.5/£
30-day forward exchange rate:	¥180/£

30-day pound interest rate: 2.70% p.a.

30-day yen interest rate: 6.01% p.a.

As a British exporter, you have a yen-denominated account receivable, which is your yen asset. If you do nothing to hedge the transaction foreign exchange risk, you are exposed to losses if the yen depreciates relative to the pound. In this case, the yen receivable will purchase fewer pounds when you receive the yen payment. In Chapter 3, we eliminated the transaction foreign exchange risk by selling the yen forward for pounds. The amount of pounds that will be received in 30 days from the forward contract is $(¥500,000,000)/(¥180/£) = £2,777,778$.

Now, consider the alternative money market hedge. You must acquire a yen liability that is equivalent in value to your yen asset. You borrow the present value of your yen asset and use the yen that you receive from selling your sweaters to pay off the principal and interest on your yen loan. To be hedged, you must convert the yen principal that is borrowed into pounds at the spot exchange rate. The present value of ¥500,000,000 at 6.01% p.a. is

$$¥500,000,000/(1 + (6.01/100)(30/360)) = ¥497,508,313$$

By borrowing ¥497,508,313 for 1 month at 6.01% p.a., you owe ¥500,000,000 in 30 days, which is the amount you receive for selling your sweaters. Your pound revenue is found by selling the ¥497,508,313 for pounds in the spot market at ¥179.5/£, which is

$$¥497,508,313/(¥179.5/£) = £2,771,634$$

We can compare this revenue to the revenue available from the forward hedge in 30 days by taking the future value of the £2,771,634. We can invest pounds at 2.70% p.a. Hence, the future value of the pounds received today is

$$£2,771,634 \times (1 + (2.7/100)(30/365)) = £2,777,785$$

Hence, at these interest rates and exchange rates, the money market hedging strategy is basically equivalent to the forward hedging strategy.

6.5 THE TERM STRUCTURE OF FORWARD PREMIUMS AND DISCOUNTS

Does interest rate parity hold at long horizons? This is an important question because many international investment projects involve currency exposures that extend over many years. If an exposure is longer term, the short-term money market contracts we discussed earlier might be inadequate. However, before we investigate interest rate parity over longer time frames, we need to explain the term structure of interest rates. Whereas the interest rates for short-term maturities are readily available in the marketplace, interest rates for longer maturities must be derived from the prices of coupon bonds. Long-term interest rates are useful in computing the present value of cash flows of long-term projects.

After we look at the term structures of interest rates for two currencies, we can combine them with interest rate parity to examine the term structure of the forward premiums or discounts between two currencies. That is, we investigate how international interest rate differentials change with different maturities. These computations can be useful for multinational corporations (MNCs) seeking financing in international bond markets. Recent empirical evidence suggests that covered interest rate parity does not hold perfectly at longer horizons. In Chapter 11, we discuss how MNCs can exploit these deviations from parity to lower their financing costs.

The Term Structure of Interest Rates

Spot Interest Rates

It is generally true that the time values of different monies for a particular maturity are not equal. The 1-year USD interest rate might be 5%, whereas the 1-year JPY interest rate might be 1.5%. Similarly, the time value of one currency, say the USD, at one maturity is usually not equal to the time value of the USD at a different maturity. The 1-year USD interest rate might be 5%, whereas the 30-year USD interest rate might be 7.5%.

When there are no intervening cash flows between the time a deposit is made and the maturity of the deposit, the interest rates are said to be **spot interest rates**. Interest rate parity only applies to spot interest rates. The **term structure of interest rates** for a particular currency is a description of the different spot interest rates for various maturities into the future. For shorter maturities, these spot interest rates are directly observable because they are widely quoted by banks. However, for longer maturities, we usually have to derive the spot interest rates from the market prices of coupon-paying bonds. Typically, the interest rates are quoted on an annual basis—that is, they reflect the return earned per year. To understand how to determine spot interest rates from bond prices, let's review some additional terminology associated with bond pricing.

A Review of Bond Pricing

Bonds are financial contracts that obligate the bond issuer to pay the bondholder a sequence of fixed contractual payments until the maturity of the bond. These payments represent the return of principal and interest on the principal. Most bonds with maturities of longer than 1 year have coupon payments that provide the bondholder with intervening interest payments between the purchase of the bond and the maturity date. For example, the coupon payments on U.S. government bonds and American corporate bonds are made every 6 months. A 7% bond with a final payment of $1,000 would pay $35 of coupon interest every 6 months because

$$(0.07/2) \times \$1,000 = \$35$$

The simplest bonds, though, are **pure discount bonds**. Such bonds promise a single payment of, say, $1,000 or €1,000 at the maturity of the bond. The terminal payment is called the *face value* of the bond. The bonds are sold at a discount on the face value such that the difference between the face value of the bond and the market price of the bond when it is purchased provides an interest return to the buyer. Long-maturity pure discount bonds are often called *deep-discount bonds*, *zero-coupon bonds*, or simply *zeros* to emphasize that the only cash flow to the bondholder is the final face value on the bond. Consequently, we can now define the spot interest rate as the market interest rate that equates the price of a pure discount bond to the present value of the face value of the bond.

Example 6.8 Pure Discount Bonds and Spot Interest Rates

Suppose the market price of a 10-year pure discount bond with a face value of $1,000 is $463.19. What is the spot interest rate for the 10-year maturity expressed in percentage per annum?

We want to find the spot interest rate, say $i(10)$, such that when $463.19 is invested today, it can grow at the compound rate of $i(10)$ to be equal to $1,000 after 10 years:

$$\$463.19[1 + i(10)]^{10} = \$1,000$$

The solution is

$$i(10) = (\$1{,}000/\$463.19)^{1/10} - 1 = 0.08$$

The spot interest rate for the 10-year maturity is 8% p.a., and at this rate, the future value of $463.19 in 10 years is $1,000, and the present value of $1,000 to be received 10 years from now is $463.19 today.

We can put the finding from Example 6.8 in more general terms. Let $B(n)$ equal the current market price of a pure discount bond with n periods to maturity, and let M be the face value of the bond paid at maturity. Let the spot interest rate today for maturity n be $i(n)$. Then, the market price of the bond is the present discounted value of the face value of the bond at the given spot interest rate:

$$B(n) = \frac{M}{[1 + i(n)]^n}$$

The interest rate $i(n)$ is called a *discount rate*. Mostly, the face values and the prices of bonds are available as information in the market. Then, we can calculate the spot interest rate by solving the following equation for $i(n)$:

$$[1 + i(n)]^n = \frac{M}{B(n)}$$

To solve this equation, we must raise each side to the $1/n$ power and then subtract 1 from both sides:

$$i(n) = \left[\frac{M}{B(n)}\right]^{1/n} - 1$$

Yields to Maturity

Let $B(n, C)$ denote the current market price of an n-period bond with a face value of M and a periodic coupon payment of C. The **yield to maturity** on this bond, denoted $y(n)$, is the single discount rate or interest rate that equates the present value of the n coupon payments plus the final principal payment to the current market price:

$$B(n, C) = \frac{C}{[1 + y(n)]} + \frac{C}{[1 + y(n)]^2} + \dots + \frac{C}{[1 + y(n)]^n} + \frac{M}{[1 + y(n)]^n} \quad \text{(6.13)}$$

Notice that the discount rate is the same for each of the coupons and the final principal, but 1 plus the discount rate is raised to various powers to reflect the number of periods the coupon payments are away from today.

Yields to maturity are straightforward to calculate for a variety of maturities, and market participants often discuss the **yield curve**. Just as the term structure of interest rates refers to the relationship between maturity and spot interest rates for different maturities, the yield curve is the relationship between maturity and the yields on bonds of those maturities. When the yield curve slopes upward, the term structure of interest rates slopes upward as well.

Exhibit 6.5 presents yield curves for the U.S. dollar (USD), the euro (EUR), the British pound (GBP), and the Japanese yen (JPY) that prevailed on January 18, 2011. Note that the yen interest rates are the lowest at all maturities, and the interest rates for the yen's shorter maturities are

Exhibit 6.5 Yield Curves for Four Currencies

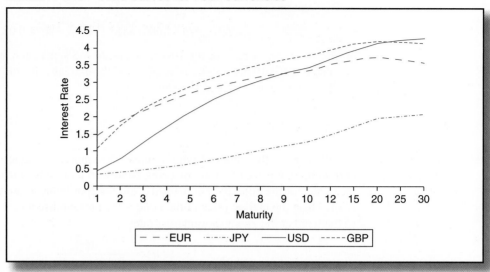

Notes: The yield curve data are taken from swap rates (see Chapter 21) for different currencies reported in the *Financial Times* for January 18, 2011. These rates are comparable to yields to maturity for domestic bonds. On the vertical axis, the yields are expressed in annualized terms. The horizontal axis displays the maturity expressed in years.

lower than the interest rates for longer maturities. Consequently, we say that the yield curve for the yen is rising, or upward sloping. Note that the yield curves for all other currencies are also upward sloping, which is what is typically observed.

Deriving Long-Term Spot Interest Rates

For pure discount bonds, the yield to maturity is the spot interest rate for that maturity because there are no cash flows between now and the maturity date. When there are intervening coupon payments and the spot interest rates for different maturities are not all equal, there must be a difference between the yield to maturity on the bond and the spot interest rate for the maturity of the bond.

Example 6.9 Spot Interest Rates Versus Yields to Maturity

Consider a 2-year bond with face value equal to $1,000, an annual coupon of $60, and a market price of $980. Suppose the 1-year spot interest rate, $i(1)$, is 5.5%. We use this to take the presnet value of the first coupon payment. Then, the 2-year spot interest rate, $i(2)$, is found by solving

$$\$980 = \frac{\$60}{1.055} + \frac{\$1,060}{1 + i(2)^2}$$

and the answer is $i(2) = 7.1574\%$.

The yield to maturity is a complicated average of the spot interest rates for the various maturities of the coupon payments and the final repayment of principal. It would be the discount rate $y(2)$ that solves[7]

$$\$980 = \frac{\$60}{[1 + y(2)]} + \frac{\$1{,}060}{[1 + y(2)]^2}$$

The value of $y(2)$ is 7.11%, which is intermediate between the two spot rates but much closer to $i(2)$ because most of the cash flows of the bond occur in the second year.

The solution procedure applied here indicates that spot interest rates are the appropriate discount rates for the cash flows that take place at a particular maturity. The logic of this conclusion is clearer if you think of a long-term bond with coupon payments and a final principal payment as the sum of several pure discount bonds. Consider each maturity at which a cash flow occurs to be a separate bond. The value of each pure discount bond is found by taking the present value of the single payment with the appropriate spot interest rate for that maturity. The market value of the bond is then the sum of the present values of the different promised payments.

Generally, let $i(j)$ denote the current spot interest rate for maturity j periods into the future. Consider the present value PV of a sequence of known cash flows, denoted $C(j)$, for values of j between 1 and n periods into the future. By discounting each cash flow with its appropriate pure discount rate, we find the current present value as

$$PV = \frac{C(1)}{[1 + i(1)]} + \frac{C(2)}{[1 + i(2)]^2} + \cdots + \frac{C(n)}{[1 + i(n)]^n}$$

Because calculating present values in different currencies is a fundamental part of international finance, understanding the different term structures of spot interest rates for different currencies is quite important.

Long-Term Forward Rates and Premiums

Let's develop the relationship between long-term forward exchange rates and spot exchange rates with an example. Let $i(2, ¥)$ and $i(2, \$)$ denote the spot interest rates today for Japanese yen and U.S. dollar investments, respectively, with 2-year maturities. Let S be the spot exchange rate of yen per dollar today, and let $F(2)$ denote the outright forward rate today for delivery in 2 years. If there are no opportunities for arbitrage, the outright forward rate of yen per dollar for the 2-year maturity must be

$$F(2) = S \times \frac{[1 + i(2, ¥)]^2}{[1 + i(2, \$)]^2} \qquad (6.14)$$

To see why this must be true, consider that a Japanese investor must be indifferent between investing in yen for 2 years and getting $[1 + i(2, ¥)]^2$ for each yen or converting the yen into dollars and getting $1/S$ dollars for each yen, investing these dollars for 2 years to have $(1/S)[1 + i(2, \$)]^2$ dollars after 2 years, and contracting to sell these dollars forward at $F(2)$ to get a yen return of $F(2)(1/S)[1 + i(2, \$)]^2$. Equating these returns and solving for $F(2)$ gives Equation (6.14). Example 6.10 is a numeric example that illustrates these issues.

---

[7]In this simple example, we can analytically solve for $y(2)$, but when there are many periods involved, the yield to maturity must typically be found with computational numeric methods. One easy way is with Microsoft Excel. The yield to maturity is the internal rate of return (IRR) on the negative cash flow incurred when the bond is purchased followed by the positive cash flows from holding the bond to maturity.

Example 6.10 The 2-Year Forward Rate

Let the spot exchange rate be ¥110/$, and let the spot interest rates for the 2-year maturity be $i(2, \$) = 5\%$ p.a. and $i(2, ¥) = 4\%$ p.a. Suppose you invest ¥10,000,000 in a 2-year yen pure discount bond. At the end of 2 years, your investment will grow to

$$¥10,000,000 \times (1.04)^2 = ¥10,816,000$$

At the current spot exchange rate, the dollar cost of ¥10,000,000 is

$$¥10,000,000/(¥110/\$) = \$90,909.09$$

If you invest $90,909.09 in a 2-year dollar pure discount bond, at the end of 2 years, you will have

$$\$90,909.09 \times (1.05)^2 = \$100,227.27$$

This analysis indicates that you can either invest $90,909.09 today to buy ¥10,000,000 and invest it for 2 years to have ¥10,816,000, or you can invest the $90,909.09 in the dollar bond for 2 years to get $100,227.27. You would be indifferent between the two investments if the forward sale of ¥10,816,000 for dollars provides you with the same dollar return as investing directly in dollars. That is, if the forward rate satisfies

$$¥10,816,000/F(2) = \$100,227.27$$

Solving this equation for the forward rate gives

$$F(2) = ¥10,816,000/\$100,227.27 = ¥107.9147/\$$$

or, rounding to the nearest one-hundredth of a yen, $F(2) = ¥107.91/\$$. If the forward exchange rate quoted today for transactions in 2 years is greater than ¥107.91/$, a dollar investor would receive more dollars by investing in the dollar bond than by investing in the yen bond. Investors of yen would also receive more yen by investing in the dollar bond than by investing in the yen bond. They would, of course, have to sell the dollars forward for yen. This is the same type of arbitrage argument that was used earlier when short-term interest rate parity was developed. Analogously, if the forward exchange rate quoted today for transactions in 2 years is less than ¥107.91/$, a dollar investor would receive more dollars by investing in the yen bond and contracting to sell yen forward for dollars than by investing directly in the dollar bond. Investors of yen would also receive more yen by investing in the yen bond than by investing in the dollar bond and contracting to sell dollars forward.

What would happen if the forward rate did not satisfy Equation (6.14), implying that there was a difference in returns available in the market? For example, suppose that the dollar and yen interest rates and the spot and forward exchange rates favored investing in the dollar bond over the yen bond. Investors would move funds out of Japanese yen bonds and into U.S. dollar bonds. If investors sold yen bonds, the prices of the yen bonds would fall, and their yields would rise. As money flowed out of Japan to invest in dollar bonds, the dollar would strengthen relative to the yen, causing the spot exchange rate of yen per dollar to rise. As additional dollars flowed into the dollar bond market, the prices of dollar bonds would rise, causing their yields to fall. Finally, the forward rate of yen per dollar would fall as investors sold dollars forward to acquire yen in the future. All four effects make investing in the yen asset more attractive and investing in the dollar asset relatively less attractive.

Notice that we have demonstrated how long-term investment considerations would move the outright forward exchange rate quoted today for delivery n periods from now to be equal to the spot rate today adjusted for the relative returns on pure discount bonds between now and n periods from now in the two currencies (in yen per dollar):

$$F(n) = S \times \frac{[1 + i(n, ¥)]^n}{[1 + i(n, \$)]^n}$$

Theoretically, this is the way that long-term forward contracts should be priced.

Of course, throughout this discussion, we have ignored bid–ask spreads on the transactions in the bond market as investors buy and sell bonds and on the transactions in the spot and forward foreign exchange markets. These transaction costs become larger as the maturities lengthen. They are also the source of the development of currency swaps, which are discussed in Chapter 21.

6.6 SUMMARY

This chapter investigates the relationship between nominal interest rates for two currencies and the corresponding spot and forward exchange rates. When the money markets are free from arbitrage, this relationship between these four variables is called *interest rate parity*. The main points in the chapter are the following:

1. The nominal interest rate is the time value of money. The future value (FV) of an amount of money is obtained by multiplying by 1 plus the interest rate: $[FV = \text{cash flow} \times (1 + i)]$. The present value ($PV$) today of an amount of money in the future is obtained by dividing by 1 plus the interest rate: $PV = \dfrac{\text{Future cash flow}}{1 + i}$.

2. Covered interest arbitrage is done in four steps: borrowing one currency, converting to a second currency, investing in the second currency, and selling the interest plus principal on the second currency in the forward market for the first currency.

3. When domestic and foreign interest rates and spot and forward exchange rates are in equilibrium such that no covered interest arbitrage is possible, the interest rates and exchange rates are said to satisfy interest rate parity.

4. With exchange rates expressed directly as domestic currency per unit of foreign currency, interest rate parity is satisfied when the forward premium or discount on the foreign currency equals the interest differential between the domestic and foreign interest rates divided by 1 plus the foreign interest rate.

5. The external currency market is an interbank market for deposits and loans that are denominated in

currencies that are not the currency of the country in which the bank is operating.

6. Bid–ask spreads in the external currency market (with the bank bidding for deposits and offering an interest rate on loans) are quite small in normal periods.

7. In the presence of transaction costs, interest rate parity is characterized by two inequalities, indicating that covered interest arbitrage leads to losses in both directions. That is, neither lending nor borrowing in a particular currency at the start of the attempted arbitrage leads to profits.

8. The empirical evidence indicates that interest rate parity holds during tranquil periods and for short maturities. During turbulent periods, persistent apparent arbitrage opportunities may arise, as was evident during the 2007 to 2010 crisis.

9. These profit opportunities may merely reflect the differential credit risks of the institutions quoting prices in the market. Credit risk or default risk is the chance that a counterparty will default on its side of a commitment.

10. Exchange controls involve taxes a government imposes on foreign investments, or regulatory restrictions on the use of foreign exchange. Political risk arises when investors rationally believe a government may impose some form of exchange controls or taxes during the life of the investment or even seize the assets of investors. Both exchange controls and political risk can lead to perceived interest rate parity violations that cannot actually be exploited.

11. Transaction exchange risk can be hedged with money market hedges. A money market hedge establishes a

foreign currency–denominated asset or liability that offsets the underlying transaction exposure. If interest rate parity is satisfied, a money market hedge is identical to a forward market hedge.

12. The only cash flow to the bondholder of a pure discount bond is the final face value of the bond. Spot interest rates are the discount rates that equate the prices of pure discount bonds to the present values of the face values of the bonds. Spot interest rates are the appropriate discount rates for cash flows with no uncertainty that take place at a particular maturity.

13. The term structure of interest rates for a particular currency represents the different spot interest rates for various future maturities.

14. A bond's yield to maturity is the single common discount rate that equates the present value of the sequence of all coupon payments and principal payments to the current price of the bond.

15. Using the spot exchange rate and the domestic and foreign spot interest rates for a particular maturity, we can derive the forward rate for that maturity.

QUESTIONS

1. Explain the concepts of present value and future value.

2. If the dollar interest rate is positive, explain why the value of $1,000,000 received every year for 10 years is not $10,000,000 today.

3. Describe how you would calculate a 5-year forward exchange rate of yen per dollar if you knew the current spot exchange rate and the prices of 5-year pure discount bonds denominated in yen and dollars. Explain why this has to be the market price.

4. If interest rate parity is satisfied, there are no opportunities for covered interest arbitrage. What does this imply about the relationship between spot and forward exchange rates when the foreign currency money market investment offers a higher return than the domestic money market investment?

5. It is often said that interest rate parity is satisfied when the differential between the interest rates denominated in two currencies equals the forward premium or discount between the two currencies. Explain why this is an imprecise statement when the interest rates are not continuously compounded.

6. What do economists mean by the external currency market?

7. What determines the bid–ask spread in the external currency market? Why is it usually so small?

8. Explain why the absence of covered interest arbitrage possibilities can be characterized by two inequalities in the presence of bid–ask spreads in the foreign exchange and external currency markets.

9. Describe the sequence of transactions required to do a covered interest arbitrage out of Japanese yen and into U.S. dollars.

10. Suppose you saw a set of quoted prices from a U.S. bank and a French bank such that you could borrow dollars, sell the dollars in the spot foreign exchange market for euros, deposit the euros for 90 days, and make a forward contract to sell euros for dollars and make a guaranteed profit. Would this be an arbitrage opportunity? Why or why not?

11. The interest rates on U.S. dollar–denominated bank accounts in Mexican banks are often higher than the interest rates on bank accounts in the United States. Can you explain this phenomenon?

12. What is a money market hedge? How is it constructed?

13. Suppose you are the French representative of a company selling soap in Canada. Describe your foreign exchange risk and how you might hedge it with a money market hedge.

14. What is a pure discount bond?

15. What is the term structure of interest rates? How are spot interest rates determined from coupon bond prices?

16. How does a coupon bond's yield to maturity differ from the spot interest rate that applies to cash flows occurring at the maturity of the bond? When are the two the same?

PROBLEMS

1. In the entry forms for its contests, Publisher's Clearing House states, "You may have already won $10,000,000." If the Prize Patrol visits your house to inform you that you have won, it offers you $333,333.33 each and every year for 30 years. If the interest rate is 8% p.a., what is the actual present value of the $10,000,000 prize?

2. Suppose the 5-year interest rate on a dollar-denominated pure discount bond is 4.5% p.a. and the interest rate on a similar pure discount euro-denominated

bond is 7.5% p.a. If the current spot rate is $1.08/€, what forward exchange rate prevents covered interest arbitrage?

3. Carla Heinz is a portfolio manager for Deutsche Bank. She is considering two alternative investments of EUR10,000,000: 180-day euro deposits or 180-day Swiss franc (CHF) deposits. She has decided not to bear transaction foreign exchange risk. Suppose she has the following data: 180-day CHF interest rate of 8% p.a.; 180-day EUR interest rate of 10% p.a.; spot rate of EUR1.1960/CHF; and 180-day forward rate of EUR1.2024/CHF. Which of these deposits provides the higher euro return in 180 days? If these were actually market prices, what would you expect to happen?

4. If the 30-day yen interest rate is 3% p.a., and the 30-day euro interest rate is 5% p.a. What is the magnitude of the forward premium or discount on the yen?

5. Suppose the spot rate is CHF1.4706/$, and the 180-day forward rate is CHF1.4295/$. If the 180-day dollar interest rate is 7% p.a., what is the annualized 180-day interest rate on Swiss francs that would prevent arbitrage?

6. As a trader for Goldman Sachs, you see the following prices from two different banks:

   1-year euro deposits/loans: 6.0%–6.125% p.a.
   1-year Malaysian ringgit deposits/loans: 10.5%–10.625% p.a.
   Spot exchange rates: MYR4.6602/EUR–MYR4.6622/EUR
   1-year forward exchange rates: MYR4.9500/EUR–MYR4.9650/EUR

   The interest rates are quoted on a 360-day year. Can you do a covered interest arbitrage?

7. As an importer of grain into Japan from the United States, you have agreed to pay $377,287 in 90 days after you receive your grain. You face the following exchange rates and interest rates: spot rate, ¥106.35/$; 90-day forward rate, ¥106.02/$; 90-day USD interest rate, 3.25% p.a.; and 90-day JPY interest rate, 1.9375% p.a.
   a. Describe the nature and extent of your transaction foreign exchange risk.
   b. Explain two ways to hedge the risk.
   c. Which of the alternatives in part b is superior?

8. You are a sales manager for Motorola and export cellular phones from the United States to other countries. You have just signed a deal to ship phones to a British distributor, and you will re-

ceive £700,000 when the phones arrive in London in 180 days. Assume that you can borrow and lend at 7% p.a. in U.S. dollars and at 10% p.a. in British pounds. Both interest rate quotes are for a 360-day year. The spot rate is $1.4945/£, and the 180-day forward rate is $1.4802/£.
   a. Describe the nature and extent of your transaction foreign exchange risk.
   b. Describe two ways of eliminating the transaction foreign exchange risk.
   c. Which of the alternatives in part b is superior?
   d. Assume that the dollar interest rate and the exchange rates are correct. Determine what sterling interest rate would make your firm indifferent between the two alternative hedges.

9. Suppose that there is a 0.5% probability that the government of Argentina will nationalize its banking system and freeze all foreign deposits indefinitely during the next year. If the dollar deposit interest rate in the United States is 5%, what dollar interest would Argentine banks have to offer in order to attract deposits from foreign investors?

10. If the market price of a 20-year pure discount bond with a face value of $1,000 is $214.55, what is the spot interest rate for the 20-year maturity expressed in percentage per annum?

11. Consider a 2-year euro-denominated bond that has a current market price of €970, a face value of €1,000, and an annual coupon of 5%. If the 1-year spot interest rate is 5.5%, what is the 2-year spot interest rate?

12. Consider some data drawn from Exhibit 6.5. The 1-year rates can be viewed as spot interest rates, and the 2-year rates are yields to maturity in annualized percent. The spot exchange rate is ¥132.192/£.

	U.K.	Japan
1 year	1.105	0.370
2 year	1.770	0.430

What should be the 2-year forward rate to prevent arbitrage?

13. Go to the Web site of the British Bankers' Association (BBA). Find out which banks are on the panel for the dollar, the euro, the yen, and the Australian dollar.

BIBLIOGRAPHY

Akram, Farooq, Dagfinn Rime, and Lucio Sarno, 2008, "Arbitrage in the Foreign Exchange Market: Turning on the Microscope," *Journal of International Economics* 76, pp. 237–253.

Baba, Naohiko, and Frank Packer, 2009a, "From Turmoil to Crisis: Dislocations in the FX Swap Market Before and After the Failure of Lehman Brothers," *Journal of International Money and Finance* 28, pp. 1350–1374.

_____, 2009b, "Interpreting Deviations from Covered Interest Parity During the Financial Market Turmoil of 2007-08," *Journal of Banking and Finance* 33, pp. 1953–1962.

Cheung, Yin-Wong, and Xingwang Qian, 2010, "Capital Flight: China's Experience," *Review of Development Economics* 14, pp. 227–247.

Coffey, Niall, Warren B. Hrung, Hoai-Luu Nguyen, and Asani Sarkar, 2009, "The Global Financial Crisis and Offshore Dollar Markets, 2009," *Current Issues in Economics and Finance* 15, Federal Reserve Bank of New York.

Domowitz, Ian, Jack Glen, and Ananth Madhavan, 1998, "Country and Currency Risk Premia in an Emerging Market," *Journal of Financial and Quantitative Analysis* 33, pp. 189–216.

Griffoli, Tommaso Mancini, and Angelo Ranaldo, 2010, "Limits to Arbitrage During the Crisis: Funding Liquidity Constraints and Covered Interest Parity," Swiss National Bank Working Paper 2010–14.

Ma, Guonan, and Robert N. McCauley, 2008, "The Efficacy of China's Capital Controls—Evidence from Price and Flow Data," *Pacific Economic Review* 13, pp. 104–123.

Shleifer, Andrei, and Robert W. Vishny, 1997, "The Limits of Arbitrage," *Journal of Finance* 52, pp. 35–55.

Speculation and Risk in the Foreign Exchange Market

*J*apanese investors, like Mrs. Watanabe in Chapter 2, have faced perennially low Japanese yen interest rates for years. They consequently have found high-yielding bonds denominated in Australian and New Zealand dollars quite attractive. More recently, retail aggregator accounts have been introduced that allow private Japanese investors to speculate in foreign exchange markets using forward contracts. A 2010 Bank for International Settlements (BIS) study by Michael King and Dagfinn Rime estimates that Japanese retail investors trade over $20 billion a day in foreign exchange markets.

This chapter examines how investors quantify expected returns and risks associated with speculative foreign exchange investments. If an investor chooses not to hedge (or "cover") the exchange risk on a foreign money market investment, the return is uncertain and will be high if the foreign currency appreciates or low if the foreign currency depreciates. Our discussion of uncovered investments in the foreign money market uses some basic statistical methods that are commonly used to explain empirical evidence about investment returns in all asset markets. The Appendix to Chapter 3 and Appendix 7.3 in this chapter provide the necessary background.

7.1 SPECULATING IN THE FOREIGN EXCHANGE MARKET

Uncovered Foreign Money Market Investments

In Chapter 6, we examined covered foreign money markets investments and found that if interest rate parity is satisfied, the domestic currency rate of return from investing in a foreign money market and covering the foreign exchange risk is the domestic currency interest rate. What happens if an investor does not cover the foreign exchange risk? Let's look at an example.

Example 7.1   Kevin Anthony's Uncovered Pound Investment

Recall the situation in Example 6.2 in which Kevin Anthony, a portfolio manager, was considering several ways to invest $10,000,000 for 1 year. The data are as follows:

> USD interest rate: 8.0% per annum (p.a.)
> GBP interest rate: 12.0% p.a.
> Spot exchange rate: $1.60/£

Remember that if Kevin invests in the USD-denominated asset at 8%, after 1 year he will have $10,000,000 × 1.08 = $10,800,000.

Suppose Kevin invests his $10,000,000 in the pound money market, but he decides not to hedge the foreign exchange risk. As before, we can calculate his dollar return in three steps.

Step 1. Convert dollars into pounds in the spot market. The $10,000,000 will buy

$$\frac{\$10{,}000{,}000}{\$1.60/£} = £6{,}250{,}000$$

at the current spot exchange rate. This is Kevin's pound principal.

Step 2. Calculate pound-denominated interest plus principal. Kevin can invest his pound principal at 12%, yielding a return in 1 year of

$$£6{,}250{,}000 \times 1.12 = £7{,}000{,}000$$

Step 3. Sell the pound principal plus interest at the spot exchange rate in 1 year:

$$\text{Dollar proceeds in 1 year} = £7{,}000{,}000 \times S(t{+}1, \$/£)$$

By choosing not to hedge the foreign exchange risk, the dollars Kevin receives from his investment in the pound money market are determined by the value of the future exchange rate.

Let's denote the $/£ current spot rate by $S(t)$ and the future spot rate by $S(t{+}1)$. Following the three steps in Example 7.1, the dollar return from investing 1 dollar in a pound money market investment, $r(t{+}1)$, is

$$r(t{+}1) = \frac{1}{S(t)} \times [1 + i(£)] \times S(t{+}1) \tag{7.1}$$

where $i(£)$ denotes the pound interest rate. In Example 7.1, we obtain

$$r(t{+}1) = \frac{1}{\$1.60/£} \times 1.12 \times S(t{+}1) = 0.7 \times S(t{+}1).$$

Notice that $0.7 = \dfrac{£7{,}000{,}000}{\$10{,}000{,}000}$ is the ratio of the amount of future pounds Kevin will have to the amount of dollars he invests today. The return on Kevin's investment is risky because the value of the future exchange rate is not known today. Kevin might also be interested in the excess return to this investment, denoted $\text{exr}(t{+}1)$—that is, the return over and above what he could earn risk free domestically. The excess return (exr) is

$$\text{exr}(t{+}1) = \frac{S(t{+}1)}{S(t)} \times [1 + i(£)] - [1 + i(\$)] \tag{7.2}$$

$$= S(t{+}1) \times 0.7 - 1.08$$

where $i(\$)$ is the dollar interest rate.

Speculating with Forward Contracts

The Break-Even Spot Rate

The future exchange rate for which Kevin breaks even between the pound and the domestic money market investments is the exchange rate, S^{BE}, that sets Equation (7.2) equal to zero:

$$S^{BE} = S(t) \times \frac{[1 + i(\$)]}{[1 + i(£)]} \tag{7.3}$$

Hence, Kevin's break-even rate is $S^{BE} = 1.08/0.7 = \$1.5429/£$.

From Chapter 6, recognize that Equation (7.3) is the formula for the forward rate! Consequently, if the foreign currency appreciates such that the future exchange rate is above the forward rate, Kevin makes a positive excess return, but if the future exchange rate is less than the forward rate, Kevin has a negative excess return. Therefore, it is not surprising that Kevin can also speculate on the direction of the pound exchange rate using forward contracts.

Comparing Forward Market and Foreign Money Market Investments

Forward contracts are pure bets—that is, no money changes hands when a forward contract is made. To make this forward contracting situation more concrete, let Mr. Buy represent the person who buys pounds forward with dollars from Ms. Sell, who represents the person who sells pounds forward for dollars. Mr. Buy will pay $F(t)$ dollars in 1 year for every pound he buys forward, and he will sell each pound in the future spot market for dollars at $S(t+1)$. Ms. Sell, on the other hand, will buy her pounds in the future spot market at a dollar price of $S(t+1)$, and she will sell each pound to Mr. Buy for $F(t)$. Therefore, on a per-pound basis, the dollar profits and losses are as follows:

$$\text{Mr. Buy's dollar profit or loss} = S(t+1) - F(t)$$
$$\text{Ms. Sell's dollar profit or loss} = F(t) - S(t+1)$$

These dollar profits and losses are graphed in Exhibit 7.1 as a function of $S(t+1)$. Notice that the dollar profit of the person buying foreign currency forward is the dollar loss of the person selling foreign currency forward, and vice versa.

How does this **forward market investment** compare with Kevin Anthony's pound foreign money market investment? Because Kevin invests in the pound money market, the relevant comparison is with Mr. Buy's purchase of pounds in the forward market. We first express Mr. Buy's profits on a per-dollar basis by dividing by $S(t)$:

$$\text{Forward Market return (per dollar)} = \text{fmr}(t+1) = \frac{S(t+1) - F(t)}{S(t)} \tag{7.4}$$

where we define the **forward market return** (per dollar) in Equation (7.4) as $\text{fmr}(t+1)$. Because the excess return can be viewed as the return on a strategy in which Kevin borrows dollars in the domestic money market and invests them in the pound money market, it is analogous to a forward contract in which no money changes hands up front. Clearly, the two returns must be closely related, as both investments are exposed to changes in the value of the pound. In fact,

$$\text{fmr}(t+1) \times [1 + i(£)] = \frac{S(t+1)}{S(t)}[1 + i(£)] - [1 + i(\$)]$$

Intuitively, because the forward contract sells £1 in the future, but Kevin's strategy invests pounds today, we must make a future value adjustment. We must scale up the forward market return by $[1 + i(£)]$ to compare it to a money market investment because 1 pound today is worth $[1 + i(£)]$ pounds in the future. Mathematically, you can verify this relation by replacing $F(t)$ in the expression for $\text{fmr}(t)$ by its value in terms of the spot exchange rate and interest rates predicted by covered interest rate parity [see Equation (7.3)].

Exhibit 7.1   Profits and Losses from Forward Market Speculation

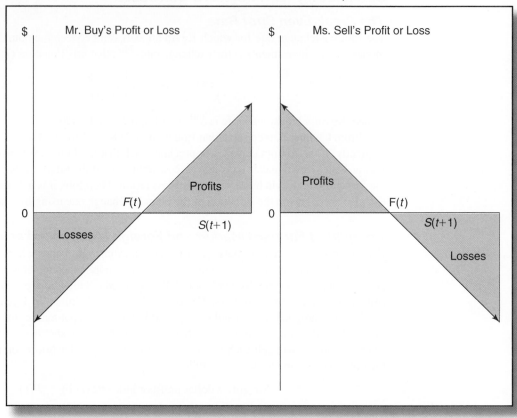

Currency Speculation and Profits and Losses

The uncertainty about future exchange rates makes currency speculation risky. We now show how to characterize expected losses and profits on speculative currency investments.

Quantifying Expected Losses and Profits

To quantify our uncertainty about future returns, we use conditional probability distributions as in Chapter 3. Recall that we view today as being time t, and remember that the *conditional probability distribution* of the spot exchange rate for some time in the future, as in Exhibit 3.1, describes the conditional probabilities associated with all the possible exchange rates that may occur at that time *conditioned on* all the information that is available today. The collection of all information that is used to predict the future value of an economic variable is typically called an **information set**. Also, recall that we refer to the expected value (the mean) of this probability distribution as the *conditional expectation of the future exchange rate*. We denote the conditional expectation at time t of the future spot exchange rate of dollars per pound at time $t+1$, for instance, 1 year from now, as $E_t[S(t+1, \$/\£)]$.

In Chapter 3, we argued that the distribution of exchange rate changes is relatively well described by a normal (that is, a bell-shaped) distribution, at least for exchange rates between the currencies of developed countries. As we will argue later in this chapter, there are times when conditional distributions of future exchange rates are fat tailed and skewed. For now, though, we'll stick to the normal distribution because it often works well. Hence, in addition to the mean of the conditional distribution of the future spot exchange rate, we must also specify its standard deviation. Now we are ready to quantify the probability of losses and gains. Let's illustrate by revisiting Kevin Anthony's example.

Example 7.2 Kevin Anthony's Probability of Loss

Suppose Kevin expects the pound to depreciate relative to the dollar by 3.57% over the next year. Then, the conditional expectation of his future spot rate in 1 year is

$$\$1.60/\pounds \times (1 - 0.0357) = \$1.5429/\pounds$$

which makes the conditional expectation of his uncertain dollar return equal to

$$\pounds 7,000,000 \times \$1.5429/\pounds = \$10,800,300$$

This return is essentially the same as the return from his dollar investment because $\$1.5429/\pounds$ is the break-even future exchange rate (S^{BE}) that equalizes the returns on dollar and pound investments.[1]

Suppose Kevin thinks that the rate of appreciation of the pound relative to the dollar is normally distributed. From the symmetry of the normal distribution, he knows that there is a 50% probability that he will do better than the dollar investment and there is a 50% probability that he will do worse.

Kevin might also be interested in knowing the probability that he will lose some of his dollar principal. At what future value of the spot exchange rate $S(t+1, \$/\pounds)$ will Kevin just get his $10,000,000 principal back? This value—let's call it $\hat{S}$—satisfies

$$(\pounds 7,000,000) \times \hat{S} = \$10,000,000$$

from which we find

$$\hat{S} = \frac{\$10,000,000}{\pounds 7,000,000} = \$1.4286/\pounds$$

Kevin can calculate the probability that the future exchange rate will be lower than $\$1.4286/\pounds$. To perform such a calculation, he needs to determine the standard deviation of the payoff on his investment. Suppose he thinks that the standard deviation of the rate of appreciation of the pound relative to the dollar over the next year is 10%. Because 10% of $\$1.60/\pounds$ is $\$0.16/\pounds$, the standard deviation of the conditional distribution of the future spot exchange rate is $\$0.16/\pounds$ (see Chapter 3). He can calculate the probability of losing money by creating a **standard normal random variable**. A standard normal random variable has a mean of 0 and a standard deviation of 1, which we denote with $N(0, 1)$, and we can calculate it by subtracting the mean of the future spot rate and dividing by the standard deviation. Thus,

$$\frac{S(t+1, \$/\pounds) - \$1.5429/\pounds}{\$0.16/\pounds}$$

has a mean of 0 and a standard deviation of 1. We graph such a standard normal distribution in Exhibit 7.2. Then, the value of the standard normal variable associated with a zero rate of return is

$$\frac{\$1.4286/\pounds - \$1.5429/\pounds}{\$0.16/\pounds} = -0.7144$$

From the probability distribution of a standard normal, we find that there is a 23.75% probability that a $N(0, 1)$ variable will be less than -0.7144, or equivalently that $S(t+1)$, $\$/\pounds$ will be less than $\$1.4286/\pounds$. In the graph in Exhibit 7.2, the area below the curve to the left of -0.7144 is 23.75% (the total area sums to 1). Hence, 23.75% is the chance that Kevin will actually lose some of his dollar principal over the course of the next year.

---

[1]The $300 difference is due to the rounding of the exchange rate to the fourth digit.

Exhibit 7.2 Standard Normal Distribution

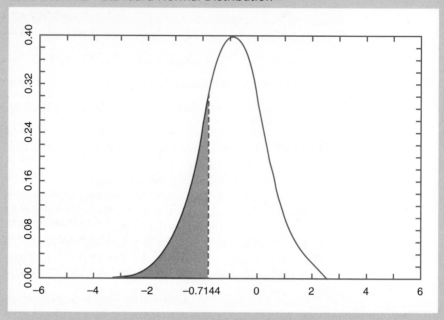

Notes: The horizontal axis represents possible values for a standard normally distributed variable (say, x). The vertical axis represents the value of the normal distribution function (say, y) for each x. In fact,

$y = \dfrac{1}{\sqrt{2\pi}}\, e^{-\frac{1}{2}x^2}$, where e is 2.71828. The area below -0.7144 represents 23.75% of the total area, which sums to 1.

Lessons from History: The Variability of Currency Changes and Forward Market Returns

At this point, one can think of the conditional probability distribution as reflecting the subjective beliefs of an individual investor, an importer or an exporter, about the uncertain future exchange rate. The next section discusses theories that determine a value for the conditional mean of the distribution. Here we review historical data to inform us about the width of the distribution. Kevin used 10% for the rate of appreciation of the pound versus the dollar. If the true number were larger, the conditional distribution for the future exchange rate would be more dispersed, and the probability that he would lose some of his principal would be larger than 23.75%.

Exhibit 7.3 shows the standard deviations of percentage changes in exchange rates and forward market returns for three exchange rates versus the U.S. dollar and the corresponding non-dollar cross rates calculated with over 30 years of actual data. The three currencies are the euro (using data on the Deutsche mark before 1999), the British pound, and the Japanese yen. Note that the annualized volatilities of percentage changes in the exchange rate reported in column 1 are indeed around 10% (somewhere between 9.25% and 12.37%). In other words, Kevin Anthony guessed about right, and the computation in Example 7.2 is realistic.

The second column of Exhibit 7.3 presents the variability of forward market returns [fmr(t), see Equation (7.4)]. Note that only the first two lines are returns from the perspective of a U.S. investor; for the other currency pairs, we follow the usual conventions, so that the

Exhibit 7.3   Standard Deviations of Monthly Exchange Rate Changes and Forward Market Returns

Exchange Rate	Standard Deviation	
	Exchange Rate % Change	Forward Market Return
$/€	11.17	11.25
$/£	10.57	10.70
¥/$	11.66	11.81
¥/€	11.34	11.42
£/€	9.25	9.35
¥/£	12.37	12.49

Notes: The table uses data from February 1976 to April 2010. The DEM replaces the euro before January 1999. The exchange rate % change is $s(t+1) = \dfrac{S(t+1) - S(t)}{S(t)} \times 100$ and the forward market return is $100 \times$ $[s(t+1) - fp(t)]$ with $fp(t) = \dfrac{F(t) - S(t)}{S(t)}$. We annualize the monthly standard deviations by multiplying by the square root of 12, as is typical in financial markets. The data were obtained from Reuters and Global Insight.

investor is either yen- or pound-based. The variability of the forward market returns is of the same order of magnitude as the variability of the exchange rate changes themselves. Clearly, speculating in the foreign exchange market is not without risk of loss.

7.2 UNCOVERED INTEREST RATE PARITY AND THE UNBIASEDNESS HYPOTHESIS

Covered interest rate parity maintains that a domestic money market investment and a foreign money market investment have the same domestic currency return as long as the foreign exchange risk in the foreign money market investment is "covered" using a forward contract. Two related theories predict what may happen when exchange rate risk is, by contrast, not hedged. **Uncovered interest rate parity** maintains that the "uncovered" foreign money market investment, which has an uncertain return because of the uncertainty about the future value of the exchange rate, has the same *expected* return as the domestic money market investment. The **unbiasedness hypothesis** states that there is no systematic difference between the forward rate and the expected future spot rate and that, consequently, the expected forward market return is zero. In this section, we develop both of these hypotheses in more detail.

Uncovered Interest Rate Parity

If we take the expected value of the return to investing 1 dollar in the pound money market, as described in Equation (7.1), we find

$$E_t[r(t+1)] = \frac{1}{S(t)} \times [1 + i(£)] \times E_t[S(t+1)]$$

Because the current spot rate, $S(t)$, and the interest rate, $i(£)$, are in the time t information set, the expectation applies only to the future exchange rate.

Uncovered interest rate parity is the hypothesis that the expected return on the uncovered foreign investment equals the known return from investing 1 dollar in the dollar money market $[1 + i(\$)]$. If uncovered interest rate parity is true, there is no compensation to the uncovered investor for the uncertainty associated with the future spot rate, and expected returns on investments in different money markets are equalized. Equivalently, the speculative return on borrowing 1 dollar and investing it in the pound money market, $\text{exr}(t+1)$ [see Equation (7.2)], is expected to be zero, given current information.

Let's go back to the portfolio manager Kevin Anthony. The interest rate on the pound is 12%, but the interest rate on the dollar is only 8%. Uncovered interest rate parity suggests that it would be naïve to think that pounds therefore constitute a great investment for Kevin. In fact, the high yield on pounds implies that the market anticipates the pound to depreciate by just enough that the expected dollar return to currency speculation in the pound market is also 8%. In particular,

$$\frac{1}{\$1.60/\pounds} \times [1 + 0.12] \times E_t[S(t+1)] = 1 + 0.08$$

or

$$E_t[S(t+1)] = \frac{1.08}{1.12} \times 1.60 = \$1.5429/\pounds$$

That is, the pound is expected to depreciate by 3.57%:

$$\left(\frac{\$1.5429/\pounds - \$1.60/\pounds}{\$1.60/\pounds} \right) = -0.0357$$

The Unbiasedness Hypothesis

When the forward rate equals the expected future spot rate, the forward rate is said to be an **unbiased predictor** of the future spot rate. This equality is summarized by the unbiasedness hypothesis:

$$F(t,\$/\pounds) = E_t[S(t+1,\$/\pounds)] \tag{7.5}$$

Covered interest rate parity and uncovered interest rate parity imply the unbiasedness hypothesis, which can be seen as follows (with S and F always referring to $\$/\pounds$ exchange rates):

$$\underbrace{E_t\left[\frac{S(t+1)}{S(t)}\right][1 + i(\pounds)] = [1 + i(\$)]}_{\text{Uncovered Interest Rate Parity}} = \underbrace{\frac{F(t)}{S(t)}[1 + i(\pounds)]}_{\text{Covered Interest Rate Parity}} \tag{7.6}$$

By eliminating $S(t)$ and $[1 + i(\pounds)]$ from both sides of the exterior equations, we recover the unbiasedness hypothesis. To better understand the concept of an unbiased prediction, we must first understand the concept of a forecast error.

Forecast Errors

Whenever you predict something that is uncertain, such as the future spot rate, there will inevitably be a forecast error. A **forecast error** is the difference between the actual future spot exchange rate and its forecast. One way to measure the magnitude of forecast errors is to examine their standard deviation. We cannot just measure the average forecast error because very large errors in either direction would tend to cancel each other out, potentially resulting in a small average error. Because the standard deviation squares the errors, large errors result in a large standard deviation. In Exhibit 7.3, we showed that percentage changes in exchange rates and forward market returns are very variable. This large variability suggests that the forecast errors in predicting exchange rates, using either the current exchange rate or the forward rate as the forecast, are very variable. Forecasts from commercial firms that sell exchange rate forecasts also have large standard deviations, and no one forecasting firm seems to be very successful over time.

The Soros Saga

Is it reasonable to expect exchange rate forecasts to be characterized with large variability? We think the answer is yes because exchange rates are the relative prices of currencies, and currencies are assets. Thus, exchange rates are asset prices, and we should expect exchange rates to behave very much like other asset prices, such as stock prices, which are also very difficult to predict. If exchange rates were easy to predict, lots of easy money would be made betting that one currency would strengthen relative to another.

Unbiased Predictors

An unbiased predictor implies that the expected forecast error is zero. In our setting, we forecast the future spot rate using the forward rate so that the forecast error is the difference between the two: $S(t+1) - F(t)$. The unbiasedness hypothesis states nothing about the magnitude of the forecast errors, which can be large or small and can vary over time. Instead, it has two important implications. First, given your current information, you should expect the forecast error to be zero. Second, on average, the forecast errors of an unbiased predictor may sometimes be negative and sometimes positive, but they are not systematically positive or negative, and they will average to zero.[2] If a forecast is biased, however, and you know what the bias is, you can improve your forecast by taking into account the bias. Currency speculators seek to exploit such biases.

The Unbiasedness Hypothesis and Market Efficiency

The unbiasedness hypothesis in Equation (7.5) is often identified with market efficiency. In efficient capital markets, investors cannot expect to earn profits over and above what the market supplies as compensation for bearing risk. An inefficient market is one in which profits from trading are not associated with bearing risks and are therefore considered extraordinary. The definition of **market efficiency** incorporates the hypotheses that people process information rationally and that they have common information on relevant variables that may help predict exchange rates. Together, these assumptions ensure that people have common expectations of the future.

To link the unbiasedness hypothesis more explicitly with market efficiency, recall the example of Mr. Buy and Ms. Sell. Mr. Buy's profit or loss from purchasing pounds forward, $S(t+1) - F(t)$, was equal but opposite in sign to Ms. Sell's profit or loss from selling pounds forward, $F(t) - S(t+1)$.

Notice that if the forward rate were a biased predictor of the future spot rate, and people had the same expectation of the future spot rate, one side of the forward contract, either Mr. Buy or Ms. Sell, would expect a profit on the contract, and the other party to the forward contract would expect a loss. Hence, the argument goes, because no one would willingly enter into a forward contract if they expected to lose money, forward rates must be unbiased

---

[2]The second implication follows from the first because of a famous statistical theorem called the Law of Iterated Expectations.

predictors of future spot rates if the market is efficient. That is, both Mr. Buy and Ms. Sell must both expect zero profits:

$$E_t[S(t+1, \$/£) - F(t, \$/£)] = 0 = E_t[F(t, \$/£) - S(t+1, \$/£)]$$

The unbiasedness hypothesis does run into a consistency problem when viewed from two different currency perspectives simultaneously. If it holds in dollars per pound, it must be violated when viewed from pounds per dollar. Appendix 7.1 analyzes this so-called Siegel paradox, demonstrating that it is not important in practice.

Uncovered interest rate parity and the unbiasedness hypothesis do take a narrow view of market efficiency, however. Because currency speculation involves risk taking, isn't it conceivable that there is a positive expected return to be made from speculating in the foreign exchange market? As long as the expected return is commensurate with the risk taken, earning an expected return would not be inconsistent with market efficiency.

7.3 RISK PREMIUMS IN THE FOREIGN EXCHANGE MARKET

You might be surprised by the fact that many rational people, like either Mr. Buy or Ms. Sell, are quite willing to enter contracts expecting a loss. Consider the purchase of fire insurance. Suppose you want to buy fire insurance for 1 year on your $250,000 home. The insurance company charges you today and promises to pay you in the future if you suffer a certain type of loss—in this case, loss due to fire. Suppose everyone agrees that the probability of fire destroying your home is 0.1%. What insurance premium would you be willing to pay? If you are risk neutral, you would just be willing to pay the expected loss:

$$\$250,000 \times \frac{1}{100} \times 0.1 = \$250$$

However, if you confronted many people with this question, they would be willing to pay more than $250 because they are risk averse. If they do, they willingly enter a contract with an expected loss because the expected value of the insurance (given the probability of a fire) is only $250.

Similarly, going back to our earlier example, either Mr. Buy or Ms. Sell may be paying the other person a **risk premium** in order to avoid further harm from large exchange rate movements. For example, Ms. Sell may be selling pounds forward because she is the treasurer of a large multinational corporation (MNC) that is expecting future pound revenues. Remember that the forward rate is $1.5429/£. Even if Ms. Sell expects the future spot rate to be higher than $1.5429/£, she might still choose to hedge because there is a lot of uncertainty about the future value of the pound.

What Determines Risk Premiums?

The risk premium on an asset is the expected return on the asset in excess of the return on a risk-free asset. In this case, the excess return can be thought of as the uncovered foreign money market return, which we called exr$(t+1)$. Denoting the foreign exchange risk premium by rp, we have $rp(t) = E_t[\text{exr}(t+1)]$. Different assets can have different risks, and assets that are riskier must offer higher expected returns in order to induce investors to hold them. You may think that the riskiness of an investment in an asset is determined by the uncertainty associated with the asset's payoff. For example, the risk premium on currency speculation must be linked to the variability of exchange rate changes. After all, the conditional distribution of the future exchange rate will be wider the more variable such changes are. However, this is not the case. The reason is that investors care about the expected return and risk of their whole portfolio of assets, not necessarily about the risk of an individual asset viewed in isolation.

Modern portfolio theory postulates that risk-averse investors like high expected returns on their portfolios, but they dislike a high variance in their portfolios. (That is, they don't like the value of their portfolios to go up and down very much.[3]) The question then becomes: How does the return on an individual asset contribute to the variance of the kinds of portfolios investors are likely to hold? It turns out that if there are many assets in the portfolio, part of the variance of an asset's return does not contribute to the portfolio's variance. This leads to an important decomposition of the uncertainty of the return on any asset.

Systematic and Unsystematic Risk

The uncertainty of a return can always be decomposed into a part that is *systematic* and a part that is *unsystematic*, which is also called *idiosyncratic*. That is,

Individual asset return uncertainty = Systematic risk + Idiosyncratic uncertainty

Systematic risk is the risk associated with an asset's return arising from the covariance of the return with the return on a large, well-diversified portfolio. The **covariance** of two random variables describes how the two variables move together, or *covary*, with each other. Often, we describe how things covary with each other in terms of **correlation** coefficients that are bounded between -1 and $+1$. If the returns on two assets are perfectly correlated (that is, they always perfectly move in the same direction), their correlation coefficient is 1. By contrast, if the assets are not at all correlated (neither moves at all in relation to the other), their correlation coefficient is 0. If the coefficient is -1, the two asset returns always move in opposite directions. The correlation coefficient is the covariance of the two variables divided by the product of their standard deviations.

The large, well-diversified portfolio that investors should hold according to finance theory is called the **market portfolio**.[4] The market portfolio is the value-weighted collection of all available financial assets in the market as a whole.

How does this decomposition relate to risk premiums? If the return on the asset contains only idiosyncratic uncertainty, there will be no increase in the expected return on the asset due to the uncertainty of the return. It will not command a risk premium! The asset will be priced to yield an expected return equal to the return on risk-free assets. An asset has only idiosyncratic uncertainty if its return does not covary with the returns on other assets.

These statements follow from a fundamental insight of portfolio theory: Idiosyncratic uncertainty can be diversified away. Even though investors do not like the uncertainty of their total portfolio and demand risk premiums on assets that contribute to the variance of the portfolio, assets whose returns contain only idiosyncratic uncertainty do not contribute to the variance of the portfolio and, consequently, do not command any risk premium. Because idiosyncratic uncertainty is diversifiable in large portfolios, it is also called *diversifiable uncertainty*, or *diversifiable risk*. Because systematic risk measures how much an asset's return co-moves with the market, it cannot be diversified away, and the risk involved commands a risk premium. For example, the variance of an individual stock return is partly driven by macroeconomic events such as the business cycle and interest rates that affect every stock. Such risks are systematic. The variance of the stock return is also partially driven by **idiosyncratic risks** that affect only that particular stock, such as the quality of the firm's management.

---

[3]We have previously discussed the variance of a random variable and indicated that it is a measure of the dispersion of the probability distribution. Graphically, the square root of the variance (the standard deviation) is associated with the width of a bell-shaped curve.

[4]Appendix 7.2 provides a review of portfolio theory and related statistical concepts, such as covariance, correlations, and betas, to allow you to examine the arguments implying that covariances among returns are the main sources of portfolio variance.

The CAPM

The theories we have been discussing are the foundation of the **capital asset pricing model (CAPM)**. William F. Sharpe was awarded the Nobel Prize in Economics in 1990 for its development. The CAPM holds that it is the covariance of an asset's return with the return on the market portfolio that determines the asset's systematic risk and hence its risk premium. The model also provides an easy-to-implement procedure to put an actual number on the risk premium, which we describe in detail in Chapter 13.

According to the CAPM, the systematic risk of an individual asset is fully described by its **beta** with respect to the market portfolio. The formula for the beta is simple:

$$\text{Beta on asset } i = \frac{\text{Covariance (Asset return } i, \text{ Market portfolio return)}}{\text{Variance (Market portfolio return)}}$$

Higher betas indicate higher systematic risk, and the CAPM postulates that

$$\text{Risk premium on asset } i = (\text{Beta on asset } i) \times (\text{Risk premium on market portfolio})$$

What is the intuition for the prediction about expected returns of the CAPM? Think of the return on the risk-free asset as the compensation provided to an investor for the time value of money that is required by the investor because the investor sacrifices the use of the money for a certain period. The investor requires compensation in excess of the risk-free rate (that is, a risk premium) if the beta of the asset is positive, as are the betas of most equity investments. Assets with positive betas contribute to the variance of the market portfolio, and the larger the beta, the riskier the asset and the higher its expected return must be. Notice that if an asset has a negative beta because the return on the asset is negatively correlated with the return on the market portfolio, the expected return on the asset is less than the risk-free rate. Investing in an asset that covaries negatively with the return on the market portfolio provides an investor with portfolio insurance. When the rest of the investor's portfolio is doing poorly, the asset with the negative covariance generally pays high returns, and when the rest of the investor's portfolio pays high returns, the asset with the negative covariance generally pays relatively low returns. Investing in this asset thus dampens the volatility of the return on the total portfolio. Risk-averse investors are willing to "pay" for this reduction in the volatility of their overall portfolio by accepting an expected return that is less than the risk-free interest rate.

Applying the CAPM to Forward Market Returns

Because a forward contract is an asset, there is potential for a risk premium. How will this bias the forward rate as a predictor of the future spot rate? Taking a position in a forward contract involves no investment of funds at the point in time when the contract is set, and it is not necessary to compensate the investor for the time value of money. But the dollar profits and losses on the forward contract can still covary systematically with the dollar return on the market portfolio. Hence, if the profitability of Mr. Buy's purchase of foreign currency at the forward exchange rate covaries positively with the dollar return on the market portfolio, Mr. Buy will view the forward contract as risky and will demand an expected profit. As noted previously, though, Ms. Sell's profits and losses on the forward contract are the opposite of Mr. Buy's profits and losses. Hence, if Mr. Buy's dollar profit is positively correlated with the dollar return on the market portfolio, the covariance of the dollar profit on Ms. Sell's side of the forward contract is negatively correlated with the dollar return on the market portfolio. In this case, when Ms. Sell enters into the contract, she obtains an asset that reduces the variability of her overall portfolio. She consequently willingly holds this contract at an expected loss. Again, this is like portfolio insurance. From Ms. Sell's perspective, the expected loss is balanced by the fact that the forward contract performs well when the rest of her portfolio does poorly. Consequently, there can be a risk premium that causes the forward rate to be a biased predictor of the future spot rate. According to the CAPM, such a risk premium should depend on the beta of the (excess) return to currency speculation.

Formal Derivation of CAPM Risk Premiums (Advanced)

The CAPM in Symbols

Let the dollar return for a 1-year holding period for an arbitrary asset j be $R_j(t+1)$, and let the risk-free return be $[1 + i(t, \$)]$. The CAPM predicts that the risk premium on an asset is equal to the beta of the asset multiplied by the amount by which the expected return on the market portfolio, $R_M(t+1)$, exceeds the return on the risk-free asset:

$$E_t\{R_j(t+1) - [1 + i(t, \$)]\} = \beta_j E_t\{R_M(t+1) - [1 + i(t, \$)]\} \qquad (7.7)$$

The beta of the jth asset is the covariance of the return on asset j with the return on the market portfolio, σ_{jM}, divided by the variance of the return on the market portfolio, σ_{MM}:

$$\beta_j = \frac{\sigma_{jM}}{\sigma_{MM}}.$$

Here, the variance (covariance) is a conditional variance (covariance) because it is based on the information at time t.

The CAPM and Forward Market Returns

Let's derive the implications of the CAPM for the risk premium on an unhedged investment of dollars in the British pound money market. The uncovered excess return was defined in Equation (7.2), and we review it here for convenience:

$$\text{exr}(t+1) = \frac{S(t+1, \$/£)[1 + i(t, £)]}{S(t, \$/£)} - [1 + i(t, \$)] = R_£(t+1) - [1 + i(t, \$)]$$

From Equation (7.7), the CAPM gives the expected excess return on this uncertain dollar investment:

$$E_t[\text{exr}(t+1)] = \beta_u E_t\{R_M(t+1) - [1 + i(t, \$)]\} \qquad (7.8)$$

The beta on the uncovered pound investment is

$$\beta_u = \frac{\text{COV}_t[R_£(t+1), R_M(t+1)]}{\text{VAR}_t[R_M(t+1)]}$$

where COV_t and VAR_t are shorthand for conditional covariance and variance, respectively, and the interest rates do not enter the expression because they are in the time t information set.

The forward market return also satisfies a CAPM relationship:

$$E_t[\text{fmr}(t+1)] = \beta_F E_t\{R_M(t+1) - [1 + i(t, \$)]\} \qquad (7.9)$$

Here, β_F is the beta on the forward contract to buy foreign currency in the forward market and sell it subsequently in the future spot market. Recall from Section 7.1 that $\text{fmr}(t+1) = \dfrac{\text{exr}(t+1)}{1 + i(t, £)}$. Therefore, $\beta_F = \dfrac{\beta_u}{1 + i(t, £)}$. In other words, the expected returns on forward market contracts and money market investments are proportional because they have the same fundamental risk exposure but invest a different number of units.

Equations (7.8) and (7.9) indicate that forward rates will be biased predictors of future spot rates if there is systematic risk associated with the profits on a forward contract. In the case of the dollar/pound example, if the dollar weakens relative to the pound when the dollar payoff on the market portfolio is high, the risk premium would be positive, and the forward rate would be below the expected future spot rate. You would expect to profit by buying pounds forward, and you would expect to suffer a loss by selling pounds forward. If, on the other hand, the dollar strengthens relative to the pound when the dollar return on the market portfolio is high, the beta on the forward contract would be negative. Thus, the forward rate would be above the expected future spot rate, and there would be an expected loss from buying pounds forward and an expected gain from selling pounds forward.

7.4 UNCOVERED INTEREST RATE PARITY AND THE UNBIASEDNESS HYPOTHESIS IN PRACTICE

Taking a stand on whether uncovered interest rate parity and the unbiasedness hypothesis actually hold is important when international financial managers make decisions. This section reviews situations in which this issue arises.

Situations Where Premiums Matter

International Portfolio Management

When a European portfolio manager buys Japanese equities, he hopes the Japanese equity market will perform well, but he is also exposed to foreign exchange risk in the yen–euro market. As we discuss in detail in Chapter 13, the return on a foreign bond and/or equity can be decomposed into two components: the (local) return on the foreign asset and the currency return. Global money managers may decide to speculate on a currency, or they may decide to hedge the currency risk. This decision is greatly affected by whether they believe in the validity of uncovered interest rate parity and the unbiasedness hypothesis.

The Cost of Hedging

Multinational corporations often hedge their transaction foreign exchange risk using forward contracts. Clearly they may be willing to pay a premium to insure against this risk. The following *Point–Counterpoint* makes a link between the unbiasedness hypothesis and a practical hedging situation. In a nutshell, when unbiasedness holds, multinationals effectively do not pay premiums to hedge their transaction foreign exchange risk. Of course, as we argued in Section 7.3, the existence of a premium is not necessarily inconsistent with market efficiency and may be fair compensation for risk insurance. Note also that an MNC may benefit from such premiums. For example, if the long position in a particular currency commands a premium, an MNC that hedges a short position will earn the risk premium.

Exchange Rate Forecasting

Forecasting exchange rates is difficult, but it remains an activity that attracts many resources and much brainpower in the real world. If the unbiasedness hypothesis holds, the best forecast of the future exchange rate can be read from a table in your daily *Financial Times* or *Wall Street Journal* because the answer lies in the forward rate. Chapter 10 examines the success of different forecasting models relative to the forward rate.

Exchange Rate Determination

Chapter 10 discusses some popular exchange rate determination theories. It turns out that many of the well-known theories linking exchange rate values to fundamentals such as trade balances, money supplies, and so forth, assume that uncovered interest rate parity holds. But if it does not hold, the validity of these theories is immediately in doubt. On the other hand, the empirical evidence that we present in Section 7.5 has motivated some macroeconomists to supplement macro-models with time-varying foreign exchange risk premiums.

POINT–COUNTERPOINT

The Cost of Hedging[5]

Ante and Freedy's Uncle Fred is holding forth during dinner at the annual Handel family gathering at his estate in Chappaqua, New York. Uncle Fred is in the export–import business, is very well traveled, and loves recounting his on-the-road war stories. After a hilarious account of how a Dutch business associate recommended checking out the Walletjes (the red light district) in Amsterdam as the high point of Dutch architecture, he suddenly turns to Ante and Freedy: "Hey, how's that international finance class going? I hope well, because I've got a question for you from my business. Suppose I owe 10 million Swedish kronor, payable in 1 month. My company has the cash to buy kronor now, or it could wait until later. I figure we should put the money wherever in the world it would earn the highest interest rate, but my treasurer, an MBA hotshot, tells me that high interest rates are irrelevant because if the krona interest rate is higher than the dollar interest rate, the krona is expected to fall in value relative to the dollar. When I ask her what I should do, she says that it doesn't matter. 'Flip a coin,' she says. Is this why I'm paying her such a high salary? Anyway, young fellows, what do you think?"

As usual, Ante is quickest to respond: "You're absolutely right, Uncle Fred, you should fire that MBA. I am convinced that you will earn a higher return if you put your cash balances in the currency that has the highest interest rate. That way, you will lower the effective dollar cost of your foreign payables."

Freedy shakes his head. "Have you been sleeping in class, Ante? Remember the theory of uncovered interest rate parity? The MBA is right. On average, dollar returns will be equalized in different countries. If Uncle Fred puts his money in kronor when the interest rate is high, the krona will likely depreciate, wiping out the interest rate gain. Maybe he could make it easier on himself and just buy the kronor in the forward market."

"Hmm, this is a useful argument. Let's have our grappa in the living room. Maybe that will bring your thoughts together," sighs Uncle Fred. As they walk toward the comfortable, Italian-designed sofas, Suttle Trooth joins them from the kitchen.

"Hey guys, I overheard your conversation, and are you ever confused," says Suttle. "Let me explain to Uncle Fred what is going on. I brought some paper and a pencil because I want to write down a few things."

"Consider what Uncle Fred is saying," continues Suttle. "Suppose he keeps his money in dollars. Then, Uncle Fred incurs currency risk because he will have to convert the dollars into kronor 1 month from now at the exchange rate of $S(t+1, \$/\text{SEK})$. The dollar cost in 1 month of the krona payable will be

$$\text{SEK10 million} \times S(t+1, \$/\text{SEK})$$

If he converts his dollars now, he will not face any currency risk because he will know exactly how many kronor to convert so that they grow to SEK10 million in 1 month. That amount will be the present value of the SEK10 million, or

$$\text{SEK10 million} \times \frac{1}{1 + i(\text{SEK})}$$

The current dollar cost of this amount of kronor is

$$\text{SEK10 million} \times \frac{1}{1 + i(\text{SEK})} \times S(t, \$/\text{SEK})$$

---

[5]This *Point–Counterpoint* is motivated by the discussion in Kenneth Froot and Richard Thaler (1990).

Chapter 7   Speculation and Risk in the Foreign Exchange Market   **219**

Because the first cost is dollars in 1 month and the second cost is dollars today, to compare the alternative strategies, we have to take both costs to the same point in time. Taking the future value in dollars of the second strategy gives

$$\text{SEK10 million} \times \frac{1}{1 + i(\text{SEK})} \times S(t, \$/\text{SEK}) \times [1 + i(\$)]$$

At this point, Freedy interjects, "Hey, those terms involving interest rates and the spot rate are equal to the forward rate, right?"

"Very good, Freedy, you've got it," replies Suttle. "The strategy of converting into kronor now is equivalent to a strategy of buying kronor in the forward market. Therefore, we can compare the performance of Uncle Fred's possible strategies by comparing the future exchange rate with the forward rate. Suppose dollar interest rates are higher than krona interest rates, in which case the krona trades at a forward premium. Then, Uncle Fred's proposal would have him not hedge, and he would keep his money in dollars. That strategy works great *if* the future USD/SEK exchange rate turns out to be lower than the forward rate. If it does, Uncle Fred's *ex post* costs will be relatively low."

"Very interesting, but all these equations do not appear to answer my question, now do they?" grumbled Uncle Fred.

"Hold on. I am not done yet," says Suttle. "Let's think about what you'd lose by hedging. We can call this the *cost of hedging*, if you wish. *Ex post*, the cost of having hedged can be either positive or negative because it will equal

$$F(t, \$/\text{SEK}) - S(t{+}1, \$/\text{SEK})$$

If the forward rate is higher than the future spot rate, you would indeed have been better off not to hedge and to have just taken the currency risk. Of course, you cannot necessarily know when this will occur, and there will certainly be instances in which the future spot rate ends up higher than the forward rate (when the SEK appreciates more than the forward rate indicates), in which case your *ex post* cost of hedging will be negative because you have higher costs by having not hedged. Now, what the MBA is trying to tell you is that the expected value of the cost of hedging is zero in an efficient market with no risk premium:

$$E[F(t, \$/\text{SEK}) - S(t{+}1, \$/\text{SEK})] = 0$$

This relationship is also known as the unbiasedness hypothesis. Equivalently, whether interest rates are higher or lower abroad does not matter because currency changes, on average, correct for this. If the unbiasedness hypothesis is correct, it won't matter whether you hedge or do not hedge your exposure. Also, Uncle Fred, your strategy won't make money on average because sometimes you will hedge and sometimes you will not, but the expected difference between the two is zero. So the expectation of the difference in the cost of the two strategies can be viewed as the expected cost of hedging, and it is zero—if unbiasedness holds."

Ante excitedly interjects, "But who says the market is efficient? These equations are derived by some ivory tower academics. Why should we expect them to characterize actual markets where real people have to trade?"

"Well, there is something to that point, I must admit," answers Suttle. "Some econometric tests have rejected the unbiasedness hypothesis, and the estimates actually indicate that Uncle Fred's high-yield strategy may work. But that need not mean the market is inefficient. If Uncle Fred does not hedge, he is exposed to currency risk. In other asset markets, such as equities, investors are compensated for taking on risk by receiving a higher expected return than the risk-free rate. We call this higher expected return a *risk premium*. There are probably risk premiums in the currency markets, too. If indeed there is a risk premium, there is an expected cost or an expected return to hedging. Suppose that a relatively high interest rate is providing compensation for both expected currency depreciation but also for risk. Uncle Fred's unhedged strategy is then associated with currency exposure when such exposure is very risky. To make this more concrete, suppose the dollar interest rate is higher than the krona interest rate. Uncle Fred won't hedge because he thinks $E[F(t) - S(t+1)] > 0$. There is a positive cost to hedging. But is that wise? Uncle Fred is not in the foreign exchange investment business, exchange rates are quite volatile, and not hedging may really hurt the bottom line, if the currency moves against him. When you hedge, you buy security! Don't you agree, Uncle?" asks Suttle, turning to see Uncle Fred comfortably snoring on the Italian sofa.

7.5 EMPIRICAL EVIDENCE ON THE UNBIASEDNESS HYPOTHESIS

In this section, we derive statistical tests of whether forward rates have historically been unbiased predictors of future spot rates and apply them to exchange rate data. The discussion uses basic statistics reviewed in Chapter 3 and **regression analysis**. (Appendix 7.3 provides a primer on regression tests.)

The Quest for a Test

A proper econometric test of the unbiasedness hypothesis transforms Equation (7.5) by dividing by $S(t, \$/\pounds)$ on both sides and by subtracting 1—with 1 written as $S(t, \$/\pounds)/S(t, \$/\pounds)$—from both sides of the equation.[6] This is possible because the spot exchange rate at time t, $S(t, \$/\pounds)$, is in the investors' information set.

$$
\begin{aligned}
fp(t, \$/\pounds) &\equiv \frac{F(t, \$/\pounds) - S(t, \$/\pounds)}{S(t, \$/\pounds)} \\
&= \frac{E_t[S(t+30, \$/\pounds) - S(t, \$/\pounds)]}{S(t, \$/\pounds)} \equiv E_t[s(t+30, \$/\pounds)]
\end{aligned}
\qquad \textbf{(7.10)}
$$

In Equation (7.10), we use a 30-day (1-month) forward contract, as in the empirical test reported in the next section. The left-hand side of Equation (7.10) is recognized as the 30-day forward premium (fp) or discount on the pound. The right-hand side of Equation (7.10) is the expected rate of appreciation or depreciation of the pound relative to the dollar (s). Equation (7.10) states that the unbiasedness hypothesis requires the forward premium or discount on the pound to be equal to the market participants' expectations about the rate of appreciation or depreciation of the pound relative to the dollar over the course of the next 30 days. If the hypothesis holds, the expected return to currency speculation will be exactly zero.

Incorporating Rational Expectations into the Test

The most difficult problem in testing the unbiasedness hypothesis is that it contains a variable that cannot be observed by a statistician: the conditional expectation of the rate of appreciation of the pound relative to the dollar. This conditional expectation is formed by market participants on the basis of their information set. Hence, in order to test the unbiasedness hypothesis, a statistician must specify how investors and speculators form their expectations. Typically, when statisticians are confronted with an unobservable variable, they make an auxiliary assumption to develop a test of the underlying hypothesis.

As in most other areas of financial economics, the most popular auxiliary assumption is that investors have **rational expectations**. If investors have rational expectations, they do not

---

[6]Because spot rates and forward rates move together over time in a very persistent fashion, a test in levels of the variables would almost always fail to reject the unbiasedness hypothesis, even when the hypothesis was false (see Engel, 1996).

make systematic mistakes, and their forecasts are not systematically biased. When investors have rational expectations, we can decompose the realized (observed) rate of appreciation into its conditional expectation plus an error term that does not depend on time t information:

$$s(t+30, \$/£) = E_t[s(t+30, \$/£)] + \varepsilon(t+30) \qquad (7.11)$$

Realized appreciation = Expected appreciation + Forecast error

The error term can be viewed as news that moved the exchange rate, but the news, by definition, was unanticipated by rational market participants at time t.

Rational expectations imply that both the conditional mean, $E_t[\varepsilon(t+30)]$, and unconditional mean, $E[\varepsilon(t+30)]$, of the error term, $\varepsilon(t+30)$, in Equation (7.11), are zero. Because it reflects unanticipated news, $\varepsilon(t+30)$ should not be correlated with anything in the information set. Substituting the unbiasedness hypothesis of Equation (7.10) into Equation (7.11), we obtain

$$s(t+30, \$/£) = fp(t, \$/£) + \varepsilon(t+30) \qquad (7.12)$$

In Equation (7.12), one observable variable, the realized rate of appreciation, equals another observable variable, the forward premium, plus an unobservable error term whose conditional mean is zero. This equation can be used for two tests of the unbiasedness hypothesis.

A Test Using the Sample Means

Because the average or mean forecast error in Equation (7.12) should be zero, we can easily test the weakest implication of the unbiasedness hypothesis: The unconditional mean of the realized rate of appreciation should equal the unconditional mean of the forward premium.[7] The equality of these means or averages constitutes the **null hypothesis** (the hypothesis that is assumed to be true and is tested using data and a test statistic). Intuitively, to test the hypothesis, we compare the two sample means and check whether the difference between them is small or large in a statistical sense.

Data on Rates of Appreciation and Forward Premiums

The equality of the mean rate of appreciation and the mean forward premium is examined in Exhibit 7.4, which reports the results for all possible exchange rates between the dollar, the euro (the Deutsche mark before 1999), the British pound, and the Japanese yen. The data are expressed in annualized percentage terms. Consequently, the value of −2.82 for the mean rate of change of the dollar relative to the yen indicates that during the sample period, the dollar weakened relative to the yen at an average annual rate of 2.82%. The sample means of the realized rates of appreciation range from −3.70% for the yen value of the pound to 2.81% for the pound value of the euro. We can conclude that the mean of a time series is significantly different from zero at the 95% confidence level if the sample mean is more than 1.96 standard errors from zero. Said differently, we are then 95% sure that the true mean is not zero. The standard error of the sample mean depends on the volatility of the time series and the number of observations.[8] In all cases, the volatilities of the rates of appreciation are large. The large volatility of the realized rate of appreciation inflates the standard errors associated with the mean rate of appreciation, making it difficult to precisely estimate the mean. Thus, not a single mean rate of depreciation is sufficiently large relative to its standard error that we can be more than 90% confident that it is significantly different from zero.

---

[7] The sample mean of a time series x_t using T observations is $\frac{1}{T}\sum_{t=1}^{T} x_t$.

[8] The usual standard error of the sample mean for a time series is $\sigma/\sqrt{T}$, where $\sigma^2 = \sum_{t=1}^{T}(x_t - \hat{\mu})^2/T$ denotes the sample variance of the series, and $\hat{\mu}$ denotes the sample mean of the series. For this to be the correct standard error, the time series must be serially uncorrelated, that is, the observation at time t must not be correlated with the observation at time $t+1$. The standard errors reported here are slightly different because they are calculated using the methods of Hansen (1982) and accommodate both serial correlation and conditional heteroskedasticity (see Chapter 2).

Exhibit 7.4 Means of Monthly Rates of Appreciation, Forward Premiums, and the Differences Between the Two

	Mean		
Exchange Rate	**Rate of Appreciation** **(S.E.)** **Conf.**	**Forward Premium** **(S.E.)** **Conf.**	**Difference** **(S.E.)** **Conf.**
$/€	2.04	1.45	0.58
	(1.98)	(0.25)	(2.02)
	0.70	1.00	0.23
$/£	−0.41	−2.24	1.62
	(1.93)	(0.23)	(1.99)
	0.17	1.00	0.59
¥/$	−2.82	−3.31	0.48
	(2.05)	(0.23)	(2.13)
	0.83	1.00	0.18
¥/€	−1.44	−1.86	0.42
	(2.03)	(0.18)	(2.07)
	0.52	1.00	0.16
£/€	2.81	3.50	−0.69
	(1.64)	(0.25)	(1.67)
	0.91	1.00	0.32
¥/£	−3.70	−5.34	1.65
	(2.29)	(0.19)	(2.34)
	0.89	1.00	0.52

Notes: The table uses data from February 1976 to April 2010. Before 1999, the DEM replaces the euro. The monthly data are expressed as annualized percentage rates. The standard error (s.e.) measures the uncertainty we have about the accuracy of our estimate of the sample average. If we had an infinite amount of data, the standard error would be zero. As a technical note, the standard errors allow for conditional heteroskedasticity and two lagged autocorrelations in the errors. The confidence level (Conf.) of the test that the mean is zero is below the standard error. A confidence level of 0.90 indicates that we can be 90% sure that the null hypothesis of a zero mean is false.

The sample means of the forward premiums range from −5.34% for the yen value of the pound to 3.50% for the pound value of the euro. Because the volatilities of the forward premiums are much smaller than those of the rates of appreciation, all the sample means of the forward premiums are large relative to their respective standard errors. Hence, we can be quite confident that all the unconditional means of the forward premiums are not zero. For example, the pound appears robustly at a forward discount relative to all other currencies.

The Test

The third column of Exhibit 7.4 tests the hypotheses that the means of the 1-month forward premiums are equal to the means of the 1-month rates of appreciation on a currency-by-currency basis. The third column is labeled "Difference" to indicate that it represents the (*ex post*) rate of appreciation minus the (*ex ante*) forward premium. If the null hypothesis is true, the mean of the difference should be zero. In no case is there sufficient evidence to reject the null hypothesis with 90% confidence. The largest confidence level is only 0.59 for the dollar value of the pound. Of course, here again, the volatilities of the realized rates of appreciation make it difficult to precisely estimate the differences of the means.[9]

---

[9]Because of triangular arbitrage, only three of the six statistical tests we conducted provide independent information. When we do a joint test for the difference between the mean rate of appreciation of the euro relative to the three other currencies and the three corresponding average forward premiums, we also fail to reject that the differences are jointly zero.

In sum, there is essentially no evidence to suggest that the unconditional means of the forward premiums differ from the unconditional means of the rates of appreciation. Because the difference between $s(t+1)$ and $fp(t)$ is the forward market return, our test results imply that, on average, forward market returns are zero.

High-Interest-Rate Currencies Depreciate

The zero unconditional means of the differences between the rates of appreciation and the forward premiums are also consistent with an important fact of international finance: Countries with high nominal interest rates have currencies that tend to depreciate in value over time relative to the currencies of countries with low nominal interest rates. From our discussion of interest rate parity in Chapter 6, you know that the forward premium on a foreign currency is equal to the interest differential between the domestic currency and the foreign currency. Hence, failure to reject the unbiasedness hypothesis with the test of unconditional means supports the proposed fact quite strongly. For example, the average forward discount on the euro in terms of the yen is 1.86%, which implies that the euro (formerly DEM) interest rates were on average 1.86% higher than JPY interest rates. Exhibit 7.4 demonstrates that these higher euro interest rates were providing compensation for the average depreciation of the euro relative to the yen, which was 1.44%, not much smaller than 1.86%.

One interesting aspect of the differences reported in Exhibit 7.4 is that with the exception of the dollar/euro pair, the high-interest-rate currencies do appear to depreciate less than the forward discount indicates. In other words, forward market returns from long positions in weak currencies are, typically, on average positive. Lustig et al. (2009) and Jylhä et al. (2010) have argued that these positive returns for weaker currencies reflect risk premiums, either because these currencies are more exposed to global risk factors or because the inflation environment in these countries is riskier. Yet, Exhibit 7.4 suggests that the statistical evidence for these premiums remains weak.

In assessing the validity of the unbiasedness hypothesis, it is important to remember that this first test is a very weak implication because it considers only the overall average performance of the theory. We can also derive tests that examine the implications of the theory at different points in time. Such an approach is important because it corresponds to what someone would do in an active international portfolio management situation.

Regression Tests of the Unbiasedness of Forward Rates

A straightforward way to use additional information to test the unbiasedness hypothesis is to use regression analysis. Suppose we write Equation (7.12) in the form of a regression, as in the following equation:

$$s(t+30) = a + b\,fp(t) + \varepsilon(t+30) \tag{7.13}$$

Here, a is the intercept, and b is the slope coefficient of the regression. The unbiasedness hypothesis implies that $a = 0$ and $b = 1$ because with these substitutions, Equation (7.13) reduces to Equation (7.12).

The regression tests of the unbiasedness hypothesis are presented in Exhibit 7.5, which presents the estimated parameters and their standard errors for regressions using the same six exchange rates as in Exhibit 7.4. The standard errors are presented in parentheses below the estimated coefficients. The confidence levels of the tests that $a = 0$ and that $b = 1$ are presented below the standard errors. Values of the confidence level that are above 0.90 indicate that we can reject the null hypothesis with 90% confidence.

Exhibit 7.5 Regression Tests of the Unbiasedness Hypothesis
$$s(t+30) = a + b\, fp(t) + \varepsilon(t+30)$$

| | Coefficients on Regressors | | |
Currency	Const. (S.E.) Conf. ($a = 0$)	Forward Premium (S.E.) Conf. ($b = 1$)	R^2
\$/€	3.26 (2.31) 0.84	−0.84 (0.81) 0.98	0.004
\$/£	−3.84 (2.24) 0.91	−1.68 (0.82) 1.00	0.016
¥/\$	−10.03 (2.67) 1.00	−2.18 (0.64) 1.00	0.023
¥/€	−4.46 (2.30) 0.95	−1.62 (0.87) 1.00	0.008
£/€	4.70 (2.56) 0.93	−0.54 (0.65) 0.98	0.003
¥/£	−17.17 (5.34) 1.00	−2.52 (0.84) 1.00	0.020

Notes: The table uses data from February 1976 to April 2010. The euro replaces the Deutsche mark (DEM) from 1999 onward. Data on rates of appreciation and the forward premiums are annualized. The parameter estimates are obtained using ordinary least-squares regression for each equation. The standard error (s.e.) is in parentheses below the estimate. The confidence level (Conf.) of the test is below the standard error. The tests are that the constant is 0 and that the slope coefficient is 1. The last column reports the R^2: how much of the variation in $s(t+30)$ is explained by the variation in $fp(t)$. The standard errors correct for heteroskedasticity and allow for serial correlation (2 lags) in the error terms.

Notice that all six of the estimated values of b are significantly different from unity. Perhaps more surprisingly, notice that all the estimated slope coefficients are negative. The estimated values of b range from −2.52 for the yen value of the pound to −0.54 for the pound value of the euro. Consequently, the regressions suggest the existence of a **forward rate bias**; the forward rate does not equal the expected future spot rate. The regression evidence thus qualifies the use of the unbiasedness hypothesis. Treasurers in MNCs and global portfolio managers must realize that there is a potential cost to hedging foreign currency risk because the forward rate is not necessarily the best forecast of the future exchange rate.

Because negative values of b are found in the cross-rate regressions as well, the explanation of this phenomenon for the dollar exchange rates should not be sought in a story about common movements of the dollar relative to other currencies, nor could it be due strictly to U.S. policy. Apparently, the explanation must encompass the behavior of all major foreign exchange markets.

Notice also that the explanatory power of the regressions, which is measured by the R^2 values, is quite low. The largest R^2 is 2.3%. The appropriate way to interpret this finding is that there is some ability of the forward premium to predict the rate of appreciation, but the unanticipated component in the rate of appreciation is large relative to its predictable component.

Interpreting the Forward Bias

The unbiasedness regression generates a forecast for the future changes in exchange rates and hence also for the forward market return

$$E_t[s(t+1)] = \hat{a} + \hat{b}fp(t) \quad \text{or} \quad E_t[s(t+1) - fp(t)] = \hat{a} + (\hat{b} - 1)fp(t) \qquad (7.14)$$

Note that $s(t+1) - fp(t)$ is nothing but the forward market return, the return to a long forward position in the foreign currency.

People familiar with the results of the unbiasedness regressions just presented often argue that the negative slope coefficients imply that currencies trading at a forward discount will strengthen, in contrast to the prediction of the unbiasedness hypothesis, which implies that discount currencies are going to weaken. Unfortunately, this interpretation of the regression is wrong because it ignores the value of the constant term in the regression.

Exhibit 7.6 shows the importance of the constant in the regression, using the yen/dollar equation as an example. We consider a forward discount on the dollar of 3.31%, the sample average (see Exhibit 7.4), implying that Japanese yen interest rates were on average approximately 3.31% less than U.S. dollar interest rates. On the first line of Exhibit 7.6, we repeat the prediction of the theory: If the dollar is at a 3.31% discount, it should be expected to depreciate by 3.31%. If we were to use the regression and ignore the constant as in the computation on the second line, the prediction is a 7.22% appreciation of the dollar, so that the dollar indeed gives a higher yield and is expected to appreciate substantially.

However, the correct interpretation is on the third line of Exhibit 7.6, which uses the regression with the estimated coefficients as in Equation (7.6) to determine an estimate of expected dollar depreciation or appreciation. The dollar is now expected to weaken, but only by 2.82%. This is the average depreciation of the dollar over the sample period (see Exhibit 7.4), and most importantly, it is lower than the depreciation the forward discount suggests. However, the regression still implies that a speculator should buy dollars forward if he believes the prediction of the regression will be borne out. That is,

$$E_t[\text{fmr}(t+1)] = E_t[s(t+1) - fp(t)]$$
$$(\text{Expected forward market return}) = -2.82\% - (-3.31\%)$$
$$= 0.49\%$$

Exhibit 7.6 Interpreting the Unbiasedness Regression

	$fp(t)$	a	b	$E_t[s(t+1)]$	$E_t[\text{fmr}(t)]$
Uncovered Interest Rate Parity	−3.31%	0	1	−3.31%	0%
Naive Interpretation	−3.31%	0	−2.18	7.22%	10.53%
Actual Interpretation	−3.31%	−10.03	−2.18	2.82%	0.49%
(large discount)	−5.00%	−10.03	−2.18	−0.87%	5.87%

Notes: The four different lines compare expected exchange rate appreciation using information in the forward premium and three different assumptions. The first line assumes uncovered interest rate parity holds. The second line uses the regression reported in Exhibit 7.5 for ¥/$ but sets the constant equal to 0. The third line uses the actual regression results. In the fourth line, we consider a larger forward discount. All the percentages are annualized.

The expected forward market return from buying dollars forward is positive! When the forward discount is unusually large, there can be an expected dollar appreciation, and the expected return from going long dollars increases substantially. The last line in Exhibit 7.6 demonstrates this for a forward discount of 5%.

7.6 ALTERNATIVE INTERPRETATIONS OF THE TEST RESULTS

In this section, we examine three possible explanations of the results from the preceding section: market inefficiency, the presence of a foreign exchange risk premium, and peso problems.

Market Inefficiency

The evidence against the unbiasedness hypothesis suggests that interest rate differentials may contain information about future exchange rates that can be profitably exploited. Both academic analysts and foreign exchange professionals have explored models that link future exchange rate changes to interest rate differentials and other easily available information (such as past exchange rates) to predict future exchange rates (see, for example, Villanueva, 2007).

Exploiting the Forward Bias and Carry Trades

To exploit the forward bias, we can use the regression to find a value for the expected return on a forward position, just like in Equation (7.14). If the expected return is positive (negative), the strategy goes long (short) the foreign currency. While some professional currency managers likely follow such quantitative strategies, deviations from unbiasedness made a much less sophisticated trade popular, namely the **carry trade**.

The idea is simple: Borrow in low-yield currencies such as the yen, and invest in high-yield currencies such as the Australian dollar. The strategy is called "carry" as the carry represents the interest rate differential between the high- and the low-yield currencies. If the exchange rate does not change in value, the investor simply earns the carry. An equivalent strategy is to go long currencies trading at a discount and go short currencies trading at a premium. Again, the naïve idea is that the investor earns the forward discount (the carry) if the future spot rate happens to equal the current spot rate.

Example 7.3 A Carry Trade

Suppose Mrs. Watanabe in Japan faces a spot exchange rate of ¥100/$ and a 3-month forward rate of ¥99.17/$. The dollar is trading at an annualized discount in the forward market of

$$4 \times \frac{99.17 - 100}{100} = -3.32\%$$

From covered interest rate parity, we know that this is approximately the interest rate differential between 3-month yen and dollar external currency market investments.

Because the dollar is cheaper in the forward market, Mrs. Watanabe simply buys dollars forward, hoping the spot exchange rate will not change very much. Her eventual return can be decomposed as follows:

$$\text{fmr}(t+1) = s(t+1) - fp(t) = s(t+1) + \frac{3.32\%}{4}$$

The forward discount or carry of $\frac{3.32\%}{4}$ gives her an 83-basis-point cushion. As long as the dollar does not depreciate by more than 83 basis points over the course of the next 3 months, Mrs. Watanabe comes out ahead. Of course, the unbiasedness hypothesis holds that the dollar should be expected to depreciate by exactly 83 basis points!

The carry trade cannot work if the unbiasedness hypothesis holds. Yet, the strategy is different from exploiting the information in the regressions we ran, as it entirely ignores the information in the constant term (see our discussion in the previous subsection). Exploiting the forward bias as implied by regressions makes you primarily invest in currencies where the discount is unusually large relative to historical data, whereas the carry trade simply invests in currencies with high forward discounts (or high interest rates) relative to other currencies.

In Chapter 2, we reported that professional investment firms (such as hedge funds) account for an increasingly larger share of currency market volumes. Over the past decade, a number of hedge funds and other professional investors have started to view investing in currencies as an asset class in its own right. One of the most popular strategies among such investors is the carry trade. Galati et al. (2007) document how carry trade activity increased in the first decade of the 21st century. They also suggest that it may potentially affect currency values by putting upward (downward) pressure on high-yield (funding) currencies and may raise concerns of financial instability, should the carry trade suddenly "unwind," that is, should the low-interest currencies actually suddenly appreciate.

The carry trade is now viewed as one of the standard currency strategies. For example, in 2006, Deutsche Bank created a carry trade index, easily investable for all types of investors, including retail investors, at a fixed fee. Deutsche Bank's strategy involves making a diversified investment in equally weighted long or short positions in 10 possible currencies versus the U.S. dollar. The 10 currencies are the euro and the currencies of Australia, Canada, Denmark, Great Britain, Japan, New Zealand, Norway, Sweden, and Switzerland. The strategy involves going long in the three currencies that trade at the steepest forward discounts versus the U.S. dollar (that is, currencies traded in countries where money market yields are higher than those in the United States) and going short in the three currencies that trade at the highest forward premiums versus the U.S. dollar (that is, currencies traded in countries where money market yields are lower than those in the United States). The long or short positions are determined at the beginning of each month and are closed at the end of each month.

Have carry trades been profitable? To judge the profitably of trading strategies, we must introduce some important financial jargon.

Households as Carry Traders?

While you may think that the carry trade is best reserved for professional currency investors, we already pinpointed Mrs. Watanabe in Japan as a retail investor often engaging in carry trades. She is not the only retail investor practicing the carry trade. In Eastern Europe, many households, likely unwittingly, have turned their mortgages into carry trades. Because interest rates in Hungary and Poland were much higher than interest rates on the euro, and especially the Swiss franc, financial institutions started offering mortgages and other loans expressed in foreign currency, mostly Swiss franc. Central bank data reveal that over 50% of mortgages in Hungary are expressed in Swiss francs! The practice is also widespread in Austria, where 13% of households hold Swiss franc–denominated mortgages, even though the interest differential with the euro is not very large (see Beer et al., 2010). The authors of this study mention that the Austrian households taking out such loans are richer and may be more financially literate than average households. Yet, it is very doubtful that an average household fully understands the risks involved. While they may experience substantial savings on interest costs in the short run, any appreciation of the foreign currency increases the loan amount to be paid off. These risks were painfully realized in Hungary during the first half of 2010, when the forint experienced a 15% depreciation relative to the Swiss franc and, at the same time, Hungarian house prices fell.

Sharpe Ratios and Leverage

To judge the usefulness of a trading strategy, we can compute the economic profits or returns it generates. Because different strategies may have different risks, it is customary to compare the Sharpe ratios of various investment strategies. The Sharpe ratio essentially represents the excess return per unit of volatility. Correcting for volatility is especially important for currency strategies, as they often employ "leverage." The following analysis reviews the important concepts of leverage and the Sharpe ratio.

The Return on Capital at Risk and Leverage

An investor has a particular amount of capital available to invest, and ultimately we are interested in the return on that capital. However, a forward contract does not necessitate an upfront investment because it is just a bilateral contract with a bank, which means the investor can put more capital at risk than she owns. Because banks want to know that their counterparties can deliver on the contracts, the actual trading strategy typically is to invest the available capital in relatively riskless securities, such as Treasury bills, to absorb potential losses, and then invest possible gains.

If there is exactly $1 invested in a Treasury bill for every dollar bought or sold in the forward foreign exchange market, the excess return on the trading strategy, that is, the return over and above the return on the Treasury bill, equals the return on "capital at risk." If forward contracts pertain to more dollars than there are in a riskless account, the trading strategy uses **leverage**. For example, if for every $1 in the riskless account, $2 of forward contracts are made, the leverage ratio is 100%:

$$\text{Leverage} = \frac{\text{Capital at risk} - \text{Capital owned}}{\text{Capital owned}}$$

$$= \frac{\$2 - \$1}{\$1} = 100\%$$

Using leverage in a trading strategy scales up both its returns and its risk. Leverage implies that we should focus on the risk–return trade-off when investigating the profitability of trading strategies. The most popular measure is the **Sharpe ratio**, named after Nobel laureate William F. Sharpe:

$$\text{Sharpe ratio} = \frac{\text{Average excess return}}{\text{Standard deviation of excess return}}$$

Currency Strategies in Practice

The Sharpe ratio in the U.S. stock market is often estimated to be 0.30 to 0.40, meaning that the average annualized excess return is between 5% and 6% and the annualized standard deviation is 15%. Studies find that regression-based foreign exchange strategies produce Sharpe ratios similar and even higher than those available in stock markets, offering a reason for the increase in professional currency managers noted earlier. Bekaert (2011) reports that the assets under management reflected in the Barclay Currency Trader Index (BCTI), an index tracking currency funds, grew from under $5 billion to over $25 billion between 2000 and the end of 2007. Pojarliev and Levich (2008) report that the returns and Sharpe ratios on the BCTI initially were quite attractive but have tended to diminish over time, especially over the last few years of the 2000s. However, they identify several currency managers who produced returns with very attractive Sharpe ratios and also outperformed naïve currency strategies, such as the carry trade index.

Although these results are interesting, it is important to realize that past performance need not repeat itself and that currency investing is risky. In particular, in Chapter 3, we indicated that the distribution of currency changes exhibits "fat tails"; that is, extreme outcomes (both positive and negative) are more likely than a normal distribution predicts. If a currency strategy's return exhibits fat tails, the Sharpe ratio might not adequately reflect the risk–return trade-off.

The global crisis in 2008 proved a wake-up call for the abnormal risks embedded in the carry trade. The Deutsche Bank index performed abysmally, losing more than 20% of its value. This means that a currency fund with a 3-to-1 leverage ratio would have generated a negative return of −80%; in other words, it would have been essentially wiped out. Not surprisingly, many currency funds closed in 2008. Moreover, daily returns on the carry trade index during 2008 were extremely highly correlated with stock returns, suggesting that carry trades do suffer from systematic risk exposure. However, 2008 was not the first time that the carry trade experienced a quick and dramatic unwind. The strategy suffered large losses during the Asian financial crisis of 1997, and again in 1998 when Russia roiled international financial markets by defaulting on its debt in August, the hedge fund Long Term Capital Management collapsed in September, and the yen appreciated very sharply in October. The events in 2008 rekindled interest in two alternative explanations of the forward bias and carry trade returns: risk premiums and peso problems.

Risk Premiums

In the discussion of risk premiums earlier in this chapter, we noted that there are good theoretical reasons that the unbiasedness hypothesis may not hold. Nevertheless, the estimated slope coefficients are quite far from the values implied by the unbiasedness hypothesis. In fact, the regression results imply risk premiums on foreign currency investments must be large and more volatile than expected rates of appreciation, as we show in an advanced section.

Let's illustrate the ideas with a numerical example. Let the forward discount on the pound relative to the dollar be 2%. However, a bank believes that the pound is expected to appreciate by 3%. What risk premium does the bank expect to earn from investing in pounds? The risk premium is

$$rp(t) = E_t[fmr(t+1)] = E_t[s(t+1) - fp(t)] = 3\% - (-2\%) = 5\%$$

Note that the risk premium is larger than both the expected rate of appreciation and the forward discount. For this forecast to be consistent with a risk explanation, we must believe that the pound is so risky that it not only offers a 2% interest rate premium but also is expected to appreciate by 3%, so that in total, it offers a 5% expected excess return to investors. Is this plausible? We end this section by briefly summarizing the academic debate on whether risk drives the "forward bias."

The Variability of the Risk Premium[10] *(Advanced)*

The volatilities of forward premiums on the major currencies are about 3% (on an annualized basis). It turns out that the regression evidence presented in Exhibit 7.5 implies that both the volatilities of expected exchange rate changes and risk premiums are often (much) larger than the volatilities of forward premiums. Let's see why.

The regression states that

$$E_t(s_{t+1}) = a + b\, fp_t$$

The variance of expected exchange rate changes is therefore

$$\text{VAR}[E_t[s(t+1)]] = \text{VAR}[a + b\, fp(t)] = b^2 \text{VAR}[fp(t)]$$

Hence, if $b^2 > 1$, which is the case for all pairs involving the yen and the \$/£ pair, expected exchange rate changes are more variable than forward premiums. To find the variance of the risk premium, recall that the risk premium is simply the expected forward market return. Therefore,

$$rp(t) = E_t[\text{fmr}(t+1)] = E_t[s(t+1)] - fp(t) = a + (b-1)fp(t)$$

Hence,

$$\text{VAR}[rp(t)] = (b-1)^2\, \text{VAR}[fp(t)]$$

Consequently, as long as b is negative, which is the case for all currencies, the implied variance of the risk premium is not only larger than the variance of the forward premium, but it is also larger than the implied variance of the expected exchange rate changes.

Is It Risk?

If risk premiums are more variable than expected currency appreciation, a particular movement in the interest rate may more likely be driven by a change in the risk premium than by a change in the expected rate of appreciation of the currency. This is counterintuitive to most economists, who think that most of the forward premium variation reflects expected currency depreciation.

A number of economists (see Frankel and Froot, 1990; and Chinn and Frankel, 2002) have argued that survey data on forecasts of rates of appreciation from market professionals are closely related to forward premiums. The survey data are therefore biased forecasts of rates of appreciation, and the researchers say this indicates that market participants are irrational. There are, however, multiple problems with survey data. Survey participants may not have the proper incentive to tell the truth. In addition, faced with a disparity of forecasts, a statistician must choose something that represents the "market's forecast." Typically, the median forecast is chosen. Ideally, however, we are interested in the marginal investor's expectation. Why is the median of the survey's responses an indication of the opinion of the marginal investor? This calls into question the representativeness of the surveys analyzed in these academic studies.

Nevertheless, basic formal models of risk, such as the CAPM, have a hard time generating risk premiums as variable as implied by the regressions (see, for example, Bekaert, 1996; and Giovannini and Jorion, 1989). The recent global crisis has rekindled interest in the dynamics and economic sources of carry trade returns. The carry trade appears to have attractive long-run returns that trickle in slowly as the "carry" more than compensates for the depreciation of the high-yield currencies. Occasionally, though, a sudden and steep carry trade unwind happens, where the low-yield currencies appreciate sharply, exposing carry traders

---

[10]Fama (1984) was the first to recognize that the estimated slope coefficients in tests of the unbiasedness hypothesis can be interpreted to provide information about the variability of risk premiums and of expected rates of appreciation.

to big losses. Thus, it is said that the carry trade appears to pick up nickels in front of a bull-dozer. Statistically, this means the strategy's returns are not normally distributed but exhibit fat tails and negative skewness. Most investors obviously dislike such return properties, and they are not adequately captured by the Sharpe ratio.

Recent academic studies focus on these dynamic properties of carry trade returns to provide new risk-based explanations. Unwinds of the carry trade tend to happen at bad economic times, and it is conceivable that people become dramatically more risk averse when they might lose their job or face large investment losses. Because the returns to carry trades are correlated with such macroeconomic risks, they command a positive risk premium [see Verdelhan (2010) for a recent example of such a model]. Other research focuses on the behavior of traders. Brunnermeier et al. (2009) stress that when a carry trade unwind happens, investment managers face margin calls and may have difficulty funding their levered positions. Their clients may withdraw money as well. These forces cause the managers to unwind their positions, selling the high-yield currencies and buying the low-yield currencies, and in doing so, they exacerbate the losses on the carry trade. If the unwind is bad enough, the investment managers may go out of business. Knowing that this might happen causes an insufficient allocation of risky capital to the carry trade, keeping the returns higher than they should be. This explanation combines the presence of risk premiums with the idea of limits to arbitrage we encountered before.

The new explanations also rely on the fact that there are infrequent disastrous returns to the carry trade. These events by themselves can provide a potential explanation of the forward bias, as we now discuss.

Problems Interpreting the Statistics

Unstable Coefficients in the Unbiasedness Hypothesis Regressions

Exhibit 7.7 presents rolling estimates of the slope coefficients from Equation (7.13) to characterize its dynamics. The first estimate uses the first 5 years of monthly data. The next estimate results from rolling the data forward by 1 month and re-estimating the regression, again with 5 years of data.

In the regression analysis of the unbiasedness hypothesis, the estimates of the slope coefficient, b, are very far from 1, but Exhibit 7.7 indicates that there is dramatic instability in these coefficients across 5-year intervals. During the major appreciation of the dollar relative to the other major currencies in the early 1980s, the estimated slope coefficient decreased from −5 to −10. Clearly, this was probably because of the unexpectedly strong appreciation of the dollar and not a response to an increase in the variability of risk premiums. The large carry trade unwinds in the 2007 to 2008 period increased the coefficients towards 1. This evidence indicates a potential problem with the assumption of rational expectations underlying the statistical analysis. We next explain how this might happen.

Peso Problems

A phenomenon called the **peso problem** arises when rational investors anticipate events, typically dramatic, that do not occur during the sample or at least do not occur with the frequency that investors expect. Peso problems invalidate statistical inference conducted under the rational expectations assumption based on data drawn from the period.

The peso problem got its name from considering problems that would have arisen in analyzing Mexico's experience with fixed exchange rates. During 1955 to 1975, the Mexican authorities successfully pegged the peso–dollar exchange rate at MXP12/USD. Suppose we assume that the market sets the forward rate in such a way that it is an unbiased predictor of the future spot rate—that is, we assume that the unbiasedness hypothesis holds. Now, let's see if a statistician would conclude that the forward rate is an unbiased or a biased predictor using the Mexican data.

Exhibit 7.7 Rolling Monthly 5-Year Regression: Monthly Spot Rate Percentage Change Versus Monthly Forward Premium, February 1976–April 2010

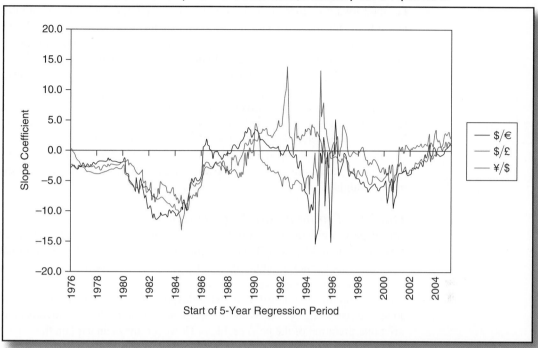

Let S_{peg} be the peso–dollar exchange rate at which the Mexican authorities are currently pegging. Let $S_{dev} > S_{peg}$ be the rate that the Mexican authorities will choose if they devalue the peso. Suppose that the market knows S_{dev}, and let $prob(t)$ be the probability that the market assigns to the event that the peso will be devalued during the next month. Then, the 1-month forward rate is an unbiased predictor of the future spot rate when it is the probability-weighted average of the two possible events:

$$F(t) = E_t[S(t+1)] = (1 - prob(t))S_{peg} + prob(t)\, S_{dev}$$

The forward rate is the probability of no devaluation multiplied by the current exchange rate plus the probability of a devaluation multiplied by the new exchange rate. As the market's assessment of the strength of the government's commitment to the peg changes over time, $prob(t)$ will change, and so will the forward rate. As long as the devaluation does not materialize, the dollar will trade at a forward premium relative to the peso (in pesos per dollar, $F > S_{peg}$), and peso money market investments will carry higher interest rates than dollar investments.

Suppose the Mexican authorities successfully peg the peso to the dollar between time T_0 and time T_2, when they eventually devalue the peso. Suppose also that the market knew during the time period between T_0 and T_2 that the Mexican authorities might devalue the peso at any time. If the statistician takes data from an interval of time during which no devaluation occurs, say, between T_0 and T_1, where $T_1 < T_2$, and compares forward rates with realized future spot rates, she will conclude that the forward rate is a biased predictor of the future spot rate. During the statistician's sample, the realized future spot rate is always below the forward rate. Hence, the statistician rejects the null hypothesis that the forward rate is an unbiased predictor of the future spot rate. The statistician has rejected the null hypothesis, but the null hypothesis is true.

How did the statistician go wrong? In other words, what led to the peso problem in this case? When we do statistical analysis on a financial time series using the rational expectations assumption, we assume that a reasonably long sample of returns is representative of the true distribution of returns that investors thought they faced when they made their investments. For the forward market example, we would assume that the *ex post* spot rates reflect all the possible events that investors thought might happen when they entered into their forward contracts. If there are important events that investors thought might happen but that did not happen, or if relatively rare events happened too frequently, the historical sample means, variances, and correlations in the data may tell us very little about the means, variances, and correlations of returns that investors thought they faced. The historical means, variances, and correlations may also be relatively uninformative about the moments that investors will face in the future. It is in this sense that the past performance of foreign investments may be poor indicators of the returns that investors can expect in the future.

In the case of the Mexican peso, even though the forward rate seemed to be a biased predictor of the future spot rate over 20 years, the devaluation eventually occurred in 1976, thereby validating the prediction embedded in the forward rate.

The Peso Problem and Carry Trades

For the peso problem to explain the evidence regarding carry trade returns and the forward bias we discussed before, the peso events must be anticipated by market participants and, when they occur, they should wipe out the gains accrued before so that excess returns from currency speculation average out to zero. Burnside et al. (2011) claim that even the 2008 disastrous returns do not suffice to make this true. They argue that carry traders can hedge the downside risk using options without sacrificing all their returns, which is inconsistent with a strict interpretation of the peso problem. However, they can explain the carry trade returns if they assume agents become very risk averse when an unwind happens. It appears that time-varying risk premiums remain critical to explain speculative currency returns.

Swedish Interest Rates of 500%

During currency crises, short-term interest rates often become exorbitantly high while long-term interest rates increase only a little, which means there is a large inversion of the term structure of interest rates. This peculiar pattern occurred in Sweden at the height of a currency crisis in Europe in 1992. The Riksbank, Sweden's central bank, raised its marginal lending rate on overnight borrowing to a staggering 500% p.a.—its highest level ever. The marginal lending rate is the rate that applies to the "last resort" financing offered by the Riksbank to Swedish financial institutions when other sources of overnight liquidity have dried up. The marginal lending rate typically provides a ceiling for the overnight market interest rate. Although only a small fraction of the Riksbank's borrowers had to pay the high rate, it still caused the *average* bank borrowing rate to rise to 38%. While interest rates rose on securities of all maturities, the term structure became sharply *inverted*, with 3-month treasury bills yielding 35% and 6-month bills yielding 30%.

Does an interest rate of 500% p.a. make any sense at all? In fact, imposing high interest rates is a tactic that central banks have used successfully since Premier Raymond Poincaré first used it in France in 1924 to prevent speculation against the franc. (This event came to be called "Poincaré's Bear Squeeze.") With the high borrowing rate, the Swedish government made speculation against the krona prohibitively expensive. It turns out that we can fully understand these interest rate hikes if we use our theory of uncovered interest rate parity and the idea behind the peso problem.

Although the Swedish krona was pegged against the ECU, let us assume for simplicity that it was pegged against the DEM (which had by far the largest weight in the ECU basket). A large fraction of the higher krona interest rates can be accounted for by what is often called a **devaluation premium**—that is, an interest rate that reflects the expected depreciation of a currency. Furthermore, devaluation premiums can also explain the inverted yield curve.

Let's revisit our simple model for exchange rate expectations. For the Swedish krona, there are two possible events:

1. A devaluation with probability of occurrence equal to prob
2. No devaluation with probability of occurrence equal to (1 − prob)

When the Swedish central bank successfully holds the peg, the exchange rate remains equal to the current spot rate. Let $Z\%$ denote the magnitude in percentage terms of a devaluation of the krona versus the DEM if the pegged exchange rate does not hold. Then, interest rate differentials tell us something about the probability of devaluation, prob, and the percentage magnitude of the devaluation, $Z\%$. Consider the expected returns in Swedish krona on two investments for a period of n days, with interest rates measured at annual rates and with exchange rates measured in Swedish krona per Deutsche mark as follows:

$$\text{Krona investment: } 1 + i(\text{SKR})\frac{n}{360}$$

$$\text{DEM investment: } \frac{\left[1 + i(\text{DEM})\frac{n}{360}\right] \times E_t[S(t+n)]}{S(t)}$$

According to uncovered interest rate parity, these two investments yield the same expected return. Because there are two possible events for the krona—a devaluation or no devaluation—the expected spot rate is simply

$$E_t[S(t+n)] = (1 - \text{prob}) \times S(t) + \text{prob} \times S(t) \times (1 + Z\%)$$

Therefore, by equating the two rates of return, substituting for the expected spot rate, and solving for the intensity of the devaluation (which is the probability of the devaluation multiplied by the size of the devaluation), we find

$$\text{prob} \times Z\% = \frac{1 + i(\text{SEK})\frac{n}{360}}{1 + i(\text{DEM})\frac{n}{360}} - 1$$

or by placing the right-hand side over a common denominator, we find

$$\text{prob} \times Z\% = \frac{\left[i(\text{SEK})\frac{n}{360}\right] - \left[i(\text{DEM})\frac{n}{360}\right]}{1 + i(\text{DEM})\frac{n}{360}}$$

Consequently, if krona interest rates are higher than Deutsche mark interest rates, there is a chance of a devaluation of some magnitude. The higher the interest differential, the higher the market assesses the chance and/or the magnitude of a devaluation.

Now, suppose at the height of a currency crisis, prob (the likelihood of a devaluation) is very close to 1, say, 0.8. Speculators are quite confident the currency will be devalued, but they are not absolutely sure it will be. Consequently, the interest rate differentials can be used to infer the expected percentage magnitude of the currency devaluation:

	$i(\text{SEK})$	$i(\text{DEM})$	prob $\times Z\%$	$Z\%$, if prob = 0.8
1 Month	35%	4%	2.57%	3.22%
3 Months	20%	4.5%	3.83%	4.79%

These numbers do not look unreasonable at all.

Why do devaluation expectations of a few percentage points lead to such high interest rates, and why is the effect so much larger for short maturities than for long ones? The inverted yield curve and the large magnitude of the short interest rates are simply a consequence of annualizing interest rates. To make this concrete, suppose that international investors expect a 5% devaluation within a week. Whatever Swedish money market investments they hold, they face an imminent capital loss of 5%. Investors will consequently demand higher interest rates to protect themselves against this possibility. If the interest rate applies to a 1-year maturity, this interest rate increase will be approximately 5%. But when the investment is very short term (such as 1 week), an extra 5% p.a. only means a small increase in the actual return. This won't compensate investors for the capital losses they will suffer as a result of a devaluation. Let the probability of a devaluation be 0.8, and let the DEM interest rate be 3% at the weekly horizon and 5% at the annual horizon. Whatever the investment, prob $\times Z = 0.8 \times 5\% \equiv 4\%$. According to the formula, we have:

$$\text{Devaluation premium} = \text{1-week investment} = \text{1-year investment}$$

$$4\% = \frac{i(\text{SEK, 1 week})\dfrac{7}{360} - 3\%\dfrac{7}{360}}{1 + 3\%\dfrac{7}{360}} = \frac{i(\text{SEK, 1 year}) - 5\%}{1 + 5\%}$$

Hence, i(SEK,1 week) will have to increase by much more than i(SEK,1 year) to compensate for the expected devaluation of 4%. In particular, we can solve for i(SEK,1 week) = 208.83% p.a., and i(SEK, 1 year) = 9.20% p.a. Clearly, the yield curve would be very inverted in this case.

7.7 SUMMARY

This chapter analyzes speculative currency investments. Its main points are as follows:

1. Speculators in currency markets can either borrow currencies they think will weaken while lending currencies they think will strengthen or buy the strengthening currency in the forward market. Speculative currency strategies are only successful when the currency predicted to weaken actually weakens more than the forward rate predicts.
2. Exchange rates are asset prices and are therefore difficult to forecast.
3. The expected return and volatility of a speculative currency investment depend on the mean and the standard deviation, respectively, of the conditional distribution of the future spot exchange rate.
4. Uncovered interest rate parity states that the expected return on an unhedged investment of domestic currency in the foreign money market equals the domestic money market return.
5. The unbiasedness hypothesis states that the forward rate equals the expected future spot rate— that is, what the market expects the spot rate to

be on the day your forward contract comes due, $F(t) = E_t[S(t+1)]$. The average forecast error of an unbiased predictor is zero when the average is computed over a large enough sample of forecasts.
6. Both uncovered interest rate parity and the unbiasedness hypothesis are consistent with a narrow view of market efficiency—that is, that there is no expected return to currency speculation. A broader view of market efficiency maintains that the expected profits from a trading strategy should merely compensate the investor for the risk she has taken.
7. The capital asset pricing model (CAPM) provides a theoretical reason why forward rates would be biased predictors of future spot rates and yet the market would still be considered to be efficient. The bias would be attributable to a risk premium, arising from the correlation between forward market returns and the market portfolio return.
8. Whether uncovered interest rate parity and the unbiasedness hypothesis hold has important implications for portfolio management, exchange rate forecasting, and theories of exchange rate determination.

9. If the expected future spot exchange rate and the forward rate differ, hedging transaction exchange risk produces a different revenue or cost than that expected to occur without hedging.

10. If investors have rational expectations, they do not make systematic mistakes when forecasting exchange rates. The actual future rate of appreciation then equals its conditional expectation plus an error term that has a conditional mean of 0; that is, only news makes future exchange rates different from their expected values.

11. The weakest implication of the unbiasedness hypothesis is that the unconditional mean of the forward premium should equal the unconditional mean of the realized rate of appreciation. The data appear consistent with the fact that high-interest-rate or forward-discount currencies tend to depreciate relative to low-interest-rate or forward-premium currencies.

12. Regression tests of the unbiasedness hypothesis indicate that it is strongly inconsistent with the data: Slope coefficients in regressions of the *ex post* rate of appreciation on the forward premium are negative rather than equal to 1. This implies that the forward rate is a biased predictor of the future spot rate.

13. The carry trade goes long in high-yield currencies selling at a forward discount and goes short in low-yield currencies selling at a forward premium.

14. Exploiting the forward bias and carry trades has offered attractive historical returns and Sharpe ratios. These returns may reflect market inefficiency, a risk premium, or a peso problem.

15. A peso problem arises when rational investors anticipate events that do not occur during the sample, or at least not do not occur with the frequency they expect. In such a situation, statistical analysis of returns can be badly biased.

16. In fixed-rate regimes, interest rate differentials provide information about the intensity of a devaluation—that is, the probability of the devaluation multiplied by its magnitude.

QUESTIONS

1. What are two ways to speculate in the currency markets without investing any money up front?

2. What do financial economists mean when they discuss the conditional expectation of the future spot exchange rate?

3. What is the main determinant of the variability of forward market returns?

4. Describe how you construct the uncertain yen-denominated return from investing 1 yen in the Swiss franc money market.

5. What is a hedged foreign currency investment? What happens if you hedge your return in Question 4?

6. What does it mean for the 90-day forward exchange rate to be an unbiased predictor of the future spot exchange rate?

7. Why is it true that the hypothesis that the forward exchange rate is an unbiased predictor of the future spot exchange rate is equivalent to the hypothesis that the forward premium (or discount) on a foreign currency is an unbiased predictor of the rate of its appreciation (or depreciation)?

8. It is often claimed that the forward exchange rate is set by arbitrage to satisfy (covered) interest rate parity. Explain how interest rate parity can be satisfied and how the forward exchange rate can be set by speculators in reference to the expected future spot exchange rate.

9. It is sometimes asserted that investors who hedge their foreign currency bond or stock returns remove the foreign exchange risk associated with the investment, reduce the volatility of their domestic currency returns, and thus get a "free lunch" because the mean return in domestic currency remains the same as the mean return in the foreign currency. Is this true or false? Why?

10. It is often argued that forward exchange rates should be unbiased predictors of future spot exchange rates if the foreign exchange market is efficient. Is this true or false? Why?

11. What is the prediction of the CAPM for the relationship between the forward exchange rate and the expected future spot exchange rate?

12. If the CAPM explains deviations of the forward exchange rate from the expected future spot exchange rate, explain why one party involved in a forward contract would be willing to enter into a contract with an expected loss.

13. Why is it only the covariance of an asset's return with the return on the world market portfolio that determines whether there is a risk premium associated with the asset's expected return?

14. What is the rational expectations hypothesis, and how is it applied to tests of hypotheses about expected returns in financial markets?

15. Suppose that the forward premium equals the conditional expectation of the future rate of appreciation of the foreign currency relative to the domestic currency. If we form the average realized rate of appreciation from a large sample of data and compare it to the average forward premium, what should be true?

16. Explain how you would use a regression to test the unbiasedness hypothesis.

17. Suppose you regress the realized rate of appreciation of a foreign currency on a constant and the forward premium on the foreign currency. What interpretation can you give to the estimated slope coefficient? If the slope coefficient is negative, is it true that the forward premium is predicting the wrong sign for the rate of appreciation?

18. What does a negative slope coefficient in an unbiasedness regression imply about the variability of risk premiums relative to variability of expected rates of appreciation?

19. What is a carry trade?

20. What is a Sharpe ratio?

21. Do carry trades contain risks that may not be reflected in their Sharpe ratios?

22. What is a peso problem? Explain the term within the context of its original derivation. Now, explain how peso problems can generally plague the study of financial market returns.

23. How can you use interest rate differentials to understand the probability of a devaluation and the potential magnitude of the devaluation?

PROBLEMS

1. Over the next 30 days, economists forecast that the pound may weaken relative to the dollar by as much as 7%, or it may strengthen by as much as 6%. The possible rates of change are -7%, -5%, -3%, -1%, 0%, 2%, 4%, and 6%. If these values are equally likely, what are the mean and standard deviation of the future spot exchange rate if the current rate is $\$1.5845/\pounds$?

2. Consider the following hypothetical facts about Mexico: The peso recently lost over 40% of its value relative to the dollar. Over the course of the next 90 days, there is a 35% chance that the Mexican government will lose control of the economy. If it does, the peso will lose 33% of its value relative to the dollar, and the Mexican stock market will fall by 39%. Alternatively, the U.S. Congress may vote to help Mexico by offering collateral for Mexican government loans. In that case, the peso will appreciate 27% relative to the dollar, and the Mexican stock market will rise by 29%. As a U.S. investor with no current assets or liabilities in Mexico, you have decided to speculate. Calculate your expected dollar return from investing dollars in the Mexican stock market for the next 90 days.

3. Suppose that the 90-day forward rate is $\$1.19/\text{\euro}$, the current spot rate is $\$1.20/\text{\euro}$, and you expect the future spot rate in 90 days to be $\$1.21/\text{\euro}$. What contract would you make to speculate in the forward market by either buying or selling $\text{\euro}10{,}000{,}000$? What is your expected profit? If the standard deviation of the 90-day rate of appreciation of the euro

relative to the dollar is 3%, what range covers 95% of your possible profits and losses?

4. Suppose the rate of appreciation of the dollar relative to the yen over the next 90 days is normally distributed with a mean of -1% and a standard deviation of 3%. Use a spreadsheet program to graph the distribution of the future yen–dollar exchange rate. If the current spot exchange rate is ¥99/\$, and the 90-day forward rate is ¥98.30/\$, describe the distribution of yen profits or losses from selling $\$5{,}000{,}000$ forward?

5. Suppose that the spot exchange rate is $\$1.55/\pounds$, that the beta on a forward contract to buy pounds with dollars is 1.5, and that the expected excess dollar rate of return on the market portfolio is 7%. What is the expected profit or loss on a forward purchase of $\pounds1{,}000{,}000$? Explain how this can be an equilibrium.

6. Suppose the estimated slope coefficient in a regression of the rate of depreciation of the dollar relative to the yen on a constant and the forward discount on the dollar is -2, and the standard deviation of the forward discount, measured on an annualized basis, is 2.5%. What is a lower bound for the variability of the risk premium in the yen–dollar forward market?

7. Suppose the British pound (GBP) is pegged to the euro (EUR). You think there is a 5% probability that the GBP will be devalued by 10% over the course of the next month. What interest differential would prevent you from speculating by borrowing GBP and lending EUR?

8. Argentina's monetary stabilization plan in 1991 included introducing a currency board that tied the Argentine peso (ARS) to the U.S. dollar at an exchange rate of ARS1/USD1. On June 21, 2000, the 3-month interest rates quoted by Argentine banks were 6.71% in USD and 7.33% in ARS. Suppose the difference reflected some probability that the currency board would be abandoned and the peso devalued, and investors think a 10% devaluation to ARS1.10/USD is possible. What is the probability of this happening if uncovered interest rate parity

holds? In early 2001, confidence in the currency board eroded and interest rates soared to well over 10%. What is the possibility of a 10% devaluation if the 3-month interest rates are 20% in ARS and 6.0% in USD?

9. The British bank Barclays has developed an exchange-traded note that pays off the Barclays Capital Intelligent Carry Index™. Look up information on this index on the Web. Explain why you like or dislike Barclays's strategy.

BIBLIOGRAPHY

Beer, Christian, Steven Ongena, and Marcel Peter, 2010, "Borrowing in Foreign Currency: Austrian Households as Carry Traders," *Journal of Banking and Finance* 34, pp. 2198–2211.

Bekaert, Geert, 1996, "The Time Variation of Risk and Return in Foreign Exchange Markets: A General Equilibrium," *Review of Financial Studies* 9, pp. 427–470.

_____, 2011, "Valuing Currency Management: TOM vs. U.S. Commerce Bank," Columbia CaseWorks No. 100310.

Brunnermeier, Markus, Stefan Nagel, and Lasse Pedersen, 2009, "Carry Trades and Currency Crashes," Chapter 5 in *NBER Macroeconomics Annual 2008*, Cambridge, MA: National Bureau of Economic Research.

Burnside, Craig, Martin Eichenbaum, Isaac Kleshchelski, and Sergio Rebelo, 2011, "Do Peso Problems Explain the Returns to the Carry Trade?" *Review of Financial Studies*, forthcoming.

Chinn, Menzie, and Jeffrey A. Frankel, 2002, "Survey Data on Exchange Rate Expectations: More Currencies, More Horizons, More Tests," in Bill Allen and David Dickinson, eds., *Monetary Policy, Capital Flows and Financial Market Developments in the Era of Financial Globalisation: Essays in Honour of Max Fry*, London: Routledge.

Engel, Charles, 1996, "The Forward Discount Anomaly and the Risk Premium: A Survey of Recent Evidence," *Journal of Empirical Finance* 3, pp. 123–191.

Fama, Eugene, 1984, "Forward and Spot Exchange Rates," *Journal of Monetary Economics* 14, pp. 319–338.

Frankel, Jeffrey, and Kenneth Froot, 1990, "Exchange Rate Forecasting Techniques, Survey Data, and Implications for the Foreign Exchange Market," in D. Das, ed., *Current Issues in International Trade and International Finance*, Oxford, U.K.: Oxford University Press.

Froot, Kenneth A., and Richard H. Thaler, 1990, "Foreign Exchange," *Journal of Economic Perspectives* 4, pp. 179–192.

Galati, Gabriele, Alexandra Heath, and Patrick McGuire, 2007, "Evidence of Carry Trade Activity," *BIS Quarterly Review* 3, pp. 27–41.

Giovannini, Alberto, and Philippe Jorion, 1989, "The Time-Variation of Risk and Return in the Foreign-Exchange Stock Markets," *Journal of Finance* 44, pp. 307–325.

Hansen, Lars Peter, 1982, "Large Sample Properties of Generalized Method of Moments Estimators," *Econometrica* 50, pp. 1029–1054.

Jylhä, Petri, Jussi-Pekka Lyytinen, and Matti Suominen, 2010, "Arbitrage Capital and Currency Carry Trade Returns," Helsinki School of Economics Working Paper W-459.

King, Michael, and Dagfinn Rime, 2010, "The $4 Trillion Question: What Explains FX Growth Since the 2007 Survey?" *BIS Quarterly Review*, December, pp. 27–42.

Lustig, Hanno, Nikolai Roussanov, and Adrien Verdelhan, 2009, "Common Risk Factors in Currency Markets," National Bureau of Economic Research Working Paper W14082.

Pojarliev, Momtchil, and Richard M. Levich, 2008, "Do Professional Currency Managers Beat the Benchmark?" *Financial Analysts Journal* 64, pp. 18–32.

Sharpe, William F., 1964, "Capital Asset Prices: A Theory of Market Equilibrium Under Conditions of Risk," *Journal of Finance* 19, pp. 425–442.

Siegel, Jeremy J., 1972, "Risk, Information, and Forward Exchange," *Quarterly Journal of Economics* 86, pp. 303–309.

Verdelhan, Adrien, 2010, "A Habit-Based Explanation of the Exchange Rate Risk Premium," *Journal of Finance* 65, pp. 123–145.

Villanueva, O. Miguel, 2007, "Forecasting Currency Excess Returns: Can the Forward Bias Be Exploited?" *Journal of Financial and Quantitative Analysis* 42, pp. 963–990.

Appendix 7.1

The Siegel Paradox

Suppose we consider Blake Bevins, Kevin Anthony's British counterpart, who is investing in the dollar money market. Let $\bar{S}(\pounds/\$)$ and $\bar{F}(\pounds/\$)$ denote the pound/dollar spot and forward exchange rates, so at each point of time $\bar{S}(\pounds/\$) = \dfrac{1}{S(\$/\pounds)}$. Now, apply Equation (7.5) from the British perspective, $\bar{F}(t) = E_t[\bar{S}(t+1)]$. But, of course, $\bar{F}(\pounds/\$) = \dfrac{1}{F(\$/\pounds)}$, so that

$$E_t[\bar{S}(t+1, \pounds/\$)] = \frac{1}{F(t, \$/\pounds)}$$

$$= \frac{1}{E_t[S(t+1, \$/\pounds)]}$$

So, for the unbiasedness hypothesis to hold from both the British and American perspectives, it must be the case that

$$E_t[\bar{S}(t+1, \pounds/\$)] = E_t\left[\frac{1}{S(t+1, \$/\pounds)}\right]$$

$$= \frac{1}{E_t[S(t+1, \$/\pounds)]}$$

However, we know the latter equality is false because of a statistical property known as Jensen's inequality.[11]

Rather than get mired in statistical jargon, let's work out a simple numeric example. Suppose Kevin and Blake agree on the following possible scenarios for the future exchange rate:

	$S(t+1, \$/\pounds)$	$\bar{S}(t+1, \pounds/\$) = \dfrac{1}{S(t+1, \$/\pounds)}$	Probability
Scenario 1	1.50	0.6667	0.714
Scenario 2	1.65	0.6061	0.286

From Kevin's perspective, the expected future $\$/\pounds$ exchange rate is

$$\begin{aligned} E_t[S(t+1, \$/\pounds)] &= 0.714 \times \$1.50/\pounds \\ &\quad + 0.286 \times \$1.65/\pounds \\ &= \$1.5429/\pounds \end{aligned}$$

This is the forward rate derived earlier. According to Blake, the expected $\pounds/\$$ rate is

$$\begin{aligned} E_t[\bar{S}(t+1, \pounds/\$)] &= 0.714 \times \pounds0.6667/\$ \\ &\quad + 0.286 \times \pounds0.6061/\$ \\ &= \pounds0.6493/\$ \end{aligned}$$

Is this consistent with the $\$1.5429/\pounds$ rate? The answer is no because

$$0.6493 \neq \frac{1}{1.5429} = 0.6481$$

We see that when the unbiasedness hypothesis is considered from the two different currency perspectives, it leads to an inconsistency. We cannot have two different forward rates in the market! This little conundrum is known as the Siegel paradox because Jeremy Siegel (1972) was the first to point out this inconsistency.

Whereas some have argued that the Siegel paradox invalidates the unbiasedness hypothesis as a reasonable theory, note that the difference between 0.6481 and 0.6493 is small: In percentage terms, it represents less than a 0.2% difference. Hence, we will ignore the Siegel paradox for the remainder of this book. Moreover, it is possible to formulate versions of the unbiasedness hypothesis either using logarithmic exchange rates or using real values that resolve the Siegel paradox (see Engel, 1996).

---

[11]In fact, because $f(x) = \dfrac{1}{x}$ is a convex function, Jensen's inequality implies $E_t\left[\dfrac{1}{S(t+1)}\right] > \dfrac{1}{E_t[S(t+1)]}$.

Appendix 7.2

The Portfolio Diversification Argument and the CAPM

If an investor places all her wealth in only one asset, the asset's expected return and variance are the mean and variance of the investor's portfolio. The purpose of this appendix is to review how the mean and variance of a portfolio are determined when there is more than one asset in the portfolio. To do this easily, we must develop some notation. Let R_i be the return on asset i and denote the expected value or mean return on asset i as $E(R_i)$. Let σ_{ij} denote the covariance between the returns on asset i and asset j. Covariance is a measure of the degree to which two returns move together, and it is found by taking the expectation of the product of deviations of the returns from their respective means:

$$\sigma_{ij} = E\left[[R_i - E(R_i)][R_j - E(R_j)]\right]$$

Because the covariance involves the product of two random variables and the order of multiplication is unimportant, $\sigma_{ij} = \sigma_{ji}$. Also, from the definition of variance, which is the expected value of the squared deviation around the mean, we have

$$\sigma_{ii} = E\left[[R_i - E(R_i)]^2\right]$$

The square root of the variance is the standard deviation. Often, people find it more intuitive to think in terms of correlations between returns on assets rather than covariances because the correlation is a number between −1 and 1. The correlation coefficient, ρ_{ij}, is defined to be the covariance divided by the product of the standard deviations of the two assets:

$$\rho_{ij} = \frac{\sigma_{ij}}{\sqrt{\sigma_{ii}}\sqrt{\sigma_{jj}}} \tag{7A.1}$$

Now, we can examine the mean and variance of the return on a portfolio of several assets. Let w_i denote the share of the investor's wealth that is invested in asset i. Let's also begin with just two assets in the portfolio. Suppose the investor puts a share of her wealth equal to w_1 in asset 1 and the remainder of her wealth in asset 2, such that $w_2 = 1 - w_1$.

The actual return on the portfolio, R_p, will be the weighted average of the returns on the two assets, where the weights are the shares of invested wealth:

$$R_p = w_1 R_1 + w_2 R_2 \tag{7A.2}$$

Hence, to find the mean return on the portfolio, we take the expectation of the realized return in Equation (7A.2), and we find

$$E(R_p) = w_1 E(R_1) + w_2 E(R_2)$$

Just as the actual return is a weighted average of the actual individual returns, the expected return on the portfolio is the same weighted average of the expected returns on the assets.

The variance of the return on the portfolio $V(R_p)$ is the expectation of the squared deviation of the return from its mean, as in the following:

$$V(R_p) = E\Big[[(w_1 R_1 + w_2 R_2) \\ - (w_1 E(R_1) + w_2 E(R_2))]^2\Big] \tag{7A.3}$$

By multiplying out and rearranging the terms in Equation (7A.3), we find that

$$V(R_p) = w_1^2 E\left[[R_1 - E(R_1)]^2\right]$$
$$+ w_2^2 E\left[[R_2 - E(R_2)]^2\right]$$
$$+ 2w_1 w_2 E\left[[R_1 - E(R_1)][R_2 - E(R_2)]\right]$$
$$V(R_p) = w_1^2 \sigma_{11} + w_2^2 \sigma_{22} + 2w_1 w_2 \sigma_{12}$$

Let's do a calculation with some real numbers to see how the mean and variance of a portfolio are related to the means and variances of the individual assets. Suppose that the expected return on asset 1 is 9%, and its standard deviation is 22%, whereas the expected return on asset 2 is 11%, and its standard deviation is 24%. Suppose also that the correlation between the returns on the two assets is 0.4, and from Equation (7A.1), we find that the covariance between the two returns is $\sigma_{12} = (0.4)(0.22)$ $(0.24) = 0.02112$.

Now, we can calculate the mean and variance of any portfolio composed of assets 1 and 2. Suppose we put 35% of our wealth in asset 1 and 65% in asset 2. The mean return on our portfolio is then

$$E(R_p) = (0.35)(0.09) + (0.65)(0.11) = 0.1030$$

and the variance of the return on our portfolio is

$$V(R_p) = (0.35)^2(0.22)^2 + (0.65)^2(0.24)^2$$
$$+ 2(0.35)(0.65)(0.02112) = 0.039875$$

The standard deviation of our portfolio is therefore $\sqrt{0.039875} = 0.1997$ or 19.97%.

The ratio of the mean to the standard deviation of an asset or a portfolio is a measure of the trade-off an investor faces between return and risk. For asset 1, the ratio of mean to the standard deviation is $09\%/22\% = 0.41$, and for asset 2, it is $11\%/24\% = 0.46$. For the portfolio, the ratio of the mean to the standard deviation is $10.30\%/19.97\% = 0.52$. By diversifying across the two assets, we have improved our risk–return trade-off. Also, note that the standard deviation of the portfolio is lower than the standard deviation of either asset. Diversification makes some risk disappear.

Because there are many more than two assets in the world, we next want to examine what happens if we put a small amount of our wealth in each of N assets. To further simplify the analysis, let's put an equal share, $w_i = (1/N)$, in the N different assets. The portfolio's mean return is just the weighted sum of the expected returns on the N assets, as in Equation (7A.2):

$$E(R_p) = \sum_{i=1}^{N} w_i E(R_i) = \sum_{i=1}^{N} \frac{E(R_i)}{N}$$

Consequently, the portfolio's mean return is the average of the mean returns on the N assets.

The variance of the return on an N-asset portfolio is as follows:

$$V(R_p) = E\left[\sum_{i=1}^{N} w_i[R_i - E(R_i)] \right.$$

$$\left. \sum_{i=1}^{N} w_i[R_i - E(R_i)] \right] \qquad \text{(7A.4)}$$

If you multiply out the terms involving the summations on the right-hand side of Equation (7A.4), you will find that you must take the sum of the expectations of N^2 terms. There will be N variances that arise from the multiplication of the return on an asset with itself, and there will be $N(N - 1)$ other terms involving covariances. So, there will be $N(N - 1)/2$ distinct covariance terms because $\sigma_{ij} = \sigma_{ji}$. In Equation (7A.4), the weights are multiplied by each other, but because the weights on the equal-weighted portfolio are the same, each of the N^2 terms in Equation (7A.4) is multiplied by $1/N^2$. Therefore,

$$V(R_p) = \frac{1}{N^2} \sum_{i=1}^{N} \sigma_{ii} + \frac{2}{N^2} \sum_{i=1}^{N-1} \sum_{j=i+1}^{N} \sigma_{ij} \qquad \text{(7A.5)}$$

The double summation term, $\sum_{i=1}^{N-1} \sum_{j=i+1}^{N} \sigma_{ij}$, is multiplied by 2 because the summation involves only the distinct $N(N - 1)/2$ covariances. Let's define the average variance as

$$\Lambda_i = \frac{1}{N} \sum_{i=1}^{N} \sigma_{ii}$$

and the average covariance as

$$\Lambda_{ij} = \frac{1}{N(N - 1)/2} \sum_{i=1}^{N-1} \sum_{j=i+1}^{N} \sigma_{ij}$$

Equation (7A.5) implies that the portfolio variance can be written as

$$V(R_p) = \frac{1}{N}\Lambda_i + \left(1 - \frac{1}{N}\right)\Lambda_{ij} \qquad \text{(7A.6)}$$

Notice that as N gets large in Equation (7A.6), the importance of the average variance goes to zero. Thus, as N gets large, the variance of the return on a highly diversified portfolio is driven to be equal to the average covariance of the assets in the portfolio. If asset returns were uncorrelated, the average covariance would be zero, and a highly diversified portfolio would produce an essentially riskless return, even though each of the individual asset returns was itself quite variable. Notice also that assets with negative covariances are very important because they reduce the average covariance of the portfolio.

From Equation (7A.6), it is clear that the individual variance of an asset will not affect the overall variance of the portfolio, and the individual variance consequently should not affect the expected return that a risk-averse investor demands to hold that particular asset. This intuition leads directly to the CAPM as a relationship describing how expected returns are determined. Essentially, the CAPM builds on the intuition that an investor will add an asset to his portfolio until he cannot further improve the risk–return trade-off of the portfolio. We elaborate on this intuition in Chapter 13.

Although the large portfolio in our analysis was arbitrary, the fundamental insight of the CAPM was that with a few additional assumptions, it would have to be the case that, in equilibrium (that is, when all investors are happily holding the existing assets in the marketplace at their current prices, without feeling the need to trade them), the well-diversified portfolio that every investor would hold would be the market portfolio. All investors would hold some fraction of their wealth in the market portfolio, with more risk-averse investors holding smaller fractions and more risk-tolerant investors holding larger fractions and possibly borrowing to invest in the market.

Appendix 7.3

A Regression Refresher

In Section 7.5, we tested the unbiasedness hypothesis with a linear regression model:

$$y(t+1) = a + bx(t) + \varepsilon(t+1)$$

where the dependent (or explained) variable $y(t+1)$, which was the rate of appreciation, $s(t+1)$, is regressed on an independent (or explanatory) variable, $x(t)$, which was the forward premium, $fp(t)$. The regression describes how variation in $y(t+1)$ can be explained linearly by variation in $x(t)$. We want to find values of the parameters, a and b, that make $a + bx(t)$ as close to $y(t+1)$ as possible. The fit is unlikely to be perfect, so there will be an error (or disturbance) term, as indicated by $\varepsilon(t+1)$.

Econometricians have developed several methods to find "estimates," or values, for the parameters, a and b, given data on $y(t+1)$ and $x(t)$. For any given sample of data, these estimates are just numbers and are typically represented by $\hat{a}$ and $\hat{b}$. With such estimates, we can compute the actual errors, called *residuals*, that the model makes in predicting $y(t+1)$:

$$\hat{\varepsilon}(t+1) = y(t+1) - \hat{a} - \hat{b}x(t)$$

The formula by which the data are transformed into an actual estimate is called an **estimator**, and the most

popular estimator for the linear regression model is the **OLS estimator**. OLS stands for *ordinary least squares* because the estimator minimizes the sum of the squared residuals. That is, the estimates of a and b are such that the sum of the squared residuals, $\sum_{t=1}^{T} \hat{\varepsilon}(t+1)^2$, is as low as possible, and we are assuming that we have $T+1$ total observations, of which only T will be used in the regression.

To illustrate this concretely, let's go back to the actual monthly data on dollar/euro exchange rates and forward premiums used for Exhibit 7.5, which were between February 1976, and April 2010. The monthly exchange rate changes represent our $y(t+1)$ observations; the forward premiums represent our $x(t)$ observations. We have to be careful with the timing to match up, say, the April 2001 exchange rate change with the forward premium for the end of March 2001.

Exhibit 7A.1 presents a scatter plot of the data, with the exchange rate changes on the vertical axis and the forward premiums on the horizontal axis. The OLS regression line through this scatter plot minimizes the sum of the squared deviations between the actual data and the regression line. The corresponding fitted values that lie on the regression line are also on the graph.

Exhibit 7A.1 Regression Residuals with Fitted Values

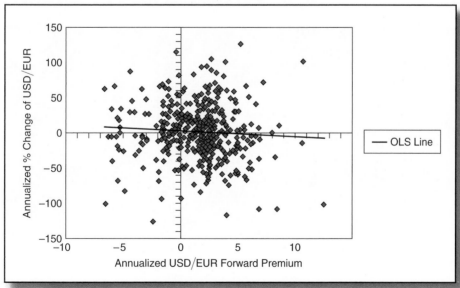

Concretely, the OLS estimator resulting from this procedure for the slope of the line is

$$\hat{b} = \frac{\frac{1}{T}\sum_{t=1}^{T}[y(t+1) - \bar{y}][x(t) - \bar{x}]}{\frac{1}{T}\sum_{t=1}^{T}[x(t) - \bar{x}]^2}$$

where $\bar{y} = (1/T)\sum_{t=1}^{T}y(t+1)$ and $\bar{x} = (1/T)\sum_{t=1}^{T}x(t)$ are the sample means, and $\hat{a} = \bar{y} - \hat{b}\bar{x}$ is the constant. Note that the numerator of $\hat{b}$ represents an estimate of the covariance between $y(t+1)$ and $x(t)$, whereas the denominator represents an estimate of the variance of $x(t)$. Hence, the slope coefficient b is the covariance of the dependent variable and the independent variable divided by the variance of the independent variable:

$$b = \frac{\text{cov}[y(t+1), x(t)]}{\text{var}[x(t)]}$$

When we carry out the actual regression with the data given in Exhibit 7A.1, we find:

$$\hat{a} = 3.26 \quad \hat{b} = -0.84$$
$$(2.31) \quad\quad (0.81)$$
$$[0.84] \quad\quad [0.98]$$
$$R^2 = 0.004\%$$

Note that we annualized the constant $\hat{a}$ by multiplying by 12.

An OLS regression also yields a standard error for the estimates, which gives an idea of how confident we are in the estimates. We report standard errors in parentheses below the parameter estimates as shown in the previous equation; that is, the standard error of $\hat{a}$ is 2.31, for example. Even if $y(t+1)$ and $x(t)$ are totally independent, they may appear to be related just by chance. Use of the standard error together with the coefficient estimate allows computation of a confidence level for b to be different from a particular value. For example, the unbiasedness hypothesis in the context of the regression model represents the null hypothesis $\hat{b} = 1$. We would like to know whether $\hat{b}$ is close to or far away from 1 in a statistical sense.

If we want to test whether b is 1, we compute the square of $\hat{b} - 1$ divide by the standard error of $\hat{b}$. Let us introduce the test statistic z:

$$z = \left[\frac{\hat{b} - 1}{se(\hat{b})}\right]^2$$

If $\hat{b}$ is truly close to 1, the value of z should be small, and if the true value of b is not equal to 1, the z statistic should be large. However, the true b may be far from 1, but the estimate may be very noisy—that is, the standard error may be big. In this case, our test statistic z will be small as well. In our sample regression, the standard error for $\hat{b}$ is 0.81; hence, $z = 5.1602$. Standard errors are inversely related to the size of the sample, and our sample here is quite long, so that z is relatively large. But at what value of z do we reject the null hypothesis?

If the sample is large, econometricians have actually figured out that the statistic z should follow a particular

Exhibit 7A.2 Chi-Square Distribution

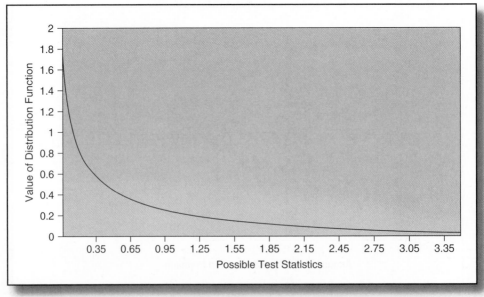

statistical distribution if the null hypothesis is correct. In our case, this distribution is a chi-square distribution with one degree of freedom. Exhibit 7A.2 graphs a $\chi^2(1)$ distribution. Even if the null hypothesis is true, sometimes, by chance, large values of z might occur, but they are not very likely. The higher z is, the less likely it is that z comes from a $\chi^2(1)$ distribution. In fact, only 5% of the observations of $\chi^2(1)$ distribution should be above 3.841. Hence, if our test statistic yields a value higher than 3.841, we are more than 95% confident that the null hypothesis is rejected because there is more than a 95% chance that a $\chi^2(1)$ variable is lower than the z statistic.

Statisticians often focus on "5% level" tests. The value 3.841 is called the critical value of the $\chi^2(1)$ distribution for a 5% test, and when z exceeds the critical value, we say that the null hypothesis is rejected at the 5% level. In the chapter itself, we primarily focus on these confidence levels. In this example, the confidence level is 0.98. We report these confidence levels in square brackets above. Consequently, we quite confidently reject the hypothesis.

The null hypothesis does not necessarily have to be about just one coefficient. We can also test multiple restrictions together (for instance, $\hat{a} = 0$ and $\hat{b} = 1$), and the resulting statistic will follow a chi-square distribution with degrees of freedom equal to the number of restrictions tested.

Finally, the regression output typically also provides the R^2 statistic. This statistic measures how much of the variation of the dependent variable is explained by the regression model. Concretely, it is computed as the variance of $\hat{a} + \hat{b}x(t)$ divided by the variance of $y(t+1)$. The R^2 is very low in our example because the regression is predictive: We use a variable at time t to predict changes in an asset price at time $t+1$. Most of the variation in the exchange rate will be driven by news that is by definition unpredictable. In Exhibit 7A.1, the poor R^2 is obvious as the data points are often quite far away from the regression line.

Chapter 8

Purchasing Power Parity and Real Exchange Rates

*I*n a speech in October 2010, U.S. Treasury Secretary Timothy Geithner accused China of deliberately maintaining an exchange rate that undervalues the yuan relative to the dollar to help China's export industries. To discuss undervaluation, you obviously need a benchmark that provides the correct value of a currency. One popular benchmark model is **purchasing power parity (PPP)**.[1] PPP links exchange rates to the prices of goods in different countries, and this chapter explores these relations in depth.

Why should you study the theory of purchasing power parity? First, PPP provides a baseline forecast of future exchange rates that is usually considered whenever it is necessary to forecast future cash flows in different currencies, especially when inflation rates differ across these countries. Consequently, PPP plays a fundamental role in corporate decision making, such as the international location of manufacturing plants, and other international capital budgeting issues. Second, understanding the theory of purchasing power parity is important because deviations from PPP significantly affect the profitability of firms. For example, pricing products internationally, analyzing long-term international contracts, hedging the cash flows of an ongoing international operation, and evaluating the performance of foreign subsidiaries all require an analysis in terms of deviations from PPP. Third, PPP is particularly useful in assessing cost-of-living differences across countries. If you are going to work in a different country, and your salary is denominated in a foreign currency, you would like to know what standard of living you will experience.

As we will see when we look at the data, PPP does not hold very well in the short run. The deviations from the theory are sometimes so large that some economists dismiss the theory, at least as far as the determination of exchange rates is concerned. Nevertheless, for the world's major currencies, we will also see that PPP has some validity in the long run. It even works reasonably well over shorter horizons, whenever inflation dominates the economic environment.

Because purchasing power parity involves comparing the **purchasing power** of a money within a country to the purchasing power of that money when spent in a different country, we need to examine how to measure these purchasing powers. When economists convert from monetary magnitudes into units of purchasing power, they say they are converting from nominal units into real units. This chapter also introduces the real exchange rate. You will see that deviations from PPP can also be described as fluctuations in real exchange rates.

To understand these ideas, we first need to discuss price levels and price indexes.

---

[1]Dornbusch (1988) notes that the earliest references to the subject are from 16th-century Spain and 17th-century England. Swedish economist Gustav Cassel (1916) is generally credited with coining the name for the theory.

8.1 PRICE LEVELS, PRICE INDEXES, AND THE PURCHASING POWER OF A CURRENCY

The General Idea of Purchasing Power

Economists usually measure the purchasing power of a country's currency in two steps:

1. First, economists calculate the monetary value, or **nominal price**, of a typical bundle of consumption goods in a country. We call this the price of the country's consumption bundle, and it represents the country's **price level**. Specifically, the price level is the weighted average of the nominal prices of the goods and services consumed in the economy. The weights of the goods and services usually represent the percentage shares of the goods and services in the consumption bundle. That is, if shoes constitute 1% of the typical consumer's budget, the price of shoes receives a weight of 0.01 in constructing the weighted average of all prices. When the price level of an economy is rising, **inflation** is occurring. Conversely, when the price level is falling, **deflation** is occurring.

2. Second, economists figure out what the purchasing power of the country's money is—that is, what a unit of currency will actually buy, given the price level in the country. To do this, they take the reciprocal, or inverse, of the price level. Taking the reciprocal of the price level gives the purchasing power of the currency. The purchasing power measures the amount of goods that can be purchased per unit of currency.

Calculating the Price Level

Rather than associate the price level with a country, for notational purposes, we associate the price level with the currency of a country. Hence, for the United States, we can write the price level as

$$P(t, \$) = \sum_{i=1}^{N} w_i P(t, i, \$)$$

where $P(t, i, \$)$ represents the dollar price of good i at time t, w_i represents the weight or consumption share of good i, and $P(t, \$)$ is the dollar price level, the weighted average of the dollar prices of the N different goods and services.

For example, the price level in the United States or Japan indicates how many dollars or yen it takes to purchase the consumption bundle of goods and services in either country. It might take something like $15,000 to purchase the consumption bundle in the United Sates and ¥1,600,000 to purchase a similar bundle in Japan. This is why the price level is also known as the cost of living.

Calculating a Price Index

Unfortunately, governments usually do not provide information on consumer price levels. Instead of reporting data on price levels, governments usually provide information on price indexes. A **price index** is the ratio of a price level at one point in time to the price level in a designated base year. Typically, the ratio of the two price levels is multiplied by 100. That is, the dollar price index in year $t+k$ with year t as a base year is

$$PI(t+k, \$) = \left(\frac{P(t+k, \$)}{P(t, \$)} \right) \times 100 = \left(\frac{\sum_{i=1}^{N} w_i P(t+k, i, \$)}{\sum_{i=1}^{N} w_i P(t, i, \$)} \right) \times 100$$

Because price indexes are ratios of price levels at different points in time, they directly reflect the amount of inflation (that is, the percentage change in the average of all

Exhibit 8.1 Price Indexes for the G7 Countries, 1960–2010

Year	United States	Canada	France	Germany	Italy	Japan	United Kingdom
1960	27.6	24.6	17.2	39.4	9.8	21.2	13.2
1970	36.1	32.3	25.2	50.9	14.0	36.9	19.6
1980	76.5	69.7	63.3	82.6	51.0	87.2	70.7
1985	100.0	100.0	100.0	100.0	100.0	100.0	100.0
1990	121.4	124.1	116.3	107.7	131.2	107.0	133.4
1995	141.7	139.2	129.9	126.2	168.6	113.5	158.4
2000	159.0	150.0	138.0	133.9	188.3	115.2	179.9
2005	179.4	167.8	151.8	144.9	212.0	112.4	202.1
2008	197.8	179.0	161.1	154.5	227.8	114.3	219.3
2009	197.1	179.5	161.2	155.0	229.5	112.7	224.0
2010	199.3	181.1	162.6	155.8	231.3	111.7	228.2

Note: Data are from the Organization for Economic Cooperation and Development's Main Economic Indicators.

nominal prices) between the base year (in the denominator of the ratio) and the current year (in the numerator of the ratio). If the price index today is 115, we know that prices are 15% higher than they were in the base year, and economists say the cost of living has increased by 15% because it takes 15% more money to purchase the consumption bundle.

Exhibit 8.1 provides some information on consumer price indexes for the G7 countries—the United States, Canada, France, Germany, Italy, Japan, and the United Kingdom—from 1960 to 2010. We can use these data to understand the historical inflationary experiences in these countries.

Example 8.1 Calculating an Annual Rate of Inflation

Notice that if the base year in a price index for year t, $PI(t)$, is the same as the base index for the next year, $PI(t+1)$, the ratio of the two price indexes measures 1 plus the rate of inflation between the 2 years because the two base-year price levels will cancel each other out:

$$\frac{PI(t+1)}{PI(t)} = \frac{P(t+1)}{P(t)} = [1 + \pi(t+1)]$$

where $\pi(t+1) \equiv \dfrac{P(t+1) - P(t)}{P(t)}$.

Now, let's use the data in Exhibit 8.1 to determine the British rate of inflation between 2008 and 2009. The values of the U.K. price indexes for 2008 and 2009 were 219.3 and 224.0, respectively. We find the percentage rate of inflation by subtracting 1 from the ratio of the price indexes and multiplying by 100:

$$\left(\frac{224.0}{219.3} - 1\right) \times 100 = 2.1\%$$

Example 8.2 Calculating the Cumulative Rate of Inflation

How do we determine the total amount of inflation between 1985 and 2010 for the United States, and how can we calculate the average annual rate of inflation during that same period? First, because 1985 is the base year, we know that 1985 = 100. Because the U.S. price index in 2010 was 199.3, we know that the average dollar prices of goods and services in 2010 were 99.3% higher than were the prices in 1985. Over the 25 years, prices increased at a compound annual rate of inflation of 2.79% because

$$\left(\frac{199.3}{100}\right)^{1/25} = 1.0279$$

Internal Purchasing Power

Now that we know how to measure a country's price level and inflation's impact on it, we can discuss the purchasing power of a dollar, first internally in the United States and then externally outside the United States. The units of the **internal purchasing power** of a dollar are the amount of goods and services that can be purchased with a dollar in the United States. That is, the amount of goods that corresponds to the purchasing power of 1 dollar is measured by taking the reciprocal of the U.S. price level. Because the units of the U.S. price level are dollars per U.S. consumption bundle, the units of purchasing power (the reciprocal of the price level) are U.S. consumption bundles per dollar. The internal purchasing power of a dollar at time t is $1/P(t, \$)$.

Example 8.3 Calculating the Purchasing Power of $1,000,000

Suppose the price level in the United States is $15,000 for the average consumption bundle. What is the purchasing power of $1,000,000?

The purchasing power of 1 dollar is $(1/\$15,000)$, so the purchasing power of $1,000,000 is

$$\frac{1}{\$15,000/\text{consumption bundle}} \times \$1,000,000 = 66.67 \text{ consumption bundles}$$

In other words, $1,000,000 is enough to purchase 66.67 consumption bundles.

External Purchasing Power

The units of the **external purchasing power** of a dollar are the amount of goods and services outside the United States that can be purchased with a dollar, say, in the United Kingdom. Therefore, calculating the external purchasing power of a dollar in Britain involves two steps. First, it is necessary to purchase some amount of pounds with the dollar. Second, it is necessary to examine the purchasing power of those pounds in Britain.

One dollar buys $1/S(t, \$/£)$ pounds if $S(t, \$/£)$ represents the spot exchange rate of dollars per pound. The purchasing power of the pound may be measured by taking the reciprocal of the price level in Britain, $1/P(t, £)$, which represents the number of consumption bundles that can be bought per pound in Britain. Therefore, the external purchasing power of the dollar in Britain is

$$\frac{1}{S(t, \$/\pounds)} \times \frac{1}{P(t, \pounds)}$$

We check the units on the external purchasing power calculation:

$$\frac{\text{Pounds}}{\text{Dollar}} \times \frac{\text{U.K. consumption bundles}}{\text{Pound}} = \frac{\text{U.K. consumption bundles}}{\text{Dollar}}$$

as is required by the concept of the external purchasing power of a dollar in Britain.

Now that we can calculate the purchasing power of the dollar in two countries, we can examine what happens when we equate the two.

8.2 Absolute Purchasing Power Parity

The Theory of Absolute Purchasing Power Parity

One version of PPP, called **absolute purchasing power parity**, states that the exchange rate will adjust to equalize the internal and external purchasing powers of a currency. The internal purchasing power is calculated by taking the reciprocal of the price level, and the external purchasing power is calculated by first exchanging the domestic money into the foreign money in the foreign exchange market and then calculating the purchasing power of that amount of foreign money in the foreign country. Hence, the prediction of absolute PPP for the dollar–pound exchange rate is found by equating the internal purchasing power of a dollar to the external purchasing power of a dollar:

$$\frac{1}{P(t, \$)} = \frac{1}{S^{\text{PPP}}(t, \$/\pounds)} \times \frac{1}{P(t, \pounds)} \tag{8.1}$$

where $S^{\text{PPP}}(t, \$/\pounds)$ signifies the dollar–pound exchange rate that satisfies the PPP relation. By solving Equation (8.1) for $S^{\text{PPP}}(t, \$/\pounds)$, we find

$$S^{\text{PPP}}(t, \$/\pounds) = \frac{P(t, \$)}{P(t, \pounds)} \tag{8.2}$$

You should think of absolute PPP as a theory that makes a prediction about what the exchange rate should be given the price levels in two countries. Equation (8.2) predicts that the dollar–pound exchange rate should be equal to the ratio of the price level in the United States to the price level in the United Kingdom. The key here is that differences in prices across countries should be reflected in the relative price of the currencies—that is, in the exchange rate. Later, we examine how well or poorly the theory works by comparing actual exchange rates to the predictions of PPP. First, let's explore the foundations of the theory of absolute PPP.

Goods Market Arbitrage

Suppose the internal purchasing power of the dollar is less than its external purchasing power in a foreign country. What could you do to make a profit? If the dollar buys more goods abroad than it does at home, it ought to be possible to take some amount of dollars, buy goods abroad, ship the goods to the United States, and sell them for more dollars than your original dollar expenditure.

To demonstrate this arbitrage, consider the following example.

Example 8.4 A Goods Market Arbitrage

Suppose that the U.S. price level is \$15,000/consumption bundle and that the U.K. price level is £10,000/consumption bundle. Let the exchange rate be \$1.40/£. Rather than compute the purchasing power of 1 dollar, consider the internal and external purchasing powers of \$1 million. As we saw earlier, the internal purchasing power of \$1 million in the United States is

$$\$1,000,000 \times \frac{1}{\$15,000/\text{consumption bundle}} = 66.67 \text{ consumption bundles}$$

The external purchasing power of \$1 million in the United Kingdom is found in two steps. First, convert the \$1 million into pounds to get

$$\$1,000,000 \times \frac{1}{\$1.40/£} = £714,286$$

Then, find the purchasing power of £714,286 in the United Kingdom:

$$£714,286 \times \frac{1}{£10,000/\text{consumption bundle}} = 71.43 \text{ consumption bundles}$$

Because the external purchasing power of the dollar in the United Kingdom is higher than the internal purchasing power of the dollar in the United States, we can profit by buying goods in the United Kingdom and shipping them to the United States for resale. If we buy goods in the United Kingdom, we can purchase 71.43 consumption bundles with our \$1 million. If we sell the 71.43 consumption bundles in the United States at \$15,000/consumption bundle, we will receive

$$(71.43 \text{ consumption bundles}) \times (\$15,000/\text{consumption bundle}) = \$1,071,450.$$

Thus, by buying goods at low prices and selling goods at high prices, we have generated a 7.145% rate of return on our \$1 million investment.

Example 8.4 demonstrates another way of looking at PPP. If absolute PPP holds, the costs of the consumption bundles in different countries are equal when expressed in a common currency. When absolute PPP does not hold, there is a potential opportunity for goods market arbitrage. Such goods market arbitrage would, of course, be subject to somewhat larger transaction costs than the financial arbitrages we discussed in previous chapters. For example, there would be transaction costs associated with the physical shipment of goods between countries. Also, if you attempted to do this type of goods market arbitrage, you would obviously have to buy a particular commodity versus a consumption bundle.

8.3 THE LAW OF ONE PRICE

The Perfect Market Ideal

If markets are competitive, we should not be able to make a profit buying and reselling goods between countries. In fact, if there were no transaction costs, arbitrage would drive the price of any good quoted in a common currency to be the same around the world. The a certain percentage with the Red Tab to protect their trademark. The quality of the jeans is no different."

Ante continues, "Hey, if the jeans really are the same, and if there is a 93% difference between the CAD price of the U.S. jeans and the CAD price of the Canadian jeans, why don't we get a truck, go around to Sears stores in the U.S., buy jeans, drive back to Canada, and sell the jeans here. If we sold 10,000 pairs of jeans, we'd make CAD361,500. That would be a pretty nifty profit."

Freedy thinks for a minute and says, "Do you ever pay attention in class? Remember PPP and the law of one price. We would not make a profit. Renting the truck would cost money, it would take time to get the jeans, and nobody would buy them from you on the street. They wouldn't believe that the jeans weren't stolen. Fundamentally, goods market arbitrage ensures that there are no abnormal profits."

Ante retorts, "PPP is a useless theory. Goods markets aren't at all like asset markets. Goods markets are totally inefficient, so exchange rates really bear no relationship to goods prices because you can't arbitrage in the goods market."

Freedy shouts back, "Oh yeah? Well, I think PPP is pretty elegant economics, and people wouldn't have talked about it for nearly 100 years if it didn't work quite well."

Ante responds, "Elegant schmelegant! What's the point of learning something that just doesn't work?"

Suttle, although somewhat mesmerized by two young women trying on jeans in the women's department, responds slowly to the escalating argument. "Look guys, you are both right and both wrong. Freedy, you're right: The PPP theory is good basic economics. But it isn't the whole story. There is some validity to Ante's point, too: Arbitrage in the goods market is a lot more costly than arbitrage in asset markets."

To make the point, he pulls out his iPhone to check some prices on the Web. "Look here. At Amazon.com, the list price of Levi's 501's is USD48.00, but they are on sale for USD34.99. Let's check the Levi's Web site. There, the same 501's list for USD46.00, but they are on sale for USD37.00. So, even in the United States and on the Web where it took a minute to check the prices, we still see price differences. Also, remember that although the exchange rate is now CAD1.05/USD, it wasn't too long ago that it was CAD1.30/USD. At that exchange rate and with a list price of USD48.00, the Canadian dollar price that satisfies the law of one price would be CAD62.40. That's still below CAD74.99, but we're getting closer."

Suttle continues, "What Ante is proposing is exactly how goods arbitrage makes PPP work in the long run. If Sears sets its Canadian dollar price too high, someone will set up a business to exploit the price differential, which moves us closer to the law of one price because that person will undercut Sears' price to attract customers. Of course, as Freedy argued, setting up such a business is costly, and if Sears Canada starts losing sales, they can drop their price. Notice also that Sears Canada only sells a couple of Levi's styles. So, maybe they know that the price is high, and they're just waiting for someone like Ante who absolutely needs a new pair of jeans and can't wait for delivery from a Web site."

Ante smiles and says, "Well, maybe we should set up the business anyway! But one thing I do remember from our international finance class is that changes in exchange rates cause big changes in relative prices across countries. I guess a big move in the exchange rate while we are setting up our business could get us into serious trouble. I'm not sure I want the foreign exchange risk."

Suttle nods, "Yes, you're right about that. Changes in exchange rates can create big changes in relative prices, and people respond to such changes by shifting their consumption patterns. Managers try to find different suppliers, and they may even relocate production facilities to cheaper countries. All this takes some time. Maybe if we look at the data, we'll get an idea for how well or poorly the PPP theory works in the short run and the long run."

Overvaluations and Undervaluations of Currencies

Before we look at actual exchange rates and PPP predictions, we first need to discuss some additional terminology. A currency is said to be **overvalued** if its external purchasing power is greater than its internal purchasing power. An **undervalued** currency's external purchasing power is less than its internal purchasing power. Because purchasing power parity makes one prediction for the actual exchange rate between two currencies, if currency A is overvalued relative to currency B, currency B must be undervalued relative to currency A.

An easy way to remember which currency is overvalued and which currency is undervalued is to add the phrase "on foreign exchange markets" to the statement. For example, the dollar is "overvalued on foreign exchange markets" if the dollar's external purchasing power is greater than its internal purchasing power.[3]

Example 8.5 Overvaluation of the Dollar Implies Undervaluation of the Pound

In this example, we check our ability to manipulate internal and external purchasing powers by verifying that if the dollar is overvalued relative to the pound, as in Example 8.4, the pound must be undervalued relative to the dollar.

Recall that the dollar price level is \$15,000/consumption bundle, the pound price level is £10,000/consumption bundle, and the exchange rate is \$1.40/£. The statement that the dollar is overvalued relative to the pound implies that the external purchasing power of the dollar is greater than its internal purchasing power. As in Example 8.4, we calculate the external purchasing power of \$1 million in the United Kingdom as

$$\$1,000,000 \times \frac{1}{\$1.40/£} \times \frac{1}{£10,000/\text{consumption bundle}}$$

$$= 71.43 \text{ consumption bundles}$$

This is larger than the internal purchasing power of \$1 million in the United States, which is

$$\$1,000,000 \times \frac{1}{\$15,000/\text{consumption bundle}} = 66.67 \text{ consumption bundles}$$

Thus, the dollar is overvalued on the foreign exchange market. Now, let's look at the pound. Is the pound over- or undervalued on the foreign exchange market? The internal purchasing power of £1,000,000 is

$$£1,000,000 \times \frac{1}{£10,000/\text{consumption bundle}} = 100 \text{ consumption bundles}$$

but the external purchasing power of the pound in the United States is

$$£1,000,000 \times \frac{\$1.40}{£} \times \frac{1}{\$15,000/\text{consumption bundle}}$$

$$= 93.33 \text{ consumption bundles}$$

---

[3]The terms *overvalued* and *undervalued* are also employed in discussions of the relationship of a particular exchange rate to other theories of exchange rate determination. An overvalued currency must weaken on the foreign exchange markets to return to the prediction of the theory, and an undervalued currency must strengthen.

Because the internal purchasing power of the pound is greater than its external purchasing power, the pound is undervalued on the foreign exchange market. Hence, the statement that the dollar is overvalued relative to the pound is equivalent to the statement that the pound is undervalued relative to the dollar.

Predictions Based on Overvaluations and Undervaluations

The logic of overvaluations and undervaluations of currencies leads to predictions of currency depreciation or appreciation. If a currency is overvalued on foreign exchange markets, it must weaken, or suffer depreciation, on the foreign exchange markets if the exchange rate is to return to the prediction of PPP. This weakening, or depreciation, of the currency lowers its external purchasing power and returns the external purchasing power of the currency to its internal purchasing power. Conversely, a currency that is undervalued on foreign exchange markets must strengthen, or experience an appreciation, on foreign exchange markets if its external purchasing power is to increase to equal its internal purchasing power. Of course, apart from currency appreciations and depreciations, differences in the rates of inflation can also reestablish the PPP relationship.

Example 8.6   Using PPP Deviations to Predict Currency Appreciations

If the yen is undervalued relative to the euro, what prediction would you make regarding the movement of the exchange rate (in yen per euro) if you think a correction back to PPP is imminent? If the yen is undervalued (on foreign exchange markets) relative to the euro, the external purchasing power of the yen in Europe is less than the yen's internal purchasing power in Japan. This can be corrected by an appreciation, or strengthening, of the yen relative to the euro, which causes the exchange rate measured in yen per euro to fall.

The MacPPP Standard

Shortly, we will examine data on absolute PPP using conventional consumer price indexes (CPIs). One criticism of using CPI data is that the consumption bundles of the different countries are not the same. Fortunately, *The Economist* calculates implied PPP exchange rates for a large number of countries, using a bundle of goods that is the same around the world—namely, a McDonald's Big Mac sandwich.

There are several advantages to using the Big Mac as an index of prices. First, McDonald's strives to make the sandwich the same way in all its outlets. Just as with the consumer price level, there are particular weights that McDonald's places on each item in the Big Mac, and these weights are the same across countries. Specifically, the commodity bundle is "two all-beef patties, special sauce, lettuce, cheese, pickles, and onions on a sesame seed bun." Second, McDonald's uses local suppliers for the goods entering the index, which reduces the role of international transportation costs.

Each spring since 1986, *The Economist* has had its correspondents sample the prices of Big Macs in local currencies in a large number of countries. Implied PPP exchange rates for various currencies relative to the dollar are calculated by taking the ratio of the local currency price of the Big Mac to its average dollar price in four U.S. cities.

Although the Big Mac PPP standard, called **MacPPP**, may seem somewhat silly in light of the fact that one cannot transport fresh Big Macs across countries, the deviations of actual exchange rates from the implied PPP values are actually about the same size as those that arise using more conventional consumer price indexes. Also, the degree of overvaluation or undervaluation of particular currencies has been used by *The Economist* to make a few interesting predictions that have had some accuracy, as you will see.

Exhibit 8.2 gives MacPPP values for 2010 from *The Economist*. The first column shows the prices of Big Macs in the local currencies of the countries in which they are sold. For example, the average price of a Big Mac in the United States was $3.58, whereas it cost ¥333.40 in Japan. The second column gives the dollar price of a Big Mac in the different countries calculated as the local currency price of a Big Mac divided by the exchange rate of local currency per dollar. This is the price that an American traveling in that country might calculate.

Because the yen–dollar exchange rate was ¥94.18/$, the dollar cost of a Big Mac in Japan was

$$\frac{(¥333.40/\text{Big Mac})}{(¥94.18/\$)} = \$3.54/\text{Big Mac}$$

The most expensive Big Mac for a person paying in U.S. dollars was in Norway, where it cost $6.87. The cheapest Big Mac for a dollar purchaser was in China, where it cost only $1.83.

The Implied MacPPP Rates

The third column of Exhibit 8.2 gives implied PPP exchange rates of the currency versus the dollar. This is the ratio of the local currency price of the Big Mac to the dollar price of the

Exhibit 8.2 MacPPP in 2010

		Big Mac Prices		Exchange Rates		
		Local Currency	Dollars	PPP	Actual	% Under (−)/Over (+) Valuation against the Dollar
United States[a]	dollar	3.58	3.58	1.00	1.00	
Australia	dollar	4.30	4.30	1.20	1.08	11%
Britain[b]	pound	2.27	3.48	1.58	1.53	−3%
Canada	dollar	4.10	4.06	1.14	1.01	13%
China	yuan	12.51	1.83	3.49	6.84	−49%
Egypt	pound	13.26	2.37	3.70	5.59	−34%
Euro area[c]	euro	3.48	4.62	1.03	1.33	29%
Hungary	forint	754.37	3.75	210.72	201.17	5%
Indonesia	rupiah	20,559.06	2.28	5,742.75	9,017.13	−36%
Japan	yen	333.40	3.54	93.13	94.18	−1%
Malaysia	ringgit	6.76	2.12	1.89	3.19	−41%
Mexico	peso	31.32	2.56	8.75	12.24	−28%
Norway	kroner	42.94	6.87	11.99	6.25	92%
Poland	zloty	8.42	2.86	2.35	2.95	−20%
Russia	ruble	69.78	2.39	19.49	29.19	−33%
Saudi Arabia	riyal	10.03	2.67	2.80	3.76	−25%
South Africa	rand	17.96	2.44	5.02	7.36	−32%
South Korea	won	3,330.75	3.00	930.38	1,110.25	−16%
Switzerland	franc	6.64	6.16	1.86	1.08	72%
Taiwan	dollar	73.97	2.36	20.66	31.35	−34%
Thailand	baht	70.12	2.16	19.59	32.46	−40%
Turkey	lire	5.51	3.71	1.54	1.49	4%
U.A.E.	dirham	10.98	2.99	3.07	3.67	−16%

[a]Average of New York, Chicago, San Francisco, and Atlanta.
[b]Exchange rate: dollars per pound.
[c]Weighted average of member countries. Exchange rate: dollars per euro.

Note: Data are from *The Economist*, online edition, May 17, 2010, and author's calculations.

Big Mac in the United States, except for Britain and the euro area, in which case the implied PPP is expressed in dollars per pound and dollars per euro, respectively. The fourth column provides the actual exchange rate measured in local currency per dollar, except for the British pound and the euro, which are again expressed as dollars per pound and dollars per euro. For Big Macs to satisfy the law of one price, implied PPP exchange rates in the third column should equal the actual exchange rates in the fourth column. The fact that they do not indicates that the local currencies are either overvalued or undervalued relative to the dollar.

Overvaluations and Undervaluations

The fifth column presents the overvaluation or undervaluation of the local currency in percentage points defined as the percentage appreciation or depreciation of the dollar required to return the actual exchange rate to the implied PPP value. For example, the Canadian dollar is 13% overvalued because with the actual exchange rate at CAD1.01/$, a 13% appreciation of the dollar versus the CAD would be required to increase the exchange rate to the implied PPP value of CAD1.14/$. Similarly, the Swiss franc is 72% overvalued because with an actual exchange rate at CHF1.08/$, a 72% appreciation of the U.S. dollar relative to the Swiss franc would be required to increase the exchange rate to the implied PPP value of CHF1.86/$.

The average of the emerging market valuations relative to the dollar is −25%, indicating that the average emerging market currency is 25% undervalued versus the dollar. These undervaluations are consistent with the fact that Big Macs also contain some labor, which is less expensive in emerging markets than in the United States. If we take the ratio of the local currency price of the Big Mac in Thailand to the price in Malaysia, we find the PPP prediction of the Thai baht price of the Malaysian ringgit, which is THB10.37/MYR. The actual exchange rate is THB10.18/MYR, implying that the ringgit is only 2% undervalued relative to the baht.

Predicting British Heartburn

At this point, you might be feeling that PPP often does not work well. Before you decide that the theory is totally bunk, it is important to realize that *The Economist* made surprisingly accurate predictions using its MacPPP standard.

For example, in April 1991, *The Economist* noted that the implied PPP of the Deutsche mark relative to the British pound was DEM2.58/£. However, the central parity of the two currencies in the European Exchange Rate Mechanism (ERM) was DEM2.95/£ when Britain entered the ERM in October 1990. Given this difference of more than 14% between the implied PPP and the central parity, *The Economist* noted that the pound was overvalued, and the Deutsche mark was undervalued. *The Economist* also suggested that the British Treasury would eventually get "severe heartburn" if it tried to defend the actual exchange rate rather than devalue the pound within the ERM.

The logic of the argument is as follows: As we discussed in Chapter 5, the ERM required countries to buy their currencies with foreign currencies if the currency weakened by a certain amount relative to the central parity. The maximum deviation of the pound from its central parity with the DEM was DEM2.78/£ (6% below the central parity), which is substantially above the MacPPP value. Thus, if the pound began to weaken in the ERM to correct its overvaluation, the British Treasury would be forced to buy pounds with Deutsche marks. Given the limited amount of DEM that the Bank of England had in its international reserves, the market could force a devaluation of the pound by borrowing pounds and lending Deutsche marks. Investors would expect to profit from the devaluation because the pounds they would borrow would be easy to repay with the appreciated Deutsche marks they would own. The only way this would not occur would be if pound-denominated interest rates were increased sufficiently by the Bank of England to make it unattractive to borrow pounds and attractive for investors to hold pound-denominated assets.

Indeed, in September 1992, British authorities were essentially forced to withdraw from the ERM. From September 15 to September 16, the exchange rate fell from DEM2.7912/£

to DEM2.7500/£, and the authorities chose to abandon the ERM rather than increase pound interest rates and sell additional international reserves. After they abandoned the ERM and allowed the exchange rate to float, the pound weakened further and by September 28, it stood at DEM2.51/£. Before abandoning the ERM, it is estimated that the Bank of England lost over $12 billion of international reserves trying to defend the pound. Because these are resources that could have been used to pay for British government spending, not only did the British Treasury get a bad a case of heartburn, so did British taxpayers.

The Econometric Evidence

More formal statistical studies by economists also support the usefulness of MacPPP. Cumby (1996) finds that deviations from MacPPP are temporary. After allowing for a constant deviation, he estimates that one-half of the deviation from parity disappears in 1 year. Cumby's evidence also indicates that both the exchange rate and the prices of the burgers are adjusting to eliminate the deviation. The prediction is that a 10% undervalued currency tends to appreciate over the next year by 3.5%. Clements and Lan (2010) confirm that exchange rate forecasts using MacPPP have value, especially at 2- or 3-year horizons.

Parsley and Wei (2007) study the components of the Big Mac and infer that local labor costs account for 45.6% of its price. Section 8.6 addresses how such non-traded goods can affect PPP calculations. Parsley and Wei also find a very high correlation between PPPs calculated with Big Mac prices and those from CPI data, to which we now turn.

8.5 EXCHANGE RATES AND ABSOLUTE PPPS USING CPI DATA

Interpreting the Charts

One disadvantage of the MacPPP analysis is its comparatively short time span because *The Economist* only started calculating MacPPP in 1986. Exhibits 8.3 through 8.7 present data for actual exchange rates and the predictions of absolute PPP calculated from consumer price indexes for several of the world's major currencies. The solid line represents the actual exchange rate, and the dashed line is the implied exchange rate from the prediction of PPP.

Overvaluations and Undervaluations

In examining the deviations from PPP in Exhibits 8.3 through 8.7, it is important to remember how the exchange rate is quoted. For example, the pound and euro exchange rates are quoted directly as the amount of dollars it takes to purchase 1 pound or 1 euro, whereas the other exchange rates relative to the U.S. dollar are quoted indirectly as the amount of that currency that it takes to purchase 1 dollar. The PPP prediction for the dollar–pound exchange rate is therefore $P(t, \$)/P(t, £)$, whereas the PPP predictions for the indirect quotes relative to the dollar are the ratios of the foreign price levels to the U.S. price level. Hence, the dollar is undervalued when the actual exchange rate $S(t, \$/£)$ is above the PPP prediction, $P(t, \$)/P(t, £)$, because the dollar must strengthen relative to the pound if the undervaluation (on foreign exchange markets) is to be corrected. For the yen/dollar rate, the dollar is overvalued when the actual exchange rate, $S(t, ¥/\$)$, is above the PPP prediction, $P(t, ¥)/P(t, \$)$, because the dollar must weaken relative to the yen if the overvaluation of the dollar (on foreign exchange markets) is to be corrected by a movement in the exchange rate.

Fixing When PPP Held

The data in Exhibits 8.3 through 8.7 begin in January 1973 and end in January 2010. Because the prices of goods are obtained as consumer price indexes rather than price levels, it is necessary to take a stand on when the actual exchange rate satisfied the PPP relationship in order for the units of the ratio of the prices to correspond to the units of the exchange rate. The data are plotted such that absolute PPP is assumed to have held on average during the decade of the 1980s.

Analyzing the Data

How well or poorly does the theory of absolute PPP work? Clearly, there are large and persistent deviations of actual exchange rates from the predictions of PPP.

Dollar–Pound

The data for the $/£ rate in Exhibit 8.3 indicate that the pound was 30.2% overvalued in October 1980, but by February 1985, it was 43.8% undervalued.[4] Because the ratio of the price levels in the two countries changed only slightly over this period, almost all of the change is due to the movement of the exchange rate from $2.40/£ to $1.10/£. Once the dollar peaked in strength in 1985, though, it began to depreciate, and by October 1990, the pound was again more than 25% overvalued relative to the dollar. Just prior to the beginning of the financial crisis in November 2007, the pound was 30.5% overvalued, and at the end of the sample in January 2010, the pound was 9.6% overvalued.

Dollar–Euro

Exhibit 8.4 presents the dollar–euro data, where the exchange rate data prior to 1999 use the dollar–Deutsche mark exchange rate. The extreme overvaluation of the dollar relative to the PPP prediction that peaks in 1985 is repeated here. In February 1985, the dollar was

Exhibit 8.3 Actual USD/GBP and PPP Exchange Rates

Notes: The solid line is the actual exchange rate, and the dashed line is the PPP rate. Data are from the International Monetary Fund's International Financial Statistics.

---

[4]The percentage overvaluation or undervaluation of the denominator currency is computed as the percentage change in the exchange rate that is required to return to the PPP value. For example, if the actual exchange rate is $1.50/£, and the PPP exchange rate is $1.80/£, the pound is 20% undervalued because the appreciation of the pound required to go from the actual exchange rate to the PPP exchange rate is $[(\$1.80/£)/(\$1.50/£) - 1] = 20\%$.

Exhibit 8.4   Actual USD/EUR and PPP Exchange Rates

Notes: The solid line is the actual exchange rate, and the dashed line is the PPP rate. Data are from the International Monetary Fund's International Financial Statistics.

overvalued by 40.7% because this is the amount the dollar would have had to weaken if the actual exchange rate were to adjust to its PPP value. This is precisely what happened over the course of the next 2 years.

For the $/€ rate, the implied PPP value in January 1973 was $0.62/€, and in January 2010, it was $1.17/€. This is a cumulative weakening of the dollar relative to the Deutsche mark and then the euro of 88.7%, or 1.7% per year.[5] This increase in the PPP exchange rate indicates that U.S. inflation was on average 1.7% per year higher than German inflation during this 37-year period. Notice that the exchange rate satisfied PPP at the start of the euro in 1999. Subsequently, the dollar strengthened substantially relative to the euro, and in October 2000, the euro was 25.9% undervalued relative to the prediction of PPP. The euro then began to strengthen, and its overvaluation peaked in July 2008, prior to the peak of the financial crisis.

Yen–Dollar

The data for the yen–dollar exchange rates in Exhibit 8.5 differ somewhat from the previous ones. First, notice that the PPP line is upward sloping from 1973 to 1977, and then it is downward sloping thereafter. Because the PPP line corresponds to $P(t, ¥)/P(t, \$)$, the positive slope indicates that Japanese inflation was higher than U.S. inflation during the first part of the sample, whereas the negative slope of the ratio of the price levels indicates that Japanese inflation was lower than U.S. inflation during the second part of the sample.

The data on the ¥/$ rate indicate that the dollar was undervalued in October 1978 by 39%, with the implied PPP rate at ¥253/$ and the actual rate at ¥182/$. By February 1985, the dollar was 26.4% overvalued. Once the dollar peaked in strength in 1985, though, it began to depreciate relative to the yen. At the end of the sample in January 2010, at a PPP

---

[5]To find the annualized rate of appreciation of the euro, we solve for a in the following equation. $(\$0.62/€)(1+a)^{37} = \$1.17/€$ or $a = \{[(\$1.17/€)/(\$0.62/€)]^{1/37} - 1\} = 0.017$.

Exhibit 8.5 Actual JPY/USD and PPP Exchange Rates

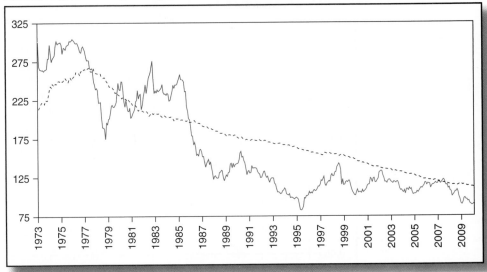

Notes: The solid line is the actual exchange rate, and the dashed line is the PPP rate. Data are from the International Monetary Fund's International Financial Statistics.

value of ¥111.6/$, the dollar was undervalued relative to the yen by 20% because the actual exchange rate was ¥91.11/$. In other words, those converting dollars into yen for expenditures in Japan found that their purchasing power was quite a bit lower than they were used to in the United States.

Canadian Dollar–U.S. Dollar

Exhibit 8.6 presents data for countries that share a common border, and here PPP works slightly better. The data for the Canadian dollar versus the U.S. dollar indicate that the maximal deviation from PPP was a 29.4% overvaluation of the U.S. dollar relative to the Canadian dollar in February 2002.

The overall flatness of the PPP line indicates that although U.S. and Canadian inflation rates were not identical period by period, they averaged essentially the same value over the sample period. Thus, the nominal weakening of the Canadian dollar during the 1990s led directly to a deviation from PPP, but by June 2004, the Canadian dollar had strengthened to restore PPP. The subsequent strengthening of the Canadian dollar returned the currencies to parity, which implies a 10% undervaluation of the U.S. dollar.

Mexican Peso–U.S. Dollar

All the exchange rates that have been discussed so far are for major developed countries. The last exchange rate we'll look at is the Mexican peso relative to the dollar, in Exhibit 8.7, where the exchange rates are in new pesos per dollar. Notice the periods of long stability when Mexico pegged the peso to the dollar, and the collapses of the fixed rates when devaluations occurred.

Note that the vertical scale is now a logarithmic one, in which the same vertical increment measures the same multiplicative increase or percentage rate of change. We need to use this graphical technique in order to see the early years of the period because the exchange rate (measured in current units) went from MXN0.0125/$ in 1973 to MXN14.58/$ in 2010. This is an increase of 116,640% over the 37 years, or 21% per year. The fact that the dollar was overvalued by only 8% relative to the peso after this enormous movement in the exchange rate is a

Exhibit 8.6 Actual CAD/USD and PPP Exchange Rates

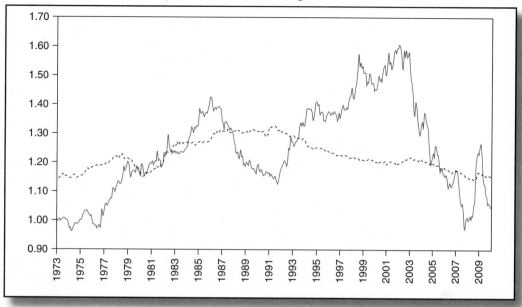

Notes: The solid line is the actual exchange rate, and the dashed line is the PPP rate. Data are from the International Monetary Fund's International Financial Statistics.

Exhibit 8.7 Actual MXN/USD and PPP Exchange Rates

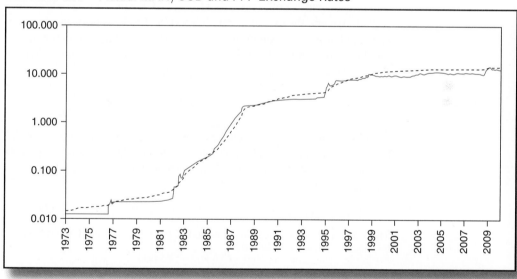

Notes: The solid line is the actual exchange rate, and the dashed line is the PPP rate. Data are from the International Monetary Fund's International Financial Statistics.

testimony to the long-run validity of PPP. The overvaluations of the peso prior to the 1976 and 1982 devaluations are also clearly present in the data. The data indicate that the peso was overvalued by 41% in August 1976, which is the maximum for the sample, and by 40% in January 1982 prior to the devaluations, whereupon it was subsequently undervalued by 13% in 1976 and 39% in 1982 after the devaluations. In November 1994, the data indicate that the peso was 21.3% overvalued when the market forced the devaluation known as the Mexican Peso Crisis.

8.6 EXPLAINING THE FAILURE OF ABSOLUTE PPP

Exhibits 8.6 through 8.7 show that there are large, persistent deviations of actual exchange rates from the predictions of absolute PPP. Because PPP is ultimately based on the law of one price, we know that anything that causes deviations from it can also cause deviations from PPP. As we saw, the factors causing deviations from the law of one price are quite numerous, including tariffs, quotas, and transaction costs. But there are other factors that cause deviations from absolute PPP.

Changes in Relative Prices

Changes in the relative prices of goods can cause deviations from PPP if price indices do not have the same weights across countries. To see this, suppose all goods are traded and assume that the prices of all goods satisfy the law of one price. Now, assume that tastes differ across countries so that expenditure shares on goods differ and let the price levels reflect the differences in consumption bundles. Typically, the residents of a country consume a larger share of the goods and services produced in that country than of imported goods and services. Consequently, the price indexes of each country will have a larger weight on goods produced at home and a smaller weight on imported goods. Changes in the relative prices will then lead to deviations from PPP.

A Burgers-and-Sushi World

Consider a simple example of the problem of changes in relative prices. Suppose there are only two countries, the United States and Japan, and to keep things really simple, assume that people consume only two goods, hamburgers and sushi. Let the United States produce only hamburgers, with a dollar price of $10, and let Japan produce only sushi, with a yen price of ¥5,000. Assume the exchange rate is ¥100/$. The U.S. price level will put a weight of 60% on the dollar price of hamburgers because U.S. consumers prefer hamburgers to sushi and a weight of 40% on the dollar price of sushi (the yen price of sushi divided by the yen–dollar exchange rate). Thus, the U.S. price level will be

$$P(t, \$) = 0.60 \times \$10 + 0.40 \times \frac{¥5,000}{¥100/\$} = \$26$$

Now, suppose the Japanese price level places a weight of 35% on the yen price of hamburgers (the dollar price of hamburgers multiplied by the yen–dollar exchange rate) because Japanese prefer sushi and a weight of 65% on the yen price of the sushi. Thus, the Japanese price level will be

$$P(t, ¥) = 0.35 \times (¥100/\$) \times \$10 + 0.65 \times ¥5,000 = ¥3,600$$

The ratio of the price level in Japan to the price level in the United States is

$$\frac{P(t, ¥)}{P(t, \$)} = \frac{¥3,600}{\$26} = ¥138.5/\$$$

Thus, even though the law of one price is satisfied in each country, the dollar appears to be 38.5% undervalued on the foreign exchange market. The problem is the difference in consumption shares. You should convince yourself that if the consumption shares were the same in both countries and if the law of one price held, then PPP would be satisfied.

It is now straightforward to understand how a change in relative prices can cause a change in the deviation between the exchange rate and measured PPP even though all goods are traded and all prices satisfy the law of one price. Suppose that there is a shift in demand away from U.S. hamburgers and toward Japanese sushi. With no changes in the supplies of the two goods, the relative price of sushi must rise both in the United States and in Japan. The increase in the relative price can be accomplished by an appreciation of the yen relative to the dollar, with no change in the dollar price of hamburgers and no change in the yen price of sushi. Suppose the yen appreciates to ¥90/$. With unchanged dollar prices of hamburgers and yen prices of sushi, the appreciation of the yen decreases the yen price of hamburgers in Japan and increases the dollar price of sushi, thereby making sushi relatively more expensive in both Japan and the United States. The U.S. price level will now be

$$P(t, \$) = 0.60 \times \$10 + 0.40 \times \frac{¥5,000}{¥90/\$} = \$28.22$$

and the Japanese price level will now be

$$P(t, ¥) = 0.35 \times (¥90/\$) \times \$10 + 0.65 \times ¥5,000 = ¥3,565$$

The ratio of the price level in Japan to the price level in the United States is

$$\frac{P(t, ¥)}{P(t, \$)} = \frac{¥3,565}{\$28.22} = ¥126.33/\$$$

Thus, even though the law of one price continues to be satisfied in each country, the dollar now appears to be 40.4% undervalued on the foreign exchange market because $(126.33 - 90)/90 = 0.404$. The shift in demand toward Japanese goods and away from U.S. goods causes the apparent undervaluation of the dollar to increase, but there is no opportunity for a goods market arbitrage.

Non-Traded Goods

Similar problems with absolute PPP arise when there are changes in the relative prices of traded and non-traded goods. Earlier in the chapter, we noted that when transaction costs are prohibitive, goods become non-traded. Because these goods are also included in the consumption bundles of individuals in the different countries, the prices of non-traded goods affect the price levels of the countries. Changes in the relative prices of traded and non-traded goods in two countries will cause deviations from absolute PPP that do not represent arbitrage opportunities.

Housing

Housing and other types of real estate are particularly important non-traded goods. If the price of housing in a country rises, with the price of other goods held constant, the relative price of housing rises, and the internal purchasing power of the country's money falls. Nevertheless, there need be no effect on the exchange rate. Consequently, after an increase in the relative price of housing in a country, the currency of that country will appear more overvalued (or less undervalued) on foreign exchange markets than before the increase in housing prices.

Technological Change

Why would the relative prices of non-traded goods rise compared to traded goods? Differential rates of technological change, which are also called productivity improvements, provide one answer. As the personal computer industry has aptly demonstrated over the past 25 years, improvements in technology in a competitive market force the prices of PCs to fall rapidly over time. The same is true of goods in other markets. If technology increases faster in traded goods industries than in non-traded goods industries, which is reasonable to expect if non-traded goods are services, we would expect that the relative price of non-traded goods would rise over time. This effect, known as the Harrod-Balassa-Samuelson effect, can impart a systematic bias in PPP calculations.[6]

---

[6]Harrod (1933), Balassa (1964), and Samuelson (1964) demonstrated that differential rates of technological change could produce systematic deviations from PPP. Canzoneri et al. (1999) and Lothian and Taylor (2008) provide empirical support for the idea.

PPP Deviations and the Balance of Payments

Our last explanation for deviations from absolute PPP is that they arise as equilibrium changes in the relative prices of goods across countries in a process that involves the balance of payments. The balance of payments of a country represents the aggregate amounts of goods and services that are bought and sold between the residents of a country and the rest of the world. We studied the accounting aspects of the balance of payments in Chapter 4. In Chapter 10, we formally discuss the relationship between deviations from PPP and the balance of payments. Here, we merely note that when a currency is overvalued relative to a PPP calculation, the external purchasing power of that currency increases, which shifts the nation's expenditures from domestic to foreign goods. This weakens the competitive position of domestic firms relative to foreign firms.

8.7 COMPARING INCOMES ACROSS COUNTRIES

Before we leave the subject of absolute PPP, we want to examine one particularly important use of PPP data: comparing nominal incomes across countries. Let's consider an extended example to make things easier.

Comparing Incomes in New York and Tokyo

The Salary Offers

Suppose you are considering working in New York for Citigroup and have been offered $100,000 per year. Goldman Sachs has also offered you a job working in Japan for the next 2 years at ¥15,000,000 per year. Suppose you are indifferent between living in New York and living in Tokyo. Either sounds okay to you. The question then becomes, which job makes you better off financially—working in New York or Tokyo?

A Naïve Calculation

You might be tempted to make the decision by simply comparing the dollar value of the yen salary offer to the dollar salary of your New York offer by converting the yen salary into dollars at the current exchange rate. If the current exchange rate is ¥100/$, the ¥15,000,000 is worth $150,000. If you used this approach, you would accept the job offer to work in Japan.

Incorporating Purchasing Power

By now, you should realize that this is a naïve calculation because if you must live and work in Japan, you will not purchase goods with $150,000. You will spend your yen salary to purchase goods and services that are sold in Japan and priced in yen, just as you would spend your dollar salary in New York to buy goods and services that are priced in dollars. To do a proper salary comparison, you must determine the command over goods and services that you will have based on the purchasing powers of the nominal salaries in each country. If you knew the price level in the United States, $P(t, \$)$, you could divide your $100,000 salary offer by the price level to determine its command over goods and services. Similarly, if you knew the price level in Japan, $P(t, ¥)$, you could divide your ¥15,000,000 salary by the Japanese price level to determine its command over goods and services in Japan. From a financial viewpoint, you would be indifferent between working in New York and working in Japan if the purchasing powers of your two salaries were the same—that is, if

$$\frac{(\$100{,}000 \text{ salary})}{P(t, \$)} = \frac{(¥15{,}000{,}000 \text{ salary})}{P(t, ¥)}$$

Working with the PPP Rate

What if the prices levels are not available, but the PPP exchange rate is available? Multiplying on both sides of the previous equation by the price level in Japan gives

$$(\$100{,}000 \text{ salary}) \times \frac{P(t, ¥)}{P(t, \$)} = ¥15{,}000{,}000 \text{ salary}$$

This equation states that you would be indifferent between the two jobs if your dollar salary multiplied by the PPP exchange rate, $[P(t, ¥)/P(t, \$)]$, equals your yen salary offer. Suppose the PPP exchange rate is ¥160/\$. To achieve the same purchasing power in Japan as you would have in the United States, you need a salary of

$$(¥160/\$) \times \$100{,}000 = ¥16{,}000{,}000$$

But your offer is only ¥15,000,000.

Alternatively, if you divide your yen salary offer by the PPP exchange rate of yen per dollar, you get a dollar equivalent of your yen salary. Then, when you determine your command over goods and services by mentally dividing the dollar equivalent salary by the dollar price level, the resulting units are consumption bundles in Japan. The implied dollar salary is

$$\frac{¥15{,}000{,}000}{¥160/\$} = \$93{,}750$$

This calculation states that the purchasing power you would have in Japan from a ¥15,000,000 salary is equivalent to the purchasing power that you would have in the United States from a \$93,750 salary. As you can see, if the PPP exchange rate were ¥160/\$, you should turn down the offer to work in Japan or demand a higher yen salary.[7]

Given the occasional large percentage differences between actual exchange rates and implied PPP exchange rates that we saw in Exhibits 8.3 through 8.7, converting a foreign currency–denominated salary into dollars using an actual exchange rate versus a PPP exchange rate will sometimes produce quite substantively different results. The numerical example in this section demonstrates that if the dollar is undervalued relative to the foreign currency, the dollar-equivalent salary of a foreign currency offer is lower when you use the PPP exchange rate rather than the actual exchange rate.

Conversely, whenever the dollar is overvalued relative to a foreign currency, converting a foreign currency salary into dollars with the actual exchange rate will result in a smaller dollar salary than if the PPP exchange rate were used. However, although your salary in dollars will seem low, the dollar prices of goods and services purchased in the country will also seem quite low relative to comparable items in the United States. In such cases, dividing by the implied PPP exchange rate again provides a better estimate of the standard of living that you will face in the country, were you to be stationed there and paid in the foreign currency. This is particularly important if you are considering job offers in emerging market countries, whose currencies often appear to be undervalued relative to the dollar.

Comparing GDPs Using PPP Exchange Rates

Exhibit 8.8 presents a comparison of gross domestic product (GDP) per capita for the Organization for Economic Cooperation and Development (OECD) countries in 2008, measured in U.S. dollars, using a 3-year average of current exchange rates in the first column and PPP exchange rates in the second column.

---

[7]Ong and Mitchell (2000) use this approach with MacPPP rates to compare academic salaries across countries.

Exhibit 8.8 GDP per Capita for OECD Countries in 2008 Using Exchange Rates and PPP Values

OECD Country	In U.S. Dollars, Based on Market Exchange Rates	In U.S. Dollars, Based on PPP Exchange Rates
Australia	48,569	39,056
Austria	49,527	37,858
Belgium	47,151	35,288
Canada	44,995	39,014
Czech Republic	20,719	24,631
Denmark	62,054	36,808
Finland	50,775	35,809
France	44,450	33,098
Germany	44,519	35,432
Greece	31,174	28,896
Hungary	15,363	19,732
Iceland	52,610	36,994
Ireland	59,944	41,493
Italy	38,384	31,195
Japan	38,456	34,132
Korea	19,115	27,658
Luxembourg	117,967	84,713
Mexico	10,194	14,517
Netherlands	53,094	41,063
New Zealand	30,142	27,444
Norway	94,572	58,599
Poland	13,861	17,294
Portugal	22,951	23,283
Slovak Republic	17,537	22,141
Spain	34,971	31,455
Sweden	51,709	36,790
Switzerland	64,885	42,783
Turkey	10,275	13,959
United Kingdom	42,378	35,620
United States	47,186	47,186

Source: Data are from the Organization for Economic Cooperation and Development's statistical database.

The last row indicates that the United States produced final goods and services in 2008 that were worth $47,186 per person. When the currency of a country is stronger in foreign exchange markets than its PPP exchange rate, as in the case of the Japanese yen, the dollar value of the country's GDP per capita when measured by current exchange rates is larger than when measured by PPP exchange rates. Notice that the dollar value of Japan's GDP falls from $38,456 per capita in the first column to $34,132 in the second column. The fact that the euro strengthened considerably relative to the dollar between 2004 and 2008 and was overvalued relative to PPP leads the European countries to have higher incomes measured at actual exchange rates rather than in PPP. Conversely, because non-traded goods are relatively inexpensive in emerging markets, their PPP exchange rates typically imply that their currencies are stronger versus the dollar than the actual exchange rates imply. Thus, the dollar value of the country's GDP per capita when measured by PPP exchange rates is larger than when measured by actual exchange rates.

The discussion in this section about comparing incomes across countries strongly suggests that the PPP exchange rates are the appropriate ones to use when comparing standards of living across countries.

Section 8.6 discusses reasons why absolute PPP generally will not hold. In addition, Exhibits 8.3 through 8.7 demonstrate that currencies are often substantially undervalued and overvalued relative to the predictions of absolute PPP calculated using CPI data. Another form of PPP, called **relative purchasing power parity**, takes market imperfections into account, and it acknowledges that because of these imperfections, a consumption bundle will not necessarily have the same value from country to country. However, according to the theory of relative PPP, exchange rates adjust in response to differences in inflation rates across countries to leave the differences in purchasing power unchanged over time. If the percentage change in the exchange rate just offsets the differential rates of inflation, economists say that relative PPP is satisfied. To help you better understand these concepts, let's begin with a numerical example.

Example 8.7 The Warranted Change in the Exchange Rate

Suppose, as in Example 8.4, that the price level in the United States is initially \$15,000/U.S. consumption bundle, the price level in the United Kingdom is initially £10,000/U.K. consumption bundle, and the exchange rate is \$1.40/£. We determined that absolute PPP is violated. The pound is undervalued on foreign exchange markets because the implied PPP exchange rate of

$$\frac{\$15{,}000}{£10{,}000} = \$1.50/£$$

is not equal to the actual exchange rate. The pound would have to strengthen relative to the dollar by 7.14% to correct its undervaluation because

$$\frac{\$1.50/£}{\$1.40/£} = 1.0714$$

Now, suppose that during the following year, the rate of U.S. inflation is 3%, and the rate of U.K. inflation is 10%. From the definition of *inflation*, we know that the new price level in the United States is 3% higher:

$$\$15{,}000 \times 1.03 = \$15{,}450$$

and the new price level in the United Kingdom is 10% higher:

$$£10{,}000 \times 1.10 = £11{,}000$$

Hence, the new implied PPP exchange rate is

$$\frac{\$15{,}450}{£11{,}000} = \$1.4045/£$$

If the pound remains 7.14% undervalued on the foreign exchange market, as it was before, the pound must weaken relative to the dollar for relative PPP to be satisfied. The new exchange rate should equal

$$S(t{+}1, \$/£) = \frac{\$1.4045/£}{1.0714} = \$1.3109/£$$

This keeps the ratio of the PPP exchange rate to the actual exchange rate at 1.0714, as before. The pound depreciates relative to the dollar by 6.36% because the actual exchange rate moves to \$1.3109/£ from \$1.40/£, and

$$\frac{\$1.3109/£}{\$1.40/£} = 0.9364 = 1 - 0.0636$$

Notice also that 0.9364 is the ratio of 1 plus the U.S. rate of inflation divided by 1 plus the U.K. rate of inflation because

$$\frac{1.03}{1.10} = 0.9364$$

Intuitively, the pound is losing purchasing power over goods and services due to U.K. inflation of 10% per year, and the dollar is losing purchasing power over goods and services due to U.S. inflation of 3% per year. A 6.36% depreciation of the pound relative to the dollar is therefore required to make the loss of the pound's external purchasing power equal to the loss of its internal purchasing power.

A General Expression for Relative PPP

The example in the preceding section demonstrates that relative PPP requires that 1 plus the rate of appreciation of the pound relative to the dollar should equal 1 plus the rate of inflation in the United States divided by 1 plus the rate of inflation in the United Kingdom.

The Logic of Relative PPP

Relative PPP is derived from the following economic reasoning: Inflation lowers the purchasing power of money. If the amount of inflation in the foreign country differs from the inflation rate in the domestic country, a change in the nominal exchange rate to compensate for the differential rates of inflation is warranted so that the loss of internal purchasing power due to domestic inflation equals the loss of external purchasing power due to foreign inflation and the change in the exchange rate. If the change in the exchange rate satisfies this warranted change, relative PPP is satisfied.[8]

A Symbolic Representation of Relative PPP

In general symbolic terms, let $s(t+1, \mathrm{DC/FC})$ denote the percentage rate of change of the domestic currency (denoted DC) per unit of foreign currency (denoted FC) from time t to $t+1$, and let $\pi(t+1, \mathrm{DC})$ and $\pi(t+1, \mathrm{FC})$ represent the corresponding rates of domestic and foreign inflation, respectively; then relative PPP requires that

$$1 + s(t+1, \mathrm{DC/FC}) = \frac{1 + \pi(t+1, \mathrm{DC})}{1 + \pi(t+1, \mathrm{FC})} \qquad (8.3)$$

---

[8]It was this formulation of the theory that Cassel (1918) called *purchasing power parity*. Cassel was writing about the reestablishment of exchange rates after World War I because foreign exchange markets had closed during the war. Prior to the war, the countries of the world were on the gold standard, and their exchange rates were fixed. Cassel wrote:

> The general inflation which has taken place during the war has lowered this purchasing power in all countries, though in a different degree, and the rate of exchange should accordingly be expected to deviate from their old parities in proportion to the inflation of each country. At every moment the real parity is represented by this quotient between the purchasing power of the money in one country and the other. I propose to call this parity *"purchasing power parity"* (p. 413).

If we subtract 1 from each side of Equation (8.3) and place terms over a common denominator, we get

$$s(t{+}1, \text{DC/FC}) = \frac{\pi(t{+}1, \text{DC}) - \pi(t{+}1, \text{FC})}{1 + \pi(t{+}1, \text{FC})} \qquad (8.4)$$

Equation (8.4) states that the rate of appreciation of the foreign currency relative to the domestic currency is equal to the difference between the domestic rate of inflation and the foreign rate of inflation divided by 1 plus the foreign rate of inflation.

Because $[1 + \pi(t{+}1, \text{FC})]$ is often close to 1 if the foreign inflation rate is low, some presentations of relative PPP ignore this term in the denominator of Equation (8.4) and state that relative PPP requires equality between the rate of appreciation of the foreign currency relative to domestic currency and the difference between the domestic and foreign inflation rates. Equation (8.4) indicates that this statement is an approximation, albeit a pretty good one if the foreign inflation rate is small.

Of course, because the graphs in Exhibit 8.3 indicate that deviations from absolute PPP change over time, relative PPP also does not hold in the data. The rate of change of the exchange rate does not equal the inflation differential between two currencies.

Relative PPP with Continuously Compounded Rates of Change (Advanced)

The discussion of relative PPP suggests ignoring the denominator of Equation (8.4) as a reasonable approximation. We encountered a similar approximation in the discussion of interest rate parity in Chapter 6. There, we noted that if we measure the forward premium on the foreign currency and the domestic and foreign interest rates in continuously compounded terms, it is exactly correct to state that interest rate parity requires equality between the forward premium on the foreign currency and the interest differential between the domestic and foreign interest rates. Analogously, if we measure the rate of appreciation of the foreign currency relative to the domestic currency and the domestic and foreign inflation rates as continuously compounded rates of change, relative PPP requires equality between the rate of appreciation of the foreign currency and the difference between the domestic and foreign rates of inflation. We demonstrate this equality by using the dollar–pound exchange rate and the respective rates of inflation.

If there are obstacles to international trade that prevent absolute PPP from holding, we can introduce a factor k such that the internal purchasing power of the money equals k times the external purchasing power of the money:

$$\frac{1}{P(t, \$)} = k \times \frac{1}{S(t, \$/£)} \times \frac{1}{P(t, £)} \qquad (8.5)$$

where $S(t, \$/£)$ denotes the actual exchange rate and not the implied PPP value. By rearranging Equation (8.5), we have

$$\frac{S(t, \$/£) \times P(t, £)}{P(t, \$)} = k \qquad (8.6)$$

If the amount of overvaluation or undervaluation of the dollar relative to the pound is the same at time $t{+}1$, we have

$$\frac{S(t{+}1, \$/£) \times P(t{+}1, £)}{P(t{+}1, \$)} = k \qquad (8.7)$$

Hence, the ratio of Equation (8.6) to Equation (8.7) is

$$\frac{S(t+1, \$/\pounds)}{S(t, \$/\pounds)} \times \frac{P(t+1, \pounds)/P(t, \pounds)}{P(t+1, \$)/P(t, \$)} = 1 \qquad (8.8)$$

Now, if $s(t+1, \$/\pounds)$ denotes the continuously compounded rate of change of the dollar–pound exchange rate over the time interval from t to $t+1$, then $[S(t+1, \$/\pounds)/ S(t, \$/\pounds)] = \exp[s(t+1, \$/\pounds)]$. Similarly, let $\pi(t+1, \pounds)$ and $\pi(t+1, \$)$ now denote the continuously compounded rates of inflation over the time interval from t to $t+1$ in the pound and dollar prices of goods, respectively. Then, $P(t+1, \pounds)/P(t, \pounds) = \exp[\pi(t+1, \pounds)]$, and $P(t+1, \$)/P(t, \$) = \exp[\pi(t+1, \$)]$. Substituting these exponential expressions into Equation (8.8) gives

$$\frac{\exp[s(t+1, \$/\pounds)] \times \exp[\pi(t+1, \pounds)]}{\exp[\pi(t+1, \$)]} = 1 \qquad (8.9)$$

If we apply the rules for taking natural logarithms from the appendix to Chapter 2 to Equation (8.9), we find

$$s(t+1, \$/\pounds) + \pi(t+1, \pounds) - \pi(t+1, \$) = 0$$

or, rearranging terms, we find

$$s(t+1, \$/\pounds) = \pi(t+1, \$) - \pi(t+1, \pounds) \qquad (8.10)$$

Equation (8.10) expresses relative PPP in its continuously compounded version. The rate of appreciation of the pound versus the dollar equals the rate of dollar inflation minus the rate of pound inflation when all the rates of change are continuously compounded.

8.9 THE REAL EXCHANGE RATE

While discussions of purchasing power parity have been around since the early twentieth century, the concept of the **real exchange rate** is much newer, as it entered the jargon of international finance in the late 1970s. Nonetheless, the real exchange rate is important because it influences the competitiveness of firms, which is explored in Chapter 9. Here, we introduce the concept of the real exchange rate.

The Definition of the Real Exchange Rate

The real exchange rate, say, of the dollar relative to the euro, will be denoted $RS(t, \$/\text{€})$. It is defined to be the nominal exchange rate multiplied by the ratio of the price levels:

$$RS(t, \$/\text{€}) = \frac{S(t, \$/\text{€}) \times P(t, \text{€})}{P(t, \$)} \qquad (8.11)$$

Notice that the real exchange rate would be 1 if absolute PPP held because the nominal exchange rate, $S(t, \$/\text{€})$, would equal the ratio of the two price levels, $P(t, \$)/P(t, \text{€})$. Similarly, if absolute PPP is violated, the real exchange rate is not equal to 1. Also, the real exchange rate is constant if relative PPP holds, as we see in the next example.

Because the real exchange rate is not equal to 1 in Example 8.8, absolute PPP does not hold. But because relative PPP holds in Example 8.8, the deviations from absolute PPP are constant in percentage terms. This keeps the real exchange rate constant. If deviations from absolute PPP vary over time, relative PPP does not hold, and the real exchange rate fluctuates.

Example 8.8   A Constant Real Exchange Rate

Suppose that the U.S. price level is initially \$15,000/U.S. consumption bundle and the price level in Europe is initially €11,000/European consumption bundle. With the nominal exchange rate equal to \$1.30/€, the real exchange rate equals

$$RS(t, \$/€) = \frac{\$1.30/€ \times €11,000}{\$15,000} = 0.9533$$

Suppose that over the next year, there is 4% inflation in the United States, there is 8% inflation in Europe, and the nominal exchange rate changes so that relative PPP is satisfied. Then, as Equation (8.3) indicates, the new nominal exchange rate is

$$S(t, \$/€) = \frac{\$1.30/€ \times 1.04}{1.08} = \$1.2519/€$$

The euro weakens by 3.7%. With 4% U.S. inflation, the new U.S. price level is \$15,600 = \$15,000 × 1.04, and with 8% European inflation, the new European price level is €11,880 = €11,000 × 1.08. The new real exchange rate is the same as it was before, because

$$RS(t{+}1, \$/€) = \frac{\$1.2519/€ \times €11,880}{\$15,600} = 0.9533$$

Essentially, the real exchange rate describes deviations from absolute PPP, and changes in the real exchange rate represent deviations from relative PPP.

Real Appreciations and Real Depreciations

Of course, when the concept of the real exchange rate took hold, people naturally began to refer to **real appreciations** and **real depreciations** of different currencies. The concepts of real appreciations and real depreciations are useful because they help us describe real exchange risk, the topic of Chapter 9.

In Chapter 2, we defined the percentage rate of change in the nominal exchange rate of the dollar relative to the pound by $s(t{+}1, \$/£) = [S(t{+}1, \$/£) - S(t, \$/£)]/S(t, \$/£)$. If the percentage change in $S(t, \$/£)$ was positive, we called it a nominal appreciation of the pound. We also defined a nominal appreciation of the pound by $a(t{+}1, \$/£) = s(t{+}1, \$/£)$, when $s(t{+}1, \$/£) > 0$. Similarly, we defined a nominal depreciation of the pound by $d(t{+}1, \$/£) = -s(t{+}1, \$/£)$, if $s(t{+}1), \$/£ < 0$. For example, if the percentage change in the dollar–pound exchange rate was –5%, we said that the pound depreciated by 5%.

The Percentage Change in the Real Exchange Rate

We can define the percentage rate of change in the real exchange rate by

$$rs(t{+}1, \$/£) = \frac{RS(t{+}1, \$/£) - RS(t, \$/£)}{RS(t, \$/£)} \tag{8.12}$$

If the right-hand side of Equation (8.12) is positive, we have a real appreciation of the pound:

$$ra(t{+}1, \$/£) = rs(t{+}1, \$/£), \text{ if } rs(t{+}1, \$/£) > 0$$

and if the real exchange rate falls, we have a real depreciation of the pound:

$$rd(t+1, \$/£) = -rs(t+1, \$/£), \text{ if } rs(t+1, \$/£) < 0$$

Because the ratio of the new real exchange rate to the old real exchange rate equals 1 plus the rate of change of the real exchange rate, we have

$$[1 + rs(t+1, \$/£)] = \frac{RS(t+1, \$/£)}{RS(t, \$/£)} \qquad (8.13)$$

To understand what leads to real appreciations and depreciations, we must substitute the definition of the real exchange rate from Equation (8.11) into Equation (8.13):

$$[1 + rs(t+1, \$/£)] = \frac{[S(t+1, \$/£) \times P(t+1, £)/P(t+1, \$)]}{[S(t, \$/£) \times P(t, £)/P(t, \$)]} \qquad (8.14)$$

Now, we group the exchange rate terms, the pound price-level terms, and the dollar price-level terms together to get the following:

$$[1 + rs(t+1, \$/£)] = \frac{[S(t+1, \$/£)/S(t, \$/£)] \times [P(t+1, £)/P(t, £)]}{[P(t+1, \$)/P(t, \$)]}$$

After substituting the definitions of the ratios of variables at time $t+1$ to those at time t, we find

$$[1 + rs(t+1, \$/£)] = \frac{[1 + s(t+1, \$/£)] \times [1 + \pi(t+1, £)]}{[1 + \pi(t+1, \$)]} \qquad (8.15)$$

The left-hand side of Equation (8.15) is 1 plus the percentage rate of change of the real dollar–pound exchange rate. The right-hand side equals 1 plus the percentage rate of change of the nominal dollar–pound exchange rate multiplied by 1 plus the U.K. rate of inflation, $\pi(t+1, £)$, divided by 1 plus the U.S. rate of inflation, $\pi(t+1, \$)$.

What Leads to Real Appreciations or Depreciations

Because the real exchange rate is composed of three variables that can all move simultaneously, many combinations of changes lead to a real appreciation of the pound. The three basic movements are as follows:

1. An increase in the nominal exchange rate ($\$/£$), that is a nominal appreciation of the pound, holding the dollar prices and pound prices of goods constant.
2. An increase in the pound prices of goods, holding the exchange rate and the dollar prices of goods constant.
3. A decrease in the dollar prices of U.S. goods, holding the exchange rate and the pound prices of goods constant.

Because relative PPP implies a constant real exchange rate, we know that $rs(t+1, \$/£) = 0$ in this case. We can therefore use this information to solve Equation (8.15) to find that the required percentage change in the nominal exchange rate that just keeps the real exchange rate constant is

$$[1 + s(t+1, \$/£)] = \frac{[1 + \pi(t+1, \$)]}{[1 + \pi(t+1, £)]} \qquad (8.16)$$

Equation (8.16) provides the warranted percentage rate of change of the dollar–pound exchange rate that leaves the real exchange rate unchanged. If the nominal appreciation is larger than the amount that is warranted by the right-hand side of Equation (8.16), there is a real appreciation of the pound. Conversely, if the actual rate of appreciation of the pound relative to the dollar falls short of the warranted amount on the right-hand side of Equation (8.16), there is a real depreciation of the pound.

Example 8.9   A Variable Real Exchange Rate

When the real exchange rate was constant in Example 8.8, the annual U.S. rate of inflation was 4%, the annual European rate of inflation was 8%, and the dollar–euro exchange rate offset the inflation differential, with the euro depreciating by 3.7%. Suppose that the euro actually depreciates in nominal terms by 2% relative to the dollar during the year of these inflations. Is this nominal depreciation of the euro associated with a real depreciation of the euro or a real appreciation?

From Equation (8.16), we know that the warranted rate of depreciation of the euro relative to the dollar is 3.7% because

$$\frac{[1 + \pi(t{+}1, \$)]}{[1 + \pi(t{+}1, \text{€})]} = \frac{1.04}{1.08} = 0.963 = 1 - 0.037$$

Because the nominal rate of depreciation of the euro relative to the dollar is only 2%, there has been a real appreciation of the euro. The new real exchange rate is now greater than it was before. With the new nominal exchange rate of

$$(\$1.30/\text{€}) \times (1 - 0.02) = \$1.2740/\text{€}$$

the new real exchange rate is

$$RS(t{+}1, \$/\text{€}) = \frac{\$1.2740/\text{€} \times \text{€}11{,}880}{\$15{,}600} = 0.9702$$

The old real exchange rate was 0.9533. There is a real appreciation of the euro, and there is a real depreciation of the dollar, even though the dollar appreciated relative to the euro in nominal terms. The nominal dollar value of the euro just did not fall enough when compared to the respective rates of inflation of the two currencies. Because the euro only weakened by 2% instead of the 3.7% that was warranted by the inflation differential, the euro actually strengthened in real terms.

Notice from Equation (8.15) that real appreciations and real depreciations can occur even if the nominal exchange rate does not change. If the exchange rate is fixed between two currencies, but the prices of goods measured in these currencies rise at different rates because of differences in inflation, the high-inflation country will experience a real appreciation of its currency, and the low-inflation country will experience a real depreciation.

Trade-Weighted Real Exchange Rates

To this point, we have considered only bilateral real exchange rates. Many governments calculate a **trade-weighted real exchange rate**. The numerator of a trade-weighted real exchange rate contains the sum of the nominal exchange rates for different currencies multiplied by the price levels of different countries weighted by the proportion of trade conducted with that country. A trade-weighted real exchange rate makes good economic sense because a given currency rarely strengthens or weakens relative to all foreign currencies by the same amount, and real exchange rates are critical determinants of international trade. For example, if we are interested in describing the extent to which a depreciation of the domestic currency would affect a country's trade balance, we must know how much trade the country is doing with other nations and how much the depreciation is increasing the relative prices of the goods of those countries.

8.10 SUMMARY

This chapter explores the theory known as purchasing power parity and a related concept, the real exchange rate. The main points in the chapter are as follows:

1. Absolute PPP states that the nominal exchange rate adjusts to equate the internal purchasing power of a nation's currency to the external purchasing power of that currency.

2. The internal purchasing power of a currency is the amount of goods and services that a unit of the currency can buy in the country that issues that money. The consumer price level of a country measures the amount of money that is necessary to purchase a typical bundle of consumption goods in that country. The internal purchasing power of a currency is consequently the reciprocal of the price level.

3. The external purchasing power of a currency is the amount of goods and services that a unit of the money can buy in a foreign country after converting from the domestic money into the foreign money.

4. Inflation (increases in a nation's price level) lowers the purchasing power of a country's currency. In contrast, deflation (decreases in a nation's price level) increases the purchasing power of a country's currency.

5. The law of one price means that the price of a commodity denominated in a particular currency is the same wherever in the world the good is being sold. If markets are competitive and there are no transaction costs or information costs, goods market arbitrage drives the price of the good quoted in a common currency to be the same around the world.

6. Violations of the law of one price are caused by transaction costs; barriers to trade such as tariffs, quotas, and government regulations; and non-competitive markets. When transaction costs or barriers to trade in international markets are prohibitive, goods become non-traded. For these goods, the law of one price won't hold.

7. A currency is said to be overvalued on foreign exchange markets if its external purchasing power is greater than its internal purchasing power. A currency is undervalued on foreign exchange markets if its external purchasing power is less than its internal purchasing power. Overvalued currencies must weaken to return to the prediction of PPP, whereas undervalued currencies must strengthen to return to PPP.

8. Deviations from absolute PPP are large and persistent. For the major currencies, deviations from PPP of 35% or more are not uncommon, and such discrepancies between the market exchange rate and the PPP prediction often persist for 5 or more years. In the long run, however, the deviations tend to subside and reverse sign.

9. Equilibrium changes in relative prices, especially between the prices of traded and non-traded goods, explain some of the observed deviations from absolute PPP.

10. The theory of relative purchasing power acknowledges that a consumption bundle will not necessarily be the same from country to country. However, it holds that exchange rates will adjust in response to differential inflation rates occurring in countries.

11. The real exchange rate of a domestic currency relative to a foreign currency is defined to be the nominal exchange rate (in domestic currency per unit of foreign currency) multiplied by the ratio of the price levels in the two countries:

$$ RS = \frac{S(DC/FC) \times P(FC)}{P(DC)} $$

12. If the percentage change in the nominal exchange rate (domestic currency per unit of foreign currency) exceeds the rate of change that is warranted by differential inflation rates between two countries (that is, the differential inflation rate that satisfies relative PPP), there is a real appreciation of the foreign currency and a real depreciation of the domestic currency.

QUESTIONS

1. What does the purchasing power of a money mean? How can it be measured?

2. Suppose the government releases information that causes people to expect that the purchasing power of a money in the future will be less than they previously had expected. What will happen to the exchange rate today? Why?

3. What is the difference between a price level and a price index?

4. What do economists mean by the law of one price? Why might the law of one price be violated?
5. What is the value of the exchange rate that satisfies absolute PPP?
6. If the actual exchange rate for the euro value of the British pound is less than the exchange rate that would satisfy absolute PPP, which of the currencies is overvalued and which is undervalued? Why?
7. What market forces prevent absolute PPP from holding in real economies? Which of these represent unexploited profit opportunities?
8. Why is it better to use a PPP exchange rate to compare incomes across countries than an actual exchange rate?
9. What is relative PPP, and why does it represent a weaker relationship between exchange rates and prices than absolute PPP?
10. What is the real exchange rate, and how are fluctuations in the real exchange rate related to deviations from absolute PPP?
11. If the nominal exchange rate between the Mexican peso and the U.S. dollar is fixed, and there is higher inflation in Mexico than in the United States, which currency experiences a real appreciation and which experiences a real depreciation? Why? What is likely to happen to the balance of trade between the two countries?

PROBLEMS

1. If the consumer price index for the United States rises from 350 at the end of a year to 365 at the end of the next year, how much inflation was there in the United States during that year?
2. As a wheat futures trader, you observe the following futures prices for the purchase and sale of wheat in 3 months: $3.00 per bushel in Chicago and ¥320 per bushel in Tokyo. Delivery on the contracts is in Chicago and Tokyo, respectively. If the 3-month forward exchange rate is ¥102/$, what is the magnitude of the transaction cost necessary to make this situation not represent an unexploited profit opportunity?
3. Suppose that the price level in Canada is CAD16,600, the price level in France is EUR11,750, and the spot exchange rate is CAD1.35/EUR.
   a. What is the internal purchasing power of the Canadian dollar?
   b. What is the internal purchasing power of the euro in France?
   c. What is the implied exchange rate of CAD/EUR that satisfies absolute PPP?
   d. Is the euro overvalued or undervalued relative to the Canadian dollar?
   e. What amount of appreciation or depreciation of the euro would be required to return the actual exchange rate to its PPP value?
4. Suppose that the rate of inflation in Japan is 2% in 2011. If the rate of inflation in Germany is 5% during 2011, by how much would the yen strengthen relative to the euro if relative PPP is satisfied during 2011?
5. One of your colleagues at Deutsche Bank thinks that the dollar is severely undervalued relative to the yen. He has calculated that the PPP exchange rate is ¥140/$, whereas the current exchange rate is ¥105/$. Because interest rates are 3% p.a. lower in Japan than in the United States, he thinks that this is a good time to speculate by borrowing yen and lending dollars. What do you think?
6. Suppose that you are trying to decide between two job offers. One consulting firm offers you $150,000 per year to work out of its New York office. A second consulting firm wants you to work out of its London office and offers you £100,000 per year. The current exchange rate is $1.65/£. Which offer should you take, and why? Assume that the PPP exchange rate is $1.40/£ and that you are indifferent between working in the two cities if the purchasing power of your salary is the same.
7. Suppose that in 2011, the Japanese rate of inflation is 2%, and the German rate of inflation is 5%. If the euro weakens relative to the yen by 10% during 2011, what would be the magnitude of the real depreciation of the euro relative to the yen?
8. Pick a particular brand of appliance, like a Bosch dishwasher with certain features, and use the Internet to compare its prices across countries. Be sure to have exactly the same style of appliance in each country. How different are the prices when expressed in a common currency?
9. Go to the International Monetary Fund's Web site at www.imf.org, find the Data and Statistics tab, locate World Economic Outlook (WEO) data, and download the "Implied PPP conversion rate" for the Indonesian rupiah and the Philippines peso versus the dollar. Calculate a rupiah per peso PPP rate and compare it to the actual exchange rate. Which currency is overvalued, and by how much?

BIBLIOGRAPHY

Balassa, Bela, 1964, "The Purchasing Power Parity Doctrine: A Reappraisal," *Journal of Political Economy* 72, pp. 584–596.

Broda, Christian, and David E. Weinstein, 2008, "Understanding International Price Differences Using Barcode Data," National Bureau of Economic Research Working Paper No. 14017.

Canzoneri, Matthew B., Robert E. Cumby, and Behzad Diba, 1999, "Relative Labor Productivity and the Real Exchange Rate in the Long Run: Evidence for a Panel of OECD Countries," *Journal of International Economics* 47, pp. 245–266.

Cassel, Gustav, 1916, "The Present Situation of the Foreign Exchanges," *Economic Journal* 26, pp. 319–323.

——————, 1918, "Abnormal Deviations in International Exchanges," *Economic Journal* 28, pp. 413–415.

Clements, Kenneth W., and Yihui Lan, 2010, "A New Approach to Forecasting Exchange Rates," *Journal of International Money and Finance* 29, pp. 1424–1437.

Cumby, Robert E., 1996, "Forecasting Exchange Rates and Relative Prices with the Hamburger Standard: Is What You Want What You Get with McParity?" National Bureau of Economic Research Working Paper No. 5675.

Dornbusch, Rudiger, 1988, "Purchasing Power Parity," in R. Dornbusch, ed., *Exchange Rates and Prices*, Cambridge, MA: The MIT Press.

Engel, Charles, and John Rogers, December 1996, "How Wide Is the Border?" *American Economic Review* 86, pp. 1112–1125.

Harrod, Roy, 1933, *International Economics*, London: Nisbet and Cambridge University Press.

Imbs, Jean M., Haroon Mumtaz, Morten O. Ravn, and Hélène Rey, 2010, "One TV, One Price?" *Scandinavian Journal of Economics* 112, pp. 753–781.

Lothian, James R., and Mark P. Taylor, 2008, "Real Exchange Rates over the Past Two Centuries: How Important Is the Harrod-Balassa-Samuelson Effect?" *The Economic Journal* 118, pp. 1742–1763.

Okun, Arthur, 1981, *Prices and Quantities*, Washington, DC: Brookings Institution.

Ong, Li Lian, and Jason D. Mitchell, 2000, "Professors and Hamburgers: An International Comparison of Real Academic Salaries," *Applied Economics* 32, pp. 869–876.

Parsley, David C., and Shang-Jin Wei, 2007, "A Prism into the PPP Puzzles: The Micro-Foundations of Big Mac Real Exchange Rates," *The Economic Journal* 117, pp. 1336–1356.

Samuelson, Paul, 1964, "Theoretical Notes on Trade Problems," *Review of Economics and Statistics* 46, pp. 145–154.

The Economist, "Big MacCurrencies," April 1991, April 2000, April 2006, May 2010.

Chapter 9

Measuring and Managing Real Exchange Risk

In May 2009, the Australian mineral extraction company, Rio Tinto Ltd., contracted with Japan's largest steel company, Nippon Steel, on a U.S. dollar (USD) price that Nippon would pay for iron ore over the next year. Given the severity of the global recession, the USD price was 33% lower than the previous price. Exchange rates provided a benefit to both companies. Over the previous year, the Australian dollar weakened relative to the U.S. dollar by 18%, whereas the Japanese yen had strengthened relative to the U.S. dollar by 10%. Because Rio Tinto's extraction costs in Australian dollars were essentially constant, the exchange rate change mitigated its loss of profit from a lower export price. Similarly, although the yen prices of finished steel were down in Japan, the strengthening of the yen lowered Nippon's costs in addition to the reduced USD price of iron ore and thus mitigated its loss of profit. The situations of these two firms are examples of how changes in exchange rates can affect the profitability of a firm, in this case positively. This chapter examines how firms respond to this "real exchange risk" with their pricing, marketing, and production policies.

In general, such changes in profitability arise because of fluctuations in real exchange rates. We develop the concept of real exchange risk by first demonstrating how the real exchange rate arises naturally in understanding the profitability of exporters and importers. Then we examine how to share real exchange risk in a long-term contract. Whenever firms from different countries that do not share a common currency enter into a long-term contract, real exchange risk must be allocated in some way. Next, we examine why firms violate the law of one price when selling in the domestic and foreign markets; that is, they "price-to-market." We also explore how firms' prices should respond optimally to fluctuations in real exchange rates. Fluctuations in real exchange rates also make foreign subsidiaries more or less profitable. We explore how to design a compensation system for foreign subsidiaries that rewards good management and not just luck due to favorable movements in real exchange rates. The chapter ends with some general advice for how managers can respond to changes in real exchange rates.

9.1 HOW REAL EXCHANGE RATES AFFECT REAL PROFITABILITY

To understand how changes in the real exchange rate affect a firm's profitability, we consider the **real profitability** of a firm, which is the purchasing power of a firm's nominal profits. It is obtained by dividing the firm's nominal profits by the price level. A firm's shareholders care only about the firm's real profits, not its nominal profits, because ultimately, they care only about how much they can consume—not how much money they have.

The Real Profitability of an Exporting Firm

Consider the real profitability of Apples Galore, a U.S. exporter that sells apples in both the United States and Britain. Suppose that Apples Galore produces apples in the United States and incurs only dollar costs. Let's begin by calculating its nominal profit.

Calculating a Firm's Nominal Profit

Apples Galore's nominal profit is the sum of its domestic sales and foreign sales minus its nominal costs:

$$\text{Nominal profit} = \text{Dollar revenue from U.S. sales} + \text{Dollar revenue from U.K. sales} - \text{Dollar costs}$$

Dollar revenue from its U.S. sales is the dollar price of apples, $P(A, \$)$, multiplied by the quantity of apples the firm sold, $Q(A, \text{U.S.})$:

$$\text{Dollar revenue from U.S. sales} = P(A, \$) \times Q(A, \text{U.S.})$$

Dollar revenue from U.K. sales is the nominal exchange rate ($\$/£$) multiplied by the pound price of apples, $P(A, £)$, multiplied by the quantity of apples sold in the United Kingdom, $Q(A, \text{U.K.})$:

$$\text{Dollar revenue from U.K. sales} = S(\$/£) \times P(A, £) \times Q(A, \text{U.K.})$$

Apples Galore's dollar cost of production is the average dollar cost per apple, $C(A, \$)$, multiplied by the total quantity of apples it sold in both the U.S. and U.K. markets:

$$\text{Dollar cost of production} = C(A, \$) \times [Q(A, \text{U.S.}) + Q(A, \text{U.K.})]$$

Relative Prices and Components of Real Profit

Apples Galore's real profit is its nominal profit divided by the U.S. price level, $P(\$)$. We'll consider U.S. revenue, U.S. costs, and U.K. revenue, in that order. The first term is

$$\text{Real revenue from U.S. sales} = \frac{P(A, \$) \times Q(A, \text{U.S.})}{P(\$)} = \frac{P(A, \$)}{P(\$)} \times Q(A, \text{U.S.})$$

On the right-hand side is the **relative price** of apples in the United States multiplied by the quantity of apples. The relative price affects the **demand curve** for apples and determines, along with other variables like people's income, how many apples will be sold. Think of Apples Galore as setting its relative price to determine how much it will be able to sell. To keep the relative price of apples constant, the firm must ensure that the nominal price of the apples increases at the U.S. rate of inflation.

Next, consider Apples Galore's real costs. Divide dollar costs by the U.S. price level:

$$\text{Real costs} = \frac{C(A, \$)}{P(\$)} \times [Q(A, \text{U.S.}) + Q(A, \text{U.K.})]$$

Total real cost is the average real cost per apple, $[C(A, \$)/P(\$)]$, multiplied by the amount of apples sold in both countries. If its nominal average cost per apple increases at the U.S. rate of inflation, its real average costs are constant.

A Firm's Real Export Revenue

Now, consider Apples Galore's real export revenue. Divide its nominal export revenue by the price level in the United States:

$$\text{Real revenue from U.K. sales} = \frac{S(\$/\pounds) \times P(A,\pounds) \times Q(A, \text{U.K.})}{P(\$)}$$

If we multiply and divide the firm's real export revenue by the U.K. price level, $P(\pounds)$, and rearrange terms, we have

$$\text{Real revenue from U.K. sales} = \frac{S(\$/\pounds) \times P(\pounds)}{P(\$)} \times \frac{P(A,\pounds)}{P(\pounds)} \times Q(A, \text{U.K.})$$

Apples Galore's real export revenue involves three real terms. The first is the real exchange rate, $[S(\$/\pounds) \times P(\pounds)/P(\$)]$; the second is the relative price of apples in the United Kingdom, $[P(A,\pounds)/P(\pounds)]$; and the third is the quantity of apples sold in the United Kingdom, $Q(A, \text{U.K.})$.

When Apples Galore sets its U.K. relative price, the demand curve determines the amount of apples sold. Over time, if the U.K. demand curve does not change, Apples Galore will sell the same amount of apples if it keeps its relative price constant. This requires increasing the pound price of apples by the same percent as the U.K. rate of inflation. In this situation, if the real exchange rate is also constant, Apples Galore gets the same U.S. real revenue. Clearly, a real appreciation of the pound increases real revenue from the United Kingdom and allows the firm to become more competitive there because it can lower its relative price of apples.

How the managers of the firm choose to respond with their relative prices to changes in the real exchange rate is known as **exchange rate pass-through**. We will study more about pricing in the face of real exchange rate changes in Section 9.4. Now, though, let's consider the nature of risk that a firm faces from real exchange rate changes.

9.2 REAL EXCHANGE RISK AT EXPORTERS, IMPORTERS, AND DOMESTIC FIRMS

The phenomenon whereby the profitability of a firm can change because of fluctuations in the real exchange rate is called **real exchange risk** (or **operating exposure** or **economic exposure**). The Apples Galore example focuses on an exporting firm, but firms that sell products domestically and have imported costs also experience real exchange risk. Why is this so?

The value of a firm is represented by the present value of its expected future profitability. If there are changes in exchange rates that affect a firm's cash flows, either through changes in the demand for its products or through changes in the costs of its inputs, the firm faces a real exchange risk. Before we examine discounted profitability, let's examine how changes in real exchange rates cause changes in a firm's profitability.

In general, a real depreciation of the domestic currency hurts importing firms and helps exporting firms. A firm can even have an exposure to real exchange rates without having direct exposure to foreign currency cash flows because, for example, a real appreciation of the domestic currency hurts domestic import–competing firms who must then compete against less expensive imports. Because many firms have important imported parts and materials, real exchange rate changes can also affect the cost structure of a firm. Exactly how a firm is affected depends on the firm's type of business—that is, it depends on whether it is a net exporter, a net importer, or an import competitor. It also depends on the firm's competitive situation, by which we mean the degree of monopoly power that the firm commands for its products.

The Real Exchange Rate Risk of a Net Exporter

Suppose an exporting firm faces a nominal depreciation of the foreign currency. If the firm does nothing, the depreciation of the foreign currency lowers the nominal value of export revenue. The firm can avoid this decrease in profitability by increasing the foreign currency price of its product, but its ability to do so will be limited by the firm's competitive situation. Because the foreign demand for the firm's product depends on the product's relative price in the foreign country, we know that the firm will sell less of its product if it raises the price in the foreign country by more than the foreign rate of inflation. However, if the magnitude of the depreciation of the foreign currency *just equals* foreign inflation minus domestic inflation [that is, if relative purchasing power parity (PPP) holds], then increasing the nominal foreign price of the product in the foreign market by the same amount as at the foreign rate of inflation will cause the domestic currency value of the firm's foreign revenue to increase at the domestic rate of inflation. Thus, the firm's real revenue from exporting would not be affected.

Example 9.1 A Greek Cell Phone Exporter

Olympia Communication Exporters (OCE) manufactures cellular phones in Greece and sells them in the United States. This year, OCE priced its phone at $79.00 and sold 2,000,000 phones at an average exchange rate of $1.25/€. Hence, OCE's euro revenue this year is

$$\frac{\$79.00}{\text{phone}} \times (2{,}000{,}000 \text{ phones}) \times \frac{1}{\$1.25/\text{€}} = \text{€}126{,}400{,}000$$

Economists are forecasting 5.5% inflation for the United States and 1% inflation for Europe. They also expect the dollar to weaken to

$$\frac{\$1.3057}{\text{€}} = \frac{\$1.25}{\text{€}} \times \frac{1.055}{1.01}$$

and this change just offsets the inflation differential and leaves the real exchange rate unchanged. If the U.S. demand curve is constant, what dollar price should OCE charge if it wants to earn the same real revenue and sell the same quantity of phones in the United States?

The answer is that the price of a phone should increase by 5.5%, to

$$(\$83.35/\text{phone}) = (\$79.00/\text{phone}) \times (1.055)$$

in which case, the nominal revenue will increase to

$$\frac{\$83.35}{\text{phone}} \times 2{,}000{,}000 \text{ phones} \times \frac{1}{\$1.3057/\text{€}} = \text{€}127{,}670{,}981$$

Notice that €127,670,981 is 1% higher than €126,400,000. An increase of 1% in nominal revenue is required to keep the firm's real revenue constant.

A Competitive Dilemma

Any increase in the exchange rate above $1.3057/€, the value that kept the real exchange rate constant in Example 9.1, creates a dilemma for Olympia Communication Exporters. If the firm does not increase the price of its phone above $83.35, the euro value of the company's revenue will decrease. However, if the company increases the price of its phone above the U.S. rate of inflation, the firm will sell fewer phones. Either way, though, a real appreciation of the euro hurts OCE's real profitability.

The choice that OCE should make in terms of raising its U.S. relative price depends on its competitive situation. We know that OCE will be less profitable after a real depreciation of the dollar, but we don't know by how much. A major factor determining the firm's response is the elasticity of its demand curve. **Elasticity** measures the percentage change in the quantity of the product demanded when the percentage relative price of the product changes. The more *inelastic* a product's demand curve, the less the quantity sold falls when its price rises. In contrast, the more *elastic* a product's demand curve, the more the quantity sold falls when the product's price rises. In other words, the more elastic the demand curve, the more likely it is that consumers will switch products or not buy the product at all when the relative price increases. In addition, the more competitive the market is for a product, the more elastic is the product's demand curve.

Because cellular phones are manufactured by many different companies around the world and because consumers are quite price sensitive, the market is quite competitive. Hence, it is unlikely that OCE would have much market power to raise its relative price without suffering a large fall in its sales. Thus, it is likely that OCE would not increase its price very much above what is warranted by U.S. inflation. However, if the OCE phone has some unique features that make the demand for its phone more inelastic (that is, less responsive to price changes), the company will not lose as much profitability because it can pass through more of the change in the exchange rate to the product's price.

The Real Exchange Risk of a Net Importer

The next example demonstrates how the real profits of a **net importer**—that is, a firm with more imported inputs than exports—are affected by a change in the real exchange rate.

Has Real Appreciation Hurt Chinese Exporters?

The November 6, 2010, U.S. edition of *The Economist* carried an article entitled "Nominally Cheap or Really Dear? The Yuan–Dollar Exchange Rate." The article noted that U.S. officials complain about an undervalued yuan that gives Chinese exporters a competitive advantage. In comparing changes in costs across countries, however, *The Economist* argued that it is not the change in the nominal exchange rate that is important but, instead, the change in the real exchange rate. Furthermore, the article noted that measuring real appreciation of the yuan versus the dollar using relative nominal unit labor costs, defined as "the price of labour per widget," makes good sense. Between 2005 and 2010, the nominal yuan appreciated by 24% versus the dollar, whereas Chinese unit labor costs increased by 21% relative to U.S. unit labor costs. The combination of the nominal appreciation and the relative increase in unit labor costs implies a 50% real appreciation of the yuan. The profitability of Chinese exporters has surely been squeezed during this 5-year period.

The debate about the undervalued yuan continued in early 2011 during a state visit to the United States by Chinese President Hu Jintao. U.S. Treasury Secretary Timothy Geithner continued to argue for faster nominal appreciation of the yuan, while in Geneva, Heiner Flassbeck, Director of the United Nations Conference on Trade and Development's Division on Globalization and Development Strategies, held a press conference on January 19, 2011, stating that according to his calculations based on unit labor costs, the Chinese currency "is not undervalued" because it has appreciated in real terms by 100% since 1995. U.S. politicians remain unconvinced.

Example 9.2 A Malaysian Airline Company

Trans-Malaysian Airlines (TMA) flies mostly domestic routes within Malaysia. Its imported fuel costs $3.50/gallon. Last year, TMA imported 250,000,000 gallons of fuel, and the Malaysian ringgit–U.S. dollar exchange rate was MYR4/USD. Thus, TMA's nominal fuel costs were

$$\frac{\$3.50}{gallon} \times 250{,}000{,}000 \text{ gallons} \times \frac{MYR4}{USD} = MYR3.5 \text{ billion}$$

Last year, TMA's nominal revenues minus its other ringgit costs were MYR4.0 billion, and its profit was

$$MYR4.0 \text{ billion} - MYR3.5 \text{ billion} = MYR0.5 \text{ billion}$$

Suppose TMA is regulated and cannot increase its MYR ticket price by more than the Malaysian rate of inflation, which is 15% this year. If holding the relative price constant results in the same demand for its flights, then TMA will have the same number of passengers this year, it will need the same amount of fuel, and its revenue will increase by 15%. Suppose that its other ringgit costs also increase by 15%. However, suppose the dollar price of fuel increases by the U.S. rate of inflation, which is 4%. By how much will real profits fall if there is a 10% real appreciation of the dollar relative to the ringgit?

Let's first calculate the new nominal MYR/USD exchange rate implied by the 10% real appreciation of the dollar. Because Malaysian inflation (15%) is higher than U.S. inflation (4%), the dollar should appreciate in nominal terms even if there is no real dollar appreciation. One plus the warranted rate of nominal dollar appreciation due strictly to the inflation differential is (1.15/1.04). The new nominal exchange rate must be 10% higher than this to induce a 10% real appreciation of the USD, so the new nominal exchange rate will be

$$\frac{MYR4}{USD} \times \frac{1.15}{1.04} \times 1.10 = \frac{MYR4.8654}{USD}$$

The new price of fuel is $3.50/gallon $\times$ 1.04 = $3.64/gallon. Because the same number of gallons will be required, new fuel costs will be

$$\frac{\$3.64}{gallon} \times 250{,}000{,}000 \text{ gallons} \times \frac{MYR4.8654}{USD} = MYR4.428 \text{ billion}$$

TMA's ringgit revenues and its other costs are now 15% higher, due to inflation in Malaysia. Because revenues net of other costs were MYR4.0 billion last year, this year, they will be MYR4.0 billion $\times$ 1.15 = MYR4.6 billion. Hence, nominal profits will be

$$MYR4.6 \text{ billion} - MYR4.428 \text{ billion} = MYR0.172 \text{ billion}$$

Recall that TMA's nominal revenues last year were MYR0.5 billion. As you can see, instead of nominal profits increasing by 15% as they would have without the real depreciation of the ringgit, nominal profits have actually fallen by 65.6% because $-0.656 = [(0.172 - 0.5)/0.5]$. Notice also that real profits have fallen by 70.1% because $-0.701 = [((0.172/1.15) - 0.5)/0.5]$.

A real appreciation of the dollar clearly has a severe effect on the real profitability of TMA because it increases TMA's costs, and the regulation prevents the company from passing any of its increased costs due to a change in the exchange rate on to its customers in the form of higher prices.

Of course, an increase in the relative price of tickets decreases the demand for air travel. If TMA could increase its relative price, it would have to decide how much of the real appreciation of the dollar it could pass through to its customers in the form of higher ringgit prices. The answer depends on the elasticity of TMA's demand curve. The less competitive the market, the less responsive consumers are to increased fares, and the more TMA's increased costs could be passed on to customers in the form of higher ticket prices.

The Real Exchange Risk of an Import Competitor

The firms we have described so far all engage in operational transactions that require the exchange of foreign currency. Therefore, each firm directly experiences a change in profitability with a change in the real exchange rate. It may seem surprising to you, however, that a firm can have an exposure to real exchange risk even though the company has no explicit cash flows denominated in foreign currency. Consider the following example of an **import competitor**.

Example 9.3   Miami Beach Restaurants

Restaurants in Miami Beach, Florida, accept only dollars from their customers. They buy all their food from suppliers who accept only dollars, and they pay their employees in dollars. Consequently, the restaurants have no explicit foreign currency cash flows and no foreign currency–denominated assets and liabilities. Nevertheless, the Miami Beach restaurants experience fluctuations in their profitability because the demand from their patrons depends on the value of the dollar on the foreign exchange markets.

For example, when the dollar is weak and European currencies are strong, more European tourists enjoy vacations in Miami Beach because U.S. vacations are relatively inexpensive from the European perspective. Likewise, when the dollar is weak on foreign currency markets, more U.S. residents vacation in Miami Beach because European trips are relatively more expensive. Hence, demand for the restaurants' services is high when the dollar is weak. In contrast, when the dollar is strong, Americans view European vacations as relative bargains, and Europeans view trips to the United States as relatively expensive. As a result, relatively fewer American and European tourists travel to Miami, and restaurant profitability falls when the dollar is strong. As you can see, changes in the real exchange rate can alter the demand for products that are neither exported nor imported, such as restaurant meals.

Measuring Real Exchange Risk Exposure

Most nominal exchange rate changes are large relative to the associated changes in the price levels of countries. Hence, most changes in the nominal exchange rate are highly correlated with changes in the real exchange rate, especially in the short run. Most large changes in the nominal exchange rate are therefore associated with changes in relative prices, and most nominal exchange rate changes generate a fair amount of real operating exposure. Real exchange rates affect a firm's operating cash and its current profitability, but they also affect its future profitability. Thus, real exchange rate exposure must include future periods as well as the current period.

The Present Value of a Firm's Profits

Let $CF(j)$ represent the expected value of a firm's after-tax profits for j periods in the future, and let r represent the appropriate discount rate. Then, the present value of the firm's future after-tax profits is

$$V = \sum_{j=1}^{\infty} \frac{CF(j)}{(1 + r)^j}$$

Real exchange risk measures the change in V in response to an unexpected change in the real exchange rate.

We focus on the unanticipated change in the real exchange rate because the effects of any anticipated change would already be incorporated into the market value of the firm. By considering the present value of the firm's profits, we recognize that changes in the exchange rate are persistent and thus have effects on future profitability. A real strengthening of the domestic currency is bad for a net exporter in the current period. Moreover, because changes are so persistent, next period's profits are also likely to be low because the domestic currency is expected to continue to be strong. The next example works through a case in which the change in the real exchange rate is expected to persist indefinitely.

Example 9.4 A French Cheese Exporter

Fromagerie du Provence exports sheep's milk cheese to the United States. Last year, Fromagerie du Provence sold 1.5 million kilos of cheese at $10 per kilo, for total revenue of $15 million. The company had dollar costs of $1 million associated with its U.S. distribution network, which left it with $14 million in net revenue earned from its U.S. exports. Because the average exchange rate was $1.40/€, Fromagerie du Provence's net export revenue in euros was equal to

$$\$14{,}000{,}000/(\$1.40/€) = €10{,}000{,}000$$

The company's euro-denominated costs were €8 million, and it has no sales outside the United States. Hence, its euro-denominated profits were €2 million = €10 million − €8 million.

Suppose financial analysts forecast a constant real exchange rate and recognize that if the company maintains a constant relative price in the United States, it will sell the same amount of cheese every year. Suppose nominal costs in the United States and France are also expected to rise at the respective rates of inflation, in which case real costs are constant.

In this situation, the purchasing power of real net revenue in today's dollars will be $14 million every year in the future. With a constant real exchange rate, the real euro profits will be €2 million. If the real discount rate is 8%, the real value of the firm in terms of its discounted future profits will be the following infinite sum:[1]

$$\frac{€2{,}000{,}000}{1.08} + \frac{€2{,}000{,}000}{1.08^2} + \cdots = \frac{€2{,}000{,}000}{0.08} = €25{,}000{,}000$$

---

[1]This particular infinite sum is a perpetuity, which is straightforward to evaluate. The appendix to Chapter 15 describes how the perpetuity formula is derived.

Suppose analysts also think that if the real dollar–euro exchange rate changes, the change will be permanent. In this situation, we can consider how a 1% appreciation of the euro would affect the value of the firm. First, let the new nominal exchange rate be $(\$1.40/€) \times 1.01 = \$1.414/€$, which we can consider to be a real appreciation of the euro as well because prices are being held constant as the company does not respond to real appreciations. If Fromagerie du Provence does not adjust its cheese price, the appreciation of the euro would lower the company's net revenue by 1%, to

$$\$14,000,000/(\$1.414/€) = €9,900,990$$

and its euro profits would fall to

$$€9,900,990 - €8,000,000 = €1,900,990$$

which is a decrease of 5%.

An unanticipated 1% real appreciation of the euro that was expected to be permanent would therefore lower all future net revenues to €1,900,990. Thus, the value of the firm would decrease to $(€1,900,990/0.08) = €23,762,375$, or by 5%.

Notice that the real exposure of Fromagerie du Provence arises from its large net dollar revenues and the assumed permanence of the exchange rate change. Extrapolating from our 1% change, we see that a 10% real depreciation of the dollar, which is not an extreme event, would cause the value of the firm to decrease by 50%. Of course, this example treats the change in the real exchange rate as permanent. This assumption conflicts with the empirical evidence presented in Chapter 8, which shows that although changes in real exchange rates are highly persistent, they appear to reverse themselves slowly over time. Thus, the actual exposure would be less than what is calculated here.

POINT–COUNTERPOINT

On Producing BMWs in the United States

It is December, and Ante, Freedy, and Suttle are driving through South Carolina on their way to Florida for a quick vacation when Ante spots the BMW plant in Spartanburg. Ante blurts out, "Why on earth would a high-quality German company like BMW want to sully their reputation by producing cars in South Carolina? They must have gotten enormous tax breaks to induce them to locate there."

Freedy steadies the steering wheel and replies, "What do you mean? American workers are every bit as good as German workers. They're cheaper, too, at current exchange rates. From the German perspective, German workers cost over €30 per hour, while Americans work for €24.50. Obviously, BMW saw a cost advantage. BMW is also very zealous about its quality. It wouldn't build a facility if it wasn't sure that it could produce high-quality cars."

Ante can hardly control himself as he shouts, "That cost advantage will quickly evaporate if the dollar strengthens versus the euro."

Suttle, who had been sleeping in the backseat, says, "Guys, there are elements of truth in what both of you are saying. It is true that BMW looks at the costs of workers when making a plant location decision. It also tries to get as many tax breaks from the local authorities as possible. After all, it has invested over $1.7 billion in the South Carolina plant during the past 10 years and is providing thousands of jobs directly, not to mention the jobs of parts suppliers. But Ante is certainly right that an appreciation of the dollar versus the euro would raise the perceived euro-denominated cost to BMW of producing products in the United States because the workers there are unlikely to take a pay cut just because the dollar strengthens. Nevertheless, you're both missing a major point."

Suttle continues, "One of the main reasons BMW built the Spartanburg plant is foreign exchange risk. If BMW builds a car in Germany and exports it to the United States, BMW has euro costs and dollar revenues. BMW loses a lot of profit when the dollar weakens because BMW cannot increase the dollar price of the car to offset the depreciation of the dollar. The potential loss is huge because the entire dollar revenue of the car is exposed to the exchange rate. On the other hand, if BMW builds a car in the United States and sells it there, BMW incurs dollar costs and dollar revenues. A depreciation of the dollar still creates a loss of value when the profits are converted into euros, and there is still pressure to increase the dollar price of the car to offset dollar depreciation, but the real exchange rate exposure is only on BMW's profit, its dollar revenues minus its dollar costs."

Suttle finishes by saying, "Ante, you're also right that BMW took a big risk that the quality of the cars would be up to the standards of the cars produced in Germany. But that was a risk worth taking because of the enormity of the foreign exchange risk."

9.3 SHARING THE REAL EXCHANGE RISK: AN EXAMPLE

This section examines an extended case that is designed to help you understand how real exchange risk can be shared between firms that do not share a common currency.

Safe Air Evaluates an International Supply Contract

John Cromwell is the 54-year-old CEO of Safe Air, Inc., a U.S. corporation that sells compressed air tanks with face masks to U.S. fire departments. Safe Air's masks are the best available, and Cromwell has often stated that Safe Air has no expertise in manufacturing air tanks. It consequently has always purchased tanks from an external supplier.

Safe Air's board of directors has begun to question Cromwell's leadership because earnings have been declining. Cromwell thinks he is too young to retire and being forced out by the board would be humiliating. In order to cut costs, he solicited bids from potential suppliers of tanks. In particular, Metallwerke, A.G., a German firm that manufactures air tanks, submitted an attractive contract that offered dollar pricing. Cromwell is intrigued by the possibility of locking in long-term dollar prices from a low-cost foreign supplier. He has evaluated the quality of Metallwerke's tanks and thinks they are as good as, if not superior to, that of Safe Air's current U.S. supplier. If the Metallwerke air tank works better than his current tank, he knows that fire departments will probably pay more for the improved performance.

The Indexing Formula

Although Metallwerke quoted a dollar price, Gerhard Spiegel, the CEO of Metallwerke, wants to sign a 10-year contract that sets a base dollar price for the tank and provides an **indexing formula** that allows for annual changes in the base dollar price under certain contingencies: (1) The base dollar price will be increased at the annual rate of inflation, as indicated by the U.S. producer price index; and (2) if the euro appreciates relative to the dollar, the percentage change in the base dollar price will equal the U.S. rate of inflation plus an additional percentage equal to one-half the rate of appreciation of the euro versus the dollar.

In the past, Safe Air's cost of the basic air tank has mostly increased with the U.S. rate of inflation, and Safe Air has typically been able to pass this increased cost along to its fire department customers by increasing its retail price at the rate of inflation. But occasionally, Safe Air's cost increases from its suppliers have exceeded the U.S. rate of inflation, resulting in several unprofitable periods. Cromwell knows that fire departments are quite sensitive to price, which limits his ability to pass along cost increases. He also does not think that the board of directors at Safe Air will tolerate another unprofitable period without a change in senior management.

The Consultant's Task

You are a consultant, trying to help Cromwell decide what to do. As he talked to you on the telephone yesterday about Metallwerke's offer, you could sense his concerns. While Spiegel's initial base price is quite attractive, Cromwell wonders if there is a way to redesign the contract to be more favorable to Safe Air, and he wants you to find it. You know that the profitability of both firms must be considered in any long-term contract. You also know that somebody must bear the risk that the euro will strengthen relative to the dollar. But something about the current contract seems fishy. If a strong euro is so bad for Metallwerke, shouldn't a weak euro be good? Why isn't this mentioned in any way?

As a consultant to Safe Air, your task is to evaluate the desirability of this contract, to redesign it to be more favorable to Safe Air, and to figure out some way of explaining the issues to Cromwell and possibly to the company's board of directors.

Basic Data and Analysis

Based on data from Cromwell, you have set out some basic prices and notations (the zeros indicate current-period values) related to the Metallwerke proposal:

Safe Air's contractual base purchase price $= B(0, \$) = \$400$ per tank
Safe Air's other variable production costs $= C(0, \$) = \$313$ per tank
Safe Air's retail sales price $= T(0, \$) = \$856$ per tank
Safe Air's profit margin $= M(0, \$) = 20\%$
U.S. price level $= P(0, \$) = \$140$ per U.S. general good
Exchange rate $= S(0, \$/€) = \$1.40/€$
German price level $= P(0, €) = €100$ per German general good
Metallwerke's profit margin $= M(0, €) = 20\%$
Metallwerke's production cost $= C(0, €) = €238$ per tank

Profitability Under a Simple Contract with Constant Prices

Let's first look at the profitability of the firms if they were to sign a long-term contract that simply fixes the dollar price of the tank at $400, no matter what the exchange rate. This is a contract that Cromwell would like because he wants to lock in a dollar price. Assuming that the sales price of the tank is kept constant at $400, Exhibit 9.1 shows the risks the two companies face under three alternative scenarios corresponding to three exchange rates: $1.40/€, $1.54/€ (which represents a 10% appreciation of the euro), and $1.26/€ (which represents a 10% depreciation of the euro).

Because Exhibit 9.1 assumes that the nominal exchange rate is changing with nominal prices fixed, the real exchange rate is also changing by 10%. Exhibit 9.1 indicates that each firm earns a 20% profit margin at $1.40/€. The ratio of Safe Air's retail sales price to its production costs is

$$\frac{\$856}{(\$400 + \$313)} = 1.20$$

Exhibit 9.1 Profitability When the Price per Tank Is Contractually Fixed

	Safe Air (dollars)			Metallwerke (euros)		
	$1.26/€	$1.40/€	$1.54/€	$1.26/€	$1.40/€	$1.54/€
Sales						
Exported				317	286	260
Local	856	856	856			
Costs of Goods Sold						
Imported	(400)	(400)	(400)			
Local	(313)	(313)	(313)	(238)	(238)	(238)
Operating Profit	143	143	143	79	48	22
Profit Margin	20%	20%	20%	33.2%	20%	9.2%

The ratio of Metallwerke's euro sales price to its production costs is

$$\frac{\$400/(\$1.40/€)}{€238} = 1.20$$

We know that the profit margin of each firm will be constant if their sales prices increase at the same rates as their costs of production. But because the $400 Metallwerke charges Safe Air doesn't change with the exchange rate in Exhibit 9.1, Metallwerke's profit margin falls to 9.2% when the euro strengthens by 10%. On the other hand, Metallwerke's profit margin rises 33.2% when the euro weakens by 10%. In other words, with a constant dollar price, if the euro strengthens, Safe Air won't suffer, but Metallwerke will see its profits decline drastically. By contrast, if the euro weakens, Safe Air won't be any more profitable, but Metallwerke will be very profitable. What should the two companies agree to do?

Exhibit 9.2 provides an analysis of the profitability of the two firms under Metallwerke's proposed contract. As in Exhibit 9.1, exchange rates can change, but nominal prices other than the tank price are held constant.

Now, Safe Air pays 5% more, or $420 total, when the euro strengthens by 10%. This causes Safe Air's profit margin to fall to 16.8%, but it causes Metallwerke's profit margin to rise to 14.7% (from 9.2% in Exhibit 9.1). Notice, though, that the increased profitability of Metallwerke when the euro weakens is not shared with Safe Air.

Sharing the Exchange Rate Risk with Constant Prices

Let's examine a contract that shares the foreign exchange risk. Exhibit 9.3 demonstrates what happens if the firms share the exchange rate risk equally. As before, if the euro strengthens, the base price of the tank increases by one-half the percentage rate of the euro appreciation. If the euro depreciates, though, the base price of the tank decreases by one-half the percentage rate of euro depreciation.

Exhibit 9.2 Profitability Under Metallwerke's Proposed Contract

	Safe Air (dollars)			Metallwerke (euros)		
	$1.26/€	$1.40/€	$1.54/€	$1.26/€	$1.40/€	$1.54/€
Sales						
Exported				317	286	273
Local	856	856	856			
Costs of Goods Sold						
Imported	(400)	(400)	(420)			
Local	(313)	(313)	(313)	(238)	(238)	(238)
Operating Profit	143	143	123	79	48	35
Profit Margin	20%	20%	16.8%	33.2%	20%	14.7%

Exhibit 9.3 Profitability Under a Contract That Shares Real Exchange Risk

	Safe Air (dollars)			Metallwerke (euros)		
	$1.26/€	**$1.40/€**	**$1.54/€**	**$1.26/€**	**$1.40/€**	**$1.54/€**
Sales						
Exported				302	286	273
Local	856	856	856			
Costs of Goods Sold						
Imported	(380)	(400)	(420)			
Local	(313)	(313)	(313)	(238)	(238)	(238)
Operating Profit	163	143	123	63.6	48	35
Profit Margin	23.5%	20%	16.8%	26.7%	20%	14.7%

In this case, the price Safe Air pays per tank when the euro weakens by 10% is $380, and Safe Air's profit margin increases to 23.5%. Metallwerke still has increased its profitability, but only to a margin of 26.7%.

Analyzing Contracts When Inflation and Real Exchange Rates Are Changing

Exhibits 9.1 through 9.3 hold the prices of labor and the retail price of the tank constant. In such a situation, the change in the nominal exchange rate *is* a change in the real exchange rate. When other prices are moving, however, it is important to distinguish contractually between movements in nominal and real exchange rates. It will turn out that if the base price increases at the U.S. rate of inflation, only movements in the real exchange rate are a source of risk. The key thing to remember is that as long as a nominal variable like the retail price of the tank or the cost of production changes at the rate of inflation, real values are constant.

In the situation in the case, it is reasonable to assume that Safe Air will only be able to raise its retail price by the U.S. rate of inflation. It is also reasonable to assume that their other costs will be increasing at the U.S. rate of inflation. Similarly, Metallwerke's costs are likely to increase at the German rate of inflation, but its euro revenue will be affected both by the change in the dollar price of the tank and by the rate of change of the dollar–euro exchange rate. Thus, we only need to focus on what happens to the base price of the tank.

In doing the analysis, it will be useful to have some notation for the percentage rates of change of several key variables. The percentage rate of change of any variable Z from period 0 to period 1 is $\%Z = [Z(1) - Z(0)]/Z(0)$. Let's define the following variables:

Rate of change of the contractual base dollar price $= \%B(\$)$
U.S. rate of inflation $= \pi(\$) = \%P(\$)$
German rate of inflation $= \pi(€) = \%P(€)$
Rate of change of the dollar–euro exchange rate $= \%S(\$/€)$

We place an R before a real variable.

Safe Air's Real Cost per Tank

In period 1, the base dollar price per tank that Safe Air pays will increase by $\%B(\$)$, and the U.S. price level will increase by $\pi(\$)$ because of inflation. Hence, the period 1 real imported cost for Safe Air will be

$$RB(1, \$) = \frac{B(1, \$)}{P(1, \$)} = \frac{B(0, \$) \times (1 + \%B(\$))}{P(0, \$) \times (1 + \pi(\$))} = RB(0, \$) \times \frac{(1 + \%B(\$))}{(1 + \pi(\$))}$$

Increases in the base price that are larger (smaller) than the U.S. rate of inflation increase (decrease) real imported part costs.

Metallwerke's Real Revenue per Tank

The real revenue per tank for Metallwerke is the dollar price per tank the company charges Safe Air, divided by the $\$/€$ exchange rate, and divided by the German price level. In period 1, Metallwerke's new real revenue will be

$$
\begin{aligned}
RR(1, €) &= \frac{B(1, \$)/S(1, \$/€)}{P(1, €)} \\
&= \frac{B(0, \$) \times (1 + \%B(\$))/[S(0, \$/€) \times (1 + \%S(\$/€))]}{P(0, €) \times (1 + \pi(€))} \\
&= RR(0, €) \times \frac{(1 + \%B(\$))}{(1 + \pi(€)) \times (1 + \%S(\$/€))}
\end{aligned}
$$

Only if the percentage change in the base price satisfies

$$
(1 + \%B(\$)) = (1 + \pi(€)) \times (1 + \%S(\$/€))
$$

will Metallwerke's real revenue be constant. Notice that this analysis indicates that Metallwerke would like to increase the base price of the tank to offset both the German rate of inflation and any appreciation of the euro relative to the dollar. But this is not how the proposed contract is written.

Designing a Contract That Shares the Real Exchange Risk

It is possible to share real exchange risk almost equally between two parties. Recall that the percentage change in the real exchange rate is

$$
(1 + \%RS(\$/€)) = \frac{(1 + \%S(\$/€)) \times (1 + \pi(€))}{(1 + \pi(\$))}
$$

Here $\%RS$ represents the real rate of appreciation (if positive) or depreciation (if negative) of the euro relative to the dollar. Then, one way to share the risk is to let the base dollar price of the product increase one for one with the U.S. rate of inflation and make an additional adjustment to the base price for changes in the real exchange rate. Equal sharing of the risk would make the base price higher by one-half of any real appreciation of the euro relative to the dollar, but would make the base price lower by one-half of any real depreciation of the euro relative to the dollar:

$$
(1 + \%B(\$)) = (1 + \pi(\$)) \times (1 + (\%RS(\$/€)/2))
$$

Now, Safe Air's real cost is

$$
RB(1, \$) = RB(0, \$) \times \frac{(1 + \%B(\$))}{(1 + \pi(\$))} = RB(0, \$) \times (1 + (\%RS(\$/€)/2))
$$

It is constant if the real exchange rate is constant, $\%RS(\$/€) = 0$. It increases by one-half of any real appreciation if the euro strengthens relative to the dollar, when $\%RS(\$/€) > 0$, but it decreases by one-half of any real depreciation if the euro weakens relative to the dollar, when $\%RS(\$/€) < 0$.

Now, consider Metallwerke's real revenue under the revised contract. We know that

$$
RR(1, €) = RR(0, €) \times \frac{(1 + \%B(\$))}{(1 + \%S(\$/€)) \times (1 + \pi(€))}
$$

which we can rewrite substituting the new terms of the contract as

$$RR(1, €) = RR(0, €) \times \frac{(1 + \pi(\$)) \times [1 + \%RS(\$/€)/2]}{(1 + \%S(\$/€)) \times (1 + \pi(€))}$$

Because $(1 + \%RS(\$/€)) = (1 + \%S(\$/€)) \times (1 + \pi(€))/(1 + \pi(\$))$, we have

$$RR(1, €) = RR(0, €) \times \frac{(1 + \%RS(\$/€)/2)}{(1 + \%RS(\$/€))} \approx RR(0, €) \times (1 - \%RS(\$/€)/2)$$

The approximation works well for small percentage changes.[2] Consequently, Metallwerke's real revenue goes up by one-half of any real depreciation of the euro when $\%RS < 0$, and it goes down by one-half of any real appreciation of the euro when $\%RS > 0$.

Understanding the Contract

The reason that the redesigned contract shares the real exchange risk is that if the euro appreciates relative to the dollar by more than is warranted by the differential rates of inflation, Metallwerke's real revenue falls. The redesigned contract forces the nominal base price to increase in this situation, which causes Safe Air to bear part of the loss. But if the euro weakens relative to the dollar by more than the inflation differential, Metallwerke's real revenue rises. The redesigned contract makes Metallwerke share this gain with Safe Air by lowering the rate at which the dollar base price is increasing.

Would the Redesigned Contract Be Adopted?

Whether the redesigned contract would actually be adopted by the firms as a way of sharing real exchange risk depends on several factors. For example, real exchange rate changes may be correlated with other production costs for the two firms. Suppose that Safe Air's workers demand higher wages when the dollar is weak because their purchasing power decreases. Safe Air would face additional cost pressure when the euro is strong and would not like to see the price of the tank increased very much. This might lead both firms to use a number less than one-half in the formula. Alternatively, it is possible that Safe Air has foreign competitors in the United States who price more aggressively when the dollar is strong and who fade away when the dollar is weak. In this case, Safe Air might like the risk-sharing coefficient to be larger than one-half.

Relative Bargaining Strength

The last issue that determines how the contract will be written is the relative bargaining strength of the two firms. As the contract was initially written, Metallwerke received all the benefit of a strong dollar, and when the dollar was weak, Safe Air still had to share part of the cost. This may be the best that Cromwell can do, given his precarious position with the board of directors. If Spiegel knows that his initial base price is attractive, he may be able to force Cromwell to accept a current benefit in exchange for possible problems in the future. In contrast, if Metallwerke really needs Safe Air's business, Spiegel might be more willing to accept a fixed-price contract and bear the risk while hoping that the dollar will strengthen.

---

[2]Note that $\dfrac{(1 + \%RS(\$/€)/2)}{(1 + \%RS(\$/€))} = 1 - \dfrac{\%RS(\$/€)/2}{(1 + \%RS(\$/€))}$. Hence, for small percentage changes, the denominator on the right-hand side is close to 1.

Another aspect of managing real exchange risk is the phenomenon of **pricing-to-market**, which simply means that producers charge different prices (measured in the same currency) for the same good in different countries. Examples of pricing-to-market abound. Apple's iPads and iPhones are often cheaper in the United States than in other countries. However, comparisons are complicated by the fact that the United States allows Apple to sell iPhones only through certain telecom service providers, AT&T and Verizon, who in turn subsidize the cost of the phone while locking the consumer into a 2-year service contract. Other countries, such as Hong Kong and Singapore, require the factory to unlock the phone so that the consumer may use it with any telecom service provider.

The Economist on July 14, 2001, noted that handbags manufactured by the French luxury goods producer Louis Vuitton cost 40% more in Japan than in Europe at that time. Enterprising Hong Kong merchants tried to arbitrage this differential by sending employees to purchase handbags in Europe for resale in Japan, much to the chagrin of the French handbag maker. The problem in Europe was how to tell an arbitrageur from a legitimate tourist. Do you draw the line at the purchase of five bags or 10?

In both examples, the producers sell a unique product in high demand. The goal of this section is to understand why producers in markets that are less than fully competitive price to market. We do this by examining how a monopolist responds to fluctuations in real exchange rates.[3]

Pricing-to-Market by a Monopolist

A Monopolistic Exporter

Consider the problem of a domestic **monopolist**, a sole producer who sells a non-storable good to both the domestic market and the foreign market. The monopolist faces a different demand curve in each market, and as the price of the product increases in each market, the monopolist will sell fewer units there. We can think of the monopolist as choosing the domestic and foreign prices of the goods it will supply to each market and letting the quantities it sells in each market be determined by the respective demand curves, or alternatively, we can think of the monopolist as choosing the quantities to supply to each market with the demand curves then determining the prices.

Example 9.5   A Monopolist Seller in Two Markets

Demand Curves

Suppose a monopolist faces the same linear demand curve in the domestic and foreign markets. The domestic demand curve is

$$Q = 1,000 - P$$

where Q is the quantity sold in the domestic market, and P is the domestic relative price. At a price of zero, the monopolist could sell 1,000 units. As the monopolist

---

[3]The issues in this section are explored more formally in Marston (1990), which provides a static, one-period profit maximization, and in Kasa (1992), which provides a dynamic formulation of the problem.

increases the price, the number of units sold decreases until none are sold at a price of 1,000. The demand curve in the foreign market is similarly

$$Q^* = 1,000 - P^*$$

where Q^* represents the quantity sold in the foreign market at the foreign relative price of P^*.

Domestic and Foreign Revenues

From the domestic demand curve, we find that $P = 1,000 - Q$, and revenue from domestic sales is

$$P \times Q = (1,000 \times Q) - Q^2$$

From our earlier analysis, we know that when the monopolist sells output in the foreign market, the domestic real value of revenue from foreign sales is the real exchange rate, RS, multiplied by the foreign relative price, multiplied by foreign sales. By substituting $P^* = 1,000 - Q^*$, we find

$$RS \times P^* \times Q^* = (RS \times 1,000 \times Q^*) - RS \times Q^{*2}$$

Cost of Production

Suppose that the **marginal cost** of production is constant, and let this per-unit cost of production be 500. Then the total cost of production is the per-unit cost multiplied by the total quantity produced for sale in each of the two markets:

$$500 \times (Q + Q^*)$$

Profit-Maximizing Quantities

A profit-maximizing monopolist produces an amount of a good such that the **marginal revenue** earned from each market is equal to the common marginal cost.[4] The marginal revenue from domestic sales is $1,000 - 2Q$, and the marginal revenue from the foreign market is $RS \times 1,000 - RS \times 2Q^*$. Thus, the monopolist should sell a quantity in the domestic market that satisfies

$$1,000 - 2Q = 500$$

or, by solving for Q, we find

$$Q = (1,000 - 500)/2 = 250$$

The optimal quantity in the foreign market satisfies

$$RS \times 1,000 - RS \times 2Q^* = 500$$

or, once again solving for Q^*, we find

$$Q^* = [1,000 - (500/RS)]/2$$

The Equilibrium with RS = 1

Suppose that the real exchange rate is initially equal to 1. In this case, the monopolist should sell 250 in each market by charging the relative price of 750 in each country. The total real profit would be

$$(750 \times 250) + (750 \times 250) - [500 \times (250 + 250)] = 125,000$$

---

[4]Marginal revenue is the derivative of total revenue with respect to the quantity sold.

Exhibit 9.4 summarizes this equilibrium in the domestic and foreign markets.

Exhibit 9.4 A Monopolistic Exporter

The Equilibrium with a Real Appreciation

Now, suppose there is a 20% real appreciation of the foreign currency such that the new real exchange rate is 1.2. The real appreciation benefits the exporting monopolist because total real revenue in the foreign country is now

$$1.2 \times (1,000 - Q^*) \times Q^*$$

How will the monopolist respond to this new environment? By equating the foreign marginal revenue to the unchanged domestic marginal cost of 500 and solving for Q^*, we find

$$Q^* = [1,000 - (500/1.2)]/2 = 291.7$$

Exhibit 9.5 summarizes the new foreign equilibrium.

Exhibit 9.5 A Monopolistic Exporter When $RS = 1.2$

In order to sell the 291.7 units in the foreign market, the monopolist must lower the foreign price per unit to

$$P* = 1,000 - 291.7 = 708.3$$

Because the marginal cost of production is constant, the domestic price per unit remains at 750, and the domestic sales remain at 250.

Notice that although the foreign currency appreciates by 20%, the monopolist only decreases the relative price in the foreign market by 5.6% because the ratio of the new foreign price to the old foreign price is

$$708.3/750 = 0.944$$

The 5.6% pass-through reduction in the relative foreign price resulting from the 20% appreciation of the foreign currency is quite small. Put differently, the domestic currency price that is equivalent to the new foreign price multiplied by the real exchange rate has increased drastically from 750 to

$$1.2 \times 708.3 = 850$$

Because the actual domestic price stays constant at 750, the law of one price is now violated.

Violations of the Law of One Price

Exhibit 9.5 demonstrates that whenever demand curves differ across countries, a monopolist finds it in his interest to violate the law of one price. Because the demand curves depend only on the relative price of the product in the consumer's country and not on the relative prices in other countries, these deviations from the law of one price do not trigger arbitrage in the goods markets. Implicit in the formulation of the demand curves are some costs that prevent arbitrage.

The real appreciation of the foreign currency makes the monopolist more profitable. Even if the monopolist lowered the foreign relative price by the full amount of the foreign currency appreciation to $625 = 750/1.2$, in which case, the law of one price would not be violated, the monopolist's profits would still increase because foreign sales would increase to $375 = 1,000 - 625$. At these prices and quantities, total profit would increase to

$$(750 \times 250) + (1.2 \times 625 \times 375) - [500 \times (250 + 375)] = 156,250$$

or by 25%, because the ratio of new profit to old profit is $156,250/125,000 = 1.25$. But the monopolist can do even better by violating the law of one price. At the new optimal prices and quantities, total profit increases to

$$(750 \times 250) + (1.2 \times 708.3 \times 291.7) - [500 \times (250 + 291.7)] = 164,583.3$$

or by 31.7%, because the ratio of new profit to old profit is $164,583.3/125,000 = 1.317$. By acting optimally, the exporting monopolist exploits the real appreciation of the foreign currency to become even more profitable.

A Monopolistic Net Importer

Now, consider how a monopolist who is a net importer responds to changes in the real exchange rate.

Example 9.6   A Monopolist with Imported Costs

The Demand Curve

Consider a monopolist who faces a domestic demand curve given by

$$Q = 1,000 - P$$

where Q is the quantity demand at the domestic relative price, P.

Domestic and Foreign Costs

The cost of production involves a domestic cost per unit of C and a foreign cost per unit of C^*. Total cost is the sum of domestic costs, $C \times Q$, and the domestic value of foreign costs, which is total foreign costs, $C^* \times Q$, multiplied by the real exchange rate, RS. Hence, total real domestic costs are

$$(C \times Q) + (RS \times C^* \times Q)$$

Because $P = 1,000 - Q$, total revenue is

$$P \times Q = 1,000 \times Q - Q^2$$

and marginal revenue is $1,000 - 2Q$. Marginal cost is $C + (RS \times C^*)$.

The Equilibrium

Suppose that initially $C = 250$, $C^* = 200$, and $RS = 1$. Then, the profit-maximizing decision of the monopolist is to set marginal revenue equal to marginal unit cost:

$$1,000 - 2Q = 250 + (1 \times 200) = 450$$

or, solving for Q, we find

$$Q = (1,000 - 450)/2 = 275$$

The monopolist would produce 275 units and sell them in the domestic market at the relative price of 725. The initial equilibrium is given in Exhibit 9.6.

Exhibit 9.6   A Monopolist with Imported Costs

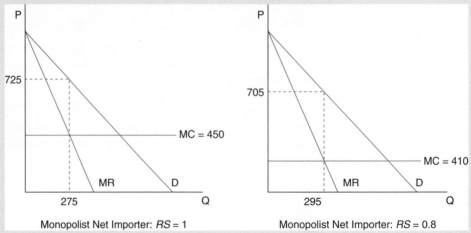

Monopolist Net Importer: $RS = 1$ Monopolist Net Importer: $RS = 0.8$

A Real Depreciation

Now, suppose there is a 20% real depreciation of the foreign currency such that the new real exchange rate is 0.8. This causes the domestic value of the monopolist's foreign costs to fall by 20% to $0.8 \times 200 = 160$. Because marginal cost falls to $250 + 160 = 410$ (versus 450), the monopolist increases his production. The optimal quantity now sets the old marginal revenue, $1,000 - 2Q$, equal to the new marginal cost:

$$1,000 - 2Q = 250 + (0.8 \times 200) = 410$$

or

$$Q = (1,000 - 410)/2 = 295$$

In order to sell 295 units, the monopolist decreases the domestic relative price to 705.

Pass-Through Pricing

How much of the cost saving shown in the preceding section is passed through to consumers? The monopolist's marginal cost has fallen by 8.9% because the ratio of new marginal cost to the old is $(410/450) = 0.911$. But the reduction in the domestic price is only 2.8% because the ratio of the new price to the old price is $(705/725) = 0.972$. Thus, once again, the pass-through is much less than one for one. In this case, the monopolist increases his profits because the real depreciation of the foreign currency lowers the cost of his imports. With a real exchange rate of 1, profits were

$$(725 \times 275) - [(250 \times 275) + (1 \times 200 \times 275)] = 75,625$$

With a real exchange rate of 0.8, profits are

$$(705 \times 295) - [(250 \times 295) + (0.8 \times 200 \times 295)] = 87,025$$

Notice that profits have risen by 15.1% because the ratio of new profits to old profits is $(87,025/75,625) = 1.151$. If the monopolist had passed through the full cost saving of 8.9% from the exchange rate to the domestic price, the new price would have been $0.911 \times 725 = 660.5$, and the new quantity sold would have been $1,000 - 660.5 = 339.5$. Hence, profits would have been

$$(660.5 \times 339.5) - [(250 \times 339.5) + (0.8 \times 200 \times 339.5)] = 85,045$$

As you can see, the monopolist's profits would, again, increase (from 75,262 to 85,045) with the complete pass-through of the reduction in foreign costs to the domestic price. However, the monopolist can do better by passing less of the savings on to consumers. Instead, he charges domestic consumers a relatively higher price per unit than with complete pass-through and produces fewer units, thereby earning 87,025 instead of just 85,045.

Empirical Evidence on Pricing-to-Market

The examples just examined demonstrate what could happen in monopolistic environments. Although there are few monopolists in actual markets, economists do generally find strong evidence that the exports of various countries are priced to market, suggesting that firms do have some market power.

For example, in their comprehensive review of the literature, Goldberg and Knetter (1997) found that the elasticity of U.S. import prices to changes in exchange rates was typically about 0.5. In other words, a 10% depreciation of the dollar was associated with a 5% increase in the dollar prices of imports. Foreign exporters consequently received about 5% less in their currencies after the dollar depreciation. For other Organization for Economic Cooperation and Development (OECD) countries, Campa and Goldberg (2005) found pass-through elasticities of 0.46 over one quarter rising to 0.64 over the longer term. They also found that pass-through elasticities seem to be declining over time.

A more recent study by Marazzi and Sheets (2007) found that pass-through to U.S. import prices has fallen from the 0.5 reported earlier to 0.2 in the 2000s. Although understanding why pass-through has fallen is a difficult problem, the economists attribute the change to a reduced share of commodity-intensive industrial supplies in U.S. imports and the increased presence of Chinese exports in the U.S. market. Because China was pegging the yuan to the dollar during this period, any depreciation of the dollar versus third currencies that would have potentially led to an increase in dollar prices of third-country exports to the United States was held in check by competition from China.

The studies discussed earlier use relatively aggregated data. Gopinath and Itskhoki (2010) use micro data from the U.S. Bureau of Labor Statistics for the period of 1994 to 2005 to investigate pass-through in the manufacturing sector because this is where they expect to see imperfect competition and imperfect pass-through. Gopinath and Itskhoki note that it takes time for firms to adjust their prices, and they consequently investigate how often prices change and by what amount over a 24-month period. The primary findings are that firms that adjust more frequently also have greater pass-through, and high-frequency adjusters have a pass-through of 0.4, whereas low-frequency adjusters have a pass-through of 0.2.

Another study, conducted by Nakamura and Steinsson (2009), uncovered a potential bias in earlier analyses of pass-through. Nakamura and Steinsson note that, in micro data, product replacement is quite frequent, whereas price changes are infrequent. Consequently, firms adjust their prices as they introduce new products. When Nakamura and Steinsson take this product replacement bias into account, they find that the price of non-oil U.S. imports respond by 0.6% to 0.7% for a 1% change in the real exchange rate, whereas prices of U.S. exports respond by roughly 0.8%. These findings show both more pass-through and more symmetry across imports and exports than previous studies.

9.5 EVALUATING THE PERFORMANCE OF A FOREIGN SUBSIDIARY

The fact that fluctuations in real exchange rates affect the profitability of international businesses severely complicates the process of evaluating the performance of managers of foreign subsidiaries.[5] We know that a real depreciation of the local currency, that is, the currency of the country in which the foreign subsidiary resides, hurts the performance of a net importing company because it increases the company's costs. Conversely, a real depreciation of the local currency improves the operating performance of a net exporting company because it increases the company's revenues.

Because fluctuations in real exchange rates are large and difficult to forecast, the operating performance of foreign subsidiaries is quite variable. How can we design a system to determine good management from bad management in such an environment?

---

[5]The approach in this chapter is based on the analysis in Lessard and Sharp (1984).

Three Types of Subsidiaries

Consider the initial situations of three different Japanese subsidiaries operating in Thailand, where the local currency is the baht. The three firms are ThaiComp, which is a net importer; WeRToys, which is a net exporter; and RiceNoodle, which neither imports nor exports.

The Net Importer

ThaiComp imports personal computer (PC) parts, assembles the PCs in Thailand, and sells most of its PCs in Thailand. ThaiComp exports some computers to Malaysia, Indonesia, and China. Because the computer maker is a net importer, its costs increase more than its revenues when there is a real depreciation of the baht. The Japanese owners of ThaiComp then experience an additional loss in real terms when they convert baht profit into yen.

The Net Exporter

WeRToys produces and exports toys. Although it also sells some toys in the local Thai market, and it, too, has some imported inputs, WeRToys's export sales produce a large fraction of its revenues. Consequently, its operating performance improves with a real depreciation of the baht, but its Japanese owners experience less of this increase in real profitability when the yen strengthens.

The Neutral Firm

RiceNoodle is a restaurant chain that serves the Thai market. It has no export revenues, no direct foreign costs, and no foreign competition. Consequently, RiceNoodle's real profit, which is its baht profit divided by the Thai price level, should not be affected by changes in the real exchange rate. However, a real depreciation of the baht relative to the yen does adversely affect the real value of RiceNoodle's profits for the company's Japanese owners.

Initial Operating Profitability

Exhibit 9.7 shows the operating profits earned by the three firms when the real exchange rate of baht per yen equals 1. The real revenues, real costs, and real operating profits are presented, along with the percentage of total revenue that each category represents. Real units are found by deflating nominal variables denominated in baht by the Thai price level. Exhibit 9.7 indicates that each firm has real revenue of 2,303. Notice that RiceNoodle gets 100% of this revenue from sales in Thailand. ThaiComp gets 70% of its real revenue in the local Thai

Exhibit 9.7 Operating Profit with a One-to-One Real Exchange Rate Between the Baht and the Yen

	RiceNoodle		ThaiComp		WeRToys	
	Real Baht	**% of Sales**	**Real Baht**	**% of Sales**	**Real Baht**	**% of Sales**
Sales						
Exported	0	0	696	30	1,607	70
Local	2,303	100	1,607	70	696	30
Costs of Goods Sold						
Imported	0	0	(900)	(39)	(825)	(36)
Local	(1,725)	(75)	(825)	(36)	(900)	(39)
Local Fixed Costs	(350)	(15)	(350)	(15)	(350)	(15)
Operating Profit in Real Baht	228	10	228	10	228	10
Operating Profit in Real Yen	228	10	228	10	228	10

market and 30% from exports out of Thailand. In contrast, WeRToys gets 30% of its real revenue from the Thai market and 70% from exports. Each firm initially has real costs of goods sold equal to 1,725. Of this, ThaiComp's local costs are only 825, whereas its imported costs are 900. These figures are reversed for WeRToys, whose local costs are 900 and whose imported costs are 825. All three firms have real local fixed costs of 350. By subtracting costs of goods sold and fixed costs from total revenue, we find that each firm has an initial real operating profit of 228, which is 10% of real revenue.

The last line of Exhibit 9.7 evaluates the real operating profit of the three subsidiaries in real yen by dividing by the real exchange rate. Although this conversion has no effect when the real exchange rate is 1, a real depreciation of the baht involves an increase in the real exchange rate of baht per yen and a consequent lowering of real profitability when the baht are converted into yen. So, even though RiceNoodle is not exposed directly to foreign exchange risk, the Japanese owners of RiceNoodle still suffer a decline in yen revenue when there is a real depreciation of the baht (as we will see in Exhibit 9.8).

Actual Versus Forecasted Operating Results

If we want to evaluate the performance of a foreign subsidiary's managers, we first need to look at the subsidiary's expected operating results. This represents the managers' best forecasts of what will happen in the upcoming year and how the subsidiaries will respond to changing economic circumstances. For simplicity, assume that Exhibit 9.7 also represents what is expected to happen during the coming year—that managers expect the same real earnings in the year to come, and they do not expect the real exchange rate to change. (Of course, in actual practice, managers generally expect these variables to change.)

Exhibit 9.8 presents the actual operating results for the three firms in the following year during which there is a 10% real appreciation of foreign currencies relative to the Thai baht. Thus, the real exchange rate is now 1.1. Let's examine how each firm is doing.

RiceNoodle's Results

RiceNoodle's real sales are down somewhat relative to what was expected, but its costs are also lower. Real operating profit is 199, down 12.7% from 228. Because the change in the real exchange rate is not supposed to affect RiceNoodle, the local Thai managers must accept

Exhibit 9.8 Actual Operating Profit After a 10% Real Appreciation of the Yen

	RiceNoodle		ThaiComp		WeRToys	
	Real Baht	% of Sales	Real Baht	% of Sales	Real Baht	% of Sales
Sales						
Exported	0	0	830	35	1,900	75
Local	2,188	100	1,526	65	648	25
Costs of Goods Sold						
Imported	0	0	(980)	(42)	(945)	(37)
Local	(1,656)	(76)	(810)	(34)	(969)	(38)
Local Fixed Costs	(333)	(15)	(349)	(15)	(355)	(14)
Operating Profit in Real Baht	199	9	217	9	279	11
% Change in Real Baht Profit	(12.7)		(4.8)		22.4	
Operating Profit in Real Yen	181	9	197	9	254	11
% Change in Real Yen Profit	(20.6)		(13.5)		11.4	

responsibility for the shortfall in baht profit relative to what was forecast. Presumably, this would affect the current compensation these managers receive, and continued substandard performance of this kind would probably result in a change in local management. Notice also that real operating profit in yen is even lower because of the real depreciation of the baht. Real operating profit in yen is now 181, down 20.6% from 228. Now, let's consider the other two firms.

Results at ThaiComp and WeRToys

Exhibit 9.8 indicates that the 10% real appreciation of the yen has hurt the profitability of ThaiComp. Real baht operating profit has fallen by 4.8%, to 217 from 228. The increase in imported costs has caused operating profit to fall to 9% of sales from 10%. In contrast, the real baht operating profit of WeRToys has risen by 22.4%, from 228 to 279, and its operating profit is now 11% of total revenue.

The last two lines of Exhibit 9.8 show how converting the baht operating profits of the foreign subsidiaries into real yen by dividing by the real exchange rate lowers the profitability of these firms as well. ThaiComp's real operating profit in yen has fallen by 13.5%, and the good performance of WeRToys, when evaluated in Thai baht, is reduced to an 11.4% increase when converted to real yen.

A naïve interpretation of these annual performances (either in real baht or real yen) would award a substantial bonus to the managers of WeRToys, who produced a profit that impressively exceeded what was forecast. Of course, headquarters would recognize that WeRToys had a favorable operating environment, in light of the unanticipated 10% real depreciation of the baht. Nevertheless, the local managers of WeRToys would argue that some of the increase in operating performance was due to superior management. They would try to take as much credit for this good performance as possible, arguing that a 22.4% increase in real baht profitability cannot be due strictly to chance.

Evaluating the performance of ThaiComp would be a problem. The managers of ThaiComp would claim that the firm's poor performance was due strictly to the real depreciation of the baht. A debate might ensue regarding whether a 4.8% fall in profitability should be expected for this type of firm operating in this adverse environment.

Comparing the Optimal Response with No Response by Managers

The previous section highlights the problem of evaluating the performance of the foreign subsidiaries only with *ex post* information. Because we know ThaiComp will do relatively poorly and WeRToys will do relatively well when the baht suffers a real depreciation, merely observing the direction of the change in operating profit gives no indication of how well the firms' managers are performing. What we need to know is how poorly ThaiComp would be expected to do and how well WeRToys would be expected to do, contingent on a 10% real depreciation of the baht.

Comparisons with No Operating Responses

One starting point would be to evaluate the operating performance of the firms if there were no operating responses by their managers. This perspective is presented in Exhibit 9.9.

With no operating responses, the firms would charge the same relative prices in their local and export markets. They would presumably sell the same quantities, and they would have the same costs of production as in their respective expected budgets in Exhibit 9.7. Differences in sales, costs of goods sold, and profitability would arise merely because each of the figures associated with international transactions—export sales and imported costs—would be multiplied by the new real exchange rate of 1.1.

Exhibit 9.9 Operating Profit After a 10% Real Appreciation of the Yen: No Response by Managers

	RiceNoodle		ThaiComp		WeRToys	
	Real Baht	% of Sales	Real Baht	% of Sales	Real Baht	% of Sales
Sales						
Exported	0	0	766	32	1,768	70
Local	2,303	100	1,607	68	696	30
Costs of Goods Sold						
Imported	0	0	(990)	(42)	(908)	(37)
Local	(1,725)	(75)	(825)	(35)	(900)	(37)
Local Fixed Costs	(350)	(15)	(350)	(15)	(350)	(14)
Operating Profit in Real Baht	228	10	208	8	306	12
% Change in Real Baht Profit	0		(8.8)		34.2	
Operating Profit in Real Yen	207	10	189	8	278	12
% Change in Real Yen Profit	(9.2)		(17.1)		21.9	

Now, look at Exhibits 9.7 and 9.9. Comparing the two exhibits shows that a 10% real depreciation of the baht, with no operating response by managers, would cause ThaiComp's operating profit in real baht to fall from 228 to 208. The fall of 20 arises because imported costs rise from 900 to 990, or 20 more than the increase in exports from 696 to 766. WeRToys's real baht operating profit would rise from 228 to 306. The increase of 78 arises because at the original one-to-one exchange rate, export revenue (1,607) exceeds imported costs (825) by 782, and the exchange rate has increased by 10%.

It's critical for the Thai managers of the three firms to understand how their imports and exports are affected by real exchange rates changes. In other words, they need to think through what their reactions will be. By responding appropriately to these changes, the firms should be able to achieve higher profits than those shown in Exhibit 9.9.[6]

Comparisons with Optimal Responses

Earlier in this chapter, we indicated that the firms' responses to a real depreciation of the baht would involve an appropriate pricing-to-market strategy. That is, in response to a real depreciation of the baht, the firms should try to shift some sales from the Thai market to the export market. This could be accomplished by increasing the relative price charged in the Thai market and decreasing the relative price charged in the export market. The increase in the import costs of production also dictates reducing the overall quantity of production for ThaiComp because its costs have increased more than the benefit of additional international sales. WeRToys, on the other hand, should expand production.

Exhibit 9.10 provides this contingent forecasting information associated with the managers' anticipated responses to a 10% real depreciation of the baht.

Notice that revenues from export sales are higher for ThaiComp and WeRToys than in Exhibit 9.9 and that their revenues from local sales are lower than in Exhibit 9.9. Also, Thai-Comp's local costs of production and imported costs of production are lower in Exhibit 9.10 than in Exhibit 9.9. These lower costs reflect the decreased output of the firm. Overall, with an optimal response by ThaiComp to the real depreciation of the baht, the operating profit in

---

[6]Marston's (2001) research indicates that the first-order effect of a real depreciation with an optimal operating response is still given by the effect of the real exchange rate on the net exposure of the firm because the firm has already optimized quantities it is selling in each market. Hence, changes in the quantities produced and sold in the different markets will not produce large improvements in operating profit.

Exhibit 9.10 Operating Profit After a 10% Real Appreciation of the Yen: Managers Respond Optimally

	RiceNoodle		ThaiComp		WeRToys	
	Real Baht	% of Sales	Real Baht	% of Sales	Real Baht	% of Sales
Sales						
Exported	0	0	815	35	1,848	74
Local	2,303	100	1,522	65	644	26
Costs of Goods Sold						
Imported	0	0	(969)	(41)	(920)	(37)
Local	(1,725)	(75)	(807)	(35)	(913)	(37)
Local Fixed Costs	(350)	(15)	(350)	(15)	(350)	(14)
Operating Profit in Real Baht	228	10	211	9	309	12
% Change in Real Baht Profit	0		(7.5)		35.5	
Operating Profit in Real Yen	207	10	192	9	281	12
% Change in Real Yen Profit	(9.2)		(15.8)		23.2	

real baht is 211, which is 1% higher than the corresponding value in Exhibit 9.9. WeRToys, the net exporter, can also do better. Exhibit 9.10 indicates that WeRToys can produce an operating profit in real baht of 309, which is slightly better than the corresponding value of 306 in Exhibit 9.9.

Who Deserves a Bonus?

The question of which of the three Thai companies deserves a bonus is now easily assessed. Exhibit 9.11 compares the actual operating results (shown in Exhibit 9.8) after a 10% real appreciation of the yen to the anticipated operating responses (shown in Exhibit 9.10) that are contingent upon the same 10% real appreciation of the yen. Notice that only ThaiComp's

Exhibit 9.11 Actual Versus Optimal Operating Profit After a 10% Real Appreciation of the Yen

	RiceNoodle Real Baht		ThaiComp Real Baht		WeRToys Real Baht	
	Optimal	Actual	Optimal	Actual	Optimal	Actual
Sales						
Exported	0	0	815	830	1,848	1,900
Local	2,303	2,188	1,522	1,526	644	648
Costs of Goods Sold						
Imported	0	0	(969)	(980)	(920)	(945)
Local	(1,725)	(1,656)	(807)	(810)	(913)	(969)
Local Fixed Costs	(350)	(333)	(350)	(349)	(350)	(355)
Operating Profit in Real Baht	228	199	211	217	309	279
% Change in Real Baht Profit	0	(12.7)	(7.5)	(4.8)	35.5	22.4
Operating Profit in Real Yen	207	181	192	197	281	254
% Change in Real Yen Profit	(9.2)	(20.6)	(15.8)	(13.5)	23.2	11.4

actual results are better than the optimal result. Managers can do better than they anticipate because they have additional information and can respond to it.

RiceNoodle's local sales were less than anticipated, but so were its costs. Unfortunately, its operating profit falls short of what was expected, conditional on operating in the new environment.

WeRToys actually sold more goods than was anticipated, both in Thailand and as exports from Thailand. Unfortunately, all of its costs, imported, local, and fixed, were higher than they should have been. Its overall profit of 279 falls substantially short of the 309 that should have been produced.

ThaiComp, on the other hand, was operating in an adverse environment. Its actual local revenues were higher, as were its exports. Its imported costs and its local fixed costs were also higher than expected. Overall, though, ThaiComp's real operating profit of 217 exceeds the 211 that was forecast for this situation. After converting to real yen, its operating profit of 197 exceeds the contingent value of 192. Clearly, the management of ThaiComp deserves a bonus for their superior performance.

Assessing the Long-Run Viability of a Subsidiary

The contingent forecasting approach can be used to assess the long-run viability of a subsidiary as it is currently being managed. Suppose that, at the real exchange rate of 1, the Thai baht is currently 10% undervalued relative to the Japanese yen. We know that in the long run, such an undervaluation is likely to be corrected. This will provide a favorable shock to the profitability of ThaiComp, the net importer, as the baht strengthens in real terms; but it will hurt the long-run profitability of WeRToys, the net exporter.

Exhibit 9.12 provides the anticipated operating responses for the three firms, contingent on a 10% real depreciation of the yen to a new real exchange rate of 0.9 in baht per yen. The figures incorporate the optimal operating responses of each firm.

RiceNoodle has no exposure to real exchange rates, so its real operating profit in Thailand is anticipated to remain at 228 baht. However, when the profits are converted into real yen, the appreciation of the baht raises the value to 253 yen.

Compared to the base case in Exhibit 9.7 with a real exchange rate of 1, the real appreciation of the baht increases ThaiComp's real operating profit in Thailand from 228 to 251.

Exhibit 9.12 Operating Profit After a 10% Real Depreciation of the Yen: Managers Respond Optimally

	RiceNoodle		ThaiComp		WeRToys	
	Real Baht	% of Sales	Real Baht	% of Sales	Real Baht	% of Sales
Sales						
Exported	0	0	574	25	1,361	65
Local	2,303	100	1,687	75	745	35
Costs of Goods Sold						
Imported	0	0	(822)	(36)	(725)	(34)
Local	(1,725)	(75)	(838)	(37)	(878)	(42)
Local Fixed Costs	(350)	(15)	(350)	(15)	(350)	(17)
Operating Profit in Real Baht	228	10	251	11	153	7
% Change in Operating Profit	0		10.1		(32.9)	
Operating Profit in Real Yen	253	10	279	11	170	7
% Change in Real Yen Profit	11		22.4		(25.4)	

When this is converted to real yen, the real profits increase to 279, which is 22.4% higher than the base case.

In contrast, a real appreciation of the baht hurts WeRToys. Even with optimal operating responses, the firm's real operating profit in Thailand would be expected to fall from 228 in the base case to 153. The conversion to real yen increases this to 170 yen, but this still represents a 25.4% fall in real operating profit. Because the operating margin is now only 7%, WeRToys looks like a marginal business unless an alternative operating strategy can be found to increase its profitability.

9.6 STRATEGIES FOR MANAGING REAL EXCHANGE RISK

Given that real exchange rates fluctuate, how should the management team of a large multi-national firm respond to various real exchange risks? The most important point is that managers must recognize that the influences of real exchange rates are pervasive. They directly affect foreign pricing and domestic costs of foreign imports, but they also affect the nature of competition between firms in different countries.

Obviously, financial managers must understand these risks, but hedging against adverse real exchange risks is complicated. Consequently, we devote Chapter 17 to a more formal analysis of that issue. Here, we merely note that financial hedging can help by assuring the firm of cash flow when changes in exchange rates would otherwise make the firm unprofitable.

It is also important for marketing and operations managers to understand the nature of real exchange risks that the firm faces. The managers of the firm must be aware that fluctuations in real exchange rates will create problem situations and profit opportunities that call for appropriate managerial responses.

Transitory Versus Permanent Changes in Real Exchange Rates

One key element that influences a firm's optimal response to a given change in the real exchange rate is the length of time that the change in the real exchange rate is expected to persist. How long a real depreciation is expected to last can affect both the amount of the exposure and managers' possible responses to that exposure. The time frame of the change in the exchange rate affects the firm's response because it is costly to change the operations of the firm. The next sections explore how managers can respond to real exchange rates in a dynamic way.

Production Management

How can a firm's production processes be designed to reflect real foreign exchange risk? Certainly, the production schedule, the sourcing of inputs, and even the location of production facilities ought to be sensitive to prospective fluctuations in real exchange rates.

Production Scheduling

Production scheduling must be sensitive to the real exchange rate because its fluctuations affect the demand for the firm's products. Many firms use changes in inventory to meet their transitory fluctuations in demand because it is usually less costly to run a smooth production process than a fluctuating one. Inventories accumulate during periods of slack demand, and inventories fall during periods of high demand, but production remains steady. In Example 9.5, we saw how a real appreciation of the foreign currency motivates a monopolist to increase its exports to foreign markets. In that example, per-unit costs were constant. However, if per-unit costs increase with the amount of production because of overtime pay and increased maintenance costs related to machines, the monopolist can earn more revenue in the foreign market simply by selling more of the product out of inventory than by increasing production. The major factor that determines by how much the firm will increase the sale of its goods from inventory versus increasing production depends on the persistence of the change in the real exchange rate. The more persistent the change, the longer the firm expects to have high demand, and the more the firm will want to increase its production rather than sell out of inventory. If the change in the exchange rate were perceived as permanent, the firm would want to permanently adjust its prices and production.

Input Sourcing

Sources of materials and intermediate parts in the production process should be sensitive to the real exchange rate. When the domestic currency is strong, domestic companies should use foreign inputs because they are relatively inexpensive. But these foreign sources should be lined up in advance to take full advantage of the fluctuations in exchange rates.

One mitigating influence that prevents manufacturers from changing between domestic and foreign suppliers is the value the firm puts on its long-term relationships with its suppliers. Having a stable and reliable source of parts or materials is a valuable asset. If the firm shifts to a foreign supplier today, there is no guarantee that its current domestic supplier will still be interested in servicing the firm's business in the future. Thus, managers must assess how long the domestic currency is expected to remain strong. If the firm switches too quickly to a foreign supplier in response to a transitory real appreciation of the domestic currency, it may ultimately end up with no domestic suppliers or with unreliable suppliers when the domestic currency depreciates and foreign supplies are no longer competitively priced.

Using foreign suppliers can also either mitigate or exacerbate a firm's exposure to real exchange risk. For example, if a firm is exporting a lot to a country that has a foreign supplier for its intermediate inputs, using the foreign supplier would mitigate the real exchange risk. But if using the foreign supplier adds a new source of real exchange risk because the firm has no exposure to that currency, the domestic firm's managers must think about this dimension as well as the respective domestic and foreign costs.

Plant Location

If a multinational firm has production operations in several countries, it is natural for the managers to shift production among the plants to minimize costs. As real exchange rates fluctuate, the firm should increase production in countries whose currencies have depreciated in real terms, and it should decrease production in countries whose currencies have strengthened in real terms. However, because opening a plant abroad represents a long-term investment, management should be reasonably sure that the current cost advantage that the country enjoys is not likely to be undone by a real appreciation of the foreign currency. It may be that the currency has experienced a temporary real depreciation that is likely to be reversed within a few years.

In the 1990s, Japanese and European car manufacturers such as Toyota and BMW invested in U.S. production facilities to hedge against the adverse effects of a real depreciation of the dollar. With their production facilities located in the market of their sales, only their profits were exposed to the risk of dollar depreciation. In contrast, when these firms merely export products to the United States, their revenues are entirely exposed to possible losses if the dollar depreciates.

A firm's ability to shift production around the world is also limited by the cost structure of its plants. If a firm operates a plant that is too small, it loses the economies of scale it could have obtained by operating a larger plant, and this increases its costs per unit. Thus, instead of limiting its real exchange risk by operating smaller plants in different countries, a firm might choose to achieve economies of scale by operating a single large plant.

A good example of this situation occurred after Jaguar was privatized in 1984. At the time, Jaguar had only one plant, which was located in the United Kingdom. Because over 50% of its sales were made in the United States, when the dollar weakened in the late 1980s, Jaguar's revenues plummeted. One way to limit the exposure of Jaguar's U.S. dollar revenue stream would have been to build a production facility in the United States. But the economies of scale Jaguar needed to remain profitable didn't allow for this.

In 1989, Jaguar became the takeover target of General Motors and Ford. These companies realized that Jaguar was more valuable as part of a larger company than as an independent entity. Ford subsequently purchased Jaguar and began sourcing additional parts from the United States. Unfortunately, even after massive capital investments, Jaguar never achieved the profitability that Ford predicted, and in 2009, Ford sold Jaguar to Tata Motors of India.

Marketing Management

How can marketing strategy and pricing policy be designed to offset real foreign exchange risk? Pricing policies, promotional strategies, market entry decisions, and even product development should be designed with exchange rate changes in mind.

Pricing Policies

We have already discussed some specific examples of pricing-to-market. In general, however, when a currency depreciates, exporters to that country face a trade-off: They can maintain either their profits or their market shares, but not both. If the firm increases its foreign currency price to maintain its profit, it will lose sales to foreign rivals. If the firm maintains a given foreign currency price, it will maintain its market share but lose profit. Research indicates that the optimal thing for firms to do lies somewhere between the two extremes. Faced with a real depreciation of the foreign currency, an exporter typically increases its relative price in the foreign country but not by the full percentage of the depreciation. The firm loses market share and earns a smaller profit on all sales.

A couple of factors affect this strategy, however. One is the elasticity of demand for the exporter's product. If demand is highly elastic, the firm's loss of market share will be large when the product's price is increased. In this case, the exporter needs to lean toward not increasing its prices. By contrast, if demand is highly inelastic, the exporter can afford to increase its prices by a greater amount. Another factor has to do with the nature of the firm's cost structure. For example, if there are important economies of scale in production, the firm's costs will increase significantly if it reduces production. Hence, the firm will hold down foreign price increases in response to a foreign currency depreciation to keep the demand for its products high. In contrast, if the firm's costs are less affected when the company loses market share, the firm may be able to reduce the quantities it produces and increase its prices.

The Frequency of Price Adjustments

Another marketing consideration that should be addressed is the frequency of price adjustments. Demand for a product often depends on the stability of its price. Consumers want to be able to compare items in different stores, and this takes time. Potential customers want to know nominal prices in advance, and this requires advertising. Customers hate surprise price increases. Given that consumers like price stability, foreign exporters are faced with the decision of how frequently to adjust prices in response to exchange rate changes. Firms consequently develop boundaries for exchange rate fluctuations that will not trigger a change in the firm's foreign currency prices. Then, only sufficiently large changes in exchange rates cause the firm to change its product price.

Market Entry Decisions

Firms often introduce new products in foreign markets when the foreign currencies are strong in real terms. Doing so allows a firm to set a comparatively low foreign currency price for a product so that it can better compete and become an established player in the market. For example, the large real appreciation of the dollar from 1980 to 1985 gave Honda and Toyota a golden opportunity to penetrate the U.S. market with low dollar prices that translated into high yen revenues. The Japanese companies were able to establish a reputation in the United States for providing high-quality, low-priced cars. This reputation persisted in the United States, even after a substantial real appreciation of the yen.

Brand Loyalty

Brand loyalty describes a situation in which consumers continue to purchase a brand they have purchased in the past even though it costs more now.[7] Developing brand loyalty clearly helps in situations of real exchange risk because consumers will not switch to competitors' products that enjoy a temporary pricing benefit from a favorable fluctuation in the exchange rate. Thus, it is important for a domestic company to develop loyal customers—especially when it's facing competition from abroad. But the firm must also recognize that in entering a foreign market, it will have to win over the customers who are loyal to brands in their home countries. That said, entering a foreign market when the foreign currency is strong in real terms makes a lot of sense because the firm can use advertising campaigns and low foreign prices to get consumers to try its product without sacrificing too much profit. Establishing a large foreign market share when the foreign currency is strong in real terms means that a large number of foreign customers will have tried the firm's product. These foreign customers will not all be lost when the foreign currency depreciates in real terms and the firm is forced to raise foreign currency prices.

The discussion in this section is summarized in Exhibit 9.13.

Exhibit 9.13 A Checklist for Managers of Real Exchange Risk

Production Inputs—Source inputs from suppliers in countries suffering real depreciations of their currencies.

Production Location—Shift production to plants located in countries suffering real depreciations of their currencies or countries with low-cost production.

Pricing-to-Market—Allow a real appreciation of the foreign currency to increase the profitability of foreign sales but lower foreign prices to expand market share.

Market Entry—Begin selling in foreign markets after a real appreciation of the foreign currency.

Brand Loyalty—Create loyal customers who will not "buy foreign" when the domestic currency strengthens in real terms.

Price Consistently—Recognize that exchange rates will be more volatile than prices of goods. Be prepared for short-run swings in profitability due to exchange rates.

Hedging—Use derivaties securities such as forward contracts or options to hedge foreign exchange risk to assure cash flow when changes in exchange rates would make the firm unprofitable.

Currency of Denomination of Debt—Denominate long-term debt in foreign currencies in which the firm has substantial assets or sales to reduce exposure to foreign exchange risk.

---

[7]Is brand loyalty a rational phenomenon? Whenever consumers cannot easily find out information about how a new product will perform without experiencing the product, it is costly for consumers to switch brands. In such a situation, brand loyalty is a rational economic phenomenon. Economists use the term *experience goods* for this situation, and in such markets, future demand depends on current market share. See Froot and Klemperer (1989) for a formal analysis of these effects.

9.7 SUMMARY

This chapter introduces the idea of real exchange risk. The main points in the chapter are as follows:

1. Real exchange risk, which is also called real operating exposure and real economic exposure, is the variability in the present value of a firm's profits that is caused by unpredictable fluctuations in real exchange rates.
2. A real depreciation of the domestic currency makes domestic exporters and import competitors more profitable because it shifts demand to the domestic market.
3. Real exchange risk is present in any long-term contract between parties from two countries that do not share a common currency. Making product prices in the contract contingent upon the real exchange rate helps firms share the real operating risk.
4. The pass-through to product prices from changes in real exchange rates is not one-to-one if goods markets are not perfectly competitive because producers optimally adjust their profits in response to fluctuations in the real exchange rate.
5. Evaluating the performance of a foreign subsidiary is complicated by fluctuations in real exchange rates. Establishing contingent forecasts based on optimal responses by managers can help determine how they have performed under a variety of exchange rate scenarios.
6. Managers can utilize pricing, promotional, and product development strategies to help reduce real exchange risks. The extent to which they are able to utilize these strategies depends on a firm's economies of scale and the elasticity of its demand curve.
7. Fluctuations in real exchange rates affect the cost of operating in different countries. A firm's input sources and plant location decisions need to take this into account.

QUESTIONS

1. As the vice president of finance for a U.S. firm, what do you say to your production manager when he states, "We shouldn't let foreign exchange risk interfere with our profitability. Let's simply invoice all our foreign customers in dollars and be done with it."
2. What do economists mean by *pricing-to-market*?
3. Why does a monopolist not charge the same price for the same good in two different countries?
4. What determines how much a foreign producer allows the dollar price of a product sold in the United States to be affected by a change in the real exchange rate?
5. Why is the pass-through from changes in exchange rates to changes in the prices of products not one-for-one?
6. Given that real exchange rates fluctuate, when would be the best time to enter the market of a foreign country as an exporter to that market?
7. You have been asked to evaluate possible sites for an Asian production facility that will manufacture your firm's products and sell them to the Asian market. What real exchange rate considerations should you entertain in your evaluation?
8. Why is it important for an exporter to understand the distinction between a temporary change in the exchange rate and a permanent change in determining whether to respond to a real depreciation of the home currency with increased production or sales out of inventories?

PROBLEMS

1. If there is 10% inflation in Brazil, 15% inflation in Argentina, and the Argentine peso weakens by 21% relative to the Brazilian real, by how much has the peso strengthened or weakened in real terms? What effect do you expect that this change in the real exchange rate would have on trade between the two countries?

2. Suppose that you have one domestic production facility that supplies both the domestic and foreign markets. Assume that the demand for your product in the domestic market is $Q = 2,000 - 3P$, and in the foreign market, demand is given by $Q^* = 2,000 - 2P^*$. Assume that your domestic marginal cost of production is 600. If the initial real

exchange rate is 1, what are your optimal prices and quantities sold in the two markets? By how much will you change the relative prices of your product if the foreign currency appreciates in real terms by 10%? What will you do to production?

3. How would you respond in Problem 2 if the marginal cost of production were increasing? Why?

4. Suppose you are a monopolist who faces a domestic demand curve given by $Q = 1,000 - 2P$. Your domestic cost of production involves domestic costs per unit of 300 and a foreign cost per unit produced of 150. If the real exchange rate is 1.1, what would be the price you would charge and the quantity you would sell? How do these variables change when the real exchange rate increases by 10%?

5. Use a program like Crystal Ball to generate Monte Carlo simulations of the profits of Safe Air and Metallwerke under various contracting clauses.

6. In 2008, Endo Pharmaceuticals, a U.S. firm, signed a 5-year contracted with Novartis, a Swiss firm, to obtain the exclusive U.S. marketing rights for Voltaren Gel, an anti-inflammatory useful in treating osteoarthritis. Search the Internet for information about the contract. Who bore the real exchange risk?

BIBLIOGRAPHY

Campa, José Manuel, and Linda S. Goldberg, 2005, "Exchange Rate Pass-Through into Import Prices," *Review of Economics and Statistics* 87, pp. 679–690.

Froot, Kenneth A., and Paul D. Klemperer, 1989, "Exchange Rate Pass-Through When Market Share Matters," *American Economic Review* 79, pp. 637–653.

Goldberg, Pinelopi Koujianou, and Michael M. Knetter, 1997, "Goods Prices and Exchange Rates: What Have We Learned?" *Journal of Economic Literature* 35, pp. 1243–1272.

Gopinath, Gita, and Oleg Itskhoki, 2010, "Frequency of Price Adjustment and Pass-Through," *Quarterly Journal of Economics* 125, pp. 675–727.

Kasa, Kenneth, 1992, "Adjustment Costs and Pricing-to-Market: Theory and Evidence," *Journal of International Economics* 32, pp. 1–30.

Lessard, Donald R., and David Sharp, 1984, "Measuring the Performance of Operations Subject to Fluctuating Exchange Rates," *Midland Corporate Finance Journal* 2, pp. 18–30.

Marazzi, Mario, and Nathan Sheets, 2007, "Declining Exchange Rate Pass-Through to U.S. Import Prices: The Potential Role of Global Factors," *Journal of International Money and Finance* 26, pp. 924–947.

Marston, Richard C., 1990, "Pricing-to-Market in Japanese Manufacturing," *Journal of International Economics* 29, pp. 217–236.

_____, 2001, "The Effects of Industry Structure on Economic Exposure," *Journal of International Money and Finance* 20, pp. 149–164.

Nakamura, Emi, and Jón Steinsson, 2009, "Lost in Transit: Product Replacement Bias and Pricing to Market," manuscript, Columbia University.

The Economist, July 14, 2001, "A Different Kind of Package Holiday," U.S. edition, www.economist.com/node/693553.

Chapter 10

Exchange Rate Determination and Forecasting

*D*uring January 2006, the value of the dollar in terms of the Japanese yen hovered around ¥117.00/$. On February 7, 2011, it was ¥82.38/$. In 5 years, the dollar lost about 30% of its value relative to the yen. What drives such extraordinary changes in relative currency valuations, and can we predict their direction and magnitude? On the one hand, the answer must be yes because financial institutions devote substantial resources to producing forecasts for their clients, and forecasting firms successfully market currency forecasts. However, the answer may be no because economic models often fail to explain exchange rate movements after the fact.

Corporations use currency forecasts in a variety of contexts: quantifying foreign exchange risk, setting prices for their products in foreign markets, valuing foreign projects, developing international operational strategies, and managing working capital. International portfolio managers use exchange rate forecasts to evaluate the desirability of investing in particular foreign equity and bond markets and whether to hedge the associated currency risks.

Should managers purchase currency forecasts? If markets are relatively efficient, it should be difficult to produce better short-term forecasts than forward exchange rates portend or better long-term forecasts than uncovered interest rate parity predicts. Yet, we saw evidence in Chapter 7 that these parity conditions do not always hold, especially in the short run. Therefore, currency forecasts are potentially valuable. This motivates our discussion of the two essential techniques that are used to forecast exchange rates: fundamental analysis and technical analysis. Because of the dramatic currency crises in a number of developing countries with pegged systems in the 1990s, forecasts in these systems are of special interest, and we discuss them separately.

10.1 PARITY CONDITIONS AND EXCHANGE RATE FORECASTS

The covered interest rate parity (CIRP) relationship, discussed in Chapter 6, links forward rates, spot rates, and interest rate differentials. Uncovered interest rate parity (UIRP), discussed in Chapter 7, which is sometimes referred to as the *international Fisher relationship* (named for the eminent American economist Irving Fisher), links expected exchange rate changes and interest rate differentials, whereas the unbiasedness hypothesis links forward rates and expected future exchange rates. Purchasing power parity (PPP), discussed in Chapter 8, provides a link between inflation rates and rates of change of exchange rates. To close the loop between expected future exchange rate changes, forward rates, interest rates, and rates of inflation, we need another well-known relationship: the *Fisher hypothesis*. After discussing the Fisher hypothesis, we demonstrate how all the parity conditions together lead to a world in which currency forecasting is not necessary. This hypothetical world constitutes an interesting benchmark for judging the potential value of currency forecasts.

The Fisher Hypothesis

Interest Rates and Inflation

The interest rates we have discussed thus far are nominal interest rates. That is, they promise a nominal or money rate of return. For example, if the 1-year dollar interest rate is 3%, you receive $1.03 in 1 year for every dollar you deposit today. Fisher (1930) noted that nominal interest rates should reflect expectations of the rate of inflation. This is easy to understand.

Your happiness with the 3% return will depend on how prices evolve over the year. If prices increase by less than 3%, the purchasing power of your $1.03 is greater than the purchasing power of your $1.00 today. You experience a positive real return. Conversely, if prices increase by more than 3%, your purchasing power is lower. You realize a negative real return. Thus, if you expect prices to increase by more than 3% over the course of the year, you are reluctant to accept a 3% deposit rate because the 3% return is insufficient to maintain the purchasing power of the money you are lending.

Recall from Chapter 8 that if $P(t)$ denotes the U.S. price level at time t, $\dfrac{\$1}{P(t)}$ is the purchasing power of 1 dollar. Inflation, the rate of increase of the price level, drives down the purchasing power of the money. Lending money to receive future nominal interest exposes the lender to the risk of loss of purchasing power during the time of the loan because of inflation.

Real Rates of Return

As a lender, you care about the real return on your investment, which is the return that measures your increase in purchasing power between two periods of time. If you invest $1, you sacrifice $\dfrac{\$1}{P(t)}$ real goods now. But in 1 year, you get back $\dfrac{1+i}{P(t+1)}$ in real goods, where i is the nominal rate of interest. We calculate the *ex post* real return, denoted by r^{ep}, by dividing the real amount you get back by the real amount that you invest:

$$1 + r^{ep} = \frac{\left(\dfrac{1+i}{P(t+1)}\right)}{\left(\dfrac{1}{P(t)}\right)} = \frac{(1+i)}{\left(\dfrac{P(t+1)}{P(t)}\right)} = \frac{1+i}{1+\pi} \tag{10.1}$$

where $P(t+1)/P(t)$ is 1 plus the rate of inflation between time t and $t+1$, $\pi(t+1)$. If we subtract 1 from each side of Equation (10.1), we have

$$r^{ep} = \frac{(1+i)}{(1+\pi)} - \frac{(1+\pi)}{(1+\pi)} = \frac{i-\pi}{1+\pi}$$

which is often approximated as

$$r^{ep} \approx i - \pi \tag{10.2}$$

Equation (10.2) states that the *ex post* real interest rate equals the nominal interest rate minus the actual rate of inflation.[1] Hence, if the nominal interest rate is 3% and the actual rate of inflation is 2%, the *ex post* real interest rate is 1%.

The Ex Ante *Real Interest Rate*

Because the inflation rate is uncertain at the time an investment is made, the real rate of return on a loan is uncertain. By taking the expected value of both sides of Equation (10.2), conditional on the information set at the time of the loan, we derive the lender's expected real rate of return, which is also called the **expected real interest rate**, or the *ex ante* real interest rate, which we denote r^e:

$$r^e = E_t[r^{ep}] = i(t) - E_t[\pi(t+1)] \tag{10.3}$$

If we rearrange the terms in Equation (10.3), we have

$$i(t) = r^e + E_t[\pi(t+1)] = r^e + \pi^e \tag{10.4}$$

where we define π^e as expected inflation, $E_t[\pi(t+1)]$.

Equation (10.4) states that the nominal interest rate is the sum of the expected real interest rate and the **expected rate of inflation**. This decomposition of the nominal interest rate is often referred to as the **Fisher hypothesis**, or the *Fisher equation*.

Example 10.1 The Expected Real Interest Rate in Mexico

Suppose the nominal interest rate in Mexico is 10%, and the expected rate of inflation in Mexico is 7%. What is the expected real rate of return in Mexico?

From Equation (10.3), we have

$$r^e = 10\% - 7\% = 3\%$$

By investing pesos at a nominal interest rate of 10% when the expected rate of inflation is 7%, the investor expects to earn a 3% real rate of return. The investor expects to have 3% more purchasing power over goods and services at the end of the year for every peso invested.

If expected real interest rates are similar across countries, countries with high expected inflation rates will have high nominal interest rates, and countries with low expected inflation rates will have low nominal interest rates. The real interest rate is important because it influences investment decisions. Firms borrow money and invest in projects only if the expected real rate of return on the investment is greater than the real interest rate.

The Fisher hypothesis is a reasonable approximation for thinking about a long-run link between inflation and interest rates. Exhibit 10.1 graphs average long-term government bond yields on the vertical axis versus average inflation rates on the horizontal axis for 16 countries between 1990 and 2010. As the Fisher hypothesis suggests, the relationship is clearly positive, and the slope of the regression line is insignificantly different from 1. That is, for each additional 1% of inflation, the nominal government bond yield is about 1% higher. Hence, for long-term averages, real interest rates appear to be equal across countries. The intercept on the vertical axis of 2.40% is also a reasonable estimate of the real interest rate. We discuss this graph in more detail later.

---

[1]There is no approximation in going from Equation (10.1) to Equation (10.2) if one uses continuously compounded interest rates and rates of inflation. See the appendix to Chapter 2 for a review of continuous compounding.

Exhibit 10.1 Average Long-Term Government
Bond Yields and Inflation Rates

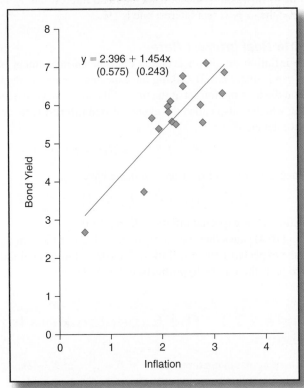

$y = 2.396 + 1.454x$
(0.575) (0.243)

Notes: The vertical axis measures average government bond yields
for 1990–2010. The horizontal axis measures the average annual
inflation rate over the same period. The diamonds represent 16
countries: Australia, Austria, Belgium, Canada, Denmark, France,
Germany, Ireland, Italy, Japan, the Netherlands, New Zealand, Sweden,
Switzerland, the United States, and the United Kingdom. The line
represents a regression of yield (y) on inflation (π). The standard
error of the estimate is between parentheses. Data are from the
International Monetary Fund's International Financial Statistics.

The International Parity Conditions

The covered interest rate parity (CIRP), uncovered interest rate parity (UIRP), and
purchasing power parity (PPP) relationships, together with the Fisher hypothesis, are
sometimes referred to as the **international parity conditions**. To review these conditions, consider the numeric example in Exhibit 10.2, which examines exchange rates,
interest rates, and expected inflation rates for the United Kingdom and Switzerland.
Exchange rates are measured as Swiss francs per British pound, CHF/GBP, and the horizon
is 1 year.

CIRP

At the bottom of Exhibit 10.2, the nominal interest differential is 2%. From covered interest
parity, we can relate the interest differential to the forward premium:

$$\text{Forward premium} = \frac{\text{Forward rate} - \text{Spot rate}}{\text{Spot rate}}$$

Exhibit 10.2 An Example of International Parity Conditions: The United Kingdom and Switzerland

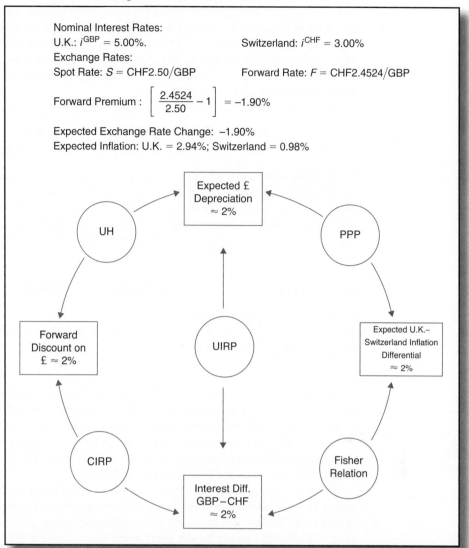

Nominal Interest Rates:
U.K.: $i^{GBP} = 5.00\%$.   Switzerland: $i^{CHF} = 3.00\%$
Exchange Rates:
Spot Rate: $S = CHF2.50/GBP$ Forward Rate: $F = CHF2.4524/GBP$

Forward Premium : $\left[\dfrac{2.4524}{2.50} - 1 \right] = -1.90\%$

Expected Exchange Rate Change: −1.90%
Expected Inflation: U.K. = 2.94%; Switzerland = 0.98%

Notes: UH = unbiasedness hypothesis; PPP = purchasing power parity; CIRP = covered interest rate parity; UIRP = uncovered interest rate parity (international Fisher relation).

The 1-year forward premium is −1.90%. Because the U.K. interest rate is higher, its currency is at a discount in the forward market to prevent arbitrage.

UIRP or Unbiasedness

If the forward rate is an unbiased predictor of the future spot rate, the forward discount on the pound means that the market expects the pound to depreciate by the amount of the forward discount, which brings us to the top of the diagram. We could have also moved to the top directly by observing that the higher pound interest rate means British investors in Swiss francs must expect a capital gain on holding Swiss francs to increase their expected return up to the higher pound return.

PPP

Relative PPP requires that the expected change in the exchange rate reflects the differential in inflation rates, so if the British pound is expected to weaken versus the Swiss franc, British inflation is expected to be higher than Swiss inflation by about 2%. This brings us to the right-hand side of Exhibit 10.2, where the inflation differential is 1.96% (also about 2%). (The small difference in percentage calculations arises because we are using inflation rates calculated in simple percentage terms. The percentage changes are identical if the computations use continuously compounded rates.)

To see this, remember from Chapter 8 that relative PPP predicts

$$\frac{S(t+1)}{S(t)} - 1 = \frac{1 + \pi(\text{SW})}{1 + \pi(\text{U.K.})} - 1 = \frac{\pi(\text{SW}) - \pi(\text{U.K.})}{1 + \pi(\text{U.K.})}$$

Because of the presence of U.K. inflation in the denominator, the inflation differential is slightly larger than the percentage rate of change of the exchange rate. Now we know that inflation is the fundamental reason for the higher British nominal interest rates observed in the first place. U.K. expected inflation is higher than Swiss expected inflation, which brings us back to the bottom of the exhibit if expected real interest rates are equal through the Fisher relationship.

Real Interest Rates and the Parity Conditions

Real Interest Rate Parity

What are the real interest rates in the United Kingdom and Switzerland? According to Equation (10.3), the real interest rate is

$$r^e = i - \pi^e$$

Plugging in the numbers for both the United Kingdom and Switzerland gives real interest rates of about 2% in both cases.[2] This is no coincidence. If the parity conditions all hold simultaneously, real interest rates are equal across countries. If uncovered interest rate parity and PPP hold, the nominal interest rate differential between the United Kingdom and Switzerland reflects only an expected inflation differential. Then, by rearranging terms, we find that the real return is the same in each country.

In a world where all the parity conditions hold, multinational business would be rather simple. International pricing would be easy because prices in foreign countries would move in line with domestic prices after converting currencies. The expected real cost of borrowing would be the same everywhere in the world. Finally, if a company wanted to know what the future exchange rate was likely to be—for example, to help quantify its transaction exposure—the best predictor for the future exchange would be the forward rate because the unbiasedness hypothesis holds. International investors would not need to worry about predicting currency values either. A higher nominal interest rate in one country would simply reflect the fact that the country's currency was expected to depreciate.

Testing Real Interest Rate Parity

Unfortunately, the world is not as simple as just described. From the empirical evidence discussed in previous chapters, we know that the international parity conditions, except CIRP, are best viewed as long-run relationships. In the short run, there are significant deviations from these conditions. Because PPP deviations are sizable and prolonged, identical nominal returns

---

[2]The small differences arise because Exhibit 10.2 does not make approximations so that $r^e = \frac{i - \pi^e}{1 + \pi^e}$.

represent very different real returns for investors in different countries. Our discussion of the forward bias in Chapter 7 implies that returns in different currencies can have different currency risk premiums. In the long run, we know that PPP holds better and that high interest rate currencies depreciate relative to low interest rate currencies. Hence, it would seem more likely that real interest rate parity holds in the long run. Real returns across countries can also differ because of political risks or the threat of capital controls, which prevent investors from taking advantage of higher returns in other countries. This is particularly true in developing countries.

Studies have found that real interest rate parity holds neither in the short nor the long run. Consider Exhibit 10.1, which at first blush seems largely consistent with real interest rate parity. The world interest rate is 2.40%, and if the slope of the regression line is actually 1, each percent of additional expected inflation implies an extra percent of nominal bond yield, keeping real interest rates the same across countries. However, the estimated slope coefficient is 1.45 instead of 1.00. This suggests that higher inflation countries have higher real interest rates. For example, if a country has an expected inflation rate of 3%, the regression line predicts a nominal bond yield of $2.40\% + 1.45 \times 3\% = 6.75\%$, and a real rate of $6.75\% - 3\% = 3.75\%$. Now, consider a country with an expected inflation rate of 5%. Following the same computations, we find that the country's real rate is 4.65%, almost 1% higher than the real rate of the low-inflation country.

Of course, real interest rate differentials between countries reflect differential risks, but they also offer multinational businesses opportunities—for example, opportunities to reduce costs of funds or to invest excess cash more profitably. Knowing the source of an observed real interest rate differential is important to making the right decisions. When the parity conditions break down, forecasting becomes important. The next section reviews the types of forecasting techniques managers use.

10.2 CURRENCY FORECASTING TECHNIQUES

While there may be as many exchange rate forecasting techniques as there are exchange rate forecasters, Exhibit 10.3 organizes them into meaningful categories. The parity conditions suggest the forward rate as a predictor. If no forward market exists for a particular currency, nominal interest rates and UIRP can be used to extract a market-based forecast. Other forecasting techniques do not rely directly on the predictions embodied in forward rates and interest rates and can be split into two main categories: *fundamental analysis* and *technical analysis*. We briefly describe these in turn and end this section with a discussion of how to evaluate the quality of a forecast. Sections 10.3 and 10.4 then provide more detail about these two forecasting techniques.

Fundamental Exchange Rate Forecasting

Some forecasters predict exchange rates using **fundamental analysis** typically based on formal economic models of exchange rate determination, which link exchange rates to macroeconomic fundamentals such as money supplies, inflation rates, productivity growth rates, and the current account. The models involve parameters that govern the relationship between the exchange rate and the fundamentals. For example, if the current account deficit as a percentage of gross domestic product (GDP) increases by $x\%$, the model predicts that the domestic currency will depreciate relative to the foreign currency by b multiplied by $x\%$. The parameter b has to be determined, and this is typically accomplished by estimating the relationship from the data using econometric techniques such as regression analysis. Alternatively, some forecasters simply examine economic information and use educated analysis

Exhibit 10.3 Categories of Exchange Rate Forecasting Techniques

to derive an exchange rate forecast based on their judgment of future macroeconomic relationships. Fundamental analysis is typically concerned with multiyear forecasts because the fundamental economic forces operate at longer horizons.

Exchange Rate Forecasting with Technical Analysis

Technical analysis is usually used for short-term forecasts. Technical analysts use only past exchange rate data, and perhaps some other financial data, such as the volume of currency trade, to predict future exchange rates. Consequently, all the information about the future exchange rate is assumed to be present in past trading behavior and past exchange rate trends.

The original technical analysts were called *chartists* because they studied graphs of past exchange rates. Now, technical analysis refers to the use of any type of financial data to predict future exchange rates outside the confines of a fundamental model. Some technical analysts employ sophisticated econometric techniques to discover what they hope are predictable patterns in exchange rates. Therefore, we distinguish between chartists and *statistical technical analysts*.

Why Technical Analysis Might Work

Technical analysis is often derided in academic circles because it is not based on any economic theory and is thought to be inconsistent with efficient markets. Nevertheless, it is important to discuss technical analysis for four reasons.

First, forex dealers and currency fund managers make extensive use of technical analysis (see, for example, Gehrig and Menkhoff, 2006). Second, fundamental analysis has some inherent problems. Fundamental forecasters must pick the right exchange rate model. Then, the model's fundamental variables must be forecast. Moreover, the macroeconomic inputs to fundamental analysis are not all available at frequent intervals. Some variables are measured weekly, some monthly, and some only quarterly or even annually, and the measurements are often poor (recall the discussion of the statistical discrepancy in the balance of payments in Chapter 4) and are frequently subject to revision. The data used by technical analysts are of much higher quality and are available much more frequently, often on a daily or even intra-daily basis.

The third reason technical analysis may have forecasting ability is that the forward rate may not be an unbiased predictor of the future spot rate, even in an efficient market. Chapter 7 argues that rational risk premiums can separate forward rates from expected future spot rates.

Moreover, we see differences of opinion on the future direction of exchange rates, even among relatively specialized foreign exchange experts. Consequently, it is conceivable that technical analysis might uncover a predictable component in exchange rate changes not present in forward rates.

A fourth reason technical analysis may have value is that if a sufficiently large segment of the trading world is using technical analysis, demands and supplies to trade currencies will be buffeted by these traders even if they are irrational. A truly rational trader would therefore need to know technical analysis to understand why irrational traders are doing what they are doing.

Evaluating Forecasts

What constitutes a good forecast? In general, it depends on how the forecast will be used. Ultimately, exchange rate forecasts are "good" when they lead to "good" decisions. Next, we distinguish three dimensions of the forecast quality.

Accuracy

One dimension is the accuracy of the forecast. Suppose that today is time t, and we are forecasting over a k-period horizon (say k months). Let $S(t+k)$ be the actual exchange rate at time $t+k$, and let $\hat{S}(t+k)$ be the forecast at time t. The closer $\hat{S}(t+k)$ is to $S(t+k)$, the more accurate the forecast, and the smaller the forecast error:

$$e(t+k) = S(t+k) - \hat{S}(t+k)$$

Of course, we cannot judge a forecaster by just one forecast because he or she may have just been lucky. Instead, we need a substantial record of forecasts and realizations to allow statistical analysis. We cannot judge the accuracy of the forecasting record by simply taking the average forecast error because huge errors with opposite signs could end up with a small average error.

The two summary measures most frequently used to judge accuracy of forecasts are the **mean absolute error (MAE)** and the **root mean squared error (RMSE)**:

$$\text{MAE} = \frac{1}{T}\sum_{t=1}^{T} |e(t+k)|$$

$$\text{RMSE} = \sqrt{\frac{1}{T}\sum_{t=1}^{T} e(t+k)^2}$$

where T is the total number of available observations. The MAE is the average of the absolute values of the forecast errors. The RMSE is the square root of the average squared forecast errors. It has the same units as the standard deviation of exchange rate changes.

In comparing forecasts, a number of obvious benchmarks come to mind. For example, we could simply replace the forecast with the current exchange rate or with the current forward rate for maturity k. We hope that a forecaster's MAE or RMSE is smaller than such simple forecasts. If it weren't, why would we need to pay money for it?

Forecast accuracy is economically meaningful in a number of settings. For example, suppose Liberty Shipping, a U.S. firm, is evaluating a foreign investment project that will generate foreign currency profits. Liberty Shipping must forecast the future dollar cash flows generated by the project by converting future foreign currency profits into future dollars that will be discounted at an appropriate discount rate to determine whether the investment project will be profitable. Suppose that its calculations lead Liberty Shipping to accept the project and make the investment. Then, however, a currency crisis erupts in the country in which Liberty Shipping invested, and the currency depreciates significantly. If local competition prevents Liberty Shipping from passing through the currency loss in the form of higher local prices, the currency crisis will depress the company's dollar earnings, and the investment decision will have been a disaster. Here accuracy matters. A more accurate assessment of the future would have led Liberty Shipping to forgo the investment.

Even if the foreign currency appreciates after the investment is made and the investment decision looks good, forecasting accuracy still matters. A better exchange rate forecast might have caused the firm to invest more in the foreign country. Pricing decisions and long-term strategic planning are other examples in which the accuracy of exchange rate forecasts matters a great deal. Note that in many of these cases, firms may be more concerned with predicting the real exchange rate rather than the nominal exchange rate.

Being on the Right Side of the Forward Rate

There are situations in which accuracy may not be the most relevant quality measure. Simply being on the right side of the forward rate is enough. If the forecast relative to the forward rate suggests a long position in the forward market, and the future exchange rate is indeed above the forward rate, the forecast was on the right side of the forward rate. Conversely, if the forecast relative to the forward rate suggests a short position in the forward market, and the future exchange rate is below the forward rate, the forecast was not on the right side of the forward rate. We illustrate this with an example.

Example 10.2   Currency Forecasts at Fancy Foods

Chapter 3 introduced the situation of Fancy Foods, which owes Porky Pies £1,000,000 in 90 days. The current exchange rate is $1.50/£, and the forward rate is $1.53/£. To decide whether to hedge its currency exposure, suppose Fancy Foods can enlist the services of two forecasting companies, Forexia and Trompe Le Monde. Forexia predicts that the exchange rate will be $1.65/£, whereas Trompe Le Monde predicts that the exchange rate will be $1.51/£. After 90 days, the exchange rate turns out to be $1.55/£. Which forecast is more accurate? Which forecast is more economically useful to Fancy Foods?

To find out, let's examine how Fancy Foods uses forecasts in its hedging decision. Suppose Fancy Foods hedges when the forecast of the future spot rate is above the forward rate, and it does not hedge when the forecast is less than the forward rate because it thinks the dollar cost of the pounds will be lower than if it uses the forward rate. The following table summarizes the situation:

	Forexia	Trompe Le Monde
Forecast	$1.65/£	$1.51/£
Forecast Relative to Forward Rate (forward rate: £1.53/$)	Higher	Lower
Decision	Hedge	Do not hedge
Forecast Error	−$0.10/£	$0.04/£
Ex Post Cost Relative to Forward Rate	Zero	Positive

So, although Trompe Le Monde's forecast turns out to be more accurate, it leads Fancy Foods not to hedge because it predicts an exchange rate lower than the forward rate. Because the pound actually appreciates to a level above the forward rate, not hedging proves costly. Not hedging would cost Fancy Foods £1,000,000 × $(1.55 − 1.53)/£ = $20,000. The prediction of Forexia, which is quite inaccurate, would lead Fancy Foods to hedge, which *ex post* leads to a lower pound cost than if the pounds had to be purchased at the future spot rate.

Example 10.2 shows that it is often more important to be on the correct side of the forward rate than to be accurate. It is also important to realize that the relevant benchmark is the forward rate, not the current spot rate, because the forward rate is the currently available rate for future transactions.

To evaluate a forecasting record, the percentage of times the forecaster was on the correct side of the forward rate seems to be a natural indicator. Because just flipping a coin could lead to a 50% correct record, this "percentage correct signals" statistic should be strictly larger than 50% for the forecaster's services to add value to your decision-making process. We can view this as a test of market timing ability.[3]

Profitability

Technical analysts assert that the percentage-correct-signals metric does not accurately measure how well they perform. They claim that they can give valuable advice and should not be required to be right more than 50% of the time. This is true because the overall size of the profits and losses a company earns as a result of the advice matters, too. A technical forecaster's performance may be characterized by a relatively small number of successful forecasts in which large profits are made and a relatively large number of incorrect predictions in which small losses are incurred. As long as you do not lose too much money when you are wrong and you make a lot of money when you are right, you can be wrong more than 50% of the time and still be valuable.

To evaluate forecasters on this basis, we can simply compute the profits or losses made based on a forecaster's advice and compare those returns to the returns on alternative investments that do not require forecasts. Again, it is important to determine that the profits are not simply due to chance. We illustrate this later in the chapter. We are now ready to examine fundamental and technical forecasts in more detail.

10.3 FUNDAMENTAL EXCHANGE RATE FORECASTING

This section examines forecasting techniques that rely on models of exchange rate determination and fundamental economic factors. From the parity conditions, we know that exchange rates are likely to be influenced by interest differentials, relative price levels, and inflation rates. Interest rates and the current account are the most talked-about fundamental factors, judging from countless articles in the financial press.

We first review the poor performance of fundamental models of exchange rates in predicting future exchange rates. This poor performance is not surprising from the perspective of two main approaches to exchange rate determination: the **asset market approach** and an equilibrium

---

[3]Henriksson and Merton (1981) developed market timing tests for stock market returns, where forecasters predict the stock market to go up or down. However, stock returns are expected to be positive, so always predicting the market to go up is likely to lead to a better-than-50%-correct forecasting record. Similarly, if it rains on 80% of the days, a weather forecaster has an 80% success rate by always forecasting rain. Analogously, if during the period that you record the forecasting performance, the forward rate is consistently below the spot rate, a forecaster who ends up with a 100% correct forecasting record may have superior forecasting knowledge or may have simply failed to change his forecast, and this laziness led to the perfect record. Because the market direction did not change, there is little information on timing the market in this sample. Henriksson and Merton show how to correct for such a bias. Basically, you should add the proportion of correct forecasts conditional on the eventual spot rate being above the forward rate to the proportion of correct forecasts conditional on the eventual spot rate being below the forward rate. If the sum of these proportions is higher than 1, there is evidence of market timing ability. Indeed, our lazy forecaster, who just got lucky, would end up with a score of 1.0 and would not be dubbed a forecasting genius with such a test.

model linking current accounts, real exchange rates, and interest rates. We discuss each in turn. We also discuss an increasingly popular method to forecast exchange rates over longer horizons, building on PPP.

Forecasting Performance of Fundamental Exchange Rate Models

Forecasting Models and Benchmarks

In a famous 1983 article, Meese and Rogoff analyze the forecasting power of fundamental models of exchange rate determination. The models link the current spot rate to relative money supplies, interest differentials, relative industrial production, inflation differentials, and the difference in cumulated trade balances, which represents the level of net foreign assets. They estimate the parameters of these models and use them to predict future exchange rate values. Because the fundamental information is not known when the forecast is made, these predictions would normally necessitate forecasting the fundamentals first, so that the forecast is truly "out of sample." However, Meese and Rogoff use actual values for the future fundamentals combined with the parameters to predict the exchange rate. This approach gives the fundamental models an advantage relative to the other models considered, which use only current information to predict future exchange rates. As benchmarks, they considered several alternative models, including the random walk $[\hat{S}(t{+}k) = S(t)]$, where, again, the caret symbol denotes a forecast today for horizon k, the unbiasedness hypothesis $[\hat{S}(t{+}k) = F(t, k)]$, and several statistical models that link the current exchange rate to past exchange rates and past values of other variables.

Computing the root mean squared error (RMSE) for the predictions at various horizons, Meese and Rogoff found that the random walk model beat all the other models in the majority of the cases considered. Particularly surprising was that the fundamental models did not even perform better at longer horizons. This result has been confirmed by a large number of researchers over the years and continues to puzzle international economists (see Rogoff, 2009).

Recent research by Meese and Prins (2011) points to the importance of order flow in the short-run determination of exchange rates and market fundamentals in the longer run. They find that market fundamentals do a poor job of explaining the time series movements of exchange rates, especially at short horizons, whereas fundamentals perform better cross-sectionally and at longer horizons.

Given the poor performance of fundamental models in forecasting exchange rates, we provide only a cursory overview of the major models. However, fundamental models still provide useful insights, and, as we will see, it may not be so surprising that they are beaten by a random walk model in forecasting exchange rates.

The Asset Market Approach to Exchange Rate Determination

UIRP and the Exchange Rate

Let's revisit the theory of Chapter 7 to see what it has to say about the *level* of the exchange rate:

$$S(t) = \frac{1 + i^*(t)}{1 + i(t)} E_t[S(t{+}1)] \tag{10.5}$$

where the exchange rate is expressed in domestic currency per foreign currency, i^* is the foreign interest rate, and i is the domestic interest rate. Everything else equal, an increase in the domestic (foreign) interest rate lowers (increases) $S(t)$; that is, the domestic currency appreciates (depreciates). However, "everything else equal" involves keeping expected values of the future exchange rate constant. Of course, changes in interest rates likely also affect exchange rate expectations. More intuition can be gained rewriting Equation (10.5) as

$$\ln[S(t)] = i^*(t) - i(t) + E_t[\ln[S(t+1)]] \tag{10.6}$$

where $\ln[S(t)]$ is the logarithm of the level of the exchange rate. This equation uses the continuously compounded form of uncovered interest rate parity.[4] Equation (10.6) also will determine the exchange rate next period, and so on into the future, which suggests that not only current but also expected future values of interest rates may affect the current exchange rate.

The Exchange Rate as an Asset Price

Just as the equity value of a firm is the expected discounted value of all future cash flows accruing to the firm's shareholders, the exchange rate is easily linked to current and future fundamentals. The asset market approach to exchange rate determination recognizes that the exchange rate is the relative price of two monies, and it notes that monies are assets, which makes the exchange rate an asset price. Hence, exchange rates should fluctuate quite randomly, and the value of an exchange rate of, say, dollars per euro should be determined by people's willingness to hold the outstanding supplies of dollar-denominated and euro-denominated assets. These demands, in turn, depend on the expectations of the future values of these assets.

To capture this idea, we view the exchange rate as a weighted average of the current fundamental and its expected future value. The equity price of a stock can also be thought of as the value of the current cash flow (the dividend) and the discounted expected value of the future equity price, the price at which you can sell the stock in the future.

$$\ln[S(t)] = (1 - a)\,\text{fund}(t) + aE_t[\ln[S(t+1)]] \tag{10.7}$$

In Equation (10.7), fund(t) is the generic name we use to indicate the value of market fundamentals at time t, and the coefficient a is a discount factor that is less than 1 but may be very near 1.

Equation (10.7) states that the exchange rate depends on current fundamentals and on what people think the exchange rate will be in the next period. If we iterate Equation (10.7) one step forward to solve for $\ln[S(t+1)]$ and plug the result back into that equation, we obtain the following:

$$\ln[S(t)] = (1 - a)\,\text{fund}(t) + aE_t[(1 - a)\,\text{fund}(t+1) + aE_{t+1}[\ln[S(t+2)]]] \tag{10.8}$$

Because expectations at time t of expectations at some future time reduce to expectations at time t, as in $E_t[E_{t+1}[\ln[S(t+2)]]] = E_t[\ln[S(t+2)]]$, iterating Equation (10.8) forward leads to:[5]

$$\ln[S(t)] = (1 - a)\,\text{fund}(t) + (1 - a)\sum_{j=1}^{\infty} a^j E_t[\text{fund}(t+j)] \tag{10.9}$$

Hence, the current exchange rate embeds all information about current and expected future fundamentals, and the exchange rate changes as the fundamentals change or as we get news about future fundamentals. Note that even a small change in current fundamentals may induce a large change in the exchange rate if it also changes the expected value of all future

---

[4]To derive this equation, simply go back to Chapter 6, Equation (6.5), and replace $\ln[F]$ by $E_t[\ln[S(t+1)]]$.

[5]This property of expectations is known as the *law of iterated expectations*, and it follows from the fact that we necessarily have less information now (at time t) than we will have in the future (at time $t+1$).

fundamentals. Thus the value of the exchange rate may move a lot in response to what seems to be a small piece of news.

The Monetary Approach

While many exchange rate models fit this framework, the best-known asset market model is the monetary exchange rate model. In this model, the menu of assets is fairly simple. There are distinct demands for non-interest-bearing domestic and foreign currencies. The demand for nominal money arises from the demand for **real money balances**. That is, people are only concerned with the real value of the nominal money they are holding.

The fundamentals in this model are a simple function of relative money supplies and relative real income levels in the two countries. The model implies that the domestic currency weakens if the domestic money supply increases today or if news arrives that leads people to believe that the future domestic money supply will increase. In contrast, the domestic currency strengthens if the foreign money supply increases today or if news arrives that causes people to think that foreign money supplies will be higher in the future. These effects arise directly from the influence an increased supply of money has on prices with the demand for money held constant. Higher prices in turn weaken the currency because PPP is assumed to hold. The domestic currency also weakens if domestic real income falls, if foreign real income rises, or if news arrives that causes people to expect lower domestic real growth or faster foreign real growth. Real income positively affects the demand for real money balances because the higher the real income, the greater the number of monetary transactions required to support the real transactions of an economy. Hence, a decrease in real income lowers the demand for real balances and given a fixed money supply, causes an increase in prices to lower the *real* money supply. The increase in prices therefore weakens the currency through the PPP channel.

Sticky Prices and Overshooting

The predictions of the monetary model are quite reasonable at long horizons, but as a short-run theory, the monetary model's reliance on PPP is questionable. An important extension of the monetary model relaxes the assumption of PPP, assuming that nominal prices of goods are "sticky" and do not adjust immediately to an increase in the money supply or to other shocks that hit the economy (see Dornbusch, 1976). Models with sticky prices predict more volatility in nominal and real exchange rates than occurs in the monetary model because asset prices, including the exchange rate, do all of the immediate adjusting to the shocks that hit the economy, whereas nominal goods prices only adjust slowly over time.

Consider how the economy responds to a permanent increase in the money supply in such a model. According to the monetary model, in the long run, an increase in the money supply causes a depreciation of the domestic currency by the same percentage that the money supply increases. What happens in the short run? Because asset prices are flexible, the asset markets will remain in equilibrium. Now, we know that an increase in the nominal money supply with goods prices fixed must increase the supply of real balances. For the money market to remain in equilibrium, the demand for real balances must increase. This can be accomplished by an increase in real income, but real income is unlikely to adjust quickly. Another channel is a decrease in the nominal interest. A lower interest rate positively affects the demand for money because it decreases the opportunity cost of holding real money balances.

Thus, the increase in the money supply causes the domestic interest rate to fall (and fall below the foreign interest rate). Because the monetary exchange rate model also assumes uncovered interest rate parity, the domestic currency must be expected to appreciate when the domestic interest rate is less than the foreign interest rate. But if people are rational, they know that, in the long run, the domestic currency will be weaker than it was before the increase in the money supply. The only path for the exchange rate that allows for a long-run depreciation of the domestic currency and an expected appreciation in the short run is for the domestic currency to immediately weaken by more than it will weaken in the long run. Thus, the exchange rate overshoots its new equilibrium: The exchange rate (in domestic currency per unit of foreign currency) jumps up when the money supply is increased and subsequently falls over time toward its new higher equilibrium value.

Why the Random Walk Works

Engel and West (2005) point out that the random walk model outperforming fundamental models of the exchange rate may not necessarily imply that these models are false. While their arguments are sophisticated, Equation (10.7) hints at the main argument. If the discount factor is close to 1, the equation implies that $\ln[S(t)] \approx E_t[\ln(S(t+1))]$. But that is the random walk model! The authors argue that, in many practical cases, the discount factor is indeed close to 1 and that, moreover, the fundamentals themselves behave like random walks. Together, this implies that the current exchange rate adequately reflects the expected value of future fundamental values. However, for this to be true, the exchange rate should also predict future fundamental values. Engel et al. (2007) show that this is indeed the case. They also document that novel forecasting techniques that efficiently exploit the information across fundamentals in multiple countries predict exchange rates out of sample better than the random walk model. Finally, at longer horizons, such as 3 to 4 years in the future, fundamental models do have predictive power for exchange rates (see, for example, Mark, 1995).

News and Exchange Rates

One implication of Engel and West's interpretation of the performance of the monetary exchange rate model is that *exchange rate changes* are unpredictable, but they should still reflect news about fundamentals. If there is news about the money supply or real income, and it does not change the exchange rate in the required direction, this would be strong evidence against the fundamentals model. Several authors have used high-frequency data on exchange rates and macroeconomic announcements to investigate how exchange rates react to macroeconomic news (see Andersen et al., 2003, 2007; and Faust et al., 2007). The studies are careful to measure the *announcement news* by subtracting from the reported number an estimate of its expected value according to a survey by Money Market Services (MMS). Every week, MMS records forecasts by some 40 money managers at financial institutions regarding all macroeconomic indicators. One prediction of the monetary exchange rate model is borne out in the data. The dollar indeed appreciates relative to positive news about U.S. real income, as revealed by news about U.S. GDP, retail sales, and construction spending. Currency markets also prove efficient in that the news is incorporated into prices quickly (typically in less than 15 minutes). However, the studies reveal a somewhat strange reaction to news about inflation and increases in the money supply: The dollar appreciates, whereas it should depreciate according to the monetary exchange rate model. One interpretation is that the appreciation reflects anticipation of an aggressive monetary policy response to the higher inflation; that is, if monetary policy sharply raises interest rates in response to positive inflation news, the exchange rate should indeed be expected to appreciate (see Clarida and Waldman, 2008).

The Real Exchange Rate, the Real Interest Rate Differential, and the Current Account

The popular press often mentions that high real interest rates go hand in hand with "strong" real exchange rates. We first show that such a relationship is implied by a real version of uncovered interest rate parity and "mean-reverting" real exchange rates. We also assess whether the relationship holds up empirically. The popular press also often mentions a strong link between the current account and exchange rates, suggesting that a current account deficit should put downward pressure on the exchange rate. However, even casual observation suggests that this link does not always hold. After all, the United States has run a current account deficit for a very long time and has had spells during which the dollar appreciated strongly even while the current account worsened. We briefly describe an equilibrium model that simultaneously determines the level of the (real) exchange rate and the current account balance.

Converting UIRP to Real Terms

To see why the level of the real exchange rate should be related to the differential between the real interest rates on different currencies, we need to convert uncovered interest rate parity from a relationship between nominal interest rates and nominal rates of depreciation into a relationship between real interest rates and expected real rates of depreciation. To do so, let's rearrange Equation (10.6) and subtract the expected inflation differential between the home and foreign countries, $E_t[\pi(t+1) - \pi^*(t+1)]$, from both sides of the uncovered interest rate parity expression:

$$i(t) - E_t[\pi(t+1)] - (i^*(t) - E_t[\pi^*(t+1)])$$
$$= E_t[\ln[S(t+1)]] - \ln[S(t)] - E_t[\pi(t+1) - \pi^*(t+1)]$$

Note that the inflation rates should be continuously compounded, as we are working with logarithmic exchange rates. Of course, $\ln[S(t+1)] - \ln[S(t)]$ will be close in practice to the simple percentage change in the exchange rate, which we usually define as $s(t+1)$.

From the definitions of the real interest rate and of the rate of change of the real exchange rate, this equation reduces to the following:

$$r^e(t) - r^{e*}(t) = E_t[\ln[RS(t+1)] - \ln[RS(t)]] \tag{10.10}$$

where $r^e(t)$ denotes the domestic real interest rate, $r^{e*}(t)$ denotes the foreign real interest rate, and $\ln[RS(t)]$ denotes the logarithm of the real exchange rate. Equation (10.10) indicates that when the foreign real interest rate is greater than the domestic real interest rate, the right-hand side of Equation (10.10) is negative and the domestic currency is expected to appreciate in real terms.

To link the expected real interest rate differential to the *level* of the real exchange rate instead of the expected rate of change of the real exchange rate, we must explain the idea of mean reversion.

Mean Reversion

A mean-reverting process is always expected to move back or be pulled toward its unconditional mean. A random walk is a good example of a process that is *not* mean reverting. Whether the exchange rate is unusually high or low does not matter in forecasting future exchange rates; your best predictor remains the current exchange rate. In a mean-reverting process, whether the current exchange rate is above or below the long-run mean is what drives the direction of the forecast. When you are above the mean, you should be expected to be pulled back toward the mean, so the forecast of the expected exchange rate change should be *negative*. When you are experiencing unusually low real exchange rates, you should expect to be pulled toward the mean, so your forecast of the change in the real exchange rate should be positive. Let's use $\overline{RS}$ as our estimate of the long-run mean for the logarithm of the real exchange rate. This could be the long-run historical average, but may also be implied by a theoretical model. The idea of mean reversion implies

$$E_t[\ln[RS(t+1)] - \ln[RS(t)]] = \kappa[\ln(RS(t) - \overline{RS}] \tag{10.11}$$

and κ is a negative number. Substituting Equation (10.10) into Equation (10.11) gives

$$r^e(t) - r^{e*}(t) = \kappa[\ln[RS(t)] - \overline{RS}] \tag{10.12}$$

Equation (10.12) indicates that when the real exchange rate is above its long-run equilibrium—that is, when $\left[\ln[RS(t)] - \overline{RS}\right] > 0$ and the domestic currency is weak (recall that the exchange rate is expressed in domestic currency per foreign currency)—the real interest rate in the home country is smaller than the real interest rate in the foreign country because κ is negative. Hence, we have demonstrated that when the dollar is weak in real terms relative to foreign currencies, the real interest rate on dollar assets should be below the real interest rate on the foreign currency assets. Conversely, when real interest rates in the United States are relatively high, the dollar should be strong in real terms and expected to depreciate.

Empirical Evidence

Academic researchers who have examined the relationship between the real value of the dollar and the real interest rate differential have found the relationship to be weak.[6] In Exhibit 10.4, we look at recent evidence for the dollar from 1992 to 2010. The solid line in Exhibit 10.4 represents an equally weighted real exchange rate of the dollar relative to 15 major currencies expressed as foreign currency per dollar. Hence, increases (decreases) in the real exchange rate in Exhibit 10.4 represent real appreciations (depreciations) of the dollar relative to foreign currencies. The dotted line in Exhibit 10.4 represents the U.S. real interest rate defined from long-term bond yields minus an equally weighted average of the real interest rates on the other 15 countries' long-term bonds. Our estimate for expected inflation is simply current annual inflation.

It is apparent from Exhibit 10.4 that when the U.S. real interest rate seems relatively high compared to foreign real interest rates, the dollar is relatively strong in real terms. Also, conversely, when the U.S. real interest rate differential is relatively low, the dollar is relatively weak. The correlation between the two time series is 0.70.

Exhibit 10.4 The Real Exchange Rate and the Real Interest Differential

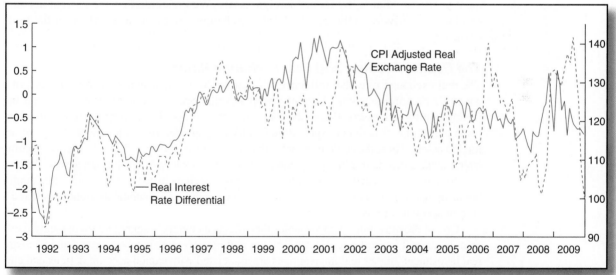

Notes: The solid line is the real exchange rate calculated as an equally weighted average of the real exchange rates of 15 currencies versus the U.S. dollar using consumer price indexes (CPIs) as the price levels. The dotted line is the U.S. real interest rate minus the equally weighted average real interests of the 15 countries. The countries are Australia, Austria, Belgium, Canada, Denmark, France, Germany, Ireland, Italy, Japan, the Netherlands, New Zealand, Sweden, Switzerland, and the United Kingdom. Data are from the International Monetary Fund's International Financial Statistics.

[6]For example, Meese and Rogoff (1988) and Edison and Pauls (1993) perform various statistical tests that are designed to find the relation between real exchange rates and the real interest rate differential. Each pair of authors concludes that the relation is very weak. Baxter (1994) finds statistical support for a long-run relation but not a short-run relation between the level of the real exchange rates and real interest rate differentials. The more recent evidence remains mixed; see, for instance, Chakrabarti (2006), who finds no link, and Sollis and Wohar (2006), who do find a link.

The Real Exchange Rate and the Balance of Payments

Now that we have successfully linked real interest rate differentials and the level of the real exchange rate, albeit more in the long run than the short run, we are in a position to discuss how other important market fundamentals help to simultaneously determine the real exchange rate and the current account of the balance of payments. Recall from Chapter 4 that the balance of payments is an identity in which the sum of the current account and the capital account must be zero. Hence, the value of the current account surplus or deficit equals the value of the capital account deficit or surplus, respectively. The real exchange rate and other variables adjust to ensure that the balance of payments balances. Hence, economic shocks to the accounts of the balance of payments affect the real exchange rate.

These shocks may come from the "real" side of the balance of payments, the trade balance, which records exports and imports, and from the "financial" side of the balance of payments, the capital account, which records purchases and sales of assets. Models of the real exchange rate recognize that real exchange rates affect these two parts of the balance of payments differently, as we now discuss in detail.[7]

The Trade Balance and Real Exchange Rates

When currencies strengthen in real terms, foreign goods become less expensive than domestic goods. Hence, a real appreciation is typically associated with a deterioration of the trade balance—that is, a rise of imports relative to exports. Conversely, a real depreciation of a country's currency enhances a country's competitiveness in world markets and improves the trade balance. In this case, exports typically increase relative to imports.

Remember that the current account of the balance of payments is the trade balance plus the flows of income that are generated by a country's net international investment position—that is, by its net foreign assets. We conclude that the current account is related negatively to the country's real exchange rate through its effect on the trade balance.

The Capital Account and Real Exchange Rates

The real exchange rate also influences the capital account, which measures changes in a country's net foreign assets. A country with a capital account deficit (surplus) is acquiring (losing) net foreign assets. Remember, also, that the excess of a country's gross national income over its gross national expenditure is related by an identity to the rate of change of net foreign assets. Thus, the economic forces that determine a country's desired excess of income over expenditures determine the country's acquisition or loss of net foreign assets. When a country's income exceeds its expenditures, or when savings exceeds investment, the country builds up net foreign assets. This requires that the country run a capital account deficit and a current account surplus.

One of the most important variables that affects a country's aggregate saving and investment is the real interest rate. Because higher real interest rates increase saving and decrease real investment, higher real interest rates are associated with capital account deficits and current account surpluses. From the previous section, we know that higher real interest rates are also associated with temporarily higher real exchange rates so that the currency can be expected to depreciate in real terms over time. This is also important for the demand for assets because it ensures that the perceived rate of return on assets denominated in different currencies is the same. Thus, we have another relationship between the real exchange rate and the balance of payments, but this time, real appreciations are associated with current account surpluses.

---

[7]An interesting formal model that simultaneously determines both the real exchange rate and the current account is the seminal analysis of Mussa (1984).

Equilibrium

Clearly, the current account and the real exchange rate are determined in a complex equilibrium. On the one hand, a real appreciation of the home currency causes imports to rise relative to exports, which lowers the current account surplus. On the other hand, a real appreciation of the home currency is associated with an expected real depreciation and thus with a higher real interest rate at home than abroad. The increase in the real interest rate decreases investment and increases saving, which creates a larger current account surplus. Just as supply and demand for any good force an equilibrium price and quantity, the opposing forces of the real exchange rate on the current account through a "goods" channel and a "savings and investment" channel lead to an equilibrium real exchange rate and an equilibrium current account balance. Hence, a particular current account balance may be consistent with various levels of the real exchange rate. Also, variables that shift demand between domestic and foreign goods and variables that affect savings and investment will cause the equilibrium to change.

Let's give a few examples of how certain economic variables can affect the equilibrium. An increase in government spending or a decrease in taxes that causes a budget deficit increases aggregate demand in the economy. The real interest rate increases to reduce private investment and encourage private saving. The domestic currency strengthens in real terms to allow increased purchases from abroad, and the current account turns to deficit. Thus, although an observer who only sees the high real interest rate might think the country is attracting capital, the capital account is actually in surplus.

These effects of government spending are consistent with the experience of the United States in the early 1980s. When President Reagan increased government spending and decreased taxes, real interest rates increased, the dollar experienced a massive real appreciation, and U.S. current account deficits grew to unprecedented levels.

How would new information that signals increases in future GDP affect the equilibrium? The news encourages firms to invest more today; likewise, consumers feel wealthier, so they want to consume more. To ration investment and consumption, it will again be the case that for every possible current account balance, a stronger domestic currency is required. In equilibrium, there will be a real appreciation and a current account deficit. The counterpart of the current account deficit is an inflow of foreign capital, which finances some of the investment and allows consumption to be higher than it otherwise could be. An example of this effect is the sustained strength of the dollar from 1995 through 2000 and the corresponding large U.S. current account deficits. These effects were thought to be the result of the attractive growth potential associated with the U.S. economy during the information technology boom.

PPP-Based Forecasts

In Chapter 8, we showed that purchasing power parity (PPP) is a reasonably good long-term model for the exchange rate. It is fair to say that PPP-based models, with some whistles and bells, are currently the most popular fundamental exchange rate models. Most brokers and banks have developed "fair value" exchange rate models. Typically, rather than relying completely on PPP, which predicts a real exchange rate of exactly 1, they attempt to adjust this value for various effects, such as the productivity trends described in Chapter 8. This is particularly important for developing countries, which otherwise may have persistently undervalued exchange rates. The models then use the deviation between the current value and the fair value of the exchange rate to predict the direction of change.

A number of academic studies have examined the forecasting prowess of related models. Jordà and Taylor (2009), for example, define the fundamental real exchange rate simply to be its long-run mean. Their evidence suggests that a 10% real overvaluation leads to a 2% monthly nominal depreciation prediction, everything else equal, and they find some evidence that the effect becomes stronger if the deviation becomes very large. Yet, when they use this information in a trading strategy, it performs poorly. However, they claim that using fundamental information in this way is helpful in reducing the tail risks of a carry strategy, even during the disastrous 2008 period. Clements et al. (2010) also find that PPP deviations have forecasting power for nominal exchange rates at medium to long horizons using the Big Mac index to define the theoretical real exchange rate. They also stress that many countries show very persistent over- or undervaluations, so that the theory must be adjusted for an expected long-run real exchange rate (also taken to be the historical average). They also demonstrate that when the real exchange rate reverts back to its long-run mean, it is primarily the nominal exchange rate that adjusts, not relative price levels. Wu and Hu (2009) find evidence that a PPP model adjusted for the Harrod-Balassa-Samuelson effect (productivity differences across countries, see Chapter 8) beats the random walk model in out-of-sample forecasts, especially at medium and long forecasting horizons.

10.4 TECHNICAL ANALYSIS

Whereas fundamental forecasters use macroeconomic data to forecast future exchange rates, technical analysts focus entirely on financial data. Next, we examine different technical forecasting methods in order of increasing sophistication: chartism, filter rules, regression analysis, and non-linear analysis. Active currency managers tend to primarily use technical analysis, and we end the section discussing their performance.

Pure Technical Analysis: Chartism

Chartists graphically record the actual trading history of an exchange rate and then try to infer possible future trends based on that information alone. Exhibit 10.5 graphs a daily exchange rate series, which we use to introduce some chartist terminology.

A **support level** is any chart formation in which the price has trouble falling below a particular level. A **resistance level** is any chart formation in which the price of an instrument has trouble rising above a particular level. Support levels and resistance levels define a trading range, which might be short term, medium term, or long term. When a trading range is broken, a sudden rise or fall in prices is expected and is called a **breakout**.

Chartists argue that a number of different patterns in data clearly signal future trends. One well-known pattern is the "head and shoulders," which indicates a pending fall in the exchange rate once "the neckline is pierced." Clearly, chartists do not believe in efficient financial markets but in markets that are driven by irrational whims that induce prolonged trends of rising or falling prices that are predictable.

Potentially Spurious Patterns

Because chartists rely on graphs to detect trends rather than on statistics, the patterns they identify may be spurious. For example, Exhibit 10.5 does not represent data corresponding to an actual exchange rate. The data are an artificial series based on the random walk model that we generated using a random number generator. The **random walk** model implies that $E_t[S(t+1)] = S(t)$. Thus, the model states that the best predictor for the future exchange rate is today's exchange rate, and the best prediction for the change in the exchange rate is zero.

Trading on a Random Walk

If exchange rates truly follow random walks, potentially profitable trading strategies nonetheless do present themselves. For example, whenever the forward rate does not equal the current spot rate, the forward rate would not be equal to the expected future spot rate, and you would have an incentive to speculate in the forward market. For example, if the euro is at a discount relative to the dollar $(F(t) < S(t))$, and if the $/€ exchange rate follows a random

Exhibit 10.5 Exchange Rate Patterns Described by Chartists

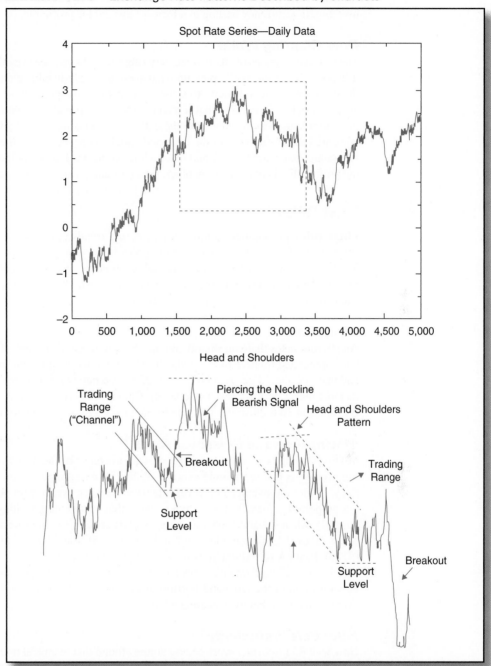

Notes: The top graph shows a daily exchange rate series (about 250 days per year) over a time span of 20 years. The graph appears to display some clear trends. The bottom panel investigates these short-term trends more closely by lifting the part in the box at the top and blowing it up. The apparent trends are then interpreted using chartist jargon.

walk, there is an expected profit to be made from buying euros forward. This is true because the future exchange rate at which you expect to sell euros for dollars in the future, which would be the current spot rate, is higher than the forward rate at which you can buy future euros with dollars today. Random walk behavior of exchange rates is consistent with the regression evidence from Chapter 7 regarding the unbiasedness hypothesis. That evidence suggests that investing in a currency trading at a forward discount is profitable.

Does Charting Work?

The recommendations of chartists are very subjective. As you see from the graph in Exhibit 10.5, it is possible for the eye to pick up what seem to be predictable patterns that are simply not there. Moreover, it is difficult to statistically analyze the predictions chartists make. For example, we must formalize what it means to see a head-and-shoulders pattern or another rule in a formula that can be applied to the data. One interesting study by Chang and Osler (1999) compared the profitability of the head-and-shoulders pattern with other trend-predicting rules. Although Chang and Osler found that trading on the head-and-shoulders patterns is profitable, the profitability is dominated by other, simpler trading rules, which we discuss next.

Filter Rules

Filter rules are popular methods for detecting trends in exchange rates. In general, filter rules are trading strategies based on the past history of an asset price that provide signals to an investor as to when to buy and sell currencies. We investigate two often-used techniques, which we describe from the perspective of a dollar-based investor who is examining exchange rates in dollars per foreign currency.

x% Rules

An $x\%$ rule states that you should go long (buy) in foreign currency after the foreign currency has appreciated relative to the dollar by $x\%$ above its most recent trough (or support level) and that you should go short (sell) in foreign currency whenever the currency falls $x\%$ below its most recent peak (or resistance level). Common $x\%$ rules are 1%, 2%, and so forth. Panel B of Exhibit 10.6 illustrates this rule for an upward trend of the currency.

Moving-Average Crossover Rules

Moving-average crossover rules use moving averages of the exchange rate. An n-day moving average is just the sample average of the last n trading days, including the current rate. A (y, z) moving-average crossover rule uses averages over a short period (y days) and over a long period (z days). The strategy states that you should go long (short) in the foreign currency when the short-term moving average crosses the long-term moving average from below (above). Common rules use 1 and 5 days (1, 5), 1 and 20 days (1, 20), and 5 and 20 days (5, 20). Panel A of Exhibit 10.6 shows how the short-run moving-average line, which in this case is the exchange rate itself because we are using a 1-day rule, more rapidly picks up the upward trend in the left-hand portion of the graph and cuts through the long-run moving-average line from below, signaling a buy.

Filter Rule Profitability

How well do filter rules work? Early studies found that technical trading rules generated statistically significant profits, which were unlikely to be generated by chance (see, for example, LeBaron, 1999). However, the sample period in these studies was dominated by long swings in the value of the dollar, which appreciated substantially in the first half of the 1980s before depreciating substantially in the second half of the 1980s.[8] Newer work by Pukthuanthong-Le et al. (2007) finds that the era of easy profits from simple trend-following strategies is over, at least for the major currencies. These authors show that the average profits generated by three moving-average rules for the Japanese yen, Deutsche mark, British pound, and Swiss franc over the 1975 to 1994 period are highly statistically significantly different from zero. The

---

[8]Engel and Hamilton (1990) developed a statistical model that clearly identifies these long swings.

Exhibit 10.6 How Filter Rules Work

Notes: In Panel A, the solid line represents the actual exchange rate, $S(t)$, which serves as the short-run moving average (SRMA). The dashed line is the long-run moving average (LRMA), averaging the current and past exchange rates. In Panel B, we graph only the exchange rate and illustrate the use of an $x\%$ filter rule.

profits range from 6.20% per year for the Swiss franc to 13.94% for the yen, and the standard error for these averages is about 2.7%. For most currencies, we can be very confident that these profits are different from zero.[9] The Canadian dollar generated positive but insignificant profits. Over the 1995 to 1999 period, the yen is the only currency with positive (and significant) profits, and for the 2000 to 2006 period, no currencies generate significantly positive profits. The authors interpret these results as indicating that foreign exchange markets have become more efficient over time, although it is puzzling that this process would have taken so long. They also demonstrate that over the 2000 to 2006 period, less liquid currencies, such as the New Zealand dollar, and emerging market currencies, such as the Brazilian real, the South African rand, and the Russian ruble, do generate significant profits when simple moving-average rules are followed. The Mexican peso generates positive but insignificant profits.

Regression Analysis

The evidence against the unbiasedness hypothesis presented in Chapter 7 suggests that interest rate differentials may contain information about future exchange rates that can be profitably exploited. Both academic analysts and foreign exchange professionals have explored

---

[9]To establish the confidence level formally as in Chapter 7, we divide the average by its standard error, square the resulting statistic, and check where this value lies in a chi-square distribution with 1 degree of freedom. For example, the statistic for the Swiss franc profits is $(6.20/2.7)^2 = 5.27$. Given a chi-square distribution with 1 degree of freedom, we have 97.8% confidence that the profits are different from zero.

regression models that link future exchange rate changes to interest rate differentials and other easily available information (such as past exchange rates) to predict future exchange. Essentially, the regression uses future returns on forward market positions [fmr(t); see Chapter 7] as the dependent variable and current information, such as the forward premium [$fp(t)$], and other variables as the independent variables. The fitted value of the regression can then be interpreted as the expected return on a long forward position.

In a trading strategy, the regression framework is used each trading period to find a value for the expected forward market return. If the expected return is positive (negative), the strategy goes long (short) in the foreign currency.

Non-Linear Models

Increased computing and mathematical and statistical sophistication have led researchers and practitioners to use more complex models to forecast exchange rates. Going beyond simple linear regression models as discussed earlier, researchers have, for example, tried to model the idea that as currencies move further from fundamentals (such as their PPP values) or as the volatility of the exchange rate increases, interest rate differentials may work less well as predictors of future exchange rate changes (see, respectively, Jordà and Taylor, 2009; and Clarida et al., 2009). Going beyond simply prespecifying the trading rules, more recent studies have applied sophisticated computer techniques, such as genetic algorithms, to search for optimal trading rules. Without going into details, these techniques apply a Darwinian-like, natural selection process to filter rules applied to past data that eventually breeds the "best" trading rules. (The *Point–Counterpoint* feature in this chapter discusses these kinds of "non-linear" forecasting techniques in more detail.) Neely et al. (1997) found that adhering to such trading rules was, indeed, profitable. In a subsequent study conducted in 2001, Neely and Weller found that additional information about central bank interventions further improved profitability.

POINT–COUNTERPOINT
Chaos, Genetic Engineering, and Neural Networks

"Come on, Ante. It will not be that bad," Freedy implored. Ante could not shake off the dreadful prospect of seeing Covis Estello at their high school reunion. Although the brothers acknowledged that Covis was smart, they had often made fun of him in high school, frequently calling him Mr. Super-Geek. Now, Ante was holding an article from the newspaper describing Mr. Estello's prowess in developing systems to trade currencies. Estello's expertise was apparently in the area of chaos theory and neural network systems, and he had reputedly "trained" different models using "genetic algorithms."

"I have no clue what he's doing, but he seems to be able to predict currency values, and he is clearly way richer than we will ever be," Ante lamented.

Freedy sighed and cautioned, "Come on, you know predicting currency values is incredibly difficult. I actually think he may just be lucky. Foreign exchange markets are very efficient. It's very hard to make abnormal returns in these markets. I think Covis used some mathematical hocus-pocus to convince investors to give him money, took some risks with other peoples' money, and got lucky. If I'm right, we'll soon see an article titled, 'The Rise and Fall of Estello.'"

"Well, that won't happen before our class reunion, and besides, to me his profits demonstrate that markets are totally inefficient," retorted Ante. "Clearly, super-nerd Covis must have devised some complex system to find trends in exchange rates, and now he is making oodles of money while we are studying efficient markets!"

At that moment, Suttle Trooth agitatedly rushed into the room. "Hey guys, did you read the article about Covis? What a success story! Come on, Ante, aren't you happy with our old friend's success?" Suttle smirked as he saw Ante frowning. Freedy immediately asked, "Please explain to us what all this math junk is about. If the foreign exchange market is efficient, how can Covis make so much money?"

Suttle relaxed and said, "Well, these are very complex issues. If markets are efficient, you're right that it would be quite difficult to make tons of money trading currencies. There certainly wouldn't be any easy trends to exploit. But even if we believe in efficient markets, the theories we studied in school make a number of doubtful or at least brave assumptions. First of all, speculating in currency markets exposes you to risk, and any profits may just be compensation for bearing currency risk. Remember, the risk premium can move around and change signs. If that is the case, predictable patterns in exchange rates, picked up by Estello's system, may just reflect time-varying risk premiums—that is, he goes long in currencies that are especially risky. If this is the case, it would not be surprising that one of these days he may suffer a serious loss.

"Second," continued Suttle, "economists often assume that all traders have the same information, act in their self-interest, and agree on the model generating exchange rates and the market fundamentals. We all know that this is not literally true. For example, some commercial banks use the superior information they have from the flow of forex orders they take from their multinational clients. This might help them get an idea of short-run patterns. In U.S. equity markets, such trading by brokers is called front-running, and it is illegal, but in the unregulated currency markets, anything goes. Other economic models have so-called 'noise traders' who trade based on reasons other than their private information. Smart people can exploit the 'noise traders' who systematically lose money. Noise traders could be acting irrationally, but they could also be a central bank that is not profit maximizing and therefore could be exploited.

"Work in psychology and economics now shows all sorts of behavioral biases that may lead to non-rational trading behavior that more rational traders could exploit. Furthermore, we know that exchange rates are influenced by monetary policy, and many relevant elements of policy making are really not publicly known. It is possible that some experts learn more about these policies or they can predict policy changes better than others. Finally, even if you are right in the long run, the market might turn against you in the short run. A trader must have sufficient capital to ride out a string of losses, or he may go broke before the profits start rolling in."

"But how exactly does Covis make money?" Freedy interjected.

Suttle answered, "Well, I do not know much about the mathematical models he uses except for the fact that they are inherently non-linear—that is, they involve cubic and quadratic functions and the like. A chaos system, which is one of the models mentioned in the article, is actually a deterministic system with no news or shocks at all. The future is thought to be a deterministic, non-linear function of the past. If you can figure out the relationship, you can perfectly predict the future. Although chaos theory seems to have some useful applications in biology and physics (it's apparently great in explaining fluid dynamics), I haven't seen any really useful applications in economics and finance.

"News is what drives asset prices! Moreover, chaos systems are extremely sensitive to initial conditions and yield vastly different predictions, depending on small perturbations to initial conditions. How will Covis ever know he has found the right system? A small data error could lead him astray. However, I see more of a future in these neural network systems," continued Suttle. "A neural network is another kind of non-linear model, where depending on the outcome of some criterion (say above or below 0), a particular function gets switched on. From what I can tell, genetic algorithms are tools to help determine the best trading rules for a given set of historic data. They are really a computer research procedure that uses the Darwinian principle. Essentially, the computer randomly generates a number of potential trading rules. The best trading rules ('survival of the fittest') have the best chance of surviving to the next round (they 'reproduce'). These rules are mixed with some randomly generated new rules (there is 'mutation'). Eventually, the program identifies trading rules that are very profitable.

"What is problematic about all these models," continued Suttle, "is that they require lots of parameters. For a particular sample of data, it will always be the case that some non-linear function describes the data very well. The key issue is whether it works in the real world with real trading and real money. And even if it does work well for a while, is it really skill, or is it simply luck? That may take years to figure out. Hence, I'm not so sure that Covis has any particular skill. The jury is still out. Moreover, if he is successful, and there is something in the data the market participants did not know, his trading will make markets more efficient, which will kill the profit opportunity. Undervalued currencies will be bought and overvalued currencies will be sold."

Freedy shouted, "See, I told you, in the end, markets are efficient! Unfortunately, Ante, Covis will still be the man at the school's reunion." Ante just sighed.

Evaluating Forecasting Services

One way to ascertain whether profits are being made in the foreign exchange market using technical analysis is to look at the forecasting records of actual forecasting services. Forex advisory services are a diverse lot. All of them generate exchange rate forecasts, but their clienteles, techniques, and forecast horizons differ. Unfortunately, there exists scant empirical evidence on the forecasting ability of such services. However, that is changing because currencies are more and more viewed as an asset class and the number of active currency traders, mostly organized as hedge funds, has grown considerably over the past decade. Because many of these currency traders report returns to various indices, we can analyze their performance. If such funds fail to forecast exchange rates, they should not consistently produce high returns!

Pojarliev and Levich (2008) conducted a study on the returns earned by currency managers reporting to the Barclay Currency Traders Index (BCTI) between January 1990 and December 2006. All of these returns are reported net of fees. Hedge funds typically charge a fixed fee of 2% and a variable fee of 20% on the performance over a benchmark (which can be zero or the Treasury bill return). The study first tries to establish what techniques the currency managers use: Do they use the carry strategy, do they follow trends, or do they trade based on fundamentals? To do so, the investigators use historical data to create returns to carry-trade, trend-following, and fundamental strategies for the major currencies, and they use regression analysis to investigate whether the returns of the various managers correlate with these benchmark returns. The majority of the funds (and the average index) appear to follow trend-following strategies; many also show positive carry exposure, but there is not much of a link with the return on fundamental strategies. The average excess return earned over 34 different managers with relatively long track records between 2001 and 2006 is 5.45%, and the average (annual) Sharpe ratio is 0.47, which is higher than the Sharpe ratio generated by the equity market. Pojarliev and Levich also check whether the managers outperform the benchmark returns. Deutsche Bank, among others, has introduced easily tradable funds that mimic the simple strategies represented by the benchmarks. For an investor, it would make little sense to pay the heavy fees hedge funds charge for exposure to an index that can be bought for a small fixed fee. Pojarliev and Levich find that only eight of the 34 managers significantly outperform a combination of benchmark indices that best describes their investment style.

Taylor Rules Currencies[10]

FX Concepts is one of the largest currency hedge funds in the world, with assets under management of close to $15 billion. John R. Taylor founded FX Concepts in 1981 as a currency forecast firm, selling forecasts to banks and pension funds. His firm gained notoriety when he correctly predicted the precipitous decline of the dollar at the end of 1985. In 1989, he started an investment fund, investing in developed market currencies using mostly sophisticated trend-following systems. During the turmoil in Europe's currency markets in 1992, Mr. Taylor's fund returned 43%. Nevertheless, later in the 1990s, Mr. Taylor experienced firsthand that trend-following systems for developed currencies have a tougher time making money,

as he experienced more and more competition from other active currency traders. Since the early 2000s, FX Concepts expanded its strategies to include one focusing on the carry trade and one focusing on volatility movements. The firm also expanded the set of traded currencies to include emerging markets. FX Concepts now trades over 30 currency pairs relative to the dollar in its Global Currency Program. Both the generation of currency forecasts and the construction of the portfolios use quantitative techniques. FX Concepts has now also ventured into commodities and fixed-income securities, but trading currencies and forecasting currency values remain its core business activities.

10.5 PREDICTING DEVALUATIONS

So far, we have discussed currency forecasting for floating exchange rates; however, more than 70% of currency systems in the world do not fit into this category. We now focus our discussion on the special forecasting problems that arise in pegged systems, but we note that many of these ideas also apply to the target zones and currency boards discussed in Chapter 5.

In a pegged system, one must forecast whether there will be devaluation, and, if so, how large it will be. We first review the major theories on why pegged systems break down. Then, we discuss various forecasting techniques, both in situations where good financial data are available and in cases where they are lacking. We also recount the currency devaluations that occurred in Europe in 1992, Mexico in 1994 to 1995, and Southeast Asia in 1997 and the havoc they wrought.

What Causes a Currency Crisis?

The failure of a pegged exchange rate is typically the result of a successful speculative attack leading the currency to experience a large devaluation [which happened many times during the European Monetary System (EMS)] or to be floated (as happened in Mexico in 1994). For multinational businesses, such occurrences are very important not only because the companies have direct currency exposures in the devaluing countries, but also because currency crises are usually accompanied by economic upheaval. This can lower the value of the local assets that the companies own, affect their production, and adversely affect their local and worldwide sales. There are two main reasons pegged currencies succumb to speculative pressures.

Macroeconomic Conditions

The seminal work of Krugman (1979) and Flood and Garber (1984) argues that if a government follows policies inconsistent with its currency peg, a speculative attack is unavoidable.

---

[10]We rely on information from FX Concepts's Web site and the article by Nielsen (2008).

Speculators will attack the system and attempt to profit by selling the local currency and buying the foreign currency. The country's central bank will lose foreign reserves defending the peg until a critical level of low reserves is reached, at which point the bank is forced to abandon the peg. Whereas initial models focused on expansionary monetary policies, expansionary fiscal policies can also lead to speculative attacks.

These models argue that devaluations are predictable. Growing budget deficits, fast money growth, and rising wages and prices should precede them. If prices rise faster in the local economy than foreign prices are rising while the nominal exchange rate remains unchanged, the local currency is appreciating in real terms. Hence, currency overvaluations should also be a signal of an imminent crisis. The combination of government budget deficits and real exchange rate overvaluations also usually leads to large current account deficits. Consequently, if the theory is correct, speculative pressures should be predictable from economic data.

Self-Fulfilling Expectations

The second explanation for why pegged currencies succumb to speculative pressures recognizes that speculative attacks sometimes seem to come out of the blue. The crisis may be a self-fulfilling prophecy caused by the "animal spirits" of investors, as the famous economist John Maynard Keynes once phrased it.

Although the formal models outlining these ideas are too abstract to recount here, consider the following argument: Suppose a significant group of investors simply starts speculating against a currency, which causes a substantial capital outflow from the country under attack. Other investors, seeing the capital outflow, think the currency will collapse, so they, too, sell the currency, leading to yet more capital outflow. If the central bank becomes overwhelmed, and the country's currency is devalued, this validates the fears of investors, even though there was no fundamental economic reason for dropping the peg.[11]

More recent studies on the issue recognize that deteriorating fundamentals may still play a role. For example, the worsening of the country's employment rate may make defending the nation's currency more costly and may eventually lead to a crisis. However, the actual occurrence and timing of the crisis are still determined by the animal spirits of speculators.

Contagion

The phenomenon known as **contagion** is an increase in the probability that a speculative attack on a currency will occur merely as a result of other currency crises. For example, in September 1992, the British pound first devalued and then left the EMS altogether. The pound suffered a large depreciation in value relative to most European currencies. A few months later, speculators attacked the Irish punt, which was still in the EMS, and the Irish authorities were forced to devalue as well. Because Ireland did not appear to be experiencing any economic problems, many market observers ascribed the Irish devaluation to contagion from the United Kingdom.

If speculative attacks are merely self-fulfilling prophesies, contagion is easy to understand. If speculators successfully attack one currency, they may as well try another. Nevertheless, contagion may be a rational response and even predictable for a variety of reasons. For example, when the British pound devalues but the Irish punt does not devalue, the Irish punt experiences a real appreciation relative to the pound. Because a real appreciation adversely affects the competitive position of Irish exporters, it causes economic and political

---

[11]Technically, such self-fulfilling attacks are possible in models with multiple equilibriums. There is a stable equilibrium in which the government follows the right policies consistent with the peg, but there is also another equilibrium in which the speculators attack the currency and the government accommodates the lower exchange rate. See, for example, Obstfeld (1986) for the theory, Jeanne (1997) for an empirical test, and Kaminsky (2006) for a survey of the literature.

pressure to devalue [see Glick and Rose (1999) for a general analysis of how international trade helps spread currency crises].

Another situation in which contagion is rational but the first crisis is not the cause of the second crisis arises when two currencies are attacked sequentially because the second country is experiencing similar negative macroeconomic conditions or is following similar inconsistent policies.

Empirical Evidence on the Predictability of Currency Crises

The theory on currency crises clearly suggests that certain macroeconomic signals predict devaluations or currency crises. What macroeconomic variables have proved useful predictors of devaluations? Although the many empirical studies do not always agree, a number of economic variables consistently show up as useful predictors. These include PPP-based measures of currency overvaluation, current account balances and monetary growth rates (see Eichengreen et al., 1995; and Kaminsky et al., 1998).

A number of economists and investment banks have built econometric models to predict currency crashes using similar economic variables. The model is estimated using data from various countries on past devaluations. The input of current values of the macroeconomic variables associated with a country then delivers the probability of a devaluation occurring. Some models in this class [for instance, that by Bekaert and Gray (1998)] combine financial data, such as interest rate differentials, and other macroeconomic information, such as cumulative inflation differentials. If liquid financial markets exist, information about forward rates or interest rates, currency option prices, and so on may prove useful in terms of forecasting devaluations. After all, the market prices should rapidly reflect all new economic information.

Finally, the recent global crisis, which started in the banking system, has renewed interest in the links between banking and currency crises. Kaminsky and Reinhart (1999) find that problems in the banking sector typically precede currency crises, as do Burnside et al. (2001) specifically for the Asian crisis. Kaminsky and Reinhart also claim that financial liberalization and the removal of capital controls play a systematic role, but Glick and Hutchison (2005) marshal empirical evidence that capital controls fail to stave off speculative attacks.

The Rocky 1990s: Currency Crises Galore

In 1992, speculators attacked a number of currencies in Europe, severely undermining and casting doubt on the progress toward monetary union in Europe. An exasperated Michel Sapin, French finance minister, was quoted in the *New York Times* on September 24, 1992, as saying, "I will fight, we will fight, France and Germany will fight this speculation, which is based on no economic fundamentals. During the French Revolution such speculators were known as 'agioteurs' and they were beheaded."

But this was only the beginning of the very rocky decade. At the end of 1994, the Mexican peso collapsed, and in its wake, other emerging market currencies and stock markets wobbled. In 1997, several Southeast Asian countries were forced to abandon their pegs relative to the dollar. We now chronicle these watershed events.

1991 to 1993 Currency Turmoil in Europe
As discussed in Chapter 5, in December 1991, representatives from the European Community (EC) countries signed the Treaty of Maastricht, which mapped out the road to a monetary union. While the euro was eventually successfully introduced in 1999, the Exchange Rate Mechanism (ERM) currencies and currencies in its periphery, looking to join at a later stage, witnessed several currency crises before and after the signing of the Maastricht Treaty. Exhibit 10.7 provides a detailed time line of the events showing 2 tumultuous years, with a

Exhibit 10.7 A Rocky Start to EMU

November 1991: Devaluation of the Finnish markka relative to the ECU

December 1991: Signing of the Maastricht Treaty

June 2, 1992: Denmark referendum rejects Maastricht Treaty

September 8, 1992: Finnish markka drops ECU peg

September 16, 1992: Black Wednesday, British pound forced out of ERM

September 17, 1992: Italian lira suspended from ERM; devaluations of Spanish peseta and Portuguese escudo

September 20, 1992: French referendum (narrowly) accepts Maastricht Treaty; Spain reimposes previously lifted capital controls

November–December 1992: Maastricht Treaty now ratified by all countries, except Britain and Denmark; Swedish and Norwegian kronor ECU pegs dropped; peseta and escudo further devalued

January 1993: Devaluation of Irish punt

May 1993: Peseta and escudo devalue once more; Danish referendum accepts Maastricht Treaty

July 1993: Heavy speculative pressure against weak ERM currencies, including the French franc

August 1993: Britain ratifies Maastricht; ERM bands widened to 15%

End of 1993: Speculative pressures ease

plethora of successful and unsuccessful speculative attacks. These events constitute a good case study of what factors may drive currency crises, and they may hold lessons for the future.

A big factor driving these events was the uncertainty surrounding the ratification of the Maastricht Treaty, which had to take place in several European countries. The first referendum in Denmark rejected the Treaty, showing that many European citizens had serious doubts about the desirability of monetary union. In several crises, trade links played a role. For example, Finland, Sweden, and Norway had adopted pegs to the European currency unit (ECU), hoping to strengthen their application for EC membership and signaling their determination to keep inflation down. In November 1991, the collapse of the former Soviet Union obliterated a large portion of Finland's foreign trade, and the markka devalued by 12.3%. The 10% devaluation of the Irish punt on January 30, 1993, was likely partially caused by the major pound depreciation following Black Wednesday, Britain being Ireland's major trade partner. It is possible that the disappearance of capital controls played a role as well. On January 1, 1993, Ireland lifted capital controls and started to rely on interest rates as its main defense mechanism against speculative attacks. From then onward, the punt faced almost continuous speculative pressure. Portugal made use of its remaining capital controls (which would have to be lifted as part of the road to monetary union), and Spain reintroduced capital controls in September 1992 to defend their currencies. However, both the escudo and the peseta were devalued multiple times.

Perhaps the most important lesson of this episode is the difficulty of keeping fixed exchange rates in a region where different countries experience very different economic shocks. The main culprit of the currency troubles undoubtedly was the 1990 reunification of East and West Germany. Germany struggled to absorb the Eastern Länder into the German economy. Inflation surged from increased demand and from wage increases in the former East Germany that exceeded growth in productivity. Moreover, the German money supply increased dramatically from the conversion of Ostmarks, the money of East Germany, into Deutsche marks at a one-for-one exchange rate, even though the purchasing power of the Ostmark was significantly less than that of the Deutsche mark. Sizable budget deficits arose when the government chose to finance the costs of the transition without raising taxes.

The Ostmark conversion, the loose fiscal policy, and the emergence of inflation worried the Bundesbank, Germany's largely independent central bank that has been obsessed with maintaining price stability ever since the hyperinflation of the 1920s. The Bundesbank stepped hard on the brakes and implemented a tight monetary policy of low money growth and high interest rates. The high interest rates in Germany caused a capital inflow and drove up the value of the mark.

The other countries in the EMS were confronted with a dilemma: either raise interest rates to stay in the EMS and appreciate versus the dollar and other major currencies along with the Deutsche mark while seeing their economies suffer in the short run or keep interest rates low to stimulate their economies and risk future devaluation and possible failure of the European Monetary Union (EMU). With Britain in deep recession and other economies heading there, participants in the financial markets began to sense a dwindling belief in the commitment to the EMU. Therefore, it is not surprising that economic news would be a major determinant of the extent of speculative pressures. When there were signs of the Bundesbank beginning to ease interest rates in May 1993, coupled with positive economic figures, speculative pressures on the French franc dissipated, leading to a virtual convergence of French short- and long-term interest rates to German levels. Ultimately, the Bundesbank stubbornly sticking to its high-interest-rate monetary policy and the release of disconcerting macroeconomic statistics caused a full-blown crisis in July and August of 1993 that led to the widening of the ERM bands from 2.25% to 15%.

1994 to 1995: The Mexican Crisis and the Tequila Effect

As we discussed in Chapter 5, in the mid-1990s, Mexico operated a crawling band exchange rate system. However, on December 20, 1994, the ceiling of the band was raised by approximately 13% in an attempt to stop the heavy losses of foreign exchange reserves sustained since mid-November. But the losses continued, and on December 22, 1994, the government effectively floated the peso.

Unfortunately, this currency crisis was only the beginning. Investors around the world and Mexican residents dumped Mexican bonds and equities, putting enormous pressure on the exchange rate. The peso halved in value, as did the equity market. Interest rates spiked up. What was worse, in the course of 1994, the Mexican government had, as a signal of its commitment to the exchange rate band, issued bonds called Tesobonos. Tesobonos are Mexican Treasury bills denominated in dollars but paid in pesos. In effect, Tesobonos protect investors from currency risk. At the end of 1994, the value of the Tesobonos outstanding was more than three times the value of the remaining foreign currency reserves of the Bank of Mexico, and despite very high Tesobonos interest rates, private foreign investors were reluctant to invest in Mexico. Mexico faced a very acute liquidity crisis, which threatened to affect other emerging markets as well.

With the private sector no longer willing to provide funds to Mexico, the IMF and the Clinton administration, drawing on funds from the U.S. Treasury's Exchange Stabilization Fund, put together a bailout package worth some $50 billion that saved Mexico. Notably, the U.S. Congress had voted down support for Mexico. The Mexican currency crisis was a watershed event for emerging markets. Since the early 1990s, many emerging markets had witnessed large portfolio inflows from the developed world. The currency crisis in Mexico and its adverse effects on equity markets seemed to cause foreign capital to dry up not only for Mexico but also for other emerging markets, from Latin America to Asia and Eastern Europe. This spillover of the Mexican crisis to other countries came to be known as the Tequila Effect and caused many economists and policymakers to reevaluate the benefits of unbridled capital flows. Nevertheless, Mexico managed to rebound rather quickly, and the loans provided in the bailout package were duly repaid.

1997: The Southeast Asian Crisis

Since 1980, the countries of Southeast Asia, the so-called Asian Tigers, had engineered an economic miracle, growing their real GDPs by over 7% per year. But there were some uncanny parallels between their macroeconomic fundamentals and those of Mexico just before the crisis. Mexico had been running large current account deficits in the years preceding the currency crisis. For some of the Asian Tigers, their high economic growth also went hand-in-hand with growing current account imbalances. The current account imbalances were worst for Thailand, followed by Malaysia, the Philippines, Korea, and Indonesia. The other Asian countries—Taiwan, Singapore, China, and Hong Kong—on the other hand, ran current account surpluses or very small deficits. These countries all had relatively fixed exchange rate systems in place. Whereas Hong Kong was the only country running a currency board with dollars, other countries were formally pegging their exchange rate to a basket of currencies. However, the effective weight of the U.S. dollar in the basket was so high that the countries were essentially pegged to the U.S. dollar.

We show the historic evolution of some of these currencies relative to the dollar in Exhibit 10.8 in which the values of the currencies are normalized to equal 100 in January 1997. All five currencies were within 10% of 100 during 1995 to 1996. In fact, the Malaysian ringgit moved in a 10% range of MYR(2.5 to 2.7)/USD for most of the years between 1990 and 1997. The Thai baht was effectively fixed in a narrow range of THB(25.2 to 25.6)/USD from 1990 until 1997. In the Philippines, the peso was practically fixed at PHP26.2/USD from spring 1995 until the beginning of 1997. The other countries followed more flexible exchange rate regimes.

Exhibit 10.8 indicates that these currencies experienced sharp depreciations in the second half of 1997. Thailand was the first country to be hit by the crisis. Intervention could not stem the outflow of capital in the first half of 1997, and by early July, the authorities

Exhibit 10.8 Asian Exchange Rates

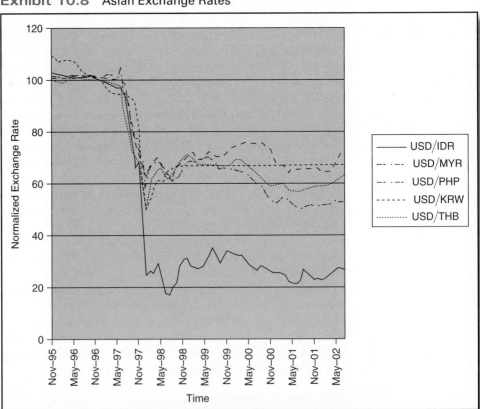

Notes: The exchange rates are normalized to equal 100 in January 1997. The currencies are the U.S. dollar values of the Indonesian rupiah (IDR), the Malaysian ringgit (MYR), the Philippine peso (PHP), the Korean won (KRW), and the Thai baht (THB).

were forced to let the baht float (or, rather, sink). Indonesia quickly became engulfed in the regional financial crisis, and its authorities allowed the rupiah to float freely in mid-August 1997. Sharp currency depreciations also occurred in Malaysia and the Philippines. Korea was the last to be hit by the crisis. Despite repeated exchange market intervention in the summer and autumn and a firming of interest rates, the Korean won's slide could not be arrested. By late November, the country seemed on the brink of defaulting on its short-term external liabilities.

All the countries facing currency crises were very heavily exposed to short-term foreign currency–denominated debt (typically dollars), but Korea was by far the most exposed. In June 1997, outstanding, short-term, foreign currency–denominated debt was more than 300% of Korea's official reserves. In Thailand and Indonesia, this ratio was also well over 100%. Of course, once the crisis hit and the currency depreciated, the value of the debt burden in local currency exploded.

The currency crises in Southeast Asia had wide repercussions, leading to corporate restructuring and bankruptcies. Rich businesspeople became poor overnight, fueling a thriving market for secondhand luxury goods. More importantly, economic growth was hampered, especially in Thailand and Korea, and unemployment rose. The Asian currency crises became real economic crises, causing the Asian miracle to come to a screeching halt.

Different Paths During The Financial Crisis: The Icelandic Króna Versus the Latvian Lat[12]

During the global financial crisis of 2007 to 2010, many currencies experienced large depreciations relative to the dollar and other safe haven currencies. Imagine a currency speculator looking at the economies of Iceland and Latvia after the collapse of Lehman Brothers in September 2008 as the severity of the global financial crisis became ever clearer. It was obvious that these economies would not weather the global financial crisis unscathed. In fact, the economic statistics in both countries contained multiple indications of overheated economies, ready for a hard landing in the dire economic times to come. Would these economies follow the same path, and more importantly, could money be made speculating against their currencies?

Latvia joined the European Union in 2004 and had been growing at break-neck speed. GDP grew by 10.4% per year during 2004 to 2007, and wages had exploded. Because Latvia eventually wanted to join the euro zone, its currency, the lat, was pegged to the euro. High Latvian inflation thus resulted in a substantial real appreciation of the lat, just as happened in Argentina in 2001. The consumption boom and loss of competitiveness contributed to large current account deficits, which were easily financed by inflows of foreign capital. A sudden stop of these capital inflows, though, would imply a drastic reorganization of the economy. As the financial crisis began to unfold, the lat was thus viewed

as a prime candidate for devaluation versus the euro, and the success of a speculative attack surely appeared high.

Iceland's problems were mostly of their own making. After Iceland liberalized its banking system in 2001, three Icelandic banks, Kaupthing, Glitnir, and Landsbanki, went on a lending spree, borrowing in international markets and lending both in domestic and international markets. The economy boomed, and by 2007, the United Nations ranked Iceland first on its index of most developed countries, with a GDP per capita of close to $70,000. Its nickname of "the Nordic Tiger" seemed wholly appropriate. As in Latvia, the economic boom put pressure on wages and made Reykjavik look like a gold rush town. To finance their lending spree, the Icelandic banks attracted lots of European deposits, offering high yields on online accounts. Best known among these was the Icesave product from Landsbanki that offered British and Dutch residents high interest rates on pound and euro deposits, respectively.

The Icelandic króna was a freely floating currency, and during the boom years from 2001 to 2007, the euro strengthened only 1.6% per year versus the króna. As the crisis began to unfold in the first half of 2008, though, the króna price of the euro increased 31%. The Central Bank of Iceland reported in 2008 that foreign debt of the three banks was over five times Iceland's GDP. By September 2008,

---

[12]For additional details on the Icelandic banking crisis, see Beim (2009).

Iceland's external debt reached close to 14 times its export revenue. Clearly, a full-blown financial and economic crisis would be kind to neither Iceland nor the króna.

The crisis did hit with a vengeance in both countries. Yet, the outcome for currency speculators betting on a devaluation of the lat and depreciation of the króna could not have been more different. Anyone buying euros with krónur on September 12, 2008, the Friday before Lehman collapsed, would have made 13.7% by the end of the month when the exchange rate hit ISK145/EUR and Glitner Bank was nationalized. Holding that position for another week would have proved very beneficial because during the first week of October, financial markets began to doubt whether the other Icelandic banks could survive and depositors began a run on the banks. When Landsbanki collapsed on October 6, 2008, the Icelandic deposit insurance scheme could not cover the bank's total deposits, and the Icelandic government chose to fully cover only domestic deposits.[13] The króna began to depreciate rapidly, and by October 9, 2008, the last reported spot trade was at ISK340/EUR before the Icelandic authorities halted trading in the currency because no international banks would serve as counterparties. The Icelandic government imposed exchange controls and capital controls, which have not yet been lifted at the time of writing (although there is a plan to do so in the near future). Eurostat reports that Iceland's per capita GDP fell 9.2% in 2009. The major depreciation of the króna may help Iceland's economy recover because all Icelandic products and services, including tourism, are now on sale.

The financial crisis also threw Latvia into a severe recession. GDP fell 4.2% in 2008 and 18% more in 2009. Capital flows dried up, but the lat did not budge. The government refused to devalue and intervened to defend the currency. Despite losing massive official reserves, the government stood firm, and speculators betting against the lat have so far been thwarted. Without a devaluation of the lat, Latvia's economy will face severe adjustment costs, including large reductions in nominal wages to regain its international competitiveness.

10.6 SUMMARY

This chapter focuses on the determination and forecasting of exchange rates. The main points of the chapter are as follows:

1. Currency forecasts are useful in the international aspects of project evaluation, strategic planning, pricing, working capital management, and the analysis of portfolio investments.

2. The Fisher hypothesis states that the nominal interest rate equals the real interest rate plus the expected rate of inflation.

3. When all the international parity conditions hold, currency forecasting models have little value: The forward rate is the best predictor for the future spot rate, the current real exchange rate is the best predictor of the future real exchange rate, and costs of funding and returns to investment are equalized in real terms across countries (that is, real interest rates are equalized across countries).

4. Empirical evidence rejects the notion of the equality of real interest rates across countries.

5. The two main forecasting techniques are fundamental analysis and technical analysis.

6. Fundamental analysis links exchange rates to fundamental macroeconomic variables such as GDP growth and the current account either through a formal model or through judgmental analysis.

7. Technical analysis uses financial data, such as past exchange rate data, to predict future exchange rates.

8. The root mean squared error (RMSE) can be used to judge the accuracy of forecasts. The percentage of correct signals relative to the forward rate can be used to judge the usefulness of hedging. The profits generated by using the forecasts can also be used to gauge their quality.

9. The asset market approach to exchange rate determination views the exchange rate as an asset price. Its value then depends on current fundamentals

---

[13]The British and Dutch governments decided to compensate their citizens who lost money in the Icelandic deposit schemes and are now suing the Icelandic government. The British government even froze Icelandic assets under the provision of an anti-terrorist law because they viewed the actions of the Icelandic government to be an attempt to harm the United Kingdom. In January 2011, several former Landsbanki executives were arrested in Iceland on allegations of market manipulation.

(such as relative money supplies and output levels of countries) and expected values of future economic fundamentals. Any change in current fundamentals or news about future fundamentals changes the exchange rate.

10. Two of the most often-mentioned determinants of exchange rates are real interest rate differentials and current account balances. These variables are simultaneously determined.

11. The complexity of the relationships that determine the current account and the exchange rate may explain why fundamental exchange rate models perform rather poorly in forecasting future exchange rates.

12. Chartists record the actual trading history of an exchange rate and try to infer possible trends based on that information alone. It is unlikely that the naked eye can pick up trends in a randomly fluctuating series.

13. Filter rules, such as $x\%$ and moving-average rules, are trading rules designed to detect trend behavior in exchange rates. Although early empirical studies focusing on data from the 1980s found strong trends in exchange rates, more recent work has a more difficult time uncovering trend behavior.

14. More sophisticated technical analysis uses regression analysis or other econometric techniques to link exchange rates to financial data, such as forward premiums. Whether the trading strategies based on this analysis are profitable and demonstrate market inefficiency has not been resolved.

15. When an exchange rate is pegged, multinational businesses must assess the probability and magnitude of a possible devaluation. Poor macroeconomic fundamentals, such as an overvalued currency, high money growth rates, and large current account deficits, are warning signs of an imminent devaluation. To make devaluation predictions, formal models employ macroeconomic information, financial information (such as interest rate differentials), or both.

QUESTIONS

1. What is the difference between the *ex ante* and the *ex post* real interest rate?

2. Suppose that the international parity conditions all hold and a country has a higher nominal interest rate than the United States. Characterize the forward premium (or discount) on the dollar, the country's inflation rate compared to the United States, the expected rate of currency appreciation or depreciation versus the dollar, and the country's real interest rate compared to the U.S. real interest rate.

3. How do fundamental analysis and technical analysis differ?

4. Would technical analysis be useful if the international parity conditions held? Why or why not?

5. Describe three statistics you should obtain from a currency-forecasting service in order to judge the quality of its currency forecasts.

6. Does a large increase in the domestic money supply always lead to a depreciation of the currency?

7. Is a current account deficit always associated with a strong real exchange rate (that is, one in which the currency is overvalued compared to the PPP prediction)?

8. Describe how three macroeconomic fundamentals affect exchange rates.

9. Which simple statistical model yields some of the best exchange rate predictions available? What does this imply for the value of models of exchange rate determination to multinational businesses?

10. What is chartism?

11. What is an $x\%$ filter rule?

12. What is a moving-average crossover rule?

13. Have currency traders been successful in exploiting their exchange rate forecasts?

14. Are devaluations of pegged exchange rates totally unexpected?

15. Construct a list of a country's economic statistics you would assemble to help determine the probability of a devaluation of its currency within the coming year.

PROBLEMS

1. Suppose the 1-year nominal interest rate in Zooropa is 9%, and Zooropa's expected inflation rate is 4%. What is the real interest rate in Zooropa?

2. You were recently hired by the Doolittle Corporation corporate treasury to help oversee its expansion into Europe. Blake Francis, the CFO, wants to hire a foreign exchange forecasting company. Blake has asked you to evaluate three different companies, and he has obtained information on their past performances. Out of a total of 50 forecasts for the

$/€ rate, the companies reported the number of times they correctly forecast appreciations and depreciations:

	Correct Down Forecasts	Correct Up Forecasts
Morrissey Forex Advisors	20	5
Pixie Exchange Land	20	4
FOREX Cures	12	12

There are a total of 35 dollar appreciations (down periods) and 15 dollar depreciations (up periods) in the sample. Blake wants to know two things:

a. Can anything be said about the companies' forecasting ability with the available data?

b. What additional information should Blake try to obtain in order to form a better judgment?

3. Mini-Case: Currency Turmoil in Zooropa

Fad Gadget has never worked so hard in his entire life. It is near midnight, and he is still poring over statistics and tables. Fad recently joined Smashing Pumpkins, a relatively young but fast-growing British firm that produces and distributes an intricate device that turns fresh pumpkins into pumpkin pie in about 30 minutes. Recently, the firm has started exporting to Zooropa. Some of the largest and tastiest pumpkins are grown in Zooropa, and its population boasts the highest per capita pumpkin consumption in the world. A recent analysis of the pumpkin market in Zooropa has left the company's senior managers very impressed with the profit potential.

Although Zooropa consists of 10 politically independent countries, their currencies are linked through a system called the Currency Rate Linkage System (CRLS) that works exactly like the former Exchange Rate Mechanism (ERM) of the EMS before the currency turmoil started in September 1992. The anchor currency is the banshee of Enigma, the leading country in Zooropa.

Initial contacts with importers in Zooropean countries indicated that they typically insist on payment in their own local currency. About a week ago, Cab Voltaire, the CEO of Smashing Pumpkins, expressed concerns about this development and asked Fad to lead a research team to further examine the present state of the currency system of Zooropa. Cab viewed the outlook for the banshee relative to the pound quite favorably and did not predict any substantial depreciation of the banshee against any other major currency. However, the precarious economic situation of some of the countries

in Zooropa and the growing importance of speculative pressures in Zooropa's currency markets last week suddenly made him suspicious about the possibility of realignments within the system. He even doubted the long-term viability of the system. Cab instructed Fad to examine the following issues:

- Which currencies in the system exhibit the highest realignment risk?
- If a currency realigns and gets devalued, what are the effects on our sales and profit margins in this particular country? Can we take the realignment possibility into account in our pricing?
- Suppose a currency is forced to leave the CRLS. What are the effects on exchange rates, interest rates, and the outlook for sales in that country? What is the likelihood of this occurring for the different countries?

Fad Gadget felt nervous. A meeting was scheduled with Cab the day after tomorrow. He wanted to write a thorough and insightful report. At the last management meeting, he had the uneasy feeling that some senior managers doubted his abilities. Some managers were naturally suspicious of a young Australian newcomer with his MBA. His earring and punk hairdo did not exactly help either. His team of analysts had already assembled a table with relevant macroeconomic and financial data (see Exhibit 10.9). "If only I could use this to rank the different countries according to realignment risk," he thought. Place yourself in Fad Gadget's shoes and see what your ranking is.

4. Web Problem: Go to www.oanda.com/currency/big-mac-index. Oanda reports the last available Big Mac index but then updates the exchange rates on a regular basis to compare them with the PPP-based exchange rates. What are currently the most undervalued and overvalued exchange rates? How would you use this information in forecasting exchange rates?

5. Mini Case: Valuing Currency Management: TOM Versus U.S. Commerce Bank

On February 19, 2009, an arbitral tribunal found that U.S. Commerce Bank (USCB) Analytics, a wholly owned subsidiary of USCB Corporation, a large U.S.-based bank, had breached an exclusivity provision of its joint venture (JV) agreement with Trend Ontledings Maatschappij (TOM), a Dutch currency management business. Consequently, TOM claimed USCB was obligated to compensate the firm for lost earnings that would have accrued to TOM during the life of the JV.

Exhibit 10.9 Zooropa in Numbers

Country	Currency's CRLS Position	Currency's Over / Undervaluation %	Reserves, Import Coverage	Budget Deficit as % of GDP	Inflation Rate, %	GDP Growth, %
Sinead	−6	−10	9	−1.9	3.6	2.4
Carmen	−36	−12	3.1	−2.3	2.7	2.0
Marquee	16	11	8.2	−4.9	5.7	2.0
Fries	−3	11	11.7	−5.4	9.5	2.8
Ney	−22	−2	2.5	−2.1	2.2	2.1
Helpisink	31	−18	1.3	−5.5	2.1	1.6
Benfica	30	−16	1.5	−3.4	3.5	1.6
Che ora	−90	3	2.6	−4.6	3.6	−0.8
Vachement	27	2	0.5	−11.3	5.2	1.3

Notes: The CRLS position measures the general strength or weakness of a currency within the target zone. A value of −100 means that the currency is at its lower bound and is weak relative to all other currencies in the zone. A value of 100 means that the currency is at its upper bound and is strong relative to all other currencies in the zone. The currency's over-/undervaluation is relative to the prediction of purchasing power parity (PPP). It is computed by taking the percentage deviation from the prediction of PPP of the currency versus the banshee, the central rate in the system. A positive number means the currency is overvalued relative to PPP. Import coverage calculates the ratio of foreign exchange reserves at the central bank to average monthly imports. This indicates how many months of imports could be purchased by the foreign exchange reserves held at the central bank. The inflation rate and GDP growth rate are in percentage per annum.

Established in 2006, the JV was to last for a minimum of 4 years. USCB was responsible for marketing the JV to third-party clients including central banks, institutional investors, and corporate clients. TOM was responsible for providing the investment management expertise by delivering a low-return, low-volatility, alpha currency investment product. TOM had a long history of quantitative trading in the currency markets. In the 1970s, TOM was thought to be the first firm to apply computerized trading to exchange rate markets. Successful partnerships with a number of U.S. banks in the 1980s and early 1990s made Geert Rijkaard, TOM's founder, one of the richest men in the world. Because the firm's strategy focused on European currencies relative to the dollar, the arrival of the euro in 1999 led to a suspension of TOM's trading activities. However, after adapting its models to focus on the euro/dollar pair, TOM started trading again in 2004 and began actively looking for partners that could help market the product.

However, as a result of the contract breach, TOM had terminated the JV on July 30, 2007. TOM claimed that it was owed in excess of $300 million from USCB. Both parties assembled teams of experts to make their cases to the tribunal. The tribunal would then use the information provided by these experts as the basis for making a decision as to the amount of damages owed to TOM.

Although all names used here are fictitious, the story is based on a real-world case. A Columbia CaseWorks case written by Bekaert (2011) provides more details. It lays out the analysis by TOM's team to motivate the $300 million damages number, relying largely on the detailed business plan at the time the JV was formed. The case further describes several key exhibits assembled by USCB's team. Its first task at hand was to simply figure out what kind of currency manager TOM was: Does it follow trends, trade on fundamentals, or run a carry strategy? The team also believed it would be important to study the relative investment performance of the JV and did so using actual data from the Barclay Currency Traders Index. Given the large number of currency funds that were available to investors, the JV's ability to win clients and grow its AUM would undoubtedly be closely linked to its performance, both in absolute terms and relative to other currency funds. Finally, simply generating a plausible track record of returns suitable for use in projections raised interesting issues. For example, TOM's team had resorted to using paper returns (meaning returns from a trading strategy that had not been used in actual trading yet) to pull together a long return record. To learn more about this case, please go to www4.gsb.columbia.edu/caseworks/ and look for the Valuing Currency Management case.

BIBLIOGRAPHY

Andersen, Torben G., Tim Bollerslev, Francis X. Diebold, and Clara Vega, 2003, "Micro Effects of Macro Announcements: Real Time Price Discovery in Foreign Exchange," *American Economic Review* 93, pp. 38–62.

―――――――, 2007, "Real-Time Price Discovery in Global Stock, Bond and Foreign Exchange Markets," *Journal of International Economics* 73, pp. 251–277.

Baxter, Marianne, 1994, "Real Exchange Rates and Real Interest Differentials: Have We Missed the Business Cycle Relationship?" *Journal of Monetary Economics* 33, pp. 5–37.

Beim, David, 2009, "Landsbanki Islands," Columbia Case-Works No. 090304.

Bekaert, Geert, 2011, "Valuing Currency Management: TOM vs. U.S. Commerce Bank," Columbia CaseWorks No. 100310.

Bekaert, Geert, and Stephen Gray, 1998, "Target Zones and Exchange Rates: An Empirical Investigation," *Journal of International Economics* 45, pp. 1–35.

Burnside, Craig, Martin Eichenbaum, and Sergio Rebelo, 2001, "Prospective Deficits and the Asian Currency Crisis," *Journal of Political Economy* 109, pp. 1155–1197.

Chakrabarti, Avik, 2006, "Real Exchange Rates and Real Interest Rates Once Again: A Multivariate Panel Cointegration Analysis," *Applied Economics* 38, pp. 1217–1221.

Chang, P.H. Kevin, and Carol L. Osler, 1999, "Methodical Madness: Technical Analysis and the Irrationality of Exchange-Rate Forecasts," *Economic Journal* 109, pp. 636–661.

Clarida, Richard H., Josh Davis, and Niels Pedersen, 2009, "Currency Carry Trade Regimes: Beyond the Fama Regression," *Journal of International Money and Finance* 28, pp. 1375–1389.

Clarida, Richard H., and Daniel Waldman, 2008, "Is Bad News About Inflation Good News for the Exchange Rate?" in John Campbell, ed., *Asset Prices and Monetary Policy*, Chicago: University of Chicago Press.

Clements, Kenneth W., Yihui Lan, and Shi Pei Seah, 2010, "The Big Mac Index Two Decades On: An Evaluation of Burgernomics," *International Journal of Finance and Economics*, http://onlinelibrary.wiley.com/doi/10.1002/ijfe.432/full.

Dornbusch, Rudiger, 1976, "Expectations and Exchange-Rate Dynamics," *Journal of Political Economy* 84, pp. 1161–1176.

Edison, Hali J., and B. Dianne Pauls, 1993, "A Re-assessment of the Relationship Between Real Exchange Rates and Real Interest Rates: 1970–1990," *Journal of Monetary Economics* 31, pp. 165–187.

Eichengreen, Barry, Andrew K. Rose, and Charles Wyplosz, 1995, "Exchange Market Mayhem: The Antecedents and Aftermaths of Speculative Attacks," *Economic Policy* 21, pp. 251–312.

Engel, Charles M., and James Hamilton, 1990, "Long Swings in the Dollar—Are They in the Data and Do Markets Know It?" *American Economic Review* 80, pp. 689–713.

Engel, Charles, Nelson C. Mark, and Kenneth D. West, 2007, "Exchange Rate Models Are Not as Bad as You Think," *NBER Macroeconomics Annual* 22, pp. 381–441.

Engel, Charles, and Kenneth D. West, 2005, "Exchange Rates and Fundamentals," *Journal of Political Economy* 113, pp. 485–517.

Faust, Jon, John H. Rogers, Shing-Yi B. Wang, and Jonathan H. Wright, 2007, "The High-Frequency Response of Exchange Rates and Interest Rates to Macroeconomic Announcements," *Journal of Monetary Economics* 54, pp. 1051–1068.

Fisher, Irving, 1930, *The Theory of Interest as Determined by Impatience to Spend Income and Opportunity to Invest It*, New York: MacMillan.

Flood, Robert, and Peter Garber, 1984, "Collapsing Exchange Rate Regimes, Some Linear Examples," *Journal of International Economics* 17, pp. 1–13.

Gehrig, Thomas, and Lukas Menkhoff, 2006, "Extending Evidence on the Use of Technical Analysis in Foreign Exchange," *International Journal of Finance and Economics* 11, pp. 327–338.

Glick, Reuven, and Michael Hutchison, 2005, "Capital Controls and Exchange Rate Instability in Developing Countries," *Journal of International Money and Finance* 24, pp. 387–412.

Glick, Reuven, and Andrew K. Rose, 1999, "Contagion and Trade: Why Are Currency Crises Regional?" *Journal of International Money and Finance* 18, pp. 603–617.

Henriksson, Roy D., and Robert Merton, 1981, "On Market Timing and Evaluation Performance, 2: Statistical Procedures for Evaluating Forecasting Skills," *Journal of Business* 54, pp. 513–533.

Jeanne, Olivier, 1997, "Are Currency Crises Self-Fulfilling? A Test," *Journal of International Economics* 43, pp. 263–286.

Jordà, Òscar, and Alan M. Taylor, 2009, "The Carry Trade and Fundamentals: Nothing to Fear but FEER Itself," NBER Working Paper No. 15518.

Kaminsky, Graciela L., 2006, "Currency Crises: Are They All the Same?" *Journal of International Money and Finance* 25, pp. 503–527.

Kaminsky, Graciela L., Saul Lizondo, and Carmen M. Reinhart, 1998, "Leading Indicators of Currency Crises," *IMF Staff Papers* 45, pp. 1–48.

Kaminsky, Graciela L., and Carmen M. Reinhart, 1999, "The Twin Crises: The Causes of Banking and Balance of Payments Problems," *American Economic Review* 89, pp. 473–500.

Krugman, Paul, 1979, "A Model of Balance of Payments Crises," *Journal of Money and Credit and Banking* 11, pp. 311–325.

LeBaron, Blake, 1999, "Technical Trading Rule Profitability and Foreign Exchange Intervention," *Journal of International Economics* 49, pp. 125–143.

Mark, Nelson, 1995, "Exchange Rates and Fundamentals: Evidence on Long-Horizon Predictability," *American Economic Review* 85, pp. 201–218.

Meese, Richard, and John Prins, 2011, "On the Natural Limits of Exchange Rate Predictability by Fundamentals," manuscript, Princeton University.

Meese, Richard, and Kenneth Rogoff, 1983, "Empirical Exchange-Rate Models of the Seventies—Do They Fit Out of Sample?" *Journal of International Economics* 14, pp. 3–24.

——————, 1988, "Was It Real? The Exchange Rate Interest Rate Differential Relation over the Modern Floating Rate Period," *Journal of Finance* 43, pp. 933–948.

Mussa, Michael, 1984, "The Theory of Exchange Rate Determination," in J.F.O. Bilson and R.C. Marston, eds., *Exchange Rate Theory and Practice*, Chicago: University of Chicago Press.

Neely, Christopher, and Paul Weller, 2001, "Technical Analysis and Central Bank Intervention," *Journal of International Money and Finance* 20, pp. 949–970.

Neely, Christopher, Paul Weller, and Robert Dittmar, 1997, "Is Technical Analysis in the Foreign Exchange Market Profitable? A Genetic Programming Approach," *Journal of Financial and Quantitative Analysis* 32, pp. 405–426.

Nielsen, Bo, 2008, "Taylor Rule Currencies, Not to Be Confused with the Other Guy," Bloomberg.com, www.bloomberg.com/apps/news?pid=newsarchive&sid=awPlkg9zw9Wk&refer=home.

Obstfeld, Maurice, 1986, "Rational and Self-Fulfilling Balance of Payments Crises," *American Economic Review* 76, pp. 72–81.

Pojarliev, Momtchil, and Richard M. Levich, 2008, "Do Professional Currency Managers Beat the Benchmark?" *Financial Analysts Journal* September/October, pp. 18–32.

Pukthuanthong-Le, Kuntara, Richard M. Levich, and Lee R. Thomas III, 2007, "Do Foreign Exchange Markets Still Trend?" *Journal of Portfolio Management* Fall, pp. 114–118.

Rogoff, Kenneth, 2009, "Exchange Rates in the Modern Floating Era: What Do We Really Know?" *Review of World Economics* 145, pp. 1–12.

Sapin, Michel, 1992, "Quote of the Day," *The New York Times*, September 24, p. A6.

Sollis, Robert, and Mark E. Wohar, 2006, "The Real Exchange Rate–Real Interest Rate Relation: Evidence from Tests for Symmetric and Asymmetric Threshold Cointegration," *International Journal of Finance and Economics* 2, pp. 139–153.

Wu, Jyh-Lin, and Yu-Hau Hu, 2009, "New Evidence on Nominal Exchange Rate Predictability," *Journal of International Money and Finance* 28, pp. 1045–1063.

Chapter 11

International Debt Financing

*I*n 2010, Reliance Industries, an energy company and India's biggest company by market value, raised $1.5 billion in the global bond markets, helped by two American banks (Bank of America Merrill Lynch and Citibank) and two British banks (HSBC and RBS). The banks directly approached investors in Singapore, Hong Kong, London, and the United States, and demand for the bonds was overwhelming, allowing aggressive pricing. This **global bond** deal was lauded as one of the corporate bond deals of the year in the February 2011 issue of *Euromoney*, a magazine specializing in international finance. The deal vividly illustrates how large companies use the international debt markets to pull in as many investors as possible to meet their financing needs. If Reliance had tried to raise $1.5 billion in India, it would have faced a much higher cost of funding, and it might not have been able to raise nearly as much capital at the same terms.

The goal of this chapter is to describe the various funding sources for debt that are available to multinational corporations (MNCs) in an increasingly globalized world and to examine what makes MNCs choose particular options. It is critical for a financial manager to understand the various worldwide markets that can be tapped to borrow money, and this chapter covers important institutional details regarding international bonds and bank lending. At the same time, it is also important to realize that free lunches are hard to get, and we carefully discuss how to compare different debt options with different characteristics (e.g., in terms of maturity and currency denomination) on an apples-to-apples basis.

11.1 THE GLOBAL SOURCES OF FUNDS FOR INTERNATIONAL FIRMS

The sources of funds for an MNC (and its subsidiaries) can be split into two major categories: cash that is internally generated by the MNC and cash that is externally provided from the debt markets or the equity markets. Exhibit 11.1 surveys the various sources of funds for an MNC, starting on top with internal sources of funds reinvested in the company.

The potential sources of external capital are extremely wide ranging. Both bonds and stocks (debt and equity financing) can be issued by a firm and sold to investors, typically through the financial intermediation of an investment bank. These externally issued securities are often tradable in secondary markets.

In contrast, loans are obtained from specialized financial intermediaries, typically commercial banks, and the lender monitors the financial behavior of the firm to make sure she

Exhibit 11.1 Sources of Long-Term Capital for a Multinational Corporation

will get repaid. For all three types of external sources of funds (bank loans, debt securities, and equity), MNCs and their affiliates can tap either domestic or international markets. *Euromarket* refers to the external, or offshore, market for borrowing and lending that we first encountered in Chapter 6.

A foreign affiliate of an MNC can obtain funds from within the MNC or from the same external sources as mentioned in Exhibit 11.1. The affiliate's external borrowing ability may be enhanced when the parent company guarantees the loan. In addition to using debt and equity, MNCs often transfer funds across their affiliates by leading and lagging the payments of intracompany accounts.[1]

The Financing Mix Around the World

The financial appetites of countries differ, and their firms use a different mix of funds to finance their activities. This is, of course, reflected in the way local affiliates of MNCs finance themselves. By and large, internally generated cash is the main source of funding for an MNC.

---

[1]The use of leading and lagging payments to transfer funds between affiliates of an MNC is explicitly discussed in Chapter 19.

It is well known that public markets (equity and bonds) dominate the financial mix in the United States, whereas the bond market is the largest source of funds in Japan; in Europe, loans dominate as a financing source. These financing mixes are in constant flux and depend both on market conditions and more structural factors.

For example, the Japanese corporate finance model of the 1970s and 1980s, in which companies relied heavily on bank funds and banks, in turn, invested heavily in equities, led to a banking and economic crisis in the 1990s, which continued into the 2000s. As the Japanese economy suffered falling product prices (deflation), the Japanese stock and real estate markets crashed, which eroded the capital base of many banks. Simultaneously, many bank loans became nonperforming, further eroding the health of the banking system.

With banks unable or unwilling to supply new loans, Japanese MNCs entered international markets. It is fair to say that the high-quality Japanese MNCs, such as Sony, Toyota, and Canon, were much less affected by the crisis of the 1990s than were purely domestic firms. In fact, it is conceivable that the increased access to bond markets by well-performing companies, such as many export-oriented companies, worsened the balance sheet of the banks because their lending was concentrated to companies with a lower ability to repay their debts.

In Europe, there seemed to be a slow trend away from bank financing prior to the recent global financial crisis. The desire of banks to decrease leverage after the crisis implies that the size of the worldwide banking sector will shrink. With firms deleveraging, there was a marked slowdown in both bank lending and bond issuance. Nevertheless, debt financing in the form of either bonds or bank loans dominates the external financing that corporations seek. We now take a closer look at the different types of debt instruments that exist in global capital markets.

11.2 THE CHARACTERISTICS OF DEBT INSTRUMENTS

The main characteristics differentiating debt instruments are their currency of denomination, their maturity, the nature of their interest payments, their tradability, and their international character. This large variety of debt instruments arose as companies sought various ways to minimize their debt payments and avoid financial distress. Financial distress occurs when debt repayment is stopped or has become difficult. Although financial distress need not always lead to bankruptcy, it may make it more difficult and more costly for a firm to get financing, and it can adversely affect a firm's share price and the demand for its products.

Currency of Denomination

When a purely domestic company issues debt denominated in a foreign currency, it faces the risk that the foreign currency will appreciate relative to the domestic currency, which would increase the cost of repaying the debt. However, for an MNC, it is quite natural to borrow in different currencies because the firm's revenues are also likely denominated in foreign currencies.

Centralized Versus Decentralized Debt Denomination

A U.S.–based MNC may, for example, prefer incurring dollar-denominated debt and, therefore, "centralize" its debt financing. We illustrate this **centralized debt denomination** model in Exhibit 11.2, using the example of a U.S. MNC with Swiss and Australian subsidiaries. Note that the debts for both the parent company and its foreign subsidiaries are denominated in dollars.

Exhibit 11.2 Centralized and Decentralized Debt Denomination

Note: The arrows indicate the direction of payment flows, either revenues or interest payments going from one entity to the other.

Alternatively, the parent company may maintain a **decentralized debt denomination** model, borrowing in the countries and currencies where the subsidiaries operate or to which it exports. In the decentralized model, also illustrated in Exhibit 11.2, the debt service payments (interest payments and principal repayment) are denominated in the currency in which the subsidiary's operating profits are generated. This is an example of balancing foreign assets against foreign liabilities and is often called a **balance-sheet hedge**.

From the perspective of an MNC, its foreign subsidiary is an asset that generates foreign currency profits. To hedge the risk of the foreign currency depreciating, which decreases the asset's value, a corporation should have an equivalent liability denominated in that foreign currency. In this way, foreign currency debt forms a natural hedge for the cash flows from the subsidiary's operations.

Consider the example shown in Exhibit 11.2. Suppose the Australian dollar appreciates relative to the U.S. dollar. In the decentralized model, the Australian dollar debt becomes more costly to service in terms of the U.S. dollar. However, as long as the appreciation does not coincide with a major recession that reduces the demand for Australian products, the USD value of the AUD operating profits is also higher. Because the AUD operating profits are used to pay off the AUD debt, the firm is not adversely affected. Now, suppose the Australian dollar weakens. This puts a strain on the subsidiary's operating profits when expressed in U.S. dollars. But again, it does not make the AUD debt more of a burden for the parent company. Hence, the decentralized model naturally hedges foreign exchange risk.

In contrast, with the centralized model, if the AUD depreciates, the USD value of the subsidiary's operating profits goes down, which reduces the USD profits the parent firm earns. With debt denominated in USD, the debt becomes more difficult to pay. Of course, as we have learned, it is possible for an MNC following the centralized model to hedge against such a situation using forward contracts.

Is Issuing Debt in Low-Interest-Rate Countries a Good Idea?

This is surely not necessarily the case because a loan denominated in a currency in which the MNC does not generate cash flows brings with it exchange rate uncertainty. If uncovered interest rate parity (UIRP) holds, the expected cost of the loan in local currency should equal the cost of a domestic currency loan. Yet, MNCs often do rightfully borrow in unusual currencies for a variety of reasons, which we discuss in detail in Section 11.6.

Debt Portfolios

If you are the manager of an MNC, you could decide to issue debt in several currencies in order to diversify your company's currency exposure. Nonetheless, when MNCs source debt in other currencies, they typically hedge the currency risk. This can be done using forward contracts or currency swaps.

Maturity

Companies tend to structure their borrowing so that large principal repayments are not clustered together. That helps limit their refinancing risk: They do not have to come up with a large amount of cash at a point in time when cash flows are potentially low and market conditions for issuing more debt are unfavorable. For example, Almeida et al. (2009) show that firms whose long-term debt was largely maturing in the 2008 to 2009 credit squeeze reduced investment by 25% more than otherwise similar firms without such refinancing needs. To avoid such problems, firms spread out the due dates on loans and debt instruments. Some firms engage in maturity matching. They attempt to finance current assets (such as accounts receivable and inventories) with short-term debt and to finance fixed assets (investments) with long-term debt.

When companies issue long-term debt, the maturity is typically governed by standards in the particular debt market in which they issue the debt or by investor demand. For example, Eurobonds mostly mature in less than 10 years and typically in exactly 5 years. By contrast, U.S. corporate bonds can have quite long maturities, typically 20 to 30 years. In fact, when the maturity is less than 10 years, the bonds are called *notes*. In 2010 to 2011, many corporations started to issue very long-dated debt. Norfolk Southern, a U.S. railway operator, sold $250 million worth of 100-year bonds in August 2010. The 100-year maturity issue is not the first of its kind. In 1993, the Walt Disney Company issued $300 million worth of 100-year bonds. The Disney 100-year bonds were immediately dubbed "Sleeping Beauties" after the fairy tale princess and heroine in the popular Disney animated film by the same name (because she slept for 100 years under a magic spell). At the end of 2010, the Mexican government also issued 100-year U.S. dollar–denominated bonds.

Of course, the record for the longest maturity goes to perpetual bonds, or consols, which never pay back the face value of the bond. HSBC, a British bank, sold $3.4 billion worth of perpetuals in mid-2010; and in early 2011, several units of Tata, the Indian conglomerate, issued or planned on issuing several dollar-denominated perpetual bounds, starting with a $500 million issue by Tata Steel. Such long-dated bonds are interesting to institutional investors with long-dated liabilities such as pension funds and insurance companies, but might the flurry of activity in long-dated issues also be explained by issuers trying to lock in the low interest rates prevailing after the crisis? To think about this formally, we need to think about the relationship between short- and long-term interest rates, which we do in the next section.

The Nature of Interest Rate Payments: Fixed-Rate Versus Floating-Rate Debt

Borrowers pay the interest on debt instruments at regular intervals (for example, annually or semiannually), and the amount may be fixed (**fixed-rate debt**), or it may vary, or float, over time (**floating-rate debt**), based on changes in the prevailing reference interest rate, typically a short-term borrowing rate in the interbank market such as LIBOR (see Chapter 6).

When to Use Floating-Rate Debt

The choice between fixed-rate and floating-rate debt depends on a variety of factors. When short-term interest rates are below long-term interest rates, you might be tempted to conclude that MNCs should choose floating-rate debt to reduce their immediate funding costs. However, higher long-term rates likely reflect investors' expectations that short-term rates will rise, so it is not at all clear that *ex post* the company will save on financing costs. Let's illustrate this with a numeric example.

Example 11.1   Cost of Debt Comparisons Across Maturities

Dig-It-Up is a Canadian mining company that wants to borrow CAD2,000,000 for 2 years. Dig-It-Up is able to borrow at the following zero-coupon annual interest rates:

	1 Year	2 Years
CAD	3%	5%

As Chapter 6 notes, if Dig-It-Up borrows for 2 years, its only payment would be the principal plus the compound interest at maturity:

$$CAD2,000,000 \times [1 + 0.05]^2 = CAD2,205,000 \qquad (11.1)$$

If the company does not want to incur either interest rate or currency risk, it should lock in a loan for 2 years at the 5% rate. However, the 3% 1-year rate looks more attractive initially. Wouldn't borrowing the money for 1 year at a 3% interest rate and then renewing the loan for another 1 year lower the cost of debt for Dig-It-Up?

The problem, of course, is that we do not know what the interest rate will be 1 year in the future. After 1 year, Dig-It-Up would have to repay the loan plus 3% interest. It would do so by borrowing that amount with another 1-year loan, at the prevailing interest rate, whatever it is. After 2 years, Dig-It-Up would then have to repay the principal plus interest. That is, with the unknown future interest rate denoted as i_{fut}, the total repayment would be

$$\text{CAD2,000,000} \times [1 + 0.03] \times [1 + i_{\text{fut}}] \qquad \text{(11.2)}$$

Comparing Equation (11.2) with Equation (11.1) demonstrates that the second option involves interest rate risk. The second alternative could turn out to be cheaper, but it might not. The break-even rate that makes the *ex post* cost of the two loans the same satisfies

$$[1 + 0.03] \times [1 + i_{\text{fut}}] = 1.05^2$$

By solving for i_{fut}, we find

$$i_{\text{fut}} = 1.05^2/1.03 - 1 = 7.04\%$$

As long as the 1-year interest rate 1 year from now remains below 7.04%, the company would be better off having borrowed sequentially in the short-term markets rather than in the longer term market. This might look like an extreme change in the prevailing interest rate, but such a change can, indeed, happen. If the firm borrows in the short term, it risks having to refinance in 1 year at a rate higher than 7.04%.

The Expectations Hypothesis

The **expectations hypothesis**, or *expectations theory*, of the term structure is the best-known theory governing the relationship between long rates and expected future short rates. In fact, the expectations theory maintains that the break-even rate is exactly the rate that the market expects for future short-term borrowing. If this were not the case, many companies would borrow short term, and short-term rates would increase because of the heavy demand for funds borrowed.

The theory also implies that long-term interest rates are a weighted average of the current short-term rate and expected future short-term rates. In the example, the long-term rate, 5%, is in between the current short rate of 3% and the higher expected future short rate of 7.04%. In this case, Dig-It-Up should be indifferent between borrowing short term and long term. Why? Because the savings the company realizes at the start of the borrowing period will be lost when short-term rates rise later on, as expected. By the same token, issuing a short-maturity or a long-maturity bond should lead to the same debt costs, on average.

The empirical evidence regarding the expectations hypothesis is mixed, however. The theory holds up better in the United Kingdom than in the United States, Germany, or Japan. Bekaert et al. (2007) argue that although there is some statistical evidence against the theory, the deviations are economically small. That said, it is possible that borrowing at a floating rate—which is what Dig-It-Up would essentially be doing if it took out two short-term loans—would give the company a natural hedge if its cash flows were positively correlated with interest rates. In other words, the company is likely to experience high-interest-rate expenses on its floating debt when its revenues are high and low-interest-rate expenses when its revenues are poor.[2] Large companies and MNCs can also constantly modify the fixed-rate versus floating-rate composition of their debt by making use of the interest rate swap markets. In fact, as we will see in Chapter 21, they frequently do.

---

[2]Ang et al. (2008) document that although cash flows tend to be procyclical, nominal interest rates are actually countercyclical, but real interest rates are procyclical.

Faulkender (2005) examined why firms in the United States issued fixed- or floating-rate debt. He found evidence that firms tend to issue more floating-rate debt when the yield curve is steep and more fixed-rate debt when the yield curve is flat. This is consistent with a naïve market timing strategy aiming to lower short-term debt costs. Faulkender surmises, partly based on interviews with corporate treasurers, that some managers seek to lower short-term interest rate expenses in order to report higher quarterly earnings, whereas others really believe that they can anticipate future interest movements and genuinely lower debt costs with such market timing behavior.

Tradability of Debt

Intermediated and Direct Debt

When debt is intermediated, financial institutions such as commercial or investment banks first attract funds from investors and then make loans, possibly to MNCs. One of the major trends in recent years has been for large MNCs to issue bonds directly to investors. The process whereby corporate borrowing takes the form of a tradable security issued in the public market, rather than a non-tradable loan provided by financial intermediaries, is called **financial disintermediation**. Note that even though financial institutions do not provide the funds directly to corporations issuing bonds, they typically still play an intermediary role in selling the securities to the investing public.

Financial disintermediation occurs for many reasons. Deregulation, such as that in the United States in 1981 and Japan in 1986, removed restrictions that had allowed banks to attract low-cost funds from depositors. Stricter regulation of bank capital (for example, through the Basel Accord requirements, discussed later in the chapter) pushed up banks' costs of funds and gave them an incentive to seek profits on activities not recorded on their balance sheets, such as intermediating the selling of securities. Finally, the information revolution also means that information regarding any company can be found much more easily than in the past, which is a necessary ingredient for a successful direct debt market.

Private Placements

Privately placed bonds lie between bank loans and publicly traded bonds. **Private placement bonds** are not sold to the market at large but are placed privately with sophisticated, well-endowed investors, such as pension funds, life insurance companies, or university endowments. Consequently, they are less tradable than standard bonds. In the United States, private placements are regulated by the Securities Act of 1933 and must conform to a number of conditions to ensure that the investors are sufficiently informed and qualified to judge the merits of the investment.

The International Character of Debt

In Chapter 6, we encountered the external capital market. An *external debt market* involves debt sold to investors outside the borders of the country issuing the currency in which the debt is denominated. In contrast, an *internal debt market* involves debt that is denominated in the currency of the host country and sold within that country.

In the long-term debt markets, it is customary to distinguish between domestic and international bonds. **Domestic bonds** are issued and traded within an internal debt market. **International bonds** are traded outside the country of the issuer. There are two types of international bonds. **Foreign bonds** are issued in a domestic market by a foreign borrower, denominated in the domestic currency, marketed to domestic residents, and regulated by the domestic authorities. Over the years, various foreign bonds have earned nicknames. For example, there are Yankee bonds in the United States, bulldog bonds in the United Kingdom, Samurai bonds in Japan, Matadors in Spain, and Rembrandts in the Netherlands.

The other type of international bond is a **Eurobond**, which is denominated in one or more currencies but is traded in external markets outside the borders of the countries issuing the currencies.

We can split up bond issues in a particular country with the following diagram:

	Issued by Residents	Issued by Non-Residents
Domestic Currency	A. Domestic bond	B. Foreign bond
Foreign Currency	C. Eurobond	D. Eurobond

The sum of segments B and D comprises the *external*, or *cross-border*, bond market. The international bond market comprises segments B, C, and D. The next section provides much more detail on the international bond market.

11.3 A TOUR OF THE WORLD'S BOND MARKETS

Size and Structure of the World Bond Market

Exhibit 11.3 reports the amounts outstanding in the world's various bond markets for the years 2000 and 2010. In most countries, government bonds constitute the most important segment of the bond market. The largest government market in 2000 was in the United States with over USD8 trillion outstanding. In 2010, the Japanese government bond market became similar in size to the United States, but the U.S. data for 2010 exclude agency debt, which is now included in the corporate category. Together with Euroland, these countries account for more than 75% of the global bond market. Government bonds are defined broadly and include federal, state, and local government issues. In emerging markets, government issues made up 72% of total local currency debt in 2000, with this share decreasing to less than 50% by 2010. Overall, countries with large government sectors tend to have large government bond markets.

Corporations can issue bonds in the domestic or international bond markets. However, the domestic bond market is still the larger of the two. With USD7.8 trillion outstanding in 2000 and over USD14 trillion in 2010, the U.S. corporate bond market is the largest in the world, but other markets have seen rapid development in this segment recently. The international bond market represents almost 30% of the global bond market, but this share has been rapidly growing over time, as Exhibit 11.4 shows.

Because of its growing importance, we devote a separate subsection to the international bond market. We first discuss some important features of domestic bond markets, which will prove useful when we discuss international bonds.[3]

Domestic Bond Markets

Domestic bonds are regulated by the domestic governments of the countries in which they are issued. These agencies include the Securities and Exchange Commission (SEC) in the United States, the Financial Services Authority (FSA) in the United Kingdom, and the Ministry of Finance (MOF) and the Financial Services Agency (FSA) in Japan.

---

[3]In the following section, we use Bank for International Settlements statistics on "debt securities." These include securities with a maturity of less than 1 year, which are typically called "money market" securities, rather than "bonds."

Exhibit 11.3 The Size and Structure of the World Bond Market (in billions of U.S. dollars)

Panel A: End of 2000

Country	Total Outstanding	% World Bond Mkt	Government U.S. $ bn	Government % of Gov	Corporate U.S. $ bn	Corporate % of Corp	Foreign U.S. $bn	Foreign % of For	Eurobond US $ bn	Eurobond % of Total
United States	15,417.5	49.1	8,025.9	46.0	4,515.9	57.4	495.4	60.8	2,380.3	45.3
Euroland	6,223.8	19.8	3,125.0	17.9	1,027.7	16.9	0.0	0.0	1,771.1	33.7
Japan	5,549.3	17.7	3,995.6	22.9	973.0	12.4	72.6	8.9	508.1	9.7
United Kingdom	1,065.3	3.4	416.7	2.4	70.6	0.9	122.3	15.0	455.7	8.7
Canada	540.6	1.7	385.0	2.2	103.4	1.3	0.4	0.0	51.8	1.0
Switzerland	277.5	0.9	45.6	0.3	89.1	1.1	113.4	13.9	29.4	0.8
Australia	182.1	0.6	69.7	0.4	80.5	1.0	6.6	0.8	30.3	0.6
Total Developed	29,804.1	95.0	16,314.6	93.5	7,422.5	94.4	815.1	100.0	5,251.9	100.0
Emerging Markets	1,598.7	5.0	1,161.7	6.5	437.0*	5.6	NA	NA	NA	NA
Total	31,402.8	100.0	17,476.3	100.0	7,859.5	100.0	815.1	100.0	5,251.9	100.0

Panel B: End of 2010

Country	Total Outstanding	% World Bond Mkt	Government U.S. $ bn	Government % of Gov	Corporate U.S. $ bn	Corporate % of Corp	International U.S. $ bn	International % of For
United States	31,841.6	35.7	10,326.9	29.2	14,754.6	52.1	6,760.1	26.4
Euroland	23,871.9	26.7	6,377.0	18.0	6,364.6	22.5	10,559.1	41.3
Japan	12,835.5	14.4	10,536.0	29.8	1,921.0	6.8	378.5	1.5
United Kingdom	4,514.5	5.1	1,223.2	3.5	326.8	1.2	2,964.5	11.6
Canada	1,928.7	2.2	931.4	2.6	405.1	1.4	592.2	2.3
Switzerland	701.5	0.8	115.1	0.3	142.1	0.5	444.3	1.7
Australia	1,393.2	1.6	253.7	0.7	591.0	2.1	548.5	2.1
Total Developed	77,938.3	87.3	30,235.5	85.4	24,931.2	88.0	23,130.8	90.4
Emerging Markets	11,341.6	12.7	5,151.9	14.6	3,390.0	12.0	1,367.3	5.3
Total	89,279.9	100.0	35,387.4	100.0	28,321.2	100.0	25,574.3	100.0

Notes: Data for Panel A is from Merrill Lynch, *Size and Structure of the World Bond Market: 2001*, April 2001. In the United States, agency debt is included in the government category. Panel B is compiled from data in the *BIS Quarterly Review*, December 2010, Tables 12–16. Corporate issuance comprises domestic bonds by corporations and financial institutions. International issues by international agencies and offshore centers are not part of the developed or emerging market category totals. The BIS makes no distinction between foreign bonds and Eurobonds. Agency debt is not included in the government category for the United States.

*Asia only.

In the United States, a company issuing debt securities to the public in amounts greater than $1.5 million is required to prepare and file a registration statement with the SEC that includes a financial history of the company, the state of its existing business, and how the funds raised through the public offering are to be used. After the registration statement is filed with the SEC, there is a waiting period of 20 days during which the SEC reviews the accuracy and completeness of the registration statement. The issue is then priced and sold. Exceptions to this rule include short-term securities maturing within 9 months and private placements.

New public issues in Japan must be approved by the MOF. The registration process forces the issuers to maintain records of the owners of corporate and government bonds, thereby facilitating the calculation and payment of accrued interest. Registration also facilitates tax collection on the semiannual interest that the bonds pay.

Unlike the United States and Japan, governments and corporations in most western European countries issue bearer bonds, which are not registered in the name of a specific

Exhibit 11.4   The Internationalization of the World
                   Bond Market

Source: Merrill Lynch, *Size and Structure of the World Bond Market: 2001*, April 2001, along with author computations based on data from *BIS Quarterly Review*, June 2007 and June 2010.

owner. Historically, the bearer would actually cut an interest coupon from the bond's certificate and redeem the value of the coupon at the banking institution listed on the bond as a paying agent. The principal advantage of such bearer bonds was that they retain the anonymity of the bondholder, which makes them perfect for tax evasion. Because it is inconvenient to present bond coupons for payment of interest, bearer bonds were usually issued with annual coupons. Currently, bearer bonds usually operate by book entry, whereby investors buy and sell their interests in a global note representing the entire bond issue that is held by a custodian.

Domestic bond market prices and yield quotation conventions and withholding taxes differ from country to country. In many countries, corporate bonds are traded over the counter by commercial and investment banks as well as listed on the local stock exchange.

The International Bond Market

The Foreign Bond Market
Foreign bonds are issued by non-residents in a country's domestic capital market and are subject to domestic regulations rather than the trading conventions of the borrower's country. For example, in the United States, foreign bonds must go through the SEC's registration process, a costly process that requires disclosure of financial information.

To make the U.S. bond market more competitive with the less-regulated Eurobond market, the SEC allowed shelf registration (since 1982) and instituted Rule 144A (since 1990). With **shelf registration**, an issuer can preregister a securities issue and then shelve the securities for later sale, when financing is actually needed. As such, foreign companies can issue bonds quickly in the United States when they need financing, but they still must disclose lots of information, which some borrowers might find expensive and/or objectionable. Through **Rule 144A**, qualified institutional investors in the United States can invest in private placement issues that do not have to meet the strict information disclosure requirements of publicly traded issues.

In 2010 and 2011, the Samurai foreign bond market was particularly "hot," as Fujikawa (2011) notes. As one example, in early 2011, South Korea's KT Corporation, a telecom company, issued a 2-year JPY20 billion Samurai bond.

The Eurobond Market[4]

Eurobonds (which are issued simultaneously in the capital markets of several nations) need not comply with the regulatory restrictions that apply to domestic issues. For example, in March 2010, America Movil, Latin America's largest mobile operator, issued a $2 billion Eurobond with a 10-year maturity, a 5% semiannual coupon that sold at $993.56 per $1,000 face value. The bonds were sold by an international group of banks led by J.P. Morgan, Citigroup, and Goldman Sachs.

Although major MNCs, national and regional governments and their agencies, and supranational organizations, such as the World Bank, the Asian Development Bank, and organizations associated with the European Union, all issue Eurobonds, the most important borrowers in the international bond market (which combines Eurobonds and foreign bonds) are financial institutions. Exhibit 11.5 shows that financial institutions accounted for well over 75% of the $26.8 trillion of outstanding bonds in June 2010. Corporate borrowers have about $2 trillion outstanding, governments about $3.4 trillion, and international institutions about $0.9 trillion.

A withholding tax on interest payments in the U.S. domestic and foreign bond markets fueled the growth of the Eurobond market in the 1960s. Because taxes could be avoided on bearer bonds, investors were willing to accept lower yields on them. Many U.S. firms took advantage of this opportunity to lower their funding cost. The financial infrastructure in London (where most of the trading in Eurobonds takes place) and the liquidity of the London market have also helped the Eurobond market flourish. Although these withholding taxes and other regulations have since been abolished, the Eurobond market continues to thrive

Exhibit 11.5 Borrowers in the International Bond Market (amounts outstanding, September 2010, in billions of USD)

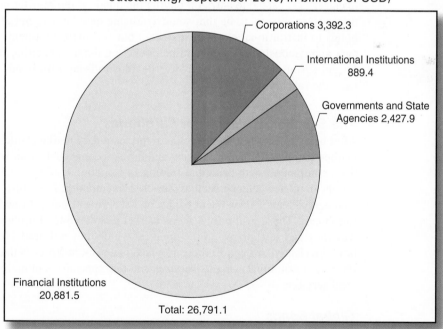

Source: Compiled from *BIS Quarterly Review*, December 2010, Tables 12A–12D.

---

[4]For a comprehensive study of the Eurobond market between 1980 and 2000, see Claes et al. (2002).

because, unlike any other capital market, it remains largely untaxed, unregulated, and convenient. Despite attempts to improve the competitive position of the U.S. bond market relative to the Eurobond market via shelf registration, Rule 144A, and so forth, the SEC disclosure requirements and registration procedure remain time consuming and costly for some U.S. and non-U.S. issuers.

The Primary Market for Eurobonds

When a bond issue is large, the borrower often benefits by issuing the bonds in a variety of locations. A borrower wanting to issue a Eurobond contacts an investment bank to serve as **lead manager** (or *bookrunner*) of a group of investment and commercial banks, or **syndicate**, that bring the bonds to market. From 1980 to 2000, more than 90% of Eurobond issues were coordinated by a single bookrunner. The lead manager usually invites co-managers to form a managing group to help negotiate terms with the borrower, ascertain market conditions, and manage the issuance.

A subset of the banks in the syndicate serve as underwriters for the issue. That is, they commit their own capital to buy the issue from the borrower at a discount, which is called the underwriting spread. Most of the underwriters are also part of the group that sells the bonds to the investing public. The various members of the underwriting syndicate receive a portion of the spread, depending on the number and the type of functions they perform. The lead manager obviously receives the full spread, but a bank serving only as a member of the selling group receives a smaller portion.

Since 1989, most Eurobond syndicates have used the fixed-price re-offer method to issue bonds. In this system, syndicate members agree to sell bonds only at a predetermined price until the lead manager feels the deal is largely placed, or until the market moves significantly. Then "the deal breaks syndicate," and bonds are free to trade at whatever level the market sets, depending on supply and demand. However, the lead manager is expected to carry on buying the bonds at the re-offer price. One problem with this system appears to be that some syndicate members do not attempt to distribute the bonds to institutional or retail investors but sell their allotments back to the lead manager anonymously, in the meantime pocketing the underwriting fees. It takes about 5 to 6 weeks from the date the borrower decides to issue Eurobonds until the net proceeds from the sale are received.

The Secondary Market for Eurobonds

After being issued, Eurobonds trade in the secondary market, which is an over-the-counter market, comprising market makers and brokers connected by an array of telecommunications equipment, with principal trading in London. Trading is also done in other major European money centers, such as Zurich, Luxembourg, Frankfurt, and Amsterdam. Many commercial banks, investment banks, and securities trading firms hold large portfolios of Eurobonds. These institutions act as market makers in the Eurobond market quoting two-way (buy and sell) prices on the bonds at which they will trade. Most Eurobond transactions are cleared through Euroclear, which is a bank in Brussels that is owned by the many financial institutions using its services and that specializes in multiple cross-border settlement services.

Global Bonds

A 10-year $1.5 billion offering by the World Bank in 1989 was the first global bond issued simultaneously in a domestic market and in the Eurobond market. This is particularly important in the United States because U.S. investors can generally only buy Eurobonds after a 40-day waiting period due to the fact that they are not registered. Borrowers issuing global bonds must be large and creditworthy, and they must borrow in actively traded currencies.

Miller and Puthenpurackal (2005) analyzed a large number of global bond issues and found that such bonds lower borrowing costs by approximately 20 basis points relative to non-global bonds.

Dragon Bonds

A **Dragon bond** is a Eurobond targeted at the Asian market (outside Japan) with Asian syndication. Lehman Brothers launched Dragon bonds in November 1991 with an issue by the Asian Development Bank. Whereas Dragon bonds are launched during Asian market hours and listed in Hong Kong and Singapore, they are cleared in Europe through major clearance organizations such as Euroclear and Clearstream. Secondary market trading is also still concentrated in Europe, primarily in London.

The Blurring of the Distinctions in the International Bond Market

The acceleration of globalization, including tax harmonization, financial deregulation, and the widespread relaxation of capital controls, has blurred traditional distinctions between domestic and international bonds, especially in Euroland. Panel A of Exhibit 11.3 uses the official definitions of the Bank for International Settlements (BIS), which has long been a leading source for international debt statistics. It divides the Eurobond market according to the currency of issue. However, the increased globalization of the world's bond markets has caused what were once distinctive market features to be more common across markets. In addition, global consolidation of the financial service industry and opportunities for foreign intermediaries to participate fully in domestic issuance make national distinctions somewhat nebulous. Finally, some statistical offices do not provide sufficient information to distinguish between foreign and traditional Eurobonds. As a result, the more recent BIS data used in Panel B no longer make this distinction.

The Types of Debt Instruments in the International Bond Market

Three main types of bonds are issued in the international bond market. We discuss them in the order of their relative importance and end the section by discussing the currency denomination of international bonds.

Straight Fixed-Rate Issues

Straight fixed-rate bond issues have a set maturity date at which the issuer promises to repay the principal or face value of the bond. During the life of the bond, fixed coupon payments, which are a percentage of the face value, are paid as interest to the bondholders. These bonds are sometimes called *bullet bonds*.

A special category of straight fixed-rate bonds is zero-coupon bonds, which are sold at a discount from face value and do not pay any coupon interest. At maturity, the investor receives the full face value. Zero-coupon bonds have been denominated primarily in U.S. dollars and Swiss francs. Zero-coupon bonds are attractive to investors who want to avoid the risk of reinvesting coupon receipts at possibly lower interest rates. Under U.S. tax law, interest on a zero-coupon bond is taxable as it accrues, even though there is no actual cash flow to the investor.

Exhibit 11.6 shows that the vast majority of international bonds outstanding in both 2000 and 2010 were straight fixed-rate bonds, with a share of about 70%.

Floating-Rate Notes

Floating-rate notes (FRNs) constitute about 30% of the total amount of international bonds outstanding. FRNs are typically medium-term bonds, with maturities between

Exhibit 11.6 Types of International Bonds Issued in the Marketplace (in billions of U.S. dollars)

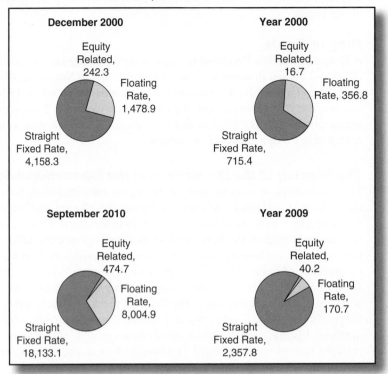

Note: The pies on the left represent amounts outstanding, whereas the pies on the right refer to new issues during that particular year.

Source: BIS Quarterly Review, December 2010, Table 13B.

1 and 10 years and with coupon payments indexed to a reference interest rate. Common reference rates are 3-month and 6-month LIBOR, and coupons are paid quarterly or semi-annually, consistent with the maturity underlying the reference rate. Most companies pay a spread above the relevant LIBOR rate, which reflects the company's credit risk (see Section 11.5). For example, in February 2011, Anheuser-Busch Inbev, the Belgian beer company, issued a 5-year FRN that paid 55 basis points (0.55%) over the 3-month USD LIBOR at a price of $998.17 per $1,000 face value. The discount to face value increased the effective spread.

At the beginning of every 3-month period, the next quarterly coupon payment is *reset* to be $\frac{1}{4} \times (\text{LIBOR} + 0.55\%)$ of face value, where LIBOR is an annual percentage rate. As an example, suppose the 3-month U.S. dollar LIBOR is 2.5%. Then, the interest paid on a $1,000 face value FRN is

$$\tfrac{1}{4} \times (0.0250 + 0.0055) \times \$1,000 = \$7.63$$

Equity-Related Bonds

As Exhibit 11.6 shows, equity-related bonds are a small component of the international bond market. This category of bonds consists of two closely related securities: convertible bonds and bonds with warrants. A **convertible bond** is a straight bond that is convertible into equity prior to maturity. The bondholder has the option to convert the bond into a certain number of shares, which is fixed when the bond is issued. Alternatively, the bond can have an attached

warrant, which grants the bondholder the right to purchase a certain amount of common stock of the company at a specified price. Investors accept lower coupon rates on convertible bonds than on comparable straight fixed-coupon bonds because of the added option value of the conversion feature. Bonds with warrants differ in that the warrant is detachable and can trade separately from the bond.

The difference between the market value of the convertible bond and that of the straight bond involves the value of the conversion option. Companies often issue convertible bonds and warrants when it is difficult to assess the riskiness of the debt, such as when the firm is involved in projects with very uncertain cash flows or when investors are worried that managers may not act in their interests. The convertible bond gives investors a piece of the equity action when the projects turn out to be successful. While rapidly growing firms with heavy capital expenditures find the lower interest rates paid on these bonds to be particularly helpful, convertible bonds are not cheap debt because the firm also issues a valuable conversion option.

In international markets, convertible bonds were very popular in the 1980s among Japanese companies. Many of the embedded equity options subsequently proved to be worthless when the Japanese bull market crashed toward the end of the 1980s.

Currency of Denomination

Historically, U.S. dollar–denominated bonds dominated international bond markets. As Exhibit 11.7 indicates, euro-denominated bonds now dominate. The only other currencies in which bonds are widely denominated are the pound, yen, and Swiss franc (in that order).

A special type of international bond is a **dual-currency bond**, which became popular in the mid-1980s. A dual-currency bond is a straight fixed-rate bond issued in one currency, say yen, which pays coupon interest in that same currency, but the promised repayment of principal at maturity is denominated in another currency, say U.S. dollars. The interest rates on these bonds are often higher than those on comparable straight

Exhibit 11.7   Currency of Issuance in the International Bond Market (September 2010, outstanding amounts, in billions of U.S. dollars)

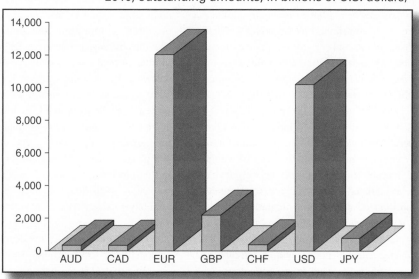

Source: Compiled based on *BIS Quarterly Review*, December 2010, Table 13B.

fixed-rate bonds. The amount of the dollar principal repayment at maturity is set when the bond is issued. Frequently, however, the amount allows for some appreciation of the stronger currency.

The dual-currency bond can be viewed as a combination of a straight yen bond and a long-term forward contract to sell the dollar principal back for yen. The yen market value of a dual-currency bond should therefore equal the sum of the present value of the yen coupon stream discounted at the yen market rate of interest plus the present value in yen of the dollar principal converted to yen at the forward exchange rate and discounted at the yen market rate of interest. Whether the bond is a good investment *ex post* depends on the movement of the dollar relative to the yen over the life of the bond.

Japanese firms have historically been large issuers of dual-currency bonds, with coupon payments in yen and the principal repayment in U.S. dollars. Use of yen/dollar dual-currency bonds can be an attractive way for Japanese MNCs to establish or expand U.S. subsidiaries. The yen proceeds can be converted to dollars to finance the capital investment in the United States, and during the early years, the coupon payments can be made by the parent firm in yen. At maturity, the dollar principal repayment can be made from dollar profits earned by the subsidiary.

On Dim Sum and Original Sin

Bond markets in developing countries are still relatively underdeveloped, especially when considering local currency–denominated debt. In developed countries, the local currency–denominated bond market represents more than 130% of gross domestic product (GDP), although it represents barely over 20% of GDP in developing economies (see Burger et al., 2010). International economists have dubbed this inability of corporations and governments in developing countries to issue debt denominated in their own currency as "original sin."

Original sin has been blamed for many global economic malaises. It contributed to the crises in Mexico, Southeast Asia, and Russia (or at least made their consequences worse, when depreciating currencies exacerbated the debt burdens). Some have even argued that original sin was one of the root causes of the 2007 to 2010 global crisis. In the years preceding the crisis, the global supply of savings increased substantially. This "global savings glut," as Federal Reserve Chairman Bernanke (2005) called it, originated partly in emerging economies, many of which ran sizable current account surpluses. Lacking well-developed local financial markets, their savings were channeled to more developed financial markets, particularly to the United States. The desire to build up official reserves following the crises of the 1990s certainly also played a role. These forces allowed the United States to run high current account deficits and contributed to what macro-economists called significant "global imbalances" (see Caballero et al., 2008).

Foreign demand for U.S. Treasury bonds may have helped lower their yields, which in turn contributed to excessive leverage by U.S. financial institutions and stoked the global financial crisis. It is conceivable that better developed financial markets in developing economies could have resulted in a more even distribution of the "global savings glut." From this perspective, developing financial markets in developing countries, including local currency–denominated bonds, may contribute to global financial stability.

The first signs of recovery after the global financial crisis seem to indicate that "original sin" may be on its way out. Many corporations and governments in developing countries have been able to raise significant sums of money in international bond markets, issuing bonds in their own currency. For example, one of Latin America's deals of 2010 according to *Euromoney* was the Republic of Chile's 10-year bond issue, with a U.S. dollar tranche of $1 billion and a Chilean peso tranche equivalent to $556 million. On the corporate side, Emgesa, a Colombian electric power company, issued a global bond (equivalent to USD400 million) in January 2011 that was denominated in Colombian pesos (even though all payments will be made in USD) with buyers nicely spread out over the United States, Latin America, and Europe.

Clearly, investors in the developed world now show an appetite for local currency–denominated debt issued by emerging market companies. So, surely, Chinese debt must be in high demand? Unfortunately, strict capital controls prevent foreign investors from buying China's domestic yuan debt. Fortunately, the Chinese government is allowing, even encouraging, an offshore yuan market to develop, especially in Hong Kong. Foreign investors can now feast on "Dim Sum" bonds, which are issued in Hong Kong but denominated in Chinese yuan. While the issuers are typically Chinese companies, this need not be the case. Another "deal of the year" for 2010, according to *Euromoney*, was VTB Bank's CNY1 billion Dim Sum 3-year notes. VTB Bank is a Russian, state-owned bank!

In early 2011, Dim Sum bonds began to run out of steam as the Chinese government made it more difficult to put the yuan raised through such bonds to work in China. Several companies, especially Chinese real estate groups such as Evergrande Real Estate, started to issue so-called "synthetic yuan bonds," which are denominated in yuan but trade in dollars. Surprisingly, the Chinese government imposes fewer restrictions on deploying money raised that way in mainland China investments (see Stein, 2011).

11.4 INTERNATIONAL BANKING

The growth and increasing integration of the world economy since the end of World War II has been paralleled by an expansion of global banking activities as commercial banks have followed their customers into foreign markets. We use two criteria to differentiate international from domestic banking activities: the location and the counterparty. If either the borrower or the depositor is a non-resident, the transaction is viewed as international. However, a transaction is also typically categorized as international if it occurs in a non-domestic currency. Exhibit 11.8 reports the international claims (lending) for the majority of the world's banks, categorized by borrowing country.

Exhibit 11.8 Consolidated Foreign Claims of Reporting Banks (by borrowing country, in billions of U.S. dollars), June 2010

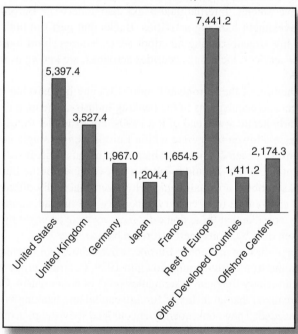

Note: This exhibit was constructed using data from Table 9A, Consolidated Foreign Claims of Reporting Banks on Individual Countries, *BIS Quarterly Review*, December 2010, pages A54–A61.

These claims are on a worldwide consolidated basis, covering all "international" contractual lending by the head office and its branches and subsidiaries. More specifically, it includes

- Cross-border claims in all currencies (that is, the borrower is a foreign entity relative to the bank's country)
- Local claims (the borrower is domestic but borrows in non-local currencies)
- Local currency positions of reporting banks' foreign affiliates with local residents

The five main countries of international banking activity are the United States, the United Kingdom, Germany, Japan, and France. This reflects the roles of New York, London, Frankfurt, Paris, and Tokyo as major international financial centers, and it also correlates with the sizes of these countries' economies. Lots of activity also happens in offshore banking centers, with the Cayman Islands accounting for more than 30%.

In this section, we first offer a brief survey of banks as important multinationals. We then summarize some important international banking regulations, known as the BIS standards. Finally, we survey the different organizational forms through which international banks assist their multinational clients, clarifying the differences between, for example, branches, subsidiaries, and offshore banking centers.

Banks as MNCs

Commercial banks usually develop a complete line of financial services to facilitate the overseas transactions of their customers. In addition to commercial credit, these ancillary financial services include trading in foreign currency spot, forward, option, and swap markets; risk management services; international trade financing; and working capital and cash management.

Unlike domestic banks, international banks participate in the Eurocurrency market and are frequently members of international loan syndicates, lending out large sums of money to MNCs or governments. International banks also underwrite Eurobonds and foreign bonds, which are investment banking activities. Banks that perform both traditional commercial banking and investment banking functions are called **merchant banks**. Banks that provide a wide array of services, including securities activities, are known as **universal banks**, or **full-service banks**.

The formation of the European Union (EU) and intensifying global competition have led to mergers and acquisitions in the banking industry. The merger and acquisition activity was particularly hectic at the end of the 1990s. For example, following the formation of the EU, banks were allowed to operate within Europe using a single banking license instead of needing licenses in each country in which they did business. It was generally expected that this relaxation in the rules would result in a consolidation of the European banking industry, as large banks gobbled up small banks. However, that really did not happen. By and large, banks didn't consolidate from country to country, but instead, consolidated *within* countries. It is certainly possible that these domestic mergers were an effort by domestic banks to stave off being taken over by "foreigners" (foreign banks).

The exception was in Central Europe, where almost all the major banks are in foreign hands. When the Iron Curtain came down in 1989, Central Europe was stuck with an inefficient and rudimentary financial system after years of communism. Central European governments soon realized that an influx of foreign capital and banking know-how and technology were badly needed. They consequently encouraged the foreign acquisition of their domestic banks. Somewhat surprisingly, the large international banks were not the main acquirers, but rather a number of medium-sized players with regional focus. These included a number of Austrian banks, such as Erste Bank, Bank Austria (owned by the Italian bank UniCredit), and Raiffeisen International, and a small Belgian bank, KBC.

The global economic integration process has transformed the banking sector from a localized, heavily regulated sector into one of the most global sectors in the world. Bekaert et al. (2011) measure how close market valuations of various industries in different countries are to global averages. They argue that under fairly mild assumptions, globally integrated and interconnected sectors would show smaller differences. By this measure, in 1980 to 1984, the banking sector was one of the most "local" and segmented sectors in the world; in 2000 to 2005, it was one of the most globalized sectors in the world. The BIS's "80th Annual Report" (2010) shows that international lending (the international claims studied in Exhibit 11.8) as a percentage of total lending steadily increased for most countries over the first decade of the 21st century.

At the same time, the banking sector also became a larger part of the economy, both in terms of market valuation and value added (with the exception of Japan, where the banking sector collapsed after the crisis in the early 1990s), after successive waves of consolidation. In hindsight, the 2007 to 2010 crisis taught us that the banking sector probably became too big and too highly leveraged. The 2010 BIS annual report computed the banking sector's precrisis leverage ratio to be on the order of 18. That is, for every dollar of equity, a typical bank would have $19 of assets. Some banks were much more levered than this average ratio. Clearly, even a small shock to asset values can bring such thinly capitalized banks to the brink of insolvency. Moreover, the international interconnections enabled the spillover of stress across borders. Here we simply note that the crisis had a profound effect on the sector. A number of banks, such as Bank of America and Wells Fargo, became larger by gobbling up (close to) bankrupt rivals. Governments in several countries took equity stakes in banks, which, to date, have not been fully divested. (The U.S. government sold its final stake in Citigroup in December 2010.) All of these developments have had a profound effect on the relative size and identity of the top global banks. Exhibit 11.9 lists the 25 largest banks in the

Exhibit 11.9 The Largest Banks Ranked by Market Capitalization

Ranking March 2010	Bank	Country	Assets (in billions of USD)	Market Capitalization (in billions of USD)
1	ICBC	China	1,428.46	242.23
2	China Construction Bank	China	1,106.20	184.32
3	HSBC Holdings	UK	2,355.83	178.27
4	Bank of America	USA	2,223.30	167.63
5	JPMorgan Chase	USA	2,031.99	166.19
6	Bank of China	China	1,016.31	147.00
7	Wells Fargo	USA	1,253.65	141.69
8	Banco Santander	Spain	1,438.68	107.12
9	Citigroup	USA	1,856.65	96.54
10	BNP Paribas	France	2,952.22	86.67
12	Royal Bank of Canada	Canada	608.05	78.17
13	Commonwealth Bank	Australia	500.20	75.10
14	Mitsubishi UFJ Financial	Japan	1,999.58	72.17
15	Westpac Banking Group	Australia	519.03	70.99
16	Bank of Communications	China	392.83	57.34
17	Barclays	UK	2,223.04	56.15
18	Toronto-Dominion Bank	Canada	517.28	55.43
19	Banco Bradesco	Brazil	281.40	54.50
20	AZN Banking	Australia	420.52	53.72
21	Lloyds Banking Group	UK	1,650.78	50.25
22	National Australia Bank	Australia	574.41	48.80
23	BBVA-Banco Bilbao Vizcaya	Spain	760.32	48.20
24	Bank of Nova Scotia	Canada	460.93	47.26
25	US Bancorp	USA	281.18	46.89

Source: "The Global 2000," Forbes.com, April 2010.

world, based on market capitalization. The top 10 include five Anglo-Saxon banks and three Chinese banks. The ascent of the Chinese banks is a relatively recent phenomenon, which results not only from the rapid development of the Chinese economy and the relatively high valuation of its stock market, but also from China being relatively insulated from the 2007 to 2010 global crisis.

Bank Consolidation Gone Awry

In 2007, Barclays, the 17th-largest bank, bid €63.9 billion for ABN AMRO, the 26th-largest bank with 4,500 branches across 53 countries. This bid was topped by a consortium led by Royal Bank of Scotland (RBS; the ninth-largest bank), which bid €70.5 billion. Under the RBS bid, Fortis NV of Belgium would take ABN AMRO's Dutch operations and its wealth and asset management operations, Banco Santander Central Hispano SA would take ABN AMRO's Brazilian and Italian operations, and RBS would get the rest, including ABN AMRO's investment banking arm. This deal was the largest in the financial industry to date.

A look behind the scenes of this acquisition reveals how bad business decisions can not only bankrupt a business, but also imperil the economy at large. RBS went from a small Scottish retail bank to one of the largest banks in the world in less than 20 years, mostly through aggressive acquisitions that included the takeover of Nat-West, a large British bank in 2000. While many of the acquisitions were value enhancing, the ABN AMRO deal

proved to be the swan song. RBS appeared not to realize how deeply exposed ABN AMRO was to subprime mortgages. As the crisis unfolded, losses at ABN AMRO started to mount. Moreover, Fortis, the Belgian-Dutch acquirer, found it increasingly hard to fund itself in the money markets, as its own exposures to toxic assets became more transparent. In September 2008, in the middle of the integration process between ABN AMRO and RBS and the separation process of assets with Fortis, the problems at both ABN AMRO and Fortis became so severe that the banks were partly nationalized and the Fortis bank split again into Belgian and Dutch parts, with the Belgian part being sold to France's BNP Paribas. In October 2008, RBS's corporate clients lost confidence in the bank and started to withdraw deposits. The bank had to be bailed out by the U.K. government, who took an equity stake that it had to increase to 84% by November 2009! As part of the recovery process, many of RBS's acquisitions will undoubtedly be unwound.

Types of International Banking Offices

Exhibit 11.10 provides an overview of the organizational forms that banks may use for their international banking activities.

Exhibit 11.10 Orginization Structure of International Banking

	International Bank							
Characteristic	Domestic Bank	Correspondent Bank	Representative Office	Foreign Branch	Subsidiary/ Affiliate Bank	Offshore Bank	International Banking Facility	Edge Act Bank
Location	Domestic	Foreign	Foreign	Foreign	Foreign	Foreign	Domestic	Domestic
Loans/deposits to foreigners	No	—	No	Yes	Yes	Yes	Yes	Yes
Separate legal entity	No	—	No	No	Yes	No	No	Yes

Note: This exhibit was inspired by Exhibit 6.2 in Eun and Resnick (1997), p. 145

Correspondent Banks

When commercial banks do not have their own banking operation in a major financial center, they establish a correspondent relationship with a local bank to conduct trade financing, foreign exchange services, and other activities on their behalves. Correspondent relationships allow a bank to service its multinational corporate clients without having to locate their banking personnel in many countries. However, the **correspondent bank** may not be able to give the same level of services as it would if it had its own facilities.

Representative Offices

A **representative office** is a small service facility that is staffed by parent bank personnel and designed to assist the clients of the parent bank in their dealings with the bank's correspondents or with information about local business practices and credit evaluation of the MNC's foreign customers. Although it does not provide direct banking functions to the MNCs, it represents a higher level of service than pure correspondent banking.

Foreign Branches

A **foreign branch** is legally part of the parent bank, but it operates like a local bank. A foreign branch allows the parent bank to offer its domestic, foreign, and international customers direct, seamless service in multiple countries. However, setting up a foreign branch is much more expensive than partnering with a correspondent bank. Foreign branch banks are also subject to both the banking regulations of their home countries *and* the countries in which they operate. However, foreign branches of U.S. banks are not subject to U.S. reserve requirements and are not required to have federal deposit insurance, which guarantees depositors up to $250,000 if the bank fails. Banks fund the Federal Deposit Insurance Corporation (FDIC) by paying insurance premiums expressed as a percentage of their deposits. Hence, both reserve requirements and deposit insurance drive up the cost of funds for banks and would prevent branches of U.S. banks from operating on the same level playing field as the local banks. Conversely, when a foreign bank locates a branch in the United States, the branch is treated like a domestic bank, and it is subject to all the same U.S. regulations.

Subsidiary and Affiliate Banks

Like a branch, a **subsidiary bank** is also wholly or partly owned by a parent bank, but it is incorporated in the foreign country in which it is located. An **affiliate bank** is only partly owned but not controlled by a foreign parent bank. Affiliate and subsidiary banks are subject to the banking laws of the countries in which they are incorporated. Prior to the repeal of the Glass Steagall Act in 1999, that meant, for example, that a U.S. parent bank was prohibited from engaging in investment banking activities, but its subsidiaries located abroad were not. Nevertheless, U.S. parent banks generally preferred to expand their operations overseas via branch banks.

Offshore Banking Centers[5]

An **offshore banking center** is a center that satisfies most of a number of conditions. First, the bulk of financial activity on both sides of the bank's balance sheet—that is, both borrowing and lending—is offshore, that is with non-residents as counterparties. Second, the transactions are typically initiated outside the financial center. Third, the majority of the financial institutions involved are controlled by non-residents doing business primarily with non-residents. Finally, the centers typically offer low or zero taxation, moderate or light financial regulation, banking secrecy, and anonymity on transactions.

Offshore banking centers can be found in the Bahamas, Bahrain, Bermuda, the Cayman Islands, Jersey, Hong Kong, the Netherlands Antilles, Panama, Singapore, Vanuatu, and

---

[5]See, for instance, "Offshore Financial Centers" (2002).

the West Indies, among other countries. Offshore banks engage in foreign currency loans, the floating of Eurobonds, over-the-counter trading in derivatives, and deposit taking from individual customers seeking to lower their tax liabilities. In some countries, international banks establish "shell branches," which have only a very limited physical presence in these nations—sometimes only post office boxes!

Clearly, a lack of financial regulation can lead to tax evasion and financial crime. Consequently, various international organizations, such as the BIS, the Organization for Economic Cooperation and Development (OECD), and the European Union, have joined forces in an effort to supervise the activities taking place in these centers. A major impetus to these efforts was the collapse of BCCI (Bank of Credit and Commerce International) in 1991. For years, BCCI (dubbed by some as the "Bank of Crooks and Criminals International") laundered drug money, faked loans, and hid losses without regulators noticing.

In the wake of the terrorist attacks of September 2001, the United States substantially expanded its antiterrorism legislation, including the power to seize money from foreign banks doing business in the United States, without notifying the foreign government. So far, the new tool has primarily been used in fraud and money-laundering cases. However, in 2009, the U.S. government forced UBS, a Swiss bank, to disclose the names of a number of accounts held by tax-evading U.S. citizens, an apparent violation of Swiss banking secrecy laws.

Edge Act Banks
Edge Act banks are federally chartered subsidiaries of U.S. banks that are physically located in the United States but are allowed to engage in a full range of international banking activities. Such activities include accepting deposits from foreign customers, trade financing, and transferring international funds. Edge Act banks are not prohibited from owning equity in U.S. corporations, as are domestic commercial banks. Consequently, U.S. parent banks own foreign subsidiaries and affiliate banks through an Edge Act setup.

International Banking Facilities
An **international banking facility (IBF)** is a separate set of asset and liability accounts that is segregated on the parent bank's books, so it is not a unique physical or legal entity. Any U.S.-chartered depositary institution (including a U.S. branch, a subsidiary of a foreign bank, or a U.S. office of an Edge Act bank) can operate an IBF. An IBF operates as a foreign bank in the United States and is consequently not subject to domestic reserve requirements or FDIC insurance regulation. However, IBFs may only accept deposits from non-U.S. citizens and make loans to foreigners. The bulk of an IBF's activities relate to interbank business.

The U.S. Federal Reserve established IBFs in an effort to allow U.S. banks to recapture business lost to offshore banks. Other countries created similar institutions. Examples include the Japanese Offshore Market (JOM) and the Bangkok International Banking Facilities in Thailand. These initiatives, along with the relaxation of financial regulations worldwide to allow offshore banking activities to be conducted by domestic banks, have slowed the growth of genuine offshore banking activities.

International Banking Regulation

The increasing globalization of the world's financial markets and the growth of international banking activities created the need for an international supervisory framework to prevent failures in one banking system from spilling over into other countries and to prevent a race to the bottom in bank regulation. Recall that banks hold capital (equity capital and other reserves) to protect depositors against losses. A bank's assets consist of the securities it buys and the loans it provides. The liabilities of the bank are the deposits it accepts from its customers, the borrowing the bank does in securities markets, and the bank's equity capital. The important role banks play in allocating capital in most countries makes their business losses resulting from companies not repaying their loans a regulatory concern, and most countries require banks to have a minimum capital-to-asset ratio as a safety cushion against losses.

The failure of one bank can set off a bank run—as worried depositors withdraw funds at many banks. Worse, bank failures in one country can lead to a global financial crisis or at least spill over into other countries. To mitigate this "systemic risk," the risk that the entire financial system can fail as a result of the failure of one bank or a few banks, central banks desire international regulation to ensure that an adequate level of capital is maintained in the international banking system. Nevertheless, bank runs have occurred regularly, and the existing regulations did not stave off the 2007 to 2010 banking crisis.

In addition, the variety of different national regulations potentially gives an unfair advantage to banks from countries with laxer regulatory standards, which could decrease the safety of the international banking system overall. International regulations create a more level playing field. A case in point occurred during the 1980s when central bankers from the G10 countries became worried that increased international competition in the banking industry due to globalization and deregulation had eroded the capital base of international banks. Japanese banks, for example, had aggressively built up their international loan portfolios by making low-cost loans. These banks gained market share, but subsequently, many of them went bankrupt. This background set the stage for the 1988 Basel Accord.

International Capital Adequacy: The 1988 Basel Accord

The **Basel Accord** of 1988 requires internationally active banks in the G10 countries to hold capital equal to at least 8% of a basket of assets measured in different ways, according to their riskiness. The accord was put together by the Basel Committee on Banking Supervision, a committee of banking supervisory authorities that was established in 1975 by the central banks of the G10 countries. It consists of senior banking supervisors and representatives of the central banks of Belgium, Canada, France, Germany, Italy, Japan, Luxembourg, the Netherlands, Sweden, Switzerland, the United Kingdom, and the United States. It usually meets at the BIS in Basel, Switzerland.

The 1988 Basel Accord was primarily concerned with default or credit risk. To measure the riskiness of a bank's asset portfolio, the assets are classified into four buckets, according to debtor category. The first category requires no capital charge and consists of items such as Treasury bills and bonds, which have zero credit risk. Claims on other banks receive only a 20% weighting, meaning that only 20% of the claim is counted against the 8% capital requirement. Some claims receive a 50% weighting, but virtually all claims on the non-bank private sector receive a 100% weight and hence the full capital charge.

One difficulty in establishing the riskiness of a bank's activities is that many bank activities are not recorded on the balance sheet. These so-called off-balance sheet activities involve trading financial instruments and generating income from fees and loan sales. Good examples include foreign exchange trading activities and interest rate and currency swaps. The Basel Accord attempted to establish ways to measure the riskiness of these activities, using complex conversion factors. Over time, it was also recognized that the regulatory framework should not only apply to credit risk but to market risk as well. Market risk is the risk of losses in trading positions when prices move adversely. In 1996, the Basel Accord was amended, and trading positions in bonds, equities, foreign exchange, and commodities were removed from the credit risk category and given explicit capital charges. During the 1990s, well over 100 countries adopted the measures set forth in the Basel Accord, making it the world standard on banking regulation.

A New Capital-Adequacy Framework or Basel II

The Basel Accord was also subject to criticism. First, the simple bucket approach with a flat 8% charge for loans made to the private sector gave banks an incentive to move high-quality assets off their balance sheets. The enormous growth in **asset securitization**—the packaging of assets or obligations (mortgages or car loans, for example) into securities for sale to third parties—played a large role in this development. Banks found that they could sell a portfolio of higher-quality loans for an amount slightly greater than the value of the original loans, making the banks profits and reducing their capital charges. Of course, the practice also reduced the average quality of bank loan portfolios. Second, financial institutions gradually developed more sophisticated models to measure risk than the simple approach adopted in the Basel Accord. Finally, the 1988 accord did not sufficiently recognize the use of techniques to mitigate credit risk, such as collateral, guarantees, or hedges.

In response to these criticisms, the Basel Committee started work on a new accord, Basel II, in 1999, hoping to implement it in each country by the end of 2006. The new accord has three pillars. The first pillar still requires the bank capital ratio (the ratio of bank capital to risk-weighted assets) to be 8%. However, now three types of risk are explicitly and separately recognized: credit risk, market risk, and operational risk. This last risk category is new. Operational risk is the risk of direct or indirect loss resulting from inadequate or failed internal processes, people, and systems or from external events, such as computer failure, poor documentation, or fraud.

Changes to the old accord had already allowed banking institutions to choose between the Basel Committee guidelines to measure market risk or to use internally developed models. In 1994, JPMorgan made its internally developed model (RiskMetrics) publicly available and introduced the *VaR* terminology. VaR stands for **value at risk**. It measures the dollar loss that a given portfolio position can experience with 5% probability over a given length of time. If the weekly VaR is $100,000, it means that the position (or set of positions) could lose $100,000 in about 1 out of 20 weeks. Using the logic developed in Chapter 3, the VaR depends on the conditional volatility of the underlying asset returns. Importantly, internal models of risk take into account the risk reduction allowed by holding a diversified portfolio of imperfectly correlated assets.

For credit risk measurement, the new accord gives banks two options: They can use either a standardized approach for credit risk measurement or an "internal-rating-based approach." The standardized approach maintains the old framework, but now the differentiated risk weightings are based on a rating provided by an external credit assessment institution. Moreover, these weightings take into account the use of collateral, guarantees, and hedging techniques. Under the internal-ratings-based approach, banks are allowed to use their internal estimates of creditworthiness to assess the credit risk of their portfolios, subject to strict methodological and disclosure standards.

The second pillar of the accord involves a supervisory review process. That is, bank supervisors must ensure that each bank has sound internal processes in place to assess capital adequacy commensurate with its risks. The final pillar stresses market discipline through disclosure. The new accord describes disclosure requirements related to the internal risk assessment methods a bank uses to compute its capital adequacy. This information is essential to ensure that market participants (including the multinational clients of the banks) better understand the bank's risk profile and solvency.

Basel III and the Crisis[6]

By 2006, Basel II had been implemented by the European Union; in the United States, the implementation literally ran aground when the global financial crisis hit. The crisis nonetheless laid bare many deficiencies of the old system. For example, the internal-ratings-based approach underestimates true capital needs because most quantitative models overestimate the power of diversification to reduce risk. During a crisis, many assets lose value together,

---

[6]See, for example, Eubanks (2010) and information on the Web site of the BIS.

and many banks hold similar positions, which increases the riskiness of bank portfolios. These problems were abundantly clear in the crisis.

The BIS, together with central banks and supervisory authorities, have tried to draw lessons from the crisis in developing a new capital adequacy framework, called Basel III. While not fully finalized yet, its major features are already known. First, core capital is defined more narrowly as retained earnings and common shares, which proved the only real buffer banks had during the crisis, and the amount of such capital banks must hold is being increased from 2% to 4.5%. Second, Basel III proposes a "capital conservation buffer," also in the form of core capital (2.5% of the bank's risk-weighted assets), as a cushion against future periods of stress. Third, Basel III recommends that local authorities require a countercyclical capital buffer such that when the economy is doing well and lending is less risky, banks are forced to hold more capital to avoid excessive risk taking and to build up a capital buffer that can be drawn upon in periods of stress. Fourth, because the crisis entailed a drying up of market liquidity, regulators want to trace and monitor funding liquidity of banks. Fifth, leverage played a huge role in the financial crisis. As we noted earlier, the banking sector is the most leveraged industry in the world. There are plans to introduce a maximum leverage ratio.

All of these changes are scheduled to be gradually phased in over several years. In the meantime, many countries worry about inconsistencies between the new international rules and their own, mostly new, banking regulation. In the United States, for example, the Dodd–Frank Wall Street Reform and Consumer Protection Act was signed into law by President Barack Obama on July 21, 2010, and it contains many provisions regarding bank regulation, including capital requirements. Senator Dodd explicitly worried about international regulatory arbitrage with financial institutions shopping for the weakest regulator.

11.5 INTERNATIONAL BANK LOANS

In addition to tapping the bond markets, MNCs can also obtain loans from their banks. We next discuss several of the options and end with a discussion of how the differences between alternative financing options have become blurred.

Eurocredits

In Chapter 6, we discussed the interbank market known as the Eurocurrency market—the market where banks borrow from and lend to each other for short periods of time outside the jurisdiction of their countries. Banks operating in the Eurocurrency market are known as **Eurobanks**. Eurobanks not only make short-term loans but also extend them to other financial institutions and to corporations, sovereign governments, and international organizations at medium to longer maturities. These long-term debts are known as **Eurocredits**.

Two characteristics differentiate Eurocredits from similar debt instruments offered by domestic banks. First, the loans tend to be extended by a syndicate of banks that share the risk of the loan. Second, Eurocredits are typically issued at floating interest rates. That is, the rate charged is typically LIBOR plus a spread that reflects the credit risk of the borrower.

Example 11.2 The Role of Floating-Rate Debt

Suppose BNP Paribas pays 1.85% on dollar deposits with 6-month maturities and lends dollars for 6 months at 1.95% earning a 10-basis point spread. Also, assume that BNP Paribas has extended a 5-year Eurocredit denominated in dollars to the Swedish company Ericsson. Ericsson borrows for 5 years because it may need capital long term, and it may be concerned about an increase in **credit spreads** or that it could be denied credit when it tries to roll over short-term debt. Assume that the 5-year U.S. Treasury bond yield is 5%. If the interest rate on the loan is fixed, BNP Paribas will charge 5% plus a spread to account for Ericsson's credit risk. If the rate is floating, BNP Paribas will charge LIBOR (that is, 1.95%) plus a credit spread, but the rate will be reset every 6 months.

Suppose that the credit spread both for a 5-year floating-rate loan and for a fixed-rate loan to Ericsson is 1%. At first glance, it would appear that BNP Paribas might be better off to offer Ericsson a fixed-rate loan. The bank would then not only earn the credit spread but also earn the difference between the short-term and long-term interest rates (5% versus 1.85%).

Many banks practice this maturity transformation; that is, taking in short-term deposits and providing long-term loans, which is sometimes called "riding the yield curve." However, this strategy is not without risk. It works only if average long-term rates are higher than short-term rates. Whereas this tends to be true in most countries, on average, it is not always true. In fact, we already discussed how the expectations hypothesis theory states that when short-term rates are lower than long-term rates, the market anticipates an increase in short-term rates. Hence, by extending a fixed-rate loan, BNP Paribas incurs the risk that short-term interest rates will rise and that in the future, it must pay its depositors a much higher interest rate than the current 1.85%, and even higher than the 5% + 1% = 6% they obtain from Ericsson.

By extending a floating-rate loan, BNP Paribas simply cashes in the credit spread on the Ericsson loan as long as the firm continues to pay interest on the loan. Hence, floating-rate loans protect banks against interest rate risk while protecting firms from rollover risk.

Types of Eurocredits

There are two main types of Eurocredits: term credits and revolving credits. A *term loan* has a fixed maturity and a fixed amount. In contrast, a *credit line* allows the borrower to withdraw as a loan any amount of money up to a fixed limit. In a term loan, the borrower has a fixed draw-down period over which it may take up the loan. A term credit does not involve any other regular expenses except for the interest rate expense. With revolving credit, the borrower has the right to borrow up to a "committed" amount at the prevailing interest rate, plus a preset credit spread during an agreed-upon period specified in the loan. However, the bank charges a commitment fee for the unused portion of the committed amount.

For instance, a borrower may have the right to issue 6-month promissory notes worth up to CHF50 million at an interest rate of 6-month LIBOR plus 1.00% per annum. This is similar to a standard credit line, except that it cannot be revoked during the lifetime of the loan. The commitment of the credit line is potentially very valuable when a company's credit standing deteriorates. Because an MNC can always borrow elsewhere if the market-required spread drops, the fixed spread can be viewed as an option contract.

Syndicates

A syndicate consists of a group of banks that take different roles in the debt-arranging process:

- The lead manager negotiates with the borrower on terms and conditions and prepares a placement memorandum that describes the borrower's financial condition and gives details about the proposed loan. The lead manager then invites other banks to participate in the loan.

- Because the funding is not yet arranged at the time of the negotiations, the lead manager often contacts a smaller number of managing banks to underwrite the loan—that is, to guarantee to make up for the shortage of funds if there is a shortage.
- The banks that provide the actual funding are called *participating banks*.
- The *paying agent* is the bank that receives the service payments from the borrower and distributes them to the participating banks.

Any given bank can play multiple roles. For instance, the lead bank is almost invariably also the largest underwriter (hence the name *lead manager*) and often provides funding as well. The main objective of syndication is to spread the risks of default. Because of the paying agent system, if the borrower defaults, the default is considered against all banks of the syndicate. This structure ensures that the borrower does not pay off the larger banks while ignoring the smaller debt holders. As in domestic banking, the borrower often signs promissory notes, one for each payment. The advantage of receiving promissory notes is that they are tradable. That is, if the lending bank needs funds, it can pass on the promissory note to another financial institution as security for a new loan, or it can sell the promissory note.

If demand by other banks to take part in the loan is good, then the borrower can potentially increase the amount of the loan. On the other hand, if there is insufficient demand, the managing banks (with the lead manager) may have to make up the difference. If the managing banks have previously guaranteed to the borrower the full amount of the proposed loan, the credit is said to be "fully underwritten." On the other hand, if the credit is on a "best efforts" basis, the managing banks have only promised to try their best. If there is not sufficient demand in the latter case, the size of the loan may be scaled down, or the terms may be changed.

Fees and Borrowing Costs

There are several types of costs to a Eurocredit borrower in addition to the obligation to repay the loan principal. These costs can be divided into two categories: periodic costs and the up-front cost.

The up-front cost is typically a one-time fee of 1.0% to 2.5% of the total amount of the credit, which is paid to the lead manager and managing banks for organizing and managing the loan. This amount is deducted from the principal; that is, a 1% fee means that the borrower receives only 99% of the face value of the loan. In practice, the managing banks pass along a portion of this fee to the participating banks.

Periodic costs include the interest paid on the amount of the credit actually in use. If the interest agreement calls for 6-month LIBOR plus a 1.5% spread, the borrower makes periodic interest payments on the amount of the credit drawn (that is, the amount of the loan the borrower has actually received) equal to the new 6-month LIBOR established at the beginning of the current 6-month period, plus 1.5%. In addition, there will be a commitment fee (probably in the range of 0.25% to 0.75%) to be paid periodically on the unused portion of the credit in the case of a revolving credit. Finally, there is usually a small fee paid to the paying agent bank to cover administrative expenses. In summary:

$$\text{Periodic costs} = (\text{Amount of total credit drawn}) \times (\text{Reference rate} + \text{Spread}) \\ + (\text{Amount of total credit not drawn}) \times (\text{Commitment fee}) \\ + \text{Agent fee}$$

The reference rate is usually LIBOR for floating-rate loans or the long-term high-quality government bond rate for fixed-rate loans. The spread depends on the default risk of the borrower, the political risk in the borrower's country, the maturity, and the up-front cost.

Many large banks have increasingly specialized in managing loans as middlemen. That is, they lead manage syndicated loans to receive up-front fees for their management services, and afterward, they sell off much of their loan share to smaller banks or thrift institutions. This practice stems not only from the comparative advantage of some banks in providing management services, but also from the new Basel Committee regulatory guidelines discussed earlier.

In principle, the fees are compensation for the services of the intermediaries, while the spread is a compensation for default risk. However, one can trade a higher up-front fee for a lower spread and vice versa. For instance, borrowers often accept a high up-front fee in return for a lower spread because the spread is sometimes seen as a quality rating. Importantly, both fees and credit spread must be taken into account to determine the effective cost of a loan, as we demonstrate in Section 11.6.

History and Size of Eurocredits

Exhibit 11.11 shows international syndicated credit facilities signed for selected years. At the beginning of the 1980s, the international syndicated loan market was well established. What is remarkable is the importance of borrowers from developing countries as opposed to developed markets. Equally striking is how the market almost completely dried up around 1985. We come back to these facts in Chapter 14 because they are intimately related to the Debt Crisis, a phenomenon that dominated the economies of many developing countries in the 1980s. After 1990, the market picked up again and grew dramatically for the next 17 years, with borrowers increasingly coming from the developed markets and the corporate sector. For example, in the mid-1990s, the new loans primarily refinanced outstanding loans or financed acquisitions, infrastructure projects, or the restructuring of national industries such as telecommunications. In 2000, a syndicated loan of $30 billion, the largest ever, supported the hostile takeover of Mannesmann A.G. by Vodafone. In 2006, the total market size exceeded $2 trillion and continued to grow until the global financial crisis of 2007 to 2010.

While syndicated deals totaled a record $2.7 trillion in 2007, the market collapsed during the financial crisis. The decline was much sharper for developed countries than for emerging markets. Chui et al. (2010) argue that the collapse was due to both demand and supply factors. For example, the crisis largely wiped out the demand for acquisition finance, which often is facilitated using Eurocredits. At the same time, many banks curtailed the supply of credit because it became more difficult to securitize loans. Giannetti and Laeven (2010) argue that banks particularly reduced loans to foreign borrowers; that is, there was a "flight home" effect during the crisis. De Haas and Van Horen (2011) claim that banks were retreating from markets where they had less information about the borrowers.

The Secondary Market

Another major development since the early 1980s has been the increasing tendency for banks to trade Eurocredits in the secondary market. The main impetus for this market was the debt

Exhibit 11.11   International Syndicated Credits (in billions of U.S. dollars)

	1980	1985	1995	2000	2006	2009
Total	82.8	19.0	370.2	1,464.9	2,121.2	1,022.6
Developed Countries	39.9	9.5	329.4	1,331.7	1,822.3	792.7
Developing Countries	41.9	9.3	40.8	94.5	237.6	195.4

Note: The two numbers do not necessarily add to the total because of two omitted categories, "offshore centers" and "international institutions."

Source: *BIS Quarterly Review*, various issues.

problem of developing countries in the 1980s. In addition, the Basel agreements on capital adequacy also presented many banks with the choice of increasing capital or removing assets from their balance sheets by selling in the secondary market.

The Euronote Market

The Euronote market is a clear example of the blurring of the distinctions between loan and security markets. The main distinction in this market is between short-term Euronotes (Euro-commercial paper and other short-term paper) and medium-term notes, although the option to issue short-term paper included in several medium-term note programs creates some overlap between the two market segments in terms of actual drawings.

Euronotes

International banks responded to the competition from the Eurobond market by creating facilities for sales of short-term, negotiable promissory notes, called **Euronotes**. In a basic Euronote facility, a syndicate of banks commits to distribute the borrower's notes (the "Euronotes") for a specified period, typically 5 to 7 years, with maturities ranging between 1, 3, 6, and 12 months. If the notes are underwritten, the syndicate banks stand ready to buy them at previously guaranteed rates. Such facilities have names, such as note issuance facility (NIF), standby note issuance facility (SNIF), or revolving underwriting facility (RUF). They give borrowers long-term continuous access to short-term money underwritten by banks at a fixed spread. Euronotes are more flexible than floating-rate notes and are usually cheaper than syndicated loans. Banks eager to beef up their earnings without fattening their loan portfolios (which would then require them to add expensive equity capital) made Euronote facilities an important segment of the Euromarket. More recently, the notes have appeared in non-underwritten form, called Euro-commercial paper (Euro-CP).

Euro Medium-Term Notes

Since the mid-1980s, a growing number of firms have been bypassing financial intermediaries and issuing **Euro-medium-term notes (Euro-MTNs)** directly to the market. Euro-MTNs bridge the maturity gap between Euro-CP and longer-term international bonds, with maturities as short as 9 months to as long as 10 years.

The first basic characteristic of a Euro-MTN is that the notes are offered continuously or periodically rather than all at once, like a bond issue, which gives issuers the flexibility to take advantage of changes in the shape and level of the yield curve and of the specific needs of investors with respect to amount, maturity, currency, and interest rate form (fixed or floating). Second, unlike conventional underwritten debt securities, medium-term notes can be issued in relatively small denominations, which makes them more flexible than the Eurobond and Eurocredit markets. Third, the costs of setting up a Euro-MTN program are much smaller than the total cost of a Eurobond issue, although its basic characteristics (coupon structure rates, maturity) are similar. Fourth, medium-term notes are not underwritten; securities firms place the paper as agents instead. Fifth, unlike public bond issues, the amounts and timing of medium-term notes sales are not disclosed. Such a lack of visibility allows companies to raise funds quickly and discreetly, without the risk of a complex public offering.

For example, suppose an MNC optimally needs USD10 million of 6-month money, USD21.0 million of 16-month money, and USD15.5 million of 24-month money. The bond market—with its high issuance costs—could not economically supply such small or precise amounts of debt, but a Euro-MTN program offers the flexibility to accomplish this precise financing need. As a concrete example, in February 2011, TeliaSonera AB, a Swedish telecom company, issued a €750 million 9-year note, under its existing €9 billion Euro-MTN program.

Exhibit 11.12 Top Arrangers of International Debt

Jan, 1, 2010–Dec. 31, 2010	2010				2009	
Firm	Volume ($ Million)	Rank	Mkt Share	Deal Count	Rank	Mkt Share
Barclays Capital	271,165	1	8.2	787	1	8.2
Deutsche Bank AG	243,584	2	7.4	1013	3	6.3
JP Morgan	214,715	3	6.5	856	2	6.6
HSBC Bank PLC	184,511	4	5.6	790	4	6.0
UBS	146,430	5	4.5	548	13	2.7
BNP Paribas Group	138,562	6	4.2	621	7	4.8
Credit Suisse	134,321	7	4.1	536	11	3.6
Bank of America Merrill Lynch	129,107	8	3.9	469	8	4.2
RBS	127,983	9	3.9	623	6	5.2
Citigroup	120,195	10	3.7	493	5	5.4
Goldman Sachs & Co	114,323	11	3.5	351	10	3.9
Morgan Stanley	104,766	12	3.2	413	9	4.2
UniCredit Group	90,706	13	2.8	356	14	2.4
Credit Agricole CIB	81,639	14	2.5	345	15	2.4
Societe Generale	76,146	15	2.3	270	12	2.8
RBC Capital Markets	59,935	16	1.8	421	23	1.2
WestLB AG	53,923	17	1.6	414	24	1.1
Natixis	52,488	18	1.6	205	22	1.3
Intesa Sanpaolo SpA	46,067	19	1.4	125	19	1.5
DZ Bank AG	45,994	20	1.4	394	18	1.6
Industry Total	**3,288,250**		**100%**	**9,829**		**100%**

Source: Bloomberg 2010 Global Fixed Income League Tables, International Bonds Table.

The Major Debt Arrangers

The success of Euronotes and Euro-MTNs has blurred the line between bond and loan markets. As a result, today, the loan and securities divisions of most major financial institutions are no longer separate and distinct. When an MNC must raise money, bankers may offer the MNC loans or the opportunity to issue a Eurobond or initiate a Euronote facility. In arranging security issues, banks earn fee income. Whereas loans allow banks to earn the spread between the interest rate they charge and the interest they pay depositors in addition to fee income, they also incur a capital charge in the BIS capital adequacy framework, which banks may want to avoid. In fact, there appears to be a trend toward relationship lending, where banks provide loans only when the borrower conducts securities or advisory business with the bank.

Exhibit 11.12 shows the top 20 global debt arrangers. "Debt" in the table combines Eurocredits, international bonds, and medium-term notes. The top 20 banks account for close to 60% of the market in arranging global debt. Not surprisingly, there is regional specialization; for example, Deutsche Bank is the number one when western European borrowers are considered; but JPMorgan Chase has been in the top five for quite some time.

11.6 COMPARING THE COSTS OF DEBT

In this section, we first review how the costs of debt of various instruments can be compared. We then reflect on the fundamental sources of the costs of debt. This brings us to the topic of a firm's credit risk and how banks measure it. Finally, we reflect on how firms can minimize their costs of debt in international financial markets and illustrate this process with some examples.

In examining the cost of alternative debt instruments, it is important to compare "oranges with oranges." In Chapter 6, we reviewed the term structure of interest rates. Interest rates for short maturities may be lower or higher than interest rates for longer maturities. Similarly, Chapter 6 revealed interest rates on different currencies to be very different. According to the expectations theory of interest rates and foreign exchange, these differences reflect expected movements in asset prices, which should eventually equalize the cost of debt for a given maturity. We illustrated how low-interest-rate currency debt does not mean cheap debt, and we used a numeric example to show how debt costs of different maturities cannot be compared (see Example 11.1).

As you can see, it is important to compare debt instruments of nearly similar amounts that have the same maturity and cash flow patterns, are expressed in the same currency, and share the same interest rate structure. Take, for example, Eurobonds versus U.S. bonds: Because fixed-rate Eurobonds normally pay their coupons once a year, whereas U.S. bonds pay semiannually, to compare the cost of debt between the two, the interest rates have to be expressed on the same basis. A semiannual yield can be annualized by using the formula

$$\text{Annual yield} = (1 + \text{Semiannual yield})^2 - 1$$

Typically, the semiannual yield will be expressed in per annum terms; that is, to obtain the semiannual yield, one takes the annualized yield and divides by 2. For example, suppose that a Eurobond carries an annual interest rate cost of 7.00%, and a U.S. corporate bond carries an interest rate of 6.95%. Both have a maturity of 5 years; but in the U.S. corporate bond market, coupons are paid semiannually, whereas in the Eurobond market, coupons are paid annually. To compare the two bonds, we must therefore annualize the U.S. corporate bond rate:

$$\text{Semiannual yield} = \frac{6.95\%}{2} = 3.457\%$$

$$\text{Annual yield} = (1 + 0.03475)^2 - 1 = 7.07\%$$

So, this U.S. corporate bond actually has a slightly higher interest rate cost.

The All-in-Cost Principle

To compare alternative debt securities, the **all-in-cost (AIC) principle** is typically used. The AIC is the discount rate or internal rate of return that equates the present value of all the future interest rate and principal payments to the net proceeds (face value minus fees) received by the issuer.

To illustrate the AIC principle, let's consider a Eurobond issued by GE Capital (in 2002). The bond has a face value of €2 billion; the maturity is 5 years; the price is €995.18 per €1,000 face value; the coupon is 5.125%; and the fees are 0.275%. To compute the AIC, we must trace the actual cash flows to and from GE Capital, which look as follows:

GE CAPITAL'S CASH FLOW (IN MILLIONS OF EUROS)		
Year	**Cash Flows**	**Present Value of Cash Flows at 5.30%**
0	1,984.86	1,984.86
1	(102.50)	(97.34)
2	(102.50)	(82.44)
3	(102.50)	(87.79)
4	(102.50)	(83.37)
5	(2,102.50)	(1,624.03)
		0.00

The net proceeds of the loan are less than €2,000 million for two reasons: GE Capital must pay 0.275% on €2,000 million (which is €5.5 million!) in fees to pay for the syndication, and the bond sold for 99.518% of face value. Hence, the net amount is

$$\text{€2,000 million} \times [0.99518 - 0.00275] = \text{€1,984.86 million}$$

The annual coupon payment is simply €2,000 million × 0.05125 = €102.50 million; the last payment (year 5) reflects the repayment of the principal plus the last coupon payment.

The AIC is the internal rate of return of all the cash flows; in other words, it is the interest rate that makes the initial proceeds equal to the present value of all the future payments GE Capital must make. In mathematical terms, the internal rate of return, y, solves

$$1,984.86 = \frac{102.50}{(1 + y)} + \frac{102.50}{(1 + y)^2} + \frac{102.50}{(1 + y)^3} + \frac{102.50}{(1 + y)^4} + \frac{2,102.50}{(1 + y)^5}$$

Software programs such as Excel have built-in commands (IRR) that compute internal rates of return for a given set of cash flows. In this example, $y = 5.30\%$. The right-hand column of the cash flow table presents the present values for each cash flow at 5.30% and demonstrates that they sum to zero. Because the present value of the cash outflows equals the net proceeds of the loan, GE Capital is said to have an AIC of 5.30%. If GE Capital wants to borrow in dollars, at fixed interest rates, for 5 years, it should try to borrow at the lowest possible AIC.

Components of the AIC

The AIC has three components: the "default-free" interest rate, the credit spread, and transaction costs. The default-free interest rate is the rate available on risk-free government securities of the same maturity. For the GE Capital example, the relevant government rate would be the 5-year rate on Bunds, German government bonds, which was 4.67% at the time GE Capital issued the bond. Hence, GE Capital paid 5.30% − 4.67% = 0.63%, or 63 basis points above the government rate.

This differential has two sources. The first is simply transaction costs. The fees that GE Capital paid to arrange the bond reduced its net proceeds and increased the effective interest rate payable on the loan. To see how much these transaction costs contribute, we compute the rate the company would pay if the fees were zero. The internal rate of return becomes 5.24%. Hence, transaction costs add only 5.30% − 5.24% = 0.06%, or 6 basis points to the AIC of the loan. Nevertheless, this is a significant cost because it amounts to €5.5 million.

The final component of the cost is the credit spread, the difference between the borrowing cost of the government and the borrowing cost of GE Capital, which in this case is 5.24% − 4.67% = 0.57%, or 57 basis points. The credit spread reflects the market's assessment of the ability of the company to repay its debt and is typically closely associated with a company's **credit rating**.

To sum up, the cost of a loan can be split up into three components:

$$\text{Total cost} = \text{Risk-free rate} + \text{Credit spread} + \text{Transaction cost}$$
$$5.30\% = 4.67\% + 0.57\% + 0.06\%$$

Credit Ratings

Companies compete in providing information on the creditworthiness of corporate and government borrowers. Moody's Investors Service and Standard & Poor's (S&P) are the best-known credit-rating organizations that provide credit ratings on U.S. domestic bonds and most international bonds, too. They classify bond issues into categories based on the creditworthiness of the borrower. The ratings are based on an analysis of current information regarding the likelihood of default and the specifics of the debt obligation. The ability of a firm to service its debt depends on the firm's financial structure, its profitability, the stability of its cash flows, and its long-term growth prospects. The ratings only reflect creditworthiness—not exchange rate uncertainty.

In addition to Moody's and S&P, the European Rating Agency (Eurorating) and the Japan Credit Rating Agency (JCR) are major rating agencies. Until a few years ago, the capital markets in Europe and Japan were less "credit risk" sensitive than the U.S. capital market, making it possible to tap the capital market without an official rating. The corporate bond and Eurobond markets have now matured to the point that this has become very difficult.

Rating Schemes

The rating schemes used by Moody's and S&P are summarized in Exhibit 11.13. Moody's rates bonds into nine major categories, from Aaa, Aa, A, Baa, and Ba down to C; S&P uses AAA, AA, A, and BBB down to C. Ratings of Aaa to Baa for Moody's and AAA to BBB for S&P are known as investment-grade ratings. For these issues, interest payments and principal appear safe at the time of the rating. Many prominent institutional investors such as pension funds are only allowed to purchase investment-grade bonds. As a result, MNCs have a huge incentive to achieve investment-grade ratings. For bonds rated lower than investment grade, investors should assign some substantial probability to future payment problems, and hence, these issues are called "speculative." Within each of the nine categories, Moody's has three numeric modifiers, 1, 2, and 3, to place an issue, respectively, at the upper, middle, or lower end of the category, whereas S&P uses + and − modifiers.

Government borrowers are called **sovereign borrowers**. Sovereign borrowing is a sizable portion of the international bond market. In rating a sovereign borrower, S&P analyzes

Exhibit 11.13   Credit Ratings for Bond Issuers

Credit Quality	Standard & Poor's	Moody's
Investment Grade		
	AAA	Aaa
Highest quality	AA+	Aa1
	AA	Aa2
High quality	AA−	Aa3
	A+	A1
Highest middle quality	A	A2
	A−	A3
	BBB+	Baa1
Middle quality	BBB	Baa2
	BBB−	Baa3
Speculative Grade		
	BB+	Ba1
Predominantly speculative	BB	Ba2
	BB−	Ba3
	B+	B1
Low quality	B	B2
	BB−	B3
Very low quality	CCC	Caa
Highly speculative	CC	Ca
Lowest quality	C	C
In Default		
	D	

Note: Data are from the Web sites of Standard & Poor's and Moody's.

its degree of political and economic risk, which we discuss in Chapter 14. The rating assigned to a sovereign government is particularly important because it affects the ratings applied to corporations within that country.

Rating Agencies Receive an F During the Crisis

Rating agencies suffered severe criticism during the crisis. First, large numbers of securitized investments, based on subprime mortgage loans, received investment-grade (even the highest) ratings and afterward turned out to be worthless. While it is possible that the rating agencies did not fully understand these complex securities, there is no doubt that investors were misled about the safety of these investments. Second, Moody's and Standard & Poor's maintained at least A ratings on AIG and Lehman Brothers up until mid-September of 2008. Lehman Brothers declared bankruptcy on September 15, 2008; the federal government provided AIG with its first of four multibillion-dollar bailouts the next day. Not surprisingly, the rating agencies have been investigated by the SEC and the U.S. government regarding the role they played in the crisis. After all, the agencies are paid by the bank or company issuing the security and asking for a rating. This business model generates an obvious conflict of interest, as the rating agencies may not be inclined to give their clients a bad rating, thereby jeopardizing future revenues. In any case, the performance of the rating agencies during the crisis surely deserves a failing grade.

Minimizing the Cost of Debt Internationally

Why Source Debt Internationally?

This chapter illustrates the rich diversity of global debt markets. Nevertheless, we have also cautioned that this world of opportunities does not necessarily mean that an MNC can easily lower its cost of capital by sourcing debt internationally. There may be other reasons than "price" to issue offshore. For example, as indicated before, large companies in emerging markets may face a relatively illiquid and small funding market at home and can access more complete, liquid, and diversified funding sources abroad. Companies worried about future refinancing needs may find it useful to diversify funding sources. While liquidity crises may be correlated across countries, it is likely that some countries are less affected than others. Companies may also source debt in different currencies simply to hedge foreign currency revenues.

If an MNC wants to minimize its fixed-interest cost of debt for a given maturity and currency of denomination, the AIC measured in the headquarters' currency is the correct number to minimize. We already discussed that when UIRP does not hold, sourcing debt in low-interest-rate countries may be less costly. If the low-interest-rate currency does not appreciate as predicted by the interest rate differential, the MNC will have lowered its cost of debt. This also entails risk. An unexpected appreciation of the currency beyond the built-in appreciation implied by the forward rate will increase the MNC's cost of debt relative to borrowing at home.

Many companies issue debt in foreign currencies but hedge the currency risk. In the previous section, we learned that the AIC has three components. Hence, there are three channels through which foreign borrowing can lower the AIC:

1. Transaction costs are lower.
2. The credit spread is lower.
3. The "hedged" foreign interest rate is lower than the local risk-free rate.

Whereas the first channel is pretty easy to understand, it will be helpful to go back to the Dig-It-Up example to illustrate the second and third channels.

Example 11.3 International Credit Spreads and the AIC

Suppose we supplement the data for 1-year borrowing for Dig-It-Up, the Canadian MNC from Example 11.1, as follows:

	LIBOR (r)	Dig-It-Up's Rates (i)
CAD	2.50	3.00
AUD	4.75	5.00

The column labeled Dig-It-Up's Rates refers to the actual 1-year borrowing rates that Dig-It-Up faces in both markets compared to the LIBOR rates that are for AAA credits. Hence, Dig-It-Up faces a 50-basis point credit spread in CAD, but only a 25-basis point spread in AUD. In what currency should Dig-It-Up borrow if the borrowing transaction costs are similar? Because Dig-It-Up is Canadian based, if it borrows in AUD, it must hedge the currency risk by buying AUD forward. Assume that the spot rate is AUD1.10/CAD. If covered interest rate parity holds, the forward rate will be

$$F = S \times \frac{[1 + r(\text{AUD})]}{[1 + r(\text{CAD})]} = \frac{\text{AUD}1.10}{\text{CAD}} \times \frac{1.0475}{1.025} = \frac{\text{AUD}1.1241}{\text{CAD}}$$

The relevant interest rates for the covered interest rate parity (CIRP) relation are the LIBOR rates, $r(\text{AUD})$ and $r(\text{CAD})$.

Because interest rate parity is satisfied, we know that an AAA company borrowing at 4.75% in Australia dollars would face an effective Canadian dollar interest rate of 2.50% when hedging the AUD currency risk by buying the necessary AUD funds in the forward market to pay off the loan. Of course, if CIRP were not to hold, this is another way to capitalize on different borrowing costs across countries. For the developed countries, we argued that CIRP holds up very well, but for many emerging markets, this may not be the case.

However, Dig-It-Up does not have an AAA credit rating, and so it faces the higher borrowing costs displayed in the table. The "hedged" CAD borrowing cost for Dig-It-Up when borrowed in AUD can be calculated by examining the hedged costs of repayment. Dig-It-Up would borrow AUD1.10 to get CAD1. It would owe interest at 5%, and it can hedge the AUD interest and principal payment by buying AUD at the forward rate of AUD1.1241/CAD. Its hedged borrowing cost will therefore be

$$\text{AUD}1.10 \times [1 + 0.05] \times \frac{1}{\text{AUD}1.1241/\text{CAD}} - 1 = 2.75\%$$

Note that 2.75% is lower than 3.00% by 25 basis points, the cost of borrowing directly in CAD. The reason is that Dig-It-Up faces a credit spread in Australia that is 25 basis points lower than in Canada!

Example 11.3 suggests that in efficient, integrated markets, credit spreads ought to be equalized across countries; otherwise, companies should all borrow in the countries where credit spreads are lowest and then hedge the exchange rate risk. This reasoning is correct for the example, but the statement is generally only true for "multiplicative" credit spreads rather than the "absolute" credit spreads that are commonly used. The absolute credit spread simply reflects the difference between the company's interest rate and the risk-free rate, whereas the multiplicative spread is somewhat smaller, reflecting the (gross) rate at which the risk-free rate must be scaled up to obtain the company's interest rate. Our example lists absolute credit spreads (designated acsp):

$$\text{acsp}(\text{CAD}) = i(\text{CAD}) - r(\text{CAD}) = 0.50\%$$
$$\text{acsp}(\text{AUD}) = i(\text{AUD}) - r(\text{AUD}) = 0.25\%$$

However, the credit spreads across currencies are really only comparable when expressed in multiplicative form. The multiplicative credit spread (mcsp) in this case is defined as

$$1 + i(\text{CAD}) = [1 + \text{mcsp}(\text{CAD})] \times [1 + r(\text{CAD})]$$
$$1 + i(\text{AUD}) = [1 + \text{mcsp}(\text{AUD})] \times [1 + r(\text{AUD})]$$

Only if mcsp(CAD) = mcsp(AUD) will the cost of borrowing in CAD and in AUD while hedging the currency risk be equivalent. To see this, note that the cost of borrowing in AUD, while hedging the currency risk, is

$$[1 + i(\text{AUD})] \times \frac{S(\text{AUD}/\text{CAD})}{F(\text{AUD}/\text{CAD})}$$

with S and F representing the spot and forward rates. Using CIRP, we obtain

$$[1 + i(\text{AUD})] \times \frac{[1 + r(\text{CAD})]}{[1 + r(\text{AUD})]} = [1 + \text{mcsp}(\text{AUD})] \times [1 + r(\text{CAD})]$$

This value equals $[1 + i(\text{CAD})]$ only if mcsp(AUD) = mscp(CAD). For our example, note that

$$\text{mcsp}(\text{CAD}) = \frac{1.03}{1.025} - 1 = 0.49\%$$

$$\text{mcsp}(\text{AUD}) = \frac{1.05}{1.0475} - 1 = 0.24\%$$

In other words, absolute or multiplicative credit spreads are almost indistinguishable when interest rates are low. However, at higher interest rate levels, discrepancies between relative and absolute credit spreads increase.

Example 11.4 Credit Spreads at High-Interest-Rate Levels

Suppose the 1-year interest rate on Mexican pesos (for an AAA credit) is 50% and that a multinational corporation faces a 1-year MXN borrowing cost of 60%. Hence, the absolute credit spread is acsp(MXN) = 60% − 50% = 10%, and the multiplicative credit spread is

$$\text{mcsp}(\text{MXN}) = 6.67\% = \left[\frac{1 + 0.60}{1 + 0.50} - 1 \right] \times 100$$

The risky company's borrowing cost in the United States will be identical to its borrowing cost in Mexico as long as its multiplicative credit spread in the United States is also 6.67%. If the USD interest rate for an AAA credit is 5%, the USD interest rate equivalent to 60% in Mexico is 1.05 × 1.0667 = 12%. Hence, the absolute credit spread in U.S. dollars that is equivalent to an absolute credit spread of 10% in Mexican pesos is only 12% − 5% = 7%!

Credit Spreads Across Countries

There are many reasons companies face different (multiplicative) credit spreads in different markets. One reason is that credit perceptions differ across markets. For example, in the not-so-recent past, European and Japanese retail investors were less concerned about credit risks, especially when the brand-name products produced by an MNC were familiar in the market-place. Ford Motor Credit, for example, successfully raised €1.5 billion in the international bond markets in 2003 even though some U.S. credit analysts were worried about a deterioration of Ford's creditworthiness. European retail and institutional investors were obviously less concerned. As a result, Ford was able to lower the yield offered on the bonds relative to what it would have been in the U.S. corporate bond market.

How could such credit spread differentials persist? If credit spreads are larger in one country than in another, investors would like to sell short securities in countries with low credit spreads (where security prices are high) and invest in comparable securities in coun-tries with high credit spreads (where security prices are low) while hedging their currency risk. This arbitrage is not so easy for several reasons. First, transactions costs can be signifi-cant when the securities are traded in the secondary market. Second, the arbitrage is risky because the company involved may go bankrupt, in which case finding out what the securi-ties are actually worth could take a long time. Also, the arbitrageur will still be left with an open forward contract that must be paid. This leaves the arbitrageur exposed to currency risk. Nevertheless, such attempted arbitrage clearly takes place in international markets, and, as it does, the credit rate differentials between local and international markets narrow.

Finally, there are cyclical variations in credit spreads that are not necessarily perfectly correlated across countries. Credit spreads tend to be countercyclical, widening in economic downturns and falling in economic booms. MNCs can react to such cycles in an effort to exploit them, but, in general, opportunities to lower the cost of debt through credit spread arbitrage are decreasing over time because of the ongoing globalization process.

Empirical Evidence

A number of academic studies have tried to systematically examine why firms source debt internationally and, more specifically, whether they exploit deviations from covered and/or uncovered interest rate parity. In fact, McBrady and Schill (2007) studied the currency composition of international bonds issued by governments and government agencies, finding concrete evidence that they try to source debt in the currencies that produce the lowest AICs after hedging. This is concrete evidence that yield arbitrage is one motive for international bond issues, as these governments do not tend to have a hedging motive for sourcing debt in different currencies. McBrady et al. (2010) show that large firms with high ratings attempt to exploit covered yield differentials across countries. The yield benefits appear small, less than 10 basis points on average. The fact that emerging-market and non-investment-grade issuers do not take advantage of such opportunities is simply due to the fact that hedging the cash flows in the currency they want (e.g., through swaps) is too expensive for them, swamping the yield advantage. The authors also demonstrate some evidence of opportunistic behavior in firms issuing in low-yield currencies when the interest differential is particularly large. In both cases, the yield differentials dissipate after issuances, suggesting that international bond issuances may in fact help enforce interest rate parity (both covered and uncovered) at longer horizons.

Black and Munro (2010) largely confirm these findings for Asian-Pacific borrowers. They note that the bulk of foreign borrowing is hedged into local currency using derivative markets or is used as a hedge against foreign currency income (for exporters for instance). They also show that many non-investment-grade borrowers in the markets they study es-cape a poorly developed local market by borrowing offshore. Brown et al. (2009) focus on loans to small businesses in Eastern Europe, where foreign currency borrowing has increased substantially over the past decade. They find that firms with foreign currency revenues borrow more in foreign currency. They cannot confirm "carry trade behavior" (unhedged borrowing in low-interest-rate currencies) but do show that when banks (e.g., foreign banks) have less access to information about a firm's revenue streams, more foreign currency borrowing occurs.

POINT–COUNTERPOINT

Financing Chocolate Globalization

When Suttle bursts into Freedy's room one sunny afternoon, he finds Ante and Freedy glued to the computer screen, surrounded by heaps of paper. "Hey guys, fancy a quick afternoon coffee?" Freedy and Ante both sigh, and Freedy says, "I am afraid we've got to really continue working because we must finish this case for tomorrow's class on corporate finance. And, unfortunately, we are not making much progress right now."

"Well, maybe I can help. What is it about?" Suttle asks. Ante throws a small package of papers Suttle's way. "Here, read for yourself," says Ante. "The more I learn about finance, the less I understand what the heck is going on." Suttle is soon engaged in reading the case while Ante and Freedy wrestle with their spreadsheets.

The case is about the financing of an acquisition of a private U.S. chocolate company, Worshey's, by a Swiss, multinational food product company, Cote D'Argent, with its own line of chocolate products. The financial team of Cote D'Argent is looking at three possibilities: a straight Eurobond in euros, a straight Eurobond denominated in yen, and a yen/euro dual-currency bond. All bonds have a maturity of 5 years, with annual coupons. The case asks which type of bond the company should pick and why. It also asks why there might be differences in financing costs across the three different instruments. Suttle finds it so fascinating that he starts to really investigate the numbers of the case. The details on the three bonds are as follows:

Face Value	Euro Eurobond €100 million	Yen Eurobond ¥14 billion	Yen/Euro Dual-Currency Eurobond ¥14 billion
Price as a % of face value	100%	101%	98%
Fees	1.25%	0.90%	0.90%
Coupon (annual)	4.10%	1.00%	2.00%
Final redemption	Par	Par	€104.90 million

The two yen-related bonds would be arranged through a syndicate run by Kozuma, a Japanese investment bank. Kozuma is negotiating aggressively with Cote D'Argent to consider the yen instruments. Kozuma is also suggesting that Cote D'Argent should immediately hedge out the currency risk by using forward contracts and is offering the following exchange rates (in yen/euros): Spot rate: 140.00; Forward rates: 1-year, 136.78; 2-year, 133.03; 3-year, 128.87; 4-year, 124.50; 5-year, 120.12. The Eurobond issue would be run by a syndicate headed by Kneutsche Bank, a German universal bank.

After digesting the numbers, Suttle asks, "What are your conclusions so far?" Ante excitedly points toward the spreadsheets onscreen: "Either the case is not realistic, or we have made a huge mistake: The dual-currency bond is too good to be true! I first thought that taking on yen debt would be great: The interest rate is so low! However, Freedy convinced me that Cote D'Argent might not want to take on currency risk, and the low interest rates simply reflect the fact that the euro trades at a huge forward discount relative to the yen. You can see from the forward exchange rates that there is a large implicit yen appreciation, from ¥140/€ to almost ¥120/€. So, we decided to compute the cost of debt for hedged cash flows using the forward exchange rates to convert yen into euros."

"Wow, I am impressed," Suttle says. "Did you also take the fees into account?"

"Oh yeah!" answers Freedy, "We computed the all-in cost as you should. Here are our spreadsheets."

Suttle takes a peek at the spreadsheets, which present Cote D'Argent's cash flows:

Year	(¥/€) Rates	I. Euro Eurobond Euro Cash Flows	II. Yen Eurobond Yen Cash Flows	II. Yen Eurobond Euro Cash Flows	III. Yen/Euro Dual-Currency Eurobond Yen Cash Flows	III. Yen/Euro Dual-Currency Eurobond Euro Cash Flows
0	140.00	98.75	14,014	100.10	13,594	97.10
1	136.78	(4.10)	(140)	(1.02)	(280)	(2.05)
2	133.03	(4.10)	(140)	(1.05)	(280)	(2.10)
3	128.87	(4.10)	(140)	(1.09)	(280)	(2.17)
4	124.50	(4.10)	(140)	(1.12)	(280)	(2.25)
5	120.12	(104.10)	(14,140)	(117.72)	(280)	(107.23)
All-In Costs		4.38%		4.11%		3.73%

Note: The year 0 cash flows are price as a percentage of face value minus fees. The interest rate on the euro Eurobond is 4.1%, the interest rate on the yen Eurobond is 1%, and the yen interest rate on the dual-currency Eurobond is 2%. Euro cash flows are calculated with the respective exchange rate in column 2. The final payment on the dual-currency Eurobond is €104.90 plus the euro value of the yen interest payment.

Suttle inquires, "So, the AIC is the internal rate of return that equates the present value of the future cash outlays with today's euro revenues, net of fees, right?"

"Yeah, of course," shouts Ante. "Maybe you can tell me why the dual-currency bond is so cheap. Clearly, Kozuma either made a mistake, or they are plain stupid to have given Cote D'Argent a deal like that. If Japanese investors really invest in this bond, they must be pretty irrational."

Freedy interjects, "Well, I think that is the wrong perspective. Perhaps the Japanese investors simply want some exposure to long-term euro risk, plus they are getting a nice coupon. They might be betting that the €104.90 million that they are getting back in 5 years will be still worth ¥14,000 million, in which case they get a great deal, relative to the 1% bond. But the forward value of the €104.90 million is only €104.90 million × ¥120.12/€ = ¥12,601 million, so they are definitely taking a risk."

After Suttle takes another look at the spreadsheets, he summarizes the situation: "I think your computations are right, and yes, both yen alternatives are cheaper than the euro alternative, with the dual-currency bond clearly offering the lowest cost of debt to Cote D'Argent. The company should use that bond to finance the acquisition."

"Why can there be such substantial differences? I think there are grains of truth in what both of you are saying," continues Suttle. "It is possible that Japanese investors, which are probably the target market for the dual-currency bonds, are indeed blinded by the high yen coupon rate because interest rates in Japan are very close to zero. They are likely aware of the currency risk, though. Japanese investors are really betting on the euro being stronger than implied by forward rates.

"I believe there is some empirical evidence for the fact that high-yield currencies do not depreciate by as much as implied by forward exchange rates, but it is not clear that investors would like to speculate on this with a bond," says Suttle. "Besides, smart investors could try to set up an arbitrage with the dual-currency bond. The yield is too low, so you'd like to sell the bond and 'buy' the underlying cash flows in, say, Treasury markets and exchange rate markets. However, such arbitrage is not risk free because Cote D'Argent may default on the bond. Moreover, transaction costs in long-date forward contracts are high. Also, there might not be a very liquid secondary market for these bonds. Hence, I am not so worried about the 27-basis point difference between the yen Eurobond and the euro Eurobond. It might be due to a difference in credit perceptions in Europe and Japan and may be hard to arbitrage. Cote D'Argent's chocolate is really popular in Japan, so some investors might very well like to buy the company's bonds. It is also striking that the fees Kozuma demands are lower than the fees for the euro Eurobond. It may be that this is part of a relationship-banking ploy. Kozuma might be keen to work with Cote D'Argent in an effort to do other, more profitable business with the company later on. However, the fact that the dual-currency bond is another 40 basis points cheaper is surprising. It is possible that for some Japanese investors, the dual-currency bond is advantageous from a tax or competitive viewpoint. For example, the dual-currency bond may be viewed as entirely domestic, even though, in truth, it is not."

"All right, Suttle. I think we've got it solved. Let's go for coffee," Ante declares.

"And let's have a nice bar of Cote D'Argent chocolate with it," Freedy yells. "What I really wonder about is why such a fine chocolate company would want to acquire such a horrible Worshey's product."

"You Euro-snob," shouts Ante. "I love my Worshey's!"

11.7 SUMMARY

This chapter analyzes debt financing in a global world. Its main points are the following:

1. Debt is only one source of funds for MNCs. MNCs can also issue equity or finance projects using their internally generated funds.
2. Debt instruments differ in currency of denomination, maturity, nature of interest rate payments, tradability, and international character.
3. Under a decentralized debt-denomination model, MNCs issue debt in different currencies to hedge the cash flows they earn in these currencies from their foreign subsidiaries. If the debt is centralized—that is, issued in the currency of the MNC's headquarters—the profits from the MNC's foreign subsidiaries are subject to additional currency risk.
4. Issuing debt in low-interest-rate currencies does not reduce a company's debt costs if international markets are efficient.
5. MNCs can issue short-term or floating-rate debt, or they can issue long-term fixed-rate debt. As with the currency of denomination, there is no free lunch here: If short-term rates are lower than long-term rates, this may be an indication of impending interest rate increases.
6. MNCs can borrow from a financial institution, in which case the debt is called *intermediated debt*.

Alternatively, they can issue securities to investors in the capital markets. The trend toward direct issues is called *financial disintermediation*.

7. International bonds are traded outside the country of the issuer. If they are issued in a particular domestic bond market, they are called *foreign bonds*. If they are issued simultaneously in various markets, outside the specific jurisdiction of any country, they are called *Eurobonds*.
8. The foreign bond and Eurobond markets make up about 30% of the global bond market.
9. Because foreign bonds are subject to local regulations, in some countries, such as the United States, they require a lengthy registration process.
10. Eurobonds are placed among investors with the help of a syndicate of financial institutions.
11. The acceleration of globalization, including tax harmonization, financial deregulation, and the relaxation of capital controls, has blurred traditional distinctions between domestic and international bonds. Global bonds, for example, are issued simultaneously in a domestic market and in the Eurobond market.
12. Bonds can have a fixed interest rate (straight issues), no interest at all (zero-coupon bonds), or a floating interest rate that varies with LIBOR rates. Convertible bonds allow the holder to convert the

bonds into shares, or stock. Dual-currency bonds are issued in one currency and pay interest in that currency, but the final principal payment is in another currency.

13. Banks are MNCs and are subject to international banking regulation in the form of capital adequacy standards set by the Basel Committee.

14. To engage in international banking activities, banks may use correspondent banks, representative offices, foreign branches, affiliate banks, or subsidiary banks. These different organizational forms determine the degree of service and control exercised by the parent bank.

15. Offshore banking centers conduct international banking activities in a "lightly" regulated setting. International banking activities can also be organized in the United States via an Edge Act bank or international banking facility.

16. Eurocredits are long-term bank loans extended by a syndicate of banks in countries other than the country in whose currency the loans are denominated. Most Eurocredits are of the floating-rate variety, with the interest rates set at a spread above LIBOR.

17. Euronotes and Euro-medium-term notes give borrowers access to short- or long-term loans via the intermediation of financial institutions. These securities blur the distinctions between debt and loan markets.

18. To compare the cost of debt across markets, debt instruments must have approximately the same maturity, be expressed in the same currency, and be of the same rate structure (fixed or floating), and their interest rates must be expressed on the same basis (that is, annualized appropriately).

19. The all-in cost (AIC) is the discount rate, or internal rate of return, that equates the present value of all future interest rate and principal payments to the net proceeds received by the issuer. The AIC can be split up into three components: the risk-free rate, the credit spread, and transaction costs.

20. S&P and Moody's rate the credit risk of debt instruments based on the creditworthiness of the borrower.

21. MNCs should minimize the AIC of their debts expressed in the local currency of the country in which they are headquartered. Opportunities to reduce these costs appear to be related to differences in credit spreads across countries.

22. As markets become more internationally integrated, opportunities to lower the cost of capital in global markets may diminish.

QUESTIONS

1. What are the three main sources of financing for any firm?
2. What is the difference between a centralized and decentralized debt denomination for an MNC?
3. Will an MNC issuing debt in low-interest-rate currencies necessarily lower its cost of funds? Why?
4. Should an MNC borrow primarily short term when short-term interest rates are lower than long-term interest rates? Or should it keep the maturity the same but use a floating-rate loan rather than a fixed-rate loan? Explain.
5. What is financial disintermediation?
6. What are the two main segments of the international bond market, and what types of regulations apply to them?
7. What is the difference between a foreign bond and a Eurobond?
8. Why might U.S. investors continue to purchase Eurobonds, despite the fact that the U.S. corporate bond market is well developed?

9. What is a global bond, and what role does the global bond market play in the blurring of the distinctions in the international bond market?
10. What are the differences between a straight bond, a floating-rate note, and a convertible bond?
11. What is a dual-currency bond?
12. What kind of activities do international banks engage in?
13. Why is there a need for international banking regulation?
14. What are the differences between credit risk, market risk, and operational risk?
15. What is systemic risk?
16. Which activity would require the largest capital charge under the 1988 Basel Accord: a loan to another bank or a loan to a large MNC? Would this necessarily be true under the Basel II rules?
17. What is VaR?
18. What is the difference between a foreign branch and a subsidiary bank?

19. What is an offshore center?
20. What is the difference between an Edge Act bank and an international banking facility?
21. What is the difference between a Eurocredit, a Euronote, and a Euro-medium-term note?
22. Why are Eurocredits not extended by one bank but by a large syndicate of banks?
23. What is the all-in cost of a 5-year loan? What are its main components?
24. What is a credit rating? What is a credit spread?
25. Should corporations issue bonds in countries where they face the lowest credit spreads? Be very specific about the concept of credit spread you use.

PROBLEMS

1. In 1985, R. J. Reynolds (RJR for short) acquired Nabisco Brands and financed the deal with a variety of financial instruments, including three dual-currency Eurobonds. The first dual-currency bond, lead-managed by Nikko, raised JPY25 billion (equivalent to USD105.5 million at the time of issue). Coupons were paid in yen, but the required final principal payment was not JPY25 billion but USD115.956 million. The coupon was 7.75%, even though a comparable fixed-rate Euroyen bond at that time carried only a 6.375% coupon. The actual 5-year forward rate at the time was around JPY200/USD.
   a. Given the "fat" coupon, is this bond necessarily a great deal for the investors?
   b. At maturity, in August 1990, the exchange rate was actually JPY144/USD. Was the bond a good deal for investors?

2. GBA Company wishes to raise $5,000,000 with debt financing. The funds will be repaid with interest in 1 year. The treasurer of GBA Company is considering three sources:
   i. Borrow USD from Citibank at 1.50%
   ii. Borrow EUR from Deutsche Bank at 3.00%
   iii. Borrow GBP from Barclays at 4.00%
   If the company borrows in euros or British pounds, it will not cover the foreign exchange risk; that is, it will change foreign currency for dollars at today's spot rate and buy foreign currency back 1 year later at the spot rate prevailing then. The GBA Company has no operations in Europe.

   A representative of GBA contacts a local academic to provide projections of the spot rates 1 year in the future. The academic comes up with the following table:

Currency	Spot Rate	Projected Rate 1 Year in the Future
USD/GBP	1.50	1.55
USD/EUR	0.95	0.85

   a. What is the expected interest rate cost for the loans in EUR and GBP?

   b. What are the projected USD/GBP rate and USD/EUR rate for which the expected interest costs would be the same for the three loans?
   c. Should the country borrow in the currency with the lowest interest rate cost? Why or why not? Would your answer change if GBA did generate cash flows in the United Kingdom and continental Europe?

3. FE Company wishes to raise $1,000,000 with debt financing. The treasurer of FE Company considers two possible instruments:

   i. A 2-year floating-rate note at 1% above the 1-year dollar LIBOR rate on which interest is paid once a year
   ii. A 2-year bond with an interest rate of 5%

   Currently, the dollar LIBOR is 1.50%.
   a. Is it obvious which security the Treasurer should pick?
   b. Suppose the Treasurer believes that the 1-year LIBOR rate 1 year from now will rise to 4.50%. Which security has the lowest expected AIC if borrowing fees are similar for the two instruments?

4. K3 Company wants to borrow $100 million for 5 years. Investment bankers propose to either do a syndicated Eurocredit or issue a Eurobond. The Eurocredit would be denominated in dollars, but the Eurobond would be denominated in different currencies for different markets (these issues are called tranches):

   Terms: Syndicated Eurocredit
   Amount: USD100 million
   Up-front fees: USD1.25%
   Interest rate: Interest payable every 6 months; LIBOR plus 1.00%
   Terms: Eurobond
   Tranche 1: USD 50 million, Interest rate: 3.50%
   Tranche 2: ¥5,952 million (equivalent of USD50 million), Interest rate 1.5%

   a. What are the net proceeds in USD for K3 for the Eurocredit loan?

b. Assuming that the 6-month LIBOR in USD is currently at 2.00%, what is the effective annual interest cost for K3 for the first 6 months of the loan?

c. Compute an effective annualized interest rate cost (all-in cost) for the USD tranche of the Eurobond.

d. What information would you need to obtain the dollar all-in cost of the yen tranche?

e. What elements would you take into account to choose between the two possibilities?

5. Suppose Intel wishes to raise USD1 billion and is deciding between a domestic dollar bond issue and a Eurobond issue. The U.S. bond can be issued at a 5-year maturity with a coupon of 4.50%, paid semiannually. The underwriting, registration, and other fees total 1.00% of the issue size. The Eurobond carries a lower annual coupon of 4.25%, but the total costs of issuing the bond runs to 1.25% of the issue size. Which loan has the lowest all-in cost?

6. Web Question: In 2010, Coca-Cola FEMSA, a bottler in Mexico, issued a $500 million 10-year bond. Look up more details about this issue. What type of bond is it? How was it rated? What is the credit spread associated with the bond?

BIBLIOGRAPHY

Almeida, Heitor, Murillo Campello, Bruno Laranjeira, and Scott Weisbenner, 2009, "Corporate Debt Maturity and the Real Effects of the Panic of August 2007," working paper.

Ang, Andrew, Geert Bekaert, and Min Wei, 2008, "The Term Structure of Real Rates and Expected Inflation," *Journal of Finance* 63, pp. 797–849.

Bank for International Settlements, 2010, "80th Annual Report," www.bis.org/publ/arpdf/ar2010e.htm.

Bekaert, Geert, Campbell Harvey, Christian Lundblad, and Stephan Siegel, 2011, "What Segments Equity Markets?" forthcoming *Review of Financial Studies.*

Bekaert, Geert, Min Wei, and Yuhang Xing, 2007, "Uncovered Interest Rate Parity and the Term Structure of Interest Rates," *Journal of International Money and Finance* 26, 1038–1069.

Bernanke, Ben S., 2005, "Global Savings Glut and the US Current Account Deficit," Homer Jones Lecture, St. Louis, MO, April 14.

Black, Susan, and Anella Munro, 2010, "Why Issue Bonds Offshore?" Bank of International Settlements Working Paper No. 334.

Bloomberg Finance, 2010, "Global Fixed Income League Tables," http://about.bloomberg.com/pdf/gfi.pdf.

Brown, Martin, Steven Ongena, and Pinar Yeşin, 2009, "Foreign Currency Borrowing by Small Firms," working paper.

Burger, John D., Francis E. Warnock, and Veronica Cacdac Warnock, 2010, "Investing in Local Currency Bond Markets," National Bureau of Economic Research Working Paper No. 16249.

Caballero, Ricardo J., Emmanuel Farhi, and Pierre-Olivier Gourinchas, 2008, "An Equilibrium Model of 'Global Imbalances' and Low Interest Rates," *American Economic Review* 98, pp. 358–393.

Chui, Michael, Dietrich Domanski, Peter Kugler, and Jimmy Shek, 2010, "The Collapse of International Bank Finance During the Crisis: Evidence from Syndicated Loan Markets," *BIS Quarterly Review* September, pp. 39–49.

Claes, Anouk, Mark J.K. De Ceuster, and Ruud Polfliet, 2002, "Anatomy of the Eurobond Market, 1980–2000," *European Financial Management* 8, pp. 373–386.

De Haas, Ralph, and Neeltje Van Horen, 2011, "Running for the Exit: International Banks and Crisis Transmission," working paper.

Eubanks, Walter W., 2010, "The Status of the Basel III Capital Adequacy Accord," Congressional Research Service Report for Congress, October 28.

Eun, Cheol, and Bruce Resnick, 1997, *International Financial Management,* Boston: Irwin-McGraw-Hill.

Faulkender, Michael, 2005, "Hedging or Market Timing? Selecting the Interest Rate Exposure of Corporate Debt," *Journal of Finance* 60, pp. 931–961.

Fujikawa, Megumi, 2011, "Japan Samurai-Bond Issuance on the Rise," MarketWatch.com, March 2.

Giannetti, Mariassunta, and Luc Laeven, 2010, "The Flight Home Effect: Evidence from the Syndicated Loan Market During Financial Crises," working paper.

McBrady, Matthew R., Sandra Mortal, and Michael J. Schill, 2010, "Do Firms Believe in Interest Rate Parity?" *Review of Finance* 14, pp. 695–726.

McBrady, Matthew R., and Michael J. Schill, 2007, "Foreign Currency-Denominated Borrowing in the Absence of Operating Incentives," *Journal of Finance* 86, pp. 145–177.

Merrill Lynch, April 2001, *Size and Structure of the World Bond Market: 2001,* New York: Merrill Lynch.

Miller, Darius P., and John J. Puthenpurackal, 2005, "Security Fungibility and the Cost of Capital: Evidence from Global Bonds," *Journal of Financial and Quantitative Analysis* 40, pp. 849–872.

"Offshore Financial Centers," June 2002, International Monetary Fund background paper.

Stein, Peter, "Behind the Yuan Bond Boom: Dollars," *Wall Street Journal,* January 24, 2011.

"Walt Disney Company's Sleeping Beauty Bonds—Duration Analysis," 1994, Harvard Business School case, 9-294-038.

Chapter 12

International Equity Financing

*W*hen a company lists its shares on a stock market, it seeks to access capital from a wide pool of investors. Apart from this **primary market** at the time of an initial public offering, the daily trading of a corporation's shares among investors (the **secondary market**) provides an objective, forward-looking valuation of the company's activities. This activity determines the cost of additional equity capital: The more investors are willing to pay for a company's shares, the cheaper will be additional capital when the company issues additional shares. Consequently, everything that affects stock market prices is important for a capital-hungry multinational corporation (MNC). (However, we leave a formal discussion of the international cost of capital to Chapter 13.) Another benefit of listing on a public stock exchange is that the presence of a stock market price can be used to align the interests of managers with the interests of shareholders in management compensation schemes.

This chapter examines how and why MNCs list their shares on international equity markets. Most MNCs list their shares on the stock exchanges of the countries in which they are headquartered. However, many MNCs also list their shares on stock exchanges located in other countries. For example, in 2010, the total value of shares traded in the stock of Nokia on the New York Stock Exchange (NYSE) exceeded $70 billion. Such a large volume for a single company is not unusual for the NYSE. For instance, IBM's total NYSE trading volume during 2010 was well over $150 billion. Nevertheless, Nokia, which is one of the world's premier mobile phone companies, is headquartered in Finland, in contrast to IBM, which is a U.S. company. Even though U.S. investors can directly buy Nokia stock on the Finnish stock exchange in what is called *cross-border trading*, Nokia must find this international ("cross-exchange") stock listing valuable. Why? After first giving you a tour of the world's stock exchanges and how they work, we explore the advantages and disadvantages of cross-listing.

12.1 A TOUR OF INTERNATIONAL STOCK MARKETS

The Size of Stock Markets

Exhibit 12.1 indicates that the U.S. stock market capitalization was about 31% of the world's stock market capitalization at the end of 2010. The second-largest market is that of Japan, which is followed by China, the London Stock Exchange (which combines the exchanges of the United Kingdom and Italy), and India.[1]

---

[1]Because not all exchanges in the world are part of the World Federation of Exchanges, from which we pull the data, we miss some reasonably sizable markets, such as New Zealand and the Czech Republic.

Exhibit 12.1 Market Capitalizations of Stock Exchanges

	Market Capitalization (in millions of U.S. dollars)						Market Type
	1991 (% of world total)		2000 (% of world total)		2010 (% of world total)		
United States	4,087,660	36.03%	15,104,037	46.82%	17,283,452	31.41%	Developed
Japan	3,130,863	27.60%	3,157,222	9.79%	4,099,606	7.50%	Developed
China	2,028	0.02%	580,991	1.80%	4,027,840	7.34%	Emerging
London Stock Exchange	NA	NA	NA	NA	3,613,064	6.58%	
United Kingdom	987,952	8.71%	2,567,992	7.99%			Developed
Italy	158,865	1.40%	768,364	2.38%			Developed
India	47,730	0.42%	148,064	0.46%	3,228,455	5.88%	Emerging
Euronext	NA	NA	NA	NA	2,930,072	5.34%	Developed
Belgium	71,319	0.63%	182,481	0.57%			Developed
France	348,083	3.07%	1,446,634	4.48%			Developed
Netherlands	136,158	1.20%	640,456	1.99%			Developed
Portugal	9,613	0.08%	60,681	0.19%			
Hong Kong	121,986	1.08%	623,398	1.93%	2,711,316	4.94%	Developed
Canada	266,874	2.35%	841,385	2.61%	2,170,433	3.95%	Developed
Brazil	42,759	0.38%	226,152	0.70%	1,545,566	2.82%	Emerging
Australia	145,511	1.31%	372,794	1.16%	1,454,491	2.65%	Developed
Germany	393,454	3.47%	1,270,243	3.94%	1,429,719	2.60%	Developed
Switzerland	173,881	1.53%	792,316	2.46%	1,229,357	2.24%	Developed
Spain	147,928	1.30%	504,219	1.56%	1,171,625	2.13%	Developed
Korea	96,373	0.85%	171,587	0.53%	1,091,912	1.99%	Emerging
OMX Nordic	NA	NA	NA	NA	1,042,154	1.90%	Developed
Denmark	44,841	0.40%	107,666	0.33%			Developed
Estonia	NA	NA	1,846	0.01%			
Finland	14,271	0.13%	293,635	0.91%			Developed
Iceland	NA	NA	4,439	0.01%			Developed
Latvia	NA	NA	563	0.00%			
Lithuania	NA	NA	1,588	0.00%			
Sweden	100,913	0.89%	328,339	1.02%			Developed
Russia	244	0.00%	38,922	0.12%	949,149	1.73%	Emerging
South Africa	168,497	1.49%	204,952	0.64%	925,007	1.69%	Emerging
Taiwan	124,864	1.10%	247,602	0.77%	838,401	1.53%	Emerging
Singapore	47,367	0.42%	152,827	0.47%	647,226	1.18%	Developed
Mexico	98,178	0.87%	125,204	0.39%	454,345	0.83%	Emerging
Malaysia	58,627	0.52%	116,935	0.36%	408,689	0.74%	Emerging
Indonesia	6,823	0.05%	28,834	0.08%	360,388	0.66%	Emerging
Saudi Arabia	48,213	0.42%	67,171	0.21%	353,410	0.64%	Not specified
Chile	27,984	0.25%	60,401	0.19%	341,799	0.62%	Emerging
Turkey	15,703	0.14%	69,659	0.22%	307,052	0.56%	Emerging
Norway	22,043	0.19%	65,034	0.20%	295,288	0.54%	Developed
Thailand	35,815	0.32%	29,489	0.09%	277,732	0.51%	Emerging
Israel	6,176	0.05%	64,081	0.20%	227,614	0.41%	Developed
Colombia	4,036	0.04%	9,560	0.03%	208,502	0.38%	Emerging
Poland	144	0.00%	31,279	0.10%	190,232	0.35%	Emerging
Philippines	11,386	0.10%	51,554	0.16%	157,321	0.29%	Emerging
Austria	7,689	0.07%	29,935	0.09%	126,032	0.23%	Developed
Peru	1,118	0.01%	10,562	0.03%	103,348	0.19%	Emerging
Luxembourg	11,308	0.10%	34,016	0.11%	101,129	0.18%	Developed
Iran	34,282	0.30%	34,041	0.11%	86,642	0.16%	Not specified
Egypt	2,651	0.02%	28,741	0.09%	84,277	0.15%	Emerging
Greece	13,118	0.10%	110,839	0.34%	67,586	0.12%	Developed
Argentina	18,509	0.16%	166,068	0.51%	63,910	0.12%	Frontier
Ireland	NA	NA	81,882	0.25%	60,368	0.11%	Developed
Jordan	2,512	0.02%	4,943	0.02%	30,864	0.06%	Frontier
Hungary	505	0.00%	12,204	0.04%	27,708	0.05%	Emerging

(continued)

Exhibit 12.1 Market Capitalizations of Stock Exchanges (*Continued*)

	Market Capitalization (in millions of U.S. dollars)						Market Type
	1991 (% of world total)		2000 (% of world total)		2010 (% of world total)		
Sri Lanka	1,936	0.02%	1,074	0.00%	19,924	0.04%	Frontier
Slovenia	NA	NA	2,547	0.01%	9,384	0.02%	Frontier
Mauritius	312	0.00%	1,331	0.00%	7,753	0.01%	Frontier
Cyprus	1,290	0.01%	11,516	0.04%	6,834	0.01%	Not specified
Malta	NA	NA	2,009	0.01%	4,194	0.01%	Not specified
Bermuda	NA	NA	2,146	0.01%	1,535	0.00%	Frontier
Total World Market	**11,345,733**		**32,260,433**		**54,884,333**		

Notes: The data are taken from the World Federation of Exchanges, Datastream, and the S&P/IFC database. The indications "Developed," "Emerging," and "Frontier" are from Morgan Stanley Capital International.

The relative market capitalizations of the different exchanges around the world are in constant flux, however. At one point in the 1980s, Japan's stock market was the world's largest. The dominance of Japan's stock market was also somewhat artificial because cross-holding grossly inflated the numbers.

Cross-holding refers to the practice of one firm owning shares in another firm. If both of these firms are listed on an exchange, and one calculates total market capitalization by merely multiplying the total number of shares outstanding by the market price per share, the market capitalization will be overstated because part of the value of the shares is essentially double-counted. Let's illustrate this with a hypothetical example.

Example 12.1 Cross-Holding of Shares

Assume that Companies A and B are each worth $100. Hence, the total market capitalization of the two companies is $200. Suppose both companies are fully equity financed, so we can represent their balance sheets as follows:

Company A		Company B	
Assets	**Liabilities**	**Assets**	**Liabilities**
$100	$100	$100	$100

Here, liabilities represent owner's equity, and assets represent plant and equipment. If there is no intercorporate share ownership, $200 represents the true value of the assets of both companies and, consequently, the true value of their shares. Now, suppose Company A issues $50 in new shares and buys $50 of the outstanding shares of Company B in the secondary stock market. Whereas the balance sheet of Company B remains unchanged, the balance sheet of Company A becomes

Company A		
	Assets	**Liabilities**
Physical Assets	$100	$150
Investment in Co. B	$50	

Therefore, the market capitalization of Company A increases by 50%, to $150, and total market capitalization of shares that have been issued by corporations increases by 25%, to $250. Of course, the true value of the assets remains $200 because no new assets were created by this transaction. To get the correct market capitalization, one must value only the shares that are held by the public, in which case we find a valuation of $50 for Company B and $150 for Company A, for a total of $200.

Cross-holding is especially common in Japan and in many European countries, such as Germany and Belgium, where banks are permitted to hold substantial and sometimes controlling interests in non-banking firms. The institutions that construct the major international stock market indices, such as Morgan Stanley Capital International (MSCI), now routinely correct for such cross-holdings.

Exhibit 12.1 also confirms two important recent trends. First, stock exchanges have consolidated across countries, which we discuss in more detail later. Second, the stock markets of a number of developing countries, such as China, India, Brazil, and Korea, have become among the largest in the world.

Emerging Stock Markets

In the early 1990s, emerging countries embarked on a trade and financial liberalization process. They relaxed restrictions on the foreign ownership of assets and improved capital market regulations. The results were dramatic. Not only did capital flows to emerging markets increase dramatically, but their composition changed substantially, as equity and fixed income investments increasingly replaced commercial bank debt. For example, in 1985, Mexico's equity market capitalization was 0.71% of gross domestic product (GDP), and foreigners' only access was through the Mexico Fund traded on the NYSE. After liberalizing its markets, by 2001, Mexico's equity market capitalization had risen to over 20% of GDP, and U.S. investors directly held about 25% of the market.[2] Currently, the Mexican stock market represents 45% of GDP.

Stock markets of developing countries are often referred to as **emerging markets**, and the young stock markets of the least developed countries are called **frontier markets**. In the far right column of Exhibit 12.1, we use the classification system of MSCI.[3]

In 1991, the largest emerging markets, each representing between 0.85% and 1.50% of world market capitalization, were Mexico, Korea, South Africa, and Taiwan. At that time, because of a political boycott, foreigners were not able to invest in South Africa (making its shares not "investable"), and its stock was not part of any established index. Since then, the most striking development has been the rapid growth of the stock markets of Brazil, Russia, India, and China, the emerging economic superpowers. Together, they represent almost 18% of the world market capitalization at the end of 2010. Of the markets dominating in 1991, Korea, South Africa, and Taiwan are still similar in size to Russia (about 1.5% to 2% of world market capitalization), but they are substantially smaller than Brazil, China, and India. It should be noted that Korea has been on the cusp of joining the list of developed markets and may do so soon.

China remains a special case. It now has three different stock exchanges—in Shanghai, Shenzhen, and Hong Kong. The Hong Kong market has been in existence for so long and Hong Kong is sufficiently high income that the Hong Kong market is actually considered a separate, developed market. The two mainland exchanges have grown spectacularly, despite being relatively closed to foreign investors. The following *Chinese Stock Markets* box provides more details.

Overall, emerging markets have become a much more important part of the world stock market since 1991. This happened in two waves. First, emerging markets did not perform as well as the U.S. stock market in the 1990s, which is reflected in their overall lower percentage of market capitalizations by 2000. While the United States and other developed markets experienced spectacular growth in the "dot-com" era, many emerging markets went through a series of crises. Second, in the first half of the past decade, many emerging equity markets appreciated considerably in value, while some markets, such as Korea, saw the number of companies listed on the exchange grow dramatically. Emerging markets also weathered the 2007 to 2010 financial crisis better than many developed markets. The fact that our numbers are measured in dollars also plays a role, as the dollar weakened considerably between 2000 and 2010, causing the U.S. market to become relatively less important over time.

---

[2]See Bekaert and Harvey (2003) for more details about the liberalization process in emerging markets.
[3]You may be surprised by finding Argentina classified as a frontier market. It was downgraded from emerging market status by MSCI in February of 2009 because of its continued capital flow restrictions.

Chinese Stock Markets

There are two stock exchanges in mainland China, Shanghai and Shenzhen. Both were founded in 1990. The Hong Kong stock exchange has a much longer history and is considered a separate developed exchange. Given its close links to China, the Hong Kong market also provides indirect access to Chinese equities through H shares and "red chips." An H share is a share of a company incorporated in mainland China but listed on the Hong Kong Stock Exchange. While regulated by Chinese law, H shares are denominated in Hong Kong dollars and trade the same as other equities on the Hong Kong exchange. Red chip stocks refer to Chinese companies incorporated outside mainland China and listed in Hong Kong. Their actual business is based in mainland China, and they are controlled, either directly or indirectly, by Chinese organizations, which are, in turn, often controlled by the local, regional, or central government.

For foreign investors, H shares and red chips may be the simplest way to invest in China, because Chinese capital controls make investing in stocks listed on the mainland exchanges rather difficult. There are two types of stocks, A shares and B shares. Originally, the A shares were quoted in renminbi and were to be traded only by local investors, and the B shares were quoted in dollars and were investable for foreigners. B shares represent only a small fraction of the total market. Various reforms have made the situation more complex. Since the end of 2002, certain foreign investors are allowed to trade in A shares under the Qualified Foreign Institutional Investor (QFII) regime. Currently, about 100 foreign institutional investors have been approved to buy and sell A shares under the QFII program, which imposes various restrictions. The total quota under the QFII program is currently USD30 billion. Since 2001, local investors can also invest in the B-share market. In December of 2006, further relaxation occurred when foreign investors were allowed to hold stakes in A shares over 10% of the market capitalization if the stake was maintained for more than 3 years.[4]

The rather minimal foreign involvement in the Chinese stock market is one significant difference between other emerging markets and the Chinese stock market. The spectacular growth of the Chinese stock market until October 2007, when the Shanghai stock index peaked at over 6,000 points, is often ascribed to the speculative fever of Chinese investors with few alternative venues for their substantial savings. Chinese investors are not allowed to invest abroad; the bond markets are relatively underdeveloped; and bank deposits offer diminutive interest rates. Real estate and the stock market are the two major investment venues. Until mid-2010, companies with A shares, which were also listed in Hong Kong and/or in the B-share market, traded at hefty premiums in the A-share market. The market capitalization of the Chinese markets also grew because of multiple initial public offerings (IPOs) by state-owned enterprises, which are often representing very large companies. On October 27, 2006, Industrial and Commercial Bank of China (ICBC) was simultaneously listed on the Hong Kong and Shanghai Stock Exchanges. It was the world's largest IPO at that time, valued at $21.9 billion. In 2010, another Chinese bank, the Agricultural Bank of China, beat the record with an IPO worth $22.1 billion. While the Chinese stock market fell substantially after October 2007 and the Shanghai index remained below 3,000 in early 2011, IPOs have kept the Chinese stock market in the top three of the world in terms of market capitalization.

Despite being one of the top stock markets in the world in terms of market capitalization, the Chinese stock market is far from well developed. For example, only 30% of the market capitalization of the listed companies is tradable (the remainder is mostly owned by government institutions). Since October 2008, the regulatory authorities have allowed margin trading of stocks and stock lending, but short selling of stocks remains difficult. Day trading is not allowed, and there are no options available on the stock market index. A futures contract was only introduced in April 2010. The Chinese market will likely remain underdeveloped until capital controls are lifted and the Chinese currency is made fully convertible.

Stock Markets and the Economy

Dividing a country's stock market capitalization by its GDP is often viewed as an indicator of stock market development. Historically, developed markets typically had larger market capitalization-to-GDP ratios than emerging markets, and within developed markets, ratios in Anglo-Saxon countries were larger than most continental European countries.

---

[4]For a more detailed time line of reforms in the Chinese stock market, see De Bondt et al. (2010).

For most emerging markets, capital market development was often a slow process, leaving many with relatively small stock markets. The Anglo-Saxon model has always relied more on bonds and equity financing than on bank financing, compared to the continental European model. It is also common for European banks to own shares of their client companies, whereas that is prohibited in the United States. Moreover, it is still the case that more enterprises in Europe are partially government owned (railroads, for example) and hence are not listed on exchanges.

While the old model still holds true on average, the 2010 picture is a bit more nuanced, as Exhibit 12.2 shows. A number of emerging markets have developed rather rapidly, while in Europe, many government companies have been privatized. After the dismantling of the Glass-Steagall Act, passed in 1933 in the United States to separate commercial from investment banking, U.S. financial institutions have become more like their European counterparts in terms of combining banking, insurance, and investment banking activities.

The capitalizations of some exchanges in continental Europe, such as Luxembourg, OMX Nordic (combining a number of Scandinavian and Baltic exchanges), and Switzerland, now represent more than 100% of the GDP in the nations in which they are located. For the London Stock Exchange, combining the United Kingdom and Italy, the 84% ratio represents a relatively high market capitalization-to-GDP ratio for the United Kingdom (well over 100%) and a relatively low one for Italy. In Asia, Hong Kong and Singapore also feature very large market capitalization-to-GDP ratios.

Exhibit 12.2 Market Capitalization as a Percentage of GDP

Developed Markets		Emerging and Frontier Markets	
Australia	119.25	Argentina	18.21
Austria	34.41	Bermuda	25.19
Canada	138.80	Brazil	76.38
Euronext	73.05	Chile	171.60
Germany	43.25	China	70.11
Greece	22.16	Colombia	73.65
Hong Kong	1,197.13	Cyprus	30.04
Ireland	29.58	Egypt	38.87
Israel	113.10	Hungary	21.95
Italy and United Kingdom	84.12	India	225.76
Japan	76.05	Indonesia	51.85
Luxembourg	193.87	Iran	25.64
Norway	71.41	Jordan	113.77
OMX Nordic	104.86	Korea	110.71
Singapore	297.74	Malaysia	186.66
Spain	89.42	Malta	53.76
Sweden	85.23	Mauritius	222.40
Switzerland	235.31	Mexico	45.25
United States	118.18	Peru	67.31
		Philippines	83.21
		Poland	43.34
		Russia	64.27
		Slovenia	20.21
		South Africa	261.00
		Sri Lanka	41.30
		Taiwan	196.35
		Thailand	88.84
		Turkey	42.12

Note: The data are for the end of 2010. Stock market capitalizations are from the World Federation of Exchanges. GDP numbers are from International Financial Statistics.

While on average, market capitalization-to-GDP ratios are smaller in emerging markets than in developed markets, there are a number of countries with ratios over 100%, including Chile, India, Jordan, Korea, Malaysia, Mauritius, South Africa, and Taiwan. Chile is the only Latin American country on this list. Its stock market development has been bolstered by a social security system requiring workers to save for retirement through several investment funds.

The Organization and Operation of Stock Markets

Legal Organization

Legally, stock markets can be organized as private or public organizations, called bourses or exchanges. A **private bourse** is owned and operated by a corporation founded for the purpose of trading securities. In many countries, several private exchanges compete with one another. This is the situation in the United States and Japan, but in most markets, one dominant exchange has emerged. In **public bourses**, the government appoints brokers, typically ensuring them a monopoly over all stock market transactions. While historically many exchanges, especially in Europe (Belgium, France, Spain, and Italy, for instance), started out as public bourses, waves of deregulation in the 1980s and 1990s resulted in the dismantling of this structure in most countries. Today, most bourses are private, although China's exchanges are quasi-state institutions. In all countries, however, bourses are typically subject to substantial government regulation.

The Globalization of Exchanges

Cross-listing, in which companies like Nokia list their shares on several exchanges around the world, has contributed substantially to the globalization of exchanges. Exchanges have also globalized simply by extending trading hours to make their markets more accessible to foreign traders located in other time zones. In addition, several exchanges have merged or created alliances with foreign exchanges to automatically cross-list their stocks.

In 2000, the stock exchanges of Amsterdam, Brussels, and Paris merged to form Euronext. Euronext then absorbed the Lisbon exchange and LIFFE, the London derivatives market. Euronext became a company listed in Paris. Its goal was to provide a pool of liquidity through a common order book, one set of clearing hours, a single settlement procedure, and one screen-based electronic system for any company listed with one of the exchanges that are part of Euronext. In March 2007, consolidation took a big leap forward with the merger of the NYSE and Euronext to form NYSE Euronext, Inc. NASDAQ (National Association of Securities Dealers Automated Quotations), the other major U.S. stock exchange, also expanded by forming the NASDAQ-OMX group, which operates seven stock exchanges in Europe (Finland, Sweden, Denmark, Iceland, Latvia, Lithuania, and Estonia) and has a stake in the Dubai stock exchange.

More mergers are in the works. In early 2011, after the London and Toronto stock exchanges announced their merger, Deutsche Börse and NYSE Euronext announced a plan to merge. Deutsche Börse owns the Frankfurt stock exchange and, together with the Swiss stock exchange operator (SWX), is co-owner of Eurex, a large derivatives exchange. Almost simultaneously, the Singapore stock exchange declared its plans to buy the Australian stock exchange. Since January 2010, the exchanges of Budapest (Hungary), Ljubljana (Slovenia), Prague (the Czech Republic), and Vienna (Austria) became equal subsidiaries of a holding company called CEESEG (Central and Eastern Europe Stock Exchange Group). While the exchanges continue to operate separately with the holding company providing financial and administrative support, it seems likely that they will eventually merge.

Consolidation is primarily a response to an increasingly competitive environment where exchanges face competition from other exchanges and alternative, mostly electronic trading systems. Such competition has also driven another major trend that makes mergers even easier going forward—**demutualization**, the process of converting exchanges from non-profit, member-owned organizations to for-profit, publicly traded companies. Examples include the Australian Stock Exchange (1998), the Toronto Stock Exchange (2000), Euronext (2000), NASDAQ (2000), Deutsche Börse (2001), and the NYSE (2005). On October 1, 2008, NYSE Euronext acquired Amex, the American Stock Exchange, to enhance its trading in U.S. options, exchange-traded funds (ETFs), closed-end funds, structured products, and cash equities.

Trading Practices

The trading practices of a market directly affect price discovery and liquidity. Price discovery is the process by which information is revealed. A good trading process leads to "fair," or "correct," prices that cannot be manipulated to the advantage of individual traders. However, stock market manipulation still exists, as the following *Stock Market Manipulation in China* box illustrates. In a liquid market, trading happens quickly, and large quantities of securities can be traded without the price being affected. Transaction costs are also low in liquid markets.

There are two major trading arrangements used by international stock markets: **price-driven trading systems** and **order-driven trading systems**. In a price-driven system, market makers stand ready to buy at their bid prices and sell at their ask prices, as in the foreign exchange market, but similar price- or quote-driven trading systems also exist for stocks. In an **order-driven trading system**, orders are batched together and then auctioned off at an equilibrium market price. Such an auction may happen once per day, a few times per day, or more continuously (e.g., facilitated by a computer). To match orders, a number of precedence rules are typically employed, such as the following:

- *Price priority:* The highest bid (buy) and the lowest ask (sell) have priority over other orders.
- *Time priority:* Orders at the same price are treated on a first-come, first-served basis.
- *Order priority:* Market orders (orders to buy or sell at the market price) have priority over limit orders (orders to buy or sell at a maximum or minimum price).

Stock Market Manipulation in China[5]

On April 1, 2003, a Beijing court handed down long-awaited sentences in one of the largest stock manipulation cases in history. Several men were convicted of manipulating the stock of China Venture Capital Group and were sentenced to jail terms ranging from 2 to 4 years and fines of up to CNY500,000. Yet the alleged masterminds of the scheme, Lu Liang and Zhu Huanliang, have not yet been captured and incarcerated.

At the beginning of 1998, China Venture Capital was a company listed on the Shenzhen Stock Exchange (one of the three stock exchanges in China), with a stock price around CNY10. In early 1998, Zhu, a major stock market player, contacted Lu, an established business journalist, to help him unwind his money-losing investment in China Venture Capital. At that time, Zhu controlled about 40% of China Venture Capital's outstanding shares.

As part of the deal, from December 1998 to May 1999, Lu began to build up his inventory of stock, buying first primarily from Zhu and eventually arranging to purchase 34.61% of the restricted shares owned by the government and assuming complete control of the board of directors. Now, Lu was ready to start the manipulation of the China Venture Capital stock in earnest. First, Lu was able to mislead the investing public with various company press releases, thereby significantly increasing the stock price. Second, Lu actively used large-size "wash trades" to increase the stock price and to produce the impression of high trading volume.[6] Apparently, Lu

---

[5]This box is based primarily on Wu and He (2003).
[6]A *wash trade* is a strategy of simultaneously buying and selling the same stock. Of course, when the manipulator sells, he hopes the stock price does not drop by more than the amount it went up when shares were bought.

gave specific instructions to his head trader to execute buy trades to attract attention and to execute sell trades while avoiding attention. As a result of this manipulation, the stock price reached over CNY84 per share. Lu then took over other companies and formed new business ventures using the stock of China Venture Capital to finance his acquisitions.

Eventually, the scheme collapsed when traders and investors began to learn the truth. Interestingly, Lu facilitated the collapse by doing an interview with a reputable finance and economics magazine, which ultimately cast light on the deception. China Venture Capital's stock price rapidly sank back to CNY10. While Lu was under house arrest, he managed to escape, and his whereabouts are unknown to this day.

Although this box is about China, it is important to note that price manipulation may occur in many less developed markets. For example, Khwaja and Mian (2005) demonstrate that brokers in Pakistan earn significantly higher returns on their trades than on trades intermediated for outside investors. They use detailed transactions to show that the returns are due to a "pump and dump" price manipulation scheme. Aggarwal and Wu (2006) in fact analyze no less than 142 stock market manipulation cases pursued by the Securities and Exchange Commission (SEC) in the United States between 1990 and 2000.

Automation and Electronic Trading

Over the past two decades, stock trading has become increasingly computerized and automated. In order-driven systems, it is straightforward to automate the trading rules adopted by the exchange to arrive at transaction prices. By recording all orders and making them public instantly, automation may appear to contribute greatly to the transparency of the market. However, this transparency has costs because of the presence of two types of traders: liquidity traders and informed traders. Liquidity traders trade for exogenous reasons, not because they have private information regarding the value of a stock. Examples of liquidity traders include retail investors who need money for a down payment on a house, pension funds or mutual funds that must invest their participants' inflows and reinvest dividends received, and index funds that track particular stock market indexes and consequently must trade the whole portfolio of stocks in the indexes. Informed traders trade on the basis of private information regarding the value of the stock.

An automated system with an open order book allows informed traders to wait behind their screens for the incoming orders of uninformed traders to obtain better pricing. Informed traders are themselves reluctant to reveal their information and consequently do not enter large orders (usually called a block) into an automatic trading system. In many countries, blocks of stock were historically traded "upstairs," meaning in offices away from the trading floor and via telephone through negotiation rather than through an automated system.

In the meantime, as in the foreign exchange market, private electronic communication networks (ECNs) have rapidly developed. An ECN lists the prices of securities trading on other exchanges and either lets its subscribers trade directly with one another or uses some form of order-crossing network. As a result, investors get slightly better buy and sell prices.

Such systems have existed for a long time. Instinet, founded in 1967 and now an independent subsidiary of Nomura, was one of the pioneers. Many investment banks also operated private crossing networks. Rapid technological developments have led to a proliferation of off-exchange trading venues, and regulatory authorities have started to regulate them. In Europe, the European Union (EU) introduced MiFID (Markets in Financial Instruments Directive), a financial law implemented in November 2007, that defined multilateral trading facilities (MTFs) and set rules regarding price and volume transparency on such venues. Chi-X Europe, a unit of Instinet, apparently attracts substantial trading volumes in the major European stocks. In the United States, the SEC has defined "Alternative Trading Systems" as alternative trading venues for securities without the formal listing requirements of an exchange. It also introduced Regulation National Market

System, known as Regulation NMS, which requires that trades anywhere be executed at the best available price.

Electronic systems clearly facilitate anonymous trading of large blocks of shares, which has allowed rapid growth in so-called "**dark pools**." Dark liquidity pools deliberately sacrifice price and volume transparency to offer anonymity to institutional and other large investors. While many of these dark pools are private companies (such as Posit/Matchnow from ITG), there are also broker-owned dark pools (such as Nomura's NX or Goldman Sachs's SIGMA X), and the exchanges are now also setting up their own dark pools to compete with the off-exchange venues. For example, NYSE Euronext operates SmartPool, and the London Stock Exchange operates Turquoise.

Electronic trading and the proliferation of trading venues also promoted the growth of high-frequency algorithmic traders, who buy and sell stocks to profit on razor thin price differences. Financial experts on microstructure have not yet agreed as to whether the new trading landscape contributes to price discovery and liquidity (see Schwartz [2010] for a discussion). On the one hand, algorithmic traders often act as liquidity providers, buying when prices are low and selling when prices are high. In fact, many exchanges pay them for their liquidity-providing services. On the other hand, both the presence of algorithmic traders and the proliferation of trading venues fragment order flow and may make prices less informative. After all, the price would be most informative and accurate if it simultaneously combines the information of as many market participants as possible, as would occur in a price auction. Many exchanges feel that these alternative trading venues free-ride on the price discovery provided by the exchanges (while their existence threatens to erode full price discovery) and that the alternative trading venues should face more regulation regarding transparency. Yet, some research suggests that trading costs have decreased over time (see Exhibit 12.4). It is likely that the debate about price discovery, transparency, and liquidity will continue for some time in academic, practitioner, and regulatory circles, and its outcome will shape the trading landscape of the future.

Examples of Trading Practices on Major Exchanges

The classic example of a price-driven stock exchange is NASDAQ, which operates a complex communications network that centralizes a geographically dispersed market. Bid and ask prices of thousands of actively traded stocks are continuously quoted by hundreds of competing NASDAQ market makers who deal in any stocks they choose. Information from ECNs is also incorporated. From computer terminals connected to NASDAQ's mainframe computer, brokers are able to see the current bid and ask prices for all NASDAQ stocks, quoted on the screen, by competing market makers (dealers). An investor's broker can execute a trade online through NASDAQ's computer or call a NASDAQ dealer with a bid or an ask price at which she wants to transact. The London Stock Exchange runs SETS (Stock Exchange Electronic Trading Service), an electronic system introduced in 1997. It also maintains active market platforms for smaller, less liquid stocks, both local and foreign ones. London is in fact a major market for international stock trading.

An example of an order-driven system is the Tokyo Stock Exchange (TSE), the largest exchange in Japan. Since 1999, the exchange switched to pure electronic trading, and it introduced a new super-fast "Arrowhead" system in early 2010. There are no dealers. Instead, the best eight bids and offers in the order book representing customers' potential trades are displayed. Trades are matched in milliseconds. The TSE sets limits on the daily stock price fluctuations based on the previous day's closing price.

The NYSE is an interesting combination of a price-driven system and an order-driven system and was recently completely redesigned. There are now three key market participants. The first are called Designated Market Makers (DMMs), which succeed the former Specialists. DDMs can also trade for their own account, but they have the responsibility to maintain a "fair and orderly" market in a particular stock, for instance, by holding physical and/or automated auctions, at the open and the close and in periods of significant imbalances. Floor Brokers, who collect orders from clients, still exist, but they may also use external ECNs to execute an order. Finally, there are Supplemental Liquidity Providers (SLPs), who are exchange members (investment banks and brokers) that generate sufficient volume (for their own accounts) to be paid for providing liquidity services. Logically, a NYSE member organization cannot act as a DDM and an SLP for the same stock.

The first European stock exchange to adopt an electronic trading system was the Paris Bourse, with its CAC (*Cotation Assistée et Continue*) system, which was later replaced by the NSC (*Nouveau Systéme de Cotation*), or Super-Cac. The market is fully automated, and there is no longer any floor trading. The Paris Bourse does allow block trades to be negotiated outside the NSC. A recent study by Lefebvre (2010) suggests that order fragmentation between the upstairs block market and the NSE system does not negatively affect liquidity on the main market. On the contrary, stocks that have an active upstairs market have higher liquidity.

Turnover and Transaction Costs

Exhibit 12.3 lists turnover on various exchanges during 1991, 2000, and 2010. **Turnover** is the total dollar volume of trade done during the year divided by the exchange's total dollar market capitalization at the end of the year. For example, if every share traded exactly once during the year, turnover would be 1, or 100%. Turnover is considered to be an indicator of liquidity, although it also reflects the arrival of news that instigates trades. In 2010, turnover in the United States of close to 200% was the highest of all developed countries; Spain and Germany also had turnover rates over 100%. In contrast, some small markets, such as Bermuda, Cyprus, and Ireland, had turnover less than 20%.

Overall, emerging markets have lower turnover than developed markets, but turnover differs greatly across emerging markets. Four emerging markets had turnover over 100% (China, Korea, Taiwan, and Turkey), but seven countries also had turnover less than 20%. Turnover is mostly higher in Asia than in Latin America and has generally increased for most countries over the past 20 years.

Turnover is inversely related to the costs of trading stocks. **Trading costs** have three components. First, the investor making a trade may have to pay brokerage commissions and other fees, which are typically relatively small, especially for large orders. Second, securities have bid and ask prices, so the investor must buy from the trader at the trader's high sell price and must sell to the trader at the trader's low bid price. Third, trading relatively large amounts when the market is illiquid creates a **market impact** in which the price the investor gets rises as the investor buys or falls as the investor sells.

Of the three components, commission costs are easiest to estimate. They tend to decrease with trade size and are minuscule for very large trades. According to Investment Technology Group (ITG), a trading and research company, commissions in 2010 account for about 10 basis points of total trading costs in developed markets and about 20 basis points in emerging markets. ITG also estimates total trading costs for various countries and country groups. Market impact costs have always been difficult to assess. This is especially true in the current trading environment, in which there are a large number of possible venues for trading. Many trades are happening within the bid–ask spread, and some traders are being paid to provide liquidity. Consequently, even the bid–ask spread component is not so trivial to estimate. Nevertheless, ITG produces regular trading cost estimates, and we reproduce some of their 2010 estimates for various countries and country groups in the last

Exhibit 12.3 Turnover in Developed and Emerging and Frontier Markets

Panel A: Developed Markets				Panel B: Emerging and Frontier Markets					
	Turnover				Turnover			Market Concentration	
	1991	2000	2010		1991	2000	2010	2000	2009
Australia	0.32		0.73	Argentina	0.26	0.04	0.06	67.6	71.9
Austria	0.92	0.31	0.39	Brazil	0.31	0.45	0.56	34.6	54.8
Bermuda	NA	0.06	0.07	Chile	0.07	0.10	0.16	67.6	48.1
Canada	0.29	0.75	0.63	China	0.40	1.24	2.00	9.5	32.5
Cyprus	0.05	0.80	0.11	Colombia	0.05	0.04	0.14	68.0	72.8
Euronext	NA	NA	0.69	Egypt	0.05	0.39	0.46	48.0	39.4
Belgium	0.09	0.21		Hungary	0.23	1.01	0.95	88.9	96.5
France	0.33	0.75		India	0.48	0.34	0.33	48.9	30.6
Netherlands	0.29	1.06		Indonesia	0.43	0.53	0.29	44.3	48.4
Portugal	0.29	0.90		Iran	0.15	0.15	0.20	NA	69.2
Germany	0.96	0.84	1.14	Jordan	0.17	0.08	0.28	58.3	69.2
Greece	0.19	0.86	0.64	Korea	0.89	3.24	1.47	18.4	33.7
Hong Kong	0.32	0.61	0.55	Malaysia	0.18	0.50	0.27	19.9	39.3
Ireland	NA	0.18	0.15	Malta	NA	0.09	0.01	NA	94.6
Israel	1.36	0.37	0.45	Mauritius	0.02	0.06	0.05	NA	61.0
Japan	0.32	0.85	0.97	Mexico	0.32	0.36	0.26	66.5	63.1
London Stock	NA	NA	0.76	Peru	0.12	0.14	0.05	67.9	65.8
Exchange				Philippines	0.13	0.16	0.14	42.7	48.7
United Kingdom	0.32	0.71		Poland	0.19	0.47	0.21	25.1	56.7
Italy	0.16	1.01		Russia	NA	0.52	0.23	93.9	66.1
Luxembourg	0.01	0.04	0.21	Saudi Arabia	0.05	0.26	0.57	67.3	58.5
Norway	0.53	0.92	0.89	Slovenia	NA	0.18	0.05	NA	79.2
OMX Nordic	NA	NA	0.89	South Africa	0.05	0.38	0.37	30.9	47.9
Denmark	0.21	0.85		Sri Lanka	0.05	0.13	0.25	68.5	46.1
Estonia	NA	0.18		Taiwan	2.93	3.97	1.08	29.5	34.6
Finland	0.11	0.70		Thailand	0.84	0.79	0.77	37.7	48.2
Iceland	NA	0.54		Turkey	0.55	2.57	1.34	43.3	50.4
Latvia	NA	0.40							
Lithuania	NA	0.13							
Sweden	0.21	1.18							
Singapore	0.38	0.60	0.45						
Spain	0.27	1.96	1.16						
Switzerland	0.40	0.77	0.64						
United States	0.53	2.11	1.76						

Notes: Computations are based on data from the World Federation of Exchanges, Datastream, and the S&P/IFC database. The numbers for 2010 use electronic order book volume but exclude negotiated deals.

column of Exhibit 12.4. The first column has data for 2005 for the developed countries and data for 2008 for the other groups. The 2008 data (the furthest we could go back) should be viewed as potentially not representative, because trading costs go up with market volatility, and markets were extremely volatile during the 2007 to 2010 global crisis. Trading costs in most developed markets are 40 to 50 basis points and have not changed much since 2005. U.S. small cap stocks are more expensive to trade (about 70 basis points), and stocks in developed Asia (excluding Japan) have become more expensive to trade since 2005 (with a trading cost of about 70 basis points). In the older emerging markets of Asia and Latin America, trading costs are now 85 to 90 basis points, whereas the costs are 110 basis points in emerging Europe and over 150 basis points in the mostly frontier markets in Africa and the Middle East.

Exhibit 12.4 Trading Costs in Emerging Markets

Country	2005 (quarter 3)	2010 (quarter 1)
United States (large cap)	40.0	38.8
United States (small cap)	75.0	71.8
United Kingdom	55.0	48.7
Japan	94.0	50.5
Canada	87.4[a]	49.4
Developed Asia (excluding Japan)	54.0	72.9
Developed Europe (excluding United Kingdom)	64.0	43.4
Emerging markets	123.7[a]	89.7
Emerging Asia	110.7[a]	85.7
Emerging Europe	145.2[a]	111.2
Emerging Latin America	150.0[a]	87.3
Emerging Africa and Middle East	145.7[a]	162.3

Notes: The data are taken from ITG's Global Trading Cost Review, 2010 (quarter 1).
The trading costs are expressed in basis points.

[a]Data are for 2008, quarter 3.

Research has shown that trading costs are "priced." That is, stocks with otherwise similar characteristics and promised cash flows trade at different prices when their trading costs and liquidity are different. Investors demand higher expected returns on stocks with higher trading costs or lower liquidity, and hence the prices of these stocks are lower. Research by Bekaert et al. (2007) suggests that financial liberalization in emerging markets has significantly lowered trading costs. Cross-country differences in trading costs thus provide an incentive to international firms to list their stocks on exchanges with lower transaction costs. Cross-listing may increase stock prices, reduce expected returns, and thus lower the firm's cost of capital, as we will see in Chapter 13.

Casablanca: From a Sleepy Place to a Thriving Modern Market?[7]

Casablanca typically conjures up the image of the classic movie starring Humphrey Bogart as Rick Blaine, an American who runs Rick's Café Américan in Casablanca, Morocco. In the early days of World War II, Morocco was a French protectorate and was thus under German control. There was active trading in "letters of transit" that allowed the bearer to travel around German-controlled Europe and to neutral Lisbon, Portugal, and then to the United States. Gambling was tolerated although it was officially banned; and special discounts were extended to Rick's friends. In short, Rick's Café could serve as a good metaphor for an emerging market: Just as Rick could "fix" the roulette wheel to help his friends, so it may be that trading practices in emerging markets are not as fair as in the developed world.

The Casablanca Stock Exchange (CSE) is a typical emerging financial market that went through momentous change between 1990 and 2000. In the 1980s, the Moroccan stock exchange was a backwater in many ways. It was a state institution, with very few listed stocks and almost no participation of individual investors in the stock market. Institutional investors would often trade blocks on the upstairs market, but this upstairs market—in which trades were based on mutual agreements—was neither transparent nor standardized. The exchange was extremely illiquid, and most stocks did not trade for weeks. Foreign investors were not prohibited from buying Moroccan stock, but foreigners stayed away because of the archaic structure, the low trading volume, and the possibilities of market manipulation.

In 1989, Morocco announced an ambitious privatization and economic liberalization program, which also included financial market reforms that would greatly alter the operation of the stock exchange starting in 1993. The stock

---

[7]The analysis in this box builds heavily on the article by Ghysels and Cherkaoui (2003).

exchange was privatized and reformed. The reforms created a dealer/market-maker structure in which more disclosure was required from both listed companies and market makers.

The new reforms began to attract foreign investors, and in 1996, the CSE was included in the International Finance Corporation (IFC) emerging markets database. The number of individual investors increased considerably, reaching 300,000 in 1996. Exhibit 12.5 shows that these reforms had a profound effect on the stock market. Trading volume and liquidity exploded. Finally, on December 17, 1996, the CSE adopted the screen-driven trading system of the Paris Bourse. It is generally believed that such structural changes should greatly affect the quality of the market and lower its cost of trading. There is no doubt, as Exhibit 12.5 amply illustrates, that the reforms immediately increased turnover and liquidity, but did trading costs fall? Unfortunately, researchers do not have data on bid–ask spreads, let alone estimates of market impact. However, Ghysels and Cherkaoui (2003) nonetheless attempted to infer what the trading costs were using the trading data of several stocks before and after the reforms. Surprisingly, Ghysels and Cherkaoui found that, at least until 1996, trading costs on the CSE actually increased after the reforms.

There are multiple interpretations of these results. Let's round up the usual suspects. First, although liquidity improved, until 1996, the CSE remained a relatively illiquid market compared to other markets, and trading was thin. Second, foreign investors (especially new arrivals) are sometimes among the least informed of market participants. *Casablanca* presents a case in point: When Captain Renault asks Rick what an ex-pat like him is doing in Casablanca, he answers that he came for his health, saying, "I came to Casablanca for the waters." Renault exclaims, "The waters? What waters? We're in the desert!" Rick laconically replies, "I was misinformed." Likewise, perhaps CSE dealers possessed a tremendous amount of market power relative to foreign traders and were able to pass along higher costs to them. A third possibility is that the Ghysels and Cherkaoui model misestimated true trading costs.

If the results are accurate, however, there are a few important lessons from this detailed example. First, jumps in turnover and trading are not necessarily associated with lower trading costs, although they typically are. Second, although reforms might encourage foreign investors to participate in a market, by themselves, they do not seem to bring down trading costs. What might have an effect on trading costs, however, is automated trading. Only after screen-driven trading was introduced to the CSE in late 1996 did transaction costs fall. Research by Domowitz et al. (2001) shows more generally that automated systems are associated with lower costs.

Exhibit 12.5 Casablanca Stock Exchange: Basic Indicators

Year	Number of Trading Sessions	Average Daily Trading Volume	Total Market Capitalization	Ratio of Market Capitalization to GDP	Market Index
1989	248	123	5.0	2.6	122.65
1990	244	510	7.8	3.5	158.68
1991	243	428	12.4	5.0	187.55
1992	248	626	17.0	6.6	207.88
1993	248	4,611	25.7	10.0	259.78
1994	251	7,235	39.0	13.1	342.39
1995	251	20,730	50.4	17.5	342.39
1996	247	19,510	75.6	23.0	447.13

Notes: From Ghysels and Cherkaoui (2003). The entries to the table provide annual summary statistics of basic indicators. The average daily volume is in millions of Moroccan dirhams (MAD), the local currency. The total market capitalization is expressed in billions of MAD, and the market index value is taken on the last day of the year.

12.2 INTERNATIONAL CROSS-LISTING AND DEPOSITARY RECEIPTS

An increasing number of MNCs are finding ways to broaden their investor bases and raise capital by cross-listing their shares on foreign exchanges. For example, Royal Dutch Shell is headquartered in Amsterdam and is listed on the Amsterdam, London, and New York exchanges. Novartis, a pharmaceutical company headquartered in Basel, Switzerland, is traded on the Swiss Exchange in Zurich and in New York.

Exhibit 12.6 Percentage of Turnover by Foreign, Cross-Listed Companies

Exchange	Turnover %	Domestic Companies Listed	Foreign Companies Listed	Exchange	Turnover %	Domestic Companies Listed	Foreign Companies Listed
Americas				**Europe-Africa-Middle East**			
Bermuda SE	5.95	14	31	Athens Exchange	7.00	277	3
BM&FBOVESPA (Brazil)	1.10	373	8	Deutsche Börse	9.89	690	75
Buenos Aires SE	32.53	101	5	Irish SE	2.10	50	9
Colombia SE	18.56	84	2	Johannesburg SE	26.07	352	45
Lima SE	20.47	199	49	London SE Group[a]	9.67	2,362	604
Mexican Exchange	8.84	130	297	Luxembourg SE	18.68	29	260
NASDAQ	9.31	2,480	298	OMX Nordic[b]	7.15	752	26
New York SE	9.76	1,799	518	Oslo Børs	22.58	195	44
TSX Group	1.31	3,654	87	Warsaw SE	2.01	569	15
Asia-Pacific				Wiener Börse	1.11	89	21
Australian SE	4.62	1,913	86				
Bursa Malaysia	1.42	948	8				
Tokyo SE Group	0.02	2,281	12				

Notes: The data are for 2010 and were provided by the World Federation of Exchanges (www.world-exchanges.org). Due to different reporting rules and calculation methods, turnover figures across exchanges are not entirely comparable. We report only the markets with foreign turnover percentages higher than 1%. We also report the total number of domestic and foreign companies that are listed.

[a]London SE Group includes Borsa Italiana.

[b]OMX Nordic includes the Copenhagen, Helsinki, Reykjavik, Riga, Stockholm, Tallinn, and Vilnius exchanges.

The number of cross-listed firms grew quickly in the 1990s. Yet, the bulk of the trading on an exchange is still mostly accounted for by domestic firms. Exhibit 12.6 shows the percentage of total value traded due to trading of foreign companies in various countries where the turnover percentage by foreign companies was over 1% in 2010. Markets with a large foreign presence include the Luxembourg exchange, the Johannesburg Stock Exchange, the Buenos Aires Stock Exchange, the Oslo exchange, and the Colombia and Lima exchanges.[8]

In the 1990s, cross-listing grew the fastest in the United States, especially at the NYSE. However, during the 2000s, growth of cross-listings in the United States stalled relative to listings on other exchanges, such as London's. Some have blamed the 2002 Sarbanes-Oxley Act, aimed at improving corporate governance and accounting standards (see Chapter 1). A number of firms even de-listed. For example, in 2007, SGL, a German graphite and carbon fiber materials maker, de-listed from the NYSE in order to cut the costs associated with complying with Sarbanes-Oxley regulations. The box summarizes academic research regarding the effects of the Sarbanes-Oxley Act on U.S. cross-listings. However, by 2010, the Bank of New York Mellon's review of the market suggests that the trend has reversed, with the majority of the new listings happening on major U.S. exchanges and on the Luxembourg exchange.

How Do Firms Cross-List?

Companies seeking a listing overseas must satisfy two requirements. First, they must comply with the standards set for cross-listing by the exchanges. For example, the Tokyo Stock

---

[8]The numbers are the value traded using the electronic order book, which exclude negotiated deals. In the United Kingdom, more than half of such deals (in total representing about 20% of value traded) involve foreign companies.

Sarbanes-Oxley Act and Cross-Listing

During the mid-2000s, the majority of new depositary receipt (DR) listings were on non-U.S. exchanges. Many felt that this shift reflected the costs of litigation and corporate governance regulations when listing in the United States in the wake of the **Sarbanes-Oxley Act** (SOX henceforth). A flurry of academic research has thoroughly studied the effects of SOX on cross-listing. Although the debate is ongoing, we summarize the results that seem robust across several studies.[9]

The first finding is that because SOX was passed, foreign firms are indeed less likely to list in the United States (as opposed to listing in, for example, the United Kingdom) than before, all else equal. The second more controversial finding is that cross-listing in the United States continues to be accompanied by positive stock market returns. In some sense, this is not surprising. Although SOX increases administrative costs, it also provides enhanced corporate governance because SOX imposes criminal and civil penalties in case of false certifications of financial statements that help protect shareholders against potentially crooked insiders (managers) better than before.

Can these two findings be reconciled? The types of firms that tend to be less likely to list are revealing: They are mostly small firms (for which compliance costs may be steep) and, particularly, firms with stronger inside control. Firms from emerging markets and from countries with weak legal protection of minority shareholders are now more likely to choose Rule 144A and Level III listings, which do not require SOX compliance (see Boubakri et al., 2010). This is consistent with the bonding hypothesis (see Section 12.3). Insiders of foreign firms, knowing that SOX makes it harder for them to extract value from minority shareholders, decide not to list in the United States. This decision is of course not in the interest of the minority shareholders. If such firms would list, the benefits to the minority holders would be higher than before SOX because agency conflicts are better mitigated than before, as Duarte et al. (2011) show.

Evidence from de-registrations from the U.S. markets also appears consistent with this interpretation. Leuz et al. (2008) studied companies that ceased SEC reporting but continued to trade publicly and showed a spike in such "going dark" actions after SOX. They found evidence suggesting that controlling insiders de-register to protect private control benefits and decrease outside scrutiny in firms with strong inside control.

Exchange listing criteria and associated fees are steeper for non-Japanese companies than for domestic companies. Second, a company that wants to cross-list must adhere to the securities regulations of the country in which it wants to list its shares. This may require registering with the country's securities commission and reconciling the company's financial accounts with the market standards of that nation.

Cross-listed stocks can be traded directly on a national stock market, but most often they are traded in the form of a **depositary receipt (DR)**, which represents a number of original shares held in custody by a financial institution in the country of the exchange. The best-known depositary receipts are American depositary receipts (ADRs) and global depositary receipts (GDRs), which we discuss next. In 2010, the first Hong Kong, Brazilian, and Indian DRs occurred. Standard Chartered, a U.K. bank, raised $590 million in the Indian offering.

American Depositary Receipts

An **American Depositary Receipt (ADR)** represents a specific number of shares in the home market that are held in custody by a U.S. depositary bank. The depositary bank converts all dividends and other payments into U.S. dollars and charges a small custodial fee for its services. The Bank of New York Mellon (BNY Mellon) dominates the ADR custodial market, but JPMorgan Chase, Citigroup, and Deutsche Bank are also important players.

---

[9]The box is based on research by Duarte et al. (2011), Doidge et al. (2009), and Leuz (2007).

Whereas most non-U.S. companies use ADRs, a minority of companies, mostly Canadian ones, use ordinary listings in which they are traded entirely like U.S. companies and face SEC registration and adherence to the reporting requirements of U.S. generally accepted accounting principles (GAAP).

Types of ADRs

The listing of foreign shares in the United States is subject to a detailed set of rules. Exhibit 12.7 gives an overview of the various types of ADRs and the rules that apply to them. Generally speaking, requirements involve registering with the SEC and furnishing an annual report with a reconciliation of financial accounts with GAAP.

A major distinction among the types of ADRs is whether the listing is associated with raising capital in the United States. No new capital is raised when firms list a Level I or Level II ADR. That is, no new shares are issued by the company. Only existing shares are being traded. **Level I ADRs** trade over the counter (OTC) in New York in what is called **pink sheet trading** and are not listed on a major U.S. stock exchange. The OTC market is composed of a network of broker/dealers who complete transactions via telephone or computer rather than in a centralized marketplace. (Pink sheets are weekly publications covering OTC securities and their market makers.) Level I ADRs face few requirements. They must register with the SEC but are not required to comply with GAAP. Basically, the firms file their home country accounting statements with adequate English translations. Well-known companies such as Switzerland's Nestlé and Japan's Nintendo are active OTC ADRs. **Level II ADRs** trade on the NYSE or NASDAQ, and hence must satisfy the exchange's listing requirements. Firms issuing Level II ADRs must register with the SEC and must also file a form to comply with GAAP ("Form 20-F"). Typically, a firm first uses a Level I ADR. Then, it moves to a Level II.

Level III ADRs trade on one of the major exchanges, and they are also issued to raise capital in the United States. This implies that the SEC disclosure and GAAP requirements are even more stringent. Finally, **Rule 144 ADRs (RADRs)** are capital-raising ADRs whereby the securities are privately placed with qualified institutional investors, such as pension funds and insurance companies. As a result, the SEC and GAAP requirements are minimal. The drawback is that RADRs are very illiquid, much like the private placements discussed in Chapter 11. RADRs can only trade through the PORTAL Alliance system, which is a screen-based automated trading system developed by the NASDAQ OMX group and a number of major financial institutions.

Another important distinction is whether the ADR is sponsored or unsponsored. Sponsored ADRs are created by the bank at the request of the foreign company that wants to cross-list. The sponsoring bank often offers ADR holders an assortment of services, including

Exhibit 12.7 Types of ADRs

	Description	Trading Location	GAAP Requirement
Level I	Unlisted	OTC pink sheets	No GAAP reconciliation required
Level II	Listed on major U.S. exchange	NYSE, AMEX, or NASDAQ	Only partial reconciliation for financials
Level III	Offered and listed on major U.S. exchange	NYSE, AMEX, or NASDAQ	Full SEC compliance, including full U.S. GAAP reconciliation for financials
Rule 144A (RADR)	Private U.S. placement to qualified institutional buyers (QIBs)	U.S. private placement market using PORTAL	No U.S. GAAP reconciliation required

Note: Data are from Miller (2000).

investment information and portions of the annual report, translated into English. The depositary fees are paid by the foreign company. Unsponsored ADRs are put in place by a U.S. financial institution, without the direct involvement of the foreign company. Consequently, the foreign company may not provide investment information on a regular basis or in a timely manner. ADR investors pay the depositary fees on unsponsored ADRs. Today, the bulk of depositary receipt programs are sponsored.

The Road to a Successful ADR Listing

The following 19 steps to a successful ADR listing in the United States are excerpted from "Solving the ADR Puzzle: The Expert Guide to Building a Successful ADR Program" (Bank of New York et al., 2002):

1. Appoint an independent accountant/auditor with expertise in international offerings and U.S. capital markets.

2. Appoint an external legal counsel specializing in U.S. securities law to advise on SEC filings, prospectus (if any), and other related matters.

3. If the listing involves a U.S. public offering, appoint an underwriter(s)/investment bank(s) with appropriate transaction experience, sector or industry knowledge, and U.S. distribution capabilities. Investment banks will often make a "pitch" for the underwriter role in what is known as a "beauty contest." An important consideration is the likelihood of good after-market support.

4. Appoint a depositary bank with a significant amount of ADR listing experience, appropriate infrastructure, a knowledgeable staff, and technical capabilities.

5. Select a financial printer, which will manage the confidential document creation, revision, SEC filings, printing, and distribution. If necessary, foreign-language translations can also be arranged by the financial printer.

6. Appoint an investor relations firm that specializes in U.S. listings of non-U.S. companies. Seek an international communications firm with experience in advising and assisting non-U.S. companies. Choose a firm with free access to senior counselors in both the United States and your country.

7. Apply for an exchange listing with the exchange on which you wish to list your stock. The procedure will differ, depending on the exchange. For example, the application to the NYSE will also involve selecting a specialist firm.

8. If the listing involves a U.S. public offering, prepare Form F-1, an SEC registration statement required for any non-U.S. company making its first offering of securities in the United States. The document describes in detail the securities and the transaction being undertaken. It will have been in preparation for several months, and it will be submitted for review and comments by the SEC's corporate finance division together with the prospectus for the offering, if any.

9. Send deposit agreement and Form F-6, submitted by the depositary bank, to the company for review. The documentation describes in detail all the activities undertaken by the depositary bank as agent on behalf of the company and has by now become standard documentation.

10. Have the investor relations firm prepare for the listing day event with detailed recommendations, including a publicity strategy, which should include a tactical plan for special events and media tour aimed at key audiences in the United States and the domestic market.

11. If the listing involves a U.S. public offering, prepare a Red Herring (preliminary prospectus). The company and underwriters print preliminary copies of the prospectus, which will be used to sell the shares to potential investors. Final prices are not contained in this document.

12. File Form F-1 (offerings only). With full and final response to SEC comments, company and counsel make final revisions to the registration statement, which the financial printer will then file with the SEC.

13. Request a CUSIP number from Standard & Poor's. This is a security identification code that provides financial intermediaries with a uniform number that identifies a company through all phases of securities processing and recording. Underwriters request a unique security identification number for the new ADR from the requisite authority.

14. Finalize an exchange listing agreement. All parties agree to the documentation, and the issuer promises to abide by the regulations of the chosen stock exchange.

15. Agree with the depositary bank on the final details of the documentation, which is then filed with Form F-6 with the SEC for review and comments. The review usually takes about 4 weeks.

16. If the listing involves a U.S. public offering, the price of the issue must be determined. Underwriters make final decisions regarding the price of the issue, taking into consideration market conditions and investor demand.

17. If the listing involves a U.S. public offering, schedule the closing, which involves the company, its underwriters (if any), the depositary, and legal counsel for all parties. The underwriters transfer the proceeds for the share sale to the company (or other selling party), and the company transfers ordinary shares to the sub-custody account of the depositary.

18. Conduct listing day events. This may involve significant promotional activities and media coverage.

19. Trading of ADRs commences!

Global Depositary Receipts

Many of the ADRs discussed so far are also part of a **global depositary receipts (GDRs)** program. GDRs are like ADRs, but they can trade across many markets and settle in the currency of each market. One important GDR program was Telmex, the Mexican telephone company, which in 1991 became the first international offering of equity shares in a public utility by a developing country. In 2010, RUSAL, a Russian mining company, raised $177 million through a GDR program, listing on NYSE Euronext Paris, the first GDR for this market. Many of the DRs listed in London and Luxembourg trade on a platform called the International Order Book. However, some of the multilateral trading facilities, such as Turquoise and Chi-X, have now also started to trade DRs.

Global depositary receipts are not always associated with existing companies seeking to increase their shareholder base and raise additional capital. They can also be associated with companies wanting to tap the equity market for the first time. Some companies issue stock locally but also target foreign investors, especially foreign institutional investors. When a firm issues shares in multiple foreign markets, sometimes simultaneously with distribution in the domestic market, the issue is part of the **Euro-equity market**. Like the Eurocurrency and Eurobond markets discussed in Chapter 11, the Euro-equity market involves international issues originated and sold anywhere in the world, making **external equity market** a more appropriate name.

Primary equity markets have become more and more globalized, with many IPOs of non-U.S. companies including a U.S. or other international listing. The wave of privatizations of government enterprises that occurred in Europe in the 1980s and in emerging markets in the 1990s is an important factor behind this development. The accompanying equity issues—such as those of British Telecom in December 1984 and YPF, Argentina's state-owned oil company, in 1993—were so large that it was desirable to involve foreign investors directly. In 2010, the Brazilian oil company, Petrobras, attempted to raise $70 billion and chose to raise $10 billion in DR form. JPMorgan Chase acted as the depositary bank for the NYSE deal.

Size and Growth of the Depositary Receipt Market[10]

While ADRs dominated the cross-listing market in the 1990s, the market is now more global. Of a total of 2,205 sponsored depositary receipt programs outstanding at the end of 2010, only 18.5% are U.S.–listed ADRs, and over 46% are now part of GDR programs.

Data from BNY Mellon indicate phenomenal growth in depositary receipt (DR) programs, with between 85 and 189 new DR programs per year every year since 1992. Part of this growth was accounted for by firms from emerging markets attempting to raise capital in the largest capital market in the world, following large-scale liberalization programs in these countries. As of the end of 2010, the BNY Mellon data indicate that India now accounts for

---

[10]Most of the data discussed here are based on data from BNY Mellon (2010).

more of the total outstanding DR programs than any other country. Russia, China, and Brazil round out the top four countries, followed closely by the United Kingdom. Each accounts for 5% to 6% of the total number of DR programs. The growing importance of Brazil, Russia, India, and China in the global economic landscape is again visible.

Russian companies primarily list on the London Stock Exchange (LSE), and Indian companies seem to prefer Luxembourg. These markets and the NYSE have the highest number of outstanding DRs. However, in terms of trading activity, the NYSE remains the largest market for DR trading by a substantial margin, representing almost two-thirds of worldwide DR trading in 2010.

Among the most actively traded DRs in the United States during 2010 were Baidu.com, a Chinese Internet company; BP, the British oil company; Vale, a Brazilian metals and mining company; Petrobras, a Brazilian oil company; and Teva Pharmaceuticals, an Israeli pharmaceutical company.

POINT–COUNTERPOINT
The Pricing of Royal Dutch and Shell

Ante is poring over the financial pages of the newspaper, searching for the prices of the ADRs for Royal Dutch and Shell, when Freedy yells, "You're not still trying to find arbitrage opportunities, are you? You know international financial markets are efficient."

Ante replies, "You may think markets are efficient, but you haven't read this article by Froot and Dabora (1999) in the *Journal of Financial Economics*. They've really uncovered a whopper of an issue. I'm going to get rich!"

Ante then lays out the facts for Freedy: "A corporate charter has linked Royal Dutch Petroleum (RDP), a Dutch company, and Shell Transport and Trading (STT), a U.K. company, since 1907. All the operating units of the two companies use the same brand name, Shell, and after cash distributions to shareholders are decided, 60% of the cash goes to RDP shareholders, and 40% goes to STT shareholders. This arrangement looks more like one company with two classes of equity. RDP is listed on nine exchanges in Europe, and its ADR trades on the NYSE in the United States. STT is listed in London, and its ADR also trades on the NYSE."

After Freedy hears the details, he asks, "So, what is the big deal? I suppose you've found some price discrepancies between the RDP price in Amsterdam and its ADR price in New York. Or is STT's London price not equal to its ADR price in New York? Which is it? You know, you've got to get the prices into a common currency, and the ADR may be for more than one share."

Ante replies, "Well, you're right about those issues. The price of one share of RDP in Amsterdam should be the price of one ADR share in New York multiplied by the €/$ exchange rate. Also, the STT ADR represents six STT shares in London, so $/ADR should equal ($/£) × (£/share) × 6. When Froot and Dabora did those calculations, the prices were usually within 2% or 3% of each other. Plus, it was hard to get the timing of the quotes on the stocks, the ADRs, and the exchange rates all at the same time. So, I know I can't make money on those tiny differences. The real issue is the difference between the prices of Shell and Royal Dutch."

Freedy takes the bait. "What do you mean? If there are X shares of RDP outstanding and Y shares of STT, and if RDP shareholders get 60% of the cash flows, and STT shareholders get 40% of the cash flows, the price of one share of RDP should equal $(Y/X) \times (60/40) \times$ (Price of one STT share). Tell me that Froot and Dabora did this and found a big difference."

Ante grins, "That is exactly right. There are 536,074,088 shares of RDP outstanding, and there are 3,314,503,242 shares of STT outstanding. So, one RDP share should have the same value as $(3{,}314{,}503{,}242/536{,}074{,}088) \times (60/40) = 9.2744$ STT shares. Or, since 6 STT shares $=$ 1 STT ADR, one RDP ADR $=$ 1.5457 STT ADR. When Froot and Dabora examined those prices, the prices were often as much as 15% different. I can drive a truck through that spread!"

As usual, Suttle is listening in and feels it is time to enter the conversation. "So, Ante, what is your big plan?" he asks.

Ante replies, "Well, if STT is selling at a 15% discount to RDP, I'll just buy STT and short RDP and pocket the difference: It is an arbitrage!"

"Ah," says Suttle. "You make it sound so easy. But what if the discount gets bigger?"

"What do you mean?" Ante asks. "I still make money, don't I?"

"Actually, Ante, if the discount gets bigger, you would lose money," says Suttle. "Remember, at some point, you have to cover your short position. If the price of RDP went up by more than the price of STT, this would widen the discount, and you would lose. You'd also lose if RDP fell in value by less than STT fell. Once there is a discount, the arbitrage is risky."

Ante replied, "Well, I'm going to have to think about that."

Epilogue

In 2005, Royal Dutch and Shell unified into Royal Dutch Shell, plc, with headquarters in The Hague. The new company now has two classes of shares, A and B shares. They trade on both the London Stock Exchange and Euronext Amsterdam and in the form of ADRs in New York. The two classes of shares have identical rights except in relation to the source of dividend income, where, for tax purposes, A shares have a Dutch source and B shares have a U.K. source.

A number of researchers have more systematically examined the price differences between ADRs and the original shares. Gagnon and Karolyi (2010) examined over 500 U.S. cross-listed securities from 35 different countries, finding very small average price differences amounting to about five basis points. However, they also note that these differences are volatile and reach extremes. Yeyati et al. (2009) also examined a wide set of cross-listings, focusing on emerging markets with some level of capital controls. They show that arbitrage is effective in eliminating substantial price differentials, especially for liquid stocks, but that capital controls do generate substantial price differentials and may effectively prevent arbitrage.

Global Registered Shares

A **global registered share (GRS)** is an ordinary share of a company that trades and transfers freely across national borders. The shares trade in the local currency of the exchanges on which they are listed and are entirely fungible across the exchanges. Unlike an ADR, a GRS is an actual share of the company, not a receipt representing the ordinary shares deposited in trust. Deutsche Bank's GRS trades on the NYSE and the Deutsche Börse, and UBS's GRS trades on the NYSE and the Swiss stock exchange.

The most famous GRS, however, was the very first one: On November 17, 1998, trading commenced for DaimlerChrysler AG shares on stock exchanges around the world. The new symbol for the first GRS was DCX. Daimler-Benz AG, the famous manufacturer of Mercedes-Benz cars, had merged with Chrysler Corporation, the smallest but most efficient of America's big three car producers, in May 1998. Daimler-Benz and Chrysler managers agreed to design and implement a global share as the only equity vehicle to be issued to all DaimlerChrysler stockholders with their merger transaction. Richard Grasso, CEO of the NYSE, hailed the event as a landmark for the globalization of stock markets, saying, "The security will trade in the United States in dollars, on the Deutsche Börse in Deutsche marks, and in 16 other markets around the world in whatever currency these markets would choose. We created for the first time a concept where equity could follow the sun" (see Karolyi, 2003).

All share registration and transfer was handled, respectively, by the U.S.–based and German-based agents/registrars. Establishment of the Europe/Asia segment required the introduction of registered shares instead of more common bearer shares in Germany. The Depositary Trust Company (DTC) in the United States and Deutsche Börse Clearing (DBC) in Germany handled the settlement and book entry of shares. To establish the GRS, the SEC approved an electronic link between DTC and DBC so that cross-border transactions could be cleared and settled in either the United States or Germany, ensuring complete transparency.

How does a GRS facility compare to an ADR? ADRs represent negotiable claims on home-market ordinary shares (in bearer or registered form) issued by a U.S. depositary bank and coordinated in the home market through a local, custodial bank affiliate. Settlement of cross-border trades takes place daily through ADR issuances or cancellations ("conversions") conducted by the depositary bank, and fees for such transactions amount to about 5 cents per share. The ADRs are, of course, quoted, traded, and settled in U.S. dollars, and dividends are paid in U.S. dollars through the bank. Finally, the depositary bank maintains ownership records and processes corporate actions.

The GRS has "fewer moving parts" and does not require the intervention of a depositary bank. The per-share fee for conversion is subsumed by a single $5 settlement cost to the DTC that is independent of the number of shares. Hence, a GRS may be less expensive to trade. At the same time, there is no depositary bank to oversee the coordination of the transfer, clearing, and settlement procedures of the GRS or to process corporate actions. In addition, ADRs provide the flexibility of bundling (or unbundling) a number of home-market shares into a receipt and, therefore, ensure that the shares trade in a price range that closely mirrors that of the company's competitors. This may help create additional liquidity. Finally, share ownership is more direct with a GRS than with an ADR. Holding a GRS gives investors the same voting privileges, rights to receive dividends, and so forth, whereas the depositary intermediary may impose certain restrictions.

Karolyi (2003) studied the DaimlerChrysler merger in detail, finding some advantages (such as greater trading activity and enhanced liquidity) but also some disadvantages. For example, the order flow and trading volume migrated from the NYSE back to the Frankfurt exchange. Also, the return volatility of DaimlerChrysler significantly increased after the issue of the GRS. Karolyi's study should temper the enthusiasm of experts who have touted the GRS as a cheaper and easier cross-border facility. In 2007, this particular cross-border marriage ended in divorce, as DaimlerChrysler sold its Chrysler unit to Cerberus Capital Management, a private equity firm, retaining only 19.9% of the company. DaimlerChrysler changed its name to Daimler AG.

12.3 THE ADVANTAGES AND DISADVANTAGES OF CROSS-LISTING

Depositary receipts (DRs) provide investors with international diversification at low cost. DRs overcome obstacles such as foreign custody arrangements and are conveniently denominated and pay dividends in the local currency. Essentially, DRs trade, settle, and clear exactly like domestic securities.

But what are the advantages for the cross-listing company? Cross-listing enhances shareholder value primarily by reducing the cost of capital (which in turn increases the stock price) and by allowing the MNC to exploit growth opportunities with additional foreign capital. Most of the empirical research has focused on foreign companies listing in the United States. Although the estimates differ somewhat across studies, the introduction of an ADR for a typical company translates into a lower cost of capital by between 0.7% and 3% (see, for example, Foerster and Karolyi, 1999; Hail and Leuz, 2009; and Miller, 2000). Cross-listing may reduce the cost of capital because it improves liquidity, provides a wider shareholder base, allows the stock to be integrated in global capital markets, and improves corporate governance, which is enforced by the country in which the MNC cross-lists. However, some have doubted the long-term benefits of cross-listing (see Sarkissian and Schill, 2009).

Cross-listing is not free, though. Money is paid in exchange fees and road shows, and more importantly, cross-listing may impose a level of scrutiny on the company's managers that they dislike. Exhibit 12.8 gives an overview of the pros and cons of cross-listing from the perspective of the cross-listing firm. The next two sections explain these benefits and costs in more detail and summarize the vast literature on the effects of cross-listing.

Exhibit 12.8 The Costs and Benefits of Cross-Listing

The benefits of cross-listing may not be limited just to the firms that cross-list. Fernandes (2009) shows that firms in the home country that do not cross-list but that are correlated with stocks that do (for example, because they are in the same industry) may also experience positive price effects. In this case, the benefits of ADR issues may "spill over" into the local market.

Why Firms Choose to Cross-List

Liquidity

It is now widely recognized that liquidity is priced in stocks. More liquid stocks have lower expected returns and hence higher prices than less liquid stocks. Thus, cross-listing on a larger, more liquid market that lowers transaction costs for investors and improves liquidity induces lower expected returns and, hence, increases the stock price.

While there is a debate about the relative importance of this liquidity effect, research has shown that typically, after listing abroad, stocks experience an increase in total trading volume and a significant decrease in home market bid–ask spreads, due in large part to competition from the new market. If trading in the foreign market also leads to more efficient price discovery and fewer opportunities to exploit insider trading, there is an additional benefit to cross-listing. Indirectly, the fact that the price effects of U.S. companies listing in Toronto, Tokyo, or European exchanges are small shows that liquidity is an important benefit of cross-listing. Nevertheless, some policymakers are quite concerned about possible adverse effects of multimarket trading. If cross-listing causes trading to migrate to the new market, firms that do not cross-list may become even less liquid as the home market traders and other people working on the local exchange are made worse off. Halling et al. (2008) found that local turnover increases for cross-listing firms based in developed markets but decreases for firms based in emerging markets.

Wider Shareholder Base

The listing of an ADR is usually thought to widen a corporation's shareholder base, and this in itself may generate a price effect. Merton (1987) developed a theory in which investors consider only a subset of the available securities when constructing their portfolios. They may be unaware of the other securities because of information problems, for example, or because the costs of trading these stocks might be prohibitive. In this case, stocks with a wide shareholder base are less risky, have lower expected returns than stocks with narrow shareholder bases, and receive higher prices.

If cross-listing through a depositary receipt literally expands the shareholder base, we should see an increase in stock price and lower expected returns going forward. This argument is particularly important because institutional investors in various countries are often restricted either legally or through their charters with respect to their foreign investments. However, cross-listed securities are often viewed as domestic investments and, hence, may be the only way that some institutional investors may diversify internationally.

Market Integration

Markets are integrated when securities of similar risk have the same expected returns, whatever the market in which they trade (see Chapter 13 for more details). A firm located in a country that is not fully integrated in the world capital markets typically faces a higher cost of capital because the firm's equity risk has to be borne mostly by investors in its own country. If the firm finds a way to make it less costly for foreign investors to hold its shares, these investors share some of the firm's risk, and therefore, the cost of capital falls.

Investment barriers segment domestic capital markets from global capital markets. Investment barriers are usually grouped into "direct" and "indirect" barriers (see Bekaert, 1995; Nishiotis, 2004). Direct barriers comprise regulatory frictions from foreign exchange controls, foreign ownership restrictions, taxes, and trading costs. For example, during much of the 1990s, the Korean authorities restricted foreign ownership in Korean companies to 10% of total market capitalization. Indirect barriers arise when countries fail to subject their companies to stringent disclosure requirements and investor protection is poor. These factors might play a large role in the investment decisions of international investors.

By cross-listing in a foreign market, a firm makes its shares more accessible to foreign investors, which can be viewed as a liberalization of the domestic equity market. In some cases, the government literally relaxes restrictions for cross-listing stocks in order to facilitate cross-border arbitrage between the stock prices in the local and foreign markets. For example, even though Chile imposed capital flow and dividend repatriation restrictions on foreign investors in the mid-1990s (that is, foreigners could not repatriate capital or dividends for at least 1 year after the initial investment), these restrictions were lifted for the many Chilean companies cross-listing in the United States during that time. The opposite occurs as well. When Brazil introduced a 2% tax on foreign bond and stock purchases in 2009 to dampen capital inflows, Brazilian ADRs suddenly became especially attractive. However, the Brazilian authorities proceeded to levy a tax on the ADR issuing company when the shares are deposited with CETIP, Brazil's custodial agency. If the Brazilian companies pass on the extra cost to the (overseas) buyers of the shares, the good deal on ADRs should disappear.

To sum up, cross-listing should lead to higher prices upon announcement of the listing and lower expected returns afterward. Consistent with this hypothesis, firms from emerging markets typically experience larger cross-listing price effects than firms from developed markets because emerging markets are more likely to be segmented from world capital markets.

Corporate Governance Signal

Indirect barriers can be reduced through better corporate governance. In corporate finance theory, it is now generally accepted that many firms are plagued by agency problems where controlling shareholders or managers try to appropriate funds from the firms. These private benefits of control may lead a firm to make suboptimal decisions (for its shareholders) with respect to investment, recruiting, and so on. In countries with poor investor protection and poor accounting standards, which includes not only emerging markets but also many European countries, these private benefits of control may be substantial and can depress stock prices.

When a firm cross-lists in a market with better investor protection, accounting standards, and disclosure requirements, firms commit themselves to an increased level of monitoring of both management and controlling shareholders. If they list in the United States, they also subject themselves to the litigious U.S. legal system. The reduction in deadweight costs resulting from agency problems increases the present value of future cash flows. The signal of improved management quality that the listing brings lowers the corporate governance discount, allowing the firm to face a lower cost of capital going forward.

This kind of reasoning, known as the "bonding hypothesis," played a major role in the NYSE listing of Kookmin Bank, the largest Korean bank, in November 2001. Kim Jung-tae, president and CEO, explains: "After Korea's financial crisis in 1997, many foreign investors were suspicious of Korean banks' books, and we wanted to clarify the situation by going abroad, especially on the NYSE. I think we have been fully tested in terms of accounting transparency and asset quality under more conservative U.S. GAAP. Our primary purpose is to be as open as possible."

Research by Doidge et al. (2004) and Reese and Weisbach (2002) argues that a substantial part of the higher valuation enjoyed by cross-listing emerging market firms is due to the corporate governance channel. Recent research by Lang et al. (2002) also suggests that more stringent disclosure requirements have an important side benefit: They improve analysts' earnings forecasts and therefore lead to more accurate prices. However, Bris et al. (2007) claim that the economic significance of the "market integration" effect is more than double that of bonding.

Capital Needs and Growth Opportunities

Companies in emerging markets and small countries often outgrow their home markets and use cross-listing to raise capital to continue to grow. In addition, the worldwide privatization boom mentioned earlier created very large companies in very capital-intensive sectors, such as telecommunication, energy, and transportation. The size of these companies, compared to their home markets, virtually required that they raise capital outside their home countries. Fast-growing emerging markets and their firms remain capital hungry. In 2010, almost $22 billion was raised through DR programs, with the BRICs accounting for more than 90% of total capital raised.

Companies that face constraints in the external financing markets can invest more only if they can generate more internal cash flows. Such a constrained firm's real investments will then be sensitive to cash flow growth. Financing constraints are most likely to exist in less financially developed markets. Lins et al. (2005) show that foreign firms listing in the United States become much less financially constrained and substantially increase funds raised in the debt and equity markets. Both access to foreign investment banks with the ability to certify the quality of a deal and greater competition among providers of underwriting services help to reduce the cost of raising external capital. Hail and Leuz (2009) assert that almost half of the increase in firm value from U.S. cross-listing is attributable to an increase in growth expectations.

Other Benefits of Cross-Listing

When SAP, a German-based software company, listed on the NYSE in 1999, it not only wanted to enhance shareholder value, but also wanted to strengthen its commercial profile in the United States. A foreign firm that has a U.S. customer base can increase brand awareness through a cross-listing, given the road show and publicity it entails and the continued increased media attention a listed security garners.

Pagano et al. (2002) found that firms with cross-listings subsequently see their foreign sales as a percentage of total sales increase by approximately 20%. Of course, it might be the case that the firms cross-listed because they planned to expand their international activities and desired access to international capital markets to facilitate the expansion of their operations.

Increasingly, ADRs play a role in cross-border acquisitions. For example, AngloGold, a South African mining company, began with a Level I ADR in June 1998 and soon after listed on the NYSE, bringing a real lion to the bell podium of the NYSE. Whereas this event clearly scored much media coverage, the main intent of the listing, according to CEO Bobby Godsell, lay elsewhere: He claimed in interviews that the firm's ADR program played a critical role in the firm's acquisition program. In 2004, AngloGold merged with the Ashanti Goldfields Corporation of Ghana to create AngloGold Ashanti, the world's second-largest gold producer.

Finally, ADRs may help in the human resource departments because they make it easier to set up a stock or stock option remuneration plan for top talent working in the United States.

Why Firms Decide Against Cross-Listing

As we have said, listing on a foreign exchange is not costless. There are direct one-time costs, such as registration and listing fees, and there are the perennial costs of additional reporting and disclosure requirements. These latter factors are the primary inhibitors that keep more companies from listing abroad. When Daimler-Benz cross-listed its stock on the NYSE, it was not happy to find out it had to disclose the pay packages of its management. German and Swiss firms also tend to "smooth" reported earnings using various hidden accounting reserves; they cannot do this under U.S. GAAP. Among other things, smooth earnings help to reduce taxes when tax rates are progressive, as demonstrated in Chapter 17.

Doidge et al. (2004) argue that cross-listing, while good for a firm, may not be beneficial for the controlling shareholders who may have to give up some of their private control benefits through the disclosure that is required under U.S. GAAP. By listing in the United States, a foreign firm increases the rights of its shareholders, especially its minority shareholders. It also constrains a controlling shareholder's ability to extract private benefits from control. From this perspective, it is not surprising that not every large foreign firm cross-lists in the United States.

Which firms cross-list? It seems likely that cross-listing will be done by firms with good growth opportunities that need funds to invest but find it difficult to finance their growth with internal funds or through debt. In these firms, the private benefits of control are relatively modest, and the controlling shareholders benefit from the firm's growth. Consequently, the growth opportunities of cross-listed firms should be valued more highly because they can better take advantage of these opportunities and because a smaller part of the cash flows of these firms is expropriated by controlling shareholders.

12.4 STRATEGIC ALLIANCES

Some projects are financed by multiple but separate companies. The best-known form of cooperation is probably the **joint venture**. A joint venture occurs when two or more independent firms form and jointly control a different entity, which is created to pursue a specific objective. The new entity tries to combine the strengths of each partner.

The joint venture is an example of a **strategic alliance**, which is an agreement between legally distinct entities to share the costs and benefits of what is hoped to be a beneficial activity. The activity typically involves large investments, but the level of collaboration is typically fairly low and is focused on a well-defined set of activities, services, or products. Strategic alliances are most appropriate for companies wanting to exchange technical expertise or when there are legal, regulatory, or cultural constraints that might prevent, say, an acquisition of one company by another.

A good example of a strategic alliance involved Novartis, a Swiss pharmaceutical company, and Vertex, a U.S. biotechnology research company. In 2001, Novartis basically funded Vertex's research with total funds involving some $215 million over 6 years and further licensing fees of up to $600 million. In exchange, Novartis retained the worldwide distribution and development and marketing rights to eight potentially marketable drugs. This example is not an isolated case. Interfirm collaborative agreements are the norm in the biotech industry, but they also occur in a broad range of other industries.

An interesting question is why certain activities are organized through strategic alliances rather than inside one firm. Why did Novartis choose to conduct this research through an arms-length contract with another firm instead of internally? Robinson (2008) suggests an intriguing possibility: Strategic alliances are more often than not used to finance "underdog projects." Underdog projects have potentially high payoffs but low success probabilities; that is, they are very risky ventures. Even though an underdog project may have equal or higher expected value compared to other projects, managers in the relevant divisions may be unwilling to supply effort, fearing that the headquarters of the firm may take resources away from the underdog project. Through an alliance with a smaller, outside firm undertaking the underdog project, a centralized, large firm (the "parent") guarantees that the project gets some basic financing because the alliance is a legally enforceable contract between two legally distinct entities. In exchange, the parent gets a fraction of the revenues the project earns while giving the stand-alone firm undertaking the underdog project options to extra funds when the project's prospects improve.

12.5 Summary

This chapter examines equity financing in a global market. The main points of the chapter are as follows:

1. A multinational corporation can obtain additional funds by issuing shares to its existing shareholders or to new shareholders. Most MNCs have shares listed on the stock market of the country in which they are headquartered, but many list their shares on several stock exchanges around the world, with the U.S. stock exchanges being most popular.

2. The largest stock markets are in the United States, Japan, and China. The U.S. market is large relative to U.S. GDP, unlike many European stock markets. In Europe, bank financing is a relatively more important source of funding for companies.

3. The emerging stock markets of developing countries developed rapidly over the past 20 years, following a process of financial liberalization. The stock markets of India, Korea, Russia, and Brazil are among the largest in the world.

4. The Chinese stock market is not yet very well developed and is not very open to foreign investors, but it has nonetheless grown spectacularly, partially through IPOs of large state-owned enterprises.

5. Most stock markets are private organizations, and many are now publicly traded corporations.

6. A trading system may be order driven or price driven. In a price-driven system, such as NASDAQ in the United States, dealers act as market markers for certain stocks and stand ready to buy at a bid price and sell at an ask price. In an order-driven system, such as the Tokyo Stock Exchange, share prices are determined in a continuous auction that brings together the supply and demand of shares. The NYSE has elements of both systems.

7. Stock markets around the world have become increasingly automated, and large numbers of alternative trading venues compete for order flow.

8. Stock markets have consolidated in response to competitive pressures to allow international investors more time to trade and to automatically cross-list shares.

9. Turnover is often viewed as a liquidity indicator, and the United States has the largest turnover of all developed stock markets.

10. Turnover is negatively related to trading costs, which consist of brokerage commissions, bid–ask spreads, and market impact.

11. Transaction costs in emerging markets are larger and turnover is generally lower than in developed markets.

12. When foreign companies list their shares in the United States, they typically use American depositary receipts (ADRs), which are held in custody by a depositary bank and represent a certain number of original shares issued in the home stock market.

13. ADR programs come in three varieties: Level I (not exchange traded), Level II (exchange traded), and Level III (exchange traded and capital raising). In addition, private placements occur through Rule 144.

14. Global depositary receipts (GDRs) are similar to ADRs. However, they can be traded on many exchanges in addition to U.S. exchanges.

15. Global registered shares (GRSs) trade simultaneously in different markets around the world, in different currencies, with the shares being completely fungible across markets.

16. Cross-listing a stock can lower a company's cost of capital through several channels, including improved liquidity and better corporate governance. It can heighten the awareness of the firm's brands, provide direct access to foreign capital, and make future capital access easier.

17. A strategic alliance is an agreement between legally distinct companies to share the costs and benefits of a particular investment.

Questions

1. What are the differences between public and private bourses?
2. What is the difference between a price-driven trading system and an order-driven trading system? Which system lends itself most easily to automation?
3. What is a dark pool?
4. Do we have a global stock market as we have a global foreign exchange market?
5. What is turnover?
6. What are the three primary components of transaction costs in trading stocks?
7. Does high turnover always signal lower transaction costs?

8. What is the difference between an ADR and a GDR?
9. What motivates companies to cross-list their shares?
10. What is the difference between a GDR and a GRS?
11. Has cross-listing been beneficial for most listed companies? If yes, why doesn't every company cross-list?
12. What is a strategic alliance?
13. What is a joint venture?

PROBLEMS

1. The following table shows how average share prices jump (in percentage) after the announcement that the stocks will be cross-listed (see Miller, 2000). The price response should be interpreted as corrected for risk and market movements that happened on the same day:

	All ADR Issues	Capital Raising	Non-Capital Raising
Emerging Markets	1.5	0.9	2.8
Developed Markets	0.9	0.7	0.9
Total	1.2	0.8	1.4

Although these numbers appear small, it is important to realize that announcements of domestic equity issues, which by definition raise capital, lead to an average negative return response of 2% to 3%. The main reason is that capital-raising equity issues are viewed as a signal by the managers that the firm may be overvalued in the stock market.

Given what you learned in this chapter, answer the following:

a. Why is there a positive price response when a company's shares are cross-listed?

b. Why might the response for emerging-market firms be larger than for developed-market firms?

c. Without knowing that equity issues in a domestic context are associated with negative price responses, is the difference between capital-raising and non-capital-raising ADRs a surprise? Why or why not?

2. Suppose you are a U.S.-based investor, and you would like to diversify your stock portfolio internationally. What advantages do ADRs offer you? Would it be wise to restrict your international portfolio only to ADRs?

3. Web Question: Go to www.adrbnymellon.com/files/MS32022.pdf, navigate to Investor Relations, and find the 2010 Annual Report. Sarkissian and Schill (2004) claim that cross-listing firms tend to prefer cross-listing in markets "close to home." Can you see evidence in favor of this hypothesis in the listing data for 2010?

BIBLIOGRAPHY

Aggarwal, Rajesh K., and Guojun Wu, 2006, "Stock Market Manipulations," *Journal of Business* 79, pp. 1915–1953.

Bank of New York, Gavin Anderson & Company, Van der Molen Specialists, PricewaterhouseCoopers, and Bowne, 2002, "Solving the ADR Puzzle: The Expert Guide to Building a Successful ADR Program," www.adrbny.com/files/2002_VDM_Guide_.pdf.

Bank of New York Mellon, 2010 "The Depositary Receipt Markets: The Year in Review," www.adrbnymellon.com/.

Bekaert, Geert, 1995, "Market Integration and Investment Barriers in Emerging Equity Markets," *World Bank Economic Review* 9, pp. 75–107.

Bekaert, Geert, and Campbell R. Harvey, 2003, "Emerging Markets Finance," *Journal of Empirical Finance* 10, pp. 3–55.

Bekaert, Geert, Campbell R. Harvey, and Christian Lundblad, 2007, "Liquidity and Expected Returns: Lessons from Emerging Markets," *Review of Financial Studies* 20, pp. 1783–1831.

Boubakri, Narjess, Jean-Claude Cosset, and Anis Samet, 2010, "The Choice of ADRs," *Journal of Banking & Finance* 34, pp. 2077–2095.

Bris, Arturo, Salvatore Cantale, and George P. Nishiotis, 2007, "A Breakdown of the Valuation Effects of International

Cross-Listing," *European Financial Management* 13, pp. 498–530.

De Bondt, Gabe J., Tuomas A. Peltonen, and Daniel Santabárbara, 2010, "Booms and Busts in China's Stock Market Estimates Based on Fundamentals," ECB Working Paper No. 1190.

Doidge, Craig, Andrew G. Karolyi, and René M. Stulz, 2004, "Why Are Foreign Firms Listed in the U.S. Worth More?" *Journal of Financial Economics* 71, pp. 205–238.

Doidge, Craig, Andrew G. Karolyi, and René M. Stulz, 2009, "Has New York Become Less Competitive than London in Global Markets? Evaluating Foreign Listing Choices over Time," *Journal of Financial Economics* 91, pp. 253–277.

Domowitz, Ian, Jack Glen, and Ananth Madhavan, 2001, "Liquidity, Volatility and Equity Trading Costs Across Countries and Over Time," *International Finance* 4, pp. 221–255.

Duarte, Jefferson, Katie Kong, Stephan Siegel, and Lance Young, 2011, "The Impact of the Sarbanes-Oxley Act on Shareholders and Managers of Foreign Firms," manuscript, Jones Graduate School of Business.

Fernandes, Nuno, 2009, "Market Liberalization at the Firm Level: Spillovers from ADRs and Implications for Local Markets," *Journal of International Money and Finance* 28, pp. 293–321.

Foerster, Stephen, and G. Andrew Karolyi, 1999, "The Effects of Market Segmentation and Investor Recognition on Asset Prices: Evidence from Foreign Stocks Listing in the U.S.," *Journal of Finance* 54, pp. 981–1013.

Froot, Kenneth, and Emile Dabora, 1999, "How Are Stock Prices Affected by the Location of Trade?" *Journal of Financial Economics* 53, pp. 189–216.

Gagnon, Louis, and Andrew G. Karolyi, 2010, "Multi-Market Trading and Arbitrage," *Journal of Financial Economics* 97, pp. 53–80.

Ghysels, Eric, and Mouna Cherkaoui, 2003, "Emerging Market and Trading Costs: Lessons from Casablanca," *Journal of Empirical Finance* 10, pp. 169–198.

Hail, Luzi, and Christian Leuz, 2009, "Cost of Capital Effects and Changes in Growth Expectations Around U.S. Cross-Listings," *Journal of Financial Economics* 93, pp. 428–454.

Halling, Michael, Marco Pagano, Otto Randl, and Joseph Zechner, 2008, "Where Is the Market? Evidence from Cross-Listings in the U.S.," *Review of Financial Studies* 21, pp. 724–761.

Karolyi, G. Andrew, 2003, "DaimlerChrysler AG, the First Truly Global Share," *Journal of Corporate Finance* 9, pp. 409–430.

Khwaja, Asia I., and Atif Mian, 2005, "Unchecked Intermediaries: Price Manipulation in an Emerging Stock Market," *Journal of Financial Economics* 78, pp. 203–241.

Lang, Mark H., Karl V. Lins, and Darius Miller, 2002, "ADRs, Analysts, and Accuracy: Does Cross Listing in the U.S. Improve a Firm's Information Environment and Increase Market Value?" *Journal of Accounting Research* 42, pp. 317–346.

Lefebvre, Jérémie, 2010, "Block Trades and Market Liquidity on Euronext Paris," manuscript, Louvain School of Management.

Leuz, Christian, 2007, "Was the Sarbanes-Oxley Act of 2002 Really This Costly? A Discussion of Evidence from Event Returns and Going-Private Decisions," *Journal of Accounting & Economics* 44, pp. 146–165.

Leuz, Christian, Alexander Triantis, and Tracy Yue Wang, "Why Do Firms Go Dark? Causes and Economic Consequences of Voluntary SEC Deregistrations," *Journal of Accounting & Economics* 45, pp. 181–208.

Lins, Karl V., Deon Strickland, and Marc Zenner, 2005, "Do Non-U.S. Firms Issue Equity on U.S. Stock Markets to Relax Capital Constraints?" *Journal of Financial and Quantitative Analysis* 40, pp. 109–133.

Merton, Robert C., 1987, "A Simple Model of Capital-Market Equilibrium with Incomplete Information," *Journal of Finance* 42, pp. 483–510.

Miller, Darius, 2000, "Return Behavior and Pricing of American Depositary Receipts," *Journal of International Financial Markets, Institutions and Money* 9, pp. 43–67.

Nishiotis, George P., 2004, "Do Indirect Investment Barriers Contribute to Capital Market Segmentation?" *Journal of Financial and Quantitative Analysis* 39, pp. 613–630.

Pagano, Marco, Ailsa Roell, and Josef Zechner, 2002, "The Geography of Equity Listings: Why Do European Companies List Abroad?" *Journal of Finance* 57, pp. 2651–2684.

Reese, William A., and Michael S. Weisbach, 2002, "Protection of Minority Shareholder Interests, Cross-Listings in the United States, and Subsequent Equity Offerings," *Journal of Financial Economics* 66, pp. 65–104.

Robinson, David T., 2008, "Strategic Alliances and the Boundaries of the Firm," *Review of Financial Studies* 21, pp. 649–681.

Sarkissian, Sergei, and Michael J. Schill, 2004, "The Overseas Listing Decision: New Evidence of Proximity Preference," *Review of Financial Studies* 17, pp. 769–809.

Sarkissian, Sergei, and Michael J. Schill, 2009, "Are There Permanent Valuation Gains to Overseas Listing?" *Review of Financial Studies* 22, pp. 371–412.

Schwartz, Robert A., 2010, "Dark Pools, Fragmented Markets, and the Quality of Price Discovery," *Journal of Trading* 5, pp. 17–22.

Wu, Guojun, and J. He, 2003, "The Life of a Manipulated Stock," manuscript, University of Houston.

Yeyati, Eduardo Levy, Sergio L. Schmukler, and Neeltje Van Horen, 2009, "International Financial Integration Through the Law of One Price: The Role of Liquidity and Capital Controls," *Journal of Financial Intermediation* 18, pp. 432–463.

Chapter 13

International Capital Market Equilibrium

A manager should allocate capital to an investment project when the present value of the net cash flows generated by the project exceeds the current investment outlay. Applying this net present value principle requires a discount rate. It is one of the hallmarks of modern finance that this discount rate—the cost of equity capital—is set by investors in the capital markets. When investors finance a firm by purchasing its equity shares, they forgo the opportunity to invest in the equities of many other firms. Therefore, investors demand to be compensated for the opportunity cost of their investment with an appropriate expected rate of return. Consequently, the manager of a firm in a capital budgeting situation should set the discount rate for a project to be the expected return for the firm's investors as if they were investing directly in that project.

Chapter 11 showed that the international bond market sets the cost of a company's debt equal to the risk-free (government) interest rate on bonds plus a risk premium to compensate for the possibility that the company may default on the debt. The appropriate rate for discounting the equity cash flows of any project similarly depends on how risky the investors in the firm view the cash flows from that particular project to be. However, thinking about risk in increasingly global equity markets is difficult because there are many more factors involved.

How, then, do investors determine the riskiness of an investment, and how do managers know the required rate of return on a risky investment? Unfortunately, there are no easy answers to these questions, and there are competing theories. This chapter develops the theories necessary to determine the cost of equity capital. It then demonstrates how these theories apply in an international context. Because investors set the cost of equity capital, we start with a detour through the fascinating world of international investing and the theory of optimal portfolio choice. The idea of portfolio diversification figures prominently, and we will argue that international diversification is highly desirable. BlackRock, the world's largest asset manager with over $3 trillion, has this advice on its iShares Web site (http://us.ishares.com/home.htm) in response to the question, "Why invest internationally?":[1]

> A strategic allocation to international securities may enhance a portfolio's risk-adjusted returns, provide portfolio diversification, and offer opportunities to seek higher performance. And when those securities are not hedged, international investing can offer pure exposure to local equity and currency returns.

Let's explore why they think this.

---

[1]BlackRock's iShares are exchange-traded funds (ETFs), which are securities that trade on stock exchanges like ordinary equity shares are managed to replicate the performance of a specific country index or industrial sector.

13.1 RISK AND RETURN OF INTERNATIONAL INVESTMENTS

The old saying "Don't put all your eggs in one basket" should entice investors to explore foreign stocks, perhaps in exotic places. As Chapter 12 indicates, global stock markets offer investors an incredible menu of choices, offering potentially higher rates of return and different types of risks. To understand the benefits and pitfalls of international investments, we must fully understand what determines risk and return in international markets. This necessitates that we understand how currency fluctuations affect international investments.

The Two Risks of Investing Abroad

When a U.S. investor is bullish about the British stock market, she must realize that investing in the British equity market also implies an exposure to the British pound. Let us analytically derive the dollar return on British equity investment. Let $S(t)$ be the $/£ exchange rate, and let $s(t+1) = [S(t+1) - S(t)]/S(t)$ indicate the rate of appreciation of the pound relative to the dollar. We are interested in the dollar rate of return on British equity, which we denote by $r(t+1, \$)$. This return will have two components: the pound rate of return on British equity, denoted by $r(t+1, £)$, and the rate of change in the value of the pound, $s(t+1)$. This reasoning is identical to the derivation of the return on a foreign money market investment in Chapter 6. In this case, however, we replace the foreign interest rate with the foreign equity rate of return. We first convert from dollars to pounds to get $1/S(t)$ pounds, which we will invest. Each pound earns the pound return $1 + r(t+1, £)$ in the equity market. Subsequently, the total pound return is sold for dollars at $S(t+1)$. Thus, the dollar return on a British equity investment is

$$1 + r(t+1, \$) = [1/S(t)] \times [1 + r(t+1, £)] \times S(t+1)$$

Subtracting 1 from each side and using $\dfrac{S(t+1)}{S(t)} = 1 + s(t+1)$ gives

$$r(t+1, \$) = [1 + r(t+1, £)] \times [1 + s(t+1)] - 1$$

or

$$r(t+1, \$) = r(t+1, £) + s(t+1) + r(t+1, £) \times s(t+1)$$

We see that the dollar rate of return on a foreign investment depends on the local equity rate of return plus the currency return plus a cross-product term (the product of the two rates of return). The cross-product term is often small relative to the other two terms because it is percentages of percentages, and it is thus often ignored.

Example 13.1   Determining the Dollar Return of a British Equity Investment

Rob Dickinson of the Catherine Wheel Fund is bullish on British equity and wants to invest $10 million in the British equity market. The spot exchange rate is $1.60/£. At that exchange rate, Rob can convert $10 million into $10/(\$1.60/£) = £6.25$ million. He then invests the £6.25 million in the British equity market. Suppose he plans to hold on to the investment for 1 year. During this time, he hopes to earn dividends plus a capital gain. Let's consider three scenarios for the return in the British equity market: an increase in the market value of the stock by 10%, a decrease of 10%, and no change.

After earning the British equity return, Rob can then sell his pound return, which is (£6.25 million) $\times$ [1 + $r(£)$], for dollars. An appreciation of the pound enhances his dollar return, and a depreciation of the pound diminishes his dollar return. Let's consider three possible scenarios for the change in the value of the pound as well: a 10% appreciation (to \$1.60/£ $\times$ 1.10 = \$1.76/£), a 10% depreciation (to \$1.60/£ $\times$ 0.9 = \$1.44/£), and no change. Consequently, there are a total of nine possible outcomes:

| | | DOLLAR–POUND EXCHANGE RATES | | |
		10% Depreciation of the Pound \$1.44/£	No Change \$1.60/£	10% Appreciation of the Pound \$1.76/£
Pound	£5.625 million (−10%)	\$8.1 million −19%	\$9.0 million −10%	\$9.9 million −1%
Stock Returns	£6.25 million (0%)	\$9.0 million −10%	\$10.0 million 0.0%	\$11.0 million 10%
	£6.875 million (+10%)	\$9.9 million −1%	\$11.0 million 10%	\$12.1 million 21.0%

Each cell illustrates the exact dollar returns—that is, the exact percentage change, including the cross-product term. If the news is all good, the pound and the British equity market both appreciate by 10%, and the approximation, which ignores the cross-product term, yields an estimated 20% return. The true number is 21% because the cross-product term is 0.10 $\times$ 0.10 = 0.01 in this case. Analogously, if the British equity market indeed increases by 10%, as Rob hopes, but at the same time the pound depreciates by 10%, then perhaps you would guess that the return would be zero, as the approximation suggests. The true answer is −1% because now the cross-product term is a negative 1%. For return horizons of 3 months or less, though, the cross-product term is small and can be ignored in computations.

The Volatility of International Investments

Exhibit 13.1 lists several characteristics of the equity markets of the G7 countries. The data are from Morgan Stanley Capital International (MSCI) for the period from January 1980 to August 2010. We first focus on the three volatility columns. Remember that volatility, Vol[r], is defined to be the standard deviation, which is the square root of the variance, Var[r]; it indicates how much returns vary around the mean or average return.

The Volatility of Currency and Equity Returns

For a U.S. investor, such as fund manager Rob Dickinson in Example 13.1, international investments appear to have two problems. First, the volatilities of equity returns in foreign currencies exceed the volatility of U.S. equity returns. In fact, the U.S. market appears to be the least volatile market, with a volatility of only 15.6%. The second-least-volatile market is the United Kingdom, with a volatility of 18.9%. The other three European markets have volatilities exceeding 20%.

Second, Exhibit 13.1 (second to last column) shows that currency changes are pretty variable themselves, with volatilities around 11%, for the most part. The only exception is the substantially lower volatility of the Canadian dollar, which is driven by the close economic

Exhibit 13.1 Characteristics of Foreign Equity Returns, 1980–2010

	Means			Volatilities		
	Market Return	Currency Return	Dollar Return	Market Return	Currency Return	Dollar Return
United States	11.52%	0.00%	11.52%	15.58%	0.00%	15.58%
Canada	10.72%	0.54%	11.73%	17.00%	6.73%	20.64%
Japan	5.21%	4.10%	9.28%	19.22%	11.76%	22.51%
United Kingdom	12.98%	−0.65%	12.17%	16.45%	10.50%	18.91%
France	12.56%	−0.21%	12.14%	20.12%	11.00%	21.93%
Germany	11.00%	1.12%	11.91%	21.13%	11.21%	23.06%
Italy	14.26%	−1.48%	12.51%	24.35%	10.89%	25.59%

Notes: The original data are monthly total equity returns (including capital gains and dividends) taken from Morgan Stanley Capital International (MSCI) for the period January 1980 to August 2010. Means and volatilities are expressed as annualized percentage rates by multiplying monthly means by 12 and monthly volatilities by $\sqrt{12}$. The market return is in foreign currency; the currency return is the change in the value of the foreign currency relative to the dollar.

ties between the United States and Canada and episodes during which Canadian monetary policy focused on exchange rate stability.

Adding Up Volatility

We know that the volatility of the exchange rate affects the volatility of the dollar return on a foreign equity. But the volatility of the dollar return on foreign equity is generally much less than the sum of the exchange rate volatility and local equity return volatility. That is, the return to a foreign investment is well approximated by the sum of a local equity return and the currency return, $r(t+1, \$) = r(t+1, \mathrm{FC}) + s(t+1)$, with FC denoting foreign currency. Volatility is not additive because it is the square root of the variance, and the variance of the sum of two variables involves their covariance. Thus,

$$\mathrm{Var}[r(t+1, \mathrm{FC}) + s(t+1)] = \mathrm{Var}[r(t+1, \mathrm{FC})] + \mathrm{Var}[s(t+1)]$$
$$+ 2\,\mathrm{Cov}[r(t+1, \mathrm{FC}), s(t+1)]$$

Recall that the covariance of two variables equals the **correlation** between the variables multiplied by the product of the two volatilities, and the correlation is a number between −1 and 1 that indicates how closely related the variations are in the two variables. Rewriting the variance as a function of the correlation, ρ, is informative:

$$\mathrm{Var}[r(t+1, \mathrm{FC}) + s(t+1)] = \mathrm{Var}[r(t+1, \mathrm{FC})] + \mathrm{Var}[s(t+1)]$$
$$+ 2\rho\mathrm{Vol}[r(t+1, \mathrm{FC})]\mathrm{Vol}[s(t+1)]$$

Suppose the correlation is 1. Then, because the variance is the square of the volatility and using $(A + B)^2 = A^2 + B^2 + 2AB$, we see that

$$\mathrm{Var}[r(t+1, \mathrm{FC}) + s(t+1)] = \mathrm{Vol}[r(t+1, \$)]^2$$
$$= \{\mathrm{Vol}[r(t+1, \mathrm{FC})] + \mathrm{Vol}[s(t+1)]\}^2$$

Hence, if $\rho = 1$, the volatility of the dollar return on foreign equity is indeed the sum of the foreign equity volatility and currency return volatility. Because of the perfect correlation, there is no natural diversification advantage to having exposure to two sources of risk. However, as long as $\rho < 1$, the total dollar volatility will be less than the sum of the two volatilities.

Exhibit 13.1 shows that the volatilities of dollar-denominated foreign equity returns are often not much above the original volatility in the local currency. This indicates that

Exhibit 13.2 Correlations of Equity Returns in Foreign Currencies with $/FC Returns

Country	Correlation
Canada	0.42
Japan	−0.02
United Kingdom	−0.09
France	−0.10
Germany	−0.09
Italy	−0.09

Notes: The original monthly data are taken from MSCI and cover the period January 1980 to August 2010.

the correlation between exchange rate changes and local equity market returns is low. It is sometimes argued that it should be negative, appealing to the competitiveness ideas of Chapter 9. When countries experience real depreciations (usually brought about by nominal exchange rate depreciations), exporting firms and import competing firms in that country experience a boost to their competitiveness and profitability, which might increase local stock market values. Under this scenario, the exchange rate and the stock market move in opposite directions. As shown in Exhibit 13.2, in most countries, the correlation between exchange rate changes and local stock market returns is indeed slightly negative.

In Canada, the correlation is positive. For such a country, the primary forces may be foreign capital flows that appreciate both the foreign currency and the stock market as investors enter the capital markets and depreciate both markets when foreign investors repatriate capital. Nevertheless, the main conclusion of Exhibit 13.2 is that dollar currency returns and foreign currency–denominated equity returns show little correlation.

Expected Returns

Average Returns

In efficient markets, risky securities should earn returns higher than the risk-free rate. In Exhibit 13.1, we also report the average (mean) returns earned in the various markets over the 31 years as a measure of the expected return, $E[r]$. If these returns are representative of true expected returns, they do not indicate that volatility is rewarded in the international marketplace. Whereas the most volatile market (Italy) does have the highest average local currency return (over 14%) and in dollars (over 12.5%), the two low-volatility markets (the United States and the United Kingdom) have relatively high average returns as well. Moreover, although Japan is a comparatively high-volatility country, it has low average stock market returns. Something else must drive average returns. We explore this issue later in this chapter.

Currency Components of Returns

Exhibit 13.1 splits up the average dollar return into the average equity return in the foreign currency and the average currency return. The currency returns range between −1.5% (Italy) and 4.1% (Japan). It should not be a surprise that countries such as Japan and Germany feature positive currency returns and that countries such as France, Italy, and the United Kingdom feature negative currency returns. In the long run, currency changes reflect nominal interest rate differentials (recall our discussion of uncovered interest rate parity in Chapter 7), and these interest rate differentials partially reflect inflation differentials. For example, Japan and Germany are both countries with historically low inflation and interest rates. In contrast, prior to the adoption of the euro, France and Italy historically experienced relatively high inflation and high nominal interest rates. The United Kingdom

Exhibit 13.3 Sharpe Ratios for the G7, 1980–2010

Country	Sharpe Ratio
United States	0.42
Canada	0.33
Japan	0.19
United Kingdom	0.38
France	0.33
Germany	0.30
Italy	0.29

Note: Ratios are computed as the average return from Exhibit 13.1 minus 5% (our estimate for the sample risk-free rate) divided by the volatilities in Exhibit 13.1.

similarly witnessed high inflation in the first part of the sample, but reformed its monetary policy in the 1990s to focus on inflation targeting.

Sharpe Ratios

Investors naturally like high returns and dislike losses. The more variable the returns, the greater is the probability of loss. Recall from Chapter 7 that the Sharpe ratio is one summary statistic of the risk–return trade-off inherent in a security or a portfolio of securities. The Sharpe ratio is measured as the average excess return relative to the volatility of the return:

$$\text{Sharpe ratio} = \frac{E[r] - r_f}{\text{Vol}[r]}$$

where r_f is the risk-free rate. It would be natural for investors to choose portfolios with high Sharpe ratios because investors want a high excess return (as measured by the numerator of the Sharpe ratio) and a low volatility (as measured by the denominator of the Sharpe ratio). The historical Sharpe ratios for the G7 countries are presented in Exhibit 13.3.

Note that the U.S. equity market produces the highest Sharpe ratio, with only the United Kingdom getting somewhat close. It is tempting to conclude that because the U.S. equity market offers the best possible Sharpe ratio, international diversification is a bust for U.S. investors. It is also tempting to conclude that Japan is the worst place to invest because it offers the lowest Sharpe ratio. The next section shows that these conclusions are naïve and erroneous.

13.2 THE BENEFITS OF INTERNATIONAL DIVERSIFICATION

Risk Reduction Through International Diversification

Exhibit 13.4 updates a classic study by Solnik (1974b) who was one of the first to demonstrate the benefits of international diversification. The horizontal axis in Exhibit 13.4 depicts the number of stocks in a particular portfolio, and the vertical axis shows the typical variance of a portfolio. For the top line, we consider a universe of only U.S. stock and compute the average variance of a typical individual U.S. stock, which is normalized to 1. Then, we consider equally weighted portfolios of two stocks (one-half each), find the average variance of this portfolio expressed as a fraction of the average variance of one stock to produce a second point on the graph, and so on.

Because of the imperfect correlation between stocks, the relative portfolio variances decline with the addition of stocks. The graph shows that the portfolio variance falls quickly as more stocks are added, but after including around 30 stocks, it becomes difficult to reduce the variance

Exhibit 13.4 The Case for International Diversification

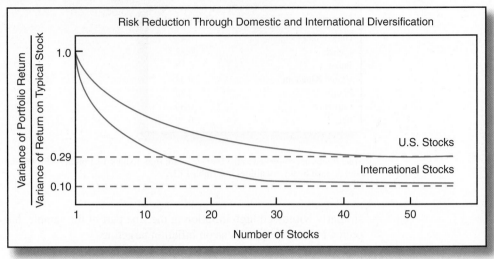

Note: Author's calculations with the assistance of Xiaoyan Zhang. The sample period is 1999 to 2008.

further. The curve finally settles at a level of about 29% of the beginning variance. In other words, more than 70% of the variance of a typical stock can be eliminated through diversification. The part of the variance that can be diversified away is called **nonsystematic variance**.

The lower line in Exhibit 13.4 repeats the exercise, but now stocks can be added from the United States and the major developed stock markets. Because there is even less correlation between U.S. and foreign stocks, the variance of the equally weighted portfolios goes down much more quickly as more stocks are added. The variance of the portfolio falls to barely 10% of the variance of a typical U.S. stock.

Recall that the appendix to Chapter 7 demonstrates that the variance of a large, equally weighted portfolio equals the average covariance among the stocks in the portfolio. Consequently, the variance of U.S. portfolios cannot be reduced further because there are systematic sources of variation that affect all stocks in the United States in the same way. The macroeconomic forces driving stock returns are factors that affect the cash flow prospects of firms and the discount rates used by investors to value these cash flows. We know that stock returns are sensitive to interest rates, which, in turn, depend on monetary policies and business cycles. Business cycles of course affect cash flow prospects, but they may also affect discount rates, as investors may become more risk averse in recessions and less risk averse during booms. These risks cannot be diversified away in a single domestic portfolio.

Notice, though, that when foreign stocks are added to the portfolio, these risks can, to some extent, be diversified away because U.S. monetary policies and business cycles are not perfectly correlated with those of the rest of the world. However, for the most part, stocks are positively correlated, so you cannot diversify away all of a portfolio's variance, no matter how many international stocks you add to the portfolio. Because the average covariance is positive, even a large portfolio of international stocks will have a positive variance. We call the variance that cannot be diversified away the **systematic variance** or **market variance**. The important insight here is that when an investor holds a diversified portfolio, a stock's contribution to the variance of the portfolio depends on its covariance relative to the other stocks in the portfolio.

Idiosyncratic Variance Changes over Time
The variance of a firm's return can be split up into an idiosyncratic component and a systematic component, with the latter variance being the source of risk. For most firms, the

idiosyncratic variance constitutes between 60% and 75% of the total variance of the firm's return. This may sound like a lot, but Exhibit 13.4 shows that this idiosyncratic variance disappears relatively quickly when a portfolio is constructed with securities that are less than perfectly correlated.

Recent research by Bekaert et al. (2010) demonstrates that idiosyncratic volatility, both in the United States and other G7 countries, seems to go through low- and high-volatility regimes. These findings provide a different interpretation of the results in Campbell et al. (2001), who argued that the general level of idiosyncratic risk in the U.S. market substantially increased from the early 1960s to 1997, whereas the level of long-run systematic risk roughly remained constant. In periods of high idiosyncratic volatility, more stocks are needed to achieve full diversification than the 30 that Exhibit 13.4 suggests.

International Return Correlations

Exhibit 13.5 reports a full correlation matrix of the stock market returns of 23 developed countries. The sample period starts in 1980 for most countries. The correlations range from 0.23 for Japan and Greece to 0.79 for Germany and the Netherlands. It is striking that the stock returns of countries that are in close geographic proximity to one another and have significant exports and imports to one another correlate more highly. This is true for Canada and the United States, and it is also true for European Union countries (in particular, Belgium, France, Germany, and the Netherlands). Ireland and the United Kingdom are also highly correlated, at 0.71; New Zealand and Australia returns have a correlation of 0.73. This suggests that trade increases correlations, presumably because importing and exporting firms are affected by the economic factors in the other countries.

Exhibit 13.5   Correlation Matrix for Developed Countries

	AT	BE	CA	DK	FR	DE	HK	IT	JP	NL	NO	SG	SP	SE	CH	UK	US	GR	PT	IE	FI	NZ
AU	0.40	0.46	0.67	0.43	0.50	0.48	0.51	0.39	0.39	0.55	0.60	0.56	0.52	0.54	0.48	0.62	0.56	0.39	0.45	0.57	0.52	0.73
AT		0.59	0.43	0.49	0.58	0.65	0.35	0.46	0.31	0.59	0.54	0.37	0.50	0.43	0.58	0.51	0.38	0.53	0.55	0.58	0.38	0.50
BE			0.50	0.61	0.74	0.70	0.36	0.54	0.42	0.75	0.64	0.42	0.57	0.53	0.67	0.64	0.56	0.50	0.59	0.66	0.40	0.42
CA				0.53	0.56	0.53	0.52	0.47	0.40	0.64	0.63	0.57	0.50	0.56	0.52	0.64	0.75	0.36	0.47	0.52	0.55	0.53
DK					0.59	0.62	0.35	0.52	0.41	0.65	0.61	0.41	0.54	0.56	0.58	0.57	0.52	0.42	0.56	0.62	0.48	0.41
FR						0.78	0.38	0.61	0.45	0.76	0.64	0.40	0.65	0.61	0.68	0.67	0.62	0.51	0.61	0.60	0.55	0.45
DE							0.42	0.57	0.38	0.79	0.60	0.43	0.63	0.66	0.72	0.61	0.60	0.50	0.59	0.63	0.57	0.46
HK								0.36	0.31	0.51	0.47	0.63	0.43	0.45	0.39	0.52	0.46	0.29	0.41	0.41	0.41	0.46
IT									0.42	0.57	0.45	0.34	0.60	0.55	0.47	0.51	0.44	0.49	0.57	0.52	0.54	0.43
JP										0.46	0.37	0.36	0.46	0.43	0.45	0.47	0.37	0.23	0.37	0.47	0.39	0.41
NL											0.70	0.52	0.62	0.66	0.74	0.75	0.71	0.49	0.64	0.70	0.56	0.55
NO												0.52	0.53	0.61	0.58	0.66	0.58	0.44	0.54	0.60	0.53	0.54
SG													0.42	0.49	0.41	0.53	0.58	0.33	0.39	0.47	0.42	0.55
SP														0.62	0.56	0.60	0.53	0.54	0.71	0.62	0.54	0.55
SE															0.58	0.60	0.60	0.44	0.59	0.59	0.67	0.57
CH																0.65	0.58	0.42	0.58	0.56	0.43	0.49
UK																	0.66	0.43	0.57	0.71	0.55	0.53
US																		0.37	0.47	0.64	0.58	0.48
GR																			0.57	0.44	0.33	0.36
PT																				0.54	0.44	0.48
IE																					0.48	0.47
FI																						0.44

Notes: The countries are Australia (AU), Austria (AT), Belgium (BE), Canada (CA), Denmark (DK), France (FR), Germany (DE), Hong Kong (HK), Italy (IT), Japan (JP), the Netherlands (NL), Norway (NO), Singapore (SG), Spain (SP), Sweden (SE), Switzerland (CH), the United Kingdom (UK), the United States (US), Greece (GR), Portugal (PT), Ireland (IE), Finland (FI), and New Zealand (NZ). The data are monthly dollar returns from MSCI for the period from January 1980 to August 2010, although for some countries, the sample starts later.

The lowest correlations are observed for Japan and Greece. Greece has a correlation of less than 0.30 with Japan and Hong Kong. The correlations with non-European countries are invariably below 40%. Even within Europe, Greece does not correlate very highly with most other markets, although the correlations are always higher than 40%. Interestingly, the highest correlation Greece has with any other country is with Portugal, another ex-emerging market. Portugal naturally correlates most closely with its neighbor and trading partner Spain.

What Drives Correlations of Returns?

Apart from trade patterns, what drives the different return co-movements we observe in Exhibit 13.5? To analyze this, it is best to first think of pure fundamental factors. Think of a country as a set of firms. Then figure that each firm is priced rationally, using a discounted cash flow analysis. In such a world, common variations in discount rates and common variations in expected cash flow growth rates will lead to correlations among the firms.

The first fundamental factor that may drive the correlations of stock returns in different countries is their industrial structures. Firms in the same industry are likely to be buffeted by the same shocks affecting cash flows and profitability. Moreover, it is likely that their systematic risks also move together, so both their discount rates and expected cash flow variations are closely related. Both Canada and Australia have many firms operating in the mining industry, for example. This might explain why Australia is highly correlated with Canada but not with Germany.

A long debate has ensued about the importance of industry factors when it comes to return correlations across countries. Some researchers have found that industry factors are starting to dominate country factors [see Brooks and Del Negro (2004) for example]. It used to be the case that country factors clearly dominated when markets were less integrated and discount rates were not highly correlated across countries. Moreover, limited trade across countries and relatively independent monetary policies implied that business cycles showed little correlation across countries, resulting in low correlations among cash flows in different countries. Consequently, policies affecting the degree of integration and the independence of business cycles appear to be important determinants of cross-country correlations. For example, the adoption of a common currency has helped synchronize business cycles in Europe. In contrast, emerging markets typically act more independently of integrated countries. This may explain why Greek stock market returns have historically not been highly correlated with the returns of other countries. If Greece continues to integrate into the European Union, we would expect these correlations to increase, but Greece's recent sovereign debt crisis obviously jeopardizes the integration process.

Finally, irrational investor behavior may induce excess correlations across equity markets, especially during crisis periods. We already talked about this contagion phenomenon in Chapter 5 and simply repeat that increased volatility may lead to temporarily increased correlations.

Asymmetric Correlations?

Because the correlations overall are so far from unity, there are ample opportunities for investors to internationally diversify their portfolios. Some investors may be less impressed and argue that they really only care about diversification when their home market is going down. Longin and Solnik (2001) confirm what casual observations may have led you to suspect: International diversification benefits evaporate when you need them the most—that is, in bear markets. To demonstrate this rather annoying fact, Longin and Solnik computed "bear market correlations" (correlations using returns below the average for both of the stock markets) and "bull market correlations" (correlations using returns above the average) for various developed markets.

The results are striking: The bear market return correlations are much higher than the bull market correlations. This finding does not justify staying at home with your equity portfolio, however. Research by Ang and Bekaert (2002) shows that these asymmetric correlations do not negate the benefits of international diversification because bear markets remain imperfectly correlated.

The Effect of International Diversification on Sharpe Ratios

Portfolio Risk and Return

Exhibit 13.3 shows the U.S. Sharpe ratio to be historically higher than the Sharpe ratios for the other G7 countries. Even so, international diversification makes perfect sense for U.S. investors. This is because it is not the Sharpe ratio of the foreign asset that the U.S. investor should care about but the Sharpe ratio of the portfolio that results from international diversification. Intuitively, because equity markets in other countries are not perfectly correlated with the U.S. market, part of their volatility disappears through portfolio diversification.

Let's consider formally how international diversification affects Sharpe ratios. Imagine putting a fraction w of your all-U.S. portfolio in international equity. Let's denote the U.S. return by r and the foreign return (in dollars) by r^*. The expected return of the new portfolio is the weighted average of the expected returns on the individual assets with the weights equal to the fractions of wealth invested in each asset, $(1 - w)E[r] + wE[r^*]$. Expected returns aggregate linearly. As we already know, volatility does not aggregate linearly. The volatility of the new portfolio equals

$$\{(1 - w)^2 \text{Var}[r] + w^2 \text{Var}[r^*] + 2w(1 - w)\text{Cov}[r, r^*]\}^{1/2}$$

Because the covariance is a function of the correlation, correlations really matter.

When Does International Diversification Improve the Sharpe Ratio?

Suppose you start with an all-U.S. portfolio. The U.S. Sharpe ratio is $E[r - r_f]/\text{Vol}[r]$, and the Sharpe ratio on the foreign equity is $E[r^* - r_f]/\text{Vol}[r^*]$. We denote the correlation between the U.S. and foreign returns as ρ. From a zero investment in foreign equities, the Sharpe ratio goes up when you add a little bit of foreign equity exposure, if the following condition holds:

$$\frac{E[r^*] - r_f}{\text{Vol}[r^*]} > \rho \frac{E[r] - r_f}{\text{Vol}[r]} \tag{13.1}$$

The appendix to this chapter proves this statement formally. Equation (13.1) states that your Sharpe ratio improves when you add a little bit of the foreign asset to your portfolio if the Sharpe ratio of the new asset is higher than the Sharpe ratio of the U.S. portfolio multiplied by the correlation between the U.S. return and the international return. In other words, the lower the correlation with the U.S. market, the lower the Sharpe ratio of the foreign market needs to be for it to become an investment that increases your Sharpe ratio. This is because markets that have low correlation with the U.S. market are the best diversifiers of a U.S. portfolio. Another way to see this is to bring ρ to the other side and notice that it is not the foreign asset's volatility that matters when computing the return to risk ratio but, rather, volatility adjusted for correlation ($\rho \text{Vol}[r^*]$). The lower ρ is, the lower this adjusted risk number becomes, and the easier it is to exceed the U.S. Sharpe ratio.

Investment Hurdle Rates

Given the correlations and volatilities provided earlier, we can compute hurdle rates on international investments for U.S.–based investors. The *hurdle rate* is the lowest possible expected foreign return that must be earned for investors with purely domestic assets to improve their Sharpe ratio when they invest in that foreign market and when the expected return on the U.S. market takes a specific value.

To find the hurdle rates, we fill in $E[r]$ in Equation (13.1) with a reasonable number (for instance, 10%), and we use the data to estimate correlations and volatilities, leaving $E[r^*]$ as an unknown variable. The minimum $E[r^*]$ we need for the Sharpe ratio with some foreign investment to be at least as large as the U.S. Sharpe ratio is the one that equates the two sides of the equation. That is,

$$\text{Hurdle rate} = \rho \frac{E[r] - r_f}{\text{Vol}[r]} \text{Vol}[r^*] + r_f$$

The hurdle rate is higher when the U.S. market has a high Sharpe ratio, the foreign market is more volatile, or there is high correlation between foreign and U.S. stock returns.

Whereas Exhibit 13.1 reports the dollar volatilities of the various international equity market returns, and Exhibit 13.3 reports their Sharpe ratios, Exhibit 13.6 reports their correlations with the U.S. market. The market returns of Canada and the United Kingdom have the highest correlations with U.S. returns, whereas Japanese and Italian market returns have the lowest correlations. For France and Germany, the correlations are about 60%.

The hurdle rates for the countries with low correlations will be low. Let's illustrate the computation of the hurdle rate for Japan, when the expected return for the United States is $10\%(E[r] = 0.10)$. The number is

$$0.05 + 0.37 \times \frac{0.10 - 0.05}{0.156} \times 0.225 = 0.0767, \text{ or } 7.67\%$$

The risk-free rate is 0.05, and the correlation between Japanese and U.S. equity returns is 0.37, the U.S. Sharpe ratio is $(0.10 - 0.05)/0.156$, and the volatility of the Japanese equity return is 0.225. Hence, a U.S. investor should put some money in Japanese equity even if he believes the expected dollar return on Japanese equity is only 7.67%.

Hurdle rates appear in Exhibit 13.7. The correct conclusion is that international diversification can easily improve performance for U.S. investors because the hurdle rates for expected dollar returns on foreign investments are low. In fact, they are lower than the expected return on the U.S. equity market in every case. It is difficult to imagine that foreign equity markets have such dramatically lower expected returns relative to the U.S. market. Italy and Japan have the lowest correlation with the United States and therefore offer the easiest performance enhancement.

Exhibit 13.6 Correlations Between Foreign and U.S. Equity Market Returns, 1980–2010

Country	Correlation
Canada	0.75
Japan	0.37
United Kingdom	0.66
France	0.61
Germany	0.60
Italy	0.43

Notes: All returns have been converted to U.S. dollars. The original monthly data are taken from MSCI.

Exhibit 13.7 Hurdle Rates for Foreign Investments

Country	E[r] = 10%	E[r] = 12%
Canada	9.96%	11.94%
Japan	7.67%	8.74%
United Kingdom	9.01%	10.61%
France	9.32%	11.05%
Germany	9.41%	11.17%
Italy	8.57%	9.99%

Notes: The hurdle rate equals $r_f + \rho \dfrac{E[r] - r_f}{\text{Vol}[r]} \text{Vol}[r^*]$. The correlation number is taken from Exhibit 13.6; the volatility numbers (in dollars) are taken from Exhibit 13.1 (both for the United States and the foreign country); r_f is set at 5%; and $E[r]$ is the U.S. expected return specified on top of the two columns. Data are from MSCI, and the sample is from January 1980 to August 2010.

How to Diversify at Home

Retail investors do not necessarily need to call a foreign broker to invest in far-flung places. Many investment vehicles can be used to accomplish international diversification. First of all, would Coca-Cola not constitute an ideal international investment? After all, Coke sells its flagship product in more than 200 countries around the world. Hence, its cash flows must be influenced by the local economies of all those countries. It was long thought that a portfolio of multinational companies would capture the benefits of international diversification. While the recent literature does indicate that the stock returns of multinational companies behave quite internationally [see, for example, Diermeier and Solnik (2001)], Rowland and Tesar (2004) find that restricting oneself to domestically traded multinational companies remains a flawed diversification strategy. The best diversification opportunities may be exactly the companies for which local factors remain important drivers of their returns.

Chapter 12 notes that many companies cross-list in the United States using American depositary receipts (ADRs). Why not simply buy these companies? Again, the problem is one of representation: The ADR companies tend to be the larger, more internationally focused companies, and they may not give full exposure to foreign stock markets.

Another possibility is to invest in **closed-end funds**, or **investment trusts**, which trade on the local equity market.

These funds represent a fixed portfolio that may invest in the world markets, sometimes restricted to a region (Latin America, for instance) or a particular country, in which case they are called **country funds**. The only way to buy into this portfolio is for the investor to buy the fund from another investor selling it. Therefore, closed-end funds can trade at prices that are different from the value of the portfolio, especially when they invest in emerging markets. Hence, it is conceivable that closed-end fund returns fail to offer the same diversification benefits as the underlying portfolio (see Section 13.6). This is not a problem with **open-end funds**, where the portfolio grows with new investments and contracts with redemptions, and the fund is not traded on an exchange. These represent the bulk of the international funds available to retail investors.

Finally, a hybrid alternative that is rapidly gaining popularity is the **exchange-traded fund (ETF)**, which trades on an exchange but where prices are kept close to the value of the underlying portfolio through arbitrage activities by a few institutional investors. Both diversified funds and funds focusing on one country, mimicking the performance of the corresponding MSCI indices, are now available. As the availability of these vehicles expands, an internationally diversified portfolio is only a phone call away for U.S. investors.

13.3 OPTIMAL PORTFOLIO ALLOCATION

We have established that diversifying internationally is likely to reduce risk and improve your Sharpe ratio. But how much should you invest internationally? This is a portfolio choice problem—one of the most fundamental finance problems, and one that brings us very close to a formula for the cost of equity capital.

To solve for the **optimal portfolio**, we must first specify feasible portfolios, which are all portfolios that use up all wealth. Let's consider the G7 example. An investor can invest in the risk-free asset or in seven different equity markets. We can represent the investor's feasible portfolios by a series of wealth fractions—the proportions of wealth devoted to each asset—and these proportions must add to 1. For example, putting 50% of your portfolio in the risk-free asset and 50% in the U.S. equity market is a feasible portfolio. The combination of all feasible portfolios constitutes the investor's menu. Of course, there is an infinite number of possible portfolios, so to figure out which portfolio is best for any investor seems like a daunting task.

Luckily, finance theory has come up with some rather simple answers. We start by defining investors' preferences regarding risk and return, and then we consider a simplified set of ingredients: one risky asset and one riskless security. After we extend the ingredients to multiple risky assets, we can solve the portfolio problem. For example, we will find that no smart investor should ever choose the 50–50 portfolio we proposed.

Preferences

In economics, preferences are typically represented by **utility functions**. Typically, a utility function mathematically links the consumption of units of real goods to a level of satisfaction. Here, we specify a utility function for the individual investor in terms of the statistical properties of the portfolio that the investor holds—that is, expected returns and portfolio variance. We assume that investors would like to generate the highest possible expected return with as little variance as possible, but each investor may have a different risk tolerance. A simple function that captures the trade-off the investors face is

$$U = E[r_p] - \frac{A}{2}\sigma_p^2$$

where the subscript p indicates the portfolio, $E[r_p]$ is the expected return on the portfolio, and σ_p is the volatility of the portfolio. The parameter A in this **mean-variance preference** function indicates the penalty the investor assigns to the variance of the portfolio. The higher A is, the more the investor dislikes variance or risk; in other words, A characterizes the investor's risk aversion.

Example 13.2   The Investor's Utility Calculation

Suppose the expected portfolio return is 9.87%, and its standard deviation is 7.84%. For an investor with $A = 4$, utility equals

$$9.87\% - \frac{1}{2} \times 4 \times (7.84\%)^2 = 9.87\% - 1.23\% = 8.64\%$$

One interpretation of this number is that the investor in this portfolio achieves the same utility as he would by investing in a completely risk-free portfolio with a return of 8.64%.

The Case of One Risky Asset

The portfolio problem is considerably simplified and much intuition is gained if we begin by restricting the set of ingredients to one single risky asset and the risk-free asset. Let's introduce some notation. Let the risk-free return be r_f, let the risky return be r, and let the weight on the risky asset be w.

If the proportion w of the portfolio is invested in the risky asset, then $1 - w$ is invested in the risk-free asset. Hence, the return on a portfolio is

$$r_p = w \times r + (1 - w) \times r_f = r_f + w \times (r - r_f)$$

The variable $r - r_f$ is the excess return. Therefore, the portfolio's expected return is $E[r_p] = r_f + w \times E[r - r_f]$, which increases linearly with the weight in the risky asset when the expected excess return is positive. To find the variance of the portfolio return, note that the risk-free rate is known with certainty. Therefore, we simply have $\sigma_p^2 = w^2\sigma^2$, where σ^2 is the variance of the risky return, r. Hence, the volatility of the portfolio is $\sigma_p = w\sigma$, and the risk of the portfolio is also linear in w. Now, use this volatility expression to substitute for w in the expected return expression, and find

$$E[r_p] = r_f + \frac{E[r] - r_f}{\sigma}\sigma_p \qquad (13.2)$$

This expression describes the relationship between the expected return on the portfolio and its standard deviation. Consequently, Equation (13.2) fully describes the "menu," or the possible risk–return combinations, for this simple case. Also, note that the relationship is of the form $y = a + bx$, with $y = E[r_p]$ and $x = \sigma_p$, which is the equation for a straight line.

We call the line describing the risk–return trade-off in the single risky asset case the **capital allocation line (CAL)** because it describes the ways capital can be allocated in the single risky asset case. The CAL is graphed in Exhibit 13.8.

Exhibit 13.8 The Capital Allocation Line

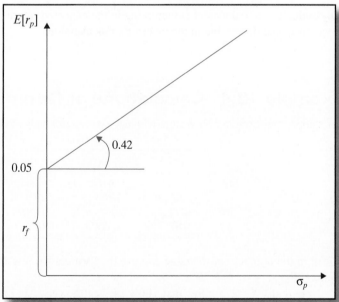

Notes: The vertical axis shows the expected return, and the horizontal axis is the standard deviation of the portfolio. The line is the capital allocation line of feasible risk–expected return patterns. It emanates at the risk-free rate (5% in this example) and slopes upward with the Sharpe ratio of the risky asset, $\frac{E(r) - r_f}{\sigma}$, as its slope.

Example 13.3 The Capital Allocation Line

Let's take the U.S. equity market as the risky asset, with expected return of 11.52%, and $\sigma^2 = (15.58\%)^2$ (see Exhibit 13.1), and let $r_f = 5\%$. Then, the CAL is given by

$$E[r_p] = 0.05 + SR \times \sigma_p, \text{ with } SR = \frac{E[r] - r_f}{\sigma} = \frac{0.1152 - 0.05}{0.1558} = 0.42, \text{ where}$$

we recognize the Sharpe ratio, SR, as the return premium per unit of risk.

The Optimal Portfolio

To find the optimal portfolio, we must combine the CAL menu with the investor's preferences. The mathematical problem can be written as

$$\max_w U = \max_w [E[r_p] - \tfrac{1}{2}A\sigma_p^2]$$

In words, we try to find the weight on the risky asset (w) that maximizes the utility function. We can substitute the expressions for $E[r_p]$ and σ_p^2 to obtain

$$\max_w [r_f + w[E[r] - r_f] - \tfrac{1}{2}Aw^2\sigma^2]$$

To solve for the optimal w, denoted w^*, we must take the derivative of this function with respect to w and set it equal to zero, in which case we find

$$E[r] - r_f - Aw^*\sigma^2 = 0$$

Solving for the optimal portfolio gives a very intuitive solution:

$$w^* = \frac{E[r] - r_f}{A\sigma^2} \tag{13.3}$$

The allocation to the risky asset is increasing in the expected return on the asset, decreasing in its variance, and decreasing in the investor's risk aversion.

Example 13.4 Calculations of Optimal Portfolios

Let's apply the formula to investors who have different levels of risk aversion:

A	w^*	$E[r_p]$ (in %)	σ_p (in %)
1.0	2.69	22.51%	41.85%
2.0	1.34	13.76%	20.92%
3.0	0.90	10.84%	13.95%
4.0	0.67	9.38%	10.46%

To fill in the numbers of the table, we use the formula for w^*, and then the expected return is $E[r_p] = r_f + w^*E[r - r_f]$ and the volatility is $\sigma_p = |w^*|\sigma$.

Note that $w^* = 1$ implies that 100% of wealth is invested in the risky asset. As risk aversion increases, the weight on the risky asset decreases, which decreases the expected return and the standard deviation. Because we stay along the CAL, the risk–return trade-off (Sharpe ratio) of the portfolio, $[E(r_p) - r_f]/\sigma_p = 0.42$, remains the same because it is the slope of the line. Exhibit 13.9 demonstrates this graphically.

Exhibit 13.9 Optimal Portfolios

Portfolio K: Long in the risky asset
        Long in risk-free asset
Portfolio L: Borrow risk-free asset to
        invest in risky asset

Note: Investors with different preferences toward risk and return invest in different portfolios, represented by different points on the capital allocation line.

For low A, we are at a point such as L. The investor is more than 100% invested in the risky asset ($w > 1$), and the investor finances this position by borrowing. For example, for $A = 1$, the investor borrows $1.69 for every dollar of his own wealth invested, and he invests the $2.69 in the stock market. For high A, the investor combines stock investing with an investment in the T-bill—that is, $w < 1$. For example, for $A = 4.0$, the investor places 67% of her wealth in the risky asset and 33% in the risk-free asset.

The Mean–Standard Deviation Frontier

What if there are multiple risky assets? Consider Exhibit 13.10. The circles represent the expected returns and standard deviations of various assets. Even with just two risky assets, many different capital allocation lines are available. After all, we could consider all feasible

Exhibit 13.10   The Mean–Standard Deviation Frontier

risky portfolios as "the risky asset." What is the optimal risky portfolio? Economist Harry Markowitz (1952) won the Nobel Prize in 1990 for showing us how to proceed.

First, we must get rid of a large number of "inefficient" portfolios by creating the **mean–standard deviation frontier**, which is the locus of the portfolios in expected return–standard deviation space that have the minimum variance for each expected return. It is therefore also often referred to as the **minimum-variance frontier**. For two assets, the frontier would have a shape similar to the one graphed in Exhibit 13.10. Imagine combining a low expected return–low variance asset (say asset X) with a high expected return–high variance asset (say asset Y). Starting from a portfolio 100% in asset X, adding some of asset Y to the portfolio increases the expected return of the portfolio in a linear fashion. However, unless assets X and Y have perfectly correlated returns, the standard deviation will not change in a linear fashion. In fact, it may even decrease at first, but in any case, when it starts to increase, imperfect correlation makes the standard deviation of the portfolio increase at a rate lower than linear, giving rise to the curved shape also seen in Exhibit 13.10.

Creating the frontier for multiple assets as in Exhibit 13.10 is the solution to a complex mathematical problem. We want to minimize the return variance for a portfolio of N securities, for each possible expected return:

$$\min_{\{w_1, \ldots, w_N\}} \left[\sum_{i=1}^{N} w_i^2 \sigma_i^2 + \sum_{i=1}^{N} \sum_{j \neq 1}^{N} w_i w_j \operatorname{cov}\left[r_i, r_j\right] \right] \Rightarrow \text{Minimum variance}$$

such that

$$\sum_{i=1}^{N} w_i = 1 \Rightarrow \text{Feasible portfolio} \quad \sum_{i=1}^{N} w_i E[r_i] = \bar{r} \Rightarrow \text{Target return}$$

By varying $\bar{r}$, we trace out the frontier. Although analytical solutions are possible, using Excel Solver is a popular way of finding minimum-variance portfolios.

Two-Fund Separation (Advanced)

Interestingly, when this problem is solved for two target returns, we are done. This is called **two-fund separation**: The minimum-variance frontier is said to be spanned (or generated) by any two minimum-variance frontier portfolios. That is, if we find two portfolios—say, portfolio X with weights $\left[w_1^X, w_2^X, \ldots, w_N^X\right]$ and portfolio Y with weights $\left[w_1^Y, w_2^Y, \ldots, w_N^Y\right]$—that are on the frontier, we can generate the whole frontier by taking combinations of these two portfolios. If there are only two assets, then the mean–standard deviation frontier can be found by simply mixing the two assets in all possible combinations with weights adding up to 1. Two-fund separation says that with multiple assets, all portfolios on the frontier can be viewed as a mix of any two frontier portfolios.

The Efficient Frontier

Once we have determined the mean–standard deviation frontier, we can focus on a rather limited set of possible portfolios. Clearly, no one will want to invest in a portfolio on the inside of the frontier: You can either lower risk at the same expected return or increase the expected return at the same risk. Also, no one will invest in a portfolio on the portion of the frontier below the global minimum-variance portfolio, which is indicated on Exhibit 13.10. The **global minimum-variance portfolio** is the portfolio with the least variance among all possible portfolios. If you are below that portfolio, you can increase expected return without increasing volatility.

What remains is the upper portion of the frontier, starting at the global minimum-variance portfolio. This set of risky portfolios is called the **efficient frontier**. It yields a large number of "efficient" risky portfolios that could be combined with a risk-free asset to form a capital allocation line.

The Mean-Variance-Efficient (MVE) Portfolio

Starting from the risk-free rate on the vertical axis of 5%, we can consider any portfolio on the mean–standard deviation frontier as a potential risky asset. We can draw a potential capital allocation line (CAL) from the risk-free rate to the risky portfolio's point on the graph. As before, the slope of the CAL is the Sharpe ratio. People with utility functions that depend positively on the expected return and negatively on the variance of the portfolio would naturally prefer higher Sharpe ratios. Once we have a CAL, we know how to optimally combine the risky portfolio with the risk-free asset from our previous analysis.

For example, consider Exhibit 13.11. It graphs the mean–standard deviation frontier for two assets, the U.S. and Japanese equity markets, using the expected return and volatility properties reported in Exhibit 13.1 and the correlation reported in Exhibit 13.6. Clearly, the "best" CAL has the steepest slope, or highest Sharpe ratio. This is the line emanating from the risk-free return to the point where the line is tangent to the mean–standard deviation frontier. This portfolio is called the **mean-variance-efficient (MVE) portfolio**, and it represents the risky portfolio that maximizes the Sharpe ratio.

The theory is surprisingly powerful. It states that there is a superior risky portfolio that all investors will prefer: Of course, preferences toward risk still differ, and investors can combine the MVE portfolio with the risk-free asset in different ways. Portfolios to the left (right) of the tangency represent the MVE portfolio for the more (less) risk-averse investors. Notice how the risky efficient frontier is completely below the CAL going through the MVE portfolio. By borrowing at the risk-free rate and investing more than 100% in the MVE portfolio, investors use leverage and can achieve a much higher expected return for the same risk than if they only considered risky assets. The actual weight on the MVE portfolio versus the risk-free asset can be determined using Equation (13.3).

Exhibit 13.11 Finding the MVE Portfolio

Notes: We form the mean–standard deviation frontier from two assets. The U.S. portfolio has a mean return of 11.52% and a standard deviation of 15.58%. The Japanese portfolio has a mean return of 9.28% and a standard deviation of 22.51%. The correlation between the two returns is 0.37. The mean-variance-efficient portfolio dominates either individual portfolio.

13.4 THE CAPITAL ASSET PRICING MODEL

This section describes the most popular model underlying computations of the cost of capital: the capital asset pricing model (CAPM). We describe its origins, provide a formal derivation and interpretation, and discuss the difference between domestic and international CAPMs.

Assumptions and Origins

The **capital asset pricing model (CAPM)** underlies all modern financial theory. It was derived by Sharpe (1964), Lintner (1965), and Mossin (1966), using principles of diversification, with simplified assumptions building on the original mean-variance optimization analytics developed by Markowitz. Markowitz and Sharpe won the 1990 Nobel Prize in economics for their efforts. The CAPM requires a long list of rather strong assumptions:

- There is a single-period investment horizon.
- Individual investors are price takers.
- Investments are limited to traded financial assets.
- There are no taxes and transaction costs.
- Information is costless and available to all investors.
- Investors are rational mean-variance optimizers.
- Expectations are homogeneous; that is, all investors agree on the expected returns, standard deviations, and covariances between security returns.

The CAPM then derives the optimal asset demands of all investors and derives restrictions on expected returns by imposing that markets have to clear (that is, supply must equal demand), implying that all assets must be willingly held. Given these assumptions, it is not surprising that the CAPM yields strong predictions:

- All investors hold the same portfolio of risky assets—the **market portfolio**.
- The market portfolio contains all securities, and the proportion of each security is its market value as a percentage of total market value.
- The risk premium on the market depends on the average risk aversion of all market participants.
- The risk premium on an individual security is a function of its covariance with the market portfolio.

Although no one literally believes that the assumptions underlying the CAPM hold in the real world, the CAPM is one of the most useful models in finance. For example, it serves as a benchmark for evaluating portfolio managers, and it provided an impetus for the development of **index funds**. Index funds are open-end funds that passively track a stock index such as the S&P 500 without trying to outperform it. Finally, the CAPM is the basis for cost-of-capital computations; it is this application of the CAPM that is most useful for this book. The next section provides a technical introduction to the main CAPM equation. The following sections help interpret it and illustrate its practical use in a global context, where exchange rate movements may complicate the model's application.

A Derivation of the CAPM (Advanced)

To derive the CAPM, recall the results of the diversification problem. We argued that adding a little bit of that new asset to a portfolio improves the investor's Sharpe ratio when Equation (13.1) holds; that is, when

$$SR_{NEW} \geq \rho \times SR_p$$

where ρ is the correlation between portfolio, p, and the new asset; SR_{NEW} is the Sharpe ratio of the new asset; and SR_p is the Sharpe ratio of the present portfolio. The correlation of the new asset return with r_p, which now contains some of the new asset, increases as we add more of the new asset, making the condition harder to satisfy. We should keep adding the asset until

$$SR_{\text{NEW}} = \rho \times SR_p \tag{13.4}$$

At that point, further additions no longer increase the Sharpe ratio; that is, we have reached the portfolio that maximizes the Sharpe ratio, implying that we have found the MVE portfolio. Thus, r_p should now be interpreted as the return on the MVE portfolio. Rewriting Equation (13.4) using the definition of the Sharpe ratio and bringing ρ to the other side gives

$$\frac{E(r_{\text{NEW}}) - r_f}{\rho \times \sigma_{\text{NEW}}} = \frac{E(r_p) - r_f}{\sigma_p}$$

Substituting $\rho = \dfrac{\text{Cov}(r_{\text{NEW}}, r_p)}{\sigma_{\text{NEW}} \sigma_p}$ gives

$$\frac{E(r_{\text{NEW}}) - r_f}{\text{Cov}(r_{\text{NEW}}, r_p)} = \frac{E(r_p) - r_f}{\sigma_p^2} \tag{13.5}$$

This relationship holds for any security i. Equation (13.5) implies that expected excess returns per unit of covariance risk are the same for all assets and are equal to $\dfrac{E(r_p) - r_f}{\sigma_p^2}$. The relevant risk for a security is its covariance with the MVE portfolio. Rewriting Equation (13.5) for security i gives

$$E(r_i) - r_f = \frac{\text{Cov}(r_i, r_p)}{\sigma_p^2} \times [E(r_p) - r_f] \tag{13.6}$$

Equation (13.6) establishes a relationship between the expected excess return on an individual asset and the expected return on the MVE portfolio.

We are almost finished. Let's review the major findings of the previous section on optimal asset allocation:

1. The efficient frontier is a set of "dominant" portfolios in risk–return space. Non-efficient portfolios would not be held by any mean-variance investor.
2. If a risk-free asset exists, one portfolio of risky securities offers the best risk–return trade-off: the MVE portfolio.

Now, if everybody is a mean-variance investor facing the same frontier, what must the MVE portfolio be for there to be no excess demand or supply for any security? It must be the market portfolio—and that is what the CAPM says! The implication is

$$E(r_i) - r_f = \frac{\text{Cov}(r_i, r_m)}{\sigma_m^2} \times [E(r_m) - r_f]$$

where the subscript m represents the market portfolio. The relationship between the expected return on an individual security and the expected return on the market portfolio depends on the statistical construct $\dfrac{\text{Cov}(r_i, r_m)}{\sigma_m^2}$, which is called the *beta* (β) of security i.

Interpreting the CAPM

The CAPM is often used as a benchmark to determine the required rate of return on risky equity capital. The CAPM provides a formula for the required rate of return on an equity investment, which is its expected rate of return, $E(r_e)$.

The CAPM Equilibrium

Equity investors require compensation for the time value of money based on the risk-free rate, r_f. In addition, they require compensation for the systematic, or non-diversifiable, risk of the investment. Systematic risk is measured by the beta of the equity, β_e, multiplied by the risk premium on the market, $[E(r_m) - r_f]$. An equity's **beta** is the covariance of the rate of return on the equity with the rate of return on the market portfolio divided by the variance of the rate of return on the market portfolio:

$$\beta_e = \frac{\text{Cov}(r_e, r_m)}{\text{Var}(r_m)}$$

Hence, the CAPM states that

$$E(r_e) = r_f + \beta_e[E(r_m) - r_f] \qquad (13.7)$$

The logic of the CAPM begins with the assumptions that investors prefer higher expected returns but are averse to risk. From the investor's perspective, risk is measured by the variance of the return on the investor's overall portfolio. Given the expected future cash flows of the assets, changes in the market prices change the assets' expected returns and their variances and covariances. In equilibrium, the market prices of assets adjust such that the expected returns on the different assets and their variances and covariances allow the market portfolio to be willingly held by investors. This will happen when the expected excess returns per unit of covariance risk are equalized across assets and are equal to the expected excess return on the market divided by its variance, as in Equation (13.5). In equilibrium, all investors are thought to be holding the market portfolio because they are assumed to have the same expectations and the same investment opportunities. The market portfolio is the MVE portfolio.

The Risk Premium on the Market

The risk premium on the market portfolio is the amount by which the expected return on the market exceeds the risk-free rate. The CAPM actually predicts that this risk premium will depend on the average risk aversion of investors and the variance of the market portfolio return. To see this, consider Equation (13.3) but applied to the market portfolio. Because every investor chooses to combine the market portfolio with the risk-free asset according to her preferences, someone with average risk aversion, say $\overline{A}$, will hold exactly the market portfolio.

$$\text{Consequently, } w^* = 1 = \frac{1}{\overline{A}} \frac{E(r_m) - r_f}{\sigma_m^2}, \text{ or}$$

$$E(r_m) - r_f = \overline{A}\sigma_m^2 \qquad (13.8)$$

Hence, the **market risk premium** balances the variance of the market portfolio to reflect the average risk aversion of the investors in the market.

Individual Expected Returns and the Role of Beta

In the CAPM equilibrium, if an equity return is not correlated with the return on the market portfolio, that equity's expected return is equal to the risk-free rate because investors do not need to be compensated for bearing the uncertainty associated with that particular return. In Equation (13.7), if $\beta_e = 0$, then $E(r_e) = r_f$. If an asset does not covary with the market portfolio, it becomes effectively riskless when it is held in a large, diversified portfolio that mirrors the market portfolio.

Equity returns that covary positively with the return on the market portfolio contribute to the variance of the return on the market portfolio. Consequently, these positive beta assets require an expected rate of return that is greater than the risk-free rate. On the other hand, an asset with a negative beta, whose return covaries negatively with the return on the market portfolio, actually reduces the overall variance of the portfolio. Investors willingly hold this asset even though its expected return is driven below the return on the risk-free interest rate in the competitive equilibrium. Most equities have positive betas, however, because the market environment tends to affect all stocks the same way.

Notice that an asset's beta measures its relative risk because the beta is the covariance of the asset's return with the return on the market portfolio divided by the variance of the return on the market portfolio. For example, if the beta is 1, the covariance of the asset's return with the return on the market portfolio equals the variance of the return on the market, and the asset's expected return is the same as the market's expected return.

Domestic Versus World CAPMs

In a **domestic CAPM**, the market portfolio is defined as the aggregate asset holdings of all investors in a particular country. Many real-world applications of the CAPM use domestic CAPMs. For example, the beta for a U.K. firm that is listed on the London Stock Exchange (LSE) would be calculated relative to the LSE value-weighted market return, and the beta for a Japanese firm that is listed on the Tokyo Stock Exchange (TSE) would be calculated relative to the TSE value-weighted market return.

What are the implications of this assumption? The domestic CAPM assumes that assets of a country are held only by investors who reside in that country. In such a case, there would be no international diversification of risk, and countries' capital markets would be completely internationally segmented. We discuss the concept of a segmented and integrated market more fully in Section 13.6. When the CAPM was first developed in the 1960s, international segmentation seemed reasonable because capital flows and portfolio investments were limited. Today, in an increasingly globalized world, it makes more sense to use an internationally diversified portfolio of securities as the market portfolio. This CAPM is called the **world CAPM**.

The Role of Exchange Rates

One major theoretical problem with using the world CAPM is that the development of the theory assumes that investors share the same expectations about the real returns on different assets. Given the observed deviations from purchasing power parity and fluctuations in real exchange rates discussed in Chapter 8, there is a substantial amount of evidence contrary to this premise. When real exchange rates fluctuate, investors in different countries have different perceptions about the real returns on different assets. Let's illustrate this with an example.

Let r_e be the real equity return on a U.S. security for a U.S.–based investor, and let r_f be the real risk-free rate in the United States. The world CAPM states

$$E(r_e) - r_f = \beta_e [E(r_m) - r_f] \qquad (13.9)$$

where r_m is the real return on the world market portfolio. Because we are defining real returns for a U.S.–based investor, they are computed relative to the U.S. consumption basket, using the U.S. price level. For example, the real rate of return on equity, r_e, can be computed by subtracting 1 from 1 plus the nominal rate of return divided by 1 plus the U.S. rate of inflation: $\dfrac{1 + r_e(\$)}{1 + \pi(\$)} - 1$. Similarly, from Chapter 10, we know that r_f, the *ex ante* real interest rate, is the expected value of the *ex post* real interest rate:

$$r_f = r_f(\mathrm{US}) = E\left[\frac{1 + i(\$)}{1 + \pi(\$)} - 1 \right]$$

where $i(\$)$ is the nominal interest rate.

Now, what is the expected real return on the same U.S. security for a German investor? The German investor cares about real German returns, hence

$$\frac{1 + r_e(\text{€})}{1 + \pi(\text{€})} = \frac{[1 + r_e(\$)](1 + s)}{1 + \pi(\text{€})}$$

with s representing the percentage change in the euro–dollar exchange rate. But the expression for the dollar-based version of the CAPM contains the real return for the U.S. investor, $\frac{1 + r_e(\$)}{1 + \pi(\$)}$. This only equals the real return for the German investor when $\frac{1 + s}{1 + \pi(\text{€})} = \frac{1}{1 + \pi(\$)}$, or $1 + s = \frac{1 + \pi(\text{€})}{1 + \pi(\$)}$. In other words, the real returns for the U.S.–based and German-based investors are identical only when purchasing power parity (PPP) holds.

What about the risk-free rate? For the German-based investor, it should be defined relative to her consumption basket. Consequently, the *ex ante* German risk-free rate is $r_f(G) = E\left[\frac{1 + i(\text{€})}{1 + \pi(\text{€})}\right] - 1$. If we assume that PPP holds, we find that $r_f(G) = E\left[\frac{1 + i(\text{€})}{(1 + s)(1 + \pi(\$))} - 1\right]$. Of course, $E\left[\frac{1 + i(\text{€})}{1 + s}\right]$ is the dollar return on an investment in the euro money market. For the real interest rates to be equalized across countries, we need more than just PPP to hold. We also need the real expected returns on money market investments to be equal across countries—that is, we need a real version of uncovered interest rate parity to hold.[2] We conclude that translating the world CAPM to the other country's perspectives works only when all the international parity conditions hold.

So far, we have focused on real returns as the theory demands. However, in practice, CAPMs are mostly applied to nominal returns. Let the nominal equity return be denoted by $r_e(\$)$, and let $i(\$)$ represent the money market interest rate in the United States. The world CAPM for the U.S.-based investor is then formulated as follows:

$$E[r_e(\$) - i(\$)] = \beta_e E[r_m(\$) - i(\$)] \tag{13.10}$$

where the equity return is earned over a short interval such as 1 month, and the interest rate is the 1-month Treasury bill rate known at the beginning of the month. For such small intervals of time, Equations (13.9) and (13.10) are indeed nearly equivalent. This is because, by definition, $r_e = \frac{1 + r_e(\$)}{1 + \pi(\$)} - 1 \approx r_e(\$) - \pi(\$)$. Moreover, $r_f = E\left[\frac{1 + i(\$)}{1 + \pi(\$)} - 1\right] \approx E[i(\$) - \pi(\$)]$. It is easy to see that the inflation rates cancel out of the equation.

Of course, the beta computation in the two equations is different, involving real returns in Equation (13.9) and nominal excess returns in Equation (13.10). Because equity returns are much more variable than inflation and interest rates, these differences are immaterial from a practical perspective.

International CAPMs (Advanced)

The conditions for the world CAPM to apply to all countries are rather stringent. With deviations from the parity conditions, theory suggests more complex models where inflation and exchange rate risks enter the expected return computation. Many models of international capital market equilibrium have been developed, but none has attained a dominant status.[3] Most models allow for currency risk premiums in one form or another.

---

[2]In Chapter 10, we derived that real interest rates are equalized across countries when PPP, uncovered interest rate parity, and the Fisher hypothesis hold.
[3]See Adler and Dumas (1983) for an early model.

An example of the most popular model in this class builds on the theories of Solnik (1974a) and Sercu (1980) and forms the counterpart to the nominal returns model in Equation (13.10):

$$E[r_j(\$) - i(\$)] = \beta_j E[r_w(\$) - i(\$)] + \sum_{k=1}^{K} \gamma_{j,k} E[s_k(t+1) - fp_k(t)] \qquad \textbf{(13.11)}$$

We assume that the dollar is the numeraire and that risk is measured for a U.S. investor.[4] The first term represents the standard world market risk; the other terms represent exchange rate risk, with s_k representing the rate of foreign currency appreciation and fp_k representing the forward premium on currency k. Exchange rates are thus measured as \$ per currency k. Recall that

$$E[s_k(t+1) - fp_k(t)] = E\left[\frac{S_k(t+1) - F_k(t)}{S_k(t)}\right],$$

which is the expected excess dollar return to a long forward market position in currency k.

The $\gamma_{j,k}$'s in Equation (13.11) measures the exposures of the j-th firm's returns to the various exchange rate risks. For example, an exporter with many unhedged foreign currency receivables may exhibit positive γ. That is, if these currencies appreciate substantially, the firm's return will be high as well. Of course, if uncovered interest rate parity holds, this model collapses to the world CAPM. To compute the cost of capital in such a setting, we must run a multivariate regression of excess returns for security j onto the world market return and various relevant currency returns. In practice, people use only a few major currencies or even a currency basket.

It is not clear whether the **international CAPM** is a better model than the world CAPM. Research by Dumas and Solnik (1995) and Zhang (2006) suggests that exchange rate risk is priced and that adding exchange rate factors to cost of capital computations is important. Other studies, such as that by Griffin and Stulz (2001), cast doubt on this conclusion. Because of the continuing academic controversy and the scant use of such models in practical capital budgeting situations, we will not discuss them further.

13.5 THE CAPM IN PRACTICE

As Chapter 15 explains in detail, firms need expected returns on their equity to get appropriate discount rates when doing capital budgeting. These expected returns represent what investors demand as compensation for giving capital to the firm. The CAPM delivers such discount rates. Let's be very concrete about how to compute the cost of equity capital.

A Recipe for the Cost of Equity Capital

Recall the CAPM equation for security j:

$$E(r_j) = r_f + \beta_{jm}[E(r_m) - r_f] \qquad \textbf{(13.12)}$$

---

[4]One problem with the many variants of the international CAPM, including the one presented here, is that the exact outcome of the cost-of-capital computation may depend on the numeraire currency.

where $\beta_{jm} = \dfrac{\text{Cov}(r_j, r_m)}{\text{Var}(r_m)}$. You find the expected nominal return on security j by taking these steps:

Step 1. Get data on the market portfolio return, the equity returns on security j, and the T-bill interest rate, r_f.

Step 2. Determine the market risk premium, $[E(r_m) - r_f]$. The market risk premium is the expected excess return on a portfolio that approximates the market portfolio.

Step 3. Obtain an estimate of β_{jm}.

Step 4. Compute the expected return on security j from Equation (13.12).

This recipe reveals three problems in applying the CAPM to a practical capital budgeting situation: the choice of a benchmark (how to measure the market portfolio), the estimation of beta, and the determination of the risk premium on the market portfolio. We discuss each in turn.

The Benchmark Problem

The Market Portfolio

One problem that has plagued the CAPM since its early development is what portfolio to use as the market portfolio.[5] The theoretically correct value of the return on the market portfolio is the value-weighted return on all assets that are available for investors to purchase. If the return on the market portfolio is measured in dollars, it would consequently include the dollar-denominated returns on the equities of all the corporations of the different countries of the world, the dollar-denominated returns on the bonds of all the corporations and the governments of these countries, and the dollar-denominated returns on real estate and assets such as gold and land.

No one has ever attempted to use this version of the theory because its data requirements are too stringent. We simply do not have all the data. More importantly, though, financial markets are too imperfect to allow us to think that highly illiquid assets, such as real estate, would be bought and sold like stocks and bonds. Because data on the returns on corporate and government bonds in many countries are also difficult to obtain, in practice, people use the CAPM as if it were a theory that relates individual equity rates of return to a market portfolio composed of only equities.

World Market Proxies

When the CAPM is applied for a particular company's project, the proxy for the market portfolio should in theory represent the well-diversified portfolio that the firm's investors are holding. In practice, many U.S. companies use the U.S. stock market index as the market portfolio. With the increasing globalization of investors' portfolios (see Section 13.6), a world market index is becoming more and more appropriate. Although the availability of data on a world market index is imperfect, there are reasonable proxies available, such as the Morgan Stanley Capital International (MSCI) Index and the Financial Times Actuaries (FTA) Index.

Getting the Benchmark Wrong

We would like to know how large a mistake is made quantitatively if we use a domestic, country-specific CAPM when the assets of the country are actually priced by investors with a world CAPM. If the assets of this country are actually priced internationally, the expected return on asset j, $E[r_j]$, satisfies the world CAPM in Equation (13.12), where r_m is the return on the world market portfolio and β_{jm} is the beta of the return on asset j with respect to the world

---

[5]This issue is often called the "Roll critique" because Roll (1977) was the first to write about the problems involved in testing the CAPM. Roll argued that statistical rejections of the theory could be incorrect if a statistician did not observe the true market portfolio.

market return. We denote this "true" expected return or cost of equity capital by COE_j^{TR}. Now, suppose we postulate incorrectly that the expected return on asset j is determined by the covariance of the return on asset j with the return on the home market portfolio, r_h, as in the following version of a domestic CAPM:

$$E(r_j) = r_f + \beta_{jh} \left[E(r_h) - r_f \right] \tag{13.13}$$

Denote the cost of equity capital number resulting from this computation by COE_j^{FA}.

To compute the error in using Equation (13.13) rather than Equation (13.12), we first compute the correct expected return on the home market portfolio. The return on the home-country market portfolio is the value-weighted return on the individual assets in the country, and hence, it will also satisfy the world CAPM, as in Equation (13.12):

$$E(r_h) = r_f + \beta_{hm} \left[E(r_m) - r_f \right] \tag{13.14}$$

Using Equations (13.12) to (13.14), we can investigate the difference between the two costs of equity capital:

$$
\begin{aligned}
COE_j^{FA} - COE_j^{TR} &= \beta_{jh}\left[E(r_h) - r_f \right] - \beta_{jm}\left[E(r_m) - r_f \right] \\
&= (\beta_{jh}\beta_{hm} - \beta_{jm})\left[E(r_m) - r_f \right]
\end{aligned}
$$

Thus, the expected return on asset j will be correct if $\beta_{jm} = \beta_{jh}\beta_{hm}$. Example 13.5 provides some insight into when this expression is likely to be right and how badly things go if it is wrong.

Example 13.5   The Nestlé Cost of Equity Capital

Stulz (1995) applies the previous analysis to derive two estimates of the expected return for the Swiss company Nestlé. Stulz estimates the beta of the Swiss franc return on Nestlé with respect to the Swiss franc return on the Swiss market portfolio (β_{jh}) to be 0.885. The beta of the Swiss franc return on Nestlé with respect to the Swiss franc return on the world market portfolio (β_{jm}) using the FTA world market index is 0.585. The beta of the Swiss franc return on the Swiss market portfolio with respect to the Swiss franc return on the world market portfolio (β_{hm}) is 0.737. Hence, the pricing error in beta from using the domestic CAPM rather than the world CAPM is

$$\beta_{jh}\beta_{hm} - \beta_{jm} = (0.885 \times 0.737) - 0.585 = 0.067$$

Stulz uses an expected excess return on the world market portfolio $[E(r_m) - r_f]$ of 6.22%, in which case the error for Nestlé from using a domestic CAPM instead of the global CAPM is $0.067 \times 6.22\% = 0.42\%$.

Thus, using local pricing instead of global pricing implies an expected return for Nestlé that is 0.42% higher than it should be. If Nestlé is priced in the world market and not the local market, its required expected return should be the risk-free return on Swiss franc bonds plus a risk premium equal to the beta with the world market portfolio multiplied by the excess return on the world market portfolio, $0.585 \times 6.22\% = 3.64\%$. If Nestlé is priced in the local market, its required expected return would be the risk-free return on Swiss franc bonds plus a risk premium equal to $3.64\% + 0.42\% = 4.06\%$.

This example demonstrates that, at least for Nestlé, the error from using a domestic CAPM when the world CAPM is appropriate does not seem to be too big. Estimation error in the betas and the mean return on the world market portfolio could easily lead one to consider discount rates that are in this range when doing sensitivity analysis. In a similar exercise, Harris et al. (2003) show that the world CAPM and the domestic CAPM led to similar cost-of-capital estimates for S&P 500 firms.

Exhibit 13.12 Estimating Beta

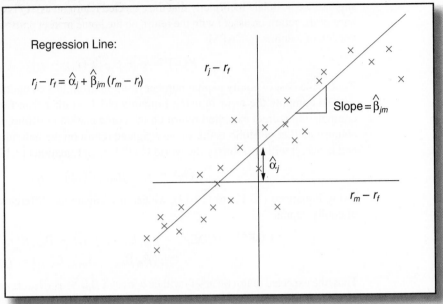

Regression Line:

$$r_j - r_f = \hat{\alpha}_j + \hat{\beta}_{jm}(r_m - r_f)$$

$r_j - r_f$

Slope $= \hat{\beta}_{jm}$

$\hat{\alpha}_j$

$r_m - r_f$

Note: The CAPM implies $\hat{\alpha}_i = 0$. The x's represent a combination of the excess return on the j-th asset and the excess return on the market portfolio.

Beta Estimation

Recall that the beta for security j is given by $\beta_j = \dfrac{\text{Cov}[r_j, r_m]}{\text{Var}[r_m]}$. Astute readers will recognize that β_j is the regression coefficient from regressing $r_j - r_f$ onto $r_m - r_f$ (see the appendix to Chapter 7). Suppose you have data on excess returns for security j, $r_j^e(t)$, and for the market, $r_m^e(t)$. You obtain β_j by running a regression:

$$r_j^e(t) = \alpha_j + \beta_j r_m^e(t) + \varepsilon_j(t)$$

where $\varepsilon_j(t)$ is the error term in the regression. Exhibit 13.12 demonstrates graphically what we would find in a regression framework.

Many firms use the CAPM in their capital budgeting analyses. They can estimate the beta of a firm directly by choosing a portfolio to represent the market portfolio that is held by their investors and run the regression just described. Firms such as Barra and Value Line do the regressions and sell the information. Typically, the regression analysis uses only 60 months of data to accommodate the possibility that the risk profiles of companies change over time.

Estimating a beta using a regression is often imprecise because a firm's returns exhibit considerable idiosyncratic volatility. That is, much of the variation in a firm's return is driven by firm-specific events. This idiosyncratic volatility reduces the fit of the regression and increases the standard errors of the estimates. Therefore, some beta providers (such as Bank of America–Merrill Lynch) shrink the estimates toward 1, which is the value we would expect without other information. Another approach is to use industry portfolios. If firms in the same industry have about the same systematic risk, their betas will be about the same as well. A portfolio of firms diversifies away a lot of idiosyncratic risk and is consequently much less variable than an individual firm's stock returns. Therefore, beta estimates from industry portfolios are more precise.

Example 13.6 Comparing Firm and Industry Betas

Yahoo's financial Web site (www.finance.yahoo.com) provides estimates of betas for free. Let's compare beta estimates obtained from there on March 21, 2011, with beta estimates obtained from Aswath Damodaran's Web site at New York University (http://pages.stern.nyu.edu/~adamodar/New_Home_Page/datafile/Betas.html) for industry portfolios. The Yahoo estimates use 5 years of individual stock returns on a monthly basis, whereas the industry estimates also use 5 years of data, but at a weekly frequency:

Firm	Yahoo Beta	Industry	Industry Beta
Ford	2.52	Automotive	1.50
McDonald's	0.40	Restaurants	1.33
Wells Fargo	1.51	Banks	0.75
Microsoft	0.95	Software	1.06
Merck	0.57	Drugs	1.11

The individual stock betas vary between 0.40 (McDonald's) and 2.52 (Ford), whereas the industry estimates are much closer to 1.0.

There are good reasons for some companies to have betas that deviate from the industry average. For instance, they may have more or less financial leverage (debt value relative to equity value). If equity holders have to pay off bondholders before laying claim to the firm's assets, their claims are riskier. Nevertheless, betas of only 0.40 for McDonald's and 2.52 for Ford are almost surely due to unusual idiosyncratic movements of the firm's stock prices over the sample period and are unlikely to give rise to reliable cost-of-capital estimates. A firm's beta also changes over time as its business changes. Microsoft used to be a growth company with a very high beta. As it has become more mature with a more steady cash flow, its beta has also converged to 1.

The Risk Premium on the Market

Historical Estimates

It is surprising how little consensus there is about the magnitude of the **equity risk premium**.[6] To estimate the risk premium, the first logical step is to look at history. Because stock returns are so volatile, it is important to take a long-run perspective. Dimson et al. (2007) collected 106 years' worth of data, and Exhibit 13.13 reproduces the historical risk premiums for 17 countries. These equity premiums vary between 4.51% for Denmark and 10.46% for Italy. The estimate for the United States is 7.41%.

Caveats

Historical estimates, even for long samples, are still prone to large sampling errors, and different subperiods give very different answers. The recent global financial crisis illustrates how sensitive risk premium estimates can be. Many stock markets decreased by 40% or more in 2008. Even with 100 years of data, such dramatic outcome would lower the average by approximately 40 basis points. When shorter time periods are relied on, the effect would be even more dramatic.

---

[6]A direct perspective on this issue can be gleaned from Ivo Welch's survey of the opinions of professional economists. Welch's 2009 survey puts the average estimate at 6%.

Exhibit 13.13 Equity Risk Premiums Around the World

Country	Arithmetic Mean	Standard Deviation
Australia	8.49	17.00
Belgium	4.99	23.06
Canada	5.88	16.71
Denmark	4.51	19.85
France	9.27	24.19
Germany[a]	9.07	33.49
Ireland	5.98	20.33
Italy	10.46	32.09
Japan	9.84	27.82
Netherlands	6.61	22.36
Norway	5.70	25.90
South Africa	8.25	22.09
Spain	5.46	21.45
Sweden	7.98	22.09
Switzerland	5.29	18.79
United Kingdom	6.14	19.84
United States	7.41	19.64
Average	**7.14**	**22.75**
World, excluding United States	**5.93**	**19.33**
World	**6.07**	**16.65**

Notes: Data from Dimson, Marsh, and Staunton (2006). The mean column reports the average return on equity in percentage per annum over and above a risk-free return for the period 1900 to 2005. The standard deviation column reports the annual standard deviation of these excess returns.

[a]Germany values omit 1922 to 1923.

Research has argued for smaller premiums going forward, even before the crisis. Brown et al. (1995) note that the equity markets of various countries have periodically closed or failed outright. If investors thought that the market might actually fail, but it did not, then the average return over a long period would be abnormally high and not a good estimate of the expected *ex ante* return. As another example, Fama and French (2002) argue that the high average realized equity returns post-World War II are greater than what was expected over the past 50 years because the *ex post* returns include "large unexpected capital gains" caused by a decline in discount rates. Claus and Thomas (2001) use analysts' forecasts to argue that the equity premium should be 3%, which is less than half the historical average.

It is certainly possible that risk premiums have permanently declined. Investing in the stock market was traditionally difficult, costly, and limited to a select few, but now better technology, improved communication, an efficient mutual fund industry, and 401(k) legislation have increased stock market participation to close to 50% of the U.S. populace. Broadening the base of equity holders spreads risks and should decrease the risk premium. A decline in the risk premium produces a capital gain in stocks, but these high past returns signal future lower expected returns. Lettau et al. (2008) ascribe a decrease in discount rates to a reduction in macroeconomic risk, as measured by the volatility of consumption and output growth, witnessed in the 1980s and 1990s (the so-called Great Moderation). However, although the 2007 to 2010 economic crisis surely implied much lower returns on equities, it also signaled the end of the Great Moderation. Given all of this, substantial uncertainty about a correct value for the risk premium remains. We propose to use an equity premium between 4% and 7%. In Chapter 15, we will use 5.5% as our point estimate.

The Need for Sensitivity Analysis

The imprecision in estimates of the equity premium combined with imprecision in the estimates of betas means that costs of equity capital are difficult to measure. In light of these difficulties, conducting **sensitivity analysis** when estimating the cost of equity capital is a good idea. Considering a range of values that are $\pm 2\%$ around the estimates of the cost of capital seems appropriate.

13.6 INTEGRATED VERSUS SEGMENTED MARKETS

In this section, we first discuss investing in emerging markets and the critical role investment barriers play. We then discuss how integrated versus segmented markets affect a company's cost of capital. We end the section by describing the phenomenon of home bias.

Investing in Emerging Markets

Exhibit 13.14 reports characteristics of annualized emerging market equity returns in dollars for the period from 1988 to 2010. The average returns vary between 5.78% for Jordan to a stellar 34.00% for Brazil. However, emerging market returns are very volatile, with most of volatilities exceeding 30%. Turkey's volatility is a whopping 59%. Nevertheless, the volatility of an index of emerging market returns measured in dollars is only 24%, which is about the same magnitude as that experienced by a developed country such as Japan.

The reduced volatility of the index reflects the low correlations across the emerging markets and the substantial benefits of diversification. The last four columns of Exhibit 13.14

Exhibit 13.14 Average Returns and Volatilities in Emerging Markets

	Average Market Return	Volatility	Correlation with U.S. Returns	Correlation with Japanese Returns	Correlation with U.K. Returns	Correlation with German Returns
Argentina	31.07	55.06	0.29	0.08	0.20	0.19
Brazil	34.00	52.77	0.40	0.29	0.35	0.32
Chile	21.85	24.61	0.45	0.20	0.36	0.35
China	6.93	37.32	0.47	0.24	0.43	0.40
Colombia	23.36	32.72	0.31	0.22	0.36	0.35
Czech Republic	18.26	29.73	0.41	0.32	0.49	0.51
Egypt	23.30	33.53	0.35	0.31	0.37	0.36
Hungary	22.23	38.27	0.60	0.36	0.61	0.61
India	16.12	31.29	0.42	0.34	0.42	0.44
Indonesia	24.32	52.42	0.33	0.19	0.24	0.30
Israel	10.60	24.61	0.54	0.25	0.48	0.52
Jordan	5.78	18.74	0.19	0.15	0.20	0.16
Korea	14.54	38.94	0.43	0.49	0.39	0.34
Malaysia	13.19	29.56	0.36	0.28	0.37	0.37
Mexico	25.32	32.19	0.57	0.32	0.42	0.43
Morocco	14.73	19.59	0.14	0.16	0.25	0.25
Pakistan	13.12	39.33	0.13	0.03	0.18	0.12
Peru	24.98	33.13	0.36	0.37	0.38	0.40
Philippines	12.75	32.20	0.41	0.25	0.32	0.34
Poland	26.31	50.49	0.43	0.35	0.43	0.43
Russia	31.62	57.17	0.48	0.38	0.49	0.37
South Africa	16.61	27.96	0.55	0.53	0.58	0.58
Sri Lanka	15.54	37.99	0.18	0.21	0.28	0.17
Taiwan	13.14	37.44	0.36	0.28	0.28	0.37
Thailand	15.90	38.96	0.46	0.36	0.37	0.39
Turkey	29.07	58.93	0.33	0.19	0.31	0.38
EM Index	16.14	24.21	0.66	0.47	0.59	0.59

Notes: For most emerging markets, the monthly data run from January 1988 to August 2010. All returns are in U.S. dollars. The last line reports characteristics for returns on the Emerging Market Index, a value-weighted average of all 26 country indexes.

report the correlations of emerging market returns with the stock returns of the United States, Japan, the United Kingdom, and Germany. The correlations are generally lower than the correlations among developed countries, but there is lots of variation. The correlations vary between 0.08 for Argentina and Japan, and 0.61 for Hungary with the United Kingdom and Germany. The lowest correlations are typically observed with Japan, with the exception of Korea, which is more highly correlated with its close neighbor than with the other developed markets.

Such low correlations should make it possible to construct low-risk portfolios. Therefore, it is not surprising that early studies showed significant diversification benefits for emerging market investments. However, these studies used market indexes compiled by the International Finance Corporation (IFC) that generally ignored the high transaction costs, low liquidity, and investment constraints associated with emerging market investments. More generally, older data may no longer be relevant given that many emerging markets imposed severe investment restrictions on foreign investors in the early 1990s. For example, in Korea, most stocks were subject to strict foreign ownership restrictions (foreign ownership was limited to 10% of market capitalization for most stocks).

Research by Bekaert and Urias (1996, 1999) showed that the returns cited in the early diversification studies using market index data could not actually be realized by foreign investors. To do so, they examined the diversification benefits U.S. investors enjoyed through investing in a variety of actually available investment vehicles for emerging markets, such as closed-end funds, ADRs, and open-end funds. These assets are easily accessible to retail investors, and investment costs are comparable to the investment costs for U.S.–traded stocks. Bekaert and Urias found that investors give up a substantial part of the diversification benefits by holding these investment vehicles relative to holding the indices.[7]

These results suggest that **investment barriers** may prevent the diversification benefits of emerging markets from being fully realized. They also make it unlikely that emerging markets satisfy the strong assumptions underlying the CAPM. In particular, emerging markets may not be completely integrated with world capital markets, making the world CAPM the wrong model to use. We now clarify the crucial distinction between integrated and segmented markets.

The Cost of Capital in Integrated and Segmented Markets

Markets are integrated when assets of identical risk command the same expected return, irrespective of their domicile. The governmental interferences with free capital markets in emerging markets can prevent market integration and effectively segment the capital markets of a country from the world capital market. If foreign investors are taxed or otherwise prohibited from holding the equities of a country, then that country's assets are not part of the world market portfolio, and that country is said to be segmented from international capital markets.

The implications of segmentation for determining the cost of capital are important. Suppose we want to figure out the expected return on the Pakistani stock market. If the Pakistani stock market is integrated with world capital markets, we can simply use the world CAPM and the world market return as the benchmark portfolio. However, such an exercise would yield a very low expected return for Pakistan because the low correlation Pakistan displays with the world market translates into a low beta. Whereas this is the right computation to make for a foreign multinational corporation (MNC) investing in Pakistan, it yields a poor estimate of the true expected market return for local investors when the market is segmented.

Harvey (1995) shows that the world CAPM provides a poor description of emerging market returns in general and that the domestic CAPM fares much better. Because the Pakistani market is segmented, all securities will be priced according to their correlation

---

[7]The reduction in benefits is only partially due to investment barriers being priced in. For open-end funds, active investment management may cause a reduction in diversification benefits. Didier et al. (2010) demonstrate that mutual fund managers tend to hold concentrated portfolios that hamper full international diversification.

with the Pakistani market portfolio, but Pakistani investors will not be able to diversify the risk of the Pakistani market. Therefore, the expected return on the Pakistani market will be a function of its own volatility. This follows from aggregating the CAPM to the market level, as in Equation (13.7):

$$E[r_j] = r_f + \beta_j E[r_{\text{pak}} - r_f] \tag{13.15}$$

for every j security in Pakistan, where r_{pak} is the return on the Pakistani market. We know that the β_j is the covariance of security j with the market portfolio; hence, we can rewrite Equation (13.15) as

$$E[r_j] = r_f + \text{Cov}(r_j, r_{\text{pak}}) \frac{E[r_{\text{pak}} - r_f]}{\text{Var}(r_{\text{pak}})}$$

The expected excess return on the market portfolio divided by its variance is called the price of covariance risk. If investors hold only equities, Equation (13.8) shows that this price of risk equals the average risk aversion of the investors in Pakistan. Let's denote this by A_{pak}. Consequently, $E[r_j] = r_f + A_{\text{pak}} \text{Cov}(r_j, r_{\text{pak}})$, and aggregating over all securities in Pakistan,

$$E[r_{\text{pak}}] = r_f + A_{\text{pak}} \text{Var}(r_{\text{pak}})$$

Therefore, in **segmented markets**, expected and, hence, average returns should be related to the variance of returns rather than to the covariance with the world market return.

Example 13.7 The Expected Return in Pakistan

From data since 2000 on Pakistani stock returns, we determine that its world market beta is 0.4265. Given a risk-free rate of 5% and a world market equity premium of 5%, full integration dictates an expected return for the Pakistani market of

$$5\% + 0.4265 \times 5\% = 7.13\%$$

While some foreign investors may find this cost-of-capital estimate low, most of the risk associated with investing in Pakistan may indeed be political in nature and idiosyncratic to Pakistan. Thus, it would not represent systematic risk.

However, if Pakistan is truly segmented, the local expected return depends on the local market volatility, which stands at 39.32% in dollar terms (see Exhibit 13.14). Suppose the average risk aversion in Pakistan is 2.0. Under a domestic CAPM for Pakistan, the expected return on the Pakistani market is

$$E[r_{\text{pak}}] = 5\% + 2.0 \, (0.3932)^2 = 35.92\%$$

Clearly, the cost-of-capital estimates from the domestic CAPM and the world CAPM are very different. The fact that the domestic CAPM expected return is so unrealistically high may suggest that the Pakistani market is not fully segmented and that part of its variability is diversifiable.

Equity Market Liberalizations

Equity market liberalizations allow inward and outward foreign equity investment. The equity market liberalizations that took place in the late 1980s and early 1990s in many emerging markets form a nice laboratory to investigate the effects of potential integration into global capital markets.

If liberalization brings about integration with the global capital market, and if the world CAPM holds, what do we expect to happen? Suppose that the country is completely segmented from world capital markets before the liberalization. In this case, it is possible for the real interest rate in the country to be quite a bit higher than the world real interest rate. Also, the risk premiums associated with the equities in that country will be dictated by the variance of the return on that country's market portfolio. As we saw in Example 13.7, these risk premiums may be quite high.

Now, suppose the country unexpectedly opens its capital markets to the world economy. Two things will happen: First, the real interest rate in the country should fall dramatically because the country's residents are now free to borrow and lend internationally, and there is additional foreign supply of capital.[8] Second, the equities of the country will now be priced based on their covariances with the return on the world market portfolio, which are likely to be much smaller than the variance of the local market. Both of these effects will reduce the discount rate on the country's assets.

A big reduction in the discount rate, of course, causes the price of an asset to rise dramatically, which provides a big rate of return to the investors holding these assets. Simply put, foreign investors will bid up the prices of local stocks in an effort to diversify their portfolios, while all investors will shun inefficient sectors.[9] Thus, equity prices should rise substantially (as expected returns decrease) when a market moves from a segmented to an integrated state.

When a market is opened to international investors, though, the country's assets may become more sensitive to world events. In other words, their covariances with the rest of the world's assets may increase. Even with this effect, it is likely that these covariances will remain much smaller than the variance of the local market. The data bear out the theory. Studies by Kim and Singal (2000), Henry (2000), Bekaert and Harvey (2000), and others show that equity market liberalizations were accompanied by positive returns to integration as foreign investors bid up local prices. Postliberalization returns, in contrast, were lower on average, as the theory predicts. While the exact estimates differ somewhat, liberalization causes the cost of capital to decline by about 1%.

An interesting parallel occurs with respect to the price of a firm's shares following the issuance of an ADR. An ADR issued by a company headquartered in a country with investment restrictions can be viewed as a sort of liberalization of investment. For example, when Chile had repatriation restrictions in place, it lifted the restrictions for those companies listing their shares overseas to allow cross-market arbitrage. When an ADR is announced, we therefore expect positive announcement returns (e.g., relative to a similar firm not introducing an ADR) and lower expected returns after the liberalization. Several studies demonstrate that this effect is typically larger than 1%, and the studies find lower costs of capital after the ADR issuance. Of course, as we discussed in Chapter 12, there are many reasons, apart from liberalization, that ADR issues may result in a positive effect on the price of equity shares.

Many studies, as surveyed in Bekaert and Harvey (2003), have investigated the effects of liberalizations on other return characteristics. First, there is no significant impact on the volatility of market returns. Indeed, it is not obvious from finance theory that volatility should increase or decrease when markets are opened to foreign investment. On the one hand, markets may become informationally more efficient, leading to higher volatility as prices quickly react to relevant information, or hot speculative capital may induce excess volatility. On the other hand, in the preliberalized market, there may be large swings from fundamental values, leading to higher volatility. In the long run, the gradual development and diversification of

---

[8]It is conceivable that before the liberalization, the government may have kept interest rates artificially low—for instance, through interest rate ceilings—in which case, the interest rate may rise upon liberalization.
[9]A more formal analysis can be found in Bekaert and Harvey (2003), which builds on work by Errunza and Losq (1985).

the market should lead to lower volatility. Second, the correlation of the return and its beta with the world market increases after equity market liberalizations, and for some countries, the increase is dramatic. This is also consistent with these liberalizing emerging markets becoming more integrated with world capital markets.

Segmentation and Integration over Time

Although the empirical studies on the financial effects of equity market liberalizations confirm the intuition predicted by the simple CAPM, this does not mean that we are now living in a globally integrated capital market. In fact, using official regulatory reforms to measure liberalization is fraught with difficulties because it is difficult to know what effectively segments a market from the global capital market. There are three different kinds of barriers. The first are legal barriers, such as foreign ownership restrictions and taxes on foreign investments. An additional complication here is that the liberalization process is typically a complex and gradual one. It took Korea almost 10 years between 1991 and 2000 to gradually remove its foreign ownership restrictions. The second are indirect barriers arising from differences in available information, accounting standards, and investor protection. The third are emerging-market-specific risks (EMSRs) that discourage foreign investment. EMSRs include liquidity risk, political risk, economic policy risk, and perhaps currency risk. In general, indirect barriers and EMSRs may make institutional investors in developed countries reluctant to invest in emerging markets and segment them from the world market.

Finally, regulatory restrictions might not have posed a barrier prior to liberalization because canny investors often find ways to circumvent them. Alternatively, there may be legal, indirect ways to access local equity markets, such as through country funds or ADRs. The Korea Fund, trading on the NYSE, is a good example; it was launched in 1986, well before the liberalization of the Korean equity market. In short, determining whether a market is segmented, integrated, or something in between is far from easy.

A Model of Time-Varying Market Integration

Given the imperfections posed by official regulatory reform dates, researchers have come up with a variety of models to determine when and to what extent markets are integrated. For example, Bekaert and Harvey (1995) build on the CAPM model to measure the degree of market integration. In **integrated markets**, the covariance with the world market should determine the expected return on the domestic market. However, if the market is truly segmented, the variance of the return on the domestic market should affect the domestic expected return. Bekaert and Harvey apply an econometric framework, which allows the degree of a country's integration with the world market to vary over time, directly to equity return data. They find that the degree of equity market integration seems to vary for all countries in the sample, but variation in the integration measure does not always coincide with capital market reforms. For example, consider the market rate of return in Greece, which is completely open to foreign investors. The market return was more sensitive to the variance of the return on the Greek market in some periods than to the covariance between the return on the Greek market and the return on the world market portfolio. In contrast, Mexico has had rather strong legal restrictions on foreign investment, which would lead us to think that the variance of Mexico's stock market ought to be important when it comes to determining its expected return. But the analysis implies that Mexico is actually quite integrated with the world market. Consistent with this analysis, Exhibit 13.14 shows that Mexican equity returns have a 57% correlation with U.S. returns, whereas we already discussed the low correlation of Greek returns with other developed markets.

Bekaert et al. (2011) follow a different approach. They compare the valuation of industry portfolios in different countries with the valuation of the same industry globally by computing earnings yields (total earnings divided by market capitalization). Under some assumptions, industry earnings yields in different countries converge toward the global earnings yields when markets are economically and financially integrated. They take the market capitalization weighted average of these earnings yields differentials for various industry portfolios to arrive at a "segmentation measure" for each country, which essentially measures the absolute difference in earnings yields with the global yield. For developed countries, these average yield differentials are 2% for 2001 to 2005, which could be generated through noise and measurement error in a fully integrated market. However, for emerging markets, these differentials were, on average, 4.3%, suggesting segmentation. Bekaert et al. also document considerable convergence of earnings yields over time and demonstrate that, apart from the regulatory liberalization process, indirect barriers (such as the quality of the regulatory and legal framework) and emerging-market-specific risks (such as the liquidity in the stock markets) play an important role in explaining variation across countries and across time in the degree of segmentation.

The Practical Implications of Segmentation and Time-Varying Integration

As a practical matter, when international managers choose a discount rate for the all-equity cash flows of a project, they must rely on a healthy dose of economic intuition and must understand the meaning of historical statistics. Let's discuss two real-world examples.[10] The first involves a Mexican company and a Swiss company bidding for the Indonesian firm PT Semen Gresik in July 1998.

Indonesia liberalized in September 1990, and PT Semen Gresik had been publicly traded for some time prior to that. In valuing PT Semen Gresik in 1998, you would have to determine an appropriate discount rate. Will any of the historical return data be of use to you? Certainly, the data prior to 1990 are worthless. The historical average rate of return will reflect both the high risk premium typical for securities in segmented countries and the one-time capital gain that occurred when Indonesia opened its international capital market.

What should you do? You should start by asking yourself what your shareholders demand as a domestic currency return if they were to invest in this project directly. If your typical shareholder is thought to be well diversified internationally, then you can attempt to determine how the domestic currency return on this foreign asset will covary with the domestic currency return on the world market portfolio. This will lead you to a domestic currency discount rate. Because PT Semen Gresik is in the cement business, the bidders could obtain a first indication by using a portfolio of either Mexican or Swiss building firms to compute an appropriate discount rate. While these firms may correctly reflect the systematic risk of globally integrated cement firms, they are not likely fully representative of the cement business in Indonesia, even after liberalization. Therefore, the beta of PT Semen Gresik's returns with respect to the world market calculated with post-1990 data should likely enter the computations as well.

Now consider the Westmore Coal Company, an actual U.S.–based firm that intended to invest $540 million in an electric power project located in Zhangze, China, in 1994. Not only were there no comparable publicly traded projects from which to compute betas, but China was a fully segmented country! As Exhibit 13.14 shows, local market volatility was very high, so the domestic discount rate would have been high, too. However, because Westmore Coal's shareholders were likely to be internationally diversified, the world CAPM should have been used. Because no data are available, the amount of risk premium that must be added to the risk-free rate becomes a business judgment. The equity risk premium should be based on the type of business that the project represents. If the business is highly cyclical and its profits are likely to covary with the return on a world market portfolio, you add more than the average risk premium. If, on the other hand, the business is highly idiosyncratic, then not

---

[10]Both examples are from Bodnar et al. (2003).

much of a risk premium may be warranted. In this case, it is likely that the power plant's cash flows in China show little correlation with the world market and that a low risk premium is called for. This may be counterintuitive because a project in China may appear risky. However, the additional risks are likely of a political nature and should be assessed separately from the project's systematic risk. We discuss political risk in Chapter 14.

Home Bias and Its Implications

Unlike what the CAPM predicts, investors in different countries are generally not very well internationally diversified. In other words, most of their portfolios have a strong home bias. **Home bias** means that British investors, for example, hold a disproportionately large share of British assets compared to the world market portfolio. Exhibit 13.15 documents home bias for equity portfolios using data from the International Monetary Fund (IMF).

The home bias in Exhibit 13.15 is measured in a "raw" and "normalized" form for 6 years between 1997 and 2005 and averaged, following Bekaert and Wang (2010). Raw

Exhibit 13.15 Characterizing Home Bias

	Raw Home Bias		Normalized Home Bias	
Least Home Biased	United States	0.386	Netherlands	0.468
	Netherlands	0.457	Norway	0.567
	Norway	0.565	Austria	0.574
	Austria	0.573	Denmark	0.630
	United Kingdom	0.626	Sweden	0.639
	Denmark	0.627	Belgium	0.664
	Sweden	0.633	New Zealand	0.687
	Belgium	0.659	Canada	0.689
	Canada	0.669	United Kingdom	0.689
	New Zealand	0.686	Argentina	0.720
	Singapore	0.717	Singapore	0.721
	Argentina	0.719	United States	0.727
	France	0.724	Finland	0.740
	Finland	0.736	France	0.757
	Italy	0.755	Italy	0.773
	Japan	0.792	Iceland	0.822
	Australia	0.814	Australia	0.829
	Iceland	0.821	Spain	0.852
	Spain	0.838	Portugal	0.876
	Portugal	0.874	Japan	0.896
	Israel	0.921	Israel	0.923
	Chile	0.957	Chile	0.960
	Venezuela	0.974	Venezuela	0.975
	Korea	0.976	Korea	0.985
	Malaysia	0.982	Malaysia	0.987
	Thailand	0.989	Thailand	0.991
Most Home Biased	Indonesia	0.997	Indonesia	0.998
Average by Group	Developed, excluding United States	0.698	Developed, excluding United States	0.715
	Emerging	0.939	Emerging	0.942
	America	0.741	America	0.814
	Europe	0.684	Europe	0.696
	Asia	0.910	Asia	0.929
	Euro zone	0.702	Euro zone	0.713

Note: Reproduced from Table 2 in Bekaert and Wang (2010).

home bias measures the difference between the portfolio share that each country invests in its own market (home market share) and the share of the country's market in the world market (world market benchmark). By this measure, the United States is by far the least home-biased market. However, this is largely true because the U.S. market represents a large fraction of the world market. The normalized home bias measure divides the raw measure by 1 – world market benchmark weight, which is nothing but the maximum bias that can occur. A fully home-biased country has a normalized measure of 1, whereas a country that invests in its own market consistent with its share in the world market has a home bias measure of zero.

Exhibit 13.15 delivers a few stark results. First, all around the world, people hold far less foreign securities than the world CAPM would dictate. Investors do not seem to take full advantage of the considerable benefits of international diversification. Second, the biases are large. Of 27 countries, only the Netherlands has a bias less than 50%. Third, the bias is much larger for emerging markets than for developed markets. This is particularly striking because the benefits of portfolio diversification are presumably larger for emerging market residents than for developed market residents, given how volatile their domestic stock markets tend to be.

Finally, it is generally known that the degree of home bias has substantially decreased over time. Cai and Warnock (2006) claim that the degree of home bias is overstated because institutional investors tend to overweight their domestic investments toward multinationals that have international exposure through their foreign operations and cash flows. Yet, even adjusting the numbers for this additional foreign exposure, home bias remains significant for most countries in the world, and it is something that is not well understood by financial economists. Let's see if Ante and Freedy can shed any light on the puzzle.

POINT–COUNTERPOINT

What Breeds Foreign Investment?

"Hmm, they are delicious," Ante sighed, while he devoured his fourth Belgian Leonidas chocolate in a row. Ante and Freedy were sitting in the salon, digesting what their father had just told them about their trust fund. Dad wanted to increase the trust's allocation to foreign equities from 15% to 30% and wondered whether Ante and Freedy knew why U.S. investors were often reluctant to invest in foreign equities, despite their obvious diversification benefits. Ante and Freedy had agreed to study the issue, and to help their thinking, they had brewed nice, frothy cappuccinos using a fancy Italian machine their father had imported.

"You know," argued Freedy, "I could think of a number of rational reasons why U.S. investors might want to be home biased. Foreign equities have currency risk and hence more volatility than U.S. equities. The U.S. market is the most efficient market in the world, and transaction costs here are lower than they are elsewhere. Plus, it is very difficult to obtain reliable accounting information on foreign companies."

"No way," mumbled Ante, while enjoying his fifth Leonidas. "These foreign equities simply are underperforming the U.S. equity market. Besides, I do not feel comfortable having our money invested in unfamiliar companies."

At this point, Suttle, who had quietly sneaked into the room when he smelled the coffee, could no longer keep quiet. "Hey, guys! I happen to have just read some articles about the home bias phenomenon. Let me fill you in. First, currency risk is not what is stopping U.S. investors from investing abroad. Because currency changes show little correlation with local equity markets, they add little to the volatility that U.S. investors face when investing in foreign equity markets. Moreover, currency volatility can be hedged. Second, arguing that the U.S. market outperforms foreign markets is short-sighted and not even true historically. Third, transaction costs may play a role, but in order to generate the observed portfolio proportions of U.S. investors, U.S. investors would have to think that the average returns on foreign stocks were 2% to 4% per annum less than the realized average returns on foreign assets. It may be that these figures represent U.S. investors' perceived transaction costs of foreign investing, but it is unlikely. Moreover, the huge volume of international capital flows is also inconsistent with the transaction costs story, as is the fact that foreign countries are home biased. Fourth, I do not like the information story: It is easy enough to obtain information on foreign companies or to set up or use local investment managers. However, it may be that the quality of the information and a poor regulatory framework in terms of investor protection and corporate governance keep out U.S. institutional investors. This may explain why foreign companies like to list ADRs and thus can be more easily included in institutional investors' portfolios."

Suttle continued, "Although these indirect barriers are clearly important, they cannot be the full story, given the cross-border flows and home biases in other countries. Clearly, direct barriers played a huge role, and many countries have only recently dismantled these barriers. In fact, there is a trend everywhere toward increased foreign holdings, so maybe investors are slowly adjusting toward rational asset allocation."

"Aha!" shouted Ante. "You do not really have a full, rational explanation for the phenomenon, do you, Suttle?"

"Well, you've got a point with that familiarity argument of yours," replied Suttle. "I just read a few articles that claim that U.S. investors even bias their domestic investments toward companies that are 'familiar' to them. One study showed that the ownership of the shares of regional telephone companies is dominated by people living in the area served by those companies. Another study showed that U.S. investment managers exhibit a strong preference for firms headquartered within a 500-mile radius of their offices."[11]

"Oh well, maybe people do not like foreign investments, but I will surely enjoy having another Italian coffee and Belgian chocolate," smirked Freedy.

Implications for Pricing

If investors are not fully internationally diversified, should we discard the world CAPM as the benchmark model? This is a difficult issue. However, it might not be necessary for every individual in the world to be fully internationally diversified for asset returns to be well described by a world CAPM. In fact, whereas it is true that emerging market returns do not look at all consistent with a world CAPM, the evidence against other stock markets is not strong. Harvey (1991) and Hodrick et al. (1999) show that a version of the CAPM in fact works well for most developed stock markets most of the time.

Time-Varying Correlations

The trend toward less home bias, and the move toward ever-increased integration, as investment barriers, both direct and indirect, are dismantled, should also increase the correlations across countries, making international diversification less viable. Exhibit 13.16 sheds some light on this issue. It reports correlations for Japan, Canada, the United Kingdom, France, and Italy with the United States for every decade since 1970 and for the past decade (until August 2010). Until 1999, the correlations increase steadily for all countries except Japan. However, for all countries, the correlations are substantially higher during 2000 to 2010 than they were previously.

---

[11]These studies are by Huberman (2001) and Coval and Moskowitz (1999), respectively.

Exhibit 13.16 Correlations Between Foreign and U.S. Equity Market Returns

	1970–1979	1980–1989	1990–1999	2000–2010	1970–2010
Canada	0.71	0.72	0.73	0.81	0.74
Japan	0.31	0.24	0.30	0.61	0.35
United Kingdom	0.45	0.56	0.58	0.85	0.57
France	0.40	0.44	0.55	0.85	0.56
Germany	0.29	0.36	0.51	0.84	0.76
Italy	0.17	0.24	0.32	0.66	0.36

Note: The data are from MSCI.

Whether the increases in correlations are due to increased market integration and, therefore, represent a permanent change is an important question. Because temporarily higher volatility in equity markets also tends to temporarily increase the correlations between markets, it is difficult to separate temporary from permanent correlation changes. The intuition for this fact is best understood if we consider two countries satisfying the world CAPM. As a consequence, part of the return variation in both countries is driven by the returns on the world market, and this joint exposure likely induces positive correlation between the returns on the two stock markets. Intuitively, if the world market movements became extremely variable, they would dominate all return variation in the two stocks, and the correlation would converge to 1. This is relevant for the numbers produced in Exhibit 13.16, as the world market volatility at the end of the 1990s, in the early 2000s, and again during the 2007 to 2010 financial crisis was indeed relatively high. A study by Bekaert et al. (2009) concludes that return correlations within Europe have permanently increased, but their tests do not reject the hypothesis that return correlations elsewhere have remained unchanged, once account is taken of temporary changes in volatility.

13.7 ALTERNATIVE COST-OF-CAPITAL MODELS

The Usefulness of the CAPM

Even though the CAPM is not without flaws, it is viewed as a reasonable model that can be used to estimate the required rates of return needed for capital budgeting. One reason is that it incorporates an important lesson about diversification: There is no evidence that firms whose returns have had high historical standard deviations have had high average returns. In fact, research by Ang et al. (2006, 2009) shows just the opposite: Stocks with high idiosyncratic standard deviations have had low average returns, both in the United States and 23 other countries.

When we consider the overall historical record, we conclude that the cost of equity capital should reflect a risk premium that compensates the firm's investors for the systematic risk present in the investment. Suppose, though, that the CAPM is wrong. In this case, it will either overstate or understate the market's required rates of return.

The Consequences of Using the Wrong Model

Managers who use the CAPM when it overstates the market's required rates of return will forgo some profitable projects with true positive net present value that should have been undertaken. Eventually, the stock market will discipline these conservative managers by viewing them as underperformers. Conversely, if the CAPM understates project risk premiums, managers using the CAPM will undertake some projects that are actually negative net present value, which will destroy shareholders' wealth. Now, the market will discipline these overly aggressive managers for their underperformance relative to what shareholders demand.

Given that the CAPM may be incorrect and that recent empirical tests have not been kind to the CAPM, is there an alternative model to compute the cost of capital? We now discuss two models that have been proposed as alternatives to the CAPM.

Factor Models and the Fama-French Model

A serious competitor to the CAPM is the **arbitrage pricing theory (APT)**, originally developed by Ross (1976).[12] The APT recognizes that the return on the market portfolio may not be the only potential source of systematic risks that affect the returns on equities. The APT postulates that other economy-wide factors can systematically affect the returns on a large number of securities. These factors might include news about inflation, interest rates, gross domestic product (GDP), or the unemployment rate. Changes in these factors affect future corporate profitability, and they may affect how investors view the riskiness of future cash flows. This, in turn, will affect how investors discount future uncertain cash flows.

When there are economy-wide factors that affect the returns on a large number of firms, the influences of these factors on the return to a well-diversified portfolio are still present. The influences of the factors cannot be diversified away. Consequently, the risk premiums on particular securities are determined by the sensitivities of their returns to the economy-wide factors and by the compensations that investors require because of the presence of each of these different risks. To determine these factor risk premiums, researchers construct factor-mimicking portfolios—portfolios that correlate very highly (ideally perfectly) with the economic factors. Because the APT is rarely used to compute costs of capital, we do not provide more details. However, over the last decade, a related factor model has gained prominence, following provocative research by Fama and French (1992).

The Value and the Small Firm Effects

In a 1992 paper, Fama and French questioned the ability of the traditional CAPM to explain the cross-section of stock returns in U.S. data. They found that the market value of a firm's market equity (ME), which is its price per share multiplied by the number of shares outstanding (or the firm's market capitalization), and the ratio of the accounting book value of a firm to its market value [book equity to market equity (BE/ME)] contribute significantly to the explanation of average stock returns.[13]

During their sample, average returns on firms with small market capitalizations were higher than could be explained by their betas with the market portfolio. Perhaps small firms suffer from a greater lack of communication between the firm's managers and its investors. This asymmetric information could lead investors to require higher rates of return from small firms. Firms that have high ratios of the book value of their equity to the market value of their equity (so-called value firms) also have higher average returns than can be explained by the CAPM and have outperformed growth stocks (stocks with a low BE/ME). Interestingly, these firms often suffer from financial distress. If financial distress tends to systematically occur when investors are more risk averse or face bad times, it may cause investors to demand a risk premium for bearing this risk.

Fama and French's findings are still the subject of great debate in the economic literature, and not everyone believes the results will hold up to further scrutiny. First, many mutual fund companies offer value funds and small-cap funds, which invest in high book-to-market

---

[12]For an introduction to the APT, see Chapter 11 of Ross et al. (2002).

[13]Although firms with higher betas tend to have higher average returns, Fama and French argue that the ability of beta to explain the cross-section of average stock returns is nil when the size of the firm's market equity and ratio of book equity to market equity are included as explanatory variables.

stocks and small-capitalization stocks, respectively. Hence, individual investors can easily diversify their portfolios along size and value characteristics. Second, Ang and Chen (2007) found little evidence of a value effect in a larger sample than the one used by Fama and French (1992), and several other authors have suggested that the size effect disappeared in the 1980s.[14]

The Fama-French Three-Factor Model (Advanced)

Based on their empirical findings, Fama and French (1995) developed a three-factor model to explain average equity returns. The first factor is the return on the value-weighted market portfolio in excess of the risk-free return, as in the CAPM. The second factor is the difference in the return on a portfolio of small firms and the return on a portfolio of big firms [small minus big (SMB)], in which the ratio of BE/ME is held constant in each portfolio. The third factor is the difference between the return on a portfolio of firms with high values of BE/ME and the return on a portfolio of firms with low values of BE/ME [high minus low (HML)], in which the size of firms is held constant in each portfolio. To find the sensitivities of a firm's equity return to the three factors, you merely run a regression, just as you do to find the beta in the CAPM. The difference is that now there are three explanatory variables instead of one. The average rates of return on the factor-mimicking portfolios can then be combined with the estimated sensitivities of the equity return to the returns on the factor-mimicking portfolios to provide an estimate of the required rate of return on the equity.

When Fama and French (1998) applied their model to international data,[15] they found that two factors—the return on the world market and a global version of the HML factor—sufficed to explain the cross-section of expected returns in 13 countries.

Example 13.8   The Cost of Equity Capital in the Fama-French Model

Suppose we want to estimate the cost of capital for a firm in Australia that has the same systematic risk as a portfolio of Australian stocks with high book-to-market levels. In Fama and French (1998), we find the following estimates:

	CAPM	TWO-FACTOR MODEL	
	Beta with Global Market	Beta with Global Market	Beta with HML Portfolio
Australian high book-to-market firms	0.84	0.90	0.59

If the current risk-free interest rate is 5%, and the world market equity risk premium is 5.93% (see Exhibit 13.13), from Equation (13.10), the required rate of return for the Australian firm from the CAPM is

$$r_{\text{AUS}} = 5\% + (0.84 \times 5.93\%) = 9.98\%$$

---

[14]To illustrate how divided the profession is on these issues, even the authors of this book disagree, with one of them arguing that there is a value effect to be explained and the other arguing that it is most likely statistical baloney. We have booked a meeting with Suttle Trooth to help us out. We will let you know the outcome in the next edition.

[15]It must be said that the empirical evidence against the CAPM was marginal at best in most countries, with the exception of the United States. Nevertheless, the new proposed model clearly improved the fit with the data.

We estimate the premium on the value factor-mimicking portfolio to be 3%. Therefore, the required equity rate of return implied by the Fama-French two-factor model is

$$r_{AUS} = 5\% + (0.90 \times 5.93\%) + (0.59 \times 3.00\%) = 12.11\%$$

Notice that the two estimates of the required rate of return on the stock are very different. This is true because value firms in Australia have historically provided higher average rates of return than the CAPM would imply. Although the Fama-French model has become quite popular, it remains an empirical model, not grounded in formal theory. With remaining doubts about the validity of the model and no good story for why the value effect would persist, the Fama-French model has not yet been widely adopted in practice.

13.8 SUMMARY

This chapter develops the theories and background necessary to determine the cost of equity capital in global financial markets. Its main points are the following:

1. To determine the international cost of equity capital, we must first determine how investors view risk in a global investments context.

2. When investing abroad, an investor must assess both the returns of the international asset in its local currency and variations in the value of the foreign currency relative to the investor's home currency.

3. The volatility of an international equity investment is mostly determined by the volatility of the local equity market. Although exchange rate changes are quite variable, they are nearly uncorrelated with local stock returns.

4. International diversification results in portfolios with risk levels much lower than what can be achieved with domestic diversification alone. The main reason is that the stock market returns of different countries are not very highly correlated with one another, despite the fact that correlations among them tend to increase during bear markets.

5. Using available data on the volatilities of different markets and the correlation among them, investors can compute a "hurdle rate" of return for foreign investments. The hurdle rate is the expected return for which a small investment in the foreign equity market, starting from an all-domestic portfolio, increases the Sharpe ratio for the portfolio.

6. Among the G7 countries, a U.S. investor can most easily improve her risk–return trade-off, as measured by the Sharpe ratio, by investing in Japan. Japan has a rather poor historical return record but features the lowest correlation with U.S. returns among G7 countries.

7. It has become easier over time to invest internationally while remaining "at home," through investment vehicles such as closed-end funds, open-end funds, ADRs, and ETFs.

8. A mean-variance investor likes high expected returns but dislikes portfolio variance. If only a risk-free asset and just one risky asset are available, she will invest more in the risky asset the lower her risk aversion, the higher the expected excess return, and the lower the variance of the risky asset.

9. The mean–standard deviation frontier collects portfolios that minimize the portfolio variance for each possible expected return. The mean-variance-efficient (MVE) portfolio is the one portfolio on the frontier that maximizes the Sharpe ratio and is hence optimal. This portfolio defines the capital allocation line, which determines how the investor mixes the risk-free asset with the optimal risky portfolio, depending on her preferences.

10. The capital asset pricing model (CAPM) states that under some simplifying assumptions, the MVE portfolio ought to be the market portfolio, which contains all securities in proportion to their market capitalization.

11. The CAPM implies that the expected return of any security equals the risk-free rate plus the beta of the security multiplied by the market risk premium. The beta of the security is the covariance of its return with the return on the market portfolio divided by the variance of the market portfolio return.

12. In an international setting, the relevant benchmark for the market portfolio should be the world market portfolio, giving rise to the world CAPM. The world CAPM ignores exchange rate risk.

13. In an international setting, investors in different countries evaluate real returns using different consumption baskets and view money market investments in other countries as risky because of exchange rate risk. Although it is possible to adjust the CAPM for these considerations, the resulting international CAPMs are rarely used in practice.

14. To use the CAPM to obtain a cost of capital, we must determine the betas, the market risk premium, and a risk-free rate. The risk-free rate is usually the Treasury bill rate. The beta is estimated from a regression of excess returns on the security in question onto excess returns on the world market portfolio. Sometimes, industry portfolios are used to reduce the sampling error in estimating the betas. The risk premium on the market portfolio is the subject of much controversy. An estimate of 4% to 7% is reasonable. In any case, any cost-of-capital estimation and project evaluation should be accompanied by a sensitivity analysis.

15. Emerging equity markets display relatively low correlations with the stock markets of developed countries. Many of the emerging markets underwent a liberalization process in the 1990s that made their stock markets fully or partially accessible to foreign investors.

16. Equity markets are integrated when assets of identical risk command the same expected return, irrespective of their domicile. The many investment barriers in place in emerging markets have effectively segmented them from the global capital market. The liberalization process, however, has led to increased asset prices, higher correlations with the world market, and lower expected returns in emerging markets.

17. The benchmark used in the cost-of-capital computation should reflect the composition of the portfolio of the investors in the company, even when the project takes place in a potentially segmented emerging market. Historical data in these emerging markets may not be very useful for a cost-of-capital analysis if the market is truly segmented or if it underwent a liberalization process that caused a structural break in the return data.

18. Even in the developed world, investors have not fully internationally diversified. Instead, their portfolios are heavily invested in their home markets. This phenomenon is known as home bias.

19. There has been a gradual increase in the correlations between the G7 countries, potentially reflecting increased economic and financial integration.

20. Whereas the CAPM is the dominant model to determine the cost of capital, Fama and French (1992, 1995, 1998) proposed an alternative factor model. In addition to the market portfolio, the Fama-French factors measure the exposure of a stock to a portfolio going long in small stocks and short in large stocks and the stock's exposure to a portfolio long in high book-to-market stocks (value stocks) and short in low book-to-market stocks (growth stocks). There is some weak empirical evidence that small stocks and value stocks have outperformed large stocks and growth stocks.

QUESTIONS

1. Is the volatility of the dollar return to an investment in the Japanese equity market the sum of the volatility of the Japanese equity market return in yen plus the volatility of dollar/yen exchange rate changes? Why or why not?

2. Why is the variance of a portfolio of internationally diversified stocks likely to be lower than the variance of a portfolio of U.S. stocks?

3. How can you increase the Sharpe ratio of a portfolio? What type of stocks would you have to add to it in order to do so?

4. Why is the hurdle rate in Section 13.2 lower for Japan than for Canada? Should U.S. investors still invest in Canada?

5. What is the mean–standard deviation frontier, and what is the mean-variance-efficient (MVE) portfolio?

6. What is the prediction of the CAPM with respect to optimal portfolio choice?

7. What is the prediction of the CAPM with respect to the expected return on any security?

8. What is the beta of a security?

9. Why might it be useful to estimate the beta for a stock from returns on stocks within its industry rather than from the stock itself?

10. What does it mean for an equity market to be integrated or segmented from the world capital market?

11. What would you expect to happen to the risk-free rate and equity returns when a segmented country opens its capital markets to foreign investment?

12. What accounts for the home bias phenomenon?

13. Suppose AZT is a small value stock and that you use both the CAPM and the Fama-French model to compute its cost of capital. Under which model is the cost of capital for AZT likely to be higher?

PROBLEMS

1. The EAFE is the international index comprising markets in Europe, Australia, and the Far East. Consider the following annualized stock return data:

Average U.S. index return:	14%
Average EAFE index return:	13%
Volatility of the U.S. return:	15.5%
Volatility of the EAFE return:	16.5%
Correlation of U.S. return and EAFE return:	0.45

   a. What would be the return and risk of a portfolio invested half in the EAFE and half in the U.S. market?

   b. Market watchers have noticed slowly increasing correlations between the United States and the EAFE index, which some ascribe to the increasing integration of markets. Given that the volatilities remain unchanged, is it possible that the volatility of a portfolio that is equally weighted between the two indexes has higher volatility than the U.S. market?

2. Let the expected pound return on a U.K. equity be 15%, and let its volatility be 20%. The volatility of the dollar/pound exchange rate is 10%.

   a. Graph the (approximate) volatility of the dollar return on the U.K. equity as a function of the correlation between the U.K. equity's return in pounds and changes in the dollar/pound exchange rate.

   b. Suppose the correlation between the U.K. equity return in pounds and the exchange rate change is 0. What expected exchange rate change would you need if the U.K. equity investment is to have a Sharpe ratio of 1.00? (Assume that the risk-free rate is 0 for a U.S. investor.) Does this seem like a reasonable expectation?

3. Suppose General Motors managers would like to invest in a new production line and must determine a cost of capital for the investment. The beta for GM is 1.185, the beta for the automobile industry is 0.97, the equity premium on the world market

is assumed to be 6%, and the risk-free rate is 3%. Propose a range of cost-of-capital estimates to consider in the analysis.

4. Thom Yorke is a typical mean-variance investor, currently invested 100% in a diversified U.S. equity portfolio with expected return of 12.46% and volatility of 15.76%. Thom is considering adding the STCMM fund to his portfolio. STCMM invests in U.S. small-capitalization, high-technology firms and has an expected return of 14.69% and a volatility of 32.5%. Thom has determined its correlation with his current portfolio to be 0.7274. He is also intrigued by the LYMF fund, which invests in several emerging markets. The expected return on the fund is only 12%; it has 35% volatility and a correlation of 0.2 with his portfolio. The correlation of the LYMF fund with the STCMM fund is 0.15. Assume that the risk-free rate is 5%.

   a. If Thom is interested in improving the Sharpe ratio of his portfolio, will he invest a positive amount in one of the funds? Which one? Carefully explain your reasoning.

   b. Suppose Thom is more risk averse than his friend, Nick Cave. Both cannot short-sell securities, and both are thinking of splitting their entire portfolio between the U.S. portfolio that Thom is currently holding, the STCMM fund, and the LYMF fund. They also do not invest in the risk-free asset and do not consider levering up risky portfolios. Compare the two investors' optimal holdings. Who will invest more in the LYMF fund, and who will invest more in the STCMM fund? Why?

5. Economists continue to be puzzled by the apparent home bias of investors across countries. With mean-variance preferences, investors ought to allocate much more of their wealth to foreign equities and bonds. Three explanations for the phenomenon are given below, all of them based on empirical facts. For each one, discuss whether the statements are true or false and in what sense they help, or fail,

to rationalize the home bias puzzle. In answering the questions, assume that investors have mean-variance preferences.

   a. Investors should not hold foreign equities because they are more volatile and have been yielding lower returns than U.S. stocks in recent years.

   b. Home bias arises because investors face an additional risk when investing internationally—namely, currency risk. Because currency risk makes returns more volatile but does not lead to a higher expected return, investing more in domestic assets is rational.

   c. Home bias arises because investors have a non-traded domestic asset that they care about as well—namely human capital. The returns to this asset can be thought of as labor income. It has been empirically determined that labor income correlates quite highly with U.S. stock returns.

6. Consider Softmike, a software company. Softmike's world market beta is 1.75. Regressing Softmike's return on the world market return and the global HML factor gives betas of 1.50 and −1.2, respectively. Assume that the world equity premium is 6%, the HML premium is 3%, and the risk-free rate is 5%. Compute the cost of equity capital using both the CAPM and the Fama-French model. Is Softmike a value company or a growth company?

7. Web Question: Estimate the cost of capital for a project that has the same risk as the cash flows earned by Google. Hint: Go to Yahoo Finance and find "key statistics" for Google.

BIBLIOGRAPHY

Adler, Michael, and Bernard Dumas, 1983, "International Portfolio Choice and Corporation Finance—A Synthesis," *Journal of Finance* 38, pp. 925–984.

Ang, Andrew, and Geert Bekaert, 2002, "International Asset Allocation with Regime Shifts," *Review of Financial Studies* 15, pp. 1137–1187.

Ang, Andrew, and Joseph Chen, 2007, "CAPM over the Long Run: 1926–2001," *Journal of Empirical Finance* 4, pp. 1–40.

Ang, Andrew, Robert Hodrick, Yuhang Xing, and Xiaoyan Zhang, 2006, "The Cross-Section of Volatility and Expected Returns," *Journal of Finance* 61, pp. 259–300.

Ang, Andrew, Robert Hodrick, Yuhang Xing, and Xiaoyan Zhang, 2009, "High Idiosyncratic Volatility and Low Returns: International and Further U.S. Evidence," *Journal of Financial Economics* 91, pp. 1–24.

Bekaert, Geert, and Campbell R. Harvey, 1995, "Time-Varying World Market Integration," *Journal of Finance* 50, pp. 403–444.

_____, 2000, "Foreign Speculators and Emerging Equity Markets," *Journal of Finance* 55, pp. 565–614.

_____, 2003, "Emerging Markets Finance," *Journal of Empirical Finance* 10, pp. 3–55.

Bekaert, Geert, Campbell R. Harvey, Christian Lundblad, and Stephan Siegel, 2011, "What Segments Equity Markets," *Review of Financial Studies*, forthcoming.

Bekaert, Geert, Robert J. Hodrick, and Xiaoyan Zhang, 2010, "Aggregate Idiosyncratic Volatility," NBER Working Paper No. 16058.

Bekaert, Geert, and Michael Urias, 1996, "Diversification, Integration and Emerging Market Closed-End Funds," *Journal of Finance* 51, pp. 835–869.

_____, 1999, "Is There a Free Lunch in Emerging Market Equities?" *Journal of Portfolio Management* 25, pp. 83–95.

Bekaert, Geert, and Xiaozheng Wang, 2010, "Home Bias Revisited," working paper.

Bodnar, Gordon M., Bernard Dumas, and Richard C. Marston, 2003, "Cross Border Valuation: The International Cost of Equity Capital," National Bureau of Economic Research Working Paper No. 6224.

Brooks, Robin, and Marco Del Negro, 2004, "The Rise in Co-movement Across National Stock Markets: Market Integration or IT Bubble?" *Journal of Empirical Finance* 11, pp. 659–680.

Brown, Stephen J., William N. Goetzmann, and Stephen A. Ross, 1995, "Survival," *Journal of Finance* 50, pp. 853–873.

Cai, Fang, and Francis Warnock, 2006, "International Diversification at Home and Abroad," NBER Working Paper No. 12220.

Campbell John Y., Martin Lettau, Burton G. Malkiel, and Yexiao Xu, 2001, "Have Individual Stocks Become More Volatile? An Empirical Exploration of Idiosyncratic Risk," *Journal of Finance* 56, pp. 1–43.

Claus, James, and Jacob Thomas, 2001, "Equity Premia as Low as Three Percent? Evidence from Analysts' Earnings Forecasts for Domestic and International Stock Markets," *Journal of Finance* 56, pp. 1629–1666.

Coval, Joshua D., and Tobias J. Moskowitz, 1999, "Home Bias at Home: Local Equity Preference in Domestic Portfolios," *Journal of Finance* 54, pp. 2045–2073.

Didier, Tatiana, Roberto Rigobon, and Sergio L. Schmukler, 2010, "Unexploited Gains from International Diversification: Patterns of Portfolio Holdings Around the World," NBER Working Paper No. 16629.

Diermeier, Jeff, and Bruno Solnik, 2001, "Global Pricing of Equity," *Financial Analysts Journal* 7, pp. 37–47.

Dimson, Elroy, Paul Marsh, and Mike Staunton, 2007, "The Worldwide Equity Premium: A Smaller Puzzle," in Rajnish Mehra, ed., *Handbook of the Equity Risk Premium*, Amsterdam: Elsevier Science, pp. 467–514.

Dumas, Bernard, and Bruno Solnik, 1995, "The World Price of Foreign-Exchange Risk," *Journal of Finance* 50, pp. 445–479.

Errunza, Vihang, and Etienne Losq, 1985, "International Asset Pricing Under Mild Segmentation: Theory and Test," *Journal of Finance* 40, pp. 105–124.

Fama, Eugene F., and Kenneth R. French, 1992, "The Cross-Section of Stock Returns," *Journal of Finance* 47, pp. 427–465.

_____, 1995, "Size and Book-to-Market Factors in Earnings and Returns," *Journal of Finance* 50, pp. 131–155.

_____, 1998, "Value Versus Growth: The International Evidence," *Journal of Finance* 53, pp. 1975–1999.

_____, 2002, "The Equity Premium," *Journal of Finance* 57, pp. 637–659.

Griffin, John M., and René M. Stulz, 2001, "International Competition and Exchange Rate Shocks: A Cross-Country Industry Analysis of Stock Returns," *Review of Financial Studies* 14, pp. 215–241.

Harris, Robert S., Felicia Marston, Dev R. Mishra, and Thomas J. O'Brien, 2003, "*Ex Ante* Cost of Equity Estimates of S&P 500 Firms: The Choice Between Global and Domestic CAPM," *Financial Management* 32, pp. 51–66.

Harvey, Campbell R., 1991, "The World Price of Covariance Risk," *Journal of Finance* 46, pp. 111–157.

_____, 1995, "Predictable Risk and Returns in Emerging Markets," *Review of Financial Studies* 8, pp. 773–816.

Henry, Peter B., 2000, "Stock Market Liberalization, Economic Reform, and Emerging Market Equity Prices," *Journal of Finance* 55, pp. 529–564.

Hodrick, Robert J., David Ng, and Paul Sengmueller, 1999, "An International Dynamic Asset Pricing Model," *International Taxation and Public Finance* 6, pp. 547–620.

Huberman, Gur, 2001, "Familiarity Breeds Investment," *Review of Financial Studies* 14, pp. 659–680.

Kim, E. Han, and Vijay Singal, 2000, "Opening Up of Stock Markets: Lessons from Emerging Economies," *Journal of Business* 73, pp. 25–66.

Lettau, Martin, Sydney Ludvigson, and Jessica Wachter, 2008, "The Declining Equity Premium: What Role Does Macroeconomic Risk Play?" *Review of Financial Studies* 21, pp. 1653–1687.

Lintner, John, 1965, "The Valuation of Risk Assets and the Selection of Risky Investments in Stock Portfolios and Capital Budgets," *Review of Economics and Statistics* 47, pp. 13–37.

Longin, François, and Bruno Solnik, 2001, "Extreme Correlation of International Equity Markets," *Journal of Finance* 56, pp. 649–676.

Markowitz, Harry, 1952, "Portfolio Selection," *Journal of Finance* 7, pp. 77–91.

Mossin, Jan, 1966, "Equilibrium in a Capital Asset Market," *Econometrica* 34, pp. 768–783.

Roll, Richard, 1977, "A Critique of the Asset Pricing Theory's Tests," *Journal of Financial Economics* 4, pp. 129–176.

Ross, Stephen A., 1976, "The Arbitrage Theory of Capital Asset Pricing," *Journal of Economic Theory* 13, pp. 341–360.

Ross, Stephen A., Randolph W. Westerfield, and Jeffrey F. Jaffee, 2002, *Corporate Finance*, 6th ed., Boston: McGraw-Hill/Irwin.

Rowland, Patrick F., and Linda L. Tesar, 2004, "Multinationals and the Gains from International Diversification," *Review of Economic Dynamics* 7, pp. 789–826.

Sercu, Piet, 1980, "A Generalization of the International Asset Pricing Model," *Revue de l'Association Française de Finance* 1, pp. 91–135.

Sharpe, William, 1964, "Capital Asset Prices: A Theory of Market Equilibrium Under Conditions of Risk," *Journal of Finance* 19, pp. 425–442.

Solnik, Bruno, 1974a, "The International Pricing of Risk: An Empirical Investigation of the World Capital Market Structure," *Journal of Finance* 29, pp. 365–378.

_____, 1974b, "Why Not Diversify Internationally Rather Than Domestically?" *Financial Analysts Journal*, pp. 48–53.

Stulz, René M, 1995, "The Cost of Capital in Internationally Integrated Markets: The Case of Nestlé," *European Financial Management* 1, pp. 11–22.

Welch, Ivo, 2009, "The Results of the Equity Premium January 2009 Survey," working paper.

Zhang, Xiaoyan, 2006, "Specification Tests of International Asset Pricing Models," *Journal of International Money and Finance* 25, pp. 275–307.

Appendix

The Mathematics of International Diversification

Here, we formally prove two results that we used in this chapter.

RISK REDUCTION

Statement:

As long as the correlation between two assets is less than 1, the standard deviation of a portfolio of the two assets will be less than the weighted average of the two individual standard deviations.

Proof: Let w and $1 - w$ denote the investment proportions in the two assets. Let σ_1 and σ_2 denote the two standard deviations of the two assets. We use two statistical properties:

1. The variance of a sum of two random variables equals the sum of the variances plus twice the covariance between the variables.
2. The correlation, ρ, between two variables is their covariance divided by the product of their standard deviations.

Hence, the variance of the portfolio with weights $\{w, 1 - w\}$ is:

$$w^2\sigma_1^2 + (1 - w)^2\sigma_2^2 + 2w(1 - w)\rho\sigma_1\sigma_2$$

We want to show

$$\{w^2\sigma_1^2 + (1 - w)^2\sigma_2^2 + 2w(1 - w)\rho\sigma_1\sigma_2\}^{0.5}$$
$$< w\sigma_1 + (1 - w)\sigma_2$$

Squaring both sides gives

$$w^2\sigma_1^2 + (1 - w)^2\sigma_2^2 + 2w(1 - w)\rho\sigma_1\sigma_2$$
$$< w^2\sigma_1^2 + (1 - w)^2\sigma_2^2 + 2w(1 - w)\sigma_1\sigma_2$$

Strict inequality follows from $\rho < 1$. Hence, when ρ is smaller than 1, the variance of the portfolio is always smaller than the variance of either asset. As a special case, if $\sigma_1 = \sigma_2 = \sigma$, the variance is minimized by setting $w = 0.5$, and the portfolio variance is $0.5[1 + \rho]\sigma^2$.

IMPROVING THE SHARPE RATIO

Statement:

If $\dfrac{E[r^*] - r_f}{\text{Vol}[r^*]} > \rho\,\dfrac{E[r] - r_f}{\text{Vol}[r]}$, the Sharpe ratio improves when an asset with return r^* is added (marginally) to the portfolio with return r. Without loss of generality, we set the return on the risk-free asset equal to 0 in our proof.

Proof: The Sharpe ratio of the portfolio with w invested in the foreign asset is

$$SR = \frac{(1 - w)E(r) + wE(r^*)}{\text{Var}(P)}$$

where $\text{Var}(P) = (1 - w)^2\text{Var}(r) + w^2\text{Var}(r^*) + 2w(1 - w)\text{Cov}(r, r^*)$.

We want to show that if the statement holds, then $\dfrac{\partial SR}{\partial w} > 0$ evaluated at $w \equiv 0$. Taking the derivative and leaving out the (positive) denominator, we obtain:

$$\frac{\partial SR}{\partial w} > 0 \Leftrightarrow (E[r^*] - E[r])\text{Var}[P]^{0.5} - E[P]$$
$$\times \frac{1}{2}\text{Var}[P]^{-\frac{1}{2}} \times [-2\text{Var}[r] + 2\text{Cov}[r, r^*]] > 0$$

Evaluating this at $w = 0$ means that P equals the U.S. portfolio. Multiplying through with $\text{Var}[P]^{0.5}$ and simplifying, we obtain

$$E[r^*]\text{Var}[r] - E[r]\text{Cov}[r, r^*] > 0$$

or

$$\frac{E[r^*]}{\text{Var}[r^*]^{0.5}} > \frac{E[r]}{\text{Var}[r]^{0.5}} \times \frac{\text{Cov}[r, r^*]}{\text{Var}[r]^{0.5}\text{Var}[r^*]^{0.5}}$$

$\uparrow$ $\uparrow$ $\uparrow$

Foreign Sharpe ratio   Domestic Sharpe ratio   Correlation, CORR(r, r^*)

Chapter 14

Country and Political Risk

On May 1, 2007, which is a traditional day for celebrating socialist causes, Venezuelan President Hugo Chavez announced that operating control of Venezuelan oil fields would transfer from international oil companies, such as Exxon Mobil and ConocoPhillips of the United States, France's Total, Norway's Statoil, and Britain's BP, to Venezuela's government-owned oil company, Petroleos de Venezuela S. A. (PDVSA). This action was a realization of **political risk**, which is the risk that a government action will negatively affect a company's cash flows. In its most extreme form, governments seize property without compensating the owners in a total **expropriation** (or **nationalization**). Venezuela offered some compensation, but Exxon Mobil and ConocoPhillips rejected the terms and filed compensation claims with the World Bank's arbitration panel. The outcome is still uncertain.

Country risk is a broader concept that encompasses both the potentially adverse effects of a country's political environment and its economic and financial environment. Understanding country risk and political risk is an important aspect of international capital budgeting and managing operations in other countries, especially developing countries.

This chapter discusses these risks and examines how they can be measured. It also explains which risks are diversifiable and which are not. Finally, it explores how multinationals, such as the international oil companies, manage the risks.

14.1 COUNTRY RISK VERSUS POLITICAL RISK

This section explores the general differences between country risk and political risk. We begin with the broader concept of country risk.

Country Risk

Country risk includes the adverse political and economic risks of operating in a country. For example, a recession in a country that reduces the revenues of exporters to that nation is a realization of country risk. Labor strikes by a country's dockworkers, truckers, and transit workers that disrupt production and distribution of products, thus lowering profits, also qualify as country risks. Clashes between rival ethnic or religious groups that prevent people in a country from shopping can also be considered country risks.

Country risk also affects investors who buy emerging market securities and the banks that lend to countries. In international bond markets, country risk refers to any factor related to a country that can cause a borrower in that country to default on a loan. The narrower risk associated with a government defaulting on its bond payments is called **sovereign risk**. Usually, the abilities of a private firm and its government to pay off international debt are highly correlated.

Financial and Economic Risk Factors

What factors enter a country risk analysis? Let's first focus on sovereign risk and consider the benefits and costs of a country defaulting on its international debt. The benefit to a government of defaulting on debt to foreigners is that the country is wealthier today. It no longer has to make interest and principal payments to foreign creditors. The chief cost to a country that defaults is loss of reputation, which undermines its future access to international capital markets. Because this reputation cost is large, a country is likely to repay its debt as long as it generates enough cash flow to do so.

Of course, if an international debt is denominated in the currency of the borrowing country, the borrowing country can always repay the debt by printing more money. But this action depreciates the local currency and is effectively equivalent to a partial default from the perspective of international investors. Thus, most developing-country debt is denominated in developed-country currencies, such as the U.S. dollar. Hence, the capacity to repay foreign debt and, consequently, the probability of default ultimately depend on the country's ability to generate foreign exchange. Nevertheless, governments sometimes refuse to pay their debts, even when they have foreign exchange available. This lack of willingness to pay is a form of political risk.

Investors use a number of economic variables to discriminate between financially sound and financially troubled countries including the following:

- The ratio of a country's external debt to its gross domestic product (GDP)
- The ratio of a country's debt service payments to its exports
- The ratio of a country's imports to its official international reserves
- A country's terms of trade (the ratio of its export to import prices)
- A country's current account deficit or its current account deficit to GDP ratio

These variables are directly related to the ability of the country to generate inflows of foreign exchange.

The ongoing European sovereign debt crisis highlights the importance of government budget deficits and public debt to GDP ratios as determinants of sovereign risk. Also, in assessing the sustainability of the fiscal situations of countries like Greece, Ireland, and Portugal, financial markets are keenly aware of the still precarious situations of various financial institutions following the 2007 to 2010 global financial crisis. Investors understand that private liabilities of failing financial institutions may be shifted to federal governments.

Factors such as inflation and real economic growth are useful as well. A country's economic health directly affects the cash flows of a multinational firm, and it may also be informative about political risk in a narrow sense. The better a country's economic situation, the less likely it is to face political and social turmoil that will inevitably harm foreign (and domestic) companies.

Political Risk Factors

This section lists the most important factors a multinational corporation (MNC) should be aware of in assessing political risk.

Expropriation or Nationalization

The most extreme form of political risk is the possibility that the host country takes over an MNC's subsidiary, with or without compensation. This is the worst-case scenario for firms. Outright expropriations used to be common: Regimes in Eastern Europe (after World War II) and in Cuba (in 1960) expropriated private businesses, both domestic and foreign. More recently, Venezuela has systematically expropriated foreign businesses as part of President Chavez's socialist revolution. In 2010, the Venezuelan government expropriated the equipment of the U.S. oil services company Helmerich & Payne, the Venezuelan operations of Owen-Illinois, a U.S. glassware manufacturer, and the Spanish agricultural firm Agroisleña.

Contract Repudiation

Governments sometimes revoke, or repudiate, contracts without compensating companies for their existing investments in projects or services. Governments default on the payments associated with the contracts, cancel licenses, or otherwise introduce laws and regulations that interfere with the contracts to which the government and the MNC agreed. For example, in 1996, Mexico's Instituto Nacional de Ecologia (INE), an agency of the federal government, awarded Tecmed, a Spanish multinational corporation, a renewable license to operate a hazardous waste landfill in Mexico. In 1998, however, the INE suddenly refused to renew the license, a realization of political risk.

In 2010, Pakistani authorities halted all operations of the $3 billion Reko Diq copper and gold project, led by Canada's Barrick Gold and Chile's Antofagasta, citing that the contract substantially undervalued the value of the project. The Supreme Court of Pakistan should come up with a decision in 2011, but existing contracts will almost surely be repudiated.

Taxes and Regulation

Governments can dramatically change the "rules of the game" that were in place when an MNC first made its investment in the host country. Examples include unexpected increases in taxes, restrictions on hiring and firing local workers, and sudden stricter environmental standards. Some industries may be more susceptible than others, especially if the foreign corporation is dominating its local competition. MNCs are also sometimes forced by governments to sell their equity stakes in local subsidiaries because of foreign ownership restrictions.

In 2010, Chile, the world's main copper producer, increased royalty rates on copper producers changing to a progressive tax from 5% to 14% rather than a flat 5% tax. Peru is now also considering an increase in royalties on mining companies.

Regulations that MNCs find particularly problematic are regulations restricting the transfer of their profits earned abroad back to their home countries. Governments not only have the power to change the tax rates on these earnings, but they can also completely block their transfer. This essentially forces the MNC to invest its funds locally, even if doing so is less profitable. Finally, governments often make decisions that can indirectly affect the cash flows of MNCs.

Exchange Controls

Another political risk factor relates to exchange controls. Governments have been known to prevent the conversion of their local currencies to foreign currencies. In general, doing business in countries with inconvertible currencies puts an MNC at considerable risk.

An interesting case is the 2002 collapse of the Argentine currency board, which effectively ended the one-for-one convertibility of pesos into dollars. The Argentine government also curtailed bank deposit withdrawals and prohibited the unauthorized export of foreign currency from the country.

Corruption and Legal Inefficiency

Highly inefficient governments with large bureaucracies can increase a company's costs of doing business. Governments may also be corrupt and demand bribes. Transparency International (TI) produces an annual "Corruption Perceptions Index" for more than 170 countries, using expert assessments and opinion surveys. In 2010, Denmark, New Zealand, and Singapore were perceived as the least corrupt countries; Somalia was perceived as the most corrupt. Russia was number 154 out of 178 countries.

TI also compiles information on which companies have the highest propensity to pay bribes and therefore undermine efforts of governments to improve governance. Multinationals from Russia, China, Mexico, and India were the worst offenders in 2008, whereas Belgian and Canadian companies had the least tendency to pay bribes.

A country's legal system is an important factor in determining the overall quality of its institutions and how attractive it is for firms to do business there. Djankov et al. (2003) gauge the quality and efficiency of the legal systems of 109 countries by measuring the time it takes to evict a tenant or clear a bounced check through the legal system. Exhibit 14.1 shows these measures for the G5 countries and for the best- and worst-performing countries on this score.

The United States and the United Kingdom seem to have the speediest legal systems among the G5 countries, but there are five countries (Uganda, Tunisia, Malawi, Swaziland, and Canada) where evicting a tenant happens even faster. In contrast, in Poland and Slovenia, it takes almost 3 years to either evict a tenant or collect on a bounced check. Such a tardy legal system is a potential risk factor for MNCs.

Ethnic Violence, Political Unrest, and Terrorism

Significant MNC losses can occur due to internal civil strife or wars. In war-torn regions across the world, companies often hire their own private armies in order to try to function normally. For example, piracy near the Somali coast has prompted some companies to hire private security firms to protect their ships. This, of course, is expensive and raises thorny legal and humanitarian issues.

Home-Country Restrictions

The politics of a company's home country can affect its cash flows from foreign operations. For example, after the Iranian Revolution in 1979, a U.S. embargo on Iran forced Coca-Cola to shut down its operations there. Coke later resumed operations in the country by the late

Exhibit 14.1 Legal System Quality

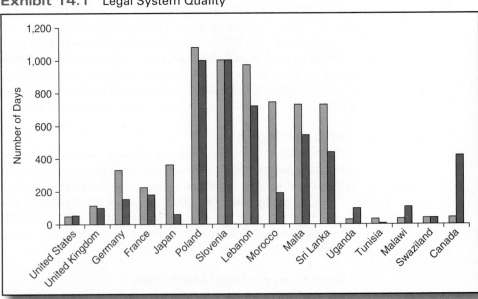

Notes: For each country, the column heights indicate numbers represent the number of days it takes to evict a tenant (on the left) or to collect a bounced check through the court system (on the right). We report numbers for the G5 countries and the five countries with the longest and shortest durations.

Source: Data from Table 6, Simeon Djankov, Rafael La Porta, Florencio Lopez-de-Silanes and Andre Shleifer, 2003, "Courts" *The Quarterly Journal of Economics* 118, 453–517.

1980s, until President Clinton reimposed the embargo in 1995. Coca-Cola now exports to Iran through subsidiaries in Ireland, thereby circumventing U.S. restrictions. However, in 2010, new U.S. and United Nations sanctions on Iran in response to its nuclear program proved a new challenge as Iranian President Ahmadinejad reacted by banning Coca-Cola and other American products from Iranian stores.

The Debt Crisis

The 1980s **Debt Crisis** was one of the defining historical episodes that made country risk analysis an important part of international banking and a critical component in international capital budgeting. It holds lessons for debt crises such as the ongoing sovereign debt crisis in Europe.

Origins of the Debt Crisis

From 1948 to the end of the 1960s, crude oil prices ranged between $2.50 and $3.00 per barrel. The Organization of Petroleum Exporting Countries (OPEC) was formed in 1960 to stabilize oil prices. In 1973, OPEC curtailed production, which sent oil prices from $3.00 per barrel to over $12.00 per barrel by the end of 1974. Over the next few years, events in Iran and Iraq led to another round of increases in the price of crude oil, with prices eventually reaching $35 per barrel in 1981. Because these prices are all nominal, current-year prices, it helps to adjust them for inflation. In 1981, oil prices reached $85.00 per barrel measured in 2010 dollars.

Exhibit 14.2 summarizes how such a boon for oil-producing countries eventually led to a Debt Crisis for the developing countries. Rather than match the increases in income generated by the oil price jumps in 1973 and 1974 with increases in consumption and investment spending, the OPEC countries saved by making loans to international banks, often in the form of dollar deposits in the Eurocurrency markets at floating interest rates. The banks in turn loaned these "petrodollars," as they were called at the time, to developing countries, typically in the form of loans called eurocredits that were quoted at a spread above the floating interest rate they paid to the OPEC countries.

Banks viewed the lending as profitable and relatively riskless for three reasons. First, the loans were made at a spread over the banks' borrowing costs. Thus, the banks were not exposed to interest rate risk, as they would have been if they had borrowed short term and had lent at long-term fixed rates. Second, the banks eliminated currency risk as both the deposits and loans were in dollars. Third, the banks syndicated the loans, taking diversified exposures to a number of countries to avoid too much exposure to a single country. As a result, during the 1970s, the debt of non-OPEC developing countries owed to banks in industrialized countries, especially banks in the United States, increased significantly.

A mix of external shocks affecting industrialized countries and developing countries in the early 1980s and macroeconomic mismanagement in developing countries triggered the actual Debt Crisis. In contrast to the response to the first oil shock, the oil shock of the late 1970s was met with a staunchly anti-inflationary monetary policy in a number of countries, particularly in the United States under Paul Volcker, Chairman of the Board of Governors of the Federal Reserve System. The macroeconomic situation in the developed world was now totally different: Real interest rates were high, the global economy was in recession, and the dollar was strong. This situation contributed to low prices of commodities on the world markets and low demand for the exports of developing countries.

With the huge dollar appreciation and high dollar interest rates, the developing countries faced steep interest payments in dollars at the same time as their export revenues were falling. Suddenly, the default risk of the loan portfolios of international banks had greatly increased. The situation was exacerbated by the fact that developing countries had not used the money they borrowed very productively and had run unsustainable economic policies.

Exhibit 14.2 The Origins of the Debt Crisis

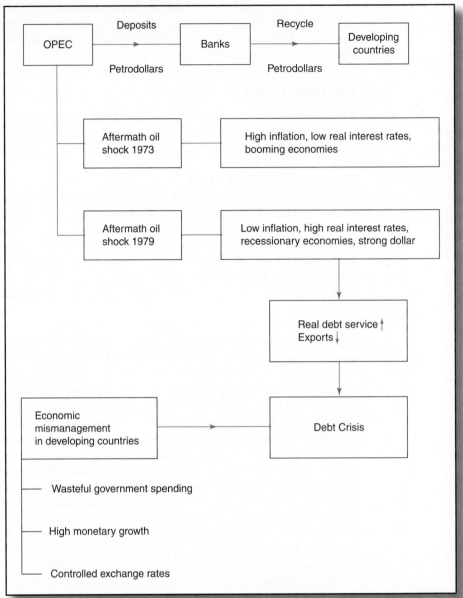

Ironically, however, the Debt Crisis actually started in Mexico, an oil-exporting country. On August 12, 1982, Mexico announced that it could no longer make its scheduled payments on its foreign debt. Mexico requested loans from foreign governments and the International Monetary Fund (IMF), and it started negotiating with its commercial bank creditors. It was the start of a prolonged and deep crisis. By the end of the year, 24 other countries had requested restructuring on their commercial bank debts.

The debt of developing countries threatened to undermine the global financial system because many large banks, in particular the largest U.S. banks, had considerable exposures to Mexico and other debt-ridden developing countries—exposures that exceeded their capital. Moreover, developing countries lost access to much-needed international capital for a decade. As a result, they failed to register any substantive economic growth during the 1980s.

Managing the Debt Crisis

At the beginning of the Debt Crisis, the banks mistook the Debt Crisis for a "liquidity" problem. They were betting that the developing countries were only temporarily unable to repay their debts. The hope was that economic recovery plus sensible economic policies in developing countries guided by the IMF would make the debt problem disappear. Advisory committees, composed of the large banks, industrial-country governments, and the IMF, arranged debt reschedulings and the extension of new credit.

The **Baker Plan**, instituted in 1985 and named for U.S. Treasury Secretary James Baker, relied heavily on countries agreeing to change their economic policies following guidelines set by the IMF. Although some successful financing packages were agreed upon, economic growth did not revive and the debt-rescheduling agreements proved a failure.

According to a number of academic observers, the developing countries' reluctance to repay their debts was justified because they were suffering from "**debt overhang**"—the notion that a country saddled with a huge debt burden has little incentive to implement economic reforms or stimulate investment because the resulting increase in income will simply be appropriated by the country's creditors in the form of higher debt payments.[1] From this perspective, it is not surprising that some countries (Peru and Brazil, for example) stopped or severely restricted repaying their debts altogether.

By 1987, it became clear that the banks were not going to be repaid in full, and most resorted to attempts to decrease their exposure to high-debt developing countries. At the same time, facing mounting debt stocks, many countries started to adopt debt-reducing policies. Stimulated by an active secondary market in developing-country debt, debt buybacks and debt–equity swaps proved popular.

In a **debt buyback**, the country repays a loan at a discount. In a **debt–equity swap**, an MNC that is willing to directly invest in a country buys the debt of the country in the secondary market at a discount from face value. The MNC then presents the debt to the country's government and receives local currency (equal to the face value of the debt or at a discount less than the market discount). The MNC then uses the local currency to make the equity investment in the country. Many MNCs used debt–equity swaps to lower the cost of their investments. Debt–equity swaps were a central element of the efforts of Peru, Chile, and Argentina to privatize their government-operated industries. For example, in 1994, Peru offered debt–equity swaps in two government-owned and -operated mining companies, Tintaya and Cajamarquilla.

Some of the Debt Crisis debt-reduction arrangements were even accompanied by developmental aid for the troubled countries. For example, an international organization buying debt in the secondary market would exchange the debt for local currency at the country's central bank. The organization would then use the proceeds to finance development projects of an environmental, health, or educational nature. However, in addition to such "debt-for-do-good" swaps, there were also interesting "debt-for-do-bad" swap proposals. For example, in the mid-1980s, Colombian drug lords offered to buy back their country's debt in return for immunity from prosecution. The proposal was rejected.

Several economists argue that when a country uses its own resources to buy back its troubled debt at a discount, the country's creditors are the only ones that benefit. Here we use a simple numeric example to illustrate the main argument.

---

[1] In Chapter 16, this debt overhang argument will resurface when we consider the investment incentives of private companies in severe financial distress.

Example 14.1 Debt Buybacks in Brazar

Suppose that the country of Brazar has an outstanding debt of $100 billion. Creditors all agree that there is only a 25% probability that the debt will be repaid. They also estimate that if the country defaults, it will be possible to seize $20 billion of Brazar's international assets for distribution to creditors. Suppose the debt is payable next year, and to keep things simple, let the market interest rate be 0. What is the market value of the debt? We know that the value of the debt must be the expected value of the repayments:

$$V = 0.25 \times \$100\,\text{billion} + 0.75 \times \$20\,\text{billion} = \$40\,\text{billion}$$

Hence, $1 of debt sells for $0.40 in the market.

Suppose that the government of Brazar has $8 billion that it could use to buy back the debt. Given the steep 60% discount, Brazar may reason that a buyback is a good investment because it retires a dollar of debt for $0.40. Can Brazar buy back $20 billion of face-value debt with $8 billion? The answer is no because creditors must be indifferent between selling the debt to Brazar in the buyback and holding the debt for the next year. They will figure out the new price of the debt after the buyback.

To determine how much Brazar must pay to buy back $20 billion of debt, we must first determine the new price of debt. Let's assume that the amount that is recoverable in the bad state of the world remains $20 billion.[2] The new value of the debt is, therefore,

$$V_{\text{new}} = 0.25 \times \$80\,\text{billion} + 0.75 \times \$20\,\text{billion} = \$35\,\text{billion}$$

Hence, given that $80 billion of debt remains outstanding, the price per dollar of debt rises to $\frac{35}{80} = 0.4375$, or $0.4375 per dollar of debt. The creditors will want to sell only at this price. Who gains in this scenario? Let's consider the different parties:

- Brazar pays $0.4375 \times \$20\,\text{billion} = \$8.75$ billion, not $8 billion and it reduces the market value of its debt from $40 billion to $35 billion, or by $5 billion.
- The creditors who sell their debt to the government realize a capital gain of 3.75 cents on the dollar. In sum, they gain $0.0375 \times \$20\,\text{billion} = \$0.75$ billion.
- The creditors who hold out (do not sell) also receive a capital gain of 3.75 cents per dollar, for a total of $0.0375 \times \$80\,\text{billion} = \$3$ billion.

The conclusion is pretty clear: The government overpaid by $3.75 billion ($8.75 − $5.00). Notice that the gain is nicely split up among the creditors who sell to the government and the holdout creditors.

A famous case that confirms this theory is the Bolivia debt buyback of 1988. The following box discusses this case in more detail.

The Bolivia Debt Buyback

In March 1988, Bolivia received $34 million from an anonymous group of countries to buy back part of its commercial bank debt. Whereas the market value of the debt before the buyback was around $50 million, the market value of debt after the buyback was $43.4 million, even though $34 million had been spent to reduce the debt. The reason was that the buyback increased the price of the debt on the secondary market from around 7 cents to the dollar

---

[2]In reality, the country must use resources to repay the debt, which would likely reduce this amount. Research by Bulow and Rogoff (1988, 1991) shows that this effect is unlikely to overturn the main result of the example.

to over 11 cents to the dollar. Although debt prices fluctuated daily, let's fix some prices to get a concrete idea of what happened.

Suppose the price just before the debt buyback is 7.25 cents on the dollar. The total outstanding face value of the debt was $670 million. Hence, the market value of the debt was $0.0725 \times \$670$ million $= \$48.575$ million. The Bolivian government paid 11 cents on the dollar to buy back $308 million worth of debt. So, it paid $0.11 \times \$308$ million $= \$33.88$ million, about $34 million. However, the secondary market price of Bolivian debt then remained at or above 11 cents per dollar, so the value of the remaining debt was 0.11 ($670 million $-$ $308 million) $= \$39.82$ million. Essentially, Bolivia paid $34 million to reduce the market value of its debt by a paltry $8.755 million.

Clearly, commercial bank creditors reaped the bulk of the benefits.

The solution to this problem is to eliminate the debt entirely so that there are no holdout creditors benefiting from the debt buyback scheme. In March 1993, Bolivia eliminated $170 million of its commercial bank debt, leaving less than $10 million outstanding. The whole operation (primarily a debt buyback at 16 cents to the dollar) was financed by donations. Some banks, such as JPMorgan, chose to channel the money received into conservation and environmental projects run by the Nature Conservancy and the World Wildlife Fund. Although the whole operation clearly seemed a success, Bolivia still ended up with an outstanding debt of no less than $3.5 billion to various multilateral organizations, including the World Bank.

The Brady Plan

After years of muddling through the Debt Crisis, it became obvious that the developing countries faced not just a lack of liquidity but were actually insolvent. In 1989, the **Brady Plan**, developed by then U.S. Treasury Secretary Nicholas Brady, put pressure on banks to offer some form of debt relief to developing countries. The Brady Plan also called for an expansion in secondary market transactions aimed at debt reduction. In addition, the IMF and the World Bank were urged to provide funding for "debt or debt service reduction purposes." The first Brady package was arranged for Mexico in July 1989.

Negotiating a debt-reduction agreement is complex because numerous banks are involved, and "free-rider" problems exist. For example, small banks could refuse to put up new money, yet they still benefit from their share of interest rate payments that the new money makes possible. In the Brady Plan, each bank could choose the restructuring option that it found most suitable from a menu of possibilities established in a debt-reduction agreement between the debtor-country government and its creditor banks. The creditor banks, because of their large number, were represented by a bank advisory committee. In order to mitigate free-rider problems, no bank could opt out. Among the options available to the banks were the following:

- *Buybacks:* The debtor country was allowed to repurchase part of its debt at an agreed discount (a debt-reduction option).
- *Discount bond exchange:* The loans could be exchanged for bonds at an agreed discount, with the bonds yielding a market rate of interest.
- *Par bond exchange:* The loans could be exchanged at their face value for bonds yielding a lower interest rate than the one on the original loans.
- *Conversion bonds combined with new money:* Loans could be exchanged for bonds at par that yield a market rate, but banks had to provide new money in a fixed proportion of the amount converted (an option for banks unable or unwilling to participate in debt reduction or debt service reduction).

The Brady Plan ended up securitizing the debt into easily tradable bonds, called **Brady bonds**. Quite a few Brady bonds have "official enhancements" attached to them, such as collateral provisions, often in the form of U.S. Treasury zero-coupon bonds. (Collateral is an asset pledged as security for the repayment of a loan.) The Brady Plan agreements also included financing arrangements to pay for the collateral and other up-front debt-reduction costs.

Sources included the IMF, the World Bank, the Inter-American Development Bank, and the Japanese government, which would typically provide funds only if the country adhered to an IMF-supported structural adjustment program. Such a program typically involved economic policy recommendations such as currency devaluation, the lifting of export and import restrictions, the balancing of government budgets, and removal of price controls and state subsidies.

For many countries, the Brady bond market soon replaced the market for secondary bank loans and provided the impetus to a thriving emerging market bond market. Not only do sovereign borrowers now tap international bond markets, but investors from industrialized countries have also started to invest in the local bond and money markets of many formerly heavily indebted developing countries. As a consequence, sovereign credit ratings have become more important (see Section 14.3). Johnson and Boone (2010) have even proposed Brady bonds to help resolve the current debt crisis in Greece and Ireland in Europe, which they feel are *de facto* insolvent. It is indeed possible that the European crisis will follow a similar pattern to the Debt Crisis in the 1980s, where early measures aimed at avoiding debt write-downs and providing new loans to the crisis countries prove futile and debt restructuring eventually becomes necessary.

14.2 INCORPORATING POLITICAL RISK IN CAPITAL BUDGETING

When MNCs undertake international investments, they must forecast their future cash flows and discount them at an appropriate risk-adjusted discount rate. There is much confusion and disagreement about how political risks should enter these computations. Some researchers suggest using a discount rate adjustment to account for political risk; others feel that political risk should affect only cash flow projections.

Adjusting Expected Cash Flows for Political Risk

Consider a multinational corporation with a shareholder base that is globally diversified. In this case, the discount rate should reflect only international, systematic risks. Chapter 13 showed that systematic risks are typically related to how an MNC's return in a particular country covaries with the world market return. If the risk of loss from political risk does not covary with the world market return, no adjustment to the discount rate is necessary. Positive covariation between the cash flows from the project and the world market return increases the required global discount rate. Consequently, unless political risk, which adversely affects the MNC's investment returns, is systematically high when the world market return is low, political risk should not enter the calculation of the discount rate. Instead, the company's cash flows should be adjusted for the presence of political risk.

To fully understand this argument, consider a simple scenario. Suppose a company takes out an insurance policy against political risk and that the policy covers all contingencies and has no deductible. In this case, a company would simply compute its expected cash flows as if there were no political risk and then subtract the insurance premium it must pay each year from the cash flows of the project. The cash flows would then be discounted at the usual discount rate. It is, indeed, possible to purchase **political risk insurance**, and in some countries, such insurance is even subsidized by the government. (However, it is seldom the case that an investment can be fully insured. We discuss insurance and other ways companies can mitigate political risks in Section 14.4.)

If a company chooses not to purchase political risk insurance, when it forecasts its future cash flows, it must incorporate into the calculation how its cash flows might be affected by various political risks, such as expropriation, unexpected taxation, and so forth. In the following example, we show how this can be done.

Example 14.2 Oconoc's Project in Zuenvela

Suppose Oconoc, an American oil company, wants to do a joint project with Atauz Petrol, an oil company in Zuenvela. Oconoc's contribution to the project is $75 million, and Oconoc predicts that the project will yield it $50 million per year for 2 years. However, Zuenvela has a very unstable political system and, in the past, has witnessed widespread strikes. The president of Zuenvela, Ugo Vezcha, has expressed some dismay with the management of Atauz Petrol, and he has hinted that he might renationalize the company, which would have drastic consequences for Oconoc's cash flows. Given this information, the managers of Oconoc think that the probability that the government will expropriate the project is 12% each year. Furthermore, if the government interferes, the cash flows will be zero from then onward.

Exhibit 14.3 presents this analysis in a simple diagram. If there were no political risk, the value of the project would be easy to calculate. With a 10% discount rate, the present value of the project is

$$V = \frac{\$50 \text{ million}}{1.1} + \frac{\$50 \text{ million}}{1.1^2} = \$86.78 \text{ million}$$

The project should be undertaken because its value, $86.78 million, is greater than its cost, $75 million.

However, the political risk adjustments change the computation considerably. Let's follow Exhibit 14.3 to make the adjustments. For the first year, there are two scenarios. With 0.88 chance, the cash flow of $50 million will be realized, and with 0.12 chance, the project will return 0. For the second year, there are three scenarios: (1) expropriation in the first year implies no second-year cash flows and has probability of 0.12; (2) no expropriation in the first year but expropriation in the second year and no cash flows has probability of $0.88 \times 0.12 = 0.1056$; and (3) no expropriation at all, which has probability of $0.88 \times 0.88 = 0.7744$. Bringing it all together, we obtain:

$$V = \frac{(0.88 \times \$50 \text{ million}) + (0.12 \times 0)}{1.1}$$
$$+ \frac{(0.88^2 \times \$50 \text{ million}) + (0.12 \times 0.88) \times 0 + (0.12 \times 0)}{1.1^2}$$
$$= \$40 \text{ million} + \$32 \text{ million} = \$72 \text{ million}$$

Exhibit 14.3 Adjusting the MNC's Cash Flows for Political Risk

Notes: Expected cash flows are $50 million in period 1 and period 2. There is a 12% chance each period that the host government will expropriate the project. In this case, the cash flow to the MNC is 0.

Hence, the value of the project is now less than its cost, and the project should not be undertaken. If Oconoc's managers find it difficult to figure out the probability of expropriation, they can still do an informative analysis: They can find the expropriation probability, p, that would cause the project to have a net present value (NPV) of 0 by solving

$$-\$75 \text{ million} + \frac{(1-p)\$50 \text{ million}}{1.1} + \frac{(1-p)^2 \$50 \text{ million}}{1.1^2} = 0$$

Such an equation can be solved analytically for the two-period case here, but it soon becomes difficult to calculate for a large number of periods. However, because p is in the interval [0, 1], trial and error can yield a solution relatively quickly. Alternatively, in Microsoft Excel, the Goal Seek function can solve the equation. The solution is $p = 9.48\%$. Hence, if management believes the expropriation probability is lower than 9.5%, it should take on the project.

Example 14.3   The Infinite Cash Flow Case

Most investments in the oil business generate cash flows over much longer periods of time than just 2 years. Let's investigate the extreme case that an oil investment generates an expected $50 million (m) per year forever. The value of the project, not taking into account political risk, is

$$\frac{\$50 \text{ m}}{1+r} + \frac{\$50 \text{ m}}{(1+r)^2} + \frac{\$50 \text{ m}}{(1+r)^3} + \ldots = \frac{\$50 \text{ m}}{r}$$

With a discount rate of 10%, the value of the project is $500 million.

How much will political risk reduce the value of the project? Let's assume that the probability of an adverse political event, again denoted by p, is constant over time. Note that the expected cash flow generated by the project now decreases with time because it is less and less certain that the government won't seize the revenues earned from the project:

$$V = \frac{\$50 \text{ m}(1-p)}{1+r} + \frac{\$50 \text{ m}(1-p)^2}{(1+r)^2} + \frac{\$50 \text{ m}(1-p)^3}{(1+r)^3} + \ldots$$

where p is the probability of expropriation ($p = 0.12$), and r is the discount rate ($r = 10\%$). To compute this infinite sum, we can use a trick we have used before. If $S = 1 + \lambda + \lambda^2 + \lambda^3 + \ldots$ and $\lambda < 1$, it is true that $S = \frac{1}{1-\lambda}$. In our case, we have

$$V = \frac{\$50 \text{ m}(1-p)}{1+r}[1 + \lambda + \lambda^2 + \ldots]$$

with $\lambda = \frac{1-p}{1+r}$. Hence, we obtain

$$V = \frac{\$50\,\text{m}(1-p)}{1+r} \times \frac{1}{1 - \dfrac{1-p}{1+r}} = \frac{\$50\,\text{m}(1-p)}{r+p}$$

$$= \frac{\$50\,\text{m}(1-0.12)}{0.10+0.12} = \$200 \text{ million}$$

With 12% probability of expropriation each period, the value of the project is reduced dramatically to $200 million.

General Formulas

In general, if the expropriation risk is idiosyncratic, capital budgeting analysis must be adjusted for political risk as follows:

Step 1. Compute the discount rate, r, and future expected cash flows for period t, $C(t)$, as usual, without expropriation risk.

Step 2. Compute a series of expropriation probabilities, $p(t)$, for each future period.

Step 3. Let $\prod_{n=0}^{t-1}(1 - p(t-n))$ be shorthand notation for $(1 - p(t))(1 - p(t-1))$ $\ldots(1 - p(1))$, which is the probability that at time t, there has not yet been any expropriation.

For an investment of I, compute the *NPV* as

$$NPV = -I + \sum_{t=1}^{T} \frac{C(t)\prod_{n=0}^{t-1}(1 - p(t-n))}{(1+r)^t} \tag{14.1}$$

The formula assumes *total* expropriation. However, in many cases, the MNC might actually receive at least some compensation or experience only a reduction in its cash flow. If this is the case, additional terms are necessary to reflect these additional cash flows with their corresponding probabilities.

In the previous example, we had

- Infinite cash flows
- The same cash flows every period (C)
- The same probability of expropriation in each period

The formula then becomes

$$V = C \times \frac{1-p}{r+p}$$

This represents a rather extreme estimate of the effect of political risk. It assumes that the MNC receives no compensation and that the political risk will be present forever. However, in the case of an imminent crisis, it is likely that the political risk outlook will improve after a few years, so p will decrease over time if the crisis is resolved favorably.

Adjusting the Discount Rate Instead of Cash Flows

A popular alternative method is to initially ignore political risk and project an MNC's cash flows under the rosy scenario that no expropriation takes place, but then apply a discount rate scaled up to account for political risk. As the following example and formulas show, such a method can indeed yield exactly the same solution, as long as the new discount rate is

$$r^* = \frac{r + p}{1 - p} \tag{14.2}$$

Note that this formula is valid only in the special case we discussed—that is, the case in which cash flows occur forever and a constant probability of expropriation is assumed—and that a dramatically higher discount rate must be used. In our example, the discount rate adjusted for political risk is 25.0%. That is more than double the original 10% rate. However, as we just explained, it may well be the case that a country's political risk is unusually high for a short period of time during a crisis, but if the crisis is weathered, the MNC's managers expect the situation to normalize after a few years. The next example shows how to deal with a situation in which political risk subsides over time.

Example 14.4   Decreasing Political Risk

Suppose that Oconoc judges political risk to be negligible after 1 year. Either the company will be expropriated in the first year, or the populace of Zuenvela will have elected a more business-friendly president. In this case, the value of the project is

$$V = \frac{\$50 \text{ m} \times 0.88}{1 + r} + \frac{\$50 \text{ m} \times 0.88}{(1 + r)^2} + \frac{\$50 \text{ m} \times 0.88}{(1 + r)^3} + \cdots$$

The first cash flow calculation accounts for the probability of an adverse political event, but cash flows from the second period onward assume that there is no further political risk. However, the probability is only 0.88 that there are any positive cash flows from the second period onward. Hence, the value of the project is

$$V = \frac{\$44 \text{ million}}{0.10} = \$440 \text{ million}$$

Under this scenario for political risk, adjusting the discount rate from 10% to 11.36% would yield the "correct" discount rate. The new rate of 11.36% is the solution for r^* of $440 = \frac{50}{r^*}$.

More realistically, some probability of an expropriation after a first, tumultuous year would remain. Suppose the probability of expropriation decreases from 12% to 1% after the first year. We now obtain

$$V = \frac{\$50 \text{ m} \times 0.88}{1.1} + \frac{0.88 \times 0.99 \times \$50 \text{ m}}{1.1^2} + \frac{0.88 \times 0.99^2 \times \$50 \text{ m}}{1.1^3} + \cdots$$

$$= \frac{\$44 \text{ m}}{1.1} + \frac{\$43.56 \text{ m}}{1.1^2} \left[1 + \frac{0.99}{1.1} + \left(\frac{0.99}{1.1}\right)^2 + \cdots \right]$$

Applying our infinite sum formula with $\lambda = \frac{0.99}{1.1} = 0.9$, we obtain

$$V = \frac{\$44 \text{ m}}{1.1} + \frac{\$43.56 \text{ m}}{1.1^2} \times \frac{1}{1 - 0.9} = \$400 \text{ million}$$

The remaining political risk reduces the value of the project further from $440 million to $400 million. Hence, the discount rate that would yield the correct project value would satisfy $400 = \frac{50}{r^*}$, implying $r^* = 12.50\%$. It is unlikely that one can guess the correct political risk–adjusted discount rate in this case.

Discount Rates for Emerging Markets and Political Risk

In Chapter 13, we argued that the discount rate for emerging market investments should be computed using the world capital asset pricing model (CAPM), if the investing company has globally diversified investors. Because many emerging markets show relatively low correlations with the world market, the standard procedure may lead to relatively low discount rates for emerging market investments, which strikes many practitioners and economists as counterintuitive. In fact, a practice has developed to adjust the standard CAPM-based discount rates with a number of fudge factors to make them more palatable (that is, higher). We discuss this in more detail in the *Point–Counterpoint* feature in this chapter. Of course, many of the perceived risks of investing in emerging markets are political in nature, and we argue here that from the perspective of global investors, idiosyncratic political risks should be perfectly diversifiable and, consequently, should not affect discount rates.

In reality, however, emerging markets are not yet fully integrated with global capital markets, and therefore, it is possible that the CAPM does not capture all systematic risk factors. Perhaps political risk is one of these factors. Nevertheless, if the cost of capital is computed from the perspective of an MNC with globally diversified shareholders, political risk should affect the discount rate only if it affects global discount rates and represents a global systematic risk.[3] Although recent crises in emerging financial markets, such as the 1998 Russia crisis, may have spilled over into other emerging markets and even have adversely affected the stock market performance in developed markets, hard evidence for such global contagion remains elusive. Therefore, it remains best to view political risk as country-specific risk that can be diversified away by global investors. For that reason, we recommend not adjusting the discount rate for pure political risk and using only business risk to increase the magnitude of the discount rate above the risk-free rate. This may imply that emerging market investments require surprisingly low discount rates. However, political risk does reduce the value of the project because it reduces the cash flows that the MNC expects to receive in the future.

14.3 COUNTRY AND POLITICAL RISK ANALYSIS

This section begins by discussing how one might acquire information on the factors that lead to various **country risk ratings**. It then discusses some of the organizations that provide political risk analysis. Finally, the section discusses sovereign credit ratings and information about default probabilities that is incorporated in market prices of government bonds.

Country Risk Ratings

The capital budgeting analysis in the previous section requires information about political risk probabilities and alternative expropriation scenarios. Many organizations analyze the risk factors associated with doing business in countries around the world and come up with risk ratings for most countries. Some of these risk-rating organizations focus on financial and economic risks and others on political risk. As explained earlier in the chapter, political risks must be treated and managed differently than economic and financial risks.

How important political risk is relative to business risk depends on the particular activity of an MNC in a country. Imagine an MNC that establishes a foreign manufacturing plant to capitalize on cheap production costs and exports the goods produced to other countries. This

---

[3]Andrade (2009) develops a model where country defaults are more likely to occur during global economic downturns, and political risk thus affects discount rates.

MNC will be relatively less subject to local economic risk than it might otherwise be because its customers are primarily outside the country. In other words, only the firm's costs—not its revenues—will be affected by economic risk. That said, the MNC might be quite vulnerable to political risks. In contrast, a firm that actually creates a local customer base in a foreign country might need to focus relatively more on economic risks because by creating local jobs and satisfying local customers, it may be less exposed to political risks. As you can see, ratings that do not distinguish between political and economic hazards are less useful for MNCs.

Political Risk Analysis

The primary objective of political and country risk analysis is to forecast losses stemming from these risks. Most risk-rating services forecast by linking certain measurable attributes to future political risk events.

Exhibit 14.4 shows two examples. Analysts have noted that ethnic conflicts in a country tend to adversely affect foreign investors, including MNCs. They have also noted that a good predictor of future ethnic conflict is the presence of ethnic fractionalization. For example, it is hard to imagine ethnic strife in a homogeneous country such as Sweden, but it is very likely to occur in Nigeria, where there are more than 250 different ethnic groups, several different religions, and at least five different languages spoken. Consequently, ethnic fractionalization is used as a risk attribute. Similarly, left-wing governments may be associated with actions that harm foreign investors, such as stricter labor regulations or outright nationalization. Countries with unstable governments and frequent, forced elections have a higher probability of electing left-wing officials within a particular period than countries with stable governments. This is true even if a right-wing government may be in power currently. Consequently, the frequency of government changes is used as a risk attribute. Generally, political risk services examine indicators of political risk, such as the following:

- Political stability (for example, the number of different governments in power over time)
- Ethnic and religious unrest; the strength and organization of radical groups
- The level of violence and armed insurrections; the number of demonstrations
- Enforcement of property rights
- The extent of xenophobia (fear of foreigners); the presence of extreme nationalism

Exhibit 14.4 Risk Attributes and Political Risk Analysis

Societal Attribute:	Ethnic fractionalization	Frequency of government changes
Political Choice/Action:	Ethnic conflict	Left-wing government
Effective Outcome:	Civil strife damages	Labor regulations and nationalization
Loss to the MNC:	Damage to facilities	Increased costs Loss of total investment

Note: Political risk analysis uses measurable "risk attributes" (at top) to predict risk events for MNCs (bottom).

The different political variables are then weighted and added to provide one country score. Of course, such weightings should be adjusted for a particular MNC's situation, which is not always possible. It is also clear that the relative importance of certain risk events has changed over time. For example, the Overseas Private Investment Company (OPIC), which is the U.S. government's political risk insurance company, has seen a distinct change in the nature of the claims it has paid over time. In the 1960s, there were a significant number of expropriations; in the 1970s and 1980s, there were many cases regarding inconvertible currencies; during the 1990s, the majority of claims were paid for damages due to civil strife.

There are, however, risk-quantifying approaches besides the attribute approach. Political Risk Services Group (PRS Group), a New York–based firm, forecasts the three most likely governments (regimes) to be in power in a country over 18 months to 5 years in the future, and it predicts how these governments will behave. Whereas PRS Group focuses on future risks, some ratings services focus on current conditions only. Of course, it is often the case that countries with precarious current political conditions also face high future political risks. It is important to realize that country and political risk analyses ultimately produce probabilistic forecasts. A high-risk country need not experience a political risk event. Let's examine some actual rating services in more detail.

Some Examples of Ratings Systems

Institutional Investor publishes a biannual country credit rating based on information provided by leading international banks. The banks grade each country (except their home countries) on a scale of 0 to 100, with 100 representing those with the least chance of default. The individual responses are weighted using a formula that gives more importance to responses from banks with greater worldwide exposure and more sophisticated country-analysis systems. The factors to which bankers pay the most attention in producing the country rating are its debt service, its political and economic outlook, its financial reserves, and its current account and trade account balances with other countries.

The composite risk indicator of the Economist Intelligence Unit (EIU), a sister company to the magazine *The Economist*, encompasses four types of risk: political risk, economic policy risk, economic structure risk, and liquidity risk. It is compiled for 100 countries on a quarterly basis. The political risk component is of the attribute type and includes two subcategories: political stability (war, social unrest, orderly political transfer, politically motivated violence, and international disputes) and political effectiveness (change in government orientation, institutional effectiveness, bureaucracy, transparency/fairness, corruption, and crime). The three other categories involve a mix of subjective elements, using opinions of country experts and objective economic statistics. For example, the EIU's economic policy category focuses on a country's monetary policy, fiscal policy, exchange rate policy, and trade and regulatory policies. The economic structure category assesses solvency using information on growth, savings, debt structure, and the current account balance. Finally, the liquidity risk category examines the imbalance between a country's assets and liabilities versus the rest of the world, using various economic statistics (such as the country's short-term debt as a percentage of its exports).

The magazine *Euromoney* provides an overall country risk score based on nine individual variables that carry different weights. The two most important indicators, each with 30% weighting, are political risk and economic performance. The political risk assessment is based on scores given by country experts and banking officers, assessing government stability, regulatory environment, corruption, risk of a country's non-payment of loans, trade-related finance and dividends, and the non-repatriation of capital. The economic performance variable combines information on bank, monetary, and currency stability; budget deficits; unemployment; and economic growth. The other indicators include indicators about the amount and status of the country's debt and its access to local and international finance.

Other examples include S. J. Rundt & Associates, which relies on a global network of associates to provide country risk scores, and Control Risks Group (CRG), which provides assessments of political risk and travel risk (focusing on terrorism, crime, and so on). The IHS Energy Group's Political Risk Ratings focus primarily on risks for the oil and gas industry.

The PRS Group's ICRG Rating System

PRS produces the *International Country Risk Guide (ICRG)* monthly, along with the *Political Risk Yearbook*, and country fact sheets and data sets. We now focus on the ICRG ratings because they can be split up into economic, financial, and political risk components and their various subcomponents. The ICRG ratings, available since 1980, are developed from 22 underlying variables. The political risk measure is based on 12 different subcomponents, and the financial and economic risk measures are based on five subcomponents each. Exhibit 14.5 presents the different components and the points assigned to them in the ICRG system.

Exhibit 14.5 The ICRG Risk Components

POLITICAL RISK COMPONENTS	
Component	Points (max.)
Government stability	12
Socioeconomic conditions	12
Investment profile	12
Internal conflict	12
External conflict	12
Corruption	6
Military in politcs	6
Religious tensions	6
Law and order	6
Ethnic tensions	6
Democratic accountability	6
Bureaucracy quality	4
Maximum total points	**100**
FINANCIAL RISK COMPONENTS	
Component	Points (max.)
Foreign debt as a percentage of GDP	10
Foreign debt service as a percentage of XGS*	10
Current account as a percentage of XGS*	15
Net liquidity as months of import cover	5
Exchange rate stability	10
Maximum total points	**50**
ECONOMIC RISK COMPONENTS	
Component	Points (max.)
GDP per head of population	5
Real annual GDP growth	10
Annual inflaction rate	10
Budget balance as a percentage of GDP	10
Current account balance as a percentage of GDP	15
Maximum total points	**50**
*XGS = exports of goods and services.	

Notes: XGS, exports of goods and services. From *International Country Risk Guide*, published by the PRS Group, Inc. Copyright © 2010. The PRS Group, Inc., www.prsgroup.com.

Financial and Economic Risk Factors

The financial and economic risk assessments are based solely on objective economic data. ICRG collects statistics on the variables listed in Exhibit 14.5 and then uses a fixed scale to translate particular statistics into risk points. For example, countries with foreign debt ratios smaller than 5% of GDP obtain a perfect 10 score on that indicator, whereas countries with a debt ratio of over 200% receive a score of 0.

The financial risk measure clearly aims to assess a country's ability to pay its foreign debts. The indicators measure (1) a country's outstanding foreign debt to GDP ratio, (2) its foreign debt service as a percentage of its exports, (3) its current account balance as a percentage of its exports, (4) its official reserves divided by its average monthly merchandise imports, and (5) exchange rate volatility. ICRG considers both large depreciations and appreciations of a currency to be "risky," but the former are considered the more risky of the two. The economic risk rating views highly developed countries (those with high levels of GDP per capita)—with high economic growth, low inflation, sound fiscal balances, and positive current balances—as having low economic risk.

The Political Risk Components

Unlike the financial and economic risk indicators, the political risk rating depends on subjective information, with ICRG editors assigning points on the basis of a series of preset questions for each risk component. The various subcomponents are shown in Exhibit 14.5. Following Bekaert et al. (2005), we organize the 12 components into four categories, based on their content but also on an analysis of how correlated different components are across countries and time, and we show some example scores in Exhibit 14.6. We group the "law and order," "bureaucratic quality," and "corruption" variables into a "quality of institutions" measure. The "law and order" variable separately measures the quality of the legal system ("law") and the observance of the law ("order"). "Bureaucratic quality" measures the institutional quality and the strength of the bureaucracy, which can help provide a cushioning effect in case governments change. "Corruption" can add directly to the cost of doing business in a particular country, for instance, because bribes must be paid. However, the corruption variable also captures the actual or potential corruption in the form of excessive patronage, nepotism, job reservations, "favors-for-favors," secret party funding, and suspiciously close ties between politics and business. ICRG uses the length a government has been in power as an early indicator of potential corruption.

A second grouping is "conflict" or "political unrest." The variables belonging in this category are "internal conflicts" (an assessment of internal political violence in the country), "external conflict" (an assessment of external disputes, ranging from full-scale warfare to economic disputes, such as trade embargoes), "religious tensions" (an assessment of the activities of religious groups and their potential to evoke civil dissent or war), and "ethnic tensions" (an assessment of disagreements and tensions between various ethnic groups that may lead to political unrest or civil war).

The sum of the subcomponents "military in politics" and "democratic accountability" is a good measure of the democratic tendencies of a country, which are correlated with political risk. A military takeover or threat of a takeover might represent a high risk if it is an indication that the government is unable to function effectively. This signals that the environment is unstable for foreign businesses. The democratic accountability category measures how responsive the government is to its citizens.

"Government stability" depends on a country's type of governance, the cohesion of its governing party or parties, the closeness of the next election, the government's command of the legislature, and the popular approval of the government's policies. We group "government stability," "socioeconomic conditions," and "investment profile" into one category, called "Policies." The "socioeconomic conditions" subcomponent attempts to measure the general public's satisfaction, or dissatisfaction, with the government's economic policies. Socioeconomic conditions cover a broad spectrum of factors, ranging from infant mortality and medical provision to housing and interest rates. Within this range, different factors have different weights in different societies.

Of particular interest for MNCs is the "investment profile" category. It has four subcategories, including the risk of expropriation or contract viability, taxation, repatriation, and labor costs. For particular projects, the investment profile category can suffice to assess an MNC's pure political risk.

Overall Ratings

The points on the 12 categories within the "political risk" measure add up to 100, which constitutes the score for the political risk index. Analogously, the financial and economic risk indexes each carry 50 points. ICRG creates an overall index by adding up the three subindexes and by dividing by 2 so that the top score is 100. When all the subcomponents have been scored, ICRG then assigns the following degrees of risk to the composite score:

Very high risk	00.00% to 49.9%
High risk	50.00% to 59.9%
Moderate risk	60.00% to 69.9%
Low risk	70.00% to 79.9%
Very low risk	80.00% to 100%

The composite score is only an assessment of the country's current country risk situation. In addition, ICRG provides 1-year and 5-year risk forecasts. These forecasts include a worst-case forecast, a most-probable forecast, and a best-case forecast. The ICRG calls the difference between the worst- and best-case forecasts "risk stability" because it is an indication of the volatility of risk.

Example 14.5   A Cross-Country Example of ICRG's Political Risk Ratings

Exhibit 14.6 lists the political risk ratings and their subcomponents for a number of countries in Southeast Asia. For comparison, we also present the G5 countries, the country ranked the highest (Norway), and the country ranked the lowest (Somalia). Among the Southeast Asian countries, Singapore and Brunei have low overall country risk, whereas Myanmar has relatively high overall country risk.

Suppose a large U.S. MNC is considering setting up a textile production facility in Southeast Asia and is exploring options in Indonesia, Malaysia, Myanmar, and Vietnam. Among these four countries, Malaysia has the best overall political risk situation, followed by Vietnam. Indonesia and Myanmar have the most risk overall. Note that these similar overall ratings hide very different performances on the subgroup measures discussed earlier. If democratic tendencies are important, both Myanmar and Vietnam score very poorly relative to Indonesia. However, Indonesia's political institutions are of poor quality, pulling down its overall score.

Suppose the CEO is particularly concerned about the repatriation of profits in the future and about the possibility that corruption will erode profits. We can specifically tailor the ICRG system to this situation by giving more weight to the "investment profile" and "corruption" categories.

The last column in Exhibit 14.6 uses the subcategories to create an alternative political risk index in which only the investment profile and corruption categories are considered. In this last column, we simply added the investment profile and corruption scores for each country and reweighted the index to be between 0 and 100. Because the "investment profile" category receives double the points of corruption, the new index puts two-thirds of its weight on "investment profile" and one-third on "corruption," and it assigns a 0 weight to all other categories. Using this system, Indonesia becomes the least risky country in which to invest, whereas it only ranked third behind Malaysia and Vietnam using the overall political risk index.

Exhibit 14.6 Country and Political Risk Ratings for Selected Countries

Country	Overall Country Risk	Political Risk	Quality of Institutions	Conflict	Democratic Tendencies	Policies	Investment Conditions / Corruption
United States	76.8	81.5	81.3	83.3	83.3	79.2	88.9
United Kingdom	76.0	80.5	84.4	77.8	100.0	75.0	80.6
France	74.5	78.0	81.3	73.6	95.8	75.0	88.9
Germany	82.3	83.0	87.5	84.7	100.0	73.6	91.7
Japan	82.0	80.5	84.4	84.7	83.3	73.6	88.9
Norway	91.0	89.0	93.8	88.9	100.0	83.3	91.7
Somalia	36.0	24.0	9.4	34.7	16.7	22.2	16.7
Brunei	87.5	82.5	68.8	93.1	45.8	90.3	77.8
Indonesia	67.8	60.5	50.0	61.1	62.5	63.9	66.7
Malaysia	78.5	73.0	59.4	77.8	79.2	72.2	63.9
Singapore	82.5	84.5	84.4	87.5	58.3	90.3	91.7
Vietnam	68.3	65.5	53.1	83.3	33.3	63.9	58.3
Myanmar	51.8	46.5	34.4	66.7	8.3	44.4	22.2
Philippines	72.3	62.5	46.9	70.8	66.7	59.7	61.1
Thailand	68.8	56.0	40.6	58.3	62.5	58.3	52.8

Notes: The ratings are taken from ICRG's Web site (www.prsgroup.com/ICRG.aspx). The data are for July 2010. Subgroup ratings were computed as the sum of the points for the several subcategories and normalizing, so that 100 would mean a perfect score (no risk).

Country Credit Spreads

In Chapter 11, we defined the credit spread on a corporate bond as the difference between the yield on the bond and the yield on a comparable Treasury bond that is not subject to default risk. When a sovereign borrower issues bonds in its own currency, there is usually no default risk because the government can simply print money to pay back the debt holders. When sovereign borrowers issue bonds in a different currency, though, a default is possible because the government must earn foreign exchange to pay off the bondholders.

Government defaults have occurred regularly in international bond markets throughout the past 200 years. Defaults occurred in Russia (1998) and Argentina (2001), and more recently in Belize (2007) and Ecuador (2008). Because of possible default, the yields offered on international bonds are higher than the yields on the government bonds of the developed country issuing the currency. The difference between the two is called the **country credit spread**. For example, if the yield on a 5-year U.S. Treasury bond is 6%, and the yield on a 5-year dollar bond issued by the Brazilian government is 9%, the Brazilian country credit spread is 3%. These spreads, which vary over time in secondary markets, are, of course, an indication of country risk.

Sovereign Credit Ratings

Today, major international rating agencies, such as Moody's, Standard & Poor's, and Fitch, are rating more and more sovereign bond issues as the markets for them continue to grow. Exhibit 14.7 reports the March 2011 ratings on long-term foreign currency debt, provided by Standard & Poor's. Recall that an investment grade rating extends from AAA to BBB. While most developed countries are rated investment grade, Greece lost its investment grade status in 2010. Other countries involved in the European sovereign debt crisis, such as Ireland, Portugal, Spain, and Italy, are still investment grade, but not AAA. Whereas the debt of many developing countries is rated as "junk debt"—for example, Argentina (B), Ukraine (B+), and

Exhibit 14.7 Sovereign Credit Ratings by Standard & Poor's

Abu Dhabi	AA	Fiji Islands	B–	The Netherlands	AAA
Albania	B+	Finland	AAA	New Zealand	AA+
Angola	B+	France	AAA	Nigeria	B+
Argentina	B	Gabonese Republic	BB–	Norway	AAA
Aruba	A–	Georgia	B+	Oman	A
Australia	AAA	Germany	AAA	Pakistan	B–
Austria	AAA	Ghana	B	Panama	BBB–
Azerbaijan	BB+	Greece	BB+	Papua New Guinea	B+
Bahamas	BBB+	Grenada	B–	Paraguay	B+
Bahrain	BBB	Guatemala	BB	Peru	BBB–
Bangladesh	BB–	Guernsey	AAA	Philippines	BB
Barbados	BBB–	Honduras	B	Poland	A–
Belarus	B	Hong Kong	AAA	Portugal	BBB
Belgium	AA+	Hungary	BBB–	Qatar	AA
Belize	B	Iceland	BBB–	Romania	BB+
Benin	B	India	BBB–	Russian Federation	BBB
Bermuda	AA	Indonesia	BB	Saudi Arabia	AA–
Bolivia	B	Ireland	A–	Senegal	B+
Bosnia and Herzegovina	B+	Isle of Man	AAA	Serbia	BB
Botswana	A–	Israel	A	Singapore	AAA
Brazil	BBB–	Italy	A+	Slovakia	A+
Bulgaria	BBB	Jamaica	B–	Slovenia	AA
Burkina Faso	B	Japan	AA–	South Africa	BBB+
Cambodia	B+	Jordan	BB	Spain	AA
Cameroon	B	Kazakhstan	BBB	Sri Lanka	B+
Canada	AAA	Kenya	B+	Suriname	B+
Cape Verde	B+	Korea	A	Sweden	AAA
Chile	A+	Kuwait	AA–	Switzerland	AAA
China	AA–	Latvia	BB+	Taiwan	AA–
Colombia	BBB–	Lebanon	B	Thailand	BBB+
Cook Islands	BB–	Liechtenstein	AAA	Trinidad and Tobago	A
Costa Rica	BB	Lithuania	BBB	Tunisia	BBB–
Croatia	BBB–	Luxembourg	AAA	Turkey	BB
Cyprus	A	Macedonia	BB	Uganda	B+
Czech Republic	A	Malaysia	A–	Ukraine	B+
Denmark	AAA	Malta	A	United Kingdom	AAA
Dominican Republic	B	Mexico	BBB	United States	AAA
Ecuador	B–	Mongolia	BB–	Uruguay	BB
Egypt	BB	Montenegro	BB	Venezuela	BB–
El Salvador	BB–	Morocco	BBB–	Vietnam	BB–
Estonia	A	Mozambique	B+		

Notes: This table is extracted from Standard and Poor's Web site (www.standardandpoors.com) and represents the agency's 2011 ratings for long-term foreign currency debt of the various sovereign borrowers. The best rating is AAA; the worst is D.

Vietnam (BB–)—countries such as Brazil, Chile, China, Korea, and Malaysia now receive investment-grade ratings.

An increasing number of firms in developing countries are also being rated as they seek to diversify their funding sources and access a wider investor base. Credit ratings of private companies generally fall at or below the credit ratings of the governments of the countries in which the firms are domiciled. This "sovereign ceiling" makes sense in the case of foreign currency debt because the sovereign has first claim on available foreign exchange and controls the ability of residents to obtain funds to repay creditors. Although there are more and more exceptions to this rule, sovereign ratings remain a significant determinant of the credit rating assigned to corporations (see Durbin and Ng, 2005; and Borensztein et al., 2007).

Why Is Sovereign Credit Risk Different?

Sovereign defaults are different from a company going bankrupt because it is very difficult to take a country to court, and there are no formal bankruptcy proceedings in place for sovereigns. Nonetheless, sovereigns still worry about the consequences of defaulting because of the following issues:

- The assets of the country located in the jurisdiction of a creditor may be seized. For example, in early 1986, the Peruvian government brought home some $700 million worth of gold and silver it had been holding abroad. This was around the time it was restricting payments on its debt to a certain percentage of the country's export revenues.
- The country will not be able to borrow as readily in the future, and if it manages to borrow, its borrowing costs may be higher.
- The country could find its ability to engage in international trade severely curtailed.
- Default may make economic crises worse, for example, by causing a run on banks and exacerbating capital flight.

Panizza et al. (2009) thoroughly review the costs of sovereign default and suggest the costs are rather moderate and short lived, but Andrade and Chhaochharia (2010) estimate the costs to be more substantial.

As we have explained, the benefit to defaulting is that the debt is no longer serviced. Servicing the debt can be painful if the country's income is low. One country that has reneged on foreign obligations numerous times is Argentina. In 1930, an economic crisis led to a military coup that ended 70 years of parliamentary government and led to a forced debt restructuring. Argentina defaulted again after Mexico declared a debt moratorium in 1982. Finally, on Christmas Eve, 2001, Argentina defaulted on $150 billion in foreign debt. The country then restructured its debt. The Argentine government offered a deal in which 76% of the defaulted bonds were exchanged for new bonds worth between 25% and 35% of the original value and with longer maturities. Payments on some of these bonds are indexed to the future economic growth of Argentina. In 2010, some of the holdout bondholders accepted another exchange offer. Yet some holdouts continue to litigate to receive full payment, and Argentina remains ostracized from the international capital markets. It has not issued a sovereign bond in foreign jurisdictions since its 2001 default.

Taking Governments to Court

Bilateral investment treaties (BITs) help investors avoid legal problems associated with sovereign debt. A few decades ago, when foreign investors and multinationals were hurt by the actions of a foreign government, they had to rely on the foreign government's laws or persuade their own governments to intervene on their behalf. To encourage international capital investment, countries have recently begun entering into treaties with each other, promising mutual respect for and protection of investments in each other's territory. A BIT allows an individual investor to make his or her claims directly against a nation at a private international arbitration tribunal consisting of three independent arbitrators. The administering organization for many of these disputes is the **International Center for the Settlement of Investment Disputes (ICSID)**, an arm of the World Bank. More than 2,500 BITs have been signed, most after 1990, and there are over 120 cases pending with the ICSID.

The standards of protection offered by BITs are quite broad. Indeed, the ICSID has made a number of precedent-setting arbitration awards. BIT arbitration now reaches far beyond cases in which expropriation or nationalization has occurred. It also encompasses any government action that deprives an investor of all or part of the economic value of an investment. This includes intangible assets such as contractual rights.

We already mentioned the example of INE, an agency of the federal government of Mexico, refusing to renew Tecmed's license to operate a hazardous waste landfill. Tecmed argued that this act constituted an expropriation of its investment that was contrary to the provisions of the 1996 Spanish–Mexican BIT, and the company brought the case before the ICSID. The tribunal agreed and ordered Mexico to pay Tecmed damages in excess of $5 million plus compound interest.

Although there have been a number of cases in which investors such as Tecmed have won, there have also been cases in which investors have lost. In some instances, the issues involved are not simple but cut across a broad set of societal and cultural lines. For example, in January 1997, the U.S.-based waste disposal company Metalclad Corporation filed a complaint with the ICSID, alleging that the Mexican state of San Luis Potosi had violated a number of North American Free Trade Agreement (NAFTA) provisions when it prevented the company from opening a multimillion-dollar hazardous waste treatment and disposal site it had built near Guadalcazar. The site had previously been contaminated in 1990 when a Mexican company illegally dumped 55,000 drums—about 20,000 tons—of hazardous waste in a valley a few kilometers away from Guadalcazar. The drums were filled with industrial waste from Mexico City and other urban areas, and they were not covered or properly stored.

Metalclad had negotiated with the Mexican federal government to clean up the site in return for using it as a waste treatment and disposal site. The Mexican federal government saw Metalclad as a company that would clean up a horrible mess, but the local government and the people of Guadalcazar were not so sure. The Governor of San Luis Potosi denied Metalclad the permit to operate when he rezoned the area of the site part of an ecological zone in response to an environmental impact assessment that revealed that the plant site lay atop an ecologically sensitive underground alluvial stream.

The Metalclad case raises complex social, legal, and economic issues. Perhaps the local population should have been consulted about the plans for establishing a toxic waste treatment facility in the area, but they never were. Legally, the case was brought against the Mexican federal government in defiance of a ruling by a local state, a factor that frightens environmentalists. "The decision is proof that NAFTA and the environment are at odds, and that municipalities will have a tough time turning away garbage if foreign corporations are involved," said Michelle Swenarchuk of the Canadian Environmental Law Association.[4] Although Metalclad sought $90 million in damages, the company received only $16.7 million. Grant Kesler, the CEO of Metalclad, stated, "This is a token amount of money that doesn't really reflect the value of the project." The company estimated that it had spent more than $20 million in planning, permitting, and construction. "The biggest losers of all," Mr. Kesler added, "are the people of Mexico who continue to have to live in a country that produces 10 million tons of hazardous waste a year and has only one facility in the whole country to handle it."[5]

Whether BITs are beneficial remains an open question. Yackee (2010) claims that there is only weak evidence that BITs meaningfully influence foreign direct investment (FDI) decisions; moreover, BITs are not strongly correlated with political risk rankings, and providers of political risk insurance do not really take BITs into account when making underwriting decisions. One potential reason is that litigation is often costly, and the outcome surely is uncertain. For example, in a recent case, Commerce Group Corp (CGC), a Wisconsin-based company, saw its case against the government of El Salvador, demanding $100 million in compensation, dismissed by an ICSID panel, stating that the dispute was not within its jurisdiction. CGC explores and produces precious metals in El Salvador, especially in the Sebastian Gold Mine, under a 1987 exploitation concession granted by the government of El Salvador. In order to mine and process gold ore, environmental permits from the El Salvador Ministry of Environment and Natural Resources are required. On September 13, 2006, the Ministry revoked the required permits, thereby effectively terminating CGC's right to mine and process gold, which led to the claim for damages.

---

[4]See Scoffield (2000).
[5]See DePalma (2000).

Historical Background: Brady Bonds

Although the majority of Brady bonds have been retired, Brady bonds remain an important and liquid component of the emerging debt market. Mexico issued the first Brady Bond in February 1990, converting $48.1 billion of its eligible foreign debt to commercial banks into two types of the bonds. The principal on both types of bonds was fully collateralized in the form of U.S. Treasury zero-coupon bonds held at the Federal Reserve Bank of New York. Mexico also guaranteed investors that 18 months' worth of interest payments would be paid on the bonds by depositing that amount as collateral with the New York Fed. Most other Brady deals were quite similar to Mexico's. Brady deals were concluded for over 20 countries, including Argentina, Brazil, Jordan, Nigeria, and Poland.

The vast majority of outstanding Brady bonds are U.S. dollar denominated, and they tend to have very long maturities (20 to 30 years). The bonds are evenly divided between fixed and floating-rate instruments. Brady bonds lend themselves to the same valuation techniques applied to more conventional fixed-income securities. The price of a given bond represents the present value of its stream of future payments. However, as we hinted earlier in the chapter, Brady bonds have a number of special features:

- *Principal collateral:* All par and discount bonds are collateralized by U.S. Treasury zero-coupon securities having similar maturities.
- *Interest collateral:* For some bonds, the government issuing the Brady bonds deposits money with the New York Federal Reserve Bank in amounts covering 12 to 18 months' of interest payments on a "rolling" basis.
- *Sovereign portion:* The remaining cash flows are subject to sovereign risk.

The collateral enhancements imply that the difference between the yield-to-maturity on the Brady bond and a U.S. Treasury bond of comparable maturity (sometimes called the "blended" yield) cannot really be viewed as a country spread. Therefore, bond traders compute the "stripped yield," based on the yield-to-maturity of the unenhanced interest stream after removing the present value of the U.S. Treasury zero-coupon bond that collateralizes the principal and the present value of the guaranteed interest stream. This stripped yield is truly based on the credit quality, or sovereign risk, of the issuing nation.

Bonds sometimes also include detachable warrants or recovery rights predicated on a country's economic performance. Mexico's Value Recovery Rights (VRRs), for example, were based on numerous variables, including oil prices, GDP, and oil production levels. In June 2003, Mexico retired the last of $35 billion in Brady bonds, drawing an end to its disastrous debt default of the early 1980s.

Analyzing a Brady Bond

Consider a Brady bond with an annual coupon of 7% issued by Peru with 10 years remaining until maturity. Assume that the par value of the bond and the following year's coupon payments are collateralized by U.S. Treasury bonds. Exhibit 14.8 contains all the information necessary to value the bond. If the Peruvian government does not default, the investor in this bond receives $7 (per $100 par) each year and receives $107 of interest and principal 10 years from now.

If this were a bond issued by the U.S. government, we would value it as in Chapter 6 by taking the present value of each year's promised cash flows with the appropriate spot interest rate from Exhibit 14.8. The value of such a hypothetical U.S. Treasury bond would be

$$\text{Value} = \frac{7}{1 + 0.035} + \frac{7}{(1 + 0.0410)^2} + \ldots + \frac{107}{(1 + 0.065)^{10}} = 105.3724$$

Exhibit 14.8 Analyzing a Brady Bond

Year	Dollar Cash Flows	Dollar Spot Rates	Present Value of the Cash Flows
1	7	3.50	6.76
2	7	4.10	6.46
3	7	4.65	6.11
4	7	5.05	5.75
5	7	5.55	5.34
6	7	5.85	4.97
7	7	6.05	4.64
8	7	6.25	4.31
9	7	6.35	4.02
10	107	6.50	57.00

Notes: The bond is trading at a price of $92 (per $100 par value) and carries a coupon of 7%. The second column lists the cash flows accruing to the bondholder when Peru does not default on its obligation. The third column lists the dollar spot interest rates. The fourth column computes the present value of the future cash flows, using these spot interest rates.

Instead, the price of the Peruvian Brady bond is only $92. To analyze this bond, let's start by computing the yield-to-maturity, ignoring the collateral. Recall that the yield-to-maturity is the one yield that makes the present value of the cash flows equal to the price:

$$92 = \frac{7}{1 + ytm} + \frac{7}{(1 + ytm)^2} + \ldots + \frac{107}{(1 + ytm)^{10}}$$

Solving this equation gives $ytm = 8.20\%$. By substituting 105.3724 for 92 above, we can also compute the yield-to-maturity on our hypothetical U.S. Treasury bond, which is $ytm = 6.26\%$.

From these computations, you might conclude that the country spread is $8.20\% - 6.26\% = 1.94\%$. However, this is incorrect because the 8.20% is a "blended," not a stripped, yield. The 8.20% yield does not take into account the fact that parts of the cash flows in the bond are collateralized and hence are risk free.

Let's value the collateral, the first coupon payment and the par value of the bond, with the USD spot interest rates:

$$\text{Value of collateral} = \frac{7}{1.035} + \frac{100}{1.065^{10}} = 60.0359$$

The price of $92 per $100 of par value consists of $60.0359 for the cash flows collateralized by U.S. Treasury bonds and $31.9641 = $92 - $60.0359 for the other cash flows. These other cash flows are nine coupons of $7 each, which the Peruvian government promises to pay. The stripped yield therefore solves

$$31.9641 = \frac{7}{(1 + ytm)^2} + \frac{7}{(1 + ytm)^3} + \ldots + \frac{7}{(1 + ytm)^{10}}$$

Note that the first non-collateralized cash flow occurs in the second year. The solution for *ytm* in this equation is 12.88%. Hence, a better estimate of the country spread is $12.88\% - 6.26\% = 6.62\%$.[6]

---

[6]This calculation is not entirely correct because the timing of the cash flows in the 6.26% computation is more tilted toward the 10-year horizon (because there is a par value payment then) than in the computation for the Peruvian non-collateralized flows. To correct for that, we would have to compute the yield-to-maturity on a U.S. bond with a cash flow pattern similar to that of the non-collateralized portion of the Peruvian bond. To do so, we must first price the cash flows of $7 from year 2 to year 10 with the U.S. spot interest rates, and then we would compute the yield-to-maturity. It so happens that this yield is only 5.82%, so the country spread is even higher than the stripped yield indicates.

Country Spreads and Political Risk Probabilities

Country spreads are often used in capital budgeting to account for political risk. It is not obvious how to do so.

First, recall that the country spread is an indication of the default risk of a sovereign bond. Although a government might default on its bonds as a result of a political event, this does not necessarily mean that it will also expropriate the assets of the MNCs that lie within its borders.

Second, even if political risk and sovereign default risk are highly correlated, the nature of Brady bonds is such that the probabilities of default are not easily recovered from the yield spreads. It is best to use an example to illustrate the point. Consider the Peruvian bond we analyzed earlier. What is the probability that the Peruvian government will default each year? We can estimate this probability by making some additional assumptions. We first assume that when the Peruvian government reneges on the debt, it will pay foreign debt holders nothing. This is clearly unrealistic. In most cases of sovereign default, a restructuring happens (the Brady deals are but one example), so that foreign debt holders still recover some of their investment. In a 2008 report, Moody's computed an average historical recovery rate of about 35%. For the sake of this example, though, we set this recovery value to 0. (The next subsection considers the case of non-zero recovery values.) We also assume here, for simplicity, that the probability of default is constant over time.

The cash flow diagram for the Peruvian bond is simple. The first period, it pays $7 for sure because that payment is collateralized. Therefore, it should not enter our computations at all. However, there is still a probability that the Peruvian government will default (for instance, on other bonds) in that year. We denote this probability by p. The second year, there is a probability of $(1 - p)^2$ that the bond will not be in default, and there is a probability of $(1 - p)p$ that there will be a default. This is the same reasoning used in Exhibit 14.3. For the third year, the probability of no default is $(1 - p)^3$, and the probability of default is $(1 - p)^2 p$. Following this same argument until the 10th year, it must be the case that

$$31.9641 = (1 - p)^2 \frac{7}{1.041^2} + (1 - p)^3 \frac{7}{1.0465^3} + \ldots + (1 - p)^{10} \frac{7}{1.065^{10}}$$

Here, we equate the value investors assign to the bond with the present value of the expected cash flows, discounted at U.S. risk-free rates. We can do this because the possibility of default is taken into account in the probabilities, and we assume that default is an idiosyncratic risk. As before, this equation can be solved for p, the probability of default. We find $p = 6.34\%$. If we believe sovereign risk as reflected in this default probability is perfectly correlated with the political risk embedded in a cash flow analysis for capital budgeting, this is the probability we should use.

Default Probabilities with Positive Recovery Values

In the previous section, we computed the probability of default by using the formula

$$\text{Stripped Price} = \sum_{j=1}^{10} \frac{CF(j)(1 - p)^j}{[1 + i(j)]^j} \tag{14.3}$$

In Equation (14.3), the stripped price is the dollar price of the bond after subtracting the value of the collateral; $CF(j)$ is the promised dollar cash flow at time j; $i(j)$ is the USD spot interest rate for period j; and p is the default probability. The assumptions are that the default probability is constant over time and the recovery value upon default is 0.

In most cases of sovereign defaults, foreign investors have recovered some of their money after the governments renegotiated the terms of the debt jointly with investors and representatives of the World Bank and the IMF.[7] How much is recoverable depends on economic conditions. The recovery values are likely to change over time. When there is the possibility of recovery under default, the formula in Equation (14.3) becomes more complex:

$$\text{Stripped Price} = \sum_{j=1}^{10} \frac{CF(j)(1-p)^j + R(j)p(1-p)^{j-1}}{[1+i(j)]^j} \tag{14.4}$$

where $R(j)$ is the expected recovery value for the bond in period j, conditional upon default at that time.

Let's apply this formula to the Peruvian bond example. The stripped bond promises nine payments of $7 per $100 par over 9 years. We computed the stripped price to be 31.9641. When there was no recovery, the default probability was 6.34%. Because recovery values increase the expected cash flows, the default probability will now be higher. In other words, assuming zero recovery underestimates the probability of the risk event occurring.

Let's work through an example. Assume that the Peruvian bond has the following expected recovery values: periods 1 and 2 = 8; periods 3 and 4 = 4; and period 5 and thereafter = 0. Recall that the first coupon payment is collateralized. However, the Peruvian government can still announce that it will no longer service its debt and that it will default in period 1. We must now find a p that solves the following equation:

$$31.9641 = \frac{8 \times p}{1+0.035} + \frac{7 \times (1-p)^2 + 8 \times p(1-p)}{1.041^2}$$
$$+ \frac{7 \times (1-p)^3 + 4 \times p(1-p)^2}{1.0465^3} + \frac{7 \times (1-p)^4 + 4 \times p(1-p)^3}{1.0505^4}$$
$$+ \frac{7 \times (1-p)^5 + 0 \times p(1-p)^4}{1.0555^5} + \cdots + \frac{7 \times (1-p)^{10}}{1.065^{10}}$$

Solving this equation yields $p = 7.20\%$. This compares to an estimated p of only 6.34%, when recovery values were assumed to be 0.

CASE STUDY

The Mexican Peso Crisis and Country Risk

Determining the default probabilities related to Brady bonds is not always easy because their cash flows extend over such long periods of time. Let's revisit the country risk related to Tesobonos, securities issued by the Mexican government in the 1990s. Let's also discuss the correlation between currency risk and country risk in the context of the Mexican peso crisis in 1995.

In the early 1990s, Mexico regained access to international capital flows and started to run a current account deficit. Domestic savings began to decline in a situation much like the United States in the mid-2000s. In fact, it was jokingly suggested that Mexico was not

---

[7]One problem has been that smallish minorities of creditors often block restructuring deals to which large majorities agree. Recently, some sovereign issuers have included "collective-action clauses" in their bonds that prevent this from happening.

only economically integrating with the United States but had also adopted the bad spending habits of U.S. citizens, as Mexican citizens were incurring substantial credit card debts. The Mexican current account deficit worsened over time, reaching 8% of Mexico's GDP by 1994. At the time, Mexico had a crawling peg exchange rate system (see Chapter 5), but the nominal exchange rate did not fully adjust with Mexican inflation. As a result, Mexico experienced a real appreciation, which further eroded Mexico's competitive trade position and encouraged Mexican consumers to buy international goods.

There were two other important developments in Mexico. First, Mexico had a weak banking system. Mexican banks had been privatized in the early 1990s, and they subsequently went on a lending boom. Non-performing loans as a share of total loans increased from less than 5% in 1990 to around 10% in 1994. To keep its banks afloat, Mexico's central bank could not let interest rates rise too much. To do so would have threatened the economy and led to even more non-performing loans. (At higher interest rates, borrowers with bad credit are the ones who still want to borrow money.)

Given Mexico's precarious economic situation, the demand for pesos was low. In order to prevent the peso from falling in value, Mexico's central bank used sterilized intervention. That is, because the bank was forced to use its foreign reserves to buy pesos, it simultaneously bought domestic bonds, increasing their prices and keeping their yields low. Understandably, foreign investors were not thrilled with the Mexican government's high-risk, low-yielding peso-denominated securities (called "Cetes"). This led to a second major development: From 1993 onward, the Mexican government started to rely more and more on the newly created Tesobonos to finance its public debt.

Tesobonos are Treasury bills issued by the Mexican government, just as Cetes are, but they are effectively U.S. dollar denominated. That is, although both the purchase amount and the principal payment are denominated and made in pesos, the principal payment is fully indexed to the change in the exchange rate between the dollar and the peso.

Let's consider an example using a 3-month Tesobonos. Suppose the yield on the Tesobonos is 5%. If the Mexican peso exchange didn't change in value, the investor would receive

$$1 + \frac{0.05}{4} = \text{MXN}1.0125$$

after 3 months. Suppose though that the Mexican peso devalues by 5% over the 3-month period. Then, the amount paid to the investor will be

$$\left(1 + \frac{0.05}{4}\right) \times 1.05 = \text{MXN}1.063125$$

Note that this represents a 25.25% (6.3125 × 4) return on an annualized basis. While Tesobonos provided investors with protection against peso devaluation, they also guaranteed that a devaluation of the peso would be extremely costly to Mexico. In that sense, by shifting heavily toward short-term financing indexed to the dollar, the Mexican government signaled that it would not let the peso devalue. On December 30, 1994, $48.9 billion of Tesobonos were outstanding, and about one-third of them were held by foreigners.

The year 1994 was an election year for Mexico, and it proved disastrous for the country, both economically and politically. Economically, the current account worsened, the central bank steadily lost reserves, and foreign investors bought only Tesobonos. Politically, 1994 was turbulent as well. Early in the year, the Chiapas Indians rebelled, and the presidential candidate most likely to win the election, Luis Donaldo Colosio, was murdered. This turmoil increased the political risk in Mexico, making it less attractive for international investors.

The situation became untenable on December 20, 1994. With international reserves in short supply, the Mexican government tried to devalue the peso by 13.67%, from MXN3.4662/$ to MXN3.94/$. However, the devaluation proved insufficient, and the

Mexican government was forced to let the Mexican peso float. By the end of December 1994, the peso sank to above MXN5.20/\$, and by March 1995, it was trading above MXN6/\$. Interest rates on both Cetes and Tesobonos shot up. The central bank's official international reserves were insufficient to cover the amount of Tesobonos coming due in the following months. It became clear that Mexico faced an acute liquidity crisis. As we discussed in Chapter 10, the Mexican government was bailed out by a U.S. Treasury and IMF support package at the end of January 1995. The last Tesobonos were issued on February 17, 1995.

The Tesobonos and Cetes securities offer a unique opportunity to study the interaction of country risk and currency risk. The standard Mexican Treasury bills (Cetes) must reward investors for both currency risk and country risk; Tesobonos, however, need only reward investors for country risk because they are indexed to the U.S. dollar. Note that this approach assumes equal default and recovery rates for the two types of bonds, which may not be true. A country may choose to default and pay less on bonds that it perceives to be held by more international investors.

To put these ideas into symbols, let the U.S. interest rate be denoted by i_{US}, the Cetes rate by i_{CET}, and the Tesobonos rate by i_{TB}. The interest rates are all deannualized. Furthermore, we denote the country premium or country spread by copr and the currency or devaluation premium by cupr. We then define

$$1 + i_{CET} = (1 + i_{US}) \times (1 + \text{copr}) \times (1 + \text{cupr}) \qquad \textbf{(14.5)}$$
$$1 + i_{TB} = (1 + i_{US}) \times (1 + \text{copr})$$

Note that we define country and currency premiums multiplicatively rather than additively (see Chapter 11). The country risk premium is, of course, directly related to default probabilities. Let p be the probability that the Mexican government will not repay the Tesobonos investors, in which case we assume that recovery of interest and principal is 0. Then, it must be the case that

$$1 + i_{US} = (1 + i_{TB}) \times (1 - p) + 0 \times p \qquad \textbf{(14.6)}$$

That is, the expected return on a U.S. T-bill investment or a Tesobonos investment is the same, taking default into account. After combining Equations (14.5) and (14.6), we obtain

$$1 + \text{copr} = \frac{1}{1 - p}$$

Equivalently, $p = \dfrac{\text{copr}}{1 + \text{copr}}$. The country risk premium embedded in Tesobonos provides immediate information on political risk probabilities.

Domowitz et al. (1998) studied 3-month and 6-month currency and country premiums in Mexico in 1993 and 1994. They found currency premiums, which averaged 7% to 8%, to be much bigger than country premiums, which averaged around 2.5%. They also found currency and country premiums to be only weakly positively correlated. Nevertheless, the correlation between the currency premiums and the country risk premium becomes extreme when it matters—that is, when the country is on the brink of a currency and/or debt crisis. This is vividly illustrated in Exhibit 14.9, which shows currency and country spreads before and during Mexico's 1994 to 1995 currency crisis.[8]

---

[8]Note that the country and currency premiums in the exhibit are annualized. That is, we multiplied them by 4 because we used 3-month Cetes and Tesobonos. When additive country and currency premiums are reported, one typically uses the annualized interest rates reported in the exhibit, so that the country risk spreads are already annualized. This annualization is not harmless. Three-month securities harbor information about currency and country risk within the 3-month period, not beyond. Consequently, the default probabilities reported in the last column use the actual 3-month country spreads (that is, the numbers in column 8 divided by 4). If we were to use annualized probabilities, the numbers would be higher. If the term structure of interest rates is relatively flat, these annualized probabilities will give a good indication of default risk over a 1-year period. However, in times of crisis, we often observe a downward-sloping term structure of interest rates, and the use of short-term rates may overestimate annual default probabilities.

Exhibit 14.9 Country and Currency Premiums Around the Mexican Currency Crisis

		3 MONTH INTEREST RATES			SPREADS		
EXCHANGE RATE		U.S.	Mexico		Country Risk Premium	Currency Risk Premium	Default Probability
Month	Peso/$ Spot	T-bill	Cetes	Tesobonos			
Dec-93	3.1070	3.054	10.370	5.090	2.021	5.569	0.5026
Jan-94	3.1065	2.992	10.890	4.670	1.666	6.148	0.4147
Feb-94	3.1900	3.435	9.340	5.050	1.601	4.237	0.3987
Mar-94	3.3586	3.538	10.120	6.790	3.223	3.274	0.7994
Apr-94	3.2700	3.940	16.450	7.750	3.773	8.535	0.9344
May-94	3.3200	4.260	16.770	7.190	2.899	9.411	0.7196
Jun-94	3.3900	4.240	17.000	7.000	2.731	9.828	0.6781
Jul-94	3.4000	4.354	17.190	7.250	2.865	9.763	0.7111
Aug-94	3.3785	4.655	13.820	7.240	2.555	6.463	0.6348
Sep-94	3.3955	4.768	13.100	6.790	1.998	6.205	0.4971
Oct-94	3.4335	5.121	14.350	6.730	1.589	7.494	0.3956
Nov-94	3.4475	5.423	14.760	7.500	2.049	7.126	0.5097
Dec-94	5.0750	5.682	31.990	10.490	4.741	20.950	1.1710
Jan-95	5.7350	5.902	38.000	24.980	18.800	12.250	4.4890
Feb-95	5.8750	5.870	57.000	16.990	10.960	38.380	2.6670

Notes: The original source is Bloomberg, but the first five columns were taken from Froot (1995). The last three columns represent the authors' own computations. The risk premiums are annualized, but the default probability applies to a 3-month horizon, and is in percent.

In the beginning of 1995, Mexico suffered from extreme country and currency risk, with the currency premium exceeding 35% and the country premium exceeding 10%. This suggests that taking into account political risk should also affect the translation of foreign currency cash flows into dollar cash flows. This correlation between the two risks is mostly ignored in capital budgeting. Ignoring it, however, typically leads to conservative estimates of expected cash flows. Let us illustrate this with a numeric example.

Example 14.6   Stars and Bars Subsidiary Sale

Suppose it is the end of 1999, and Stars and Bars, a U.S. company, is planning to sell its Argentine subsidiary in 2 years. Given its projections for the local economy and the subsidiary's projected revenues and costs, the expected sales price is 50 million pesos. While the peso is trading at $1 per peso because of the Argentine currency board, Stars and Bars assigns a 20% chance to a collapse of the currency board regime, which will lead to a 25% devaluation of the peso. Hence, the expected dollar sales price is

$$\left(\text{ARS50 million} \times \frac{\$1.00}{\text{ARS}} \times 0.80 \right) + \left(\text{ARS50 million} \times \frac{\$0.75}{\text{ARS}} \times 0.20 \right)$$
$$= \$47.5 \text{ million}$$

Alternatively, note that the expected dollar–peso rate is $\$0.95/ARS = (1.00 \times 0.80) + (0.75 \times 0.20)$. Political risk analysts are also arguing that there is a 10% chance of total expropriation, in which case Stars and Bars would lose the full value of its subsidiary.

Following the recipe of this book, the expected cash flows are adjusted to reflect the expropriation probability:

$$(\$47.5 \text{ million} \times 0.90) + (0 \times 0.10) = \$42.75 \text{ million}$$

However, it is quite unlikely that expropriation will happen while the currency board is still in place. It is more likely that when Argentina gets into economic difficulties, it may first lift the currency board and devalue the currency. Then, if things get worse, it may also expropriate foreign investments. Hence, a more realistic scenario analysis is as follows:

	Probability	Dollar Sales Price
No devaluation, no expropriation	80%	$50 million
25% devaluation, no expropriation	10%	$37.5 million
25% devaluation and expropriation	10%	$0

The expected sales price now becomes:

$$(\$50 \text{ million} \times 0.80) + (\$37.5 \text{ million} \times 0.10) + (0.0 \times 0.10) = \$43.75 \text{ million}$$

The analysis that ignored the correlation between political and currency risk underestimated expected cash flows by $1 million.

Epilogue

If Stars and Bars sold before the end of 2001, it would have received the full $50 million. However, at the end of January 2002, the currency board had collapsed, and the peso's value was reduced to $0.7143 per peso!

POINT–COUNTERPOINT

Cable Television in Argentina

"You are so naïve!" shouted Ante at Freedy. "That discount rate you've come up with is much too low. This is an emerging market, for crying out loud, so there has got to be an adjustment for political risk in your discount rate!"

Ante and Freedy already regretted having chosen to be in the same group to solve their international finance cases. Their case discussion on the Continental–Fintelco deal was due tomorrow, and they could simply not agree on the discount rate to be used for the cash flow analysis.

The case concerned Continental Cablevision, the third-largest U.S. cable operator, which was seeking to acquire a 50% stake in Fintelco, the number 3 cable company in Argentina, in early 1994. At the time, Carlos Menem, Argentina's president, had overseen a profound transformation of Argentina's economy from a state-dominated closed economy suffering from hyperinflation to an open, deregulated economy in which the peso was pegged to the dollar through a currency board, and many state-owned companies had been privatized. Many risk factors remained. The stock market had been extremely volatile; inflation had been higher in Argentina than in the United States, leading to a loss of competitiveness; and presidential elections were scheduled for 1995. As part of the deregulation program, a treaty was in the works that would allow U.S. investors to own up to 100% of Argentine cable systems and 25% of broadcast television stations.

Ante and Freedy had worked hard on the case and had come up with a set of expected dollar cash flows. The only thing left to do was to discount them at an appropriate rate. Because they were supposed to value Fintelco assuming an all-equity deal, Freedy had suggested simply using the standard CAPM formula (see Chapter 13):

$$E[r_{\text{fin}}] = r_f + \beta_{\text{fin}} E[r_m - r_f]$$

where r_f is the risk-free rate, $E[r_m - r_f]$ is the risk premium on the world market, and β_{fin} is Fintelco's beta with the world market.

Freedy had suggested using a beta estimated from data on publicly traded U.S. cable companies. The number was 1.08. Although Ante agreed with the use of a world market risk premium and a beta appropriate for cable companies, he had read a few articles on cost of capital computations for emerging markets and felt that two adjustments were necessary.

First, he wanted to increase the risk-free rate with the Brady bond country spread. The articles he read suggested that this was an appropriate adjustment for the political risk present in emerging markets. This would increase the discount rate by 3.5% in 1994. Second, he did not feel it would be appropriate to compare the cash flow risk of U.S. companies with the cash flow risk of Argentine companies. However, he had not been able to find data on publicly traded cable companies in Argentina. The beta of the Argentine market as a whole seemed to be quite unstable and had moved from being negative in the 1980s to close to 1.00 the past 5 years. Nevertheless, he felt they had to somehow adjust for the huge volatility of the Argentine market, which had been running over 60% on an annualized basis in the years before the time of the deal. One of the articles he read had suggested scaling up the beta for local companies with the ratio of the volatility of the local market to the volatility of the U.S. or world market.[9]

Freedy shouted at Ante, "If anything, my discount rate is too high! If we could compute betas of the local Argentine cable companies, they would be really low. I think that it provides a unique chance for the U.S. shareholders of Continental to diversify their cash flow risks."

Cousin Suttle Trooth leisurely walked into the room of the quarreling brothers, his smirk betraying a tired déjà vu feeling. "Did I hear someone mention political risk adjustments? I know all about that! I once did a summer internship for OPIC, a U.S. political risk insurer," said Suttle.

Ante and Freedy simultaneously gasped: "You can insure your investments for political risk?"

"Sure you can," replied Suttle. "And it is done quite often, too."

Freedy, reasoning quickly, burst out: "Aha! So I am right. You do not need a discount rate adjustment!"

"Hold on, Cousin, it is not that simple!" said Suttle. "First of all, you should, of course, subtract any insurance premium from the expected cash flows. If your case says there was no insurance, you must still take political risk into account. In fact, full insurance is hard to get anyway. And there have been many cases in which political risk events wiped out whole investments. It is really an extremely bad negative cash flow scenario that many cash flow projections forget to take into account. So making no adjustment at all is probably worse than making an adjustment through the discount rate."

Ante was getting really agitated. "So, these professor guys talking about Brady bond spreads and risk premium adjustments do not know what they are talking about? Come on!" he said.

"Well, no, I did not say that," Suttle argued back. "It is very difficult to figure out what political risk events may occur, what their probabilities are, and whether there will be some compensation when they do occur. Therefore, some quite knowledgeable people have suggested that it is easier to scale up the discount rate with something that captures political risk in some sense like the country spread. However, it is quite hard to do even that right. Moreover, Freedy is absolutely right that the betas of local Argentine companies with the world market are likely low, and if the shareholders of the U.S. company are well diversified, the true discount rate should be low because the investment carries low systematic risk for them."

---

[9]Damodaran (2003), for example, suggests both to increase the risk free rate by the country spread and to increase the risk premium by some function of the volatility ratio.

"Is there anything you do not know, cousin?" Ante sighed, as he turned on the TV—cable, of course.

Epilogue

Continental Cable and Fintelco signed a joint venture agreement to go in effect in October 1994. However, Continental had trouble financing the deal because of the Mexican peso crisis. Eventually, the $80 million deal was financed using bank loans, part of them insured against political risk by OPIC.

Computing Political Risk Probabilities

In this book, we strongly recommend adjusting for political risk by changing the cash flow projections to reflect the probabilities of political risk. This, of course, requires computing the probabilities of political risk, which is easier said than done. In any case, cash flow scenarios for investments in high political risk countries should incorporate dramatic scenarios where part or all of the investment is lost due to a political risk event. To estimate political risk probabilities, we recommend using as much information as possible. There are essentially three sources of information that can be used, two of which we have already discussed extensively:

- Country credit spreads
- Political risk analysis and political risk ratings
- Political risk insurance premiums

Even when a company does not intend to use political risk insurance or finds it unavailable for its project, the rates quoted for the insurance can be a useful indication. It can tell a firm's capital budgeting group about how much should be subtracted from expected cash flows to account for political risk. It is also possible that political risk insurance products provided by government organizations are priced below private market rates, in which case they should be purchased when available. We will discuss political risk insurance in Section 14.4, but now we discuss how to use country spreads and political risk ratings.

Using Country Spreads to Compute Political Risk Probabilities

Major currency–denominated bonds provide a market-determined assessment of a country's default risk that promptly reacts to new information. Although we do not recommend scaling up the costs of capital using a country spread, we do recommend analyzing these securities to uncover default probabilities, as we illustrated earlier. In addition, when available, securities of different maturities should be examined to potentially detect horizon effects in a country's default probability.

We have already indicated some disadvantages of country spreads. In particular, the country risk premium reflects the ability and willingness of a country to repay debt; therefore, it reflects both political and economic risks. In addition, sovereign bond spreads may be influenced by the risk appetites of international investors, which have nothing to do with the likelihood of a political risk event in the bond-issuing country. Finally, countries that face elevated political risks, such as African countries, are least likely to have any outstanding market debt because their ability to borrow from the rest of the world is limited.

Using Political Risk Ratings

Some of the political risk rating systems assign numeric scores to narrowly defined subcategories of political risk. Therefore, they are likely to be more informative than country spreads about the exact political risks a multinational corporation faces.

The subcategory risk ratings have two major disadvantages. First, because they are not determined by market forces, little is known about how well the ratings truly predict political risk events. In addition, credit rating companies are often accused of lagging behind events and not being able to predict actual defaults. Second, although the ratings are numeric, they are not expressed in units (such as probabilities of expropriation or percentage discount rates) that are useful for capital budgeting purposes. The scores must somehow be converted into such units. Unfortunately, there simply does not seem to be an accepted method for accomplishing this; the following box describes some recent research that goes in the right direction.

Credit Spreads, Political Risk Ratings, and Capital Budgeting

Recent academic research on sovereign spreads, computed either from bonds or from credit default swaps (see Chapter 21), dramatically shows why unadjusted spreads cannot be used to infer political risk probabilities.[10] These articles determine what factors drive the cross-country and temporal variation in credit spreads, invariably finding that local macroeconomic conditions and, importantly, global risk factors (such as U.S. credit spreads) play an important role. This implies that the use of credit spreads leads to a double counting of risk factors. Macroeconomic risk factors should already be accounted for in the usual cash flow analysis, whereas global risk factors presumably should already be part of the usual discount rate factor. Therefore, it makes no economic sense to simply add a sovereign credit spread to a discount factor obtained from, say, the world CAPM. Only the part of the sovereign spread that is driven by pure political risk factors is useful to enter political risk computations. Bekaert et al. (2011) attempt to derive a "political risk spread" by cleansing credit spreads from the effects of other factors (macroeconomic risks, global and liquidity risks). To do so, they use regression analysis and data on these factors and on political risk ratings (from ICRG). Of the variation in spreads that the model explains, about 40% is due to political risk factors, with the remainder due to other factors. Using their model, they can then use political risk ratings to predict a value for the credit spread, associated with political risk, which they call the "political risk spread." Because political and other risk factors are positively correlated, they compute two versions of the spread, a narrow spread (assuming no correlation) and a wide spread (accounting for other factors correlated with political risk). Their analysis effectively turns political risk ratings into percentage discount rate units. For example, during the Argentine crisis, credit spreads rose to over 1,500 basis points, but the model of Bekaert et al. (2011) predicts a narrow political risk spread of about 550 basis points and a wide spread of about 770 basis points.

14.4 MANAGING POLITICAL RISK

Political risk management means more than computing the probability of political risk events occurring. Even after a project is accepted and implemented, political risk must continue to be monitored. An MNC should develop a strategy that minimizes the chances that political risk events will materialize. They should also determine what actions they will take if political risk events do materialize. We discuss these strategies and others in the following sections.

Structuring an Investment

When political risk is a factor, an MNC should structure its investment so as to minimize the chance that political risk events will adversely affect its cash flows. Here is a short list of actions that could be taken:

- **Rely on unique supplies or technology:** The MNC can make a government takeover difficult without its cooperation by relying on unique supplies coming in from its

---

[10]See Borri and Verdelhan (2011), Hilscher and Nosbusch (2010), Longstaff et al. (2011), Özatay et al. (2009), and Remolana et al. (2008).

headquarters or unique technology that is difficult to operate without the collaboration of the MNC.

- **Use local resources:** When the MNC hires local labor or borrows funds locally, it reduces the government's incentive to close down the plant.
- **Bargain with the government:** Prior to making a major investment in a particular country, the MNC can improve its position by negotiating an agreement with the host country regarding how profits the MNC earns will be taxed and converted to foreign currency. Developing relationships with government officials can come in handy if a political risk event occurs and a settlement must be negotiated. Nevertheless, bargaining with the current government can also backfire when the government turns over.
- **Hire protection:** In the case of kidnapping possibilities or violence—for example, because of local warfare—MNCs can hire bodyguards or, at the extreme, employ private military companies for protection. With conflicts raging all around the globe, private military companies have become an important global business in their own right. Many private military companies are no longer small companies built by a few veteran soldiers but are sophisticated companies that offer a wide range of services. The oldest and most respected private military companies in the industry, MPRI, DynCorp, and Vinnell, have been purchased by industrial giants moving into the growing private military company market. MPRI was purchased by L3, DynCorp was purchased by CSC, and Vinnell was purchased by Northrop Grumman. Other well-known groups include Xe, formerly known as Blackwater; Control Risks Group; and Janusian, part of the Risk Advisory Group, with portfolios of services including crisis management, kidnap and extortion management, fraud and insurance investigation, countersurveillance, and the defense of personnel and assets.
- **Focus on the short term:** Anshuman et al. (forthcoming) formally motivate front-loading cash flows in cases where expropriation risk is high. If possible, the MNC can try to repatriate cash flow early. It can also sell assets to local investors or the government in stages rather than reinvesting funds for the long haul.

Insurance

Perhaps the clearest indication that political risk is a cash flow risk is that it is an insurable risk. If MNCs can fully insure against all possible risk events and are fully compensated for their losses, subtracting the insurance premium from the expected cash flows suffices to account for political risk. The reality is much different, however. Full insurance is impossible to purchase. Because cash flows are uncertain, it is typically difficult to insure an amount more than the current investment. Nevertheless, political risk insurance is available from an increasingly wide variety of sources.

There are three potential sources of political risk insurance: international organizations aimed at promoting foreign direct investment (FDI) in developing countries, government agencies, and the private market. Among international organizations providing insurance, the World Bank's Multilateral Investment Guarantee Agency (MIGA), the Inter-American Development Bank (IDB), and the Asian Development Bank (ADB) are the best known. Most Organization for Economic Cooperation and Development (OECD) countries have national agencies that provide domestic companies with political risk insurance. Examples include the Overseas Private Investment Corporation (OPIC; United States), Nippon Export and Investment Insurance (Japan), the Export Development Corporation (EDC; Canada), the Export Credits Guarantee Department (ECGD; United Kingdom), and the Export Finance and Insurance Corporation (EFIC; Australia). The private market has grown significantly and now includes firms such as Lloyd's, American International Group (AIG), Sovereign Risk Insurance Ltd., and Zurich Emerging Markets Solutions.

Coverage is typically provided for three types of political risk events:

- Currency inconvertibility and non-transferability coverage protects companies against losses in case a company is unable to convert its foreign earnings to its home currency or otherwise transfer the earnings out of the host country. Currency inconvertibility and non-transferability coverage does not protect an investor against the devaluation of a country's currency.
- Expropriation coverage protects MNCs and lenders against confiscation, expropriation, nationalization, and other acts by the host government that adversely affect the MNC's cash flows. In addition to outright acts of nationalization and confiscation, "creeping expropriation" (a series of acts that cumulatively expropriate), discriminatory legislation, the deprivation of assets or collateral, the repudiation of a concession, and the failure of a sovereign entity to honor an arbitration award issued against it can also be included in expropriation coverage.
- War and political violence coverage compensates a company when war or civil disturbances cause damage to the MNC's assets or cash flows. Political violence coverage does not cover losses due to labor strife or student unrest without a political objective. Political violence coverage has come back into the spotlight since the September 11, 2001, terrorist attacks on the United States.

Seldom is it true that 100% of losses are covered. Private insurers almost always impose limits on the amount of coverage they provide. We now discuss two of the most important publicly provided political insurance programs: the OPIC in the United States and the MIGA run by the World Bank.

Political Risk Insurance for U.S. Companies

The U.S. government provides political risk insurance through the **Overseas Private Investment Corporation (OPIC)**. OPIC was established in 1971 as a self-sustaining government development agency. Its mission is to mobilize U.S. private capital and technological knowledge to aid the economic and social development of less developed countries with a particular focus on countries in transition from non-market to market economies. OPIC carries out this mission by providing financing through direct loans and loan guarantees and by leveraging private capital, using OPIC-supported funds. However, here, we focus on its third task—the provision of political risk insurance.

By charging market-based fees for its products, OPIC operates at no net cost to taxpayers. While it has issued thousands of contracts and paid close to $1 billion in claims, it has earned a profit in each year of its operation. OPIC has built up substantial reserves of about $5 billion. All its guaranty and insurance obligations are backed by its own reserves and by the full faith and credit of the U.S. government. OPIC insurance can cover up to $250 million per project for up to 20 years, and it can insure up to 90% of an eligible investment. For FDI, OPIC typically issues insurance commitments equal to 270% of the initial investment, with 90% representing the original investment and 180% to cover future earnings.

OPIC offers the three standard types of coverage: insurance against the risk of expropriation, political violence, and currency inconvertibility. OPIC has paid out claims under all three types of losses during its long history. With terrorist acts becoming more prevalent, OPIC has also started to offer stand-alone terrorism insurance. Terrorism coverage protects against violent acts with the primary intent of achieving a political objective, undertaken by individuals or groups that do not constitute national or international armed forces. OPIC has also started to support more and more small businesses in recent years, sometimes at reduced rates. OPIC's political risk insurance and financing have helped U.S. businesses of all sizes invest in more than 150 emerging markets and developing nations worldwide.

Political Risk Insurance in Emerging and Transitioning Economies

In 1988, the World Bank established the **Multilateral Investment Guarantee Agency (MIGA)** to promote development by facilitating investment in emerging and transitioning economies. MIGA provides political risk insurance for projects that cannot be easily covered elsewhere. In addition to the three types of risks covered by most other insurers (the risk of expropriation, political violence, and currency inconvertibility), MIGA also offers breach-of-contract insurance, a relatively new product that protects investors from losses arising from the host government's breach or repudiation of a contract with the investor. The investor must be able to invoke a dispute resolution mechanism (for example, an international arbitration) and obtain an award for damages. MIGA will pay compensation if the dispute resolution mechanism fails due to host government actions.

As of 2010, MIGA had issued more than 950 contracts worth more than $22 billion. Its largest exposures are in Ukraine (12.8%), Russia (12.7%), and Turkey (8.6%). As an example of its 2010 activities, MIGA issued guarantees totaling $1.8 million to the Sierra Investment Fund and the ManoCap Soros Fund of Mauritius covering their equity investment in Dragon Transport Ltd., a transport and logistics company in Sierra Leone. The coverage is for a period of up to 10 years against the risks of transfer restriction, expropriation, and war and civil disturbance. The project consists of the design and development of a national distribution, warehousing, and trading transport company in Freetown, Sierra Leone. The company will provide transport services to the Sierra Leonean market with a focus on the distribution of fish, ice, and other perishables. While small, this project fits in well with two focal points of MIGA's recent activities: developing infrastructure in sub-Saharan Africa and promoting investment in war-torn areas.

Public Versus Private Insurance

Private insurers are playing an increasingly important role in the political risk insurance market. Nonetheless, public-sector insurers remain seemingly indispensable players, especially when it comes to long-term investment insurance in high-risk countries. Taxpayers may wonder why their tax dollars support an agency that provides a service that can be easily provided by private financial service companies. The basic idea is that political risk insurance facilitates FDI in less developed countries and that FDI benefits both the developing countries and the countries that invest in them to the extent that governments should promote it.[11] Assuming that this is true, why then does OPIC have an advantage over, say, AIG? There are two related reasons.

First, the existence of a government-backed or international agency–backed political risk insurance program acts as a deterrent to rogue countries. When an OPIC or MIGA policy is in place, the host government that interferes with an investment risks retribution from the United States or the World Bank. In other words, OPIC and other public insurers provide an umbrella of protection that helps to correct a market failure in the ability of host countries to make long-term commitments to honor contracts. Without such a policy in place, host countries find it harder to resist domestic pressures to confiscate large amounts of foreign capital invested within their borders. In that sense, the presence of public political risk insurance allows foreign investment projects to launch where they otherwise would never have been launched.

Second, when there is a claim, most public insurers try to recover the money from the respective governments of the countries in which the political risk event occurred. The claim then becomes the public debt of these developing countries to the U.S. government (in the case of OPIC) or another developed country. These governments have much more clout than private parties to recover their claims. For example, they can seize assets of the host countries on their territory, put pressure on the governments in trade matters, discourage further foreign direct investments, and so forth. It is striking that OPIC has operated for more than three

---

[11]In economic jargon, FDI is a public good that generates positive externalities, benefits beyond those that accrue to the private parties involved (see Moran, 2003).

decades on a self-sustaining basis, managing a recovery rate of over 90% on its settlements. It is difficult to fathom that private-sector insurance providers would be able to replicate the deterrent function of the public-sector insurance providers or that their recovery rates for damages would compare favorably.

We now return to Oconoc's oil project in politically unstable Zuenvela to illustrate how political risk insurance affects capital budgeting.

Example 14.7 Political Risk Insurance at Oconoc

Barring political risk, the Oconoc project is very valuable, requiring a $75 million investment but generating a present value of $86.78 million. However, when political risk is taken into account, the NPV of the project becomes negative. Oconoc now considers obtaining political risk insurance from OPIC. OPIC has special rates for oil- and gas-sector companies. The ranges of the rates quoted on its Web site (www.opic. gov) for oil and gas development and production on March 29, 2011, are as follows:

Coverage	Rate Range
Inconvertibility	$0.20–$0.40
Expropriation	$1.35–$1.60
Political violence	$0.65–$0.85
Interference with operations	$0.35–$0.55

These rates are annual base rates per $100 of coverage. The actual rate depends on the particular situation in the country. Because the situation in Zuenvela is precarious, we assume that its rates are at the top of the range. Consequently, full coverage on all four types of coverage would cost $3.40 per $100 of coverage. Even though Oconoc may be particularly worried about expropriation, it might prefer to obtain full insurance because an unstable political situation can lead to riots and civil unrest, which can also jeopardize operations.

Let us assume that Oconoc takes out full coverage (that is, all four policies) and negotiates with OPIC to insure for $50 million. This is only two-thirds of the investment, rather than the more typical 90%, but it helps reduce the cost of the insurance. Given this situation, the annual insurance premium is $0.034 \times \$50$ million = $1.70 million.

Exhibit 14.10 describes the new cash flow pattern, which can be compared with that of Exhibit 14.3. In period 1, if there is an expropriation, Oconoc gets paid $50 million by OPIC, so its expected cash flows for that period are identical whether the political risk event is realized or not. Of course, this event then prevents Oconoc from continuing its operations and earning another $50 million in period 2. Moreover, Oconoc must pay the insurance premium of $1.70 million, which reduces its cash flow to $48.30 million. This is true whether or not expropriation occurs. The probability that the cash flow in the second period is realized is still only 0.88. Consequently, the present value computation using the discount rate of 10% becomes

$$V = \frac{\$48.30 \text{ million}}{1.1} + 0.88 \times \frac{\$48.30 \text{ million}}{1.1^2} = \$79.036 \text{ million}$$

Hence, the project now has a NPV of $4.036 million, so Oconoc should proceed with the project.

Does the fact that Oconoc turns a negative NPV project into a positive NPV project mean that the insurance company loses for sure? That is, for the insurance company, the

Exhibit 14.10   Political Risk Insurance and Capital Budgeting

Notes: Expected cash flows are $50 million in period 1 and period 2. There is a 12% chance that the host government will appropriate the project. However, the company takes out political risk insurance, insuring $50 million at a $1.70 million premium per year. That is 48.30 = 50 − 1.70.

expected value of the insurance claim must be negative. If this is true for all of the company's policies in different countries, and if the probabilities that we used accurately reflect the true probability of a risk event, then it seems as if OPIC should have to rely heavily on tax money. But as we learned, this is not the case. OPIC is actually profitable. The reason is that OPIC, in the case of expropriation, will simply turn the money it paid to Oconoc into a U.S. government claim on the Zuenvela government and use political pressure to recover its money. As history shows, OPIC's record in recovering money from offending host countries has been phenomenal.

Project Finance

At the end of the 13th century, a leading merchant bank in Florence, Italy, financed the development of silver mines in Devon, England, which were owned by the English Crown. In exchange for paying all the operating costs, the bank received a 1-year lease for the total output of the mines. However, if the extracted ore did not suffice to recover the bank's costs, it could seek no recourse from the Crown. This is an early example of **project finance**.

Project finance has two main characteristics. First, it is specific to a particular project, and second, the providers of the funds receive a return on their investment only from the cash flows generated by the project. For debts, there is no recourse to a parent corporation—only to the project's cash flows.

The project finance market has grown considerably in recent years. It is particularly prevalent in terms of power, telecom, infrastructure, and oil and gas projects. Project finance deals are typically long term, with maturities mostly extending beyond 10 years and often beyond 20 years.

Famous examples of project finance transactions include the $16 billion Channel Tunnel (the "Chunnel") connecting France and the United Kingdom and the $4.4 billion Berlin–Brandenburg International airport. Although deals in developed countries still dominate, a growing number are taking place in developing countries. However, issuing bonds to finance projects in developing countries is sometimes problematic because of the "sovereign ceiling" that applies to credit ratings for such bonds (see Section 14.3). If the country is not investment grade, it is difficult for the project finance bond to obtain an investment-grade rating, and without that, most institutional investors will not invest in these bonds.

Example 14.8 Petrozuata

Petrozuata was a joint venture between Maraven, a subsidiary of Venezuela's government-owned oil company, Petroleos de Venezuela S. A. (PDVSA), and ConocoPhillips, a U.S. oil company. Petrozuata was established in 1997 to develop the Orinoco oil belt in central Venezuela, the largest-known heavy and extra-heavy oil accumulation in the world. The project initially involved a $2.4 billion investment. It was part of PDVSA's long-term plan to expand domestic oil and gas production in Venezuela, which could not be accomplished without foreign funding.[12]

Directing investments to Venezuela at that time was not obvious for a foreign oil company. In 1976, oil companies in Venezuela were the victims of a great deal of political turmoil. The Venezuelan government nationalized the domestic oil industry, integrating the Venezuelan assets of the multinationals Royal Dutch Shell, Exxon Mobil, ConocoPhillips, and Gulf, among others, with those of PDVSA. According to some estimates, the government compensation package for the foreign oil companies amounted to only about 25% of the market value of their assets. In the early 1990s, the Venezuelan economy continued to depend heavily on its oil revenues, and it had witnessed two (failed) military coups.

Because the project was so large, planning its financing was complicated. Eventually, PDVSA decided to fund 60% of the project with debt and 40% with equity financing. Petrozuata's planning team also decided that project financing should be used on a stand-alone non-recourse basis. Moreover, the deal contained a special feature called a "cash waterfall."

The cash waterfall worked like this: Petrozuata's customers would deposit their dollar-denominated funds from the purchase of refined oil and by-products into an off-shore account maintained by Bankers Trust, a U.S.-based bank. Bankers Trust would then disburse the cash according to a payment hierarchy, ensuring that the project debt would be serviced before money would be transferred to Venezuela to pay off the project's equity holders. It was hoped that this structure would help mitigate political risk and result in lower funding costs. By keeping dollar cash flows out of Venezuela, foreign exchange controls imposed by the Venezuelan government could not undermine the repayment of the debt.

The team considered bank loans, public bonds, and Rule 144A Bonds (private placement bonds, which we discussed in Chapter 11) as possible debt options to finance the deal. Of the three alternatives, the 144A bonds would raise money most quickly because they could be underwritten within a 6-month period and did not require an initial disclosure to the Securities and Exchange Commission (SEC). The main problem with this route, however, was that Rule 144A bonds can only be bought by institutional investors, and many institutional investors can buy only investment-grade debt.

At the time, PDVSA was a very well-run company. However, it had the same credit rating as Venezuela: a B rating from Standard & Poor's and Ba2 from Moody's. Even though the revenue cash flows from the project were protected by the cash waterfall structure, the Venezuelan government could still expropriate Petrozuata's oil fields. Consequently, some political risk remained. Eventually, the deal closed in June 1997. Petrozuata issued $1 billion worth of bonds with three different maturities in the Rule 144A market. S&P rated Petrozuata BBB–, Moody's rated it Baa1, and Duff and Phelps rated it BBB+ (investment grade). Therefore, the project was able to exceed the sovereign rating of the country, partly due to the special project finance structure.

---

[12]See Esty (1999) for additional information.

The financing of the deal was considered a success, and the project itself proceeded smoothly at first. However, President Chavez had other ideas. Chavez initially meddled with the internal affairs of PDVSA, firing half of its workers, including nearly all the well-respected senior managers in 2003. In practice, this turned the control of PDVSA over to the presidency.

Then, on May 1, 2007, President Chavez announced that Venezuela was taking over control of all oil-production projects in the Orinoco belt. Romero (2007) reports that Chavez stated, "Today is the end of that era when our natural riches ended up in the hands of anyone but the Venezuelan people." The international oil companies were allowed to remain as minority partners, but, as we mentioned before, Exxon Mobil and ConocoPhillips decided to take the case to an international tribunal, with the outcome still uncertain. In 2008, the majority of the bondholders reached an agreement with PDVSA, in which PDVSA bought back bonds linked to the Petrozuata project, paying accrued and unpaid interest as well as 33% of the redemption premium specified in the original bond issue.

The MidAmerican Energy Holdings Case

In the mid-1990s, two Indonesian subsidiaries of MidAmerican Energy Holdings Company entered into contractual arrangements with the wholly state-owned Indonesian electricity company PLN, the wholly state-owned natural resources company Pertamina, and the government of Indonesia. Under the contract terms, the subsidiaries were supposed to develop and operate a separate geothermal field, owned by Pertamina, for 42 years. The contracts also involved an energy sales contract, providing that PLN would purchase electricity generated from the field, and they established "unused capacity" fees even when no electricity was purchased. The development was to happen in stages. General Suharto had been governing Indonesia for over 30 years, and Indonesia was viewed as a stable country with low political risk. MidAmerican nevertheless took out political risk insurance policies with both OPIC and Lloyd's.

In September 1997, the Indonesian government issued a presidential decree essentially stopping the further development of the power projects, even though one of them was near completion. In 1998, PLN failed to make the first payment due under its contractual obligation. Moreover, the Indonesian government made it publicly clear that it viewed the power projects as unnecessary. As discussions with the Indonesian government proved fruitless, MidAmerican started arbitration proceedings, according to the stipulations in the contracts. In October 1999, the arbitration tribunal established that the Indonesian government had breached its contract with the MidAmerican subsidiaries and violated international laws it had signed and was therefore liable for damages to the two subsidiaries in the aggregate amount of $577 million. The government's defense was to assert that the contract was established as the result of corruption. Interestingly, the Indonesian government accused all international companies involved in power projects of "KKN" (corruption, cronyism, and nepotism), while trying to cancel the deals.

In the meantime, MidAmerican filed insurance claims, and by November 1999, OPIC and Lloyd's had paid a total of $290 million, with OPIC's share being $217.5 million. As a matter of normal practice, paid OPIC claims become the responsibility of the host country's government, making the claim paid to MidAmerican effectively Indonesian government debt to the U.S. government. From then on, the U.S. government started to pressure the Indonesian government to pay. Successors to Suharto continued to claim that MidAmerican had cut a corrupt deal involving members of the Suharto family. The prospect of reduced foreign investment and strained relations with the United States finally made the Indonesian government capitulate. By mid-2001, the Indonesian government agreed to pay OPIC most, if not all, of the original claim.

14.5 Summary

This chapter discusses how MNCs can measure and manage political and country risk. Its main points are the following.

1. Country risk refers to the potentially adverse impact of a country's economic and political environment on an MNC's cash flows. Political risk is a special case of country risk in which a government or political action negatively affects a company's cash flow. Country risk and political risk are also closely associated with the ability and willingness of a government to repay its foreign debt holders. The risk of nonpayment is often referred to as sovereign risk.

2. Political risk factors include the risk of expropriation, contract repudiation, currency controls that prevent the conversion of local currencies to foreign currencies, and laws that prevent MNCs from transferring their earnings out of the host country. Corruption, civil strife, and war are also risk factors.

3. Country risk analysis became prevalent after the Debt Crisis began in 1982. Many developing countries had borrowed heavily from commercial banks in developed countries, using floating-rate dollar debt. When both interest rates and the value of the dollar shot up, many countries could no longer service their debts.

4. It soon became clear that many countries suffered from debt overhang: They failed to attract new investment as most of the benefits were feared to accrue to the creditors.

5. Many countries attempted to reduce their debt burdens by using debt–equity swaps and debt buybacks. Some fear that these operations merely provided windfall gains for the creditors.

6. The 1989 Brady Plan finally resolved the Debt Crisis by providing for some form of debt relief—securitizing the debt in the form of Brady bonds and stimulating economic reforms.

7. To take political risk into account in capital budgeting, we must forecast the effects it will have on expected cash flows. However, we need not adjust the discount rate for political risk because most global companies operate in open, integrated markets. From this perspective, political risk is diversifiable and does not require a discount rate adjustment—only a cash flow adjustment.

8. Only rarely will adjusting the discount rate instead of a company's cash flows yield the same result as a cash flow analysis.

9. Organizations such as Euromoney, Institutional Investor, Economist Intelligence Unit, and Political Risk Services Group produce country risk ratings for most countries in the world.

10. Both quantitative and qualitative information obtained from experts is used to evaluate country and political risks.

11. The ICRG system contains many subcomponents that can be used to tailor a risk measure to the particular situation a multinational corporation faces.

12. Although country risk ratings provide useful information, it is difficult to translate the information into political risk probabilities. Country risk spreads can be more easily converted into political risk probabilities, but they are not available for most countries. Moreover, care must be taken with respect to collateralized cash flows and maturity effects.

13. Most political risk analysis ignores the fact that currency crises and political risk events often occur simultaneously.

14. In capital budgeting, MNCs should not only take into account political risk, but also should take other actions to mitigate the chances of being affected by political risk events. Examples include relying on unique supplies or technologies, doing business with local lenders and workers, having good working relationships with local and national governments, and front-loading cash flows.

15. MNCs can purchase political risk insurance from either private-sector or public-sector insurers.

16. Public-sector insurers, such as OPIC in the United States and the World Bank's MIGA, are important players in the political insurance market. Some believe that they play a special role because their presence is a deterrent to rogue government actions. In addition, public-sector insurers of large developed countries can put political pressure on foreign governments to pay claims made against them.

17. Insurance is typically available for currency inconvertibility, expropriation, and war and political violence. It is not typically possible to insure all the expected cash flows from an investment.

18. Project financing is a method of financing that is specific to a particular project in which the providers of the funds are repaid only from the cash flows generated by the project.

QUESTIONS

1. Describe the differences between country risk and political risk. What is sovereign risk?
2. What economic variables would give some indication of the country risk present in a particular country?
3. Suppose an MNC is considering investing in Bolivia. Will an overall assessment of Bolivia's country risk suffice to understand the political risk present in the investment?
4. What are three political risk factors?
5. When, where, and why did the Debt Crisis start?
6. What is debt overhang?
7. What is a debt buyback? Why was a program of debt buybacks not sufficient to resolve the Debt Crisis?
8. What were the main characteristics of the Brady Plan?
9. Why should the discount rate not be adjusted for political risk?
10. What are some examples of organizations that provide country risk ratings?
11. How can we use current quantitative information to predict future political events, such as expropriation?
12. Suppose a multinational corporation is particularly worried about ethnic warfare in a few countries in which it is considering investing. Do country risk ratings have information on this particular risk?
13. Can Panama issue a bond denominated in dollars at the same terms (that is, at the same yield) as the U.S. government? Why or why not?
14. What stops governments from defaulting on loans or bonds held by foreigners?
15. What is a Brady bond?
16. How is a political risk probability related to a country spread?
17. What are Cetes? What are Tesobonos?
18. What are the three main types of political risk covered by political risk insurance?
19. What are some organizations or firms that provide political risk insurance?
20. How is it possible to embed political risk insurance in a capital budgeting analysis?
21. What is project finance?

PROBLEMS

1. In February 1994, Argentina's currency board was in place, and 1 peso was exchangeable into 1 dollar. The following interest rates were available:

   U.S. LIBOR 90 days: 3.25%
   Peso 90-day deposits: 8.99%
   Dollar interest rate in Argentina, 90-day deposits: 7.10%

   The latter two rates were offered by Argentine banks. What risk does the difference between the 7.10% dollar interest and 3.25% LIBOR reflect? What risk does the difference between the rate on 90-day pesos and 90-day dollar deposits by Argentine banks reflect?

2. Consider the numbers in the previous question. Assume that if the peso were to depreciate, investors figure it will depreciate by 25%. Also, assume that if the Argentine bank were to default on its dollar obligations, it would pay nothing to investors. Compute the probability that the peso will devalue and the probability that there will be a default.

3. Consider a 10-year Brady bond issued by Brazil. The coupon payment is 6.50%, and the par value has been collateralized by a U.S. Treasury bond.

   The current price of the bond is $98 (per $100 in par value). Compute the (blended) yield-to-maturity for the bond. What is the stripped yield? Assume that the spot rates on the dollar are the ones reported in Exhibit 14.8.

4. At the height of the Mexican peso crisis in January 1995, the default probabilities on U.S. dollar-denominated emerging-market bonds were quite high. A British investment bank, assuming that these bonds would pay 15 cents on the dollar upon default, calculated a 61% chance of default on Venezuelan bonds. Consider a bond with 5 years left to maturity, paying a coupon of 12%. The par value is 80% collateralized by American Treasury bonds. Assume that the U.S. interest rate is 5% for all maturities. What is the price of a bond with $100 par?

5. Badwella United Company (BUC) is worried that its banana plantation in El Salvador will be expropriated during the next 2 years. However, BUC, through an agreement with El Salvador's central bank, knows that compensation of $100 million will be paid if the plantation is expropriated. If the expropriation does not occur, the plantation will be worth $400 million 2 years from now. A wealthy

El Salvadoran has just offered $160 million for the plantation. BUC would have used a discount rate of 23% to discount the cash flows from its Honduran operations if the threat of expropriation were not present. Evaluate whether BUC should sell the plantation now for $160 million. (Hint: Set up a diagram.)

6. You are the chief financial officer of Clad Metal, a U.S. multinational with operations throughout the world. Your capital budgeting department has presented a proposal to you for a 5-year ore-extraction project in Mexico. The expected year-end net dollar cash flows are as follows:

Year	Net Cash Flow
1	$100,000
2	$200,000
3	$250,000
4	$250,000
5	$250,000

The initial required investment in plant and equipment is $500,000, and the cost of capital is 16%.

a. What is the present value of the project? Should the project be undertaken?

b. You notice that the proposal does not include any analysis of political risk, but you are concerned about potential expropriation of the investment. Therefore, you decide to call a meeting to discuss political risk. Who would you invite to this meeting? What information or data would you need? How would you arrive at a political risk probability estimate?

c. Assume that, at the end of the meeting, you decide that the probability of expropriation is between 5% and 7%. Also assume that there is no compensation in the case of expropriation. Would you approve the project?

d. Given the possibility of expropriation, might you want to reconsider converting Mexican peso expected cash flows at forward rates?

7. Web Question: How will the political turmoil in a number of Middle East countries in early 2011, such as Egypt, affect political risk? Try to use Web resources on ratings and spreads to come up with a quantitative answer.

BIBLIOGRAPHY

Andrade, Sandro C., 2009, "A Model of Asset Pricing Under Country Risk," *Journal of International Money and Finance* 28, pp. 671–695.

Andrade, Sandro C., and Vidhi Chhaochharia, 2010, "How Costly Is Sovereign Default? Evidence from Financial Markets," working paper.

Anshuman, V. Ravi, John Martin, and Sheridan Titman, forthcoming, "Sovereign Risk and Investing in Emerging Markets," *Journal of Corporate Finance*.

Bekaert, Geert, Campbell R. Harvey, and Christian Lundblad, 2005, "Does Financial Liberalization Spur Growth?" *Journal of Financial Economics* 77, pp. 3–55.

Bekaert, Geert, Campbell R. Harvey, Christian Lundblad, and Stephan Siegel, 2011, "Political Risk, Country Spreads, and the Cost of Capital," working paper.

Borensztein, Eduardo, Kevin Cowan, and Patricio Valenzuela, 2007, "Sovereign Ceilings 'Lite'? The Impact of Sovereign Ratings on Corporate Ratings in Emerging Market Economies," International Monetary Fund Working Paper No. 07/75.

Borri, Nicola, and Adrien Verdelhan, 2011, "Sovereign Risk Premia," manuscript, MIT.

Bulow, Jeremy, and Kenneth Rogoff, 1988, "The Buyback Boondoggle," *Brookings Papers on Economic Activity* 2, pp. 675–698.

_____, 1991, "Sovereign Debt Repurchases: No Cure for Overhang," *Quarterly Journal of Economics* 106, pp. 1219–1235.

Damodaran, Aswath, 2003, "Country Risk and Company Exposure: Theory and Practice," *Journal of Applied Finance* 13, pp. 63–76.

DePalma, Anthony, 2000, "Mexico Is Ordered to Pay a U.S. Company $16.7 Million," *New York Times*, August 31, p. C4.

Djankov, Simeon, Rafael La Porta, Florencio Lopez-de-Silanes, and Andrei Shleifer, 2003, "Courts," *The Quarterly Journal of Economics* 118, pp. 453–517.

Domowitz, Ian, Jack Glen, and Anath Madhavan, 1998, "Country and Currency Risk Premia in an Emerging Market," *Journal of Financial and Quantitative Analysis* 33, pp. 189–216.

Durbin, Erik, and David Ng, 2005, "The Sovereign Ceiling and Emerging Market Corporate Bond Spreads," *Journal of International Money and Finance* 24, pp. 631–649.

Esty, Ben C., 1999, "Petrozuata: A Case Study on the Effectual Use of Project Finance," *Journal of Applied Corporate Finance* 12, pp. 26–42.

Froot, Kenneth, 1995, "Futures on the Mexican Peso," Harvard Business School Case N9-296-004.

Hilscher, Jens, and Yves Nosbusch, 2010, "Determinants of Sovereign Risk: Macroeconomic Fundamentals and the

Pricing of Sovereign Debt," *Review of Finance* 14, pp. 235–262.

Johnson, Simon, and Peter Boone, 2010, "Brady Bonds for the Eurozone," www.Project-Syndicate.org, September 15.

Longstaff, Francis A., Jun Pan, Lasse H. Pedersen, and Kenneth J. Singleton, 2011, "How Sovereign Is Sovereign Credit Risk?" *American Economic Journal: Macroeconomics* 3, pp. 75–103.

Moran, Theodore H., 2003, "On the Reauthorization of OPIC," Testimony to the Committee on International Relations, U.S. House of Representatives.

Özatay, Fatih, Erdal Özmen, and Gülbin Sahinbeyoglu, 2009, "Emerging Market Sovereign Spreads, Global Financial Conditions and U.S. Macroeconomic News," *Economic Modelling*, 26, pp. 526–531.

Panizza, Ugo, Federico Sturzenegger, and Jeromin Zettel- meyer, 2009, "The Economics and Law of Sovereign Debt and Default," *Journal of Economic Literature* 47, pp. 1–47.

PRS Group, 2010, *International Country Risk Guide*, East Syracuse, NY: The PRS Group, Inc.

Remolana, Eli M., Michela Scatigna, and Eliza Wu, 2008, "The Dynamic Pricing of Sovereign Risk in Emerging Markets: Fundamentals and Risk Aversion," Bank for International Settlements and University of New South Wales Working Paper.

Romero, Simon, 2007, "Chavez Takes Over Foreign- Controlled Oil Projects in Venezuela," *New York Times* online edition, May 2, www.nytimes.com/2007/05/02/ world/americas/02venezuela.html.

Scoffield, Heather, 2000, "NAFTA Ruling Raises Environ- mental Questions; Mexico Ordered to Pay California-Based Metalclad $16.7-Million After Municipality Blocks Plans for a Hazardous Waste Dump," *The Globe and Mail*, September 1, p. B5.

Yackee, Jason W., 2010, "Do Bilateral Investment Treaties Promote Foreign Direct Investment? Some Hints from Alternative Evidence," University of Wisconsin Legal Studies Research Paper No. 1114.

Chapter 15

International Capital Budgeting

*O*n January 10, 2010, the 186-year-old British candy company, Cadbury, agreed to be taken over by the American company, Kraft Foods, for $19 billion. How did Kraft determine that this was the right amount to pay? Why did Cadbury accept the offer? Answering these questions requires a methodology to value Cadbury with or without the merger. This chapter explains how corporations assess such future profitability. Our methodology is **adjusted net present value (ANPV)** analysis. The ANPV methodology can be used in **capital budgeting** when corporations make investment decisions and determine the valuations of international projects.

We also find the ANPV methodology particularly useful when valuing a project done by a foreign subsidiary. We use a multistep approach that begins with the discounted cash flows to the subsidiary and then makes the adjustments necessary to determine whether the project is worthwhile from the parent corporation's point of view. The first sections of this chapter describe why the ANPV approach provides correct international valuations. We then apply the ANPV approach to an extended case involving International Wood Products, Inc., a company that has seen a substantial increase in its exports to Europe and consequently must decide whether to locate a production subsidiary in Spain or expand its operations in New Hampshire.

15.1 AN OVERVIEW OF ADJUSTED NET PRESENT VALUE

This section provides an overview of valuation done with adjusted net present value (ANPV) analysis. This is not the only way to do valuations or capital budgeting. Chapter 16 compares alternative methods, such as the weighted average cost of capital (WACC) method and the flow-to-equity (FTE) method. Although each method can be correctly applied to answer the same capital budgeting question, some methods are easier to apply in different situations. Our view is that the ANPV approach lends itself to international applications most easily.

The basic principal of capital budgeting is that all projects with positive ANPVs should be accepted. For mutually exclusive projects, the one with the highest ANPV should be undertaken. Modern financial theory develops the ANPV of a project in several steps, as discussed in the following sections.

Step 1: Discount the Cash Flows of the All-Equity Firm

The first step in deriving an ANPV is to calculate the net present value (NPV) of the project's cash flows under the hypothetical scenario in which the project is financed entirely with equity. Any benefits or costs associated with how the project is financed are valued at a later stage. Thus, in the first step, we are not concerned about the amount of debt issued to finance the project. The effects of the project on the firm's eventual capital structure or its debt–equity ratio are considered in later stages. At this point, we are only concerned that the value of the cash coming into the firm from the perspective of the firm's shareholders is greater than the value of the cash going out of the firm.

The project's all-equity NPV is the sum of all discounted expected future revenues minus the sum of current and discounted expected future costs and investments. The revenues and costs must be measured on an incremental, after-tax, cash flow basis. All cash flows should be measured in the same currency, and the discount rate must be appropriate for the currency of denomination of the cash flows.[1] The discount rates used for the all-equity NPV of the project should reflect both the time value of the money in which the forecasts are denominated and any risk premium that the firm's equity holders demand. Chapter 13 argues that a risk premium arises when the return on the project covaries with the return on a well-diversified international portfolio, in which case the cash flows from the project contain non-diversifiable risk.

Example 15.1   The Vincenzo Uno Project

Suppose that an Italian company, Vincenzo Uno, has a project with the following expected cash flows:

Annual revenue	€1,000,000
Annual cost	−€600,000
Operating income	€400,000
Corporate tax (0.34 tax rate)	−€136,000
After-tax profits	€264,000

If the discount rate for this project is 10%, the present value of these perpetual expected profits is as follows:[2]

$$\frac{€264,000}{1.10} + \frac{€264,000}{1.10^2} + \frac{€264,000}{1.10^3} + \ldots = \frac{€264,000}{0.10} = €2,640,000$$

Suppose that the initial investment required to generate these cash flows is €2,750,000. Then, the NPV of this project to Vincenzo Uno is negative:

$$€2,640,000 - €2,750,000 = -€110,000$$

Because the project has a negative NPV to the all-equity firm, it would not be undertaken unless additional benefits are available. Later examples in this chapter explore these benefits.

---

[1]Chapter 13 examines the choice of the discount rate for a project. Here we take the discount rate as given. Chapter 16 explores issues related to the currency of denomination of the forecasts.
[2]Perpetuity formulas are discussed in the appendix to this chapter.

Step 2: Add the Value of the Financial Side Effects

The second part of an ANPV analysis adds the **net present value of financial side effects (NPVF)** that arise from accepting the project. Generally, these effects arise from the following:

- The costs of issuing securities
- Tax deductions associated with the type of financing instrument used (including the tax deductibility of interest paid on debt)
- The costs of financial distress
- Subsidized financing from governments

These financial side effects are discussed in more detail later in the chapter.

Step 3: Value Any Real Options

The third part of an ANPV analysis adds the present value of any **real options (RO)** that arise from doing the project. Real options involve the ability to adjust the scale of the project in response to future information, such as closing a gold mine if the price of gold falls or scraping a factory if future demand is too low.

A special case of a real option is a **growth option**, which arises when a firm undertakes a project and obtains an option to do another project in the future. The option to do the second project adds value to the first project. The classic example of a growth option is the ability to do a sequel to a movie. After assessing the profitability of the first movie in a potential series, studio executives decide if it's worthwhile to make a sequel. Part of the benefit of doing the original movie comes in the form of an option to do the sequel only if the original is successful. These investment options are valuable and should be taken into account when deciding whether to do the first movie.

Although real options can be considered as part of the all-equity cash flows in step 1 of the ANPV, we break them out separately for two reasons. First, the value of such options is often difficult to quantify, and second, they are always positive and hence add value to the project. If the ANPV of the project is positive without adding the value associated with real options, the ANPV will only be *more* positive after considering the options.

In summary, the adjusted net present value (ANPV) of a project is the net present value (NPV) of the cash flows of a hypothetical, all-equity project, plus the net present value of financing side effects (NPVF), plus the present value of any real options (RO) that the project offers:

$$\text{ANPV} = \text{NPV} + \text{NPVF} + \text{RO} \tag{15.1}$$

The ANPV is the enterprise value of the project of the firm. The equity value is found by subtracting the value of debt from the ANPV.

Next, we examine the cash flows associated with each of the items in an ANPV in detail.

15.2 DERIVING THE NPV OF FREE CASH FLOW

The first part of an ANPV analysis determines the discounted expected value of the project's future **free cash flows (FCF)**.[3] Free cash flow at time t, FCF(t), is the profit that is available for distribution to those who have supplied capital to the firm. The corporation

---

[3]This section provides only a limited overview of the link between accounting concepts and the determination of free cash flow. See Koller et al. (2005) for a reconciliation of the accounting statements of a corporation and the determinants of the corporation's free cash flow.

uses FCF to provide returns on the investments that various classes of investors have made in the firm.

FCF is defined to be the after-tax, incremental operating earnings from the project plus any non-cash accounting charges, such as **depreciation**, minus investments that the firm makes to produce future profit. These investments are of two types: increases in the firm's capital expenditures and increases in the firm's net working capital. **Capital expenditures** increase or replace the firm's property, plant, and equipment. The firm's **net working capital** is the cash, inventory, and net short-term assets that the firm must have to run its business. Both of these investments are discussed in more detail shortly.

The firm's managers decide what to do with the firm's FCF. If the firm is all-equity financed, FCF can be used in three ways: It can be paid out immediately to stockholders as dividends, it can be used to repurchase shares, or it can be retained in the firm. If the managers choose to retain the FCF, they can plan to pay the future value of today's FCF to shareholders as future dividends or as a **liquidating dividend**. A liquidating dividend is the value of final cash that the owners of a firm receive when it goes out of business. Alternatively, the managers can use the accumulated free cash flow to finance future projects.

As long as the firm earns an appropriate rate of return on its retained free cash flow, the firm need not pay out the FCF to the shareholders when it is realized. But if the management of the firm chooses not to pay out the FCF, it may develop excess cash, called **financial slack**. Firms with financial slack are often poorly managed and have high agency costs. **Agency costs** arise when managers do not have an incentive to act in the interests of shareholders. With too much financial slack, managers are tempted to spend the extra money on negative NPV projects or perks for themselves, such as larger offices or company jets. Financial slack can also reduce managers' incentives to find ways to make the company operate more cost-effectively. If the firm has issued debt, the FCF can be used to pay the interest and principal on the debt.[4] Remember, though, that the first part of an ANPV analysis ignores debt and its associated interest payments, the side effects of which will be introduced later in the chapter.

Incremental Profit

As we noted earlier, free cash flow represents the **incremental profit** of the project. When we make an investment, we are interested in how much new cash is coming into the firm in return. Focusing on incremental cash flows is important because changing how an international corporation operates can cannibalize some of the firm's existing business. For example, when the German car manufacturer BMW decided to build a U.S. manufacturing facility in the Greenville-Spartanburg area of South Carolina, the investment was worthwhile only if the discounted expected profits from producing and selling cars in the United States were larger than both the cost of constructing the new plant and the possible lost profits on export sales from Germany to the United States. If BMW thought it could export the cars that it was formerly exporting to the United States to another country, all the production from the company's new U.S. plant would have been considered incremental. In this case, the discounted expected profitability of the proposed U.S. plant would have been the only factor influencing the decision. On the other hand, if BMW thought that it would not be able to find a new market for the cars it was formerly exporting to the United States, the lost profit on these exports would have been a cost of establishing the new U.S. plant. This latter situation describes **export cannibalization**.

---

[4]See Jensen (1986) for a discussion of the use of debt in mergers and acquisitions. Jensen argues that debt disciplines the management by providing incentives to find efficiencies in generating operating cash flow that allows the debt to be repaid.

Exhibit 15.1   Deriving Free Cash Flow

Step 1.	Subtract costs from revenues:
	Revenue − Costs = Earnings before interest and taxes (EBIT)
Step 2.	Subtract taxes on earnings:
	EBIT − Taxes on EBIT = Net operating profit less adjusted taxes (NOPLAT)
Step 3.	Add back non-cash costs:
	NOPLAT + Accounting depreciation = Gross cash flow (GCF)
Step 4.	Subtract investments made to increase future profitability:
	GCF − Change in net working capital (ΔNWC) − Capital expenditures (CAPX) = Free cash flow (FCF)

Because forecasting free cash flow is separable from discounting it, we first consider each forecasting step in detail before discussing discounting. At this point, we consider all flows to be denominated in the same currency, which involves forecasting exchange rates. The steps needed to forecast free cash flow are summarized in Exhibit 15.1.

Deriving Free Cash Flow

Revenues and Costs

Forecasts of revenue, the price of a product times the amount sold, depend on the corporation's economic environment. Demand for the product depends on the company's pricing and advertising policies, on the competitive nature of its industry, and on macroeconomic factors in the countries where the company's sales occur. Future exchange rates will affect the value of the firm's future revenues. Exporters will be helped by depreciation of the home currency, and import competitors will be hurt by appreciation of the home currency.

The costs of operating a project include the costs of raw materials and labor, which are measured as the costs of goods sold (CGS). The managerial expenses, advertising, and other fixed costs of the project must also be subtracted. These are measured by the selling and general administrative expenses (SGA) of running the business. The final cost that must be subtracted is the accounting cost, measured by depreciation expense. Each of these costs is subtracted from revenues when calculating earnings.

If a firm imports raw materials or intermediate parts, its costs depend on exchange rates. A depreciation of the home currency drives up the cost of imports. Forecasting future costs involves understanding how wages and the prices of inputs will evolve in the economy in which the firm is manufacturing and how much it will cost to distribute the product around the world. It also involves understanding how any productivity-enhancing investments will affect the firm's future costs.

EBIT and NOPLAT

The pretax operating income that a firm would have if it had no debt is its **earnings before interest and taxes (EBIT)**:

$$\text{EBIT} = \text{Revenue} - \text{Cost of goods sold (CGS)} - \text{Selling and general administrative expenses (SGA)} - \text{Accounting depreciation}$$

Interest expense is not deducted from EBIT because we are valuing the project as if it has no debt in its capital structure. Because interest expense is a cost in most countries' accounting systems, however, one has to be careful to construct EBIT correctly from the firm's accounting statements. EBIT is found by adding taxes paid and interest to the after-tax income on the income statement.

After EBIT is calculated, we subtract the cash value of taxes that would actually be paid on EBIT to find an after-tax value of net operating profit. **Net operating profit less adjusted taxes (NOPLAT)** equals EBIT minus the taxes that would be paid on EBIT:

$$\text{NOPLAT} = \text{EBIT} - \text{Taxes on EBIT}$$

In practice, calculating the taxes on EBIT from actual income statements involves adding back the taxes the firm did not have to pay because it deducted interest expenses, subtracting any taxes on interest income that the firm earned, and subtracting any taxes incurred on non-operating income. (The value of "tax shields" arising from the ability to deduct interest payments on debt is discussed in Section 15.3.)

Free Cash Flow

After NOPLAT is derived, free cash flow is only a few short steps away. Because depreciation is an accounting expense, but not an actual cash flow, we must add depreciation to NOPLAT to generate gross cash flows:

$$\text{Gross cash flow (GCF)} = \text{NOPLAT} + \text{Accounting depreciation}$$

To go from gross cash flow to free cash flow involves subtracting two types of investments. We first subtract capital expenditures (CAPX), which are the firm's purchases of additional property, plant, or equipment that are required to do the project.

CAPX is typically large in the initial stages of the project. Eventually, the planned capital expenditures in future years will merely be whatever is necessary to maintain the plant and equipment by replacing what is wearing out, which we refer to as *economic depreciation*. In many presentations of valuations, it is assumed for the later stages of a project that CAPX equals depreciation. One must be careful, though, because there may be a big difference between accounting depreciation, which is related to the book value of the firm, and the actual economic depreciation that future CAPX represents. If CAPX is replacing the existing plant and equipment as it wears out, and if there is inflation, the nominal value of CAPX will differ from the depreciation recorded on the firm's books.

The second investment that must be subtracted from GCF to obtain FCF is changes in net working capital (NWC).[5] If the project involves expected additions to NWC, these investments will use cash and must be subtracted from GCF. Thus, free cash flow is

$$\text{FCF} = \text{GCF} - \text{CAPX} - \Delta \text{NWC}$$

Discounting Free Cash Flows

Because expected free cash flows are future values, we must discount them to determine their present value. Let the discount rate that is appropriate for the riskiness of the all-equity future cash flows be denoted r. Then, if the initial capital expenditures associated with the project are included in the initial year's free cash flow, the NPV of the project, on an all-equity basis, is

$$\text{NPV}(t) = \sum_{k=0}^{\infty} \frac{E_t[\text{FCF}(t+k)]}{(1 + r)^k} \qquad (15.2)$$

Although the discount rate in Equation (15.2) is assumed to be constant, in general, the discount rate is not required to be the same for each period in the future. The appropriate discount rate for each future period can be different. In this case, we can denote the rate that is appropriate for discounting expected time $t+k$ cash flows to time t as $r(t, k)$.

---

[5]Management of net working capital is reviewed in Chapter 19, where we more formally discuss the idea that increases in net working capital are investments that a firm is making in its future profitability.

Different discount rates can reflect differences in the time value of money for different periods in the future. The importance of this adjustment to Equation (15.2) will be demonstrated in the Consolidated Machine Tool Company capital budgeting case that is considered in Chapter 16.

Calculating the Terminal Value of a Project

The summation of discounted expected free cash flows in Equation (15.2) goes into the indefinite future because we think of the equity of a firm as being infinitely lived. Because our ability to forecast is limited, after developing explicit forecasts for a few years in the future, we are forced to assume that expected free cash flow will settle down, either to a constant value or, more typically, to growth at some constant rate such as the expected rate of inflation. Thus, after the explicit forecasting period, we calculate a **terminal value** for the project that represents the discounted present value of expected future free cash flows in the years extending into the indefinite future beyond the explicit forecast period using perpetuity formulas because we are assuming constant growth.

Suppose that we develop explicit forecasts for the next 10 years. Let the final explicit forecast of free cash flow at time t for 10 years in the future be $E_t[\text{FCF}(t+10)]$. Let's assume that future free cash flow grows at the rate g, and let the discount rate for these perpetual cash flows be r.[6] The starting value in year 11 is higher than the expected free cash flow in year 10 by $(1 + g)$. From the perpetuity formula for a growing cash flow, we know that

$$\text{Terminal value in year 10} = \frac{E_t[\text{FCF}(t+10)](1 + g)}{(r - g)}$$

After calculating the terminal value in year 10, we discount it to year 0 by dividing by $(1 + r)^{10}$:

$$\text{Terminal value in year 0} = \frac{\text{Terminal value in year 10}}{(1 + r)^{10}}$$

The growth rate of g should primarily reflect the expected rate of inflation in the currency of the forecasts because the project's real capacity will eventually be met. Additional real investments will have to be made to produce additional real goods. If there is a forecast of real growth without such additional investments, it would be under the assumption that the firm will be able to maintain its market share and its profitability as the world economy grows by installing replacement capital that is more productive than the old capital. If no new capital expenditures are planned and CAPX is just offsetting depreciation, the physical plant and equipment will not be capable of growing indefinitely unless the replacement CAPX is more productive. It makes sense to limit the assumed growth to the rate of inflation unless you are sure that the firm can install more efficient capital as old capital is replaced. If there is real growth and the forecast of real growth rate is 2%, with a forecast of inflation of 4%, we would forecast that free cash flow would grow at 6.08%, because

$$(1 + 2\%) \times (1 + 4\%) = (1 + 6.08\%)$$

Another way of determining the terminal value involves understanding when the firm's return on investment is expected to settle down to the competitive level predicted by the required rate of return that investors demand on capital employed by the firm. This approach to terminal values is discussed in Chapter 16.

---

[6]The appendix to this chapter provides a derivation of the perpetuity formula used in deriving the terminal value.

15.3 FINANCIAL SIDE EFFECTS

While the NPV of a project's free cash flow is usually the primary source of a project's value, it is not the only source. Side effects from financing the project can add significant value to the project. These financial side effects arise from the costs of issuing securities, from the tax deductions that certain types of financing provide, from the costs of financial distress associated with issuing debt, and from the subsidized financing that governments offer to entice corporations to locate in particular countries or regions. We discuss each of these issues in turn.

The Costs of Issuing Securities

When a corporation does not have enough resources from its current and previously generated free cash flows to finance a new project, it must turn to outside investors for additional resources. This process is costly for a number of reasons.

The investment bankers must be compensated for acting as financial intermediaries in issuing securities either to the public or to private investors. This compensation includes monetary fees, but it also includes an **underwriting discount**, or spread. The underwriting discount between what the corporation receives from issuing the securities and what the public pays for the securities is often a large part of the compensation of the investment bank that underwrites the issue.

Lee et al. (1996) investigated these costs as a function of the amount raised for initial public offerings (IPOs) of equity. They found that the percentage costs decrease as the amount of money raised increases, indicating that some economies of scale are achieved. Nonetheless, the costs are still large. According to the researchers, the flat expenses charged by underwriters averaged 3.69% of the amount raised, and gross spreads averaged 7.31% across the 1,767 IPOs studied.

Tax Shields for Certain Securities

When a firm issues debt, the interest paid on the debt is deductible for tax purposes because the government views interest as a legitimate cost of doing business. The value of the ability to deduct interest payments for tax purposes is called an **interest tax shield**. Because debt financing reduces a firm's income taxes, issuing debt increases the value of the corporation, at least for small amounts of debt.

To find the value of the interest tax shield, consider the following scenario. Suppose that the market interest rate on a one-period loan of principal D is r_D. Let the corporate income tax rate be τ. Then, in the first period, the corporation borrows D, and it repays $(1 + r_D)D$ in the second period. Because the interest payment is deductible, the corporation also gets a tax deduction of $\tau r_D D$ in the second period. The present value of these flows using the market interest rate as the discount rate is

$$D - \frac{(1 + r_D)D}{(1 + r_D)} + \frac{\tau r_D D}{(1 + r_D)} = \frac{\tau r_D D}{(1 + r_D)} \tag{15.3}$$

Equation (15.3) demonstrates that the value of a loan at market interest rates is 0 in the absence of tax deductions or subsidies from the government. When interest is deductible, there is a valuable interest tax shield. If there were only benefits associated with issuing debt, the corporation would be entirely debt financed. Something else must be going on. We will examine the costs of debt later in this chapter, but first, we consider how adding debt to the capital structure of Vincenzo Uno's project changes its desirability.

Example 15.2 Vincenzo Uno's Tax Shield

Let's return to Example 15.1 and examine what happens if Vincenzo Uno issues some debt to finance the project. Suppose the company issues €500,000 of debt at 6% per annum. Also, assume that Vincenzo Uno will allow this debt to be outstanding for the indefinite future. The tax shield of $\tau r_D D$ derived in Equation (15.3) now occurs in every period into perpetuity. Hence, the discounted present value of the perpetual tax shield is

$$\frac{\tau r_D D}{(1 + r_D)} + \frac{\tau r_D D}{(1 + r_D)^2} + \frac{\tau r_D D}{(1 + r_D)^3} + \ldots = \tau D$$

With a corporate tax rate of 34%, the value of the tax shield is

$$0.34 \times €500,000 = €170,000$$

Because the net present value, assuming all-equity financing, was −€110,000, the value of the project is now positive, and Vincenzo Uno should do it by issuing both debt and equity.

The Discount Rate for Interest Tax Shields

The basic principle of ANPV analysis is that expected values of future cash flows should be discounted at the appropriate discount rate that reflects the riskiness of the cash flows. In Equation (15.3), we violated this procedure by discounting the promised cash flows with the actual market interest rate. We can reconcile the two approaches in the following way. Suppose that δ is the probability of default on the debt, and if the company defaults, it will pay nothing to its creditors. Then the expected payment is the probability-weighted average of the two possible payments:

$$(1 - \delta) \times (1 + r_D)D + \delta \times 0 = (1 - \delta) \times (1 + r_D)D$$

and the expected tax deduction for interest expense is

$$(1 - \delta) \times \tau r_D D + \delta \times 0 = (1 - \delta) \times \tau r_D D$$

Suppose that the events that will cause the firm to default are idiosyncratic to the firm. Then the appropriate discount rate for the expected debt cash flows is the risk-free interest rate, r_F. Thus, to find the value of a debt, the expected future values should be discounted at the risk-free rate. The value of a one-period debt is therefore

$$D - \frac{(1 - \delta)(1 + r_D)D}{(1 + r_F)} + \frac{(1 - \delta)\tau r_D D}{(1 + r_F)} \qquad (15.4)$$

The expression in Equation (15.4) reduces to the expression in Equation (15.3) when we recognize that the market sets the interest rate to reflect the probability of default:

$$(1 - \delta) \times (1 + r_D) + \delta \times 0 = (1 + r_F) \qquad (15.5)$$

Substituting from Equation (15.5) into Equation (15.4) gives Equation (15.3).

Costs of Financial Distress

The presence of interest tax shields suggests that a firm should be financed completely with debt because the bigger the debt, the larger is the tax shield. This cannot be right because we do not observe firms acting this way. Firms limit their leverage because **costs of financial distress** offset the benefits of the interest tax shields.

Direct Costs of Financial Distress

Financial distress arises when a firm has difficulty meeting its commitments to its bondholders. A firm defaults on its debts when it is unable or unwilling to make the required interest or principal payments on its debts. A bankruptcy proceeding may result, with the assets of the firm being formally transferred from the stockholders to the bondholders. Bankruptcy is costly because the legal, consulting, and accounting fees associated with the process eat away at the value of the company. Academic studies of the direct costs of financial distress find that they are typically around 3% of the market value of the firm.[7]

Indirect Costs of Financial Distress

The indirect costs of financial distress refer to the loss of a firm's value that occurs because people believe the company may fail in the future. For example, some potential customers will avoid a firm's product if they fear after-sales service will not be there. Suppliers will also be less willing to deal with the firm and may be unwilling to extend it credit, demanding that it pay cash for its purchases. This adversely affects the ability of the firm to manage its cash flow and increases the firm's required investments in its net working capital. Other indirect costs of financial distress occur on the managerial side of the business. The firm will have trouble attracting and retaining a high-quality, skilled labor force because no one will want to develop firm-specific human capital. Managers also might spend significant time looking for other jobs. These indirect costs of financial distress are more abstract and therefore more difficult to measure than direct costs.

The Equilibrium Amount of Debt

We know that a firm should issue debt up to the point at which the marginal benefit of the debt from the interest tax shield is equal to the marginal costs of financial distress. This is demonstrated in Exhibit 15.2. The marginal benefit of the debt is constant and is given by the tax shield. The marginal cost of debt is increasing. Initially, these costs are low, but eventually they escalate. To find the total benefits and total costs of issuing debt, we need to evaluate the areas under the marginal benefit and marginal cost curves.

Exhibit 15.2 shows that the marginal cost of financial distress is essentially 0 when the firm first begins to take on debt, but it increases as the firm issues more debt. If the marginal cost of financial distress eventually increases quickly as the firm approaches its optimal capital structure, as in Exhibit 15.2, the total cost of financial distress, which is the area under the marginal cost curve, will be minimal and can essentially be ignored in valuing the firm. The value of issuing debt is then just the interest tax shield. Of course, it is always better to attempt to value the costs of financial distress by understanding how issuing debt adversely affects the ability of the firm to operate in world markets

Subsidized Financing

When a manufacturing company decides to build a plant in a foreign country, the company is often able to get regions of the country, or even entire countries, to compete for the jobs that will be brought to the area. The governments and municipalities of these countries and

---

[7]Some classic articles on the costs of bankruptcy include White (1983) and Altman (1984); for a more recent discussion, see Kalay et al. (2007).

Exhibit 15.2 The Benefits and Costs of Debt

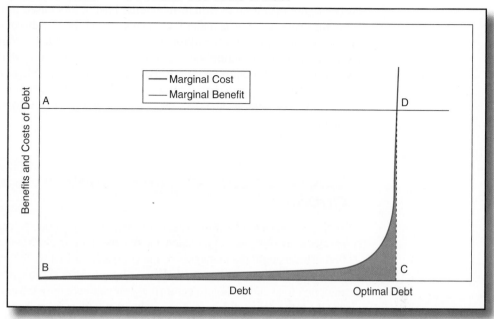

Note: The rectangle ABCD is the total benefit of the debt. The shaded area under the marginal cost curve is the total cost of the debt.

regions will often offer subsidies to the corporation in the form of lower corporate taxes for a number of years. Alternatively, the subsidies might be loans made at below-market interest rates because such subsidies are less obvious to taxpayers.

Interest subsidies add value to a project. The appropriate discount rate for an interest subsidy is simply the market interest rate on the debt of the corporation. Why? Because the corporation is just as likely to default on a subsidized loan from the government as it is on a normal loan at market interest rates. Let's derive an analytical representation of the value of a subsidized loan. Suppose a corporation can borrow a principal of D for one period at a subsidized interest rate of $r_S < r_D$, which, as before, is the market interest rate on the corporation's debt. The corporation repays $(1 + r_S)D$ and gets the interest tax shield of $\tau r_S D$ in the second period. The present value of the cash flows of the subsidized debt using the market interest rate on the corporation's debt is therefore

$$D - \frac{(1 + r_S)D}{(1 + r_D)} + \frac{\tau r_S D}{(1 + r_D)} = \frac{(r_D - r_S)D}{(1 + r_D)} + \frac{\tau r_S D}{(1 + r_D)} \qquad (15.6)$$

Equation (15.6) demonstrates that the value of a subsidized loan is the present value of the interest subsidy, which is the difference between the interest paid on a market loan and the interest on the subsidized loan, plus the present value of the actual interest tax shield. In both cases, the present value is taken at the corporation's market interest rate.

15.4 REAL OPTIONS

As noted in Section 15.1, real options also add value. A good example of how real options add value to international investments was a 1989 decision by Procter & Gamble (P&G) to purchase Phebo, a privately held Brazilian company. At the time, Phebo was the 13th-largest

Brazilian cleaning and personal care products company (see Procter & Gamble, 1991), and P&G was not operating in Brazil. In valuing Phebo, P&G used projected future free cash flows for Phebo's products under P&G management. P&G's discounted cash flow analysis indicated that a price of $91 million was appropriate for Phebo. P&G also recognized that there was significant option value from owning and operating Phebo. The idea was that P&G would learn about operating in Brazil and would be able to expand its presence in Brazil if the Phebo acquisition went well and the Brazilian economy improved.[8] Let's examine how a real option can affect the valuation of Vincenzo Uno, which we introduced in Example 15.1.

Example 15.3 Vincenzo Uno's Abandonment Option

Suppose Vincenzo Uno forecasts that it will either generate €1,250,000 or €750,000 in sales in its first year of operation and that the sales levels are equally likely. After the first year, though, the managers of the company will know for sure which of the two sales levels will persist into the indefinite future. Also, assume that the managers have an option to abandon the project if first-year sales are only €750,000. Finally, assume that the scrap value of the plant and equipment will be €1,425,000.

What should Vincenzo Uno do, given the two different sales scenarios? We summarize the situation with the following table that indicates cash flows in year 1 and in all future years if the project is abandoned in the bad state:

	Year 1		Future Years	
	Good State	Bad State	Good State	Bad State
Annual cash inflows	€1,250,000	€750,000	€1,250,000	0
Annual cash costs	−€600,000	−€600,000	−€600,000	0
Operating income	€650,000	€150,000	€650,000	0
Corporate tax (0.34 tax rate)	−€221,000	−€51,000	−€221,000	0
Unlevered free cash flow	€429,000	€99,000	€429,000	0

Thus, in 1 year, the project will have either of two values. In the good state, the project will be worth that year's free cash flow plus the value of the perpetuity from continuing in the good state, or

$$€429,000 + €429,000/0.10 = €4,719,000$$

On the other hand, in the bad state, the project will be abandoned and will be worth that year's free cash flow plus the scrap value of the machinery, or

$$€99,000 + €1,425,000 = €1,524,000$$

Because these valuations are equally likely, the discounted expected value of the project is

$$[0.5(€4,719,000) + 0.5(€1,524,000)]/1.10 = €2,837,727$$

---

[8]An additional source of value to the project arose from the fact that part of the investment was done with a debt-equity swap. P&G purchased Brazilian government dollar-denominated debt in the secondary market that was trading at a significant discount, presented the debt to the Brazilian government, and received in value more cruzeiros than could have been obtained by purchasing cruzeiros with those dollars at the market exchange rate. Countries do such swaps to encourage foreign direct investment.

Because this is more than the cost of the project, which is €2,750,000, Vincenzo Uno would undertake the project even without the benefits of debt.

Notice that in the first year, the value of doing the project in the bad state in perpetuity is the discounted value of receiving €99,000 in all future periods, or

$$€99,000/0.1 = €990,000$$

Thus, the abandonment option increases the value of the project in year 1 in the bad state by €1,425,000 − €990,000 = €435,000. Because there is a 50% chance of this happening, the value of the project increases by

$$[0.5(€435,000)]/1.10 = €197,727$$

This is the difference between the value of the project with the abandonment option, which is €2,837,727, and the value of the project without the abandonment option, which is €2,640,000, as in Example 15.1.

Problems with the Discounted Cash Flow Approach

The previous section shows that management's real options are important when doing project valuation. The problem with discounted cash flow analysis is that it usually ignores these options. As a result, projects tend to be undervalued. This problem exists whenever a manager can take a discretionary action in the future that affects the cash flows of a project. The ANPV approach adds in the value of real options as a separate valuation term.

Within an international context, perhaps the most important option involves the decision to enter a foreign market. Many factors need to be considered, such as changing costs and prices, changing real exchange rates, and the timing of the market entry. Similarly, the decision to exit the foreign market involves costs and depends on the real exchange rate. One important aspect of market entry is the competition: Does the competition also have the option of entering the same market? There is often a first-mover advantage related to establishing a product in a new market. In such a situation, the value of a firm's option to wait to enter can be competed away (see Grenadier, 2002). Option pricing can help value projects, given these situations.

POINT–COUNTERPOINT

Valuing a Project Using Discounted Cash Flows Versus a Ratio Analysis

Freedy is poring over the income statement of German firm Bayer, trying to develop a spreadsheet model of the discounted free cash flows of the company. He has a meeting with Ante in a few minutes, and he is trying to justify an investment by the Handel Brothers Trust Fund in the American depositary receipt of Bayer, which is listed on the NYSE. Ante asked him to find three or four undervalued equities that would make good investments. For Freedy, the equity value of a firm is found by subtracting the value of its debt from the enterprise value of the firm, which is the present discounted value of the firm's all-equity free cash flow plus any adjustments for debt and growth options. He thinks an undervalued equity has stock market value less than this predicted equity value. He also knows Ante doesn't necessarily do valuations this way.

Suddenly, Ante bursts into the room, sees Freedy's spreadsheets, and shouts, "What are you doing? I only wanted some sensible **ratio analysis**. Discounted free cash flow analysis never works. The valuations always depend on bogus assumptions about the terminal value. On Wall Street, they just check the **price–earnings (P/E) ratio**, and they buy low P/E stocks and sell high P/E stocks. You'll never make an investment if you stick to that discounted cash flow stuff."

Freedy, feeling a bit overwhelmed by his brother's tirade, meekly responds, "Well, I'm a value investor. When I invest, I want to see expected future profits discounted at some sensible required rate of return and know that I'm not paying too much for a stock. Think about all the people who got burned investing in dot-coms in 2000. The managers of those firms would explain to investors that they had 'good ratios' of stock prices to future earnings, but nobody at those firms even had a plan for becoming profitable. It was all a bubble. Ratio analysis is simply stupid."

As Suttle Trooth is walking by, he hears the brothers arguing and asks, "What's all the fuss about?" Both brothers talk at once, and Suttle realizes what's up. He says, "Well, I like doing a discounted cash flow analysis in some situations and a ratio analysis in others. Let's think about the relationship between them. We know that in a rational world, the stock price reflects the discounted expected payoffs to the stockholders. In fact, we know that higher P/E ratios are produced either by faster growth or lower required rates of return on the equity.

"A discounted cash flow analysis is a scientific tool," says Suttle, "but you've got to have the right forecasts to go into the tool. Otherwise, you'll get a garbage-in, garbage-out result. You've really got to understand the sources of a firm's profitability. Does a firm's production process give it a cost advantage that is sustainable? Are there barriers to entry in the market that significantly affect the firm's competitive situation? Have its marketing campaigns generated loyal customers? Is its accounting accurate and an honest reflection of reality? What do we think of the quality of the firm's management team? These are some of the forces that determine profitability, both now and in the future."

"Lots of times," continues Suttle, "analysts become comfortable with the nature of an industry and realize that its firms are all trading at prices around a certain multiple of some measure of current or projected future earnings. The analysts can then make their suggested trades based on P/E ratios, and they can be fairly sure that in the short run, they're in the right ballpark. Nevertheless, ratio analysis is just a quick, summary statistic. It's still necessary to do the due diligence of free cash flow analysis to really value a company."

The brothers looked at each other and smiled. Suttle was on target once again.

15.5 PARENT VERSUS SUBSIDIARY CASH FLOWS

The cash flows from a foreign subsidiary can differ substantially from the cash flows that can ultimately accrue to the parent. Consequently, we must be clear about whose ANPV we are evaluating. The fundamental point of free cash flow analysis is to determine the net present value of the cash that is available for distribution to the ultimate shareholders of the corporation. Hence, the parent's perspective is the most relevant for our analysis. If taxes, regulations, and foreign exchange controls severely limit the amount of funds that can be transferred from the foreign subsidiary to the parent, the project is less valuable than if it were being done by an independent company that owned the project inside the country.

Of course, the parent's free cash flows from a foreign subsidiary can also substantially exceed the subsidiary's free cash flow because of **royalty payments**, **licensing agreements**, and **overhead management fees**. Subsidiaries must pay these costs to the parent corporation. Hence, the subsidiary's income is reduced by these costs, but the parent's income is enhanced.

In addition, if the parent is selling intermediate parts to the subsidiary, the subsidiary's cost of goods sold includes the amount of profit that is included in the transfer pricing of the intermediate parts. Clearly, this profit enhances the value of the subsidiary from the parent company shareholder's perspective.

Although the parent's perspective is ultimately what we want to value, it is often easiest to do international capital budgeting with a three-step approach. We begin with the subsidiary's viewpoint of free cash flow and then consider how the cash flows change when the parent's viewpoint is taken into account. Finally, we adjust for financial side effects and growth options. We now consider these three steps in detail.

A Three-Step Approach to Determining the Value of a Foreign Subsidiary

The first step in deriving the value of a foreign subsidiary to the parent corporation involves conducting the NPV cash flow analysis of the foreign subsidiary as if it were an independent, all-equity firm. This analysis provides the value that an independent company would place on the foreign project if it were licensed to use the technology of the parent corporation. Hence, the royalty payments, licensing fees, and other overhead management fees that the subsidiary must pay the parent are just costs of doing business.

Second, we consider the cash flow implications from the parent's perspective. Several issues are important at this point. First, the dividends that the subsidiary will pay to the parent will incur withholding taxes because foreign governments tax the repatriation of profits. These taxes essentially reduce the value of the free cash flow that accrues to the parent relative to what accrues to the subsidiary by the percentage tax rate. From the parent's perspective, though, the after-tax values of the royalty payments, licensing fees, and management fees that the subsidiary pays the parent provide profits that increase the parent's valuation of the foreign subsidiary. We must also include any profits on sales of intermediate parts from the parent to the subsidiary. Finally, we must watch for cannibalization of exports to the market served by the subsidiary, as discussed in Section 15.2.

In the third step, we must adjust the value of the project for the net present value of financing side effects and possible growth options. Often, there will be loans and subsidies that must be valued. Opportunities for additional growth in the future will also typically be present. These three steps are now demonstrated in an extensive case analysis.

15.6 THE CASE OF INTERNATIONAL WOOD PRODUCTS

International Wood Products, Inc. (IWPI) is considering whether to build a Spanish manufacturing facility to serve its European market. IWPI is U.S.–based and manufactures wooden tables and chairs. The stylishly designed furniture has found its way into better European homes, and the company forecasts that European demand for its furniture is likely to increase significantly over the next 10 years. IWPI is currently exporting to Europe from its New Hampshire manufacturing plant. Because European demand for the company's products has been growing at 10% per year for the past 5 years, the New Hampshire plant is now operating at 100% of capacity. Hence, this is an appropriate time for IWPI to consider establishing a new European production facility.

Although Spain is not centrally located in Europe, the availability of skilled Spanish workers at relatively low wages makes locating in Spain desirable. In addition, the Spanish government is offering a 10-year, €30 million loan at an attractive interest rate of 3% per annum. The interest payments on the loan would be due annually at the end of the year, and the repayment of principal would be a final payment at the end of year 10.

IWPI-Spain's Free Cash Flows

Initial Investments

IWPI's managers have discovered a manufacturing facility outside of Madrid, Spain, that can be acquired for €100 million. They estimate that the total cost of equipping the plant with the necessary machines would be €73 million. An initial investment in cash and inventory would require another €5.66 million. Hence, the total initial expenditure on the project is

$$€100 \text{ million} + €73 \text{ million} + €5.66 \text{ million} = €178.66 \text{ million}$$

At the spot exchange rate of $1.40/€, the total initial dollar investment is therefore

$$€178.66 \text{ million} \times \$1.40/€ = \$250.12 \text{ million}$$

After the acquisition, training the Spanish workforce to meet IWPI's high quality standards will take time, and IWPI forecasts that only one-half of the first year's European demand will be met by the Spanish facility.

Forecasting Total Revenue

Exhibit 15.3 presents forecasts of revenue for the next 10 years for IWPI-Spain. Line 1 indicates that growth in European demand is expected to be 10% in the first year; to increase to 12% by the third year, as new showrooms are opened throughout Europe; and then to decline to 1% by year 10, as the market becomes saturated. Line 2 translates these growth forecasts into forecasts of unit sales. Because the current European demand for IWPI's furniture is 40,000 units, 10% growth in year 1 implies expected sales of 44,000 units. One-half of this, or 22,000 units, will be produced in Spain. Thereafter, IWPI plans to satisfy the entire European demand from the Spanish plant. By the 10th year, the Spanish plant expects to produce slightly more than 76,000 units. The Madrid facility is sufficiently large that this growth can be accommodated without a major expansion of plant and equipment.

The current dollar price of a typical unit of IWPI furniture is $3,430, and IWPI charges an analogous euro price, which at the current exchange rate is

$$\$3,430/(\$1.40/€) = €2,450$$

Sales in the parts of Europe that do not use the euro will be priced in local currencies, but the retail prices will be dictated by the euro price. This retail price is expected to increase at the euro rate of inflation. The forecasts in Line 3 of Exhibit 15.3 indicate that IWPI expects the euro rate of inflation to first increase before falling to 2% from year 4 into the indefinite future.

Line 5 of Exhibit 15.3 forecasts euro revenue by multiplying the expected euro price per unit in Line 4 by the expected number of units sold in Line 2. Revenue forecasts increase from €55.52 million in the first year to €236.04 million in 10 years.

Exhibit 15.3 Revenue Forecasts for IWPI-Spain

	Year in the Future									
	1	2	3	4	5	6	7	8	9	10
1. Real Growth Rates of Unit Sales	10%	11%	12%	10%	8%	6%	4%	3%	2%	1%
2. Unit Sales	22,000	48,840	54,701	60,171	64,985	68,884	71,639	73,788	75,264	76,017
3. Euro Inflation Rates	3%	4%	3%	2%	2%	2%	2%	2%	2%	2%
4. Euro Price per Unit	2,524	2,624	2,703	2,757	2,812	2,869	2,926	2,985	3,044	3,105
5. Total Euro Revenue (millions) (Line 2) × (Line 4)	55.52	128.18	147.87	165.91	182.76	197.60	209.62	220.22	229.12	236.04

Exhibit 15.4 Forecasts of Additions to Net Working Capital and Capital Expenditures for IWPI-Spain

					Year in the Future						
	0	1	2	3	4	5	6	7	8	9	10
1. Total Revenue (Exhibit 15.3, Line 5)		55.52	128.18	147.87	165.91	182.76	197.60	209.62	220.22	229.12	236.04
2. Stock of NWC (year 0 given, then 10.5% of Line 1)	5.66	5.83	13.46	15.53	17.42	19.19	20.75	22.01	23.12	24.06	24.78
3. Addition to NWC (Line 2 year i − Line 2 year $(i-1)$)		0.17	7.63	2.07	1.89	1.77	1.56	1.26	1.11	0.93	0.73
4. Capital Expenditures	173.00	10.58	11.01	11.34	11.56	11.80	12.03	12.27	12.52	12.77	13.02
5. Depreciation		10.28	10.90	11.56	12.23	12.92	13.62	14.33	15.06	15.81	16.57

Notes: All numbers are in millions of euros. Capital expenditures are the nominal spending necessary to keep the real capital stock constant.

Forecasting Net Working Capital, Capital Expenditures, and Depreciation

Exhibit 15.4 presents forecasts of investments that IWPI-Spain must make to maintain its productivity and satisfy the demand for its products. These investments are presented now because they determine accounting depreciation, which is a cost of doing business but not a cash outflow.

The first investment is net working capital, the cash and inventory that the firm needs to conduct its business. The initial stock of net working capital is €5.66 million, and we assume that net working capital is expected to be 10.5% of total revenue. Line 1 of Exhibit 15.4 presents the total revenue forecasts, and the required stocks of net working capital are in Line 2. The additions to net working capital are presented in Line 3 and represent the increases in the stocks from year to year. For example, 10.5% of the first year's total revenue is €5.83 million, which is greater than the initial €5.66 million. Hence, the first-year investment is

$$€5.83 \text{ million} - €5.66 \text{ million} = €0.17 \text{ million}$$

Line 4 of Exhibit 15.4 presents the forecasts of capital expenditures (CAPX). Annual nominal CAPX is required to offset economic depreciation, that is, the wearing out of plant and equipment. Management anticipates that economic depreciation as a percentage of the real capital stock will coincide with the percentage associated with accounting depreciation, derived below. But, as the plant and equipment wear out, the nominal euros that must be spent to keep the real capital stock constant increase with inflation.

The Spanish tax authorities require straight-line accounting depreciation with a 3% per year allowance for plant and 10% per year allowance for equipment. Because plant represents 58% (€100 million out of €173 million) of the initial CAPX and equipment represents 42% (€73 million out of €173 million), accounting depreciation in the first year is $(0.03 \times 0.58) + (0.10 \times 0.42) = 5.94\%$ of initial CAPX (€173 million), or €10.28 million. We assume that CAPX in year 1 is also 5.94% of initial CAPX, but 3% more must be spent due to inflation. Hence, CAPX in year 1 is €10.58 million. In later years, CAPX grows with the euro rate of inflation, $\pi(t+k, €)$, because purchasing the same 5.94% of the real plant and equipment gets progressively more expensive:

$$\text{CAPX}(t+k) = \text{CAPX}(t+k-1) \times (1 + \pi(t+k, €))$$

Line 5 of Exhibit 15.4 presents the forecasts of accounting depreciation, which are related to the forecasts of CAPX. Until the initial plant and equipment are fully depreciated, which will take 33 years for plant and 10 years for equipment, depreciation in year $t+k$ is the same as last year's depreciation plus 5.94% of last year's CAPX. Hence, depreciation follows

$$\text{Depreciation}(t+k) = \text{Depreciation}(t+k-1) + 0.0594 \times \text{CAPX}(t+k-1)$$

Forecasting Total Costs

Exhibit 15.5 forecasts total costs for IWPI-Spain, which include variable costs and fixed costs. Variable cost per unit has three components. Labor costs in Line 1.a begin at €702. Materials sourced in Europe, presented in Line 1.b, are forecast to cost €665 per unit in the first year. Intermediate parts sourced from the parent company, IWPI-U.S., are presented in Line 1.c and are forecast to cost €407 per unit in the first year. Labor costs, the price of European materials, and the euro price of U.S. parts are each forecast to increase at the euro rate of inflation. For imported parts, this assumption is consistent with the dollar prices of the parts being expected to increase at the dollar rate of inflation and the $/€ exchange rate being expected to satisfy relative purchasing power parity (see Chapter 8). Total variable cost in Line 2 represents the estimated number of units sold in a particular year (Line 2 of Exhibit 15.3) multiplied by the sum of the per-unit variable labor costs and the two material costs. Total variable cost is forecast to increase from €39.03 million in the first year to €165.93 million in 10 years.

The next part of Exhibit 15.5 forecasts the costs associated with the royalty and the overhead allocation agreements between IWPI-U.S. and IWPI-Spain. The royalty fee paid by IWPI-Spain to its parent, in Line 3, is 5% of total revenue. The overhead allocation fee paid to the parent corporation for accounting and other managerial assistance, in Line 4, is 2% of total revenue. Because these fees are constant percentages of total revenue, they grow with total revenue.

Fixed costs and direct overhead expenses of IWPI-Spain are presented in Line 5 of Exhibit 15.5. These begin at €1.59 million and increase at the euro rate of inflation. Depreciation, calculated in Exhibit 15.4, is the last cost and is presented again for completeness as Line 6.

Total cost in Line 7 of Exhibit 15.5 is the sum of total variable cost in Line 2, the royalty fee in Line 3, the overhead allocation fee in Line 4, the overhead expenses in Line 5, and depreciation in Line 6. Total costs are forecast to increase from €54.78 million in the first year to €200.98 million in 10 years.

Exhibit 15.5 Cost Forecasts for IWPI-Spain

| | \multicolumn{10}{c}{Year in the Future} | | | | | | | | | |
	1	2	3	4	5	6	7	8	9	10
1. Variable Cost per Unit										
a. Labor	702	730	752	767	782	798	814	830	847	864
b. Materials Sourced in Europe	665	692	712	727	741	756	771	786	802	818
c. Parts Purchased from IWPI-U.S.	407	423	436	445	454	463	472	481	491	501
2. Total Variable Cost (Lines 1.a + 1.b + 1.c) × (Exhibit 15.3, Line 2)	39.03	90.11	103.95	116.63	128.48	138.91	147.36	154.81	161.07	165.93
3. Royalty Fees @ 5% of Total Revenue (0.05 × Exhibit 15.3, Line 5)	2.78	6.41	7.39	8.30	9.14	9.88	10.48	11.01	11.46	11.80
4. Overhead Allocation @ 2% of Total Revenue (0.02 × Exhibit 15.3, Line 5)	1.11	2.56	2.96	3.32	3.66	3.95	4.19	4.40	4.58	4.72
5. Overhead Expenses	1.59	1.65	1.70	1.74	1.77	1.81	1.84	1.88	1.92	1.96
6. Depreciation (Exhibit 15.4, Line 5)	10.28	10.90	11.56	12.23	12.92	13.62	14.33	15.06	15.81	16.57
7. Total Cost (Lines 2 + 3 + 4 + 5 + 6)	54.78	111.64	127.56	142.21	155.96	168.17	178.21	187.17	194.83	200.98

Note: All numbers except the per-unit values in Line 1 are in millions of euros.

Exhibit 15.6 Forecasts of After-Tax Profit for IWPI-Spain

	Year in the Future									
	1	**2**	**3**	**4**	**5**	**6**	**7**	**8**	**9**	**10**
1. Total Revenue (Exhibit 15.3, Line 5)	55.52	123.18	147.87	165.91	182.76	197.60	209.62	220.22	229.12	236.04
2. Total Cost (Exhibit 15.5, Line 7)	54.78	111.64	127.56	142.21	155.96	168.17	178.21	187.17	194.33	200.98
3. Earnings Before Interest and Tax (EBIT) (Line 1 − Line 2)	0.74	16.54	20.30	23.69	26.80	29.43	31.41	33.05	34.29	35.06
4. Corporate Income Tax @ 35% (0.35 × Line 3)	0.26	5.79	7.11	8.29	9.38	10.30	10.99	11.57	12.00	12.27
5. Earnings After Tax (NOPLAT) (Line 3 − Line 4)	0.48	10.75	13.20	15.40	17.42	19.13	20.41	21.48	22.29	22.79

Note: All numbers are in millions of euros.

Forecasting Net Operating Profit Less Adjusted Taxes (NOPLAT)

Exhibit 15.6 forecasts NOPLAT. Line 1 reproduces the forecasts of total revenues from Line 5 of Exhibit 15.3. Line 2 reproduces the forecasts of total costs from Line 7 of Exhibit 15.5. The difference between total revenue and total cost is earnings before interest and taxes (EBIT), which is presented in Line 3. With a Spanish corporate income tax rate of 35%, Line 4 gives corporate taxes as 35% of EBIT. Line 5 presents after-tax earnings or NOPLAT, which start at €0.48 million in the first year and increase to €22.79 million in 10 years.

Forecasting IWPI-Spain's Free Cash Flow

Exhibit 15.7 presents the forecasts of IWPI-Spain's free cash flow. The first line presents after-tax earnings (NOPLAT), derived in Line 5 of Exhibit 15.6. To NOPLAT we add the accounting depreciation in Line 6 of Exhibit 15.5 because accounting depreciation was subtracted as a cost, but it is not a cash flow. The firm's investments, the change in its net working capital and its capital expenditures, from Lines 3 and 4 of Exhibit 15.6, are then subtracted. The results in Line 5 of Exhibit 15.7 are the forecasts of free cash flow (FCF). The initial FCF is negative and represents the initial cost of the project. Forecasts of FCF start at zero in year 1 and grow to €25.60 million in year 10.

The Net Present Value of IWPI-Spain

The forecasts of free cash flow must then be discounted to the present. The discount rate reflects a 4.5% nominal interest rate on 10-year German government bonds (the risk-free euro interest rate), a beta for the project of 1.2, and an equity risk premium of 5.5%:

$$11.1\% = 4.5\% + (1.2 \times 5.5\%)$$

Hence, the discount factor for year k in the future is $1/(1 + 0.111)^k$, and these values are given in Line 6 of Exhibit 15.7. Multiplying these discount factors by the forecasts of free cash flow in Line 5 gives the present values of the free cash flows in Line 7. The sum of these present values plus the terminal value provides the net present value of the project.

Deriving the Terminal Value

The terminal value in Line 8 of Exhibit 15.7 represents the discounted present value of all expected future free cash flows in years 11 and beyond into the indefinite future. The year 0 value of the terminal value is calculated to be €100.17 million. This terminal value is calculated in two steps. First, the terminal value of free cash flow in year 10 is taken to be a perpetuity that is growing at the long-run euro rate of inflation of 2%. The perpetuity must

Exhibit 15.7 Net Present Value of Project Free Cash Flows for IWPI-Spain

	Year in the Future										
	0	1	2	3	4	5	6	7	8	9	10
1. Earnings After Tax (NOPLAT) (Exhibit 15.6, Line 5)		0.48	10.75	13.20	15.40	17.42	19.13	20.41	21.48	22.29	22.79
2. Depreciation (Exhibit 15.4, Line 5)		10.28	10.90	11.56	12.23	12.92	13.62	14.33	15.06	15.81	16.57
3. Change in NWC (Exhibit 15.4, Line 3)	5.66	0.17	7.63	2.07	1.89	1.77	1.56	1.26	1.11	0.93	0.73
4. Capital Expenditures (CAPX) (Exhibit 15.4, Line 4)	173.00	10.58	11.01	11.34	11.56	11.80	12.03	12.27	12.52	12.77	13.02
5. Free Cash Flow (FCF) (Lines $1 + 2 - 3 - 4$)	−178.66	0.00	3.02	11.35	14.17	16.77	19.16	21.21	22.91	24.39	25.60
6. Discount Factors (@ 11.1% per annum)	1.00	0.90	0.81	0.73	0.66	0.59	0.53	0.48	0.43	0.39	0.35
7. Present Value of FCF (Lines 5×6)	−178.66	0.00	2.45	8.28	9.30	9.91	10.19	10.15	9.87	9.46	8.94
8. Terminal Value	100.17										
9. NPV of the Project (sum of Line 7 + Line 8)	0.05										

Notes: All numbers except the discount factors are in millions of euros. The terminal value is the discounted value of free cash flow from years 11 to infinity, calculated as a perpetuity growing at the euro rate of inflation of 2%.

be discounted at 11.1%, and its starting value in year 11 will be 2% higher than the expected value of the free cash flow in year 10. That is, the terminal value in year 10 is

$$\frac{(€25.60 \text{ million}) \times (1 + 0.02)}{(0.111 - 0.02)} = €286.95 \text{ million}$$

Second, the terminal value in year 10 is discounted to year 0 by dividing by $(1 + 0.111)^{10}$:

$$\text{Terminal value in year } 0 = \frac{€286.95 \text{ million}}{(1 + 0.111)^{10}} = €100.17 \text{ million}$$

Notice that IWPI forecasts 2% growth in free cash flow into the indefinite future, which is the expected euro rate of inflation. This reflects IWPI's assessment that the Spanish plant and equipment can only produce 76,000 units. Consequently, free cash flow cannot grow faster than inflation without additional investments.

The last line of Exhibit 15.7 adds the present values of the free cash flows in Line 7 and the terminal value in Line 8 to obtain an initial net present value of the project of €0.05 million. This is the value that an independent all-equity Spanish company that was licensed by IWPI would place on the cash flows coming from IWPI-Spain. Such a company would have a zero net present value project. The projected value of the free cash flows in years 1 to infinity would just be worth what the company would pay in the initial year.

The Parent Company's Perspective

This section considers how the value of a project changes when we take the perspective of the U.S. parent corporation. We first adjust for differences in taxes because the U.S. parent owes U.S. taxes on the dividends it receives, but it also receives some tax credits. More importantly, many items that were costs to the subsidiary provide profit to the parent. This additional profit substantially enhances the parent's value of the project. Throughout this section, we continue to present the analysis in euros, although we note that U.S. taxes must be paid in dollars.

Forecasting the Dividends Received by IWPI-U.S.

We assume that the dividends IWPI-Spain pays to its parent company, IWPI-U.S., will equal its annual free cash flow. The amount that IWPI-U.S. receives depends on both Spanish and U.S. tax laws. Exhibit 15.8 demonstrates that IWPI-U.S. initially receives 10% less than IWPI-Spain pays because the Spanish government imposes a 10% withholding tax on dividends paid by subsidiaries to their parent corporations.

Calculating the U.S. Foreign Tax Credit

Under U.S. tax law, IWPI-U.S. can claim a foreign tax credit for the withholding tax that is paid on the international dividends it receives. IWPI-U.S. also receives a tax credit for a portion of the Spanish income tax paid by IWPI-Spain. The portion of the Spanish tax that becomes a U.S. tax credit is determined by the deemed paid credit, which is discussed shortly. These tax credits help to offset the IWPI-U.S. income tax liability in the United States on the dividend income it receives from its Spanish subsidiary. Exhibit 15.9 presents the U.S. foreign tax credit, and Exhibit 15.10 derives the potential U.S. tax liability.

Exhibit 15.8 Dividends Received by IWPI-U.S.

	Year in the Future									
	1	2	3	4	5	6	7	8	9	10
1. Dividend Paid to IWPI-U.S. (Exhibit 15.7, Line 5)	0.00	3.02	11.35	14.17	16.77	19.16	21.21	22.91	24.39	25.60
2. Spanish Withholding Taxes @ 10% (0.10 × Line 1)	0.00	0.30	1.14	1.42	1.68	1.92	2.12	2.29	2.44	2.56
3. After-Tax Dividend Rec'd by IWPI-U.S. (Line 1 − Line 2)	0.00	2.72	10.22	12.76	15.09	17.24	19.09	20.62	21.95	23.04

Note: All numbers are in millions of euros.

Exhibit 15.9 Calculation of Foreign Tax Credit for IWPI-U.S.

	Year in the Future									
	1	2	3	4	5	6	7	8	9	10
1. Net Income to IWPI-Spain (Exhibit 15.6, Line 5)	0.48	10.75	13.20	15.40	17.42	19.13	20.41	21.48	22.29	22.79
2. Dividend Paid by IWPI-Spain (Exhibit 15.8, Line 1)	0.00	3.02	11.35	14.17	16.77	19.16	21.21	22.91	24.39	25.60
3. Income Tax Paid by IWPI-Spain (Exhibit 15.6, Line 4)	0.26	5.79	7.11	8.29	9.38	10.30	10.99	11.57	12.00	12.27
4. Deemed Paid Credit to IWPI-U.S. for Income Taxes Paid by IWPI-Spain [(Line 2/ Line 1) × Line 3] if Line 2 < Line 1; Line 3, otherwise	0.00	1.63	6.11	7.63	9.03	10.30	10.99	11.57	12.00	12.27
5. Withholding Tax Paid (Exhibit 15.8, Line 2)	0.00	0.30	1.14	1.42	1.68	1.92	2.12	2.29	2.44	2.56
6. Total Foreign Tax Credit (Line 4 + Line 5)	0.00	1.93	7.25	9.05	10.71	12.22	13.11	13.86	14.44	14.83

Note: All numbers are in millions of euros.

Exhibit 15.10 Calculation of U.S. Tax Liability of IWPI-U.S.

	Year in the Future									
	1	**2**	**3**	**4**	**5**	**6**	**7**	**8**	**9**	**10**
1. Grossed-up Foreign Dividend Received (Exhibit 15.8, Line 3 + Exhibit 15.9, Line 6)	0.00	4.64	17.46	21.81	25.80	29.46	32.21	34.48	36.39	37.88
2. Tentative U.S. Tax Liability @ 34% (0.34 × Line 1)	0.00	1.58	5.94	7.41	8.77	10.02	10.95	11.72	12.37	12.88
3. Available Foreign Tax Credit (Exhibit 15.9, Line 6)	0.00	1.93	7.25	9.05	10.71	12.22	13.11	13.86	14.44	14.83
4. Net U.S. Tax Owed (Line 2 − Line 3, if Line 2 > Line 3)	0.00	0.00	0.00	0.00	0.00	0.00	0.00	0.00	0.00	0.00
5. Excess Foreign Tax Credit (Line 3 − Line 2, if Line 2 < Line 3)	0.00	0.35	1.31	1.64	1.94	2.20	2.16	2.13	2.07	1.95

Note: All numbers are in millions of euros.

The most important part of Exhibit 15.9 is the calculation of the **deemed-paid credit** in Line 4. If the ratio of the dividend paid by IWPI-Spain to its after-tax income is less than 1, only that corresponding fraction of the income tax paid by IWPI-Spain is allowed as a credit against U.S. taxes owed by IWPI-U.S. For example, Line 1 of Exhibit 15.9 shows that the year 2 forecast of after-tax income (NOPLAT) of IWPI-Spain is €10.75 million. Because of its investments in CAPX and the change in net working capital that must be made in that year, IWPI-Spain will not pay its full after-tax income as a dividend. In Line 2 of Exhibit 15.9, we see that the year 2 forecast of IWPI-Spain's free cash flow is €3.02 million, and this amount will be paid to the parent as a dividend. Consequently, even though IWPI-Spain expects to pay €5.79 million in Spanish income taxes, only €1.63 million is allowed as a U.S. foreign tax credit because this is the same proportion of the income tax as the income paid by IWPI-Spain to its parent as a dividend:

$$\frac{\text{Dividend of €3.02 million}}{\text{Net income of €10.75 million}} \times \text{Spanish tax of €5.79 million} = \text{Credit of €1.63 million}$$

The reason that only €1.63 million of the Spanish income tax of €5.79 million is allowed as a foreign tax credit is that the U.S. government recognizes that only that fraction of the income of the foreign subsidiary was paid to the parent. After year 5, the dividend paid is forecast to be larger than the subsidiary's net income because of increases in depreciation relative to CAPX, so the full Spanish tax is credited. The sum of the deemed-paid credit (Line 4) and the dividend withholding tax (Line 5) gives the foreign tax credit in Line 6 of Exhibit 15.9.

Calculating the U.S. Income Tax Liability for IWPI-U.S.

Exhibit 15.10 calculates whether IWPI-U.S. will owe additional U.S. income tax on the dividends it receives from IWPI-Spain or whether there will be excess foreign tax credits that can be used to offset the U.S. income tax IWPI-U.S. owes on other foreign income. Line 1 presents the **grossed-up dividend**, which is the sum of the actual dividend received (Exhibit 15.8, Line 3) plus the foreign tax credit (Exhibit 15.9, Line 6).

In year 2, the dividend received after paying the Spanish withholding tax is €2.72 million. The foreign tax credit in year 2 is €1.93 million. Hence, for U.S. tax purposes, the grossed-up dividend is €2.72 million + €1.93 million = €4.65 million. Because the U.S. corporate income tax rate is 34%, the U.S. corporate income tax on this amount would be

$$0.34 \times \text{€4.65 million} = \text{€1.58 million}$$

If the tentative U.S. tax liability is less than the available foreign tax credit, calculated in Exhibit 15.9 and presented in Line 3 of Exhibit 15.10, then no additional U.S. tax is owed. This analysis is evaluated in Line 4. Line 5 of Exhibit 15.10 subtracts the U.S. tax liability from the available foreign tax credit to calculate the excess foreign tax credit. These excess foreign tax credits can be used by IWPI-U.S. to offset U.S. income taxes owed on other foreign income.

Calculating the Net Present Value of After-Tax Dividends Received by IWPI-U.S.

Now, we can calculate the after-tax value of the dividends received by IWPI-U.S. In Exhibit 15.11 the present value of after-tax dividends received by IWPI-U.S. is €160.84 million. This present value includes a terminal value, calculated as a perpetuity, growing at 2% and discounted at 11.1%:

$$€90.15 \text{ million} = \frac{€23.04 \text{ million} \times 1.02}{(0.111 - 0.02) \times (1.111)^{10}}$$

Because the present value of the dividends is less than the €178.66 million total cost of the project, if dividends were the only source of value, the NPV of the project would be negative, and it would not be undertaken. But, there are additional sources of value. IWPI-U.S. receives royalties and overhead allocation fees that add value to the project.

Forecasting the Royalty and Overhead Allocation Fees

The royalty fee in Line 1 of Exhibit 15.12 is forecast to be 5% of total revenue, which was calculated in Exhibit 15.3. The Spanish government extracts a 10% withholding tax on royalty payments, in Line 2, in recognition of the fact that the royalty payment is income to the parent, exactly like a dividend. The overhead allocation fee in Line 3 of Exhibit 15.12 is also a cost to the subsidiary and a profit to the parent. It is forecast to be 2% of total revenue, and the Spanish government extracts a 14% withholding tax on such payments, as is calculated in Line 4. Line 5 of Exhibit 15.12 sums the after-withholding-tax values of the royalty and overhead fees, which provide forecasts of income to IWPI-U.S. The tentative U.S. corporate tax liability of 34% is calculated in Line 6, based on the gross of foreign tax royalties and fees received, because the U.S. government gives a tax credit for the Spanish withholding taxes. Line 7 presents the excess foreign tax credit that is available from Exhibit 15.10. The net U.S. tax owed is calculated in Line 8. IWPI receives a tax credit for the two withholding taxes and can use the excess foreign tax credit from its dividends.

Exhibit 15.11 Net Present Value of After-Tax Dividends for IWPI-U.S.

					Year in the Future						
	0	1	2	3	4	5	6	7	8	9	10
1. After Tax Value of Dividends to IWPI-U.S. (Exhibit 15.8, Line 3 − Exhibit 15.10, Line 4)		0.00	2.72	10.22	12.76	15.09	17.24	19.09	20.62	21.95	23.04
2. Discount Factors (@ 11.1% per annum)	1.00	0.90	0.81	0.73	0.66	0.59	0.53	0.48	0.43	0.39	0.35
3. Present Value of After-Tax Dividends (Line 1 × Line 2)		0.00	2.20	7.45	8.37	8.92	9.17	9.14	8.88	8.51	8.04
4. Terminal Value of Dividends	90.15										
5. NPV of After-Tax Dividends (sum of Line 3 + Line 4)	160.84										

Notes: All numbers except the discount factors are in millions of euros. The terminal value is the discounted value of dividends from years 11 to infinity, calculated as a perpetuity growing at the euro rate of inflation of 2%.

Exhibit 15.12 Net Present Value of After-Tax Royalty and Overhead Allocation Fees Received by IWPI-U.S.

					Year in the Future						
	0	1	2	3	4	5	6	7	8	9	10
1. Royalty Fee @ 5% of Total Revenue (Exhibit 15.5, Line 3)		2.78	6.41	7.39	8.30	9.14	9.88	10.48	11.01	11.46	11.80
2. Spanish Withholding Tax @ 10% (0.10 × Line 1)		0.28	0.64	0.74	0.83	0.91	0.99	1.05	1.10	1.15	1.18
3. Overhead Fee @ 2% of Total Revenue (Exhibit 15.5, Line 4)		1.11	2.56	2.96	3.32	3.66	3.95	4.19	4.40	4.58	4.72
4. Spanish Withholding Taxes @ 14% (0.14 × Line 3)		0.16	0.36	0.41	0.46	0.51	0.55	0.59	0.62	0.64	0.66
5. After-Tax Fees Received by IWPI-U.S. (Line 1 − Line 2 + Line 3 − Line 4)		3.45	7.97	9.20	10.32	11.37	12.29	13.04	13.70	14.25	14.68
6. Tentative U.S. Tax Liability @ 34% (0.34 × (Line 1 + Line 3)		1.32	3.05	3.52	3.95	4.35	4.70	4.99	5.24	5.45	5.62
7. Excess Foreign Tax Credit from Dividends (Exhibit 15.10, Line 5)		0.00	0.35	1.31	1.64	1.94	2.20	2.16	2.13	2.07	1.95
8. Net U.S. Tax Owed (Line 6 − Line 2 − Line 4 − Line 7)		0.89	1.70	1.06	1.02	0.99	0.96	1.19	1.39	1.60	1.82
9. After-Tax Value of Fees to IWPI-U.S. (Line 5 − Line 8)		2.57	6.27	8.14	9.30	10.38	11.33	11.85	12.31	12.65	12.86
10. Discount Factors (@ 11.1% per annum)		0.90	0.81	0.73	0.66	0.59	0.53	0.48	0.43	0.39	0.35
11. Present Value of After-Tax Fees (Line 8 × Line 9)		2.31	5.08	5.94	6.10	6.13	6.02	5.67	5.30	4.91	4.49
12. Terminal Value of Fees	50.31										
13. NPV of After-Tax Fees (Sum of Line 11 + Line 12)	102.26										

Notes: All numbers except the discount factors are in millions of euros. The terminal value is the discounted value of fees from years 11 to infinity, calculated as a perpetuity growing at the euro rate of inflation of 2%.

For example, in year 2, IWPI-U.S. receives €7.97 million of after-withholding-tax fees, based on €8.97 million of gross income. This gross income generates a tentative U.S. tax liability of €3.05 million. But IWPI-U.S. paid withholding taxes of €0.64 million on the royalty and €0.36 million on the overhead, for which it receives foreign tax credits. IWPI-U.S. can also use the €0.35 million of excess foreign tax credits associated with the income tax on its dividends, calculated in Exhibit 15.10, to offset U.S. tax owed. The net result is a tax liability of

$$€3.05 \text{ million} - €0.64 \text{ million} - €0.36 \text{ million} - €0.35 \text{ million} = €1.70 \text{ million}$$

Subtracting the actual U.S. tax liability in Line 8 of Exhibit 15.12 from the after-tax fees received in Line 5 gives the after-tax value of the fees to IWPI-U.S. shown in Line 9. These profits are also discounted at 11.1% per annum, and the discount factors are again presented in Line 10. Multiplying the expected values in Line 9 by the discount factors in Line 10 gives the present values of the fees in Line 11. The terminal value of the fees for years 11 to the indefinite future discounted to year 0 is €50.31 million, and it is calculated just like the terminal value of dividends. The net present value of the fees, which is the sum of the discounted values in Line 11 and the terminal value in Line 12, is €102.26 million.

Forecasting the Profits Earned from Intermediate Goods

Because IWPI-U.S. sells intermediate parts to IWPI-Spain, additional profit accrues to IWPI-U.S. Exhibit 15.13 calculates the net present value of these export profits. Export revenue is

Exhibit 15.13 Net Present Value of After-Tax Profit on Intermediate Goods Sold by IWPI-U.S. to IWPI-Spain

					Year in the Future						
	0	**1**	**2**	**3**	**4**	**5**	**6**	**7**	**8**	**9**	**10**
1. Unit Sales (Exhibit 15.3, Line 2)		22,000	48,840	54,701	60,171	64,985	68,884	71,639	73,788	75,264	76,017
2. Per-Unit Price of Exported Parts (Exhibit 15.5, Line 1.c)		407	423	436	445	454	463	472	481	491	501
3. Export Revenue of IWPI-U.S. (Line 1 × Line 2)		8.95	20.67	23.85	26.76	29.48	31.87	33.81	35.52	36.95	38.07
4. Before-Tax Profit @ 16% Margin (0.16 × Line 3)		1.43	3.31	3.82	4.28	4.72	5.10	5.41	5.68	5.91	6.09
5. U.S. Corporate Tax @ 34% (0.34 × Line 4)		0.49	1.12	1.30	1.46	1.60	1.73	1.84	1.93	2.01	2.07
6. After-Tax Profit (Line 4 − Line 5)		0.95	2.18	2.52	2.83	3.11	3.37	3.57	3.75	3.90	4.02
7. Discount Factors (@ 11.1% per annum)		0.90	0.81	0.73	0.66	0.59	0.53	0.48	0.43	0.39	0.35
8. Present Value of After-Tax Profits (Line 6 × Line 7)		0.85	1.77	1.84	1.85	1.84	1.79	1.71	1.62	1.51	1.40
9. Terminal Value of Profits	15.73										
10. NPV of After-Tax Profits (sum of Line 8 + Line 9)	31.91										

Notes: All numbers except Lines 1 and 2 and the discount factors are in millions of euros. The terminal value is the discounted value of profits from years 11 to infinity, calculated as a perpetuity growing at the euro rate of inflation of 2%.

calculated in Line 3 as the product of the euro price of exported parts per unit in Line 2 multiplied by the unit sales forecast in Line 1.

The profit margin on these export sales is known to be 16%, and this is calculated in Line 4. U.S. corporate income tax on this profit is 34% in Line 5, and the after-tax profits are presented in Line 6. The present value of these expected profits on export sales is €31.91 million.

Valuing the Financial Side Effects

IWPI-U.S. also gets value from the financial side effects associated with the project. The Spanish government is offering a subsidized loan, and the interest payments provide valuable interest tax shields. When the Spanish government loan is repaid, IWPI-U.S. also plans to issue perpetual debt. Let's begin with the valuation of the interest tax shields in Exhibit 15.14.

Interest Tax Shields

The interest rate on the Spanish government loan is 3% per annum, the principal on the loan is €30 million, and the maturity of the loan is 10 years. Hence, for the next 10 years, IWPI-Spain will make annual interest payments of

$$0.03 \times €30 \text{ million} = €0.9 \text{ million}$$

These interest payments are valuable because they are tax deductible. Consequently, they increase the value of the project each year by the Spanish tax rate multiplied by the interest payment:

$$0.35 \times €0.9 \text{ million} = €0.315 \text{ million}$$

Exhibit 15.14 Net Present Value of Interest Tax Shields

						Year in the Future						
	0	1	2	3	4	5	6	7	8	9	10
1. Tax Rate × Interest Paid		0.315	0.315	0.315	0.315	0.315	0.315	0.315	0.315	0.315	0.315
2. Discount Factors (@ 6.00% per annum)		0.94	0.89	0.84	0.79	0.75	0.70	0.67	0.63	0.59	0.56
3. Present Value of Interest Tax Shields (Line 1 × Line 2)		0.30	0.28	0.26	0.25	0.24	0.22	0.21	0.20	0.19	0.18
4. Terminal Value of Tax Shields	8.97										
5. NPV of Interest Tax Shields (sum of Line 3 + Line 4)	11.29										

Note: All numbers except the discount factors are in millions of euros.

If IWPI-Spain were certain that it would make these interest payments, the tax shields should be discounted at the euro risk-free interest rate. In a more likely scenario, though, the interest payments would not be risk free because there would be a probability of IWPI-Spain failing and being forced into bankruptcy. If there is a bankruptcy probability, the firm's debt will not be risk free, and the firm will not expect to make the full value of the interest payments.

Suppose that IWPI-U.S. knows from its investment bankers that if it were to issue 10-year bonds, it would borrow euros at an interest rate that is 150 basis points above the euro risk-free rate of 4.5%. Thus, IWPI-Spain's euro-denominated market interest rate is 4.5% + 1.5% = 6%. The increase in the required interest rate above the risk-free rate reflects the market's assessment of possible default by IWPI.

If the risk of default on the Spanish government loan is the same as the risk of default on a market loan, then 6.0% is the appropriate rate to discount the interest tax shields. The present value of these interest tax shields is the sum of the numbers in Line 3, or €2.32 million.

If IWPI-U.S. issues €30 million of debt in year 11 at its market interest rate of 6%, and if this debt is expected to grow each year at the euro rate of inflation of 2%, the terminal value of the interest tax shields would be

$$\text{Terminal value of interest tax shield} = \frac{0.35 \times 0.06 \times €30 \text{ million} \times (1.02)}{(0.06 - 0.02) \times (1.06^{10})}$$

$$= €8.97 \text{ million}$$

The full value of the interest tax shield is therefore €2.32 million + €8.97 million = €11.29 million. This calculation no doubt overstates the value of debt to the corporation because it ignores the costs of financial distress.

Interest Subsidies
IWPI-U.S. also obtains value from the interest subsidy provided by the Spanish government. If IWPI had to borrow €30 million at its market interest rate of 6.0% per annum, its annual interest payment would be

$$0.06 \times €30 \text{ million} = €1.8 \text{ million}$$

Because the Spanish government only charges 3% per annum, IWPI's actual interest payment is €0.9 million. Therefore, the annual interest savings is

$$€1.8 \text{ million} - €0.9 \text{ million} = €0.9 \text{ million}$$

Exhibit 15.15 Net Present Value of Interest Subsidy

		Year in the Future									
	0	**1**	**2**	**3**	**4**	**5**	**6**	**7**	**8**	**9**	**10**
1. Interest Subsidy		0.90	0.90	0.90	0.90	0.90	0.90	0.90	0.90	0.90	0.90
2. Discount Factors (@ 6.00% per annum)		0.94	0.89	0.84	0.79	0.75	0.70	0.67	0.63	0.59	0.56
3. Present Value of Interest Subsidy (Line 1 × Line 2)		0.85	0.80	0.76	0.71	0.67	0.63	0.60	0.56	0.53	0.50
4. NPV of Interest Subsidy (sum of Line 3)	6.62										

Note: All numbers except the discount factors are in millions of euros.

Exhibit 15.15 values this subsidy using the firm's market interest rate of 6.0%. The net present value of the interest subsidy is €6.62 million.

The Full ANPV of IWPI-Spain

The initial cost of the IWPI-Spain project is €178.66 million. This is the sum of the initial capital expenditures for plant and equipment and the initial investment in cash and inventory. Exhibit 15.11 calculates that the net present value of the after-tax dividends that will be returned to IWPI-U.S. from IWPI-Spain is €160.84 million. Line 13 of Exhibit 15.12 calculates the net present value of after-tax royalty and overhead fees as €102.26 million. Line 10 of Exhibit 15.13 calculates the net present value of after-tax profits on the sale of intermediate export goods as €31.91 million. The value of the interest tax shield on the loan from the Spanish government is €11.29 million, and the value of the interest subsidy is €6.62 million. Upon adding together all the costs and benefits of the project, we find

$$
\begin{aligned}
\text{ANPV of IWPI-Spain} = {} & -€178.66 \text{ million in initial costs} \\
& +€160.84 \text{ million from dividends} \\
& +€102.26 \text{ million from royalties and fees} \\
& +€31.91 \text{ million from exports} \\
& +€11.29 \text{ million from the interest tax shield} \\
& +€6.62 \text{ million from the interest subsidy} \\
= {} & €134.26 \text{ million}
\end{aligned}
$$

At the current exchange rate of $1.40/€, the dollar value to IWPI-U.S. of setting up a Spanish subsidiary is

$$(\$1.40/€) \times €134.26 \text{ million} = \$187.97 \text{ million}$$

The initial cost of the project is

$$(\$1.40/€) \times €178.66 \text{ million} = \$250.12 \text{ million}$$

Thus, by investing $250.12 million, IWPI-U.S. is purchasing a series of uncertain, risky cash flows worth

$$\$250.12 \text{ million} + \$187.97 \text{ million} = \$438.09 \text{ million}$$

The $438.09 million is the enterprise value of the project, which is the sum of the value of debt and equity. Because IWPI is able to borrow €30 million = $42 million from the Spanish government, the equity value of the project is $396.09 million. Shareholders also only need to invest €148.66 million. So, by investing $208.12 million = $1.40/€ × €148.66 million of shareholders' wealth, the shareholders are able to almost double their wealth. This is clearly a good managerial decision unless the opportunity cost of lost export sales is too large.

Cannibalization of Export Sales

The final part of the valuation of IWPI-Spain involves the possibility that IWPI-U.S. may not have another market for the 40,000 units it is currently exporting to Europe. If it does not have another market, the lost profit on these exports is a cost of creating the Spanish subsidiary.

Exhibit 15.16 presents the net present value of the after-tax profit on sales of 40,000 units between the current year and the indefinite future. Units exported are held constant in Line 1, except in year 1, because IWPI-U.S. is currently exporting its maximum capacity from the New Hampshire manufacturing facility. Lost sales in the first year are 18,000 units because the Spanish facility will produce 22,000 units, and total European demand is 44,000. Hence, IWPI-U.S. can export 22,000 units to Europe and will only lose profit on 40,000 − 22,000 = 18,000 units.

Prices per unit are given in Line 2 and correspond to the euro prices forecast in Exhibit 15.3, Line 4. Export revenue is given in Line 3 as the euro price per unit multiplied by the number of units exported. Line 4 presents the profit on these export sales, assuming a profit margin of 16%, the same profit margin as on the intermediate part exports. Line 5 calculates the IWPI-U.S. corporate income tax liability as 34% of the profits in Line 4. After-tax profits are reported in Line 6. Because these are forecasts of risky euro cash flows, it is again appropriate to discount them at 11.1% per annum. The discount factors are presented in Line 7.

Multiplying the discount factor by the after-tax profit provides the present values of each of the cash flows in Line 8. Line 9 presents the year 0 value of the terminal value, which is calculated as a perpetuity growing at the euro rate of inflation of 2% and discounted at 11.1%.

Exhibit 15.16   Net Present Value of After-Tax Profit on Lost Export Sales by IWPI-U.S.

					Year in the Future						
	0	**1**	**2**	**3**	**4**	**5**	**6**	**7**	**8**	**9**	**10**
1. Unit Export Sales		18,000	40,000	40,000	40,000	40,000	40,000	40,000	40,000	40,000	40,000
2. Price per Unit (Exhibit 15.3, Line 4)		2,524	2,624	2,703	2,757	2,812	2,869	2,926	2,985	3,044	3,105
3. Export Revenue (Line 1 × Line 2)		45.42	104.98	108.13	110.29	112.50	114.75	117.04	119.38	121.77	124.20
4. Before-Tax Profit @ 18% Margin (0.16 × Line 3)		7.27	16.80	17.30	17.65	18.00	18.36	18.73	19.10	19.48	19.87
5. U.S. Corporate Tax @ 34% (0.34 × Line 4)		2.47	5.71	5.88	6.00	6.12	6.24	6.37	6.49	6.62	6.76
6. After-Tax Profit (Line 4 − Line 5)		4.80	11.09	11.42	11.65	11.88	12.12	12.36	12.61	12.86	13.12
7. Discount Factors (@ 11.1% per annum)		0.90	0.81	0.73	0.66	0.59	0.53	0.48	0.43	0.39	0.35
8. Present Value of After-Tax Profits (Line 6 × Line 7)		4.32	8.98	8.33	7.64	7.02	6.44	5.92	5.43	4.99	4.58
9. Terminal Value of Profits	51.31										
10. NPV of After-Tax Profits (sum of Line 8 + Line 9)	114.95										

Notes: All numbers except Lines 1 and 2 and the discount factors are in millions of euros. The Terminal Value is the discounted value of profits from years 11 to infinity calculated as a perpetuity growing at the euro rate of inflation of 2%.

The sum of the cash flows in Line 8 and the terminal value of lost profits from year 11 to the indefinite future in Line 9 is the net present value of the after-tax profits from lost export sales. In Line 10, the year 0 value of the after-tax profits on all lost sales is €114.95 million.

Because the ANPV of the project without lost export sales was €134.26 million, even if IWPI-U.S. does not have another market for its current exports, it should still establish IWPI-Spain, although the increase in the enterprise value of the firm is now substantially smaller

$$(\text{€}134.26 \text{ million} - \text{€}114.95 \text{ million}) = \text{€}19.31 \text{ million}$$

15.7 SUMMARY

In this chapter, we develop the adjusted net present value (ANPV) approach to capital budgeting, and we apply the ANPV approach to value a foreign subsidiary. The important points in the chapter are the following:

1. Corporations use capital budgeting to decide how to allocate funds for investment projects, and they should accept all projects with a positive ANPV.

2. The first part of an ANPV calculates the net present value (NPV) of the project's free cash flows assuming the project is financed entirely with equity. Any benefits or costs associated with issuing debt are valued later. The discount rate should reflect the riskiness of the project's free cash flows.

3. The second part of an ANPV analysis adds the net present value of financial side effects (NPVF) associated with the project, which arise from the direct costs of issuing securities, from taxes or tax deductions because of the type of financing instrument used, from the costs of financial distress, and from subsidized financing provided by governments.

4. The third part of an ANPV analysis adds the present value of any real options that arise from doing the project.

5. Free cash flow is the profit available for distribution to a firm's shareholders and is defined as the after-tax operating earnings of the corporation, plus any non-cash accounting charges, minus the investments of the firm. These investments involve increases in the firm's net working capital and capital expenditures on property, plant, and equipment.

6. The pretax operating income that a firm would have if it had no debt is EBIT (operating earnings before interest and taxes):

$$\begin{aligned} \text{EBIT} = \text{Revenue} &- \text{Costs of goods sold} \\ &- \text{Selling and general administrative} \\ &\quad \text{expense} - \text{Depreciation} \end{aligned}$$

7. Net operating profit less adjusted taxes (NOPLAT) equals EBIT minus taxes on EBIT.

8. The terminal value of a project represents the present value of all expected future free cash flows in the years extending into the indefinite future beyond the explicit forecast horizon of the project and can be calculated using perpetuity formulas.

9. If a corporation does not have enough free cash flow to finance a project, it must turn to outside investors for additional resources. The costs of raising funds must be subtracted from the value of the project.

10. When a firm issues debt, the interest payments on the debt are tax deductible because the government views interest as a cost of doing business. Thus, debt financing reduces a corporation's income taxes and increases the value of the corporation. The value of the ability to deduct interest payments for tax purposes is called an interest tax shield.

11. The costs of financial distress refer to the loss of firm value that occurs because the firm may experience bankruptcy. These costs include direct costs due to bankruptcy and indirect costs due to the following: loss of customers who choose not to purchase the firm's products, problems with suppliers who have no long-term interest in the firm, inability of the firm to hire and retain high-quality managers and skilled workers, and poor investment decisions managers may make when the firm faces possible bankruptcy in the future.

12. The value of a subsidized loan is the difference between the interest payments on a loan of the same size at market interest rates and the interest payments on the subsidized loan discounted to the present by the market's required rate of return on the debt.

13. If, when a firm undertakes a project, it obtains an option to do another project in future, the option value of the second project adds value to the first project. In international finance, an important example of

such a growth option is the decision to enter a foreign market to sell a firm's products.

14. Because there can be a substantial difference between the cash flows from a project that accrue to a foreign subsidiary versus the cash flows that can ultimately be paid to the parent company, a three-step approach to international capital budgeting is appropriate. The first step involves doing an NPV free cash flow analysis on the foreign subsidiary as if it were an independent all-equity firm, recognizing that the royalty payments, licensing fees, and management fees that the subsidiary must pay the parent are costs to the subsidiary. The second step involves valuing the free cash flow of the subsidiary from the parent's perspective, including the withholding taxes on the dividends repatriated to the parent, and then adding back the after-tax value of royalty payments, licensing fees, and management fees paid by the subsidiary, along with any profits on the sale of intermediate parts to the subsidiary. The third step involves adjusting the value of the project for the net present value of the project's financial side effects and growth options.

15. The cannibalization of exports to the market that will be served by a foreign subsidiary can substantially reduce the value of establishing the subsidiary. These lost exports could be from the parent or from another foreign subsidiary in a different country.

QUESTIONS

1. Can an investment project of a foreign subsidiary that has a positive net present value when evaluated as a stand-alone firm ever be rejected by the parent corporation? Assume that the parent accepts all projects with positive adjusted net present values.
2. How do licensing agreements, royalties, and overhead allocation fees affect the value of a foreign project?
3. Why does an adjusted net present value analysis treat the present value of financial side effects as a separate item? Isn't interest expense a legitimate cost of doing business?
4. What is meant by the net present value of the financial side effects of a project?
5. Why is it costly to issue securities?
6. What is an interest tax shield? How do you calculate its value?
7. What is an interest subsidy? How do you calculate its value?
8. What are growth options? Provide an example of one in an international context.
9. What is the difference between EBIT and NOPLAT?
10. Why is it important to understand and manage net working capital?
11. What does CAPX mean, and why is it a firm's engine of growth?
12. Why is it sometimes assumed that CAPX equals depreciation in the later stages of a project? How does expected inflation affect this assumption?
13. What is the terminal value of a project? How is it calculated?
14. What is meant by the cannibalization of an export market?
15. What are the primary sources of value to IWPI-U.S. in establishing a Spanish subsidiary?
16. Why are the profits on exports of intermediate parts by IWPI-U.S. to IWPI-Spain included in the value of the project?
17. What risks are present in the IWPI-Spain project? How do they affect the value of the project?

PROBLEMS

1. What percentage of the adjusted net present value of the IWPI-Spain project arises from the dividends that will occur more than 10 years in the future?
2. How sensitive is the value of IWPI-Spain to the assumed discount rate of 11.1%? What happens to the value of the project if the rate is 12.1% instead?
3. What would be the terminal values of the dividends from IWPI-Spain if they were expected to grow in real terms at 1% rather than 0%? How would this growth arise?
4. How much does the value of IWPI-Spain, viewed as a stand-alone firm, change if the royalty fee is increased by 1% and the overhead allocation fee is reduced by 1%? What is the change in value to IWPI-U.S.? What is the source of this change in value?

5. **Valuing Metallwerke's Contract with Safe Air, Inc.**

Consider the discounted expected value of the 10-year contract that Metallwerke may sign with Safe Air in Chapter 9. In the initial year of the deal, Metallwerke sells an air tank to Safe Air for $400. It costs €238 to produce an air tank. The current exchange rate is $1.40/€. Assume that 15,000 air tanks will be sold the first year. Make the following other assumptions in your valuation:

a. The demand for air tanks is expected to grow at 5% for the second year, 4% for the third and fourth years, and 3% for the remaining life of the contract.

b. Euro-denominated costs are expected to increase at the euro rate of inflation of 2%.

c. The base dollar price of the air tank will be increased at the U.S. rate of inflation plus one-half of any real depreciation of the dollar relative to the euro, but the base dollar price will be reduced by one-half of any appreciation of the dollar relative to the euro. The U.S. rate of inflation is expected to be 4%.

d. The dollar is currently not expected to strengthen or weaken in real terms relative to the euro.

e. The German corporate income tax rate is 30%.

f. The appropriate euro discount rate for the project is 12%.

g. Metallwerke typically establishes an account receivable for its customers. At any given time, the stock of the account receivable is expected to equal 10% of a given year's revenue.

h. Accepting the Safe Air project will not require any major capital expenditures by Metallwerke.

Can you determine the value of the contract to Metallwerke?

6. **Deli-Delights Inc.**

Deli-Delights Inc. is a U.S. company that is considering expanding its operations into Japan. The company supplies processed foods to storefront delicatessens in large cities. This requires Deli-Delights to have a centralized production and warehousing facility in each of these cities. Deli-Delights has located a possible site for a Japanese subsidiary in Tokyo. The cost to purchase and equip the facility is ¥765,000,000. Perform an ANPV analysis to determine whether this is a good investment, under the following assumptions:

a. The average per-unit sales price will initially be ¥410.

b. First-year sales will be 15 million units, and physical sales will then grow at 10% per annum for the next 3 years, 5% per annum for the 3 years after that, and then stabilize at 3% per annum for the indefinite future.

c. First-year variable costs of production will be ¥225 per unit of labor and $1.75 per unit of imported semi-finished goods. Administrative costs will be ¥300 million.

d. Depreciation will be taken on a straight-line basis over 20 years.

e. Retail prices, labor costs, and administrative expenses are expected to rise at the Japanese yen rate of inflation, which is forecast to be 1%. Dollar prices of semi-finished goods are expected to rise at the U.S. dollar rate of inflation, which is expected to be 4%.

f. The yen/dollar exchange rate is currently ¥85/$, and the yen is expected to appreciate at a rate justified by the expected inflation differential between the yen and dollar rates of inflation.

g. There will be a 4% royalty paid by the Japanese subsidiary to its U.S. parent.

h. The Japanese corporate income tax rate is 37.5%, and there is a 10% withholding tax on dividends and royalty payments.

i. The yen-denominated equity discount rate for the project is 13%.

j. Net working capital will average 6% of total sales revenue.

k. Capital expenditures will offset depreciation.

l. All of the Japanese subsidiary's free cash flow will be paid to the parent as dividends.

m. The corporate income tax rate for the United States is 34%.

n. Deli-Delights Inc. has sufficient other foreign income that will allow it to fully utilize any excess foreign tax credits generated by its Japanese subsidiary.

o. Deli-Delights Inc. does not plan to issue any debt associated with this project.

7. Web Question: Go to http://investor.google.com and find Google's latest annual income statement. Determine its free cash flow. If you discount its free cash flow as a perpetuity growing at rate g, and you discount at 12%, what perpetual growth rate justifies Google's current market price?

BIBLIOGRAPHY

Altman, Edward I., 1984, "A Further Empirical Investigation of the Bankruptcy Cost Question," *Journal of Finance* 39, pp. 1067–1089.

Grenadier, Steven, 2002, "Option Exercise Games: An Application to the Equilibrium Investment Strategies of Firms," *Review of Financial Studies* 15, pp. 691–721.

Jensen, Michael C., 1986, "Agency Costs of Free Cash Flow, Corporate Finance and Takeovers," *American Economic Review* 76, pp. 323–329.

Kalay, Avner, Rajeev Singhal, and Elizabeth Tashjian, 2007, "Is Chapter 11 Costly?" *Journal of Financial Economics* 84, pp. 772–796.

Koller, Tim, Marc Goedhart, and David Wessels, 2005, *Valuation: Measuring and Managing the Value of Companies*, 4th ed., Hoboken, NJ: John Wiley and Sons.

Lee, Inmoo, Scott Lockhead, Jay Ritter, and Quanshui Zhao, 1996, "The Costs of Raising Capital," *Journal of Financial Research* 19, pp. 59–74.

Procter & Gamble, 1991, "Procter & Gamble in Brazil," Procter & Gamble case.

White, Michelle J., 1983, "Bankruptcy Costs and the New Bankruptcy Code," *Journal of Finance* 38, pp. 477–488.

Appendix

Deriving the Value of a Perpetuity

This appendix derives perpetuity formulas that are used to calculate the terminal value of a sequence of growing free cash flows. Recall that a perpetuity is an infinite sum. Suppose that the growth rate is g so that each cash flow forecast is $g\%$ higher than the previous value, that each cash flow is discounted at r, and that we are deriving a terminal value for year 10. Thus, based on the forecast of free cash flow in year 10, which we denote $E_t[FCF(t+10)]$, we have

Terminal value = PV of cash flows in years 11
in year 10   + 12 + 13 + ...

$$= \frac{E_t[FCF(t+10)](1 + g)}{(1 + r)}$$

$$+ \frac{E_t[FCF(t+10)](1 + g)^2}{(1 + r)^2}$$

$$+ \frac{E_t[FCF(t+10)](1 + g)^3}{(1 + r)^3} + ...$$

To evaluate this infinite sum, define $\lambda = [(1 + g)/(1 + r)]$, and move the common term, $E_t[FCF(t+10)][(1 + g)/(1 + r)]$, outside the brackets. Then, we have

Terminal value in year 10

$$= \frac{E_t[FCF(t+10)](1 + g)}{(1 + r)}[1 + \lambda + \lambda^2 + ...]$$

Clearly, for this infinite sum to be a finite number, it must be the case that $\lambda < 1$, which requires that $g < r$. Thus, the growth rate of expected future free cash flows must be less than the discount rate. We know that the value of the infinite sum is $\frac{1}{(1 - \lambda)}$. After substituting for the infinite sum and for λ, we have

$$\text{Terminal value in year 10} = \frac{E_t[FCF(t+10)](1 + g)}{(r - g)}$$

Chapter 16

Additional Topics in International Capital Budgeting

Siemens, the German company known for its expertise in electrical engineering and electronics, has 277,000 employees outside of Germany. If its Brazilian subsidiary would like to expand its operations in anticipation of growth throughout Latin America, someone in German headquarters must decide whether the projected benefits outweigh the costs. Will the analysis be done in euros or Brazilian reals? Will it matter? This chapter addresses such questions.

International capital budgeting can be done in two basic ways: either by forecasting future foreign currency cash flows and then discounting them with a foreign currency discount rate or by converting the foreign currency cash flows into forecasts denominated in the domestic currency and then discounting them with a domestic currency discount rate. The two values should be the same when expressed in a common currency. However, that doesn't always happen in practice unless the two methods are used with the same implicit assumptions. The chapter considers an international capital budgeting case that demonstrates how easy it is to get different values with the two methods for discounting foreign currency cash flows and what assumptions are required to ensure that the methods are equivalent.

This chapter also discusses several important topics that extend and complement the basic international capital budgeting analysis presented in Chapter 15. In that chapter, we developed a framework for international capital budgeting using adjusted net present value (ANPV) analysis. In this chapter, we consider two alternative approaches. First, we discuss how to value a project using the weighted average cost of capital (WACC) approach to capital budgeting. Then, we examine the flow-to-equity (FTE) approach to capital budgeting, which is a third way of valuing projects. We discuss situations in which firms might prefer to use WACC or FTE, we explore the limitations of the different approaches, and we determine when a WACC or an FTE analysis is equivalent to an ANPV analysis.

It is well known that valuations often hinge on assumptions about terminal values. We examine what happens if we assume that current expansion of the firm and future competition drive the return on investment equal to the cost of capital into the indefinite future. How fast can the firm grow, and what is its terminal value?

We also examine how to value tax shields and subsidies on a firm's foreign currency loans, and we analyze a case in which a firm must choose between several different subsidized borrowing opportunities denominated in different currencies. The chapter discusses how the presence of outstanding debt can lead to conflicts of interest between the company's bondholders and stockholders. Finally, we briefly note that international differences in accounting standards must be taken into account when valuing corporations in different countries.

Chapter 15 reviewed some of the basic principles of international capital budgeting and project evaluation. We emphasized the importance of estimating the correct cash flows. We also advocated using the ANPV approach to value foreign projects.

The ANPV Approach

In the ANPV analysis, we first find the value of the unlevered, or all-equity, firm or project (which in this chapter we refer to as V_U) by discounting the expected value of the free cash flows. The discount rate, r_A, was the appropriate risk-adjusted required rate of return on the assets of the firm or the assets associated with the project. Then, we explored sources of additional value from the net present value of financial side effects and from the value of real options. Adding these various sources of value gives the value of the levered firm or project (which we call V_L).

Two Valuation Alternatives to ANPV

Capital budgeting is also done with the **weighted average cost of capital (WACC)** approach and the **flow-to-equity (FTE)** approach. When properly used, the three approaches are equivalent. We introduced the ANPV approach first because we like the way it identifies the economic sources of value. Nevertheless, the WACC approach is probably most widely used, and there are times when the FTE approach is most easily calculated. Hence, it is important to understand all three approaches, as well as their limitations.

The WACC approach to capital budgeting involves forecasting the all-equity free cash flows and then finding the value of the levered firm by discounting the all-equity free cash flows at an appropriate WACC. This is denoted r_{WACC}, and it is the weighted sum of the after-tax required rate of return on the firm's debt, r_D, and the required rate of return on the firm's equity, r_E. The market value of the equity is then found by subtracting the market value of the debt from the value of the levered firm.

The FTE approach finds the value of the equity directly by discounting the forecasts of the flows to equity holders at the appropriate risk-adjusted required rate of return on the equity, r_E. Then the value of the levered firm can be found by adding the value of the debt to the value of the equity.

The WACC Approach to Capital Budgeting

The WACC approach is a one-step method that works well for projects that have stable debt–equity ratios. An important point to remember about WACC is that if it is used for international projects, the weights should be specific to the international project and not to the overall firm. Unfortunately, some firms mistakenly use the same weighted average cost of capital (r_{WACC}) as the discount rate in all their capital budgeting decisions. To understand the logical foundations of WACC and its potential pitfalls, let's examine the derivation of r_{WACC} and how it can be used to value a firm.

WACC Without Taxes

Consider the value of a firm that has assets that are expected to yield cash flows of Y per year in perpetuity. If the riskiness of these cash flows dictates that they be discounted at r_A, we know from our ANPV analysis of Chapter 15 that the value of the unlevered firm is

$$V_U = \frac{Y}{(1 + r_A)} + \frac{Y}{(1 + r_A)^2} + \frac{Y}{(1 + r_A)^3} + \frac{Y}{(1 + r_A)^4} + \ldots = \frac{Y}{r_A} \qquad (16.1)$$

If the firm has no debt, the value of the equity, E, must be equal to the value of the unlevered firm, V_U.

Now, suppose that the firm issues some debt. Nobel Laureates Modigliani and Miller (1958, 1961) noted that in the absence of taxes, the presence of debt cannot change the value of the firm. Hence, without taxes, the value of the levered firm, V_L, equals the value of the unlevered firm. In other words, issuing debt does not create wealth—it merely transfers cash flows from the stockholders to the bondholders. If D represents the market value of the firm's debt, and if E_L represents the market value of the firm's levered equity, then because all of the firm's cash flows must go to either the bondholders or the stockholders, we know that the value of the debt plus the value of the equity must be the value of the firm:

$$V_L = D + E_L \tag{16.2}$$

We also know that the income of the firm must be paid to either the bondholders or the stockholders.[1] Thus, for a firm with income of Y, we have

$$Y = r_A V_L = r_D D + r_E E_L \tag{16.3}$$

Let the fraction of the value of the firm that is financed by debt be D/V_L, and let the fraction of the value of the firm that is financed with equity be E_L/V_L. Then, if we divide Equation (16.3) by the value of the levered firm, V_L, we find that the return on the firm's assets is split proportionately to the bondholders and the stockholders:

$$r_A = \frac{D}{V_L} r_D + \frac{E_L}{V_L} r_E \tag{16.4}$$

Equation (16.4) indicates that the return on the firm's assets is a weighted average of the return on the firm's debt and the return on the firm's equity. The weights reflect the percentages of the valuation of the firm that are financed with debt and equity. Essentially, investors view the firm as a portfolio of assets, with the return on the assets of the firm as the overall portfolio return and the debt and equity as the individual investments. Without taxes, the weighted average cost of capital, r_{WACC}, is the same as the rate of return on the assets of the firm, r_A.

As the firm changes its leverage, the rate of return on its assets remains constant. Because stockholders get paid only after the bondholders are paid, changing the firm's leverage changes the required rate of return on the equity. We can understand this relation by solving Equation (16.4) for r_E:

$$r_E = \frac{V_L}{E_L} r_A - \frac{D}{E_L} r_D = \frac{E_L + D}{E_L} r_A - \frac{D}{E_L} r_D = r_A + \frac{D}{E_L} [r_A - r_D] \tag{16.5}$$

Equation (16.5) indicates that the higher the leverage ratio, D/E_L, the higher the required rate of return on the firm's equity. This makes sense because as the firm issues more debt, less of the firm's cash flow is available to pay the stockholders, which makes their position more risky.

WACC with Taxes

When interest payments can be deducted from a firm's taxes, the firm must only make the after-tax interest payments on its debts. In this situation, as we saw in Chapter 15, issuing debt adds value to the firm. Let the corporate tax rate be τ, and let r_D be the required rate of return on the firm's debt. Then, because interest payments are tax deductible to the corporation, the after-tax required rate of return on the firm's debt is $(1 - \tau)r_D$. We will also let Y represent the after-tax cash flow of the firm, in which case the value of the unlevered firm is unchanged.

---

[1] We are discussing payouts of the firm's income as if the firm pays all free cash flow immediately. If a firm retains earnings over and above its investments in capital expenditures and the change in net working capital, the firm must invest those earnings appropriately, or it will destroy value.

Assume that the firm issues an amount of debt to finance the project equal to D and assume that this debt will be perpetually outstanding. Then, from our ANPV analysis in Chapter 15, the present value of the interest tax shield is the discounted sum of the perpetual interest deduction,

$$\frac{\tau r_D D}{(1 + r_D)} + \frac{\tau r_D D}{(1 + r_D)^2} + \frac{\tau r_D D}{(1 + r_D)^3} + \ldots = \frac{\tau r_D D}{r_D} = \tau D \qquad (16.6)$$

The ANPV of the levered firm is the value of the unlevered firm plus the value of the interest tax shield:

$$V_L = V_U + \tau D \qquad (16.7)$$

Now, as before, the cash flows of the firm must be split between the bondholders and the stockholders, but only the after-tax interest is required to be paid:

$$Y = r_D(1 - \tau)D + r_E E_L \qquad (16.8)$$

The weighted average cost of capital, r_{WACC}, is defined as the discount rate that sets the value of the levered firm equal to the discounted present value of the expected, after-tax, all-equity cash flows. For a firm that has a perpetual expected after-tax income of Y, we have

$$V_L = \frac{Y}{r_{WACC}} \qquad (16.9)$$

If we solve Equation (16.9) for $Y = r_{WACC} V_L$ and then substitute this result for Y in Equation (16.8), and finally divide by V_L, we find the value of the WACC:

$$r_{WACC} = \frac{D}{V_L}(1 - \tau)r_D + \frac{E_L}{V_L}r_E \qquad (16.10)$$

Equation (16.10) states that the firm's WACC is the weighted sum of the after-tax required rate of return on the firm's debt and the required rate of return on the firm's equity.

Why r_{WACC} Must Be Less Than r_A

Notice that the weighted average cost of capital, r_{WACC}, is necessarily less than the rate of return on a firm's assets, r_A, because the value of the levered firm, $V_L = Y/r_{WACC}$, is larger than the value of the unlevered firm, $V_U = Y/r_A$. This insight is important in capital budgeting because in both the ANPV and WACC analyses, the all-equity cash flows are in the numerator. The value of financial side effects is added separately in an ANPV analysis, whereas the WACC analysis includes them in one step.

Why Use WACC?

To understand the intuition for using r_{WACC} as the discount rate for a firm's expected all-equity free cash flows in capital budgeting analyses, consider an example. Suppose a firm has a potential project that provides an expected constant infinite stream of income in each future period. Let the expected value of the annual after-tax cash flow from the project be Y, and let the funds needed to undertake this investment project be I. Now, suppose that the fraction D/V_L of the financing for the project will be done with debt, and the fraction E_L/V_L of the financing for the project will be done with equity.

Some of the income from the project must first be paid to the bondholders to provide the required rate of return on the firm's debt, but the firm only loses the after-tax value of the interest payments because interest is tax deductible:

$$\text{Income paid to bondholders} = r_D(1 - \tau) \times (\text{Value of debt in the project})$$
$$= r_D(1 - \tau) \times (D/V_L)I$$

The rest of the income from the project is paid to the stockholders and provides the return on the firm's equity.[2] If this income is just what the stockholders expected to receive and is equal to their risk-adjusted required rate of return, then

$$\text{Income paid to stockholders} = r_E \times (\text{Value of equity in the project}) = r_E \times (E_L/V_L)I$$

From the perspective of the firm, adding the income paid to the bondholders and the income paid to the stockholders exhausts the income from the project:

$$\text{Income from project} = [r_D(1 - \tau)(D/V_L) + r_E(E_L/V_L)]I = r_{\text{WACC}}I \qquad \textbf{(16.11)}$$

Now, recognize that a project is a zero net present value investment if the income from the project, Y, just equals the weighted average of the required returns to the firm's bondholders and stockholders, $r_{\text{WACC}}I$. If $Y = r_{\text{WACC}}I$, the net present value (NPV) of the project when discounted at r_{WACC} is 0,

$$\text{NPV} = \frac{Y}{r_{\text{WACC}}} - I = 0$$

If the rate of return on the project provides more expected income than ($r_{\text{WACC}}I$), the project's rate of return is larger than r_{WACC}, and the project is positive NPV. If the project's rate of return is smaller than r_{WACC}, the project is not a positive NPV project and should not be done.

Example 16.1   WACC Valuation of Teikiko Printing Co.

Suppose that the Teikiko Printing Co. is considering an investment of ¥20 billion in a modernization project. Assume that the company's stockholders require an 8% rate of return, that the company's bondholders require a 4% rate of return, that the Japanese corporate tax rate is 30%, and that 45% of the project will be financed by debt and 55% will be financed with equity.

The previous analysis has equipped us to answer two questions:

- What is Teikiko Printing's WACC?
- What perpetual annual income must the project generate if the project is to be viable, in the sense of being at least a zero net present value investment?

From Equation (16.10), we find that Teikiko Printing's WACC is

$$r_{\text{WACC}} = [0.45 \times (1 - 0.30) \times 0.04] + [0.55 \times 0.08] = 0.0566$$

or 5.66%.

From Equation (16.11), Teikiko Printing will be able to provide the required compensation to its bondholders and its stockholders if the annual income from the project is

$$0.0566 \times ¥20\,\text{billion} = ¥1.132\,\text{billion}$$

In this case, the project has a zero net present value because the value of the project, which is the perpetual income divided by the WACC, equals to the cost of the project:

$$\frac{¥1.132\,\text{billion}}{0.0566} = ¥20\,\text{billion}$$

Teikiko should invest in the project only if it is expected to generate at least ¥1.132 billion per year.

---

[2]We are intentionally ignoring the possibility of reinvestment of earnings in the firm. This makes no difference as long as the reinvested earnings are invested in zero NPV projects.

Deriving r_A from r_D and r_E

One reason people like the WACC approach to capital budgeting is that it uses the rates of return on traded securities, and the debt and equity shares of the firm. In contrast, the ANPV analysis requires the rate of return on the firm's underlying assets. To derive the required rate of return on the firm's assets, we first equate the two values of the levered firm in Equations (16.2) and (16.7):

$$E_L + D = V_L = V_U + \tau D \tag{16.12}$$

The value of the equity plus the value of the debt must equal the value of the levered firm, which is the value of the unlevered firm plus the interest tax shield. Rearranging Equation (16.12) gives

$$V_U = E_L + (1 - \tau)D \tag{16.13}$$

Because $Y = r_A V_U$ and because the income must be distributed to the bondholders and the stockholders as in Equation (16.8), we can use Equation (16.13) to derive

$$r_A[E_L + (1 - \tau)D] = r_D(1 - \tau)D + r_E E_L \tag{16.14}$$

By solving Equation (16.14) for r_A, we find

$$r_A = \frac{D}{[E_L + (1 - \tau)D]}(1 - \tau)r_D + \frac{E_L}{[E_L + (1 - \tau)D]}r_E \tag{16.15}$$

Once again, the return on the firm's assets is a weighted average of the returns on the firm's debt and equity. The denominator of the weights is the value of the unlevered firm. The weight on the after-tax cost of debt is the ratio of debt to the unlevered firm value, and the weight on the required rate of return on equity is the ratio of the market value of equity to the unlevered firm value. If the firm has accurate estimates of the required rate of return on its levered equity, r_E, and the required rate of return on its debt, r_D, then Equation (16.15) provides the required rate of return on the assets in the ANPV analysis.

Equation (16.15) can also be solved for r_E to get

$$r_E = r_A + \frac{(1 - \tau)D}{E_L}(r_A - r_D) \tag{16.16}$$

Because $r_A > r_D$, Equation (16.16) indicates how leverage increases the required rate of return on the equity of the firm above the required rate of return on the assets of the firm in the presence of an interest deduction for corporate income tax.

Example 16.2   ANPV Valuation of Teikiko Printing

In Example 16.1, Teikiko's WACC was 5.66% when the required rate of return on its debt was 4% and the required rate of return on its equity was 8%. The project was zero NPV because the value of the project just equaled its cost, or ¥20 billion. Now, let's use an ANPV analysis to check our logic.

The value of the debt is 45% of the value of the project or

$$0.45 \times \text{¥20 billion} = \text{¥9 billion}$$

and the value of the equity is

$$\text{¥20 billion} - \text{¥9 billion} = \text{¥11 billion}$$

From Equation (16.16), the required rate of return on the project's unlevered assets is

$$r_A = \frac{¥9}{¥11 + [(1 - 0.30)¥9]}(1 - 0.30)0.04 + \frac{¥11}{¥11 + [(1 - 0.30)¥9]}0.08$$
$$= 0.0654$$

or 6.54%. An ANPV analysis of the project discounts the project's annual after-tax income of ¥1.132 billion at 6.54%, adds the value of the interest tax shield to get the value of the levered project, and subtracts the cost of the project. From Equation (16.7), the ANPV of the project is

$$\frac{¥1.132 \text{ billion}}{0.0654} + (0.30 \times ¥9 \text{ billion}) - ¥20 \text{ billion} = 0$$

The project has a zero ANPV, which was the conclusion of the WACC analysis.

Pros and Cons of Using WACC

The derivation of r_{WACC} presupposes that the project will perpetually provide the expected level of cash flows. It also assumes that the firm continuously monitors the value of its debt and adjusts the debt to keep the ratio of debt to total firm value, D/V_L, constant (see Miles and Ezzell, 1980). Hence, using a constant r_{WACC} in some situations is incorrect and leads to valuation mistakes. For example, you should not use a constant r_{WACC} if the project's leverage is changing, which is often the case in leveraged buyouts, for example.[3] Equation (16.16) indicates that changing leverage changes the required return on the firm's equity, which in turn changes the WACC. In situations of changing leverage, it is better to assume that the rate of return on the firm's assets is constant rather than the WACC.

In the ANPV analysis in Chapter 15, we clearly stated that the discount rate is a project-specific concept. Similarly, in international capital budgeting using a WACC analysis, the cost of capital should be specific to the international project. Using the same WACC for all projects is particularly troublesome for international capital budgeting applications in which foreign currency cash flows are converted into domestic currency and then discounted with a domestic currency discount rate. The nature of cash flow uncertainty when operating in a foreign country, along with the uncertainty of foreign exchange rate changes, can alter the riskiness of the cash flows. As a result, the riskiness of foreign cash flows can be different from the riskiness of domestic cash flows, even if the two projects are similar.

The Flow-to-Equity Method of Capital Budgeting

The third approach to capital budgeting is the flow-to-equity (FTE) method, which is based on the fact that the equity value of a firm is the present discounted value of the expected cash flows to stockholders, discounted at the required rate of return on the equity, r_E. In our analysis, we treated Y as the value of the perpetual after-tax cash flow to the all-equity firm. If the firm has perpetual debt of D, the stockholders do not receive Y each period. The stockholders must first pay the interest on the debt, but they can deduct the interest payments and pay less in taxes. Thus, the stockholders can expect to receive $Y - (1 - \tau)r_D D$ each period.

---

[3]In a leveraged buyout (LBO), a firm is converted from a publicly traded corporation into a private corporation. The purchasers of the outstanding equity often use large amounts of debt, which they plan on paying down over time.

By discounting the value of what stockholders expect to receive at the required rate of return on the equity, we find the value of the levered equity:

$$E_L = \frac{Y - (1 - \tau)r_D D}{(1 + r_E)^1} + \frac{Y - (1 - \tau)r_D D}{(1 + r_E)^2} + \frac{Y - (1 - \tau)r_D D}{(1 + r_E)^3} + \ldots$$

$$= \frac{Y - (1 - \tau)r_D D}{r_E} \tag{16.17}$$

The Equivalence of FTE to Other Approaches

For the firm with perpetual cash flows that we've been discussing in this chapter, it is straightforward to demonstrate that the FTE approach is equivalent to the WACC approach. If it is, then $E_L + D = V_L = Y/r_{WACC}$. Let's assume that this is true and confirm that we can produce the same WACC. We begin by rearranging Equation (16.17) by multiplying both sides by r_E and moving the debt terms to the other side:

$$Y = r_E E_L + (1 - \tau) r_D D \tag{16.18}$$

Dividing on both sides of Equation (16.18) by the value of the levered firm, V_L, we find

$$\frac{Y}{V_L} = \frac{r_E E_L + (1 - \tau)r_D D}{V_L} = r_{WACC} \tag{16.19}$$

Thus, by assuming that the levered firm value is the same in the two cases, we have demonstrated that we produce the same value of r_{WACC}. Thus, the equity value derived from the FTE method is consistent with the equity value found in the WACC analysis.

Example 16.3   FTE Valuation of Teikiko Printing Co.

Let's find the equity value of the Teikiko Printing Co. from the previous examples, using the flow-to-equity method of valuation. Remember that the project's expected annual after-tax income to the all-equity firm was ¥1.132 billion and that it was zero NPV and cost ¥20 billion. The required rates of return are 4% on the debt and 8% on the equity. The firm will issue ¥9 billion of debt. With this information, what is the value of the levered equity from the FTE approach?

Because the corporate tax rate is 30%, the expected annual after-tax income to the stockholders of the firm is

$$\text{¥1.132 billion} - (1 - 0.30) \times 0.04 \times \text{¥9 billion} = \text{¥0.880 billion}$$

This income is expected to be paid perpetually. We find the discounted present value of the cash flows to stockholders by dividing by the required rate of return on the equity:

$$\frac{\text{¥0.880 billion}}{0.08} = \text{¥11 billion}$$

Thus, the FTE approach to capital budgeting tells us that the Teikiko's equity is worth ¥11 billion. This is the amount of money that the stockholders would have to contribute to the project because they can borrow ¥9 billion. Because the cost of the project to the stockholders is equal to the value of the project to the stockholders, the project has a zero net present value.

The Pros and Cons of Alternative Capital Budgeting Methods

In Chapter 15 and the first part of this chapter, we presented three capital budgeting methods: the adjusted net present value (ANPV), the weighted average cost of capital (WACC), and the flow-to-equity (FTE) methods. If used appropriately, the three methods give the same present value of a project.

We stressed the ANPV approach because it categorizes the sources of value and thus lets a manager make an informed decision about the economic profitability of a project versus other sources of value coming from financing and growth. The ANPV approach also provides a great way to discuss risk management and the desirability of hedging foreign exchange risk, which we do in Chapter 17. In addition, the ANPV approach works well for international projects, such as the project being considered by International Wood Products, Inc. (discussed in Chapter 15), in which the firm knows the level of debt. It is also straightforward to value subsidized financing, which is often missed in a WACC analysis. Sometimes, though, the other approaches are easier to use.

The ANPV approach assumes that the manager knows the level of debt in future periods. If, instead, managers are planning to keep the debt–equity ratio constant, as is assumed in the WACC approach, then calculating an ANPV is problematic because the amount of debt depends on the amount of equity and vice versa. Conversely, if the level of debt is going to be changing over time because the firm has subsidized debt that will not be replaced, for example, then the leveraged equity required rate of return, r_E, will be changing, even if the risk-adjusted rate of return on the assets of the firm, r_A, is constant. With changing future values of r_E, both WACC and FTE are difficult to apply. ANPV works best in such situations. Because each of the three methods works well in different situations, it is important to have them all in your tool kit.

16.2 FORECASTING CASH FLOWS OF FOREIGN PROJECTS

The Choice of Currency

Generally, a significant part of the revenue earned by international projects is denominated in foreign currencies because the project's products are sold throughout the world. Multinational corporations also typically have costs that are denominated in foreign currencies because they source raw materials and intermediate goods in a global market.

Because an international project's cash flows are denominated in different currencies, the first decision in an international valuation is whether to do the valuation using forecasts denominated in a foreign currency or in the domestic currency. Later in the chapter, an extended case demonstrates how international capital budgeting can be done in either currency. We also examine what it takes for the two approaches to result in the same domestic currency value.

As discussed in Chapter 15, we can use a straightforward approach to find the value of a foreign project by forecasting the future foreign currency cash flows and discounting them to the present, using an appropriate foreign currency discount rate. The current value of the foreign project in domestic currency is then determined by multiplying the present value denominated in the foreign currency by the current spot exchange rate between the two currencies. One problem with this approach is that it is sometimes difficult to determine the appropriate foreign currency discount rate.

The second way to determine the value of a foreign project is to forecast the foreign currency value of the cash flows and then multiply them by the corresponding forecasts of future exchange rates. The result is a measure of the expected future domestic currency value of the foreign cash flows. Then, using an appropriate domestic currency discount rate to take the present values gives the current value of the foreign project in domestic currency.

Reconciling the Two Methods for Discounting Foreign Cash Flows

To see the equivalence of the two methods for discounting foreign cash flows, let $X(t+k)$ be the foreign currency cash flow at time $t+k$, which is k years in the future, and let $S(t+k)$ be the exchange rate of domestic currency per unit of foreign currency at time $t+k$. Then, $E_t[X(t+k)]$ is the forecast, or expected value of the future foreign currency cash flow, and $E_t[S(t+k)]$ is the forecast, or expected value, of the future exchange rate. Let $r(FC, k)$ and $r(DC, k)$ be the appropriate risk-adjusted discount rates in the foreign currency and domestic currency, respectively, that are used to discount the expected cash flows generated in year $t+k$ back to year t.

Using the first method for discounting foreign cash flows takes the foreign currency denominated present value of the future cash flow, which is $\dfrac{E_t[X(t+k)]}{[1 + r(FC, k)]^k}$, and converts this into domestic currency by multiplying by $S(t)$. Hence, the domestic currency denominated present value of the future foreign currency cash flow is $\dfrac{S(t)E_t[X(t+k)]}{[1 + r(FC, k)]^k}$.

The second method for discounting foreign cash flows is based on using a domestic currency forecast of the future foreign currency cash flows and then applying a domestic currency discount rate. You can think of this as directly forecasting the product of the exchange rate and the foreign currency cash flow, $E_t[S(t+k)X(t+k)]$, and then using a home currency discount rate. As a practical matter, no one does this. Instead, we first calculate the foreign currency forecasts and then multiply by the forecasts of the exchange rate, $E_t[S(t+k)]E_t[X(t+k)]$, to get the domestic currency value of the future cash flows. We then take the present value using the domestic currency discount rate, $r(DC, k)$. Thus, the domestic currency denominated present value of the future foreign currency cash flow using the second method is $\dfrac{E_t[S(t+k)]E_t[X(t+k)]}{[1 + r(DC, k)]^k}$.[4]

Equating the two methods of discounting the value of future foreign currency cash flows gives

$$\frac{S(t)E_t[X(t+k)]}{[1 + r(FC, k)]^k} = \frac{E_t[S(t+k)]E_t[X(t+k)]}{[1 + r(DC, k)]^k} \qquad (16.20)$$

Simplifying Equation (16.20) by dividing both sides by the expected foreign currency cash flow and the current exchange rate and multiplying both sides by 1 plus the discount factors raised to the k power gives

$$[1 + r(DC, k)]^k = [1 + r(FC, k)]^k \frac{E_t[S(t+k)]}{S(t)} \qquad (16.21)$$

Equation (16.21) indicates that the two approaches are the same when the discount rates satisfy a parity condition exactly like uncovered interest rate parity, which is discussed in Chapter 7. The foreign currency discount rate will be higher than the domestic currency discount rate if the foreign currency is expected to depreciate relative to the domestic currency, in which case $E_t[S(t+k)] < S(t)$.

---

[4]If you are forecasting the product of the exchange rate and the foreign currency cash flow, the domestic currency discount rate is slightly different unless the exchange rate and the foreign currency cash flow are uncorrelated.

It is important to notice that the discount rates will usually be different for different time periods. We know that unless the term structures of interest rates in the two currencies are flat, the expected rate of appreciation will be different for different periods. Therefore, if the discount rate is the same across maturities in one currency, it cannot be the same across maturities in the other.

The next section examines the valuation of a foreign project using the two methods. We consider an international capital budgeting case in which expected changes in real exchange rates play a role in the valuation of a foreign project.

16.3 CASE STUDY: CMTC's AUSTRALIAN PROJECT

It was early Friday evening in St. Louis, Missouri, and Donna Elichalt was still staring at her computer screen. Donna had recently been promoted from financial analyst to assistant treasurer for international operations of the Consolidated Machine Tool Company (CMTC) with sales in 39 countries and manufacturing operations in seven countries.

Elichalt had been asked by CMTC's chief financial officer (CFO) to evaluate a capital budgeting request from CMTC's Australian subsidiary. The project was the largest request that she had ever analyzed. Rather than a weekend away from the office, it now was beginning to look as though she would be at the office all night.

The Australian Investment Proposal

CMTC's Australian plant manager, Rod Wickens, had submitted a proposal to spend 47 million Australian dollars to reengineer his plant with new robotics and other computerized machinery. At the current exchange rate of USD1.35/AUD, the request was for USD63.45 million. Such an expenditure would severely cut into the free cash flow of the Australian subsidiary and would eliminate any possibility of a dividend from Australia this year. In his proposal, Wickens indicated that the investment in new equipment promised significant cost savings in the future. He also argued that the project's cost would be partially offset by the sale of old equipment for AUD11.83 million.

Elichalt had met Wickens on several occasions, and while she thought he probably did production well, she wasn't sure that he really understood the importance of a proper discounted cash flow analysis of investment projects. Wickens usually wanted to do any project that lowered his future costs, especially if the payback on the project was within 5 years. He often justified this attitude with statements such as "CMTC can't be profitable if our costs are higher than our competitors' costs."

The Australian plant was not CMTC's oldest, but Elichalt knew that CMTC planned to close the Australian plant in 10 years, when it would expand CMTC's operations in China. With low Chinese labor costs and growing demand for machine tools, operating from China made sense. Elichalt consequently knew that only 10 years of expected cash flows from the Australian plant would need to be considered.

In his proposal to reengineer the plant, Wickens indicated that the current AUD costs of production were AUD45.375 million per year. He argued that AUD costs of production would probably increase at the Australian rate of inflation for the remaining life of the plant. On the other hand, Wickens argued that after the reengineering of the plant, manufacturing costs could be expected to be 90% of the old costs in the first year, 85% in the second year, and 80% in the remaining years of the plant's existence. Elichalt wondered if such expected cost savings justified the project's large initial expenditure.

Because Wickens had not provided any explicit future cash flow projections, Elichalt's first job was to forecast the after-tax AUD cash flows of the project. She then needed to discount these expected cash flows to the present, using appropriate discount factors. She wasn't sure whether to discount the expected cash flows in Australian dollars or to first convert the expected cash flows into U.S. dollars. If she wanted to discount the cash flows in U.S. dollars, she would need forecasts of future exchange rates, whereas if she discounted them in Australian dollars, she would just have to get the AUD discount rate right.

Gathering the Economic Data

To begin her analysis, Elichalt had placed a call to the economic analysis group at Golder Sax, an investment bank, to get interest rate data and forecasts of inflation rates for Australia and the United States. Elichalt's contact at Golder Sax easily provided both USD and AUD interest rates, which are in Exhibit 16.1. The analyst indicated that these term structures of interest rates referred to the spot interest rates in each currency that are the pure discount bond yields in the respective currencies.[5] The analyst indicated that the annual forecasts of AUD and USD inflation rates included in Exhibit 16.1 were the consensus forecasts of business economists.

Expected 1-Year Real Interest Rates

The Golder Sax analyst also included annual expected real interest rates for each currency. He showed how they were derived from the market-determined nominal interest rates for different maturities and the forecasts of future inflation rates to reflect the expected real return on a one-period investment that begins a number of years in the future. That is, $r^e(t, k)$ is the 1-year real rate of return that is expected to prevail k years in the future. Let $i(t,k)$ be the k-year spot nominal interest rate at time t for payoffs k years in the future, and let $\pi^e(t, k)$ be the expected annual rate of inflation at time t for year $t+k$. One unit of currency borrowed for k years generates a liability of $[1 + i(t, k)]^k$ that must be paid in the future at time $t+k$. The one unit of borrowed currency can be invested in the $(k-1)$-year bond to get a payoff of $[1 + i(t, k-1)]^{k-1}$ at time $t+k-1$. When that payoff is received, the proceeds from investing in the $(k-1)$-year bond can be invested at the 1-year interest rate, $i(t+k-1, 1)$, that will be known at the end of year $t+k-1$ and will pay off at the end of year $t+k$. Because the strategy requires no investment today, the expected return must equal the expected cost, ignoring risk premiums. Thus,

$$\{1 + E_t[i(t+k-1, 1)]\} [1 + i(t, k-1)]^{k-1} = [1 + i(t, k)]^k \qquad \text{(16.22)}$$

Exhibit 16.1   Information on Australian and U.S. Interest Rates and Inflation Rates

	Year in the Future									
	1	2	3	4	5	6	7	8	9	10
1. USD Spot Rates	1.50	2.19	2.70	3.07	3.36	3.61	3.83	4.02	4.19	4.34
2. AUD Spot Rates	12.78	11.77	11.14	10.66	10.29	9.97	9.70	9.46	9.25	9.07
3. USD Expected Inflation	1.25	2.13	2.33	2.44	2.50	2.54	2.57	2.59	2.61	2.63
4. AUD Expected Inflation	7.00	5.50	5.00	4.75	4.60	4.50	4.43	4.38	4.33	4.30
5. USD Expected Real Rates	0.25	0.75	1.35	1.70	2.00	2.75	2.50	2.70	2.90	3.00
6. AUD Expected Real Rates	5.40	5.00	4.65	4.30	4.00	3.75	3.50	3.30	3.10	3.00

Notes: The term structures of interest rates are the spot rates appropriate for discounting a known future cash flow k years in the future. The expected inflation rates represent analysts' forecasts. The expected real interest rates are derived in Equation (16.24).

---

[5]Chapter 6 explains the term structure of spot interest rates and the relationship between bond prices and pure discount bond yields.

The Fisher equation implies that 1 plus the expected nominal interest rate can be broken into 1 plus the expected real interest rate multiplied by 1 plus the expected rate of inflation, or

$$\{1 + E_t[i(t+k-1, 1)]\} = [1 + r^e(t, k)][1 + \pi^e(t, k)] \qquad (16.23)$$

Substituting from Equation (16.23) into Equation (16.22) and solving for $[1 + r^e(t, k)]$ gives

$$[1 + r^e(t, k)] = \frac{[1 + i(t, k)]^k}{[1 + i(t, k-1)]^{k-1}[1 + \pi^e(t, k)]} \qquad (16.24)$$

These real interest rates will later be linked to the expected real depreciation of the Australian dollar.

Book Value and Depreciation

To begin the task of constructing expected cash flows, Elichalt checked with CMTC's accounting department and determined that the book value of the Australian plant's existing equipment was AUD10.5 million. Hence, the sale of the old equipment would generate some taxable income. Accounting had also informed Elichalt the old equipment had 5 years of remaining accounting depreciation and that straight-line depreciation was being used. The new equipment would be depreciated on a straight-line basis over the course of 10 years. Finally, the accounting group noted that a 40% tax rate was the appropriate rate to apply to the AUD cash flows. Armed with this information, Elichalt knew that she could generate appropriate forecasts of AUD cash flows. Only the discount rate remained to be settled.

Discounted Cash Flows

As she reached for her well-thumbed copy of Bekaert and Hodrick's *International Financial Management*, Elichalt remembered that they advocated using equity discount rates that reflect both the spot nominal interest rates for each period and the riskiness of the individual project's equity cash flows. Elichalt knew that historically the AUD profits of the Australian subsidiary, when converted into USD, were quite similar to the USD equity returns of other CMTC plants. Hence, she knew that a USD equity risk premium of 5.5% seemed appropriate when discounting expected USD cash flows from the Australian subsidiary.

But Elichalt also knew that Wickens would want to see an analysis done in Australian dollars. This raised the question of whether it mattered if the analysis were done in U.S. dollars or in Australian dollars. Elichalt didn't relish a clash with Wickens or the CFO on Monday.

Case Solution

Elichalt's solution proceeds in several logical steps. First, Exhibit 16.2 presents the AUD after-tax cash flows in millions of AUD forecast for the current year and the next 10 years. Each of the lines is explained below. Then, Exhibit 16.3 presents forecasts of expected USD per AUD exchange rates that are used in Exhibit 16.4 to derive the expected dollar cash flows from the project. These are discounted using USD equity discount rates. Exhibit 16.5 then demonstrates how the analysis can be done directly in Australian dollars.

Initial Cash Flows

Line 1 of Exhibit 16.2 gives the net investment, which is the initial outlay of AUD47 million minus the after-tax value from selling the old equipment. Selling the old equipment for AUD11.83 million partially offsets the project's initial cost, but because the market price of

Exhibit 16.2 Projected Project Cash Flows in Millions of Expected Australian Dollars

					Year in the Future						
	0	**1**	**2**	**3**	**4**	**5**	**6**	**7**	**8**	**9**	**10**
1. Net Investment	−35.70										
2. Old Cost		48.55	51.22	53.78	56.34	58.93	61.58	64.31	67.12	70.03	73.04
3. New Cost		43.70	43.54	43.03	45.07	47.14	49.26	51.45	53.70	56.02	58.43
4. After-Tax Cost Saving		2.91	4.61	6.45	6.76	7.07	7.39	7.72	8.05	8.40	8.76
5. Old Dep. Tax Shield		−0.84	−0.84	−0.84	−0.84	−0.84					
6. New Dep. Tax Shield		1.88	1.88	1.88	1.88	1.88	1.88	1.88	1.88	1.88	1.88
7. AUD Cash Flow	−35.70	3.95	5.65	7.49	7.80	8.11	9.27	9.60	9.93	10.28	10.64

the old equipment is greater than its AUD10.5 million book value, CMTC generates taxable income. The after-tax benefit is the price of the old equipment minus the income tax rate multiplied by the difference between the sale price and the book value of the old equipment:

$$\text{AUD11.83 million} - 0.40 \times (\text{AUD11.83 million} - \text{AUD10.5 million})$$
$$= \text{AUD11.30 million}$$

Thus, CMTC's net investment is

$$\text{AUD35.70 million} = \text{AUD47 million} - \text{AUD11.30 million}$$

The After-Tax Cost Savings of the Project

Line 2 of Exhibit 16.2 shows forecasts of the plant's old costs. As Wickens indicated, old costs are expected to increase at the AUD rate of inflation for years 1 through 5. Thus, if $\pi^e(t, k, \text{AUD})$ is the forecast at time t of the annual AUD rate of inflation k years in the future, old costs in year $t+k$ are expected to be

$$\text{Old costs in } k \text{ years} = [1 + \pi^e(t, k, \text{AUD})] \times [\text{Old costs in } (k\text{--}1) \text{ years}], k = 1, \ldots, 10$$

For example, costs in year 0 are AUD45.375 million and the expected AUD rate of inflation in year 1 is 7%. Thus, first-year costs are expected to be

$$\text{AUD45.375 million} \times 1.07 = \text{AUD48.55 million}$$

Line 3 of Exhibit 16.2 shows forecasts of new costs. These were generated according to the percentage savings that Wickens predicted over the next 10 years:

$$\text{New costs in year 1} = 0.90 \times (\text{Old costs in year 1})$$
$$\text{New costs in year 2} = 0.85 \times (\text{Old costs in year 2})$$
$$\text{New costs in year } k = 0.80 \times (\text{Old costs in year } k), k = 3, \ldots, 10$$

Line 4 of Exhibit 16.2 shows the expected after-tax cost savings, which are the differences between the forecasts of old costs and new costs for year k multiplied by one minus the tax rate of 40%. It is assumed that the new equipment will produce machine tools that are identical to the ones that CMTC would have sold but that the new equipment will do so more cheaply. CMTC consequently forecasts that it will sell exactly as many machine tools in the future if the investment is made, but each machine tool it sells will generate more profit because it will be produced at lower cost. Of course, because CMTC will be more profitable, it will have to pay income tax on the additional profit. Hence, the after-tax value of the cost savings, listed in Line 5 of Exhibit 16.2, provides the primary benefit of the project.

Depreciation Tax Shields

Depreciation of equipment is an accounting cost that reduces the before-tax income of the firm. If the firm generates a before-tax cash flow of Y and takes depreciation of Dep, the before-tax income of the firm is $(Y - Dep)$. If the corporate tax rate is τ, the firm's after-tax income is $(1 - \tau)(Y - Dep)$. Because depreciation is not a cash flow, we must add Dep to after-tax income to get the firm's after-tax cash flow:

$$(1 - \tau)(Y - Dep) + Dep = (1 - \tau)Y + \tau Dep$$

Depreciation provides a tax benefit to the project, which is often called the depreciation tax shield, equal to the tax rate multiplied by depreciation. Line 5 of Exhibit 16.2 recognizes that when the old equipment is sold, CMTC will lose the remaining 5 years of depreciation tax shields associated with the old equipment. With the straight-line method of depreciation, the lost depreciation expense in years 1 through 5 would be one-fifth (20%) of the book value of the equipment, which is AUD10.5 million. Hence, the firm will lose a depreciation tax shield of

$$(0.40) \times (0.20) \times (\text{AUD}10.5 \text{ million}) = \text{AUD}0.84 \text{ million}$$

in each year of the first 5 years of the project.

Because the firm is purchasing new equipment, it will generate new depreciation tax shields, which are given in Line 6 of Exhibit 16.2. The new depreciation tax shield recognizes that the life of the equipment is 10 years. Hence, 10% of the value of the purchase will be deducted in each of the next 10 years, and the tax rate multiplied by this value provides the new depreciation tax shield:

$$(0.40) \times (0.10) \times (\text{AUD}47 \text{ million}) = \text{AUD}1.88 \text{ million}$$

The Total Expected After-Tax Cash Flows in Australian Dollars

The expected total after-tax AUD cash flows of the project are given in Line 7 of Exhibit 16.2. The year 0 value is net investment in Line 1. The cash flows in years 1 through 10 are the sums of the after-tax cost savings in Line 4 and the depreciation tax shields in Lines 5 and 6. To determine whether or not the project is acceptable, we must take the present value of these cash flows, either in Australian dollars or in U.S. dollars, after converting them to expected U.S. dollars.

The equipment is assumed to be fully depreciated and of zero economic value after the end of the 10-year forecast period. If this were not the case, some terminal value or residual salvage value of the equipment would be available as an additional benefit of the project.

Forecast Future Spot Rates

Expected future spot exchange rates are easily constructed from the current spot rate and the term structures of spot interest rates in each currency that are supplied in Exhibit 16.1. Let $S(t)$ denote the current spot rate of USD per AUD, which is USD1.35/AUD. Let $i(t, k, \text{AUD})$ denote the nominal AUD k-year spot interest rate at time t. For example, the 5-year AUD interest rate is 10.29% in Exhibit 16.1. Let $i(t, k, \text{USD})$ denote the nominal USD k-year spot interest rate at time t and notice that the 5-year USD interest rate is 3.36% in Exhibit 16.1. Then, from interest rate parity, a k-year forward rate of USD per AUD that was quoted at time t for delivery in year $t+k$ would satisfy

$$F(t, k) = S(t) \times \frac{[1 + i(t, k, \text{USD})]^k}{[1 + i(t, k, \text{AUD})]^k} \qquad \textbf{(16.25)}$$

Substituting the current spot rate and the 5-year interest rates into Equation (16.25), we find an implicit forward rate at time t for year $t+5$ of

$$\frac{\text{USD}1.35}{\text{AUD}} \times \frac{(1.0336)^5}{(1.1029)^5} = \frac{\text{USD}0.98}{\text{AUD}}$$

Exhibit 16.3   Forecasts of U.S. Dollar–Australian Dollar Exchange Rates from Interest Rate Parity

	0	1	2	3	4	5	6	7	8	9	10
					Year in the Future						
1. USD/AUD	1.35	1.22	1.13	1.07	1.02	0.98	0.94	0.92	0.90	0.88	0.87
2. Rate of AUD Depreciation		10.00	7.12	5.61	4.65	3.89	3.29	2.73	2.28	1.84	1.61

Because AUD nominal interest rates are substantially higher than USD nominal interest rates, the Australian dollar is at a large discount in the forward market.

In the absence of information about a risk premium in the forward foreign exchange market, Equation (16.25) can be used to generate expected future spot exchange rates. That is, we can assume that the implicit forward rates are unbiased predictors of future spot rates:

$$F(t, k) = E_t[S(t+k)] \qquad (16.26)$$

Line 1 of Exhibit 16.3 presents expected future spot exchange rates constructed in this way from Equations (16.25) and (16.26) using the data of Exhibit 16.1. Line 2 expresses the annual expected rates of depreciation of the Australian dollar relative to the U.S. dollar implicit in these forecasts. These will be used in a later analysis.

Assuming that the future spot exchange rates and the AUD cash flows from the project are independent, the expected after-tax AUD cash flows of the project, $E_t[X(t+k, \text{AUD})]$, can be converted into expected USD cash flows by multiplying by the forecast of the exchange rate in year $t+k$ from Exhibit 16.3:

$$\text{Expected value at time } t \text{ of U.S. dollars in year } t+k = E_t[X(t+k, \text{AUD})] \\ \times E_t[S(t+k)] \qquad (16.27)$$

For example, the forecast for year 1 of the AUD after-tax cash flow from Exhibit 16.2 is AUD3.95 million, and the forecast of the exchange rate for year 1 from Exhibit 16.3 is USD1.2150/AUD. Hence, the forecast of USD value of the AUD cash flows in year 1 is

$$\text{AUD3.95 million} \times \frac{\text{USD1.2150}}{\text{AUD}} = \text{USD4.80 million}$$

The present value of the expected USD cash flows calculated in Equation (16.27) is found by discounting them at USD equity discount rates, $r_E(t, k, \text{USD})$:

$$\text{Present value at time } t \text{ of expected USD in year } t+k$$
$$= \frac{E_t[X(t+k, \text{AUD})] \times E_t[S(t+k)]}{[1 + r_E(t, k, \text{USD})]^k} \qquad (16.28)$$

The U.S. Dollar Discount Rates

The choice of appropriate USD discount rates for the expected USD cash flows involves two considerations. First, from the spot interest rates, we know that the time value of money is not the same across maturities. Thus, the USD equity discount rates should also reflect this fact. The second consideration is that the projected USD cash flows are not risk free. Because the realized profits from the Australian subsidiary are equity cash flows, it is appropriate to discount the expected cash flows with discount rates that reflect the riskiness of the equity. We are told that Elichalt thinks that a 5.5% USD equity risk premium is appropriate.

Exhibit 16.4 Net Present Value of the Project in Millions of U.S. Dollars

					Year in the Future						
	0	**1**	**2**	**3**	**4**	**5**	**6**	**7**	**8**	**9**	**10**
1. AUD Cash Flows	−35.70	3.95	5.65	7.49	7.80	8.11	9.27	9.60	9.93	10.28	10.64
2. USD/AUD	1.35	1.22	1.13	1.07	1.02	0.98	0.94	0.92	0.90	0.88	0.87
3. USD Cash Flows	−48.20	4.80	6.38	7.98	7.92	7.92	8.75	8.81	8.92	9.06	9.23
4. USD Discount Rates		7.00	7.69	8.20	8.57	8.86	9.11	9.33	9.52	9.69	9.84
5. USD Present Values	−48.20	4.49	5.50	6.30	5.70	5.18	5.19	4.72	4.31	3.94	3.61
USD NPV @ Variable Rates = 0.74					USD NPV @ 9.84% = −0.86						

Consequently, the appropriate USD equity discount rates are the USD nominal risk-free interest rates plus 5.5%:

$$r_E(t, k, \text{USD}) = i(t, k, \text{USD}) + 5.5$$

These USD equity discount rates are presented in Line 4 of Exhibit 16.4.

The Net Present Value of the Project in U.S. Dollars

The present values corresponding to Equation (16.28) are presented in Line 5 of Exhibit 16.4. The sum of these present values is USD0.74 million. Because the project is positive NPV, it should be accepted.

How Incorrect Discounting Leads to Problems

Often in actual capital budgeting analyses, a single discount rate is used for all the future cash flows. If a 10-year project is being analyzed, the 10-year discount rate is used for all years. Sometimes this is an innocuous assumption, if the term structure of interest rates is reasonably flat, but it is not innocuous in this case. Exhibit 16.4 indicates that if each of the 10 years of expected USD cash flows is discounted by the 10-year USD equity discount factor, which is 9.84%, the project has a negative NPV of –$0.86 million.

The project is negative NPV when this incorrect method is used because the term structure of USD interest rates is upward sloping. An upward-sloping term structure of spot interest rates indicates that expected future USD short-term nominal interest rates are higher than current short-term interest rates. Hence, longer-term expected USD cash flows require higher discount rates than nearer-term cash flows. If the expected USD profits from the early years of the project are discounted by the high USD rate of return that is appropriate only for discounting cash flows in year 10, the present value of the project is penalized needlessly.

The Net Present Value of the Project in Australian Dollars

The previous analysis derives the net present value of the project in U.S. dollars by discounting the expected USD cash flows with USD equity discount rates. It is also possible to derive a USD NPV for the project by first discounting the expected AUD cash flows with appropriate AUD equity discount rates, $r_E(t, k, \text{AUD})$:

Present value at time t of expected AUD in year $t+k$

$$= \frac{E_t[X(t+k, \text{AUD})]}{[1 + r_E(t, k, \text{AUD})]^k} \tag{16.29}$$

The USD NPV of the project can subsequently be found by multiplying the AUD NPV by the current spot rate of USD per AUD:

$$\text{USD present value at time } t \text{ of expected AUD in year } t+k$$

$$= \frac{E_t[X(t+k, \text{AUD})]}{[1 + r_E(t, k, \text{AUD})]^k} \times S(t) \tag{16.30}$$

If the two methods of deriving a USD NPV are to provide the same value, the expression in Equation (16.28) must equal the expression in Equation (16.30) from which we find the following equality:

$$\frac{E_t[X(t+k, \text{AUD})]}{[1 + r_E(t, k, \text{AUD})]^k} \times S(t) = \frac{E_t[X(t+k, \text{AUD})] \times E_t[S(t+k)]}{[1 + r_E(t, k, \text{USD})]^k} \tag{16.31}$$

The relation between the AUD discount rate and the USD discount rate in Equation (16.31) can then be written as

$$[1 + r_E(t, k, \text{AUD})]^k = [1 + r_E(t, k, \text{USD})]^k \times \frac{S(t)}{E_t[S(t+k)]} \tag{16.32}$$

By solving Equation (16.31) for the AUD discount rate, we find

$$r_E(t, k, \text{AUD}) = [1 + r_E(t, k, \text{USD})] \times \left(\frac{S(t)}{E_t[S(t+k)]}\right)^{1/k} - 1 \tag{16.33}$$

From the derivation of the expected rates of depreciation of the Australian dollar relative to the U.S. dollar in Exhibit 16.3, we know that we can calculate

$$\frac{S(t)}{E_t[S(t+k)]} = \frac{[1 + i(t, k, \text{AUD})]^k}{[1 + i(t, k, \text{USD})]^k} \tag{16.34}$$

We can substitute these market-determined forecasts in Equation (16.34) into Equation (16.33). Alternatively, we could use proprietary forecasts of expected rates of appreciation of the U.S. dollar relative to the Australian dollar, but we should have a reason why our proprietary forecasts differ from the market forecasts. In either case, we generate the necessary AUD discount rates.

Notice that the expected rate of depreciation of the Australian dollar relative to the U.S. dollar over the next k years, when expressed at an annual rate as in Equation (16.33) by taking the $(1/k)$-th power of the ratio of the current spot rate to the expected future spot rate, is just the ratio of 1 plus the spot nominal interest rate on the Australian dollar for k years in the future to 1 plus the spot nominal interest rate on the U.S. dollar for k years in the future:

$$\left(\frac{S(t)}{E_t[S(t+k)]}\right)^{1/k} = \frac{[1 + i(t, k, \text{AUD})]}{[1 + i(t, k, \text{USD})]} \tag{16.35}$$

By substituting from Equation (16.35) into Equation (16.33), we find

$$r_E(t, k, \text{AUD}) = [1 + r_E(t, k, \text{USD})] \times \frac{[1 + i(t, k, \text{AUD})]}{[1 + i(t, k, \text{USD})]} - 1 \tag{16.36}$$

The values of the AUD equity rates of return that satisfy Equation (16.36) are given in Line 2 of Exhibit 16.5.

When the expected AUD cash flows are discounted at these required equity rates of return, the NPV of the project is AUD0.55 million. Multiplying the AUD NPV by the current exchange rate of USD1.35/AUD gives the USD NPV of $0.74 million. Notice that this is the

Exhibit 16.5 Net Present Value of the Project in Millions of Australian Dollars

					Year in the Future						
	0	1	2	3	4	5	6	7	8	9	10
1. AUD Cash Flow	−35.70	3.95	5.65	7.49	7.80	8.11	9.27	9.60	9.93	10.28	10.64
2. AUD Discount Rates		18.89	17.79	17.09	16.57	16.15	15.81	15.51	15.25	15.02	14.82
3. AUD Present Values	−35.70	3.33	4.07	4.67	4.22	3.84	3.84	3.50	3.19	2.92	2.67

AUD NPV @ Variable Rates = 0.55
Corresponding USD NPV = 0.74

AUD NPV @ 14.82% = 2.15
Corresponding USD NPV = 2.90

same value we found by discounting the expected USD cash flows at the USD required rate of return.

An Incorrect Approach—Again

We demonstrated that if the expected USD cash flows are discounted at the common discount rate associated with the 10-year maturity, the project would have a negative USD NPV. This occurred because using a common discount rate ignores expected changes in USD interest rates, which in this case are expected to increase over time.

Analogously, we get the wrong present value for the project if each of the 10 years of expected AUD cash flows is incorrectly discounted by the common 10-year AUD discount rate, which is 14.82%. If we discount with this common rate, the project has an even larger positive NPV in Australian dollars. Exhibit 16.5 indicates that this value is AUD2.15 million, which is $2.90 million when converted at the current exchange rate.

The reason the value of the project is higher when this incorrect method is used is that the term structure of AUD interest rates is downward sloping. A downward-sloping term structure indicates that future short-term nominal AUD interest rates are expected to be lower than current short-term interest rates. Hence, longer-term AUD cash flows should be discounted at lower discount rates, and nearer-term AUD cash flows should be discounted at higher rates. If the expected AUD profits from the early years of the project are discounted by the low AUD rate of return that is appropriate only for year 10 cash flows, the value of the project appears to be more favorable than it actually is.

The Expected Real Depreciation of the Australian Dollar

The nominal interest rates for the two currencies imply that the Australian dollar is expected to depreciate relative to the U.S. dollar in nominal terms, as demonstrated in Exhibit 16.3. Given the expected rates of inflation from Exhibit 16.1, we can also determine that the Australian dollar is expected to depreciate relative to the U.S. dollar in real terms. This is demonstrated in Exhibit 16.6. Knowing that the Australian dollar is expected to weaken in real terms is important because it implies that the forecast USD cash flows from the project that might be generated from an assumption of relative purchasing power parity would seriously overvalue the project.

Exhibit 16.6 Forecasts of Real Depreciation of the AUD

				Year in the Future						
	1	2	3	4	5	6	7	8	9	10
1. Depreciation per Year	4.89	4.05	3.15	2.49	1.92	1.45	0.97	0.58	0.19	0.00
2. Compounded	4.89	8.74	11.61	13.82	15.47	16.70	17.50	17.98	18.14	18.14

Using purchasing power parity (PPP) to forecast foreign currency cash flows is appropriate only if relative purchasing power parity is expected to hold in all future periods. If one of the currencies is strong in real terms and is expected to depreciate, as is the Australian dollar in this case, then PPP forecasts will be invalid.

Recall that the expected rate of real depreciation of the Australian dollar relative to the U.S. dollar is defined as the percentage change in the real exchange rate. The real exchange rate in this situation is the nominal exchange rate of USD/AUD multiplied by the Australian price level divided by the U.S. price level:

$$RS(t) = \frac{S(t)P(t, \text{AUD})}{P(t, \text{USD})}$$

Let the percentage change in the real exchange rate be $rs(t+1)$, and let the actual rates of inflation be $\pi(t+1, \text{USD})$ and $\pi(t+1, \text{AUD})$. Then

$$rs(t+1) = \frac{[S(t+1)P(t+1, \text{AUD})/P(t+1, \text{USD})]}{[S(t)P(t, \text{AUD})/P(t, \text{USD})]} - 1$$

$$= \frac{[1 + s(t+1)][1 + \pi(t+1, \text{AUD})]}{[1 + \pi(t+1, \text{USD})]} - 1$$

To generate expected rates of real depreciation, we can substitute expected values for actual values, using the expected rates of nominal appreciation derived in Exhibit 16.3 and the expected USD and AUD rates of inflation in Exhibit 16.1.

The calculations in Exhibit 16.6 indicate that the AUD is expected to weaken in real terms by 4.89% in the first year. The expected rate of real depreciation subsequently declines until it reaches 0.19% in year 9 and 0% in year 10. Exhibit 16.6 also shows the cumulative, expected percentage change in the real exchange rate. Given the nominal interest rates and the expected rates of inflation associated with two currencies, the financial markets are predicting that the Australian dollar will weaken in real terms relative to the U.S. dollar by 18.14% over the next 10 years. If the valuation of the project did not allow for this real depreciation of the Australian dollar, the value of the project would be severely overstated. Notice from the real interest rates in Exhibit 16.1 that the expected real depreciation of the AUD is associated with a currently high Australian real interest rate and a currently low U.S. real interest rate. Over time, the real interest differential is forecast to close as the Australian dollar weakens.

Chapter 9 notes that changes in real exchange rates often substantively affect the profitability of foreign operations. There is nothing in the present case that captures this important aspect of forecasting. This does not mean that the effect is unimportant. We merely left it out to simplify the discussion.

16.4 TERMINAL VALUE WHEN RETURN ON INVESTMENT EQUALS r_{WACC}

This section presents an alternative way to determine the terminal value of a project. In Chapter 15, we argued that terminal values in capital budgeting valuations should consider the rate at which the firm will grow in the long run and should discount the firm's growing free cash flow at the firm's cost of capital. If an explicit forecast for a 10-year horizon is available, the perpetuity formula for a cash flow growing at rate g, discounted at rate r, implies that the terminal value in year $t+10$, denoted TV($t+10$), is

$$\text{TV}(t+10) = \frac{\text{FCF}(t+11)}{(r - g)} \tag{16.37}$$

where $FCF(t+11) = FCF(t+10) \times (1 + g)$ is the expected value at time t of free cash flow in year $t+11$, which is g percent higher than the last explicit forecast. Notice that if we are doing a WACC analysis, we set $r = r_{WACC}$, whereas if we are doing an ANPV analysis, we set $r = r_A$, and we would handle the interest tax shields of perpetual debt separately.

Although calculating the terminal value in such a way is perfectly correct, it requires an understanding of the firm's nominal growth rate into the indefinite future. One assumption is that nominal growth will be only due to inflation because any real growth would require on-going investment by the firm. In such a situation, people often assume that the firm's capital expenditures are just equal to depreciation because the firm must be investing enough to keep its physical capital stock constant. To keep things simple, we adopt this convention below, in which case any investments are new investments. The firm's free cash flow (FCF) then equals its net operating profit (NOPLAT) minus new investments (INVEST). Recall from Chapter 15 that investments are in capital expenditures (CAPX) and changes in net working capital (ΔNWC).

Equilibrium Rate of Return on Investment

An alternative way of deriving terminal values involves developing explicit forecasts up to the point at which you think the firm's return on investment equals its weighted average cost of capital, r_{WACC}. This is a sensible condition because if the firm is earning a return on its investments that is larger than its cost of capital, either the firm should expand or, more likely, competitors will notice the above-average returns and enter the industry, thereby driving down the rate of return on invested capital. In the first part of this section, we assume that there is no expected inflation. Later, we add expected inflation to the analysis.

The Return on Investment and the Plowback Ratio

If there is no expected inflation, the **return on investment (ROI)** is simply the change in a firm's future operating profit divided by its investment:

$$ROI(t+1) = \frac{NOPLAT(t+1) - NOPLAT(t)}{INVEST(t)} \quad \text{(16.38)}$$

Because free cash flow is the difference between current net operating profit and investments, we can write

$$FCF(t) = NOPLAT(t) - INVEST(t) = NOPLAT(t) \times \left[1 - \frac{INVEST(t)}{NOPLAT(t)} \right] \quad \text{(16.39)}$$

In Equation (16.39), the ratio of investment to net operating profit is called the *reinvestment ratio*, or the **plowback ratio**, which we denote $PB(t)$. The plowback ratio is the fraction of operating profits that management reinvests in the firm.

If we multiply both sides of Equation (16.38) by $INVEST(t)$ and divide both sides by $NOPLAT(t)$, we find

$$ROI(t+1) \times \frac{INVEST(t)}{NOPLAT(t)} = \frac{NOPLAT(t+1) - NOPLAT(t)}{NOPLAT(t)} \quad \text{(16.40)}$$

The left-hand side of Equation (16.40) is the return on investment multiplied by the plowback ratio, and the right-hand side is the rate of growth of the cash flows:

$$ROI(t+1) \, PB(t) = g$$

This makes perfect sense. A firm's income grows faster, the higher the rate of return on its investments, and the more of its previous income the firm chooses not to pay its shareholders.

The Terminal Value Calculation

If we substitute for FCF $(t+1)$ in Equation (16.37) using Equation (16.39), we find

$$TV(t+10) = \frac{\text{NOPLAT}(t+11) \times [1 - \text{PB}(t+11)]}{r - g} \tag{16.41}$$

From Equation (16.40), $[1 - \text{PB}] = [1 - g/\text{ROI}] = [\text{ROI} - g]/\text{ROI}$. A key insight is that if a firm has exhausted all its positive NPV projects, then the firm's return on investment will just equal its cost of capital. Thus, we should set $\text{ROI} = r$, and by substituting into the expression for terminal value in Equation (16.41), we find

$$TV(t+10) = \frac{\text{NOPLAT}(t+11)\left(\dfrac{r - g}{r}\right)}{(r - g)} = \frac{\text{NOPLAT}(t+11)}{r} \tag{16.42}$$

This expression looks like a no-growth perpetuity, but NOPLAT and FCF are actually growing at rate g.

Example 16.4 Conundrum Corporation's Terminal Value

Assume that the Conundrum Corporation has a weighted average cost of capital of 10%, and suppose that the final year of a 10-year forecast for Conundrum's NOPLAT is $100 million. If Conundrum just invests enough to offset depreciation, we know free cash flow in year $t+10$ will also be $100 million. With no inflation and no real growth, $100 million will also be the forecast of free cash flow in all future periods. Hence, the terminal value in year $t+10$ of future cash flows beginning in year $t+11$ is

$$TV(t+10) = \frac{\$100\,\text{m}}{1.1} + \frac{\$100\,\text{m}}{1.1^2} + \frac{\$100\,\text{m}}{1.1^3} + \ldots = \frac{\$100\,\text{m}}{0.1} = \$1,000 \text{ million}$$

Now, suppose that every year, Conundrum reinvests 20% of its net operating profits in new projects. What is Conundrum's growth rate if these new investment projects are zero NPV?

Because $\text{ROI} = r$ when projects are zero NPV, we use Equation (16.40) to find Conundrum's growth rate:

$$g = r \times \text{PB} = 10\% \times 20\% = 2\%$$

We can find the new terminal value in two ways. We know that Conundrum invests 20% of NOPLAT or $20 million. Hence, the last explicit forecast is FCF$(t+10) =$ $80 million. Free cash flow in year $t+11$ will be 2% higher because the firm is growing at 2%, so FCF$(t+11) =$ $80 million $\times$ 1.02 = $81.6 million. Equation (16.37) indicates that the terminal value is a perpetuity starting at $81.6 million, growing at 2%, and discounted at 10%. Thus,

$$TV(t+10) = \frac{\$81.6 \text{ million}}{0.10 - 0.02} = \$1,020 \text{ million}$$

Alternatively, we can calculate the terminal value using Equation (16.42). In year t+11, NOPLAT will be 2% higher than year t+10 's $100 million, or $102 million. Thus,

$$\text{TV}(t+10) = \frac{\$102 \text{ million}}{0.10} = \$1,020 \text{ million}$$

Notice that the terminal values are the same; furthermore, they are $20 million higher than the no-growth terminal value. This is exactly what is required for firm value not to change because $20 million of free cash flow was invested in year t+10.

Terminal Value with Perpetual Growth and with Expected Inflation

In the Conundrum Corporation example, there is no expected inflation. When there is expected inflation, we must modify not only the cost of capital, but also the terminal value calculation in Equation (16.42). The easiest way to do this is to recognize that the firm's nominal required rate of return can be decomposed, as in the Fisher equation, into a required real return and expected inflation:

$$1 + R_{\text{WACC}} = (1 + r_{\text{WACC}}) \times (1 + \pi^e) \qquad \textbf{(16.43)}$$

In Equation (16.43), R_{WACC} is the firm's nominal weighted average cost of capital, r_{WACC} is the firm's real weighted average cost of capital, and π^e is the expected rate of inflation. Let's assume that the expected rate of inflation is 5%, and we continue to assume that the real weighted average cost of capital is 10%. Then, the nominal weighted average cost of capital is 15.5%, since $(1.155) = (1.10) \times (1.05)$.

Exhibit 16.7 demonstrates what happens when there is inflation and growth using the Conundrum parameters as examples. In Panel A, the plowback ratio is 0, so there are no net investments. All nominal cash flows grow at the 5% rate of inflation. The terminal value in year t+10 is again $1,000 million because

$$\text{TV}(t+10) = \frac{\$105 \text{ m}}{1.155} + \frac{\$110.3 \text{ m}}{1.155^2} + \ldots = \frac{\$105 \text{ m}}{0.155 - 0.05} = \$1,000 \text{ million}$$

In Panel B, the firm has a plowback ratio of 20%, and it earns a 10% real return on investment. This means that real growth, g, will be 0.02% = 20% × 10%. NOPLAT will be 2% higher each year in the future because more real goods are being produced, but each of those goods will be sold at 5% higher prices. Hence, all of the firm's nominal cash flows will grow at 7.10% = $(1.02) \times (1.05) - 1$. The terminal value in year t+10 can be found by discounting the forecasts of growing free cash flow with the nominal weighted average cost of capital:

$$\text{TV}(t+10) = \frac{\$85.7 \text{ m}}{1.155} + \frac{\$91.8 \text{ m}}{1.155^2} + \frac{\$98.3 \text{ m}}{1.155^3} + \ldots = \frac{\$85.7 \text{ m}}{0.155 - 0.071} = \$1,020 \text{ million}$$

where $85.7 million = ($100 million − $20 million) × 1.071. Notice that this terminal value is $20 million higher than in the no plowback case exactly because the firm earns the required real rate of return on its investment, 10%, and $20 million was taken from year t+10 to begin the growth process. The overall value of the firm has not changed. The $20 million taken from free cash flow in year t+10 is returned in the present value of future free cash flows. Thus, when there is inflation and growth, we can find the terminal value by taking the terminal value with no net investment and adding the value of zero NPV investments made in year t+10:

$$\text{TV}(t+10) = \frac{\text{NOPLAT}(t+10) \times (1 + \pi^e)}{R_{\text{WACC}} - \pi^e} + \text{Net investments } (t+10)$$

The *Point–Counterpoint* explores Panel C of Exhibit 16.7.

Exhibit 16.7 Terminal Values in Year 10 with Inflation and Growth

Panel A: Terminal Value with Inflation

			Year					
Inputs			**10**	**11**	**12**	**13**	**14**	**15**
Inflation	5%	NOPLAT	100.0	105.0	110.3	115.8	121.6	127.6
Required Real ROI	10%	Net Investment	0.0	0.0	0.0	0.0	0.0	0.0
Actual Real ROI	10%	Free Cash Flow	100.0	105.0	110.3	115.8	121.6	127.6
Plowback Ratio	0%	NPV	100.0	90.9	82.6	75.1	68.3	62.1
Nominal WACC	15.5%							
		NOPLAT Growth		5.0%	5.0%	5.0%	5.0%	5.0%
		FCF Growth		5.0%	5.0%	5.0%	5.0%	5.0%
		Real Growth		0.0%	0.0%	0.0%	0.0%	0.0%
	Terminal Value in Year 10		**1000**					

Panel B: Terminal Value with Growth and Inflation

			Year					
Inputs			**10**	**11**	**12**	**13**	**14**	**15**
Inflation	5%	NOPLAT	100.0	107.1	114.7	122.8	131.6	140.9
Required Real ROI	10%	Net Investment	20.0	21.4	22.9	24.6	26.3	28.2
Actual Real ROI	10%	Free Cash Flow	80.0	85.7	91.8	98.3	105.3	112.7
Plowback Ratio	20%	NPV	80.0	74.2	68.8	63.8	59.1	54.8
Nominal WACC	15.5%							
		NOPLAT Growth		7.1%	7.1%	7.1%	7.1%	7.1%
		FCF Growth		7.1%	7.1%	7.1%	7.1%	7.1%
		Real Growth		2.0%	2.0%	2.0%	2.0%	2.0%
	Terminal Value in Year 10		**1020**					

Panel C: Terminal Values in Year 10 Under Different ROIs and Plowback Ratios

		Actual Real ROI						
		0.07	**0.08**	**0.09**	**0.1**	**0.11**	**0.12**	**0.13**
	0	1,000	1,000	1,000	1,000	1,000	1,000	1,000
	0.05	988	994	999	1,005	1,011	1,017	1,023
	0.10	975	986	998	1,010	1,022	1,035	1,048
Plowback Ratio	0.15	960	977	996	1,015	1,035	1,055	1,076
	0.20	943	968	993	1,020	1,048	1,078	1,109
	0.25	925	956	990	1,025	1,063	1,104	1,147
	0.30	905	943	985	1,030	1,079	1,133	1,192

POINT–COUNTERPOINT

Does Faster Growth Lead to More Value?

It's springtime in Washington, D.C., and the Handel brothers are walking with Suttle by the Potomac River enjoying the cherry blossoms. Out of the blue, Ante says, "You know, Freedy, I think we've got to invest more of our retirement portfolio in growth companies. Faster growth leads to higher profits, and higher profits provide better returns. That means we'll be able to retire earlier."

Freedy is a little taken aback because his mind is on the cherry trees, but he manages to reply, "Ante, you just don't get it, do you? Managers who increase growth are only wasting shareholders' cash. I like nice stable cash flows from value companies. They have great products and good profits, and they return lots of cash to shareholders. Growth just destroys value."

Ante argues, "Well, in Bekaert and Hodrick's book, faster growth translates into higher terminal values because you're dividing the last forecast of free cash flow by $r - g$. A larger g makes the denominator smaller, and that makes the terminal value bigger, so faster growth leads to more value."

Freedy counters, "Those investments for growth came from free cash flow that could have been paid out to shareholders. I want money now, not some promise of money in the future that never materializes."

Suttle knows that an argument is brewing and says, "When we get back to the hotel, let's revisit the part in Bekaert and Hodrick's book where they discuss growth and terminal values. I think it's Example 16.4." Later, Suttle shows the brothers that real growth depends on the plowback ratio multiplied by the actual real rate of return on investment.

"So, I'm right!" exclaims Ante. "If a firm invests more, it grows faster." Freedy, red in the face, argues, "But the firm is worth less because they aren't paying out the money now."

At this point, Suttle says, "Ante, you're right that a higher plowback ratio leads to more growth, and Freedy, you're wrong that the firm can't be worth more. But, Ante, you're wrong, too. Whether growth increases firm value or not depends on the firm's return on investment relative to its WACC. Look at Panel C of Exhibit 16.7. The different cells refer to Conundrum's terminal value depending on their plowback ratio and their actual real return on investment. Remember, Conundrum's real cost of capital was 10%. The Exhibit clearly shows that plowing back higher percentages of NOPLAT decreases value if the firm earns less than its cost of capital, while value increases if the firm earns more than the cost of capital."

"The interesting column is when Conundrum's return on investment just equals its cost of capital. Suppose Conundrum changes its plowback ratio from 20% to 30%. Equation (16.40) indicates that the firm's real growth rate will increase from 2% to 3%. So, Ante is right, more plowback leads to more growth. The additional investment in year $t+10$ is 10% of $100 million, or $10 million. Thus, free cash flow in year $t+10$ falls from $80 million to $70 million. The terminal value calculation is now done by recognizing that free cash flow will be growing at 8.15% $(1.03 \times 1.05 - 1)$ and is discounted at 15.5%:

$$\text{Terminal value in year } t+10 = \frac{\$70 \text{ million} \times 1.0815}{0.155 - 0.0815} = \$1,030 \text{ million}$$

"Notice that this is $10 million higher than before," says Suttle, "which is the amount of the additional investment."

After Suttle presents his analysis, he says, "Growth does lead to increases in value, but only if the real return on investment is larger than the real WACC does the firm's value increase by more than the amount of the investment."

16.5 TAX SHIELDS ON FOREIGN CURRENCY BORROWING

When a corporation borrows foreign currency, it gets an interest deduction just as if it borrows in the home currency. But when the loan is repaid, the corporation may experience either a capital gain (if the home currency strengthens in value relative to the foreign currency) or capital loss (if the home currency weakens relative to the foreign currency). The capital gains are treated as income to the firm and are subject to tax. The capital losses are deductible for tax purposes and provide additional tax shields. This section first explores the theory associated with these capital gains and losses. It then analyzes the borrowing possibilities of Banana Computers.

The Tax Implications of Borrowing in a Foreign Currency

Suppose a U.S. corporation borrows foreign currency at time t for 1 year. Let the foreign currency principal and interest be denoted $D(FC)$ and $i(FC)$, respectively. If the exchange rate, $S(t)$, is dollars per foreign currency, the dollar value of the principal is $S(t) \times D(FC)$. In 1 year, the firm will repay the foreign currency principal plus interest, and it will be able to deduct the dollar value of the actual interest paid. A weakening of the dollar increases the amount of interest paid, and a strengthening of the dollar decreases the amount of interest paid. Thus, the actual interest deduction at time $t+1$ will be $S(t+1) \times i(FC) \times D(FC)$.

Changes in the exchange rate will also affect the dollar value of the repayment of the foreign currency principal, which is $S(t+1) \times D(FC)$ dollars. If the dollar has strengthened versus the foreign currency, $S(t+1) < S(t)$, in which case the corporation will repay fewer dollars of principal than it borrowed. The difference between the dollar amount borrowed and the dollar amount repaid, $[S(t) - S(t+1)] \times D(FC)$, is the corporation's capital gain. Because capital gains are income to the firm, the firm will have to pay income tax on this capital gain.

Conversely, if the dollar has weakened versus the foreign currency, $S(t+1) > S(t)$, and the corporation repays $S(t+1) \times D(FC)$ dollars, which is more dollars than it borrowed. The difference between the dollar amount repaid and the dollar amount borrowed, $[S(t+1) - S(t)] \times D(FC)$, is the firm's capital loss. The firm will be able to deduct that loss from its income, which allows the firm to pay less income tax.

Because interest rates differ across countries, there are expected changes in exchange rates, and consequently, there are expected capital gains and losses when borrowing foreign currencies. The expected taxes on capital gains are necessary to prevent the firm from having an incentive to borrow in high interest rate currencies to get larger interest tax shields. Because high interest rate currencies are expected to depreciate relative to the home currency, the borrower expects to have a capital gain on the repayment of principal. The capital gain tax offsets the higher interest tax shield and prevents the existence of a tax incentive to borrow in high interest rate currencies.

The next section presents an analysis of a case in which Banana Computers is confronted with alternative foreign currency borrowing opportunities. Banana uses an ANPV analysis to find the best one.

Foreign Currency Borrowing by Banana Computers

If projects are mutually exclusive, ANPV analysis dictates that the firm should accept the project with the largest ANPV. One situation in which this type of analysis arises is when an importer is buying goods with subsidized financing provided either by the exporter or by the exporter's government. If the imported goods are really the same from country to country, the importer's problem is just to find the best financing. An ANPV analysis of the financing takes account of the interest tax shields as well as any capital gain taxes or capital loss subsidies that arise from changes in exchange rates. This section provides a concrete demonstration of these effects.

Banana's Borrowing Possibilities

Suppose Banana Computers, a U.S. company, wants to buy some computer hard drives from either a German manufacturer or a Japanese manufacturer. From Banana's perspective, the hard drives are the same, but the financing is different. The German company has arranged for Banana to borrow EUR300 million for 8 years at an annual interest rate of 3.5%. This rate is below the 8-year, risk-free euro interest rate of 5%. The Japanese manufacturer has also arranged for Banana to borrow JPY36,000 million for 8 years at an even lower interest rate of 1.5%.

The 8-year, risk-free yen interest rate is 2.5%. At the current exchange rate of JPY120/EUR, the principals on the loans are identical because

$$(\text{JPY}120/\text{EUR}) \times \text{EUR}300 \text{ million} = \text{JPY}36{,}000 \text{ million}$$

Both exporters require repayment with equal annual installments. Amortization is the process of repaying the principal on a long-term debt over time. Because interest is paid only on outstanding principal, amortizing a loan with equal annual payments means that the borrower pays more interest in the earlier years of the loan and more principal in the later years.[6]

If the hard drives are identical, which foreign loan should Banana take? Alternatively, should Banana borrow in dollars at its market rate of 6% when the risk-free dollar interest rate is 4%? At the spot exchange rate of USD1.0909/EUR, the dollar principal would be

$$(\text{USD}1.0909/\text{EUR}) \times \text{EUR}300 \text{ million} = \text{USD}327.27 \text{ million}$$

Exhibits 16.8 through 16.10 present the ANPV cash flow analyses associated with the dollar loan, the euro loan, and the yen loan, respectively.

The Dollar Loan

The dollar loan is the most straightforward and is the benchmark to which the other loans can be compared. Exhibit 16.8 indicates that eight annual payments of USD52.70 million are required to repay the USD327.27 million principal at an interest rate of 6%. Because interest is paid only on the outstanding balance, the first interest payment is

$$0.06 \times \text{USD}327.27 \text{ million} = \text{USD}19.64 \text{ million}$$

By year 8, only USD49.72 million of principal is outstanding, so the last interest payment is

$$0.06 \times \text{USD}49.72 \text{ million} = \text{USD}2.98 \text{ million}$$

The ANPV analysis values the expected after-tax dollar cash flows that are received or paid in each year. In the first year, Banana receives the $327.27 million as the principal of the loan. In future years, the cash outflow is the sum of the interest paid and the principal repaid

Exhibit 16.8 The Value of a Dollar Loan

					Years in the Future				
	0	1	2	3	4	5	6	7	8
Dollar Payments on the USD327.27 Million Loan									
Interest @ 6%		19.64	17.65	15.55	13.32	10.96	8.45	5.80	2.98
Principal		33.07	35.05	37.15	39.38	41.76	44.25	46.91	49.72
Total		52.70	52.70	52.70	52.70	52.70	52.70	52.70	52.70
Expected Dollar Cash Flows Associated with the USD Loan									
Interest		−19.64	−17.65	−15.55	−13.32	−10.96	−8.45	−5.80	−2.98
Principal	327.27	−33.07	−35.05	−37.15	−39.38	−41.75	−44.25	−46.91	−49.72
Interest Tax Shield		6.68	6.00	5.29	4.53	3.73	2.87	1.97	1.01
Dollar Cash Flows	327.27	−46.03	−46.70	−47.42	−48.17	−48.98	−49.83	−50.73	−51.69
NPV of Dollar Cash Flows @ 6%	26.42								

Notes: All cash flows are in millions of dollars and are rounded to two decimal places. Inflows are positive, and outflows are negative.

---

[6]In Microsoft Excel, the command PMT(*rate, nper, pv, fv, type*) returns the value of an annual payment associated with borrowing an amount, *pv*, at an interest rate, *rate*, for *nper* years with future value *fv*. *type* indicates whether the payments are at the beginning or the end of the year. The commands IPMT and PPMT provide the breakdown of the payment into interest and principal.

minus the interest tax shield. With a corporate tax rate of 34%, the deductibility of interest paid provides an interest tax shield in the first year equal to

$$0.34 \times \text{USD19.64 million} = \text{USD6.68 million}$$

The amount by which the present value of the future after-tax payments associated with the loan is less than the value of the principal borrowed is the ANPV of the loan. These debt cash flows should be discounted at Banana's market-debt interest rate of 6%. Exhibit 16.8 indicates that the ability to borrow USD327.27 million at 6% is worth USD26.42 million.

The Euro and Yen Loans

Exhibit 16.9 presents the analysis of the euro loan. We see that eight annual payments of EUR43.64 million are required to amortize the EUR300 million principal at an interest rate of 3.5%. Because interest is paid on the outstanding balance, the first interest payment is

$$0.035 \times \text{EUR300 million} = \text{EUR10.50 million}$$

By year 8, only EUR42.17 million of principal is outstanding, so the final interest payment is

$$0.035 \times \text{EUR42.17 million} = \text{EUR1.48 million}$$

Exhibit 16.10 presents the analysis of the yen loan. Here, eight annual payments of JPY4,809.02 million are required to amortize the JPY36,000 million principal at an interest rate of 1.5%. The first interest payment is

$$0.015 \times \text{JPY36,000 million} = \text{JPY540 million}$$

In year 8, the outstanding principal is JPY4,737.96 million, so the final interest payment is

$$0.015 \times \text{JPY4,737.96 million} = \text{JPY71.07 million}$$

Comparing the Foreign Currency Loans

Because Banana Computers is a U.S. company, it can compare the values of the two subsidized deals by converting the expected future foreign currency cash flows into expected future dollars, using expected future exchange rates. Exhibits 16.9 and 16.10 use uncovered

Exhibit 16.9 The Value of a Subsidized Euro Loan

					Years in the Future				
	0	**1**	**2**	**3**	**4**	**5**	**6**	**7**	**8**
Euro Payments on the EUR300 Million Loan									
Interest @ 3.5%		10.50	9.34	8.14	6.90	5.61	4.28	2.90	1.48
Principal		33.14	34.30	35.50	36.75	38.03	39.36	40.74	42.17
Total		43.64	43.64	43.64	43.64	43.64	43.64	43.64	43.64
Expected USD/EUR from Interest Rate Parity with i(USD) = 4% and i(EUR) = 5%									
Exchange Rate	1.0909	1.0805	1.0702	1.0600	1.0499	1.0399	1.0300	1.0202	1.0105
Expected Dollar Cash Flows Associated with the Euro Loan									
Interest		−11.35	−10.00	−8.63	−7.24	−5.83	−4.41	−2.96	−1.49
Principal	327.27	−35.81	−36.71	−37.63	−38.58	−39.55	−40.55	−41.56	−42.61
Interest Tax Shield		3.86	3.40	2.93	2.46	1.98	1.50	1.01	0.51
Capital Gains Subsidy or Tax		−0.12	−0.24	−0.37	−0.51	−0.66	−0.81	−0.98	−1.15
Dollar Cash Flows	327.27	−43.42	−43.55	−43.70	−43.87	−44.06	−44.27	−44.50	−44.75
NPV of Dollar Cash Flows @ 6%	54.31								

Notes: All cash flows are in millions and are rounded to two decimal places. In the top panel, the currency is the euro; in the bottom panel, it is the dollar.

Exhibit 16.10 The Value of a Subsidized Yen Loan

				Years i	n the Fut	ure			
	0	**1**	**2**	**3**	**4**	**5**	**6**	**7**	**8**
Yen Payments on the JPY36,000 Million Loan									
Interest @ 1.5%		540.00	475.96	410.97	345.00	278.04	210.07	141.09	71.07
Principal		4,269.02	4,333.06	4,398.06	4,464.03	4,530.99	4,598.95	4,667.94	4,737.96
Total		4,809.02	4,809.02	4,809.02	4,809.02	4,809.02	4,809.02	4,809.02	4,809.02
Expected JPY/USD from Interest Rate Parity with i(USD) = 4% and i(JPY) = 2.5%									
Exchange Rate	110.00	108.41	106.85	105.31	103.79	102.29	100.82	99.36	97.93
Expected Dollar Cash Flows Associated with the Yen Loan									
Interest		−4.98	−4.45	−3.90	−3.32	−2.72	−2.08	−1.42	−0.73
Principal	327.27	−39.38	−40.55	−41.76	−43.01	−44.29	−45.62	−46.98	−48.38
Interest Tax Shield		1.69	1.51	1.33	1.13	0.92	0.71	0.18	0.25
Capital Gains Subsidy or Tax		0.19	0.39	0.61	0.83	1.06	1.29	1.54	1.80
Dollar Cash Flows	327.27	−42.47	−43.10	−43.73	−44.38	−45.03	−45.70	−46.37	−47.05
NPV of Dollar Cash Flows @ 6%	50.75								

Notes: All cash flows are in millions and are rounded to two decimal places. In the top panel, the currency is the yen; in the bottom panel, it is the dollar.

interest rate parity, calculated using the risk-free interest rates, to generate forecasts of future exchange rates. It is assumed that the term structures of interest rates are flat in each of the currencies. In Exhibit 16.9, the spot exchange rate of dollars per euro is USD1.0909/EUR, and the forecast of the exchange rate k years in the future is

$$E_t[S(t+k)] = (\text{USD}1.0909/\text{EUR}) \times [1.04/1.05]^k$$

Because the dollar interest rate is less than the euro interest rate, the dollar is expected to appreciate relative to the euro. The expected dollar appreciation implies that capital gains are expected on the repayment of the euro principal. The capital gain arises because it takes fewer dollars to repay the euro principal, which increases the income of Banana Computers. The associated capital gains taxes reduce the value of the deal.

In Exhibit 16.10, the spot exchange rate of yen per dollar is JPY110/USD, and the forecast of the exchange rate k years in the future is

$$E_t[S(t+k)] = (\text{JPY}110/\text{USD}) \times [1.025/1.04]^k$$

Because the yen interest rate is less than the dollar interest rate, the dollar is expected to weaken relative to the yen. Hence, Banana Computers expects to pay more dollars to repay the yen principal than the amount of dollars it borrows after the conversion of the yen principal at the current exchange rate. Banana therefore expects to take capital losses on the repayment of the yen principal. Because these expected capital losses are tax deductible, they enhance the value of the deal.

With a U.S. corporate tax rate of 34%, the interest tax shield is 34% of the expected dollar interest paid on either the euro loan or the yen loan, just as in the case of a dollar loan. For example, in year 1, interest on the euro loan is €10.50 million, and the expected spot rate is $1.0805/€. Expected dollar interest is therefore $1.0805/€ × €10.5 million = $11.35 million. The interest tax shield is 0.34 × $11.35 million = $3.86 million. In the case of the euro loan, the capital gains tax is 34% of the difference between the dollar value of the principal borrowed and the dollar value of the principal repaid. For example, the principal repaid in year 1 is €33.14 million, and the expected capital gains tax is $0.34 \times €33.14 \times \left(\dfrac{\$1.0909}{€} - \dfrac{\$1.0805}{€} \right) = \$0.12$ million. For the yen loan, the tax deductibility of the capital loss provides a subsidy of 34% of the difference between the dollar value of the principal repaid and the dollar value of the principal borrowed.

As in the case of the dollar loan, the ANPV analysis takes the present value of the expected after-tax dollar cash flows that are received or paid in each year using the discount rate of 6% because the future expected dollar cash flows have the same risk characteristics as dollar debt. In the first year, Banana receives the $327.27 million as the principal of the loan. For foreign currency loans, the dollar cash outflow in future years is the sum of the interest paid and principal repaid, minus the interest tax shield and plus any capital gains tax or minus any capital-loss subsidy. The amount by which the present value of the future payments is less than the value of the principal borrowed is the ANPV of the loan.

Exhibit 16.9 indicates that the ANPV of the euro loan is $54.31 million, whereas Exhibit 16.10 indicates that the ANPV of the yen loan is $50.75 million. Both of these dominate the dollar loan because they are subsidized. Because only one loan can be taken, Banana should take the euro loan. By taking the euro loan, Banana adds $54.31 million to the value of the corporation.

16.6 CONFLICTS BETWEEN BONDHOLDERS AND STOCKHOLDERS

Whenever a firm issues debt, potential conflicts of interest arise between the bondholders and the stockholders. These conflicts are one of the difficult-to-quantify aspects of the costs of **financial distress**. Rather than attempt to quantify the nature of these costs, we merely examine how they arise in an international context. You should remember that the managers of a firm are assumed to be acting in the interests of the shareholders—that is, maximizing shareholder value. This is the natural perspective because the shareholders are the ultimate owners of the firm, and the managers report to the board of directors, who represent the shareholders.

The Incentive to Take Risks

The first conflict between bondholders and stockholders arises because the managers of a firm that is near bankruptcy, who are acting in the interests of the stockholders, have an incentive to invest in very risky projects. The projects might even be ones that have a negative net present value.

To understand these incentives, consider a U.S. firm with debt that has a face value of $500 and that is trying to choose between two mutually exclusive international investment projects. The variance of the return on one project is low, whereas the variance of the return on the other is high. For ease of exposition, assume that there are only two possible states of the world that affect the projects: Either the foreign currency will appreciate versus the dollar, implying that the projects will be successful, or the foreign currency will depreciate, and the projects will provide poor returns. Assume that each of the two possible states of the world has a 50% possibility. To simplify the arguments, we ignore discounting throughout.

The Low-Variance Project
If the firm accepts the low-variance project, the value of the firm, its equity, and its bonds in the different states of the world can be summarized as follows:

LOW-VARIANCE PROJECT				
	Probability	Value of Firm	Value of Equity	Value of Bonds
Foreign Currency Depreciation	0.5	$500	0	$500
Foreign Currency Appreciation	0.5	$600	$100	$500

If the firm accepts the low-variance project, the expected value of the firm is

$$0.5 \times \$500 + 0.5 \times \$600 = \$550$$

The cash flows from the project are sufficient to cover the firm's outstanding debt in either state of the world, so the debt is riskless. Because the firm always generates enough cash to repay the debt, the debt is worth its face value of $500 whether the dollar appreciates or depreciates. Equity, on the other hand, will be worthless if the dollar strengthens because the firm generates only enough funds to repay the bondholders. However, the equity will be worth $100 if the dollar weakens. The expected value of equity is therefore

$$0.5 \times \$0 + 0.5 \times \$100 = \$50$$

The High-Variance Project

If the firm takes the high-variance project, the values of the firm, its equity, and its debt can be described as follows:

	HIGH-VARIANCE PROJECT			
	Probability	Value of Firm	Value of Equity	Value of Bonds
Foreign Currency Depreciation	0.5	$400	0	$400
Foreign Currency Appreciation	0.5	$650	$150	$500

If the firm undertakes the high-variance project, the expected value of the firm is

$$0.5 \times \$400 + 0.5 \times \$650 = \$525$$

If the dollar strengthens, though, the cash flows from the project will be insufficient to cover the firm's $500 outstanding debt, and the value of the debt will be $400. If the dollar depreciates, the full value of the debt can be repaid, and it will be worth $500. The expected value of debt is therefore

$$0.5 \times \$400 + 0.5 \times \$500 = \$450$$

On the other hand, equity will again be worthless if the dollar strengthens, but equity will be worth $150 if the dollar weakens. The expected value of equity is therefore

$$0.5 \times \$0 + 0.5 \times \$150 = \$75$$

Clearly, because the two projects are mutually exclusive, if the firm's managers act in the interest of the stockholders, they will undertake the inferior, high-variance project because it maximizes the value of the firm's equity. The key insight is that because the firm is currently levered, the stockholders gain when the dollar weakens but they do not lose when the dollar strengthens. By taking the high-variance project, the managers of the firm transfer $25 of value from the bondholders to the stockholders. Notice, though, the managers also destroy an additional $25 of firm value. By accepting the wrong project from the perspective of the firm as a whole, the managers are said to have engaged in **asset substitution**.

The Underinvestment Problem

If a firm is near bankruptcy, managers who act in the interest of stockholders often do not have an incentive to make investments that would increase the overall value of the firm because too much of the increase in the firm's value is captured by the existing bondholders. This is known as **underinvestment**. To understand this scenario, examine the following situations.

A Firm Without a New Project

Suppose that a firm has outstanding bonds with face value of $500, and its cash flows without a new project are as follows:

FIRM WITHOUT A NEW PROJECT				
	Probability	Value of Firm	Value of Equity	Value of Bonds
Dollar Appreciation	0.5	$400	0	$400
Dollar Depreciation	0.5	$600	$100	$500

The expected value of the firm's assets is

$$0.5 \times \$400 + 0.5 \times \$600 = \$500$$

Because the firm does not have enough to repay the bonds in the bad state of the world, the expected value of the firm's bonds is

$$0.5 \times \$400 + 0.5 \times \$500 = \$450$$

As the residual claimants to the firm's cash flows, the expected value of the equity is

$$0.5 \times \$0 + 0.5 \times \$100 = \$50$$

A Firm with a New Project

Now, suppose that the managers of this firm have an opportunity to invest in a project that costs $100 of equity. Suppose that the cash flows of the firm with the new project would be as follows:

FIRM WITH A NEW PROJECT				
	Probability	Value of Firm	Value of Equity	Value of Bonds
Dollar Appreciation	0.5	$500	0	$500
Dollar Depreciation	0.5	$760	$260	$500

If the firm accepts the project, the expected value of the firm increases by $130, to

$$0.5 \times \$500 + 0.5 \times \$760 = \$630$$

Because the firm now has enough resources to repay the bonds, the expected value of the firm's bonds is $500:

$$0.5 \times \$500 + 0.5 \times \$500 = \$500$$

The stockholders remain the residual claimants to the firm's cash flows, and the expected value of the equity of the firm is

$$0.5 \times \$0 + 0.5 \times \$260 = \$130$$

What has been accomplished by investing the additional $100 of shareholders' equity? First, the value of the firm has increased by $130. Consequently, this is a positive NPV project for the firm as a whole. But will the stockholders want the managers to invest in this project? The answer is no.

Earlier, we determined that the value of equity without an investment in the new project is $50. With the new project, equity value rises to $130. Hence, from the stockholders' perspective, they invest $100, but they see their equity value increase by only $80. The problem is, of course, that the existing bondholders of the firm are reaping a substantial benefit from the new project. Their bonds increase in value by $50, from $450 to $500.

In this situation, as in the previous section, managers who are acting in the interests of stockholders and are maximizing shareholder value do not make a correct investment decision. If the manager does not take this investment project, this is a true cost of financial distress because the project is positive NPV for the firm as a whole.

Underinvestment in Emerging Market Crises

Economists think that the problems associated with underinvestment partially explain the prolonged nature of the Debt Crisis in the 1980s. The governments of emerging-market countries with large outstanding foreign debts could not credibly commit not to tax the positive returns to investments made in their countries. Thus, because managers of firms perceived that too much of the return on investment would be captured by the governments to repay the foreign loans due to the debt overhang, no one wanted to invest in these countries. Without investments, the countries could not grow and could not generate enough tax revenues to allow the governments to repay the foreign debts. Debt forgiveness, in the form of the Brady Plan, helped to overcome the problems and allowed growth to resume.

Other Managerial Problems Caused by Financial Distress

The previous section demonstrates that stockholders might not want to contribute new equity to a project that has a positive NPV if too much of the benefit of the new project will go to existing bondholders. A natural counterpart to this idea is that stockholders would like to see cash distributed from the firm when it is near financial distress. Of course, when cash is distributed from the firm, the market value of the firm's stock will fall, but it will fall less than the value of any cash dividends because bondholders will suffer some of the loss, as well.

The managers of a firm that is close to financial distress also have an incentive to misrepresent the financial condition of the firm to keep creditors at bay. The firm may be forced to cut its capital expenditures by doing less maintenance than is desirable, and its research and development expenditures may be slashed. Such actions buy time for the current managers, but they may destroy the value of the firm's assets.

16.7 INTERNATIONAL DIFFERENCES IN ACCOUNTING STANDARDS

Historically, international valuations were often complicated because accounting standards differed significantly across countries. However, over the past 10 years, a large number of countries (well over 80) have endorsed **international financial reporting standards (IFRS)**, which were developed by the International Accounting Standards Board.[7] While a number of firms have used IFRS voluntarily for quite a while, mandatory adoption started in a large number of countries, including the European Union (EU), in 2005. Adoption rates differ across countries but now exceed over 90% of the firms in many developed and some emerging countries. Because mandatory adoption of IFRS is limited to consolidated accounts and smaller firms often get an exemption, some firms in countries with mandatory IFRS adoption continue to report under local accounting standards. Nevertheless, IFRS opens up the possibility of providing investors and analysts with transparent financial statements that can be easily compared across countries. While the United States has not formally adopted IFRS yet, the U.S. Securities and Exchange Commission (SEC) has, since 2009, allowed cross-listed companies to either use U.S. **generally accepted accounting principles (GAAP)** or IFRS. Moreover, in 2008, it set out a roadmap for possible IFRS adoption by U.S. publicly traded companies to be completed by 2015 for large companies and by 2017 for small companies.

---

[7]For a discussion of the key differences between U.S. GAAP and IFRS, see Chapter 21 of Koller et al. (2005).

Before jumping for joy and thinking that comparisons across countries will be easy in the future, it is important to think about some issues raised by Ball (2006), who argues, "All accounting accruals (versus simply counting cash) involve judgments about future cash flows. Consequently, there is much leeway in implementing accounting rules. . . . Achieving uniformity in accounting standards seems easy in comparison with achieving uniformity in actual reporting behavior" (p. 27). Ball notes that while many countries use the metric system, the weight of the butcher's thumb on the scale differs across countries and is constrained by the eye of the customer, the butcher's concern for reputation, and the monitoring mechanisms of state and private systems. So too will it be with international accounting. The roles of auditors, regulators, courts, boards, analysts, rating agencies, the press, and others who use financial information in overseeing the financial reporting of corporations differ across countries and over time in a specific country. Hence, it is unlikely that uniformity in accounting rules will be followed quickly by uniformity in accounting practice. Hail et al. (2010), in an exhaustive survey on IFRS, also conclude that diversity in accounting standards may be the expected outcome of diversity in the institutional infrastructures of different countries.

Empirical Effects of IFRS Adoption

Despite Ball's (2006) criticism, a large literature has tried to uncover the benefits and costs of IFRS adoption. First, while IFRS should be expected to harmonize accounting standards across countries, as Ball argues, differences in accounting practices will remain and comparability may not be perfect. For U.S. firms, it is often argued that U.S. GAAP and IFRS are not so different to begin with and have been converging over time. Yet, some recent studies document rather large differences in terms of important financial results. For example, Henry et al. (2009) claim that an important economic concept like the return on equity may substantially differ across the two systems for a large set of firms. Second, better accounting standards may lead to more and better quality disclosure of information about the firm's projects and economic earnings. This, in turn, should be associated with positive market outcomes, such as improved liquidity (as investors feel more secure trading the stock) and larger investments by foreign investors. Both effects may induce lower costs of capital for the firm. In their survey of the empirical literature, Hail et al. (2010) claim that these effects are surely not observed for all firms in all countries adopting IFRS. They find that mandatory adopters experience the most positive effects upon adoption in those countries where local accounting standards are most different from IFRS, but where legal enforcement is strong. Yu (2010) demonstrates that international mutual funds increase their investments in firms reporting under IFRS, thereby helping to further integrate markets. Yet, the expected effect for U.S. firms may be more minor, as U.S. GAAP is arguably an as good or better accounting standard than IFRS. At the same time, the transition costs of adopting a new accounting system are likely steep, especially for large firms. The SEC estimated these costs for the largest firms to be $32 million for the first 3 years of adoption. The firms likely to benefit the most from worldwide IFRS adoption are, of course, multinational firms, which may look forward to using one single standard for financial reporting across all their markets.

16.8 SUMMARY

This chapter examines advanced international capital budgeting. The main points in the chapter are as follows:

1. The weighted average cost of capital, r_{WACC}, is defined as the weighted sum of the after-tax required rate of return on the firm's debt and the required rate of return on the firm's equity, where the weights represent the percentage of the firm's value financed with debt versus equity. Discounting all-equity free cash flows at r_{WACC} provides a correct valuation only when the riskiness of the cash flows and the ability of the project to support debt are the same as those of the overall corporation.

2. The flow-to-equity (FTE) approach discounts the after-tax free cash flows to stockholders at the

required rate of return on the equity to derive the equity value of a project.

3. The adjusted net present value (ANPV) method works well when a firm knows the level of its debt in future periods. If the ratio of debt to value is more likely to be constant, the weighted average cost of capital (WACC) approach or FTE approach may be easier to use.

4. The domestic currency value of a foreign project can be found either by discounting the expected foreign currency cash flows with an appropriate foreign currency discount rate and then converting them into domestic currency using the current spot exchange rate, or by forecasting future exchange rates, multiplying them by the expected value of the future foreign currency cash flows, and then discounting them using a domestic currency discount rate.

5. The Consolidated Machine Tool Company (CMTC) case demonstrates the importance of using different discount rates for different future horizons. Furthermore, expected rates of real appreciation between currencies can substantively affect international valuations.

6. The terminal value of a project can be calculated by assuming that the rate of return on an investment will fall, because of competition, to the weighted average cost of capital.

7. When determining the tax shields associated with borrowing foreign currency, you must take account of taxes on expected capital gains or tax shields on expected losses due to the expected appreciation or depreciation of the domestic currency relative to the foreign currency.

8. The presence of debt can give rise to conflicts between a firm's stockholders and bondholders. The firm's managers can engage in asset substitution or underinvestment. Asset substitution occurs when the managers invest in projects that are more risky than bondholders expected. Underinvestment occurs when managers refuse to take on low-risk projects that would increase the firm's value because too much of the value from the project accrues to the bondholders.

9. Differences in accounting conventions across countries must be taken into account when doing international capital budgeting.

QUESTIONS

1. Why should the required rate of return for a capital budgeting problem be project specific? Doesn't the firm just have to satisfy an overall cost-of-capital requirement?

2. What is the conceptual foundation of the flow-to-equity approach to capital budgeting?

3. What is the weighted average cost of capital?

4. Should a firm ever accept a project that has a negative NPV when discounted at the weighted average cost of capital?

5. Can you do capital budgeting for a foreign project using a domestic currency discount rate? Explain your answer.

6. Why might it be important to use period-specific discount rates when doing capital budgeting?

7. Why is it necessary to consider forecasts of real currency appreciation and depreciation when doing international capital budgeting?

8. What is the rate of return on invested capital? How is it calculated?

9. If you borrow a foreign currency, what interest deduction would you receive on your taxes?

10. If you borrow a foreign currency, are there any capital gains taxes to worry about?

11. Why might a manager accept a high-variance, low-value project instead of a low-variance, high-value project?

12. Why would a manager not accept a positive net present value project?

PROBLEMS

1. Suppose that the required rate of return on a firm's debt is 8%, the corporate tax rate is 34%, and the required rate of return on the firm's equity is 15%. If the firm finances its projects with 40% debt, what is the firm's WACC?

2. Suppose that U.K. Motors Ltd. is considering an investment of £30 million to develop a new factory.

Assume that its stockholders require a 22% rate of return, that its bondholders require a 9% rate of return, that the U.K. corporate tax rate is 40%, that 35% of the project will be financed by debt, and that 65% of the project will be financed with equity. What must be the annual income from the project if it is to be a zero net present value investment?

3. If the risk-free rate is 5%, the firm's required rate of return on its debt is 6%, the equity beta is 1.4, the equity risk premium is 5.5%, the corporate tax rate is 34%, and the debt–equity ratio is 0.5, what is the expected rate of return on the assets of the firm that is predicted by the capital asset pricing model (CAPM)?

4. Suppose that a firm's corporate headquarters thinks that the appropriate dollar rate of return on investments in Japan is 18% per annum. If the dollar is expected to weaken relative to the yen by 4% per annum, what is the Japanese yen required rate of return on the expected yen cash flows?

5. Which is a better deal: borrowing at 1% in yen when the risk-free yen interest rate is 3% and the firm's market-debt rate is 4%, or borrowing in euros at 3% when the risk-free euro interest rate is 5% and the firm's market-debt rate is 6%? Assume that uncovered interest rate parity holds and that the corporate tax rate is 34%.

6. Consider a firm that owes $700 to its bondholders facing the following two mutually exclusive projects:

PROJECT A		
	Probability	Value of Firm
Dollar Appreciation	0.5	$700
Dollar Depreciation	0.5	$800

PROJECT B		
	Probability	Value of Firm
Dollar Appreciation	0.5	$650
Dollar Depreciation	0.5	$830

If the managers are operating in the interest of the stockholders, which project will the firm take? Why?

7. Suppose that a firm has $700 of bonds outstanding, and its cash flows without a new project will be as follows:

FIRM WITHOUT A NEW PROJECT		
	Probability	Value of Firm
Dollar Appreciation	0.5	$600
Dollar Depreciation	0.5	$800

Suppose that the cash flows of the firm with a new project that costs $60 would be as follows:

FIRM WITH A NEW PROJECT		
	Probability	Value of Firm
Dollar Appreciation	0.5	$700
Dollar Depreciation	0.5	$840

If the managers are acting in the interests of the shareholders, will they accept this project? Why or why not?

8. Web Question: Go to www.vodafone.com and determine the outstanding amounts of debt and equity. If the required rate of return on its debt is 75 basis points over the 10-year U.K. Treasury yield, its equity beta is 0.75, and the equity premium is 5.5%, what is Vodafone's weighted average cost of capital? *Hint:* Don't forget to find the U.K. tax rate.

BIBLIOGRAPHY

Ball, Ray, 2006, "International Financial Reporting Standards (IFRS): Pros and Cons for Investors," *Accounting and Business Research, International Accounting Policy Forum* 36, pp. 5–27.

Hail, Luzi, Christian Leuz, and Peter Wysocki, 2010, "Global Accounting Convergence and the Potential Adoption of IFRS by the US (Part I): Conceptual Underpinnings and Economic Analysis," *Accounting Horizons* 24, pp. 355–394.

Henry, Elaine, Stephen Lin, and Ya-wen Yang, 2009, "The European–US 'GAAP GAP': IFRS to U.S. GAAP Form 20-F Reconciliations," *Accounting Horizons* 23, pp. 121–150.

Koller, Tim, Marc Goedhart, and David Wessels, 2005, *Valuation: Measuring and Managing the Value of Companies*, 4th ed., New York: Wiley.

Miles, James A., and John R. Ezzell, 1980, "The Weighted Average Cost of Capital, Perfect Capital Markets and Project Life," *Journal of Financial and Quantitative Analysis* 15, pp. 719–730.

Modigliani, Franco, and Merton Miller, 1958, "The Cost of Capital, Corporation Finance, and the Theory of Investment," *American Economic Review* 48, pp. 261–297.

_____, 1961, "Dividend Policy, Growth, and the Valuation of Shares," *Journal of Business* 34, pp. 411–433.

Yu, Gwen, 2010, "Accounting Standards and International Portfolio Holdings: Analysis of Cross-Border Holdings Following Mandatory Adoption of IFRS," manuscript, Harvard University.

Chapter 17

Risk Management and the Foreign Currency Hedging Decision

*F*irms hedge foreign exchange risk by using instruments such as forward and futures foreign exchange contracts, interest rate and currency swaps, and foreign currency options and by choosing to denominate assets and liabilities in foreign currencies. For example, Infosys, an Indian software firm, has a six-person Treasury team in Bangalore, India, that routinely hedges its currency risk one to two quarters ahead. The risk is substantive because the firm has most of its costs in Indian rupees and 98% of its revenue in foreign currencies. Infosys estimates that it loses 40 basis points of profit margin for each 1% that the Indian rupee depreciates against the U.S. dollar. This chapter examines why a firm would want to use these financial instruments to hedge foreign exchange risk.

We first show that hedging would be desirable for a risk-averse entrepreneur because it reduces the variance of profits. However, in a modern, publicly held corporation, the benefits of hedging are less clear. Indeed, the logic of Modigliani and Miller (1958, 1961) implies that hedging is irrelevant as investors can always undo any hedging a corporation does. Nevertheless, there are modern arguments for and against hedging, and we know that the assumptions of Modigliani and Miller probably do not hold for most situations.

After reviewing the Modigliani–Miller arguments, we examine three arguments against hedging: that hedging is costly, that hedging is impossible for equity-like cash flows, and that hedging increases the costs of financial distress by exposing bondholders to a possible bait and switch. However, hedging can be valuable!

Hedging is valuable because it can reduce the future taxes that a firm expects to pay. Hedging can lower the costs of financial distress, and it can improve the investment decisions the firm will face in the future. When there is asymmetric information between the managers of a firm and its stockholders, hedging may also affect the ability of stockholders to evaluate the quality of the management.

We end the chapter by taking a look at the practice of hedging. As a case study, we examine the logic behind Merck's decision to hedge its foreign exchange risk with foreign currency options. Then, we examine academic studies and surveys that have sought to determine why firms actually hedge.

This section examines the desirability of **hedging** foreign exchange risk in two situations: in an entrepreneurial venture and in a modern publicly held corporation. Hedging foreign exchange risk is one type of **risk management**. Generally, risk management is the use of **derivative securities** to take positions in financial markets that offset the underlying sources of risks that arise in a company's normal course of business. Derivative securities, or *derivatives* for short, are discussed in more detail in Chapter 20; they include financial contracts such as forwards, futures, swaps, and options whose value depends on the value of an underlying asset price. Taking positions in derivatives that increase in value when the firm would take a loss or decrease in value when the firm would experience a gain reduces the variance of the firm's profits.

Hedging in an Entrepreneurial Venture

One persistent theme of this book is that future foreign exchange rates are uncertain. The volatility of foreign exchange rates implies that firms choosing not to hedge foreign exchange risk will experience more volatility in their cash flows than firms choosing to hedge foreign exchange risks. This volatility makes it harder to predict the profitability of firms, in the sense that the forecast errors are bigger. While reducing the volatility of future cash flows might seem like a good reason to hedge, the volatility of foreign exchange rates provides a necessary but not a sufficient condition for a modern corporation to hedge foreign exchange risk. To understand why this is so, we must understand the goals of management and how these goals are affected by hedging.

The first time students encounter discussions of hedging, they are often surprised that reducing uncertainty is not a sufficient condition for hedging. One reason for this opinion may be that students tend to think of themselves as individual entrepreneurs facing the foreign exchange risks, and they react to the situation as risk-averse individuals. It turns out that in this case, their intuition is actually right.

Reducing the uncertainty of a firm's future cash flows does provide an appropriate motivation for hedging foreign exchange risk if the firm is privately owned and its owner-managers are risk averse. A risk-averse person prefers his or her cash inflows to have a higher mean and a lower variance. Because an entrepreneur's profits are a significant part of the entrepreneur's wealth, entrepreneurs are unable to diversify away such risks through transactions in their own portfolios. Hence, if forward rates are unbiased predictors of future spot rates, **risk-averse entrepreneurs** will choose to hedge their future foreign currency cash flows because doing so will reduce the variance of the flows without changing their expected values in the domestic currency. Therefore, reducing the variance of future profits would increase the entrepreneur's expected utility.[1]

Hedging in a Modern Corporation

For publicly held corporations, simply reducing the uncertainty of future cash flows by hedging becomes problematic. To understand why, let's review the sources of value

---

[1]Chapter 7 indicates that whether forward rates are unbiased predictors of future spot rates is still unresolved. If the forward rate is a biased predictor but the bias is due to an equilibrium risk premium, investors in forward contracts experience either an expected profit or loss, depending on the position in the contract. In either case, the expected value of the profit or loss provides compensation for the riskiness of the position. If the bias in the forward contract is due to market inefficiency, the entrepreneur would possibly face a nontrivial trade-off between a reduced variance of profits and a reduced expected value of profits.

of a corporation using the adjusted net present value (ANPV) approach developed in Chapter 15:

$$
\begin{aligned}
\text{ANPV} = \quad &\text{Present value of future after-tax cash flows for the all equity firm} \\
&+ \text{Present value of future interest tax shields} \\
&+ \text{Present value of interest subsidies} \\
&- \text{Present value of the costs of financial distress} \\
&+ \text{Present value of the firm's real options}
\end{aligned}
$$

To derive the equity value of the firm, we must subtract the market value of debt from the ANPV of the firm's overall value:

$$\text{Equity value of the firm} = \text{ANPV} - \text{Market value of the firm's debt}$$

If the goal of a corporation's management is to maximize stockholders value, hedging and other risk management activities should increase the equity value of the firm to be worthwhile. Consequently, these activities must affect one or more of the terms in the ANPV, or it must decrease the market value of the debt. Later on in this chapter, we will examine how the ANPV terms can be affected by hedging.

The Hedging-Is-Irrelevant Logic of Modigliani and Miller

In this section, we review the logic of the **Modigliani–Miller proposition** regarding the valuation of cash flows from a corporation. Modigliani and Miller argued that a corporation's financial policies, such as issuing debt, hedging foreign exchange risk, and other purely financial risk management activities, do not change the value of the firm's assets unless these financial transactions lower the firm's taxes, affect its investment decisions, or can be done more cheaply than individual investors' transactions can be done.

The reason that reducing the uncertainty of future cash flows, *per se*, does not lead to a rationale for hedging is that it may not change investors' perceptions of the firm's systematic risk. We know from modern portfolio theory that the required rate of return on the equity cash flows of a corporation does not depend on the standard deviation of the firm's cash flows but only on the systematic risk associated with those cash flows. The fact that a firm's cash flows are uncertain is a necessary but not a sufficient condition for discounting the cash flows at a discount rate higher than the risk-free interest rate. Hence, unlike the case of an entrepreneurial firm, if hedging merely reduces the unsystematic risk of the corporation's cash flows while leaving unchanged both the systematic risk and the expected value of the cash flows, hedging will not have any effect on the firm's value. Investors will still discount the same expected cash flows at the same required rate of return that is appropriate for the firm's systematic risk.[2]

Modigliani and Miller also argued that, if individuals have the same investment opportunities as firms, investors can "undo" the financial transactions of corporations. In other words, individuals can adjust the leverage of their portfolios to the levels they want. They can also buy and sell foreign exchange forward contracts or option contracts to match their desired hedging levels—regardless of the firm's preferred hedging level. Notice in each of these situations that transaction costs and taxes must be the same for both the corporation and the individual.

---

[2]Essentially, the value of the hedged firm equals the value of the unhedged firm plus the value of any forward contracts. If the forward rate is an unbiased predictor of the future spot rate, the forward contracts have zero value when initiated. If the forward rate is biased, but the bias is due to an equilibrium risk premium, the forward contracts have value, and hedging changes the firm's expected cash flows. But hedging also changes the firm's systematic risk such that the expected value of the hedged firm is unchanged.

Because major corporations command better foreign exchange rate terms than the individual investors—that is, they transact at smaller bid–ask spreads—there is a rationale for corporations to hedge *for* investors. But we could easily argue that major institutional investors, such as the mutual fund investment companies Fidelity and Vanguard, who invest on behalf of individual investors, can deal in the foreign exchange market on terms comparable to, or even better than, those of a major corporation. As a result, we should look for reasons other than transaction costs as to why a firm might want to hedge.

17.2 ARGUMENTS AGAINST HEDGING

First, though, we take up three arguments against hedging. The first argument is that hedging is costly. The second argument against hedging is that most foreign exchange risk is equity related. Equity risk is long term in nature and effectively impossible to hedge away. The third argument is that hedging can create bad incentives. Let's look at each of these arguments in turn.

Hedging Is Costly

One frequently encountered argument against hedging is that it is costly, so firms should avoid doing it. People who make this argument often have in mind an incorrect notion of the cost of hedging. They argue that if the firm is selling foreign currency in the forward market, a forward discount on the foreign currency is a cost of hedging because the domestic currency forward price of foreign currency is less than the spot price. Conversely, a forward premium is viewed as providing a benefit or profit from hedging when the firm is selling foreign currency forward. In contrast, a forward premium is thought to increase the costs of the firm if it is buying foreign currency in the forward market.

This argument was first discussed in Chapter 3, where we noted that the argument is incorrect because it reflects an irrelevant accounting perspective on the nature of costs rather than an appropriate economic perspective. We know that the forward rate differs from the current spot rate because of differences in interest rates. The foreign currency cash flow is occurring in the future, not today. This makes the current spot rate irrelevant when it comes to valuing the future foreign currency cash flow unless the cash flow is first discounted to the present.

A True Hedging Cost: The Bid–Ask Spread

Bid–ask spreads are typically larger in the forward market than in the spot market. Thus, one of the true costs of hedging is that the costs of transacting in the forward market typically exceed the costs of transacting in the spot market. This incremental cost is small for near-term transactions. In near-term transactions, the difference is only a few hundredths of a percent of the current spot rate. But the bid–ask spread widens as one contracts more distantly in the future. In this sense, the cost of forward hedging increases with the maturity of the contract.

The Employee Cost

An additional cost of hedging is that a firm must use employees to determine the types and sizes of various hedging instruments. These employees must then be monitored to prevent them from engaging in speculative behavior. Their compensation also must not be based on the profitability of their transactions alone. Otherwise, they will be motivated to speculate, and they will take off hedges that become profitable so that they can book accounting profits. Of course, this will expose the underlying risk that was being hedged. The following example illustrates how this works.

Example 17.1 Incorrectly Booking Profit on a Hedge

Suppose that a firm will receive 5,000,000 Swiss francs in 1 year. Let the 1-year forward rate be CHF1.50/USD. Suppose the treasurer makes a forward contract to sell CHF5,000,000 such that the firm will receive

$$\frac{\text{CHF5,000,000}}{\text{CHF1.50/USD}} = \text{USD3,333,333.33}$$

in 1 year. Now, let 6 months pass and suppose that the 6-month forward rate is CHF1.70/USD. The value of the firm's underlying Swiss franc asset has fallen from USD3,333,333.33 to

$$\frac{\text{CHF5,000,000}}{\text{CHF1.70/USD}} = \text{USD2,941,176.47}$$

for a loss of USD392,156.86. Remember, though, that the firm is hedged because it sold the CHF5,000,000 forward, and the forward contract to sell CHF5,000,000 at CHF1.50/USD has increased in value by USD392,156.86.

If the treasurer of the company were trying to maximize profit on the contracts he makes, he could enter the 6-month forward market, say, by purchasing CHF5,000,000 to offset the firm's existing forward contract that has 6 months left to maturity. The dollar profit on this transaction would equal the fall in the forward rate of dollars per Swiss franc multiplied by the contractual amount of Swiss francs:

$$\left[\frac{1}{\text{CHF1.5/USD}} - \frac{1}{\text{CHF1.7/USD}}\right] \times \text{CHF5,000,000} = \text{USD392,156.86}$$

Because this is a hedging situation, we know that the dollar value of the CHF5,000,000 account receivable has fallen in value by this same amount. If the firm's cost accountants decide that the treasurer should receive a profit of USD392,156.86, the loss on the receivable must be booked somewhere. If the sales division is allocated the corresponding loss, some serious incentive problems will arise in terms of getting the treasurer to hedge correctly.

Instead of hedging, the treasurer will begin to speculate. Taking off the hedge by buying CHF5,000,000 in the 6-month forward market would lock in the "profit" for the treasurer, but it would expose the firm's original, underlying Swiss franc asset to the risk that the Swiss franc might weaken even more. It is unlikely that the treasurer of a corporation has the ability to make profitable calls about the direction of exchange rates. If he or she does, the person should be working for an investment bank or hedge fund, where this ability can be leveraged and where investors are hoping for superior performance.

Now, let's examine the second argument against hedging.

Hedging Equity Risk Is Difficult, if Not Impossible

People sometimes argue that it is effectively impossible for a corporation to hedge the change in the value of its equity with a change in the exchange rate because the value of equity is the present discounted value of an infinite series of cash flows. To understand this argument, let's consider an example.

The Weehawken Widget Project

Consider the situation of Weehawken Widget Works, a U.S. firm that has the opportunity to invest in a U.K. project. If the company spends $1,900 today, its project will return either £125 or £75 of free cash flow with equal probability for every year from next year into the infinite future. (Later, we treat each pound as £1 million to make the argument more forceful, but for now, let's just keep things simple.) The expected value of the cash flow each year is

$$0.5 \times £75 + 0.5 \times £125 = £100$$

If the appropriate pound discount rate is 10% per annum, the present value of the project is

$$\frac{£100}{1.1} + \frac{£100}{1.1^2} + \frac{£100}{1.1^3} + \ldots = \frac{£100}{0.1} = £1,000$$

If the current spot exchange rate is $2/£, the dollar present value of the project is

$$(\$2/£) \times £1,000 = \$2,000$$

To find the net present value (NPV) of the project, we must subtract its cost, which is $1,900. Hence, if Weehawken's investors pay $1,900 today, they obtain a project with a discounted expected value of $2,000. Accepting the project causes the value of Weehawken to increase by $100.

Changes in the Project's Value over Time

Now, let's see how the value of the project changes over time. Suppose, for simplicity, that the exchange rate in each year can either increase or decrease by $0.20/£ with equal probability. Then, next year, the exchange rate will be either $2.20/£ or $1.80/£. If forward rates are unbiased forecasts of future spot rates, the current forward rates for all maturities will be $2.00/£. Let's assume that the dollar discount rate for Weehawken's cash flows is also 10% and that the discount rates do not change over time. Finally, let's also assume that the realization of the project cash flow is independent of the realization of the exchange rate. These assumptions are simplistic, but they allow us to easily make the necessary calculations.

Exhibit 17.1 provides the four possible values for the project in 1 year, where by the value of the project we mean the payoff on the project in the first year, plus the ongoing value of the project, plus any gains or losses from hedging. For example, if the exchange rate turns out to be $2.20/£ and the project returns £125, the value of the project at time $t+1$ is

$$\underset{\text{Term A}}{[(\$2.20/£) \times £125]} + \underset{\text{Term B}}{[(\$2.20/£) \times £1,000]} = \$2,475$$

Term A represents the dollar value of the time $t+1$ pound cash flow, and Term B is the dollar value of the infinite stream of future expected pound cash flows that still has a present value of £1,000. In general, if $S(t+1, \$/£)$ is the dollar–pound exchange rate and $CF(t+1, £)$ is the pound cash flow at time $t+1$, the dollar value of the unhedged project at time $t+1$ is

$$[S(t+1, \$/£) \times CF(t+1, £)] + [S(t+1, \$/£) \times £1,000]$$

Exhibit 17.1 The Value of Weehawken's Project with Unhedged Cash Flows

		Possible Future Exchange Rates	
		$2.20/£	**$1.80/£**
Possible Pound Returns	£125	$2,475	$2,025
	£75	$2,365	$1,935

Exhibit 17.2 The Value of Weehawken's Project with 1-Year Hedged Cash Flows

		Possible Future Exchange Rates	
		$2.20/£	**$1.80/£**
Possible Pound Returns	£125	$2,455	$2,045
	£75	$2,345	$1,955

The Project's Value with 1 Year of Hedged Cash Flows

Now, suppose Weehawken hedges 1 year of pound cash flows by selling the expected value of next year's cash flow, £100, at the 1-year forward rate of $2.00/£. The possible values of the project, including the time $t+1$ cash flow, are given in Exhibit 17.2 and are found just as they were in Exhibit 17.1. If the exchange rate turns out to be $2.20/£ and the project returns £125, the value of the project at time $t+1$ is

$$\underset{\text{Term C}}{[(\$2.00/£) \times £100]} + \underset{\text{Term D}}{[(\$2.20/£) \times £25]} + \underset{\text{Term B}}{[(\$2.20/£) \times £1{,}000]} = \$2{,}455$$

Term C represents the dollar value of the forward sale of pounds. Term D is the dollar value of the extra pound return that was not sold forward and that must therefore be sold in the spot market. Term B is, once again, the dollar value of the infinite stream of future expected pound cash flows that has a present value of £1,000. If the project returns only £75, Weehawken will have to purchase £25 in the spot market to deliver on the forward contract. In general, the value of the project at time $t+1$ with 1 year of hedged cash flows is

$$[(\$2.00/£) \times £100] + \{S(t+1, \$/£) \times [CF(t+1, £) - £100]\} + [S(t+1, \$/£) \times £1{,}000]$$

By rearranging this expression, we see that it is the dollar value of the underlying unhedged pound asset plus the dollar return on a forward contract to sell £100 at $2.00/£:

$$[S(t+1, \$/£) \times CF(t+1, £)] + [S(t+1, \$/£) \times £1{,}000]$$
$$+ [(\$2.00/£) - S(t+1, \$/£)] \times £100$$

By comparing the entries in Exhibit 17.1 with those in Exhibit 17.2, we see that the forward hedge transfers $20 from the good state of the world, in which the pound strengthens, to the bad state of the world, in which the pound weakens. This $20 represents the difference between the forward rate and the future exchange rate multiplied by the expected cash flow, which is sold forward.

The Project's Value with 2 Years of Hedged Cash Flows

Now, suppose that Weehawken hedges by selling the first and second years of expected future pound revenue in the forward market, and under our assumptions, the 2-year forward rate at time t is also $2.00/£. The possible values of the project at time $t+1$, including the time $t+1$ cash flow, are given in Exhibit 17.3. If the exchange rate turns out to be $2.20/£ and the project returns £125, the value of the project at time $t+1$ is

$$\underset{\text{Term C}}{[(\$2.00/£) \times £100]} + \underset{\text{Term D}}{[(\$2.20/£) \times £25]} + \underset{\text{Term E}}{\left[\frac{(\$2.00/£) \times £100}{1.1}\right]}$$

$$+ \underset{\text{Term F}}{\left[\frac{(\$2.20/£) \times £1{,}000}{1.1}\right]} = \$2{,}436.82$$

Exhibit 17.3 The Value of Weehawken's Project with 2-Year Hedged Cash Flows

		Possible Future Exchange Rates	
		$2.20/£	**$1.80/£**
Possible Pound Returns	£125	$2,436.82	$2,063.18
	£75	$2,326.82	$1,973.18

Terms C and D are again the dollar value of the 1-year forward contract and the dollar value of the extra pounds that must be sold in the spot market. Term E is the present value of the payment on the 2-year forward contract that has 1 year remaining, and Term F is the dollar value of the unhedged £100 perpetuity whose first cash flow begins 2 years from now discounted at the constant dollar discount rate of 10%. By making the 2-year forward contract, Weehawken transfers an additional ($20/1.1) = $18.18 from the good state, in which the pound strengthens, to the bad state, in which the pound weakens. The $18.18 represents the present value of the profit on a forward contract that could be locked in at time $t+1$ because the 1-year forward rate at that time would equal the spot rate of $2.20/£ because the two interest rates are assumed to be equal to each other.[3]

The Project's Value with an Infinite Sequence of Hedged Cash Flows

Say that Weehawken makes an infinite sequence of forward contracts at time t—that is, if it contracts to sell £100 in every year from time $t+1$ to the infinite future at the assumed forward rates of $2.00/£. The fully hedged values of the project at time $t+1$ are given in Exhibit 17.4. If the exchange rate turns out to be $2.20/£, and the project returns £125, the dollar value of the fully hedged project at time $t+1$ is

$$
\overbrace{[(\$2.00/£) \times £100]}^{\text{Term C}} + \overbrace{[(\$2.20/£) \times £25]}^{\text{Term D}} + \overbrace{\left[\frac{(\$2.00/£) \times £100}{1.1}\right]}^{\text{Term E}}
$$

$$
+ \overbrace{\left[\frac{(\$2.00/£) \times £100}{1.1^2}\right]}^{\text{Term G}} + \overbrace{\left[\frac{(\$2.00/£) \times £100}{1.1^3}\right]}^{\text{Term H}} + \ldots = \$2,255
$$

Terms C and D are, once again, the values of the 1-year forward contract and the extra pounds that must be sold in the spot market. Term E represents the dollar value of the 2-year forward contract that has 1 year remaining. Terms G and H represent the present value

Exhibit 17.4 The Value of Weehawken's Project with Infinitely Hedged Cash Flows

		Possible Future Exchange Rates	
		$2.20/£	**$1.80/£**
Possible Pound Returns	£125	$2,255	$2,245
	£75	$2,145	$2,155

---

[3]Because £100 was sold forward at time t for each of 2 years, at $t+1$, the present value of the profit or loss on the forward contract that could be locked in by buying £100 in the 1-year forward market is

$$
£100 \times \left[\frac{F(t, 2) - F(t+1, 1)}{(1 + i(t+1, 1))}\right] = £100 \times \left[\frac{(2.00/£) - (2.20/£)}{1.1}\right] = -\$18.18
$$

in dollars of previously made forward contracts to sell £100 that now have 2 and 3 years remaining to maturity, and so on, into the indefinite future.

Of course, an infinite number of forward-contract maturities are not available to the firm in the real world. Also, the bid–ask spreads in the forward market start to widen with maturities beyond a few years. Hence, Weehawken would not be able to sell pounds forward at $2/£ for all maturities because the transaction costs would cause the rates to be lower and lower for future maturities. Consequently, it is possible to mitigate the fluctuations in the value of the pound revenue stream due to foreign exchange rates, but it is not possible to eliminate them completely.

The Project's Value with an Equity Hedge

An alternative way to hedge this situation would be for Weehawken to do a sequence of 1-year forward contracts in which it sells £1,100 forward, which is the expected future value of the equity in 1 year. The possible returns on the project at time $t+1$ in this case are actually the same as those in Exhibit 17.4, but they are calculated differently. The dollar value of the project at time $t+1$ would be

$$\overset{\text{Term I}}{[(\$2.00/£) \times £1,100]} - \overset{\text{Term J}}{\{S(t+1, \$/£) \times [£1,100 - CF(t+1, £)]\}}$$

$$+ \overset{\text{Term K}}{[S(t+1, \$/£) \times £1,100]}$$

Term I is the dollar value of the forward sale of £1,100. Term J subtracts the realization of the pound cash flow at time $t+1$ from the £1,100 that was sold forward to determine a net amount of pounds that must be purchased in the spot market to deliver the pounds that were sold forward. Weehawken would have only the return on the project at time $t+1$ as a pound cash flow and would have to purchase the rest in the spot market. Term K is the dollar value of the £100 into perpetuity that Weehawken still expects to receive. By rearranging terms and canceling, we can rewrite the value of the pound perpetuity as

$$(\$2.00/£) \times £1,100 + S(t+1, \$/£) \times [CF(t+1, £) - £100]$$

which is the same value as the sequence of infinite forward contracts. For example, when the spot exchange rate at time $t+1$ is $2.20/£ and the cash flow is £125, the value is $2,255, as before. The problem with this approach to hedging is that Weehawken must sell in the 1-year forward market more than 10 times the amount of pounds that it expects to receive in the next period. Then, after 1 year, it must enter the spot market and purchase a large amount of pounds to deliver on the forward contract.

In order to see the problem with this strategy more clearly, remember that the additional value to the firm from this project is only $100, which is the original $2,000 of projected cash flows minus the $1,900 initial cost. To put the issue in better perspective, think of each pound as representing 1 million pounds, with the value of the project representing the firm's entire value. Then, Weehawken would have an initial equity value of $2 billion. Initial investors would have invested $1.9 billion, and the firm's positive NPV project would increase its value to $2 billion. It is questionable whether a bank would allow a firm with an equity value of $2 billion to make a 1-year forward sale of £1.1 billion or a 1-year purchase of $2.2 billion. It is in this sense that the firm would have difficulty fully hedging the cash flows.

Reality Is More Complicated

The equity cash flows we have just examined are quite simple, fluctuating between only two values, year in and year out, and the firm confidently forecasts that this pattern will persist forever. Neither the dollar discount rate nor the pound discount rate fluctuates in the example, and the exchange rate is a simple process with an expected value that depends on the realization of the exchange rate.[4] In a more realistic equity project, the pattern of cash flows would involve forecasts of growth and the possibility of total loss. The real profitability of the foreign project also would probably be related to the real exchange rate. In the simple example, however, Weehawken's nominal pound cash flows were simply being converted into dollars by the nominal exchange rate.

As you can see, the world is much more complicated and more uncertain than the Weehawken example indicates. Nevertheless, Weehawken's situation provides an important intuition: Because much of the value of a firm's equity is due to its cash flows in the relatively far distant future, Weehawken cannot fully hedge even simple equity cash flows.

Hedging Can Create Bad Incentives

Of course, as investors in firms, we must be aware of how changes in hedging policies can be used to the advantage of one class of stakeholders and the disadvantage of others. Chapter 16 describes how equity stockholders prefer projects with high variances to projects with low variances, especially when the firm is near financial distress. One way that a firm can increase the variance of its cash flows is to stop a hedging program that is already in place. For example, if a firm has foreign currency revenues and is having difficulty meeting its fixed obligations, it can leave the foreign currency cash flows unhedged and hope for a strengthening of the foreign currency. In such a situation, any weakening of the foreign currency when the firm is unhedged simply creates additional losses, most of which are borne by the firm's bondholders.

Of course, even though a firm is actively engaged in a financial hedging program, the financial officers who are in charge of the hedging program must be supervised to prevent them from speculating with the firm's money. Such a temptation would surely grow as the firm gets closer to financial distress.[5] After all, what better way is there to come up with the principal on a bond issue than to try to make some money in the "casinos" of foreign exchange futures and options markets? The chief financial officer (CFO) of a firm facing financial distress might think exactly this way.

In light of the arguments mentioned, some managers say that the firm simply should not try to hedge. But there are other arguments that support hedging. It is to those that we now turn.

17.3 ARGUMENTS FOR HEDGING

This section examines how hedging can enhance the value of a firm by affecting the various terms in an ANPV analysis. We begin by demonstrating that hedging can increase the after-tax value of a firm's cash flows under certain conditions.

Hedging Can Reduce the Firm's Expected Taxes

Hedging can increase the value of a firm by reducing its expected future income taxes. One way that expected income taxes can be decreased is by making sure that the firm does not experience losses. When a firm is unprofitable, it owes no current tax, but it does

---

[4]We specified only the first year of the time series process for the exchange rate with plus or minus $0.20 increments. Obviously, the increments to this process cannot be constant because the exchange rate cannot be negative, but the expected value can depend on the current realization.

[5]An interesting example of this phenomenon is provided by Ross et al. (2007, p. 458), who relate the following story. When Federal Express encountered severe financial difficulty a few years after its inception, Frederick Smith, the founder, is reputed to have taken $20,000 of corporate funds to gamble in Las Vegas. He apparently won enough money to save the firm from bankruptcy. Had he lost, the firm would have gone bankrupt, and the creditors of the firm would have received $20,000 less.

not get an immediate refund from the government. Instead, the firm generates a **tax-loss carry-forward** that allows it to offset the losses that were incurred against future income. Thus, the firm pays less tax in the future. But, a tax-loss carry-forward is an accounting convention that only allows a firm to offset $1 of future income against $1 of loss incurred today. Because the economic value of $1 of income in the future is worth less than $1 of income today, due to the time value of money, having $1 of future tax-loss carry-forward is not as valuable as avoiding $1 of tax today. Hence, there is a reason for avoiding losses today.

Tax-loss carry-forwards also usually have a statutory time limit. They cannot be extended beyond a certain future date. Any unused tax-loss carry-forwards simply expire if the firm is unable to generate sufficient taxable income by the expiration date. The fact that tax-loss carry-forwards can expire unused provides another reason for avoiding losses today. Consequently, if hedging can help a firm avoid losses, it is valuable. Avoiding financial losses also increases the probability that a firm's tax shields from depreciation and interest payments can be fully utilized in the future.

Finally, hedging reduces expected future taxes if the tax code is convex. A **convex tax code** imposes a larger tax rate on higher incomes and a smaller tax rate on lower incomes. Exhibit 17.5 provides a hypothetical convex tax code.

Although the corporate tax rates in many countries are a flat percentage of income, if the firm loses money, and those losses are not refunded immediately at the same rate as the rate for positive income, the tax function is effectively convex. Example 17.3, which appears a little later in the chapter, demonstrates this principal. Graham and Smith (1999) simulate the provisions of the U.S. tax code and find that, on average, it is convex. They find that a 5% reduction in volatility of taxable income implies a 5.4% reduction in expected tax liability.

In the presence of a convex tax code, a firm prefers to pay tax on its expected income with certainty rather than to determine its expected tax by taking the probability weighted average of the taxes on possible incomes in the uncertain future states of the world. Because hedging allows the firm to shift income across different states of the world, hedging reduces expected taxes and increases the firm's value. Some examples will help to clarify this discussion.

Exhibit 17.5   A Convex Income Tax

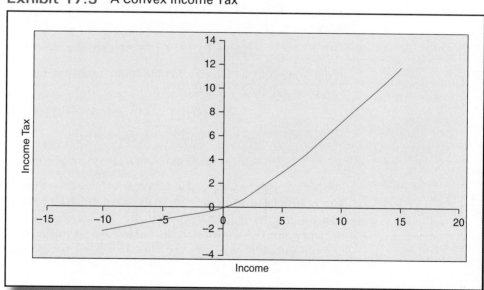

Example 17.2 Starpower's Swiss Project with Non-Convex Taxes

Assume that a U.S. firm, Starpower, has a project that provides revenue of CHF40,000,000 in 1 year. Starpower's project costs $19,000,000, and we assume this amount is paid in 1 year. Although the dollar cost of the project will be paid with certainty and the Swiss franc revenue from the project will be received with certainty, the dollar revenue from the project is uncertain because the future spot exchange rate is uncertain. Let's assume that there are only two possible future spot exchange rates. Either the spot rate in 1 year will be $0.55/CHF with 50% probability, or it will be $0.45/CHF, also with 50% probability. If Starpower is unhedged, it will experience a positive income of $3,000,000 with 50% probability because

$$[(\$0.55/CHF) \times CHF40,000,000] - \$19,000,000 = \$3,000,000$$

or Starpower will experience a loss of $1,000,000 because

$$[(\$0.45/CHF) \times CHF40,000,000] - \$19,000,000 = -\$1,000,00$$

The expected dollar value of Starpower's before-tax income on the unhedged project is therefore the probability weighted average of the two possibilities:

$$[0.5 \times \$3,000,000] + [0.5 \times (-\$1,000,000)] = \$1,000,000$$

Suppose that the tax rate is 35% and that the government also will immediately subsidize 35% of all losses. That is, the government refunds $35\% \times \$1,000,000 = \$350,000$ to the firm in the event of a loss. The expected value of Starpower's after-tax income on the unhedged project is the probability weighted average of the after-tax cash flows:

$$[0.5 \times \$3,000,000 \times (1 - 0.35)] + [0.5 \times (-\$1,000,000) \times (1 - 0.35)]$$
$$= \$650,000$$

Suppose that Starpower has the opportunity to hedge its CHF cash flow by selling CHF40,000,000 at the 1-year forward rate of $0.50/CHF. Note that this forward rate is also the expected future spot rate because

$$[0.5 \times (0.55/CHF)] + [0.5 \times (0.45/CHF)] = \$0.50/CHF$$

If Starpower fully hedges, it will receive

$$(\$0.50/CHF) \times CHF40,000,000 = \$20,000,000$$

of dollar revenue no matter what the future exchange rate turns out to be. Hence, Starpower will have a sure income of

$$\$20,000,000 - \$19,000,000 = \$1,000,000$$

Consequently, Starpower's after-tax income will be

$$\$1,000,000 \times (1 - 0.35) = \$650,000$$

Notice, in this example, that although hedging allows the firm to reduce the variance of its income while keeping its expected income the same, hedging provides no after-tax gain. Starpower's expected after-tax income is the same whether the firm hedges or not. This situation occurs because the tax treatment of losses is identical to the tax treatment of gains. The tax schedule is linear, not convex.

Example 17.3 Starpower's Swiss Project with Convex Taxes

Consider the same project as in Example 17.2, but now suppose that Starpower can claim only a 25% refund on its losses while the firm is taxed at a 35% rate on its positive income. With these tax rates, the expected value of the after-tax income on the unhedged project falls to

$$[0.5 \times \$3,000,000 \times (1 - 0.35)] + [0.5 \times (-\$1,000,000) \times (1 - 0.25)]$$
$$= \$600,000$$

The firm's expected tax bill is the difference between the expected before-tax income of \$1,000,000 and the expected after-tax income of \$600,000, or

$$\$1,000,000 - \$600,000 = \$400,000$$

Equivalently, the firm's expected tax bill is the probability weighted average of taxes that will be paid in the good state (35% of \$3 million) minus subsidies that will be received in the bad state (25% of \$1 million):

$$[\$0.5 \times \$1,050,000] - [0.5 \times \$250,000] = \$400,000$$

When Starpower has the ability to hedge, it takes no losses in this example, and its after-tax income is unchanged from the previous example. We calculated that Starpower's after-tax income was \$650,000, which implies that the firm expects to pay taxes of only

$$\$1,000,000 - \$650,000 = \$350,000$$

if it hedges versus the \$400,000 in taxes it expects to pay if it does not hedge. By reducing its expected income tax payment, Starpower increases its expected after-tax value by \$50,000.

What happens to the expected tax saving if we increase the volatility of Starpower's income while leaving the expected value of its income the same? It will turn out that the expected tax savings from hedging increases. Next, we show how this is so.

Example 17.4 Starpower's Swiss Project with a Larger Variance

Let the possible equally probable values of the future exchange rate be \$0.60/CHF and \$0.40/CHF. The forward rate remains \$0.50/CHF. The unhedged dollar income from Starpower's project will now be either

$$[(\$0.60/CHF) \times CHF40,000,000] - \$19,000,000 = \$5,000,000$$

or

$$[(\$0.40/CHF) \times CHF40,000,000] - \$19,000,000 = -\$3,000,000$$

The expected value of Starpower's before-tax income remains \$1,000,000 because

$$[0.5 \times \$5,000,000] + [0.5 \times (-\$3,000,000)] = \$1,000,000$$

The expected value of the after-tax income on the project if Starpower does not hedge is now

$$[0.5 \times \$5,000,000 \times (1 - 0.35)] - [0.5 \times (\$3,000,000) \times (1 - 0.25)]$$
$$= \$500,000$$

Consequently, if Starpower does not hedge, it expects to pay tax of

$$\$1,000,000 - \$500,000 = \$500,000$$

On the other hand, if Starpower hedges as before, it sells CHF40,000,000 forward, has income of $1,000,000, and after-tax income of $650,000. The firm pays only $350,000 of tax instead of the $500,000 of expected tax if it does not hedge. Starpower saves $150,000 of expected tax payments when the possible returns on the project are $5,000,000 and –$3,000,000 versus the $50,000 of expected tax saving when the possible returns on the project were $3,000,000 and –$1,000,000. Hence, the more volatile Starpower's income, the greater is the expected tax saving from hedging.

The tax benefit of hedging also increases if the convexity of the tax rates is greater. In our two-state example, greater convexity amounts to a greater difference between the tax rate on positive income and the refund rate on losses.

Example 17.5   Starpower's Swiss Project with a More Convex Tax Schedule

Suppose in Example 17.3 that positive income is taxed at a rate of 45% instead of 35%, whereas losses are again refunded at the 25% rate. Then, if Starpower does not hedge, its expected after-tax income is

$$[0.5 \times (\$5,000,000) \times (1 - 0.45)] + [0.5 \times (-\$3,000,000) \times (1 - 0.25)]$$
$$= \$250,000$$

Hence, the firm now expects to pay tax of

$$\$1,000,000 - \$250,000 = \$750,000$$

If Starpower hedges by selling CHF40,000,000 forward at $0.50/$, it will again pay taxes on the $1,000,000 of sure income, giving it an after-tax income of

$$\$1,000,000 \times (1 - 0.45) = \$550,000$$

When Starpower hedges, it pays $450,000 of tax instead of the expected tax of $750,000 when it does not hedge. Starpower therefore saves $300,000 of expected tax payments.

General Principles

Examples 17.2 through 17.5 illustrate some general principles. First, risk management or hedging has definite tax benefits when the tax code is convex. Progressive tax rates on positive income are one source of convexity in tax codes. Most countries, though, do not have progressive corporate income taxes on positive income. The same percentage tax rate is applied to all positive income and to losses. But other factors in tax codes, such as tax-loss carry-forwards, alternative minimum taxes, and investment tax credits, do impart convexity to tax schedules in their treatment of losses and their encouragement to undertake certain transactions.

The general principles revealed by the examples are that the tax benefits of hedging require the tax code to be convex and are larger the more convex, or progressive, is the tax code, and the more volatile is a firm's pretax income.

Hedging Can Lower the Costs of Financial Distress

Hedging can increase the value of a firm by reducing the expected costs of financial distress (see Smith and Stulz, 1985). Chapter 15 explains that the costs of financial distress are the losses of value that a firm experiences because it may experience bankruptcy in the future. These costs are distinct from the losses of value experienced by a firm that trigger an actual default or a declaration of bankruptcy. As explained in Chapter 15, the costs of financial distress include the direct costs of bankruptcy, such as the legal and administrative expenses. But they also include indirect costs, such as a firm's inability to make binding commitments to its customers, suppliers, workers, and managers and vice versa. In addition, the managers of a firm may be led to act selfishly in the interest of stockholders at the expense of bondholders. Hedging reduces the probability that a firm will encounter financial distress and thus mitigates these problems.

Graham and Rodgers (2002) find that by reducing costs of financial distress, hedging allows firms to take on more debt. In their sample of firms, the increase in value due to the additional interest tax shields averages 1.1% of firm value.

Hedging Can Improve the Firm's Future Investment Decisions

Chapter 16 describes how firms that are near financial distress can be led to reject a positive NPV project because too much of the return on the project accrues to the bondholders and not enough to the stockholders. If hedging avoids the fall in firm value that would place the firm in a state in which it would make such a poor investment decision, then hedging improves the firm's future investment decisions.

More generally, Bolton et al. (2011) develop a dynamic model that builds on the intuition of Froot et al. (1993) demonstrating that imperfections in capital markets provide a strong rationale for hedging. Whenever externally generated funds for investment projects are more costly to the firm than internally generated funds from retained earnings, hedging increases the firm's value by providing it with a reliable, less volatile stream of internally generated cash, which it can use to finance its research and development and capital expenditures. Hedging provides a source of cash flow that allows a firm to exercise its investment opportunities and its growth options at the point in time when it is optimal to invest.

The Basic Logic of the Argument

Suppose that a firm does not hedge. Then, variability in cash flow from assets in place will be reflected in variability in free cash flow to equity holders. Now, remember that free cash flow to equity cannot be negative. If free cash flow to equity were to begin to be negative, the firm would either have to raise cash externally, or it would have to cut back on the firm's investment policy. Because variability in investment or research and development is generally undesirable, the firm would normally use external capital markets to finance investment, when the firm has insufficient internally generated cash. However, in imperfect capital markets, the marginal cost of raising external funds may increase with the amount of funds raised. In that case, the firm will find it optimal to cut back on investments and research and development when internally generated cash flow is low. If the firm hedges, it can avoid the shortfall in internally generated cash and avoid the drop in investment.

Asymmetric Information Is the Problem

The managers of a firm usually know more about the firm's future prospects than investors do. This asymmetric information consequently makes it difficult and sometimes impossible for financial markets to price a firm's new offerings of debt or equity. This uncertainty leads investors to demand a premium for financing new projects, and the premium may increase with the amount of funds the company is trying to raise. As a result, the cost of raising externally generated funds is high, and firms prefer to finance their investment projects from internally generated funds.

A corporation in an industry that relies heavily on internally generated funds for its investment projects should definitely consider instituting a hedging program. This appears to be Merck's rationale for hedging, as we will see later in the chapter.

Hedging Can Change the Assessment of a Firm's Managers

Another argument for financial hedging that relies on asymmetric information between the managers of the firm and its stockholders has been offered by DeMarzo and Duffie (1995). Stockholders must gauge the quality of the managers based on their observations of the firm's profitability and earnings, as disclosed in its accounting data. From this perspective, hedging makes good sense at first glance. Hedging reduces the amount of "noise" in earnings data that is not due to actions of the managers. In other words, hedging increases the informational content of a firm's profits about a manager's ability. DeMarzo and Duffie demonstrate that in this situation, the accounting treatment of hedging and the optimal hedging policy are intimately linked. Because managers are better able to gauge the different financial risks the company faces, they have an incentive to hedge these risks to reduce the variability of the firm's earnings and, with that, the variability of their own income stream, which will be linked to the firm's earnings. A manager does not want to face an unexpected currency depreciation that adversely affects the firm's profits.

The disclosure of information, though, will make stockholders better able to gauge the true ability of a manager. Stockholders can then make the managers' compensation more sensitive to the firm's performance. To avoid this additional variability in their income, managers may choose not to hedge. If the additional informational content of hedged earnings is sufficiently high, the stockholders may optimally decide not to disclose the firm's hedging activities, to give managers an incentive to hedge.

POINT–COUNTERPOINT

Asymmetric Information and the Pecking Order

Ante, Freedy, and Suttle are visiting Berlin, strolling by the Brandenburg Gate, discussing the fall of the Berlin Wall and the collapse of communism in 1989. Freedy says, "Isn't capitalism great? Look at all the new buildings in what used to be East Germany." Ante replies, "The buildings are cool, and the architecture is fantastic, but capitalism would be a lot better if we could just stop managers from ripping off investors. I don't know why anybody buys equity." Freedy says, "What's the big deal, Ante? Equity markets are efficient. Any information that is out there pretty quickly finds its way into market prices." Ante, getting hot under the collar, blurts, "Well, if that's true, why do Bekaert and Hodrick argue that asymmetric information is a big deal in risk management? If managers know more than investors when it comes to risk management, they also know more than investors when it comes to issuing equity. The managers would issue equity when it is overvalued, and they would buy back equity when it is undervalued. Markets are stupid!"

At this point, Suttle sees that the brothers are about to really get into it, so he feels it is necessary to intervene. "Hey, you guys need to understand something," says Suttle. "Markets can't know everything. Indeed, there is good reason to think that managers know more than the stockholders about the prospects of the firm. Some pretty good economists have figured out the implications of these ideas for corporate finance."

"For example," says Suttle, "Ross (1977) developed one of the first models of corporate finance to rely on asymmetric information. In the Ross model, managers know the prospects of the firm better than the financial markets. Without a signal from the managers, investors view all firms as the same. To signal a firm's good prospects, the managers of the good firm must do something that is costly and cannot be mimicked by the managers of the firms with poorer prospects. Managers can signal the prospects of the firm to the capital markets by choosing an appropriate level of debt. Thus, Ross argues that the firms with good prospects signal this information by taking on more debt than firms with bad prospects. This action is an effective signal because bankruptcy is costly. A high-debt firm that has good prospects is less likely to incur bankruptcy costs than a similarly levered firm with poorer prospects."

Freedy and Ante smile at how loquacious Suttle can be. Ante pipes up, "That's fine for debt, but I was talking about equity." Suttle replies, "Well, Stewart Myers wrote two important papers extending this asymmetric information intuition to the decision to issue equity. His **'pecking order' theory of financing**[6] states that investments should be financed with the least information-sensitive source of funds. Myers argues that managers are better informed about the prospects of their firm than the capital markets, but the capital markets understand this. Managers consequently will not want to issue equity to finance a project when they think the firm is undervalued by capital markets. In fact, they will try to issue equity when it's overvalued. Because capital markets understand this logic, capital markets will view issuing equity as a very bad signal.

"The pecking order for financing investments is the result. Internally generated cash is used first because no explanation has to be given to the capital markets about why or how it is being used. Debt is the next source of finance because the cash flows paid to the debt holders are fixed and insensitive to future cash flows of the firm. Firms without enough internally generated funds but good future prospects should issue debt. Resorting to equity to finance investment projects is the least preferred method because it is such a bad signal. Consequently, only firms with insufficient internally generated funds and no ability to issue debt will rely on issuing equity."

Freedy and Ante grab Suttle and say, "Come on. We've had enough of this asymmetric information economics. Let's go get a good German bratwurst. We're hungry!"

17.4 THE HEDGING RATIONALE OF REAL FIRMS

Only a few firms have actually written down why they chose to institute a hedging program and to explain the logic of their analysis. This section first describes Merck's decision to use foreign currency options to hedge its foreign currency revenue.[7] We then discuss the findings of Brown (2001) who reports on the management of foreign exchange risk at HDG Inc., a pseudonym for a U.S.–based durable goods manufacturer.

---

[6]See Myers (1984) and Myers and Majluf (1984).
[7]Merck's decision is described in detail in Lewent and Kearney (1990). At the time of the analysis, Ms. Lewent was Merck's vice president and treasurer, and in 2006, she was executive vice president and chief financial officer. The following section summarizes their argument.

Merck's Hedging Rationale

At the time that Merck decided to institute a hedging policy in 1988, it had sales of $6.6 billion in a pharmaceutical industry with total sales of roughly $103.7 billion. No one firm in the industry commanded more than a 5% share of total sales. Approximately 50% of Merck's revenue came from foreign sales of its drugs. Merck had approximately 70 subsidiaries around the world that imported semi-finished product and were responsible for finishing, marketing, and distributing final product in the countries in which they were incorporated. The competitive nature of the business dictated that final sale prices were usually denominated in local currencies. In addition, many of the local prices were regulated. Therefore, if a local currency weakened relative to the dollar, Merck had limited ability to increase the local price of its products.

The dividends repatriated from Merck's foreign subsidiaries formed a substantial fraction of its earnings and profits. It was from these internally generated funds that Merck usually financed its research and development and its capital expenditures.

Merck's decision to hedge came in the mid-1980s, following a rough patch when the dollar strengthened. The dollar appreciation really hurt Merck; the company developed a sales index that measured the strength of the dollar relative to a basket of currencies weighted by the revenue it produced in that currency. The index declined from a base level of 100 in 1978 to 60 in 1984. During that time, Merck experienced a cumulative loss of revenue of approximately $900 million. In response, Merck cut back on its research and development and investment projects.

However, after reviewing the performance of the firm during this period, Merck's managers decided that this was a flawed decision. One important aspect of the competitive nature of the industry is its emphasis on the development of new drugs. By decreasing its research and development, Merck risked becoming uncompetitive in the global marketplace.

Merck's Five-Step Procedure

Merck first considered using an **operating currency hedge**, that is, shifting the company's operations across countries to provide a better balance between the costs and revenues denominated in different currencies. Unfortunately, because Merck wanted to conduct most of its research and development in the United States as well as keep its corporate headquarters there, this option was not really feasible.

Merck then developed a five-step procedure to help decide whether to hedge with financial contracts and what types of financial hedges to choose. The five steps were as follows:

1. Develop forecasts of the distributions of future exchange rates to determine the probabilities of adverse movements in exchange rates.
2. Assess the impact of exchange rate changes on the firm's 5-year strategic plan.
3. Decide whether to hedge the firm's exchange rate exposure.
4. Select the appropriate hedging instruments.
5. Simulate alternative hedging programs to determine those most cost effective, given the risk tolerance of Merck's managers.

We next consider the factors that enter into each of these steps.

Step 1: Develop Forecasts of the Distributions of Future Exchange Rates to Determine the Probability of Adverse Movements Related to Them

Merck considered four main factors in determining the probability of future changes in exchange rates: economic fundamentals, government interference in the setting of exchange rates, past exchange rates, and professional forecasts. Lewent and Kearney (1990) note that the economic fundamentals include variables such as the trade balance deficit, international capital flows, and government budget deficits, which are used to define an "equilibrium" exchange rate, but they are not specific about the equilibrium model. Merck's model also recognizes that central bankers often set explicit or implicit target zones for currency prices, which they stand ready to defend with intervention. In addition, Lewent and Kearney note that the Merck model is "mean reverting" in the sense that when there have been several large movements of the exchange rate in the same direction, the probability of future movements in that direction is reduced. The idea is that such a large movement in the nominal exchange rate would most surely be associated with a large movement in the real exchange rate. Such a large change in the real exchange rate would create forces in the trade balance that would limit the likelihood of an additional change in the same direction. The fourth factor affecting Merck's assessment of future exchange rates involved obtaining the opinions of various professional forecasting services. The staffs of the world's major investment and commercial banks routinely supply forecasts of future exchange rates.

Step 2: Assess the Impact of Exchange Rate Changes on the Firm's 5-Year Strategic Plan

Merck's second step involved assessing the impact of adverse changes in exchange rates on the firm's strategic plan. This involved examining cash flow and earnings projections for 5 years into the future under various exchange rate scenarios. These forecasts had to incorporate the effects that past profitability would have on the firm's future investment decisions.

Step 3: Decide Whether to Hedge the Firm's Exchange Rate Exposure

The issue here is whether the firm generates enough cash in all states of the world to pursue its research and development (R&D) and investments. Suppose that in some scenarios, exchange rate movements are forecast to adversely affect the firm's operating profits so that they fall below the level needed to finance its desired R&D and capital expenditures. How, then, will the firm finance its investment projects? The firm could turn to the external capital markets for financing, but the firm may find it difficult to raise the needed funds at reasonable required rates of return in those states of the world when it is unprofitable. Financial markets might ascribe the lack of profitability not to adverse fluctuations in exchange rates, but to poor managerial decisions. In the latter case, the firm's managers will find it difficult to pursue the projects they believe will keep the firm competitive. Hedging would prevent this from happening.

Examining the cash flow projections in the previous step gave Merck an idea about the likelihood that it would encounter adverse circumstances and how these situations would affect the firm's future investment decisions. Merck came to the conclusion that it should hedge against exchange rate volatility because a large proportion (typically 50% or more) of the company's earnings are generated overseas, and the volatility of the cash flows potentially adversely affects the firm's ability to execute its strategic plan—namely invest in R&D. In addition, the pharmaceutical industry has a very long planning horizon, one that reflects the complexity of the research involved as well as the lengthy process of product registration. It often takes more than 10 years between the discovery of a product and its market launch. Success in the industry generally requires a continuous, long-term commitment to a steadily increasing level of research funding. In this regard, it made sense for Merck to hedge.

Step 4: Select the Appropriate Hedging Instrument

The available financial hedging instruments are forward and futures contracts, foreign currency debts, currency swaps, and currency options. Forward foreign exchange contracts, futures contracts, foreign currency debt, and currency swaps "fix" the value of domestic currency that will be received in the future in return for a *given* amount of foreign currency delivered. In other words, the amount of the domestic currency received cannot be increased or decreased. In contrast, put options provide insurance against a strengthening of the dollar against the foreign currency because they give the firm the right, but not the obligation, to sell foreign currency at a contractual price. (We discuss put options in Chapter 20.) The firm can either exercise this right or, if the exchange rate in the market is better, it can experience higher dollar payoffs by ignoring its option. Of course, the firm must pay the option premium for this privilege. Merck decided that it was unwilling to forgo the potential gains if the dollar weakened, so options were the company's preferred hedging vehicle.

Step 5: Simulate Alternative Hedging Programs to Determine Those Most Cost Effective, Given the Risk Tolerance of Merck's Managers

After deciding to hedge with options, the issue of how exactly to implement a 5-year hedging plan remained to be determined. Several questions had to be addressed, including the following: What term of the hedge is appropriate? Should it be multiyear or year-by-year? What strike prices (contractual exchange rates) should the put options have? What percentage of income should be covered? In other words, can the firm afford partially to "self-insure" its risks—that is, to leave part of the exposure unhedged, thereby reducing current expenditures to implement the hedge?

Merck used a privately developed Monte Carlo simulation model to analyze these questions. A Monte Carlo simulation model generates alternative cash flow scenarios and exchange rates. From the simulations, Merck determined that (1) it should hedge for several years, using long-term options, (2) it should use "out-of-the-money" options[8] as a means of reducing costs, but the options should not be "too far" out of the money, and (3) it should partially self-insure.

Merck's strategy worked well throughout the 1990s, as its profitability remained high and its stock price went from $12.40 in the beginning of 1990 to $90.50 a share in terms of current prices (that is, adjusted for stock splits) in December 2000. As the general market fell in the early 2000s, Merck's stock price fell also. Then, unfortunately, one of Merck's most important pain-relief drugs, Vioxx, had to be taken off the market in 2004, when it was reported that Vioxx caused heart attacks. Although Merck vowed to fight all the subsequent lawsuits, its stock price suffered when the firm lost in court. By June 2006, the stock price had fallen to $36.43 per share. By December 2007, the price was back to $60.67 per share, but during the financial crisis, Merck's share price fell to $23.45 in April 2009, and it was only $31.08 in March 2011.

Analysis of Hedging at HDG Inc.

Brown (2001) describes what he learned spending 3 months during 1998 observing the foreign exchange hedging operations in the Treasury Department of HDG Inc. (a pseudonym), which is a U.S. durable goods manufacturer. The company operates in more than 50 countries, and foreign sales account for just under half of its 1997 revenue of $10 billion.

Oversight, Control, and Operations

The overall structure of HDG's risk management operations is typical of how multinational corporations organize the operations. The Board of Directors has broad oversight and ultimate responsibility for HDG's foreign exchange policies. The Finance Committee, which reports to the Board of Directors, does quarterly and annual policy reviews and performance reviews, while the Foreign Exchange Management Committee (FXMC), which is chaired by the CFO and reports to the Finance Commitee, provides most of the oversight. The FXMC

---

[8]Foreign currency options are covered in Chapter 20. An out-of-the-money option means that the strike price, which is the contractual exchange rate in the option, is fewer dollars per foreign currency than the current exchange rate.

meets monthly, and its primary function is to review foreign exchange exposures and formally approve the hedging strategy of the firm. Hedging strategy essentially means the types of derivative hedges and their amounts.

The Accounting and Control Group reports to the FXMC and has the responsibility to confirm foreign exchange transactions including all derivative trades. Importantly, none of the employees of this group are allowed to enter trades on the firm's behalf, which is a safeguard against rogue trading.

The Treasury Foreign Exchange Group also reports to the FXMC and has operational responsibility for foreign exchange risk management. These employees are responsible for executing the approved hedging strategy. This group consists of 11 full-time employees, and HDG management estimates that their foreign exchange risk management operations cost $1.5 million annually, which is roughly split between employee compensation and overhead for systems and space. Clearly, no one is getting rich working at HDG's foreign exchange operations.

HDG's Motivations for Risk Management

Brown first investigated whether HDG was speculating or hedging. In an interview with the Manager of Foreign Exchange, this explanation was offered to Brown (2001): "We do not take speculative positions, but the extent (to which) we are hedged depends on our views" (p. 413). While Brown found no evidence of active trading, HDG clearly thinks that it can sometimes beat the market.

We noted earlier that convexity of the tax code is a possible motivation for hedging. Brown (2001) found the historical data provided by HDG to indicate consistent profitability of sufficient magnitude that the tax code is essentially linear. Hence, this potential motivation did not apply. Analogously, HDG has relatively large cash holdings and low debt, implying that hedging to avoid costs of financial distress is also not a motivation.

The relatively large cash holdings also appeared to Brown to be sufficient to fund HDG's possible investment projects, making Merck's motivation for hedging less compelling as well. Although this situation may have been the case during the time period examined by Brown, the 1990s were considerably different than the 1980s, and it is not obvious that this motivation for hedging can be dismissed.

Brown (2001) notes that the stated goal of HDG's hedging program is "to increase the certainty of operating margins" (p. 417). He argues that, in practice, HDG management seeks to minimize the impact of changes in exchange rates on reported earnings to have earnings grow linearly. Such "earnings smoothing" is difficult to rationalize in a perfect information world, but with asymmetric information, it can be value enhancing. Brown also spoke to the firm's outside equity analysts, and although they were aware that HDG had a hedging program, they were generally not well informed about the specifics of the program. It was just expected that HDG would manage its exposure and avoid large losses.

A second positive motivation for hedging at HDG centers on competitiveness. It is thought that the hedging program allows the local managers to price competitively without sacrificing margins. Such a motivation may arise if HDG has little competitive ability to pass-through exchange rate changes to its customers and the nature of competition requires consistent competitive product pricing. The relatively short-term horizon (generally less than 1 year) of hedges suggests that this explanation is not very important.

The last motivation that Brown (2001) mentions is the facilitation of internal contracting. One of the primary responsibilities of HDG's forex group is to establish the "hedge rate." This exchange rate is a weighted average of various forward and option hedges and serves as a basis of internal planning and evaluation. The regional managers lobby the central treasury for a "better" hedge rate. Brown (2001) quotes the Manager of Foreign Exchange who stated, "I spend more time managing managers than I do managing currencies" (p. 425). Chapter 9 explored the issue of assessing the performance of foreign subsidiaries. This quote indicates that it is a difficult task to accomplish.

Until recently, it was difficult to obtain data on a firm's use of derivatives. Accountants treated many hedges as off–balance sheet items, and because only balance sheets and income statements tend to get reported, gathering information about hedge activity and trends had to be done some other way. Some scholars used survey data, and others directly read the footnotes of annual reports and other regulatory filings. More recently, reporting standards have changed, and more information is directly obtainable in computer databases. We discuss each of these sources of information in turn.

Information from Surveys

Nance et al. (1993) were among the first to use surveys to attempt to determine the characteristics of firms that actively hedge versus those that do not. Their findings provide some support for the framework developed in this chapter.

In particular, Nance, Smith, and Smithson find that firms with large R&D expenditures are active hedgers. This may be because it is more difficult for high-R&D firms to raise external financing either because their principal assets are intangible and cannot be used as collateral or because there is more asymmetric information about the quality of their new projects. There is also some evidence that more highly levered firms (ones with larger debt–equity ratios) hedge more. Firms that are highly levered do not want to encounter financial distress, so they actively manage their risks to prevent it.

One interesting finding is that firms with higher dividend payouts are also more likely to hedge. Apparently, these firms have a substantial amount of free cash flow and are not constrained in a traditional sense. Yet managers may view a dividend policy as a commitment to the firm's stockholders that cannot be violated. Hedging allows the firm both to maintain its dividend policy and to fund its future investments.

The Wharton/CIBC Survey

A Wharton/CIBC Survey, conducted by Bodnar et al. (1998), obtained responses from 399 non-financial firms on their use of derivatives and their risk management practices. Bodnar et al. found that 83% of large firms and only 12% of small firms used derivatives to hedge. The fact that the larger firms in the study tended to hedge and the smaller ones tended not to hedge is consistent with the argument that the cost of hedging contains a fixed cost. Only when a firm is sufficiently large to overcome the fixed costs of hedging does the firm institute a hedging policy.

The foreign exchange exposures of the firms in the study varied widely. Some 40% of the firms with foreign exchange exposure reported that their foreign currency revenues constituted at least 20% or more of their total revenues. Almost 40% of firms reported that their foreign currency expenses were 20% or more of their total expenses. On the other hand, 60% of the firms reported that their total foreign currency revenues and expenses were effectively balanced. It is possible that these firms were naturally operationally hedged.

The Wharton/CIBC Survey does not explicitly explore the reasons for hedging, but it nonetheless offers some insights. The results indicate that firms employed only partial hedges and did not hedge very far into the future. In fact, Bodnar et al. (1998) found that firms with a significant amount of regularly recurring foreign exchange exposure tended to hedge only a small fraction of their exposure. Most of the firms used short-term hedges; the vast majority of the hedges matured in 90 days or less. One potential explanation for this phenomenon is that the transaction costs of longer-term hedges are higher.

Finally, the Wharton/CIBC Survey finds that some firms use derivatives more for speculative purposes than for hedging. In fact, Bodnar et al. (1998) find that a little under one-third of firms using derivatives reported that their market view of exchange rates leads them to do so at least occasionally. Pramborg (2005) finds similar evidence for firms in Korea and Sweden.

Empirical Analysis of Why Firms Hedge

Géczy et al. (1997) examined the footnotes of firms' annual reports and their periodic reports to the Securities and Exchange Commission (SEC) for 372 non-financial Fortune 500 firms in 1990 to determine their use of currency derivatives. Approximately 41% of these firms used currency swaps, forwards, futures, options, or combinations of these derivative instruments. The econometric analysis indicates that firms with greater growth opportunities are more likely to use currency derivatives for hedging purposes. This finding is consistent with the notion that firms use derivatives to reduce the volatility of their cash flow to avoid being in a situation in which they might otherwise be precluded from investing in one of their growth opportunities.

Géczy et al. (1997) also found an important difference between firms that had foreign currency exposures because they had foreign operations and firms that had foreign operations and also had foreign currency debt. R&D expenses were high among the group of firms that did not have foreign currency debt, but R&D expenses were no longer a significant determinant of the use of currency derivatives for the firms with debt. This suggests that issuing debt in a foreign currency can serve the same function as hedging.

Bartram et al. (2009) examine data from 50 countries and 7,319 companies that cover about 80% of the global market capitalization of non-financial firms. They find that tax factors and high leverage are important reasons for the use of any financial derivative. Additionally, they find that larger and more profitable firms use financial derivatives, consistent with there being a fixed cost. Firms with high market values relative to book values also have a lower probability of using financial derivatives and foreign exchange derivatives in particular, which is inconsistent with the theoretical prediction that growth firms would want to assure themselves of adequate cash flow to fund investment projects. Finally, firms with larger foreign exchange exposures, larger foreign currency debts, and equity listings in a foreign country have a higher probability of using foreign exchange derivatives. This is consistent with the earlier finding in Allayannis and Ofek (2001) that the levels of firms' foreign sales and trade are the only determinants of the amount of currency hedging that firms do.

Financial Effects of Hedging

While the aforementioned studies explore why and how much firms hedge, Allayannis and Weston (2001) attempt to quantify whether firms that use foreign currency derivatives have an increased market value compared to firms that do not use derivatives. Allayannis and Weston find evidence consistent with the hypothesis that hedging increases a firm's value by a little under 5%. This conclusion must be considered with some caution because it assumes that some managers are smart and increase the value of their firms while others are not acting in the best interests of the firm's owners. The alternative hypothesis is that the econometrician has failed to hold constant all the aspects that make the firms different.

A related question is why foreign exchange exposure and equity value appear to be so poorly linked. A number of studies have regressed individual firm equity returns on returns on the overall market return and rates of change in exchange rates typically finding small or insignificant exchange rate exposures. Bartram et al. (2010) offer an explanation. First, they show that exchange rate pass-through and operational hedging are important, and they estimate that each of these channels reduces equity exposure by 10% to 15%. Use of foreign exchange derivatives and foreign currency debt reduces exposure by an additional 40%.

Chapter 18

Financing International Trade

International trade has been conducted for over 2,000 years. A host of institutional arrangements, some of them quite elaborate, have developed over the years to facilitate such activity. Major international banks, in particular, are key players in bringing together importers and exporters. This chapter introduces and describes these institutional relationships.

The chapter first introduces the fundamental problems of international trades. Then it examines the important documents that control the ownership and insurance of goods that are being shipped internationally. Commercial banks require these documents when they provide financing to importers and exporters. We then look at alternative payment methods and a variety of ways in which exports can be financed. Governments often have special export–import banks that provide subsidized financing and insurance to promote international trade.

For example, in November 2009, the U.S. Export–Import Bank announced that it would lend $80.66 million to Electrica del Valle de Mexico (EVM), a subsidiary of France's EDF Energies Nouvelle, which is building a wind farm in Oaxaca, Mexico. EVM was purchasing the wind turbines from Clipper Windpower, a small U.S. manufacturer with a sole production facility in Cedar Rapids, Iowa. The sale of the turbines to EVM represented Clipper's first international sale. EVM was able to obtain a 14-year term loan priced at 100 basis points over 7-year U.S. Treasury notes. Because Clipper Windpower was too small to offer financing to EVM directly, and because bank and bond financing may have proven too expensive at the time, the deal probably would not have gotten done without the Export-Import Bank's assistance. It is difficult to assess how much of a subsidy the loan represents.

The chapter concludes with a discussion of countertrade and the host of ways goods can be traded more or less directly for other goods.

18.1 THE FUNDAMENTAL PROBLEM WITH INTERNATIONAL TRADE

Shipping goods across a country as large as the United States poses many complex logistical and financial problems. Shipping goods across international borders creates a host of additional complications.

Exhibit 18.1 describes the fundamental situation: An importer in Canada, Jean Claude Richot Men's Apparel, Inc., would like to buy some sweaters from a Scottish exporter of wool sweaters, Albemarle's Scottish Sweaters. Because it takes time to ship the sweaters

Exhibit 18.1 An Example of the Fundamental Problem in International Trade

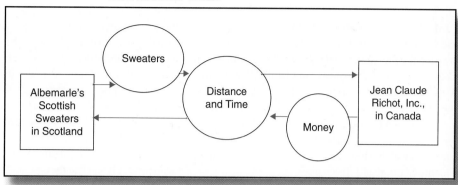

internationally, the sweaters cannot be delivered from the Scottish exporter to the Canadian importer immediately after an agreement is reached to purchase the goods. Either the Canadian importer or the Scottish exporter must own the sweaters during the time they are being shipped. Consequently, either the exporter or the importer must engage in some method of financing because the goods cannot be sold immediately after production.

When the shipment and sale of goods occur within a single country, there is a common jurisdiction and system of courts that adjudicates contractual disputes between buyers and sellers. When goods are shipped across borders, though, additional legal complexities arise. One such complexity relates to collecting on delinquent accounts. Differences in languages, cultures, accounting standards, and other information issues make it quite difficult, in some cases, to assess who is a good credit risk and who is not. The International Chamber of Commerce, which we discuss in the following box, attempts to overcome some of these problems.

Of course, exporters, like other producers, must obtain financing during the manufacturing process. They can finance their production in a number of ways: from retained earnings, with bank loans, by issuing securities, or by obtaining advanced payments from importers.

Techniques for handling these international financing issues and credit transactions differ across countries and industries and have evolved over time.[1] Firms within the same industry can use a variety of methods, depending on the competitive pressures specific to the individual firm. For example, established exporters who are the international leaders of their industry are in a better position to demand more stringent payment terms from importers than other exporters. A single firm might also use different strategies, depending on its customer. For example, the policy that an exporting firm finds appropriate when dealing with an importer located in a developed country will probably not be appropriate for importers located in a developing country. This chapter explores alternative ways that firms deal with such financing and credit issues to establish overall credit policies. Before discussing these issues, however, we cover the documents that banks and other intermediaries use to control the ownership of the goods, the insurance, and the billing processes.

---

[1]Greif (1993) describes how some eleventh-century traders known as the Maghribi developed an institutional coalition to overcome the problems inherent in international trade. The Maghribi were Jewish traders who were operating in the Muslim western Mediterranean. Greif notes, "Agents provided merchants with many trade-related services, including loading and unloading ships; paying the customs, bribes and transportation fees; storing the goods; transferring the goods to market; and deciding when, how, and to whom to sell the goods, at what price, and at which credit terms" (p. 528).

The International Chamber of Commerce

The **International Chamber of Commerce (ICC)**, based in Paris, was founded in 1919 with the goals of promoting international trade and investment, opening international markets for goods and services, and facilitating the free flow of capital between countries. The original members of the ICC were private companies in Belgium, Britain, France, Italy, and the United States. Membership has expanded dramatically, and today, the ICC is a world business organization with thousands of member companies and associations in more than 130 countries.

The activities of the ICC include setting rules and standards for international trade, arbitration and other forms of dispute resolution, and business self-regulation; making the political case for open trade and the market economy system; fighting corruption; and combating commercial crime. Each year, the ICC International Court of Arbitration hears hundreds of cases from around the world. The disputes are quite varied; examples include differences over the supply of steel pipes, the liquidation of a bank, the interpretation of a shareholders' agreement, the insurance for a film, and the construction of a shopping center.

One of the ICC's most important activities is setting standards for commercial contracts. This includes establishing the meaning of acronyms used internationally. The acronyms indicate who pays the costs of shipping, insurance, and import duties. On January 1, 2011, the eighth edition of the ICC publication *INCOTERMS* came into effect. It groups these terms into four different categories. The *E* terms, as in *EXW* for "ex works," indicate the goods are available to the buyer at the seller's premises. The *F* terms, such as *FAS* for "free alongside ship" and *FOB* for "free on board," indicate that the price quoted by the seller includes delivery of the goods to a carrier appointed by the buyer. The *C* terms, including *CFR* for "cost and freight," and *CIF* for "cost, insurance, and freight," imply that the exporter's quoted price includes the cost of transportation to the named port of destination for CFR and that the cost of insurance is also included in the price, in addition to the transportation charges for CIF. The *D* terms refer to delivery specifics. *DAT* for "delivered at terminal" implies that the exporter's quoted price includes the cost of transportation and unloading from the transportation vehicle, which could be a plane or a ship, at a particular terminal or port. *DAP* for "delivered at place" is similar except the buyer must pay for the unloading.

The ICC's Uniform Customs and Practice for Documentary Credits (UCP 500) consists of a set of rules banks use to finance billions of dollars of world trade annually. The ICC is also leading the charge to establish standards for e-commerce. For example, a supplement to UCP 500, called the eUCP, was added in 2002 to create standards for electronic international trade documents. In addition, the ICC's codes on advertising and marketing influence both national legislation and the rules adopted by professional associations.

18.2 INTERNATIONAL TRADE DOCUMENTS

This section examines several of the important documents of international trade. International banks require many of these documents when financing international trade. The documents include bills of lading, which come in various types; commercial invoices; packing lists; insurance certificates; consular invoices; and certificates of analysis. Exhibit 18.2 provides a summary of the documents and their definitions.

Bills of Lading

A **bill of lading (B/L)** is a contract issued to an exporter of goods by the shipping company (also called a *common carrier*) that will transport the goods to their destination. The bill of lading serves several purposes, but most importantly, it documents that the exporter's goods have been received by the carrier.

The bill of lading contains the contractual terms between the carrier and the shipper (exporter). It describes the kind and quantity of goods being shipped, who the shipper (also called the *consignor*) is, who the importer (also called the *consignee*) is, the ports of loading and discharge, the carrying vessel, and the cost of the shipping. A **negotiable bill of lading**

Exhibit 18.2 Documents of International Trade

Bill of Lading A contract issued to an exporter or a shipper of goods by the company that will transport the goods from the place of shipment to the destination.

Commercial Invoice A detailed description of merchandise being sold, including the unit prices of the items and the number of items that are being shipped as well as the financial terms of the sale, including the amount due from the buyer and any charges to the buyer arising from insurance and shipping.

Packing List A description of merchandise to be exported, including the containers in which the goods are packed, the contents of each container, and the total number of containers.

Insurance Documents indicating that the owner of goods will be compensated in the event that the goods are damaged, destroyed, or stolen when being transported internationally.

Consular Invoice A document that must be filled out by an exporter in consultation with the consulate of the importing country that is located in the exporting country; it provides information to customs officials in the importing country, with the goal of preventing false declarations of the value of the merchandise.

Certificate of Analysis A document which assures an importer and possibly government officials that a shipment meets certain standards of purity, weight, sanitation, or other measurable characteristics.

is the most common form. It can be used to transfer title or ownership of goods between different parties.

In our example, Albemarle's Scottish Sweaters receives a bill of lading from its shipping company. If Jean Claude Richot, Inc., had already paid for the sweaters, a negotiable B/L would indicate that Jean Claude Richot, Inc., should receive the sweaters upon their arrival in Canada.

Straight Bill of Lading

In its simplest form, a **straight bill of lading** states that a carrier has received merchandise from a shipper (a consignor) and will deliver the merchandise to a designated party (the consignee). A straight bill of lading is not title to the goods and is consequently not required for the consignee to obtain delivery of the merchandise. Because it is not a title to the merchandise, a straight bill of lading is not negotiable and cannot be used to transfer title of the goods to a third party. Consequently, it cannot serve as collateral with a commercial bank and is used only when no export or import financing is desired. A straight bill of lading is used when goods have been paid for in advance, when the exporter is financing the shipment and retaining title to the goods, or when the shipment is between affiliated parties of the same corporation.

Order Bill of Lading

If the transfer of title to goods is desired, or if some form of third-party financing is desired, an **order bill of lading** is used. Because most export transactions do involve financing, order bills of lading are most common. An order bill of lading consigns the goods to a party named in the contract, which is usually the exporter because the exporter wants to retain title to the goods until payment from the importer has been received. The exporter can endorse the order bill of lading on the reverse side to transfer title of the goods to a specific party designated in the endorsement. At the destination, the carrier of the goods delivers the goods only to the party bearing the endorsed order bill of lading, who surrenders it to the carrier.

Having an order bill of lading is tantamount to having the title to the goods. This means that the goods can be used as collateral for bank loans. Banks are willing to lend to the party bearing an endorsed order bill of lading. In addition, the goods are usually fully insured. An order bill of lading is also required with a documentary credit or for discounting drafts, as we will see later in the chapter. Discounting is simply the taking of the present value of the payment promised in the draft.

On-Board Versus Received-for-Shipment Bills of Lading

Bills of lading have several unique characteristics. An **on-board bill of lading** indicates that goods have been placed on a particular vessel for shipment. This is the type of bill of lading that is usually used in a documentary credit. An alternative form is a **received-for-shipment bill of lading**, which indicates only that the merchandise is at the dock awaiting transport. A received-for-shipment bill of lading is not an acceptable document in a bank financing unless it has been explicitly authorized in a documentary credit. A received-for-shipment bill of lading is issued by the carrier upon receipt of the merchandise. It is easily converted into an on-board bill of lading when it is stamped appropriately with the name of the vessel, dated, and signed or initialed by an authorized representative of the carrier. The reason a received-for-shipment bill of lading is not acceptable in bank financing is that no one knows for sure when the goods will be shipped.

Clean Versus Foul Bills of Lading

A bill of lading contains information on the status of the merchandise when it is received by the carrier. A **clean bill of lading** indicates that the carrier believes the merchandise was received in good condition after an external visual inspection. Carriers are not responsible for formal evaluations of the condition of the merchandise. In contrast, a **foul bill of lading** indicates that the carrier's initial inspection uncovered some damage that occurred before the goods were received by the carrier for shipment. Foul bills of lading are typically not negotiable because no one knows the extent of the damage to the merchandise.

Commercial Invoices

A **commercial invoice**, issued by an exporter and given to an importer, contains a detailed description of the merchandise, including the unit prices of the items and the number of items being shipped. The invoice also specifies the financial terms of the sale, including the amount due from the importer and any charges to the importer arising from insurance and shipping.

In the example that we have been following, the total number of sweaters of all types might be 7,500, and if each sweater costs $200, the total invoice would be for $1,500,000. Notice that in this case, the U.S. dollar is used as the currency of invoice even though neither party to the transaction is in the United States. Alternatively, the transaction could be denominated in British pounds, the currency of the exporter, or in Canadian dollars, the currency of the importer.

Packing Lists

Because goods shipped internationally are often prepackaged in a container, the shipper must include a **packing list**. This list contains a description of the merchandise to be exported, including the containers in which the goods are packed, the contents of each container, and the total number of containers. In our example, the packing list would contain a description of the numbers and types of sweaters.

Insurance

Merchandise that is shipped internationally is invariably insured. The insurance documents must be signed by an authorized representative of the insurance company, its agents, or its underwriters. (An insurance broker's signature is unacceptable.) The insurance must either be issued in the name of the consignee or in the name of the exporter, who can then endorse the policy to the consignee. The value of the insurance must be expressed in the same currency as the currency of the invoice. Otherwise, there would be transaction foreign exchange risk.

Open Insurance Policies

Firms that do a substantial amount of exporting can purchase insurance policies that are described as "open," or "floating." Such a policy automatically covers all the exports of a firm, which eliminates the necessity of arranging coverage for each individual export order. In such cases, the evidence of insurance is an insurance certificate that the insurance company supplies. The entry of information on the insurance certificate should conform exactly to the information describing the merchandise on the bill of lading, the commercial invoice, and, if it is required, the consular invoice.

Consular Invoice

Imports into many countries require a **consular invoice** filled out by the exporter in consultation with the importing country's consulate located in the exporting country. A consular invoice provides information to customs officials in the importing country, with the goal of preventing false declarations of the value of the merchandise. Failing to fill out such forms correctly can lead to fines and substantial delays in the clearing of goods through customs. A consular invoice is sometimes combined with a **certificate of origin** of the goods, which indicates the source of the goods.

Certificates of Analysis

A **certificate of analysis** is sometimes required to assure an importer that a shipment meets certain standards of purity, weight, sanitation, or other measurable characteristics. These documents may be required by the health or other officials of the importing country, especially when it comes to food and drug imports. Certificates of analysis may be issued by private organizations or by governments.

18.3 METHODS OF PAYMENT

Ideally, an exporter wants to be paid when the importer orders the goods, especially if they are being made to order. Prepayment helps finance the production of the goods and assures the exporter of his profit. Moreover, if the exporter must finance the production of a highly customized good, the exporter will usually demand that the importer bear some of the cost. Importers, on the other hand, prefer to pay as late as possible. If an importer can pay the exporter after being paid by the final buyer of the product, the exporter essentially finances the importer's inventory until it is sold.

This section examines the different methods available for an importer to pay an exporter, ranging from cash in advance, which is the least risky from the exporter's perspective, to documentary credits and documentary collections and to open accounts, which are increasingly risky methods of payment from the exporter's point of view.

Cash in Advance

Cash-in-advance transactions require the importer to pay the exporter before the goods are shipped, implying that the exporter does not have to finance the goods during their shipment. For exporters, cash in advance is obviously the least risky policy. The importer must finance the purchase of the goods, incurs the cost of shipping them, and bears the risk of their being damaged in transit.

Cash in advance is used primarily with high credit-risk trading partners and in countries in which political risks are large. If a credit rating agency, such as Dun & Bradstreet, has given a foreign importer a low credit rating, or if a credit insurance agency has removed the foreign firm from its list of eligible firms, the exporter may demand cash in advance. Also, if the exporter thinks the importer may have difficulty securing foreign currency because the importer's government might close the foreign exchange market during the time of shipment, the exporter may demand cash in advance. If the importer is unable to get trade finance, negotiations between the exporter and the importer might break down.

Because few importers are willing to pay for goods in advance, international banks developed a method of securing payment that substitutes the bank's credit risk for the importer's credit risk. This method is the documentary credit.

Documentary Credits

Documentary credits (D/Cs) are designed to solve the problems caused by the fact that importers and exporters want to pay and be paid at different times.[2] Documentary credits also provide a way for exporters to finance the production of their goods. With a documentary credit, at least one commercial bank stands between the importer and the exporter. The exporter must assess the credit risk of this international bank, not the credit risk of the importer. Because the involvement of commercial banks in the transaction is extensive, using a documentary credit is the most expensive method of payment.

Exhibit 18.3 presents an example of a documentary credit associated with the transaction between an importer, Jean Claude Richot Men's Apparel, Inc., and an exporter, Albemarle's Scottish Sweaters, written by the importer's bank, Bank of Quebec.

Drafts

A D/C is created when an importer asks its commercial bank to write a letter to an exporter on behalf of the importer. In the D/C, the importer's bank indicates that it will honor a draft, drawn on it, if the exporter satisfies certain conditions set forth in the D/C. The draft is a written order by the bank to pay the exporter and may be either a **sight draft** or a **time draft**.

Exhibit 18.4 presents an example of a time draft. The time draft indicates that the Bank of Quebec will pay $1,500,000 to Albemarle Scottish Sweaters 3 months after the date the D/C was written, at which time the draft can be presented to the bank. The account of Jean Claude Richot, Inc. will be charged for the payment. If the draft is a sight draft, the bank is obligated to pay the draft any time it is presented, as long as the documents associated with the D/C are in order.

If a bank accepts a time draft, the draft becomes a **banker's acceptance (B/A)**, where the bank agrees to pay the face value of the draft at maturity, or may pay a discounted value immediately. More details follow later.

Once the documentary credit is established, it becomes a financial document that substitutes the credit of the bank for the credit of the importer. The conditions that the exporter must satisfy in order to be paid include providing formal documentary evidence that the goods have been shipped, that the freight has been paid, and that the goods have been insured.

Advantages of Documentary Credits to Exporters

Documentary credits offer a number of advantages to exporters:

1. The most important advantage of a D/C is that it substitutes the creditworthiness of the bank for the credit risk of the importing firm. If the exporter satisfies the requirements of the D/C, the exporter will be paid by the bank.
2. Establishing a documentary credit enhances the probability that the exporter will not experience delays in payment due to the imposition of foreign exchange controls or

---

[2]In the United States, a documentary credit is often referred to as a letter of credit (L/C).

Exhibit 18.3   A Documentary Credit

Irrevocable
Documentary Credit

Est. 1847

Bank of Quebec

860 Rene-Levesque Blvd W
Montreal, PQ H3B4A5 CA

International Division   Commercial D/C Department   www.boq.com

Documentary Credit No.: 0087349824   Amount: USD1,500,000   Date: July 3, 2011

This number must be mentioned
on all drafts and correspondence.

. Albemarle's Scottish Sweaters   . Bank of Edinburgh
. Edinburgh, Scotland   . Edinburgh, Scotland
.   .

Dear Madame or Sir:

   By order of   Jean Claude Richot Men's Apparel, Inc.

and for the account of   SAME

we hereby authorize you to draw on   Ourselves

up to an aggregate amount of   One Million, Five Hundred Thousand, U.S. Dollars

Available by your drafts at   Ourselves, but not before October 3, 2011

Accompanied by
Signed invoice in triplicate
Packing list in triplicate
Full set of clean ocean bills of lading, made out to order of shipper, blank endorsed, marked freight prepaid
and notify: Jean Claude Richot Men's Apparel, Inc., Montreal, dated on board not later than July 30, 2011.
Insurance policy/certificate in triplicate for 110% of invoice value, covering all risks.

Covering: Shipment of sweaters, as per buyer's order no. 86354011, dated June 15, 2011, from Edinburgh,
Scotland port C.I.F. to Montreal, Quebec, CANADA.
Partial Shipments not permitted.
Transshipment is not permitted.
Documents must be presented within 7 days after the board date of the bills of lading, but in any event not
later than August 7, 2011.

Drafts must be drawn and negotiated not later than August 3, 2011
**All drafts drawn under this credit must bear its date and number and the amounts must be endorsed
on the reverse side of this Documentary Credit by the negotiating bank. We hereby agree with the
drawers, endorsers, and bona fide holders of all drafts drawn under and in compliance with the terms
of this credit, that such drafts will be duly honored upon presentation to the drawee. This credit is subject to the uniform customs and practice for documentary credits (International Chamber of Commerce
Publication No. 500)**

Francois Montblanc
Commercial Credit Officer
Bank of Quebec

other political risks. Countries are well aware of the importance of international trade.
As a result, governments generally permit banks to honor existing documentary credits.
Failing to do so severely damages a country's reputation and its ability to borrow in
international financial markets in the future.

Exhibit 18.4   An Example of a Time Draft

not before October 3, 2011	July 3, 2011 Montreal, Quebec, Canada
INDICATE ABOVE WHETHER PAYABLE ON DEMAND, ARRIVAL, OR OTHER TIME LIMIT	DATE AND LOCATION

PAY TO THE ORDER OF   ALBEMARLE'S SCOTTISH SWEATERS   USD 1,500,000

ONE MILLION, FIVE HUNDRED THOUSAND UNITED STATES DOLLARS

JEAN CLAUDE RICHOT'S IMPORTED MEN'S APPAREL, INC.
VALUE RECEIVED AND CHARGE TO ACCOUNT OF

TO   Bank of Quebec
860 Rene-Levesque Blvd W, Montreal, PQ, H3B4A5 CA

No.   D/C No. 0087349824

Robert Rochambeau, Treasurer
Jean Claude Richot, Inc.

3. A D/C reduces the uncertainty of a transaction by clearly establishing the acts that the exporter must carry out in order to receive payment.
4. Because a D/C is a legally binding document between a bank and an exporter, the exporter is protected if the importer desires to cancel the contract during the production process. This is especially important if the goods are being made to order.
5. A D/C makes it easy for an exporter to receive early payment because a time draft can be accepted by the bank, which creates a banker's acceptance.

Advantages of Documentary Credits to Importers

Documentary credits also have advantages from the importer's perspective:

1. The foremost advantage for an importer is that a D/C clearly indicates a time frame by which the goods must be shipped. The importer knows that the exporter must ship the goods by a certain date and must provide certain documents to the bank if the exporter wants to be paid. The importer is thus assured of having the goods when they are needed for the importer's production process or for resale in the importer's market.
2. Another advantage of a D/C from the importer's perspective is that the importer's bank assumes responsibility for checking the documents provided by an exporter. Hence, if the exporter does not properly ship the goods, the bank will not pay the exporter, and the importer is protected from having to pay for goods that are not valuable. If the importer takes possession of the goods and it is discovered that there is a problem with the shipment that should have been caught by examining the shipping documents, the bank is responsible for this oversight.
3. The fact that a D/C substitutes the bank's credit standing for the importer's credit standing means that the importer may be able to command better payment terms. A D/C may be required by some exporters if they cannot get cash in advance.
4. If some form of prepayment is required by an exporter, an importer is better off depositing money in an escrow account at its domestic bank than with a foreign company. If the exporter encounters some difficulty that limits its ability to follow through on its contractual commitments, the importer can recover its deposit from a local bank more easily than it could from the foreign exporter.

Attributes of Documentary Credits

A documentary credit can be either revocable or irrevocable. A **revocable D/C** is a means of arranging payment, but it provides no guarantee of payment. The importer reserves the right to revoke the D/C at any time prior to the presentation of the draft by the exporter to the bank. A revocable D/C establishes that the importer has a working business relationship with a reputable bank. It also establishes that the transaction is one that is legitimately eligible for scarce foreign exchange if there is a crisis in the importer's country. Hence, it is useful for transactions between related affiliates of a multinational corporation to assure that exchange controls do not disrupt the importing process. It is less expensive than an irrevocable D/C.

Most documentary credits between unrelated parties are irrevocable. An **irrevocable D/C** cannot be revoked unless all parties, including the exporter, agree to the revocation. International transactions between parties not well known to each other are typically conducted with irrevocable documentary credits. Otherwise, much of the benefit of substituting the credit of the bank for the credit of the importer would be lost. Once an irrevocable documentary credit has been received, the exporter is assured that it will be paid by the importer's bank if it performs certain tasks by certain dates in the future.

A documentary credit can also be confirmed or unconfirmed. A **confirmed documentary credit** is one in which a second commercial bank agrees to honor the draft presented by the exporter. Typically, the bank that issues the documentary credit is from the country of the importer. Two issues arise from the perspective of the exporter. First, although the issuing bank may be a reputable international bank, it is still subject to the legal jurisdiction of the importing country and may not be well known to the exporter. Second, the exporter might ultimately want to present the draft to a bank in the exporting country. By having a bank in the exporting country confirm the D/C, the exporter obtains a guarantee that a domestic bank that the exporter trusts will accept the responsibility for paying the draft. Of course, the second bank will demand some additional compensation for the confirmation of the D/C, and this increases transaction costs.

In summary, the three primary types of documentary credits, in decreasing order of security to the exporter, are (1) an irrevocable, confirmed D/C; (2) an irrevocable, unconfirmed D/C; and (3) a revocable D/C. Choosing among these three and who pays for the increased cost of the deal depends on the bargaining strength of the importer and the exporter. Making the deal more secure for the exporter makes the deal more expensive because banks charge additional fees. This added expense must be paid either by the importer, who agrees to a higher cost, or by the exporter, who accepts a lower price. Of course, if the exporter demands the most stringent terms and forces the importer to pay the transaction costs, the exporter risks losing business to lower-cost exporters willing to take greater risks.

Summary of the Creation and Use of a D/C and a B/A

As we have seen, international trade can be handled in a number of different ways. This section provides a summary diagram of some complex transactions—the creation and use of a documentary credit with the discounting of a draft to create a banker's acceptance. Exhibit 18.5 provides a general diagram of the transactions involved:

1. The importer orders goods from the exporter and asks whether the exporter is willing to ship the goods under a documentary credit containing a time draft.
2. The exporter and importer agree to ship the goods under a documentary credit. The two parties negotiate the price of the goods and the other aspects related to how the goods will be shipped.
3. The importer applies for a documentary credit to its commercial bank, designated in Exhibit 18.5 as "Bank IMP."
4. Bank IMP issues the documentary credit, with the exporter named as the beneficiary. The D/C specifies the information associated with the deal and is sent to an advising bank, "Bank EXP," in the exporter's country.
5. Bank EXP advises the exporter that the documentary credit has arrived. If the exporter so desires, Bank EXP confirms the documentary credit for a fee and adds its guarantee to Bank IMP's guarantee.

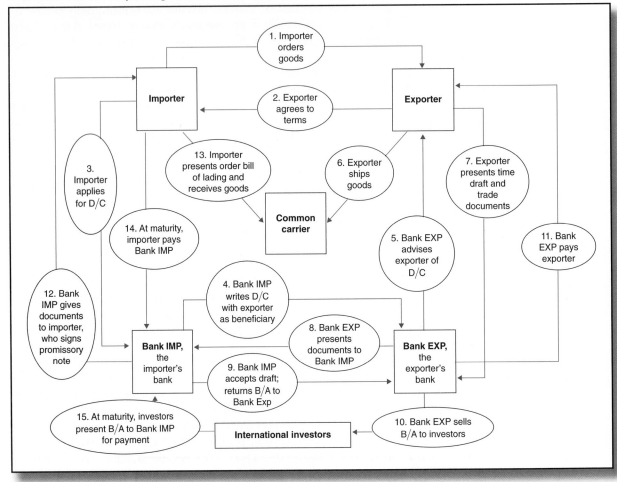

6. The exporter ships the goods to the importer using a common carrier.

7. The exporter presents a time draft, with a maturity of, say, 90 days in the future, to Bank EXP. The draft is drawn on Bank IMP, as specified in the D/C from Bank IMP. The exporter also presents the documents required by the D/C, including the order bill of lading. The exporter endorses the order bill of lading "in blank" so that the title of the goods passes to the holder of the endorsed bill of lading, which is Bank EXP at this point.

8. Bank EXP presents the draft and the export documents to Bank IMP, which accepts the draft and takes possession of the documents. A banker's acceptance, B/A, with a maturity of 90 days is created.

9. Either Bank IMP returns the accepted draft to Bank EXP, or Bank EXP could ask for the discounted cash value of the B/A, in which case Bank IMP would deduct a discounting fee. The interest rate in the B/A market is used to take the present value.

10. Assuming that Bank EXP receives the B/A, it now either gives the B/A to the exporter or pays the exporter. In the latter case, Bank EXP can either hold the B/A in its own portfolio or sell the B/A to an investor in the international financial markets.

11. Normally, the exporter receives the discounted cash value for the B/A less any bank charge for a discounting fee rather than wait for 90 days to receive a cash payment.

12. Bank IMP informs the importer that the documents have arrived. The importer either signs a promissory note or follows through with some mutually agreed-upon plan for paying Bank IMP, at which point Bank IMP releases the documents, including the order bill of lading, to the importer. Often, the maturity of the promissory note is the same as the maturity of the B/A, which is 90 days in this case.
13. When the goods arrive, the importer collects them from the common carrier, using the order bill of lading.
14. At the maturity of the promissory note, the importer pays Bank IMP.
15. At the maturity of the B/A, Bank IMP pays the holder of the matured banker's acceptance. The investor receives the face value of the B/A. The holder may present the B/A directly to Bank IMP, or it may have Bank EXP collect the amount through its normal banking relationships with Bank IMP.

Documentary Collections

Firms can avoid directly assessing the creditworthiness of their trading partners by using a **documentary collection**. With a documentary collection, the exporter retains control of the goods until the importer has paid or is legally bound to pay for them, and the exporter gets banks involved in the collection process, although the degree of responsibility banks bear for assuring payment to the exporter in a documentary collection is not as high as with a confirmed documentary credit. Documentary collections are also less expensive than documentary credits.

When conducting an export transaction through documentary collection, the exporter uses a remitting bank as its agent to collect the payment from the importer. The exporter ships the merchandise to the importer, but the exporter retains title to the goods. The exporter next presents the shipping documents and a draft or bill of exchange that is drawn on the importer to the remitting bank. The remitting bank (the agent of the exporter) sends the documents, the draft, and the instructions to a bank in the importer's country. This bank is called the collecting, or presenting, bank, and it could be a foreign branch of the remitting bank or a correspondent bank in the foreign country. The collecting, or presenting, bank notifies the importer that the documents are available and that they may be obtained when the importer complies with the terms of the documentary collection.

The exporter instructs its remitting bank that the payment should be collected from the importer in one of two ways, either as a **documents against payment (D/P) collection** or as a **documents against acceptance (D/A) collection**. Under a D/P collection, the importer must pay the amount of the sight draft to the collecting bank before the documents are released. When the funds are received, they are transmitted to the remitting bank for payment to the exporter. The exporter consequently does not give up control of the merchandise until payment is received by the collecting bank.

Under a D/A collection, the exporter extends credit to the importer in the following way. The collecting bank presents a time draft to the importer, who must sign it, date it, and write *accepted* across it. The shipping documents are then released to the importer. By accepting the draft, the importer acknowledges his legal obligation to pay the face amount of the draft at maturity, which is usually 30, 60, or 90 days after the date of the acceptance. An accepted draft is known as a **trade acceptance**. It can be retained by the collecting bank on behalf of the exporter for presentation to the importer at maturity, or it may be returned to the exporter. At maturity, the draft is presented by the collecting bank to the importer, who must pay the face amount. The funds are then transmitted to the remitting bank for payment to the exporter. With a D/A collection, the exporter gives up title to the goods in exchange for the legally binding commitment of the importer to pay the trade acceptance. Hence, it is important for the exporter to understand the creditworthiness of the importer.

Advantages of Documentary Collections

From an exporter's perspective, the documents against acceptance collection create a negotiable trade acceptance, which is an enforceable debt instrument. Not only is the importer legally bound to pay, but the exporter can sell the trade acceptance in the short-term money market to obtain financing. Of course, the sale of a trade acceptance is done at a discount that reflects both the time value of the money in which the acceptance is denominated and the money market's perception of the default risk of the importer.

Exporters often find that they are paid more promptly when using documentary collections rather than just invoicing the importers because importers are more responsive to their local banking communities than to the invoices of the exporter. The documentary collection does add the expenses of the remitting and collecting banks to the process, but these transaction costs are lower than the expenses involved in establishing a documentary credit.

Disadvantages of Documentary Collections

The chief disadvantage of a D/A collection arises because the banks are only acting as the agents of the exporter and are not obligated to pay, as they are with a documentary credit. The exporter consequently bears the importer's default risk.

How might the deal break down? One way is if the importer refuses to take ownership of the shipment after inspecting the shipping documents. The importer consequently refuses to pay the sight or time draft. Or it might happen if, from the viewpoint of the importer, there is a document discrepancy. Documents are rejected by importers for a variety of reasons. The invoice price may not be the price that the importer agreed to in the sales contract. The goods may have been shipped late or incorrectly packaged. Sometimes, importers will use documentary discrepancies that are otherwise superficial as a reason to refuse shipment when they have changed their minds about the deal because their business has slowed down. In such a circumstance, if the exporter is not able to reconcile the issue with the importer, the exporter is forced either to warehouse the goods until another foreign buyer is located or the exporter must pay to have the goods reshipped. Sometimes, even though the exporter has a trade acceptance that is signed by the importer, getting paid by the importer entails a lengthy and costly legal battle in the importing country's courts.

Finally, because the exporter is extending credit to the importer, the exporter must bear the political risk of the importer's country. Situations can arise, having nothing to do with the importer, that prevent the exporter from being able to repatriate funds at the maturity of the trade credit. For example, the government of the importing country might impose delays or prohibit the payment of foreign exchange to foreign corporations. Delays can also arise when foreign exchange is rationed by a country's central bank, and the importer or the collecting bank must wait in the queue to buy convertible currencies.

Sales on Open Account

Demanding cash in advance poses the least risk to the exporter, but it imposes the most financial burden on the importer. At the other extreme, exporters allow **sales on open account**, which poses the most risk to the exporter. Under an open account arrangement, the exporter establishes an account for the importer, who is allowed to order goods, which are either produced to order or shipped from inventory at the instruction of the importer. The payment for the goods is based on an invoiced amount, but there is no particular date in the future when the payment must be made. In other words, the exporter extends trade credit on certain terms to the importer. There is typically a discount offered from the invoiced amount if payment is made within a certain number of days. In contrast, the invoice indicates that overdue payments carry additional interest and financial service charges. The terms of such accounts must be negotiated and are subject to the competitive pressures of the industry.

Open accounts are used primarily between related affiliates of the same multinational corporation, but they also arise when exporting and importing firms have long-standing relationships or when the importer's credit rating is high. Open accounts offer importers more flexibility with regard to their financing, which can enhance an exporter's sales, and transaction costs are lower because banks are not involved in the process.

The open account method of payment is risky to the exporter, though, because an unpaid invoice is the only evidence of an importer's indebtedness to an exporter. If an importer fails to pay, the exporting firm must use the importing country's courts to attempt to enforce payment. It is possible that a court in the importing country might decide that an unpaid open account invoice is not an enforceable debt instrument. In that case, the exporter will have no rights in a bankruptcy proceeding against an insolvent importer.

An exporter is also exposed to political risks of foreign exchange controls that may prevent a solvent importer from fulfilling its promise to pay. Before granting an open account to an importer, exporters should monitor the macroeconomic and political developments in the importer's country. The exporter wants to avoid problems with blocked funds, which arise when a currency is inconvertible into other currencies. We will discuss this further in Chapter 19.

18.4 FINANCING EXPORTS

Now that we have seen how payments can be arranged between importers and exporters, let's examine how exporters can obtain financing while they are awaiting payment from importers. Exhibit 18.6 lists the six methods that we will study, starting with the exporter arranging a bank line of credit, the most popular financing method among U.S. exporters according to surveys. We also cover discounting of a banker's acceptance, another popular method, and end with export factoring. The entire array of financial products, including loans and insurance policies or guarantees that facilitate international sales, is often referred to as "**trade finance**."

Bank Line of Credit

Exporters often finance their accounts receivable from importers with a bank line of credit. The terms of this type of loan agreement allow the borrower to draw up to a prespecified maximum amount during a given time period at a stated interest rate. The line of credit is generally renewable, usually annually. Although the exporter's normal revenue stream is thought to be the primary source of repayment of interest and principal associated with the line of credit, banks may require that the exporter designate assets to serve as collateral. The bank may also require the exporter to purchase insurance designating the bank as beneficiary and covering the value of the exports.

Exhibit 18.6   Methods of Export Financing

1. Bank line of credit
2. Discounting of a banker's acceptance
3. Buyer credit
4. Receivables purchase
5. Limited-recourse financing—forfaiting
6. Export factoring

Banker's Acceptances

In Section 18.3, we saw how the use of a time draft in a documentary credit creates the opportunity for the creation of a banker's acceptance. The bank stamps and signs the draft as accepted, indicating that it will pay the face value of the draft at maturity. The accepted draft can then be discounted either by the issuing bank or in the money market. Given the current and historical importance of this method of export financing, let's examine the creation, use, and pricing of a banker's acceptance in more detail.

There are two types of banker's acceptances. As we have seen, a documentary acceptance is created by the use of a time draft in a documentary credit. A **clean acceptance** is created under a separate credit agreement, without an underlying documentary credit between the exporter and the bank. The bank agrees to accept a certain number of time drafts for various amounts that are submitted by the exporter. The bank then immediately discounts the drafts to provide financing for the exporter. At maturity, the exporter repays the face amounts of the drafts to the bank.

Using a banker's acceptance to finance exports involves two associated costs: the acceptance commission charged by the bank and the discount due to the time value of money. Typical acceptance commissions for medium-sized companies range between 0.75% and 2% of the face value of the draft. When setting the negotiable commission rate, the bank assesses the creditworthiness of the company, any country risk factors that affect the exporter's business, and the bank's competitive position. Whether the exporter or the importer bears the cost of the acceptance commission depends on their respective competitive negotiating strengths.

Eligible Versus Ineligible Banker's Acceptances

In the United States, the Federal Reserve regulates the market for banker's acceptances. A distinction is drawn between eligible and ineligible banker's acceptances. If a bank sells an **eligible banker's acceptance**, it does not have to maintain reserves against the proceeds of the sale. On the other hand, if the bank sells an **ineligible banker's acceptance**, the bank must keep the proceeds of the sale on reserve with the Federal Reserve in a non-interest-bearing account. Clearly, if banks want to use the proceeds of the B/A for future lending, they must sell an eligible B/A.

The eligibility requirements for banker's acceptances are as follows:

1. The tenor, or maturity, of the B/A must not be greater than 180 days, although it is possible to seek an exception.
2. The acceptance must be created within 30 days of the date of shipment of the export goods.
3. The transaction must be between two separate legal entities either within the United States, between a U.S. firm and a foreign firm, or between two foreign firms.
4. The eligible B/A cannot be renewed at maturity unless a legitimate delay occurs in the transaction that is being financed.
5. During the transaction, only one B/A is allowed to be outstanding, although the importer and the exporter can finance the transaction, just not for an overlapping interval of time.
6. The B/A cannot be drawn without recourse to the second party in the transaction. In other words, if the bank that accepts the B/A defaults, the holder of the B/A must have recourse to the drawer of the B/A (that is, the party ultimately responsible for paying the bank).
7. The B/A must not be used to finance trade with any country for which trade is prohibited by the U.S. Department of the Treasury.

Buyer Credit

When expensive capital equipment is being purchased, an exporter sometimes arranges for a financial institution or a syndicate of financial institutions to grant credit to the importer in what is known as a **buyer credit**. By arranging credit for the importer, the exporter is ultimately paid cash up front, and the financial intermediaries bear most of the importer's default risk.

Setting up a typical buyer credit involves several steps. First, the exporter and the importer must agree to a commercial contract for which the importer can pay a down payment of 10% to 20% of the face value of the invoice. Then, the exporter must agree to provide part of the financing to the importer, which allows the bank to establish an analogous agreement with the importer in a commercial contract. The exporter must insure the goods with an export credit insurer and assign the insurance policy to the bank. After delivery of the goods, the bank either purchases the signed promissory notes of the importer from the exporter or grants a direct loan to the importer. In either case, the exporter receives its cash right then. Notice that the buyer credit is a contract between the bank and the importer, so there can be no recourse against the exporter by the bank if the importer defaults. Consequently, the credit of the exporter is unaffected by the transaction.

Buyer credits are much longer-term contracts than banker's acceptances. The maturity can be from 4 to 12 years, and the interest rate in the contract typically floats with a spread over LIBOR. The spread reflects the riskiness of the importer and the bank's competitive position, including its potential to win other business associated with the deal. Other costs of a buyer credit include an arrangement fee and an annual commitment fee of 0.25% to 0.75% on the unused portion of the loan.

Selling Accounts Receivable

If an exporter wants to raise cash, it can sell drafts or invoices related to its accounts receivable to a financial intermediary. The sale could be on a recourse or non-recourse basis. In the United States, it is usually done with recourse to the exporter. That is, the exporter remains financially liable for the payments that the importer is scheduled to make should the importer default in the future. Typically, the accounts receivable must also be insured. European customs are somewhat different. In these markets, a method of export finance developed to allow financing without recourse to the exporter.

Limited-Recourse Financing: Forfaiting

In limited-recourse financing, the financial intermediary purchases the promissory notes of the importer from the exporter at a discount. The term **forfaiting** is often used interchangeably with the term *note purchase* to describe this financing technique.[3] The forfaiter must assess and ultimately bear all the commercial and political risks of the project. Typically, the forfaiter removes the commercial risk by requiring the guarantee of the importer's government or its bank (which may be government owned).

Exporters often use limited-recourse financing, or forfaiting, to finance medium-term projects for importing countries that have substantial commercial and political risk. In such a financing, the exporter receives cash, and the financial intermediary bears the risks without recourse to the exporter unless the exporter fails to fulfill its contractual commitments or commits fraud. If the exporter fulfills its contractual terms, it does not have to worry about getting paid.

Forfaiting describes the practices of European banks and their subsidiaries in various countries such as Germany, Switzerland, Austria, and the United Kingdom. Banks in these countries were requested to finance capital goods exports to eastern European countries and needed to develop expertise in assessing the risks of delayed payments. Although the techniques were

---

[3]The expression derives from the French phrase *forfait et sans garanties*, which means that the legal right of recourse (to the exporter) has been forfeited, or surrendered.

developed to deal with eastern European countries when they were state controlled, they can be applied more broadly.

The Mechanics of Forfaiting

Let's examine several stages of a typical forfaiting transaction.

First, the exporter and the importer agree on a commercial transaction that covers a fixed interval of time. The exporter agrees to ship various amounts of goods to the importer at various points in time in return for periodic payments made against the progress of the project.

Second, the exporter and the forfaiter negotiate financing in which the forfaiter discounts the payments promised by the importer at a fixed discount rate. The exporter receives the discounted amount when the promissory notes of the importer are delivered to the forfaiter. The forfaiter charges the exporter an additional standby fee of 0.1% or 0.125% per month between the time that a commitment is made to the exporter and the time that the exporter delivers the notes. The forfaiter must arrange to have the funds available when the exporter presents the notes, which might require the forfaiter to borrow and deposit the funds in the short-term money market.

Third, the importer signs a sequence of promissory notes obligating it to pay the exporter certain sums, usually every 6 or 12 months, contingent upon the exporter performing certain functions related to the project. The notes are usually guaranteed by the importer's government or bank. In Europe, this irrevocable guarantee is referred to as an **aval**. With this guarantee, all subsequent holders of the note view the importer's government or its bank as the primary obligor to the note.

Fourth, the importer delivers the notes to the exporter. The exporter then endorses the notes "without recourse" and sells them to the forfaiter at the agreed-upon discount.

Fifth, the forfaiter endorses the notes and sells them in the money market. Investors know that the notes are the liabilities of both the importer's bank and the forfaiting institution, but it is the latter whose credit risk is of most concern.

The final step involves investors presenting the notes to the importer or its bank at maturity. If both of these default on the scheduled payments, the investor turns to the forfaiter for payment because the forfaiter provides a guarantee with its endorsement.

Essentially, the forfaiting institution provides two services to the exporter: country risk assessment and financial intermediation in the money market. In its role as country risk assessor, the forfaiter must price the default risks of different countries. In its role as a financial intermediary, the forfaiter packages discounted notes in various maturities for sale to the money market. Because the forfaiter guarantees the notes it sells, the success of the forfaiter ultimately depends on its ability to price the default risks of countries.

Export Factoring

A technique for financing exports that is closely related to forfaiting is export factoring. An **export factor** is a company that performs credit risk investigations and collects funds from the accounts receivable of other firms. In international trade, factors provide both of these services to exporters. They may also provide financing of exporters' accounts receivable.

An example is the International Factors Group (IF-Group) of companies. When dealing with the International Factors Group of companies, one IF-Group member acts as the export factor, which deals with the exporter's country; the second member of the IF-Group, the import factor, handles credit risk cover and collection in the importer's country. *Credit risk cover* is the amount that the factor accepts as a risk that an individual buyer may be financially unable to pay.

Factors perform several services for exporters. The primary service is credit investigation. During the negotiations between an exporter and a foreign importer, the exporter provides information to the factor about the potential importer and the nature of the deal under negotiation. The factor uses its network of local affiliates in various countries, which are usually in partnership with local banks, to perform a credit check on the importer. The factor may also be asked to provide a guarantee to the exporter, which stipulates that if the importer defaults, the factor pays the bill.

Factors give two types of credit approvals: order approvals and revolving credit lines. With an order approval, the factor provides the approval for a specific shipment by the exporter to an importer. With a revolving credit line, the exporter obtains advance approval for what is anticipated to be the maximum shipment to an importer for a given period of time. If the factor buys the receivables of the exporter at a discount, it is the responsibility of the factor to collect payment from the importer. The factor's local affiliate adheres to the standard collection practices in the particular countries involved.

If an exporter is small, a factor can also perform various accounting functions for the exporter. These include providing a monthly statement of cash flows, including all sales to the factor, commissions paid, and other debits and credits. The factor also provides statements of the credit lines outstanding for various importers, notices of disputes with any importers over specific invoices, and reports on outstanding risk exposures classified by importer and whether the factor guarantees the invoice.

Methods of Payment

Factors pay exporters in a variety of ways. One is on a collection basis. Under this arrangement, the exporter gets paid when the factor receives funds from the importer. Exporters also get paid by factors when the importer is declared insolvent or when a specific political event in the contract occurs that prevents the importer from paying.

The exporter may also receive payment on an average collection basis, which reflects the past experience of the factor collecting from an importer. The factor calculates the average number of days that a particular exporter's customers have taken to pay and remits payment to the exporter in the following month, based on that average experience. For example, if an importer pays earlier or later than average, the exporter receives interest from or pays interest to the factor.

Funds can also be remitted on a maturity basis. Under this method, the factor calculates the weighted-average maturity date of all invoices maturing in a particular month, adds a specified number of collection days, and pays the sum of that month's invoices on that date. For example, suppose Invoice A for \$50,000 is due on September 1, Invoice B for \$25,000 is due on September 30, and 10 days are added for collection. Then, the exporter would receive \$75,000 on September 21 because the weighted average of the payments times is

$$(50/75) \times (1\,\text{day}) + (25/75) \times (30\,\text{days}) + 10\,\text{days} = 20.67\,\text{days}$$

Past-due interest is charged to the exporter for any receivable outstanding at the end of the month.

An exporter can arrange for financing either through the factor handling the servicing of the exports or from another financial intermediary, such as a commercial bank. Factors structure their lines of credit somewhat differently than do commercial banks. Factors agree with exporters on a percentage of exports that will be advanced to the exporter, in contrast to the set credit limit established by a commercial bank. The percentage advanced from factors to exporters varies between 70% and 90%, depending on the financial characteristics of the exporter. Exporters like this arrangement because it gives them additional capital to exploit growth opportunities without having to recontract with a financial intermediary. Exporters pay for this growth option, however, because factors charge slightly higher interest rates than banks.

In addition, exporters and factors can involve a second financial intermediary in a **tripartite arrangement**. Under a tripartite arrangement, the factor services the exporter, which assigns any credit balances due from the factor to a financial intermediary that provides funds to the exporter.

Government Sources of Export Financing and Credit Insurance

The governments of countries that have substantial export sectors have developed specialized financial intermediaries to provide export finance, insurance, and possibly subsidies to their exporters. In trade finance, they are known as export credit agencies (ECA). The Export-Import Bank of the United States is discussed in the following section. Other examples include China Eximbank, the Compagnie Française d'Assurance pour le Commerce Extérieur (COFACE), the Japan Bank for International Cooperation, and the Export-Import Bank of India.

Export subsidies serve several purposes: They provide credit to exporters or their customers when private markets fail; they offer loans to exporters at below-market interest rates; and they provide insurance or guarantees at below-market prices. Ultimately, the subsidies are paid by the taxpayers of the country. Governments justify these subsidies by claiming that they are designed to promote employment and to keep their exporters technologically competitive, especially in light of the subsidies that other countries offer their exporters. Some criticize ECAs as providers of corporate welfare.

Ex-Im Bank

The Export–Import Bank of the United States, commonly called **Ex-Im Bank**, is an independent U.S. government corporation involved in financing and facilitating U.S. exports. Ex-Im Bank offers a variety of guarantees and financing for short-term (180 days or less), medium-term (181 days to 5 years), and long-term (more than 5 years) export transactions.

Ex-Im Bank's charter requires that it not compete with private-sector lenders. Rather, it provides export financing that private-sector lenders do not offer. For example, Ex-Im Bank assumes credit risks and country risks that the private sector is unwilling to accept. It also provides working capital guarantees that help exporters with their financing prior to their shipping products abroad. In addition, it provides export credit insurance and offers loan guarantees and direct loans to importers of U.S. products.

The majority of Ex-Im Bank's resources are devoted to long-term financing. Its two major programs involve direct loans and financial guarantees. These programs facilitate the export of construction projects, such as power plants, and the production of other long-term capital goods, such as commercial aircraft and locomotives. Ex-Im Bank's medium-term programs primarily benefit the exporters of agriculture, construction, general aviation, mining, and refining equipment; its short-term programs primarily benefit producers of small manufactured goods, such as consumer goods and replacement parts.

Ex-Im Bank operates under a number of political and economic constraints. Its long-term loans are made directly to foreign borrowers wanting to purchase long-lived U.S. exports. The maturity of the credit cannot be longer than the economic life of the export good. The loans are dollar denominated, and principal and interest must be repaid in dollars. Repayment typically occurs semi-annually, with the first payment due after delivery of the goods or start-up of the project.

Ex-Im Bank typically deals in amounts of $5 million or more, and all Ex-Im Bank loans are required to have "reasonable assurance of repayment." Ex-Im Bank consequently may require a foreign borrower to obtain an unconditional guarantee from its government or an internationally respected bank. Ex-Im Bank also requires a borrower to demonstrate that its project is technically feasible.

PEFCO

Ex-Im Bank often works in cooperation with the **Private Export Funding Corporation (PEFCO)**, which is a private corporation whose mission is to make dollar loans to foreign purchasers of U.S. exports. PEFCO was created in 1971 by a consortium of private banks, an investment bank, and several large industrial firms. PEFCO acts either as a direct lender or as a secondary market buyer of export loans originated by lenders. Its programs cover short-term, medium-term, and long-term export finance. To be eligible for financing by PEFCO, loans must be protected against nonpayment under an appropriate guarantee or insurance policy issued by Ex-Im Bank or by a guarantee issued by the U.S. Small Business Administration. Because PEFCO loans are insured by Ex-Im Bank and because the attorney general of the United States has ruled that Ex-Im Bank's liabilities are general obligations of the United States backed by the full faith and credit of the federal government, PEFCO can borrow at interest rates close to U.S. Treasury rates. However, PEFCO's rates are set higher than those on U.S. Treasury bonds to reflect both the cost of PEFCO's funds and a margin for risk. For example, with typical PEFCO financing, an importer of, say, U.S. airplanes, borrows from a commercial bank at short-term maturities, from Ex-Im Bank at long-term maturities, and from PEFCO at medium-term maturities.

Export Credit Insurance

Although exporters who offer more favorable credit terms to importers are more likely to win business, exporters and their banks want to be repaid. Thus, if the commercial or political risk of a deal is too large, the private credit market may not finance the deal.

Because the extension of credit to importers is often an important part of a deal, governments have stepped in to provide insurance to cover export financing. The insurance protects an exporter or an exporter's bank against losses due to commercial and political risks. Of course, here, again, it is ultimately the taxpayers of the exporter's country who are subsidizing the export market. In the United States, the Ex-Im Bank offers a variety of ways to insure exports. In China, the China Export & Credit Insurance Corp., or **SINOSURE**, was established in 2001 to insure exports. Over the last 10 years, SINOSURE has supported exports, domestic trade, and investments with a total value of more than USD290 billion involving thousands of policyholders and hundreds of medium- and long-term projects.

The Global Financial Crisis and the Trade Finance Gap[4]

During the 2007 to 2010 financial crisis, global trade collapsed as exports fell over 20% from peak (early 2008) to trough (early 2009). The main factor behind the collapse was undoubtedly the global recession accompanying the crisis, which reduced overall demand. Creeping protectionism may also have played a role. Several studies have argued that the collapse was made worse by a fall in the supply of trade finance (the trade finance gap): Stress in the financial system caused financial institutions to cut back on trade finance to exporting firms. Trade finance has proved vulnerable in earlier crises, such as the Southeast Asia crisis in the late 1990s and the Argentina crisis in 2001. Surveys suggest that the supply of trade finance decreased during the recent crisis (although by far less than the volume of trade) and its price (that is, the credit spreads charged) increased, with emerging markets being most affected. In fact, the uncertainty brought about by the crisis likely increased the demand for trade finance, as trading partners resorted to more formal bank-intermediated instruments in order to reduce the higher expected probability of default in open account trades, where exports are fully exposed to the credit risk of the importer.

There are several reasons why the crisis may have caused the supply of trade finance to decrease, including increased uncertainty about the credit risk of counterparties, the liquidity crisis causing banks to cut trade finance credit lines, which are short term in nature, and the moral suasion of authorities on banks to lend their funds domestically. Showing that there is an actual decrease in the supply of trade finance in the face of large demand shocks is actually quite difficult to do. Yet, a number of careful academic studies strongly suggest the supply of trade credit was indeed a critical factor during the crisis. Chor and Manova (2010) show that countries with tighter credit conditions suffered a larger decline in exports to the United States during the crisis, and these effects were most apparent in sectors that had

---

[4]See Wynne (2009) and Chauffour and Farole (2009) for more details.

the least access to trade credit from trade partners, controlling for other factors. Paravisini et al. (2010) use detailed data from Peru, allowing them to compare firms exporting the same product to the same destination but borrowing from different banks. Banks that relied heavily on foreign currency–denominated loans reduced the supply of credit, causing their client firms to export less (accounting for 15% of the reduction in exports) and some firms to exit certain product–destination markets.

In any case, governments and international organizations were keenly aware of the potentially dire consequences of a collapse in trade finance and intervened through a variety of channels. Most notably, the London summit of the G20 in April 2009 offered $250 billion in support for trade finance through export credit and investment agencies and multilateral development banks. The International Finance Corporation (IFC) doubled its Global Trade Finance Program (which provides guarantees) and offered substantial additional liquidity support. Many individual countries took unilateral actions, such as Norway's government pumping $7.2 billion into its cash-strapped export credit institution, Eksportfinans. It seems that governments have learned the lesson of the Great Depression in the 1930s, when protectionist trade policy exacerbated the downturn.

POINT–COUNTERPOINT

On Bicycles and Countertrade

Ante and Freedy are in Vienna, Austria, visiting their Aunt Helga. After the collapse of the former Soviet Union, Helga realized that the central European and eastern European regions would see a big increase in international trade. Along with German and English, Helga had learned Polish and Russian, which allowed her to move comfortably around the region as a consultant, setting up trading operations for corporations in these emerging markets.

Helga wanted some advice from Ante and Freedy: "I've gotten a call from a Ukrainian bicycle manufacturer that wants to import some gears from the Italian company Campagnolo. I called Campagnolo, and they said they don't export to such companies unless the importer gets a documentary credit from a major international bank. I checked with the Ukrainians, and they said their banks charge too much for a D/C. Do you have any suggestions?"

Ante said, "Yeah, let them pay cash in advance. That'll make Campagnolo happy."

Freedy seized the moment to squash his brother. "Oh sure, these Ukrainians have mountains of hard currency sitting around, waiting to be paid to their shareholders, so the bicycle company will just dip into its massive stockpile of cash and buy the gears. Silly me!"

Ante felt embarrassed when he realized how impractical his suggestion was, but he tried again, "Okay, cash in advance is impractical, and a D/C is too expensive. Maybe the Italians will accept a documentary collection."

Helga interjected, "I've already been down that route with Campagnolo's CFO, and he said no dice. He thinks the credit risk is too high. I think these Ukrainian bikes are really high quality. There has got to be another way to do this deal."

Of course, Suttle Trooth was traveling with his cousins, and he had been listening in. Suttle offered the following insight: "Helga, there is always another way. Why don't you contact a major importer of bicycles here in Vienna or up in Berlin, and get them to look at the Ukrainian bikes? If they like the quality, they can contract with the Ukrainians to buy the bicycles, but part of the contract will pay Campagnolo for the gears that will be exported to the Ukraine. In fact, a major bicycle distributor probably even has an open account with Campagnolo. Gears will go to the Ukraine, bikes will go to Berlin, and Campagnolo will increase its accounts receivable from the Berlin bike distributor. It's easy." Helga was impressed with Suttle's assessment of the situation. She asked, "Does that transaction have a name?"

Suttle replied, "Yes, it's a form of countertrade."

Countertrade emerged in the 1960s as a way to facilitate East–West trade, and its complexity continues to evolve to this day. Countertrade makes it possible for exporters and importers to exchange goods and services without necessarily having to use money as a medium of exchange. Countertrade does not describe one particular type of international transaction, however, but a related set of activities that encompasses various types of barter. It can occur between two or more parties, involve one or more contracts, and use money or not.

The United Nations estimates that at least 25% of all international trade involves some form of countertrade. The **Global Offset and Countertrade Association (GOCA)** holds semi-annual conferences and supports a Web site (www.globaloffset.org) devoted to the practice. Some representative member companies of the GOCA include Boeing, Cisco Systems, Embraer, General Dynamics, General Electric, Motorola, and Raytheon.

One quintessential example of an early countertrade involved PepsiCo, which began operating in the Soviet Union in 1974. PepsiCo agreed to license several Soviet-owned bottling plants and to supply them with cola concentrate. In return for its concentrate, PepsiCo agreed to become the exclusive importer to the United States of the Soviet Union's Stolichnaya vodka.

Exhibit 18.7 lists the specific types of countertrade, of which there are two broad categories (see Hammond, 1990). Within each category are three subcategories. The first category contains transactions that are designed to avoid the use of money. These include barter, clearing arrangements, and switch trading. The second category of transactions uses money or credit and is designed to impose commitments on the exporter. These transactions include buybacks, counterpurchases, and offsets. We examine each of the six types of countertrade in turn.

Transactions Without Money

Barter and Clearing Arrangements

International barter involves the transfer of goods or services from a party in one country to a party in another country in return for some other good or service. Trade is balanced in the sense that the value of what is being exported equals the value of what is being imported. Although money is not involved, money may be the numeraire that determines the values of the goods. However, the difficulty in valuing various goods and the disagreements that can ensue about their equivalence have led to the decline of barter as an instrument of international trade.

Clearing arrangements allow barter to be conducted on credit. Under a clearing arrangement, each of the two parties to a transaction agrees to import a certain value of goods and services from the other. A clearing account is established, and imports and exports are debited and credited over time. If the contract has a specified end date, the two parties can settle any nonzero, residual balance with a final shipment of goods or a money payment at the end of the specified period.

Exhibit 18.7 Types of Countertrade

Trades Without Money	Trades Involving Money or Credit
Barter	Buybacks
Clearing arrangements	Counterpurchases
Switch trading	Offsets

Switch Trading

Switch trading involves a third party, a switch trader, who facilitates the eventual clearing of an imbalance of trade between two partners to a bilateral clearing arrangement. Often, governments are involved in the creation of a clearing arrangement. If one of the countries generates an imbalance of trade, and no hard currency is available to offset the imbalance, it may be sold at a discount to a switch trader, who uses the account to purchase goods in the country that has run the trade balance deficit. The switch trader then resells the goods on world markets.

For example, Brazil and Romania might agree to exchange Brazilian coffee for Romanian fertilizer during the coming year, with the intention of balancing trade by year end. If the value of Romania's coffee imports exceeds the value of its fertilizer exports, a switch trader could purchase the clearing balance from Brazil with hard currency. The switch trader would then have the right to purchase other Romanian goods with the clearing balance, and these goods would be exported to the world market.

Some critics of switch trading note that there is no guarantee that Romania would not be dumping its manufactured goods, where *dumping* is defined as selling goods internationally for less than they cost to produce. If dumping is occurring, though, it is being done indirectly by a third party, the switch trader, and not directly by the manufacturer. Other critics note that by failing to establish a foreign distribution network, countries such as Romania, in our example, never learn how to make their products more attractive to foreign buyers.

Countertrade Involving Money or Credit

Buybacks

A **buyback** involves an agreement in which an exporter of physical capital agrees to accept payment in the form of the output of a plant that the exporter helps to construct and equip in a foreign country. There are three varieties of buybacks. In one, the exporter receives products directly from the factory that was constructed, and these products may be similar to what the exporter also produces. The exporter must be aware that the increased supply of the foreign product could drive down its world price, with adverse consequences on the exporter's other markets. This is what PepsiCo realized would happen with its deal in the Soviet Union if it accepted cola produced in the Soviet Union. Hence, the company bought back vodka instead. In another variety of buyback, the exporter receives resultant products that are unrelated to the exporter's industry. Here the problem is that the exporter has less ability to assess the value of the products and no marketing network. In a third type of buyback, the exporter receives a mix of resultant products and other products of the country.

A famous example of a buyback is the agreement by several western European countries to supply the Soviet Union with the pipe, compressors, controls, and other equipment necessary to build a natural gas pipeline from the Soviet Union to western Europe. The payment for the pipeline was natural gas delivered through the pipeline to western Europe over several years.

Counterpurchases

A **counterpurchase** is similar to a buyback, except the exporter purchases totally non-resultant products from the importer. For example, in 2010, Venezuela and Belarus entered into a bilateral country deal in which billions of dollars of oil and natural gas would be sent from Venezuela to Belarus in future years and Belarus would in turn build public housing complexes and a factory to manufacture tractors and trucks in Venezuela.

Offsets

An **offset** is a requirement of an importing country that the price of its imports be offset in some way by the exporter. Offsets are common in contracts for weapons and contracts for other large expenditures, such as power-generating facilities. The exporter agrees to purchase goods in the importer's country, to increase its imports from that country, to transfer technology to the country, or to conduct additional direct foreign investment in the country in return for setting up the facility. For example, in a multiyear contract, signed in 2004, the Lockheed Martin Corporation of Fort Worth, Texas entered into an offset trade with the United Arab Emirates (UAE), which purchased 80 F16 fighter planes called Desert Falcons—a deal worth $6.4 billion. The offset included Lockheed agreeing to invest $160 million in a gas pipeline running from Qatar to UAE and then on to Pakistan.

The set of issues involved in various forms of countertrade has expanded to the point where some people now prefer to talk in terms of **compensatory trade**, or "mandated reciprocity." For example, the Web site for the Beijing Investment Guide (www.chinavista.com/beijing/invest/invest-types.html) describes compensatory trade in the following way:

> Compensatory trade enterprises are ones in which overseas partners provide equipment and technology and are bound to purchase a certain quantity of the finished products for exportation. Purchase of the equipment and technology can be made on the installment plan. Agreed upon negotiation by both parties of the compensatory trade enterprises, the loans for purchasing and importing the equipment and technology can be paid back in kind with other products as well as the finished equipment and technology as approved of when forming the compensatory trade enterprises.

Clearly, this is countertrade, and as such, parties involved in these complex international trade deals must understand that they may be entering into a long-term deal that will involve many future rounds of not only trade but additional negotiations.

18.6 SUMMARY

This chapter examines some of the institutional details related to how international trade is conducted and financed. The main points in the chapter are as follows:

1. The shipping documents of international trade include bills of lading, commercial invoices, packing lists, insurance certificates, consular invoices, and certificates of analysis.
2. A straight bill of lading instructs a common carrier to deliver merchandise to a designated party, known as the consignee. An order bill of lading transfers the title of goods. An on-board bill of lading indicates that goods have been placed on a particular vessel for shipment, whereas a received-for-shipment bill of lading indicates only that the merchandise is at the dock awaiting transport. A clean bill of lading indicates that a carrier believes the merchandise in question was received in good condition, whereas a foul bill of lading indicates that a carrier's initial inspection of the merchandise in question uncovered some damage before the merchandise was received for shipment.
3. Exporters issue to importers commercial invoices that provide a description of the merchandise, including the unit prices of the items, the number of

items shipped, and the financial terms of the sale, including the amount due from the buyer and any charges to the buyer arising from insurance and shipping. A packing list indicates how the specific goods are stored in various containers.
4. A firm that does a substantial amount of exporting can purchase open, or floating, insurance policies that automatically cover all of the firm's exports. This eliminates the need for the exporter to arrange insurance coverage for each order.
5. A consular invoice, filled out by an exporter in consultation with the consulate of the importing country, provides information to customs officials that prevents false declarations of the value of the merchandise.
6. Certificates of analysis are sometimes required by documentary credits to assure an importer that a shipment meets certain standards of purity, weight, sanitation, or other measurable characteristics.
7. The different methods of payment available for an importer include cash in advance, open account, documentary collections, and documentary credits.
8. Cash in advance requires an importer to pay an exporter before the goods in question are shipped.

The importer must finance the purchase of the goods and must bear the risk that the goods will not be exactly what is ordered.

9. An open account arrangement allows an importer to order goods and pay an invoiced amount at some time in the future. The exporter extends trade credit to the importer, which finances the importer's purchase.

10. A documentary collection is an instrument that allows an exporter to retain control of the goods until the importer has paid for them or is legally bound to pay for them and that involves a bank in the collection process.

11. With a documentary credit, also called a letter of credit, banks stand between the importer and the exporter, and the exporter must assess the credit risk of the international banks. Because the involvement of banks in the transaction is extensive, the documentary credit is the most expensive of the methods of payment, but a confirmed irrevocable documentary credit is also the safest for the exporter.

12. A banker's acceptance is a document, tradable in financial markets, that is created when a bank stamps and signs a time draft indicating that the bank will pay the face value of a draft at maturity.

13. Exporters can obtain financing through a bank line of credit, through the discounting of a banker's acceptance, by setting up a buyer credit, by arranging a receivables purchase, from limited-recourse financing, and through export factoring.

14. Major exporting countries have export–import banks that offer a variety of programs that subsidize the exports of their countries. The subsidies include providing credit either directly to an exporter or its customers when the private market fails to do so, loans at below-market interest rates, and credit insurance or guarantees at below-market prices.

15. Countertrade refers to various trade agreements that involve contractual links between exports of a good or service and imports of a good or service. The various forms of countertrade include barter, clearing arrangements, switch trading, buybacks, counterpurchases, and offsets.

QUESTIONS

1. What is the fundamental financing problem in international trade?
2. What is a bill of lading? Explain the difference between a straight bill of lading and an order bill of lading.
3. What is the difference between a clean bill of lading and a foul bill of lading?
4. What are the purposes of a commercial invoice and a packing list?
5. What do the INCOTERMS acronyms FOB, FAS, CFR, and CIF mean?
6. How can an exporter insure against the loss of value of goods while they are being shipped internationally?
7. Why might a country require an exporter to acquire a consular invoice in order to clear the customs of an importing country?
8. Why would a certificate of analysis be important for shipping goods internationally?
9. What are four different methods by which an importer can pay an exporter? List them in increasing order of risk to the exporter.
10. True or false: In a documentary collection, the remitting bank is the agent of the importer.
11. What is the difference between a documents against payment collection and a documents against acceptance collection?

12. How is a trade acceptance created? Whose liability is it? Can it be sold in the international money market?
13. What is meant by a document discrepancy? How might one arise? How can it be resolved?
14. How is a documentary credit created, and what are its advantages to exporters and importers?
15. What is a confirmed documentary credit? Why would an exporter demand a confirmed, irrevocable documentary credit? What are the costs of using a documentary credit?
16. What is the most straightforward way for an exporter to finance its accounts receivable?
17. What is a banker's acceptance? How is one created? Whose liability is it?
18. What is the difference between an eligible and an ineligible banker's acceptance, and what are the eligibility requirements?
19. How is a buyer credit arranged?
20. What is forfaiting? How does it work? Why did it arise?
21. What is export factoring? What services does a factor perform for an exporter?
22. What are the differences between receiving payment on a collection basis, on an average collection basis, and on a maturity basis?

23. How does an export–import bank work? Who ultimately pays for the services of an export–import bank?
24. What are the major programs of the U.S. Ex-Im Bank?
25. What are the six different types of countertrade? Describe them.
26. How would a clearing arrangement work between the Ukraine and Lithuania, whereby the Ukraine exports grain and Lithuania exports shoes?
27. There are major natural resource deposits in the People's Republic of China (PRC). How might a buyback arrangement work in which the PRC purchases earthmoving equipment from the Japanese firm Komatsu?
28. The Indonesian government is concerned that it may contribute to the country's balance-of-trade deficit if it follows through with plans to import a large order of trucks from Germany that will be used to develop Indonesian timber resources. How might the Indonesian government use a counterpurchase to its advantage?
29. Web Question: Go to the Trade Finance magazine Web site at www.tradefinancemagazine.com and report on the latest innovations in trade finance.
30. Web Question: Visit the following Web site: www.pitc.gov.ph/contracts/qinetiq.pdf. What type of international trade is described in this contract? What is the rationale for such a contract?

BIBLIOGRAPHY

Chauffour, Jean-Pierre, and Thomas Farole, 2009, "Trade Finance in Crisis: Market Adjustment or Market Failure," manuscript, The World Bank.

Chor, Davin, and Kalina Manova, 2010, "On the Cliff and Back? Credit Conditions and International Trade During the Financial Crisis," manuscript, Singapore Management University.

Greif, Avner, 1993, "Contract Enforceability and Economic Institutions in Early Trade: The Maghribi Traders' Coalition," *American Economic Review* 83, pp. 525–548.

Hammond, Grant T., 1990, *Countertrade, Offsets, and Barter in International Political Economy*, London: Pinter.

International Chamber of Commerce, 2011, *INCOTERMS 2010*, ICC Publication No. 715.

Paravisini, Daniel, Veronica Rappoport, Philipp Schnabl, and Daniel Wolfenzon, 2010, "Dissecting the Effect of Credit Supply on Trade: Evidence from Matched Credit-Export Data," manuscript, Columbia Business School.

Wynne, Mark A., 2009, "The Financial Crisis, Trade Finance, and the Collapse of World Trade," working paper, Federal Reserve Bank of Dallas.

Chapter 19

Managing Net Working Capital

*T*his chapter discusses the management of short-term assets and liabilities within a multi-national corporation. The assets consist of cash, marketable securities, inventories, and accounts receivable. The liabilities consist of short-term debt and accounts payable. We begin by discussing net working capital, an investment that a firm must manage well to ensure its future profitability. The next topic is international cash management, which is followed by a discussion about how foreign affiliates transfer funds to their parent corporations.

When related affiliates buy goods and services from each other, the prices charged are called *transfer prices*. This chapter explores how different transfer pricing policies can shift a firm's income and income tax burdens around the world and how governments attempt to regulate these shifts. The effect of transfer pricing policies on managerial incentives is also considered. Governments watch transfer prices very closely as large tax payments can be shifted across jurisdictions. For example, in September 2006, GlaxoSmithKline (GSK), the U.K. headquartered global pharmaceutical firm, agreed to settle a transfer pricing dispute with the U.S. Internal Revenue Service (IRS) by paying $3.1 billion in back taxes, interest, and fines. The IRS argued that GSK charged its American subsidiary too much for Zantac, the blockbuster ulcer treatment drug, resulting in lower profitability for the American subsidiary and lower taxes for the IRS.

We also address techniques for mitigating problems associated with blocked funds. Finally, we discuss the management of a firm's accounts receivable and its inventories in an international environment.

19.1 THE PURPOSE OF NET WORKING CAPITAL

Every corporation maintains a stock of current assets and current liabilities to buffer the inflows and outflows of cash generated by the firm's business. **Working capital**, or current assets, is the collection of cash, marketable securities, accounts receivable, and inventories held by a firm at any point in time. By subtracting the value of a firm's current liabilities, which are the corporation's short-term debts and its accounts payable, from its stock of working capital, we arrive at its **net working capital**:

$$\text{Net working capital} = \text{Cash} + \text{Marketable securities} + \text{Accounts receivable} \\ + \text{Inventories} - \text{Short-term debt} - \text{Accounts payable}$$

642

If a firm can be managed with a smaller stock of net working capital, cash can be paid to shareholders. Thus, one goal of management is to run a corporation efficiently in order to minimize the need for net working capital.

Increases in net working capital are investments that a firm makes to produce cash in the future. This is perhaps most easily understood when you think about inventories.

Inventories as Assets

The stock of a firm's inventory includes raw materials, goods that represent work-in-progress, and finished goods. Raw materials and work-in-progress are necessary because all goods take time to produce. Finished goods inventories are necessary because demand is stochastic, and orders are placed randomly by customers.

Firms typically find that costs of production are lower if production is smoothed over time. If a firm tries to match its production to its demand, the firm will have to pay its workers overtime wages and ask its suppliers to expedite shipments when demand is high, both of which increase costs. If a firm does not meet orders, it will incur backlog costs because frustrated customers will be less likely to do business with the firm in the future. Hence, stockpiling inventory can help minimize the cost of production and prevent the loss of future sales, both of which increase profitability. Thus, increasing a firm's inventory is as much of an investment as if the firm were purchasing a new machine to enhance its production and future profits. Of course, as with all other investments, management must decide on the appropriate level of inventories to allow the right rate of return to the capital that is invested in the inventories. We address this issue later in the chapter.

Other Current Assets

Increases in cash, marketable securities, and accounts receivable should also be viewed as investments the firm is making in the operation of its business. For example, suppose Reagon Optical Products sells contact lenses to a pharmacy on credit. This increases Reagon's accounts receivable because the value of the sale, which increases accounts receivable, is worth more than the decrease in Reagon's inventory. Hence, Reagon's net working capital increases. However, the actual revenue from the sale will only be collected in the future, which means that Reagon is making an investment. For example, Reagon could have induced its customer to pay today by lowering the price of the contact lenses. The fact that the transaction takes place on credit indicates that Reagon's long-run profitability is enhanced by selling the contact lenses at the higher price and financing the sale with an extension of credit to the buyer.

Short-Term Liabilities

Accounts payable and other short-term borrowings generate resources and conserve cash. If a firm needs additional raw materials, and it uses internally generated cash to buy them, no additional funds are needed from outside investors. Hence, there is no change in net working capital because the value of the raw materials, or additional inventory, is equal to the value of the cash paid for them.

Likewise, if a firm takes out a short-term bank loan to purchase inventory, it does not have to tap the long-term debt market or the equity market. Again, however, the firm's net working capital does not change because the increase in its inventory of raw materials matches the increase in its short-term liabilities.

Another way a company can obtain goods for its inventory without using the assets of the firm is to buy on trade credit from its suppliers. This action generates an account payable. Once again, inventories rise, but the firm's *net* working capital has not changed because the increase in working capital is offset by a corresponding increase in the firm's short-term liabilities.

Of course, as noted earlier, firms try to hold enough net working capital to smooth out the production–sales cycle. This implies that there is an optimal amount of net working capital a firm should have on hand. Having excessive cash or short-term assets is costly if the investments earn a lower rate of return than shareholders could earn. Also, excessive cash can lead to severe agency problems between the shareholders and the managers, which is also very costly. Now that we've explored the importance of managing net working capital, let's look at how to manage net working capital in an international context.

19.2 INTERNATIONAL CASH MANAGEMENT

The goals of an international money manager of a multinational corporation are (1) to establish control over the cash resources of the organization, (2) to invest excess short-term funds in an optimal way, and (3) to obtain short-term financing at the lowest cost. Establishing control over the cash resources of an organization necessitates creating a reporting system that provides timely and accurate information. When the information is available, the international cash manager can try to improve upon the cash disbursements to and collections from its foreign affiliates. By synchronizing the flows of funds, the international cash manager can lower the cost of moving funds among them. These goals are no different than those of a purely domestic cash manager who transfers money from one account to another (or from one subsidiary to another) so that the firm has an optimal amount of working capital. However, there are constraints on international cash management that domestic managers do not face.

Constraints on International Cash Management

An international cash manager of a multinational corporation often encounters constraints that do not arise in a purely domestic corporation. These constraints include government restrictions on the transfers of funds, taxes that depend on the type of fund transfer, transaction costs in the foreign exchange market, and problems maintaining the liquidity of all foreign affiliates.

We first discussed blocked funds in Chapter 18. **Blocked funds** arise when the government of a foreign country makes the nation's currency completely inconvertible. Foreign exchange controls that impose unattractive foreign exchange rates can also constrain a firm. Host countries also impose taxes on the repatriation of funds from a foreign affiliate to its parent. These taxes often differ, depending on whether the transfer of funds consists of dividends, service fees, or royalty payments. Such taxes can have a constraining effect on a firm's international cash management as well.

Of course, transaction costs are incurred whenever funds are converted from one currency into another. These transaction costs include the fees charged by banks as well as the bid–ask spread that banks use to generate profits, the loss of interest that occurs during the time that funds are withdrawn from one bank and are deposited in another bank, and other transaction fees, such as cable charges. Chapter 2 notes that these transaction costs are quite small for transactions involving the major currencies of the world. Even if transaction costs are a small percentage, too frequent movement back and forth between currencies unnecessarily increases transaction costs. Also, for minor currencies, the transaction costs are larger. The final constraint on an international cash manager is the need to ensure that each of the firm's foreign affiliates maintains an adequate amount of cash to make it liquid enough to function efficiently.

Cash Management with a Centralized Pool

Economists have long noted that short-term cash and liquid assets satisfy the needs of firms that arise from both the transactions and precautionary demands for money. The **transactions**

demand for money arises because a firm realizes that it has some expenditure that will be incurred in the near future. The **precautionary demand for money** arises because a firm may need to purchase something due to an unanticipated change in its environment.

Just as an inventory of finished goods buffers the production process and lowers costs, an inventory of cash provides a buffer that lowers the costs of doing business due to the mismatch between inflows and outflows of funds. Of course, holding cash balances and short-term, highly marketable securities has costs. The rates of return on these assets are lower than the rates of return on longer-term assets precisely because these assets are liquid. Holding cash provides flexibility, but the cost of this flexibility is the forgone interest that could have been earned by holding longer-term, less liquid assets.

By centralizing the management of short-term cash balances of its foreign affiliates, a multinational corporation (MNC) can reduce the transaction costs incurred in moving cash around the world, and it can minimize the overall amount of cash needed by the organization. The savings in transaction costs arise from utilizing a multilateral netting system. The savings in the overall level of cash balances arise from exploiting the stochastic nature of the precautionary demand for money by centralizing the holdings of cash. We now consider these issues in detail.

Short-Term Cash Planning

To illustrate the management of a firm's centralized cash pool, consider an MNC that has European affiliates operating in Great Britain, Denmark, the Netherlands, and Spain. Exhibit 19.1 presents the daily cash reports of each European affiliate, as they might be transmitted to the company's central cash pool located, say, in Geneva, Switzerland. At the

Exhibit 19.1 Daily Cash Reports of an MNC's European Affiliates (in thousands of euros)

Date: October 21, 2011
British Affiliate
Current Cash Position: +200

Five-Day Forecasts

Day	Receive	Pay	Net
+1	200	100	100
+2	150	500	−350
+3	100	150	−50
+4	200	100	100
+5	150	100	50
Net for period			−150

Date: October 21, 2011
Danish Affiliate
Current Cash Position: −100

Five-Day Forecasts

Day	Receive	Pay	Net
+1	300	200	100
+2	400	400	0
+3	600	250	350
+4	100	300	−200
+5	200	300	−100
Net for period			150

Date: October 21, 2011
Dutch Affiliate
Current Cash Position: +250

Five-Day Forecasts

Day	Receive	Pay	Net
+1	450	700	−250
+2	400	100	300
+3	200	700	−500
+4	450	200	250
+5	400	300	100
Net for period			−100

Date: October 21, 2011
Spanish Affiliate
Current Cash Position: +150

Five-Day Forecasts

Day	Receive	Pay	Net
+1	600	100	500
+2	500	100	400
+3	400	100	300
+4	200	700	−500
+5	100	200	−100
Net for period			600

Note: The cash flows for each of the affiliates are converted into euros at current exchange rates.

Exhibit 19.2 Consolidated Daily Cash Reports of an MNC's European Affiliates (in thousands of euros)

	Daily Cash Balances, October 21, 2011		
	Closing Balance	**Minimum-Desired Balance**	**Surplus (Deficit) Cash Balance**
British	200	100	100
Danish	−100	200	−300
Dutch	250	300	−50
Spanish	150	250	−100
European Total			−350

Notes: The "closing balance" is taken from Exhibit 19.1. The "minimum-desired balance" is typically set by the parent company in consultation with the management of the local affiliate. The "surplus (deficit) cash balance" represents the difference between the "closing balance" and the "minimum-desired balance."

close of business each day, the local treasurer of each affiliate would e-mail the information to the central office in Geneva. The reports are denominated in a single currency—in this case, the euro. The reports indicate that the British affiliate has €200,000 on hand, which it could spend immediately without drawing on its short-term line of credit. The Danish affiliate has borrowed €100,000, either from the central pool or from a bank. The Dutch and Spanish affiliates have cash balances of €250,000 and €150,000, respectively.

Exhibit 19.2 relates each European affiliate's existing cash balances to its previously agreed-upon, desired cash position, which is the minimum amount of cash the affiliate needs on a daily basis. Exhibit 19.2 also calculates the MNC's overall cash surplus or deficit. From Exhibit 19.2, we learn that the British affiliate's current cash balance of €200,000 is €100,000 over its minimum desired cash balance. The Danish affiliate's desired cash balance is €200,000, and it is €300,000 below this level because it previously borrowed €100,000. The Dutch affiliate is €50,000 below its desired cash balance of €300,000. Finally, the Spanish affiliate's cash balance of €150,000 places it €100,000 below its desired level. Overall, across the four European affiliates, there is a deficit of €350,000.

Managing Surpluses and Deficits

Once the information in Exhibits 19.1 and 19.2 is collected, the central office must decide how to invest any surpluses and how to cover any deficits. Excess cash can be invested in a variety of short-term money market instruments, and short-term borrowing can be done through banks or in the commercial paper market. In either case, the firm faces several choices. Most important are the currency of denomination and the maturity of the investment or the debt. The appropriate choices depend on the interest rates in different currencies, the expectations of the financial manager about the rates of appreciation and depreciation of one currency relative to another, the amount of foreign exchange risk that the organization is willing to bear, and the manager's forecasts of future short-term cash needs of the different affiliates.

For example, suppose the central office thought that a weakening of the Danish krone relative to the euro was imminent. If nominal interest differentials (the Danish krone rate minus the euro rate) did not adequately reflect their expected rate of depreciation of the krone, the central office could instruct the Danish affiliate to borrow additional kroner by drawing on its line of credit. An alternative way of discussing this situation recognizes that the minimum desired balance expressed in Exhibit 19.2 should be adjusted downward in light of the interest rates and the expectations of depreciation. Having the Danish affiliate borrow kroner provides funds to be invested. These extra kroner would be invested in the euro and other currencies that were expected to strengthen relative to the krone.

Forecasts of Cash Flows

Exhibit 19.1 provides information on the forecasted cash receipts and cash disbursements each affiliate expects to have over the following 5 days. The managers of each affiliate generate daily 5-day rolling forecasts of their cash flow needs and share this information with the central office. These 5-day forecasts help the central office improve profitability in at least three ways.

First, the forecasts can be checked for accuracy. The more accurate the forecasts, the better the firm can manage its resources. Hence, helping the affiliates to improve their forecasts should improve the operating cash needs of each affiliate by reducing its precautionary cash balances.

Second, the 5-day forecasts allow the central office to assess the short-term needs of each affiliate in light of the transaction costs related to exchanging different currencies and the interest rates and possible changes in exchange rates that may occur. For example, Exhibit 19.1 shows that the British affiliate is currently sitting on a lot of cash and is forecasting an inflow on day 1, but it has a large payment due on day 3. On net, over the 5 days, it expects to have to borrow. Given the costs of converting between pounds and euros and the losses possible due to adverse currency movements, it probably does not make sense to have the British affiliate transfer funds out of the country.

The third use of the 5-day forecasts is to generate overall forecasts of the net cash flows of the European affiliates. This provides the central office with information that can be used to assess the maturity and currency of denomination of investments and short-term borrowing. For example, Exhibit 19.3 aggregates the information from Exhibit 19.1 and demonstrates that the four European affiliates are forecasting positive cash flows for the next 3 days, but the cash flow forecasts are negative on days 4 and 5. Hence, this is not an appropriate time to place surplus funds in an investment with a 1-week maturity. Instead, the short-term surpluses should be invested in overnight interest-bearing accounts in anticipation of the need for funds later in the week.

Multilateral Netting Systems

Coordinating the worldwide production and distribution of the many products produced in tandem by the firm's affiliates makes for a large volume of transactions and a heavy flow of funds between them. Of course, the greater the flow of funds, the larger the transaction costs. Although the transaction costs differ with the particular country, it is estimated that they vary between 0.25% and 1.5% of the amount of funds transferred. Thus, there is an incentive for the MNC to avoid fund transfers between affiliates.

The firm can save money on these transactions by using a **multilateral netting system**, just like the multilateral netting described in Chapter 2. Multilateral netting extends the concept of bilateral netting to several affiliated parties with commensurate cost savings.

Exhibit 19.3 Consolidated 5-Day Cash Forecasts of an MNC's European Affiliates (in thousands of euros)

	British	Danish	Dutch	Spanish	Total
Day 1	100	100	−250	500	450
Day 2	−350	0	300	400	350
Day 3	−50	350	−500	300	100
Day 4	100	−200	250	−500	−350
Day 5	50	−100	100	−100	−50
5-day Total	−150	150	−100	600	500

Notes: The forecasts are taken from Exhibit 19.1. The 5-day total is the sum of the individual forecasts.

Exhibit 19.4 The Cash Flows of an MNC's Affiliates Before Multilateral Netting (in thousands of euros)

Receiving Affiliate	Paying Affiliate				Total Receipts	Net Receipts (Payments)
	British	**Dutch**	**Spanish**	**Danish**		
British	—	3,000	7,000	4,000	14,000	5,000
Dutch	1,000	—	3,000	3,000	7,000	(3,000)
Spanish	5,000	6,000	—	2,000	13,000	(1,000)
Danish	3,000	1,000	4,000	—	8,000	(1,000)
Total Payments	9,000	10,000	14,000	9,000	42,000	—

Exhibit 19.4 presents a typical month's cumulative cash flows before any multilateral netting for the European affiliates of a multinational corporation. Without multilateral netting, each of the affiliates would make three payments, and each would accept three receipts. For example, the Spanish affiliate owes €4,000,000 to the Danish affiliate, €7,000,000 to the British affiliate, and €3,000,000 to the Dutch affiliate. In turn, the Spanish affiliate has booked receivables of €2,000,000 from the Danish affiliate and is owed €5,000,000 from the British affiliate and €6,000,000 from the Dutch affiliate. If the Spanish affiliate made all these payments and accepted all the receipts, there would be €14,000,000 of payments and €13,000,000 of receipts. Under bilateral netting, the Spanish affiliate sends €2,000,000 (€7,000,000 − €5,000,000) to the British affiliate, and the outstanding debts are cancelled. Because the gross debt of €12,000,000 is not transferred, the cost saving is the transaction costs on €10,000,000.

Multilateral netting can do even better. By examining the intracompany payment matrix in Exhibit 19.4, we see that the British affiliate has a net receipt of €5,000,000, whereas the other three European affiliates have net payments. The Dutch affiliate owes a net amount of €3,000,000, and the Danish and Spanish affiliates owe a net amount of €1,000,000. Transactions costs are minimized by having each of the European affiliates make just one net payment to the British affiliate. This is summarized in Exhibit 19.5.

Notice in Exhibit 19.4 that there would be €42,000,000 of total transactions between the four affiliates if all affiliates made all their gross payments. If transaction costs in the foreign exchange market average 0.4%, total transaction costs in this example, without multilateral netting, would be

$$0.004 \times €42,000,000 = €168,400$$

Exhibit 19.5 Cash Flows After Multilateral Netting (in thousands of euros)

However, with the multilateral netting shown in Exhibit 19.5, the total payment between the affiliates is reduced to €5,000,000, which generates transaction costs of only

$$0.004 \times €5,000,000 = €20,000$$

This is a significant savings for the company. In addition, many MNCs facilitate the process of multilateral netting by establishing a foreign subsidiary to serve as a netting center in a country with minimal foreign exchange controls. It is also possible to outsource the netting (and other cash management services) to a bank or other third party. Not surprisingly, Internet-based netting services have also appeared recently.

Using a Centralized Cash Management System to Reduce Precautionary Cash Demands

Centralized cash management also allows the MNC to exploit differences in the precautionary demands for money in their affiliates that arise from the uncertain timing of future cash inflows and outflows. Uncertainty in the demand for future cash is described with a probability distribution. Suppose the affiliates' cash demands are normally distributed. Then, we know that if an affiliate holds cash balances that exceed the mean of the probability distribution by 2 standard deviations, there is slightly less than a 2.5% probability that the affiliate's demand for cash will exceed its available cash.

Let's again consider the British, Danish, Dutch, and Spanish affiliates of the MNC in the multilateral netting example. If each affiliate describes its precautionary demand for cash with a probability distribution, the overall organization can reduce the total demand for cash while still satisfying the demands of each affiliate by exploiting the fact that the demands for cash from the different affiliates will not be perfectly correlated in the future.

To be concrete, suppose that if each affiliate were to operate independently, each would desire to hold cash balances equal to its mean demand for cash plus two standard deviations of the distribution. Exhibit 19.6 presents a hypothetical summary of these positions. The total demand for cash of each affiliate equals its mean demand, or what it expects to pay in the near term, plus cash balances equal to two standard deviations of its possible future expenditures. For example, the Spanish affiliate forecasts that it expects to spend €2,500,000, but it needs an additional $2 \times €1,150,000 = €2,300,000$ to be 97.5% sure that it will not be caught short of cash in the future. Consequently, the Spanish affiliate's total demand for cash is €4,800,000. The sum of the total demands for cash of the four European affiliates is €14,300,000.

Now, let's centralize the cash balances at a regional cash management office. What level of cash balances must the central office hold to be sure both that it can meet the expected demands of its affiliates and that it will meet contingent demands for cash 97.5% of the time? To answer this question, recognize that the central office is concerned with

Exhibit 19.6 European Affiliates' Demands for Cash

	Mean Demand for Cash	One Standard Deviation	Total Demand for Cash
British	€1,000,000	€750,000	€2,500,000
Danish	€2,000,000	€900,000	€3,800,000
Dutch	€1,500,000	€850,000	€3,200,000
Spanish	€2,500,000	€1,150,000	€4,800,000
Total	€7,000,000		€14,300,000

Notes: The first two columns list the affiliates' mean demands for cash and their standard deviations. For example, the British affiliate expects to use €1,000,000 in the coming month, but it may need as much as €1,000,000 + 2 × €750,000 = €2,500,000 to cover unexpected contingencies with 97.5% probability. The third column reports the sum of the mean and two standard deviations.

the sum of the demands for cash from the four affiliates. Because each demand for cash is normally distributed, the demand for cash of the central office will also be normally distributed. The mean demand for cash will therefore be the sum of the mean demands of the four affiliates:

$$€1,000,000 + €2,000,000 + €1,500,000 + €2,500,000 = €7,000,000$$

The savings in cash balances arise if the precautionary demands for money are less than perfectly correlated with each other. If the precautionary demands for cash are completely uncorrelated, we know that the variance of the sum of four random variables is the sum of their variances. Hence, the standard deviation of the demand for money of the central office is the square root of the sum of the four variances:

$$[(€750,000)^2 + (€900,000)^2 + (€850,000)^2 + (€1,150,000)^2]^{0.5} = €1,848,648$$

If the central office wants to be 97.5% sure of meeting the aggregate demand for cash of the four affiliates, it must hold

$$€7,000,000 + (2 \times €1,848,648) = €10,697,296$$

Consequently, the central office can hold

$$€14,300,000 - €10,697,296 = €3,602,704$$

less cash than the sum necessary if each of the affiliates forms its demand for cash independently. If the individual affiliates' precautionary demands for cash are positively correlated, the cash saving will be commensurately less than €3.6 million; but, if the individual affiliates' precautionary demands for cash are negatively correlated, the cash savings will be more than €3.6 million.

Limits to Centralization

The 2007 to 2010 global financial crisis caused corporations to rethink their desire for centralized cash management. If even the largest banks have the potential to default, MNCs must diversify this default risk. During the crisis, Faurecia, the European automotive parts manufacturer, which operates in 32 countries, found that having access to local banks in countries like India facilitated its access to loans that it would otherwise not have been able to obtain from its developed country banks. In a Cash Management Debate in *Euromoney* (2010), Faurecia's Treasurer argued, ". . . corporates may want to concentrate on picking specific banks for certain specialist products, and not trying to get their main corporate bank to provide everything, to spread the counterparty risk" (p. 130).

19.3 CASH TRANSFERS FROM AFFILIATES TO PARENTS

Foreign affiliates of a multinational corporation transfer cash to the parent headquarters primarily as dividends, royalties, management fees, and payments related to the sale of goods and their transfer prices. Government officials in host countries prefer to see the free cash flows of foreign affiliates reinvested in the host country rather than paid as dividends to the shareholders of the MNC. On the other hand, host country governments also recognize that a direct investment by a multinational corporation brings with it valuable technology, capital, managerial skills, and jobs. Payments made by foreign affiliates to their parents in the form of royalties for patents and fees for services are usually recognized as legitimate business expenses of the foreign affiliate and hence reduce corporate income taxes. Because host governments apply different tax rates to different types of income being repatriated, MNCs try to minimize these taxes by doing advance planning before establishing an affiliate.

International Dividend Cash Flows

Dividend payments make up the bulk of international cash flows transferred from foreign affiliates to their parent corporations. For U.S. parent corporations, dividends typically represent more than 50% of all remittances. The primary determinants of a firm's dividend policy for a foreign affiliate include the profitability of the affiliate, its investment opportunities, taxes in the host country and the home country, and foreign exchange and political risks.

If a foreign affiliate is profitable, it will be generating cash that could be paid to the parent as a dividend, whereas if it is unprofitable, it will be unable to pay dividends without accessing capital markets to fund these payments. If the investment opportunities of the foreign affiliate are good, the foreign affiliate's earnings should be reinvested because the overall firm wants to undertake as many positive net present value projects as possible. If the foreign affiliate is generating a substantial amount of free cash flow, the parent may want to institute a dividend policy for the subsidiary. A dividend policy requires the corporation to declare a quarterly or annual dividend equal to a certain percentage of its foreign earnings.

Tax Planning

Host country governments tax the income of foreign affiliates directly and withhold additional taxes on the repatriation of dividends. **Tax planning** is the process of minimizing the firm's taxes by choosing when to repatriate funds. The firm should shift its dividends into the future if the firm thinks that the withholding tax on the dividends is going to be reduced. Of course, the firm must be able to reinvest the funds to generate a reasonable expected rate of return if it is going to shift the profits into the future. In addition, the parent corporation often receives a tax credit for the foreign taxes it has paid on its dividends. The tax credit is worth more to the firm if the firm is profitable and paying taxes to the home country. Otherwise, the foreign tax credit would be worthless.

Dealing with Political Risk

The political environments of foreign affiliates can change significantly from year to year. Consequently, it is advantageous for a multinational corporation to have an established dividend policy that it can easily defend if government officials of the host country question it. Without such a policy or a history of dividend payments, an MNC may have difficulty explaining the reason for any given year's dividend payment.

For example, if the host country is having difficulty financing its balance of payments, it may appear to the government that the MNC's dividend payment is actually an attempt by the company to export capital from the country in a time of crisis. Even if a government blocks the dividends and no transfers can be made, MNCs find it to their advantage to declare a dividend in order to establish its validity in case the government later relaxes its foreign exchange restrictions.

Some corporations also set a "common" dividend repatriation rate for all their foreign affiliates in different countries. This approach establishes that the shareholders of the parent corporation demand a certain share of the earnings of all of the corporation's foreign subsidiaries and are not merely trying to take capital out of one particular country.

Dealing with Foreign Exchange Risk

If a parent corporation thinks that a depreciation of a foreign currency is imminent, it can try to accelerate the payment of dividends from its foreign affiliate. Conversely, if it is likely that the foreign currency will strengthen, the foreign affiliate can try to delay the dividends. This is part of the normal cycle of speculative activity in which a multinational corporation can engage. The idea of leading and lagging payments is discussed later in the chapter.

Other Factors Affecting Dividend Policy

Of course, if a foreign affiliate is a joint venture with a foreign partner, the dividend policy must be decided in consultation with the corporation's foreign partner. The costs related to negotiating a dividend payout year in and year out will tend to lead to stability in the dividend policy. Firms tend to change their dividend policies only when all parties involved perceive that there has been a permanent change in earnings.

International Royalty and Management-Fee Cash Flows

Royalties are payments made to the owners of a technology, a patent, or a trademark for the use of the technology or the right to manufacture under the patent or trademark. Royalty payments are pure profits in the sense that the firm receiving them performs no current services and incurs no current costs to receive the payment. Thus, royalties can be a substantial source of income for the receiving firm.

For example, Yum! Brands owns the KFC, Taco Bell, and Pizza Hut brands and is the world's largest restaurant chain. Yum! licenses the restaurant names to franchisees and has over 38,000 restaurants in 110 countries. It has three divisions: United States, China, and International. Its 2009 Annual Report states that Yum! Restaurants International, which operates outside the United States and China, provided over $650 million in franchise fees that required minimal capital investment on the part of the parent corporation.

Parent corporations also assess fees for services provided to their affiliates, including management and technical consulting services, and for the overhead costs associated with day-to-day operations the parent performs for the foreign affiliate. These costs include the foreign affiliate's shares of the research and development costs, legal and accounting costs, the salaries of the corporate management, and the costs of general advertising and public relations. Often, the fees associated with the parent's overhead are based on the affiliate's sales. In other circumstances, the overhead charges are based on a pro rata sharing of all the MNC's fixed costs.

Repatriation in a Joint Venture

Designing a repatriation schedule in a joint venture is especially important because it establishes the rules by which future payments can be made and curtails the problems associated with negotiating between foreign partners whose future interests might not be aligned. Because the MNC often supplies technological and design expertise as well as capital to its affiliate in the host country, it is compensated with a royalty or fee for the technology, which is the affiliate's cost. In light of this fact, the division of profits in the joint enterprise may give a somewhat smaller share of net income to the foreign company than would be dictated by the percentage of capital that it invested to create the joint venture.

Tax Advantages of Royalties and Fees

Royalties and fees often have income tax advantages over dividends because most countries withhold taxes on dividends but not necessarily on royalties and fees. Consequently, when an affiliate pays a dividend to its parent, it does so after paying local income taxes and the withholding tax on the dividend. Under U.S. tax law, the parent obtains tax credits both for the local income tax paid and for the withholding tax paid. However, if the foreign affiliate's combined tax rate is greater than the parent's tax rate, some of the tax credit may be lost.

In contrast, royalties and fees are paid out of pretax income, and if there is a withholding tax, the tax rate is often lower than the rate levied on dividends. Of course, the royalties and fees received by the parent are income, so the parent must pay income taxes on them to the home country.

Transfer Pricing and Cash Flows

Firms charge their affiliates **transfer prices** when selling goods and services to them. Consequently, these prices are not directly determined by market forces, and it is often difficult to determine whether a particular transfer price is close to what would be set in a competitive market. This is especially true of semi-finished manufactured goods for which there is literally no alternative market. Because a higher transfer price shifts income and tax payments from the affiliate that is paying the price to the affiliate that is receiving the price, transfer pricing is a politically contentious issue. Governments often argue that MNCs use transfer pricing to avoid paying income taxes, withholding taxes, and tariffs. Governments consequently establish rules and regulations that specify whether a transfer price is appropriate.

Shifting Income and Tax Burdens Between Countries

Let's examine how a multinational corporation could use transfer prices to lessen its income tax. Consider Exhibit 19.7, which shows how a low transfer price (shown in Panel A) affects a company's taxes on net income versus a high transfer price (shown in Panel B). The manufacturing affiliate is located in the home country, where the corporate income tax rate is 30%, and the distribution affiliate is located in a foreign country, where the corporate income tax rate is 60%.

The analysis is conducted on a per good sold basis. From the perspective of the company as a whole, it costs $1,800 to produce and sell the good. The original cost of goods sold that is incurred by the manufacturing affiliate is $1,500, and operating expenses are $200 for the manufacturing affiliate and $100 for the distribution affiliate. The good can ultimately be sold for $3,200. Let's assume that these numbers cannot be changed by different transfer policies. Hence, there is $3,200 − $1,800 = $1,400 of taxable income for the consolidated company. The transfer price determines what share of this income accrues to the manufacturing affiliate, what share accrues to the distribution affiliate, and how much total tax is paid.

Exhibit 19.7   Effects of High and Low Transfer Prices on Net Income

Panel A: Low-Transfer-Price Policy

	Manufacturing Affiliate (30% tax rate)	Distribution Affiliate (60% tax rate)	Consolidated Company
Sales	$2,200	$3,200*	$3,200*
Less Cost of Goods Sold	1,500*	2,200	1,500*
Less Operating Expenses	200*	100*	300*
Taxable Income	$ 500	$ 900	$1,400*
Less Income Taxes	150	540	690
Net Income	$ 350	$ 360	$ 710

Panel B: High-Transfer-Price Policy

	Manufacturing Affiliate (30% tax rate)	Distribution Affiliate (60% tax rate)	Consolidated Company
Sales	$2,600	$3,200*	$3,200*
Less Cost of Goods Sold	1,500*	2,600	1,500*
Less Operating Expenses	200*	100*	300*
Taxable Income	$ 900	$ 500	$1,400*
Less Income Taxes	270	300	570
Net Income	$ 630	$ 200	$ 830

Note: The numbers marked with an asterisk are the true revenues and costs and do not change with different transfer prices. All other numbers change with different transfer prices.

The Effect of a Low Transfer Price

In Exhibit 19.7, Panel A, the manufacturing affiliate charges a low transfer price of $2,200. Its expenses are $1,500 plus $200, so its taxable income is $500. The manufacturing affiliate pays the 30% income tax of $150 and has after-tax net income of $350. The distribution affiliate pays $2,200 for the goods and has expenses of $100. After selling the goods for $3,200, the distribution affiliate has before-tax income of $900. With a 60% tax rate, it pays $540 of income tax. Thus, the consolidated company has taxable income of $1,400, on which it pays income tax of $690, which works out to be a tax rate of 49.3%. That leaves net income of $710 for the consolidated company.[1]

The Effect of a High Transfer Price

Now, suppose the manufacturing affiliate charges a high transfer price of $2,600, as in Panel B of Exhibit 19.7. The manufacturing affiliate now has taxable income of $900; it pays income tax of $270; and its net income is $630. The distribution affiliate pays $2,600 for the goods, which reduces its taxable income to $500. Its income tax is now $300, which reduces its net income to $200. The consolidated company now pays income tax of $570 on the same taxable income of $1,400, which implies a 40.7% tax rate. The net income of the consolidated company therefore increases to $830. By shifting $400 of income from the regime with the 60% tax rate to the regime with the 30% tax rate, the company saves $30\% \times \$400 = \$120$. This represents an increase in net income from $710 to $830.

Notice that the increase in the transfer price also shifted income from the distribution affiliate to the manufacturing affiliate. This obviously would still be the case if the tax rates in the two countries were the same. However, the net income of the consolidated company would not change when moving from a low transfer price to a high transfer price. This shift in income can affect managerial incentives as we explain below. To see the shift in income, let the tax rate be 30% in both countries. The income tax of the distribution affiliate would fall to $270 under the low-transfer-price policy, which would cause its net income to increase to $630. The net income of the consolidated company would be $980, which is 70% of $1,400. Increasing the transfer price to $2,600 would again cause the taxable income of the distribution affiliate to fall to $500, but with a 30% tax rate, its net income would increase to $350. The net income of the manufacturing affiliate would be $630, and the net income of the consolidated company would be $980. The increase in the transfer price effectively shifts funds from the distribution affiliate to the manufacturing affiliate.

Transfer Pricing Regulations

Governmental tax authorities are aware of the incentives that multinational corporations face to manipulate transfer prices to avoid taxes. Economists have even been able to demonstrate that the effects are in the data.[2]

Tax regulations and court cases in each country have established a body of law for determining whether a transfer price is appropriate. In the United States, the IRS specifies that an appropriate transfer price is one that reflects an "arm's-length price"—that is, one that would

---

[1] A more complete analysis of this issue would examine the ultimate effect of different transfer pricing policies on the ultimate cash flows of the parent corporation. Such an analysis would involve consideration of the dividends that are actually paid to the parent and the foreign tax credits that the parent can use to offset tax owed to the home country tax authority, as in Chapter 15.

[2] See Bartelsman and Beetsma (2003) for empirical evidence that much of a unilateral increase in corporate taxes in OECD countries is lost because of decreases in reported income. The empirical work in Clausing (2003) also indicates that after controlling for other variables that affect trade prices, a lower country corporate tax rate is associated with lower U.S. intrafirm trade export prices to that country and higher import prices from that country, which is consistent with shifting income to the low-tax country. Similar results for Hong Kong are reported by Feenstra and Hanson (2004).

be observed in a sale of the good or service to an unrelated customer.[3] The IRS recognizes five methods that can be used to establish an arm's-length price. The methods are presented here, in decreasing order of general acceptance to tax authorities:

1. The comparable uncontrolled price method
2. The resale price method
3. The cost-plus method
4. The comparable-profits method
5. Other acceptable methods

The Organization for Economic Cooperation and Development (OECD) also recommends these methods for its member countries.

The most accurate evidence of an arm's-length price is to demonstrate that the transfer price is equivalent to a comparable uncontrolled price. Uncontrolled prices are straightforward to determine if the good or service that is being transferred between related affiliates is also being sold by the MNC to an unrelated corporation or if two unrelated corporations trade a similar good or service. However, in practice, it is often difficult to document two transactions that are identical in all features. This problem is particularly difficult when goods are made to order.

The resale price approach to establishing an arm's-length price starts with the retail price to the corporation's customers, subtracts an appropriate profit for the distribution unit, and uses the net price as the allowable selling price for the manufacturing unit. However, if the distributor is adding a great deal of value to the ultimate sale of the product, either by physically altering the product or by providing extensive distribution services, it is difficult to determine the appropriate profit markup the distributor should be paid. Hence, this method is often used when the distributor does not add a substantial amount of value to the product.

The cost-plus method begins with the costs of the manufacturing unit. An appropriate markup for the profit of that unit is added to the manufacturing costs to arrive at the transfer price that should be paid by the distribution unit. Of course, determining a manufacturer's costs is no minor matter. For example, correctly allocating the manufacturer's fixed costs across the various products it produces is paramount if this method is to be used. Whenever possible, the gross markup is based on a comparable uncontrolled sale.

The comparable-profits method involves comparing the profitability of businesses engaging in similar activities to the profitability of the organization doing the transfer pricing. This method can be used in combination with one of the other methods. It works well unless the organization setting the transfer price is trading valuable intangible products, such as computer software. In this case, the corporation likely bore a significant amount of risk to develop the product and therefore deserves to earn a premium on it.

Other methods can be used when none of the other four is appropriate. The conditions for the application of such an alternative method basically require that the firm supply supporting documents that make the case why none of the other methods applies and why the approach chosen is reasonable. An alternative method is often adopted in conjunction with one of the other four if products that are not routinely traded and difficult to value are being transferred.

Although both the government of the importing country and the government of the exporting country can readily observe transfer prices, it is far more difficult to observe the actual costs of the exporting affiliate. Hence, if the political forces that are currently executing the

---

[3]Section 482 of the U.S. Internal Revenue Code contains provisions that regulate transfer pricing in the United States. Under this law, the IRS can reallocate gross income, deductions, credits, and allowances between related corporations to prevent tax evasion or to more accurately reflect the income of the different parties. As with other aspects of the tax code, if the IRS restates income, the burden of proof is on the taxpayer to demonstrate that the actions of the IRS are arbitrary or unreasonable.

Of course, in setting its transfer pricing policy, an MNC must be aware that it risks being charged with tax evasion if its transfer prices do not meet the arm's-length test. Clearly, ethical considerations matter in the setting of transfer prices. A firm must also be aware that possible future tax penalties, litigation, and bad publicity are the potential costs of setting transfer prices too aggressively.

Using Transfer Pricing to Deal with Foreign Exchange Quotas

Some countries set quotas on the amount of foreign exchange available for importing goods into the country. This makes the value of a unit of foreign exchange to a foreign affiliate in that country higher than the stated market price. However, the MNC can partially correct the economic distortion by lowering the transfer price. In this situation, a low transfer price allows the foreign subsidiary to import a greater quantity of goods into the country for a given amount of foreign currency. Conversely, high transfer prices can be used to access blocked funds, as we will discuss shortly.

Transfer Pricing in Joint Ventures

When a multinational corporation enters into a joint venture with a local corporation rather than setting up a wholly owned foreign subsidiary, the MNC is less likely to be able to utilize transfer pricing to its advantage. Like governments, joint-venture partners are likely to question manipulated transfer prices. For example, as we saw in Exhibit 19.7, a high transfer price charged to a joint-venture company will adversely affect the income it earns. This can lead to conflicts between the two firms and jeopardize their venture. Because joint ventures are often expensive to set up, this is usually not a good strategy.

Strategies for Dealing with Blocked Funds

In a fixed exchange rate system, devaluation pressures may cause the country's international reserves to dwindle, and the government may decide to ration access to foreign exchange rather than devalue its currency. An MNC operating in such a country experiences the rationing of foreign exchange along with anyone else holding the local currency who wants to buy foreign currency. This gives rise to the problem of blocked funds, which can be severe for an MNC. For example, an MNC's affiliate operating inside the country might need to acquire foreign currency to purchase imported raw materials or semi-finished goods integral to its production process. Without these goods, the affiliate might have to shut down its production. The foreign affiliate is also likely to be prohibited from making royalty and fee payments, except possibly at very unattractive foreign exchange rates. It is also quite likely that the parent will be unable to repatriate the affiliate's profits as dividends.

Because of these pitfalls, before investing in a foreign affiliate, a parent company should analyze the factors that might trigger a situation in which blocked funds would occur and how such a situation would affect the affiliate's profitability. The parent should also develop a contingency plan for how its foreign affiliate will operate within the country if such a problem develops.

Fronting Loans

One technique that a multinational corporation can use to increase the probability that its foreign affiliate will be able to transfer funds out of the country is to finance the foreign affiliate with a **fronting loan**. A fronting loan is a parent-to-affiliate loan that uses a large international bank as a financial intermediary. Rather than have the parent corporation lend directly to its foreign affiliate, the parent instead makes a deposit with an international bank, which makes a loan to the foreign affiliate that is equivalent to 100% of the deposited funds. From the bank's perspective, a fronting loan is risk free because the loan is fully collateralized by the parent's deposit. The bank willingly participates for a small fee, earned in the form of a spread between the deposit rate that is paid to the parent and the rate it charges the foreign affiliate.

Involving an international bank can potentially avert the adverse impact of a blocked-funds situation. Countries that ration foreign exchange often allow businesses to make some payments but not others. Interest and principal payments on intracompany loans from the foreign affiliate of an MNC operating in the country to its parent are generally given a lower priority by the government than interest and principal payments from the same foreign affiliate to an international bank in a neutral country. Although halting the payments made to large MNCs does have costs, the perceived costs are smaller than those incurred when a country stops allowing payments to major international banks.

International banks can refuse to finance a country's international trade or can hamper the government's ability to borrow funds, whereas MNCs can do little more than threaten not to invest in the country in the future. Fronting loans can also give an MNC a tax advantage. If the local government allows the foreign affiliate to take a tax deduction for interest paid on a bank loan but does not allow a tax deduction for interest paid on an intracompany loan, the use of a fronting loan creates a valuable interest tax shield.

For example, suppose a parent corporation wants to invest $1,000,000 in its foreign manufacturing affiliate. To simplify the analysis, let the parent make the transfer using a wholly owned financial affiliate that operates in a tax haven with no income tax. Suppose the financial affiliate charges a 7% interest rate on the intracompany loan. If the manufacturing affiliate cannot deduct the interest, the after-tax cost of the loan is $70,000 per year, which equals the income for the financial affiliate.

Now suppose the parent fronts the loan by transferring $1,000,000 from the financial affiliate to its foreign manufacturing affiliate. The financial affiliate would make a deposit of $1,000,000 to an international bank that would agree to pay 7% interest on the deposit. The bank, in turn, would make a loan to the foreign manufacturing affiliate, charging perhaps 8% interest. Let the income tax rate for the foreign manufacturing affiliate be 50%, and let the interest cost of the bank loan be deductible. Now, the foreign manufacturing affiliate owes $80,000 of interest to the bank, but the after-tax cost of this payment is only $40,000 because the interest payment is tax deductible. The bank gets $10,000 of income for its role as an intermediary. Once again, the financial affiliate is left with $70,000 of income, but the foreign manufacturing affiliate has to pay only $40,000 of after-tax income to achieve the transfer of $70,000 out of the country.

Reinvesting Working Capital Locally

When a government shuts off access to the foreign exchange market, it is trying to prevent capital from leaving the country. Governments also often place restrictions on nominal interest rates that can be offered in money markets. In such a situation, the yields on short-term money market instruments may produce negative real returns. When this happens, an MNC needs to try to find local investments that at least break even. The minimum goal of investing the profits of the local affiliate should be to maintain the real value of the existing principal. Toward this end, the local managers should be given the power to invest in any zero net present value investments. Because the local managers cannot be expected to be able to pick winners in the local economy, given the dire straits that it is in, any market-determined, zero net present value investment should be an acceptable investment from the parent corporation's point of view.

It is possible, however, that the firm may be able to invest in other products in the country that offer market-determined expected rates of return. These investments include the corporate bonds and the equities of other firms. If none of these investments appear to be attractive, the firm can engage in additional direct investment in the country. For example, the firm could purchase local real estate, either land or buildings. The firm can also pursue other real investments, including commodities, either for export or to add to its existing inventory, or it might construct additional facilities. Another way for a multinational corporation to use its working capital is to have a local affiliate contract with other firms operating in the country to supply goods or to perform services for the parent or its other affiliates. For example, an architectural firm in a country with blocked funds could be hired to design a factory slated to be built by the parent.

Altering the Terms of Trade

Another tactic MNCs can use to get around the inconvertibility problem was illustrated by the Radisson Hotel chain in 1990, when it began building hotels in the former Soviet Union. Radisson began its foray into the former Soviet Union by first building a hotel in Moscow that accepted only convertible currencies. Then it added others that accepted rubles. Similarly, when McDonald's opened its first two restaurants in Moscow, one accepted rubles, but the other accepted only dollars. Both cases demonstrate how the two firms tried to overcome potential problems related to blocked funds. Although Radisson and McDonald's weren't already doing business in the former Soviet Union, such a strategy could have worked for a multinational that was.

Finally, when a firm knows that it is going to be operating in a country whose money is not fully convertible, it may be able to set up a trading operation to export unrelated products from that country. That is, the firm may be able to use a countertrade strategy.

19.4 MANAGING ACCOUNTS RECEIVABLE

A critical source of a multinational corporation's working capital is its accounts receivable. Any firm that decides to issue trade credit must therefore perform five tasks within the firm or hire an outside firm to do so.[4] First, the credit risk of the customer must be assessed. Second, the terms of the credit must be determined. These terms include the length of time between the sale and the payment and any interest penalties for late payments. Third, the receivable must be financed between the production and receipt of funds from the sale. Fourth, the receivable must be collected. Fifth, the firm must bear the default risk of the companies to which it extends credit. MNCs commonly extend credit to their customers, but the problems related to managing the company's accounts receivable are more complex for the MNC than a purely domestic firm. In addition to the five tasks just mentioned, the MNC also must decide the currency of denomination of its accounts receivable.

Currency of Denomination

An MNC must decide whether its foreign sales should be denominated in the domestic currency, in the currency of the foreign customer, or possibly in a third currency. Often, MNCs are advised to price their exports in hard currencies (ones that are likely to appreciate) and to denominate their imports in soft currencies (ones that are likely to depreciate). Does this advice make sense? If the two parties to a transaction agree on the distribution of future exchange rates and face the same cost of hedging, the advice is irrelevant. The currency of denomination of the sales contract then does not matter to the parties because there is a foreign currency price for the product that both parties agree is equal to the domestic currency price of the product. Let's look at an example to see why this is true.

---

[4]See Mian and Smith (1992) for a discussion of the economics of whether these five tasks should be done within the firm or contracted outside the firm. Alternative policies include doing everything within the firm, financing the receivables with secured debt, establishing a captive financial subsidiary, using a credit information firm, using a credit collection agency, using a credit insurance company, and using non-recourse factoring or recourse factoring.

Example 19.2   Pricing Airplanes for British Airways

Suppose Boeing enters into a contract to sell planes to British Airways. If the contract is denominated in dollars, British Airways will have to pay $100,000,000 in 1 year when the planes are delivered. With the deal denominated in dollars, British Airways is also confronted with the risk that the dollar will strengthen relative to the pound. Suppose that the spot exchange rate and the 1-year forward rate are as follows:

$$\text{Spot rate} = \$1.65/\pounds$$
$$\text{1-year forward rate} = \$1.60/\pounds$$

If British Airways does not want to bear the risk that the dollar will strengthen relative to the pound, it can contract to buy dollars forward with pounds at the forward rate of $1.60/£. In this case, British Airways converts its $100,000,000 account payable into a pound-denominated account payable of

$$\$100,000,000/(\$1.60/\pounds) = \pounds62,500,000$$

Notice that if Boeing denominates the deal in pounds, with payment again in 1 year, British Airways would be indifferent between paying £62,500,000 and hedging the $100,000,000 payment. Analogously, if Boeing denominates the deal in pounds and chooses not to bear the transaction foreign exchange risk, it would generate $100,000,000 in 1 year by charging £62,500,000 for the planes and selling that amount of pounds forward for dollars.

Example 19.2 demonstrates the important point that the currency of invoice really does not matter if the two parties have the same hedging opportunities and view exchange risk symmetrically. In negotiating a deal, though, it is often the case that the two parties do not have equal access to hedging opportunities. Also, in many circumstances, there are no well-developed forward markets. Money market hedges might not be available either because of the difficulty of securing loans in the foreign currency.

When hedging is impossible, one of the parties will be forced to bear the foreign exchange risk. Once again, though, if the two parties agree on the distribution of future exchange rates, and if the cost to each of the parties of bearing the risk is the same, there will be a foreign currency price that each party agrees is equivalent to the proposed domestic currency price.

If the parties disagree about the nature of the distribution of future exchange rates, or if the perceived cost to the parties of bearing the risk is not the same, the two parties will disagree about the foreign currency price that is equivalent to the possible domestic currency price. The next example demonstrates this point.

Example 19.3   Pricing Airplanes for Bangkok Airways

Suppose that Boeing is selling planes to a new Thai company, Bangkok Airways. Boeing must choose whether to denominate the contract in U.S. dollars or Thai baht. Suppose that the spot exchange rate is THB25/$ and that there is no forward market. Suppose there is a possibility that the baht will be devalued relative to the dollar during the next year. If Boeing prices in dollars, it will charge $100,000,000, and it will expect payment in 1 year. In this case, Bangkok Airways has two choices. It can buy dollars today and invest them for 1 year if it wants to hedge, or it can bear the exchange risk that the baht will weaken relative to the dollar. In this case, we assume that it is financially infeasible for Bangkok Airways to buy dollars today because it cannot borrow the requisite amount of dollars or baht.

In order to analyze the values that the two parties attribute to the price quotes in the different currencies, we must understand each party's perceived distribution of future spot exchange rates. To summarize Bangkok Airways's and Boeing's probability distributions of future exchange rates in a simple way, assume that both parties think either the baht will remain at THB25/\$ or the baht will be devalued. Suppose Bangkok Airways thinks there is a 50% probability the exchange rate will increase to THB40/\$. Then, Bangkok Airways's expected future spot rate is

$$[0.5 \times (THB25/\$)] + [0.5 \times (THB40/\$)] = THB32.5/\$$$

Suppose Boeing also thinks that the exchange rate may increase to THB40/\$, but Boeing believes there is a 55% probability of a devaluation. Hence, Boeing's expected future spot rate is

$$[0.45 \times (THB25/\$)] + [0.55 \times (THB40/\$)] = THB33.25/\$$$

When Boeing quotes a price of \$100,000,000, Bangkok Airways expects to pay

$$(THB32.5/\$) \times \$100,000,000 = THB3,250,000,000$$

If Boeing quotes a price denominated in baht that is equivalent in expected value (from its perspective) to \$100,000,000 in 1 year, it will quote

$$(THB33.25/\$) \times \$100,000,000 = THB3,325,000,000$$

Notice that Bangkok Airways would prefer to be invoiced in dollars because its expected value of the \$100,000,000 when converted into baht is less than the sure baht payment that it would have to make if it were invoiced in baht.[5] If Bangkok Airways accepts the dollar-denominated payment, it will pay either THB2,500,000,000 if there is no devaluation or THB4,000,000,000 if there is a devaluation.

Examples 19.2 and 19.3 indicate that the decision about the currency in which to invoice cannot be made in isolation of the perceived probability distributions of future exchange rates, the opportunities that the parties have to hedge their foreign exchange risk, the determination of a local currency price for the product, and the riskiness of cash flows denominated in different currencies. If, in Example 19.3, Boeing were to place a probability on the devaluation that was lower than 50%, say 40%, its expected future spot rate would be

$$[0.6 \times (THB25/\$)] + [0.4 \times (THB40/\$)] = THB31/\$$$

Then, Boeing would quote

$$(THB31/\$) \times \$100,000,000 = THB3,100,000,000$$

---

[5]Notice that Bangkok Airways must compare a sure payment of baht in the future to an expected payment of baht in the future. To determine the baht cost today, it must take present values. Notice that Bangkok Airways will take the present value of a sure baht payment with the risk-free interest rate and the present value of an expected baht payment with an appropriate rate that reflects the systematic risk of the uncertain payment. If there is no systematic risk of the devaluation, the two payments can be compared with the baht risk-free rate. Analogously, Boeing would quote a baht price equal to the \$100,000,000 times the expected value of the baht–dollar exchange rate only if the systematic risk of a devaluation of the baht relative to the dollar were zero.

as the baht price for its planes. Bangkok Airways would happily agree to be invoiced for THB3,100,000,000 rather than for $100,000,000, and Boeing would be left with the foreign exchange risk. Notice that if the true probability of devaluation were actually 50%, Boeing would have mispriced the deal.

Leading and Lagging Payments

MNCs make use of leading and lagging payments to manage the net working capital needs of their foreign affiliates. A **leading payment** is a payment made earlier than usual; a **lagging payment** is a delayed payment. By shortening and lengthening the payment cycle between related affiliates, an MNC can affect the liquidity of its affiliates around the world. Desai et al. (2008) find that MNCs routinely shift profits from one country to another to create an internal capital market for their affiliates.

For example, suppose the British affiliate of an MNC typically sells $2 million worth of goods each month to the German affiliate of the MNC. When the sale takes place, the British affiliate extends an account receivable to the German affiliate, which books an account payable. For each additional 30 days that the accounts receivable and payable are extended, the German affiliate obtains an additional $2 million worth of financing from the British affiliate. Net working capital is increased at the British affiliate, and it is reduced at the German affiliate.

What are the determinants of leading and lagging? First, and foremost, the MNC must understand the opportunity costs associated with the net working capital of its affiliates. This interest rate must be based on a common currency, such as the dollar, and it should be calculated on an after-tax basis. Funds should then be moved from affiliates that have low opportunity costs of net working capital to affiliates that have high opportunity costs.

Of course, the interest rate at which an affiliate can borrow in the short-term money market is substantially above the interest rate at which it can lend. If all borrowing rates are above all lending rates, the movement of funds through leading and lagging is simple. Funds should be moved from affiliates that are lending to the short-term money market to affiliates that are borrowing from short-term money markets. This is done by allowing the affiliates that are borrowing to lag their payments to the affiliates that are lending and by having the affiliates that are lending accelerate their payments to the affiliates that are borrowing.

The problem is only slightly more complicated if all the affiliates have surplus funds. Then, the affiliate with the best investment opportunity should receive accelerated payments from the other affiliates. In contrast, if all the affiliates have deficits of funds and are therefore borrowing, the MNC should attempt to borrow as much as possible through the affiliate that has the lowest borrowing cost.

The following example provides a numeric illustration of this issue.

Example 19.4 Different Borrowing and Lending Rates for Different Affiliates

Suppose the dollar borrowing and lending rates for a U.S. parent and its British affiliate for 90-day periods are as follows:

	Borrowing Rate (in percent per annum)	Lending Rate (in percent per annum)
U.S. Parent	8.0	7.0
British Affiliate	8.2	6.9

At the margin, both the U.S. parent and its British affiliate can have either positive short-term funds that they want to invest or short-term borrowing requirements.

Consequently, four situations must be considered. In each of these four situations, we can determine which direction funds should flow and the return to the MNC of transferring $1 million:

1. **The U.S. parent has surplus funds, and the British affiliate must borrow:** The U.S. parent can invest funds at 7%, whereas the British affiliate borrows at 8.2%. Clearly, the U.S. parent should lend funds to the British affiliate. For each $1 million transferred for 90 days, the MNC saves

$$\$1,000,000 \times (8.2 - 7)/100 \times (90/360) = \$3,000$$

2. **The U.S. parent must borrow, and the British affiliate has surplus funds:** The U.S. parent borrows funds at 8.0%, whereas the British affiliate earns only 6.9% on its lending. Clearly, the British affiliate should lend to the U.S. parent. For each $1 million transferred for 90 days, the MNC saves

$$\$1,000,000 \times (8.0 - 6.9)/100 \times (90/360) = \$2,750$$

3. **Both the U.S. parent and the British affiliate have surplus funds:** Because both the U.S. parent and the British affiliate have funds to invest, we merely compare what they can earn. The U.S. parent can earn 7%, whereas the British affiliate can only earn 6.9%. Clearly, funds should flow from the British affiliate to the U.S. parent. For each $1 million transferred for 90 days, the MNC earns

$$\$1,000,000 \times (7 - 6.9)/100 \times (90/360) = \$250$$

4. **Both the U.S. parent and the British affiliate must borrow:** Because both the U.S. parent and the British affiliate must borrow, we merely compare their respective borrowing rates. The U.S. parent borrows at 8.0%, whereas the British affiliate borrows at 8.2%. Clearly, funds should flow from the U.S. parent to the British affiliate. For each $1 million transferred over 90 days, the corporation saves

$$\$1,000,000 \times (8.2 - 8.0)/100 \times (90/360) = \$500$$

Of course, governments are aware of the incentives that multinational corporations have to engage in leading and lagging of payments. Consequently, they regulate the credit terms that can be extended across borders.

Credit Terms

An MNC can extend credit not only to its affiliates but also to its customers. How does an MNC decide on the terms of payments for its customers?

Fundamentally, the optimal policy involves increasing the term of an account receivable and reducing the interest charge until the marginal benefit of the affiliate's increased sales equals the marginal costs imposed by the five tasks involved in managing accounts receivable (mentioned at the outset of our discussion). The better the credit terms an MNC offers, the more sales it is likely to make. In changing terms, the firm must be sure that today's sale on credit actually contributes positive expected future cash flow. Quoting easier credit terms can attract undesirable buyers who are slow to pay or who default on their payments.

Credit assessment is costly, so the longer the term of the credit, the more extensive should be the investigation of the creditworthiness of the customer. Collecting what is owed is also costly, as is financing the accounts receivable. Increasing accounts receivable uses cash that could be used to finance other productive projects, if it could be collected, and increases the default risk that the firm faces.

If an MNC has a lower cost of capital than its local customers, the MNC can increase its profits by extending relatively long credit terms to its customers and charging them financing fees. It makes sense for the MNC to finance the inventory of its customers if the MNC can charge a cheaper rate than the customer would be charged by local banks. Of course, the MNC must assess the default risk of its customers. The higher interest rate or limited borrowing capacity of a local customer might simply reflect a high default risk associated with doing business with the customer rather than a shortage of funds from local sources.

One advantage that a multinational corporation may have over a bank is that the collateral used to secure the loan may be worth more to the MNC than it is to a bank. If the account receivable is not repaid, the MNC should be able to repossess the merchandise and possibly resell it on more favorable terms than a bank could. The MNC might also have better information about the default risk of its customers than a bank has because it is in a related business.

19.5 INVENTORY MANAGEMENT

As explained earlier, inventories are held to smooth the production process and to make sure that goods are available for customers when their orders arrive. But inventory is costly for a firm to hold because the stocks of inventories are the firm's assets, and they must be financed. If the firm's cost of capital is 15% and the firm is holding $100,000,000 of inventory, its annual financing cost is $15,000,000. The inventories also must be stored in a safe place, which requires warehouses and personnel to manage the storage. The firm is also exposed to losses in the event that the inventory is stolen or destroyed as a result of a fire or another natural disaster, or if it becomes obsolete. Of course, the firm can purchase insurance to guard against these risks, but there is a direct cost of doing so. Finally, inventories can lose value if the market prices of the goods fall. Commodities such as raw materials used in manufacturing are especially vulnerable to price drops.

So how does a firm decide how much inventory to hold? Optimal inventory theory, discussed next, can help a firm formulate a policy.

Optimal Inventory Theory

A firm should increase its inventory until the marginal benefit arising from reduced production costs and increased sales revenue equals the marginal cost of storing and financing the inventories. Although the inventory management problems multinational firms face are similar to those faced by purely domestic firms, the volatility of prices and exchange rates makes determining an optimal policy even more challenging for an MNC.

Devaluation or Depreciation Risk

Managers of foreign subsidiaries are often confronted with the risk of devaluation or depreciation of the local currency. This risk raises the question of whether additional inventory from foreign suppliers should be purchased prior to a devaluation of the local currency relative to the foreign currency. A naïve answer to this question would appear to be "yes." After all, the local currency price of the inventory will rise after the devaluation. But let's examine this issue in more detail to gain insight about the balancing of marginal costs and marginal benefits.

Consider a two-period model in which a German subsidiary of a U.S. firm buys some imported goods today to place in inventory, and the subsidiary sells the goods in Germany in the next period. The German firm can borrow in euros to buy the goods, which are priced in dollars, and the company incurs a euro-denominated storage cost that increases with the amount of goods stored. Because the parent corporation is a U.S. firm, the objective of the German subsidiary is to maximize its dollar profit in the second period. Assume that the markets for both the imported goods and the final goods are competitive, so the firm cannot influence the prices of these goods by the amounts that it buys or sells.

To facilitate the analysis, let the dollar–euro exchange rate at time t be $S(t, \$/€)$, let $P(t, \$)$ be the dollar price of the imported good at time t, let $P(t, €)$ be the euro retail price of the good at time t, let $i(t, €)$ be the euro interest rate that will be paid at time $t+1$, and let $C(t+1, €)$ be the euro-denominated marginal storage cost that is increasing in the amount of inventory. Let's build up the equilibrium condition in steps.

The expected dollar revenue from selling a unit of the good next period is

$$E_t[S(t+1, \$/€) \times P(t+1, €)] \tag{19.1}$$

The expected marginal cost from buying the good on credit and storing the good for one period has two parts. The euro cost of the good at time t is $P(t, \$)/S(t, \$/€)$, which must be borrowed and repaid with interest at time $t+1$. Hence, the dollar value of the euro interest plus principal at time $t+1$ is

$$S(t+1, \$/€) \times \frac{P(t, \$)}{S(t, \$/€)} \times (1 + i(t, €)) \tag{19.2}$$

The firm must also pay the dollar value of the marginal storage cost, $S(t+1, \$/€) \times C(t+1, €)$.

The equilibrium condition that determines the optimal inventory of goods imported into Germany requires that the expected marginal dollar revenues at time $t+1$ in Equation (19.1) equal the expected dollar marginal cost in Equation (19.2) plus the expected marginal storage cost.

Consider the equilibrium implications. On the revenue side, the important point is whether the local-currency prices in the retail market, $P(t+1, €)$, will increase to keep pace with any depreciation of the local currency as $S(t+1, \$/€)$ falls with a depreciation of the euro. If retail prices are expected to increase faster than the rate of depreciation, this force would motivate managers to purchase a larger amount of inventory, other things being equal. If, on the other hand, a depreciation of the euro will be accompanied by a price freeze, the expected increase in the retail price is less than the expected rate of depreciation of the local currency. This would motivate managers to purchase a smaller amount of inventory.

Now, let's look at how a possible depreciation of the euro would affect the firm's marginal costs in Equation (19.2). If local interest rates fail to increase sufficiently to reflect the expected depreciation, the firm's marginal costs will be lower, and larger inventories should be purchased. On the other hand, if interest rates are higher than warranted by the expected depreciation, the firm's inventory carrying costs will be high, and smaller inventories should be purchased.

Finally, consider the expected marginal storage costs. If marginal costs are expected to be low, possibly because the firm's warehousing costs are fixed in nominal terms, this would cause the firm to choose larger inventories. In contrast, if the firm's workers are likely to strike for increased wages after the depreciation, smaller inventories are optimal.

In summary, the prospects of a depreciation of a local currency are insufficient in and of themselves to warrant an increase in inventories. Only by balancing the anticipated marginal benefits and anticipated marginal costs of holding the inventory can we arrive at the optimal stock. What will happen to future retail prices and whether nominal interest rates will accurately and rationally reflect the probabilities of devaluation are equally as important as the fact that the local currency is expected to depreciate.

POINT–COUNTERPOINT

Planning for a Dinjonasian Devaluation

Ante, Freedy, and Suttle are again visiting their Uncle Fred, the importer–exporter. Uncle Fred is explaining that last year, he set up a textile manufacturing plant in Tajarka, Dinjonasia. The plant produces really cheap v-neck cotton T-shirts that are the rage in California. Uncle Fred is trying to figure out how to respond to a request from his Dinjonasian plant manager, Mr. Ibrahim.

"This e-mail from Ibrahim has me puzzled," says Uncle Fred. "He thinks the Dinjonasian rupiah (DJR) is going to crater versus the dollar sometime within the next year, and I agree. The latest figures show the stock of international reserves of Bank Dinjonasia at $32 billion, and they're losing over $4 billion per month intervening in support of the rupiah. At that rate of loss, they've got less than 8 months to figure out what to do before a devaluation of the rupiah is forced upon them. Ibrahim is worried that I'll fire him when the plant is less profitable after the devaluation. Last year, he made a profit of DJR8,100,000,000, which sounds impressive, but it only converted to USD900,000 at the fixed exchange rate of DJR9,000/USD. If the rate goes to DJR12,000/USD, as the media are anticipating, he'll only produce profit of

$$\frac{\text{DJR8,100,000,000}}{(\text{DJR12,000/USD})} = \$675,000$$

Uncle Fred continues, "Ibrahim wants to speculate to protect the dollar value of his budget. The stumbling block to this plan is that the Dinjonasian government has frozen forward trading in the rupiah—basically outlawing the forward market. I understand that he could sell rupiah forward for dollars and make a killing after the rupiah crashes, but if he can't do that, what can he do? I'm obviously not going to fire him for something that is out of his control."

"Well, he should be worried about his job if all that he can think of is forward contracts," shouts Ante. "There are lots of other ways to speculate against the rupiah." "Name one," comes the cry from Freedy. "You're asleep in international finance most times I look."

Ante thinks for a second and responds, "Well, you could always have Ibrahim buy some extra inventory. Doesn't he get his cotton from Egypt? The dollar value of the cotton is set on world markets, and if he buys cotton before the devaluation, its rupiah value will increase with the devaluation."

Uncle Fred interjects, "Ante, that's a good suggestion, but what if the price of cotton falls in a few months? I've heard the Egyptians think there will be a huge harvest, and the price of cotton has consequently been trending downward for the past 2 weeks. I think cotton prices are going to fall 20% to 30% in the next 6 months. We could find ourselves with some really high-priced cotton on the books, which wouldn't look so good either. I think I'll just tell Ibrahim not to worry."

"Wait a minute," says Freedy. "Can't Uncle Fred do some leading and lagging of payments? It seems to me that he should maximize his dollar assets. That means lengthening out the Dinjonasian plant's accounts receivable that are denominated in dollars and shortening the plant's accounts payable. Uncle Fred should delay paying Ibrahim for the shirts, and Ibrahim should accelerate the payment of management fees and royalties to Uncle Fred. What would happen if everybody did that?"

Suttle interjects, "Freedy, you're right on the mark. Even though Bank Dinjonasia has tried to prevent speculation in the capital markets, all commercial firms will have an incentive to accelerate their purchases of dollars with rupiah and to delay their sales of dollars for rupiah. If you're going to buy dollars for some legitimate international trade purpose, you'd rather do it at DJR9,000/USD than at DJR12,000/USD. Similarly, if you can delay converting out of dollars into rupiah until after the devaluation, you'll get the capital gain. Of course, there may be a run on the reserves of Bank Dinjonasia, even with all the capital market controls in place. Leading and lagging international payments can have a first-order effect on the flow of international reserves, much to the displeasure of central bankers."

Ante and Freedy nod approvingly, but Uncle Fred shakes his head and interjects, "Suttle, don't you have to worry about interest rates in these strategies?"

Suttle smiles and says, "You certainly do, Uncle Fred! If the interest rates in Dinjonasia anticipate a devaluation, the leading/lagging strategy my be costly to implement and may backfire if the devaluation ultimately doesn't materialize."

19.6 SUMMARY

This chapter explores issues related to managing a multinational corporation's net working capital. The main points in the chapter are as follows:

1. Net working capital is the difference between a firm's current assets of cash, marketable securities, accounts receivable, and inventories and its current liabilities. An increase in the stock of net working capital is an investment.

2. The goals of an international money manager of a multinational corporation are to establish control over the cash resources of the organization, to invest excess short-term funds in an optimal way, and to obtain short-term financing at the lowest cost.

3. Managing cash from a centralized pool of resources can reduce a firm's costs by minimizing its transaction costs and by optimizing the currency of denomination and the maturity of any of its investments or borrowing.

4. A multilateral netting system reduces transaction costs between the affiliates of a multinational corporation by eliminating gross transfers and substituting net transfers that take account of what is owed among them.

5. The precautionary demand for money arises because a firm cannot perfectly match its current production to its current sales. A centralized cash management system can improve a multinational corporation's cash flows by exploiting the fact that the demands for cash by different affiliates are less than perfectly correlated.

6. The primary cash transfers that foreign affiliates make to their parent corporations are dividends. Other cash transfers to the parent include royalties, fees, and payments related to transfer prices. The parent should plan how it will repatriate the profits it earns from its affiliates and how it will minimize the taxes owed on the profits.

7. Transfer prices are the prices that a firm charges its affiliates when selling goods and services to them. Because transfer prices are set internally, it is often difficult to determine whether a particular transfer price is close to what would be set in a competitive market.

8. Higher transfer prices shift income and tax burdens from distribution affiliates to manufacturing affiliates. Lower transfer prices shift income and tax burdens from manufacturing affiliates to distribution affiliates.

9. In the United States, the IRS specifies that an appropriate transfer price is one that reflects an arm's-length price—that is, the price a seller would charge to an unrelated buyer.

10. Prior to investing in a foreign affiliate, a parent company should analyze the factors that might trigger blocked funds and how such a situation would affect the affiliate's profitability. The parent should also develop a contingency plan for how the affiliate would operate within the country if such a problem developed.

11. A fronting loan is a parent-to-affiliate loan that uses a large international bank as a financial intermediary. Such a loan helps an MNC avoid the adverse effects of potential blocked-funds situations and results in valuable interest tax shields.

12. A critical source of a multinational corporation's working capital is its accounts receivable. A firm that issues credit must assess the credit risk of its customers and determine the terms of the credit. The firm must also finance its accounts receivable and bear the risk associated with them and the costs of collecting them. The appropriate terms of credit balance the marginal benefits the firm receives from the increased sales it makes on credit with the marginal costs it incurs extending credit.

13. The appropriate currency of denomination of accounts receivable cannot be determined without understanding the perceived distributions of future exchange rates of each party, the opportunities that the parties have to hedge their foreign exchange risk, the determination of a local currency price for the product, and the riskiness of the cash flows denominated in different currencies.

14. Leading and lagging the payments made between its affiliates allows an MNC to affect the liquidity of the affiliates and to speculate on changes in exchange rates.

15. Stocks of inventories, consisting of raw materials, work-in-progress, and finished goods, are held to smooth production and to make sure that goods are available for customers when orders arrive. The benefits of holding inventories arise from better production planning and a reputation for reliability in supplying products. These benefits must be balanced at the margin against the storage, insurance, and financing costs inherent in holding inventories.

QUESTIONS

1. What is net working capital? Why should it be considered an investment that a firm must make to increase its future profitability?
2. What distinguishes international cash management from purely domestic cash management? In particular, what constraints arise in the international environment?
3. Why is it important for a foreign affiliate to have a well-defined dividend policy for repatriating profits to its parent corporation?
4. What is the difference between a royalty and a fee?
5. What are the determinants of leading and lagging payments between related international affiliates?
6. What principles determine the appropriateness of transfer prices under U.S. regulations?
7. How can transfer pricing be used to shift income around the world?
8. How can transfer pricing be used to avoid tariffs?
9. What are blocked funds? How can a corporation structure its foreign affiliates to mitigate problems with blocked funds?
10. What is a fronting loan? How does its structure potentially create value for a multinational corporation?
11. Why is the threat of devaluation an insufficient reason for a firm to build up its stocks of inventories?
12. What are the five tasks involved in issuing trade credit?
13. What is wrong with the rule that firms should invoice their customers in hard currencies?
14. Why does it make sense for a multinational corporation to allow its foreign customers to pay on credit if there is rationing in the foreign credit market?

PROBLEMS

1. Euroshipping Corporation maintains separate production and distribution facilities in Sweden, France, Spain, and Italy. The corporate headquarters is in France. As a consultant to the treasurer of Euroshipping, you have been asked to estimate how much money the firm could save by creating a centralized cash management pool. Currently, each affiliate maintains precautionary cash balances equal to three standard deviations above its expected demand for cash.

Affiliate	Mean Demand for Money	One Standard Deviation
Swedish	€25,000,000	€7,000,000
French	€50,000,000	€13,000,000
Italian	€35,500,000	€10,000,000
Spanish	€20,000,000	€6,000,000

By how much could Euroshipping reduce its overall demand for cash if it were to create a centralized cash pool for the four affiliates? (Assume that the cash needs are normally distributed and are independent of each other.)
2. Euroshipping is also considering developing a multilateral netting system.
   a. Given the cumulative monthly payments in the following payments matrix, derive the minimum transfers that could be made.

Euroshipping Intracompany Payments Matrix (in millions of euros)

Receiving Affiliate	Paying Affiliate			
	Swedish	French	Italian	Spanish
Swedish	—	16	14	18
French	19	—	12	15
Italian	22	7	—	11
Spanish	9	15	3	—

   b. If the transaction costs on these fund transfers are 0.45%, how much would the company save by switching to a multilateral netting system?
3. Suppose the euro borrowing and lending rates for a German parent and its Spanish affiliate for a 90-day period are as follows:

	Borrowing Rate (in percent per annum)	Lending Rate (in percent per annum)
German Parent	9.3	8.1
Spanish Affiliate	9.6	7.9

In each of the following cases, determine the direction funds should flow and the return to the MNC of transferring EUR1,000,000:
   a. The German parent has positive funds; the Spanish affiliate has negative funds.

b. The German parent has negative funds; the Spanish affiliate has positive funds.

c. The German parent has positive funds; the Spanish affiliate has positive funds.

d. The German parent has negative funds; the Spanish affiliate has negative funds.

4. Consider a situation in which a manufacturing affiliate is selling to a distribution affiliate. The relevant tax information, operating expenses, and cost of goods sold are given in the following table. Fill out the entries in the table and determine how the overall income of the consolidated company would change if it were to increase the transfer price by $500:

	Manufacturing Affiliate (35% tax rate)	Distribution Affiliate (55% tax rate)	Consolidated Company
Sales	$4,500	$5,700	
Less Cost of Goods Sold	2,600		
Less Operating Expenses	1,000	450	
Taxable Income			
Less Income Taxes			
Net Income			

5. If a manufacturing affiliate faces a 55% income tax rate, and its distribution affiliate faces a 40% income tax rate and a 15% import tariff, should transfer prices be high or low?

6. Caterpillar is selling earthmoving equipment to an Indonesian construction company. Caterpillar must choose whether to denominate the contract in U.S. dollars or in Indonesian rupiah. Suppose that the spot exchange rate is IDR9,150/$ and that there is no forward market. Suppose, too, that there is a possibility that the rupiah will be devalued relative to the dollar during the next year. If Caterpillar prices the contract in dollars, it will charge $15,000,000 and will expect to be paid in 1 year. It is also willing to discuss pricing the machines in rupiah. The Indonesian firm thinks that there is a 60% chance the exchange rate will remain the same and a 40% chance it will increase to IDR9,300/$. Caterpillar thinks that there is a 65% probability of the exchange rate remaining the same and a 35% probability that it will increase to ID9,450/$. How should the deal be priced, and who will bear the risk of devaluation of the rupiah?

7. Web Question: Go to the PwC Web site related to transfer pricing at www.pwc.com/gx/en/international-transfer-pricing and download the latest version of their manual on international transfer pricing. Determine how Venezuela handles transfer pricing and what the penalties are for non-compliance.

BIBLIOGRAPHY

Bartelsman, Eric J., and Roel Beetsma, 2003, "Why Pay More? Corporate Tax Avoidance through Transfer Pricing in OECD Countries," *Journal of Public Economics* 87, pp. 2225–2252.

Clausing, Kimberly. A., 2003, "Tax-Motivated Transfer Pricing and US Intrafirm Trade Prices," *Journal of Public Economics* 87, pp. 2207–2223.

Desai, Mihir, C. Fritz Foley, and Kristin Forbes, 2008, "Financial Constraints and Growth: Multinational and Local Firm Responses to Currency Crises," *Review of Financial Studies* 21, pp. 2857–2888.

Euromoney, 2010, "Optimizing Local, Regional and Global Cash Management," June, pp. 130–137.

Feenstra, Robert C., and Gordon H. Hanson, 2004, "Intermediaries in Entrepot Trade: Hong Kong Re-Exports of Chinese Goods," *Journal of Economics and Management* 13, pp. 3–35.

Mian, Shehzad L., and Clifford W. Smith, 1992, "Accounts Receivable Management Policy: Theory and Evidence," *Journal of Finance* 47, pp. 169–200.

Chapter 20

Foreign Currency Futures and Options

*T*his chapter considers foreign currency futures and options and demonstrates how they can be used for hedging or speculative purposes. Because the profits and losses earned on futures and option contracts, as well as those earned on forward contracts, depend on how the spot exchange rate evolves over time, all these instruments are considered **derivative securities**. Derivative securities are securities whose values depend on the values of other, more basic underlying variables—in this case, the spot exchange rate.

As with other instruments in the foreign exchange market, much of the trade in futures contracts and options is conducted by banks. Commercial and investment banks deal aggressively in foreign currency options in order to meet the demands of their corporate and institutional customers, who use them to hedge their foreign exchange risks. In addition to banks, hedge funds and other investors trade foreign currency futures and options purely for speculative purposes—that is, strictly in order to earn a profit.

This chapter begins by introducing the foreign currency futures market and discussing how futures and forward contracts differ. It then discusses hedging with futures. Sections 20.3 and 20.4 present the basics of foreign currency options and their use in risk management. Section 20.5 examines some exotic options. As we first mentioned in Chapter 3, exotic derivatives caused a large number of international firms in emerging markets to suffer substantial losses during the 2007 to 2010 global financial crisis, and it is important to understand the risks involved.

20.1 THE BASICS OF FUTURES CONTRACTS

Futures Versus Forwards

Foreign currency futures contracts allow individuals and firms to buy and sell specific amounts of foreign currency at an agreed-upon price determined on a given future day. Although this sounds very similar to the forward contracts discussed in Chapter 3, there are a number of important differences between forward contracts and futures contracts.

Exchange Trading
The first major difference between foreign currency futures contracts and forward contracts is that futures contracts are traded on an exchange, whereas forward contracts are

made by banks and their clients. Examples of futures exchanges include the CME Group with its CME Globex electronic trading platform, which trades G10 as well as a variety of emerging market currency futures; NYSE Euronext's LIFFE CONNECT, which trades dollar-euro futures and options; and the Tokyo Financial Exchange (TFX), which trades both yen-denominated futures as well as other base currency–denominated futures. With exchange trading, futures contracts are standardized by the exchange, whereas the terms of forward contracts are negotiable.

In addition, with exchange trading, orders for futures contracts must be placed during the exchange's trading hours. This used to be more of an issue when trading only occurred in the "pit" by floor traders. Now, electronic trading platforms match demand to supply over many more hours. For example, CME Globex operates 23 hours per day, only closing between 4 P.M. and 5 P.M. Central Time, during the work week. The exchange is closed from 4 P.M. Friday until 5 P.M. Sunday.

In contrast to forward contracts, where dealers quote bid and ask prices at which they are willing either to buy or sell a foreign currency, for each party that buys a futures contract, there is a party that sells the contract at the same price. The price of a futures contract with specific terms changes continuously, as orders are matched on the floor or by computer.

Standardized Amounts

Contracts on a futures exchange represent standardized amounts of currencies. Although the futures contracts cannot be tailored to a corporation's specific needs as can forward contracts, the standardized amounts are relatively small compared to a typical forward contract. If larger positions are desired, one merely purchases more contracts. The small contract sizes facilitate trade and enhance market liquidity. Some examples of the current contract sizes at the CME Group for currencies versus the dollar are JPY12,500,000, EUR125,000, CAD100,000, GBP62,500, CHF125,000, and AUD100,000. Other dollar-based contracts are also traded, ranging from the Swedish krona to the New Zealand dollar to a number of emerging market currencies, including the Mexican peso, the Brazilian real, and the Russian ruble. Cross-rate products, such as GBP/EUR or JPY/EUR, are also traded.

Fixed Maturities

In the forward market, a client can request any future maturity date, and active daily trading occurs in contracts with maturities of 30, 60, 90, 180, or 360 days. Contracts on futures exchanges have only a few maturity dates. For example, CME Group contracts mature on the third Wednesday of March, June, September, and December. These dates are fixed, and hence the time to maturity shrinks as trading moves from one day to the next, until trading begins in a new maturity. Typically, contracts are introduced 6 months before maturity. Consistent with the delivery procedures on spot foreign exchange contracts, trading in futures contracts stops at 9:16 A.M. Central Time 2 business days before the maturity day of the contract.

Credit Risk

As the box on the origins of the CME Group futures contracts indicates, banks willingly trade forward contracts with large corporations, hedge funds, and institutional investors, but they might not trade forward contracts with individual investors or small firms with bad credit risk.

One major reason why futures markets exist is the way credit risk is handled. In contrast to forward markets, in which the two counterparties must directly assess the credit risk of their counterparty, all contracts on a futures exchange are between a member of the exchange and the exchange itself. Retail clients buy futures contracts from futures brokerage firms, which in the United States must register with the **Commodity Futures Trading Commission (CFTC)** as a **futures commission merchant (FCM)**. Legally, FCMs serve as the principals for the trades of their retail customers. Consequently, FCMs must meet minimum capital requirements set

The Origins of Currency Futures

Although the Chicago Mercantile Exchange (CME), a precursor of CME Group, began trading agricultural futures contracts in 1898, the first foreign currency futures contract was not traded until 1972. It was done via the International Monetary Market (IMM), which was a subdivision of the CME. The IMM was the brainchild of Nobel Laureate Milton Friedman of the University of Chicago and Leo Melamed, the head of the CME, which was a world center for trading commodity futures. In the late 1960s, Friedman became convinced that the Bretton Woods system of fixed exchange rates was doomed. He predicted that the dollar would devalue relative to various European currencies, including the Deutsche mark, after the breakup.

Friedman wanted to profit from the situation, which he correctly foresaw, but he was frustrated by his attempts to purchase Deutsche mark–denominated forward contracts at a bank because he had no "legitimate" business purpose for doing so—aside from speculating, which banks frowned upon. Consequently, he approached Melamed about having the CME develop futures contracts for foreign currencies in which the average citizen could "vote with his dollars" on the government policies being discussed in Washington and other capitals around the world. Melamed liked the idea, and by 1972, foreign currency futures contracts were approved for trading by the Commodity Futures Trading Commission, and the IMM was born. Unfortunately for Friedman, the breakdown of Bretton Woods and the devaluation of the dollar occurred in August 1971, when President Richard M. Nixon withdrew the commitment of the United States to redeem dollars for gold—before Friedman could place his bet.

by the exchanges and fiduciary requirements set by the CFTC. In addition, if an FCM wants to trade with the CME Group, it must become a **clearing member**.

When a trade takes place on the exchange, the **clearinghouse** of the exchange, which is an agency or a separate corporation of the futures exchange, acts as a buyer to every clearing member seller and a seller to every clearing member buyer. The clearinghouse imposes margin requirements, which are also called performance bonds, and conducts the daily settlement process known as marking to market that mitigates credit concerns. These margin requirements are then passed on to the individual customers by the futures brokers.

Margins

When someone enters a forward contract, no money changes hands, and the only cash flow is at the maturity of the contract. Assessing credit risk is thus very important. When a futures contract is purchased or sold, the investor must deposit some assets into a **margin account** to fulfill the **initial margin** requirement and ensure that any future losses on the contract will be covered. These assets act as a **performance bond** because they may be confiscated if the investor loses money in the trade.[1] As futures prices change, one party to the contract experiences profits, and the other party experiences losses. The daily profits and losses are deposited to and subtracted from the margin accounts of the respective parties. This is the **marking to market** process that we will examine in detail shortly.

Clearing members of the CME clearinghouse accept margin payments in the form of cash, U.S. government obligations, securities listed on the NYSE or the American Stock Exchange (valued at 70% of their market prices), gold warehouse receipts (valued at 70% of the afternoon price of gold on the London Stock Exchange), or letters of credit of at least

---

[1]The CME Group uses the terms "margin" and "performance bond" interchangeably. In 1988, the CME Group developed the **Standard Portfolio Analysis of Risk (SPAN)** system, which calculates performance bond requirements for portfolios of positions using simulations of market prices. In discussing SPAN on its Web site, the CME Group states, "It is the official performance bond (margin) mechanism of 50 registered exchanges, clearing organizations, service bureaus and regulatory agencies throughout the world. SPAN software is utilized by a wide range of end-users, including futures commission merchants (FCMs), investment banks, hedge funds, research organizations, risk managers, brokerage firms and individual investors worldwide."

the amount required for the initial margin. It is important to realize that depositing assets in a margin account is not a payment for the futures contract. The investor still owns the assets that are in the margin account and can receive interest on monies deposited in the account.

In 2011, initial margins on the CME Group for members or hedgers were between $1,500 for the USD/GBP to $4,500 for the JPY/USD, and the **maintenance margins** were the same.[2] For speculators, the initial margins were higher. For example, the JPY/USD contract required $6,075 as initial margin and $4,500 as maintenance margin. The maintenance margin is the minimum amount that must be kept in the account to guard against severe fluctuations in the futures prices and the losses that would be incurred by one of the parties. When the value of the margin account reaches the maintenance margin, there is a **margin call**, at which point the account must be brought back up to its initial value. Because margins are intended to control risk, their magnitude depends on the size of the contract and the volatility of the currencies.

Of course, the initial margin payments must eventually reach the clearinghouse. This happens through a pyramid structure. The clearinghouse, which sits at the top of the pyramid, collects the margins from clearing member FCMs, which collect the margins from non-clearing member FCMs, which collect them from their customers and execute their trades through FCM clearing members.

Marking to Market

The system of margin accounts coupled with a process of daily marking to market ensures that the users of these contracts present little credit risk to the FCMs and thus to the clearinghouse of the exchange. To better understand the process, let's examine marking to market, using a euro futures contract. Let's assume that each contract represents €125,000.

Suppose it is September, and you buy a December euro futures contract. Buying the contract means that you "go long in December euro," and you will profit if the euro appreciates relative to the dollar. Conversely, you will take losses if the euro depreciates. You place your order to buy with your broker, and the order is executed on the futures exchange at a price at which another trader is willing to sell the identical contract. This trader could be selling for his own account, or he could be executing an order on behalf of someone who has placed an order to "short" the December euro contract.

Consider how the contractual profits and losses evolve over time and how this affects your margin account. Exhibit 20.1 provides a 7-day example. Suppose that your trade was

Exhibit 20.1   An Example of Marking to Market in the Futures Market

Day	Futures Price ($/€)	Change in Futures Price ($/€)	Gain or Loss	Cumulative Gain or Loss	Margin Account
t	1.3321	0	0		$2,000.00
$t+1$	1.3315	−$0.0006	−$75.00	−$75.00	$1,925.00
$t+2$	1.3304	−$0.0011	−$137.50	−$212.50	$1,787.50
$t+3$	1.3288	−$0.0016	−$200.00	−$412.50	$1,587.50
$t+4$	1.3264	−$0.0024	−$300.00	−$712.50	$2,000.00
$t+5$	1.3296	+$0.0032	+$400.00	−$312.50	$2,400.00
$t+6$	1.3301	+$0.0005	+$62.50	−$250.00	$2,462.50

Notes: The futures price column lists the daily settle prices in the futures market. The contract size for the euro contract is assumed to be €125,000. The initial margin is $2,000, and the maintenance margin is $1,500. The gain or loss is the change in the futures price ($/€) multiplied by the size of the contract. The cumulative gain or loss is the sum of the daily gain or loss.

---

[2]Current margin requirements may be found at www.cmegroup.com.

filled on September 16, at the end of trading, and the **settle price**, or final futures trading price, for that day for the December contract was $1.3321/€. When you purchase the December euro contract, you must place the initial margin, which is assumed to be $2,000, into your margin account. The individual who sold the euro contract to you must also place $2,000 into his or her margin account. We assume that the maintenance margin is $1,500. In other words, if the value of your margin account drops by more than $500 because of losses on your futures position, you will be required to bring the account's balance back up to the initial $2,000.

Suppose that on September 17, the dollar price of the December euro futures contract falls by $0.0006/€, to $1.3315/€. This is the new daily settle price of the contract, and it affects the balance in your margin account. Because you are long in the euro contract, and the futures price of the euro fell, money is taken out of your margin account. Conversely, the person who sold the December futures contract—that is, the one who shorted the euro—gains money. The amount taken from your margin account to be placed in the margin account of the individual who sold the euro short is the change in the settle price times the contract size:

$$(\$0.0006/€) \times €125,000 = \$75$$

This process continues every day, until the maturity date of the contract. Exhibit 20.1 indicates that if the euro futures price falls to $1.3264/€ by day t+4, you will have a cumulative loss of $712.50. Because this cumulative loss makes the value of your margin account less than the maintenance margin of $1,500, you will receive a margin call from your broker, notifying you that you have to increase your margin account back to the initial margin of $2,000. Exhibit 20.1 also indicates that funds will be credited to your margin account if the December futures price increases as it does on days t+5 and t+6. These funds could either be left in your account, as in Exhibit 20.1, or they could be withdrawn to leave the margin account at the value of the initial margin ($2,000).

On the last trading day of the futures contract, 2 business days remain before delivery. Trading the futures contract stops at 9:16 A.M. Central Time. Arbitrage guarantees that the futures price at the maturity of the contract will be equal to the spot exchange rate on that day because both the futures price and the spot price are ways of purchasing euros with dollars for delivery in 2 business days. Hence, if on the Monday before the third Wednesday of December, the spot price is $1.3421/€, the futures price will have risen by

$$1.3421/€ - \$1.3321/€ = \$0.0100/€$$

You will have had an inflow of profit equal to

$$(\$0.0100/€) \times €125,000 = \$1,250$$

Of course, because you received the $1,250 in increments, it will actually be worth something slightly more than this amount because you will have received interest on your profits.

The marking-to-market process means that entering a futures contract can be thought of as a sequence of bets on the direction of the change in the price of the contract rather than a direct future purchase of foreign currency. This is an accurate description because all gains and losses are settled every day. Each day, you face the decision of sticking with your long or short position, which is called your **open interest**, or ending the bet by taking the reverse position. If you are long one contract and you sell one contract for the same maturity, the clearinghouse simply nets your position to zero. This is the way most futures contracts are closed out.

The Pricing of Futures Contracts

Because forward and futures contracts both allow you to buy or sell foreign currency at a particular future time at an exchange rate known today, you might think that the two prices should be the same. However, because forward contracts entail no cash flows until maturity, whereas futures contracts are marked to market, the two prices can, in theory, be slightly different.

Comparing Payoffs

Let's illustrate the payoff patterns for forward and futures contracts in symbols. Let $F(t)$ be the forward price of the foreign currency at time t. Then, the payoff per unit of foreign currency at maturity, time T, depends on the future spot rate, $S(T)$. If you purchase the foreign currency forward, the payoff equals

$$S(T) - F(t)$$

You win if $S(T) > F(t)$, and you lose if $S(T) < F(t)$.

Suppose you buy a foreign currency futures contract at time t at the futures price, $f(t)$, and you hold the contract until maturity, the same time T as the maturity of the forward contract. Because the payoff dribbles in over time due to marking to market, the per-unit payoff is

Day $t+1$:	$f(t+1) - f(t)$
Day $t+2$:	$f(t+2) - f(t+1)$
Day $t+3$:	$f(t+3) - f(t+2)$
$\vdots$	
Day T:	$f(T) - f(T-1)$

If we ignore the time value of money and add up all the cash flows, the aggregate payoff is

$$[f(t+1) - f(t)] + [f(t+2) - f(t+1)] + [f(t+3) - f(t+2)] + \ldots$$
$$+ [f(T) - f(T-1)] = f(T) - f(t)$$

because the intermediate futures prices cancel out. Because arbitrage drives the futures price at maturity, $f(T)$, to equality with the spot rate on that day, $S(T)$, the payoff on the futures contract is essentially the same as the payoff on the forward contract.

Why Futures Can Differ from Forwards

The payoffs of futures contracts and forward contracts are only "essentially the same" because a slight difference in payoffs arises when we do not ignore the interest that is earned on future profits or that must be paid on future losses. Technically, if the path of short-term interest rates could be foreseen—that is, if there were no random elements in the change in future short-term interest rates—there would be an arbitrage possibility if the forward exchange rate were different from the futures price because you would know how you could invest the profits or borrow to finance your losses. However, future interest rates are not known with certainty, so forward prices and futures prices can be different, in theory. In practice, though, the price differentials are minimal, and they appear to be within the transaction costs of the forward market. Therefore, we argue that futures prices are "essentially the same" as forward prices, and we don't explore further how futures contracts are valued.

Futures Quotes

Now that you understand how futures markets work, let's examine Exhibit 20.2, which shows data on futures prices from the CME Group. The information reports trading from April 21, 2011, and the first trade, which is the **open price** on that day, for a June euro contract was $1.4505/€.

During the day, trades occurred at prices as high as $1.4631/€ and as low as $1.4487/€. The settle price was $1.4555/€, and this price represents the value weighted price for all trades conducted in the last 30 seconds before 2:00 P.M. Central Time.

Exhibit 20.2   Futures Quotes from April 21, 2011

| Contract Size | JPY12,500,000 | | | CAD100,000 | | | GBP62,500 | | | EUR125,000 | | |
| Exchange Rate | USD per 100 JPY | | | USD per CAD | | | USD per GBP | | | USD per EUR | | |
Maturity	JUN	SEP	DEC	JUN	SEP	DEC	JUN	SEP	DEC	JUN	SEP	DEC
Open Price	1.2111	1.2136	1.2193	1.0486	1.0475	1.0478	1.6387	1.6460	—	1.4505	1.4454	1.4444
High Price	1.2256	1.2261	1.2257	1.0563	1.0534	1.0502	1.6590	1.6562	—	1.4631	1.4585	1.4510
Low Price	1.2111	1.2125	1.2138	1.0472	1.0447	1.0416	1.6376	1.6356	—	1.4487	1.4447	1.4444
Settle Price	1.2232	1.2241	1.2254	1.0491	1.0463	1.0431	1.6538	1.6514	—	1.4555	1.4512	1.4468
Change in Price	0.0093	0.0093	0.0093	0.0027	0.0026	0.0024	0.0141	0.0141	—	0.0058	0.0058	0.0060
Open Interest	125,635	1,312	119	139,545	2,781	2,481	112,115	430	—	246,358	3,137	86

| Contract Size | CHF125,000 | | | AUD100,000 | | | MXN500,000 | | | EUR100,000 | | |
| Exchange Rate | USD per CHF | | | USD per AUD | | | USD per 10 MXN | | | JPY per EUR | | |
Maturity	JUN	SEP	DEC	JUN	SEP	DEC	JUN	SEP	DEC	JUN	SEP	DEC
Open Price	1.1256	1.1275	—	1.0636	1.0535	—	0.8575	—	—	119.39	—	—
High Price	1.1392	1.1393	—	1.0710	1.0578	—	0.8605	—	—	119.39	—	—
Low Price	1.1249	1.1257	—	1.0613	1.0485	—	0.8545	—	—	118.83	—	—
Settle Price	1.1324	1.1329	—	1.0681	1.0550	—	0.8580	—	—	119.02	—	—
Change in Price	0.0071	0.0072	—	0.0077	0.0076	—	0.0008	—	—	-0.38	—	—
Open Interest	71,895	123	—	146,579	—	—	172,588	—	—	7,242	—	—

Note: All contracts except the JPY/EUR are traded on the CME Group. The JPY/EUR contract is trade on ICE Futures U.S. Data sources are Thomson Reuters and the Wall St. Journal Market Data Group.

Futures Contracts for Emerging Markets

In addition to trading futures contracts on the major currencies of the world, the CME Group now trades quite a few contracts on emerging-market currencies. The first of these to be established was for the Mexican peso, which began trading in April 1995.

At that time, trading futures contracts for the Mexican peso was quite a courageous move. Mexico had just witnessed a severe currency crisis, and Larry Summers, the U.S. Secretary of the Treasury, argued that introducing Mexican peso futures would be a bad idea because it would be easier for currency speculators to bet against the Mexican peso. Moreover, when plans for the contract were unfolding, it became clear that the usual delivery procedures of the CME were incompatible with the capital controls in place in Mexico.

In addition, the CME wanted to involve the Mexican government in the process of establishing the contract. Fortunately, the Mexican minister of finance at the time, Guillermo Ortiz, a Stanford-trained economist, thought that the introduction of a CME Mexican peso futures contract fit in well with his plans to restore confidence in the Mexican government and economy and to move toward more market-oriented policies. Ortiz argued that an effective futures contract would be hugely beneficial to international trade between the United States and Mexico because it would facilitate hedging, and he did not feel it would generate excessive exchange rate volatility. In fact, Ortiz decided to lift the Mexican capital controls, making it possible for the CME to employ its usual delivery procedures for the Mexican peso contract when it launched in April 1995.

This turned out to be a good decision in facilitating the success of the contract because actual delivery of currency was used more often than is the case with major currencies. That is, many of the users of the contracts turned out to be exporters and importers who desired the actual delivery of the currencies.

For the CME, this was the beginning of an Emerging Markets division that now has contracts listed not only on the Mexican peso but also on the Brazilian real, the Russian ruble, the Czech koruna, the Hungarian forint, the Polish zloty, the Chinese renminbi, the Korean won, the Israeli shekel, the Turkish lira, and the South African rand. The CME Group now also trades euro-denominated contracts on the koruna, the forint, the zloty, the renminbi, and the lira.

The row labeled "Change in Price" in Exhibit 20.2 indicates that the new settle price is $0.0058/€ higher that the previous day's settle price.

The final row represents the open interest that is outstanding, which is 246,358. The open interest is the number of pairs of contracts bought and sold that have not yet been closed out. Notice that the largest open interest is in the contract closest to maturity. This is typically true until the contract enters the maturity month, in which case activity switches to the next-closest contract.

20.2 HEDGING TRANSACTION RISK WITH FUTURES

This section examines how futures contracts can be used to hedge exposures to transaction exchange risk. It does so in the context of an extended example.

Hedging at Nancy Foods

Suppose it is the middle of February, and Nancy Foods, an American firm, has just contracted to sell frozen quiches to Kühlerkuchen, a German firm. Nancy Foods will receive €250,000 in the middle of March and is considering hedging the exposure with futures contracts.

The Hedging Decision

First, because the contract size on the CME Group is €125,000, Nancy Foods uses two contracts. Second, Nancy Foods has to determine whether it wants to buy or sell the futures contracts. Because it has a €250,000 account receivable, which is a euro asset, Nancy Foods will lose money if the euro weakens relative to the dollar. The company will gain if the euro strengthens relative to the dollar. Consequently, to hedge its exposure, Nancy Foods must enter into futures contracts that provide profits when the euro weakens and losses when the euro strengthens. That is, Nancy Foods hedges by acquiring a euro liability whose value is equivalent to the value of the underlying receivable.

If Nancy Foods sells two euro futures contracts, it profits when the euro weakens because the dollar value of €250,000 in the futures market is going down. The company loses on the futures contract if the euro strengthens because the dollar value of €250,000 in the futures market is going up. Notice that if the maturity date of the receivable is the third Wednesday in March, the maturity of the euro asset from the underlying receivable and the euro liability represented by Nancy Foods's sale of the futures contracts are matched exactly. Hence, the company is effectively hedged.

A Numeric Example

To be concrete, let's assume that the following exchange rates are observed:

	Spot Rate	Futures Rate (March contract)
February	$1.24/€	$1.23/€
March	$1.35/€	$1.35/€

The March futures rate coincides with the spot rate because both are for the third Wednesday in March. Because Nancy Foods is exposed to euro depreciation, the company goes short two futures contracts, at the futures rate of $1.23/€. What are the final cash flows?

First, when Nancy Foods sells the euro receivables in the spot market in March, the cash flow is

$$€250,000 \times \$1.35/€ = \$337,500$$

Second, the futures contract will have lost money because Nancy Foods established a short position in the futures market, and the euro appreciated versus the dollar. The cash flow on the futures contract is the change in the futures price multiplied by the contractual amount:

$$[(\$1.23/€) - (\$1.35/€)] \times €250,000 = -\$30,000$$

Combining the cash flow from the euro receivables with the loss on the futures contracts yields a total cash flow of

$$\$337,500 - \$30,000 = \$307,500$$

The effective exchange rate at which Nancy Foods sells the euro receivables is

$$\$307,500/€250,000 = \$1.23/€$$

Thus, by transacting in the futures market, Nancy Foods effectively locks in the original futures price.

Potential Problems with a Futures Hedge

Hedging transactions exposures with futures has two obvious problems. First, futures contracts are sold only in standardized sizes (€125,000 in our example). Hence, if you need to hedge an amount that is not a multiple of the standard size, some of your risk cannot be covered. A second problem is caused by the relatively low number of delivery dates. If the maturity of your foreign currency asset or liability does not match a settlement date in the futures market, the relationship between the spot exchange rate at the time the transaction takes place and the futures price of the foreign exchange is somewhat uncertain.

Basis Risk

To provide a perfect hedge, the price of the futures contract should move one-for-one with the spot exchange rate. Then, being long in the foreign currency from an underlying transaction can be hedged by going short in the corresponding futures contract. If this is not the case, the hedge is said to suffer **basis risk**. The basis is the difference between the spot price at time t, $S(t)$, and the futures price at time t, $f(t,T)$, for maturity date at time T:

$$\text{Basis} = \text{Spot price} - \text{Futures price} = S(t) - f(t, T)$$

Mostly, we refer to a single maturity, so we will omit the T indicator.

To see how the basis affects the quality of a hedge, let's ignore the time value of money because the maturity is short, and let's consider how the value of the receivable and the hedge move over time in Exhibit 20.3. Initially, the value of the receivable per unit of foreign currency is worth $S(t)$, the value of the spot exchange rate. The problem is that you can only sell the receivable at time T at the as-of-yet unknown exchange rate $S(T)$. The uncertain change in value $S(T) - S(t)$ represents your transaction exchange risk. Column 2 in Exhibit 20.3 shows how the value of the receivable moves with the spot rate. When you hedge a foreign currency asset using the futures market, you sell the foreign currency futures. Initially, the futures contract has no value, but on day 2, the cash flows start coming in (or leaving) your margin account. We record the cumulative cash flows in the third column. The fourth column reflects the value of the hedged position: the receivable plus the cash flows earned or lost in the futures market. It is easy to see that the hedged position equals the futures rate at which you entered the contract plus the basis. Consequently, to make sure you really lock in the future rate, the basis at maturity must be zero.

Suppose we hold the contract until maturity. In that case, the futures rate converges to the spot rate; that is, the basis is zero at maturity. Then, Exhibit 20.3 shows that the hedged position is worth $f(t)$; you effectively sell the receivable at the futures rate. If the maturities of the receivable and the futures contract do not coincide, the basis will not equal zero when the futures contract is closed, and there will be basis risk. Note that the value of the hedged position has changed as follows between time t and time T:

$$f(t) + [S(T) - f(T)] - S(t) = [S(T) - f(T)] - [S(t) - f(t)]$$

Hence, the change in value in the hedged position equals the change in basis between time t and T. If the basis is zero at maturity, this change in value is perfectly known at time t. Although basis risk is typically much smaller than the risk associated with an uncovered

Exhibit 20.3 Hedging a Receivable with Futures

Time	Value of Receivable	Cumulative Value of Futures Hedge (short position)	Value of Hedged Position
t	$S(t)$	0	$S(t)$
$t+1$	$S(t+1)$	$f(t) - f(t+1)$	$f(t) + [S(t+1) - f(t+1)]$
$t+2$	$S(t+2)$	$[(f(t+1) - f(t+2)] + [f(t) - f(t+1)]$ $= f(t) - f(t+2)$	$f(t) + [S(t+2) - f(t+2)]$
⋮	⋮	⋮	⋮
T	$S(T)$	$f(t) - f(T)$	$f(t) + [S(T) - f(T)]$

Note: The hedged position reflects the sum of the previous two columns.

position, a substantial amount of risk may nevertheless remain. Risk managers often use quantitative techniques to figure out the best way to mitigate basis risk, but these techniques are beyond the scope of this book.

Example 20.1   A Euro Receivable and Basis Risk

Let's return to the situation in which Nancy Foods is contracting to sell quiches in Germany, thereby generating a €250,000 receivable. This time, assume that the contract is made in January, and payment is scheduled for early March. Now, the delivery date for the quiches does not coincide with the maturity date of the futures contract, and Nancy Foods consequently faces basis risk. We assume that the following exchange rates are observed:

	Spot Rate	Futures Rate (March contract)
January	$1.21/€	$1.22/€
March	$1.33/€	$1.325/€

To protect itself from euro depreciation, Nancy Foods sells two futures contracts at the futures rate of $1.22/€. What are the final cash flows now?

First, Nancy Foods sells the euro receivables in the spot market, receiving

$$€250,000 \times \$1.33/€ = \$332,500$$

Second, the futures contract lost money because the euro appreciated, and Nancy Foods established a short position in the futures market. The total cash flow would be

$$[(\$1.22/€) - (\$1.325/€)] \times €250,000 = -\$26,250$$

So, ultimately, the euro receivables plus the loss on the futures contract yields

$$\$332,500 - \$26,250 = \$306,250$$

The effective exchange rate at which Nancy Foods sold the euro receivables is

$$\$306,250/€250,000 = \$1.225/€$$

This does not equal the futures rate of $1.22/€ because of basis risk. The difference of $0.005/€ with the futures rate exactly reflects the basis (Spot rate − Futures rate = $1.33/€ − $1.325/€) at the time that the futures contract was closed out and the receivable sold for dollars in the spot market. In this case, basis risk had a positive effect on Nancy Foods's cash flow. That is, we have, as in Exhibit 20.3,

$$\text{Effective rate} = \text{Futures rate} + \text{Basis}$$
$$\$1.225/€ = \$1.22/€ + (\$1.33/€ - \$1.325/€)$$

After the fact, we see that Nancy Foods would have been better off not hedging at all because the euro actually appreciated, and the company had a euro receivable. If Nancy Foods wanted to hedge completely, though, the futures market works pretty well—even in the presence of basis risk.

In Section 20.3, we will look at how options allow companies to hedge while retaining some benefit from advantageous exchange rate movements. But first, we need to see how the Handel brothers are doing.

POINT–COUNTERPOINT

On Good Beer and Korunas

The Handel family reunion on Uncle Fred's estate in Chappaqua, New York, brought Ante, Freedy, and Suttle together again with their flamboyant uncle who's in the export–import business. Uncle Fred was keen to get his nephews' insights on the international financial issues he faced. After dinner, he insisted that they all meet at the bar in his den because he had something to show them. Uncle Fred poured a particularly clear lager from a funky-looking bottle and roared, "Here my friends, drink this!"

"What beer is this?" Ante inquired, "This tastes wonderful!"

"Well, my friends, this is Pilsner Kozquell, an authentic Czech lager," their uncle explained. "It is brewed under strict purity laws—only hops, yeast, malt, and water can be used. The result is very different from that chemically, carbon dioxide–infused, scrub water they make as beer in America! And guess what? This wonderful beer may soon be available in America at reasonable prices, as I am hoping to start importing the stuff! I have bid for the import license with the Czech brewery, and if everything goes well, the first shipment should arrive in 6 months."

"That's wonderful news, Uncle!" exclaimed Freedy.

"Well, there are problems," sighed their uncle. "I'm not sure I'm going to win the bid, and the brewery will take a month to decide. Moreover, they insist on being paid in Czech korunas. I've got a potentially huge koruna liability 6 months from now, and I am worried about the currency risk. I was kind of hoping you guys could help me out. What can I do to hedge this risk? At current exchange rates, my margins are not that great, and I cannot afford to pay many more dollars for the beer. On top of all that, the dollar has been weakening, and my bank is not willing to do a koruna forward contract with me. They say I've maxed out my credit limit."

"Ha," said Ante, "I would not hedge! The Czech Republic is now a member of the European Union, and it may soon adopt the euro as its currency. Because it is an emerging market, it likely still has tons of inflationary pressure, and I suspect its currency will depreciate tremendously in the run-up to adopting the euro. If that happens, your liability will be melting away in dollar terms if the dollar stays even with the euro."

"No way, Uncle! Don't take that risk!" Freedy interjected. "If the koruna moves with the euro versus the dollar, the opposite may happen. Also, the koruna might appreciate against both currencies, as people hoard it in anticipation of joining the euro monetary system. With the weak dollar, your koruna exposure is very risky now! I would use the futures market to hedge. The CME Group has futures contracts on the koruna, so you can go long in koruna futures. If the koruna appreciates, the payment for the shipment is going to cost you more dollars, but the futures position will gain money, too, offsetting the loss on the payable."

"That sounds interesting," Uncle Fred mused. "But, Suttle, tell me what you think."

Suttle reluctantly put down his glass of Pilsner Kozquell and said, "I think there is indeed a chance the koruna will depreciate as Ante claims, but I've heard that the Czech economy is doing very well, and the currency has been stable. In fact, the Czech central bank has competently adopted a modern monetary policy, and the inflation rate there has recently run at a lower rate than in the European Union. Hence, the risk of koruna appreciation versus the euro is real. The risk of euro appreciation versus the dollar is also very real. With such risks and low profit margins, some form of hedge is probably a good idea. However, it depends on your point of view. How sure are you that you will win the contract? If you hedge with a long koruna futures position and don't get the contract, you'll take losses if the koruna weakens. I think you need to look into options. Because you need to buy koruna, why not buy a koruna call option? You pay a bit of a premium, but you are hedged, and you still profit from a lower dollar payment in case the koruna depreciates. If you don't get the contract, the most you can lose is the option premium, and these options also trade at the CME."

Ante gasped: "Options? Gee, I've got to study this for our international finance exam. They're so complicated!" Uncle Fred just smiled and poured another Pilsner Kozquell lager. He knew what to do.

20.3 BASICS OF FOREIGN CURRENCY OPTION CONTRACTS

A foreign currency option contract gives the buyer of an option the right, but not the obligation, to trade a specific amount of foreign currency for domestic currency at a specific exchange rate. Foreign currency options are traded primarily over the counter (OTC) by money center banks, but they are also traded on organized exchanges. Two of the largest exchanges are the NASDAQ OMX PHLX, which was formed in 2008 when the Philadelphia Stock Exchange (PHLX) was purchased by NASDAQ OMX, and the International Securities Exchange, which is a subsidiary of Eurex.

Basic Option Terminology

The two fundamental types of options are calls and puts. A **foreign currency call option** gives the buyer of the option the right, but not the obligation, to buy a specific amount of foreign currency with domestic currency at an exchange rate stated in the contract. A **foreign currency put option** gives the buyer of the option the right, but not the obligation, to sell a specific amount of foreign currency for domestic currency at an exchange rate stated in the contract. Because the buyer of the option purchases the right to transact from the seller, the buyer must pay the seller the value of the option, which is the option's price. Market participants also refer to the option price as an **option premium**. The seller of the option is also referred to as the writer of the option.

European Versus American Options

Foreign currency option contracts have an expiration or maturity date. If the buyer of an option decides to engage in the transaction at the time specified in the option contract, she is said to have "exercised" her option. If the buyer has not exercised her option by the expiration date, the option becomes worthless. An option that can be exercised only at maturity is called a **European option**. An option that can be exercised at the discretion of the buyer at any time between the purchase date and the maturity date is called an **American option**. If an American option is exercised prior to maturity, the person is said to have engaged in **early exercise**.[3]

Strike Prices and Intrinsic Value

The exchange rate in an option contract is called the option's **strike price**, or **exercise price**. Investors commonly compare a contract's strike price with the current spot exchange rate. If some revenue could be earned by exercising the option immediately, even though the option holder cannot or might not want to exercise it, the option is said to be

---

[3]Note that the terminology describing when options can be exercised—that is, European vs. American—has nothing to do with where the options are traded or how the exchange rates are quoted. The terminology only describes the inability (European) or ability (American) of the buyer to exercise the option prior to maturity.

"in the money." If no revenue could be earned by exercising the option immediately, the option is said to be "out of the money." An "at-the-money" option has a strike price equal to the current spot rate. Traders also speak of options that are "at-the-money-forward" if the strike price is equal to the forward rate for that maturity. Option transactions can also be terminated by closing out the position in the OTC market, or by reversing the original transaction, as in the futures markets. That is, the buyer of the option can simply sell the contract on the exchange.

The immediate revenue from exercising an option is called the option's **intrinsic value**. Let K be the strike price, and let S be the current spot rate, both in domestic currency per unit of foreign currency. Then, the intrinsic value per unit of a foreign currency option can be represented as

$$\text{Call option intrinsic value: } \max[S - K, 0]$$
$$\text{Put option intrinsic value: } \max[K - S, 0]$$

Here, max denotes the operation that takes the maximum of the two numbers between the square brackets. For example, when the spot rate is smaller than the stock price ($S < K$), the call option is not worth exercising immediately, so its intrinsic value is 0, but the put option's intrinsic value is $K - S$. Now that we have examined the terminology of options, let's look at some concrete examples.

Example 20.2   A Euro Call Option Against Dollars

A euro call option against dollars gives the buyer the right, but not the obligation, to purchase a certain amount of euros, such as €1 million, with dollars at a particular exchange rate, such as $1.20/€. If the spot exchange rate of dollars per euro in the future is greater than the exercise price of $1.20/€, the buyer of the option will exercise the right to purchase euros at the lower contractual price. When exercising the option, the buyer pays the seller of the option

$$(\$1.20/€) \times €1,000,000 = \$1,200,000$$

and the seller delivers the €1,000,000. The buyer of the option can then sell the euros in the spot market for dollars at whatever spot rate, $S(\$/€)$, prevails at that time, generating dollar revenue of

$$S(\$/€) \times €1,000,000$$

Hence, the net dollar revenue generated for the buyer of the option is equal to the difference between the current spot price and the exercise price multiplied by the contractual amount. If the spot rate is $1.25/€, the net dollar revenue from exercising the euro call option on €1,000,000 is

$$[(\$1.25/€) - (\$1.20/€)] \times €1,000,000 = \$50,000$$

Note that this is the intrinsic value of the option at the time of exercise, $\max[S - K, 0]$, multiplied by the contract size. Remember that the $50,000 is purely the revenue from exercising the option. It is not the profit to the purchaser of the option because it does not subtract the cost of the option position.

Notice also that the right to buy €1,000,000 with dollars at the exchange rate of $1.20/€ is equivalent to the right to sell $1,200,000 for €1,000,000. This option is described as a dollar put option against the euro with contractual amount of $1,200,000 and a strike price of

$$€1,000,000/\$1,200,000 = 1/(\$1.20/€) = €0.8333/\$$$

These options are the same; they are just described differently.

Also, note that the buyer of the option could accept a payment of $50,000 from the seller of the option to close out the position rather than take delivery of the €1,000,000 and resell the euros in the spot market. Many option contracts are closed in this way, and this is how options on the NASDAQ OMX PHLX are settled.

Example 20.3   A Yen Put Option Against the Pound

A Japanese yen put against the British pound in a European contract gives the buyer of the option the right, but not the obligation, to sell a certain amount of yen, say ¥100,000,000, for British pounds to the seller of the option at the maturity of the contract. The sale takes place at the strike price of pounds per 100 yen, say £0.6494 /¥100. If the spot exchange rate of pounds per 100 yen at the exercise date in the future is less than the strike price, the buyer of the option will exercise the right to sell the ¥100,000,000 for pounds at the higher contractual price. When exercising the option, the buyer delivers ¥100,000,000 to the seller of the option, who must pay

$$(£0.6494/¥100) \times ¥100,000,000 = £649,400$$

Suppose that the spot exchange rate at maturity is £0.6000/¥100 yen, which is less than the strike price. Then, the buyer of the option can purchase ¥100,000,000 in the spot foreign exchange market for £600,000 and sell the yen to the person who wrote the put contract. By exercising the option, the buyer of the yen put generates pound revenue equal to the difference between the exercise price of £0.6494/¥100 and the current spot price of £0.6000/¥100 multiplied by ¥100,000,000:

$$[(£0.6494/¥100) - (£0.6000/¥100)] \times ¥100,000,000 = £49,400$$

This corresponds to the intrinsic value of the contract at maturity multiplied by the contract size—that is, Revenue $= \max[K - S, 0] \times$ Contract size. Once again, this is purely the revenue from the option contract; it is not the profit to the purchaser of the option because it does not subtract the original cost of the put option.

Notice, also, that the right to sell ¥100,000,000 for British pounds at the exchange rate of £0.6494/¥100 is equivalent to the right to buy £649,400 with yen at the exchange rate of

$$¥100,000,000/£649,400 = 1/(£0.6494/¥100) = ¥153.99/£$$

This latter option is a British pound call option against the Japanese yen.

Options Trading

Most options are traded by banks, either in the interbank market or as OTC transactions with the bank's clients. That is, transactions are done in a dealer network and are not listed on any centralized exchange. Typical OTC options use the European exercise convention. In the OTC market, though, a reasonable request by a corporate customer for any type of option with a particular strike price, maturity date, or other characteristic will be met with a price quoted by a bank. OTC options are also typically written for much larger amounts than exchange-traded options, and a much broader range of currencies is covered.

The cash flows generated by exercise of an OTC option are handled either by exchange of the relevant currency amounts 2 business days after the notification of exercise or, often, by cash settlement. In the latter case, the writer of the option compensates the buyer of the option for the revenue that the option generates when the option ends up in the money.

As with forward contracts, there is a considerable amount of counterparty risk that concerns both bank traders and corporate treasurers. Banks manage their counterparty risks by establishing maximum exposure limits to particular clients, and corporate treasurers must be aware of the risks of dealing with particular banks.

Currency Options on the NASDAQ OMX PHLX

The NASDAQ OMX PHLX trades options on spot currencies versus the U.S. dollar. The contracts specify different amounts of the underlying foreign currency: 10,000 units of foreign currency for the Australian dollar, the British pound, the Canadian dollar, the euro, the Swiss franc, and the New Zealand dollar; 100,000 units of foreign currency for the Mexican peso, the Norwegian krone, the South African rand, and the Swedish krona; and 1,000,000 Japanese yen. The expiration months are March, June, September, and December plus the 2 nearest future months. The last trading day is the third Friday of the expiring month. The exercise style is European. The settlement of all the contracts is in dollars. The option prices are quoted in U.S. cents per foreign currency unit for the currencies in which the contractual amount is 10,000 units; in 0.1 U.S. cents per unit for the currencies in which the contractual amount is 100,000 units; and in 0.01 U.S. cents for the yen. Thus, a one-point move in the option price corresponds to a gain or loss of $100 on each of the contracts. The Options Clearing Corporation serves as the official clearinghouse for options trades on the NASDAQ OMX PHLX. Let's consider an example from this market.

Example 20.4   A Euro Call Option Against Dollars

On October 1, 2010, the euro was trading at $1.3780/€. A euro call option with a strike price of "135" and a December 2010 maturity was quoted at 4.75 cents per euro. Because the strike price is expressed in cents per euro, we can convert it to dollars per euro, or $1.35/€, and a similar transformation of the option price gives $0.0475/€. For a contract size of €10,000, this option would have cost

$$(\$0.0475/€) \times €10,000 = \$475$$

While this option cannot be used to buy the euro, notice that the the cost of purchasing €10,000 at the stike price of $1.35/€ would have been

$$(\$1.35/€) \times €10,000 = \$13,500$$

Therefore, the option premium (the cost of the option) represents less than 4% of the value of the underlying contract:

$$(\$475/\$13,500) \times 100 = 3.52\%$$

Exhibit 20.4 Prices of Options on Futures Contracts

Currency	Type	Maturity	Strike Prices					
			900	950	1000	1050	1100	1150
Canadian Dollar	**Calls**	May	14.91	9.91	4.93	0.68	0.01	—
		Jun	14.91	9.93	5.04	1.20	0.08	—
		Sep	14.7	9.91	5.55	2.26	0.63	0.18
CAD100,000		May	—	—	0.02	0.77	5.10	10.09
USD cents per CAD	**Puts**	Jun	—	0.02	0.14	1.29	5.17	10.09
		Sep	0.11	0.31	0.94	2.63	5.98	10.52
			1000	1050	1100	1150	1200	1250
Swiss Franc	**Calls**	May	13.24	8.24	3.34	0.37	0.02	—
		Jun	13.24	8.27	3.73	0.96	0.17	0.05
		Sep	13.42	8.86	5.04	2.47	1.12	0.59
CHF 125,000		May	-	-	0.10	2.13	6.78	10.76
USD Cents per CHF	**Puts**	Jun	-	0.04	0.49	2.72	6.92	10.80
		Sep	0.17	0.60	1.76	4.17	7.81	11.27
			14200	14300	14400	14500	14600	14700
Euro	**Calls**	May	3.85	3.01	2.26	1.6	1.08	0.69
		Jun	4.49	3.75	3.09	2.48	1.95	1.49
		Sep	6.04	5.41	4.83	4.29	3.78	3.31
EUR125,000		May	0.30	0.46	0.68	1.05	1.53	2.14
USD Cents per EUR	**Puts**	Jun	0.94	1.17	1.59	1.93	2.40	2.94
		Sep	2.93	3.30	3.71	4.14	4.66	5.18
			1410	1460	1510	1560	1610	1660
British Pound	**Calls**	May	24.38	19.38	14.38	9.40	4.51	0.83
		Jun	24.38	19.38	14.41	9.50	4.96	1.59
		Sep	24.24	19.42	14.74	10.33	6.46	3.46
GBP62,500		May	0.02	0.02	0.01	0.02	0.13	1.45
USD Cents per GBP	**Puts**	Jun	0.01	0.01	0.04	0.13	0.53	2.21
		Sep	0.16	0.33	0.64	1.22	2.33	4.32
			1120	1170	1220	1270	1320	1370
Japanese Yen	**Calls**	May	10.32	5.38	1.26	0.16	0.03	0.01
		Jun	10.38	5.65	2.07	0.59	0.18	0.06
		Sep	10.97	6.93	3.95	2.11	1.13	0.62
JPY12,500,000		May	0.01	0.06	0.94	4.84	9.71	14.69
USD Cents per 100 JPY	**Puts**	Jun	0.07	0.34	1.75	5.26	9.85	14.73
		Sep	0.59	1.54	3.54	6.68	10.69	15.17

Note: All contracts are traded at the CME Group. Data are from Thomson Reuters and the Wall Street Journal Market Data Group.

Currency Options at the CME Group

At the CME Group, the buyer of an option is entitled to the right to buy (for a call) or to sell (for a put) the corresponding currency futures contract. Consequently, the contract sizes and expiration months follow those of the futures contracts. Trading closes on the Friday immediately preceding the third Wednesday of the contract month. Exhibit 20.4 contains examples of options quotes from the CME Group from Thursday, April 21, 2011.

Options Quotes

In Exhibit 20.4, the first column identifies the currency, the contract size, and the units in which option premiums are expressed. For example, the British pound contract size is

£62,500, and prices of the options are quoted in U.S. cents per pound. The option prices for most other currencies are also quoted in cents per unit. The exception is the Japanese yen, where the units are cents per 100 yen. The quotations for the strike prices are unusual, and the user should be aware of current futures prices to ensure a correct interpretation of the units. Most currencies, such as the euro, are quoted in $1/100$ cent per unit, as the first euro strike price is 14,200, which corresponds to an exchange rate of $\$1.42/€$. But the strike prices for the pound are quoted in $1/10$ cent per pound, as 1,510 corresponds to an exchange rate of $\$1.51/£$, and the strike prices for the yen are in $1/1,000$ cent per yen, as 1,270 corresponds to an exchange rate of $\$0.01270/¥$.

Each column related to a contract price provides the strike price in the first row followed by three rows of call prices and three rows of put prices. The three rows refer to different expiration months. The May contract is linked to the May futures contract. To check your understanding of the information provided in Exhibit 20.4, let's consider the purchase of a yen put option contract because the units are a little tricky.

Example 20.5 A Yen Put Option Against Dollars

Consider a Japanese yen put option contract with a strike price of 1,270 ($\$0.01270/¥$) and a maturity of June, which costs 5.26 U.S. cents per 100 yen. If we want to express the strike price in dollars per yen, we must first divide by 100 to convert from cents per 100 yen to cents per yen, and then we must divide by 100 again to convert from cents per yen to dollars per yen. Hence, the cost of the option goes from 5.26 cents per 100 yen to 0.0526 cents per yen, or $\$0.000526/¥$. Consequently, the buyer of the contract would pay

$$(\$0.000526/¥) \times ¥12,500,000 = \$6,575$$

to the seller of the contract at the initiation of the deal. Because the contract is an American-style option, the buyer of the contract would have the right, but not the obligation, to sell ¥12,500,000, or one futures contract, at the strike price of $\$0.01270/¥$ in the futures markets, and the seller would be obligated to purchase the yen futures contract at that price at any time before the June maturity.

Exchange-Listed Currency Warrants

Longer-maturity foreign currency options, called **currency warrants**, are sometimes issued by major corporations or investment banks and are actively traded on exchanges such as the American Stock Exchange, the London Stock Exchange, and the Australian Stock Exchange. Corporate issuers include AT&T Credit Corp., Deutsche Bank, Ford Motor Credit Co., Goldman Sachs, General Electric Credit Corp., the Macquarie Bank Ltd., the Student Loan Marketing Corp. (Sallie Mae), Société Générale, and Xerox Credit Corp. Maturities often exceed 1 year.

Currency warrants allow retail investors and small corporations that are too small to participate in the OTC markets to purchase long-term currency options. In most cases, the original issuer should not be viewed as bearing the implied currency risk. Instead, the issuer is probably hedging in the bank-dominated OTC market. The issuers are effectively buying foreign exchange options at wholesale prices and selling options to the public at a retail price. A currency warrant is generally cash settled, with the payoff clearly explained in the prospectus. Let's look at an example.

Example 20.6 Macquarie Put Warrant

Consider an Australian dollar put warrant against the U.S. dollar issued by Macquarie Bank with a maturity date of December 15, 2010, that traded on the Australian Stock Exchange. The warrant was characterized by a strike price of $0.90/AUD and a multiplier of AUD10. The payoff to the put warrant was specified as

$$\max\left[0, \frac{\text{Strike price} - \text{Spot rate}}{\text{Spot rate}}\right] \times \text{Multiplier}$$

For example, suppose the spot exchange rate was $0.85/AUD at maturity. Then, the settlement value for one warrant would have been

$$\frac{(\$0.90/\text{AUD}) - (\$0.85/\text{AUD})}{(\$0.85/\text{AUD})} \times \text{AUD10} = \$0.59$$

Note that, as is true with exchange-traded options, an investor can close out his position at any point by selling the warrant back into the market. Since the actual spot exchange rate at maturity was $1.0233/AUD, the holder of the warrant at maturity received no payoff.

20.4 THE USE OF OPTIONS IN RISK MANAGEMENT

Now that you understand the basics of foreign currency options, we can examine how they can be used to manage foreign exchange risk. The classic use of a foreign currency option contract as a hedging device arises in a bidding situation.

A Bidding Situation at Bagwell Construction

Suppose that Bagwell Construction, a U.S. company, wants to bid on the construction of a new office building in Tokyo. The Japanese developer has instructed all interested parties to submit their yen-denominated bids by June 30. Because the bids are complex contracts involving many more parameters than just the overall yen price of the contract, it will take the Japanese developer a month to evaluate the bids, and the winner will not be announced until July 31.

Bagwell management has determined that it can do the construction in Tokyo for $80,000,000, which will be paid out more or less evenly over the course of a year. If the firm gets the contract, it will receive yen revenue from the Japanese developer in five equal installments. There will be an initial yen payment on July 31, followed by four quarterly installments.

The Transaction Risk

By bidding a fixed amount of yen to do this project, Bagwell Construction incurs transaction foreign exchange risk. If Bagwell gets the project and the yen weakens relative to the dollar, the contractual yen revenue will purchase fewer dollars in the future. Notice that as soon as Bagwell bids on the contract, it acquires a transaction exposure. If the firm does nothing to hedge its contingent yen asset exposure during the time that the contracts are being evaluated and the yen weakens relative to the dollar, Bagwell's entire dollar profit could be eliminated before it even begins construction. If its strategy is to get the contract and then hedge, it could be too late.

The Problem with a Forward Hedge

Can Bagwell Construction hedge this risk with a forward contract? If Bagwell sells yen forward, it acquires an uncontingent yen liability. No matter what happens in 30 days, Bagwell will have to sell a specific amount of yen to the bank. Everything will be fine if Bagwell gets the contract. But what would happen if Bagwell sells yen forward and then fails to win the construction contract?

If the company does not get the construction job, it will still have to buy yen to fulfill the uncontingent commitment of the forward contract. If the yen strengthens such that the dollar price of yen in the spot market is higher than the contractual forward price, Bagwell will lose money because it will cost more dollars in the spot market to buy the yen to be delivered on the forward contact than the amount of dollars that the company will receive from the bank. Hence, if the yen strengthens versus the dollar, Bagwell will lose money, possibly a lot of money.

The Options Solution

Foreign exchange options provide a much better solution to Bagwell's problem of hedging in June prior to the resolution of the contract because options provide the purchaser with a contingent claim. How would an option contract work, and which option should be used?

Because Bagwell ultimately wants to sell the yen it will be paid if it gets the contract, the company should hedge by buying a yen put against the dollar. The yen put gives the buyer the right, but not the obligation, to sell yen for dollars at the strike price. Then, if Bagwell gets the contract and the yen has weakened relative to the dollar, the loss of value on the construction contract is offset by a gain in the value of the yen put. The company can sell yen from the construction contract at the exercise price, which is higher than the dollar price of yen in the spot market.

If Bagwell does not win the contract, the value of the yen put is the maximum that the firm can lose. But if at the maturity of the option, the yen has weakened relative to the dollar, the right to sell yen at a high dollar price will be valuable. Bagwell will consequently be able to recoup some of the premium that was initially paid for the option. Purchasing the option thus provides insurance against transaction risk.

Using Options to Hedge Transaction Risk

We now turn to the use of options in managing transaction exchange risk. While forwards and futures can be used, options allow the firm to hedge while retaining some of the upside potential from favorable exchange rate changes. Our next example considers an exporting situation.

Example 20.7 Exporting Pharmaceutical Products from the United States to the United Kingdom

On Friday, October 1, 2010, Pfimerc, an exporter of pharmaceutical products from the United States to the United Kingdom, knew it had an account receivable of £500,000 due on Friday, March 19, 2011. The following data were available:

Spot rate (U.S. cents per British pound): 158.34
170-day forward rate (U.S. cents per British pound): 158.05
U.S. dollar 170-day interest rate: 0.20% p.a.
British pound 170-day interest rate: 0.40% p.a.
Option data for March contracts in ¢/£:

Strike	Call Prices	Put Prices
158	5.00	4.81
159	4.52	5.33
160	4.08	5.89

Pfimerc wanted to understand how it might hedge this transaction using foreign currency options. The first thing to determine is which type of option provides a hedge. Because Pfimerc would be receiving British pounds, the transaction risk is that the pound weakens relative to the dollar. If the company does not hedge, it could experience a large loss when it sells the £500,000 in the spot market in March. The appropriate option hedge gives Pfimerc the right, but not the obligation, to sell pounds in 170 days at a contractual strike price of dollars per pound—a European pound put option.

Let's work with a strike price of 158¢/£, which costs 4.81¢/£ or $0.0481/£. Because Pfimerc wants to sell £500,000 in the future, today it must pay

$$£500,000 \times (\$0.0481/£) = \$24,050$$

If in March, the dollar value of the pound falls below the strike price of $1.58/£, Pfimerc will exercise the option to sell £500,000 at that price. Consequently, the minimum March revenue that Pfimerc will receive is

$$£500,000 \times \$1.58/£ = \$790,000, \text{ if } S(t+170) \le \$1.58/£$$

When the future spot rate exceeds the strike price, the company will sell its pounds in the future spot market, and its revenue will be

$$£500,000 \times S(t+170) > \$790,000, \text{ if } S(t+170) > \$1.58/£$$

Whether Pfimerc exercises the option or not, if it hedges with put options, it must subtract the March value of the cost of the puts that was paid in October from its March revenue to get a net revenue figure. This opportunity cost of purchasing the option is therefore

$$[\$24,050 \times (1 + i(\$))] = [\$24,050 \times (1.00094)] = \$24,073$$

where the interest factor is $(0.2/100)(170/360) = 0.00094$. Hence, the minimum net revenue that Pfimerc receives in March if it hedges with puts is

$$\$790,000 - \$24,073 = \$765,927$$

On a cents-per-pound basis, the March cost of the put option is

$$(4.81¢/£) \times (1.00094) = 4.82¢/£$$

Exhibit 20.5 summarizes the transaction risk exposure related to various strategies for selling British pounds. The horizontal axis shows possible realizations of future spot exchange rates expressed in U.S. cents per pound. The vertical axis measures the net revenue Pfimerc receives (in cents per pound), and the three different lines represent its net revenues depending on the realizations of the future exchange rate.

The 45-degree line represents the unhedged strategy. If Pfimerc chooses not to hedge, it sells pounds for dollars in the future spot market, and its revenue increases one for one with pound appreciation. But, its revenue also decreases one for one with any pound depreciation. Pfimerc's risk of loss is therefore unlimited.

The horizontal line in Exhibit 20.5 represents the strategy of hedging with a forward contract. If Pfimerc sells pounds forward at $1.5805/£, its March revenue is

$$(\$1.5805/£) \times £500,000 = \$790,250$$

On a cents-per-pound basis, Pfimerc's revenue will equal the forward rate of 158.05¢/£ no matter what future spot exchange rate is realized.

The kinked line in Exhibit 20.5 represents the net revenue from the strategy of buying the 158 March pound put. The minimum net revenue is

$$158¢/£ - 4.82¢/£ = 153.18¢/£$$

Exhibit 20.5 Hedging Pound Revenues

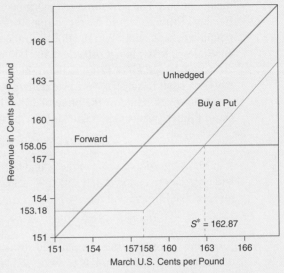

Notes: The horizontal axis presents different possible future exchange rates. The vertical axis represents the revenue in cents per pound from three different strategies. The horizontal line reflects the revenue implied by a forward contract, which is not dependent on the future exchange rate. The upward-sloping 45-degree line represents the unhedged strategy. The revenue equals the future exchange rate. The "hockey stick" line represents the revenue from hedging the receivable by buying a pound put option.

This occurs when Pfimerc exercises its puts—that is, when the future spot rate is less than or equal to 158¢/£. The option hedge provides a floor on Pfimerc's revenue while allowing it to participate in any strengthening of the pound relative to the dollar.

Notice also that the net revenue from the option hedge is below the net revenue from the forward hedge when the exchange rate in the future is below a certain exchange rate, denoted S^* in Exhibit 20.5. If the future spot rate is greater than S^*, the net revenue from the option hedge exceeds the revenue from the forward hedge. This is an example of no-free-lunch economics. If the option hedge puts a floor on your net revenue, but it allows you to participate in a possible strengthening of the pound, which increases your net revenue, the floor must be below the forward rate. Otherwise, the option strategy would strictly dominate the forward strategy.

We can determine the value of S^* by equating the two net revenues. The net revenue from the option hedge is $S^* - 4.82¢/£$, and the revenue from the forward hedge is $158.05¢/£$. Therefore, we find that S^* is

$$S^* - 4.82¢/£ = 158.05¢/£$$
$$S^* = 162.87¢/£$$

Because the current spot rate is 158.34¢/£, the pound must strengthen relative to the dollar by 2.86%—that is, to 162.87¢/£—before hedging with puts provides a higher net revenue than the forward hedge.

So should Pfimerc use the option strategy or the forward hedge strategy? To decide, the company must calculate the probability that the exchange rate in the future will exceed $S^*(¢/£)$. We discuss how this question is answered later in the chapter.

Example 20.8 Importing Watches to the United States from Switzerland

Consider the case of an importer who must pay in the exporter's currency. Here, the importer will use call options on the exporter's currency to hedge.

Suppose it is Thursday, September 16, and Orlodge, an importer of Swiss watches to the United States, has an account payable of CHF750,000 due on Wednesday, December 15. The following data are available:

Spot rate: 71.42¢/CHF
90-day forward rate: 71.14¢/CHF
U.S. dollar 90-day interest rate: 3.75% p.a.
Swiss franc 90-day interest rate: 5.33% p.a.
Option data for December contracts (¢/CHF):

Strike	Call	Put
70	2.55	1.42
72	1.55	2.40

To hedge this transaction using foreign currency options, Orlodge must first determine the type of option that provides a hedge. Because Orlodge will be paying Swiss francs in 90 days, the transaction risk is that the Swiss franc will strengthen versus the dollar, which increases the cost of the CHF750,000. To hedge, Orlodge should buy the option that gives it the right, but not the obligation, to buy Swiss francs in 90 days at a strike price of dollars per Swiss franc. This is a European Swiss franc call option.

Let's work with the December Swiss franc call option with a strike price of 72¢/CHF. The cost per unit of this contract is 1.55¢/CHF, or \$0.0155/CHF. As the buyer of the contracts, Orlodge must pay today

$$\text{CHF750,000} \times \$0.0155/\text{CHF} = \$11,625$$

If, at maturity in December, the dollar value of the Swiss franc is greater than or equal to the strike price of \$0.7200/CHF, Orlodge will exercise its option to buy CHF750,000 at that price. Consequently, Orlodge's maximum payment is

$$\text{CHF750,000} \times \$0.7200/\text{CHF} = \$540,000, \text{ if } S(t+88) \geq \$0.7200/\text{CHF}$$

At all exchange rates less than \$0.7200/CHF, Orlodge will buy francs in the spot market, and its cost will be

$$\text{CHF750,000} \times S(t+88) < \$540,000, \text{ if } S(t+88) < \$0.7200/\text{CHF}$$

Whether Orlodge exercises its option or not, if it hedges with call options, it must add the December value of the September cost of the call options to the December cost of the Swiss francs to get a total cost figure. This opportunity cost is

$$\$11,625 \times [1 + i(\$)] = \$11,625 \times (1.0094) = \$11,734$$

where the interest factor is $(3.75/100)(90/360) = 0.0094$. Hence, Orlodge's maximum December total cost if it hedges with call options is

$$\$540,000 + \$11,734 = \$551,734$$

In cents per Swiss franc, the December cost of the call option is

$$(1.55¢/\text{CHF}) \times (1.0094) = 1.56¢/\text{CHF}$$

Exhibit 20.6 Hedging Swiss Franc Costs

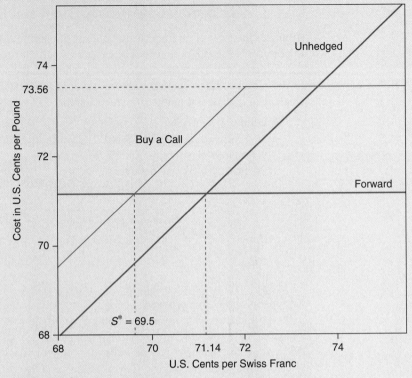

Notes: The horizontal axis presents different possible future exchange rates. The vertical axis represents the costs in cents per Swiss franc from three different strategies. The horizontal line reflects the cost implied by a forward contract, which is not dependent on the future exchange rate. The upward-sloping 45-degree line represents the unhedged strategy: The cost equals the future exchange rate. The inverted "hockey stick" line represents the cost from hedging the payable by buying a call option.

Exhibit 20.6 has possible December values of the exchange rate in cents per Swiss franc on the horizontal axis and the cost in cents per Swiss franc on the vertical axis. The different lines now represent the cost of different strategies, depending on the realization of the future exchange rates. As before, the 45-degree line represents the unhedged strategy. If Orlodge chooses not to hedge, it must buy its Swiss francs with dollars in the future spot market. Its cost will increase one for one with any strengthening of the Swiss franc versus the dollar, but its cost will also be lower, one for one, with any weakening of the Swiss franc. Its risk of loss is therefore unlimited.

The horizontal line in Exhibit 20.6 represents hedging with a forward contract. If Orlodge buys Swiss francs forward at $0.7114/CHF, its December cost is

$$\$0.7114/CHF \times CHF750,000 = \$533,550$$

On a cents-per-franc basis, Orlodge's cost will be 71.14¢/CHF no matter what spot exchange rate is realized in the future.

The kinked line in Exhibit 20.6 represents the total cost of hedging with the 72 December Swiss franc call options. The maximum total cost is

$$72.00¢/CHF + 1.56¢/CHF = 73.56¢/CHF$$

This cost arises when Orlodge exercises its call options—that is, when the future spot rate in December is greater than or equal to 72.00¢/CHF.

The option hedge provides a ceiling on Orlodge's costs, while allowing it to participate in any strengthening of the dollar relative to the Swiss franc, which can reduce the company's costs. Notice also that the total cost from the option hedge is above the total cost from the forward hedge whenever the exchange rate in the future is above S^*. If the future spot rate is less than S^*, the total cost from the option hedge is less than the cost from the forward hedge. This is another example of no-free-lunch economics: If the call option hedge puts a ceiling on your total cost, but it allows you to participate in a possible strengthening of the dollar that can reduce your costs, the ceiling must be above the forward rate.

The value of S^* equates the total costs of the two hedges. The total cost from the option hedge is $[S^* + 1.56¢/\text{CHF}]$, and the cost from the forward hedge is 71.14¢/CHF. Therefore, solving for S^* gives

$$S^* = 71.14¢/\text{CHF} - 1.56¢/\text{CHF} = 69.58¢/\text{CHF}$$

The Swiss franc must weaken by 2.58% relative to the dollar, from 71.42¢/CHF to 69.58¢/CHF, before the call option contract provides a lower cost than the forward hedge.

As Orlodge considers different strategies for dealing with the Swiss franc payable, including alternative option strategies or the forward hedge, the firm should attempt to calculate the probability that the future spot rate will be less than S^*. We will discuss this in the next section, which compares option hedges to the purchase of insurance.

Hedging with Options as Buying Insurance

In the two previous examples, option strategies hedge transaction exchange risks. Here, we consider how hedging with options is analogous to purchasing insurance. Before we do so, we summarize more generally how to hedge foreign currency receivables and payables with forward, futures, and option contracts. Exhibit 20.7 gives an overview of this discussion. It also includes some speculative option strategies that we will discuss later.

Hedging Foreign Currency Risk with Forwards and Options

Exporters who price in foreign currency generate foreign currency revenues. Their appropriate forward hedge is to sell the foreign currency receivable forward. Their appropriate option

Exhibit 20.7 Hedging and Speculating Strategies

	Underlying Transaction	
	Foreign Currency Receivable	**Foreign Currency Payable**
Forward Hedge (or futures hedge)	Sell forward (Go short)	Buy forward (Go long)

Option Hedge	Buy a put
	  Establishes a revenue floor
	  of $K - (1 + i)P$
		Buy a call
		  Establishes a cost ceiling
		  of $K + (1 + i)C$

Option Speculation	Sell a call
	  Imposes a revenue ceiling
	  of $K + (1 + i)C$ but
	  allows unlimited risk
		Sell a put
		  Imposes a liability floor
		  of $K - (1 + i)P$ but
		  allows unlimited risk

Notes: K is the strike price, C is the call option premium, P is the put option premium, and i is the appropriate deannualized interest rate factor.

hedge is to buy a foreign currency put. The put provides the right, but not the obligation, to sell the foreign currency revenue at the strike price of domestic currency per foreign currency, which establishes a floor on net revenue equal to the strike price minus the future value of the option premium.

If you buy a put option, you are not contractually committed to sell the export revenue through that option. You retain the right to sell the foreign currency in the spot market if the domestic currency value of the foreign currency exceeds the strike price. A strenghtening of the foreign currency allows your net revenue to exceed the floor established by the put option, and if the foreign currency strengthens sufficiently, your net domestic currency revenue from the option hedge can substantially exceed the revenue from the forward hedge. Nevertheless, because some money is paid up front, the net revenue from the option hedge remains less than the revenue that would have been generated if the option contract had not been purchased. Naturally, this can only be known *ex post*—that is, after the realization of future uncertain exchange rates. But, of course, the strategy must be chosen first.

For importers with foreign currency costs, the appropriate forward hedge is to buy the foreign currency forward. The appropriate option hedge is to buy a **foreign currency call option** contract. This gives you the right, but not the obligation, to buy the foreign currency at the strike price, which places a ceiling on your total costs. The ceiling on your costs is the strike price plus the future value of the option premium.

If you buy a call option, you retain the right to buy foreign currency in the spot market if the domestic currency value of the foreign currency is less than the strike price, and if the domestic currency strengthens, your cost falls below the ceiling. If the domestic currency strengthens a lot, the cost from the option hedge can be substantially less than the cost from the forward hedge. But your total cost can never be less than the cost that would have been generated if the option contract had not been purchased. Once again, this can only be known *ex post*, and, unfortunately, you must choose your strategy first.

Options as Insurance Contracts

How are the examples just discussed like insurance policies? Consider the purchase of fire insurance for a home. A homeowner pays annual premiums for insurance that provides a certain amount of coverage in the event of a fire. The quality of the coverage can be varied. The more of the home's value that the homeowner wants to protect, the more costly is the insurance. Expensive insurance completely replaces the home if it is destroyed by fire, and less expensive policies pay some fraction of the loss.

Clearly, the homeowner puts a ceiling on his possible losses by purchasing fire insurance. If there is a fire, the homeowner can repair the home, and the insurance company pays some part of the bill. But, suppose the homeowner lives in the home for 10 years, and no fires occur. *Ex post*, the homeowner will not have needed fire insurance, but he will have paid 10 years of insurance premiums. The homeowner will also have captured the appreciation in the home's value. Nevertheless, the homeowner will not be as well off as he would have been without purchasing the insurance. Of course, this does not mean that purchasing the insurance was a bad idea. It just means that the homeowner did not need the insurance when he lived in the home.

With foreign currency transaction exposures, purchasing the right type of option is like purchasing an insurance policy. Take Example 20.7, in which Pfimerc has a British pound receivable. A weakening of the pound is like a fire because it destroys part of the value of Pfimerc's pound asset. By contracting in advance with an option, some of the value is replaced. That is, if Pfimerc purchases a put option, it places a floor on the dollar value of its pound receivable, even if the pound depreciates. If, on the other hand, the pound strengthens, that is like an appreciation of the value of the home without a fire. Pfimerc ignores the put option and sells its pounds in the spot market. The put option was not needed just like the insurance policy was not needed if there was no fire.

Changing the Quality of the Insurance Policy

Can we carry the fire insurance analogy further? If a homeowner can purchase different qualities of fire insurance at different prices, is there a range of insurance quality when it comes to hedging foreign exchange risk?

Let's first consider hedging a foreign currency receivable with a put option. High-quality insurance in this context means that the floor on our domestic currency revenue is as high as possible. As we discussed, the floor is directly related to the strike price of the put option. The higher the strike price of the option, the less the foreign currency must depreciate before we can exercise the option and cut our losses. Just as insurance that covers more losses is more expensive, put options with higher strike prices are more expensive. We discuss valuation issues in more detail in the next section.

Similarly, high-quality insurance in the context of a foreign currency liability means that we would like to make the ceiling on our cost of the foreign currency as low as possible. This can be accomplished by buying call options with lower strike prices. Again, there is a trade-off because these options will be more expensive. To fully understand this, let's work through a numeric example.

Example 20.9 Purchasing Better, but More Expensive, Insurance

In Example 20.8, Orlodge was importing Swiss watches, and we worked with a December Swiss franc European call option with a strike price of 72¢ per Swiss franc. The cost to hedge the Swiss franc liability was 1.55¢/CHF. Alternatively, we could choose a December call option with a strike price of 70¢/CHF that costs 2.55¢/CHF. This more expensive "insurance" should provide a lower ceiling on the total Swiss franc cost. The trade-off is that the exchange rate, S^*, at which Orlodge has the same cost as the forward hedge is now lower. Hence, the probability of having a lower cost than the forward hedge is smaller because Orlodge gets a lower cost only if the future exchange rate is less than this new S^*.

Exhibit 20.8 presents the cost diagrams for the two option strategies with strike prices of 70¢/CHF and 72¢/CHF. The initial cost of the insurance from the call option with the lower strike price is

$$\text{CHF750,000} \times (\$0.0255/\text{CHF}) = \$19,125$$

compared to the $11,625 in Example 20.8. At maturity in December, if the dollar value of the Swiss franc is greater than or equal to the strike price of $0.70/CHF, Orlodge will exercise its option to buy CHF750,000 at that price. Consequently, the maximum that Orlodge will pay in December is

$$\text{CHF750,000} \times \$0.70/\text{CHF} = \$525,000, \text{ if } S(t+88) \geq \$0.70/\text{CHF}$$

At all exchange rates less than $0.70/CHF, Orlodge will buy Swiss francs in the spot market, and its cost will be

$$\text{CHF750,000} \times S(t+88) < \$525,000, \text{ if } S(t+88) < \$0.70/\text{CHF}$$

Of course, Orlodge must add the December value of the cost of the call options that was paid in September to the December cost of the Swiss francs to get a total cost figure. This opportunity cost is

$$[\$19,125 \times 1.0094] = \$19,305$$

Exhibit 20.8 Alternative Option Hedges

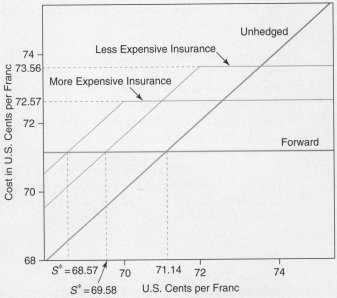

Notes: The horizontal axis represents the future exchange rate in cents per Swiss franc. The vertical axis represents the cost in cents per Swiss franc of various strategies for dealing with a Swiss franc liability. The horizontal line shows that a forward hedge locks in a cost per Swiss franc of 71.14 cents. The 45-degree line represents the unhedged strategy, and the two inverted "hockey stick" lines represent the *ex post* costs of two option strategies, struck at different strike prices.

where the interest factor is $(3.75/100)(90/360) = 0.0094$. Hence, the maximum total cost that Orlodge will pay in December if it hedges with call options is

$$\$525,000 + \$19,305 = \$544,305$$

In Example 20.8, the corresponding figure is $551,734. Hence, Orlodge has improved the quality of its insurance because its total cost is now lower in the bad states of the world in which the dollar weakens relative to the Swiss franc.

On a cents-per-franc basis, the December cost of the call option with a strike price of 70¢/CHF is

$$2.55¢/\text{CHF} \times 1.0094 = 2.57¢/\text{CHF}$$

Hence, the total cost of the liability per unit of foreign currency is, at most,

$$70¢/\text{CHF} + 2.57¢/\text{CHF} = 72.57¢/\text{CHF}$$

We can again determine the value of S^* that equates the cost of the option hedge to the cost of the forward hedge. The total cost from the option hedge is $S^* + 2.57¢/\text{CHF}$, and the cost from the forward hedge is $71.14¢/\text{CHF}$. Solving for S^* gives

$$S^* = 71.14¢/\text{CHF} - 2.57¢/\text{CHF} = 68.57¢/\text{CHF}$$

This is less than the S^* of 69.58¢/CHF in Example 20.8. With more expensive insurance, more strengthening of the dollar relative to the Swiss franc must occur before Orlodge's cost is lower than the cost of the forward hedge. Because the current spot rate is 71.42¢/CHF, the Swiss franc must weaken by 3.99%, to 68.57¢/CHF, before the call option contract with a strike price of 70¢/CHF provides a lower total cost than the forward hedge.

Speculating with Options

Examples 20.7 and 20.8 discuss hedging transaction exchange risk with options. Choosing the right strategy in these examples is tantamount to purchasing insurance. Sometimes, firms think that this insurance is too expensive. If it is, a firm can profit from a speculative strategy as long as the realized future exchange rate remains in certain regions. That is, rather than purchase insurance, you can use the option markets to sell insurance.

If purchasing a put provides insurance when you have a foreign currency receivable, then selling a call allows you to sell the foreign currency, either to the purchaser of the call option or in the spot market, and your revenue is enhanced by the option premium. Of course, you are now selling insurance to someone who may want to exercise the option.

Similarly, if purchasing a call seems too expensive when hedging a foreign currency liability, you might want to write a put. The put obligates you to buy the foreign currency at the strike price when the buyer of the put exercises that option to sell foreign currency to you. Once again, though, the option premium provides you with revenue that lowers the effective cost of your foreign currency liability.

While we illustrate these strategies, you should understand that speculating does not protect the firm's revenue from potential losses or its cost from potential increases due to exchange rate changes. Some of the large foreign exchange losses experienced by firms in the recent financial crisis arose because they were following complex versions of these speculative strategies, either through ignorance of the possible losses or an assessment that the *ex ante* risk was worth taking. We come back to this issue in Section 20.5.

Speculating on Foreign Currency Receivables

Let's illustrate these speculative strategies with the foreign currency receivable in Example 20.7. Suppose Pfimerc is scheduled to receive £500,000 in 170 days. The pound put option provides the hedge: It gives Pfimerc the right, but not the obligation, to sell pounds at a contractual strike price of dollars per pound. But suppose this put option seems expensive. Would a different option strategy allow Pfimerc to sell pounds for dollars and have the potential to generate more dollar revenue?

Pfimerc could achieve this objective by selling someone the right, but not the obligation, to buy pounds from it in exchange for dollars. This option describes a pound call option against the dollar. Because Pfimerc knows the date on which it wants to sell pounds and the amount of pounds it wants to sell, it could sell someone a European pound call option against the dollar with 170 days until maturity. When Pfimerc sells the pound call option, it generates dollar revenue in September, and this revenue enhances its dollar return in the future.

This strategy is speculative, though, because Pfimerc loses protection against downside risk. If the pound weakens substantially relative to the dollar, the purchaser of the pound call option from Pfimerc will find it to be worthless. Pfimerc will be forced to sell its pounds in the spot market precisely when the dollar value of those pounds is low. Also, its ability to participate in a strengthening of the pound versus the dollar is limited.

Suppose that at maturity the dollar–pound spot rate is above the exercise price of the call option contract. The purchaser of Pfimerc's call option will consequently want to buy pounds at the exercise price. Pfimerc will therefore have to sell the pounds at the exercise price. The company will then miss participating in any further strengthening of the pound relative to the dollar. Nevertheless, Pfimerc does take in revenue for selling the call options, and if options are expensive, this revenue can be substantial.

Example 20.10 Speculating on British Pound Receivables

To see how speculating on receivables works with actual data, let's examine the options on British pounds we used before. The March British pound call option with a strike price of 158¢/£ costs 5.00¢/£, or $0.05/£. If Pfimerc sells the call option in October, it generates revenue of

$$£500,000 \times \$0.05/£ = \$25,000$$

In March, if the dollar value of the pound is above the strike price of $1.58/£, Pfimerc will have to sell £500,000 to the option buyer, who will exercise the option to buy pounds at the strike price. Pfimerc's maximum revenue in March will therefore be

$$£500,000 \times \$1.58/£ = \$790,000, \text{ if } S\,(t{+}32) > \$1.58/£$$

At all exchange rates less than or equal to $1.58/£, the option Pfimerc sold will be worthless, so Pfimerc will sell its pounds in the spot market instead. Its revenue in March will then be

$$£500,000 \times S(t{+}32) \leq \$790,000, \text{ if } S\,(t{+}32) \leq \$1.58/£$$

In both cases, though, Pfimerc can add the March value of the October revenue from the option sale to get net revenue. This additional revenue is

$$\$25,000 \times (1 + i(\$)) = \$25,000 \times 1.00094 = \$25,024$$

where the interest factor is $(0.20/100)(170/360) = 0.00094$. Hence, the maximum net revenue that Pfimerc receives in March if it sells the call option is

$$\$790,000 + \$25,024 = \$815,024$$

On a cents-per-pound basis, the additional March revenue is

$$5.0¢/£ \times 1.00094 = 5.01¢/£$$

This is the amount of extra revenue on a cents-per-pound basis that Pfimerc can use to offset any weakening of the pound. To find the future spot exchange rate, $S^*(¢/£)$, at which Pfimerc has the same revenue as the forward rate, we equate the revenue from the two strategies:

$$S^*(¢/£) + 5.01¢/£ = 158.05¢/£$$
$$S^*(¢/£) = 153.04¢/£$$

Because the current spot exchange rate is 158.34¢/£, the pound would have to weaken by 3.35% over the next 170 days before this strategy generated lower revenue than the forward hedge. Exhibit 20.9 illustrates the revenue payoff for this speculative strategy.

Notice that there is a range of values of future spot rates over which this speculative strategy has the highest net revenue. On a cents-per-pound basis, maximum revenue from selling the option equals the strike price of 158¢/£ plus the 5.01¢/£. Consequently, the spot exchange rate in the future must be

$$158¢/£ + 5.01¢/£ = 163.01¢/£$$

before the unhedged strategy provides more revenue *ex post* than the speculative option strategy. This requires an appreciation of the pound of 2.95% over the course of 170 days. If you think that the volatility of the exchange rate is not very large, the probability of it reaching this value may not be very large.

Exhibit 20.9 Speculating with Pound Revenue

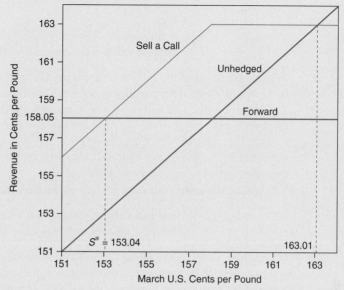

Notes: The horizontal axis represents the future exchange rate in cents per pound. The vertical axis represents the revenue in cents per pound of various strategies for selling a pound asset. The horizontal line shows that a forward hedge locks in revenue of 158.05 cents. The 45-degree line represents the unhedged strategy, and the inverted "hockey stick" line represents the *ex post* revenue from the strategy of selling a call option with a strike price of 158.

Speculating on Foreign Currency Liabilities

Exhibit 20.7 summarizes how the speculative strategies work. In the case of a foreign currency liability, you must buy foreign currency. Selling someone a **foreign currency put option** forces you to buy the foreign currency at the strike price when the buyer of the option finds it advantageous to sell foreign currency to you—that is, when the exchange rate of domestic currency per foreign currency is lower than the strike price. If the exchange rate ends up higher than the strike price, the option expires worthless, and you must buy the foreign currency in the spot market, exactly when it is relatively expensive. However, whatever happens, writing the option yields revenue, and this strategy may be advantageous when the exchange rate is not anticipated to move very far from its current value.

Options Valuation

We saw that the buyer of an option pays a premium to the seller of the option. How expensive is this type of contract? The purpose of this section is to give you an intuitive idea about how options are valued. The actual formal valuation of options is discussed in the appendix to this chapter because it is quite mathematically complex.[4]

The Intrinsic Value of an Option

Recall that the intrinsic value of an American option is the return, or revenue, generated from the immediate exercise of the option. Intrinsic value is another way of describing whether an

---

[4]An Excel spreadsheet that performs the calculations can be downloaded from Professor Hodrick's Columbia Business School Web site. Values of foreign currency options are usually discussed in terms of the Garman-Kolhagen (see Garman and Kolhagen, 1983) model, an extension of the famous Black-Scholes (see Black and Scholes, 1973) model.

option is in the money, at the money, or out of the money. So, if K is the strike price of a euro call option against the dollar, and S is the current spot exchange rate, both expressed in $/€, then

$$\text{Intrinsic value of the euro call} = S - K, \text{if } S > K$$
$$\text{Intrinsic value of the euro call} = 0, \text{if } S \leq K$$

Because the buyer of the call option must pay the seller of the option for the right to exercise it, the option's price (or its value) must be at least as great as the intrinsic value of the option. The intrinsic value of a call is positive if the strike price is below the current spot exchange rate because the buyer of the option could exercise the right to buy pounds at K and then sell euros in the spot market for the higher price S. If the strike price is higher than the spot rate, immediately exercising the option would result in a loss of money, so the intrinsic value of the option is 0. The option is out of the money.

For an American-style euro put option, we have the following relationships:

$$\text{Intrinsic value of the euro put} = K - S, \text{if } S < K$$
$$\text{Intrinsic value of the euro put} = 0, \text{if } S \geq K$$

Once again, because the buyer of the put option must pay the seller of the option for the right to exercise it, the option's price (or its value) must be at least as great as the intrinsic value of the option. The intrinsic value of a put is positive if the put's strike price is greater than the current exchange rate because the buyer of the option could exercise her right to sell euros at K, having bought euros in the spot market for the lower price S. If the strike price is lower than the spot rate, immediately exercising the option would result in a loss of money. Therefore, the option's intrinsic value is 0. The option is out of the money.

The Time Value of an Option

The **time value** of an option is the current price or value of the option minus its intrinsic value:

$$\text{Time value of an option} = \text{Option price} - \text{Intrinsic value}$$

To understand what creates time value, think about a European call option—that is, an option that can only be exercised at maturity. To be concrete, let's think of a euro call option against dollars with a maturity of 90 days.

When we introduced forward contracts in Chapter 3, we discussed the probability distribution of future spot exchange rates. Based on our information today, we do not know exactly what the exchange rate of dollars per euros will be in 90 days. Hence, we express our ignorance with a probability distribution, as in Exhibit 20.10. Exhibit 20.10 indicates that the expected value of the dollar–euro rate is $1.25/€ and that values between $1.10/€ and $1.40/€ are fairly likely, while values less than $1.00/€ and greater than $1.50/€ are possible but unlikely to happen.

Exhibit 20.10 has two strike prices, K_1 and K_2. Focus first on K_1. If you buy a European call option on the euro with strike price K_1, you have the right to buy euros at K_1 and then sell the euros in the spot market. You will only do so if the future spot exchange rate of dollars per euro is greater than the exercise price of the option in which case your dollar revenue is $S(t{+}90) - K_1$. Hence, we can write that for a European option, the euro call option price at time t, $C(t)$, is

$$C(t) = \text{Value at time } t \text{ of max}[0, S(t{+}90) - K_1]$$

To determine the value of an option, we must take the present value of the option payoff at the maturity of the contract, which is a non-trivial problem. At this point, it is sufficient to simply understand the intuition of what gives options value.

Exhibit 20.10 Different Probability Distributions of Future USD/EUR

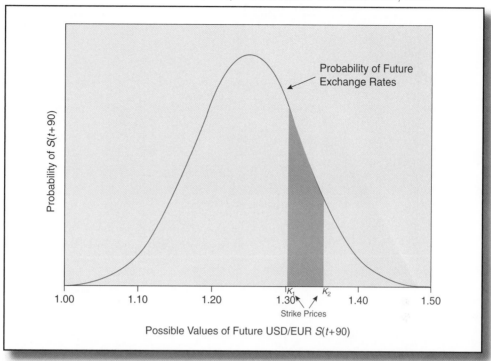

Increasing the Exercise Price

If we hold constant the maturity date of an option, we hold constant the probability distribution in Exhibit 20.10. Now, let's think about increasing the strike price of the option from K_1 to K_2. What happens to the value of the call option? It should be apparent that increasing the exercise price of a euro call must decrease the value of a call option because it removes possible states of the world over which the contract provides revenue when the strike price is lower.

The region of the probability distribution to the right of K_1 gives the probability that the call option with a strike price of K_1 will be exercised. The shaded region contains the additional probability for which the call option with strike price K_1 will be exercised relative to the probability of exercising the option with the higher strike price of K_2. So, when we increase the exercise price from K_1 to K_2, we lose the probability of generating the revenue associated with the shaded region, which makes the option with the strike price K_2 less valuable than the option with the strike price K_1.

A put option provides revenue to the buyer at expiration only if the spot rate in the future is less than the option's exercise price. Hence, increasing the exercise price of a put option must increase the value of a put option because it increases the possible states of the world over which the contract is profitable. We see this in Exhibit 20.10. The probability of exercising the option with a strike price of K_2 is the area of the probability distribution below K_2. The shaded area of Exhibit 20.10 gives the additional probability of exercising an option with strike price K_2 versus one with strike price equal to K_1.

An Increase in the Variance

How does increasing the variance of future exchange rates affect an option's value? Exhibit 20.11 compares two probability distributions—one with a small variance, associated with tranquil periods, and one with a larger variance, associated with turbulent periods. To understand how an increase in variance affects option prices, suppose we place the strike price of

Exhibit 20.11   Different Probability Distributions of Future USD/EUR

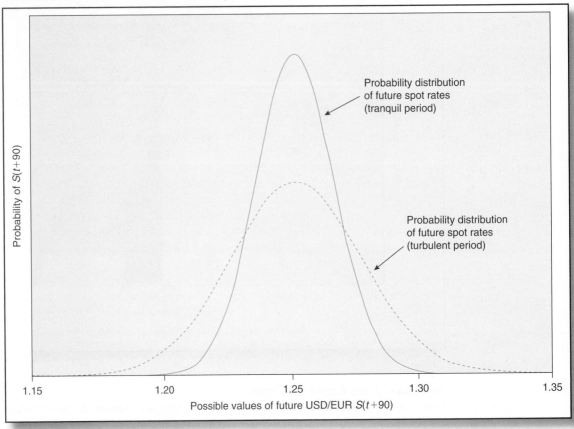

a call option at the conditional mean of the two probability distributions in Exhibit 20.11—that is, we choose $K = \$1.25/€$. The increase in the variance of the possible future exchange rate clearly increases the possible range of future exchange rates. But, because the conditional mean is still $\$1.25/€$, the probability that the option will finish in the money is still one-half because one-half of the probability distribution remains above the strike price. However, if the option does finish in the money, the distribution with the larger variance yields possibly larger payoffs, and the option will cost more. A symmetrical argument can be applied to a put option. (Can you explain how?) Therefore, an increase in the variance of future possible exchange rates increases both call and put option values.

Increasing the Time to Expiration

How does increasing the time to expiration affect an option's value? Here, it is important to distinguish clearly between American-style and European-style options. For American options, the effect is unambiguous: Increasing the time to maturity always increases an option's value because it increases the uncertainty of the spot exchange rate at maturity. When this effect is combined with the fact that the holder of a 6-month option can always treat the option as a 3-month option, we clearly see that the additional 3 months of maturity cannot hurt the payoff to the holder of the option as long as the holder of the option can exercise it early.

For European options, the situation is not so simple. Although the effect of an increase in time to maturity is technically ambiguous, in most situations, the effect of the increased uncertainty of the spot exchange rate at maturity dominates, and option prices increase. Nevertheless, this is not always true because it is possible for a European option that is currently in the money to lose value as time evolves. You would like to be able to exercise the option to lock in the revenue now, but you cannot do so prior to maturity.

Put–Call Parity for Foreign Currency Options

The fact that you can hedge and speculate with options suggests that there should be a link between the prices of the put and call options for a given strike price and the forward foreign exchange rate. Because money changes hands at the beginning of option transactions as well as at the end, the interest rate must enter the relationship as well. **Put–call parity** is the fundamental no arbitrage relationship that links the common strike price of domestic currency per unit of foreign currency, the domestic currency prices of European-style put and call options at that strike price, and the domestic currency interest rate. How can we derive this no arbitrage relationship?

Let's work with dollar–euro exchange rates. One way to unconditionally sell euros for dollars (that is, you sell euros for all realizations of the future exchange rate) is to sell at the rate of F. A synthetic way to sell euros unconditionally in the future involves two option transactions. If you purchase a euro put option against the dollar with a strike price of K, you will exercise the option whenever the dollar–euro spot exchange rate at maturity, $S(T)$, is less than K. Let your dollar cost of purchasing the put option be P. If you sell or write a call option with the same strike price of K, you give someone else the right to purchase euros from you at that strike price. She will exercise her option whenever $S(T)$ is greater than or equal to K. You will charge the purchaser of the call option C dollars today.

When both of these option transactions are done simultaneously, you will sell euros in the future at the strike price, K, no matter what happens to the future spot rate. That is, at maturity, you will unconditionally sell euros for dollars at the strike price, K, but your dollar revenue will be enhanced by the future value of the difference between the revenue from selling the call option and the cost of buying the put option, which is $(C - P)[1 + i(\$)]$. Therefore, the two option transactions create a **synthetic forward contract**, and absence of arbitrage requires that the forward exchange rate must be equal to the strike price adjusted for the future values of the revenue from selling the call minus the cost of purchasing the put. That is, put–call parity requires

$$F = K + (C - P)[1 + i(\$)]$$

If you can purchase euros in the forward market at F dollars per euro, and this price is less than the dollar price at which you can synthetically sell euros forward through the two option transactions just described, you can obviously make money. Such an arbitrage transaction is called a **conversion**.

What if the market's forward price is higher than the synthetic forward price? In this case, traders do what is called a **reversal**: They create a synthetic forward purchase of euros and contract to sell euros in the forward market. The synthetic purchase of euros can be done by buying a euro call option with strike price K, which generates a cost of C today; selling a put option with the same strike price, which brings in revenue of P today; and investing or borrowing the difference. The future profit on a reversal is therefore

$$F - K - (C - P)[1 + i(\$)]$$

When neither conversions nor reversals are profitable, the market prices satisfy put–call parity.

Of course, as with interest rate parity, put–call parity will not be an exact equality because it is difficult to do the required transactions simultaneously, and there are transaction costs. Because such costs are typically small, actual option prices are usually close to those implied by put–call parity.

Example 20.11 Putting Numbers to Put–Call Parity

To illustrate how put–call parity works, let's consider the exchange rates and options that Orlodge was facing in Example 20.8. We'll use the options with a strike price of 70¢/CHF. Note that the call option costs 2.55¢/CHF, which is more than the 1.42¢/CHF cost of the put option. We should expect the call option to cost more than the put because the call option is in the money, whereas the put option is not (the current exchange rate is 71.42¢/CHF). Put–call parity states that one can sell the Swiss franc forward at a predetermined rate in two ways: through a forward contract or through buying a put and writing a call. Recall from Example 20.8 that the forward rate is 71.14¢/CHF. The option strategy yields an effective rate of the strike price plus the net cost or revenue of the two option transactions, adjusted for the time value of money. That is, the synthetic forward rate obtained by buying a put and writing a call is

$$70¢/\text{CHF} + (2.55 \, ¢/\text{CHF} - 1.42¢/\text{CHF}) \times \left(1 + 0.0375 \times \frac{90}{360}\right) = 71.14¢/\text{CHF}$$

This is the same as the forward rate. Hence, put–call parity holds in these quotes. You can verify that it also holds for options with a 72¢/CHF strike price.

20.5 COMBINATIONS OF OPTIONS AND EXOTIC OPTIONS

Corporations and institutional investors are increasingly using options and other derivative instruments to manage their exchange rate and interest rate risks.[5] Hedge funds and other institutional investors also often want to invest in instruments that allow them to express their views about various risks and rewards in currency markets. Consequently, investment banks now design products specifically for the tastes of their clients. Often, such products represent combinations of basic put and call options that lower the cost of managing a particular risk. Options with different payoff patterns and features than the basic options discussed in this chapter are mostly referred to as **exotic options**. Some of the more standard exotic options are discussed briefly in this section.

First, though, a word of caution for the purchasers of these options. How can banks offer exotic options that seem like good deals to clients? Banks will hedge an exotic option position by doing the opposite transaction with some other counterparty or by creating synthetic options by trading the underlying assets to offset their risk. Of course, because you can't get something for nothing, purchasers of exotic options should be aware that the ability of the bank to offer such a contract indicates that the purchaser's distribution of future spot rates is probably somewhat different from the market's implied distribution of future spot rates. For example, in terms of Exhibit 20.11, if option prices seem expensive to you, it may be because the market is pricing options from a distribution with a wider conditional variance than you are using. Of course, your personal distribution of future exchange rates may differ in other ways from the market's distribution, and you may be right. But, you should be careful not to delude yourself into thinking that you are getting a good deal; you need to understand the distribution implied by market prices and the implied payoffs on your contract.

---

[5]See the discussion of current risk management practices in Chapter 17.

Range Forwards and Cylinder Options

Corporate treasurers often argue that option strategies are expensive. They dislike incurring the upfront cost of option premiums. They also encounter difficulty explaining their hedging expenses to their superiors, especially when the insurance they purchase seems to have been unnecessary after the fact. Financial institutions have proposed several solutions that retain some of the hedging features of options but reduce the upfront costs. One solution, designed in 1985 by the investment bank Salomon Brothers, is a range forward contract. A **range forward contract** allows a company to specify a range of future spot rates over which the firm can sell or buy foreign currency at the future spot rate. When the future spot rate falls outside the range, the firm sells or buys the currency at the limits of the range. For example, if the firm is selling foreign currency, it enters into a contract to sell the currency for dollars within a particular range. This creates a floor on the firm's dollar revenue in case the foreign currency weakens. However, it also creates a ceiling on the firm's dollar revenue in case the foreign currency strengthens. If the firm's treasurer thinks that the foreign currency is unlikely to strengthen, or at least not strengthen very much, she will not believe she is sacrificing any upside potential.

At exchange rates in between the limits of the range forward contract, the firm simply sells its foreign currency at the spot rate in the future. Although the firm gets some upside potential, the firm doesn't need to pay money up front for the range forward contract. Range forward contracts were quickly modified by Citibank and other financial institutions, which developed cylinder options. **Cylinder options** allow buyers to specify a desired trading range and either pay money or possibly receive money up front for entering into the contracts.

Synthesizing Cylinder Options

How can we use our knowledge of call and put options to construct synthetic cylinder options and range forward contracts when we are selling foreign currency in the future? Consider a slight modification to our derivation of put–call parity. Here, we express all exchange rates in dollars per pound, just to be concrete.

Suppose you must buy pounds in the future to pay for some British goods. It is possible to construct cylinder options or a range forward contract that allows you to buy pounds in the future at the spot rate over a particular range but places a ceiling on your costs to provide you with insurance. Unfortunately, you must also agree to have a floor on your costs that prevents you from participating fully in dollar appreciation. The ceiling on your costs is established by purchasing a call option, and the floor is established by selling a put option at a lower strike price.

Let the strike price of the put option that is sold be K_p, and let the strike price of the call option that is purchased be K_c, with $K_p < K_c$. Then, depending on the realization of the future spot rate, you will buy pounds in the following way:

If $S \leq K_p$, you buy pounds at K_p because the put you wrote is exercised.
If $K_p < S < K_c$, you buy pounds at S with no exercise of options.
If $S \geq K_c$, you buy pounds at K_c by exercising your call.

In all cases, the firm has an expense equal to the future value of the call premium, $C(K_c)$, that it purchased, and it has revenue equal to the future value of the put premium, $P(K_p)$, that it sold. Hence, its net revenue is augmented by

$$[P(K_p) - C(K_c)] \times [1 + i(\$)]$$

This additional revenue can be adjusted by changing the strike prices on the options to be either positive, negative, or zero. Because the range forward contract requires no cash flows other than the purchase of the pounds, the strike prices must be set such that $P(K_p) = C(K_c)$. The firm might propose the ceiling on its trading range, which establishes the strike price of the call, and the investment bank then sets the floor of the trading range to correspond to the strike price of a put option with the same value as the call option.

Example 20.12   A Cylinder Option Contract

Let's work with some data to create a synthetic cylinder option for a situation in which you have an inflow of foreign currency. As in Example 20.7, suppose it is October, and Pfimerc has a £500,000 account receivable due in March. The following data are available:

Spot rate (U.S. cents per British pound): 158.34
170-day forward rate (U.S. cents per British pound): 158.05
U.S. dollar 170-day interest rate: 0.20% p.a.
British pound 170-day interest rate: 0.40% p.a.
Option data for March contracts in cents per pound (¢/£):

Strike	Call Prices	Put Prices
158	5.00	4.81
159	4.52	5.33
160	4.08	5.89

In Example 20.7, Pfimerc bought the March put option with a strike price of 158¢/£ at a cost of 4.81¢/£. This established a floor on their revenue. Now, suppose that Pfimerc wants to guarantee itself the right to exchange the £500,000 in the range between \$1.58/£ to \$1.60/£. Pfimerc could purchase the 158 March put option for 4.81¢/£ and sell the 160 call option for 4.08¢/£. The net cost from the two option contracts would be 4.81¢/£ − 4.08¢/£ = 0.73¢/£, or \$0.0073/£. The future value of this net revenue using the interest rate calculated in Example 20.7 is

$$£500,000 \times \$0.0073/£ \times 1.00094 = \$3,653$$

With these two transactions, Pfimerc's dollar revenue would range from

$$(£500,000 \times \$1.58/£) - \$3,653 = \$786,347$$

if $S(\$/£) \leq \$1.58/£$ to

$$(£500,000 \times \$1.60/£) - \$3,653 = \$796,347$$

if $S(\$/£) \geq \$1.60/£$. This range of revenues can be compared to the forward contract. If Pfimerc sells pounds forward at \$1.5805/£, its March revenue is

$$\$1.5805/£ \times £500,000 = \$790,250$$

Other Exotic Options

Average-Rate Options

An **average-rate option**, which is sometimes called an Asian option, is one of the most common exotic options. The payoff on an average-rate call option on one unit of foreign currency with a strike price of K is $\max[0, \bar{S} - K]$, where $\bar{S}$ defines the average exchange rate between the initiation of the contract and the expiration date. To calculate the average exchange rate, the counterparties to the option contract must agree on a source for the data and a way of computing the average. They must decide on a time interval for the observations entering the average, which could be daily, weekly, or monthly, and they must decide whether the average is an arithmetic or geometric average.[6] At the maturity of an average-rate option, the seller of the option settles the contract by delivering the option payoff to the buyer. Because an average of future exchange rates is less volatile than the future spot rate at maturity, average-rate options are less expensive than standard European options.

Barrier Options

A **barrier option** is like a traditional option, with an additional requirement that either activates the option or extinguishes it if the exchange rate passes through a prespecified barrier exchange rate. For example, suppose the current exchange rate is $1.50/£. A 1-year, up-and-out European put option on the pound with a strike price of $1.45/£ and a barrier of $1.53/£ specifies that the holder of the option has the right, but not the obligation, to sell pounds for dollars at $1.45/£ in 1 year unless the exchange rate crosses the barrier of $1.53/£ prior to the maturity of the option. If the exchange rate crosses the barrier, the option is worthless. Such an option is desirable for people who have pound receivables because they may think that the put option hedge is not necessary if the pound strengthens during the life of the contract.

Barrier options can be either calls or puts, and there are four essential varieties. In addition to the up-and-out option described earlier, there are up-and-in, down-and-out, and down-and-in options. Each of these options specifies a barrier that either activates the option, in the cases of the up-and-in and down-and-in options, or that extinguishes the option if the barrier is crossed, in the cases of the up-and-out and down-and-out options.

Lookback Options

Suppose you want to assure yourself today that in 1 year, you will have bought foreign exchange at the minimum dollar value that occurs during the coming year. You can actually do this by purchasing a **lookback option**. For example, let S_{min} be the minimum exchange rate (in dollars per foreign currency) realized during the year, and let $S(T)$ be the exchange rate in 1 year. The payoff on the lookback call option is

$$\max[0, S(T) - S_{min}]$$

Because the minimum exchange rate may occur on the last day, $S(T)$ is at least as big as S_{min}, and the payoff can be written as $S(T) - S_{min}$. A lookback put option can be defined analogously. It allows you to sell foreign currency at the highest exchange rate of dollars per foreign currency that is realized during the life of the option. Of course, when you transact with a lookback option, you are transacting at the prices that are the most favorable to you. Hence, lookback options are more expensive than traditional call and put options.

Digital Options

The two basic **digital options**, or binary options, are cash-or-nothing and asset-or-nothing options. They can be European or American; they can be structured as a call or a put; and they are mostly cash settled. A European cash-or-nothing digital option pays off a fixed amount of money when it expires in the money and nothing otherwise. For example, suppose you buy a digital call option on the dollar/euro exchange rate with a strike price of $1.35/€ and a principal of $1,000,000. If, at expiration, the exchange rate is higher than $1.35/€, you obtain the $1,000,000; if not, the payoff is 0. The American equivalent of this digital option pays off $1,000,000 if the exchange rate reaches the $1.35/€ level any time before expiration. Obviously, such options are issued only at strike prices that are out of the money. If the payout is specified in euros (for example, €1,000,000), the option is really an asset-or-nothing option because the dollar amount represented by the euro payoff, $S(T) \times €1,000,000$, is uncertain from the perspective of the U.S. investor.

---

[6]If there are n observations, the arithmetic average is $(1/n)\sum_{i=1}^{n}S_i$, and the geometric average is $(\prod_{i=1}^{n}S_i)^{1/n}$, where $\sum$ denotes the summation operator and $\prod$ denotes the product operator.

Binary options are interesting because they are useful building blocks in the creation of complex payoff patterns. For example, an option that pays off a very large amount when the exchange rate is within a certain range (a sort of lottery payoff) can be constructed by buying and selling digital call options with different strike prices.

How KIKOs Can Knock You Out

Before the financial crisis, exporters in many emerging economies witnessed surging export volumes but not corresponding increases in profitability as many emerging-market currencies also strongly appreciated in value relative to the U.S. dollar and other major currencies. In trying to hedge their foreign exchange risk while enhancing their revenues, scores of exporters in emerging markets got badly burned by exotic derivatives during the 2007 to 2010 financial crisis. According to Dodd (2009), possibly 50,000 firms in at least 12 economies suffered derivatives losses estimated to be a staggering $530 billion.

To get an idea of what happened, let's focus on the KIKO contracts that many small and medium-size Korean firms used. The exact details of the contracts differed across countries and firms, but they all shared many features with the KIKO contracts. KIKO stands for kick in, kick out, and the contracts can be understood using a combination of put–call parity, barrier options, and leverage.

Consider the situation of Kumkang Valve, a small Korean exporter of valves that open and close oil and gas pipelines [see Lee (2009) for more on the plight of this company]. As the Korean won strengthened versus the dollar prior to the crisis, Kumkang Valve's dollar revenues became worth less and less in Korean won. Hedging foreign currency receivables could be done using a forward contract to sell dollars for won or by buying a dollar put against the won. The KIKO contract essentially combined the buying of a dollar put against won with the selling of a dollar call against won at the same strike price. We know from put–call parity that, if done for the same dollar amount, this strategy is equivalent to selling dollars forward, which is exactly what Kumkang Valve would need to do to hedge its dollar transaction exchange risk.

However, KIKOs added a few twists. First, the amount involved in the call transaction was double the amount involved in the put. This now places the company at risk if the dollar appreciates, placing the won/dollar exchange rate above the strike price; it will incur losses on the call option it sold on the dollar (while of course, its foreign exchange revenues may increase as the dollar is worth more won). Second, the KIKO contract involved a "kick-out" barrier; when the won/dollar exchange rate reaches a particular value, the gains on the put are "kicked out." This makes the dollar put option less expensive. Analogously, it also involved a "kick-in" option: The losses on the won/dollar exchange rate only kick in after the won/dollar exchange rate rises above a particular value, which in turn reduces the value of the call premium earned by the company. The KIKO contract was structured to have zero premiums at initialization. It typically involved a long series of contracts for multiple maturity months in the future. The zero premium structure probably made the contract an easier sell as no initial costs were paid, and financial accounting rules allowed it to be reported as a hedging transaction. It is likely that many companies felt the exchange rate would never hit the "kick in" loss region, as currency forecasts called for further appreciation of emerging-market currencies.

Unfortunately, these forecasts were wrong. As the global financial crisis really took off in 2008, investors flocked to the U.S. dollar as a safe haven, and many emerging-market currencies, including the Korean won, experienced steep depreciations. The "kick-in" barrier was breached, and the losses for KIKO investors started to mount. Kumkang Valve filed for bankruptcy in September 2008. Dodd (2009) claims that reports of losses on derivatives at many companies roiled the local currency markets, amplifying selling pressures. Because the OTC markets for these exotic derivatives are not transparent, the currency markets were in the dark about the total amounts of the outstanding transactions and the magnitudes of the potential losses. This lack of information may have led to uncertainty, which potentially further depressed currency values and, in turn, caused greater losses on exotic foreign exchange derivatives.

Even ignoring such potentially adverse macroeconomic effects, this episode raises many policy issues. Did the firms really understand the risks involved in the contracts? Why did they take out such large amounts of contracts? It is well known that many of these companies had bought contracts for amounts far exceeding their expected overseas revenues. Were they willingly speculating or simply fooled by the bankers structuring the deals? Should there be regulatory oversight of such complex derivatives structures? The future will tell, but in the mean time, we hope that financial managers around the world think twice before engaging in overtly complex derivative contracts.

20.6 SUMMARY

The purpose of this chapter is to develop an understanding of futures markets and foreign exchange options markets and the use of futures and options in hedging transaction exchange risks. The main points in the chapter are as follows:

1. Foreign currency futures are standardized contracts that allow one to buy or sell specific amounts of foreign currency at a price determined today, with delivery on a given day in the future. The contracts are traded on organized exchanges.
2. The clearinghouse of an exchange is the counterparty to all transactions. To guarantee that the terms of the contracts will be met, buyers and sellers must maintain margin accounts.
3. Marking to market is the process by which the clearinghouse of an exchange debits and credits the losses and profits that arise from the daily changes in futures prices to the margin accounts.
4. Futures contracts are rarely held until delivery and are closed out by simply reversing the original transaction.
5. Futures contracts are used to hedge transaction exchange risks in a fashion similar to forward contracts. To hedge a foreign currency receivable, one must go short in that foreign currency futures contract. To hedge a foreign currency payable, one goes long in the foreign currency futures contract.
6. If the maturity of a futures contract does not coincide with the maturity of the receivable or payable to be hedged, there is basis risk.
7. Foreign currency call options give the buyer of an option the right, but not the obligation, to buy a specific amount of foreign currency at the strike price, which is an exchange rate stated in the contract. Foreign currency put options give the buyer of an option the right to sell foreign currency.

8. Foreign currency options are primarily traded in the over-the-counter interbank market, but they are also traded on exchanges.
9. Option payoffs are functions of the future spot rate. The payoff on a call option is either 0 or the difference between the spot rate and the strike price, $\max[0, S(T) - K]$; for a put option, the payoff is $\max[0, K - S(T)]$.
10. The classic use of option contracts as hedges arises in bidding situations.
11. Transaction exchange risks can be hedged with an option that gives you the right, but not the obligation, to do the transaction that gives rise to the risk.
12. Purchasing foreign currency options in hedging situations is like purchasing insurance, and varying the strike price varies the quality of the insurance.
13. Increasing the strike price of a foreign currency call (put) option decreases (increases) the option's value because it removes (adds) possible states of the world over which the contract provides revenue.
14. An increase in the variance of possible future exchange rates increases the possible range of future exchange rates for any given date in the future that increases the value of both call and put options.
15. Option prices are mostly positively related to time to maturity because an increase in time to maturity primarily increases the conditional variance of the distribution of future exchange rates.
16. Put-call parity is a no arbitrage relationship between the prices of European put and call options, the forward exchange rate, and the domestic interest rate.
17. Average-rate call options have a payoff that is the maximum of the average future exchange rate minus the strike price of the option. This is only one example of a complex payoff that can be purchased through various exotic options.

QUESTIONS

1. How does a futures contract differ from a forward contract?
2. What effects does "marking to market" have on futures contracts?
3. What are the differences between foreign currency option contracts and forward contracts for foreign currency?
4. What are you buying if you purchase a U.S. dollar European put option against the Mexican peso with a strike price of MXN10.0/$ and a maturity of July? (Assume that it is May and the spot rate is MXN10.5/$.)
5. What are you buying if you purchase a Swiss franc American call option against the U.S. dollar with a strike price of CHF1.30/$ and a maturity of January? (Assume that it is November and the spot rate is CHF1.35/$.)

6. What is the intrinsic value of a foreign currency call option? What is the intrinsic value of a foreign currency put option?
7. What does it mean for an American option to be "in the money"?
8. Why do American option values typically exceed their intrinsic values?
9. Suppose you go long in a foreign currency futures contract. Under what circumstances is your cumulative payoff equal to that of buying the currency forward?
10. What is basis risk?
11. Your CEO routinely approves changes in the fire insurance policies of your firm to protect the value of its buildings and manufacturing equipment. Nevertheless, he argues that the firm should not buy foreign currency options because, he says, "We don't speculate in FX markets!" How could you convince him that his positions are mutually inconsistent?
12. Why do options provide insurance against foreign exchange risks in bidding situations? Why can't you hedge with a forward contract in a bidding situation?
13. Suppose that you have a foreign currency receivable (payable). What option strategy places a floor (ceiling) on your domestic currency revenue (cost)?
14. Describe qualitatively how changing the strike price of the option provides either more or less expensive insurance.
15. Why does an increase in the strike price of an option decrease the value of a call option and increase the value of a put option?
16. Why does an increase in the volatility of foreign exchange rates increase the value of foreign currency options?
17. How does increasing time to maturity affect foreign currency option value?
18. What is the payoff on an average-rate pound call option against the dollar?
19. Suppose the current spot rate is $1.29/€. What is your payoff if you purchase a down-and-in put option on the euro with a strike price of $1.31/€, a barrier of $1.25/€, and a maturity of 2 months? When would someone want to do this?

PROBLEMS

1. If you sold a Swiss franc futures contract at time t and the exchange rate has evolved as shown here, what would your cash flows have been?

Day	Futures Price $/CHF	Change in Futures Price	Gain or Loss	Cumulative Gain or Loss	Margin Account
t	0.7335				
$t+1$	0.7391				
$t+2$	0.7388				
$t+3$	0.7352				
$t+4$	0.7297				

2. Given the following information, how much would you have paid on September 16 to purchase a British pound call option contract with a strike price of 155 and a maturity of October?

Data for September 16

	Calls	Puts
50,000 Australian Dollar Options (cents per unit)		
64 Oct	—	0.48
65 Oct	—	0.90
67 Oct	0.22	—
31,250 British Pounds (cents per unit)		
152.5 Dec	—	4.10
155 Oct	1.50	3.62
155 Nov	2.35	—

3. Using the data in problem 2, how much would you have paid to purchase an Australian dollar put option contract with a strike price of 65 and an October maturity?
4. Suppose that you buy a €1,000,000 call option against dollars with a strike price of $1.2750/€. Describe this option as the right to sell a specific amount of dollars for euros at a particular exchange rate of euros per dollar. Explain why this latter option is a dollar put option against the euro.
5. Assume that today is March 7, and, as the newest hire for Goldman Sachs, you must advise a client on the costs and benefits of hedging a transaction with options. Your client (a small U.S. exporting firm) is scheduled to receive a payment of €6,250,000 on April 20, 44 days in the future. Assume that your client can borrow and lend at a 6% p.a. U.S. interest rate.
   a. Describe the nature of your client's transaction exchange risk.
   b. Use the appropriate American option with an April maturity and a strike price of 129¢/€ to determine the dollar cost today of hedging the transaction with an option strategy. The cost of the call option is 3.93¢/€, and the cost of the put option is 1.58¢/€.

c. What is the minimum dollar revenue your client will receive in April? Remember to take account of the opportunity cost of doing the option hedge.

d. Determine the value of the spot rate ($/€) in April that would make your client indifferent ex post to having done the option transaction or a forward hedge. The forward rate for delivery on April 20 is $1.30/€.

6. Assume that today is September 12. You have been asked to help a British client who is scheduled to pay €1,500,000 on December 12, 91 days in the future. Assume that your client can borrow and lend pounds at 5% p.a.

a. Describe the nature of your client's transaction exchange risk.

b. What is the option cost for a December maturity and a strike price of £0.72/€ to hedge the transaction? The option premiums per 100 euros are £1.70 for calls and £2.40 for puts.

c. What is the minimum pound cost your client will experience in December?

d. Determine the value of the spot rate (£/€) in December that makes your client indifferent *ex post* to having done the option transaction or a forward hedge if the forward rate for delivery on December 11 is £0.70/€.

7. Assume that today is June 11. Your firm is scheduled to pay £500,000 on August 15, 65 days in the future. The current spot is $1.75/£, and the 65-day forward rate is $1.73/£. You can borrow and lend dollars at 7% p.a. Suppose you think options are overpriced because you think the dollar will be in a tight trading range in the near future. You have been thinking about selling an option as a way to reduce the dollar cost of your pound payable.

a. If an August pound option with a strike price of 175¢/£ costs 4.5¢/£ per pound for the call and 4¢/£ for the put, what is the minimum effective exchange rate in August that you will pay? Over what range of future exchange rates will this price be achieved?

b. How much must the pound appreciate before your speculative option strategy ends up costing you more than the forward rate?

8. Upon arriving for work on Monday, you observe a violation of put–call parity. In particular, the synthetic forward price of dollars per yen is above the current forward rate. How would you capitalize on this information?

9. Use interest rate parity to demonstrate that you can represent put–call parity as

$$P - C = \frac{K}{1 + i(\$)} - \frac{S}{1 + i(€)}$$

10. On April 28, 1995, the Paine Webber Group introduced a new type of security on the NYSE: *U.S. dollar increase warrants on the yen*. At exercise, each warrant entitled the holder to an amount of U.S. dollars calculated as

Greater of (i) 0 and
(ii) $100 − [$100 × (¥83.65/$/Spot rate)]

The "spot rate" in the formula refers to the yen/dollar rate on any day during the exercise period, which extended until April 28, 1996. The 1-year forward rate on April 28 was ¥79.72/$, and the spot rate was ¥83.65/$.

a. What view on the future yen/dollar rate do investors in this security hold?

b. This security was issued at a price of $5.50. To see whether the security is fairly priced, which option prices would you want to examine?

BIBLIOGRAPHY

Black, Fischer, and Myron Scholes, 1973, "The Pricing of Options and Corporate Liabilities," *Journal of Political Economy* 81, pp. 637–659.

Dodd, Randall, 2009, "Exotic Derivatives Losses in Emerging Markets: Questions of Suitability, Concerns for Stability," International Monetary Fund Working Paper.

Garman, Mark B., and Steven W. Kolhagen, 1983, "Foreign Currency Option Values," *Journal of International Money and Finance* 2, pp. 231–237.

Lee, Yoolim, 2009, "Korean Corporations Court Bankruptcy with Suicidal KIKO Options," *Bloomberg Markets Magazine*, March 24.

Appendix

Foreign Currency Option Pricing (Advanced)

While knowledge of option pricing models is not required to be able to use the products of financial markets, decision making is enhanced if you understand how option prices are determined. This information is especially important for quotations that involve over-the-counter market prices. Option pricing models allow us to know whether the market prices that we observe are reasonable and competitive given our perceptions of the riskiness of exchange rates. Armed with an explicit model, we also can use observable option prices to determine the implied volatility of exchange rates, which enables us to quantify the market's forecast of foreign exchange risk. This should lead to improved risk management.

While option pricing models seem quite mathematically intimidating to some, a great deal of insight into how options are priced can be gained by understanding the no-arbitrage intuition from a two-state example. The binomial model assumes that at each point in time there are only two possible states to which the exchange rate can evolve.[1] The limiting case of the binomial model as the discrete time period gets smaller and smaller is the continuous time model of Garman and Kolhagen (1983), who generalized the Black-Scholes (1973) stock-option pricing model to price foreign currency options. We present the Garman-Kolhagen model below.

A Two-State Example of Arbitrage Pricing

Suppose we want to price a 1-month European call option, which allows us to purchase £100 at a strike price of \$1.52/£. Let the value of this pound call option be $C(t)$ dollars today. Our goal is to determine $C(t)$.

Let the current dollar–pound spot exchange rate be \$1.50/£, and assume that 1 month from now, the spot rate will be either \$1.55/£ or \$1.45/£. Let's also assume that the USD interest rate is 0.5% per month and that the GBP interest rate is 1% per month.

We use an arbitrage argument to value the pound call option. We create a portfolio that perfectly replicates the possible returns on the pound call option so that the option price must equal the value of the replicating portfolio to prevent arbitrage. If the current value of

the call option were greater than the value of our replicating portfolio, we could sell the call option to someone and invest in the portfolio. At maturity, we would be able to cover the outflows demanded by those who would exercise their option, and we would have wealth left over. If, on the other hand, the current value of the call option were less than the value of our replicating portfolio, we would borrow the portfolio and purchase or invest in the option. The payoff on our call option would be more than enough to offset the cost of borrowing the replicating portfolio.

To understand these arbitrage arguments, let's continue with the example. To derive our replicating portfolio we invest in £X today, and we borrow \$Y. The initial dollar cost of our replicating portfolio is therefore

$$\left[\left(\frac{\$1.50}{£} \right) \times £X \right] - \$Y$$

We must buy £X in the spot market, but we borrow \$Y, which partially offsets our dollar cost. Remember that we will get interest on our £X at 1% per month no matter what state of the world is realized in 1 month, and similarly, we will owe interest at 0.5% per month on our dollar borrowing.

If the dollar weakens, the value of the £100 call option is

$$\left[\left(\frac{\$1.55}{£} \right) - \left(\frac{\$1.52}{£} \right) \right] \times £100 = \$3.00$$

Because we have the right to buy £100 at the strike price of \$1.52/£ and we can sell the £100 in the spot market for \$1.55/£, we make \$3.00. On the other hand, if the dollar strengthens, the call option is worthless because no one wants to buy £100 at \$1.52/£ if the spot exchange rate is \$1.45/£.

From the discussion of the two payoffs on the option, we want the value of our replicating portfolio in 1 month to be

$$\left[\left(\frac{\$1.55}{£} \right) \times £X \times 1.01 \right] - [\$Y \times 1.005] = \$3.00$$

---

[1] By extending the example to multiple periods, it generalizes to become the binomial option pricing model of Cox and Rubinstein (1985).

if the dollar weakens, and if the dollar strengthens, we want the value of the portfolio to be

$$\left[\left(\frac{\$1.45}{£}\right) \times £X \times 1.01\right] - [\$Y \times 1.005] = 0$$

The previous two equations are linear in two unknowns. Consequently, there is a unique solution for £X and $Y.

Solving the second equation for £X gives

$$£X = \frac{\$Y \times 1.005}{\left(\frac{\$1.45}{£}\right) \times 1.01}$$

If we substitute this result into the first equation, we get

$$\left[\left(\frac{\$1.55}{£}\right) \times \left(\frac{\$Y \times 1.005}{\left(\frac{\$1.45}{£}\right) \times 1.01}\right) \times 1.01\right]$$
$$- [\$Y \times 1.005] = \$3.00$$

Solving this equation for $Y gives

$$\$Y = \$43.28$$

Substituting into the solution for £X gives

$$£X = £29.70$$

Hence, the cost of the replicating portfolio is

$$\left[\left(\frac{\$1.50}{£}\right) \times £29.70\right] - \$43.28 = \$1.27$$

Consequently, because this portfolio replicates the payoff on the £100 call option, the dollar cost of this option must be $1.27 to prevent arbitrage.

Suppose that the £100 call option were more expensive than $1.27, say $1.37. In this situation, selling the call option and investing the proceeds in the replicating portfolio should make money. From earlier, we know that if we borrow $43.28 and lend £29.70, we will replicate the payoffs on the £100 call option because

$$\left[\left(\frac{\$1.55}{£}\right) \times £29.70 \times 1.01\right] - (\$43.28 \times 1.005)$$
$$= \$3.00$$

and

$$\left[\left(\frac{\$1.45}{£}\right) \times £29.70 \times 1.01\right] - (\$43.28 \times 1.005)$$
$$= 0$$

Consequently, we will be able to meet the demands of the investors who purchased the call option from us. But, the cost of the replicating portfolio is only $1.27, whereas we generate $1.37 by selling the £100 call option. Clearly,

given these prices, we would try to sell as many of these call options as possible, investing the proceeds in the replicating portfolio to cover the demands of our investors, but keeping the residual for ourselves.

Conversely, if the price of the £100 call option were less than $1.27, we would make money by doing exactly the opposite set of transactions. We would buy the call options and lend the replicating portfolio. Suppose the price of the £100 call option were $1.20. If we borrow £29.70 at 1% per month, and convert the pounds into dollars, we get

$$\left(\frac{\$1.50}{£}\right) \times £29.70 = \$44.55$$

We can buy the £100 pound call option for $1.20, which leaves

$$\$44.55 - \$1.20 = \$43.35$$

to invest at 0.5% per month. In 1 month, we will have to pay back interest and principal on our pound borrowing; we can collect interest and principal on the dollars we invested; and we can collect the payoff on our pound call options. Hence, we will have either

$$-\left[\left(\frac{\$1.55}{£}\right) \times £29.70 \times 1.01\right] + (\$43.35 \times 1.005)$$
$$+ \left[\left(\frac{\$1.55}{£}\right) - \left(\frac{\$1.52}{£}\right)\right] \times £100 = \$0.07$$

or

$$-\left[\left(\frac{\$1.45}{£}\right) \times £29.70 \times 1.01\right] + (\$43.35 \times 1.005)$$
$$= \$0.07$$

Because we have generated $0.07 in both states of the world without any investment of our own money, we have a riskless arbitrage, and we would try to invest on a much larger scale.

Notice in this example that we did not need to know the probabilities associated with the possible up and down movements in the exchange rate. We only needed to know the current spot rate, the strike price, the two interest rates, and the two possible values of the future spot rate. The fact that the probabilities were irrelevant means that the expected rate of appreciation of the pound relative to the dollar was not directly relevant to determining the value of the pound call option.

You may find this to be a counterintuitive result, especially when reflecting on the earlier discussion in this chapter, which indicated that the value of a call option depends on the position of the strike price in relation to the probability distribution of the future exchange rate.

The puzzle arises because one naturally thinks that the probability distribution of future exchange rates depends on the mean rate of appreciation of one currency relative to another. While the intuition in this chapter is correct, the explanation for why the option does not depend explicitly on the mean rate of appreciation in this example is that we were able to price the option by a no-arbitrage argument. Essentially, the spot exchange rate, the interest rates, and the volatility of the process driving exchange rates implicitly characterize the future distribution. Formally, option pricing is said to rely on risk-neutral pricing.[2] Whenever we are able to develop a no-arbitrage argument, option prices will not depend explicitly on the expected rate of appreciation, and we are able to price options with risk-neutral methods.

The Binomial Option Pricing Model

The last section considered an example in which there were only two possible values for the future exchange rate. While this is clearly unrealistic over an interval as long as a month, it may not be so unreasonable over a very short time interval. **Binomial option pricing** relies on the assumption that random movements in the underlying asset, in this case the exchange rate, over short intervals are well approximated by a discrete, two-state model.[3]

To develop the intuition, let the spot exchange rate, $S(t)$, denote the domestic currency price of the foreign currency. At each discrete point in time t, it is assumed that $S(t)$ will either move up to $uS(t)$ or down to $dS(t)$ at time $t+1$. Analogously, we can assume that the domestic currency price of a call option to purchase one unit of the foreign currency, $C(t)$, will evolve up to $C(u, t+1)$ if the exchange rate increases, or down to $C(d, t+1)$ if the exchange rate decreases. If there were only one period left before the maturity of the option, we would use the logic of the numerical example to value the call option.

We could form a portfolio containing an investment of $\Delta(t)$ units of foreign currency in the foreign currency–denominated risk-free asset and $B(t)$ units of domestic currency in the domestic currency–denominated risk-free asset. Earlier, we found $B(t) < 0$, in which case we are borrowing the domestic currency. The domestic currency cost of this replicating portfolio would be

$$S(t)\Delta(t) + B(t)$$

As above, if the call price, $C(t)$, were not equal to the value of the replicating portfolio, there would be an arbitrage opportunity.

It is straightforward, although tedious, to add more periods. The simplest binomial model assumes that the possible events in each period are independent of all previous events and that the sizes of the possible increases or decreases in the exchange rate are the same in all future periods. Hence, if there are two periods remaining, there are three possible values for the exchange rate at the maturity of the option. The exchange rate can increase twice, it can decrease twice, or it can first increase and then decrease, which is the same as first decreasing and then increasing. Similarly, the price of the call option will either increase twice, decrease twice, first increase and then decrease, or first decrease and then increase. This binomial tree is illustrated in Exhibit 20A.1.

The value of the call option in the first period, $C(t)$, can then be determined by an argument that uses the technique of backward recursion. We know that in the next to the last period, we will have evolved to a particular state, and there will be only two possible events that characterize the last period. Therefore, we can use the logic of the replicating portfolio that was developed earlier to determine the possible call prices for the next to the last period. From there, we work backward to develop the possible prices in previous periods.

The Continuous Time Case

Let T be the calendar time to expiration of the option contract, and let the continuously compounded domestic and foreign interest rates for that maturity be $i(t)$ and $i^*(t)$, respectively. Let the volatility of the rate of depreciation over a small time interval h be $\sigma\sqrt{h}$. That is, σ is the annualized standard deviation, and h is the fraction of the year. In the earlier discrete time analysis, we thought of dividing the interval of time T into n periods, each of length h, where $h = T/n$. If we drive n to infinity, the period h shrinks to 0, and the exchange rate is said to follow a continuous time stochastic process. The resulting expression for the call option price is the Garman-Kolhagen version of the Black-Scholes option pricing model.

While some of you may be interested in the formal arguments that lead to the option pricing formula, we

---

[2]Remember, a risk-neutral investor is indifferent between holding an asset with a certain return and holding a different asset that has an uncertain return if its expected return is the same as the risk-free return.
[3]See Cox and Rubinstein (1985) for additional discussion of the binomial option pricing model.

Exhibit 20A.1   A Two-Period Binomial Tree

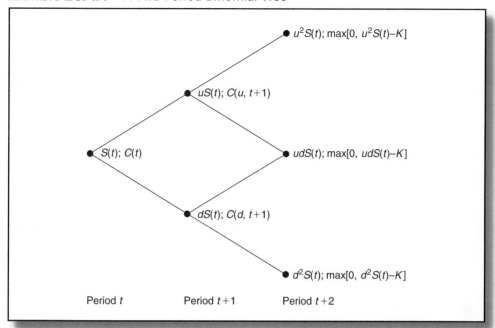

Period t Period $t+1$ Period $t+2$

will not present those here. Instead, we present the final formula and discuss some intuition. The price of a call option in the Garman-Kolhagen model is

$$C(t) = \exp(-i^*(t)T)\, S(t)\, N(d_1(t))$$
$$-\exp(-i(t)T) K\, N(d_2(t))$$

The terms $N(d_1(t))$ and $N(d_2(t))$ are probabilities associated with the cumulative standardized normal distribution. That is

$$N(d) = \int_{-\infty}^{d} \frac{1}{\sqrt{2\pi}} \exp\left(-\frac{x^2}{2}\right) dx$$

The limits of integration are

$$d_1(t) = \big[\ln[S(t)/K] + [i(t) - i^*(t)$$
$$+ 0.5\sigma^2]T\big]/\sigma\sqrt{T}$$

and

$$d_2(t) = d_1(t) - \sigma\sqrt{T}$$

Exhibit 20A.2 presents various prices for European call options corresponding to plausible values of the variables entering the Garman-Kolhagen model. The option prices and the exchange rates are expressed in U.S. cents per pound, as on the NASDAQ OMX PHLX. Hence, the spot exchange rate is measured as 150¢/£. The strike prices represent in-the-money call options with a strike price of 145¢/£, at-the-money calls with a

strike price of 150¢/£, and out-of-the-money calls with a strike price of 155¢/£. The volatilities range from 8% per annum, which is relatively low, to a more normal value of 12%, and a relatively high value of 16%. Finally, the U.S. dollar interest rate takes the values of 1%, 4%, and 7% per annum. The pound interest rate is held constant at 5% per annum.

The option prices are larger the lower is the strike price, the higher is the volatility, the higher is the U.S. interest rate, and, usually, the longer is the time to maturity. Note that for the in-the-money call options with a low U.S. interest rate and low volatility, the call option prices actually decrease with longer times to expiration. These facts will be explored in more detail later.

Notice that the replicating portfolio for the binomial option is $C(t) = S(t)\Delta(t) + B(t)$. In the continuous time case, the same expression equates the call option price to the value of the portfolio that replicates the instantaneous payoff on a call option. Hence, by comparing the option pricing formula to the price of the call option, we see that the domestic currency investment in the foreign currency risk-free asset is $\exp(-i^*(t)T)\, S(t)\, N(d_1(t))$, and the amount of domestic currency that is borrowed is $\exp(-i(t)T)\, K\, N(d_2(t))$. These amounts change continuously as the values of the parameters underlying the option prices change.

Once we have call option prices, we can use put–call parity to determine the value of put options.

Exhibit 20A.2   Garman-Kolhagen Call Option Values

Spot = 150¢/£, i£ = 5%

Vol.	Strike	i$ = 1%			i$ = 4%			i$ = 7%		
					Fraction of a Year to Maturity					
σ	K	0.25	0.50	0.75	0.25	0.50	0.75	0.25	0.50	0.75
8%	145	4.49	4.39	4.27	5.30	5.75	6.10	6.16	7.29	8.27
8%	150	1.70	2.06	2.23	2.18	2.95	3.48	2.74	4.06	5.12
8%	155	0.44	0.80	1.02	0.54	1.27	1.77	0.86	1.91	2.86
12%	145	5.53	5.99	6.26	6.24	7.24	7.98	7.00	8.61	9.92
12%	150	2.87	3.66	4.13	3.36	4.60	5.48	3.91	5.68	7.07
12%	155	1.27	2.07	2.59	1.55	2.72	3.59	1.88	3.49	4.82
16%	145	6.62	7.61	8.24	7.29	8.79	9.89	7.99	10.07	11.70
16%	150	4.04	5.29	6.09	4.54	6.25	7.47	5.09	7.31	9.03
16%	155	2.26	3.53	4.38	2.61	4.27	5.51	2.99	5.11	6.81

Note: The maturities of the options are 91 days, 182 days, or 273 days with a 365-day year.

Comparative Statics for the Call Option Price

We next consider how call option prices are affected by changes in the various variables that determine the price. The effects of changes in the underlying variables on the option prices are partial derivatives since they are derived holding the influence of the other variables constant. Often, financial market participants discuss these effects with Greek letters.

To help in understanding the nature of each partial effect, we will discuss how the price changes relative to a base case whose parameter values are the following:

> Spot exchange rate = 150¢/£
> Strike price = 152¢/£
> USD interest rate = 3% per annum
> GBP interest rate = 4% per annum
> Volatility = 12% per annum
> Time to maturity of 0.25 years

These are reasonable values that one might encounter in actual markets, and the theoretical value of a call option with these parameter values is 2.5224¢/£.

The Delta of an Option

The first partial effect examines how the call option price changes when the exchange rate changes. From the derivation of the call option price, we find

$$\frac{\partial C(t)}{\partial S(t)} = \Delta(t) = \exp(-i^*(t)T)\, N(d_1(t)) > 0$$

This expression is called the **delta** of the call option because it represents the change in the value of the derivative

asset with a small change in the value of the underlying asset. The expression is also sometimes called the "hedge ratio" because it arises from the construction of the replicating portfolio. Delta is the amount of pounds invested in the risk-free asset to replicate the payoff on the call option. Evaluating this equation at the base parameter values gives a delta of 0.4039. Hence, if the exchange rate increases from 150.00¢/£ to 150.01¢/£, the value of the call option increases by (0.4039)(0.01¢/£) = 0.0040¢/£, or from 2.5224¢/£ to 2.5264¢/£.

Exhibit 20.14 graphs the call option value as a function of the exchange rate. The slope of the curve in Exhibit 20A.3 is the delta of the call option. Notice that when the exchange rate is low relative to the strike price of 152¢/£, the call option is deeply out of the money, and the delta of the option is nearly 0 because increases in the exchange rate have only a small effect on the option value. As the exchange rate increases toward the strike price, the sensitivity of the option value to changes in the exchange rate increases. Eventually, when the exchange rate is well above the exercise price, the delta of the call option approaches 1 as the option value nearly increases one-for-one with an increase in the exchange rate. To summarize, we have found that the delta of a call option is always between 0 and 1 because the change in the option price is less than the change in the underlying spot rate.

Delta Hedging

Knowledge of the delta of an option is important for those who sell or write options because it tells them how

Exhibit 20A.3 Call Option Price

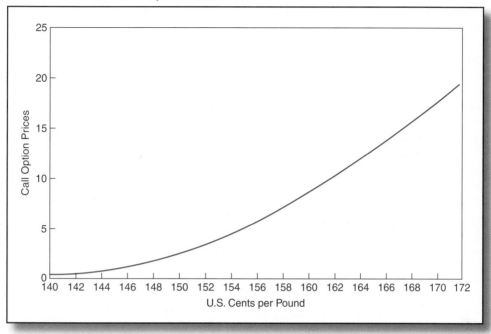

to hedge the position that they have created. Suppose we have sold call options on one million pounds, and we do not want to be exposed to losses from movements in the underlying exchange rate. Then, if the pound call option against the dollar has a delta of 0.34, we know that we must own 0.34 × £1,000,000 = £340,000 to have a hedged position. If alternatively, we have sold £1,000,000 put options whose delta is −0.48, we will have to borrow 0.48 × £1,000,000 = £480,000 to have a hedged position.

Making a market in call and put options without losing a lot of money requires the trader to be continually aware of the exposure to losses due to fluctuations in exchange rates that is inherent in the trader's portfolio at any point in time. Essentially, the trader must track the delta of his overall portfolio created through his transactions. This is not too difficult because deltas are additive. Hence, the overall exposure of the portfolio is the sum of the different deltas of each of the options that is bought or sold weighted by the amount of the position.

For example, if a trader sells a call option on £1,000,000 with a delta of 0.40 and buys another call option on £1,000,000 with different parameters whose delta is 0.45, his net exposure to small movements in the exchange rate is a delta of 0.05 = 0.45 − 0.40. Effectively, selling the one call option coupled with buying the other call option leaves the trader with a net long position of 0.05 × £1,000,000 = £50,000. The trader's

portfolio of options will lose value if the pound weakens relative to the dollar.

Many market makers attempt to remain reasonably close to **delta neutral**, which means that they actively adjust their portfolios so that they are not exposed to risk of loss from small changes in foreign exchange rates. In the previous example, in which the trader is effectively long £50,000, one way to achieve a delta-neutral position would be to sell £100,000 of call options with a delta of 0.5. Obviously, there are many ways in which a delta-neutral position could be established, and profitable market making involves trying to buy options that are undervalued and to sell options that are overvalued while managing the exposure to exchange rates and the other variables that affect option prices.

The Gamma of an Option

The **gamma of a call option** describes how the option's delta changes with a change in the underlying exchange rate:

$$\gamma(t) = \frac{\partial \Delta(t)}{\partial S(t)} = \frac{\exp(-i^*(t)T)\phi(d_1(t))}{S(t)\sigma\sqrt{T}}$$

where $\phi(z)$ represents the probability density function of the standard normal:

$$\phi(z) = \frac{1}{\sqrt{2\pi}} \exp\left(\frac{-z^2}{2}\right)$$

When the option is either deeply out of the money or deeply in the money, the gamma of the call option is near 0. When the exchange rate is near the strike price, gamma takes its largest values. When evaluated at the base parameter values given above, the delta of the option is 0.4039, and the value of gamma is 0.04. Hence, if the exchange rate changes from $150.00\text{¢}/\text{£}$ to $150.01\text{¢}/\text{£}$, the delta of the call option increases by $0.04 \times 0.01 = 0.0004$, or from 0.4039 to 0.4043.

Knowledge of the gamma of an option is important to those who sell or write options because it tells them how rapidly they must adjust their hedge ratios when the exchange rate changes. For example, if a call option that has been sold is deep in the money, the hedge ratio is near 1, and the gamma is very low. Holding the underlying asset in an amount equivalent to the amount of the call option is effectively what is required to produce a riskless position. Even if the exchange rate changes, no change in the underlying position is required.

But, if the call option is at the money, the hedge ratio is much less than 1, and the gamma is large. An increase in the exchange rate may move the delta of the option from 0.40 to 0.50. Now, if the trader had sold £1,000,000 of call options and was holding £400,000 as a hedge, the trader must buy an additional £100,000 if he does not want to bear exchange risk. An understanding of gamma helps the trader determine in advance how much of which options will have to be bought or sold after the next movement in the exchange rate.

The Elasticity of an Option
The elasticity of a call option price with respect to the exchange rate is denoted in various presentations as either omega, $\Omega(t)$, or lambda, $\lambda(t)$. Elasticity measures the percentage change in the call option price divided by the percentage change in the exchange rate:

$$\Omega(t) = \frac{\dfrac{\partial C(t)}{C(t)}}{\dfrac{\partial S(t)}{S(t)}} = \Delta(t)\frac{S(t)}{C(t)}$$

For example, the delta of the call option at the basic parameters is 0.4039, the current spot rate is $150\text{¢}/\text{£}$, and the price of the call option is $2.52\text{¢}/\text{£}$. Thus, the elasticity of this call option is $\Omega(t) = .4039 \times \dfrac{150}{2.52} = 24.04$. Hence, if the exchange rate increases by 1% to $151.5\text{¢}/\text{£}$, the price of the call option is predicted to increase by 24.04% to $3.13\text{¢}/\text{£} = (2.52\text{¢}/\text{£}) \times 1.2404$.

The elasticity of a call option is an important concept because the volatility of a call option is its elasticity

times the volatility of the exchange rate. Because the volatility of the underlying rate of appreciation is 12%, the volatility of the call option is $24.04 \times 12\% = 288.48\%$. Unhedged positions in foreign currency call options are quite volatile.

The Vega of an Option
The change in the value of a call option as volatility changes is usually referred to as the vega of the option. Increasing the volatility of exchange rates increases the value of the call option because

$$\frac{\partial C(t)}{\partial \sigma} = \exp(-i^*(t)T)\phi(d_1(t))\sqrt{T} > 0$$

The value of the call option is quite sensitive to the volatility of the exchange rate. For example, the vega of the option at the base parameters is 29. Hence, a change in volatility from 12% to 13% increases the option value by $0.01 \times 29 = 0.29$ or from $2.52\text{¢}/\text{£}$ to $2.81\text{¢}/\text{£}$.

The Rhos of an Option
The changes in the value of a call option as either the domestic or foreign interest rates change are usually referred to as the rhos of the option. The price of a foreign currency call option increases with the domestic interest rate and decreases with the foreign interest rate because

$$\frac{\partial C(t)}{\partial i(t)} = T\exp(-i(t)T)\,K\,N(d_2(t)) > 0$$

and

$$\frac{\partial C(t)}{\partial i^*(t)} = -T\exp(-i^*(t)T)\,S(t)\,N(d_1(t)) < 0$$

When these equations are evaluated at the base parameter values, their values are 0.14 and −0.15, respectively, when the interest rates are expressed as percent per annum. Thus, for example, an increase in the USD interest rate from 3% to 4% increases the option price from $2.52\text{¢}/\text{£}$ to $2.66\text{¢}/\text{£}$ or by $0.14\text{¢}/\text{£}$. Similarly, an increase in the GBP interest rate from 4% to 5% decreases the option price from $2.52\text{¢}/\text{£}$ to $2.37\text{¢}/\text{£}$ or by $0.15\text{¢}/\text{£}$.

The Theta of an Option
The last effect that we discuss is how changes in the maturity of an option affect its value. As noted earlier, increasing the time to maturity has an ambiguous effect on the call option price. Formally, we have

$$\begin{aligned}
\frac{\partial C(t)}{\partial T} = {} & -i^*(t)\exp(-i^*(t)T)S(t)\,N(d_1(t)) \\
& + i(t)\exp(-i(t)T)\,K\,N(d_2(t)) \\
& + \exp(-i^*(t)T)\,S(t)\phi(d_1(t))\sigma/(2\sqrt{T})
\end{aligned}$$

The expression may be negative for call options that are in the money ($S_t > K$) especially if they are deep in the money or the time to maturity is short. The situation is exacerbated if the foreign interest rate is well above the domestic interest rate. If the foreign interest rate were zero, an increase in time to maturity would increase the foreign currency option value.

Rather than discuss the sensitivity of call option prices to an increase in maturity, market participants are interested in the sensitivity of the price of a call option to the passage of time, which is often referred to as the option's **theta**. The theta of a call option is simply the negative of the derivative of the call option with respect to maturity, and it describes how the option price will evolve as the time remaining until maturity decays.

To examine the influence of time to maturity on call option value at the base case parameter values, we calculate the theta of the call option as 1 day elapses. The call option with 91 days to maturity is worth 2.5224¢/£, while the call option with 90 days to maturity is worth 2.5052¢/£. This corresponds with the theta of the 91-day option being −0.0171¢/£.

Implied Volatility

Since all of the variables that determine foreign currency option prices are observable except the volatility of the exchange rate, option prices can be used in conjunction with an option pricing model and the observations on the other variables to determine an **implied volatility**. This is the unique value of σ that sets the option price from the model equal to the option price observed in the market.

There are several ways that one may determine an implied volatility, but the simplest is merely to try out a value, say $\sigma = 0.11$, and see if the price from the option pricing model is higher or lower than the observed option price from the market. If the model's price is too high, we know that we must lower the implied volatility. If the model's price is too low, we must increase the implied volatility. It isn't too hard to iterate and find the unique solution.[4]

One important use of implied volatility is to determine if one option is expensive relative to another option with the same maturity but with a different strike price. Since the options are for the same maturity, they are pricing the same distribution of future spot rates, and they should have the same implied volatility. Of course, one reason that the implied volatilities may differ is that one or more of the assumptions of the option pricing model may be wrong.

SUMMARY OF THE APPENDIX

1. The theory associated with foreign currency call option pricing uses a replicating portfolio that consists of an investment in the foreign currency risk-free asset that is partially financed by borrowing the domestic currency. The payoffs on the replicating portfolio are constructed to match the payoffs on a foreign currency call option, and the value of the replicating portfolio equals the value of the option to prevent arbitrage.

2. If it is assumed that the continuously compounded rate of appreciation of the foreign currency relative to the domestic currency is normally distributed, the binomial model converges to the Garman-Kolhagen model in the limit as the number of periods between the current date and the expiration of the option goes to infinity.

3. The delta of a call option represents the change in the value of the option with a small change in the value of the underlying spot exchange rate. The expression is also sometimes called the "hedge ratio" because it is equal to the amount of foreign currency in the replicating portfolio. Delta must be between 0 and 1.

4. If a portfolio of foreign currency options does not change in value with a change in the exchange rate, the portfolio is said to be delta neutral.

5. The implied volatility of an option is the unique value of the standard deviation of the rate of appreciation that sets the option price derived from a model equal to the observed market price given observations from market prices on the other variables that affect the option pricing formula.

---

[4]Of course, most modern spreadsheet programs contain an equation solver that will do the iterations for you. Hence, it is a simple matter to let the computer determine the unique value of implied volatility.

ADDITIONAL QUESTIONS

1. Explain intuitively how foreign currency options can be replicated with portfolios of borrowing and lending in the two currencies.
2. Why do the formulas for option prices not depend explicitly on the expected rate of appreciation of one currency relative to another currency?
3. What is the Garman-Kolhagen model of foreign currency option pricing?
4. What is the delta of an option? Why is it useful?
5. What does it mean for a portfolio of options to be delta neutral?
6. What is the gamma of an option?
7. How does a change in the volatility of the rate of appreciation affect the pricing of foreign currency options?
8. Why does a change in the domestic interest rate affect the pricing of a foreign currency option? Does a change in the foreign interest rate cause any change in option prices?
9. What is the theta of an option?
10. What is the implied volatility of an option?

ADDITIONAL PROBLEMS

1. Let the current spot rate be $1.25/€, and assume that 1 month from now the spot rate will be either $1.30/€ or $1.20/€. Let the dollar interest rate be 0.4% per month, and let the euro interest rate be 0.3% per month. Develop a portfolio that replicates the payoff on a 1-month euro call option with a strike price of $1.25/€. What is the corresponding price of the euro put option with the same strike price?
2. Suppose that the price of the euro call option in Problem 1 were $0.03/€. How would you arbitrage between the market in risk-free assets and the foreign currency options market? What would you do if the price of the call option were $0.02/€?
3. Let the continuously compounded 6-month USD interest rate be 3% p.a., let the analogous JPY interest rate be 1% p.a., let the exchange rate be ¥98/$, and assume that the volatility of the continuously compounded annualized rate of appreciation of the yen relative to the dollar is 13%. Use the Garman-Kolhagen option pricing model to determine the yen price of a 6-month European dollar call option with a strike price of ¥100/$. How does your answer change if the volatility were 16% p.a.?
4. With the same variables as in Problem 3, use put–call parity to determine the yen price of the corresponding dollar put option with the same maturity and same strike price.
5. Suppose a trader sells a call option on £500,000 with a delta of 0.35 and buys another call option on £1,000,000 with different parameters whose delta is 0.55. What is his net exposure to small movements in the exchange rate? How could he cover this position?
6. Assume you are looking at prices from the NASDAQ OMX PHLX and that the price of a 3-month European AUD call option with a strike price of 92 cents per Australian dollar is 3.2¢/AUD. Suppose that the spot exchange rate is 90¢/AUD, the continuously compounded annualized dollar interest rate is 2%, and the analogous AUD interest rate is 5%. What is the implied volatility of the continuously compounded annualized rate of appreciation of the AUD relative to the dollar?
7. Suppose the implied volatilities expressed in percent per annum of yen call options against the dollar with maturities of 1, 2, and 3 months are 9%, 10%, and 11%, respectively. If you thought that the market would soon price options to have a common volatility of 10%, what position would you take in the options to expect to profit from your beliefs?

ADDITIONAL BIBLIOGRAPHY

Cox, John C., and Mark Rubenstein, 1985, *Option Markets*, Upper Saddle River, NJ: Prentice Hall.

Chapter 21

Interest Rate and Foreign Currency Swaps

In 2002, only 18% of Wal-Mart's outstanding debt had payments that fluctuated with the short-term interest rate. By 2003, it had increased the exposure of its outstanding debt to short-term interest rates to more than 40% by engaging in interest rate swaps. In 2011, Chinese authorities announced that certain banks would be allowed to offer currency swaps to their corporate clients. These corporations can now issue dollar debt and swap into renminbi debt, or vice versa.

This chapter examines interest rate and currency swaps, which are additional instruments for your risk management tool kit. We have previously discussed a number of ways of managing a firm's currency risks using derivative securities, including forward contracts in Chapter 3 and futures and options in Chapter 20. The maturities for these instruments are somewhat limited, whereas the maturities in the swap markets extend to 30 years. We have also noted that exchange rate exposures can be thought of as arising from a general mismatch between assets and liabilities denominated in different currencies. We will see how interest rate swaps allow firms to change the nature of their liabilities for a given currency from fixed to floating interest rates or from floating to fixed interest rates. Currency swaps can be used to change the currency of denomination of a firm's liabilities. Changes such as these can be desirable as the nature of a firm's business changes. Swaps also allow firms to seek out low-cost financing without sacrificing their preferred type of debt.

Section 21.1 introduces the basic ideas associated with swaps and discusses the impressive size of the swap market. Section 21.2 provides a detailed analysis of the cash flows of interest rate swaps, and Section 21.3 provides a detailed analysis of the cash flows of currency swaps.

21.1 INTRODUCTION TO SWAPS

Swaps are agreements between two counterparties to exchange a sequence of cash flows. In the modern swap market, over-the-counter dealers at major banks quote bid–ask spreads at which they are willing to do either side of a swap. The cash flows of interest rate and currency swaps are structured like the cash flows of standard bonds, and the maturities extend from 1 year to 30 years and even more. Many international financial managers now actively use swaps to manage their companies' interest rate and currency risks and for speculative purposes.

The nature of the contract between swap counterparties is usually based on the best practices suggested by the **International Swaps and Derivatives Association (ISDA)**. The ISDA is a trade organization that was chartered in 1985 and now represents more than 800 member institutions from 56 countries. Its members include most of the world's major financial institutions that deal in privately negotiated derivatives, as well as their clients who rely on over-the-counter derivatives to manage the financial market risks inherent in their core economic activities. The most important ISDA document is the ISDA Master Agreement Protocol, which controls the legal aspects of swap cash flows, such as how swaps are closed out in the event of default.

Swaps are effectively agreements between two counterparties to exchange different types of debts. Currency swaps are actually modern counterparts of parallel loans and back-to-back loans, which are still used but are much less important than currency swaps. By examining these early forms of swaps, we can understand why the market began and how it has evolved.

Parallel Loans and Back-to-Back Loans

Parallel loans originated as a means of securing low-cost funding for foreign subsidiaries and to circumvent various government regulations, such as currency controls. Another motivation of these contracts was the desire to avoid taxation on intracompany multinational transactions.

Parallel Loans

Suppose Stars and Stripes Inc., a U.S. corporation, has an Indonesian subsidiary that would like to borrow rupiah, and Java Cava, an Indonesian corporation, has a U.S. subsidiary that would like to borrow dollars. These funding needs could be met in several ways. The most direct way is for each subsidiary to simply borrow the currency it needs. But, if a subsidiary is not well known in the foreign money market, it could be assessed a high default risk premium on the loan, which would make the loan very expensive. A second way for the subsidiaries to raise funds would be for the parent of each subsidiary to borrow the currency the subsidiary needs and to make an intracompany loan. Because parent corporations are usually better credit risks, this is less costly, but the interest payments that the subsidiary makes to the parent may be subject to withholding taxes. This leads to additional expenses of borrowing.

A **parallel loan** avoids these extra expenses. In our example, the Stars and Stripes parent corporation would lend dollars to the Java Cava subsidiary operating in the United States, and the Java Cava parent corporation would simultaneously lend rupiah of equivalent value to the Stars and Stripes subsidiary operating in Indonesia. Because the loans are between entities operating in the same country, problems with the inconvertibility of currencies, exchange controls, and withholding taxes are avoided.

The two loans are separate contractual obligations of the respective parties. This means that interest and principal repayment on one of the parallel loans must be continued even if the other subsidiary defaults on a payment. For example, if the Stars and Stripes subsidiary defaults on its rupiah loan that is owed to the Java Cava parent, the Java Cava subsidiary must continue to pay dollar interest and principal to the Stars and Stripes parent. Parallel loans do not contain a "right of offset," which, in this example, would allow the Java Cava subsidiary to stop payments on the dollar loan if the Stars and Stripes subsidiary defaults on the euro loan.

Back-to-Back Loans

While similar in structure to parallel loans, **back-to-back loans** have two key differences: (1) They involve simultaneous loans between multinational parent corporations (vs. subsidiaries) in two different countries, and (2) they contain the right of offset. In terms of the corporations in our example, a back-to-back loan involves the U.S. headquarters of Stars and Stripes making a dollar loan to the Indonesian headquarters of Java Cava. Simultaneously, the Indonesian headquarters of Java Cava would make a rupiah loan of equivalent value to the headquarters of Stars and Stripes. The parent corporations would then make intracompany loans to their subsidiaries. A back-to-back loan involves only a single loan document and contains a provision for the **right of offset**, a clause that stipulates that if one party defaults on a payment, the other party can withhold corresponding payments of equal value. Because the exchange control regulations of many countries explicitly prohibit rights of offset, parallel loans are more common than back-to-back loans.

The World Bank–IBM Swap

In 1981, the World Bank and IBM engaged in one of the first currency swaps. The World Bank had substantial outstanding debt denominated in dollars as well as in Deutsche marks and Swiss francs. It considered its liabilities to be unbalanced and wanted to reduce its dollar debt and increase its Deutsche mark and Swiss franc debt. Although it could have issued additional debt in the European currencies and retired its dollar debt, the World Bank was near its official borrowing limit in the European currencies. Meanwhile, IBM had outstanding debts denominated in Deutsche marks and Swiss francs, but the company wanted the debt denominated in dollars. Why? Because much of IBM's revenue was generated in dollars, and the firm was worried that the dollar would soon depreciate, making it relatively more difficult for IBM to repay its Deutsche mark– and Swiss franc–denominated debt.

It occurred to smart financial advisors that the World Bank and IBM could both benefit by swapping their debts. The result was that the World Bank agreed to take over IBM's Deutsche mark and Swiss franc debt service in return for IBM taking over the World Bank's dollar debt service. Since then, the swap market has grown tremendously, and interest rate and currency swaps have become indispensable risk management tools for multinational corporations.

Basic Aspects of Currency Swaps and Interest Rate Swaps

A **currency swap** allows a multinational corporation to change the currency of denomination of its debts, as the World Bank and IBM did. Exhibit 21.1 presents the basic idea of a currency swap. Counterparty A is paying interest and principal on a dollar amount to Counterparty B. Counterparty B, in turn, is paying interest and principal on a yen amount to Counterparty A. At the beginning of the swap, the dollar principal is equal to the yen principal. These principals will again be exchanged at the end of the currency swap, but if the exchange rate has changed, the values of the principals will no longer be equal at the end of the swap.

Exhibit 21.1 Foreign Currency Swap Diagram

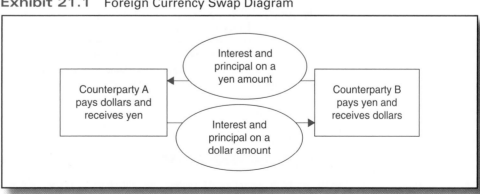

Exhibit 21.2 Interest Rate Swap Diagram

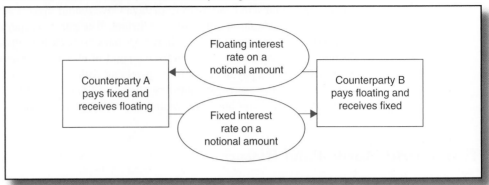

An **interest rate swap** allows a multinational corporation (MNC) to change the nature of its debt from a fixed interest rate to a floating interest rate or from a floating interest rate to a fixed interest rate. Exhibit 21.2 provides a basic interest rate swap diagram. Counterparty A is paying a fixed amount of interest on a **notional principal** to Counterparty B, and Counterparty A is receiving floating interest rate cash flows on the same notional amount from Counterparty B. The term *notional* indicates the basic principal amount on which the cash flows of the interest rate swap depend. Unlike a currency swap, no exchange of principal is necessary because the principal is an equal amount of the same currency.

The Size of the Swap Markets

The growth in the use of swaps since their introduction in the early 1980s has been truly phenomenal. Exhibit 21.3 presents Bank for International Settlements (BIS) data on the outstanding amounts of interest rate and currency swaps. Notice that the notional amount of interest rate swaps on the books of corporations and banks around the world in 2010 was $347 *trillion* dollars, whereas in 2001, the notional value of aggregate interest rate swaps was $51 trillion, an annualized growth rate of over 23%. These figures are adjusted for the obvious double-counting problem that arises because each contract is counted on the books of two counterparties. The notional value of currency swaps is significantly smaller than the notional value of interest rate swaps, but it was still an incredibly large $16.3 trillion in June 2010.

In thinking about these notional values, it is important to understand that, like forward contracts, interest rate swaps and currency swaps begin life as zero net present value contracts. That is, swaps have no market value initially because the present value of the cash

Exhibit 21.3 The Size and Growth of Interest Rate and Currency Swap Markets (amounts outstanding in billions of U.S. dollars)

	Currency Swaps		Interest Rate Swaps		Credit Default Swaps	
	Notional Amounts	Gross Market Value	Notional Amounts	Gross Market Value	Notional Amounts	Gross Market Value
June 2001	3,823	314	51,407	1,404	—	—
June 2004	7,033	442	127,570	3,562	—	—
June 2007	12,291	617	271,853	5,315	42,580	721
June 2010	16,347	1,187	347,508	15,951	30,261	1,666

Note: Data are taken from various December issues of the Bank for International Settlements *Quarterly Review*.

flows that are to be paid by one of the counterparties is exactly equal to the present value of the cash flows that are to be paid by the other counterparty. Subsequently, though, changes in interest rates and especially exchange rates imply that one of the counterparties to the swap experiences a profit and the other experiences an equivalent loss.

Exhibit 21.3 also shows that the gross market value of the outstanding interest rate swaps in 2010 was 4.59% of the notional value, or $15.951 trillion, whereas the market value of outstanding currency swaps was 7.26% of notional value, or $1.187 trillion. These are the market values of the debts that are owed between counterparties at that time.

As you can see from Exhibit 21.3, interest rate and particularly currency swaps can become quite valuable. Of course, value created on one side of a swap is a loss when viewed from the other side. So, swaps can be the source of large trading losses, especially when they are being used for speculative purposes. For example, in 1998, the hedge fund Long Term Capital Management (LTCM) lost $1.6 billion on trades in the swap markets, and it lost more than $4 billion in total, causing the Federal Reserve Bank of New York to organize a $3.6 billion bailout of LTCM counterparties to prevent a crisis [see Lowenstein (2000)]. The LTCM crisis brought home the fact that the counterparty risk of swaps can be substantial, and the same marking-to-market techniques that are used in the futures market have become common in the swap market to mitigate these risks.

Some market observers have argued that the growth rate of the swap market has been too fast and that the magnitudes outstanding in the swap markets were a financial catastrophe waiting to happen. However, the 2007 to 2010 global financial crisis taught the financial community that a rapidly growing new category of swaps, namely credit default swaps, posed a much larger danger for financial stability.

Credit Default Swaps and the Financial Crisis

The **credit default swap (CDS)** was devised by JPMorgan Chase bankers. It is essentially a bilateral insurance contract between a protection buyer and a protection seller to protect against default on a specific bond or loan issued by a corporation or sovereign (the "reference entity"). The protection buyer pays semiannual or annual insurance premiums to the protection seller. In return, when there is a default event, the protection seller transfers value to the protection buyer. Value is transferred either through physical settlement or cash settlement. If there is physical settlement, the protection buyer delivers the defaulted bond to the protection seller who pays the face amount of the referenced bond. If there is cash settlement, the protection seller pays the buyer the difference between the face value of the bond and the value of the defaulted bond. The insurance analogy is apt in the case of physical settlement because the CDS contract protects the owner of the bond in the event of default, but with cash settlement, the CDS is just another derivative contract that allows market participants to trade and transfer the credit risks of corporations and sovereigns.

The CDS market remained very small in the 1990s, but it grew exponentially in the first decade of the 21st century, reaching notional open interest of $60 trillion in 2008 (see Exhibit 21.3 for more data on outstanding amounts). The rapid growth meant that many of the contracts were speculative in nature. Institutional investors, including insurance companies, and hedge funds became major players in the CDS market. Some skeptical market observers noted that the market was entirely unregulated and was analogous to letting someone who you do not know take an insurance contract out on your house, and when it is destroyed by a fire, having the unknown person get paid the value of the house.

Substantial amounts of credit default swaps were written on subprime mortgages, and when defaults began to increase in 2007 and 2008, the dangers inherent in the CDS market soon became very clear. One of the most important sellers of CDS protection was the American International Group (AIG), one of the oldest and most venerable American insurance companies. AIG had written (sold) over $440 billion worth of CDS on corporate bonds, loans (including those of Lehman Brothers), and mortgage-backed securities. As AIG began to take losses, the firm's credit rating was downgraded and it faced massive collateral calls. In September 2008, the U.S. government arranged an $85 billion secured credit facility in one of the largest bailouts of a company in U.S. history.

Not surprisingly, in the aftermath of the crisis, governments around the world are considering regulating the over-the-counter derivative markets, asking for more transparency, clearing by central counterparties as on an exchange, and perhaps higher capital charges for derivative transactions by banks. The United States passed the Dodd–Frank act in 2010, which included financial regulation, but how the regulations will actually be concretely implemented and what the effects will be on interest rate and currency swaps remain to be seen.

21.2 INTEREST RATE SWAPS

Interest rate swaps allow corporations to manage their interest rate risk or to speculate on the direction of interest rates. In this section, we first discuss the cash flows associated with interest rate swaps. Then, we discuss why a corporation might prefer floating-rate debt to fixed-rate debt or vice versa, which is related to the issue of the choice of debt contracts in Chapter 11. We then discuss why interest rate swaps would be used in a world where many different debt contracts are available. We begin with an example of an interest rate swap between Jocko Sports and Banco Coloro.

Example 21.1   A 5-Year Interest Rate Swap

Suppose Jocko Sports is paying the floating-rate side of a dollar interest rate swap and receiving fixed interest rate payments from Banco Coloro. Let the notional principal on the 5-year swap be $25 million, and let the fixed interest rate be 8%. Because Banco Coloro pays the fixed interest rate side of the swap, it would owe 10 semiannual payments for 5 years of

$$0.5 \times 0.08 \times \$25 \text{ million} = \$1 \text{ million}$$

In return, Jocko Sports would pay Banco Coloro semiannual interest payments on $25 million at the London Interbank Offered Rate (LIBOR), that is LIBOR $\times$ $25 million.

Usually, only a net interest payment is transferred between the two parties because the currency is the same. That is, the party with the higher interest rate pays the net interest payment to the party with the lower interest rate. For example, suppose the current 6-month LIBOR is 10% p.a. Because Jocko Sports is paying the LIBOR rate of 10% and receiving the fixed rate of 8%, Jocko Sports must pay the de-annualized 2% net interest rate payment on the $25 million, or

$$0.5 \times 0.02 \times \$25 \text{ million} = \$250,000$$

Why Use Interest Rate Swaps?

Fixed Versus Floating-Rate Debt
Many corporations have revenue cash flows that are pro-cyclical, which means their revenues are high during booms and low during recessions. Short-term interest rates are also pro-cyclical. That is, short-term interest rates tend to rise during expansions in the business

cycle and fall during recessions. A corporation whose sales are pro-cyclical can afford to borrow continually in the short-term money market. The corporation does not mind making high interest rate payments during a boom because its revenues are high, too. During recessions, the corporation likes its interest costs to be low because its revenues are relatively lower as well. But if the corporation borrows at long-term fixed rates, its fixed interest costs are a higher percentage of its cash flows during contractions in business cycles than during expansions. This cyclical pattern increases the corporation's risk of default.

One danger of borrowing short term, though, is that the lender may refuse to renew the loan agreement when the circumstances of the corporation change for the worse. Hence, there is a corporate demand for long-term contracts that have floating-rate payments. Banks are happy to provide long-term contracts with floating interest rates. Although banks' liabilities are mostly short term, and the interest rates they pay on their deposits fluctuate, the banks' deposit bases are often quite stable. This allows banks to enter into relatively long-term contracts to receive floating interest rate cash flows. In addition, many investors prefer the certainty of long-term, fixed interest rate debt. Some borrowers, such as corporations with stable revenues, can afford to make fixed-rate payments during both booms and recessions. Thus, there are demands and supplies for all types of interest rate contracts, and all types of interest rate contracts exist.

Changed Circumstances

Although a company might have rationally determined that a long-run, fixed-rate debt was the right type of loan to take out when a debt was initially issued, over time, the firm's circumstances might change. For example, suppose the company subsequently forecasts that its cash flows are likely to deteriorate at a time when short-term interest rates are low. In this case, the firm can perhaps stave off its difficult financial situation by swapping out of its fixed-rate debt and into a short-term debt with a lower interest rate.

Alternatively, consider a firm that typically borrows with floating-rate debt because its cash flows are cyclical. After the firm acquires another company, the combined firm's cash flows might become much less cyclical. This could prompt the company's managers to swap from floating-rate debt to fixed-rate debt.

Views on the Future

While we have stressed the risk management role of derivative contracts, it is no secret that the treasury departments of major corporations often place bets on the direction of interest rates, currencies, and other financial variables. When managers view future short-term interest rates as unusually low, they may try to lower the company's interest costs by converting its existing fixed-rate debt into floating-rate debt. Alternatively, if they forecast that interest rates are going to rise, they may want to swap out of floating-rate debt and into fixed-rate debt. Chernenko and Faulkender (forthcoming) find empirical evidence that firms use interest rate swaps to both hedge and speculate. Speculation is particularly prevalent in firms where executive compensation contracts are more performance sensitive, a fact confirmed by survey evidence in Geczy et al. (2007).

Minimizing the Cost of Debt

As indicated in Chapter 11, corporations can fund their projects in a number of ways: via bank loans, floating-rate debt, Eurobonds, and so forth. When a company's financing needs are large, shaving a few basis points off the cost of debt can mean millions of dollars in cost savings. Hence, a large corporation figures out what kind of debt it ultimately wants, it determines the cheapest way to raise the funds, and it uses the swap market to convert the actual debt into the desired debt.

Research is beginning to find support for this view. For example, Li and Mao (2003) find that certain firms with low or no credit ratings are relegated by the markets to borrowing from banks that make floating-rate loans because the banks do not want to risk lending to these firms at fixed rates. Nevertheless, these firms can then enter into interest rate swaps as fixed-rate payers to eliminate their exposure to interest rate risk. By doing so, the lowly rated firms are able to effectively borrow at fixed rates.

Manipulating Earnings

Another use of swaps that has been discussed in the literature involves their use by management to manipulate earnings. Chernenko et al. (2007) present some empirical evidence that swap activity is partially driven by the desire of managers to manipulate the earnings of firms so as to meet their earnings forecasts and keep their pay high. If the term structure is upward sloping, initializing a fixed to floating swap increases a firm's net income by a predictable amount in the first year. However, the authors also show that financial markets at least partially discern the differences between earnings derived from normal operations versus earnings derived from this type of "window-dressing" swap activity.

The Nature of Interest Rate Swap Contracts

Major commercial and investment banks serve as market makers for interest rate swaps by quoting bid–offer rates for various maturities at which they are willing to swap fixed interest rate debts for floating interest rate debts or floating interest rate debts for fixed interest rate debts. By convention, the quotes in the dollar interest rate swap market usually use 6-month LIBOR as the base rate of the floating-rate side of the transaction. The bank's bid interest rate

Inverted Swap Spreads?

The 2007 to 2010 global financial crisis generated potentially anomalous pricing behavior in the swap markets. Since mid-2008 in the United Kingdom, and a bit later in other euro area countries and the United States, yields on long-term Treasury bonds have been higher than swap rates of the same maturity. One partial explanation is the change in relative credit risk across markets. With the global financial crisis and the sovereign debt crisis in Europe, government debt is not necessarily viewed as default free, and CDS markets charge a premium even to insure U.S. government debt. For example, on April 20, 2011, CNBC quoted premiums for 5-year CDSs on U.S. and U.K. government debt of 46 and 61 basis points, respectively. Parenthetically, the countries embroiled in the European sovereign debt crisis traded at much larger premiums, ranging from 241 basis points for Spain to 852 basis points for Greece.

At the same time, the credit risk of an interest rate swap is different than that of a bond because only the differential cash flows are at risk and the value of a swap is much less than the notional principal and varies through time (see Exhibit 21.3). Moreover, swaps are now often fully or partially collateralized with cash or government bonds, further reducing credit risk. Yet, bonds issued by banks still carry higher spreads than government bonds of a similar maturity. Can the differential risk exposure really change the sign of relative credit risk on government bonds versus interest rate swaps?

It remains somewhat puzzling why nobody would (1) borrow at LIBOR, (2) take out an interest rate swap that receives LIBOR (to pay off the LIBOR loan) and pays fixed, and (3) invest in a government bond, paying a higher interest rate than the fixed side of the interest rate swap. Perhaps this trade has become too costly, and surely not every bank can borrow at LIBOR (or hope to continue to do so for a long time). Also, while LIBOR borrowing is unsecured, the swap requires collateralization, which may be costly. Another reason is suggested by Laurence Mutkin, a Morgan Stanley interest rate strategist: The arbitrage uses up too much "balance sheet." He thinks the negative swap spreads are here to stay because they reflect an additional difference between bonds and swaps, which he calls the cost of "balance sheet rent." When an institution buys a government bond, bank capital must be used because the bond appears on the institution's balance sheet. However, swaps are off balance sheet items, so they allow long exposure to interest rates without using "balance sheet capital," and are therefore more competitively priced.

is the fixed rate that the bank is willing to pay over a given maturity in return for receiving semiannual payments corresponding to 6-month LIBOR. The bank's higher offer, or ask, interest rate is the fixed rate that the bank will receive from a counterparty over a given maturity if the bank is to pay 6-month LIBOR to that counterparty.

In the case of the U.S. dollar, the bank's fixed bid and offer interest rates are often quoted in terms of a **swap spread**—that is, a number of basis points that are added to the yield to maturity on a U.S. government bond corresponding to that maturity. The swap spread reflects differences in credit quality of the private sector relative to the U.S. Treasury and the liquidity differences in the markets.

Notional Principal

As noted earlier in this chapter, the actual interest payments in an interest rate swap are based on what is called a notional principal. The notional principal is the amount of the outstanding debts. In an interest rate swap, the underlying currency is the same for the two parties of the transaction. Hence, there is no exchange of principal at the beginning or end of the transaction because these amounts are identical and simply cancel one another out.

Bid–Ask Prices for Interest Rate Swaps

Assume that at the 5-year maturity, the market sets the price of U.S. Treasury bonds to have a yield to maturity of 5.66% p.a. Consider the following indicative bid–ask quotes on an interest rate swap. The bank structures the bid side of its swap as the yield on Treasury bonds plus a swap spread of 55 basis points. Thus, the bank is willing to pay fixed-rate interest payments to a high-quality corporate customer at

$$5.66\% + 0.55\% = 6.21\%$$

In return, the bank receives a floating-rate payment from the corporation equal to 6-month LIBOR. The bank structures the offer side of its swap as the yield on Treasury bonds plus 60 basis points. The bank is willing to receive fixed interest rate payments from a high-quality corporation for the next 5 years at

$$5.66\% + 0.60\% = 6.26\%$$

In return, the bank is willing to pay interest to the corporation at 6-month LIBOR.

Profits and Risks for Swap Dealers

To the extent that a bank successfully matches the aggregate amount of interest rate swaps for a given maturity in which it must make fixed interest rate payments with the aggregate notional amount on which it receives fixed interest rate payments from its counterparties, the bank will earn the bid–ask spread on that aggregate amount. For example, if the bank has an outstanding notional principal of $100 billion from both sides of these transactions, the bank generates $50 million in revenue per year from the 5-basis-point spread between the bid and offer rates because

$$0.0005 \times \$100\,\text{billion} = \$50\,\text{million}$$

Notice, though, that if there is a mismatch between the aggregate notional amounts on which the bank is paying the fixed rate versus receiving the fixed rate, the bank is exposed to interest rate risk. Suppose that at a particular maturity, the value of the Second National Bank of Chicago's contracts to pay LIBOR is larger than the value of Second Chicago's contracts to receive LIBOR. Second Chicago is consequently exposed to interest rate risk because an increase in LIBOR will cause losses. If short-term interest rates rise in the future, Second Chicago will be required to pay interest at a higher rate while continuing to receive contractual long-term interest payments that are fixed. Conversely, if Second Chicago enters into more contracts in which it is paying the fixed rate than in which it is receiving the fixed rate, the bank will experience losses if LIBOR falls. If short-term interest rates fall, Second Chicago must continue to pay interest at the contractually fixed high interest rate while receiving short-term interest payments that are falling.

Dealing with Credit Risks

Of course, the bid–offer rates quoted by banks typically only indicate prices at which the bank is willing to transact with other banks or counterparties with AAA credit risk ratings. Most corporate customers pose a substantial amount of default risk. Consequently, even though interest rate swaps carry the right of offset in that the bank can stop making its side of the payments if the corporation defaults on its side of the transaction, the bank will widen its bid–offer spread in dealing with less creditworthy corporate or institutional customers.

Alternatively, the bank may ask for a credit enhancement in the form of collateral, which is what the International Swaps and Derivatives Association now recommends. The amount of collateral is equal to the mark-to-market value of the swap contract.[1] The increased use of collateral is evidenced in the 2011 ISDA Margin Survey, which reported that almost 150,000 collateral agreements were in place in 2010—up from 70,892 in 2005 and up from only 12,000 in 2000.

A similar problem arises from the corporate perspective. Most corporate customers are not in the business of assessing the credit risks of banks. They therefore want their banking counterparties to have excellent credit ratings. Many commercial banks and investment banks have responded to this demand by establishing subsidiaries, the so-called special purpose vehicles (SPVs), that conduct swap transactions and providing those subsidiaries with enough capital to become AAA rated.

21.3 FOREIGN CURRENCY SWAPS

A currency swap is essentially an agreement between two parties to exchange the cash flows of two long-term bonds denominated in different currencies. The parties exchange initial principal amounts in the two currencies that are equivalent in value when evaluated at the spot exchange rate. Simultaneously, the parties agree to pay interest on the currency they initially receive, to receive interest on the currency they initially pay, and to reverse the exchange of initial principal amounts at a fixed future date.

The principal amount of one of the currencies is determined by negotiation between the two parties, and the corresponding principal amount of the other currency in the swap is set by the prevailing spot exchange rate. For example, suppose one of the parties wants to exchange $10 million with its counterparty for euros, and the spot exchange rate is $1.25/€. Then, the euro amount in the swap corresponding to the $10 million is

$$\$10 \text{ million}/(\$1.25/€) = €8 \text{ million}$$

Currency swaps usually involve both parties exchanging the interest and principal payments. If only a net interest payment from one counterparty to the other is desired, in the beginning, the counterparty that initially receives the high interest rate currency will owe funds to the counterparty that is initially receiving the low interest rate currency. Usually, the interest payments are made semiannually. As the exchange rate changes, though, the value of the fixed interest payments in the different currencies changes, and the net amount paid in the currency swap evolves.

---

[1]Johannes and Sundaresan (2007) explore the effect that collateral enhancement has on the pricing of interest rate swap contracts.

Example 21.2 Michaelone's Currency Swap with Margon Stonely

Suppose that the Italian company Michaelone is the party that initially pays €8 million and receives $10 million, as we were discussing, and the investment bank Margon Stonely is the counterparty that initially pays $10 million and receives €8 million. Then, in future periods, Michaelone will owe dollar interest to Margon Stonely on the $10 million, and Margon Stonely will owe euro interest on the €8 million to Michaelone. Suppose the maturity of the swap is 5 years, and the interest rates for that maturity are 4% on dollars and 6% on euros. Exhibit 21.4 describes the corresponding cash flows. Twice per year for 5 years, Margon Stonely, the initial receiver of euros, would owe Michaelone semiannual euro payments of

$$0.5 \times 0.06 \times €8 \text{ million} = €240,000$$

Michaelone, the initial receiver of dollars, would owe semiannual dollar payments to Margon Stonely of

$$0.5 \times 0.04 \times \$10 \text{ million} = \$200,000$$

If the exchange rate did not move from the original value of $1.25/€ by the time an interest payment was due, the euro value of the $200,000 would be €160,000 = $200,000/($1.25/€). Because this is fewer euros than Michaelone is to receive from Margon Stonely, if only a net interest payment is being made, Margon Stonely would be required to pay Michaelone the net interest payment of

$$€240,000 - €160,000 = €80,000$$

In actuality, the net interest payment made by Margon Stonely to Michaelone would depend on the evolution of the exchange rate. At a future payment date $t+k$, the net interest payment would be the €240,000 owed minus the euro value of $200,000:

$$€240,000 - \$200,000/S(t+k, \$/€)$$

Exhibit 21.4 The Cash Flows of a Currency Swap

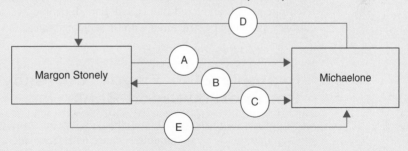

Notes: The currency swap diagram summarizes the transactions and various cash flows:

A. Margon Stonely gives $10 million to Michaelone. The U.S. dollar interest rate is 4%. Michaelone will owe semiannual interest payments of $0.5 \times 0.04 \times \$10$ million = $200,000.

B. Michaelone gives Margon Stonely €8 million in exchange for the $10 million in A. The exchange rate is $1.25/€. The euro interest rate is 6%. Margon Stonely will owe semiannual interest payments of $0.5 \times 0.06 \times €8$ million = €240,000.

C. A semiannual net interest payment of €240,000 − [$200,000/$S(t+k, \$/€)$] is made from Margon Stonely to Michaelone as long as the spot exchange rate $S(t+k, \$/€) > \$0.8333/€$. If the exchange rate falls below this value, the net payment flows from Michaelone to Margon Stonely.

D. In the final period, Michaelone must repay the $10 million to Margon Stonely.

E. In the final period, Margon Stonely must repay the €8 million to Michaelone.

Notice that if the dollar strengthened relative to the euro to an exchange rate that is smaller than $0.8333/€ = $200,000/€240,000, the euro value of the $200,000 would be greater than €240,000. Consequently, a net dollar payment would have to be made from Michaelone to Margon Stonely. For example, at the exchange rate of $0.75/€, Michaelone would owe Margon Stonely

$$\$200,000 - (\$0.75/€) \times €240,000 = \$20,000$$

Although currency swaps were originally special contracts, they have now become standardized products of financial intermediaries. The next section explains how modern currency swaps are quoted and traded.

The Mechanics of Modern Currency Swaps

As the market for U.S. dollar interest rate swaps and currency swaps grew and participants searched for ways to standardize these contracts, financial intermediaries began to quote bid–offer rates for fixed foreign currency interest rates at which they were willing to swap versus paying or receiving floating interest rate payments given by the 6-month dollar LIBOR. Consider the following quotations on 5-year fixed interest rate and currency swaps that might be offered by the Commercial Credit Bank:

U.S. Dollars: 5.25% bid and 5.35% offered against 6-month dollar LIBOR
British Pounds: 8.00% bid and 8.10% offered against 6-month dollar LIBOR

Notice that the first of these quotations for the U.S. dollar is just an interest rate swap. The second quote involves a transformation of both the currency and the interest rate. Commercial Credit is willing to pay to its counterparty either the fixed interest rate of 5.25% in U.S. dollars or 8.00% in pounds against receiving 6-month dollar LIBOR from its counterparty. Commercial Credit is also willing to receive from its counterparty the fixed interest rates of 5.35% in dollars or 8.10% in pounds against paying 6-month dollar LIBOR to its counterparty. Because Commercial Credit is willing to participate on either side of these transactions versus 6-month dollar LIBOR, one can easily structure a currency swap between fixed-rate pounds and fixed-rate U.S. dollars. Example 21.3 and Exhibit 21.5 illustrate how a currency swap can be structured with these quoted rates.

Example 21.3 Floyds' Currency Swap with Commercial Credit Bank

Suppose a large insurer such as Floyds has outstanding pound debt and wants to swap into fixed-rate dollar debt because its U.S. business has grown. Let the principal amount be £200 million, which corresponds to $360 million at a spot exchange rate of $1.8/£. Because Floyds wants to pay dollar interest to Commercial Credit Bank, Floyds will swap at an interest rate of 5.35%, the offer rate quoted by the bank when it receives dollars in return for paying interest at the 6-month LIBOR. This part of the transaction is an interest rate swap. The cash flows are represented in Part 1 of Exhibit 21.5. Because the fixed-rate payments are made semiannually, the dollar interest payments are

$$0.5 \times 0.0535 \times \$360 \text{ million} = \$9.63 \text{ million}$$

In the other part of the transaction, Floyds wants to receive pound interest payments from Commercial Credit. The bank is willing to do this at 8.00%, its bid rate, in return for receiving floating-rate dollar payments from Floyds. The cash flows for the second

Exhibit 21.5 The Cash Flows for Floyds from a Currency Swap

Time Period	Part 1		Part 2	
	Floyds Pays the $ Fixed Rate	Floyds Receives the $ Floating Rate	Floyds Pays the $ Floating Rate	Floyds Receives the £ Fixed Rate
Year 0			$360,000.000	(£200,000.000)
Year 0.5	($9,630.000)	LIBOR × $360 m	(LIBOR × $360 m)	£8,000.000
Year 1.0	($9,630.000)	LIBOR × $360 m	(LIBOR × $360 m)	£8,000.000
Year 1.5	($9,630.000)	LIBOR × $360 m	(LIBOR × $360 m)	£8,000.000
Year 2.0	($9,630.000)	LIBOR × $360 m	(LIBOR × $360 m)	£8,000.000
Year 2.5	($9,630.000)	LIBOR × $360 m	(LIBOR × $360 m)	£8,000.000
Year 3.0	($9,630.000)	LIBOR × $360 m	(LIBOR × $360 m)	£8,000.000
Year 3.5	($9,630.000)	LIBOR × $360 m	(LIBOR × $360 m)	£8,000.000
Year 4.0	($9,630.000)	LIBOR × $360 m	(LIBOR × $360 m)	£8,000.000
Year 4.5	($9,630.000)	LIBOR × $360 m	(LIBOR × $360 m)	£8,000.000
Year 5.0	($9,630.000)	LIBOR × $360 m	($360,000.000 + LIBOR × $360 m)	£200,000.000 + £8,000.000

Notes: The interest rate at which Commercial Credit receives fixed dollar payments is 5.35% p.a., and $(0.5) \times (0.0535) \times \$360$ million $= \$9.63$ million. The interest rate at which Commercial Credit makes fixed pound payments is 8.00% p.a., and $(0.5) \times (0.08) \times £200$ million $= £8$ million.

part of the transaction are under Part 2 of Exhibit 21.5. Because the fixed-rate pound payments are received semiannually, the pound interest receipts are

$$0.5 \times 0.08 \times £200 \text{ million} = £8 \text{ million}$$

Because this part of the transaction involves a change of currencies, the principal amounts are exchanged both at the beginning of the swap and in the reverse direction at the end of the 5 years. Hence, in the final period, Floyds must pay the $360 million principal in addition to its final dollar interest payment, and it will receive £200 million plus its final pound interest receipt from Commercial Credit. Notice that the dollar LIBOR receipts in Part 1 are equal to the dollar LIBOR payments in Part 2. Hence, Floyds has swapped out of fixed pound debt payments into fixed dollar debt payments. Floyds can then use the pound principal and interest received from Commercial Credit to pay the bondholders of its pound-denominated debt.

In Example 21.3, Floyds is content to transact at the quoted rates provided by Commercial Credit. But because the cash flows on a corporation's debt will typically not exactly equal the cash flows from the swap quoted by the financial intermediary, some residual foreign exchange risk can be present.

Later in this chapter, we will consider an extended example that shows how the cash flows of a swap can be adjusted to eliminate the exchange rate risk. First, though, we examine how a currency swap would have been done in the 1980s when financial intermediaries first arranged deals that allowed firms to issue bonds in one currency and then swap the cash flows with a firm that had issued bonds in a different currency. This first part of the example introduces the important concept of comparative advantage in borrowing.

Comparative Borrowing Advantages in Matched Currency Swaps

The Goodweek–Bridgerock Situation

Consider two tire companies, Goodweek and Bridgerock, which both want to issue 5-year, fixed-rate debt. Suppose Goodweek wants to raise approximately $200 million, and Bridgerock

Exhibit 21.6 Possible Bond Issues for Goodweek and Bridgerock

Goodweek Bridgerock	Dollar Bond Issues 200 Million @ 8.5% with 1.875% Fee 200 Million @ 9.5% with 1.875% Fee		Euro Bond Issues 100 Million @ 13.5% with 2.25% Fee 100 Million @ 13.75% with 2.25% Fee	
Year	Goodweek's Cash Flows	Bridgerock's Cash Flows	Goodweek's Cash Flows	Bridgerock's Cash Flows
0	196.25	196.25	97.75	97.75
1	−17.00	−19.00	−13.50	−13.75
2	−17.00	−19.00	−13.50	−13.75
3	−17.00	−19.00	−13.50	−13.75
4	−17.00	−19.00	−13.50	−13.75
5	−217.00	−219.00	−113.50	−113.75
All-In Cost	8.98%	9.99%	14.16%	14.41%

Note: Yearly cash flows are in millions of dollars or euros.

wants to raise €100 million, which is equal to $200 million at the current exchange rate of $2/€. Exhibit 21.6 shows the possible bond issues that the two firms are considering.

Investment bankers are quoting dollar interest rates of 8.5% for Goodweek and 9.5% for Bridgerock, with annual interest payments. Both companies would have to pay a 1.875% fee to the banks for their help in issuing the bonds. Hence, if $200 million of bonds were issued at par, the proceeds to the two firms would be

$$(1 − 0.01875) \times \$200 \text{ million} = \$196,250,000$$

The annual coupon payments for Goodweek would be

$$0.085 \times \$200 \text{ million} = \$17,000,000$$

Bridgerock would make annual coupon payments of

$$0.095 \times \$200 \text{ million} = \$19,000,000$$

The all-in cost (AIC) of a debt issue (see Chapter 11) is the internal rate of return on the company's cash flows given by the net proceeds to the firm in year 0 as an inflow and given the coupon interest payments made in years 1 through 5 and the final return of principal in year 5 as outflows. If Goodweek does the dollar debt issue, its AIC is 8.98%. If Bridgerock does the dollar debt issue, its AIC is 9.99%.

It is also possible for the two firms to issue euro-denominated debt, in which case the size of the issue must be €100 million in order to raise $200 million. Investment bankers are quoting euro interest rates of 13.5% for Goodweek and 13.75% for Bridgerock. In both cases, there would be a 2.25% fee, and the proceeds of the issue to either firm would be

$$(1 − 0.0225) \times €100,000,000 = €97,750,000$$

or $195,500,000 at the current exchange rate of $2/€. The annual coupon payments for Goodweek would be

$$0.135 \times €100,000,000 = €13,500,000$$

Bridgerock would make annual coupon payments of

$$0.1375 \times €100,000,000 = €13,750,000$$

Exhibit 21.6 indicates that if Goodweek does the euro debt issue, its AIC is 14.16%. If Bridgerock does its euro debt issue, its AIC is 14.41%.

How should the firms choose the currency of denomination of their bonds? We need to consider their hedging motives as well as the direct AICs of the different debts. Suppose

Goodweek would like to have euro debt because it has positive euro cash flows from the sales of its products in Europe. The euro debt would provide a partial hedge to the revenue stream from Goodweek's European sales. Suppose, analogously, that Bridgerock would like to have dollar debt because it has positive dollar cash flows from the sales of its products in the United States. Given the firms' hedging motives, each firm could issue the bonds denominated in its preferred currency. In this case, Goodweek would issue euro bonds, and Bridgerock would issue U.S. dollar bonds. But, as we will demonstrate, this is inefficient given the quoted AICs.

Absolute Versus Comparative Advantage

With the bond yields quoted in Exhibit 21.6, Goodweek has an **absolute borrowing advantage** in both currencies because its AICs are lower in both currencies, but Bridgerock has a comparative borrowing advantage when it comes to issuing euro debt. This implies that Goodweek has a comparative borrowing advantage in issuing U.S. dollar debt.

What does it mean for Bridgerock to have a **comparative borrowing advantage** in issuing euro debt? Because neither firm is borrowing at the risk-free rate, investors have demanded a default premium, which is built into the quoted rates and the AICs. If the firms borrow dollars, Bridgerock must pay 9.99%, an additional 101 basis points compared to 8.98% for Goodweek. If the two firms borrow in euros, Bridgerock must pay only an additional 25 basis points—14.41% for Bridgerock versus 14.16% for Goodweek. Because euro interest rates are higher than dollar interest rates, the euro is at a discount relative to the dollar. Consequently, a euro basis point in the future is actually worth less than a dollar basis point in the future. If the relative borrowing costs in the two currencies were the same for the two companies, the number of euro basis points corresponding to 101 dollar basis points would have to be higher, not lower, than 101.

The euro debt of Bridgerock is being priced by the market more favorably than its dollar debt, and this means Bridgerock has a comparative advantage borrowing in euros, and Goodweek has a comparative advantage borrowing in dollars. Later on, we will discuss the possible sources of these comparative advantages. For now, let's examine how both firms can benefit by issuing debt in the currency in which they have a comparatively cheaper borrowing cost and then doing a currency swap. Bridgerock will consequently issue euro debt, and Goodweek will issue dollar debt. A financial intermediary then matches up the two parties and ensures that eventually Goodweek has its desired euro debt and Bridgerock its desired dollar debt.

Using a Financial Intermediary in a Currency Swap

Can an investment bank such as Bank Carribus do the Goodweek–Bridgerock currency swap and still make money? The answer is yes because currency swaps were originally handled this way until the mid-1980s. Financial intermediaries would know of two counterparties that could benefit by swapping the interest and principal payments on bonds denominated in different currencies. The financial intermediary would arrange the swap, act as counterparty for both firms, and walk away with a handsome profit.

Exhibits 21.7 demonstrates how the cash flows for a currency swap could be structured for Goodweek, Bridgerock, and Bank Carribus. Exhibit 21.8 provides a summary diagram of the cash flows and the AICs. The currency swap begins with each firm issuing bonds denominated in the currency in which it has a comparative borrowing advantage: Goodweek issues a dollar-denominated bond to investors, and Bridgerock issues a euro-denominated bond to investors.

Bank Carribus wants each firm to make the interest and principal payments associated with the bond issue of the other company in return for receiving cash flows that are equivalent to the interest and principal payments that each firm owes its bondholders. What must be determined is how much money will change hands initially, at the beginning of the swap. This initial transfer determines the AICs of the swap to each company.

Exhibit 21.7   Swaps with Bank Carribus as the Financial Intermediary

Year	Goodweek's Cash Flows			Bridgerock's Cash Flows			Bank Carribus's Cash Flows	
	$ Bond Issue	Swap with Bank Carribus		€ Bond Issue	Swap with Bank Carribus		Net	
		Dollar	Euro		Dollar	Euro	Dollar	Euro
0	196.25	−196.25	99.83	97.75	191.57	−97.75	4.86	−2.08
1	−17.00	17.00	−13.75	−13.75	−17.00	13.75	0.00	0.00
2	−17.00	17.00	−13.75	−13.75	−17.00	13.75	0.00	0.00
3	−17.00	17.00	−13.75	−13.75	−17.00	13.75	0.00	0.00
4	−17.00	17.00	−13.75	−13.75	−17.00	13.75	0.00	0.00
5	−217.00	217.00	−113.75	−113.75	−217.00	113.75	0.00	0.00
AIC	8.98%	8.98%	13.80%	14.41%	9.60%	14.41%		

Bank Carribus's net dollar profit   0.5206

Note: All cash flows are in millions of dollars or euros.

Exhibit 21.8   Intermediated Currency Swap Diagram

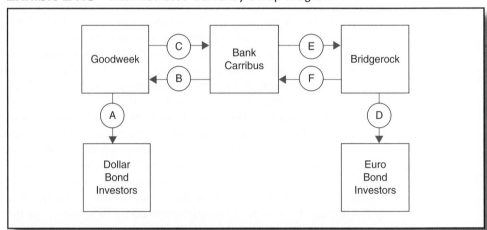

Notes: The currency swap diagram summarizes the rates of return and the various cash flows:

A. Goodweek issues $200 million of bonds to investors with 8.5% coupons. After fees of 1.875%, the AIC is 8.98%.

B. Goodweek gives the net proceeds of the bond issue, $196.25 million, to Bank Carribus in exchange for €99.83 million, which is the present value at 13.80% of the € cash flows given in C. Goodweek receives from Bank Carribus the dollar interest and principal payments that it owes to bondholders in A.

C. Goodweek makes the euro payments to Bank Carribus of the interest and principal associated with the bond issue of Bridgerock in D that has an AIC of 13.80%.

D. Bridgerock issues €100 million of bonds with 13.75% coupons. After fees of 2.25%, the company's AIC is 14.41%.

E. Bridgerock gives the net proceeds of the debt, €97.75 million, to Bank Carribus in exchange for $191.57 million, which is the present value at 9.60% of the dollar cash flows given in F. Bridgerock receives from Bank Carribus the euro interest and principal payments that it owes to bondholders in D.

F. Bridgerock makes payments to Bank Carribus of the dollar payments of interest and principal with an AIC of 9.60% associated with the bond issue of Goodweek in A.

If it participates in the currency swap, Goodweek receives dollar interest and principal from Bank Carribus that exactly match the cash flows that Goodweek owes its bondholders. In return, Goodweek pays Bank Carribus the sequence of euro cash flows associated with Bridgerock's bond issue. Bank Carribus then gives these euro cash flows to Bridgerock, and Bridgerock makes the dollar interest and principal payments to Bank Carribus that are equivalent to the cash flows associated with Goodweek's dollar debt.

The challenge for Bank Carribus is to make the swapping of these cash flows attractive to both counterparties. It can do this by quoting an AIC to Goodweek for the euro cash flows the firm will pay to Bank Carribus that is less than 14.16%, Goodweek's direct AIC. It must also quote an AIC to Bridgerock for the dollar cash flows that Bridgerock will pay Bank Carribus that is less than Bridgerock's direct borrowing cost of 9.99%. These interest rates are the opportunity costs of the respective firms of borrowing directly in their desired currencies.

Exhibit 21.7 is structured with quotes from Bank Carribus of 13.80% in euros for Goodweek and 9.60% in dollars for Bridgerock. The euro interest rate of 13.80% is used to discount the sequence of euro cash flows that Goodweek will make to Bank Carribus. In exchange for the $196,250,000 raised in the bond issue, Goodweek gets the present value of the euro cash flows discounted at 13.80%, which is €99,827,517.60. Similarly, the dollar interest rate of 9.60% is used to discount the sequence of cash flows that Bridgerock will make to Bank Carribus. In exchange for the €97,750,000 raised in its bond issue, Bridgerock gets the present value of the dollar cash flows discounted at 9.60%, which is $191,574,344.

How much does Bank Carribus make in the deal? At the initiation of the deal, Bank Carribus has a net dollar cash inflow of

$$\$196,250,000 - \$191,574,344 = \$4,675,656$$

and a net euro cash outflow of

$$€99,827,517.60 - €97,750,000 = €2,077,517.60$$

At the current spot exchange rate of $2/€, the dollar value of the euro outflow is

$$(\$2/€) \times €2,077,517.60 = \$4,155,035.20$$

Hence, Bank Carribus makes a net dollar profit of

$$\$4,675,656 - \$4,155,035.20 = \$520,620.80$$

Bank Carribus's initial euro cash flow must be negative because it must induce Goodweek to make the euro interest and principal payments associated with the Bridgerock bonds. At Bridgerock's borrowing cost of 14.41%, the net proceeds of the euro bond issue are equal in present value to the euro cash flows that Goodweek will pay to Bank Carribus. But Bank Carribus cannot give Goodweek only the net euro proceeds of Bridgerock's bond issue because that would imply an AIC for Goodweek of 14.41%. Because Goodweek can borrow directly in euros at an interest rate of 14.16%, Bank Carribus must offer Goodweek more euros up front than Bank Carribus will receive from Bridgerock's bond issue.

Bank Carribus has an initial positive dollar cash flow because it can keep some of the dollar proceeds of Goodweek's bond issue, which raises the internal rate of return on the cash flows, while offering a dollar AIC to Bridgerock that is lower than Bridgerock's opportunity cost. The reason Bank Carribus has a positive net cash flow is that the currency swap exploits the comparative borrowing ability of each firm, which allows each of the participants, including the financial intermediary, to gain.

Bank Carribus also bears the credit risk of each counterparty, and it must be compensated for bearing this risk. If either Goodweek or Bridgerock stops making its payments to Bank Carribus, Bank Carribus can stop making payments to that firm. Depending on how interest rates and exchange rates have evolved, one of the parties will owe the other a net payment. But Bank Carribus must continue to serve as the financial intermediary for the other side of the deal.

We now want to find the value of the annual euro payment that is equivalent to this euro principal, using the euro interest rate of 13.10%. It turns out that the present value of five payments of €0.28 million when discounted at 13.10% is equivalent to €0.99 million. Hence, the euro discounted present value of five payments of €0.28 million at 13.10% is equivalent to five payments of $0.50 million discounted at 8.25% when the exchange rate is $2/€. This extra euro interest is added to the €13.10 million of notional interest, and Goodweek will owe interest of €13.38 million. This provides Goodweek with an AIC of 13.93%, which is less than its direct euro borrowing cost of 14.16%.

The Transactions of Bridgerock

The transactions of Bridgerock's swap with Bank Carribus would be structured in an analogous way. Bridgerock wants dollar debt, but it issues a euro bond. Bridgerock asks Bank Carribus to make the interest and principal payments on its euro bond issue in return for letting the company make dollar-denominated interest and principal payments to the bank.

Because Bank Carribus is using the quoted interest rates, Bank Carribus would be willing to make fixed euro payments to Bridgerock at an interest rate of 13.00%. For €100 million principal, Bank Carribus would expect to pay interest of

$$0.13 \times €100 \text{ million} = €13 \text{ million}$$

Because the quoted interest rate at which Bank Carribus is willing to receive dollar payments is 8.35%, and because the dollar principal that is equivalent to €100 million is $200 million, the notional cash flows for Bridgerock involve interest of

$$0.0835 \times \$200 \text{ million} = \$16.70 \text{ million}$$

Once again, this plain-vanilla swap does not suit Bridgerock for two reasons. First, Bridgerock does not have €100 million to exchange because it raised only €97.75 million in bond proceeds. Second, Bridgerock must pay €13.75 million in annual interest to its bondholders, and Bridgerock would like to receive that much from Bank Carribus.

Consequently, the actual swap requires two adjustments: a change in the initial principals and a basis point adjustment. First, in exchange for the €97.75 million proceeds of the bond issue, Bank Carribus will give Bridgerock the equivalent value in dollars, at the exchange rate of $2/€:

$$€97.75 \text{ million} \times (\$2/€) = \$195.50 \text{ million}$$

Second, Bridgerock will require Bank Carribus to pay extra euro interest, in exchange for which Bridgerock will pay extra dollar interest to Bank Carribus. The extra euro interest that Bank Carribus must pay to Bridgerock is €0.75 million for each of the next 5 years. The present value of this amount at 13% is €2.64 million. In order to find the extra dollar interest that Bridgerock must pay each year, we convert the present value of the extra euro interest to dollars at the spot exchange rate. Thus, we get a dollar principal of

$$€2.64 \text{ million} \times (\$2/€) = \$5.28 \text{ million}$$

It turns out that the present value of five payments of $1.33 million when discounted at the dollar interest rate of 8.35% is equivalent to $5.28 million. These payments are, in turn, equivalent to five payments of €0.75 million discounted at 13% when the exchange rate is $2/€. This extra dollar interest is added to the $16.70 million of notional interest, and we find that Bridgerock will owe interest of $18.03 million. This provides Bridgerock with an AIC of 9.60%, which is less than its direct dollar borrowing cost of 9.99%.

The Transactions of Bank Carribus

The last part of Exhibit 21.10 provides the actual dollar and euro cash flows for Bank Carribus from engaging in the two swaps. At the beginning of the currency swap, Bank Carribus exchanges principal amounts that are equivalent at the spot exchange rate. The net inflow of dollars to Bank Carribus is $0.75 million, which is equivalent to its net outflow of euros, €0.38 million.

In years 1 through 5, Bank Carribus makes interest payments in dollars to Goodweek of $17 million and receives dollar interest payments from Bridgerock of $18.03 million, giving it a net dollar inflow of $1.03 million. Bank Carribus also makes interest payments in euros to Bridgerock of €13.75 million and receives euro interest payments from Goodweek of €13.38 million, giving it a net euro outflow of €0.37 million. In the fifth year, the exchange of principals occurs with each firm, but Bank Carribus has no net cash flows of either dollars or euros because the principal amounts are equal.

Because Bank Carribus is not attempting to perfectly match the future cash flows of two counterparties, it bears some risk from these two transactions due to possible fluctuations in interest rates and exchange rates. Without knowing Bank Carribus's overall portfolio of cash flows, though, we cannot know whether Bank Carribus is taking on additional risk. Since it is making a market in these transactions, it is only concerned about the net exposure it generates from all the transactions it makes.

Because Bank Carribus now experiences dollar and euro cash flows in all 5 years instead of just in the present, we must take the present values of the future cash flows to determine how much net revenue Bank Carribus has generated in the two transactions. The present value of the dollar cash inflow can be taken at the swap rate of 8.35%, because this is the swap rate at which the bank receives dollars. The dollar present value is $4.84 million. The euro cash outflow from Bank Carribus is discounted at 13%, which is the rate at which Bank Carribus pays euros. The euro present value is €1.67 million. The net of these two cash flows in dollars is

$$\$4.84 \text{ million} - [(\$2/€) \times €1.67 \text{ million}] = \$1.50 \text{ million}$$

Currency Swaps as a Package of Forward Contracts

In the 5-year swap just described, Goodweek contracts to pay euros in return for receiving dollars at various dates in the future. Bridgerock is paying dollars in return for receiving euros at various contractual dates in the future. These transactions are analogous to long-term forward contracts. Goodweek's transactions define bid prices of dollars per euro from Bank Carribus's perspective, and Bridgerock's transactions define ask prices of dollars per euro, again from the perspective of the financial intermediary.

Notice, though, that the structure of the 5-year swap has four exchanges of currencies at the same implicit forward exchange rate and a fifth exchange at a different rate. That is, the exchanges of the five interest payments are done at the same implicit forward rate, and the final return of principal is done at the original spot rate. When interest rates differ across currencies, the implicit forward rates in the swap are very different from the long-term forward rates that we have calculated in earlier chapters using the spot exchange rate and the term structures of spot interest rates. To understand the difference and to get an idea why the long-term swap market exits, let's examine how Goodweek and Bridgerock might go about hedging their transactions in the forward market.

Euro Bond Issues with Forward Hedging

Rather than doing currency swaps, both Goodweek and Bridgerock could exploit their comparative advantages in borrowing and achieve the desired currencies of denomination for their liabilities by issuing bonds in their comparatively low-cost currencies and using long-term forward contracts to hedge the bond payments. In this scenario, Goodweek issues dollar bonds and contracts to buy dollars with euros in the long-term forward market to cover the dollar interest and principal payments owed to its bondholders. Goodweek would offset its outstanding dollar liability with the forward-market contracts of a financial intermediary, like Bank Carribus, which promises to deliver dollars to Goodweek in return for the company making euro payments to the bank. Analogously, Bridgerock would issue euro bonds and contract to sell dollars forward for euros in the long-term forward market to cover its euro interest and principal payments. Bridgerock matches its euro liabilities with a sequence of euro assets that Bank Carribus delivers to the company in return for the company making dollar payments to the bank.

If the currency swap is to be preferred by both Goodweek and Bridgerock, the transaction costs in the long-term forward market must exceed those in the currency swap market. Exhibit 21.11 presents a set of bid and ask forward exchange rates such that this is indeed the case. The midpoints of the bid and ask forward rates for year k in the future are determined from covered interest rate parity using the midpoints of the dollar and euro swap rates:

$$(\$2/€) \times (1.0830/1.1305)^k$$

This is the right computation because the term structure of interest rates is assumed to be flat. The higher euro interest rate results in a substantial forward dollar discount on the euro. The forward market transaction costs are given by the percentage bid–ask spreads in the % Spread column, and they increase with maturity.

In Exhibit 21.11, Goodweek issues the dollar bond and converts the $196.25 million proceeds into €98.12 million at Bank Carribus's ask rate of $2.0002/€ in the spot market. We use the ask rate because Goodweek is selling dollars to Bank Carribus for euros. In years 1 through 5, Goodweek buys dollars from Bank Carribus with euros, which gives Goodweek euro liabilities. These transactions are done at Bank Carribus's bid rates of dollars per euro. We use the bid rates because Goodweek is contracting to buy dollars forward from Bank Carribus with euros. For example, Goodweek's first-year euro payment is

$$€8.88 \text{ million} = \$17 \text{ million}/(\$1.9143/€)$$

Goodweek's resulting euro AIC for these transactions is 13.96%. This is slightly higher than the AIC of 13.93% achieved in the currency swap, so Goodweek would prefer the currency swap.

To use the forward market hedge, Bridgerock would issue the euro bond and convert the €97.75 million proceeds into $195.48 million at Bank Carribus's bid rate of $1.9998/€ in the spot market. In years 1 through 5, Bridgerock would contract to buy euros from Bank Carribus with dollars, which gives Bridgerock dollar liabilities. These transactions would be done at Bank Carribus's forward ask rates of dollars per euro. Bridgerock's resulting dollar

Exhibit 21.11   Bond Issues Hedged in the Forward Market

Year	Bid	Dollars/Euros Midpoint	Ask	% Spread	Goodweek's Dollar Bond Hedged into Euros Dollars	Euros	Bridgerock's Euro Bond Hedged into Dollars Euros	Dollars
0	1.9998	2.0000	2.0002	0.02	196.25	98.12	97.75	195.48
1	1.9143	1.9160	1.9176	0.17	−17.00	−8.88	−13.75	−26.37
2	1.8316	1.8355	1.8393	0.42	−17.00	−9.28	−13.75	−25.29
3	1.7516	1.7583	1.7651	0.77	−17.00	−9.71	−13.75	−24.27
4	1.6742	1.6845	1.6947	1.22	−17.00	−10.15	−13.75	−23.30
5	1.5990	1.6137	1.6284	1.82	−217.00	−135.71	−113.75	−185.23
				AICs	8.98%	13.96%	14.41%	9.79%

Notes: Midpoint forward prices are $(\$2/€) \times (1.0830/1.1305)^k$, where k is the number of years in the future. Cash flows are in millions of dollars or euros. The % spread is $100 \times (\text{Ask} - \text{Bid})/[(\text{Ask} + \text{Bid})/2]$.

AIC for its euro bond issue hedged into dollars in the forward market is 9.79%, which is higher than the 9.60% achieved in the currency swap. Hence, Bridgerock would prefer the currency swap as well.

The Value of a Currency Swap

As explained earlier, currency swaps begin life as zero net present value contracts. Over time, though, as interest rates and exchange rates change, a currency swap develops a positive value to one of the counterparties, with a corresponding negative value to the other participant. Consider the perspective of Goodweek. It owes euro interest and principal to Bank Carribus and is receiving dollar interest and principal from Bank Carribus. Essentially, the currency swap gives Goodweek an asset in the form of a dollar bond with a principal of $200 million and coupons of 8.50% because it is receiving $17 million of interest; it gives Goodweek a liability in the form of a euro bond with a principal of €100 million and coupons of 13.38% because it is paying €13.38 million of interest.

Let $B(t, \$200 \text{ m}, 8.50\%)$ and $B(t, €100 \text{ m}, 13.38\%)$ represent the market prices of these dollar and euro bonds at some time, t, in the future, and let $S(t, \$/€)$ be the spot exchange rate. Then, the dollar market value of the currency swap, from Goodweek's perspective, is

$$B(t, \$200 \text{ m}, 8.50\%) - [B(t, €100 \text{ m}, 13.38\%) \times S(t, \$/€)]$$

The market value of the swap is affected by three things. It rises if the dollar strengthens relative to the euro because the dollar value of Goodweek's euro liability falls. The swap also increases in value if dollar interest rates fall or if the euro interest rates rise because these interest rate changes directly affect the present values of the fixed cash flows in the swap.

Bridgerock's perspective is the opposite of Goodweek's. Bridgerock owes dollar interest and principal, and it is receiving euro interest and principal. The currency swap consequently gives Bridgerock an asset in the form of a euro bond with principal of €100 million and coupons of 13.75% because Bridgerock receives €13.75 million of interest; the swap gives Bridgerock a liability in the form of a dollar bond with principal of $200 million and coupons of 9.015% because it pays interest of $18.03 million. If $B(t, \$200 \text{ m}, 9.015\%)$ and $B(t, €100 \text{ m}, 13.75\%)$ represent the market prices of these dollar and euro bonds at some future time, t, the euro market value of the currency swap, from Bridgerock's perspective, is

$$B(t, €100 \text{ m}, 13.75\%) - [B(t, \$200 \text{ m}, 9.015\%)/S(t, \$/€)]$$

This euro market value rises if the dollar weakens relative to the euro, if dollar interest rates rise, or if euro interest rates fall.

If either firm wants to exit the swap early, the market value of the swap determines which firm receives money. Exhibit 21.12 determines the market value of Bridgerock's swap if it decides to close out the swap after 1 year, with 4 years of interest and the final principal payment remaining. The spot exchange rate is $2.25/€, the dollar interest rate for 4-year bonds is 8%, and the euro interest rate for 4-year bonds is 12%. At these prices, the euro cash flows that Bridgerock is scheduled to receive have a present value of €105.32 million, which is greater than the face value because the euro interest rate has fallen. The dollar present value of what Bridgerock is required to pay has increased to $206.72 million because the dollar interest rate has also fallen. The net euro value of these cash flows at the spot rate is

$$€105.32 \text{ million} - [\$206.72 \text{ million}/(\$2.25/€)] = €13.44 \text{ million}$$

If Bridgerock wanted to close out the swap, Bank Carribus would pay Bridgerock €13.44 million. Of course, Bridgerock would still owe its euro bondholders.

Exhibit 21.12   Valuing a Swap to Close Out the Position

BRIDGEROCK'S EURO BOND ISSUE AND SWAP INTO DOLLARS WITH BANK CARRIBUS		
	Swap Receipts (+) and Payments (−) with Bank Carribus	
Year	Euros	Dollars
2	13.75	−18.03
3	13.75	−18.03
4	13.75	−18.03
5	113.75	−218.03
	105.32	−206.72
	PV © 12%	PV @ 8%
Euro value of the Swap at USD2.25/EUR 13.44		

Notes: The euros Bridgerock is to receive are discounted at 12%, the dollars Bridgerock is to pay are discounted at 8%, and the spot exchange rate is $2.25/€.

Note that the changes in valuation that we have discussed ignore the issue of credit risk, which is critical in advanced valuation methodologies, as exemplified by the analysis of Duffie and Singleton (1997).

The Rationale for Currency Swaps

A currency swap is a low-transaction-cost instrument for changing the currency of denomination of debt financing. This by itself does not explain why the currency swap market has grown so rapidly. The growth of the currency swap market reflects and has contributed to the increased integration of the world's international financial system. No longer are corporations tied to the financial markets of their country of residence. They can issue bonds in any currency and swap into their desired currency at the lowest AIC.

In the early days of the currency swap market, swaps were often driven by regulatory restraints and tax arbitrage opportunities. In 1985, R.J. Reynolds Tobacco Company famously took over Nabisco, lowering its costs of funding substantially by exploiting certain regulatory restrictions on Japanese institutional investors. Swaps played an integral role in making the deal work.

Differences in the way credit risks are analyzed across countries and the associated differences in spreads over risk-free rates also continue to provide an opportunity for lowering the cost of debt using swaps. When comparative borrowing advantages exist, it makes sense for the parties to issue debt in their least expensive currencies and to enter into a swap if the debts are not in the currencies of denomination that they prefer. These comparative advantages arise because institutional differences across countries lead to debt pricing that is slightly different, depending on the ultimate holder of the debt and its currency of denomination. Such differences in credit spreads amount to a market inefficiency that can be exploited for profit.

Regulations on the types of debt instruments that institutions can hold and accounting and tax differences across countries also have contributed to the growth of the swap market by providing demands for certain types of bonds that borrowers might not otherwise want to issue. Financial intermediaries who understand these demands and know borrowers who can supply the debts are then in a position to do a swap that results in lower borrowing costs for the issuer and a profit for the financial intermediary.

Why Swaps and Not Forwards?

Although we explained how long-dated forward contracts can be used to convert bonds issued in one currency into bonds denominated in a preferred currency, this method of financing is not widely used because long-dated forward markets are relatively illiquid. The bid–ask spreads of long-dated outright forward contracts begin to widen beyond a maturity of 1 year.

Banks also like swaps because the associated cash flows are just like those of bonds, and they can easily hedge the swaps in the bond markets later. In other words, if the swap book has too many dollars coming into the bank at the 5-year maturity, the bank can simply sell a 5-year bond from its portfolio to balance that risk.

Because the cash flows of forward contracts are not like the cash flows of bonds, banks find it difficult to offset their exposures in long-term outright forward contracts with other business transactions. They consequently try to make the offsetting trade directly in the forward market with a different financial intermediary, which only pushes the problem onto someone else. If it is expensive for a bank to hedge a long-term forward contract, the costs will ultimately be pushed onto the demanders of the contracts, making them more expensive and therefore less popular.

21.4 SUMMARY

This chapter examines interest rate, credit default, and currency swaps. The major points of the chapter are as follows:

1. The cash flows of swaps are structured like the cash flows of bonds. Banks act as market makers in interest rate and currency swap markets. The outstanding volume of swaps is in the trillions of dollars.

2. Precursors to currency swaps were parallel loans (simultaneous loans between an MNC and the subsidiary of another MNC in two countries) and back-to-back loans (two MNCs lending one another money in different currencies and then subsequently lending to their foreign subsidiaries within a single loan document).

3. The relatively new credit default swap is essentially an insurance contract between a protection buyer and a protection seller covering default on a specific bond or loan. Credit default swaps played a major role in the 2007 to 2010 global financial crisis, when default rates shot up.

4. Interest rate swaps allow a corporation or an institution to convert from fixed-rate debt to floating-rate debt or from floating-rate debt to fixed-rate debt, using a bank as an intermediary. No principal payments are made. The cash flows associated with interest rate swaps are based on the notional principal, which is the conceptual amount of the outstanding debt.

5. In a currency swap, the counterparties exchange principal amounts in two different currencies, and they agree to pay and receive interest on those currencies, as well as reverse the initial exchange of principal amounts at a fixed date in the future. The principal amounts are equivalent at the prevailing spot exchange rate.

6. Currency swaps can be used to exploit a company's comparative advantage in borrowing across countries and then swap into their preferred currencies of denomination.

7. Swap market transaction costs are lower than transaction costs in the long-term forward market because the structure of swaps allows banks to easily trade in the bond markets to hedge their exposures.

QUESTIONS

1. How does an interest rate swap work? In particular, what is the notional principal?
2. What is a currency swap? Describe the structure of and rationale for its cash flows.
3. What is a credit default swap? What happens in the event of default?
4. Banks quote interest rate and currency swaps using 6-month LIBOR as a basis for both transactions. How can a bank make money if it does not speculate on movements in either interest rates or exchange rates?
5. What is the AIC of a bond issue?
6. What is a comparative advantage in borrowing, and how could it arise?
7. What is basis point adjustment? Why is it not appropriate simply to add the basis point differential associated with the first currency to the quoted swap rate that the firm will pay?

8. Discuss the sense in which a 5-year currency swap is a sequence of long-term forward contracts. How do the implicit forward exchange rates in a currency swap differ from the long-term forward exchange rates for those maturities?

9. What are the determinants of the value of a currency swap as time evolves? Is it possible to close out a swap before it has reached maturity?

PROBLEMS

1. General Motors (GM) wants to swap out of $15,000,000 of fixed interest rate debt and into floating interest rate debt for 3 years. Suppose the fixed interest rate is 8.625% and the floating rate is dollar LIBOR. What semiannual interest payments will GM receive, and what will GM pay?

2. Pfizer is a U.S. firm with considerable euro assets. It is considering entering into a currency swap involving $10 million of its dollar debt for an equivalent amount of euro debt. Suppose the maturity of the swap is 8 years, and the interest rate on Pfizer's outstanding 8-year dollar debt is 11%. The interest rate on the euro debt is 9%. The current spot exchange rate is $1.35/€. How could a swap be structured?

3. At the 7-year maturity, U.S. Treasury bonds' yield to maturity is 7.95% p.a. The Second Bank of Chicago states that it will make fixed interest rate payments on dollars at the yield on Treasury bonds plus 55 basis points in exchange for receiving dollar LIBOR, and it will receive fixed interest rate payments on dollars at the yield on Treasury bonds plus 60 basis points in exchange for paying dollar LIBOR. If you enter into an interest rate swap of $10 million with Second Chicago, what will be your cash flows if you are paying the fixed rate and receiving the floating rate?

4. The swap desk at UBS is quoting the following rates on 5-year swaps versus 6-month dollar LIBOR:

   U.S. Dollars: 8.75% bid and 8.85% offered
   Swiss Francs: 5.25% bid and 5.35% offered

   You would like to swap out of Swiss franc debt with a principal of CHF25,000,000 and into fixed-rate dollar debt. At what rates will UBS handle the transaction? If the current exchange rate is CHF1.3/$, what would the cash flows be?

5. Suppose Viacom can issue $100,000,000 of debt at an AIC of 9.42%, whereas Gaz de France can issue $100,000,000 of debt at an AIC of 10.11%. Suppose that the exchange rate is $1.35/€. If Viacom issues euro-denominated bonds equivalent to $100,000,000, its AIC will be 8.27%, whereas if Gaz de France issues such bonds, its all-in cost will be 9.17%. Which firm has a comparative advantage when borrowing euros? Why?

6. Suppose in problem 5 that because of currency risk, Viacom would prefer to have dollar debt, and Gaz de France would prefer to have euro debt. How could an investment bank structure a currency swap that would allow each of the firms to issue bonds denominated in the currency in which the firm has a comparative advantage while respecting the firms' preferences about currency risks?

7. Suppose Sony issues $100,000,000 of 5-year dollar bonds. Nomura will handle the bond issue for a fee of 1.875%. Sony's bonds will be priced at par if they carry a coupon of 8.5%. As the swap trader for Mitsubishi UFJ (MUFJ), you have been quoting the following rates on 5-year swaps:

   U.S. Dollars: 8.00% bid and 8.10% offered against the 6-month dollar LIBOR
   Japanese Yen: 4.50% bid and 4.60% offered against the 6-month dollar LIBOR

   Sony would like to do the dollar bond issue, but it prefers to have fixed-rate yen debt. If MUFJ gets the proceeds of the dollar bond issue, giving Sony an equivalent amount of yen, and MUFJ agrees to make the dollar interest payments associated with Sony's dollar bonds, what yen interest payments should MUFJ charge Sony? What is Sony's all-in cost in yen? The current spot exchange rate is ¥98.50/$.

8. Assume that 1 year has passed since you entered into the transaction described in problem 4. Assume that the new spot exchange rate is CHF1.45/$ and that UBS is now quoting the following interest rates on 4-year swaps:

   U.S. Dollars: 7.50% bid and 7.60% offered against the 6-month dollar LIBOR

Swiss Francs: 6.75% bid and 6.85% offered against the 6-month dollar LIBOR

If you close out the swap in problem 4, what net dollar cash flow will you experience? Explain why this is the correct amount. You can assume that the term structures of interest rates in both currencies are flat.

9. Web Question: Go to www22.verizon.com/investor/app_resources/interactiveannual/2010/mda06.html to find an excerpt of the 2010 Annual Report of Verizon, a large telecommunications company. Determine whether they use interest rate and/or currency swaps and why.

BIBLIOGRAPHY

Bank for International Settlements (BIS), 2004, *Central Bank Survey of Foreign Exchange and Derivatives Market Activity*, Basel, Switzerland: BIS.

Chernenko, Sergey, and Michael Faulkender, Forthcoming, "The Two Sides of Derivatives Usage: Hedging and Speculating with Interest Rate Swaps," *Journal of Financial and Quantitative Analysis*.

Chernenko, Sergey, Michael Faulkender, and Nicole Thorne Jenkins, 2007, "The Market Reaction to the Strategic Use of Interest Rate Swaps," working paper.

Duffie, Darrell, and Kenneth Singleton, 1997, "An Econometric Model of the Term Structure of Interest Rate Swap Yields," *Journal of Finance* 52, pp. 1287–1323.

Geczy, Christopher, Bernadette Minton, and Catherine Schrand, 2007, "Taking a View: Corporate Speculation, Governance, and Compensation," *Journal of Finance* 62, pp. 2405–2443.

International Swaps and Derivatives Association (ISDA), 2011, *ISDA 2011 Margin Survey*, New York: ISDA.

Johannes, Michael, and Suresh Sundaresan, 2007, "Pricing Collateralized Swaps" *Journal of Finance* 62, pp. 383–410.

Li, Haitao, and Connie X. Mao, 2003, "Corporate Use of Interest Rate Swaps: Theory and Evidence," *Journal of Banking and Finance* 27, pp. 1511–1538.

Lowenstein, Roger, 2000, *When Genius Failed: The Rise and Fall of Long-Term Capital Management*, New York: Random House.

GLOSSARY

absolute borrowing advantage A situation in which one corporation's all-in costs are lower in each of two currencies than another corporation's all-in costs.

absolute purchasing power parity The idea that the exchange rate should adjust to equate the internal and external purchasing powers of a money, in which case the exchange rate, quoted as domestic currency per foreign currency, should equal the ratio between the domestic and foreign price levels.

ad valorem duties Tariffs that are quoted as a certain percentage of the export price.

adjusted net present value (ANPV) A capital budgeting technique that derives the value of a firm or project in steps, first deriving the present value of the all-equity free cash flows and then adding the present value of financial side effects and growth options.

affiliate bank A bank partly owned but not controlled by a foreign parent bank.

agency costs The costs that the owners of a firm incur because of the separation of ownership and control.

agency theory Economic models that explore the problems in corporations arising from the separation of ownership and control and that devise ways to resolve them.

AIC (all-in-cost) principle The discount rate or internal rate of return that equates the present value of all the future interest and principal payments to the net proceeds (face value minus fees) received by the issuer.

American depositary receipt (ADR) A stock certificate traded in the United States representing a specific number of shares in a company listed on a foreign stock exchange that are held in custody by a U.S. depositary bank that issues the ADR.

American option An option that can be exercised at the discretion of the buyer any time between the purchase date and the maturity date.

American quote The dollar price of a foreign currency—that is, the amount of dollars it takes to purchase one unit of the foreign currency.

anti-globalization An umbrella term encompassing separate social movements, united in their opposition to the globalization of corporate economic activity and the free trade with developing nations that results from such activity.

appreciation In discussing changes in exchange rates, the strengthening or increase in value of one currency relative to another.

arbitrage The process of earning riskless profits by simultaneously buying and selling equivalent assets or commodities.

arbitrage pricing theory (APT) An asset pricing model based on the idea that a number of economy-wide factors systematically affect the returns on a large number of securities and hence drive their expected returns.

ask rate The price (exchange rate) at which a dealer is willing to sell one currency in return for another currency. Also called the offer price.

asset market approach (to exchange rate determination) Exchange rate models that view the exchange rate as an asset price, with its value depending on current fundamentals (such as relative money supplies and output levels of countries) and expected values of future economic fundamentals.

asset securitization The packaging of assets or obligations into securities for sale to third parties.

asset substitution A situation in which managers, acting in the interests of shareholders, accept a high-variance project that may lower overall firm value but that increases shareholder value.

Association of Southeast Asian Nations (ASEAN) A regional economic and political organization that is designed to promote trade and investment in its member countries: Brunei Darussalam, Cambodia, Indonesia, Laos, Malaysia, Myanmar, Philippines, Singapore, Thailand, and Vietnam.

aval An irrevocable guarantee of the debts of an importer, usually guaranteed by the importer's government or its bank.

average-rate option An option contract in which the payoff depends on the difference between the strike price and the average exchange rate, calculated from the initiation of the contract to the expiration date.

B/A (banker's acceptance) A document, tradable in financial markets, that is created when a bank stamps and signs a time draft indicating that the bank will pay the face value of a draft at maturity.

back-to-back loan An agreement that is similar in structure to a parallel loan but in which the loans are made between the multinational parent corporations, which then lend to their subsidiaries in two different countries, and which contains the right of offset.

Baker Plan A 1985 plan that constituted a second phase of the handling of the developing country Debt Crisis. It relied heavily on countries agreeing to change their economic policies following guidelines set by the IMF in exchange for a modest amount of new loans extended to developing countries by private commercial banks and the World Bank.

balance of payments (BOP) A summary of the value of the transactions between a country's residents, businesses, and government with the rest of the world for a specific period of time, such as a month, a quarter, or a year.

balance-sheet hedge The practice of denominating debt in a currency in which a firm has revenues.

Bank for International Settlements (BIS) An international organization based in Basel, Switzerland, that promotes international monetary and financial stability and serves as a bank for the world's central banks.

barrier option A traditional option with an additional requirement that either activates the option or extinguishes it if the exchange rate passes through a prespecified barrier exchange rate.

Basel Accord An agreement between G10 countries that sets capital requirements (also known as "capital adequacy rules") for internationally active banks.

basis point adjustment The process of changing the interest rate on the side of a currency swap the client is paying away from the bank's quoted rate when the client wants to receive interest cash flows from the bank at something other than the bank's quoted rate.

basis risk The risk arising from differences between the current spot price and the futures price and the fact that the maturity of what is being hedged may not be the maturity of the futures contract.

basket of currencies A composite currency composed of various amounts of other currencies.

beta The systematic risk of an individual asset in the capital asset pricing model (CAPM). Measured as the covariance of the return on the security with the return on the market portfolio divided by the variance of the return on the market portfolio.

bid–ask spread The difference between the ask rate and the bid rate. The spread constitutes a source of profits for market makers.

bid rate The price (exchange rate) at which a dealer is willing to buy one currency in return for another currency.

bilateral investment treaty (BIT) An agreement between two countries that promises mutual respect for, and protection of, investments in each other's territory, with the purpose of encouraging international capital investment.

bilateral netting system A payment system between two parties who agree to transfer only the net amounts that are owed to each other.

binomial option pricing Model to price options that assumes that random movements in the underlying asset, over short intervals, are well approximated by a discrete, two-state model. The option is then priced by considering a portfolio of stocks and bonds, or currencies, that replicates the payoff to the option over the two states.

B/L (bill of lading) A contract issued to an exporter by a shipping company that will transport the exporter's goods to their destination.

blocked funds A problem encountered by multinational corporations when government restrictions in a host country prevent the transfer of foreign currency out of that country.

BOP *See* balance of payments.

Brady bonds Bonds issued by countries in response to the Brady Plan in which the principal and some initial interest payments are collateralized.

Brady Plan A comprehensive plan to resolve the developing countries Debt Crisis developed in 1989 by then U.S. Treasury Secretary Nicholas Brady. This plan put pressure on banks to offer some form of debt relief to developing countries. It also called for an expansion in secondary market transactions aimed at debt reduction.

breakout Term used by chartists to describe a situation when a trading range is broken and a sudden rise or fall in prices is expected.

Bretton Woods Agreement An accord signed by 44 Allied nations toward the end of World War II. It established regulations and regulatory bodies for an international monetary system, based on a target zone relative to the dollar, which itself was fixed relative to gold at $35 per ounce. The system collapsed in 1971.

buyback An agreement in which an exporter of physical capital agrees to accept payment in the form of the output of a plant, which the exporter helps to construct in a foreign country.

buyer credit An international finance method used when expensive capital equipment is imported in which the exporter arranges for a financial institution to grant credit to the importer to enable payment to the exporter.

call option *See* foreign currency call option.

cannibalization of exports The possible loss of export revenue when a foreign market is served by direct foreign investment and the former exports to that market are unable to be sold elsewhere.

capital account A major account of the balance of payments that records the purchases and sales of foreign assets by domestic residents as well as the purchases and sales of domestic assets by foreign residents.

capital adequacy rules *See* Basel Accord.

capital allocation line (CAL) A description of the feasible trade-offs between expected return and standard deviation that arise when allocating capital between a risk-free asset and a single risky asset.

capital asset pricing model (CAPM) A model in which an asset's risk premium, its expected return in excess of the risk-free rate, is determined by its beta with respect to the market portfolio times the risk premium on the market portfolio.

capital budgeting The process of valuing investments by taking their net present values and allocating capital upon that basis.

capital controls Regulations that restrict the flow of capital into and out of a country.

capital expenditures The investments in plant and equipment that a firm makes in expectation of future profitability.

capital flight An outflow of capital from a country, typically associated with a prospective devaluation of the currency or other actions by the country's government that would result in a loss of wealth for investors in that country.

capital inflow Purchases by foreign residents of the assets of a country, such as its stocks, bonds, or real estate, or the sale of foreign assets by domestic residents.

capital outflow Purchases by domestic residents of the assets of a foreign country, such as its stocks, bonds, or real estate, or the sale of domestic assets by foreign residents.

CAPX *See* capital expenditures.

carry trade Investment in a high-yield currency while borrowing in a low-yield currency (or buying the high-yield currency in the forward market relative to the low-yield currency).

cash-in-advance Export financing technique requiring the importer to pay the exporter before the goods are shipped, implying that the exporter does not have to finance the goods during their shipment.

centralized debt denomination A situation in which a multinational corporation borrows in the company's domestic currency.

certificate of analysis A document that attests to some measurable characteristics of a shipment.

certificate of origin A document that indicates the source of a shipment of merchandise.

chartism Forecasting technique (for exchange rates or other asset prices) that tries to infer possible future trends based only on information regarding the actual trading history of the asset price.

clean acceptance An export finance method in which a bank agrees to accept a certain number and amount of time drafts submitted by the exporter. The bank immediately discounts the drafts to provide financing for the exporter, and the exporter repays the face amount of the draft to the bank at maturity.

clean bill of lading A shipping contract that indicates that the carrier believes the merchandise was received in good condition, based on visual inspection.

clearing arrangements International barter conducted with the extension of credit from one party to the other.

Clearing House Interbank Payments System (CHIPS) An electronic payment system that transfers funds and settles transactions in U.S. dollars.

clearinghouse An agency or a separate corporation of a futures exchange that acts as a buyer to every clearing member seller and a seller to every clearing member buyer. The clearinghouse also settles trading accounts, collects and maintains margin monies, regulates delivery, and reports trading data.

clearing member A member of an exchange clearinghouse. The member is usually a company, which is responsible for the financial commitments of its customers for whom it clears trades.

closed-end fund An investment fund that trades on a stock exchange at a price that may differ from the net asset value of the assets of the managed portfolio.

CLS Bank A financial institution owned by the world's largest financial groups that engages in continuous linked settlement by collecting details of all the currency trades between its member banks, using multilateral netting to figure net payments for each bank and finalizing pay-ins and pay-outs to the system over a 5-hour window.

CME Group The Chicago Mercantile Exchange Group, a large futures and options exchange, that trades, among other contracts, currency futures and options on those futures.

commercial invoice A document given by an exporter to an importer that contains a detailed description of the merchandise in question, including unit prices, the number of items, and the financial terms of the sale.

Commodity Futures Trading Commission (CFTC) The government organization that regulates the U.S. futures industry.

comparative advantage The idea that international trade makes everyone better off when countries specialize in the production of goods that they produce relatively most efficiently.

comparative borrowing advantage A situation in which one corporation's ratio of all-in costs for borrowing in two currencies is lower than another corporation's ratio of all-in costs.

compensatory trade A type of complex countertrade.

conditional expectation The probability-weighted average of future events, such as possible future exchange rates, which is also the mean of a conditional probability distribution for that variable. Also called the conditional mean.

conditional mean *See* conditional expectation.

conditional probability distribution A description of possible future events and their respective probabilities of occurrence that is based on an information set at a point in time.

conditional standard deviation The square root of the variance of a conditional probability distribution of a particular variable, such as the rate of currency appreciation. Often called the conditional volatility when applied to a financial return.

conditional volatility *See* conditional standard deviation.

confirmed documentary credit (D/C) A documentary credit in which, in addition to the bank that issues the documentary credit, a second commercial bank that is usually well known to the exporter agrees to honor the draft presented by the exporter.

consular invoice A document filled out by an exporter in consultation with the local consulate of the importing country that provides information to customs officials in the importing country, with the goal of preventing false declarations of the value of the merchandise.

contagion The phenomenon in which a currency or other financial crisis spreads from one country to another merely as a result of a crisis occurring in a first country.

conversion The process of buying a foreign currency in the forward market and selling it forward with a synthetic forward contract constructed with options.

convertible bond A corporate bond that is convertible into a fixed number of equity shares of the corporation prior to maturity.

convex tax code A tax system that imposes a larger tax rate on higher incomes and a smaller tax rate on lower incomes, also called a progressive system of taxation.

corporate governance The legal and financial structure that controls the relationship between a company's shareholders and its management.

correlation A number between −1 and 1 that indicates how closely related are the random variations in two variables.

correspondent bank A bank that performs services as a proxy for financial institutions that lack an on-site presence in a particular country.

costs of financial distress   The loss of firm value from the direct costs of bankruptcy associated with legal, consulting, and accounting fees and the indirect losses associated with the possibility that the firm may go into bankruptcy.

counterpurchase   A trading activity that is similar to a buyback, except the exporter agrees to purchase goods that are not produced by the importer.

countertrade   A variety of international trade activities in which exporters and importers exchange goods and services without necessarily having to use money as a medium of exchange.

country credit spread   The difference between the yield on a bond issued by a developing country in an international currency and the government bond yield of the country that issues the international currency. This spread reflects sovereign risk.

country fund   A closed-end fund that invests in the securities of one particular country.

country risk   The risk that a country's political environment as well as its economic and financial environment may adversely affect a company's cash flows.

country risk premium   The additional yield above the risk-free rate demanded by investors in government bonds to protect them against political risk.

country risk rating   Assessments of country risk produced by a number of specialized organizations, typically for a large number of countries.

covariance   The probability-weighted average of the product of the deviations of two random variables from their means, which measures how the two random variables move together, or covary with each other.

covered interest rate arbitrage   An arbitrage that exploits deviations from covered interest rate parity.

covered interest rate parity   A no-arbitrage relationship between spot and forward exchange rates and the two nominal interest rates associated with these currencies.

crawling peg system   A target zone system wherein the bands are reset over time, typically in response to movements in inflation.

credit default swap (CDS)   A bilateral insurance contract between a protection buyer and a protection seller to protect against default on a specific bond or loan issued by a corporation or sovereign. The protection buyer pays semiannual or annual insurance premiums to the protection seller. In return, when there is a default event, the protection seller transfers money (e.g., the face value of the bond) to the protection buyer in return for the defaulted bond.

credit rating   A rating that is provided by a credit-rating firm and that indicates the creditworthiness of a corporate or government borrower.

credit spread   The difference between the borrowing cost of a corporate borrower and the borrowing cost of a risk-free government on a security with similar maturity.

credit transaction   In balance of payments accounting, any transaction that results in a receipt of funds from foreigners; in other words, any transaction that gives rise to a conceptual inflow or source of foreign currency.

cross-currency settlement risk   The risk that a financial institution will fail to deliver currency on one side of a foreign exchange transaction, even though the financial institution has received the other currency from its counterparty to the transaction. Also called Herstatt risk.

cross-holding   The practice of one firm owning shares in another firm.

cross-listing   The practice of listing shares on an exchange outside the country in which the company is headquartered.

cross-rate   An exchange rate between two currencies not involving the U.S. dollar.

currency board   An exchange rate system in which the monetary base of the domestic currency is 100% backed by a foreign reserve currency and is fully convertible into the reserve currency at a fixed rate and on demand.

currency swap   An agreement between two counterparties to exchange principals denominated in two currencies of equivalent value at the spot exchange rate and then to have one party pay interest and principal on the currency it received and the other party to pay interest and principal on the currency it received.

currency warrants   Longer maturity foreign currency options that are sometimes issued by major corporations and are actively traded on exchanges.

current account   A major account of the balance of payments that records transactions in goods and services, transactions associated with the income flows from assets, and unilateral transfers.

cylinder option   A contract that allows the buyer to specify a desired trading range in the future so that if the future spot rate falls outside of the range, the buyer transacts at the limits of the range. Unlike the range forward contract, the trading range is set to allow the buyer either to pay money or possibly to receive money up front for entering into the contract.

D/A (documents against acceptance) collection   A method of international trade in which an exporter extends credit to an importer, which acknowledges its legal obligation to pay the face amount of a draft at maturity by having the collecting bank present a time draft to the importer who must sign it, date it, and write *accepted* across it before the shipping documents are released to the importer.

dark pools   Electronic trading systems that deliberately sacrifice price and volume transparency to offer anonymity to large traders.

D/C (documentary credit)   A method of international trade in which commercial banks stand between an importer and an exporter to assure the exporter of payment after fulfilling certain requirements. In the United States, also known as a letter of credit (L/C).

debit transaction   In balance of payments accounting, any transaction that results in a payment to foreigners; in other words, any transaction that gives rise to a conceptual outflow or use of foreign currency.

debt buyback   A situation in which a country buys back its own outstanding loans at a discount.

Debt Crisis   A 1980s economic and financial crisis that occurred in a large number of developing countries after many defaulted on their loan payments to international banks and that took a full decade to be resolved.

debt–equity swap   A situation in which a multinational corporation buys the debt of a country from an original creditor at a discount, presents the debt to the debtor government, receives local currency equal to the face value of the debt, and then uses the local currency to make an equity investment in that country.

debt overhang   The notion that a country saddled with a huge debt burden has little incentive to implement economic reforms or stimulate investment because the resulting increase in income will simply be appropriated by the country's creditors in the form of higher debt payments. Also used to describe a similar situation within a firm in which the management has no incentive to undertake profitable investments because the benefits accrue mostly to bondholders.

decentralized debt denomination   A situation in which a multinational corporation borrows in the currencies in which its revenues are received.

deemed-paid credit   The amount of domestic tax credit a company receives for foreign taxes paid by one of its subsidiaries.

deficit   In balance of payments accounting, the idea that debits on a particular account are greater than credits on that account.

deflation   The rate of change of the price level when prices are falling.

delta (of an option)   The change in the value of the derivative asset with a small change in the value of the underlying asset.

delta neutral   The property of a portfolio of foreign exchange positions, of not being exposed to risk of loss from small changes in foreign exchange rates.

demand curve   A function that indicates the quantity demanded by consumers, given the relative price of a product.

demutualization   The process of converting stock exchanges from non-profit, member-owned organizations to for-profit, investor-owned, and typically publicly traded companies.

density function   The mathematical formula that describes a probability distribution.

depository receipt   *See* DR.

depreciation   In discussing changes in exchange rates, a weakening or decrease in the value of one currency relative to another.

depreciation (accounting)   Accounting deductions for corporate income tax associated with previous capital expenditures on plant and equipment.

depreciation tax shield   The amount of taxes that a corporation avoids because depreciation is a deductible expense.

derivative securities   Financial contracts, such as forwards, futures, options, and swaps, whose values depend on the values of underlying asset prices, such as exchange rates, interest rates, or stock prices.

devaluation   A change in a fixed exchange rate that increases the domestic currency price of foreign currency and thus decreases the value of the domestic currency.

devaluation premium   The part of the interest rate on a particular currency that reflects its expected depreciation relative to another currency.

digital options   Contracts that pay off an amount of cash or the value of an asset when a certain condition is met—for example, when the spot rate is lower than the strike price.

direct quote   An exchange rate quote expressed as an amount of domestic currency per unit of foreign currency.

dirty float currency system   A floating exchange rate system in which a central bank nonetheless intervenes in the foreign exchange market, buying and selling its currency to affect its foreign exchange value.

discount rates   Expected rates of return used to take present values.

documentary collection   A method of international trade, with some bank involvement, in which an exporter retains control of goods until an importer has paid or is legally bound to pay.

dollarization   The phenomenon in which use of a foreign currency drives out the domestic currency as a means of payment and as a savings vehicle.

domestic bonds   Bonds that are issued and traded within the internal market of a single country and are denominated in the currency of that country.

domestic CAPM   An application of the CAPM that assumes that the assets of a country are held only by investors who reside in that country so that the market portfolio is a local market index.

D/P (documents against payment) collection   A method of international trade in which an importer must pay the amount of a sight draft to the collecting bank before the trade documents are released.

DR (depositary receipt)   A stock certificate that represents a specific number of shares in a company listed in a foreign stock exchange that are held in custody by a depositary bank that issues the DR.

dragon bond   A Eurobond targeted at the Asian market (outside Japan) with Asian syndication.

dual-currency bond   A straight, fixed-rate bond issued in one currency, for example yen, which pays coupon interest in that same currency, but the promised repayment of principal at maturity is denominated in another currency, for example U.S. dollars.

early exercise   The exercise of an American option prior to maturity.

earnings before interest and taxes (EBIT)   Revenue minus cost of goods sold minus selling and general administrative expenses and minus accounting depreciation.

economic and monetary union (EMU)   Agreement among European Union countries to achieve an economic and monetary union. In an economic union, there is free movement of labor, goods, services, and capital. In a monetary union, a group of currencies uses a common currency and a common central bank conducts monetary policy. Also, informally used as the European Monetary Union to specifically describe the countries that abandoned their sovereign currencies in order to create the euro.

economic exposure   *See* real exchange risk.

Edge Act bank   A federally chartered subsidiary of a U.S. bank that is physically located in the United States but is allowed to engage in a full range of international banking activities. This bank can accept deposits from foreign customers, finance international trade, transfer international funds, and even own equity in U.S. corporations.

efficient frontier   The set of risky portfolios that maximize the expected return on the portfolio for each level of portfolio variance.

elasticity   The percentage change in the quantity demanded with a percentage change in the relative price of a product but defined to be a positive number.

electronic communication network (ECN)   A system that electronically collects and matches buy and sell orders and displays the best available prices.

electronic foreign exchange trading (eFX)   Electronic trading platforms that may offer multiple quotes from a number of foreign exchange dealers and that may house an electronic communication network (ECN).

eligible banker's acceptance (B/A)   A banker's acceptance that meets the requirements of the Federal Reserve and consequently does not require the bank to hold reserves against the B/A.

emerging markets   In equity trading, the stock markets of developing countries, or more generally, the countries themselves.

equity market liberalization   A policy reform that allows foreign investment in the local stock market and allows local investors to invest abroad.

equity risk premium   In general, the expected return on an equity in excess of the risk-free return, and specifically, the expected excess return on the market portfolio.

estimator   The formula for translating data into parameter estimates (of a model); see also OLS estimator.

Eurobank   A bank that operates in the Eurocurrency market, making short-term loans and extending Eurocredits to other financial institutions, corporations, sovereign governments, and international organizations.

Eurobond   An international bond that is denominated in one or more currencies but that is traded in external markets outside the borders of the countries issuing the currencies.

Eurocredit   A long-term loan granted by a syndicate of banks to a bank, a corporation, a government, or an international organization; typically issued at a spread above LIBOR.

Eurocurrency market   *See* external currency market.

Euro-equity market   A market for issuing shares in multiple foreign markets, sometimes simultaneously with distribution in the domestic market.

Euro-MTNs (Euro-medium-term notes)   Notes that are similar to Euronotes but whose maturity is longer—between 9 months and 10 years.

Euronotes   Short-term, negotiable promissory notes distributed for a borrower by an international bank over a specified period (5 to 7 years). They are more flexible than floating-rate notes and usually cheaper than syndicated loans.

European Currency Unit (ECU)   A historical currency basket in the European Monetary System composed of specific amounts of 12 different European currencies.

European Economic Community (EEC)   An agreement, created by the Treaty of Rome in 1957, between six countries (Belgium, West Germany, Luxembourg, France, Italy, and the Netherlands) to remove trade barriers between themselves and to form a "common market."

European Monetary System (EMS)   A target zone system created in 1979 for currencies of European Union countries to prevent large currency fluctuations relative to one another, which was replaced by a monetary union in 1999.

European option   An option that can be exercised only at maturity.

European quote   An exchange rate quote expressed as the amount of foreign currency needed to buy 1 dollar.

European Union (EU)   An intergovernmental union of 27 European countries that was established in 1992 by the Maastricht Treaty to promote economic and political integration.

eurozone   The group of countries that use the euro as their currency.

***ex ante* real interest rate**   Nominal interest rate minus expected inflation.

exchange controls   Government regulations that interfere with the buying and selling of foreign exchange (for example, taxes or quotas on foreign exchange transactions).

exchange rate   The relative price of two currencies, such as the Japanese yen price of the U.S. dollar, the U.S. dollar price of the British pound, or the Mexican peso price of the euro.

exchange rate pass-through   The amount that a given change in the exchange rate changes the prices of products.

exchange-traded fund (ETF)   An investment fund that trades on an exchange but whose price is kept close to the value of the underlying portfolio through arbitrage activities by a few institutional investors.

exercise price   *See* strike price.

Ex-Im Bank   The Export–Import Bank of the United States, an independent U.S. government corporation involved in financing and facilitating U.S. exports.

exotic options   Options with different payoff patterns and features than the basic call and put options.

expectations hypothesis   Theory of the term structure that holds that long-term interest rates are an appropriate weighted average of the current short-term rate and expected future short-term rates.

expected rate of inflation   The rate of change of prices of goods and services that people think may occur over some future horizon.

expected real interest rate *See ex ante* real interest rate.

expected value The probability-weighted average of future events.

export factor A company that performs credit risk investigations for exporters and collects funds from an exporter's accounts receivable while possibly providing financing to the exporter.

exports Sales of domestic goods and services to foreign residents.

expropriation The act of a government seizing property without compensating the owners for it—in particular by turning private companies into state-owned companies.

external currency market The interbank market for deposits and loans that are denominated in currencies that are not the currency of the country in which the bank is operating.

external equity market *See* Euro-equity market.

external purchasing power (of a currency) The amount of goods and services that can be purchased with the domestic currency in a foreign country.

factoring Export financing and facilitation business. *See* export factor.

Fama-French three-factor model An asset pricing model in which the factors are the excess return on the market portfolio, the excess return on a portfolio long in small stocks and short in big stocks, and the excess return on a portfolio long in high book-to-market stocks (value stocks) and short in low book-to-market stocks (growth stocks).

fat tails Property of a probability distribution in which more of the event probability is away from the mean than in the normal distribution.

Fedwire A real-time gross settlement system operated by the Federal Reserve System of the United States that instantly moves dollar balances between financial institutions.

Feldstein-Horioka puzzle The observation that countries' savings and investment expenditures are highly correlated, perhaps more than would be predicted by perfect capital mobility.

filter rules Trading rules designed to detect trend behavior in exchange rates, such as $x\%$ and moving-average rules.

financial disintermediation The process whereby corporate borrowing happens via a tradable security issued in the public market, rather than a non-tradable loan provided by financial intermediaries.

financial distress The situation where a firm is close to or perceived to be close to bankruptcy.

financial slack The presence of excess cash that is not needed to efficiently run a firm.

Fisher hypothesis Theory holding that the nominal interest rate equals the expected real interest rate plus the expected rate of inflation.

fixed exchange rate *See* pegged currency.

fixed-rate debt Debt for which the interest amount is fixed over time.

floating currency An exchange rate system in which the relative values of currencies are determined by market forces, without government interventions or restrictions.

floating-rate debt Debt for which the interest rate varies through time, according to variation in a reference rate, which is often LIBOR.

floating-rate notes (FRNs) Medium-term bonds, with maturities between 1 and 10 years and with coupon payments indexed to a reference interest rate, typically LIBOR.

flow to equity (FTE) A capital budgeting approach that finds equity value by directly discounting expected cash flows to equity holders with an appropriate risk-adjusted rate.

forecast error The difference between the actual realization of a random variable (like the future spot exchange rate) and the forecast of that random variable.

foreign bonds Bonds issued in a domestic market by a foreign borrower, denominated in the domestic currency, marketed to domestic residents, and regulated by the domestic authorities.

foreign branch of a bank A bank that is legally a part of its parent bank but operates like a local bank thereby allowing the parent bank to offer its domestic, foreign, and international customers direct, seamless service in a foreign country.

foreign currency call option A contract that gives the buyer of the option the right, but not the obligation, to buy a specific amount of foreign currency with domestic currency at an exchange rate stated in the contract.

foreign currency futures contracts Contracts, traded on futures exchanges that are similar to forward contracts and that allow one to bet on the direction of change of an exchange rate and effectively buy or sell foreign currency at an agreed-upon price, determined on a given future day.

foreign currency put option A contract that gives the buyer of the option the right, but not the obligation, to sell a specific amount of foreign currency with domestic currency at an exchange rate stated in the contract.

foreign direct investment (FDI) Occurs when a company from one country makes a significant investment that leads to at least a 10% ownership interest in a firm in another country.

foreign exchange brokers Financial intermediaries in the foreign exchange market who do not put their own money at risk but who receive a brokerage fee for matching buyers and sellers of currencies.

foreign exchange dealers Traders of currencies at commercial banks, investment banks, and brokerage firms in the major financial cities around the world.

foreign exchange market An over-the-counter market where currencies are traded.

foreign exchange reserves The foreign currency assets held by a central bank.

forfaiting Export financing technique whereby an exporter's accounts receivable are sold without recourse to the exporter.

forward contract An agreement between two parties to exchange specific amounts of two currencies at a future time at a quoted forward exchange rate.

forward foreign exchange market The over-the-counter market for the exchange of currencies at a future time at contractual prices (forward rates) agreed today. Also called the forward market.

forward market investment   A long or short position in the forward market to be closed out at the future spot rate.

forward market return   The return on a forward market investment that represents the difference between the future spot rate and the forward rate for a long contract or the negative of that for a short contract.

forward premium or discount   The difference between the forward and spot exchange rates expressed as a percentage of the spot rate. A premium specifies a positive value, and a discount specifies a negative value.

forward rate   An exchange rate in a forward contract that is quoted today for exchange of currencies at a future time.

forward rate bias   The difference between the expected future spot rate and the corresponding forward rate.

forward settlement date   The date the exchange of currencies occurs in a forward foreign exchange contract. Also called the forward value date.

forward value date   *See* forward settlement date.

foul bill of lading   A shipping contract that indicates that the carrier received the merchandise in a damaged condition, based on visual inspection.

franchising   Method to expand overseas, whereby the firm provides a specialized sales or service strategy, offers support at various levels, and may even initially invest in the franchise in exchange for periodic fees.

free cash flows (FCF)   The cash that can be returned to investors, which is gross cash flow minus investments in plant and equipment and working capital.

frequency distribution   A histogram with observations in each interval expressed as fractions of the total number of observations.

frontier markets   The young stock markets of the least-developed countries.

fronting loan   A parent-to-affiliate loan that uses a large international bank as a financial intermediary.

full-service bank   *See* universal bank.

fundamental analysis   Approach to exchange rate determination that links exchange rates to fundamental macroeconomic variables such as GDP growth and the current account either through a formal model or through judgmental analysis.

future value   The value of an investment in the future, found by multiplying the current value by 1 plus the interest rate.

futures commission merchant (FCM)   An individual or organization that accepts orders to buy or sell futures contracts or options on futures and accepts money or other assets from customers to support such orders.

gamma (of an option)   Describes how the option's delta changes with a change in the underlying exchange rate.

General Agreement on Tariffs and Trade (GATT)   A multilateral agreement, signed in 1947, that was designed to provide an international forum to encourage free trade between member states by regulating and reducing tariffs on traded goods and by providing a common mechanism for resolving trade disputes. It was superseded in 1995 by the World Trade Organization (WTO).

generally accepted accounting principles (GAAP)   Accounting standards determined in the United States by the Financial Accounting Standards Board.

global bond   A bond issued simultaneously in a domestic market and in the Eurobond market.

global depositary receipt (GDR)   A depositary receipt that trades across multiple markets and can settle in the currency of each market.

global minimum-variance portfolio   The portfolio of assets with the least variance among all possible portfolios.

Global Offset and Countertrade Association (GOCA)   An industry trade association that holds annual conferences and supports a Web site (www.globaloffset. org) devoted to the practice of countertrade.

global registered share (GRS)   An ordinary share of a company that trades and transfers freely across national borders.

globalization   The process of increasing global connectivity and integration between countries, corporations, and individuals within these nations and organizations in their economic, political, and social activities.

gold standard   An exchange rate system in which a currency is pegged to a specified amount of gold and can be exchanged for gold at the central bank.

goods market arbitrage   Buying and selling goods to make a profit without bearing risk.

government budget surplus   The difference between taxes and total government expenditures (including spending on goods and services, transfer payments, and interest on government debt). Also known as national government saving.

gross cash flows   Net operating profit less adjusted taxes plus accounting depreciation.

gross domestic product (GDP)   The market value of all final goods and services produced within a country in a given period of time.

gross national income (GNI)   The total income of an economy equal to gross domestic product plus the foreign income accruing to domestic residents minus the income from the domestic market accruing to non-residents plus unilateral transfers from foreigners.

grossed-up dividend   The value of dividends received from a foreign subsidiary plus the tax credit for taxes paid to foreign governments.

growth option   The option to do an additional project if the first project is successful. Its presence adds value to the first project.

hedge fund   An investment company that pools investors' money and invests in financial instruments to make a positive return. Hedge funds tend to be less regulated than other investment pools and seek to profit in all kinds of markets by pursuing speculative investment practices that may increase the risk of loss.

hedging The act of using financial markets, especially derivative securities, to reduce or eliminate risks arising from underlying business transactions.

Herstatt risk *See* cross-currency settlement risk.

histogram Representation of the likelihoods of the occurrences of a random variable that groups observations into intervals of equal length and records the number of observations in each interval.

home bias The phenomenon that investors of countries are not very well internationally diversified but instead own portfolios concentrated in the securities of their home markets.

idiosyncratic risk The part of the uncertainty of a return that is not systematic. *See also* systematic risk.

idiosyncratic variance The part of an asset's return that cannot be explained by pervasive factors in the economy, especially the market return.

IMF conditionality The monetary and fiscal policies and macroeconomic conditions that a country must follow if it borrows from the IMF.

implied volatility The unique value of volatility (for the underlying asset) that sets the option price from an option pricing model equal to the option price observed in the market.

import competitor A domestic company that competes for business in the domestic market with foreign competitors.

imports Purchases of foreign goods and services by domestic residents.

impossible trinity *See* trilemma.

incremental profits The additional cash that comes into a firm as a result of making an investment.

index funds Funds that passively track stock indices, such as the S&P 500, without trying to outperform them.

indexing formula A clause in a contract that requires changes in prices based on the realization of certain contingencies such as the amount of inflation or depreciation of a currency.

indirect quote An exchange rate quote expressed as an amount of foreign currency per unit of domestic currency.

ineligible banker's acceptance (B/A) A banker's acceptance that does not meet the requirements of the Federal Reserve, which consequently requires that the bank hold reserves against the B/A.

inflation A general increase in monetary prices of goods and services in an economy measured as the rate of change of the price level.

information set The collection of all information used to predict the future value of an economic variable.

initial margin The initial amount of wealth that must be placed in a margin account, as determined by the futures exchange.

institutional investors Organizations that invest pools of money on behalf of individual investors or other organizations. Examples include banks, insurance companies, pension funds, mutual funds, and university endowments.

integrated market A market where securities are priced in the global capital market.

interbank market The wholesale part of the foreign exchange and external currency markets where major banks trade.

interest rate parity *See* covered or uncovered interest parity.

interest rate swap An agreement in which two counterparties agree to exchange fixed interest payments for floating interest rate payments on the same notional principal.

interest subsidy The firm value created by the ability of a firm to borrow at an interest rate below the firm's market-determined interest rate.

interest tax shield The firm value created by the tax deductibility of interest on debts.

internal purchasing power (of a currency) The amount of goods and services that can be purchased with the domestic currency in the domestic country.

International Bank for Reconstruction and Development (IBRD) Original name of the World Bank.

international banking facility (IBF) A separate set of asset and liability accounts, used to record international transactions, that is segregated on the parent bank's books and is not a unique physical or legal entity.

international barter International trade in which the transfer of goods or services from a party in one country is made directly to a party in another country in return for some other good or service of equal value.

international bonds Bonds traded outside the country of the issuer.

international CAPM A version of the CAPM that takes exchange rate risk into account.

International Center for the Settlement of Investment Disputes (ICSID) An organization within the World Bank that administers legal disputes filed as claims under bilateral investment treaties.

International Chamber of Commerce (ICC) A world business organization based in Paris that has thousands of member companies and associations in more than 130 countries, whose activities include setting rules and standards for international trade and arbitration and other forms of dispute resolution.

International Development Association (IDA) Orgainization within the World Bank that focuses on development of the poorest countries in the world by providing low-interest loans, interest-free credits, and grants for investments in education, health, infrastructure, communications, and other activities.

International Finance Corporation (IFC) Part of the World Bank group and a global investor and advisor committed to promoting private-sector development in developing countries. One priority is the development of domestic financial markets through institution building and the use of innovative financial products.

International Financial Reporting Standards (IFRS) Accounting regulations developed by the International Accounting Standards Board.

international Fisher equation *See* uncovered interest rate parity.

international investment income account The account on the balance of payments that is associated with flows of investment income.

international investment position *See* net international investment position.

International Monetary Fund (IMF) International organization of 187 member countries, based in Washington, DC, which was conceived at a United Nations conference convened in Bretton Woods, New Hampshire, in 1944. The main goal of the IMF is to ensure the stability of the international monetary and financial system.

international parity conditions Collective name for covered interest rate parity, uncovered interest rate parity, purchasing power parity, and the Fisher hypothesis. If all these relationships hold, real interest rates are equalized across countries.

International Swap and Derivatives Association (ISDA) A derivatives trade organization, whose members include most of the world's major financial institutions, that sets standards for derivative transactions.

intertemporal budget constraint The idea that the present value of expenditures must be balanced by the present value of revenues.

intrinsic value The immediate revenue generated from exercising an option.

investment barriers Direct or indirect investment restrictions that limit or prevent foreign investors from investing in a country.

investment trust The U.K. version of a closed-end fund.

irrevocable D/C A documentary credit that cannot be revoked unless all parties, including the exporter, agree to the revocation.

joint venture An organizational form in which two or more independent firms form and jointly control a different entity, which is created to pursue a specific objective.

lagging payment A payment delayed beyond what is usual.

lag operation An exporter's method of profiting from international trade by collecting payment after a rise in the value of a foreign currency (for example, by lengthening the maturity of trade credits).

law of one price The idea that the price of a commodity in a particular currency should be the same throughout the world.

L/C (letter of credit) *See* D/C.

leading payment A payment made earlier than usual.

lead manager The main bank in a syndicate, organizing the issuance of a bond.

lead operation An importer's method of profiting from international trade by prepaying for goods before a fall in the value of the local currency.

leptokurtosis *See* fat tails.

Level I ADR An ADR that trades over the counter in New York—in what is called pink sheet trading—and is not listed on a major U.S. stock exchange.

Level II ADR An ADR that trades on the NYSE, NASDAQ, or AMEX and hence must satisfy the exchange's listing requirements.

Level III ADR An ADR that trades on one of the major exchanges in the United States and is also issued to raise capital in the United States.

leverage The use of borrowed money (or derivative securities) to increase capital at risk beyond capital owned when investing. Using leverage in a trading strategy scales up both its returns and its risk. Leverage also refers to a firm's use of debt to finance its assets.

licensing Method to enter foreign markets in which the multinational corporation gives local firms abroad the right to manufacture the company's products or provide its services in return for fees, typically called royalties.

licensing fees Fees paid to a firm for the use of a technology, copyright, or patent.

liquidating dividend The final payment to shareholders when a firm goes out of business.

liquidity The property of a market in which buyers and sellers are easily matched, making the transaction costs of trading low.

London Interbank Offer Rate (LIBOR) The external currency interest rate in London, which is the most important reference rate in international loan agreements.

lookback option An option in which the payoff depends on the difference between the spot rate at maturity and the minimum spot rate during the life of the option.

MacPPP The idea that the exchange rate quoted as domestic currency per foreign currency should equal the ratio between the domestic currency and foreign currency prices of McDonald's Big Macs.

maintenance margin The minimum value that a margin account can have before an investor gets a margin call and must bring the margin account back to the initial margin.

managed floating Currency system in which currencies in principle freely float, but where the monetary authorities nonetheless often intervene in the foreign exchange market.

margin account Deposits of cash and other assets from which losses on futures contracts are deducted and to which profits are added.

marginal cost The cost of producing the last unit of output.

marginal revenue The revenue from selling the last unit of output.

margin call A notification to an investor that his or her margin account is below the maintenance margin.

market efficiency A financial concept in which the market prices of assets reflect information available to investors such that assets offer expected returns that are consistent with rational behavior and no arbitrage possibilities. In efficient capital markets, investors cannot expect to earn profits over and above what the market supplies as compensation for bearing risk. An inefficient market is one in which profits from trading are not associated with bearing risks and are therefore considered extraordinary.

market impact The effect of a large trade on the price of a security.

market maker (in the forex market) A trader who stands ready to buy and sell particular currencies.

market portfolio The portfolio that contains all securities in proportions equal to their market values as percentages of the total market value.

market risk The exposure of a return to fluctuations in the return on the market portfolio that cannot be diversified away.

market risk premium The expected excess return on the market portfolio.

market variance The variance of the return on the market portfolio.

marking to market The process of crediting and debiting daily profits and losses on futures accounts to margin accounts.

mean The expected value of a probability distribution of a random variable, which is the probability-weighted average of future events.

mean absolute error (MAE) The average of the absolute values of forecast errors.

mean reversion The property of a time series in which the expected change in the process would move the random variable toward an unconditional mean.

mean–standard deviation frontier The locus of the portfolios in expected return–standard deviation space that have the minimum standard deviation for each expected return. Also known as the minimum-variance frontier.

mean-variance-efficient (MVE) portfolio The one portfolio on the efficient frontier that maximizes the Sharpe ratio and hence is the optimal risky portfolio for all investors with mean-variance preferences.

mean-variance preferences Representation of an investor's preferences that depend positively on the expected return of the investor's portfolio and negatively on the portfolio's variance.

median The value of a random variable for which 50% of the values will be greater and 50% will be less.

menu costs Costs of changing prices that are a source of sticky prices.

merchandise trade balance The value of exports of goods minus imports of goods on a country's balance of payments.

merchant bank A bank that performs both traditional commercial banking and investment banking functions.

minimum-variance frontier *See* mean–standard deviation frontier.

Modigliani–Miller proposition A proposition that states that a corporation's financial policies, such as issuing debt, hedging foreign exchange risk, and other purely financial risk management activities, do not change the value of the firm's assets unless these financial transactions lower the firm's taxes, affect its investment decisions, or can be done more cheaply than individual investors' transactions can be done.

monetary approach A model of exchange rate determination that highlights the relative demands and supplies for monies as assets.

monetary base The sum of a central bank's liabilities (that is, currency in circulation plus total reserves of banks at the central bank).

monetary union A system in which several countries use a common currency by official agreement, with monetary policy administered by one central bank.

money market hedge The process of acquiring foreign currency liabilities or assets in the money markets to offset underlying exposures to foreign currency receivables or payables.

monopolist The sole seller of a good or service who consequently faces a downward sloping demand curve.

moving-average crossover rule Technical trading rule that uses moving averages of the exchange rate to predict trends. An *n*-day moving average is just the sample average of the last *n* trading days, including the current rate. The strategy goes long (short) in the foreign currency when the short-term moving average crosses the long-term moving average from below (above).

Multilateral Development Banks (MDBs) Institutions that provide financial support and professional advice for economic and social development activities in developing countries. The term typically refers to the World Bank Group and four regional development banks: the African Development Bank, the Asian Development Bank, the European Bank for Reconstruction and Development, and the Inter-American Development Bank.

Multilateral Investment Guarantee Agency (MIGA) Part of the World Bank Group established in 1988 to promote development by facilitating investment in emerging and transitioning economies (for instance, by providing political risk insurance).

multilateral netting system A payment system in which only the net amounts of what is mutually owed are transferred.

multinational corporation (MNC) A company engaged in producing and selling goods or services in more than one country.

national government saving *See* government budget surplus.

national income and product accounts (NIPA) Government statements of the sources of income and the value of final production for a country.

nationalization A government takeover of a private company.

negotiable bill of lading The most common shipping contract, which can be used to transfer title or ownership of goods between parties.

net exporter A firm that has more exports than imports and benefits from a real depreciation of the home currency.

net foreign assets *See* net international investment position.

net foreign income Income that accrues to domestic residents from ownership of foreign assets and from working abroad minus the income that accrues to foreign workers who are employed domestically and to foreign owners of domestic assets.

net importer A firm that has more imports than exports and benefits from a real appreciation of the home currency.

net international investment position The difference between the value of a country's ownership of foreign assets and the value of foreign ownership of the country's assets at a given point in time. Also known as net foreign assets.

net operating profit less adjusted taxes (NOPLAT) Earnings before interest and taxes (EBIT) minus taxes on EBIT.

net present value A valuation method that discounts expected future profits and subtracts the value of investment expenditures.

net present value of financial side effects (NPVF) The firm value created by the ability to issue debt, including the value of interest tax shields and the value of interest subsidies but minus the costs of financial distress.

net private saving The difference between private saving and the private sector's expenditures on investment goods.

net working capital The value of short-term assets minus short-term liabilities necessary to run a firm.

nominal price The amount of money that is paid for a good or service.

non-sterilized intervention The buying or selling of foreign exchange by a central bank in the currency markets, which affects the money supply because the central bank does not use offsetting open market operations.

non-systematic variance The part of the variance of a return that can be diversified away. Also called idiosyncratic risk.

normal distribution A probability distribution characterized by a symmetric bell-shaped curve that is completely described by its mean and variance.

North America Free Trade Agreement (NAFTA) A free trade agreement between Canada, the United States, and Mexico.

note purchase *See* forfaiting.

notional principal The conceptual principal amount that controls the cash flows of an interest rate swap.

null hypothesis A hypothesis that is tested using data and a test statistic.

offer price *See* ask rate.

official international reserves Assets of the central bank that are not denominated in the domestic currency, that is, the sum of foreign exchange reserves, gold reserves, and IMF-related reserve assets.

official reserves account *See* official settlements account.

official settlements account The account of the balance of payments that records changes in the official reserves of a country's central bank. Also known as official reserves account.

offset The requirement of an importing country that the effective cost of its imports be offset in some way by the exporter, who must contract to purchase items from the importing country; common in large expenditure contracts for weapon systems and power-generating facilities.

offshore banking center A center that primarily services the borrowing and lending needs of foreigners. Transactions are typically initiated outside the banking center whose location is in a country with low or zero taxation, moderate or light financial regulation, banking secrecy, and anonymity of transactions.

OLS (ordinary least squares) estimator A statistical methodology that estimates the relationship between a dependent variable and one or more independent variables by minimizing the sum of squared residuals.

on-board bill of lading A shipping contract that indicates that goods have been placed on a particular vessel for shipment.

open-end fund An investment fund that grows in size with new investments and shrinks with redemptions.

open interest The total number of contracts outstanding for a particular derivative contract.

open market operation The purchase or sale of government bonds by the central bank, which is done to affect the money supply.

open price The first price at which a transaction is completed on an exchange.

operating currency hedge The process of shifting a company's operations across countries to provide a better balance between the costs and revenues denominated in different currencies.

operating exposure *See* real exchange risk.

optimal portfolio A portfolio that maximizes the utility function of an investor.

optimum currency area A collection of countries for which a monetary union is optimal in that it balances the microeconomic benefits of perfect exchange rate certainty against the costs of macroeconomic adjustment problems.

option premium The price the buyer of an option must pay to the seller or writer of the option.

order bill of lading A shipping contract that legally consigns goods to a party named in the contract.

order-driven trading system A trading system in which orders are batched together and then auctioned off at an equilibrium market price.

Organization for Economic Cooperation and Development (OECD) A group of 30 relatively rich countries that examines, devises, and coordinates policies to foster employment, rising standards of living, and financial stability.

outright forward contract A forward contract that contains only one transaction to buy or sell foreign currency.

outsourcing The shifting of non-strategic functions, such as payroll, information technology, maintenance, facilities management, and logistics, to specialist firms, sometimes in other countries, to reduce costs.

overhead management fees Fees paid by a subsidiary to a parent corporation for managerial activities such as accounting.

Overseas Private Investment Company (OPIC) The U.S. government's political risk insurance company.

overvalued currency A currency with larger external purchasing power than internal purchasing power.

packing list A description of merchandise to be exported, including the contents of each container and the total number of containers.

parallel loan A situation in which two corporations have headquarters in two different countries and each makes a loan of equivalent value to the subsidiary of the other company that operates in its country.

"pecking order" theory of financing A theory of how firms finance their investments with the least information-sensitive sources of funds: first using internally generated cash, then using debt, and finally using equity.

pegged currency A currency whose value relative to other currencies is set by the government; a currency in a fixed exchange rate system. Also known as a fixed currency.

P/E (price–earnings) ratio The ratio of stock price to earnings per share.

performance bond Assets in a margin account.

peso problem A phenomenon that arises when rational investors anticipated events that did not occur during the sample or at least did not occur with the frequency the investors expected.

pink sheet trading Over-the-counter trading of Level I ADRs in New York.

pip Trader jargon for the fourth decimal point in a currency quote.

plowback ratio The fraction of operating profits that management chooses to reinvest in a firm.

political risk The possibility of a government adversely affecting the return to a foreign investment or the cash flows of a multinational corporation (for example, by imposing exchange controls or taxes on foreign investments, or by outright expropriation).

political risk insurance Insurance against political risk provided by private firms, governments, and international organizations.

precautionary demand for money Money balances held because of the uncertain timing of future cash inflows and outflows.

present value The current value of an expected future payment, which requires discounting of the expected future payments at an appropriate risk-adjusted discount factor.

price-driven trading system A trading system in which market makers stand ready to buy at their bid prices and sell at their ask prices.

price index The ratio of the price level at a particular time to the price level in a base year multiplied by 100.

price level The price of a consumption bundle of goods and services.

pricing-to-market A situation in which a firm charges different prices for the same good in different markets.

primary market A market in which corporations raise funds by issuing securities (equities or bonds).

private bourse A stock market that is privately owned and operated by a corporation founded for the purpose of trading securities.

private equity firm A company that raises money from investors and invests in a number of individual companies, which are mostly private (that is, not traded on a stock market). Such firms typically control the management of their companies, often bringing in new teams that focus on making the overall company more valuable.

Private Export Funding Corporation (PEFCO) A private corporation whose mission is to make dollar loans to foreign purchasers of U.S. exports.

private placement bonds Bonds that are not sold to the market at large but that are placed privately with sophisticated, well-endowed investors such as pension funds, life insurance companies, or university endowments.

private saving The difference between the disposable income and consumption of the private sector.

probability distribution A description of possible future events associated with a random variable and their respective probabilities of occurrence.

project finance Financing of a particular industrial project in which the providers of the funds receive a return on their investment primarily from the cash flows generated by the project.

public bourse A stock market where the government appoints brokers, typically ensuring them a monopoly over all stock market transactions.

purchasing power The amount of goods and services that can be purchased with an amount of money.

purchasing power parity (PPP) A simple theory of the determination of exchange rates in which the exchange rate adjusts to equate the internal and external purchasing powers of a currency.

pure discount bond A bond that promises a single face value payment at the maturity of the bond.

put–call parity The fundamental no-arbitrage relationship that links the forward rate to the spot rate, the prices of European put and call options at a common strike price, and the domestic currency interest rate.

put option *See* foreign currency put option.

random walk A time series process in which the change in the variable is unpredictable. The model states that the best predictor for the future exchange rate is today's exchange rate, and the best prediction for the change in the exchange rate is zero.

range forward contract A contract that allows a company to specify a range of future spot rates over which the firm can transact in foreign currency at the future spot rate without any other cash flow. If the future spot rate falls outside of the range, the firm transacts at the limits of the range.

ratio analysis The use of financial ratios in the valuation of firms.

rational expectations Expectations of investors that do not involve systematic mistakes or systematically biased forecasts.

real appreciation An increase in the real exchange rate of the denominator currency.

real depreciation A decrease in the real exchange rate of the denominator currency.

INDEX

Boldface page number indicates glossary term.

A

ABN AMRO, 374
Account transactions in balance of payments
    capital account, **102**–103
    current account, **102**, 103–106, 119–123
    official reserves, **102**–103, 107–108
Accounting standards, international
    differences in, 585–586
Acharya, Viral V., 6, 34
Ad valorem duties, **656**
Adjusted net present value (ANPV),
    521–523, 554
    cash flow analysis, 523–527 (*See also*
        Cash flows; Flow-to-equity (FTI);
        Weighted average cost of capital
        (WACC))
    earnings before interest and taxes
        (EBIT), **525**
    financial side effects, 528–531
        costs of financial distress, **529**–530
        costs of issuing securities, 528
        discount rate for tax shields, 529
        equilibrium amount of debt, 530
        subsidized financing, 530–531
        tax shields, 528–529
    flow-to-equity (FTE), 521
    free cash flows, 526–527
    incremental profit, **524**–525
    net operating profit less adjusted taxes
        (NOPLAT), **526**
    perpetuity formula, 527n, 552
    real options, 531–534
    revenues and costs, 525
    steps in, 522–523
        discount the cash flows of all-equity
           firm, 522, 522n
        net present value of financial side effects
           (NPVF), **523**
        value any real options (ROs), **523**
    terminal value of a project, 527
    weighted average cost of capital
        (WACC), 521
Adler, Michael, 450n, 472
Affiliate banks, **375**
Affiliate-parent transfers, in cash
    management, 650–660
African Development Bank, 19
"After a Devaluation, Two African Countries
    Fare Very Differently," *Wall Street
    Journal*, 156n, 172
Agency costs, **524**
Agency theory, **11**–12
Aggarwal, Rajesh K., 406, 426
Aggregate versus individual incentives, 152
Agricultural Bank of China, 402
Ahmadinejad, 479
Aitken, Brian J., 27n, 28n, 34

Aizenman, Joshua, 144n, 172
Akram, Farooq, 187, 204
Alcalá, Francisco, 2n, 34
Algorithmic trading firms, 41
All-in-cost (AIC) principle, **385**–388
Allayannis, George, 612, 615
Allen, Franklin, 15, 34
Almeida, Heitor, 358, 397
Alternative cost-of-capital models, 428,
    466–469
Alternative trading systems, 406
Altman, Edward I., 530n, 552
AMB, 5
Amegbeto, Koffi, 156n, 172
American Depository Receipts (ADRs),
    413–416
American International Group (AIG),
    9, 727–728
American option, **683**
American quote, **46**
Amiti, Mary, 27, 34
Ammer, John, 57n
Andersen, Torben G., 95, 97, 329, 352
Andrade, Sandro C., 489n, 519
Ang, Andrew, 369n, 397, 437, 466, 468, 472
Anglo-Saxon stock market model, 402–403
AngloGold, 423
Anheuser-Busch InBev, 1, 9
Anshuman, V. Ravi, 519
Anti-globalist movement and MNCs,
    26–28
Antofagasta, 577
Appreciation, **62**, 63–65
Aracruz Celulose SA, 69n
Arbitrage, **36**
    covered interest, 179–186
    goods market, 250–251
    pricing, 714–716
    pricing theory (APT), **467**
    triangular, 49–52, 223n
ArcelorMittal, 1, 9
ARCH model, 94n
Argentina, Convertibility Plan, 158, 159
Arrowhead system, 407
Ashanti Goldfields Corporation, 423
Asian Development Bank, 19
Asian Tigers, 345–347
Ask rate, **52**
Asset market approach, to fundamental
    exchange rate forecasting analysis,
    326–327
Asset securitization, **378**
    Assets, in balance of payments, 111
Association of Southeast Asian Nations
    (ASEAN), 3, 164, 164n
Asymmetric economic shocks, 168, 169
Asymmetric information, 604
Automation and electronic trading, 406–407
Average-rate options, 708–709

B

Baba, Naohiko, 188, 204
Back-to-back loans, and swaps, **724**–725
Bai, Yan, 125, 126, 130
Baillie, Richard, 97
Baker, James, 481
Baker Plan, **481**
Baku-Tbilisi-Ceyhan (BTC) Pipeline, 31
Balance of payments (BOP), **101**–132
    account transactions in
        capital account, **102**–103
        current account, **102**, 103–106,
           119–123
        official reserves, **102**–103, 107–108
    assets in, 111
    dynamics of, 115–119
        international investment income
           account, **116**
        net international investment position,
           117–119
        net international investment position or
           net foreign assets, **116**–117
        trade account, **115**–116
    openness of international capital markets,
        125–126
    Point-Counterpoint, 123–125
    and the real exchange rate, 332
    surpluses and deficits in, 108–115
        capital and financial accounts, 110–113
        current account, 108–110
        official settlements account, 112–114
        savings and spending link to, 119–123
        worldwide statistics, 114–115
Balance of Payments Manual (IMF), 105
Balance-sheet hedge, **357**
Balassa, Bela, 267, 280
Baldwin, Richard E., 34, 169n, 172
Ball, Laurence, 7n, 8, 35
Ball, Ray, 586, 588
Banco Santander Central Hispano SA, 374
Bangkok Airways, 662n
Bank Austria, 372
Bank for International Settlements (BIS), 20,
    21, 38, 67, 83, 97, 118, 130, 362n,
    367, 376, 397, 751
    Web site, 378n
Bank holidays, 191n
Bank line of credit, 629
Bank of America, 354, 454
Bank of Credit and Commerce International
    (BCCI), 376
Bank of England, 8
Bank of Mexico, 345
Bank of New York Mellon, 412, 413, 415,
    416n, 426
Banker's acceptance (B/A), **622**, 630
Bankhaus Herstatt, 59